Peterson's® Two-Year Colleges 2018

PETERSON'S®

© 2017 Peterson's®, a Nelnet® company. All rights reserved.
Peterson's is a registered service mark of Nelnet, Inc.

Previous editions published as *Peterson's Annual Guide to Undergraduate Study* © 1970, 1971, 1972, 1973, 1974, 1975, 1976, 1977, 1978, 1979, 1980, 1981, 1982 and as *Peterson's Two-Year Colleges* © 1983, 1984, 1985, 1986, 1987, 1988, 1989, 1990, 1991, 1992, 1993, 1994, 1995, 1996, 1997, 1998, 1999, 2000, 2001, 2002, 2003, 2004, 2005, 2006, 2007, 2008, 2009, 2010, 2011, 2012, 2013, 2014, 2015, 2016

ISSN 0894-9328
ISBN: 978-0-7689-4159-3

Printed in the United States of America

10 9 8 7 6 5 4 3 2 1   19 18 17

Forty-eighth Edition

Contents

A Note from the Peterson's® Editors

For more than 50 years, Peterson's has given students and parents the most comprehensive, up-to-date information on undergraduate institutions in the United States. Peterson's researches the data published in *Peterson's Two-Year Colleges* each year. The information is furnished by the colleges and is accurate at the time of publishing.

This guide also features advice and tips on the college search and selection process, such as how to decide if a two-year college is right for you, how to approach transferring to another college, and what's in store for adults returning to college. If you seem to be getting more, not less, anxious about choosing and getting into the right college, *Peterson's Two-Year Colleges* provides just the right help, giving you the information you need to make important college decisions and ace the admission process.

Opportunities abound for students, and this guide can help you find what you want in a number of ways:

"What You Need to Know About Two-Year Colleges" outlines the basic features and advantages of two-year colleges. "Surviving Standardized Tests" gives an overview of the common examinations students take prior to attending college. "Who's Paying for This? Financial Aid Basics" provides guidelines for financing your college education. "Frequently Asked Questions About Transferring" takes a look at the two-year college scene from the perspective of a student who is looking toward the day when he or she may pursue additional education at a four-year institution. "Returning to School: Advice for Adult Students" is an analysis of the pros and cons (mostly pros) of returning to college after already having begun a professional career. "Coming to America: Tips for International Students Considering Study in the U.S." is an article written particularly for students overseas who are considering a U.S. college education. "Community Colleges and the Green Economy" offers information on some exciting "green" programs at community colleges throughout the United States, as well as two insightful essays by Mary F. T. Spilde, President, Lane Community College and Tom Sutton, Director of Wind Energy and Technical Services, Kalamazoo Valley Community College. Finally, "How to Use This Guide" gives details

on the data in this guide: what terms mean and why they're here.

- If you already have specifics in mind, such as a particular institution or major, turn to the easy-to-use **Two-Year Colleges At-a-Glance Chart** or **Indexes.** You can look up a particular feature—location and programs offered—or use the alphabetical index and immediately find the colleges that meet your criteria.

- For information about particular colleges, turn to the **Profiles of Two-Year Colleges** section. Here, our comprehensive college profiles are arranged alphabetically by state. They provide a complete picture of need-to-know information about every accredited two-year college—from admission to graduation, including expenses, financial aid, majors, and campus safety. All the information you need to apply is placed together at the conclusion of each college **Profile.** Display ads, which appear near some of the institutions' profiles, have been provided and paid for by those colleges or universities that wished to supplement their profile data with additional information about their institution.

- In addition, two-page narrative descriptions, which appear in the **Featured Two-Year Colleges** section, are paid for and written by college officials and offer great detail about each college. They are edited to provide a consistent format across entries for your ease of comparison.

Peterson's publishes a full line of books—education exploration, test prep, financial aid, and career preparation. Peterson's publications can be found at high school guidance offices, college libraries and career centers, and your local bookstore and library. Peterson's books are also available at www.petersonsbooks.com.

We welcome any comments or suggestions you may have about this publication. Your feedback will help us make educational dreams possible for you—and others like you.

Colleges will be pleased to know that Peterson's helped you in your selection. Admissions staff members are more than happy to answer questions, address specific problems and help in any way they can. The editors at Peterson's wish you great success in your college search.

The College Admissions Process: An Overview

What You Need to Know About Two-Year Colleges

David R. Pierce

Two-year colleges—better known as community colleges—are often called "the people's colleges." With their open-door policies (admission is open to individuals with a high school diploma or its equivalent), community colleges provide access to higher education for millions of Americans who might otherwise be excluded from higher education. Community college students are diverse and of all ages, races, and economic backgrounds. While many community college students enroll full-time, an equally large number attend on a part-time basis so they can fulfill employment and family commitments as they advance their education.

Community colleges can also be referred to as either technical or junior colleges, and they may either be under public or independent control. What unites two-year colleges is that they are regionally accredited, postsecondary institutions, whose highest credential awarded is the associate degree. With few exceptions, community colleges offer a comprehensive curriculum, which includes transfer, technical, and continuing education programs.

IMPORTANT FACTORS IN A COMMUNITY COLLEGE EDUCATION

The student who attends a community college can count on receiving high-quality instruction in a supportive learning community. This setting frees the student to pursue his or her own goals, nurture special talents, explore new fields of learning, and develop the capacity for lifelong learning.

From the student's perspective, four characteristics capture the essence of community colleges:

1. They are community-based institutions that work in close partnership with high schools, community groups, and employers in extending high-quality programs at convenient times and places.

2. Community colleges are cost effective. Annual tuition and fees at public community colleges average approximately half those at public four-year colleges and less than 15 percent of private four-year institutions. In addition, since most community colleges are generally close to their students' homes, these students can also save a significant amount of money on the room, board, and transportation expenses traditionally associated with a college education.

3. Community colleges provide a caring environment, with faculty members who are expert instructors, known for excellent teaching and meeting students at the point of their individual needs, regardless of age, sex, race, current job status, or previous academic preparation. Community colleges join a strong curriculum with a broad range of counseling and career services that are intended to assist students in making the most of their educational opportunities.

4. Many offer comprehensive programs, including transfer curricula in such liberal arts programs as chemistry, psychology, and business management, that lead directly to a baccalaureate degree and career programs that prepare students for employment or assist those already employed in upgrading their skills. For those students who need to strengthen their academic skills, community colleges also offer a wide range of developmental programs in mathematics, languages, and learning skills, designed to prepare the student for success in college studies.

GETTING TO KNOW YOUR TWO-YEAR COLLEGE

The first step in determining the quality of a community college is to check the status of its accreditation. Once you have established that a community college is appropriately accredited, find out as much as you can about the programs and services it has to offer. Much of that information can be found in materials the college provides. However, the best way to learn about a college is to visit in person.

During a campus visit, be prepared to ask a lot of questions. Talk to students, faculty members, administrators, and counselors about the college and its programs, particularly those in which you have a special interest. Ask about available certificates and associate degrees. Don't be shy. Do what you can to dig below the surface. Ask college officials about the transfer rate to four-year colleges. If a college emphasizes student services, find out what particular assistance is offered, such as educational or career guidance. Colleges are eager to provide you with the information you need to make informed decisions.

COMMUNITY COLLEGES CAN SAVE YOU MONEY

If you are able to live at home while you attend college, you will certainly save money on room and board, but it does cost something to commute. Many two-year colleges offer you instruction in your own home through online learning programs or through home study courses that can save both time and money. Look into all the options, and be sure to add up all the costs of attending various colleges before deciding which is best for you.

FINANCIAL AID

Many students who attend community colleges are eligible for a range of federal financial aid programs, state aid, and on-campus jobs. Your high school counselor or the financial aid officer at a community college will also be able to help you. It is in your interest to apply for financial aid months in advance of the date you intend to start your college program, so find out early what assistance is available to you. While many community colleges are able to help students who make a last-minute decision to attend college, either through short-term loans or emergency grants, if you are considering entering college and think you might need financial aid, it is best to find out as much as you can as early as you can.

WORKING AND GOING TO SCHOOL

Many two-year college students maintain full-time or part-time employment while they earn their degrees. Over the years, a steadily growing number of students have chosen to attend community colleges while they fulfill family and employment responsibilities. To enable these students to balance the demands of home, work, and school, most community colleges offer classes at night and on weekends.

For the full-time student, the usual length of time it takes to obtain an associate degree is two years. However, your length of study will depend on the course load you take: the fewer credits you earn each term, the longer it will take you to earn a degree. To assist you in moving more quickly toward earning your degree, many community colleges now award credit through examination or for equivalent knowledge gained through relevant life experiences. Be certain to find out the credit options that are available to you at the college in which you are interested. You may discover that it will take less time to earn a degree than you first thought.

PREPARATION FOR TRANSFER

Studies have repeatedly shown that students who first attend a community college and then transfer to a four-year college or university do at least as well academically as the students who entered the four-year institutions as freshmen. Most community colleges have agreements with nearby four-year institutions to make transfer of credits easier. If you are thinking of transferring, be sure to meet with a counselor or faculty adviser before choosing your courses. You will want to map out a course of study with transfer in mind. Make sure you also find out the credit-transfer requirements of the four-year institution you might want to attend.

ATTENDING A TWO-YEAR COLLEGE IN ANOTHER REGION

Although many community colleges serve a specific county or district, they are committed (to the extent of their ability) to the goal of equal educational opportunity without regard to economic status, race, creed, color, sex, or national origin. Independent two-year colleges recruit from a much broader geographical area—throughout the United States and, increasingly, around the world.

Although some community colleges do provide on-campus housing for their students, most do not. However, even if on-campus housing is not available, most colleges do have housing referral services.

NEW CAREER OPPORTUNITIES

Community colleges realize that many entering students are not sure about the field in which they want to focus their studies or the career they would like to pursue. Often, students discover fields and careers they never knew existed. Community colleges have the resources to help students identify areas of career interest and to set challenging occupational goals.

Once a career goal is set, you can be confident that a community college will provide job-relevant, technical education. About half of the students who take courses for credit at community colleges do so to prepare for employment or to acquire or upgrade skills for their current job. Especially helpful in charting a career path is the assistance of a counselor or a faculty adviser, who can discuss job opportunities in your chosen field and help you map out your course of study.

In addition, since community colleges have close ties to their communities, they are in constant contact with leaders in business, industry, organized labor, and public life. Community colleges work with these individuals and their organizations to prepare students for direct entry into the world of work. For example, some community colleges have established partnerships with local businesses and industries to provide specialized training programs. Some also provide the academic portion of apprenticeship training, while others offer extensive job-shadowing and cooperative education opportunities. Be sure to examine all of the career-preparation opportunities offered by the community colleges in which you are interested.

David R. Pierce is the former President of the American Association of Community Colleges.

Surviving Standardized Tests

WHAT ARE STANDARDIZED TESTS?

Colleges and universities in the United States use tests to help evaluate applicants' readiness for admission or to place them in appropriate courses. The tests that are most frequently used by colleges are the ACT® of American College Testing, Inc., and the College Board's SAT®. In addition, the Educational Testing Service (ETS) offers the TOEFL® test, which evaluates the English-language proficiency of nonnative speakers. The tests are offered at designated testing centers located at high schools and colleges throughout the United States and U.S. territories and at testing centers in various countries throughout the world.

Upon request, special accommodations for students with documented visual, hearing, physical, or learning disabilities are available. Examples of special accommodations include tests in Braille or large print and such aids as a reader, recorder, magnifying glass, or sign language interpreter. Additional testing time may be allowed in some instances. Contact the appropriate testing program or your guidance counselor for details on how to request special accommodations.

THE ACT®

The ACT® is a standardized college entrance examination that measures knowledge and skills in English, mathematics, reading comprehension, and science reasoning and the application of these skills to future academic tasks. The ACT® consists of four multiple-choice tests.

Test 1: English
- 75 questions, 45 minutes
- Usage and mechanics
- Rhetorical skills

Test 2: Mathematics
- 60 questions, 60 minutes
- Pre-algebra
- Elementary algebra
- Intermediate algebra
- Coordinate geometry
- Plane geometry
- Trigonometry

Test 3: Reading
- 40 questions, 35 minutes
- Prose fiction
- Humanities
- Social studies
- Natural sciences

Test 4: Science
- 40 questions, 35 minutes
- Data representation
- Research summary
- Conflicting viewpoints

Each section is scored from 1 to 36 and is scaled for slight variations in difficulty. Students are not penalized for incorrect responses. The composite score is the average of the four scaled scores. The ACT® Plus Writing includes the four multiple-choice tests and a writing test, which measures writing skills emphasized in high school English classes and in entry-level college composition courses.

To prepare for the ACT®, ask your guidance counselor for a free guidebook, "Preparing for the ACT®," or download it at www.act.org/content/dam/act/unsecured/documents/Preparing-for-the-ACT.pdf. Besides providing general test-preparation information and additional test-taking strategies, this guidebook provides full-length practice tests, including a Writing test, information about the optional Writing Test, strategies to prepare for the tests, and what to expect on test day.

DON'T FORGET TO . . .

- ❑ Take the SAT® or ACT® before application deadlines.
- ❑ Note that test registration deadlines precede test dates by about six weeks.
- ❑ Register to take the TOEFL® test if English is not your native language and you are planning on studying at a North American college.
- ❑ Contact the College Board or American College Testing, Inc., in advance if you need special accommodations when taking tests.

THE SAT®

The redesigned SAT®, which saw its first test-takers in the spring of 2016, has these sections: Evidence-Based Reading and Writing, Math, and the Essay. It is based on 1600 points—the top scores for the Math section and the Evidence-Based Reading and Writing section will be 800, and the Essay score is reported separately.

Evidence-based Reading Test
- 52 questions; 65 minutes
- Passages in U.S. and world literature, history/social studies, and science
- Paired passages
- Lower and higher text complexities
- Words in context, command of evidence, and analysis

Writing and Language Test
- 44 questions; 35 minutes
- Passages in careers, history/social studies, humanities, and science
- Argument, informative/explanatory, and nonfiction narrative passages

- Words in context, grammar, expression of ideas, and analysis

Mathematics Test

- One no-calculator section (25 minutes)
- One calculator section (55 minutes)
- Content includes algebra, problem solving and data analysis, advanced math, area and volume calculations, trigonometric functions, and lines, triangles, and circles using theorems.

Essay (Optional)

- 50 minutes
- Argument passage written for a general audience
- Analysis of argument in passage using text evidence
- Score: 3–12 (Reading: 1–4 scale, Analysis: 1–4 scale, Writing: 1–4 scale)

According to the College Board's website, the "Eight Key Changes" are the following:

- **Relevant Words in Context:** Students need to interpret the meaning of words based on the context of the passage in which they appear. The focus is on "relevant" words—not obscure ones.

- **Command of Evidence:** In addition to demonstrating writing skills, students need to show that they're able to interpret, synthesize, and use evidence found in a wide range of sources.

- **Essay Analyzing a Source:** Students read a passage and explain how the author builds an argument, supporting support their claims with actual data from the passage.

- **Math Focused on Three Key Areas:** Problem Solving and Data Analysis (using ratios, percentages, and proportional reasoning to solve problems in science, social science, and career contexts), the Heart of Algebra (mastery of linear equations and systems), and Passport to Advanced Math (more complex equations and the manipulation they require).

- **Problems Grounded in Real-World Contexts:** All of the questions are grounded in the real world, directly related to work performed in college.

- **Analysis in Science and in Social Studies:** Students need to apply reading, writing, language, and math skills to answer questions in contexts of science, history, and social studies.

- **Founding Documents and Great Global Conversation:** Students will find an excerpt from one of the Founding Documents—such as the Declaration of Independence, the Constitution, and the Bill of Rights—or a text from the "Great Global Conversation" about freedom, justice, and human dignity.

- **No Penalty for Wrong Answers:** Students earn points for the questions they answer correctly.

Check out the College Board's website at https://collegereadiness.collegeboard.org for the most up-to-date information.

Top 10 Ways Not to Take the Test

1. Cramming the night before the test.
2. Not becoming familiar with the directions before you take the test.
3. Not becoming familiar with the format of the test before you take it.
4. Not knowing how the test is graded.
5. Spending too much time on any one question.
6. Second-guessing yourself.
7. Not checking spelling, grammar, and sentence structure in essays.
8. Writing a one-paragraph essay.
9. Forgetting to take a deep breath—
10. and finally—Don't lose it!

SAT SUBJECT TESTS™

Subject Tests are required by some institutions for admission and/or placement in freshman-level courses. Each Subject Test measures one's knowledge of a specific subject and the ability to apply that knowledge. Students should check with each institution for its specific requirements. In general, students are required to take three Subject Tests (one English, one mathematics, and one of their choice).

Subject Tests are given in the following areas: biology, chemistry, Chinese, French, German, Italian, Japanese, Korean, Latin, literature, mathematics, modern Hebrew, physics, Spanish, U.S. history, and world history. These tests are 1 hour long and are primarily multiple-choice tests. Three Subject Tests may be taken on one test date.

Scored like the current SAT®, students gain a point for each correct answer and lose a fraction of a point for each incorrect answer. The raw scores are then converted to scaled scores that range from 200 to 800.

THE TOEFL® INTERNET-BASED TEST (IBT)

The Test of English as a Foreign Language Internet-Based Test (TOEFL® iBT) is designed to help assess a student's grasp of English if it is not the student's first language. Performance on the TOEFL® test may help interpret scores on the critical reading sections of the SAT®. The test consists of four integrated sections: speaking, listening, reading, and writing. The TOEFL® iBT emphasizes integrated skills. The paper-based versions of the TOEFL® will continue to be administered in certain countries where the Internet-based version has not yet been introduced. For further information, visit www.toefl.org.

WHAT OTHER TESTS SHOULD I KNOW ABOUT?

The AP® Program

This program allows high school students to try college-level work and build valuable skills and study habits in the process. Subject matter is explored in more depth in AP courses than in other high school classes. A qualifying score on an AP test—which varies from school to school—can earn you college credit or advanced placement. Getting qualifying grades on enough exams can even earn you a full year's credit and sophomore standing at more than 1,500 higher-education institutions. There are more than thirty AP courses across multiple subject areas, including art history, biology, and computer science. Speak to your guidance counselor for information about your school's offerings.

College-Level Examination Program (CLEP®)

The CLEP enables students to earn college credit for what they already know, whether it was learned in school, through independent study, or through other experiences outside of the classroom. More than 2,900 colleges and universities now award credit for qualifying scores on one or more of the 33 CLEP exams. The exams, which are 90 minutes in length and are primarily multiple choice, are administered at participating colleges and universities. For more information, check out the website at www.collegeboard.com/clep.

WHAT CAN I DO TO PREPARE FOR THESE TESTS?

Know what to expect. Get familiar with how the tests are structured, how much time is allowed, and the directions for each type of question. Get plenty of rest the night before the test and eat breakfast that morning.

There are a variety of products, from books to software to videos, available to help you prepare for most standardized tests. Find the learning style that suits you best. As for which products to buy, there are two major categories— those created by the test-makers and those created by private companies. The best approach is to talk to someone who has been through the process and find out which product or products he or she recommends.

Some students report significant increases in scores after participating in coaching programs. Longer-term programs (40 hours) seem to raise scores more than short-term programs (20 hours), but beyond 40 hours, score gains are minor. Math scores appear to benefit more from coaching than critical reading scores.

Resources

There is a variety of ways to prepare for standardized tests— find a method that fits your schedule and your budget. But you should definitely prepare. Far too many students walk into these tests cold, either because they find standardized tests frightening or annoying or they just haven't found the time to study. The key is that these exams are standardized. That means these tests are largely the same from administration to administration; they always test the same concepts. They have to, or else you couldn't compare the scores of people who took the tests on different dates. The numbers or words may change, but the underlying content doesn't.

So how do you prepare? At the very least, you should review relevant material, such as math formulas and commonly used vocabulary words, and know the directions for each question type or test section. You should take at least one practice test and review your mistakes so you don't make them again on the test day. Beyond that, you know best how much preparation you need. You'll also find lots of material in libraries or bookstores to help you: books and software from the test- makers and from other publishers (including Peterson's) or live courses that range from national test-preparation companies to teachers at your high school who offer classes.

Who's Paying for This? Financial Aid Basics

A college education can be expensive—costing more than $150,000 for four years at some of the higher priced private colleges and universities. Even at the lower-cost state colleges and universities, the cost of a four-year education can approach $60,000. Determining how you and your family will come up with the necessary funds to pay for your education requires planning, perseverance, and learning as much as you can about the options that are available to you. But before you get discouraged, College Board statistics show that 53 percent of full-time students attend four-year public and private colleges with tuition and fees less than $9,000, while 20 percent attend colleges that have tuition and fees more than $36,000. College costs tend to be less in the western states and higher in New England.

Paying for college should not be looked at as a four-year financial commitment. For many families, paying the total cost of a student's college education out of current income and savings is usually not realistic. For families that have planned ahead and have financial savings established for higher education, the burden is a lot easier. But for most, meeting the cost of college requires the pooling of current income and assets and investing in longer-term loan options. These family resources, together with financial assistance from state, federal, and institutional sources, enable millions of students each year to attend the institution of their choice.

FINANCIAL AID PROGRAMS

There are three types of financial aid:

1. Gift-aid—Scholarships and grants are funds that do not have to be repaid.

2. Loans—Loans must be repaid, usually after graduation; the amount you have to pay back is the total you've borrowed plus any accrued interest. This is considered a source of self-help aid.

3. Student employment—Student employment is a job arranged for you by the financial aid office. This is another source of self-help aid.

The federal government has four major grant programs—the Federal Pell Grant, the Federal Supplemental Educational Opportunity Grant, Academic Competitiveness Grants (ACG), and National SMART (Science and Mathematics Access to Retain Talent) grants. ACG and SMART grants are limited to students who qualify for a Pell Grant and are awarded to a select group of students. Overall, these grants are targeted to low-to-moderate income families with significant financial need. The federal government also sponsors a student employment program called the Federal Work-Study Program, which offers jobs both on and off campus, and several loan programs, including those for students and for parents of undergraduate students.

There are two types of student loan programs: subsidized and unsubsidized. The subsidized Federal Direct Loan and the Federal Perkins Loan are need-based, government-subsidized loans. Students who borrow through these programs do not have to pay interest on the loan until after they graduate or leave school. The unsubsidized Federal Direct Loan and the Federal Direct PLUS Loan Program are not based on need, and borrowers are responsible for the interest while the student is in school. These loans are administered by different methods. Once you choose your college, the financial aid office will guide you through this process.

After you've submitted your financial aid application and you've been accepted for admission, each college will send you a letter describing your financial aid award. Most award letters show estimated college costs, how much you and your family are expected to contribute, and the amount and types of aid you have been awarded. Most students are awarded aid from a combination of sources and programs. Hence, your award is often called a financial aid "package."

SOURCES OF FINANCIAL AID

Millions of students and families apply for financial aid each year. Financial aid from all sources exceeds $143 billion per year. The largest single source of aid is the federal government, which will award more than $100 billion this year.

The next largest source of financial aid is found in the college and university community. Most of this aid is awarded to students who have a demonstrated need based on the Federal Methodology. Some institutions use a different formula, the Institutional Methodology (IM), to award their own funds in conjunction with other forms of aid. Institutional aid may be either need-based or non-need based. Aid that is not based on need is usually awarded for a student's academic performance (merit awards), specific talents or abilities, or to attract the type of students a college seeks to enroll.

Another source of financial aid is from state government. All states offer grant and/or scholarship aid, most of which is need-based. However, more and more states are offering substantial merit-based aid programs. Most state programs award aid only to students attending college in their home state.

Other sources of financial aid include:

- Private agencies
- Foundations
- Corporations
- Clubs
- Fraternal and service organizations

- Civic associations
- Unions
- Religious groups that award grants, scholarships, and low-interest loans
- Employers that provide tuition reimbursement benefits for employees and their children

More information about these different sources of aid is available from high school guidance offices, public libraries, college financial aid offices, directly from the sponsoring organizations, and online at www.petersons.com/college-search/scholarship-search.aspx.

HOW NEED-BASED FINANCIAL AID IS AWARDED

When you apply for aid, your family's financial situation is analyzed using a government-approved formula called the Federal Methodology. This formula looks at five items:

1. Demographic information of the family
2. Income of the parents
3. Assets of the parents
4. Income of the student
5. Assets of the student

This analysis determines the amount you and your family are expected to contribute toward your college expenses, called your Expected Family Contribution, or EFC. If the EFC is equal to or more than the cost of attendance at a particular college, then you do not demonstrate financial need. However, even if you don't have financial need, you may still qualify for aid, as there are grants, scholarships, and loan programs that are not need-based.

If the cost of your education is greater than your EFC, then you do demonstrate financial need and qualify for assistance. The amount of your financial need that can be met varies from school to school. Some are able to meet your full need, while others can only cover a certain percentage of need. Here's the formula:

> Cost of Attendance
> − Expected Family Contribution
> = Financial Need

The EFC remains constant, but your need will vary according to the costs of attendance at a particular college. In general, the higher the tuition and fees at a particular college, the higher the cost of attendance will be. Expenses for books and supplies, room and board, transportation, and other miscellaneous items are included in the overall cost of attendance. It is important to remember that you do not have to be low-income to qualify for financial aid. Many middle and upper-middle income families qualify for need-based financial aid.

APPLYING FOR FINANCIAL AID

Every student must complete the Free Application for Federal Student Aid (FAFSA®) to be considered for financial aid. The FAFSA® is available from your high school guidance office, many public libraries, colleges in your area, or directly from the U.S. Department of Education.

Students are encouraged to apply for federal student aid on the Web. The electronic version of the FAFSA® can be accessed at http://www.fafsa.ed.gov.

The NEW Federal Student Aid ID

In order for a student to complete the online FAFSA®, he or she will need a Federal Student Aid (FSA) ID. You can get this online at https://fsaid.ed.gov/npas/index.htm. Since May 2015, the FSA ID has replaced the previously used PIN system. Parents of dependent students also need to obtain their own FSA ID in order to sign their child's FAFSA® electronically online.

The FSA ID can be used to access several federal aid-related websites, including FAFSA.gov and StudentLoans.gov. It consists of a username and password and can be used to electronically sign Federal Student Aid documents, access your personal records, and make binding legal obligations. The FSA ID is beneficial in several ways:

- It removes your personal identifiable information (PII), such as your Social Security number, from your log-in credentials.
- It creates a more secure and efficient way to verify your information when you log in to access to your federal student aid information online.
- It gives you the ability to easily update your personal information.
- It allows you to easily retrieve your username and password by requesting a secure code be sent to your e-mail address or by answering challenge questions.

It's relatively simple to create an FSA ID and should only take a few minutes. In addition, you will have an opportunity to link your current Federal Student Aid PIN (if you already have one) to your FSA ID. The final step is to confirm your e-mail address. You will receive a secure code to the e-mail address you provided when you set up your FSA ID. Once you retrieve the code from your e-mail account and enter it—to confirm your e-mail address is valid—you will be able to use this e-mail address instead of your username to log in to any of the federal aid-related websites, making the log-in process EVEN simpler for you and your parents.

When you initially create your FSA ID, your information will need to be verified with the Social Security Administration. This process can take anywhere from one to three days. For that reason, it's a good idea to take care of setting up your FSA ID as early as possible, so it will be all set when you are ready to begin completing your FAFSA®.

IMPORTANT NOTE: Since your FSA ID provides access to your personal information and is used to sign online documents, it's imperative that you protect this ID. Don't share it with *anyone* or write it down in an insecure location—you could place yourself at great risk for identify theft.

If Every College You're Applying to for Fall 2018 Requires the FAFSA®

. . . then it's pretty simple: Complete the FAFSA® after October 1, 2017, being certain to send it in before any college-imposed deadlines. (Students will now be permitted to send in the 2018–19 FAFSA® before January 1, 2018.) Students (and parents, as appropriate) are required to report income for an earlier tax year, so for the 2018–19 school year, you would report 2016 income information.

After you send in your FAFSA®, you'll receive a Student Aid Report (SAR) that includes all of the information you reported and shows your EFC. If you provided an e-mail address, the SAR is sent to you electronically; otherwise, you will receive a SAR or SAR Acknowledgment in the mail, which lists your FAFSA® information but may require you to make any corrections on the FAFSA® website. Be sure to review the SAR, checking to see if the information you reported is accurately represented. If you used estimated numbers to complete the FAFSA®, you may have to resubmit the SAR with any corrections to the data. The college(s) you have designated on the FAFSA® will receive the information you reported and will use that data to make their decision.

The CSS/Financial Aid PROFILE®

To award their own funds, some colleges require an additional application, the CSS/Financial Aid PROFILE® form. The PROFILE asks supplemental questions that some colleges and awarding agencies feel provide a more accurate assessment of the family's ability to pay for college. It is up to the college to decide whether it will use only the FAFSA® or both the FAFSA® and the PROFILE. PROFILE applications are available from the high school guidance office and on the Web. Both the paper application and the website list those colleges and programs that require the PROFILE application.

If a College Requires the PROFILE

Step 1: Register for the CSS/Financial Aid PROFILE in the fall of your senior year in high school. You can apply for the PROFILE online at http://profileonline.collegeboard.com/prf/index.jsp. Registration information with a list of the colleges that require the PROFILE is available in most high school guidance offices. There is a fee for using the Financial Aid PROFILE application ($25 for the first college, which includes the $9 application fee, and $16 for each additional college). You must pay for the service by credit card when you register. If you do not have a credit card, you will be billed. A limited number of fee waivers are automatically granted to first-time applicants based on the financial information provided on the PROFILE.

Step 2: Fill out your customized CSS/Financial Aid PROFILE. Once you register, your application will be immediately available online and will have questions that all students must complete, questions which must be completed by the student's parents (unless the student is independent and the colleges or programs selected do not require parental information), and *may* have supplemental questions needed by one or more of your schools or programs. If required, those will be found in Section Q of the application.

In addition to the PROFILE application you complete online, you may also be required to complete a Business/ Farm Supplement via traditional paper format. Completion of this form is not a part of the online process. If this form is required, instructions on how to download and print the supplemental form are provided. If your biological or adoptive parents are separated or divorced and your colleges and programs require it, your noncustodial parent may be asked to complete the Noncustodial PROFILE.

Once you complete and submit your PROFILE application, it will be processed and sent directly to your requested colleges and programs.

IF YOU DON'T QUALIFY FOR NEED-BASED AID

If you are not eligible for need-based aid, you can still find ways to lessen your burden.

Here are some suggestions:

- Search for merit scholarships. You can start at the initial stages of your application process. College merit awards are increasingly important as more and more colleges award these to students they especially want to attract. As a result, applying to a college at which your qualifications put you at the top of the entering class may give you a larger merit award. Another source of aid to look for is private scholarships that are given for special skills and talents. Additional information can be found at www.finaid.org.

- Seek employment during the summer and the academic year. The student employment office at your college can help you locate a school-year job. Many colleges and local businesses have vacancies remaining after they have hired students who are receiving Federal Work-Study Program financial aid.

- Borrow through the unsubsidized Federal Direct Loan program. This is generally available to all students. The terms and conditions are similar to the subsidized loans. The biggest difference is that the borrower is responsible for the interest while still in college, although the government permits students to delay paying the interest right away and add the accrued interest to the total amount owed. You must file the FAFSA® to be considered.

- After you've secured what you can through scholarships, working, and borrowing, you and your parents will be expected to meet your share of the college bill (the Expected Family Contribution). Many colleges offer monthly payment plans that spread the cost over the academic year. If the monthly payments are too high, parents can borrow through the Federal Direct PLUS Loan Program, through one of the many private education loan programs available, or through home equity loans and lines of credit. Families seeking assistance in financing college expenses should inquire at the financial aid office about what programs are available at the college. Some families seek the advice of professional financial advisers and tax consultants.

Frequently Asked Questions About Transferring

Muriel M. Shishkoff

Among the students attending two-year colleges are a large number who began their higher education knowing they would eventually transfer to a four-year school to obtain their bachelor's degree. There are many reasons why students go this route. Upon graduating from high school, some simply do not have definite career goals. Although they don't want to put their education on hold, they prefer not to pay exorbitant amounts in tuition while trying to "find themselves." As the cost of a university education escalates—even in public institutions—the option of spending the freshman and sophomore years at a two-year college looks attractive to many students. Others attend a two-year college because they are unable to meet the initial entrance standards—a specified grade point average (GPA), standardized test scores, or knowledge of specific academic subjects—required by the four-year school of their choice. Many such students praise the community college system for giving them the chance to be, academically speaking, "born again." In addition, students from other countries often find that they can adapt more easily to language and cultural changes at a two-year school before transferring to a larger, more diverse four-year college.

If your plan is to attend a two-year college with the ultimate goal of transferring to a four-year school, you will be pleased to know that the increased importance of the community college route to a bachelor's degree is recognized by all segments of higher education. As a result, many two-year schools have revised their course outlines and established new courses in order to comply with the programs and curricular offerings of the universities. Institutional improvements to make transferring easier have also proliferated at both the two-and four-year levels. The generous transfer policies of the Pennsylvania, New York, and Florida state university systems, among others, reflect this attitude; these systems accept all credits from students who have graduated from accredited community colleges.

If you are interested in moving from a two-year college to a four-year school, the sooner you make up your mind that you are going to make the switch, the better position you will be to transfer successfully (that is, without having wasted valuable time and credits). The ideal point at which to make such a decision is **before** you register for classes at your two-year school; a counselor can help you plan your course work with an eye toward fulfilling the requirements needed for your major course of study.

Naturally, it is not always possible to plan your transferring strategy that far in advance, but keep in mind that the key to a successful transfer is **preparation,** and preparation takes time—time to think through your objectives and time to plan the right classes to take.

As students face the prospect of transferring from a two-year to a four-year school, many thoughts and concerns about this complicated and often frustrating process race through their minds. Here are answers to the questions that are most frequently asked by transferring students.

Q Does every college and university accept transfer students?

A Most four-year institutions accept transfer students, but some do so more enthusiastically than others. Graduating from a community college is an advantage at, for example, Arizona State University and the University of Massachusetts Boston; both accept more community college transfer students than traditional freshmen. At the University at Albany, SUNY, graduates of two-year transfer programs within the State University of New York System are given priority for upper-division (i.e., junior-and senior-level) vacancies.

Schools offering undergraduate work at the upper division only are especially receptive to transfer applications. On the other hand, some schools accept only a few transfer students; others refuse entrance to sophomores or those in their final year. Princeton University requires an "excellent academic record and particularly compelling reasons to transfer." Check the catalogs of several colleges for their transfer requirements before you make your final choice.

Q Do students who go directly from high school to a four-year college do better academically than transfer students from community colleges?

A On the contrary: some institutions report that transfers from two-year schools who persevere until graduation do *better* than those who started as freshmen in a four-year college.

Q Why is it so important that my two-year college be accredited?

A Four-year colleges and universities accept transfer credits only from schools formally recognized by a regional, national, or professional educational agency. This accreditation signifies that an institution or program of study meets or exceeds a minimum level of educational quality necessary for meeting stated educational objectives.

Q After enrolling at a four-year school, may I still make up necessary courses at a community college?

A Some institutions restrict credit after transfer to their own facilities. Others allow students to take a limited number of transfer courses after matriculation, depending on the subject matter. A few provide opportunities for cross-registration or dual enrollment, which means taking classes on more than one campus.

Q What do I need to do to transfer?

A First, send for your high school and college transcripts. Having chosen the school you wish to transfer to, check its admission requirements against your transcripts. If you find that you are admissible, file an application as early as possible before the deadline. Part of the process will be asking your former schools to send official transcripts to the admission office, i.e., not the copies you used in determining your admissibility.

Plan your transfer program with the head of your new department as soon as you have decided to transfer. Determine the recommended general education pattern and necessary preparation for your major. At your present school, take the courses you will need to meet transfer requirements for the new school.

Q What qualifies me for admission as a transfer student?

A Admission requirements for most four-year institutions vary. Depending on the reputation or popularity of the school and program you wish to enter, requirements may be quite selective and competitive. Usually, you will need to show satisfactory test scores, an academic record up to a certain standard, and completion of specific subject matter.

Transfer students can be eligible to enter a four-year school in a number of ways: by having been eligible for admission directly upon graduation from high school, by making up shortcomings in grades (or in subject matter not covered in high school) at a community college, or by satisfactory completion of necessary courses or credit hours at another postsecondary institution. Ordinarily, students coming from a community college or from another four-year institution must meet or exceed the receiving institution's standards for freshmen and show appropriate college-level course work taken since high school. Students who did not graduate from high school can present proof of proficiency through results

on the the GED® Test, the HiSET® Exam, or another state-approved high school equivalency test.

Q Are exceptions ever made for students who don't meet all the requirements for transfer?

A Extenuating circumstances, such as disability, low family income, refugee or veteran status, or athletic talent, may permit the special enrollment of students who would not otherwise be eligible but who demonstrate the potential for academic success. Consult the appropriate office—the Educational Opportunity Program, the disabled students' office, the athletic department, or the academic dean—to see whether an exception can be made in your case.

Q How far in advance do I need to apply for transfer?

A Some schools have a rolling admission policy, which means that they process transfer applications as they are received, all year long. With other schools, you must apply during the priority filing period, which can be up to a year before you wish to enter. Check the date with the admission office at your prospective campus.

Q Is it possible to transfer courses from several different institutions?

A Institutions ordinarily accept the courses that they consider transferable, regardless of the number of accredited schools involved. However, there is the danger of exceeding the maximum number of credit hours that can be transferred from all other schools or earned through credit by examination, extension courses, or correspondence courses. The limit placed on transfer credits varies from school to school, so read the catalog carefully to avoid taking courses you won't be able to use. To avoid duplicating courses, keep attendance at different campuses to a minimum.

Q What is involved in transferring from a semester system to a quarter or trimester system?

A In the semester system, the academic calendar is divided into two equal parts. The quarter system is more aptly named trimester, since the academic calendar is divided into three equal terms (not counting a summer session). To convert semester units into quarter units or credit hours, simply multiply the semester units by one and a half. Conversely, multiply quarter units by two thirds to come up with semester units. If you are used to a semester system of fifteen- to sixteen-week courses, the ten-week courses of the quarter system may seem to fly by.

Q Why might a course be approved for transfer credit by one four-year school but not by another?

A The beauty of postsecondary education in the United States lies in its variety. Entrance policies and graduation requirements are designed to reflect and serve each institution's mission. Because institutional policies vary so widely, schools may interpret the subject matter of a course from quite different points of view. Given that the granting of transfer credit indicates that a course is viewed as being, in effect, parallel to one offered by the receiving institution, it is easy to see how this might be the case at one university and not another.

Q Must I take a foreign language to transfer?

A Foreign language proficiency is often required for admission to a four-year institution; such proficiency also often figures in certain majors or in the general education pattern. Often, two or three years of a single language in high school will do the trick. Find out if scores received on Advanced Placement (AP®) examinations, placement examinations given by the foreign language department, or SAT Subject Tests™ will be accepted in lieu of college course work.

Q Will the school to which I'm transferring accept pass/ no pass, pass/fail, or credit/no credit grades in lieu of letter grades?

A Usually, a limit is placed on the number of these courses you can transfer, and there may be other restrictions as well. If you want to use other-than-letter grades for the fulfillment of general education requirements or lower-division (freshman and sophomore) preparation for the major, check with the receiving institution.

Q Which is more important for transfer—my grade point average or my course completion pattern?

A Some schools believe that your past grades indicate academic potential and overshadow prior preparation for a specific degree program. Others require completion of certain introductory courses before transfer to prepare you for upper-division work in your major. In any case, appropriate course selection will cut down the time to graduation and increase your chances of making a successful transfer.

Q What happens to my credits if I change majors?

A If you change majors after admission, your transferable course credit should remain fairly intact. However, because you may need extra or different preparation for your new major, some of the courses you've taken may now be useful only as electives. The need for additional lower-level preparation may mean you're staying longer at your new school than you originally planned. On the other hand, you may already have taken courses that count toward your new major as part of the university's general education pattern.

Excerpted (and updated) from *Transferring Made Easy: A Guide to Changing Colleges Successfully,* by Muriel M. Shishkoff, © 1991 by Muriel M. Shishkoff (published by Peterson's).

Returning to School: Advice for Adult Students

Sandra Cook, Ph.D.
Associate Vice President for Enrollment Management, San Diego State University

Many adults think for a long time about returning to school without taking any action. One purpose of this article is to help the "thinkers" finally make some decisions by examining what is keeping them from action. Another purpose is to describe not only some of the difficulties and obstacles that adult students may face when returning to school but also tactics for coping with them.

If you have been thinking about going back to college, and believing that you are the only person your age contemplating college, you should know that approximately 7 million adult students are currently enrolled in higher education institutions. This number represents 50 percent of total higher education enrollments. The majority of adult students are enrolled at two-year colleges.

There are many reasons why adult students choose to attend a two-year college. Studies have shown that the three most important criteria that adult students consider when choosing a college are location, cost, and availability of the major or program desired. Most two-year colleges are public institutions that serve a geographic district, making them readily accessible to the community. Costs at most two-year colleges are far less than at other types of higher education institutions. For many students who plan to pursue a bachelor's degree, completing their first two years of college at a community college is an affordable means to that end. If you are interested in an academic program that will transfer to a four-year institution, most two-year colleges offer the "general education" courses that compose most freshman and sophomore years. If you are interested in a vocational or technical program, two-year colleges excel in providing this type of training.

SETTING THE STAGE

There are three different "stages" in the process of adults returning to school. The first stage is uncertainty. Do I really want to go back to school? What will my friends or family think? Can I compete with those 18-year-old whiz kids? Am I too old? The second stage is choice. Once the decision to return has been made, you must choose where you will attend. There are many criteria to use in making this decision. The third stage is support. You have just added another role to your already-too-busy life. There are, however, strategies that will help you accomplish your goals—perhaps not without struggle, but with grace and humor nonetheless. Let's look at each of these stages.

UNCERTAINTY

Why are you thinking about returning to school? Is it to

- fulfill a dream that had to be delayed?
- become more educationally well-rounded?
- fill an intellectual void in your life?

These reasons focus on personal growth.

If you are returning to school to

- meet people and make friends
- attain and enjoy higher social status and prestige among friends, relatives, and associates
- understand/study a cultural heritage
- have a medium in which to exchange ideas

You are interested in social and cultural opportunities.

If you are like most adult students, you want to

- qualify for a new occupation
- enter or reenter the job market
- increase earnings potential
- qualify for a more challenging position in the same field of work

You are seeking career growth.

Understanding the reasons why you want to go back to school is an important step in setting your educational goals and will help you to establish some criteria for selecting a college. However, don't delay your decision because you have not been able to clearly define your motives. Many times, these aren't clear until you have already begun the process, and they may change as you move through your college experience.

Assuming you agree that additional education will benefit you, what is it that keeps you from returning to school? You may have a litany of excuses running through your mind:

- I don't have time.
- I can't afford it.
- I'm too old to learn.
- My friends will think I'm crazy.

- I'll be older than the teachers and other students.
- My family can't survive without me to take care of them every minute.
- I'll be X years old when I finish.
- I'm afraid.
- I don't know what to expect.

And that is just what these are—excuses. You can make school, like anything else in your life, a priority or not. If you really want to return, you can. The more you understand your motivation for returning to school and the more you understand what excuses are keeping you from taking action, the easier your task will be.

If you think you don't have time: The best way to decide how attending class and studying can fit into your schedule is to keep track of what you do with your time each day for several weeks. Completing a standard time-management grid (each day is plotted out by the half hour) is helpful for visualizing how your time is spent. For each 3-credit-hour class you take, you will need to find 3 hours for class plus 6 to 9 hours for reading-studying-library time. This study time should be spaced evenly throughout the week, not loaded up on one day. It is not possible to learn or retain the material that way. When you examine your grid, see where there are activities that could be replaced with school and study time. You may decide to give up your bowling league or some time in front of the TV. Try not to give up sleeping, and don't cut out every moment of free time. Here are some suggestions that have come from adults who have returned to school:

- Enroll in a time-management workshop. It helps you rethink how you use your time.
- Don't think you have to take more than one course at a time. You may eventually want to work up to taking more, but consider starting with one. (It is more than you are taking now!)
- If you have a family, start assigning to them those household chores that you usually do—and don't redo what they do.
- Use your lunch hour or commuting time for reading.

If you think you cannot afford it: As mentioned earlier, two-year colleges are extremely affordable. If you cannot afford the tuition, look into the various financial aid options. Most federal and state funds are available to full- and part-time students. Loans are also available. While many people prefer not to accumulate a debt for school, these same people will think nothing of taking out a loan to buy a car. After five or six years, which is the better investment? Adult students who work should look into whether their company has a tuition-reimbursement policy. There are also private scholarships, available through foundations, service organizations, and clubs, that are focused on adult learners. Your public library, the Web, and a college financial aid adviser are three excellent sources for reference materials regarding financial aid.

If you think you are too old to learn: This is pure myth. A number of studies have shown that adult learners perform as well as, or better than, traditional-age students.

If you are afraid your friends will think you're crazy: Who cares? Maybe they will, maybe they won't. Usually, they will admire your courage and be just a little jealous of your ambition (although they'll never tell you that). Follow your dreams, not theirs.

If you are concerned because the teachers or students will be younger than you: Don't be. The age differences that may be apparent in other settings evaporate in the classroom. If anything, an adult in the classroom strikes fear into the hearts of some 18-year-olds because adults have been known to be prepared, ask questions, be truly motivated, and be there to learn!

If you think your family will have a difficult time surviving while you are in school: If you have done everything for them up to now, they might struggle. Consider this an opportunity to help them become independent and self-sufficient. Your family can only make you feel guilty if you let them. You are not abandoning them; you are becoming an educational role model. When you are happy and working toward your goals, everyone benefits. Admittedly, it sometimes takes time for them to realize this. For single parents, there are schools that offer support groups, child care, and cooperative babysitting.

If you're appalled at the thought of being X years old when you graduate in Y years: How old will you be in Y years if you don't go back to school?

If you are afraid or don't know what to expect: Know that these are natural feelings when one encounters any new situation. Adult students find that their fears usually dissipate once they begin classes. Fear of trying is usually the biggest roadblock to the reentry process.

No doubt you have dreamed up a few more reasons for not making the decision to return to school. Keep in mind that what you are doing is making up excuses, and you are using these excuses to release you from the obligation to make a decision about your life. The thought of returning to college can be scary. Anytime anyone ventures into unknown territory, there is a risk, but taking risks is a necessary component of personal and professional growth. It is your life, and you alone are responsible for making the decisions that determine its course. Education is an investment in your future.

CHOICE

Once you have decided to go back to school, your next task is to decide where to go. If your educational goals are well defined (e.g., you want to pursue a degree in order to change careers), then your task is a bit easier. But even if your educational goals are still evolving, do not defer your return. Many students who enter higher education with a specific major in mind change that major at least once.

Most students who attend a public two-year college choose the community college in the district in which they live. This is generally the closest and least expensive option if the school offers the programs you want. If you are planning to begin your education at a two-year college and then transfer to a four-year school, there are distinct advantages to choosing your four-year school early. Many community and four-year colleges have "articulation" agreements that designate what credits from the two-year school will transfer to the four-year college and how. Some four-year institutions accept an associate degree as equivalent to the freshman and sophomore years, regardless of the courses you have taken. Some four-year schools accept two-year college work only on a course-by-course basis. If you can identify which school you will transfer to, you can know in advance exactly how your two-year credits will apply, preventing an unexpected loss of credit or time.

Each institution of higher education is distinctive. Your goal in choosing a college is to come up with the best student-institution fit—matching your needs with the offerings and characteristics of the school. The first step in choosing a college is to determine what criteria are most important to you in attaining your educational goals. Location, cost, and program availability are the three main factors that influence an adult student's college choice. In considering location, don't forget that some colleges have conveniently located branch campuses. In considering cost, remember to explore your financial aid options before ruling out an institution because of its tuition. Program availability should include not only the major in which you are interested, but also whether or not classes in that major are available when you can take them.

Some additional considerations beyond location, cost, and programs are:

- Does the school have a commitment to adult students and offer appropriate services, such as child care, tutoring, and advising?
- Are classes offered at times when you can take them?
- Are there academic options for adults, such as credit for life or work experience, credit by examination (including CLEP), credit for military service, or accelerated programs?
- Is the faculty sensitive to the needs of adult learners?

Once you determine which criteria are vital in your choice of an institution, you can begin to narrow your choices. There are myriad ways for you to locate the information you desire. Many newspapers publish a "School Guide" several times a year in which colleges and universities advertise to an adult student market. In addition, schools themselves publish catalogs, class schedules, and promotional materials that contain much of the information you need, and they are yours for the asking. Many colleges sponsor information sessions and open houses that allow you to visit the campus and ask questions. An appointment with an adviser is a good way to assess the fit

between you and the institution. Be sure to bring your questions with you to your interview.

SUPPORT

Once you have made the decision to return to school and have chosen the institution that best meets your needs, take some additional steps to ensure your success during your crucial first semester. Take advantage of institutional support and build some social support systems of your own. Here are some ways of doing just that:

- Plan to participate in any orientation programs. These serve the threefold purpose of providing you with a great deal of important information, familiarizing you with the campus and its facilities, and giving you the opportunity to meet and begin networking with other students.
- Take steps to deal with any academic weaknesses. Take mathematics and writing placement tests if you have reason to believe you may need some extra help in these areas. It is not uncommon for adult students to need a math refresher course or a program to help alleviate math anxiety. Ignoring a weakness won't make it go away.
- Look into adult reentry programs. Many institutions offer adults workshops focusing on ways to improve study skills, textbook reading, test-taking, and time-management skills.
- Build new support networks by joining an adult student organization, making a point of meeting other adult students through workshops, or actively seeking out a "study buddy" in each class—that invaluable friend who shares and understands your experience.
- Incorporate your new status as "student" into your family life. Doing your homework with your children at a designated "homework time" is a valuable family activity and reinforces the importance of education.
- Make sure you take a reasonable course load in your first semester. It is far better to have some extra time on your hands and to succeed magnificently than to spend the entire semester on the brink of a breakdown. Also, whenever possible, try to focus your first courses not only on requirements, but also on areas of personal interest.
- Faculty members, advisers, and student affairs personnel are there to help you during difficult times—let them assist you as often as necessary.

After completing your first semester, you will probably look back in wonder at why you thought going back to school was so imposing. Certainly, it's not without its occasional exasperations. But, as with life, keeping things in perspective and maintaining your sense of humor make the difference between just coping and succeeding brilliantly.

Coming to America: Tips for International Students Considering Study in the U.S.

Introduction: Why Study in the United States?

Are you thinking about going to a college or university in the United States? If you're looking at this book, you probably are! All around the world, students like you, pursuing higher education, are considering that possibility. They envision themselves on modern, high-tech campuses in well-known cities, surrounded by American students, taking classes and having fun. A degree from a U.S. school would certainly lead to success and fortune, either back in your home country or perhaps even in the United States, wouldn't it?

It can be done—but becoming a student at a college or university in the U.S. requires academic talent, planning, time, effort, and money. While there may be only a small number of institutions of higher learning in your country, there are more than 2,900 four-year colleges and universities in the United States. Choosing one, being accepted, and then traveling and becoming a student in America is a big undertaking.

If this is your dream, here is some helpful information and expert tips from professionals who work with international students at colleges and universities throughout the United States.

Timing and Planning

The journey to a college or university in the U.S. often starts years in advance. Most international students choose to study in the U.S. because of the high quality of academics. Your family may also have a lot of input on this decision, too.

"We always tell students they should be looking in the sophomore year, visiting in the junior year, and applying in the senior year," says Father Francis E. Chambers, OSA, D.Min., Associate Director of International Admission at Villanova University. He stresses that prospective students need to be taking challenging courses in the years leading up to college. "We want to see academic rigor. Most admission decisions are based on the first six semesters—senior year is too late."

Heidi Gregori-Gahan, Assistant Provost for International Programs at the University of Southern Indiana agrees that it's important to start early. "Plan ahead and do your homework. There is so much to choose from—so many schools, programs, degrees, and experiences. It can be overwhelming."

While students in some countries may pay an agent to help them get into a school in the United States, Gregori-Gahan

often directs potential international students to EducationUSA (http://educationusa.state.gov), a U.S. State Department network of over 400 international student advising centers in more than 170 countries. "They are there to provide unbiased information about studying in the United States and help you understand the process and what you need to do."

Two to three years of advance planning is also recommended by Daphne Durham, who has been an international student adviser at Harvard, Suffolk University, Valdosta State University, and the University of Georgia. She points out that the academic schedule in other countries is often different than that of the United States, so you need to synchronize your calendar accordingly.

You will have to take several tests in order to gain admission to a U.S. school, so it's important to know when those tests are given in your country, then register and take them so your scores will be available when you apply. Even if you have taken English in school, you will probably have to take The Test of English as a Foreign Language (TOEFL®), but some schools also accept the International English Language Testing Sytem (IELTS). You will probably also have to take the SAT® or ACT® tests, which are achievement or aptitude tests, and are usually required of all students applying for admission, not just international students.

"Make sure you understand how the international admissions process works at the school or schools you want to attend," says Durham. "What test scores are needed and when? Does the school have a fixed calendar or rolling admissions?" Those are just some of the many factors that can impact your application and could make a difference in when you are able to start school.

"Every university is unique in what's required and what they need to do. Even navigating each school's different website can be challenging," explains Gregori-Gahan.

Searching for Schools

This book contains information on thousands of four-year colleges and universities, and it will be a valuable resource for you in your search and application process. But with so many options, how do you decide which school you should attend?

"Where I find a big difference with international students is if their parents don't recognize the school, they don't apply to the school," says Fr. Chambers. "They could be overlooking a lot of great schools. They have to look outside the box."

The school Gregori-Gahan represents is in Evansville, Indiana, and it probably isn't familiar to students abroad. "Not many people have heard of anything beyond New York and California and maybe Florida. I like to tell students that this is 'real America.' But happy international students on our campus have recruited others to come here."

She points out that Internet technology has made a huge difference in the search process for international students. Websites full of information, live chat, webinars, virtual tours, and admission interviews via Skype have made it easier for potential students to connect with U.S. institutions, get more information, and be better able to visualize the campus.

One thing than will help narrow your search for a school is knowing specifically what you want to study. You need to know what the course of study is called in the United States, what it means, and what is required in order to study that subject. You also need to consider your future plans. What are your goals and objectives? What do you plan to do after earning your degree?

"If you're going to overcome the hurdles and get to a U.S. school, you have to have a directed path chosen," says Durham.

The other thing that could help your search process is finding a school that is a good fit.

Fit Is Important

You want your clothing and shoes to fit you properly and be comfortable, so a place where you will spend four or more years of your life studying should also be comfortable and appropriate for you. So how can you determine if a particular school is a good fit?

"We really recommend international students visit first. Yes, there are websites and virtual tours, but there's still nothing that beats an in-person visit," says Fr. Chambers. He estimates that 50 to 60 percent of Villanova's international students visited the campus before enrolling.

"It can be hard to get a sense of a place—you're so far away and you're probably not going to set foot on campus until you arrive," says Gregori-Gahan. "There is a high potential for culture shock."

You need to ask yourself what is important to you in a campus environment, then do some homework to ensure that the schools you are considering meet those needs. Here are some things to consider when it comes to fit:

- **Location:** Is it important for you to be in a well-known city or is it a part of the United States that is unfamiliar a possibility? "Look at geographic areas, but also cost of living," recommends Durham. "Be sure to factor in transportation costs also, especially if you plan to return to your home country regularly."
- **Student population:** Some small schools have just 1,000 students while larger ones may have 30,000 students or more.
- **Familiar faces:** Is it important for you to be at a school with others from your home nation or region?

- **Climate:** Some students want a climate similar to where they live now, but others are open and curious about seasons and weather conditions they may not have ever experienced. "We do have four seasons here," says Gregori-Gahan. "Sometimes students who come here from tropical regions are concerned about the winters. The first snow is so exciting, but after that, students may not be aware of how cold it really is."
- **Amenities:** Do you want to find your own housing or choose a school where the majority of students live on campus? Is there public transportation available or is it necessary to walk or have a bicycle or car? Does the school or community have access to things that are important to you culturally and meet the traditions you want to follow?
- **Campus size:** Some campuses are tightly compacted into a few city blocks, but others cover hundreds of acres of land. "International students are amazed by how green and spacious our campus is, with blooming flowers, trees, and lots of grass," says Gregori-Gahan.
- **Academic offerings:** Does this school offer the program you want to study? Can you complete it in four years or perhaps sooner? What sort of internship and career services are available?
- **Finances:** Can you afford to attend this school? Is there any sort of financial assistance available for international students?
- **Support services:** Durham suggests students look carefully at each school's offerings for international students. "Does the school have online guidance for getting your visa? Is ESL tutoring available? Does the school offer host family or community friend programs?" She also suggests you look for campus support groups for students from your country or region.

Looking at the listings and reading the in-depth descriptions in this book can help you search for a school that is a good fit for you.

Government Requirements

The one thing that every international student must have in order to study in the United States is a student visa. Having accurate advice and following all the necessary steps regarding the visa process is essential to being able to enter this country and start school.

As you schedule your tests and application deadlines, you must also consider how long it will take to get your visa. This varies depending on where you live; in some countries, extensive background checks are required. The subject you plan to study can also impact your visa status; it does help to have a major rather than be undeclared. The U.S. State Department website, http://travel.state.gov/content/visas/english/study-exchange.html, can give you an idea of how long it will take.

In addition to the visa, you will also need a Form I-20, which is a U.S. government immigration form. You must have that form when you get to the United States.

"It's very different from being a tourist. You need to be prepared to meet with an immigration officer and be interviewed about your college," explains Durham. "Where you are going, why you are going, where the school is located, what you are studying, and so on."

You also need to keep in mind that there are reporting requirements once you are a student in the U.S. Every semester, your adviser has to report to the government to confirm that you are enrolled in and attending school in order for you to stay in the United States.

Finances

Part of the visa process includes having the funds to pay for the cost of your schooling and support yourself. Finances are a huge hurdle in the process of becoming a college student in the United States.

"It's crucial. So many foreign systems offer 'free' higher education to students. How is your family going to handle the ongoing expense of attending college for four years or longer in the United States?" Durham reiterates that planning ahead is key because there are so many details. Student loans require a U.S.-based cosigner. Each school has its own financial aid deadlines. You have to factor in your own government's requirements, such currency exchange and fund transfers.

The notion that abundant funds are available to assist international students is not true. Sometimes state schools may offer diversity waivers or there may be special scholarship opportunities for international students. But attending school in the U.S. is still a costly venture.

"We do offer financial aid to international students, but they still have to be able to handle a large portion of the costs. Full-need scholarships are not likely," explained Fr. Chambers. "Sometimes students think that once they get here, it will all work out and the funds will be there. But the scenario for the first year has to be repeated each year they are on campus.

Once You Arrive…

You've taken your tests, researched schools, found a good fit, applied, got accepted, arranged the financing, gotten your visa and I-20, and made it to the campus in the United States. Now what?

You can expect the school where you have enrolled to be welcoming and helpful, but within reason. If you arrive on a weekend, or at a time outside of the time when international students are scheduled to arrive, the assistance you need may not be available to you.

Every school offers different levels of assistance to international students. For instance, Villanova offers a full-service office that can assist students with everything from visas, to employment, to finding a place for students to stay over breaks.

Fr. Chambers attends the international student orientation session to greet the students he's worked with through the recruitment and application process. "But I rarely see an international student after that. I think that bodes well for them being integrated into the entire university."

"Those of us who work with international students are really working to help them adjust," says Gregori-Gahan. "International students get here well before school starts so they can get over jet lag. We have orientation sessions and pair them with peer advisers who help them navigate the first few days, and we assure them that we are there for them."

Students should be open to their new setting, but they should be prepared that things may not be at all how they had envisioned during their planning and searching process. "While you may think you'll meet lots of Americans, don't underestimate the importance of community with your traditional home culture and people," says Durham.

Don't Make These Mistakes

The journey to college attendance in the United States is a long one, with many steps. The experts warn about mistakes to avoid along the way.

"Not reading through everything thoroughly and not understanding what the program of study really is and what will it cost. You have to be really clear on the important details," says Gregori-Gahan.

"Every school does things differently," cautions Fr. Chambers. "International students must be aware of that as they are applying."

Durham stresses that going to school in the United States is too big a decision to leave to someone else. "Students need to know about their school—they have to be in charge of their application."

"It involves a lot of work to be successful and happy and not surprised by too many things," Gregori-Gahan says.

Hopefully now, you are more informed and better prepared to pursue your dream of studying at a college or university in the United States.

Community Colleges and the Green Economy

Community colleges are a focal point for state and national efforts to create a green economy and workforce. As the United States transforms its economy into a "green" one, community colleges are leading the way—filling the need for both educated technicians whose skills can cross industry lines as well as those technicians who are able to learn new skills as technologies evolve.

President Obama extolled community colleges as "the unsung heroes of America's education system," essential to our country's success in the "global competition to lead in the growth of industries of the twenty-first century." With the support of state governments, and, more importantly, local and international business partners, America's community colleges are rising to meet the demands of the new green economy. Community colleges are training individuals to work in fields such as renewable energy, energy efficiency, wind energy, green building, and sustainability. The programs are as diverse as the campuses housing them.

Here is a quick look at just some of the exciting "green" programs available at community colleges throughout the United States.

At Mesalands Community College in Tucumcari, New Mexico, the North American Wind Research and Training Center provides state-of-the-art facilities for research and training qualified technicians in wind energy technology to help meet the need for an estimated 170,000 new positions in the industry by 2030. The Center includes a facility for applied research in collaboration with Sandia National Laboratories—the first-ever such partnership between a national laboratory and a community college. It also provides associate degree training for wind energy technicians, meeting the fast-growing demand for "windsmiths" in the western part of the country—jobs that pay $45,000–$60,000 per year. For more information, visit http://www.mesalands.edu.

Cape Cod Community College (CCCC) in Massachusetts has become one of the nation's leading colleges in promoting and integrating sustainability and green practices throughout all campus operations and technical training programs. Ten years ago, Cape Wind Associates, Cape Cod's first wind farm, provided $50,000 to jumpstart CCCC's wind technician program—considered a state model for community-based clean energy workforce development and education. In addition, hundreds of CCCC students have earned associate degrees in environmental technology and environmental studies, as well as certificate programs in coastal zone management, environmental site assessment, solar thermal technology, and more. Visit http://www.capecod.edu/web/natsci/env/programs for more information.

At Oakland Community College in Michigan, more than 350 students are enrolled in the college's Renewable Energies and Sustainable Living program and its related courses. Students gain field experience refurbishing public buildings with renewable materials, performing energy audits for the government, and working with small businesses and hospitals to reduce waste and pollution. To learn more, visit http://www.oaklandcc.edu/est/.

Portland Community College (PCC) in Portland, Oregon, offers associate degree and certificate options in Renewable Energy Systems (RES) training, preparing technicians for solar power, wind power, fuel cell, and other renewable energy fields. Students can earn an Associate in Applied Science (A.A.S.) degree or a One-Year Certificate in EET: Renewable Energy Systems. PCC's Microelectronic Technology Department offers an A.A.S. degree and a Certificate of Completion (COC) in Solar Voltaic Manufacturing Technology. The COC provides an orientation in solar manufacturing for those who have no prior education or experience in the field, which enables students to obtain entry-level jobs in this industry and eventually complete their A.A.S. degree.

Central Carolina Community College (CCCC) in Pittsboro, North Carolina, has been leading the way in "green" programs for more than a decade. It offered a sustainable agriculture class at its Chatham campus in 1996 and soon became the first community college in the nation to offer an Associate in Applied Science degree in sustainable agriculture and the first in North Carolina to offer an associate degree in biofuels. In addition, it was the first North Carolina community college to offer a North American Board of Certified Energy Practitioners (NABCEP)–approved solar PV panel installation course as part of its green building/renewable energy program. CCC also offers an associate degree in sustainable technology, a Natural Chef culinary arts program, an ecotourism certificate, and certificates in other green programs. For more information about Central Carolina Community College's green programs, visit http://www.cccc.edu/green.

At Metropolitan Community College in Omaha, Nebraska, the Continuing Education Department in partnership with Pro-Train is offering green/renewable energy/sustainability online training courses. The courses are designed to provide students with the workforce skills necessary for many in-demand green-collar occupations. Green/Renewable Energy courses include Building Energy Efficient Level, Fundamentals of Solar Hot Water Heating, Green Building Sales (or Technical)

Professional, and more. Sustainability Green Supply Chain Training courses include Alternative Energy Operations, Carbon Strategies, Green Building for Contractors, and Sustainability 101.

Visit www.theknowledgebase.org/metropolitan/.

At Cascadia Community College in Bothell, Washington, thanks to a grant from Puget Sound Energy (PSE), students in the Energy Informatics class designed a kiosk screen that shows the energy usage and solar generation at the local 21 Acres Center for Local Food and Sustainable Living. The PSE grant supports the classroom materials for renewable energy education and the Web-based monitoring software that allows students and interested community members to track how much energy is being generated as the weather changes. For more information, visit http://www.cascadia.edu/Default.aspx.

At Grand Rapids Community College, the federally funded Pathways to Prosperity program has successfully prepared low-income residents for jobs in fields such as renewable energy. More than 200 people have completed the program, which began in 2010 thanks to a $4-million grant from the Department of Labor, and found jobs in industries ranging from energy-efficient building construction to alternative energy and sustainable manufacturing. For additional information, check out http://cms.grcc.edu/workforce-training/pathways-prosperity.

Established in 2008, the Green Institute at Heartland Community College in Normal, Illinois, supports a wide range of campus initiatives, educational programs, and community activities that are related to sustainability, energy conservation, renewable energy, recycling, retro-commissioning, and other environmental technologies. For more information, visit http://www.heartland.edu/greenInstitute/.

Most of California's 112 community colleges offer some type of green-tech classes. These include photovoltaic panel installation and repair, green construction practices, and biotechnology courses leading to careers in agriculture, medicine, and environmental forensics. Visit http://www.californiacommunitycolleges.cccco.edu/ProgramstoWatch/MoreProgramstoWatch/GreenTechnology.aspx.

Linn-Benton Community College (LBCC) in Albany, Oregon, is now offering training for the Oregon Green Technology Certificate. Oregon Green Tech is a federally funded program that is designed to prepare entry-level workers with foundational skills for a variety of industries associated with or in support of green jobs. Students learn skills in green occupations that include green energy production; manufacturing, construction, installation, monitoring, and repair of equipment for solar, wind, wave, and bio-energy; building retro-fitting; process recycling; hazardous materials removal work; and more. LBCC is one of ten Oregon community colleges to provide training for the Green Technology Certificate, offered through the Oregon Consortium and Oregon Workforce Alliance. Visit http://www.linnbenton.edu for additional information.

The Santa Fe Community College Sustainable Technology Center in New Mexico offers several green jobs training programs along with various noncredit courses. It also provides credit programs from certificates in green building systems, environmental technology training, and solar energy training as well as an Associate in Applied Science (A.A.S.) degree in environmental technology. For more information, go online to http://www.sfcc.edu/sustainable_technologies_center.

In Colorado, Red Rocks Community College (RRCC) offers degree and certificate programs in renewable energy (solar photovoltaic, solar thermal, and wind energy technology), energy and industrial maintenance, energy operations and process technology, environmental technology, water quality management, and energy audit. RRCC has made a commitment to the national challenge of creating and sustaining a green workforce and instructs students about the issues of energy, environmental stewardship, and renewable resources across the college curriculum. For more information, visit http://www.rrcc.edu/green/.

At GateWay Community College in Phoenix, Arizona, graduates of the Environmental Science program now work for the U.S. Geological Survey (USGS), the Arizona Department of Environmental Quality (ADEQ), the Occupational Safety and Health Administration (OSHA), and municipalities across the state and region, as well as private consultants and environmental organizations. For additional information, check out http://www.gatewaycc.edu/environment.

During the past 4.5 years, 17 Illinois community colleges and their partners have created 35 certificate and degree programs to prepare students for careers in green industry sectors. Over 185 courses were created and piloted, online and on-site, in communities across Illinois. The courses were created using open-source materials, with the intent to be shared with other colleges and universities through the Department of Labor's Trade Adjustment Assistance Community College and Career Training (TAACCCT) Grant Program repository.

Next you'll find two essays about other green community college programs. The first essay was written by the president of Lane Community College in Eugene, Oregon, about the role Lane and other community colleges are playing in creating a workforce for the green economy. Then, read a first-hand account of the new Wind Turbine Training Program at Kalamazoo Valley Community College in Kalamazoo, Michigan—a program that has more applicants than spaces and one whose students are being hired BEFORE they even graduate. It's clear that there are exciting "green" programs at community colleges throughout the United States.

The Role of Community Colleges in Creating a Workforce for the Green Economy

by Mary F.T. Spilde, President
Lane Community College

Community colleges are expected to play a leadership role in educating and training the workforce for the green economy.

Due to close connections with local and regional labor markets, colleges assure a steady supply of skilled workers by developing and adapting programs to respond to the needs of business and industry. Further, instead of waiting for employers to create job openings, many colleges are actively engaged in local economic development to help educate potential employers to grow their green business opportunities and to participate in the creation of the green economy.

As the green movement emerges there has been confusion about what constitutes a green job. It is now clear that many of the green jobs span several economic sectors such as renewable energy, construction, manufacturing, transportation and agriculture. It is predicted that there will be many middle skill jobs requiring more than a high school diploma but less than a bachelor's degree. This is precisely the unique role that community colleges play. Community colleges develop training programs, including pre-apprenticeship, that ladder the curriculum to take lower skilled workers through a relevant and sequenced course of study that provides a clear pathway to career track jobs. As noted in *Going Green: The Vital Role of Community Colleges in Building a Sustainable Future and Green Workforce* by the National Council for Workforce Education and the Academy for Educational Development, community colleges are strategically positioned to work with employers to redefine skills and competencies needed by the green workforce and to create the framework for new and expanded green career pathways.

While there will be new occupations such as solar and wind technologists, the majority of the jobs will be in the energy management sector—retrofitting the built environment. For example, President Obama called for retrofitting more than 75 percent of federal buildings and more than 2 million homes to make them more energy-efficient. The second major area for growth will be the "greening" of existing jobs as they evolve to incorporate green practices. Both will require new knowledge, skills and abilities. For community colleges, this means developing new programs that meet newly created industry standards and adapting existing programs and courses to integrate green skills. The key is to create a new talent pool of environmentally conscious, highly skilled workers.

These two areas show remarkable promise for education and training leading to high wage/high demand jobs:

- Efficiency and energy management: There is a need for auditors and energy efficiency experts to retrofit existing buildings. Consider how much built environment we have in this country, and it's not difficult to see that this is where the vast amount of jobs are now and will be in the future.
- Greening of existing jobs: There are few currently available jobs that environmental sustainability will not impact. Whether it is jobs in construction, such as plumbers, electricians, heating and cooling technicians, painters, and building supervisors, or chefs, farmers, custodians, architects, automotive technicians and interior designers, all will need to understand how to lessen their impact on the environment.

Lane Community College offers a variety of degree and certificate programs to prepare students to enter the energy efficiency fields. Lane has offered an Energy Management program since the late 1980s—before it was hip to be green! Students in this program learn to apply basic principles of physics and analysis techniques to the description and measurement of energy in today's building systems, with the goal of evaluating and recommending alternative energy solutions that will result in greater energy efficiency and energy cost savings. Students gain a working understanding of energy systems in today's built environment and the tools to analyze and quantify energy efficiency efforts. The program began with an emphasis in residential energy efficiency/solar energy systems and has evolved to include commercial energy efficiency and renewable energy system installation technology.

The Renewable Energy Technician program is offered as a second-year option within the Energy Management program. Course work prepares students for employment designing and installing solar electric and domestic hot water systems. Renewable Energy students, along with Energy Management students, take a first-year curriculum in commercial energy efficiency giving them a solid background that includes residential energy efficiency, HVAC systems, lighting, and physics and math. In the second year, Renewable Energy students diverge from the Energy Management curriculum and take course work that starts with two courses in electricity fundamentals and one course in energy economics. In the following terms, students learn to design, install, and develop a thorough understanding of photovoltaics and domestic hot water systems.

Recent additions to Lane's offerings are Sustainability Coordinator and Water Conservation Technician degrees. Both programs were added to meet workforce demand.

Lane graduates find employment in a wide variety of disciplines and may work as facility managers, energy auditors, energy program coordinators, or control system specialists, for such diverse employers as engineering firms, public and private utilities, energy equipment companies, and departments of energy and as sustainability leaders within public and private sector organizations.

Lane Community College also provides continuing education for working professionals. The Sustainable Building Advisor (SBA) Certificate Program is a nine-month, specialized training program for working professionals. Graduate are able to advise employers or clients on strategies and tools for implementing sustainable building practices. Benefits from participating in the SBA program often include saving long-term building operating costs; improving the environmental, social, and economic viability of the region; and reducing environmental impacts and owner liability—not to mention the chance to improve one's job skills in a rapidly growing field.

The Building Operators Certificate is a professional development program created by The Northwest Energy Efficiency

Council. It is offered through the Northwest Energy Education Institute at Lane. The certificate is designed for operations and maintenance staff working in public or private commercial buildings. It certifies individuals in energy and resource-efficient operation of building systems at two levels: Level I–Building System Maintenance and Level II–Equipment Troubleshooting and Maintenance.

Lane Community College constantly scans the environment to assess workforce needs and develop programs that provide highly skilled employees. Lane, like most colleges, publishes information in its catalog on workforce demand and wages so that students can make informed decisions about program choice.

Green jobs will be a large part of a healthy economy. Opportunities will abound for those who take advantage of programs with a proven record of connecting with employers and successfully educating students to meet high skills standards.

Establishing a World-Class Wind Turbine Technician Academy

by Thomas Sutton, Director of Wind Energy and Technical Services
Kalamazoo Valley Community College

When Kalamazoo Valley Community College (KVCC) decided it wanted to become involved in the training of utility-grade technicians for wind-energy jobs, early on the choice was made to avoid another "me too" training course.

Our program here in Southwest Michigan, 30 miles from Lake Michigan, had to meet industry needs and industry standards.

It was also obvious from the start that the utility-grade or large wind industry had not yet adopted any uniform training standards in the United States.

Of course, these would come, but why should the college wait when European standards were solidly established and working well in Germany, France, Denmark and Great Britain?

As a result, in 2009, KVCC launched its Wind Turbine Technician Academy, the first of its kind in the United States. The noncredit academy runs 8 hours a day, five days a week, for twenty-four weeks of intense training in electricity, mechanics, wind dynamics, safety, and climbing. The college developed this program rather quickly—in eight months—to fast-track individuals into this emerging field.

KVCC based its program on the training standards forged by the Bildungszentrum fur Erneuerebare Energien (BZEE)—the Renewable Energy Education Center. Located in Husum, Germany, the BZEE was created and supported by major wind-turbine manufacturers, component makers, and enterprises that provide operation and maintenance services.

As wind-energy production increased throughout Europe, the need for high-quality, industry-driven, international standards

emerged. The BZEE has become the leading trainer for wind-turbine technicians across Europe and now in Asia.

With the exception of one college in Canada, the standards were not yet available in North America. When Kalamazoo Valley realized it could be the first college or university in the United States to offer this training program—that was enough motivation to move forward.

For the College to become certified by the BZEE, it needed to hire and send an electrical instructor and a mechanical instructor to Germany for six weeks of "train the trainer." The instructors not only had to excel in their respective fields, they also needed to be able to climb the skyscraper towers supporting megawatt-class turbines—a unique combination of skills to possess. Truly, individuals who fit this job description don't walk through the door everyday—but we found them! Amazingly, we found a top mechanical instructor who was a part-time fireman and comfortable with tall ladder rescues and a skilled electrical instructor who used to teach rappelling off the Rockies to the Marine Corps.

In addition to employing new instructors, the College needed a working utility-grade nacelle that could fit in its training lab that would be located in the KVCC Michigan Technical Education Center. So one of the instructors traveled to Denmark and purchased a 300-kilowatt turbine.

Once their own training was behind them and the turbine was on its way from the North Sea, the instructors quickly turned to crafting the curriculum necessary for our graduates to earn both an academy certificate from KVCC and a certification from the BZEE.

Promoting the innovative program to qualified potential students across the country was the next step. News releases were published throughout Michigan, and they were also picked up on the Internet. Rather quickly, KVCC found itself with more than 500 requests for applications for a program built for 16 students.

Acceptance into the academy includes a medical release, a climbing test, reading and math tests, relevant work experience, and, finally, an interview. Students in the academy's pioneer class, which graduated in spring 2010, ranged in age from their late teens to early 50s. They hailed from throughout Michigan, Indiana, Ohio, and Illinois as well as from Puerto Rico and Great Britain.

The students brought with them degrees in marketing, law, business, science, and architecture, as well as entrepreneurial experiences in several businesses, knowledge of other languages, military service, extensive travel, and electrical, computer, artistic, and technical/mechanical skills.

Kalamazoo Valley's academy has provided some high-value work experiences for the students in the form of two collaborations with industry that has allowed them to maintain and/or repair actual utility-grade turbines, including those at the 2.5 megawatt size. This hands-on experience will add to the attractiveness of the graduates in the market place. Potential employers were recently invited to an open house where they could see the lab and meet members of this pioneer class.

The College's Turbine Technician Academy has also attracted a federal grant for $550,000 to expand its program through additional equipment purchases. The plan is to erect our own climbing tower. Climbing is a vital part of any valid program, and yet wind farms cannot afford to shut turbines down just for climb-training. The funds were put to use engineering, fabricating, and erecting a wind training tower that incorporated all of the necessary components to teach competency-based work at heights safety training.

When the students are asked what best distinguishes the Kalamazoo Valley program, their answers point to the experienced instructors and the working lab, which is constantly changing to offer the best training experiences. Students also consistently report that the hands-on field experience operating and maintaining the five large turbines during the course has set them apart at companies where they work.

Industry continues to tell us that community colleges need to offer fast-track training programs of this caliber if the nation is to reach the U.S. Department of Energy's goal of 20 percent renewable energy by 2030. This would require more than 1,500 new technicians each year.

The Wind Turbine Technician Academy continues the process improvements as directed by industry input. The academy not only holds the BZEE certification, it is also one of the few American Wind Energy Association (AWEA) Seal of Approval schools in the nation.

With that in mind, KVCC plans to host several BZEE orientation programs for other community colleges in order to encourage them to consider adopting the European training standards and start their own programs.

Meanwhile, applications are continuing to stream in from across the country for the next Wind Turbine Technician Academy program at Kalamazoo Valley Community College. For more information about the program, visit http://www.kvccgrovescenter.com/career/wtta.

How to Use This Guide

Peterson's *Two-Year Colleges 2017* contains a wealth of information for anyone interested in colleges offering associate degrees. This section details the criteria that institutions must meet to be included in this guide and provides information about research procedures used by Peterson's.

QUICK-REFERENCE CHART

The **Two-Year Colleges At-a-Glance Chart** is a geographically arranged table that lists colleges by name and city within the state, or country in which they are located. Areas listed include the United States, Canada, and other countries; the institutions are included because they are accredited by recognized U.S. accrediting bodies (see **Criteria for Inclusion** section).

The At-a-Glance chart contains basic information that enables you to compare institutions quickly according to broad characteristics such as degrees awarded, enrollment, application requirements, financial aid availability, and numbers of sports and majors offered. A dagger (†) after the institution's name indicates that an institution has an entry in the **Featured Two-Year Colleges** section.

Column 1: Degrees Awarded

C= *college transfer associate degree:* the degree awarded after a "university-parallel" program, equivalent to the first two years of a bachelor's degree.

T= *terminal associate degree:* the degree resulting from a one- to three-year program providing training for a specific occupation.

B= *bachelor's degree (baccalaureate):* the degree resulting from a liberal arts, science, professional, or preprofessional program normally lasting four years, although in some cases an accelerated program can be completed in three years.

M= *master's degree:* the first graduate (postbaccalaureate) degree in the liberal arts and sciences and certain professional fields, usually requiring one to two years of full-time study.

D= *doctoral degree* (research/scholarship, professional practice, or other)

Column 2: Institutional Control

Private institutions are designated as one of the following:

Ind = *independent* (nonprofit)

I-R = *independent-religious:* nonprofit; sponsored by or affiliated with a particular religious group or having a nondenominational or interdenominational religious orientation.

Prop = *proprietary* (profit-making)

Public institutions are designated by the source of funding, as follows:

Fed = *federal*

St = *state*

Comm = *commonwealth* (Puerto Rico)

Terr = *territory* (U.S. territories)

Cou = *county*

Dist = *district:* an administrative unit of public education, often having boundaries different from units of local government.

City = *city*

St-L = *state and local:* local may refer to county, district, or city.

St-R = *state-related:* funded primarily by the state but administratively autonomous.

Column 3: Student Body

M= *men only* (100% of student body)

PM = *coed, primarily men*

W= *women only* (100% of student body)

PW = *coed, primarily women*

M/W = *coeducational*

Column 4: Undergraduate Enrollment

The figure shown represents the number of full-time and part-time students enrolled in undergraduate degree programs as of fall 2016.

Columns 5–7: Enrollment Percentages

Figures are shown for the percentages of the fall 2016 undergraduate enrollment made up of students attending part-time (column 5) and students 25 years of age or older (column 6). Also listed is the percentage of students in the last graduating class who completed a college-transfer associate program and went directly on to four-year colleges (column 7).

For columns 8 through 15, the following letter codes are used: Y = yes; N = no; R = recommended; S = for some.

Columns 8–10: Admission Policies

The information in these columns shows whether the college has an open admission policy (column 8) whereby virtually all applicants are accepted without regard to standardized test scores, grade average, or class rank; whether a high school equivalency certificate is accepted in place of a high school diploma for admission consideration (column 9); and whether a high school transcript (column 10) is required as part of the application process. In column 10, the combination of the codes R and S indicates that a high school transcript is recommended for all applicants (R) or required for some (S).

Columns 11–12: Financial Aid

These columns show which colleges offer the following types of financial aid: need-based aid (column 11) and part-time jobs (column 12), including those offered through the federal government's Federal Work-Study program.

Columns 13–15: Services and Facilities

These columns show which colleges offer the following: career counseling (column 13) on either an individual or group basis, job placement services (column 14) for individual students, and college-owned or -operated housing facilities (column 16) for noncommuting students.

Column 16: Sports

This figure indicates the number of sports that a college offers at the intramural and/or intercollegiate levels.

Column 17: Majors

This figure indicates the number of major fields of study in which a college offers degree programs.

PROFILES OF TWO-YEAR COLLEGES AND SPECIAL MESSAGES

The **Profiles of Two-Year Colleges** contain basic data in capsule form for quick review and comparison. The following outline of the **Profile** format shows the section headings and the items that each section covers. Any item that does not apply to a particular college or for which no information was supplied is omitted from that college's **Profile.** Display ads, which appear near some of the institution's profiles, have been provided and paid for by those colleges that chose to supplement their profile with additional information. A star ★ next to the name of a school signifies that the school is one of the "Featured Two-Year Colleges," with a two-page in-depth description in that section of this guide and may also have an expanded profile on Peterson's website at www.petersons/com.

Bulleted Highlights

The bulleted highlights section features important information, for quick reference and comparison. The number of possible bulleted highlights that an ideal **Profile** would have if all questions were answered in a timely manner follow. However, not every institution provides all of the information necessary to fill out every bulleted line. In such instances, the line will not appear.

First Bullet

Institutional control: Private institutions are designated as independent (nonprofit), proprietary (profit-making), or independent, with a specific religious denomination or affiliation. Nondenominational or interdenominational religious orientation is possible and would be indicated.

Public institutions are designated by the source of funding. Designations include federal, state, province, commonwealth

(Puerto Rico), territory (U.S. territories), county, district (an administrative unit of public education, often having boundaries different from units of local government), city, state and local (local may refer to county, district, or city), or state-related (funded primarily by the state but administratively autonomous).

Religious affiliation is also noted here.

Institutional type: Each institution is classified as one of the following:

> **Primarily two-year college:** Awards baccalaureate degrees, but the vast majority of students are enrolled in two-year programs.

> **Four-year college:** Awards baccalaureate degrees; may also award associate degrees; does not award graduate (postbaccalaureate) degrees.

> **Upper-level institution:** Awards baccalaureate degrees, but entering students must have at least two years of previous college-level credit; may also offer graduate degrees.

> **Comprehensive institution:** Awards baccalaureate degrees; may also award associate degrees; offers graduate degree programs, primarily at the master's, specialist's, or professional level, although one or two doctoral programs may be offered.

> **University:** Offers four years of undergraduate work plus graduate degrees through the doctorate in more than two academic or professional fields.

Founding date: If the year an institution was chartered differs from the year when instruction actually began, the earlier date is given.

System or administrative affiliation: Any coordinate institutions or system affiliations are indicated. An institution that has separate colleges or campuses for men and women but shares facilities and courses is termed a coordinate institution. A formal administrative grouping of institutions, either private or public, of which the college is a part, or the name of a single institution with which the college is administratively affiliated, is a system.

Second Bullet

Setting: Schools are designated as urban (located within a major city), suburban (a residential area within commuting distance of a major city), small-town (a small but compactly settled area not within commuting distance of a major city), or rural (a remote and sparsely populated area). The phrase *easy access to...* indicates that the campus is within an hour's drive of the nearest major metropolitan area that has a population greater than 500,000.

Third Bullet

Endowment: The total dollar value of funds and/or property donated to the institution or the multicampus educational system of which the institution is a part.

Fourth Bullet

Student body: An institution is coed (coeducational—admits men and women), primarily (80 percent or more) women, primarily men, women only, or men only.

Undergraduate students: Represents the number of full-time and part-time students enrolled in undergraduate degree programs as of fall 2015. The percentage of full-time undergraduates and the percentages of men and women are given.

Category Overviews

Undergraduates

For fall 2016, the number of full- and part-time undergraduate students is listed. This list provides the number of states and U.S. territories, including the District of Columbia and Puerto Rico (or for Canadian institutions, provinces and territories), and other countries from which undergraduates come. Percentages of undergraduates who are part-time or full-time students; transfers in; live on campus; out-of-state; Black or African American, non-Hispanic/Latino; Hispanic/Latino; Asian, non-Hispanic/Latino; Native Hawaiian or other Pacific Islander, non-Hispanic/Latino; American Indian or Alaska Native, non-Hispanic/Latino are given.

Retention: The percentage of freshmen (or, for upper-level institutions, entering students) who returned the following year for the fall term.

Freshmen

Admission: Figures are given for the number of students who applied for fall 2016 admission, the number of those who were admitted, and the number who enrolled. Freshman statistics include the average high school GPA; the percentage of freshmen who took the SAT® and received critical reading, writing, and math scores above 500, above 600, and above 700; as well as the percentage of freshmen taking the ACT® who received a composite score of 18 or higher.

Faculty

Total: The total number of faculty members; the percentage of full-time faculty members as of fall 2016; and the percentage of full-time faculty members who hold doctoral/first professional/ terminal degrees.

Student-faculty ratio: The school's estimate of the ratio of matriculated undergraduate students to faculty members teaching undergraduate courses.

Majors

This section lists the major fields of study offered by the college.

Academics

Calendar: Most colleges indicate one of the following: 4-1-4, 4-4-1, or a similar arrangement (two terms of equal length plus an abbreviated winter or spring term, with the numbers referring to months); semesters; trimesters; quarters; 3-3 (three courses for each of three terms); modular (the academic year is divided into small blocks of time; courses of varying lengths are assembled according to individual programs); or standard year (for most Canadian institutions).

Degrees: This names the full range of levels of certificates, diplomas, and degrees, including prebaccalaureate, graduate, and professional, that are offered by this institution:

Associate degree: Normally requires at least two but fewer than four years of full-time college work or its equivalent.

Bachelor's degree (baccalaureate): Requires at least four years but not more than five years of full-time college-level work or its equivalent. This includes all bachelor's degrees in which the normal four years of work are completed in three years and bachelor's degrees conferred in a five-year cooperative (work-study plan) program. A cooperative plan provides for alternate class attendance and employment in business, industry, or government. This allows students to combine actual work experience with their college studies.

Master's degree: Requires the successful completion of a program of study of at least the full-time equivalent of one but not more than two years of work beyond the bachelor's degree.

Doctoral degree (doctorate; research/scholarship, professional, or other): The highest degree in graduate study. The doctoral degree classification includes Doctor of Education, Doctor of Juridical Science, Doctor of Public Health, Doctor of Philosophy, Doctor of Podiatry, Doctor of Veterinary Medicine, and many more.

Post-master's certificate: Requires completion of an organized program of study of 24 credit hours beyond the master's degree but does not meet the requirements of academic degrees at the doctoral level.

Special study options: Details are next given here on study options available at each college:

Accelerated degree program: Students may earn a bachelor's degree in three academic years.

Academic remediation for entering students: Instructional courses designed for students deficient in the general competencies necessary for a regular postsecondary curriculum and educational setting.

Adult/continuing education programs: Courses offered for nontraditional students who are currently working or are returning to formal education.

Advanced placement: Credit toward a degree awarded for acceptable scores on College Board Advanced Placement (AP®) tests.

Cooperative (co-op) education programs: Formal arrangements with off-campus employers allowing students to combine work and study in order to gain degree-related experience, usually extending the time required to complete a degree.

Distance learning: For-credit courses that can be accessed off-campus via cable television, the Internet, satellite, DVD, correspondence course, or other media.

Double major: A program of study in which a student concurrently completes the requirements of two majors.

English as a second language (ESL): A course of study designed specifically for students whose native language is not English.

External degree programs: A program of study in which students earn credits toward a degree through a combination of independent study, college courses, proficiency examinations, and personal experience. External degree programs require minimal or no classroom attendance.

Freshmen honors college: A separate academic program for talented freshmen.

Honors programs: Any special program for very able students offering the opportunity for educational enrichment, independent study, acceleration, or some combination of these.

Independent study: Academic work, usually undertaken outside the regular classroom structure, chosen or designed by the student with departmental approval and instructor supervision.

Internships: Any short-term, supervised work experience usually related to a student's major field, for which the student earns academic credit. The work can be full-or part-time, on or off-campus, paid or unpaid.

Off-campus study: A formal arrangement with one or more domestic institutions under which students may take courses at the other institution(s) for credit.

Part-time degree program: Students may earn a degree through part-time enrollment in regular session (daytime) classes or evening, weekend, or summer classes.

Self-designed major: Program of study based on individual interests, designed by the student with the assistance of an adviser.

Services for LD students: Special help for learning-disabled students with resolvable difficulties, such as dyslexia.

Study abroad: An arrangement by which a student completes part of the academic program studying in another country. A college may operate a campus abroad or it may have a cooperative agreement with other U.S. institutions or institutions in other countries.

Summer session for credit: Summer courses through which students may make up degree work or accelerate their program.

Tutorials: Undergraduates can arrange for special in-depth academic assignments (not for remediation) working with faculty members one-on-one or in small groups.

ROTC: Army, Naval, or Air Force Reserve Officers' Training Corps programs offered either on campus, at a branch campus [designated by a (b)], or at a cooperating host institution [designated by (c)].

Unusual degree programs: Nontraditional programs such as a 3-2 degree program, in which three years of liberal arts study is followed by two years of study in a professional field at another institution (or in a professional division of the same institution), resulting in two bachelor's degrees or a bachelor's and a master's degree.

Library

The name of the college's main library, plus the number of other libraries on campus will appear followed by: *Books:* number of physical and digital/electronic books; *Serial titles:* number of physical and digital/electronic serial titles; and the number of *Databases*. Also included here (if provided by the school) are the number of "Weekly public service hours" and study area information—the number of hours and days of the week open and if students can reserve study rooms.

Student Life

Housing options: The institution's policy about whether students are permitted to live off-campus or are required to live on campus for a specified period; whether freshmen-only, coed, single-sex, cooperative, and disabled student housing options are available; whether campus housing is leased by the school and/or provided by a third party; whether freshman applicants are given priority for college housing. The phrase *college housing not available* indicates that no college-owned or -operated housing facilities are provided for undergraduates and that noncommuting students must arrange for their own accommodations.

Activities and organizations: Lists information on drama-theater groups, choral groups, marching bands, student-run campus newspapers, student-run radio stations, and social organizations (sororities, fraternities, eating clubs, etc.) and how many are represented on campus.

Campus security: Campus safety measures including 24-hour emergency response devices (telephones and alarms) and patrols by trained security personnel, student patrols, late-night transport-escort service, and controlled dormitory access (key, security card, etc.).

Student services: Information provided indicates services offered to students by the college, such as legal services, health clinics, personal-psychological counseling, and women's centers.

Athletics

Membership in one or more of the following athletic associations is indicated by initials.

NCAA: National Collegiate Athletic Association

NAIA: National Association of Intercollegiate Athletics

NCCAA: National Christian College Athletic Association

NJCAA: National Junior College Athletic Association

USCAA: United States Collegiate Athletic Association

CIS: Canadian Interuniversity Sports

The overall NCAA division in which all or most intercollegiate teams compete is designated by a roman numeral I, II, or III. All teams that do not compete in this division are listed as exceptions.

Sports offered by the college are divided into two groups: intercollegiate (**M** or **W** following the name of each sport indicates that it is offered for men or women or **M/W** if the sport is offered for both men and women) and intramural. An **s** in parentheses following an **M, W or M/W** for an intercollegiate sport indicates that athletic scholarships (or grants-in-aid) are offered for men and/or women in that sport, and a c indicates a club team as opposed to a varsity team.

Standardized Tests

The most commonly required standardized tests are the ACT®, SAT®, and SAT Subject Tests™. These and other standardized tests may be used for selective admission, as a basis for counseling or course placement, or for both purposes. This section notes if a test is used for admission or placement and whether it is required, required for some, or recommended.

In addition to the ACT and SAT, the following standardized entrance and placement examinations are referred to by their initials:

ABLE: Adult Basic Learning Examination

ACT ASSET: ACT Assessment of Skills for Successful Entry and Transfer

ACT PEP: ACT Proficiency Examination Program

CAT: California Achievement Tests

CELT: Comprehensive English Language Test

CPAt: Career Programs Assessment

CPT: Computerized Placement Test

DAT: Differential Aptitude Test

LSAT: Law School Admission Test

MAPS: Multiple Assessment Program Service

MCAT: Medical College Admission Test

MMPI: Minnesota Multiphasic Personality Inventory

OAT: Optometry Admission Test

PAA: Prueba de Aptitud Académica (Spanish-language version of the SAT)

PCAT: Pharmacy College Admission Test

PSAT/NMSQT: Preliminary SAT National Merit Scholarship Qualifying Test

SCAT: Scholastic College Aptitude Test

SRA: Scientific Research Association (administers verbal, arithmetical, and achievement tests)

TABE: Test of Adult Basic Education

TASP: Texas Academic Skills Program

TOEFL: Test of English as a Foreign Language (for international students whose native language is not English)

WPCT: Washington Pre-College Test

Costs

Costs are given for the 2017–18 academic year or for the 2016–17 academic year if 2017–18 figures were not yet available. Annual expenses may be expressed as a comprehensive fee (including full-time tuition, mandatory fees, and college room and board) or as separate figures for full-time tuition, fees, room and board, or room only. For public institutions where tuition differs according to residence, separate figures are given for area or state residents and for nonresidents. Part-time tuition is expressed in terms of a per-unit rate (per credit, per semester hour, etc.) as specified by the institution.

The tuition structure at some institutions is complex in that freshmen and sophomores may be charged a different rate from that for juniors and seniors, a professional or vocational division may have a different fee structure from the liberal arts division of the same institution, or part-time tuition may be prorated on a sliding scale according to the number of credit hours taken. Tuition and fees may vary according to academic program, campus/location, class time (day, evening, weekend), course/credit load, course level, degree level, reciprocity agreements, and student level. Room and board charges are reported as an average for one academic year and may vary according to the board plan selected, campus/location, type of housing facility, or student level. If no college-owned or college-operated housing facilities are offered, the phrase *college housing not available* will appear in the Housing section of the Student Life paragraph.

Tuition payment plans that may be offered to undergraduates include tuition prepayment, installment payments, and deferred payment. A tuition prepayment plan gives a student the option of locking in the current tuition rate for the entire term of enrollment by paying the full amount in advance rather than year by year. Colleges that offer such a prepayment plan may also help the student to arrange financing.

The availability of full or partial undergraduate tuition waivers to minority students, children of alumni, employees or their children, adult students, and senior citizens may be listed.

Financial Aid

The number of Federal Work Study and/or part-time jobs and average earnings are listed. Financial aid deadlines are given as well.

Applying

Application and admission options include the following:

Early admission: Highly qualified students may matriculate before graduating from high school.

Early action plan: An admission plan that allows students to apply and be notified of an admission decision well in advance of the regular notification dates. If accepted, the candidate is not committed to enroll; students may reply to the offer under the college's regular reply policy.

Early decision plan: A plan that permits students to apply and be notified of an admission decision (and financial aid offer, if applicable) well in advance of the regular notification date. Applicants agree to accept an offer of admission and to withdraw their applications from other colleges. Candidates who are not accepted under early decision are automatically considered with the regular applicant pool, without prejudice.

Deferred entrance: The practice of permitting accepted students to postpone enrollment, usually for a period of one academic term or year.

Application fee: The fee required with an application is noted. This is typically nonrefundable, although under certain specified conditions it may be waived or returned.

Requirements: Other application requirements are grouped into three categories: required for all, required for some, and recommended. They may include an essay, standardized test scores, a high school transcript, a minimum high school grade point average (expressed as a number on a scale of 0 to 4.0, where 4.0 equals A, 3.0 equals B, etc.), letters of recommendation, an interview on campus or with local alumni, and, for certain types of schools or programs, special requirements such as a musical audition or an art portfolio.

Application deadlines and notification dates: Admission application deadlines and dates for notification of acceptance or rejection are given either as specific dates or as **rolling** and **continuous.** Rolling means that applications are processed as they are received, and qualified students are accepted as long as there are openings. Continuous means that applicants are notified of acceptance or rejection as applications are processed up until the date indicated or the actual beginning of classes. The application deadline and the notification date for transfers are given if they differ from the dates for freshmen. Early decision and early action application deadlines and notification dates are also indicated when relevant.

Admissions Contact

The name, title, and phone number of the person to contact for application information are given at the end of the Profile. The admission office address is listed in most cases. Toll-free phone numbers may also be included. The admission office fax number and e-mail address, if available, are listed, provided the school wanted them printed for use by prospective students. Finally, the URL of the institution's Web site is provided.

Additional Information

Each college that has a **Featured Two-Year College Close-Up** in the guide will have a cross-reference appended to the Profile, referring you directly to the page number of that **Featured Two-Year College Close-Up.**

Institutional Changes Since *Peterson's®* *Two-Year Colleges 2017*

Here you will find an alphabetical listing of institutions that have recently closed, merged with other institutions, or changed their name or status.

FEATURED TWO-YEAR COLLEGES

These narrative descriptions provide an inside look at certain colleges, shifting the focus to a variety of other factors that should also be considered. The descriptions provide a wealth of information that is crucial in the college decision-making equation—such as tuition, financial aid, academic programs, and life on campus. Prepared exclusively by college officials, the descriptions are designed to help give students a better sense of the individuality of each institution, in terms that include campus environment, student activities, and lifestyle. Such quality-of-life intangibles can be the deciding factors in the college selection process. The absence of any college or university does not constitute an editorial decision on the part of Peterson's. In essence, these descriptions are an open forum for colleges, on a voluntary basis, to communicate their particular message to prospective students. The colleges included have paid a fee to Peterson's to provide this information. The Close-Ups in the **Featured Two-Year Colleges** section are edited to provide a generally consistent format across entries for your ease of comparison.

INDEXES

Associate Degree Programs at Two- and Four-Year Colleges

These indexes present hundreds of undergraduate fields of study that are currently offered most widely according to the colleges' responses on *Peterson's Annual Survey of Undergraduate Institutions*. The majors appear in alphabetical order, each followed by an alphabetical list of the schools that offer an associate-level program in that field. Liberal Arts and Studies indicates a general program with no specified major. The terms used for the majors are those of the U.S. Department of Education Classification of Instructional Programs (CIPs). Many institutions, however, use different terms. Readers should refer to the **Featured Two-Year Colleges** two-page descriptions in this book for the school's exact terminology. In addition, although the term "major" is used in this guide, some colleges may use other terms, such as "concentration," "program of study," or "field."

DATA COLLECTION PROCEDURES

The data contained in the **Profiles** of Two-Year Colleges and **Indexes** were researched in winter and spring 2017 through *Peterson's Annual Survey of Undergraduate Institutions*. Questionnaires were sent to the more than 1,700 colleges that meet the outlined inclusion criteria. All data included in this edition have been submitted by officials (usually admission and financial aid officers, registrars, or institutional research personnel) at the colleges themselves. All usable information received in time for publication has been included. The omission of any particular item from the **Profiles** of Two-Year Colleges and **Indexes** listing signifies either that the item is not applicable to that institution or that data were not available. Because of the comprehensive editorial review that takes place in our offices and because all material comes directly from college officials, Peterson's has every reason to believe that the information presented in this guide is accurate at the time of printing. However, students should check with a specific college or university at the time of application to verify such figures as tuition and fees, which may have changed since the publication of this volume.

CRITERIA FOR INCLUSION IN THIS BOOK

Peterson's Two-Year Colleges 2017 covers accredited institutions in the United States, U.S. territories, and other countries that award the associate degree as their most popular undergraduate offering (a few also offer bachelor's, master's, or doctoral degrees). The term two-year college is the commonly used designation for institutions that grant the associate degree, since two years is the normal duration of the traditional associate degree program. However, some programs may be completed in one year, others require three years, and, of course, part-time programs may take a consid-erably longer period. Therefore, "two-year college" should be understood as a conventional term that accurately describes most of the institutions included in this guide but which should not be taken literally in all cases. Also included are some non-degree-granting institutions, usually branch campuses of a multicampus system, which offer the equivalent of the first two years of a bachelor's degree, transferable to a bachelor's degree–granting institution.

To be included in this guide, an institution must have full accreditation or be a candidate for accreditation (preaccreditation) status by an institutional or specialized accrediting body recognized by the U.S. Department of Education or the Council for Higher Education Accreditation (CHEA). Institutional accrediting bodies, which review each institution as a whole, include the six regional associations of schools and colleges (Middle States, New England, North Central, Northwest, Southern, and Western), each of which is responsible for a specified portion of the United States and its territories. Other institutional accrediting bodies are national in scope and accredit specific kinds of institutions (e.g., Bible colleges, independent colleges, and rabbinical and Talmudic schools). Program registration by the New York State Board of Regents is considered to be the equivalent of institutional accreditation, since the board requires that all programs offered by an institution meet its standards before recognition is granted. This guide also includes institutions outside the United States that are accredited by these U.S. accrediting bodies. There are recognized specialized or professional accrediting bodies in more than forty different fields, each of which is authorized to accredit institutions or specific programs in its particular field. For specialized institutions that offer programs in one field only, we designate this to be the equivalent of institutional accreditation. A full explanation of the accrediting process and complete information on recognized, institutional (regional and national), and specialized accrediting bodies can be found online at www.chea.org or at www.ed.gov/admins/finaid/accred/index.html.

Quick-Reference Chart

Two-Year Colleges At-a-Glance

This chart includes the names and locations of accredited two-year colleges in the United States, Canada, and other countries and shows institutions' responses to the *Peterson's Annual Survey of Undergraduate Institutions*. If an institution submitted incomplete data, one or more columns opposite the institution's name is blank. A dagger after the school name indicates that the institution has one or more entries in the *Featured Two-Year Colleges* section. If a school does not appear, it did not report any of the information.

Y—Yes; N—No; R—Recommended; S—For Some

Institution	City	Degrees Awarded	Institutional Control	Student Body	Undergraduate Enrollment	Percent Attending Part-Time	Percent 25 Years of Age or Older	Percent of Grads Going on to Four-Year Colleges	HS Equivalency Certificate Accepted	HS Transcript Required	Open Admissions	Need-Based Aid Available	Part-Time Jobs Available	Career Counseling Available	Job Placement Services Available	College Housing Available	Number of Sports Available	Number of Majors Offered
UNITED STATES																		
Alabama																		
Bevill State Community College	Jasper	C,T	St	M/W	3,806	47	25	18	Y	Y	Y	Y	Y	Y	Y	Y		16
Coastal Alabama Community College	Bay Minette	C,T	St	M/W	3,323	36												
Community College of the Air Force	Maxwell Gunter Air Force Base	T	Fed	M/W	268,763		34		Y	Y	Y				Y		N	12	49
Enterprise State Community College	Enterprise	C,T	St	M/W	3,410	45												
Gadsden State Community† College	Gadsden	C,T	St	M/W	5,018	49												
George C. Wallace Community College	Dothan	C,T	St	M/W	4,769	55												
H. Councill Trenholm State Community College	Montgomery	C	St	M/W	1,364	45	31		Y	Y	Y	Y	Y	Y	Y	N		18
Jefferson State Community College	Birmingham	C,T	St	M/W	8,943	69	29		Y	Y	S	Y	Y	Y	Y	N	1	19
J. F. Drake State Community and Technical College	Huntsville	C,T	St	M/W	996	51												
Lurleen B. Wallace Community College	Andalusia	C,T	St	M/W	1,742	41	19		Y	Y	Y	Y	Y	Y	Y	N	3	10
Marion Military Institute	Marion	C	St	M/W	457	2												
Northeast Alabama Community College	Rainsville	C,T	St	M/W	2,704	56												
Northwest-Shoals Community College	Muscle Shoals	C	St	M/W	3,752	58	15	70	Y	Y	Y	Y	Y	Y	Y	N	3	16
Reid State Technical College	Evergreen	T	St	M/W	489	58	37		Y		Y	Y	Y	Y	Y	Y		2	5
Snead State Community College	Boaz	C,T	St	M/W	2,161	29			Y	Y	Y	Y	Y			Y	5	5
Alaska																		
Alaska Career College	Anchorage	T	Prop	M/W														
Ilisagvik College	Barrow	C	St	M/W	271													
University of Alaska Anchorage, Kenai Peninsula College	Soldotna	C,T,B	St	M/W	2,733													
University of Alaska, Prince William Sound College	Valdez	C,T	St	M/W														
American Samoa																		
American Samoa Community College	Pago Pago	C,T,B	Terr	M/W	1,253	44	12	0	Y	Y		Y	Y	Y	Y	N	8	25
Arizona																		
Arizona Western College	Yuma	C,T	St-L	M/W	7,569	68	57		Y			Y	Y	Y	Y	Y	7	67
Carrington College–Mesa	Mesa	T	Prop	M/W	633	10												
Carrington College–Phoenix East	Phoenix	T	Prop	M/W	346	23												
Carrington College–Phoenix North	Phoenix	T	Prop	M/W	676													
Carrington College–Tucson	Tucson	C	Prop	M/W	357													
Chandler-Gilbert Community College	Chandler	C,T	St-L	M/W	14,630				Y				Y	Y	Y	N	6	37
Cochise County Community College District	Douglas	C,T	St-L	M/W	4,223	61	13	44	Y			R,S	Y	Y	Y	Y	3	48
Coconino Community College	Flagstaff	C,T	St	M/W	3,608	69	9		Y			Y	Y	Y	Y	N		39
Eastern Arizona College	Thatcher	C,T	St-L	M/W	6,423	69	35	3	Y			R	Y	Y	Y	Y	10	54
Estrella Mountain Community College	Avondale	C,T	St-L	M/W	9,344	67	28	0	Y			Y	Y	Y	Y	N	2	2
Mesa Community College	Mesa	C,T	St-L	M/W	20,508				Y				Y	Y	Y	N	12	54
Mohave Community College	Kingman	C,T	St	M/W	4,230	80	47		Y				Y			N		34
Penn Foster College	Scottsdale	C,T,B	Prop	M/W	24,527				Y	Y	Y					N		23
The Refrigeration School	Phoenix	T	Prop	PM	688		72					Y		Y	Y	N		1
Rio Salado College	Tempe	C,T	St-L	M/W	20,865		43		Y				Y	Y	Y	N		15
Scottsdale Community College	Scottsdale	C,T	St-L	M/W	9,551	73	29		Y				Y	Y	Y	N	12	22
Tohono O'odham Community College	Sells	C,T	Pub	M/W	206	57	74	25	Y	Y	Y				Y	N	1	6
Arkansas																		
Arkansas Northeastern College	Blytheville	C,T	St	M/W	1,416	57	45		Y		Y	R	Y	Y	Y	N	4	11
College of the Ouachitas	Malvern	C,T	St	M/W	1,328	67	50		Y	Y	Y	Y	Y	Y	Y	N		16
NorthWest Arkansas Community College	Bentonville	C,T	St	M/W	7,761				Y	Y	Y	Y	Y	Y	Y	N	6	23
Southern Arkansas University Tech	Camden	C,T	St	M/W	1,650	70	47	90	Y	Y	Y	Y	Y	Y	Y	N	8	18
University of Arkansas Community College at Morrilton	Morrilton	C,T	St	M/W	2,029	38	33		Y	Y		Y	Y	Y	Y	N		16
California																		
American River College	Sacramento	C,T	Dist	M/W	33,821													
Antelope Valley College	Lancaster	C,T	Dist	M/W	13,820													
Beverly Hills Design Institute	Beverly Hills	C,T,B	Prop	M/W														
Cañada College	Redwood City	C,T	Dist	M/W	5,433	93			Y	Y	R	Y	Y	Y	Y	N	5	45
Carrington College–Citrus Heights	Citrus Heights	T	Prop	M/W	568	8												
Carrington College–Pleasant Hill	Pleasant Hill	T	Prop	M/W	616	16												
Carrington College–Pomona	Pomona	T	Prop	M/W	406	32												
Carrington College–Sacramento	Sacramento	T	Prop	M/W	1,272	18												
Carrington College–San Jose	San Jose	T	Prop	M/W	791	7												
Carrington College–San Leandro	San Leandro	T	Prop	M/W	478	9												
Carrington College–Stockton	Stockton	T	Prop	M/W	583	6												
Cerritos College	Norwalk	C,T	Dist	M/W	22,043	67	35		Y			Y	Y	Y	Y	N	13	82
Citrus College	Glendora	C	Dist	M/W	12,780	61			Y	Y	Y	Y	Y	Y	Y		10	59
Coastline Community College	Fountain Valley	C	Dist	M/W	11,431	78	72		Y		R	Y	Y	Y	Y	N		1
College of Marin	Kentfield	C,T	Dist	M/W	5,621				Y			Y	Y	Y	Y	N	8	55
College of the Canyons	Santa Clarita	C,T	Dist	M/W	17,174	65	26		Y		R	Y	Y	Y	Y	N	10	55
College of the Desert	Palm Desert	C,T	Dist	M/W	10,285	61	33		Y			Y	Y	Y	Y	N	11	61
Columbia College	Sonora	C,T	Dist	M/W	2,424	70												
De Anza College	Cupertino	C,T	Dist	M/W	21,099	52						Y	Y	Y	Y	N	13	63

This chart includes the names and locations of accredited two-year colleges in the United States, Canada, and other countries and shows institutions' responses to the *Peterson's Annual Survey of Undergraduate Institutions*. If an institution submitted incomplete data, one or more columns opposite the institution's name is blank. A dagger after the school name indicates that the institution has one or more entries in the *Featured Two-Year Colleges* section. If a school does not appear, it did not report any of the information.

Legend: Y—Yes; N—No; R—Recommended; S—For Some

Institution	Location	Degrees Awarded	Institutional Control	Student Body	Undergrad Enrollment	% Part-Time	% 25+	% to 4-Year	HS Equiv Accepted	Open Admissions	HS Transcript Required	Need-Based Aid Required	Part-Time Jobs	Career Counseling	Job Placement	College Housing	Sports	Majors
Feather River College	Quincy	C,T,B	Dist	M/W	1,663	71	52	54	Y				Y	Y	Y	Y	9	28
FIDM/Fashion Institute of Design & Merchandising, Orange County Campus	Irvine	C,T	Prop	PW	92	7	5		N	Y	Y		Y	Y	Y	N		6
FIDM/Fashion Institute of Design & Merchandising, San Diego Campus	San Diego	C,T	Prop	PW	75	8	9		N	Y	Y		Y	Y	Y	N		3
Fullerton College	Fullerton	C,T	Dist	M/W	22,569	67	23		Y			Y	Y	Y	Y	N		13	75
Golden West College	Huntington Beach	C,T	Dist	M/W	12,394	65	29		Y	Y	R		Y	Y	Y	N		9	31
Imperial Valley College	Imperial	C,T	Dist	M/W	7,828		31		Y			R,S	Y	Y	Y	N		7	35
Los Angeles City College	Los Angeles	C,T	Dist	M/W	16,556	72	62		Y					Y	Y	N			28
Los Angeles Trade-Technical College	Los Angeles	C,T	Dist	M/W	13,194	68													
Los Angeles Valley College	Valley Glen	C,T	Dist	M/W	17,957														
Merced College	Merced	C,T	Dist	M/W	12,525		51		Y			R	Y	Y	Y	Y	N	14	71
Mt. San Antonio College	Walnut	C,T	Dist	M/W	4,690	45	.		Y			S	Y	Y	Y	Y	N	15	81
Norco College	Norco	C,T	Dist	M/W	9,399														
Orange Coast College	Costa Mesa	C,T	Dist	M/W	41,616	59	28		Y				Y	Y	Y	N		14	89
Oxnard College	Oxnard	C	Dist	M/W	7,006	72													
Palomar College	San Marcos	C	Dist	M/W	25,244		37		Y				Y	Y	Y	N		14	93
Pasadena City College	Pasadena	C,T	Dist	M/W	27,050	59													
Rio Hondo College	Whittier	C,T	Dist	M/W	18,367	78			Y				Y	Y	Y	N		11	4
San Joaquin Delta College	Stockton	C,T	Dist	M/W	15,566		31		Y				Y	Y	Y	N		18	57
San Joaquin Valley College	Bakersfield	T	Prop	M/W	864														
San Joaquin Valley College	Fresno	T	Prop	M/W	1,019														
San Joaquin Valley College	Hanford	T	Prop	M/W	275														
San Joaquin Valley College	Hesperia	T	Prop	M/W	804														
San Joaquin Valley College	Lancaster	T	Prop	M/W	328														
San Joaquin Valley College	Ontario	T	Prop	M/W	994														
San Joaquin Valley College	Rancho Cordova	T	Prop	M/W	158														
San Joaquin Valley College	Salida	T	Prop	M/W	465														
San Joaquin Valley College	Temecula	T	Prop	M/W	728														
San Joaquin Valley College	Visalia	T	Prop	M/W	1,294														
San Joaquin Valley College–Fresno Aviation Campus	Fresno	T	Prop	PM	130														
San Joaquin Valley College–Online	Visalia	T	Prop	M/W	1,005														
Santa Monica College	Santa Monica	C,T	Dist	M/W	30,830	86	22		Y	Y	Y	Y	Y	Y	Y	N		10	65
Santa Rosa Junior College	Santa Rosa	C,T	Dist	M/W	22,008		46		Y				Y	Y	Y	N		15	76
Sierra College	Rocklin	C,T	Dist	M/W	18,758	74	35		Y				Y	Y	Y	Y	13	61
Victor Valley College	Victorville	C,T	Dist	M/W															
Colorado																		
Arapahoe Community College	Littleton	C,T	St	M/W	9,383	82	38		Y				Y	Y	Y	N			28
Bel–Rea Institute of Animal Technology	Denver	T	Prop	M/W	400		39		Y	Y	Y		Y	Y		N			1
CollegeAmerica–Denver	Denver	T,B	Ind	M/W	321														
CollegeAmerica–Fort Collins	Fort Collins	T,B	Ind	M/W	120		57		Y	Y	Y			Y		N			5
Colorado Northwestern Community College	Rangely	C,T	St	M/W	1,178	54	24		Y	Y	Y		Y	Y	Y	Y	9	14
Community College of Aurora	Aurora	C,T	St	M/W	7,379	80						S	Y	Y	Y	N			13
Front Range Community College	Westminster	C,T	St	M/W	18,747	71	37		Y				Y	Y	Y	Y			30
IBMC College	Fort Collins	T	Prop	M/W	1,020		63		Y	Y	Y		Y	Y	Y	N			7
Lamar Community College	Lamar	C,T	St	M/W	777	48	19		Y	Y			Y	Y	Y	Y	7	12
Morgan Community College	Fort Morgan	C,T	St	M/W	1,474	78	25		Y			R	Y	Y	Y	N			26
Northeastern Junior College	Sterling	C,T	St	M/W	1,469	37	18	10	Y			R	Y	Y	Y	Y	8	44
Otero Junior College	La Junta	C,T	St	M/W	1,449		32	11	Y			R	Y	Y	Y	Y	7	24
Pueblo Community College	Pueblo	C,T,B	St	M/W	5,562	35	81	3	Y				Y	Y	Y	N			36
Connecticut																		
Asnuntuck Community College	Enfield	C,T	St	M/W	1,945	66	49		Y	Y	Y		Y	Y	Y	N			12
Housatonic Community College	Bridgeport	C,T	St	M/W	5,369				Y	Y	Y		Y	Y	Y	N			23
Manchester Community College	Manchester	C,T	St	M/W	6,780	68	31		Y	Y	Y		Y	Y	Y	N		4	31
Naugatuck Valley Community College	Waterbury	C,T	St	M/W	6,651	66	34		Y	Y	Y		Y	Y	Y	N			32
Norwalk Community College	Norwalk	C,T	St	M/W	5,869	65	37		Y	Y	Y		Y	Y	Y	N			34
St. Vincent's College	Bridgeport	C,T,B	I-R	M/W	763	91	67					Y	Y	Y		N			4
Three Rivers Community College	Norwich	C,T	St	M/W	4,259	67	41		Y	Y	R		Y	Y	Y	N		2	30
Tunxis Community College	Farmington	C,T	St	M/W	4,079	61													
Florida																		
Chipola College	Marianna	C,T,B	St	M/W	2,147	60													
College of Business and Technology–Cutler Bay Campus	Cutler Bay	C	Prop	M/W	117		78		Y	Y	Y			Y	Y	N			4
College of Business and Technology–Flagler Campus	Miami	C	Prop	M/W	300		78		Y	Y	Y			Y	Y	N			4
College of Business and Technology–Hialeah Campus	Hialeah	C	Prop	PM	238		81		Y	Y	Y			Y	Y	N			2
College of Business and Technology–Main Campus	Miami	C,B	Prop	M/W	10		70		Y	Y	Y			Y	Y	N			1
College of Business and Technology–Miami Gardens	Miami Gardens	C,B	Prop	M/W	113		72		Y	Y	Y			Y		N			5
College of Central Florida	Ocala	C,T,B	St-L	M/W	7,931	62	39		Y				Y	Y	Y	N		5	75
Daytona State College	Daytona Beach	C,T,B	St	M/W	12,807	62	34		Y				Y	Y	Y	N		9	52
Florida Keys Community College	Key West	C,T,B	St	M/W	1,023	63	34		Y			S	Y	Y	Y	Y			9
Florida SouthWestern State College	Fort Myers	C,T,B	St-L	M/W	16,616	66	26		Y				Y	Y	Y	Y	5	40
Gulf Coast State College	Panama City	C,T,B	St	M/W	5,483	66	39		Y				Y	Y	Y	N		4	43
Hillsborough Community College	Tampa	C,T	St	M/W	27,061	60	35		Y				Y	Y	Y	N		5	34
Miami Dade College	Miami	C,T,B	St-L	M/W	55,206	62	31		Y				Y	Y	Y	N		4	194
Pensacola State College	Pensacola	C,B	St	M/W	9,643	63			Y				Y	Y	Y	N		16	97
Seminole State College of Florida	Sanford	C,T,B	St-L	M/W	17,706	65	43	32	Y				Y	Y	Y	N		3	50
Southeastern College–West Palm Beach	West Palm Beach	T	Prop	M/W	1,063		70		Y	Y	Y			Y		N			13
South Florida State College	Avon Park	C,T,B	St	M/W	2,722	65	37		Y				Y	Y	Y	Y	6	165
Tallahassee Community College	Tallahassee	C,T,B	St-L	M/W	12,200	53	23		Y				Y	Y	Y	N		6	38

This chart includes the names and locations of accredited two-year colleges in the United States, Canada, and other countries and shows institutions' responses to the *Peterson's Annual Survey of Undergraduate Institutions*. If an institution submitted incomplete data, one or more columns opposite the institution's name is blank. A dagger after the school name indicates that the institution has one or more entries in the *Featured Two-Year Colleges* section. If a school does not appear, it did not report any of the information.

Legend: Y—Yes; N—No; R—Recommended; S—For Some

Name	Location	Degrees Awarded	Institutional Control	Student Body	Undergraduate Enrollment	Percent Attending Part-Time	Percent 25 or Older	Percent of Grads Going on to Four-Year Colleges	Open Admissions	High School Equivalency Certificate Accepted	High School Transcript Required	Need-Based Aid Available	Part-Time Jobs Available	Career Counseling Available	Job Placement Services Available	College Housing Available	Number of Sports Offered	Number of Majors Offered
Ultimate Medical Academy Clearwater	Clearwater	T	Ind	M/W	247	80				Y	Y	Y		Y	Y	N	1	7
Ultimate Medical Academy Online	Tampa	T	Ind	M/W	16,411	21	80			Y	Y	Y		Y	Y	N		7
Georgia																		
Albany Technical College	Albany	T	St	M/W	3,251	57				Y		Y				N		17
Athens Technical College	Athens	T	St	M/W	4,210	75				Y		Y	Y	Y		N		27
Atlanta Technical College	Atlanta	T	St	M/W	3,775	63				Y		Y				N		11
Augusta Technical College	Augusta	T	St	M/W	4,370	61				Y		Y	Y	Y		N		24
Bainbridge State College	Bainbridge	C,T,B	St	M/W	2,459		33		Y	S	Y	Y	Y	Y		N		33
Central Georgia Technical College	Warner Robins	T	St	M/W	7,762	69				Y		Y	Y	Y	Y	N		27
Chattahoochee Technical College	Marietta	T	St	M/W	9,999	72				Y		Y	Y	Y		N		22
Coastal Pines Technical College	Waycross	T	St	M/W	2,775	78				Y		Y				N		11
Columbus Technical College	Columbus	T	St	M/W	3,228	72				Y		Y	Y	Y		N		24
East Georgia State College	Swainsboro	C,T,B	St	M/W	3,001	23	10		N	Y	Y	Y	Y	Y	Y	Y	5	4
Emory University, Oxford College	Oxford	C	I-R	M/W	936													
Georgia Highlands College	Rome	C,T,B	St	M/W	5,994	53	20		N	Y	Y	Y	Y	Y		N	12	30
Georgia Military College	Milledgeville	C,B	Pub	M/W	8,234	44	33		Y	Y	S	Y	Y	Y		Y	10	26
Georgia Northwestern Technical College	Rome	T	St	M/W	6,016	70				Y		Y	Y	Y		N		13
Georgia Piedmont Technical College	Clarkston	T	St	M/W	4,103	78				Y		Y	Y	Y		N		27
Gordon State College	Barnesville	C,T,B	St	M/W	3,901	36	18		N	Y	Y	Y	Y	Y	Y	Y	4	45
Gupton-Jones College of Funeral Service	Decatur	T	Ind	M/W	220		71		Y	Y	Y	Y		Y	Y	N		1
Gwinnett Technical College	Lawrenceville	T	St	M/W	7,479	78				Y		Y	Y	Y	Y	N		27
Interactive College of Technology	Chamblee	T	Prop	M/W	312													
Interactive College of Technology	Gainesville	T	Prop	M/W														
Lanier Technical College	Oakwood	T	St	M/W	3,636	72				Y		Y				N		21
North Georgia Technical College	Clarkesville	T	St	M/W	2,838	68				Y		Y				N		10
Oconee Fall Line Technical College	Sandersville	T	St	M/W	1,404	74				Y		Y				N		5
Ogeechee Technical College	Statesboro	T	St	M/W	1,904	62				Y		Y				N		24
Savannah Technical College	Savannah	T	St	M/W	3,938	65				Y		Y	Y			N		16
Southeastern Technical College	Vidalia	T	St	M/W	1,563	72				Y		Y				N		13
Southern Crescent Technical College	Griffin	T	St	M/W	4,703	66				Y		Y	Y					23
Southern Regional Technical College	Thomasville	T	St	M/W	3,521	67				Y		Y	Y	Y		N		11
South Georgia Technical College	Americus	T	St	M/W	1,829	50				Y		Y						15
West Georgia Technical College	Waco	T	St	M/W	6,743	71				Y		Y	Y	Y		N		17
Wiregrass Georgia Technical College	Valdosta	T	St	M/W	3,940	76				Y		Y				N		15
Guam																		
Guam Community College	Mangilao	T	Terr	M/W	2,428	57	25		Y	Y	Y	Y	Y			N		22
Hawaii																		
Hawaii Tokai International College	Kapolei	C,T	Ind	M/W	80	1	80		N	Y	Y	Y				Y		1
Leeward Community College	Pearl City	C,T	St	M/W	7,942	58												
Idaho																		
Carrington College–Boise	Boise	T	Prop	M/W	420	10												
Eastern Idaho Technical College	Idaho Falls	T	St	M/W	676	53	56		Y	Y	Y	Y	Y	Y	Y	N		14
Illinois																		
City Colleges of Chicago, Kennedy-King College	Chicago	C,T	St-L	M/W	2,818	44	48	45	Y		Y	Y	Y	Y	Y	N	2	14
City Colleges of Chicago, Olive-Harvey College	Chicago	C,T	St-L	M/W	2,979	63			Y	Y	S	Y	Y	Y	Y	N	3	11
Coyne College	Chicago	C,T	Prop	M/W	522													
Danville Area Community College	Danville	C,T	St-L	M/W	2,704	61	38	64	Y	Y	Y	Y	Y	Y	Y	N	5	30
Elgin Community College	Elgin	C,T	St-L	M/W	9,949	68	26		Y		S		Y	Y	Y	N	8	35
Fox College	Bedford Park	T	Priv	M/W	360													
Harper College	Palatine	C,T	St-L	M/W	14,142	55	34		Y	Y	Y	Y	Y	Y	Y	N	12	66
Highland Community College	Freeport	C,T	St-L	M/W	1,857	52	29		Y	Y	R,S	Y	Y	Y	Y	N	6	26
Illinois Central College	East Peoria	C,T	St-L	M/W	9,704	64	29		Y		Y		Y	Y			11	51
Illinois Eastern Community Colleges, Frontier Community College	Fairfield	C,T	St-L	M/W	1,930	84	60		Y	Y	Y	Y	Y	Y	Y	N	4	16
Illinois Eastern Community Colleges, Lincoln Trail College	Robinson	C,T	St-L	M/W	938	57	38		Y	Y	Y	Y	Y	Y	Y	N	3	14
Illinois Eastern Community Colleges, Olney Central College	Olney	C,T	St-L	M/W	1,219	59	35		Y	Y	Y	Y	Y	Y	Y	N	3	16
Illinois Eastern Community Colleges, Wabash Valley College	Mount Carmel	C,T	St-L	M/W	4,175	88	49		Y	Y	Y	Y	Y	Y	Y	N	3	21
Illinois Valley Community College	Oglesby	C,T	Dist	M/W	3,306	57	31	64	Y		Y	Y	Y	Y	Y	N	7	42
Kankakee Community College	Kankakee	C,T	St-L	M/W	3,306	63												
Kaskaskia College	Centralia	C,T	St-L	M/W	3,665	64	30		Y	Y	Y	Y	Y	Y	Y	N	9	41
Kishwaukee College	Malta	C,T	St-L	M/W	3,775	57	26		Y		R,S	Y	Y	Y		N	4	29
Lake Land College	Mattoon	C,T	St-L	M/W	6,351	56												
Lewis and Clark Community College	Godfrey	C,T	Dist	M/W	8,179													
Lincoln College	Lincoln	C,B	Ind	M/W	1,304		22		N	Y	Y	Y	Y			Y	13	20
McHenry County College	Crystal Lake	C,T	St-L	M/W	6,561	66	32		Y		R	Y	Y	Y	Y	N	6	27
Moraine Valley Community College	Palos Hills	C	St-L	M/W	15,016	57												
Morton College	Cicero	C,T	St-L	M/W	4,397	69	25		Y	Y	Y	Y	Y	Y	Y	N	6	29
Oakton Community College	Des Plaines	C,T	Dist	M/W	8,934		39		Y	Y	R	Y	Y	Y	Y	N	10	30
Rend Lake College	Ina	C,T	St	M/W	2,489	52	26		Y	Y	Y	Y	Y	Y	Y	N	6	40
Richland Community College	Decatur	C,T	Dist	M/W	3,005	68												
Rock Valley College	Rockford	C,T	Dist	M/W	6,937	55	32		Y	Y	Y	Y	Y	Y	Y	N	4	32
Shawnee Community College	Ullin	C,T	St-L	M/W	1,819	56	27		Y	Y	Y	Y	Y	Y	Y	N	4	30
South Suburban College	South Holland	C,T	St-L	M/W	3,867		49		Y	Y	Y	Y	Y	Y	Y	N	5	23

This chart includes the names and locations of accredited two-year colleges in the United States, Canada, and other countries and shows institutions' responses to the *Peterson's Annual Survey of Undergraduate Institutions*. If an institution submitted incomplete data, one or more columns opposite the institution's name is blank. A dagger after the school name indicates that the institution has one or more entries in the *Featured Two-Year Colleges* section. If a school does not appear, it did not report any of the information.

Y—Yes; N—No; R—Recommended; S—For Some

Column key — Degrees Awarded: College Transfer Associate (C); Terminal Associate (T); Bachelor's (B), Master's (M), Doctoral (D). Institutional Control: County, District, City, State and Local; Federal; State; Commonwealth, Territory; Independent, Independent-Religious, Proprietary. Student Body: Men, Primarily Men; Women, Primarily Women; Coed.

Institution	Location	Degrees	Control	Student Body	Undergrad Enrollment	% Part-Time	% 25+	% Grads to 4-Yr	HS Equiv Cert	HS Transcript	Open Adm	Need-Based Aid	PT Jobs	Career Couns	Job Placement	College Housing	# Sports	# Majors
Spoon River College	Canton	C,T	St	M/W	1,560	52	22		Y	Y	Y	Y	Y	Y	Y	N	2	12
Vet Tech Institute at Fox College	Tinley Park	T	Priv	M/W	164													
Indiana																		
Ancilla College	Donaldson	C,T	I-R	M/W	504	24	13		Y	Y	Y	Y	Y	Y	Y	Y	13	26
International Business College	Indianapolis	T	Prop	M/W	354													
Ivy Tech Community College–Bloomington	Bloomington	C,T	St	M/W	5,885	68	41		Y		Y	Y	Y	Y	Y			44
Ivy Tech Community College–Central Indiana	Indianapolis	C,T	St	M/W	18,355	73	46		Y		Y	Y	Y	Y	Y	N	6	51
Ivy Tech Community College–Columbus	Columbus	C,T	St	M/W	2,988	76	45		Y		Y	Y	Y	Y	Y	N		46
Ivy Tech Community College–East Central	Muncie	C,T	St	M/W	6,327	64	41		Y		Y	Y	Y	Y	Y	N		55
Ivy Tech Community College–Kokomo	Kokomo	C,T	St	M/W	2,502	67	49		Y		Y	Y	Y	Y	Y	N		49
Ivy Tech Community College–Lafayette	Lafayette	C,T	St	M/W	4,862	61	36		Y		Y	Y	Y	Y	Y	N		55
Ivy Tech Community College–North Central	South Bend	C,T	St	M/W	4,984	70	49		Y		Y	Y	Y	Y	Y	N		39
Ivy Tech Community College–Northeast	Fort Wayne	C,T	St	M/W	7,376	73	45		Y		Y	Y	Y	Y	Y	N		39
Ivy Tech Community College–Northwest	Gary	C,T	St	M/W	7,845	65	48		Y		Y	Y	Y	Y	Y	N		41
Ivy Tech Community College–Richmond	Richmond	C,T	St	M/W	1,778	74	53		Y		Y	Y	Y	Y	Y	N	1	46
Ivy Tech Community College–Sellersburg	Sellersburg	C,T	St	M/W	4,585	82	51		Y		Y	Y	Y	Y	Y	N		47
Ivy Tech Community College–Southeast	Madison	C,T	St	M/W	2,408	71	40		Y		Y	Y	Y	Y	Y	N		29
Ivy Tech Community College–Southwest	Evansville	C,T	St	M/W	4,991	76	53		Y		Y	Y	Y	Y	Y	N		56
Ivy Tech Community College–Wabash Valley	Terre Haute	C,T	St	M/W	4,060	66	45		Y		Y	Y	Y	Y	Y	N	2	60
Vet Tech Institute at International Business College	Fort Wayne	T	Priv	M/W	147													
Vet Tech Institute at International Business College	Indianapolis	T	Priv	M/W	147													
Vincennes University	Vincennes	C,T,B	St	M/W	18,897	70	32		Y	Y	Y	Y				Y	7	124
Iowa																		
Des Moines Area Community College	Ankeny	C,T	St-L	M/W	22,446	70	23		Y			S	Y	Y	Y	Y	8	50
Hawkeye Community College	Waterloo	C,T	St-L	M/W	5,532	53	29		Y	Y		S	Y	Y	Y	N	10	41
Iowa Central Community College	Fort Dodge	C,T	St-L	M/W	5,634	48	16		Y	Y		R,S	Y	Y	Y	N	16	35
Northeast Iowa Community College	Calmar	C,T	St-L	M/W	4,786	72	32		Y			R	Y	Y	Y	N	7	29
St. Luke's College	Sioux City	C,T,B	Ind	M/W	259	54	44	25	N	Y		Y	Y	Y	Y	N	N	4
Southeastern Community College	West Burlington	C	St-L	M/W	2,844	54	29		Y				Y	Y	Y	Y	6	29
Western Iowa Tech Community College	Sioux City	C,T	St	M/W	6,152	63												
Kansas																		
Allen Community College	Iola	C,T	St-L	M/W	2,379		20		Y	Y	Y	Y	Y	Y	Y	Y	12	65
Barton County Community College	Great Bend	C,T	St-L	M/W	5,292	63												
Cloud County Community College	Concordia	C,T	St-L	M/W	2,038	60	26		Y	Y	Y	Y	Y	Y	Y	Y	11	19
Dodge City Community College	Dodge City	C,T	St-L	M/W	1,804				Y		Y	Y	Y	Y	Y	Y	13	70
Donnelly College	Kansas City	C,T,B	I-R	M/W	318	26	36		Y	Y	R	Y	Y	Y	Y	Y	3	4
Hesston College	Hesston	C,T,B	I-R	M/W	401	5	15		Y	Y	Y	Y	Y	Y		Y	10	13
Hutchinson Community College	Hutchinson	C,T	St-L	M/W	5,868	60	25	75	Y	Y	Y					Y	12	59
Johnson County Community College	Overland Park	C,T	St-L	M/W	19,110	68	37		Y	Y		S	Y	Y	Y	N	7	41
Manhattan Area Technical College	Manhattan	C,T	St-L	M/W	825	58	47		Y	Y	Y			Y	Y			24
Salina Area Technical College	Salina	C,T	St-L	M/W	582	63					Y	Y					N	18
Kentucky																		
Beckfield College	Florence	T,B	Prop	M/W	605													
Elizabethtown Community and Technical College	Elizabethtown	C,T	St	M/W	7,353	62												
Gateway Community and Technical College	Florence	C,T	St	M/W	4,392	70	44		Y	Y	Y			Y		N		14
Hopkinsville Community College	Hopkinsville	C,T	St	M/W	3,120	60												
Interactive College of Technology	Newport	T	Prop	M/W														
Maysville Community and Technical College	Maysville	C,T	St	M/W	3,525				Y	Y	Y	Y	Y	Y	Y	N		12
Owensboro Community and Technical College	Owensboro	C,T	St	M/W	4,001	62	36	4	Y	Y	Y	Y	Y	Y	Y	N		25
Somerset Community College	Somerset	C,T	St	M/W	6,639		80		Y	Y	Y	Y	Y			N		18
Spencerian College	Louisville	T,B	Prop	M/W	416	44	57		Y	Y			Y	Y	Y			8
Spencerian College–Lexington	Lexington	T	Prop	M/W	74		51			Y	Y		Y	Y	Y			3
Louisiana																		
Bossier Parish Community College	Bossier City	C	St	M/W	6,043	42	41		Y		Y	Y	Y	Y	Y	N	10	35
ITI Technical College	Baton Rouge	T	Prop	M/W								Y		Y	Y	N		8
Louisiana State University at Eunice	Eunice	C,T	St	M/W	2,906	52	25		Y		Y	Y	Y	Y	N		6	11
Nunez Community College	Chalmette	C,T	St	M/W	2,586	69	32		Y		S	Y	Y	Y	N			8
Southern University at Shreveport	Shreveport	C,T	St	M/W	3,240	46	29			Y	Y	Y	Y	Y	Y	N	3	36
Sowela Technical Community College	Lake Charles	C,T	St	M/W	3,241	43	26		Y	Y	Y		Y	Y	N			14
Maine																		
Beal College	Bangor	T	Prop	M/W	464	22												
Central Maine Community College	Auburn	C,T	St	M/W	3,025	60	34		N	Y	Y	Y	Y	Y	Y	Y	7	23
Kennebec Valley Community College	Fairfield	C,T	St	M/W	2,451	70												
Maine College of Health Professions	Lewiston	T	Ind	M/W	169	66	44		N	Y	Y			Y				3
Northern Maine Community College	Presque Isle	C,T	St	M/W	750	24	40		Y	Y	Y	Y	Y	Y	Y	Y	7	16
Southern Maine Community College	South Portland	C,T	St	M/W	6,045	57												
Washington County Community College	Calais	C,T	St	M/W	374													
York County Community College	Wells	C,T	St	M/W	1,827	77	34		Y	Y	Y	Y	Y			N	6	22
Marshall Islands																		
College of the Marshall Islands	Majuro	T	St	M/W	995	30	21		Y	Y	Y			Y				5
Maryland																		
Anne Arundel Community College	Arnold	C,T	St-L	M/W	13,904	72	35		Y		Y	Y	Y	Y	N		8	47
Carroll Community College	Westminster	C,T	St-L	M/W	3,362	65	24		Y	Y	Y	Y	Y	Y	N			33
Cecil College	North East	C,B	Cou	M/W	2,612	64	33		Y	Y	Y	Y	Y	Y	Y		8	42

This chart includes the names and locations of accredited two-year colleges in the United States, Canada, and other countries and shows institutions' responses to the *Peterson's Annual Survey of Undergraduate Institutions*. If an institution submitted incomplete data, one or more columns opposite the institution's name is blank. A dagger after the school name indicates that the institution has one or more entries in the *Featured Two-Year Colleges* section. If a school does not appear, it did not report any of the information.

Legend: Y—Yes; N—No; R—Recommended; S—For Some

Degrees Awarded: College Transfer Associate (C), Terminal Associate (T), Bachelor's (B), Master's (M), Doctoral (D)

Institution	Location	Degrees Awarded	Institutional Control	Student Body	Undergraduate Enrollment	% 25 Years or Older	% Attending Part-Time	% of Grads to Four-Year Colleges	HS Equiv. Cert. Accepted	HS Transcript Required	Open Admissions	Need-Based Aid Avail.	Part-Time Jobs Avail.	Career Counseling Avail.	Job Placement Services Avail.	College Housing Avail.	No. of Sports Offered	No. of Majors Offered
Chesapeake College	Wye Mills	C,T	St-L	M/W	2,112	70	29		Y	Y	Y	Y	Y	Y		N	5	34
Community College of Baltimore County	Baltimore	C,T	Cou	M/W	21,416	71			Y	Y				Y		N	8	60
Frederick Community College	Frederick	C,T	St-L	M/W	6,252	68	32		Y		R	Y	Y	Y	Y	N	7	32
Garrett College	McHenry	C,T	St-L	M/W	754	31	13		Y	Y	R	Y	Y	Y	Y	Y	8	13
Hagerstown Community College	Hagerstown	C,T	St-L	M/W	4,276	75	33		Y		S	Y	Y	Y	Y		12	29
Harford Community College	Bel Air	C,T	St-L	M/W	10,310	60	29	50	Y			Y	Y	Y	Y	N	13	58
Howard Community College	Columbia	C,T	St-L	M/W	9,163	62	35		Y		S	Y	Y	Y	Y	N	6	48
Montgomery College	Rockville	C,T	St-L	M/W	23,916	64	30	65			R	R	Y	Y	Y	N	9	44
Wor-Wic Community College	Salisbury	C,T	St-L	M/W	3,098	73	42		Y		R	R		Y	Y	N		20
Massachusetts																		
Berkshire Community College	Pittsfield	C,T	St	M/W	1,959	68	42		Y	Y	Y	Y	Y	Y	Y	N	6	20
Bunker Hill Community College	Boston	C,T	St	M/W	13,324	68			Y	Y	Y	Y	Y	Y	Y	N	4	59
FINE Mortuary College, LLC	Norwood	T	Prop	M/W	91	90	82			Y	Y	Y				N		1
Holyoke Community College	Holyoke	C,T	St	M/W	5,890	56	32		Y		Y	Y	Y	Y	Y	N	8	26
Massachusetts Bay Community College	Wellesley Hills	C,T	St	M/W	4,855	67	37	75	Y	Y	S	Y	Y	Y	Y	N	6	35
Middlesex Community College	Bedford	C,T	St	M/W	8,745	64	36		Y	Y	S	Y	Y	Y	Y	N	5	42
Mount Wachusett Community College	Gardner	C,T	St	M/W	3,961	61		32	Y	Y	Y	Y	Y	Y	Y	N	8	30
Northern Essex Community College	Haverhill	C,T	St	M/W	5,976	65	36		Y	Y	Y	Y	Y	Y	Y	N	9	61
North Shore Community College	Danvers	C,T	St	M/W	6,315	66	40	45	Y	Y	S	Y	Y	Y	Y	N	2	40
Quincy College	Quincy	C,T	City	M/W	4,732	61												
Quinsigamond Community College	Worcester	C,T	St	M/W	7,699	62	40		Y	Y	Y	Y	Y	Y	Y	N	8	54
Springfield Technical Community College	Springfield	C,T	St	M/W	5,622	58	40		Y	Y	Y	Y	Y	Y	Y	N	8	53
Michigan																		
Delta College	University Center	C,T	Dist	M/W	9,132	64	30		Y		R	Y	Y	Y	Y	N	6	65
Grand Rapids Community College	Grand Rapids	C,T	Dist	M/W	14,464	70	36		Y		Y	Y	Y	Y	Y	N	6	44
Kellogg Community College	Battle Creek	C,T	St-L	M/W	4,815	75	39		Y		S	Y	Y	Y	Y	N	5	33
Keweenaw Bay Ojibwa Community College	Baraga	C,T	Cou	M/W	77	44												
Kirtland Community College	Roscommon	C,T	Dist	M/W	1,529	69	38		Y	Y		Y	Y	Y	Y	N	3	19
Lansing Community College	Lansing	C,T	St-L	M/W	13,583	63			Y		S	Y	Y	Y	Y	N	6	114
Macomb Community College	Warren	C,T	Dist	M/W	21,734	70	36					Y	Y	Y	Y	N	11	72
Monroe County Community College	Monroe	C,T	Cou	M/W	3,144		25		Y	Y	Y	Y	Y	Y	Y	N		42
Mott Community College	Flint	C,T	Dist	M/W	8,013	73	35		Y	Y	Y	Y	Y	Y	Y	N	7	46
Muskegon Community College	Muskegon	C,T	St-L	M/W	4,506	67												
Saginaw Chippewa Tribal College	Mount Pleasant	C,T	Ind	M/W	141	60	55					Y				N		3
St. Clair County Community College	Port Huron	C,T	St-L	M/W	3,625	61			Y		Y	Y	Y	Y	Y	N	6	26
Schoolcraft College	Livonia	C,T,B	Dist	M/W	11,339	72	33		Y	Y	R,S	Y	Y	Y	Y	N	8	39
Southwestern Michigan College	Dowagiac	C,T	St-L	M/W	2,262	53	20		Y	Y	Y	Y	Y			Y	6	24
Wayne County Community College District	Detroit	C,T	St-L	M/W	16,822	85	48		Y	Y	Y	Y	Y	Y		N	5	53
Minnesota																		
Alexandria Technical and Community College	Alexandria	C,T	St	M/W	2,577		19		Y	Y	Y	Y	Y	Y		Y	4	25
Anoka-Ramsey Community College	Coon Rapids	C,T	St	M/W	8,874	62			Y	Y	S	Y	Y	Y		N	11	25
Anoka Technical College	Anoka	C,T	St	M/W	1,809	54			Y	Y	Y	Y	Y	Y	Y	N		22
Central Lakes College	Brainerd	C,T	St	M/W	4,274													
Century College	White Bear Lake	C,T	St	M/W	8,597	58	39		Y		Y	Y	Y	Y		N	13	46
Duluth Business University	Duluth	T,B	Prop	PW	111	41	59				Y			Y	Y	N		3
Dunwoody College of Technology	Minneapolis	T,B	Ind	PM	1,264	16	48		N	Y	Y	Y	Y	Y	Y	N		29
Hennepin Technical College	Brooklyn Park	C,T	St	M/W	5,299		57		Y	Y	R	Y	Y	Y	Y	N		34
Lake Superior College	Duluth	C,T	St	M/W	5,050	58	41		Y		Y	Y	Y	Y	Y	N	1	62
Mesabi Range College	Virginia	C,T	St	M/W	1,150	44	37		Y		Y	Y	Y	Y	Y	Y	7	16
Minneapolis Business College	Roseville	T	Prop	M/W	231													
Minnesota State College–Southeast Technical	Winona	C,T	St	M/W	1,961	59	46		Y	Y	Y	Y	Y			N		27
Minnesota State Community and Technical College	Fergus Falls	C,T	St	M/W	6,303	59	34	68	Y	Y	Y	Y	Y	Y	Y	Y	14	70
Minnesota State Community and Technical College–Detroit Lakes	Detroit Lakes	C,T	St	M/W	6,391	58							Y			N		21
Minnesota State Community and Technical College–Moorhead	Moorhead	C	St	M/W	6,303	59							Y			N		36
Minnesota State Community and Technical College–Wadena	Wadena	C,T	St	M/W	6,303	59							Y			N		11
Minnesota West Community and Technical College	Pipestone	C,T	St	M/W	3,182				Y	Y	Y	Y	Y				7	42
North Hennepin Community College	Brooklyn Park	C,T	St	M/W	6,847	70												
Northland Community and Technical College	Thief River Falls	C,T	St	M/W	3,599	62			Y	Y	Y	Y	Y	Y		N	13	33
Northwest Technical College	Bemidji	T	St	M/W	1,114	70												
Rainy River Community College	International Falls	C,T	St	M/W	268	20	54		Y	Y	R	Y	Y	Y	Y	Y	16	5
Ridgewater College	Willmar	C,T	St	M/W	3,563													
Mississippi																		
Copiah-Lincoln Community College	Wesson	C,T	St-L	M/W	3,157	21												
Hinds Community College	Raymond	C,T	St-L	M/W	11,469	33	29					Y	Y	Y	Y	Y	14	58
Itawamba Community College	Fulton	C,T	St-L	M/W	5,611	36												
Meridian Community College	Meridian	C,T	St-L	M/W	3,598	31	30		Y	Y	Y	Y	Y	Y	Y	Y	10	13
Missouri																		
Cottey College	Nevada	C,B	Ind	CW	326													
Crowder College	Neosho	C,T	St-L	M/W	5,710	54	30		Y	Y	Y	Y	Y	Y	Y	Y	4	46
Culinary Institute of St. Louis at Hickey College	St. Louis	T	Priv	M/W	95													
East Central College	Union	C,T	Dist	M/W	2,966	53	23		Y	Y	Y	Y	Y	Y		N	3	29
Jefferson College	Hillsboro	C,T	Dist	M/W	4,705	51												
Metro Business College	Jefferson City	T	Prop	PW	142													

This chart includes the names and locations of accredited two-year colleges in the United States, Canada, and other countries and shows institutions' responses to the *Peterson's Annual Survey of Undergraduate Institutions*. If an institution submitted incomplete data, one or more columns opposite the institution's name is blank. A dagger after the school name indicates that the institution has one or more entries in the *Featured Two-Year Colleges* section. If a school does not appear, it did not report any of the information.

Y—Yes; N—No; R—Recommended; S—For Some

Column key: Degrees Awarded (College Transfer Associate (C), Terminal Associate (T), Bachelor's (B), Master's (M), Doctoral (D)); Institutional Control; Student Body; Undergraduate Enrollment; Percent Attending Part-Time; Percent 25 Years of Age or Older; Percent of Grads Going on to Four-Year Colleges; High School Equivalency Certificate Accepted; High School Transcript Required; Open Admissions; Need-Based Aid Available; Part-Time Jobs Available; Career Counseling Available; Job Placement Services Available; College Housing Available; Number of Sports Offered; Number of Majors Offered

Institution	Location	Degrees	Control	Student Body	Enroll	%PT	%25+	%Grads→4yr	HS Equiv	HS Transcript	Open Adm	Need Aid	PT Jobs	Career Couns	Job Place	Housing	Sports	Majors
Missouri State University–West Plains	West Plains	C,T	St	M/W	1,944	49	32		Y	Y	S	Y	Y	Y	Y	Y	2	16
North Central Missouri College	Trenton	C,T	Dist	M/W	1,505	47	28		Y	Y	S	Y	Y	Y	Y	Y	3	21
Ozarks Technical Community College	Springfield	C,T	Dist	M/W	13,260				Y	Y	Y	Y	Y	Y	Y	N		34
Ranken Technical College	St. Louis	C,T,B	Ind	PM	1,743													
St. Charles Community College	Cottleville	C,T	St	M/W	6,756	51	25		Y	Y	R,S	Y	Y	Y	Y		3	27
St. Louis Community College	St. Louis	C,T	Pub	M/W	19,052	62	35		Y	Y	S		Y	Y	Y	N	5	53
Three Rivers Community College	Poplar Bluff	C,T	St-L	M/W	3,505	44	33		Y	Y	R,S	Y	Y	Y	Y	N	3	43
Vet Tech Institute at Hickey College	St. Louis	T	Priv	M/W	167													
Montana																		
Aaniiih Nakoda College	Harlem	C,T	Fed	M/W	236		66		Y	Y	Y	Y	Y	Y		N		12
Dawson Community College	Glendive	C,T	St-L	M/W	304	47												
Great Falls College Montana State University	Great Falls	C,T	St	M/W	1,674	61	54		Y	Y	Y	Y	Y	Y				15
Nebraska																		
Metropolitan Community College	Omaha	C,T	St-L	M/W	17,003	58	44		Y		R	Y	Y	Y	Y	Y		33
Mid-Plains Community College	North Platte	C,T	Dist	M/W	2,276	65	29		Y	Y	Y	Y	Y	Y	Y	Y	5	19
Nebraska Indian Community College	Macy	C,T	Fed	M/W	175	79	36	22			Y	Y	Y	Y	Y	N		5
Northeast Community College	Norfolk	C,T	St-L	M/W	5,075	58	31		Y		R,S	Y	Y	Y	Y	Y	9	73
Southeast Community College, Lincoln Campus	Lincoln	C,T	Dist	M/W	9,262	57			Y	Y	Y	Y	Y	Y		N	6	24
Southeast Community College, Milford Campus	Milford	T	Dist	PM	9,262	57			Y	Y	Y	Y	Y	Y		Y	6	14
Nevada																		
Carrington College–Las Vegas	Las Vegas	T	Prop	M/W	370	19												
Carrington College–Reno	Reno	T	Prop	M/W	327	21												
Great Basin College	Elko	C,T,B	St	M/W	3,362	73	52	75	Y	Y			Y	Y	Y	Y		35
Truckee Meadows Community College	Reno	C,T,B	St	M/W	10,873	74	37	49	Y				Y	Y	Y	N		54
Western Nevada College	Carson City	C,T,B	St	M/W	3,567	65	41	62	Y	Y	R,S	Y	Y	Y		N	1	19
New Hampshire																		
NHTI, Concord's Community College	Concord	C	St	M/W	3,700		50		Y	Y		Y	Y	Y	Y	Y	6	32
River Valley Community College	Claremont	C,T	St	M/W	1,009	77												
St. Joseph School of Nursing	Nashua	C,T	Ind	M/W	144	56												
White Mountains Community College	Berlin	C,T	St	M/W	762	60	46					Y	Y	Y		N		21
New Jersey																		
Camden County College	Blackwood	C,T	St-L	M/W	11,263	50	37		Y	Y	S	Y	Y	Y	Y	N	5	45
County College of Morris	Randolph	C,T	Cou	M/W	8,067	53	19		Y	Y	Y	Y	Y	Y	Y	N	11	34
Hudson County Community College	Jersey City	C,T	St-L	M/W	8,449	39	34		Y			Y	Y	Y	Y	N		31
Jersey College	Teterboro	C	Prop	PW	2,743		12		N	Y	Y			Y	Y			1
Mercer County Community College	Trenton	C,T	St-L	M/W	7,979	61	30		Y			Y	Y	Y	Y	N	9	51
Middlesex County College	Edison	C,T	Cou	M/W	11,673				Y	Y	Y	Y	Y	Y	Y	N	7	40
Ocean County College	Toms River	C,T	Cou	M/W	8,663	47												
Raritan Valley Community College	Branchburg	C,T	St-L	M/W	8,226	59	29					Y	Y	Y	Y	N	7	55
Rowan College at Burlington County	Pemberton	C,T	Cou	M/W	8,762													
Sussex County Community College	Newton	C,T	St-L	M/W	2,539	44	23		Y				Y	Y	Y	N	4	17
New Mexico																		
Carrington College–Albuquerque	Albuquerque	T	Prop	M/W	442	10												
Central New Mexico Community College	Albuquerque	C,T	St	M/W	24,781	71	41		Y				Y	Y	Y	N		67
New Mexico Junior College	Hobbs	C,T	St-L	M/W	3,222		52		Y			Y	Y	Y	Y	Y	10	35
San Juan College	Farmington	C,T	St	M/W	5,479	51	56		Y	Y	Y	Y	Y	Y	Y	N	4	51
Santa Fe Community College	Santa Fe	C,T	St-L	M/W	9,619	77			Y			R	Y	Y	Y	N		54
Southwestern Indian Polytechnic Institute	Albuquerque	C,T	Fed	M/W	402	14	39	1	N	Y	Y	Y	Y	Y	Y	Y	3	11
University of New Mexico–Gallup	Gallup	C,T	St	M/W	2,473	53												
New York																		
Adirondack Community College	Queensbury	C,T	St-L	M/W	3,850	44	26		Y	Y		Y	Y	Y	Y	Y	10	25
American Academy of Dramatic Arts–New York	New York	T	Ind	M/W	310				N	Y	Y	Y	Y			Y	N	1
The Belanger School of Nursing	Schenectady	C,T	Ind	PW	119	67	61	0					Y	Y		N		1
Borough of Manhattan Community College of the City University of New York	New York	C,T	St-L	M/W	26,748	32	25		Y	Y	Y	Y	Y	Y	Y		4	36
Cayuga County Community College	Auburn	C,T	St-L	M/W	4,297	62	40	41	Y	Y	Y	Y	Y	Y	Y	N	6	37
Clinton Community College	Plattsburgh	C,T	St-L	M/W	1,913	50	26	39	Y	Y		Y	Y	Y	Y	Y	4	17
Cochran School of Nursing	Yonkers	T	Ind	PW	96	86	83		N	Y	Y	Y				N		1
The College of Westchester	White Plains	C,T,B	Prop	M/W	1,021	21	40		N	Y		Y	Y	Y	Y	N		9
Columbia-Greene Community College	Hudson	C,T	St-L	M/W	1,643	59	28					R	Y	Y	Y	Y	9	17
Corning Community College	Corning	C,T	St-L	M/W	3,972	51												
Dutchess Community College	Poughkeepsie	C,T	St-L	M/W	9,348	56	16		Y	Y		Y	Y	Y	Y	Y	6	31
Erie Community College	Buffalo	C,T	St-L	M/W	2,424	24	43		Y	Y	Y	Y	Y	Y	Y	N	11	17
Erie Community College, North Campus	Williamsville	C,T	St-L	M/W	5,224	33	33		Y	Y	Y	Y	Y	Y	Y	N	11	32
Erie Community College, South Campus	Orchard Park	C,T	St-L	M/W	3,630	41	22		Y	Y	Y	Y	Y	Y	Y	N	11	20
Fashion Institute of Technology†	New York	C,T,B,M	St-L	PW	9,096	19	18		N	Y		Y	Y	Y	Y	Y	7	23
Finger Lakes Community College	Canandaigua	C,T	St-L	M/W	6,521	60	31		Y	Y		Y	Y	Y	Y	Y	9	57
Fiorello H. LaGuardia Community College of the City University of New York	Long Island City	C,T	St-L	M/W	19,332	45	34	48	Y	Y	Y	Y	Y	Y	Y	N	7	44
Genesee Community College	Batavia	C,T	St-L	M/W	6,141	59	34		Y	Y	Y	Y	Y	Y		Y	13	91
Helene Fuld College of Nursing	New York	C,T,B	Ind	PW	354	74												
Herkimer County Community College	Herkimer	C,T	St-L	M/W	3,019	42												
Island Drafting and Technical Institute	Amityville	C,T	Prop	PM	112													
Jamestown Business College	Jamestown	T,B	Prop	M/W	311	2	34		N	Y	Y	Y			Y	Y	N		4

This chart includes the names and locations of accredited two-year colleges in the United States, Canada, and other countries and shows institutions' responses to the *Peterson's Annual Survey of Undergraduate Institutions.* If an institution submitted incomplete data, one or more columns opposite the institution's name is blank. A dagger after the school name indicates that the institution has one or more entries in the *Featured Two-Year Colleges* section. If a school does not appear, it did not report any of the information.

Y—Yes; N—No; R—Recommended; S—For Some

Column key — Degrees Awarded: College Transfer Associate (C); Terminal Associate (T); Bachelor's (B); Master's (M); Doctoral (D). Institutional Control. Student Body: Men, Primarily Men, Women, Primarily Women, Coed.

Institution	Location	Degrees	Control	Student Body	Undergrad Enrollment	% Part-Time	% 25+	% Grads to 4-Yr	Open Adm	HS Equiv Accepted	HS Transcript Req	Need-Based Aid	Part-Time Jobs	Career Counseling	Job Placement	College Housing	Sports	Majors
Jamestown Community College	Jamestown	C,T	St-L	M/W	4,617	53	31	57	Y	Y	Y	Y	Y	Y	Y	Y	10	28
Jefferson Community College	Watertown	C,T	St-L	M/W	3,748	44			N	Y	Y	Y	Y	Y	Y	Y	6	35
Kingsborough Community College of the City University of New York	Brooklyn	C,T	St-L	M/W	16,195	45	25		Y	Y	Y	Y	Y	Y	Y	N	7	40
Long Island Business Institute	Flushing	C	Prop	M/W	1,118	12	86	0	N	Y	Y	Y		Y	Y	N		7
Mohawk Valley Community College	Utica	C,T	St-L	M/W	6,625	48	29		Y		S	Y	Y	Y	Y	N	13	49
Monroe Community College	Rochester	C,T	St-L	M/W	13,587	40	39		Y	Y	Y	Y	Y	Y	Y	Y	18	67
Nassau Community College	Garden City	C,T	St-L	M/W	36,408	38	23		Y	Y	Y	Y	Y	Y	Y	N	18	53
Niagara County Community College	Sanborn	C,T	St-L	M/W	5,892	42	21		Y	Y	Y	Y	Y	Y	Y	Y	10	42
Onondaga Community College	Syracuse	C,T	St-L	M/W	11,886	50												
Phillips Beth Israel School of Nursing	New York	C,T,B	Ind	M/W	254	87												
Queensborough Community College of the City University of New York	Bayside	C,T	St-L	M/W	15,569	42	22		Y	Y	Y	Y	Y	Y	Y	N	11	41
St. Joseph's College of Nursing	Syracuse	T	I-R	M/W	273	39												
Schenectady County Community College	Schenectady	C,T	St-L	M/W	6,151	64												
State University of New York College of Technology at Alfred	Alfred	C,T,B	St	M/W	3,699	9	14		N	Y	Y	Y	Y	Y	Y	Y	17	56
Sullivan County Community College	Loch Sheldrake	C,T	St-L	M/W	1,610	49	20	31	Y	Y	Y	Y	Y	Y	Y	Y	13	37
Tompkins Cortland Community College	Dryden	C,T	St-L	M/W	2,844	30	30		Y	Y	Y	Y	Y	Y	Y	Y	22	35
Trocaire College	Buffalo	T,B	Ind	PW	1,369	55												
Ulster County Community College	Stone Ridge	C,T	St-L	M/W	3,416	60	30	61	Y	Y	Y	Y	Y	Y	Y	N	7	31
Westchester Community College †	Valhalla	C,T	St-L	M/W	12,842	46	31		Y	Y	Y	Y	Y	Y	Y	N	11	49
Wood Tobe–Coburn School	New York	T	Prop	M/W	411													
North Carolina																		
Alamance Community College	Graham	C,T	St	M/W	4,459	40	48		Y	Y	Y	Y	Y	Y	Y	N		28
Caldwell Community College and Technical Institute	Hudson	C,T	St	M/W	3,805	61	62		Y	Y	Y	Y	Y	Y	Y	N	1	28
Cape Fear Community College	Wilmington	C,T	St	M/W	9,067	57	43		Y	Y	S	Y	Y	Y	Y	N	6	38
Carolinas College of Health Sciences	Charlotte	T	Pub	M/W	433	89	51		N	N	S	Y	Y	Y	Y	N		3
Carteret Community College	Morehead City	C,T	St	M/W	1,363	58	45		Y	Y	S	Y	Y	Y	Y	N		24
Catawba Valley Community College	Hickory	C,T	St	M/W	4,571	59												
Cleveland Community College	Shelby	C,T	St	M/W	2,990	66												
College of The Albemarle	Elizabeth City	C,T	St	M/W	2,052	65	56		Y	Y	Y	Y	Y	Y	Y	N	14	26
Craven Community College	New Bern	C,T	St	M/W	2,883	63			Y	Y	Y	Y	Y	Y	Y	N		36
Fayetteville Technical Community College	Fayetteville	C,T	St	M/W	11,380	63	56	22	Y	Y	S	Y	Y	Y	Y	N	3	54
Halifax Community College	Weldon	C,T	St-L	M/W	1,136	51	50			Y	Y	Y	Y			N		17
Haywood Community College	Clyde	C,T	St-L	M/W	1,794	61	50		Y	Y	Y	Y	Y	Y	Y	N	1	32
James Sprunt Community College	Kenansville	C,T	St	M/W	1,228	64	25	1	Y	Y	Y	Y	Y	Y	Y	N	2	17
Johnston Community College	Smithfield	C,T	St	M/W	3,903	60			Y	Y	Y	Y	Y	Y	Y	N	2	13
King's College	Charlotte	T	Prop	M/W	395													
Lenoir Community College	Kinston	C,T	St	M/W	2,674	61	34		Y	Y	Y	Y	Y	Y	Y	N	3	36
Living Arts College	Raleigh	C,B	Prop	M/W	578													
Martin Community College	Williamston	C,T	St	M/W	890													
Mitchell Community College	Statesville	C,T	St	M/W	3,024	62	41		Y	Y	Y	Y	Y	Y	Y	N		35
Montgomery Community College	Troy	C,T	St	M/W	818	66	38		Y	Y	Y	Y	Y	Y	Y	N		13
Piedmont Community College	Roxboro	C,T	St	M/W	1,298				Y	Y	S	Y	Y	Y	Y	N	1	23
Randolph Community College	Asheboro	C,T	St	M/W	2,696	65	25		Y	Y	Y	Y	Y		Y	N		27
Richmond Community College	Hamlet	C,T	St	M/W	2,550	56	36		Y	Y	Y	Y	Y	Y	Y	N		23
Rockingham Community College	Wentworth	C,T	St	M/W	1,779	62				Y	Y	Y	Y	Y	Y	N	4	20
Rowan-Cabarrus Community College	Salisbury	C,T	St	M/W	5,180		34		Y	Y	Y	Y	Y	Y	Y	N		24
Southwestern Community College	Sylva	C	St	M/W	2,566	65						Y	Y	Y	Y	N		28
Wayne Community College	Goldsboro	C,T	St-L	M/W	3,837	53												
Western Piedmont Community College	Morganton	C,T	St	M/W	2,933													
North Dakota																		
Bismarck State College	Bismarck	C,T,B	St	M/W	3,976	44	34		Y	Y	Y	Y	Y	Y	Y	Y	6	37
Dakota College at Bottineau	Bottineau	C,T	St	M/W	811				Y	Y	Y	Y	Y	Y	Y	Y	9	72
Lake Region State College	Devils Lake	C,T	St	M/W	1,947	74	20		Y	Y	S	Y	Y	Y		Y	7	15
Williston State College	Williston	C,T	St	M/W	1,039	40	23		Y	Y	Y	Y	Y	Y		Y	5	15
Ohio																		
Beckfield College	Cincinnati	C	Prop	M/W														
Bowling Green State University–Firelands College	Huron	C,T,B	St	M/W	2,162	57	22		Y	Y	Y	Y	Y	Y	Y	N	5	20
Bradford School	Columbus	T	Prop	M/W	443													
Central Ohio Technical College	Newark	T	St	M/W	3,566	73												
Chatfield College	St. Martin	C,T	I-R	M/W	396	50												
Cincinnati State Technical and Community College	Cincinnati	C,T	St	M/W	9,630	70												
Columbus Culinary Institute at Bradford School	Columbus	T	Priv	M/W	150													
Columbus State Community College	Columbus	C,T	St	M/W	27,109	74	43		Y		R,S	Y	Y	Y	Y	N	5	63
Davis College	Toledo	T	Prop	M/W	159	79												
Eastern Gateway Community College	Steubenville	C,T	St-L	M/W	3,024	60												
Edison State Community College	Piqua	C,T	St	M/W	3,367	76	45		Y	Y		Y	Y	Y	Y	N	4	40
ETI Technical College of Niles	Niles	T	Prop	M/W	124	50												
International College of Broadcasting	Dayton	C,T	Prop	M/W					Y	Y	Y	Y		Y	Y	N		2
Kent State University at Ashtabula	Ashtabula	C,T,B	St	M/W	2,074	43	41		Y	Y	Y	Y	Y	Y	Y	N	1	22
Kent State University at East Liverpool	East Liverpool	C,T,B	St	M/W	1,302	45	40		Y	Y	Y	Y	Y	Y	Y	N		13
Kent State University at Salem	Salem	C,T,B	St	M/W	1,673	34	35		Y	Y	Y	Y	Y	Y	Y	N		18
Kent State University at Trumbull	Warren	C,T,B,M	St	M/W	2,377	37	37		Y	Y	Y	Y	Y	Y	Y	N		22
Kent State University at Tuscarawas	New Philadelphia	C,B	St	M/W	2,035	40	30		Y	Y	Y	Y	Y	Y	Y	N	10	21
Lakeland Community College	Kirtland	C,T	St-L	M/W	7,997	68	38		Y	Y	Y	Y	Y	Y	Y	N	6	39
Lorain County Community College	Elyria	C,T	St-L	M/W	11,548	72	31		Y	Y	S	Y	Y	Y	Y	N	12	41

This chart includes the names and locations of accredited two-year colleges in the United States, Canada, and other countries and shows institutions' responses to the *Peterson's Annual Survey of Undergraduate Institutions*. If an institution submitted incomplete data, one or more columns opposite the institution's name is blank. A dagger after the school name indicates that the institution has one or more entries in the *Featured Two-Year Colleges* section. If a school does not appear, it did not report any of the information.

Degrees Awarded: College Transfer Associate (C); Terminal Associate (T); Bachelor's (B); Master's (M); Doctoral (D)

Y—Yes; N—No; R—Recommended; S—For Some

Institution	Location	Degrees Awarded	Institutional Control	Student Body	Undergraduate Enrollment	Percent Attending Part-Time	Percent 25 Years of Age or Older	Percent of Grads Going on to Four-Year Colleges	High School Equivalency Certificate Accepted	High School Transcript Required	Open Admissions	Need-Based Aid Available	Part-Time Jobs Available	Career Counseling Available	Job Placement Services Available	College Housing Available	Number of Sports Offered	Number of Majors Offered
Ohio Business College	Sheffield Village	T	Prop	M/W	350													
The Ohio State University Agricultural Technical Institute	Wooster	C,T	St	M/W	772	6	8	52	Y	Y	Y	Y	Y	Y	Y	Y	10	34
Ohio Technical College	Cleveland	T	Prop	M/W	1,072		16				Y			Y	Y			7
Rosedale Bible College	Irwin	T	I-R	M/W	89					Y		Y				Y		1
School of Advertising Art	Kettering	T	Prop	M/W	197	2	1		N	Y	Y			Y	Y	N		1
Stark State College	North Canton	C,T	St-R	M/W	12,370	73	51				Y	Y	Y	Y	Y			27
Trumbull Business College	Warren	T	Prop	M/W	159	35												
University of Cincinnati Blue Ash College	Cincinnati	C,T,B	St	M/W	5,065	36	22		Y	Y		Y	Y	Y	Y	N		32
University of Cincinnati Clermont College	Batavia	C,T,B	St	M/W	2,883	45	26		Y	Y		Y	Y	Y	Y	N	6	36
Vet Tech Institute at Bradford School	Columbus	T	Priv	M/W	163													
Virginia Marti College of Art and Design	Lakewood	T,B	Prop	M/W	108		26		N	Y				Y	Y	N		5
Oklahoma																		
Carl Albert State College	Poteau	C,T	St	M/W	2,194	40	36		Y			Y	Y	Y	Y	Y	6	24
Clary Sage College	Tulsa	C	Prop	PW	406		51		Y	Y	Y			Y	Y	N		
Community Care College	Tulsa	T	Ind	PW	623		62		Y	Y	Y	Y		Y	Y	N	N	12
Murray State College	Tishomingo	C,T	St	M/W	2,674				Y		Y				Y	Y	6	26
Oklahoma City Community College	Oklahoma City	C,T	St	M/W	12,529	64	35		Y		S	Y	Y	Y	Y	N	8	64
Oklahoma State University Institute of Technology	Okmulgee	C,T,B	St	M/W	2,397	29	28		Y	Y	Y	Y	Y			Y	7	23
Oklahoma State University–Oklahoma City	Oklahoma City	C,T,B	St	M/W	5,963		43		Y	Y	S	Y	Y	Y	Y	N		36
Oklahoma Technical College	Tulsa	C	Ind	M/W	186		56		Y	Y	Y			Y	Y	N		
Seminole State College	Seminole	C,T	St	M/W	1,634	46	25		Y		R	Y	Y	Y		Y	8	27
Tulsa Community College	Tulsa	C,T	St	M/W	16,708	66												
Oregon																		
Central Oregon Community College	Bend	C,T	Dist	M/W	5,711	56	39		Y	Y			Y	Y	Y	Y	12	56
Oregon Coast Community College	Newport	C,T	Pub	M/W	486	53	38	34	Y					Y		N		7
Rogue Community College	Grants Pass	C,T	St-L	M/W	4,901	61	45		Y	Y		Y	Y	Y	Y		5	27
Southwestern Oregon Community College	Coos Bay	C,T	St-L	M/W	2,338	52												
Sumner College	Portland	T	Prop	PW	261													
Treasure Valley Community College	Ontario	C,T	St-L	M/W	2,170	56	46		Y			Y	Y	Y	Y	Y	9	30
Pennsylvania																		
Antonelli Institute	Erdenheim	T	Prop	M/W	188													
Bradford School	Pittsburgh	T	Prop	M/W	413													
Bucks County Community College	Newtown	C,T	Cou	M/W	8,232	66	28	47	Y	Y	Y	Y	Y	Y	Y	N	12	54
Butler County Community College	Butler	C,T	Cou	M/W	3,573													
Career Training Academy	Lower Burrell	T	Prop	PW														
Community College of Allegheny County	Pittsburgh	C,T	Cou	M/W	16,092	65					R	Y	Y			N	15	115
Community College of Philadelphia	Philadelphia	C,T	St-L	M/W	30,194		54	64	Y	Y	S	S	Y	Y	Y	N	7	29
Harrisburg Area Community College	Harrisburg	C,T	St-L	M/W	18,837	71	41		Y		S	S	Y	Y	Y	N	4	69
JNA Institute of Culinary Arts	Philadelphia	T	Prop	M/W	59		30											1
Lackawanna College	Scranton	C,T	Ind	M/W	1,691	35	21		Y	Y		Y	Y	Y	Y	Y	9	32
Lansdale School of Business	North Wales	C,T	Prop	M/W	372		73			Y		Y		Y	Y	N		10
Lehigh Carbon Community College	Schnecksville	C,T	St-L	M/W	6,620	62	35	48	Y		S	Y	Y	Y	Y	N	7	62
Luzerne County Community College	Nanticoke	C,T	Cou	M/W	5,669	55			Y		R	Y	Y	Y	Y	N	10	72
Manor College	Jenkintown	C,T	I-R	M/W	622	36	31	60	N	Y		Y	Y	Y	Y	Y	4	23
Montgomery County Community College	Blue Bell	C,T	Cou	M/W	11,480	67	35	64	Y	Y	Y	Y	Y			N	13	56
New Castle School of Trades	New Castle	T	Ind	PM	503													
Northampton Community College	Bethlehem	C,T	St-L	M/W	10,067	56	33	74	Y		R,S	Y	Y	Y	Y	Y	10	64
Penn State DuBois	DuBois	C,T,B	St-R	M/W	608	21	19		N	Y		Y	Y	Y	Y	N	7	127
Penn State Fayette, The Eberly Campus	Lemont Furnace	C,T,B	St-R	M/W	643	13	16		N	Y		Y	Y	Y	Y	N	11	124
Penn State Mont Alto	Mont Alto	C,T,B	St-R	M/W	902	24	23		N	Y		Y	Y	Y	Y	Y	10	120
Penn State Shenango	Sharon	C,T,B	St-R	M/W	462	48	75		N	Y		Y	Y	Y		N	7	124
Pennsylvania Highlands Community College	Johnstown	C	St-L	M/W	2,456	65												
Pennsylvania Institute of Technology	Media	C,T	Ind	M/W	492	72	55		Y			Y	Y	Y	Y	N		17
Pittsburgh Career Institute	Pittsburgh	T	Prop	M/W	200		44			Y	Y	Y		Y	Y	Y	N		1
Pittsburgh Institute of Aeronautics	Pittsburgh	C,T	Ind	PM	368		28			Y	Y	Y			Y	Y	N		4
Pittsburgh Institute of Mortuary Science, Incorporated	Pittsburgh	C,T	Ind	M/W	193	56	53		Y	Y	Y			Y	Y	N	N		1
Pittsburgh Technical College	Oakdale	T,B	Prop	M/W	1,875		21			Y	Y	Y			Y	Y	Y	5	18
Reading Area Community College	Reading	C,T	Cou	M/W	4,090	77												
The Restaurant School at Walnut Hill College	Philadelphia	T,B	Prop	M/W	429													
Thaddeus Stevens College of Technology	Lancaster	T	St	M/W	823													
University of Pittsburgh at Titusville	Titusville	C,T	St-R	M/W	388	19	14					Y	Y	Y	Y	Y	12	13
Vet Tech Institute	Pittsburgh	T	Prop	M/W	372													
Westmoreland County Community College	Youngwood	C,T	Cou	M/W	5,554	58	34		Y			Y	Y	Y	Y		8	75
Williamson College of the Trades	Media	T	Ind	CM	270													
Puerto Rico																		
Humacao Community College	Humacao	T,B	Ind	M/W	516	25	20		Y	Y	Y	Y	Y	Y	Y	N		14
Rhode Island																		
Community College of Rhode Island	Warwick	C	St	M/W	15,101	71	38		Y	Y		Y	Y	Y	Y	Y	8	50
South Carolina																		
Aiken Technical College	Graniteville	C,T	St-L	M/W	2,357	71												
Denmark Technical College	Denmark	C,T	St	M/W	1,043	37												
Forrest College	Anderson	C,T	Prop	M/W	99	14												
Greenville Technical College	Greenville	C,T	St	M/W	11,932	60			Y	Y		Y	Y	Y	Y	N	8	35
Horry Georgetown Technical College	Conway	C,T	St-L	M/W	7,018	57	45		Y		S	Y	Y	Y	Y	N		9
Midlands Technical College	Columbia	C,T	St-L	M/W	10,946	54												

This chart includes the names and locations of accredited two-year colleges in the United States, Canada, and other countries and shows institutions' responses to the *Peterson's Annual Survey of Undergraduate Institutions*. If an institution submitted incomplete data, one or more columns opposite the institution's name is blank. A dagger after the school name indicates that the institution has one or more entries in the *Featured Two-Year Colleges* section. If a school does not appear, it did not report any of the information.

Y—Yes; N—No; R—Recommended; S—For Some

Degrees Awarded: College Transfer Associate (C); Terminal Associate (T); Bachelor's (B); Master's (M); Doctoral (D)

Institution	City	Degrees Awarded	Institutional Control	Student Body	Undergrad Enrollment	% Attending Part-Time	% 25 Years or Older	% Grads Going on to Four-Year Colleges	Open Admissions	HS Equivalency Certificate Accepted	HS Transcript Required	Need-Based Aid Available	Part-Time Jobs Available	Career Counseling Available	Job Placement Services Available	College Housing Available	Number of Sports Offered	Number of Majors Offered
Spartanburg Community College	Spartanburg	C,T	St	M/W	4,715	54	29		Y	Y	Y	Y	Y	Y	Y	N		19
Spartanburg Methodist College	Spartanburg	C,T	I-R	M/W	737	1	1	82	N	Y	Y	Y	Y	Y	Y	Y	12	5
Technical College of the Lowcountry	Beaufort	C,T	St	M/W	2,332	71												5
Tri-County Technical College	Pendleton	C,T	St	M/W	6,128	44												
Trident Technical College	Charleston	C,T	St-L	M/W	13,561	60	44		Y	Y	S	Y	Y	Y	Y	N		39
University of South Carolina Salkehatchie	Allendale	C,T	St	M/W	1,076		25			Y	Y	Y	Y			N	4	1
University of South Carolina Union	Union	C,B	St	M/W	757		33		N	Y	Y	Y	Y			N	2	5
Williamsburg Technical College	Kingstree	C,T	St	M/W	676	74	31		Y	Y	Y	Y	Y			N		5
South Dakota																		
Lake Area Technical Institute	Watertown	T	St	M/W	2,061	22	17		Y	Y	Y	Y	Y	Y	Y	N	6	27
Mitchell Technical Institute	Mitchell	T	St	M/W	1,253	33	24		Y	Y	Y	Y	Y	Y	Y	N	6	28
Sisseton-Wahpeton College	Sisseton	C,T	Fed	M/W	165	39	42		Y	Y	Y	Y	Y	Y	Y	Y		12
Southeast Technical Institute	Sioux Falls	T	St	M/W	2,047	36			Y	Y	Y	Y	Y	Y	Y	N		21
Western Dakota Technical Institute	Rapid City	T	St	M/W	1,002	35	45		Y	Y	Y	Y	Y	Y	Y	N		21
Tennessee																		
Cleveland State Community College	Cleveland	C,T	St	M/W	3,315	48	23	32	Y	Y		Y	Y	Y	Y	N	10	13
Dyersburg State Community College	Dyersburg	C,T	St	M/W	2,857	57	32			Y	Y	Y	Y	Y	Y		8	18
John A. Gupton College	Nashville	C,T	Ind	M/W	120	42												
Motlow State Community College	Tullahoma	C,T	St	M/W	5,670	43	18		Y	Y		Y	Y	Y	Y	N	9	8
Nashville State Community College	Nashville	C,T	St	M/W	8,914		55		Y	Y	Y	Y	Y	Y	Y	N		66
Southwest Tennessee Community College	Memphis	C,T	St	M/W	10,167	59												
Volunteer State Community College	Gallatin	C,T	St	M/W	8,684	45	25		Y	Y		Y	Y	Y	Y	N	3	21
Walters State Community College	Morristown	C,T	St	M/W	5,951	46	17		Y	Y	Y	Y	Y	Y	Y	N	5	20
Texas																		
Alvin Community College	Alvin	C,T	St-L	M/W	5,677	76					S	Y	Y	Y	Y	N	2	55
Amarillo College	Amarillo	C,T	St-L	M/W			36		Y		Y	Y	Y	Y	Y	N	5	83
Austin Community College District	Austin	C,T	St-L	M/W	41,543		39		Y	Y	Y	Y	Y	Y	Y	N	3	96
Blinn College	Brenham	C,T	St-L	M/W	18,747	44			Y	Y	Y	Y	Y	Y	Y	Y	10	34
Brookhaven College	Farmers Branch	C,T	Cou	M/W	13,240	82	46		Y		Y	Y	Y	Y	Y	N	4	27
Central Texas College	Killeen	C,T	St-L	M/W	19,562	78			Y		Y	Y	Y	Y	Y	N	5	48
Collin County Community College District	McKinney	C,T	St-L	M/W	29,703	68	26		Y	Y	S	Y	Y	Y	Y	N	2	49
Culinary Institute LeNotre	Houston	T	Prop	M/W	320				Y	Y	Y			Y	Y	N		3
Dallas Institute of Funeral Service	Dallas	C,T	Ind	M/W	141		52		Y	Y	Y	Y				N		1
Del Mar College	Corpus Christi	C,T	St-L	M/W	11,973	75	26		Y	Y	Y	Y	Y	Y	Y	N	10	102
El Paso Community College	El Paso	C,T	Cou	M/W	29,460	70	20		Y		Y	Y	Y	Y	Y	N	3	65
Galveston College	Galveston	C,T	St-L	M/W	2,071	76												
Hill College	Hillsboro	C,T	Dist	M/W	4,075		26		Y		Y	Y	Y	Y	Y	Y	5	62
Houston Community College	Houston	C,T	St-L	M/W	57,032	71			Y		S	Y	Y	Y	Y	N		77
Interactive College of Technology	Houston	T	Prop	M/W														
Interactive College of Technology	Houston	T	Prop	M/W														
Interactive College of Technology	Pasadena	T	Prop	M/W														
Kilgore College	Kilgore	C,T	St-L	M/W	5,666	60												
Lone Star College–CyFair	Cypress	C,T	St-L	M/W	21,636	69	25		Y	Y	R			Y		N		30
Lone Star College–Kingwood	Kingwood	C,T	St-L	M/W	12,287	69	29		Y	Y	R	Y	Y	Y		N		17
Lone Star College–Montgomery	Conroe	C,T	St-L	M/W	14,411	69	29		Y	Y	R	Y	Y	Y		N		14
Lone Star College–North Harris	Houston	C,T	St-L	M/W	16,290	71	37		Y	Y		Y	Y	Y	Y		15	22
Lone Star College–Tomball	Tomball	C,T	St-L	M/W	9,013	70	35		Y	Y	R	Y	Y	Y		N		15
Lone Star College–University Park	Houston	C,T	St-L	M/W	12,024	70	27				R		Y	Y		N		4
McLennan Community College	Waco	C,T	Cou	M/W	7,149	51	32		Y	Y	Y	Y	Y	Y	Y	N	5	26
Mountain View College	Dallas	C,T	St-L	M/W	9,068	77	37		Y	Y	Y	Y	Y	Y		N	4	11
Navarro College	Corsicana	C,T	St-L	M/W	9,230	66	19		Y	Y	Y	Y	Y	Y	Y	Y	7	46
North Central Texas College	Gainesville	C,T	St-L	M/W	9,618	68												
Northwest Vista College	San Antonio	C,T	St-L	M/W	13,218	68												
Odessa College	Odessa	C,T	St-L	M/W	5,096	68												
Panola College	Carthage	C,T	St-L	M/W	2,675	50	30			R,S	Y	Y	Y	Y	Y	Y	6	48
Paris Junior College	Paris	C,T	St-L	M/W	4,806	62	20		Y	Y	Y	Y	Y	Y		Y	8	62
St. Philip's College	San Antonio	C,T	Dist	M/W	11,604	88	34		Y	Y	Y	Y	Y			N	5	66
San Jacinto College District	Pasadena	C,T	St-L	M/W	28,998	77		42	Y	Y	Y	Y	Y	Y	Y	N	10	81
South Plains College	Levelland	C,T	St-L	M/W	9,053	49	24	95	Y	Y	Y	Y	Y	Y	Y	Y	9	57
Southwest Texas Junior College	Uvalde	C,T	St-L	M/W			19		Y	Y	Y	Y	Y	Y	Y	Y	8	14
Tarrant County College District	Fort Worth	C,T	Cou	M/W	51,688	70	34		Y		Y	Y	Y	Y	Y	N	7	42
Texarkana College	Texarkana	C,T	St-L	M/W	4,296		26		Y		Y	Y	Y	Y	Y	Y	5	40
Texas State Technical College	Waco	C,T	St	M/W	10,689	56	29	10	Y	Y	Y	Y	Y	Y	Y	Y	7	38
Trinity Valley Community College	Athens	C,T	St-L	M/W	7,120	68	44	19	Y	Y	Y	Y	Y	Y	Y	Y	7	55
Tyler Junior College	Tyler	C,T,B	St-L	M/W	11,478	49	24		Y	Y	Y	Y	Y	Y	Y	Y	11	66
Vet Tech Institute of Houston	Houston	T	Prop	M/W	216													
Victoria College	Victoria	C,T	Cou	M/W	4,000	74	37		Y	Y	Y	Y	Y	Y	Y	N	4	14
Weatherford College	Weatherford	C,T	St-L	M/W	5,637		23		Y	Y	R	Y	Y	Y	Y	Y	5	18
Western Texas College	Snyder	C,T	St-L	M/W	2,125	74												
Utah																		
AmeriTech College	Draper	C,T,B	Prop	M/W														
LDS Business College	Salt Lake City	C,T	I-R	M/W	2,191	27												
Nightingale College	Ogden	C,B	Prop	M/W														
Salt Lake Community College	Salt Lake City	C,T	St	M/W	29,901	74	33		Y			Y	Y	Y	Y	N	6	68

This chart includes the names and locations of accredited two-year colleges in the United States, Canada, and other countries and shows institutions' responses to the *Peterson's Annual Survey of Undergraduate Institutions*. If an institution submitted incomplete data, one or more columns opposite the institution's name is blank. A dagger after the school name indicates that the institution has one or more entries in the *Featured Two-Year Colleges* section. If a school does not appear, it did not report any of the information.

Y—Yes; N—No; R—Recommended; S—For Some

Name	Location	Degrees Awarded	Institutional Control	Student Body	Undergraduate Enrollment	Percent Attending Part-Time	Percent 25 Years of Age or Older	Percent of Grads Going on to Four-Year Colleges	High School Equivalency Certificate Accepted	High School Transcript Required	Open Admissions	Need-Based Aid Available	Part-Time Jobs Available	Career Counseling Services Available	Job Placement Services Available	College Housing Available	Number of Sports Offered	Number of Majors Offered
Vermont																		
Community College of Vermont	Montpelier	C,T	St	M/W	6,351		46	36	Y	Y		Y	Y	Y	Y	N		26
New England Culinary Institute	Montpelier	C,B	Prop	M/W	300	14	32		N	Y	Y	Y	Y	Y	Y	N		3
Virginia																		
Central Virginia Community College	Lynchburg	C,T	St	M/W	4,125		21		Y	Y		Y	Y	Y	Y	N		18
Dabney S. Lancaster Community College	Clifton Forge	C,T	St	M/W														
John Tyler Community College	Chester	C,T	St	M/W	10,021	76	42		Y	R		Y	Y	Y	Y	N	3	18
J. Sargeant Reynolds Community College	Richmond	C,T	St	M/W	10,375	73	41	8	Y	Y	Y	Y	Y	Y	Y	N		38
New River Community College	Dublin	C,T	St	M/W	4,477				Y	S		Y	Y	Y	Y	N	4	27
Patrick Henry Community College	Martinsville	C,T	St	M/W	2,405	50	26		Y	Y	Y	Y	Y	Y	Y	N	8	17
Piedmont Virginia Community College	Charlottesville	C,T	St	M/W	5,438				Y	S		Y	Y	Y	Y	N	8	
Rappahannock Community College	Glenns	C,T	St-L	M/W	3,463				Y			Y	Y	Y	Y		1	11
Southwest Virginia Community College	Richlands	C,T	St	M/W	2,481	53	25		Y	Y	Y	Y	Y	Y	Y	N		12
Tidewater Community College	Norfolk	C,T	St	M/W	23,946		49		Y			Y	Y	Y	Y	N	5	26
Virginia Western Community College	Roanoke	C,T	St	M/W	8,632	71	32		Y	Y	R,S	Y	Y	Y		N	3	25
Wytheville Community College	Wytheville	C,T	St	M/W	2,745		26		Y		Y	Y	Y	Y	Y	N	1	21
Washington																		
Bellingham Technical College	Bellingham	C,T	St	M/W	2,864													
Big Bend Community College	Moses Lake	C,T	St	M/W	2,016	28												
Carrington College–Spokane	Spokane	T	Prop	M/W	413													
Cascadia College	Bothell	C,T,B	St	M/W	2,759													
Clark College	Vancouver	C,T,B	St	M/W	10,477	52												
Northwest School of Wooden Boatbuilding	Port Hadlock	T	Ind	M/W				85		Y	Y			Y	Y	N		1
Olympic College	Bremerton	C,T,B	St	M/W	7,253		48		Y	S		Y	Y	Y	Y	Y	7	27
Renton Technical College	Renton	C,T,B	St	M/W	3,961	69	52			S		Y	Y	Y	Y			30
Wenatchee Valley College	Wenatchee	C,T	St-L	M/W	3,218	27												
West Virginia																		
Blue Ridge Community and Technical College	Martinsburg	C,T	St	M/W	5,599	81	73		Y	Y	Y			Y	Y	N		25
Mountain State College	Parkersburg	T	Prop	M/W	176	1												
Potomac State College of West Virginia University	Keyser	C,T,B	St	M/W	1,475	22												
West Virginia Junior College–Bridgeport	Bridgeport	C,T	Prop	M/W	150		30		Y	Y	R	Y	Y	Y	Y	N		5
Wisconsin																		
Blackhawk Technical College	Janesville	C,T	Dist	M/W	2,034	60	55	0	Y	Y	Y	Y	Y	Y	Y	N		22
Chippewa Valley Technical College	Eau Claire	C,T	Dist	M/W					Y	Y		Y	Y	Y	Y	N		37
Fox Valley Technical College	Appleton	T	St-L	M/W	10,889	78	43		Y		S	Y	Y	Y	Y	N	2	53
Gateway Technical College	Kenosha	T	St-L	M/W	8,722	84	48		Y		Y	Y	Y	Y		N		37
Madison Area Technical College	Madison	C,T	Dist	M/W	16,537	70	50		Y		S	Y	Y	Y	Y	Y	9	46
Northcentral Technical College	Wausau	C,T	Dist	M/W	4,158	65	49		Y	Y	Y	Y	Y	Y	Y	Y	6	36
University of Wisconsin–Fox Valley	Menasha	C,T	St	M/W	1,399		25	70				Y	Y	Y	Y	N	7	1
Waukesha County Technical College	Pewaukee	T	St-L	M/W	7,947	79	55		Y			Y	Y	Y	Y	N		41
Wisconsin Indianhead Technical College	Shell Lake	C,T	Dist	M/W	2,944	61	51		Y							N		19
Wyoming																		
Casper College	Casper	C,T	St-L	M/W	3,626	52	34		Y	Y	Y	Y	Y	Y	Y	Y	10	100
Central Wyoming College	Riverton	C,T	St-L	M/W	2,016	66	43	56	Y		R	Y	Y	Y	Y	Y	17	61
Eastern Wyoming College	Torrington	C,T	St-L	M/W	1,604	62	29				R	Y	Y	Y	Y	Y	4	43
Laramie County Community College	Cheyenne	C,T	Dist	M/W	4,132	58	40		Y	Y	S	Y	Y	Y		Y	11	62
Northwest College	Powell	C,T	St-L	M/W	1,664	39	25		Y	Y	Y	Y	Y			Y	9	52
Sheridan College	Sheridan	C,T	St-L	M/W	4,307	68												
Western Wyoming Community College	Rock Springs	C,T	St-L	M/W	3,392	65	33	8	Y	Y	R	Y	Y	Y	Y	Y	5	84
OTHER COUNTRIES																		
Marshall Islands																		
College of the Marshall Islands	Majuro	T	St	M/W	995	30	21			Y	Y	Y				Y		5
Palau																		
Palau Community College	Koror	C,T	Terr	M/W	627	45												

Profiles of Two-Year Colleges

NOTICE: Certain portions of or information contained in this book have been submitted and paid for by the educational institution identified, and such institutions take full responsibility for the accuracy, timeliness, completeness and functionality of such content. Such portions or information include (i) each display ad in the "Profiles" section from pages 49 through 328 that comprises a half or full page of information covering a single educational institution, and (ii) each two-page description in the "Featured Two-Year Colleges" section from pages 334 through 346.

ALABAMA

Bevill State Community College
Jasper, Alabama

- **State-supported** 2-year, founded 1969, part of Alabama Community College System
- **Rural** 245-acre campus with easy access to Birmingham
- **Coed**, 3,806 undergraduate students, 48% full-time, 59% women, 36% men

Undergraduates 1,838 full-time, 1,771 part-time. Students come from 8 states and territories; 3% are from out of state; 14% Black or African American, non-Hispanic/Latino; 2% Hispanic/Latino; 0.4% Asian, non-Hispanic/Latino; 0.3% American Indian or Alaska Native, non-Hispanic/Latino; 0.6% Two or more races, non-Hispanic/Latino; 1% Race/ethnicity unknown; 50% transferred in. *Retention:* 56% of full-time freshmen returned.
Freshmen *Admission:* 3,607 applied, 3,281 admitted, 937 enrolled.
Faculty *Total:* 286, 41% full-time, 12% with terminal degrees. *Student/faculty ratio:* 17:1.
Majors Administrative assistant and secretarial science; child-care and support services management; computer and information sciences; drafting and design technology; electrician; emergency medical technology (EMT paramedic); general studies; heating, ventilation, air conditioning and refrigeration engineering technology; industrial electronics technology; industrial mechanics and maintenance technology; instrumentation technology; liberal arts and sciences/liberal studies; registered nursing/registered nurse; salon/beauty salon management; tool and die technology; vehicle maintenance and repair technologies.
Academics *Calendar:* semesters. *Degree:* certificates and associate. *Special study options:* academic remediation for entering students, adult/continuing education programs, advanced placement credit, cooperative education, distance learning, honors programs, off-campus study, part-time degree program, services for LD students, summer session for credit.
Library Main Library plus 5 others. *Books:* 113,246 (physical); *Serial titles:* 3,563 (physical); *Databases:* 15. Weekly public service hours: 56.
Student Life *Housing Options:* coed. Campus housing is university owned. *Activities and Organizations:* drama/theater group, choral group, Student Government Association, Campus Ministries, Circle K, Outdoorsmen Club, Sigma Kappa Delta.
Costs (2016–17) *Tuition:* state resident $2808 full-time, $117 per credit hour part-time; nonresident $5616 full-time, $234 per credit hour part-time. Full-time tuition and fees vary according to course load and program. Part-time tuition and fees vary according to course load and program. *Required fees:* $711 full-time, $29 per credit hour part-time. *Room and board:* $1850. Room and board charges vary according to board plan and location. *Payment plan:* installment. *Waivers:* employees or children of employees.
Financial Aid Of all full-time matriculated undergraduates who enrolled in 2015, 2,149 applied for aid, 1,867 were judged to have need, 49 had their need fully met. 42 Federal Work-Study jobs (averaging $3224). In 2015, 40 non-need-based awards were made. *Average percent of need met:* 46%. *Average financial aid package:* $5357. *Average need-based gift aid:* $5544. *Average non-need-based aid:* $2988.
Applying *Options:* electronic application, early admission, deferred entrance. *Required:* high school transcript. *Application deadlines:* rolling (freshmen), rolling (transfers).
Freshman Application Contact Ms. Melissa Stowe, Dean of Students, Bevill State Community College, 1411 Indiana Avenue, Jasper, AL 35501. *Phone:* 205-387-0511 Ext. 5813. *E-mail:* melissa.stowe@bscc.edu. *Website:* http://www.bscc.edu/.

Bishop State Community College
Mobile, Alabama

Freshman Application Contact Bishop State Community College, 351 North Broad Street, Mobile, AL 36603-5898. *Phone:* 251-405-7000. *Toll-free phone:* 800-523-7235. *Website:* http://www.bishop.edu/.

Calhoun Community College
Decatur, Alabama

Freshman Application Contact Admissions Office, Calhoun Community College, PO Box 2216, Decatur, AL 35609-2216. *Phone:* 256-306-2593. *Toll-free phone:* 800-626-3628. *Fax:* 256-306-2941. *E-mail:* admissions@calhoun.edu. *Website:* http://www.calhoun.edu/.

Central Alabama Community College
Alexander City, Alabama

Freshman Application Contact Ms. Donna Whaley, Central Alabama Community College, 1675 Cherokee Road, Alexander City, AL 35011-0699. *Phone:* 256-234-6346 Ext. 6232. *Toll-free phone:* 800-634-2657. *Website:* http://www.cacc.edu/.

Chattahoochee Valley Community College
Phenix City, Alabama

Freshman Application Contact Chattahoochee Valley Community College, 2602 College Drive, Phenix City, AL 36869-7928. *Phone:* 334-291-4929. *Website:* http://www.cv.edu/.

Coastal Alabama Community College
Bay Minette, Alabama

- **State-supported** 2-year, founded 1965, part of Alabama Community College System
- **Small-town** 105-acre campus
- **Coed**

Undergraduates 2,139 full-time, 1,184 part-time. 3% are from out of state; 9% live on campus.
Faculty *Student/faculty ratio:* 15:1.
Academics *Calendar:* semesters. *Degree:* certificates and associate. *Special study options:* academic remediation for entering students, adult/continuing education programs, advanced placement credit, cooperative education, honors programs, internships, part-time degree program, services for LD students.
Library Austin R. Meadows Library plus 3 others. *Books:* 66,811 (physical); *Serial titles:* 2,924 (physical); *Databases:* 67. Weekly public service hours: 40.
Student Life *Campus security:* 24-hour emergency response devices and patrols, controlled dormitory access.
Athletics Member NJCAA.
Costs (2016–17) *Tuition:* state resident $4380 full-time, $117 per credit hour part-time; nonresident $7890 full-time, $234 per credit hour part-time. Full-time tuition and fees vary according to class time, course level, course load, program, and student level. Part-time tuition and fees vary according to class time, course level, course load, program, and student level. *Required fees:* $850 full-time, $29 per credit hour part-time, $29 per credit hour part-time. *Room and board:* $5800. Room and board charges vary according to board plan and housing facility.
Applying *Options:* early admission, deferred entrance. *Required:* high school transcript.
Freshman Application Contact Ms. Carmelita Mikkelsen, Director of Admissions and High School Relations, Coastal Alabama Community College, 1900 Highway 31 South, Bay Minette, AL 36507. *Phone:* 251-580-2213. *Toll-free phone:* 800-381-3722. *Fax:* 251-580-2285. *E-mail:* cmikkelsen@faulknerstate.edu. *Website:* http://www.faulknerstate.edu/.

Community College of the Air Force
Maxwell Gunter Air Force Base, Alabama

- **Federally supported** 2-year, founded 1972, part of Air University
- **Suburban** campus
- **Coed**, 268,763 undergraduate students, 100% full-time, 19% women, 81% men

Undergraduates 268,763 full-time.
Freshmen *Admission:* 31,231 applied, 31,231 admitted, 31,231 enrolled.
Faculty *Total:* 6,144, 100% full-time.
Majors Aeronautics/aviation/aerospace science and technology; airframe mechanics and aircraft maintenance technology; air traffic control; apparel and textile marketing management; atmospheric sciences and meteorology; automobile/automotive mechanics technology; avionics maintenance technology; biomedical technology; cardiovascular technology; clinical/medical laboratory technology; commercial and advertising art; communications technology; construction engineering technology; criminal justice/law enforcement administration; dental assisting; dental laboratory technology; dietetics; educational/instructional technology; educational leadership and administration; electrical, electronic and communications engineering technology; environmental health; environmental studies; finance; fire science/firefighting; health/health-care administration;

hematology technology; hotel/motel administration; human resources management; industrial technology; legal assistant/paralegal; logistics, materials, and supply chain management; management information systems; medical radiologic technology; mental health counseling; metallurgical technology; music performance; nuclear medical technology; occupational safety and health technology; office management; ophthalmic laboratory technology; parks, recreation and leisure; pharmacy technician; physical therapy technology; physiology; public relations/image management; purchasing, procurement/acquisitions and contracts management; security and loss prevention; social work; surgical technology.

Academics *Calendar:* continuous. *Degrees:* certificates and associate (courses conducted at 125 branch locations worldwide for members of the U.S. Air Force). *Special study options:* academic remediation for entering students, adult/continuing education programs, advanced placement credit, distance learning, independent study, internships, off-campus study.

Library Air Force Library Service.

Student Life *Housing:* college housing not available. *Campus security:* 24-hour emergency response devices and patrols. *Student services:* health clinic, personal/psychological counseling, legal services.

Athletics *Intramural sports:* badminton W, basketball M/W, bowling M/W, cross-country running M/W, football M, golf M/W, racquetball M/W, softball M/W, table tennis M/W, tennis M/W, volleyball M/W, weight lifting M/W.

Standardized Tests *Required:* Armed Services Vocational Aptitude Battery (ASVAB) (for admission).

Costs (2016–17) *Comprehensive fee:* Air Force Tuition Assistance (TA) provides 100% tuition and fees for courses taken by active duty personnel.

Applying *Options:* electronic application. *Required:* high school transcript, interview, military physical, good character, criminal background check. *Application deadlines:* rolling (freshmen), rolling (transfers). *Notification:* continuous (freshmen), continuous (transfers).

Freshman Application Contact Ms. Gwendolyn Ford, Chief of Admissions Flight, Community College of the Air Force, Community College of the Air Force, 100 South Turner Boulevard, Maxwell Air Force Base, Maxwell - Gunter AFB, AL 36114-3011. *Phone:* 334-649-5081. *Fax:* 334-649-5015. *E-mail:* gwendolyn.ford@us.af.mil. *Website:* http://www.au.af.mil/au/ccaf/.

Enterprise State Community College
Enterprise, Alabama

- **State-supported** 2-year, founded 1965, part of Alabama College System
- **Small-town** 100-acre campus
- **Coed**

Undergraduates 1,859 full-time, 1,551 part-time. 5% are from out of state; 7% transferred in.

Faculty *Student/faculty ratio:* 18:1.

Academics *Calendar:* semesters. *Degree:* certificates, diplomas, and associate. *Special study options:* academic remediation for entering students, accelerated degree program, adult/continuing education programs, advanced placement credit, distance learning, English as a second language, honors programs, independent study, internships, part-time degree program, services for LD students, summer session for credit.

Library Snuggs Hall.

Student Life *Campus security:* security personnel.

Athletics Member NJCAA.

Costs (2016–17) *Tuition:* state resident $3276 full-time, $117 per credit hour part-time; nonresident $6496 full-time, $232 per credit hour part-time. *Required fees:* $812 full-time. *Room and board:* $4088.

Applying *Required:* high school transcript.

Director of Admissions Mr. Gary Deas, Associate Dean of Students/Registrar, Enterprise State Community College, 600 Plaza Drive, Enterprise, AL 36330. *Phone:* 334-347-2623 Ext. 2233. *E-mail:* gdeas@eocc.edu. *Website:* http://www.escc.edu/.

Fortis College
Mobile, Alabama

Admissions Office Contact Fortis College, 7033 Airport Boulevard, Mobile, AL 36608. *Toll-free phone:* 855-4-FORTIS. *Website:* http://www.fortis.edu/.

Fortis College
Montgomery, Alabama

Admissions Office Contact Fortis College, 3470 Eastdale Circle, Montgomery, AL 36117. *Toll-free phone:* 855-4-FORTIS. *Website:* http://www.fortis.edu/.

Fortis College
Montgomery, Alabama

Admissions Office Contact Fortis College, 3736 Atlanta Highway, Montgomery, AL 36109. *Toll-free phone:* 855-4-FORTIS. *Website:* http://www.fortis.edu/.

Fortis Institute
Birmingham, Alabama

Admissions Office Contact Fortis Institute, 100 London Parkway, Suite 150, Birmingham, AL 35211. *Toll-free phone:* 855-4-FORTIS. *Website:* http://www.fortis.edu/.

Gadsden State Community College
Gadsden, Alabama

- **State-supported** 2-year, founded 1965, part of Alabama Community College System
- **Small-town** 275-acre campus with easy access to Birmingham
- **Coed**

Undergraduates 2,576 full-time, 2,442 part-time. Students come from 8 states and territories; 45 other countries; 19% Black or African American, non-Hispanic/Latino; 3% Hispanic/Latino; 0.5% Asian, non-Hispanic/Latino; 0.1% Native Hawaiian or other Pacific Islander, non-Hispanic/Latino; 1% American Indian or Alaska Native, non-Hispanic/Latino; 3% Two or more races, non-Hispanic/Latino; 0.9% Race/ethnicity unknown; 2% international; 6% transferred in; 2% live on campus.

Faculty *Student/faculty ratio:* 17:1.

Academics *Calendar:* semesters. *Degree:* certificates and associate. *Special study options:* academic remediation for entering students, adult/continuing education programs, advanced placement credit, cooperative education, distance learning, English as a second language, external degree program, honors programs, internships, part-time degree program, services for LD students, study abroad, summer session for credit. *ROTC:* Army (b).

Library Meadows Library plus 2 others. *Books:* 79,933 (physical), 62,846 (digital/electronic); *Databases:* 75.

Student Life *Campus security:* 24-hour patrols.

Athletics Member NJCAA.

Costs (2016–17) *Tuition:* state resident $2808 full-time, $117 per credit hour part-time; nonresident $5616 full-time, $234 per credit hour part-time. Full-time tuition and fees vary according to reciprocity agreements. Part-time tuition and fees vary according to reciprocity agreements. *Required fees:* $456 full-time, $19 per credit hour part-time. *Room and board:* $3600.

Applying *Options:* electronic application, early admission, deferred entrance. *Required:* high school transcript.

Freshman Application Contact Mrs. Jennie Dobson, Admissions and Records, Gadsden State Community College, PO Box 227, 1001 George Wallace Drive, Gadsden, AL 35902-0227. *Phone:* 256-549-8210. *Toll-free phone:* 800-226-5563. *Fax:* 256-549-8205. *E-mail:* info@gadsdenstate.edu. *Website:* http://www.gadsdenstate.edu/.

George Corley Wallace State Community College
Selma, Alabama

Director of Admissions Ms. Sunette Newman, Registrar, George Corley Wallace State Community College, PO Box 2530, Selma, AL 36702. *Phone:* 334-876-9305. *Website:* http://www.wccs.edu/.

George C. Wallace Community College
Dothan, Alabama

- **State-supported** 2-year, founded 1949, part of The Alabama Community College System
- **Rural** 258-acre campus
- **Coed**

Undergraduates 2,161 full-time, 2,608 part-time. Students come from 12 states and territories; 4% are from out of state; 29% Black or African American, non-Hispanic/Latino; 2% Hispanic/Latino; 0.7% Asian, non-Hispanic/Latino; 0.1% Native Hawaiian or other Pacific Islander, non-Hispanic/Latino; 0.6% American Indian or Alaska Native, non-Hispanic/Latino; 1% Two or more races, non-Hispanic/Latino; 0.1% Race/ethnicity unknown; 47% transferred in.

Faculty *Student/faculty ratio:* 19:1.

Academics *Calendar:* semesters. *Degree:* certificates, diplomas, and associate. *Special study options:* academic remediation for entering students,

adult/continuing education programs, advanced placement credit, cooperative education, distance learning, English as a second language, independent study, off-campus study, part-time degree program.
Library Learning Resources Centers.
Student Life *Campus security:* 24-hour patrols.
Athletics Member NJCAA.
Standardized Tests *Recommended:* SAT or ACT (for admission).
Costs (2016–17) *Tuition:* state resident $3450 full-time, $115 per credit hour part-time; nonresident $6900 full-time, $230 per credit hour part-time. Full-time tuition and fees vary according to reciprocity agreements. Part-time tuition and fees vary according to reciprocity agreements. *Required fees:* $810 full-time, $27 per credit hour part-time.
Financial Aid Of all full-time matriculated undergraduates who enrolled in 2015, 82 Federal Work-Study jobs (averaging $1975).
Applying *Options:* early admission. *Required:* high school transcript.
Freshman Application Contact Mr. Keith Saulsberry, Director, Enrollment Services/Registrar, George C. Wallace Community College, 1141 Wallace Drive, Dothan, AL 36303. *Phone:* 334-983-3521 Ext. 2470. *Toll-free phone:* 800-543-2426. *Fax:* 334-983-3600.
E-mail: ksaulsberry@wallace.edu. *Website:* http://www.wallace.edu/.

H. Councill Trenholm State Community College
Montgomery, Alabama

- **State-supported** 2-year, founded 1966, part of Alabama Community College System
- **Urban** 83-acre campus with easy access to Montgomery
- **Coed,** 1,661 undergraduate students, 45% full-time, 41% women, 41% men
- 26% of applicants were admitted

Undergraduates 745 full-time, 619 part-time. Students come from 2 states and territories; 66% Black or African American, non-Hispanic/Latino; 2% Hispanic/Latino; 2% Asian, non-Hispanic/Latino; 0.1% American Indian or Alaska Native, non-Hispanic/Latino; 0.1% Two or more races, non-Hispanic/Latino; 12% transferred in. *Retention:* 62% of full-time freshmen returned.
Freshmen *Admission:* 1,658 applied, 424 admitted, 351 enrolled.
Faculty *Total:* 101, 51% full-time, 16% with terminal degrees. *Student/faculty ratio:* 15:1.
Majors Accounting technology and bookkeeping; administrative assistant and secretarial science; automotive engineering technology; child-care and support services management; computer and information sciences; culinary arts; dental assisting; diagnostic medical sonography and ultrasound technology; drafting and design technology; electrician; emergency medical technology (EMT paramedic); graphic communications related; heating, ventilation, air conditioning and refrigeration engineering technology; industrial mechanics and maintenance technology; machine tool technology; manufacturing engineering technology; medical/clinical assistant; radiologic technology/science.
Academics *Calendar:* semesters. *Degree:* certificates, diplomas, and associate. *Special study options:* academic remediation for entering students, adult/continuing education programs, advanced placement credit, cooperative education, distance learning, English as a second language, external degree program, independent study, internships, part-time degree program, services for LD students, summer session for credit.
Library Trenholm State Learning Resources plus 2 others. *Books:* 10,164 (physical), 36,973 (digital/electronic); *Serial titles:* 91 (physical), 58 (digital/electronic); *Databases:* 20. Weekly public service hours: 107.
Student Life *Housing:* college housing not available. *Activities and Organizations:* Student Government Association, College Ambassadors, National Society of Leadership and Science, SkillsUSA–VICA. *Campus security:* 24-hour patrols. *Student services:* personal/psychological counseling.
Standardized Tests *Required for some:* SAT or ACT (for admission).
Costs (2017–18) *Tuition:* state resident $2856 full-time, $119 per credit hour part-time; nonresident $5712 full-time, $238 per credit hour part-time. *Required fees:* $624 full-time, $26 per credit hour part-time. *Payment plan:* installment. *Waivers:* senior citizens and employees or children of employees.
Applying *Options:* electronic application, early admission. *Required:* high school transcript. *Application deadlines:* rolling (freshmen), rolling (transfers).
Freshman Application Contact Mrs. Tennie McBryde, Registrar, H. Councill Trenholm State Community College, Montgomery, AL 36108. *Phone:* 334-420-4306. *Toll-free phone:* 866-753-4544. *Fax:* 334-420-4201.
E-mail: tmcbryde@trenholmstate.edu.
Website: http://www.trenholmstate.edu/.

Jefferson State Community College
Birmingham, Alabama

- **State-supported** 2-year, founded 1965, part of Alabama Community College System
- **Suburban** 351-acre campus with easy access to Birmingham
- **Endowment** $1.2 million
- **Coed,** 8,943 undergraduate students, 31% full-time, 61% women, 39% men

Undergraduates 2,799 full-time, 6,144 part-time. Students come from 28 states and territories; 53 other countries; 2% are from out of state; 23% Black or African American, non-Hispanic/Latino; 4% Hispanic/Latino; 2% Asian, non-Hispanic/Latino; 0.1% Native Hawaiian or other Pacific Islander, non-Hispanic/Latino; 0.3% American Indian or Alaska Native, non-Hispanic/Latino; 3% Two or more races, non-Hispanic/Latino; 0.1% Race/ethnicity unknown; 2% international; 11% transferred in. *Retention:* 57% of full-time freshmen returned.
Freshmen *Admission:* 4,739 applied, 2,624 admitted, 1,696 enrolled. *Average high school GPA:* 2.98.
Faculty *Total:* 461, 31% full-time, 8% with terminal degrees. *Student/faculty ratio:* 20:1.
Majors Accounting technology and bookkeeping; administrative assistant and secretarial science; child-care and support services management; clinical/medical laboratory technology; computer and information sciences; construction engineering technology; criminal justice/police science; emergency medical technology (EMT paramedic); engineering technology; fire services administration; funeral service and mortuary science; general studies; hospitality administration; liberal arts and sciences/liberal studies; office management; physical therapy technology; radiologic technology/science; registered nursing/registered nurse; veterinary/animal health technology.
Academics *Calendar:* semesters. *Degree:* certificates and associate. *Special study options:* academic remediation for entering students, adult/continuing education programs, advanced placement credit, distance learning, English as a second language, honors programs, independent study, internships, part-time degree program, services for LD students, summer session for credit. *ROTC:* Army (c), Air Force (c).
Library Jefferson State Libraries plus 4 others. *Books:* 80,798 (physical), 180,799 (digital/electronic); *Serial titles:* 193 (physical); *Databases:* 60. Weekly public service hours: 62.
Student Life *Housing:* college housing not available. *Activities and Organizations:* choral group, Student Government Association, Phi Theta Kappa, Sigma Kappa Delta, Jefferson State Ambassadors, Enactus. *Campus security:* 24-hour patrols.
Athletics Member NJCAA.
Costs (2017–18) *Tuition:* state resident $4500 full-time, $150 per semester hour part-time; nonresident $8070 full-time, $269 per semester hour part-time. Full-time tuition and fees vary according to course load. Part-time tuition and fees vary according to course load. *Waivers:* senior citizens and employees or children of employees.
Applying *Options:* electronic application, early admission, deferred entrance. *Required for some:* high school transcript. *Application deadlines:* rolling (freshmen), rolling (transfers). *Notification:* continuous (freshmen), continuous (transfers).
Freshman Application Contact Mrs. Lillian Owens, Director of Admissions and Retention, Jefferson State Community College, 2601 Carson Road, Birmingham, AL 35215-3098. *Phone:* 205-853-1200 Ext. 7990. *Toll-free phone:* 800-239-5900. *Fax:* 205-856-6070.
E-mail: lowens@jeffstateonline.com.
Website: http://www.jeffstateonline.com/.

J. F. Drake State Community and Technical College
Huntsville, Alabama

- **State-supported** 2-year, founded 1961, part of Alabama Community College System
- **Urban** 6-acre campus
- **Coed**

Undergraduates 484 full-time, 512 part-time. Students come from 2 states and territories; 11% transferred in. *Retention:* 41% of full-time freshmen returned.
Faculty *Student/faculty ratio:* 15:1.
Academics *Calendar:* semesters. *Degree:* certificates and associate. *Special study options:* academic remediation for entering students, cooperative education, distance learning, English as a second language, internships, part-time degree program, services for LD students.
Library S.C. O'Neal Library and Technology Center.
Student Life *Campus security:* 24-hour patrols.

Costs (2016–17) *Tuition:* state resident $3510 full-time, $117 per credit hour part-time; nonresident $7020 full-time, $234 per credit hour part-time. Full-time tuition and fees vary according to course load. Part-time tuition and fees vary according to course load. *Required fees:* $840 full-time, $28 per credit hour part-time, $28 per credit hour part-time. *Room and board:* $6300.

Financial Aid Of all full-time matriculated undergraduates who enrolled in 2015, 11 Federal Work-Study jobs (averaging $3179).

Applying *Options:* electronic application, deferred entrance. *Required:* high school transcript.

Freshman Application Contact Mrs. Kristin Treadway, Assistant Director of Admissions, J. F. Drake State Community and Technical College, Huntsville, AL 35811. *Phone:* 256-551-3111. *Toll-free phone:* 888-413-7253. *E-mail:* kristin.treadway@drakestate.edu. *Website:* http://www.drakestate.edu/.

J F Ingram State Technical College
Deatsville, Alabama

Admissions Office Contact J F Ingram State Technical College, 5375 Ingram Rd, Deatsville, AL 36022. *Website:* http://www.istc.edu/.

Lawson State Community College
Birmingham, Alabama

Freshman Application Contact Mr. Jeff Shelley, Director of Admissions and Records, Lawson State Community College, 3060 Wilson Road, SW, Birmingham, AL 35221-1798. *Phone:* 205-929-6361. *Fax:* 205-923-7106. *E-mail:* jshelley@lawsonstate.edu. *Website:* http://www.lawsonstate.edu/.

Lurleen B. Wallace Community College
Andalusia, Alabama

- **State-supported** 2-year, founded 1969, part of Alabama Community College System
- **Small-town** 200-acre campus
- **Coed,** 1,742 undergraduate students, 59% full-time, 57% women, 43% men

Undergraduates 1,035 full-time, 707 part-time. Students come from 4 states and territories; 8 other countries; 4% are from out of state; 22% Black or African American, non-Hispanic/Latino; 2% Hispanic/Latino; 0.3% Asian, non-Hispanic/Latino; 0.6% American Indian or Alaska Native, non-Hispanic/Latino; 2% Two or more races, non-Hispanic/Latino; 0.5% Race/ethnicity unknown; 0.3% international; 19% transferred in.

Freshmen *Admission:* 453 enrolled.

Faculty *Total:* 95, 58% full-time. *Student/faculty ratio:* 18:1.

Majors Administrative assistant and secretarial science; child-care and support services management; computer and information sciences; diagnostic medical sonography and ultrasound technology; emergency medical technology (EMT paramedic); forest technology; general studies; industrial electronics technology; liberal arts and sciences/liberal studies; registered nursing/registered nurse.

Academics *Calendar:* semesters. *Degree:* certificates and associate. *Special study options:* academic remediation for entering students, cooperative education, distance learning, honors programs, independent study, part-time degree program, summer session for credit.

Library Lurleen B. Wallace Library plus 3 others. Students can reserve study rooms.

Student Life *Housing:* college housing not available. *Activities and Organizations:* drama/theater group, choral group, Student Government Association, Student Ambassadors, Campus Civitan, Christian Student Ministries, Saints Angels. *Campus security:* security cameras. *Student services:* personal/psychological counseling.

Athletics Member NJCAA. *Intercollegiate sports:* baseball M(s), basketball M(s)/W(s), softball W(s).

Costs (2016–17) *Tuition:* state resident $3510 full-time, $117 per credit hour part-time; nonresident $7020 full-time, $234 per credit hour part-time. Full-time tuition and fees vary according to course load. Part-time tuition and fees vary according to course load. *Required fees:* $870 full-time, $29 per credit hour part-time. *Payment plan:* installment. *Waivers:* senior citizens and employees or children of employees.

Financial Aid Of all full-time matriculated undergraduates who enrolled in 2014, 103 Federal Work-Study jobs.

Applying *Options:* electronic application. *Required:* high school transcript. *Application deadlines:* rolling (freshmen), rolling (transfers).

Freshman Application Contact Lurleen B. Wallace Community College, PO Box 1418, Andalusia, AL 36420-1418. *Phone:* 334-881-2273. *Website:* http://www.lbwcc.edu/.

Marion Military Institute
Marion, Alabama

- **State-supported** 2-year, founded 1842, part of Alabama Community College System
- **Rural** 130-acre campus with easy access to Birmingham
- **Coed**

Undergraduates 449 full-time, 8 part-time. Students come from 36 states and territories; 54% are from out of state; 21% Black or African American, non-Hispanic/Latino; 9% Hispanic/Latino; 2% Asian, non-Hispanic/Latino; 0.4% Native Hawaiian or other Pacific Islander, non-Hispanic/Latino; 0.7% American Indian or Alaska Native, non-Hispanic/Latino; 5% Two or more races, non-Hispanic/Latino; 1% Race/ethnicity unknown; 4% transferred in; 100% live on campus. *Retention:* 41% of full-time freshmen returned.

Faculty *Student/faculty ratio:* 17:1.

Academics *Calendar:* semesters. *Degree:* associate. *Special study options:* academic remediation for entering students, English as a second language, services for LD students. *ROTC:* Army (b), Air Force (c).

Library Baer Memorial Library.

Student Life *Campus security:* 24-hour patrols.

Athletics Member NJCAA.

Standardized Tests *Required:* SAT or ACT (for admission).

Financial Aid Of all full-time matriculated undergraduates who enrolled in 2015, 29 Federal Work-Study jobs (averaging $210).

Applying *Options:* electronic application, deferred entrance. *Application fee:* $30. *Required:* high school transcript, minimum 2.0 GPA.

Freshman Application Contact Mrs. Brittany Crawford, Director of Admissions, Marion Military Institute, 1101 Washington Street, Marion, AL 36756. *Phone:* 800-664-1842. *Toll-free phone:* 800-664-1842. *Fax:* 334-683-2383. *E-mail:* bcrawford@marionmilitary.edu. *Website:* http://www.marionmilitary.edu/.

Northeast Alabama Community College
Rainsville, Alabama

- **State-supported** 2-year, founded 1963, part of Alabama Community College System
- **Rural** 117-acre campus
- **Coed**

Undergraduates 1,193 full-time, 1,511 part-time. Students come from 3 states and territories; 2% Black or African American, non-Hispanic/Latino; 8% Hispanic/Latino; 0.8% Asian, non-Hispanic/Latino; 3% American Indian or Alaska Native, non-Hispanic/Latino; 1% Race/ethnicity unknown; 13% transferred in.

Faculty *Student/faculty ratio:* 22:1.

Academics *Calendar:* semesters. *Degree:* certificates and associate. *Special study options:* academic remediation for entering students, accelerated degree program, adult/continuing education programs, advanced placement credit, cooperative education, distance learning, double majors, English as a second language, honors programs, independent study, internships, part-time degree program, services for LD students, summer session for credit.

Library Cecil B. Word Learning Resources Center. *Books:* 62,979 (physical), 47,085 (digital/electronic); *Serial titles:* 95 (physical); *Databases:* 49. Weekly public service hours: 58; students can reserve study rooms.

Student Life *Campus security:* 24-hour emergency response devices.

Costs (2016–17) *Tuition:* state resident $3450 full-time, $115 per credit hour part-time; nonresident $6900 full-time, $230 per credit hour part-time. *Required fees:* $870 full-time, $29 per credit hour part-time, $29 per credit hour part-time. *Payment plans:* installment, deferred payment.

Financial Aid Of all full-time matriculated undergraduates who enrolled in 2015, 40 Federal Work-Study jobs (averaging $2500).

Applying *Required:* high school transcript.

Freshman Application Contact Northeast Alabama Community College, PO Box 159, Rainsville, AL 35986-0159. *Phone:* 256-228-6001 Ext. 2325. *Website:* http://www.nacc.edu/.

Northwest-Shoals Community College
Muscle Shoals, Alabama

- **State-supported** 2-year, founded 1963, part of Alabama Community College System
- **Small-town** 210-acre campus
- **Endowment** $733,034
- **Coed,** 3,752 undergraduate students, 42% full-time, 57% women, 43% men

Undergraduates 1,576 full-time, 2,176 part-time. Students come from 3 states and territories; 11% Black or African American, non-Hispanic/Latino; 4% Hispanic/Latino; 0.3% Asian, non-Hispanic/Latino; 0.1% Native Hawaiian or other Pacific Islander, non-Hispanic/Latino; 0.8% American Indian or Alaska

Native, non-Hispanic/Latino; 0.3% Two or more races, non-Hispanic/Latino; 2% Race/ethnicity unknown; 0.7% international; 3% transferred in.
Freshmen *Admission:* 5,386 applied, 5,386 admitted, 988 enrolled.
Faculty *Total:* 161, 47% full-time, 5% with terminal degrees. *Student/faculty ratio:* 23:1.
Majors Administrative assistant and secretarial science; child-care and support services management; child development; computer and information sciences; criminal justice/police science; drafting and design technology; emergency medical technology (EMT paramedic); environmental engineering technology; general studies; industrial electronics technology; industrial mechanics and maintenance technology; liberal arts and sciences/liberal studies; medical/clinical assistant; multi/interdisciplinary studies related; registered nursing/registered nurse; salon/beauty salon management.
Academics *Calendar:* semesters. *Degree:* certificates and associate. *Special study options:* academic remediation for entering students, accelerated degree program, adult/continuing education programs, advanced placement credit, cooperative education, distance learning, double majors, honors programs, independent study, internships, off-campus study, part-time degree program, services for LD students, summer session for credit.
Library Larry W. McCoy Learning Resource Center. *Books:* 61,555 (physical), 38,143 (digital/electronic); *Databases:* 2. Weekly public service hours: 59.
Student Life *Housing:* college housing not available. *Activities and Organizations:* choral group, Student Government Association, Science Club, Phi Theta Kappa, Baptist Campus Ministry, Northwest-Shoals Singers. *Campus security:* 24-hour emergency response devices.
Athletics *Intramural sports:* basketball M/W, football M/W, tennis M/W.
Costs (2017–18) *Tuition:* state resident $4320 full-time, $117 per credit hour part-time; nonresident $8640 full-time, $234 per credit hour part-time. Full-time tuition and fees vary according to course load. Part-time tuition and fees vary according to course load. *Required fees:* $841 full-time, $27 per credit hour part-time. *Waivers:* senior citizens and employees or children of employees.
Financial Aid Of all full-time matriculated undergraduates who enrolled in 2016, 44 Federal Work-Study jobs (averaging $2396). *Financial aid deadline:* 6/1.
Applying *Options:* electronic application. *Required:* high school transcript. *Application deadlines:* rolling (freshmen), rolling (transfers). *Notification:* continuous (transfers).
Freshman Application Contact Mr. Tom Carter, Assistant Dean of Recruitment, Admissions and Financial Aid, Northwest-Shoals Community College, PO Box 2545, Muscle Shoals, AL 35662. *Phone:* 256-331-5263. *Fax:* 256-331-5366. *E-mail:* tom.carter@nwscc.edu.
Website: http://www.nwscc.edu/.

Reid State Technical College
Evergreen, Alabama

- **State-supported** 2-year, founded 1966, part of Alabama Community College System
- **Rural** 26-acre campus
- **Coed,** 489 undergraduate students, 42% full-time, 61% women, 39% men

Undergraduates 205 full-time, 284 part-time. Students come from 2 states and territories; 1% are from out of state; 57% Black or African American, non-Hispanic/Latino; 0.4% Hispanic/Latino; 1% American Indian or Alaska Native, non-Hispanic/Latino; 1% Two or more races, non-Hispanic/Latino.
Freshmen *Admission:* 76 applied, 76 admitted, 76 enrolled.
Faculty *Total:* 32, 63% full-time, 3% with terminal degrees. *Student/faculty ratio:* 12:1.
Majors Administrative assistant and secretarial science; electrical, electronic and communications engineering technology.
Academics *Calendar:* semesters. *Degree:* certificates and associate. *Special study options:* academic remediation for entering students, adult/continuing education programs, double majors, independent study, internships, part-time degree program, services for LD students, summer session for credit.
Library Edith A. Gray Library.
Student Life *Activities and Organizations:* Student Government Association, Phi Beta Lambda, National Vocational-Technical Society, Ambassadors, Who's Who. *Campus security:* 24-hour emergency response devices, day and evening security guard. *Student services:* personal/psychological counseling.
Costs (2016–17) *Tuition:* state resident $4212 full-time, $117 per credit part-time; nonresident $8424 full-time, $234 per credit part-time. Full-time tuition and fees vary according to course load and program. Part-time tuition and fees vary according to course load and program. *Required fees:* $1080 full-time, $30 per credit part-time. *Waivers:* senior citizens and employees or children of employees.
Financial Aid Of all full-time matriculated undergraduates who enrolled in 2015, 35 Federal Work-Study jobs (averaging $1500).

Applying *Options:* electronic application, early admission. *Required:* high school transcript. *Application deadlines:* rolling (freshmen), rolling (transfers).
Freshman Application Contact Ms. Mandy Godwin, Assistant to the Registrar, Reid State Technical College, Evergreen, AL 36401-0588. *Phone:* 251-578-1313 Ext. 148. *E-mail:* mwilson@rstc.edu.
Website: http://www.rstc.edu/.

Remington College–Mobile Campus
Mobile, Alabama

Freshman Application Contact Remington College–Mobile Campus, 828 Downtowner Loop West, Mobile, AL 36609. *Phone:* 251-343-8200. *Toll-free phone:* 800-323-8122. *Website:* http://www.remingtoncollege.edu/.

Shelton State Community College
Tuscaloosa, Alabama

Freshman Application Contact Ms. Sharon Chastine, Secretary to the Associate Dean of Student Services Enrollment, Shelton State Community College, 9500 Old Greensboro Road, Tuscaloosa, AL 35405. *Phone:* 205-391-2309. *Fax:* 205-391-3910. *E-mail:* schastine@sheltonstate.edu.
Website: http://www.sheltonstate.edu/.

Snead State Community College
Boaz, Alabama

- **State-supported** 2-year, founded 1898, part of Alabama College System
- **Small-town** 42-acre campus with easy access to Birmingham
- **Endowment** $2.6 million
- **Coed,** 2,161 undergraduate students, 71% full-time, 61% women, 39% men

Undergraduates 1,538 full-time, 623 part-time. Students come from 11 states and territories; 1% are from out of state; 6% Black or African American, non-Hispanic/Latino; 11% Hispanic/Latino; 0.8% Asian, non-Hispanic/Latino; 0.2% Native Hawaiian or other Pacific Islander, non-Hispanic/Latino; 3% American Indian or Alaska Native, non-Hispanic/Latino; 0.6% Race/ethnicity unknown; 35% transferred in. *Retention:* 61% of full-time freshmen returned.
Freshmen *Admission:* 716 enrolled.
Faculty *Student/faculty ratio:* 23:1.
Majors Business administration and management; child-care and support services management; computer and information sciences; engineering technology; general studies.
Academics *Calendar:* semesters. *Degree:* certificates and associate. *Special study options:* academic remediation for entering students, accelerated degree program, adult/continuing education programs, advanced placement credit, distance learning, independent study, internships, part-time degree program, services for LD students, student-designed majors, summer session for credit.
Library Learning Resource Center. *Books:* 6,430 (physical), 99,766 (digital/electronic); *Serial titles:* 15 (physical); *Databases:* 57.
Student Life *Housing Options:* coed. Campus housing is university owned. *Activities and Organizations:* drama/theater group, choral group, Phi Theta Kappa, Ambassadors, Student Government Association. *Campus security:* 24-hour patrols.
Athletics Member NJCAA. *Intercollegiate sports:* baseball M(s), basketball M(s)/W(s), softball W(s), tennis W(s), volleyball W(s).
Financial Aid Of all full-time matriculated undergraduates who enrolled in 2015, 45 Federal Work-Study jobs.
Applying *Options:* electronic application, early admission, deferred entrance. *Required:* high school transcript. *Required for some:* interview.
Freshman Application Contact Mr. Jason Cannon, Vice President Student Services, Snead State Community College, PO Box 734, Boaz, AL 35957-0734. *Phone:* 256-840-4150. *Fax:* 256-593-7180.
E-mail: jcannon@snead.edu.
Website: http://www.snead.edu/.

Southern Union State Community College
Wadley, Alabama

Freshman Application Contact Admissions Office, Southern Union State Community College, PO Box 1000, Roberts Street, Wadley, AL 36276. *Phone:* 256-395-5157. *E-mail:* info@suscc.edu.
Website: http://www.suscc.edu/.

Virginia College in Huntsville
Huntsville, Alabama

Freshman Application Contact Director of Admission, Virginia College in Huntsville, 2021 Drake Avenue SW, Huntsville, AL 35801. *Phone:* 256-533-7387. *Fax:* 256-533-7785. *Website:* http://www.vc.edu/.

Virginia College in Mobile
Mobile, Alabama

Admissions Office Contact Virginia College in Mobile, 3725 Airport Boulevard, Suite 165, Mobile, AL 36608. *Website:* http://www.vc.edu/.

Virginia College in Montgomery
Montgomery, Alabama

Admissions Office Contact Virginia College in Montgomery, 6200 Atlanta Highway, Montgomery, AL 36117-2800. *Website:* http://www.vc.edu/.

Wallace State Community College
Hanceville, Alabama

Director of Admissions Ms. Jennifer Hill, Director of Admissions, Wallace State Community College, PO Box 2000, 801 Main Street, Hanceville, AL 35077-2000. *Phone:* 256-352-8278. *Toll-free phone:* 866-350-9722. *Website:* http://www.wallacestate.edu/.

ALASKA

Alaska Career College
Anchorage, Alaska

- **Proprietary** 2-year
- **Urban** 20-acre campus
- **Coed**

Academics *Calendar:* continuous. *Degree:* certificates, diplomas, and associate.
Freshman Application Contact Alaska Career College, 1415 East Tudor Road, Anchorage, AK 99507. *Website:* http://www.alaskacareercollege.edu/.

Alaska Christian College
Soldotna, Alaska

Admissions Office Contact Alaska Christian College, 35109 Royal Place, Soldotna, AK 99669. *Website:* http://www.akcc.org/.

Charter College
Anchorage, Alaska

Director of Admissions Ms. Lily Sirianni, Vice President, Charter College, 2221 East Northern Lights Boulevard, Suite 120, Anchorage, AK 99508. *Phone:* 907-277-1000. *Toll-free phone:* 888-200-9942. *Website:* http://www.chartercollege.edu/.

Ilisagvik College
Barrow, Alaska

- **State-supported** 2-year, founded 1995
- **Rural** 7-acre campus
- **Endowment** $4.7 million
- **Coed**

Undergraduates Students come from 1 other state; 1% are from out of state; 2% Black or African American, non-Hispanic/Latino; 2% Hispanic/Latino; 7% Asian, non-Hispanic/Latino; 4% Native Hawaiian or other Pacific Islander, non-Hispanic/Latino; 63% American Indian or Alaska Native, non-Hispanic/Latino; 2% Race/ethnicity unknown; 3% international; 10% live on campus.
Faculty *Student/faculty ratio:* 7:1.
Academics *Calendar:* semesters. *Degree:* certificates, diplomas, and associate. *Special study options:* academic remediation for entering students, cooperative education, distance learning, double majors, English as a second language, independent study, internships, off-campus study, part-time degree program, services for LD students, summer session for credit.
Library Tuzzy Consortium Library. *Books:* 43,561 (physical), 56,345 (digital/electronic); *Serial titles:* 150 (physical). Weekly public service hours: 60; students can reserve study rooms.
Student Life *Campus security:* 24-hour emergency response devices and patrols, controlled dormitory access.
Standardized Tests *Recommended:* ACCUPLACER.
Costs (2016–17) *Tuition:* state resident $125 per credit part-time; nonresident $125 per credit part-time. Full-time tuition and fees vary according to course load and program. Part-time tuition and fees vary according to course load and program. *Required fees:* $60 per term part-time. *Room and board:* Room and board charges vary according to housing facility. *Payment plans:* installment, deferred payment.
Applying *Options:* deferred entrance. *Required:* high school transcript, minimum 2.0 GPA. *Required for some:* copy of Alaska Native Shareholder/Native American Tribal Affiliation card for Natives.
Freshman Application Contact Tennessee Judkins, Recruiter, Ilisagvik College, PO Box 749, Barrow, AK 99723. *Phone:* 907-852-1772. *Toll-free phone:* 800-478-7337. *Fax:* 907-852-1789. *E-mail:* tennessee.judkins@ilisagvik.edu. *Website:* http://www.ilisagvik.edu/.

University of Alaska Anchorage, Kenai Peninsula College
Soldotna, Alaska

- **State-supported** primarily 2-year, founded 1964, part of University of Alaska System
- **Rural** 360-acre campus
- **Coed**

Academics *Calendar:* semesters. *Degrees:* certificates, associate, and bachelor's. *Special study options:* academic remediation for entering students, adult/continuing education programs, advanced placement credit, cooperative education, distance learning, double majors, English as a second language, part-time degree program, services for LD students.
Library Kenai Peninsula College Library.
Student Life *Campus security:* 24-hour emergency response devices.
Standardized Tests *Required:* ACT, SAT or ACCUPLACER (for admission).
Costs (2016–17) *Tuition:* state resident $4608 full-time, $194 per credit part-time; nonresident $16,344 full-time, $681 per credit part-time. Full-time tuition and fees vary according to course load, degree level, location, and program. Part-time tuition and fees vary according to course load, degree level, location, and program. *Required fees:* $1176 full-time. *Room and board:* $10,868; room only: $6918. Room and board charges vary according to board plan.
Applying *Options:* electronic application. *Application fee:* $40. *Required:* high school transcript.
Freshman Application Contact Mrs. Julie Cotterell, Admission and Student Records Coordinator, University of Alaska Anchorage, Kenai Peninsula College, 156 College Road, Soldotna, AK 99669-9798. *Phone:* 907-262-0311. *Toll-free phone:* 877-262-0330. *E-mail:* jmcotterell@kpc.alaska.edu. *Website:* http://www.kpc.alaska.edu/.

University of Alaska Anchorage, Kodiak College
Kodiak, Alaska

Freshman Application Contact University of Alaska Anchorage, Kodiak College, 117 Benny Benson Drive, Kodiak, AK 99615-6643. *Phone:* 907-486-1235. *Toll-free phone:* 800-486-7660. *Website:* http://www.koc.alaska.edu/.

University of Alaska Anchorage, Matanuska-Susitna College
Palmer, Alaska

Freshman Application Contact Ms. Sandra Gravley, Student Services Director, University of Alaska Anchorage, Matanuska-Susitna College, PO Box 2889, Palmer, AK 99645-2889. *Phone:* 907-745-9712. *Fax:* 907-745-9747. *E-mail:* info@matsu.alaska.edu. *Website:* http://www.matsu.alaska.edu/.

University of Alaska, Prince William Sound College

Valdez, Alaska

- **State-supported** 2-year, founded 1978, part of University of Alaska System
- **Small-town** campus
- **Endowment** $62,630
- **Coed**

Undergraduates Students come from 1 other state; 2 other countries; 13% are from out of state; 2% live on campus.
Faculty *Student/faculty ratio:* 5:1.
Academics *Calendar:* semesters. *Degree:* certificates, diplomas, and associate. *Special study options:* academic remediation for entering students, adult/continuing education programs, advanced placement credit, cooperative education, distance learning, double majors, English as a second language, independent study, internships, services for LD students, summer session for credit.
Library Valdez Consortium Library.
Student Life *Campus security:* student patrols, controlled dormitory access, housing manager supervision.
Standardized Tests *Recommended:* SAT or ACT (for admission), ACCUPLACER.
Costs (2016–17) *One-time required fee:* $40. *Tuition:* state resident $4032 full-time, $168 per credit part-time; nonresident $4032 full-time, $168 per credit part-time. *Required fees:* $350 full-time, $100 per term part-time. *Room and board:* room only: $2527. Room and board charges vary according to housing facility. *Payment plans:* installment, deferred payment.
Applying *Options:* electronic application, early admission. *Application fee:* $25. *Required:* high school transcript.
Freshman Application Contact Dr. Denise Runge, Academic Affairs, University of Alaska, Prince William Sound College, PO Box 97, Valdez, AK 99686-0097. *Phone:* 907-834-1600. *Toll-free phone:* 800-478-8800. *Fax:* 907-834-1691. *E-mail:* drunge@pwscc.edu.
Website: http://www.pwsc.alaska.edu/.

University of Alaska Southeast, Ketchikan Campus

Ketchikan, Alaska

Freshman Application Contact Admissions Office, University of Alaska Southeast, Ketchikan Campus, 2600 7th Avenue, Ketchikan, AK 99901-5798. *Phone:* 907-225-6177. *Toll-free phone:* 888-550-6177. *Fax:* 907-225-3895. *E-mail:* ketch.info@uas.alaska.edu. *Website:* http://www.ketch.alaska.edu/.

University of Alaska Southeast, Sitka Campus

Sitka, Alaska

Freshman Application Contact Ms. Teal Gordon, Admissions Representative, University of Alaska Southeast, Sitka Campus, UAS Sitka, 1332 Seward Avenue, Sitka, AK 99835. *Phone:* 907-747-7726. *Toll-free phone:* 800-478-6653. *Fax:* 907-747-7731. *E-mail:* ktgordon@uas.alaska.edu. *Website:* http://www.uas.alaska.edu/.

AMERICAN SAMOA

American Samoa Community College

Pago Pago, American Samoa

- **Territory-supported** primarily 2-year, founded 1969
- **Rural** 20-acre campus
- **Endowment** $3.1 million
- **Coed,** 1,253 undergraduate students, 56% full-time, 67% women, 33% men

Undergraduates 702 full-time, 551 part-time. Students come from 5 other countries; 0.1% Hispanic/Latino; 0.4% Asian, non-Hispanic/Latino; 89% Native Hawaiian or other Pacific Islander, non-Hispanic/Latino; 0.2% Race/ethnicity unknown; 10% international; 0.2% transferred in. *Retention:* 100% of full-time freshmen returned.
Freshmen *Admission:* 407 applied, 407 admitted, 407 enrolled. *Test scores:* SAT critical reading scores over 500: 17%; SAT math scores over 500: 19%; SAT critical reading scores over 600: 5%; SAT math scores over 600: 2%.

Faculty *Total:* 82, 78% full-time, 9% with terminal degrees. *Student/faculty ratio:* 20:1.
Majors Accounting; agricultural business and management; agriculture; architectural drafting and CAD/CADD; art; autobody/collision and repair technology; automobile/automotive mechanics technology; business administration and management; civil engineering; construction trades; criminal justice/safety; education; electrical, electronic and communications engineering technology; family and consumer economics related; forensic science and technology; health services/allied health/health sciences; human services; liberal arts and sciences/liberal studies; marine science/merchant marine officer; music; natural resources/conservation; office occupations and clerical services; political science and government; pre-law studies; welding technology.
Academics *Calendar:* semesters. *Degrees:* certificates, associate, and bachelor's. *Special study options:* academic remediation for entering students, adult/continuing education programs, cooperative education, double majors, English as a second language, honors programs, independent study, internships, off-campus study, part-time degree program, services for LD students, student-designed majors, summer session for credit. *ROTC:* Army (b).
Library ASCC Learning Resource Center/Library plus 1 other. *Books:* 40,000 (physical); *Serial titles:* 236 (physical). Weekly public service hours: 42.
Student Life *Housing:* college housing not available. *Activities and Organizations:* student-run newspaper, Student Government Association, Phi Theta Kappa, ASCC Research Foundation Student Club, Fa'aSamoa (Samoan culture) Club, Journalism Club. *Campus security:* 24-hour patrols. *Student services:* personal/psychological counseling.
Athletics *Intramural sports:* basketball M/W, football M/W, golf M/W, rugby M, soccer M, tennis M/W, track and field M/W, volleyball M/W.
Standardized Tests *Recommended:* SAT (for admission), ACT (for admission), SAT or ACT (for admission), SAT and SAT Subject Tests or ACT (for admission), SAT Subject Tests (for admission).
Costs (2017–18) *Tuition:* territory resident $3300 full-time; nonresident $3600 full-time. Full-time tuition and fees vary according to course load. Part-time tuition and fees vary according to course load. *Required fees:* $250 full-time. *Payment plan:* installment. *Waivers:* employees or children of employees.
Financial Aid Of all full-time matriculated undergraduates who enrolled in 2015, 588 applied for aid, 588 were judged to have need.
Applying *Options:* electronic application, early admission, deferred entrance. *Application deadline:* rolling (freshmen). *Notification:* continuous (freshmen).
Freshman Application Contact Elizabeth Leuma, Admissions Officer, American Samoa Community College, PO Box 2609, Pago Pago 96799, American Samoa. *Phone:* 684-699-9155 Ext. 411. *Fax:* 684-699-1083. *Website:* http://www.amsamoa.edu/.

ARIZONA

Arizona Automotive Institute

Glendale, Arizona

Director of Admissions Director of Admissions, Arizona Automotive Institute, 6829 North 46th Avenue, Glendale, AZ 85301-3597. *Phone:* 623-934-7273 Ext. 211. *Toll-free phone:* 800-321-5861 (in-state); 800-321-5961 (out-of-state). *Fax:* 623-937-5000. *E-mail:* info@azautoinst.com. *Website:* http://www.aai.edu/.

Arizona College

Glendale, Arizona

Freshman Application Contact Admissions Department, Arizona College, 4425 West Olive Avenue, Suite 300, Glendale, AZ 85302-3843. *Phone:* 602-222-9300. *E-mail:* lhicks@arizonacollege.edu. *Website:* http://www.arizonacollege.edu/.

Arizona Western College

Yuma, Arizona

- **State and locally supported** 2-year, founded 1962, part of Arizona State Community College System
- **Rural** 640-acre campus
- **Coed,** 7,569 undergraduate students, 32% full-time, 56% women, 44% men

Undergraduates 2,456 full-time, 5,113 part-time. Students come from 28 states and territories; 26 other countries; 3% are from out of state; 2% Black or African American, non-Hispanic/Latino; 71% Hispanic/Latino; 1% Asian, non-Hispanic/Latino; 0.4% Native Hawaiian or other Pacific Islander, non-

Hispanic/Latino; 1% American Indian or Alaska Native, non-Hispanic/Latino; 2% Two or more races, non-Hispanic/Latino; 4% Race/ethnicity unknown; 2% international; 0.1% transferred in; 6% live on campus.

Freshmen *Admission:* 1,350 enrolled.

Faculty *Total:* 313, 40% full-time, 9% with terminal degrees.

Majors Accounting; agricultural business and management; agriculture; American Indian/Native American studies; architectural technology; automobile/automotive mechanics technology; automotive engineering technology; biology/biological sciences; business administration and management; CAD/CADD drafting/design technology; carpentry; chemistry; civil engineering technology; communication; community health and preventive medicine; computer and information sciences; computer graphics; construction engineering technology; construction management; criminal justice/law enforcement administration; crop production; culinary arts; data entry/microcomputer applications; dramatic/theater arts; early childhood education; electrical, electronic and communications engineering technology; elementary education; emergency medical technology (EMT paramedic); engineering; English; environmental science; family and consumer sciences/human sciences; fine/studio arts; fire science/firefighting; general studies; geology/earth science; health and physical education/fitness; heating, air conditioning, ventilation and refrigeration maintenance technology; heating, ventilation, air conditioning and refrigeration engineering technology; history; homeland security; hospitality administration; industrial technology; law enforcement investigation and interviewing; legal assistant/paralegal; logistics, materials, and supply chain management; manufacturing engineering technology; massage therapy; mathematics; music; parks, recreation and leisure facilities management; philosophy; physics; plumbing technology; political science and government; prenursing studies; psychology; radio and television broadcasting technology; radiologic technology/science; registered nursing/registered nurse; secondary education; social sciences; solar energy technology; Spanish; sport and fitness administration/management; water quality and wastewater treatment management and recycling technology; welding engineering technology.

Academics *Calendar:* semesters. *Degree:* certificates and associate. *Special study options:* academic remediation for entering students, adult/continuing education programs, advanced placement credit, cooperative education, distance learning, English as a second language, honors programs, independent study, part-time degree program, services for LD students, summer session for credit.

Library Arizona Western College and NAU-Yuma Library. *Books:* 62,780 (physical), 194,220 (digital/electronic); *Serial titles:* 521 (physical), 13,429 (digital/electronic); *Databases:* 39,599. Weekly public service hours: 64; students can reserve study rooms.

Student Life *Housing Options:* coed, men-only, women-only. Campus housing is university owned. *Activities and Organizations:* drama/theater group, student-run newspaper, radio and television station, choral group, Student Government Association, Spirit Squad, Dance Team, Matador Ambassadors, Presidential Leadership Society. *Campus security:* 24-hour emergency response devices and patrols, student patrols, late-night transport/escort service, controlled dormitory access. *Student services:* health clinic, personal/psychological counseling.

Athletics Member NJCAA. *Intercollegiate sports:* baseball M(s), basketball M(s)/W(s), football M(s), soccer M(s)/W(s), softball W(s), volleyball W(s). *Intramural sports:* cheerleading M(c)/W(c).

Standardized Tests *Required for some:* SAT or ACT (for admission).

Costs (2017–18) *Tuition:* state resident $2460 full-time, $82 per credit part-time; nonresident $9450 full-time, $315 per credit part-time. Full-time tuition and fees vary according to course load, program, and reciprocity agreements. Part-time tuition and fees vary according to course load, program, and reciprocity agreements. *Room and board:* $6570; room only: $2240. Room and board charges vary according to board plan and housing facility. *Payment plan:* installment. *Waivers:* senior citizens and employees or children of employees.

Financial Aid Of all full-time matriculated undergraduates who enrolled in 2015, 350 Federal Work-Study jobs (averaging $1500). 100 state and other part-time jobs (averaging $1800).

Applying *Options:* electronic application, early admission, deferred entrance. *Application deadlines:* rolling (freshmen), rolling (transfers).

Freshman Application Contact Nicole D. Harral, Director of Admissions/Registrar, Arizona Western College, PO Box 929, Yuma, AZ 85366. *Phone:* 928-344-7600. *Toll-free phone:* 888-293-0392. *Fax:* 928-344-7543. *E-mail:* nicole.harral@azwestern.edu.

Website: http://www.azwestern.edu/.

Carrington College–Mesa
Mesa, Arizona

- **Proprietary** 2-year, founded 1977, part of Carrington Colleges Group, Inc.
- **Suburban** campus
- **Coed**

Undergraduates 572 full-time, 61 part-time. 2% are from out of state; 6% Black or African American, non-Hispanic/Latino; 35% Hispanic/Latino; 2% Asian, non-Hispanic/Latino; 0.9% Native Hawaiian or other Pacific Islander, non-Hispanic/Latino; 15% American Indian or Alaska Native, non-Hispanic/Latino; 3% Two or more races, non-Hispanic/Latino; 0.3% Race/ethnicity unknown; 13% transferred in.

Faculty *Student/faculty ratio:* 37:1.

Academics *Calendar:* semesters. *Degree:* certificates and associate.

Applying *Required:* essay or personal statement, high school transcript, interview.

Freshman Application Contact Carrington College–Mesa, 1001 West Southern Avenue, Suite 130, Mesa, AZ 85210. *Website:* http://carrington.edu/.

Carrington College–Phoenix East
Phoenix, Arizona

- **Proprietary** 2-year, part of Carrington Colleges Group, Inc.
- **Urban** campus
- **Coed**

Undergraduates 266 full-time, 80 part-time. 2% are from out of state; 7% Black or African American, non-Hispanic/Latino; 36% Hispanic/Latino; 6% Asian, non-Hispanic/Latino; 0.9% Native Hawaiian or other Pacific Islander, non-Hispanic/Latino; 6% American Indian or Alaska Native, non-Hispanic/Latino; 2% Two or more races, non-Hispanic/Latino; 5% Race/ethnicity unknown; 14% transferred in.

Faculty *Student/faculty ratio:* 12:1.

Academics *Calendar:* semesters. *Degree:* certificates and associate.

Costs (2016–17) *Tuition:* $52,594 per degree program part-time. Full-time tuition and fees vary according to program.

Applying *Required:* essay or personal statement, high school transcript, interview.

Freshman Application Contact Carrington College–Phoenix East, 2149 West Dunlap Avenue, Suite 100, Phoenix, AZ 85021.

Website: http://carrington.edu/.

Carrington College–Phoenix North
Phoenix, Arizona

- **Proprietary** 2-year, founded 1976, part of Carrington Colleges Group, Inc.
- **Urban** campus
- **Coed**

Undergraduates 676 full-time. 3% are from out of state; 4% Black or African American, non-Hispanic/Latino; 61% Hispanic/Latino; 1% Asian, non-Hispanic/Latino; 0.4% Native Hawaiian or other Pacific Islander, non-Hispanic/Latino; 9% American Indian or Alaska Native, non-Hispanic/Latino; 1% Two or more races, non-Hispanic/Latino; 1% Race/ethnicity unknown; 14% transferred in.

Faculty *Student/faculty ratio:* 37:1.

Academics *Calendar:* continuous. *Degree:* certificates and associate.

Applying *Required:* essay or personal statement, high school transcript, interview.

Freshman Application Contact Carrington College–Phoenix North, 8503 North 27th Avenue, Phoenix, AZ 85051. *Website:* http://carrington.edu/.

Carrington College–Tucson
Tucson, Arizona

- **Proprietary** 2-year, founded 1984, part of Carrington Colleges Group, Inc.
- **Suburban** campus
- **Coed**

Undergraduates 357 full-time. 4% Black or African American, non-Hispanic/Latino; 69% Hispanic/Latino; 0.6% Asian, non-Hispanic/Latino; 0.3% Native Hawaiian or other Pacific Islander, non-Hispanic/Latino; 5% American Indian or Alaska Native, non-Hispanic/Latino; 1% Two or more races, non-Hispanic/Latino; 1% Race/ethnicity unknown; 11% transferred in.

Faculty *Student/faculty ratio:* 45:1.

Academics *Calendar:* semesters modular courses are offered. *Degree:* certificates and associate.

Applying *Required:* essay or personal statement, high school transcript, interview.
Freshman Application Contact Carrington College–Tucson, 201 North Bonita Avenue, Suite 101, Tucson, AZ 85745. *Website:* http://carrington.edu/.

Central Arizona College
Coolidge, Arizona
Freshman Application Contact Dr. James Moore, Dean of Records and Admissions, Central Arizona College, 8470 North Overfield Road, Coolidge, AZ 85128. *Phone:* 520-494-5261. *Toll-free phone:* 800-237-9814. *Fax:* 520-426-5083. *E-mail:* james.moore@centralaz.edu. *Website:* http://www.centralaz.edu/.

Chandler-Gilbert Community College
Chandler, Arizona
- **State and locally supported** 2-year, founded 1985, part of Maricopa County Community College District System
- **Suburban** 188-acre campus with easy access to Phoenix
- **Coed,** 14,630 undergraduate students

Faculty *Total:* 622, 22% full-time.
Majors Accounting; accounting technology and bookkeeping; airline pilot and flight crew; business administration and management; business administration, management and operations related; business/commerce; business, management, and marketing related; computer and information sciences; computer and information sciences and support services related; computer programming; computer programming (vendor/product certification); computer systems analysis; computer systems networking and telecommunications; criminal justice/safety; data entry/microcomputer applications; data modeling/warehousing and database administration; dietetic technology; dietitian assistant; dramatic/theater arts; electromechanical technology; elementary education; fine/studio arts; general studies; information technology; kinesiology and exercise science; liberal arts and sciences and humanities related; liberal arts and sciences/liberal studies; lineworker; massage therapy; mechanic and repair technologies related; music management; organizational behavior; physical sciences; psychology; registered nursing/registered nurse; social work; visual and performing arts.
Academics *Calendar:* semesters. *Degree:* certificates, diplomas, and associate. *Special study options:* academic remediation for entering students, advanced placement credit, English as a second language, freshman honors college, honors programs, independent study, part-time degree program, services for LD students, study abroad, summer session for credit.
Library Chandler-Gilbert Community College Library.
Student Life *Housing:* college housing not available. *Activities and Organizations:* student-run radio station, choral group. *Campus security:* 24-hour emergency response devices and patrols, late-night transport/escort service. *Student services:* personal/psychological counseling.
Athletics Member NJCAA. *Intercollegiate sports:* baseball M, basketball M/W, golf M/W, soccer M/W, softball W, volleyball W.
Costs (2017–18) *Tuition:* area resident $2064 full-time, $86 per credit hour part-time; state resident $9192 full-time, $383 per credit hour part-time; nonresident $7848 full-time, $327 per credit hour part-time. Full-time tuition and fees vary according to reciprocity agreements. Part-time tuition and fees vary according to reciprocity agreements. *Required fees:* $30 full-time, $15 per term part-time. *Payment plans:* installment, deferred payment. *Waivers:* employees or children of employees.
Applying *Options:* electronic application.
Freshman Application Contact Holly Rouse, Coordinator of Enrollment Services, Chandler-Gilbert Community College, 2626 East Pecos Road, Chandler, AZ 85225-2479. *Phone:* 480-857-5210. *E-mail:* holly.rouse@cgc.edu. *Website:* http://www.cgc.maricopa.edu/.

Cochise County Community College District
Douglas, Arizona
- **State and locally supported** 2-year, founded 1962
- **Rural** 619-acre campus with easy access to Tucson
- **Coed,** 4,223 undergraduate students, 39% full-time, 54% women, 46% men

Undergraduates 1,633 full-time, 2,590 part-time. Students come from 17 states and territories; 2 other countries; 7% are from out of state; 5% Black or African American, non-Hispanic/Latino; 48% Hispanic/Latino; 2% Asian, non-Hispanic/Latino; 0.5% Native Hawaiian or other Pacific Islander, non-Hispanic/Latino; 0.6% American Indian or Alaska Native, non-Hispanic/Latino; 3% Two or more races, non-Hispanic/Latino; 2%

Race/ethnicity unknown; 1% international; 20% transferred in; 3% live on campus. *Retention:* 63% of full-time freshmen returned.
Freshmen *Admission:* 1,422 applied, 1,422 admitted, 722 enrolled. *Average high school GPA:* 2.66.
Faculty *Total:* 321, 27% full-time. *Student/faculty ratio:* 17:1.
Majors Administrative assistant and secretarial science; adult and continuing education; agricultural business and management; air and space operations technology; airline pilot and flight crew; air transportation related; art; automobile/automotive mechanics technology; avionics maintenance technology; biology/biological sciences; building construction technology; business administration and management; chemistry; computer and information systems security; computer programming; computer science; computer systems networking and telecommunications; criminal justice/police science; crop production; culinary arts; digital communication and media/multimedia; dramatic/theater arts; early childhood education; economics; electrical, electronic and communications engineering technology; elementary education; emergency medical technology (EMT paramedic); engineering; English; equestrian studies; fire science/firefighting; general studies; health and physical education/fitness; humanities; information science/studies; intelligence; journalism; logistics, materials, and supply chain management; mathematics; mechatronics, robotics, and automation engineering; music; philosophy; physics; registered nursing/registered nurse; respiratory care therapy; social sciences; speech communication and rhetoric; welding technology.
Academics *Calendar:* semesters. *Degrees:* certificates and associate (profile includes campuses in Douglas and Sierra Vista, AZ). *Special study options:* academic remediation for entering students, adult/continuing education programs, advanced placement credit, cooperative education, distance learning, English as a second language, honors programs, independent study, internships, part-time degree program, services for LD students, summer session for credit.
Library Charles Di Peso plus 1 other. *Books:* 55,145 (physical), 40,945 (digital/electronic); *Serial titles:* 22 (physical), 7,401 (digital/electronic); *Databases:* 16. Weekly public service hours: 45.
Student Life *Housing Options:* coed, special housing for students with disabilities. Campus housing is university owned. *Activities and Organizations:* drama/theater group, choral group, Phi Theta Kappa, Table Top Games, The Art Club, Student Nurses Association, Digital Media Arts Club. *Campus security:* 24-hour emergency response devices and patrols, late-night transport/escort service. *Student services:* personal/psychological counseling.
Athletics Member NJCAA. *Intercollegiate sports:* baseball M(s), basketball M(s)/W(s), soccer W(s).
Costs (2016–17) *Tuition:* state resident $2370 full-time, $79 per credit hour part-time; nonresident $7500 full-time, $250 per credit hour part-time. Full-time tuition and fees vary according to course load, program, and reciprocity agreements. Part-time tuition and fees vary according to course load, program, and reciprocity agreements. *Room and board:* $6564. Room and board charges vary according to housing facility. *Payment plan:* installment. *Waivers:* senior citizens and employees or children of employees.
Financial Aid Of all full-time matriculated undergraduates who enrolled in 2014, 1,300 applied for aid, 1,121 were judged to have need. 72 Federal Work-Study jobs (averaging $5437). In 2014, 22 non-need-based awards were made. *Average financial aid package:* $5876. *Average need-based loan:* $3658. *Average need-based gift aid:* $3730. *Average non-need-based aid:* $1666. *Financial aid deadline:* 6/15.
Applying *Options:* electronic application, deferred entrance. *Required for some:* high school transcript. *Recommended:* high school transcript. *Application deadlines:* rolling (freshmen), rolling (transfers). *Notification:* continuous (freshmen), continuous (transfers).
Freshman Application Contact Ms. Debbie Quick, Director of Admissions and Records, Cochise County Community College District, 4190 West Highway 80, Douglas, AZ 85607-6190. *Phone:* 520-515-3640. *Toll-free phone:* 800-593-9567. *Fax:* 520-515-5452. *E-mail:* quickd@cochise.edu. *Website:* http://www.cochise.edu/.

Coconino Community College
Flagstaff, Arizona
- **State-supported** 2-year, founded 1991
- **Small-town** 5-acre campus
- **Endowment** $322,526
- **Coed,** 3,608 undergraduate students, 31% full-time, 51% women, 49% men

Undergraduates 1,134 full-time, 2,474 part-time. 1% Black or African American, non-Hispanic/Latino; 18% Hispanic/Latino; 1% Asian, non-Hispanic/Latino; 0.2% Native Hawaiian or other Pacific Islander, non-Hispanic/Latino; 18% American Indian or Alaska Native, non-Hispanic/Latino; 4% Two or more races, non-Hispanic/Latino; 2% Race/ethnicity unknown; 22% transferred in. *Retention:* 58% of full-time freshmen returned.

Freshmen *Admission:* 2,629 applied, 592 enrolled.

Faculty *Total:* 154, 22% full-time. *Student/faculty ratio:* 25:1.

Majors Accounting technology and bookkeeping; anthropology; architectural drafting and CAD/CADD; architectural engineering technology; architectural technology; area studies related; building construction technology; business administration and management; business/commerce; carpentry; computer software technology; computer technology/computer systems technology; construction management; construction trades related; corrections; corrections and criminal justice related; criminal justice/law enforcement administration; desktop publishing and digital imaging design; early childhood education; electrical, electronic and communications engineering technology; elementary education; emergency care attendant (EMT ambulance); environmental science; fine/studio arts; fire science/firefighting; forensic science and technology; general studies; hospitality administration; medical insurance/medical billing; medical office assistant; nursing assistant/aide and patient care assistant/aide; phlebotomy technology; psychology; registered nursing/registered nurse; sheet metal technology; sign language interpretation and translation; sociology; solar energy technology; visual and performing arts.

Academics *Calendar:* semesters. *Degree:* certificates and associate. *Special study options:* academic remediation for entering students, adult/continuing education programs, distance learning, honors programs, independent study, internships, part-time degree program, study abroad, summer session for credit. *ROTC:* Air Force (b).

Library Information Resources and Library Services.

Student Life *Housing:* college housing not available. *Activities and Organizations:* Art Club, Clay Club, Dance Club, Native American Club, Video Gaming Club. *Campus security:* 24-hour emergency response devices, student patrols, late-night transport/escort service, security patrols during hours of operation, electronic access throughout the campuses with security cards.

Applying *Options:* electronic application. *Application deadlines:* rolling (freshmen), rolling (transfers). *Notification:* continuous (freshmen), continuous (transfers).

Freshman Application Contact Veronica Hipolito, Director of Student Services, Coconino Community College, 2800 South Lone Tree Road, Flagstaff, AZ 86001. *Phone:* 928-226-4334 Ext. 4334. *Toll-free phone:* 800-350-7122. *Fax:* 928-226-4114. *E-mail:* veronica.hipolito@coconino.edu. *Website:* http://www.coconino.edu/.

CollegeAmerica–Flagstaff
Flagstaff, Arizona

Freshman Application Contact CollegeAmerica–Flagstaff, 399 South Malpais Lane, Flagstaff, AZ 86001. *Phone:* 928-213-6060 Ext. 1402. *Toll-free phone:* 800-622-2894. *Website:* http://www.collegeamerica.edu/.

CollegeAmerica–Phoenix
Phoenix, Arizona

Admissions Office Contact CollegeAmerica–Phoenix, 9801 North Metro Parkway East, Phoenix, AZ 85051. *Toll-free phone:* 800-622-2894. *Website:* http://www.collegeamerica.edu/.

Diné College
Tsaile, Arizona

Freshman Application Contact Mrs. Louise Litzin, Registrar, Diné College, PO Box 67, Tsaile, AZ 86556. *Phone:* 928-724-6633. *Toll-free phone:* 877-988-DINE. *Fax:* 928-724-3349. *E-mail:* louise@dinecollege.edu. *Website:* http://www.dinecollege.edu/.

Eastern Arizona College
Thatcher, Arizona

- **State and locally supported** 2-year, founded 1888, part of Arizona State Community College System
- **Small-town** campus
- **Endowment** $5.3 million
- **Coed,** 6,423 undergraduate students, 31% full-time, 56% women, 44% men

Undergraduates 1,969 full-time, 4,454 part-time. Students come from 29 states and territories; 22 other countries; 3% are from out of state; 3% Black or African American, non-Hispanic/Latino; 20% Hispanic/Latino; 0.9% Asian, non-Hispanic/Latino; 0.5% Native Hawaiian or other Pacific Islander, non-Hispanic/Latino; 7% American Indian or Alaska Native, non-Hispanic/Latino; 0.9% Two or more races, non-Hispanic/Latino; 3% Race/ethnicity unknown; 1% international; 3% transferred in; 7% live on campus.

Freshmen *Admission:* 818 applied, 818 admitted, 1,041 enrolled.

Faculty *Total:* 346, 27% full-time, 8% with terminal degrees. *Student/faculty ratio:* 19:1.

Majors Anthropology; art; art teacher education; automobile/automotive mechanics technology; biology/biological sciences; business administration and management; business, management, and marketing related; business operations support and secretarial services related; business teacher education; chemistry; civil engineering technology; commercial and advertising art; cosmetology; criminal justice/law enforcement administration; criminal justice/police science; diesel mechanics technology; drafting and design technology; dramatic/theater arts; early childhood education; elementary education; emergency medical technology (EMT paramedic); English; entrepreneurship; environmental biology; fire science/firefighting; foreign languages and literatures; forestry; geology/earth science; health and physical education/fitness; health/medical preparatory programs related; history; industrial electronics technology; industrial mechanics and maintenance technology; information science/studies; liberal arts and sciences/liberal studies; machine shop technology; mathematics; mining technology; multi/interdisciplinary studies related; music; pharmacy technician; photographic and film/video technology; physics; political science and government; premedical studies; pre-pharmacy studies; psychology; registered nursing/registered nurse; secondary education; sociology; speech communication and rhetoric; technology/industrial arts teacher education; welding technology; writing.

Academics *Calendar:* semesters. *Degree:* certificates and associate. *Special study options:* academic remediation for entering students, adult/continuing education programs, advanced placement credit, cooperative education, distance learning, double majors, independent study, internships, part-time degree program, services for LD students, study abroad, summer session for credit.

Library Alumni Library plus 1 other. *Books:* 47,622 (physical), 945 (digital/electronic); *Serial titles:* 637 (physical); *Databases:* 41. Weekly public service hours: 80; students can reserve study rooms.

Student Life *Housing Options:* men-only, women-only. Campus housing is university owned. *Activities and Organizations:* drama/theater group, choral group, marching band, Latter-Day Saints Student Association, Criminal Justice Student Association, Multicultural Council, Phi Theta Kappa, Mark Allen Dorm Club. *Campus security:* 24-hour emergency response devices, late-night transport/escort service, controlled dormitory access, 20-hour patrols by trained security personnel. *Student services:* personal/psychological counseling.

Athletics Member NJCAA. *Intercollegiate sports:* baseball M(s), basketball M(s)/W(s), football M(s), golf M/W, softball W(s), volleyball W(s). *Intramural sports:* basketball M/W, racquetball M/W, swimming and diving M/W, table tennis M/W, tennis M/W, volleyball M/W.

Financial Aid Of all full-time matriculated undergraduates who enrolled in 2015, 1,619 applied for aid, 1,419 were judged to have need, 65 had their need fully met. In 2015, 102 non-need-based awards were made. *Average percent of need met:* 28%. *Average financial aid package:* $6336. *Average need-based gift aid:* $6053. *Average non-need-based aid:* $3309.

Applying *Options:* electronic application, early admission, deferred entrance. *Recommended:* high school transcript. *Application deadlines:* rolling (freshmen), rolling (transfers). *Notification:* continuous (freshmen).

Freshman Application Contact Suzette Udall, Records Assistant, Eastern Arizona College, 615 North Stadium Avenue, Thatcher, AZ 85552-0769. *Phone:* 928-428-8904. *Toll-free phone:* 800-678-3808. *Fax:* 928-428-3729. *E-mail:* admissions@eac.edu. *Website:* http://www.eac.edu/.

Estrella Mountain Community College
Avondale, Arizona

- **State and locally supported** 2-year, founded 1992, part of Maricopa County Community College District System
- **Urban** campus with easy access to Phoenix
- **Coed,** 9,344 undergraduate students, 33% full-time, 60% women, 40% men

Undergraduates 3,124 full-time, 6,220 part-time. Students come from 1 other state; 8% Black or African American, non-Hispanic/Latino; 51% Hispanic/Latino; 4% Asian, non-Hispanic/Latino; 0.4% Native Hawaiian or other Pacific Islander, non-Hispanic/Latino; 2% American Indian or Alaska Native, non-Hispanic/Latino; 2% Two or more races, non-Hispanic/Latino; 3% Race/ethnicity unknown; 0.3% international; 7% transferred in.

Freshmen *Admission:* 1,661 enrolled.

Faculty *Student/faculty ratio:* 22:1.

Majors General studies; liberal arts and sciences/liberal studies.

Academics *Calendar:* semesters. *Degree:* certificates and associate. *Special study options:* academic remediation for entering students, adult/continuing education programs, advanced placement credit, cooperative education, distance learning, English as a second language, honors programs, independent study, part-time degree program, services for LD students, summer session for credit. *ROTC:* Air Force (c).

Library Estrella Mountain Library.

Student Life *Housing:* college housing not available. *Activities and Organizations:* Phi Theta Kappa, Men Of Color Association (MOCA), Movimiento Estudiantil Chicano de Aztlan (MEChA), Savings and Investment Club. *Campus security:* 24-hour emergency response devices and patrols, late-night transport/escort service. *Student services:* personal/psychological counseling.

Athletics *Intercollegiate sports:* cross-country running M/W, golf M/W.

Applying *Options:* electronic application.

Freshman Application Contact Estrella Mountain Community College, 3000 North Dysart Road, Avondale, AZ 85392. *Phone:* 623-935-8812. *Website:* http://www.estrellamountain.edu/.

Fortis College
Phoenix, Arizona

Admissions Office Contact Fortis College, 555 North 18th Street, Suite 110, Phoenix, AZ 85006. *Toll-free phone:* 855-4-FORTIS. *Website:* http://www.fortis.edu/.

GateWay Community College
Phoenix, Arizona

Freshman Application Contact Director of Admissions and Records, GateWay Community College, 108 North 40th Street, Phoenix, AZ 85034. *Phone:* 602-286-8200. *Fax:* 602-286-8200. *E-mail:* enroll@gatewaycc.edu. *Website:* http://www.gatewaycc.edu/.

Glendale Community College
Glendale, Arizona

Freshman Application Contact Ms. Mary Blackwell, Dean of Enrollment Services, Glendale Community College, 6000 West Olive Avenue, Glendale, AZ 85302. *Phone:* 623-435-3305. *Fax:* 623-845-3303. *E-mail:* admissions.recruitment@gccaz.edu. *Website:* http://www.gc.maricopa.edu/.

Golf Academy of America
Chandler, Arizona

Admissions Office Contact Golf Academy of America, 2031 N. Arizona Avenue, Suite 2, Chandler, AZ 85225. *Website:* http://www.golfacademy.edu/.

Mesa Community College
Mesa, Arizona

- **State and locally supported** 2-year, founded 1965, part of Maricopa County Community College District System
- **Urban** 160-acre campus with easy access to Phoenix
- **Coed,** 20,508 undergraduate students, 31% full-time, 52% women, 48% men

Undergraduates 6,404 full-time, 14,104 part-time. 6% Black or African American, non-Hispanic/Latino; 25% Hispanic/Latino; 4% Asian, non-Hispanic/Latino; 0.4% Native Hawaiian or other Pacific Islander, non-Hispanic/Latino; 4% American Indian or Alaska Native, non-Hispanic/Latino; 2% Two or more races, non-Hispanic/Latino; 8% Race/ethnicity unknown; 3% international.

Faculty *Student/faculty ratio:* 21:1.

Majors Administrative assistant and secretarial science; agribusiness; agroecology and sustainable agriculture; architectural drafting and CAD/CADD; biotechnology; business/commerce; child development; computer and information sciences; computer systems analysis; computer systems networking and telecommunications; construction/heavy equipment/earthmoving equipment operation; criminal justice/police science; criminal justice/safety; dental hygiene; design and visual communications; electrical, electronic and communications engineering technology; electromechanical technology; emergency medical technology (EMT paramedic); fashion merchandising; finance; fire science/firefighting; food service systems administration; geography; heavy equipment maintenance technology; horticultural science; industrial technology; insurance; interior design; journalism; kinesiology and exercise science; liberal arts and sciences/liberal studies; library and information science; machine tool technology; manufacturing engineering; manufacturing engineering technology; marketing/marketing management; mathematics; medical administrative assistant and medical secretary; music; music management; organizational behavior; ornamental horticulture; parks, recreation and leisure; physical sciences; pre-engineering; public relations/image management;

quality control technology; real estate; recording arts technology; registered nursing/registered nurse; teacher assistant/aide; veterinary/animal health technology; web page, digital/multimedia and information resources design; welding technology.

Academics *Calendar:* semesters. *Degree:* certificates and associate. *Special study options:* academic remediation for entering students, adult/continuing education programs, advanced placement credit, cooperative education, distance learning, English as a second language, freshman honors college, honors programs, independent study, off-campus study, part-time degree program, services for LD students, student-designed majors, study abroad, summer session for credit. *ROTC:* Army (c), Air Force (c).

Library Information Commons. Students can reserve study rooms.

Student Life *Housing:* college housing not available. *Activities and Organizations:* drama/theater group, student-run newspaper, choral group, MECHA, International Student Association, American Indian Association, Asian/Pacific Islander Club. *Campus security:* 24-hour emergency response devices and patrols, student patrols. *Student services:* personal/psychological counseling, legal services.

Athletics Member NJCAA. *Intercollegiate sports:* baseball M(s), basketball M(s)/W(s), cheerleading W(s), cross-country running M(s)/W(s), football M(s), golf M(s)/W(s), soccer M(s)/W(s), softball W(s), tennis M(s)/W(s), track and field M(s)/W(s), volleyball W(s). *Intramural sports:* basketball M/W, bowling M/W, cross-country running M/W, football M/W, softball W, track and field M/W, volleyball M/W.

Costs (2017–18) *Tuition:* state resident $2064 full-time, $86 per credit hour part-time; nonresident $7848 full-time, $327 per credit hour part-time. Full-time tuition and fees vary according to course load and reciprocity agreements. Part-time tuition and fees vary according to course load and reciprocity agreements. *Required fees:* $30 full-time, $15 per term part-time. *Payment plan:* installment. *Waivers:* senior citizens and employees or children of employees.

Applying *Options:* electronic application, early admission, deferred entrance. *Application deadlines:* 9/1 (freshmen), 9/1 (transfers). *Notification:* continuous (freshmen).

Freshman Application Contact Carmen Newland, Dean, Enrollment Services, Mesa Community College, 1833 West Southern Avenue, Mesa, AZ 85202-4866. *Phone:* 480-461-7600. *Toll-free phone:* 866-532-4983. *Fax:* 480-844-3117. *E-mail:* admissionsandrecords@mesacc.edu. *Website:* http://www.mesacc.edu/.

Mohave Community College
Kingman, Arizona

- **State-supported** 2-year, founded 1971
- **Small-town** 160-acre campus
- **Coed,** 4,230 undergraduate students, 20% full-time, 66% women, 34% men

Undergraduates 836 full-time, 3,394 part-time. Students come from 19 states and territories; 5% are from out of state; 1% Black or African American, non-Hispanic/Latino; 23% Hispanic/Latino; 2% Asian, non-Hispanic/Latino; 0.7% Native Hawaiian or other Pacific Islander, non-Hispanic/Latino; 2% American Indian or Alaska Native, non-Hispanic/Latino; 3% Two or more races, non-Hispanic/Latino; 1% Race/ethnicity unknown.

Freshmen *Admission:* 582 enrolled.

Faculty *Total:* 309, 26% full-time. *Student/faculty ratio:* 13:1.

Majors Accounting; art; automobile/automotive mechanics technology; building/construction finishing, management, and inspection related; business administration and management; computer and information sciences related; computer programming (specific applications); computer science; criminal justice/police science; culinary arts; dental assisting; dental hygiene; drafting and design technology; education; emergency medical technology (EMT paramedic); English; fire science/firefighting; heating, air conditioning, ventilation and refrigeration maintenance technology; history; information technology; legal assistant/paralegal; liberal arts and sciences/liberal studies; mathematics; medical/clinical assistant; personal and culinary services related; pharmacy technician; physical therapy technology; psychology; registered nursing/registered nurse; sociology; substance abuse/addiction counseling; surgical technology; truck and bus driver/commercial vehicle operation/instruction; welding technology.

Academics *Calendar:* semesters. *Degree:* certificates and associate. *Special study options:* academic remediation for entering students, adult/continuing education programs, cooperative education, distance learning, English as a second language, independent study, part-time degree program, summer session for credit.

Library Mohave Community College Library.

Student Life *Housing:* college housing not available. *Activities and Organizations:* Art Club, Phi Theta Kappa, Computer Club (MC4), Science Club, Student Government. *Campus security:* late-night transport/escort service.

Costs (2016–17) *Tuition:* state resident $2430 full-time, $81 per credit hour part-time; nonresident $8505 full-time, $284 per credit hour part-time. Full-time tuition and fees vary according to program. Part-time tuition and fees vary according to program. *Required fees:* $210 full-time, $7 per credit hour part-time. *Payment plans:* installment, deferred payment. *Waivers:* employees or children of employees.

Applying *Options:* electronic application, early admission, deferred entrance. *Application deadlines:* rolling (freshmen), rolling (transfers). *Notification:* continuous (freshmen), continuous (transfers).

Freshman Application Contact Mrs. Ana Masterson, Dean of Student Services, Mohave Community College, 1971 Jagerson Avenue, Kingman, AZ 86409. *Phone:* 928-757-0803. *Toll-free phone:* 888-664-2832. *Fax:* 928-757-0808. *E-mail:* amasterson@mohave.edu.
Website: http://www.mohave.edu/.

Northland Pioneer College
Holbrook, Arizona

Freshman Application Contact Ms. Suzette Willis, Coordinator of Admissions, Northland Pioneer College, PO Box 610, Holbrook, AZ 86025. *Phone:* 928-536-6271. *Toll-free phone:* 800-266-7845. *Fax:* 928-536-6212. *Website:* http://www.npc.edu/.

Paradise Valley Community College
Phoenix, Arizona

Freshman Application Contact Paradise Valley Community College, 18401 North 32nd Street, Phoenix, AZ 85032-1200. *Phone:* 602-787-7020. *Website:* http://www.pvc.maricopa.edu/.

The Paralegal Institute at Brighton College
Scottsdale, Arizona

Freshman Application Contact Patricia Yancy, Director of Admissions, The Paralegal Institute at Brighton College, 2933 West Indian School Road, Drawer 11408, Phoenix, AZ 85061-1408. *Phone:* 602-212-0501. *Toll-free phone:* 800-354-1254. *Fax:* 602-212-0502. *E-mail:* paralegalinst@mindspring.com. *Website:* http://www.theparalegalinstitute.edu/.

Penn Foster College
Scottsdale, Arizona

- **Proprietary** primarily 2-year
- **Coed,** 24,527 undergraduate students

Undergraduates Students come from 50 states and territories; 5 other countries.
Faculty *Total:* 203, 20% full-time, 5% with terminal degrees.
Majors Accounting; building construction technology; business administration and management; computer and information sciences; computer installation and repair technology; criminal justice/law enforcement administration; early childhood education; engineering technology; fashion merchandising; finance; graphic design; health/health-care administration; health information/medical records technology; hospitality administration; human resources management; industrial electronics technology; legal assistant/paralegal; marketing/marketing management; marketing research; medical/clinical assistant; retail management; roofing; veterinary/animal health technology.
Academics *Calendar:* continuous. *Degrees:* certificates, associate, and bachelor's. *Special study options:* academic remediation for entering students, accelerated degree program, distance learning, external degree program, independent study, off-campus study, part-time degree program, services for LD students.
Library Penn Foster College Online Library.
Student Life *Housing:* college housing not available. *Activities and Organizations:* Online Community-Hosted Academic Interest Groups.
Costs (2017–18) *Tuition:* $79 per credit part-time. Part-time tuition and fees vary according to course load and program. *Payment plan:* installment.
Applying *Options:* electronic application. *Application fee:* $75. *Required:* high school transcript. *Application deadlines:* rolling (freshmen), rolling (out-of-state freshmen).
Freshman Application Contact Admissions, Penn Foster College, 14300 North Northsight Boulevard, Suite 120, Scottsdale, AZ 85260. *Phone:* 888-427-1000. *Toll-free phone:* 800-471-3232.
Website: http://www.pennfostercollege.edu/.

Phoenix College
Phoenix, Arizona

Freshman Application Contact Ms. Brenda Stark, Director of Admissions, Registration, and Records, Phoenix College, 1202 West Thomas Road, Phoenix, AZ 85013. *Phone:* 602-285-7503. *Fax:* 602-285-7813. *E-mail:* kathy.french@pcmail.maricopa.edu. *Website:* http://www.pc.maricopa.edu/.

Pima Community College
Tucson, Arizona

Freshman Application Contact Terra Benson, Director of Admissions and Registrar, Pima Community College, 4905B East Broadway Boulevard, Tucson, AZ 85709-1120. *Phone:* 520-206-4640. *Fax:* 520-206-4790. *E-mail:* tbenson@pima.edu. *Website:* http://www.pima.edu/.

Pima Medical Institute
Mesa, Arizona

Freshman Application Contact Pima Medical Institute, 2160 South Power Road, Mesa, AZ 85209. *Phone:* 480-898-9898. *Toll-free phone:* 800-477-PIMA. *Website:* http://www.pmi.edu/.

Pima Medical Institute
Mesa, Arizona

Freshman Application Contact Admissions Office, Pima Medical Institute, 957 South Dobson Road, Mesa, AZ 85202. *Phone:* 480-644-0267 Ext. 225. *Toll-free phone:* 800-477-PIMA. *Website:* http://www.pmi.edu/.

Pima Medical Institute
Tucson, Arizona

Freshman Application Contact Admissions Office, Pima Medical Institute, 3350 East Grant Road, Tucson, AZ 85716. *Phone:* 520-326-1600 Ext. 5112. *Toll-free phone:* 800-477-PIMA. *Website:* http://www.pmi.edu/.

The Refrigeration School
Phoenix, Arizona

- **Proprietary** 2-year, founded 1965
- **Urban** campus
- **Coed, primarily men,** 688 undergraduate students, 100% full-time, 1% women, 99% men

Undergraduates 688 full-time. 6% are from out of state; 8% Black or African American, non-Hispanic/Latino; 20% Hispanic/Latino; 0.7% Asian, non-Hispanic/Latino; 0.6% Native Hawaiian or other Pacific Islander, non-Hispanic/Latino; 6% American Indian or Alaska Native, non-Hispanic/Latino; 2% Two or more races, non-Hispanic/Latino; 30% Race/ethnicity unknown. *Retention:* 72% of full-time freshmen returned.
Faculty *Student/faculty ratio:* 34:1.
Majors Energy management and systems technology.
Academics *Calendar:* continuous. *Degree:* certificates, diplomas, and associate.
Student Life *Housing:* college housing not available.
Freshman Application Contact Mr. John Palumbo, Regional Director of Admissions, The Refrigeration School, 4210 East Washington Street. *Phone:* 602-275-7133. *Toll-free phone:* 888-943-4822. *Fax:* 602-267-4811. *E-mail:* info@rsiaz.edu.
Website: http://www.refrigerationschool.com/.

Rio Salado College
Tempe, Arizona

- **State and locally supported** 2-year, founded 1978, part of Maricopa County Community College District System
- **Urban** campus
- **Coed,** 20,865 undergraduate students

Undergraduates Students come from 38 other countries; 4% are from out of state.
Freshmen *Admission:* 13,332 applied, 13,332 admitted.
Faculty *Total:* 1,170. *Student/faculty ratio:* 13:1.
Majors Business administration and management; computer and information sciences and support services related; computer and information sciences related; computer programming related; computer science; consumer services and advocacy; data entry/microcomputer applications; dental hygiene; information science/studies; information technology; network and system

administration; public administration; substance abuse/addiction counseling; web/multimedia management and webmaster; web page, digital/multimedia and information resources design.

Academics *Calendar:* semesters. *Degree:* certificates and associate. *Special study options:* academic remediation for entering students, accelerated degree program, adult/continuing education programs, advanced placement credit, cooperative education, distance learning, double majors, English as a second language, external degree program, honors programs, independent study, internships, part-time degree program, services for LD students, summer session for credit.

Library Rio Salado Library and Information Center.

Student Life *Housing:* college housing not available. *Campus security:* 24-hour emergency response devices, late-night transport/escort service. *Student services:* personal/psychological counseling.

Costs (2017–18) *Tuition:* state resident $2064 full-time, $86 per credit hour part-time; nonresident $5160 full-time, $215 per credit hour part-time. Full-time tuition and fees vary according to course load and reciprocity agreements. Part-time tuition and fees vary according to course load and reciprocity agreements. *Required fees:* $30 full-time, $15 per term part-time. *Payment plans:* installment, deferred payment. *Waivers:* senior citizens and employees or children of employees.

Applying *Options:* electronic application, early admission, deferred entrance. *Application deadlines:* rolling (freshmen), rolling (transfers).

Freshman Application Contact Laurel Redman, Director of Admissions, Records and Registration, Rio Salado College, 2323 West 14th Street, Tempe 85281. *Phone:* 480-517-8563. *Toll-free phone:* 800-729-1197. *Fax:* 480-517-8199.

Website: http://www.riosalado.edu/.

Scottsdale Community College
Scottsdale, Arizona

- **State and locally supported** 2-year, founded 1969, part of Maricopa County Community College District System
- **Urban** 160-acre campus with easy access to Phoenix
- **Coed,** 9,551 undergraduate students, 27% full-time, 53% women, 47% men

Undergraduates 2,563 full-time, 6,988 part-time. Students come from 9 states and territories; 25 other countries; 1% are from out of state; 4% Black or African American, non-Hispanic/Latino; 17% Hispanic/Latino; 3% Asian, non-Hispanic/Latino; 0.3% Native Hawaiian or other Pacific Islander, non-Hispanic/Latino; 5% American Indian or Alaska Native, non-Hispanic/Latino; 3% Two or more races, non-Hispanic/Latino; 7% Race/ethnicity unknown; 1% international; 10% transferred in.

Freshmen *Admission:* 1,016 enrolled.

Faculty *Total:* 485, 34% full-time, 16% with terminal degrees. *Student/faculty ratio:* 18:1.

Majors Accounting; administrative assistant and secretarial science; business administration and management; criminal justice/law enforcement administration; culinary arts; dramatic/theater arts; electrical, electronic and communications engineering technology; environmental design/architecture; equestrian studies; fashion merchandising; finance; hospitality administration; hotel/motel administration; information science/studies; interior design; mathematics; medical administrative assistant and medical secretary; photography; public administration; real estate; registered nursing/registered nurse; special products marketing.

Academics *Calendar:* semesters. *Degree:* certificates, diplomas, and associate. *Special study options:* academic remediation for entering students, adult/continuing education programs, advanced placement credit, cooperative education, English as a second language, honors programs, internships, off-campus study, part-time degree program, services for LD students, study abroad, summer session for credit.

Library Scottsdale Community College Library. Students can reserve study rooms.

Student Life *Housing:* college housing not available. *Activities and Organizations:* drama/theater group, student-run newspaper, radio station, choral group, Student Leadership Forum, International Community Club, Phi Theta Kappa, Music Industry Club, SCC ASID-Interior Design group. *Campus security:* 24-hour emergency response devices and patrols, student patrols, late-night transport/escort service, 24-hour automatic surveillance cameras. *Student services:* personal/psychological counseling.

Athletics Member NCAA, NJCAA. All NCAA Division II. *Intercollegiate sports:* baseball M, basketball M/W, cross-country running M/W, football M, golf M/W, soccer M/W, softball W, volleyball W. *Intramural sports:* archery M/W, badminton M/W, basketball M/W, racquetball M/W, track and field M/W, volleyball M/W.

Costs (2017–18) *Tuition:* state resident $1290 full-time, $86 per credit hour part-time; nonresident $4905 full-time, $327 per credit hour part-time. Full-time tuition and fees vary according to program and reciprocity agreements. Part-time tuition and fees vary according to program and reciprocity

agreements. *Required fees:* $30 full-time, $15 per credit hour part-time. *Payment plans:* installment, deferred payment. *Waivers:* senior citizens and employees or children of employees.

Financial Aid Of all full-time matriculated undergraduates who enrolled in 2015, 75 Federal Work-Study jobs (averaging $2000). *Financial aid deadline:* 7/15.

Applying *Options:* electronic application, early admission. *Application deadline:* rolling (freshmen). *Notification:* continuous (freshmen).

Freshman Application Contact Ms. Laura Krueger, Director of Admissions and Records, Scottsdale Community College, 9000 East Chaparral Road, Scottsdale, AZ 85256. *Phone:* 480-423-6133. *Fax:* 480-423-6200. *E-mail:* laura.krueger@scottsdalecc.edu.

Website: http://www.scottsdalecc.edu/.

Sessions College for Professional Design
Tempe, Arizona

Freshman Application Contact Ms. Mhelanie Hernandez, Director of Admissions, Sessions College for Professional Design, 350 South Mill Avenue, Suite B-104, Tempe, AZ 85281. *Phone:* 480-212-1704. *Toll-free phone:* 800-258-4115. *E-mail:* admissions@sessions.edu. *Website:* http://www.sessions.edu/.

South Mountain Community College
Phoenix, Arizona

Director of Admissions Dean of Enrollment Services, South Mountain Community College, 7050 South Twenty-fourth Street, Phoenix, AZ 85040. *Phone:* 602-243-8120. *Website:* http://www.southmountaincc.edu/.

Southwest Institute of Healing Arts
Tempe, Arizona

Director of Admissions Katie Yearous, Student Advisor, Southwest Institute of Healing Arts, 1100 East Apache Boulevard, Tempe, AZ 85281. *Phone:* 480-994-9244. *Toll-free phone:* 888-504-9106. *E-mail:* joannl@swiha.net. *Website:* http://www.swiha.org/.

Tohono O'odham Community College
Sells, Arizona

- **Public** 2-year, founded 1998
- **Rural** 42-acre campus
- **Endowment** $314,747
- **Coed,** 206 undergraduate students, 43% full-time, 55% women, 45% men

Undergraduates 89 full-time, 117 part-time. Students come from 7 states and territories; 2% are from out of state; 6% Black or African American, non-Hispanic/Latino; 4% Hispanic/Latino; 82% American Indian or Alaska Native, non-Hispanic/Latino; 2% Two or more races, non-Hispanic/Latino; 10% live on campus. *Retention:* 43% of full-time freshmen returned.

Freshmen *Admission:* 19 enrolled.

Faculty *Total:* 48, 35% full-time, 21% with terminal degrees. *Student/faculty ratio:* 10:1.

Majors Business administration and management; child development; computer systems analysis; early childhood education; human services; liberal arts and sciences/liberal studies.

Academics *Calendar:* semesters. *Degree:* certificates, diplomas, and associate. *Special study options:* academic remediation for entering students, adult/continuing education programs, cooperative education, double majors, part-time degree program, services for LD students, summer session for credit.

Library Tohono O'odham Community College Library plus 2 others. *Books:* 12,865 (physical), 54 (digital/electronic). Weekly public service hours: 40.

Student Life *Housing Options:* coed, men-only, women-only. Campus housing is university owned. *Activities and Organizations:* Student Senate, AISES, Archery Club. *Campus security:* 24-hour patrols. *Student services:* personal/psychological counseling.

Athletics Member NJCAA. *Intercollegiate sports:* basketball M(s)/W(s).

Costs (2017–18) *Tuition:* state resident $811 full-time, $35 per credit hour part-time; nonresident $811 full-time, $35 per credit hour part-time. Full-time tuition and fees vary according to class time, course level, course load, degree level, location, program, and student level. Part-time tuition and fees vary according to class time, course level, course load, degree level, location, program, and student level. *Required fees:* $20 full-time, $10 per term part-time. *Room and board:* $2400. *Payment plan:* installment. *Waivers:* employees or children of employees.

Applying *Options:* electronic application. *Required:* high school transcript. *Application deadlines:* rolling (freshmen), rolling (out-of-state freshmen),

rolling (transfers), rolling (early action). *Early decision deadline:* rolling (for plan 1), rolling (for plan 2). *Notification:* continuous (freshmen), continuous (out-of-state freshmen), continuous (transfers), rolling (early decision plan 1), rolling (early decision plan 2), rolling (early action).
Freshman Application Contact Jennifer Hill, Admissions, Tohono O'odham Community College, PO Box 3129, Sells, AZ 85634. *Phone:* 520-383-8401. *E-mail:* jhill@tocc.edu. *Website:* http://www.tocc.edu/.

Universal Technical Institute
Avondale, Arizona

Freshman Application Contact Director of Admission, Universal Technical Institute, 10695 West Pierce Street, Avondale, AZ 85323. *Phone:* 623-245-4600. *Toll-free phone:* 800-510-5072. *Fax:* 623-245-4601. *Website:* http://www.uti.edu/.

Yavapai College
Prescott, Arizona

Freshman Application Contact Mrs. Sheila Jarrell, Admissions, Registration, and Records Manager, Yavapai College, 1100 East Sheldon Street, Prescott, AZ 86301-3297. *Phone:* 928-776-2107. *Toll-free phone:* 800-922-6787. *Fax:* 928-776-2151. *E-mail:* registration@yc.edu. *Website:* http://www.yc.edu/.

ARKANSAS

Arkansas Northeastern College
Blytheville, Arkansas

- **State-supported** 2-year, founded 1975
- **Small-town** 80-acre campus with easy access to Memphis
- **Endowment** $187,500
- **Coed,** 1,416 undergraduate students, 43% full-time, 65% women, 35% men

Undergraduates 610 full-time, 806 part-time. Students come from 5 states and territories; 18% are from out of state; 27% Black or African American, non-Hispanic/Latino; 3% Hispanic/Latino; 0.5% Asian, non-Hispanic/Latino; 0.1% Native Hawaiian or other Pacific Islander, non-Hispanic/Latino; 0.2% American Indian or Alaska Native, non-Hispanic/Latino; 0.8% Two or more races, non-Hispanic/Latino; 5% transferred in. *Retention:* 83% of full-time freshmen returned.
Freshmen *Admission:* 501 applied, 501 admitted, 277 enrolled. *Average high school GPA:* 2.87.
Majors Business/commerce; criminal justice/police science; general studies; industrial mechanics and maintenance technology; industrial production technologies related; industrial technology; marketing/marketing management; metallurgical technology; middle school education; multi/interdisciplinary studies related; registered nursing/registered nurse.
Academics *Calendar:* semesters. *Degree:* certificates and associate. *Special study options:* academic remediation for entering students, adult/continuing education programs, advanced placement credit, distance learning, double majors, part-time degree program, summer session for credit.
Library Adams/Vines Library.
Student Life *Housing:* college housing not available. *Activities and Organizations:* drama/theater group, choral group, Gamma Beta Phi, Association of Childhood Education International, Nursing Club, Cultural Diversity, Adult Student Association. *Campus security:* 24-hour patrols.
Athletics *Intramural sports:* badminton M/W, basketball M, football M, volleyball M/W.
Costs (2016–17) *Tuition:* area resident $1876 full-time, $67 per credit hour part-time; state resident $2156 full-time, $77 per credit hour part-time; nonresident $3556 full-time, $127 per credit hour part-time. Full-time tuition and fees vary according to course load. Part-time tuition and fees vary according to course load. *Required fees:* $330 full-time, $10 per credit hour part-time, $25 per term part-time. *Payment plans:* installment, deferred payment. *Waivers:* senior citizens and employees or children of employees.
Financial Aid Of all full-time matriculated undergraduates who enrolled in 2015, 42 Federal Work-Study jobs (averaging $2500).
Applying *Options:* deferred entrance. *Recommended:* high school transcript. *Application deadlines:* rolling (freshmen), rolling (transfers). *Notification:* continuous (freshmen), continuous (transfers).
Freshman Application Contact Arkansas Northeastern College, PO Box 1109, Blytheville, AR 72316. *Phone:* 870-762-1020. *Fax:* 870-763-1654. *Website:* http://www.anc.edu/.

Arkansas State University–Beebe
Beebe, Arkansas

Freshman Application Contact Mr. Ronald Hudson, Coordinator of Student Recruitment, Arkansas State University–Beebe, PO Box 1000, Beebe, AR 72012. *Phone:* 501-882-8860. *Toll-free phone:* 800-632-9985. *E-mail:* rdhudson@asub.edu. *Website:* http://www.asub.edu/.

Arkansas State University Mid-South
West Memphis, Arkansas

Freshman Application Contact Jeremy Reece, Director of Admissions, Arkansas State University Mid-South, 2000 West Broadway, West Memphis, AR 72301. *Phone:* 870-733-6786. *Toll-free phone:* 866-733-6722. *Fax:* 870-733-6719. *E-mail:* jreece@midsouthcc.edu. *Website:* http://www.asumidsouth.edu/.

Arkansas State University–Mountain Home
Mountain Home, Arkansas

Freshman Application Contact Ms. Delba Parrish, Admissions Coordinator, Arkansas State University–Mountain Home, 1600 South College Street, Mountain Home, AR 72653. *Phone:* 870-508-6180. *Fax:* 870-508-6287. *E-mail:* dparrish@asumh.edu. *Website:* http://www.asumh.edu/.

Arkansas State University–Newport
Newport, Arkansas

Freshman Application Contact Arkansas State University–Newport, 7648 Victory Boulevard, Newport, AR 72112. *Phone:* 870-512-7800. *Toll-free phone:* 800-976-1676. *Website:* http://www.asun.edu/.

Baptist Health College Little Rock
Little Rock, Arkansas

Admissions Office Contact Baptist Health College Little Rock, 11900 Colonel Glenn Road, Suite 100, Little Rock, AR 72210-2820. *Website:* http://www.bhclr.edu/.

Black River Technical College
Pocahontas, Arkansas

Director of Admissions Director of Admissions, Black River Technical College, 1410 Highway 304 East, Pocahontas, AR 72455. *Phone:* 870-892-4565. *Website:* http://www.blackrivertech.edu/.

Bryan University
Rogers, Arkansas

Admissions Office Contact Bryan University, 3704 West Walnut Street, Rogers, AR 72756. *Website:* http://www.bryanu.edu/.

College of the Ouachitas
Malvern, Arkansas

- **State-supported** 2-year, founded 1972
- **Small-town** 11-acre campus with easy access to Little Rock
- **Coed,** 1,328 undergraduate students, 33% full-time, 57% women, 43% men

Undergraduates 439 full-time, 889 part-time. Students come from 9 states and territories; 1% are from out of state; 14% Black or African American, non-Hispanic/Latino; 4% Hispanic/Latino; 0.2% Asian, non-Hispanic/Latino; 0.1% Native Hawaiian or other Pacific Islander, non-Hispanic/Latino; 0.7% American Indian or Alaska Native, non-Hispanic/Latino; 4% Two or more races, non-Hispanic/Latino; 0.1% international; 23% transferred in.
Freshmen *Admission:* 154 enrolled.
Faculty *Total:* 98, 40% full-time, 9% with terminal degrees.
Majors Accounting; administrative assistant and secretarial science; automobile/automotive mechanics technology; business administration and management; child-care and support services management; computer and information sciences; electromechanical technology; industrial technology; legal administrative assistant/secretary; legal assistant/paralegal; liberal arts and sciences/liberal studies; licensed practical/vocational nurse training; machine tool technology; management information systems;

marketing/marketing management; medical administrative assistant and medical secretary.

Academics *Calendar:* semesters. *Degree:* certificates and associate. *Special study options:* academic remediation for entering students, accelerated degree program, advanced placement credit, cooperative education, distance learning, double majors, freshman honors college, honors programs, independent study, internships, part-time degree program, services for LD students, summer session for credit.

Library College of the Ouachitas Library/Learning Resource Center. Students can reserve study rooms.

Student Life *Housing:* college housing not available. *Activities and Organizations:* student-run newspaper. *Campus security:* 24-hour emergency response devices and patrols. *Student services:* personal/psychological counseling.

Costs (2017–18) *Tuition:* state resident $2790 full-time, $93 per credit hour part-time; nonresident $5580 full-time, $186 per credit hour part-time. Full-time tuition and fees vary according to course load and program. Part-time tuition and fees vary according to course load and program. No tuition increase for student's term of enrollment. *Required fees:* $1180 full-time, $28 per credit hour part-time. *Payment plan:* installment. *Waivers:* senior citizens and employees or children of employees.

Financial Aid Of all full-time matriculated undergraduates who enrolled in 2015, 18 Federal Work-Study jobs (averaging $2400).

Applying *Options:* electronic application, early admission, deferred entrance. *Required:* high school transcript, immunizations. *Application deadlines:* rolling (freshmen), rolling (transfers). *Notification:* continuous (freshmen), continuous (transfers).

Freshman Application Contact Janet Hunt, Student Success Coordinator, College of the Ouachitas, One College Circle, Malvern, AR 72104. *Phone:* 501-337-5000 Ext. 1194. *Toll-free phone:* 800-337-0266. *Fax:* 501-337-9382. *E-mail:* jhunt@coto.edu.
Website: http://www.coto.edu/.

Cossatot Community College of the University of Arkansas
De Queen, Arkansas

Freshman Application Contact Mrs. Tommi Cobb, Admissions Coordinator, Cossatot Community College of the University of Arkansas, 183 College Drive, DeQueen, AR 71832. *Phone:* 870-584-4471 Ext. 1158.
Toll-free phone: 800-844-4471. *Fax:* 870-642-5088.
E-mail: tcobb@cccua.edu. *Website:* http://www.cccua.edu/.

Crowley's Ridge College
Paragould, Arkansas

Freshman Application Contact Amanda Drake, Director of Admissions, Crowley's Ridge College, 100 College Drive, Paragould, AR 72450-9731. *Phone:* 870-236-6901. *Toll-free phone:* 800-264-1096. *Fax:* 870-236-7748. *E-mail:* njoneshi@crc.pioneer.paragould.ar.us. *Website:* http://www.crc.edu/.

East Arkansas Community College
Forrest City, Arkansas

Freshman Application Contact Ms. Sharon Collier, Director of Enrollment Management/Institutional Research, East Arkansas Community College, 1700 Newcastle Road, Forrest City, AR 72335-2204. *Phone:* 870-633-4480. *Toll-free phone:* 877-797-3222. *Fax:* 870-633-3840. *E-mail:* dadams@eacc.edu. *Website:* http://www.eacc.edu/.

Jefferson Regional Medical Center School of Nursing
Pine Bluff, Arkansas

Admissions Office Contact Jefferson Regional Medical Center School of Nursing, 1600 West 40th Avenue, Pine Bluff, AR 71603. *Website:* http://www.jrmc.org/.

National Park College
Hot Springs, Arkansas

Director of Admissions Dr. Allen B. Moody, Director of Institutional Services/Registrar, National Park College, 101 College Drive, Hot Springs, AR 71913. *Phone:* 501-760-4222. *E-mail:* bmoody@npcc.edu. *Website:* http://www.np.edu/.

North Arkansas College
Harrison, Arkansas

Freshman Application Contact Mrs. Charla Jennings, Director of Admissions, North Arkansas College, 1515 Pioneer Drive, Harrison, AR 72601. *Phone:* 870-391-3221. *Toll-free phone:* 800-679-6622. *Fax:* 870-391-3339. *E-mail:* charlam@northark.edu. *Website:* http://www.northark.edu/.

NorthWest Arkansas Community College
Bentonville, Arkansas

- **State-supported** 2-year, founded 1989
- **Suburban** 77-acre campus
- **Coed,** 7,761 undergraduate students

Undergraduates 2% Black or African American, non-Hispanic/Latino; 17% Hispanic/Latino; 3% Asian, non-Hispanic/Latino; 0.4% Native Hawaiian or other Pacific Islander, non-Hispanic/Latino; 2% American Indian or Alaska Native, non-Hispanic/Latino; 3% Two or more races, non-Hispanic/Latino; 3% Race/ethnicity unknown; 2% international. *Retention:* 58% of full-time freshmen returned.

Faculty *Total:* 452, 31% full-time. *Student/faculty ratio:* 18:1.

Majors Accounting; business administration and management; commercial and advertising art; computer programming; criminal justice/law enforcement administration; criminal justice/safety; culinary arts; data processing and data processing technology; drafting and design technology; early childhood education; education; electrical, electronic and communications engineering technology; emergency medical technology (EMT paramedic); environmental science; finance; fire services administration; health information/medical records technology; legal assistant/paralegal; liberal arts and sciences/liberal studies; occupational safety and health technology; physical therapy; registered nursing/registered nurse; respiratory care therapy.

Academics *Calendar:* semesters. *Degree:* certificates and associate. *Special study options:* academic remediation for entering students, accelerated degree program, adult/continuing education programs, advanced placement credit, cooperative education, distance learning, double majors, English as a second language, honors programs, independent study, internships, part-time degree program, services for LD students, student-designed majors, study abroad, summer session for credit. *ROTC:* Army (c), Air Force (c).

Library Pauline Whitaker Library plus 1 other.

Student Life *Housing:* college housing not available. *Activities and Organizations:* drama/theater group, student-run newspaper, choral group, Student Advisory Activity Council, Gamma Beta Phi, Phi Beta Lambda, Student Nurses Association, Enactus. *Campus security:* 24-hour emergency response devices and patrols. *Student services:* personal/psychological counseling.

Athletics *Intramural sports:* basketball M(c)/W(c), bowling M(c)/W(c), golf M(c), soccer M(c)/W(c), softball M(c)/W(c), volleyball W(c).

Costs (2016–17) *Tuition:* area resident $2250 full-time, $75 per credit hour part-time; state resident $3675 full-time, $123 per credit hour part-time; nonresident $3750 full-time, $125 per credit hour part-time. Full-time tuition and fees vary according to program. Part-time tuition and fees vary according to program. *Required fees:* $958 full-time, $29 per credit hour part-time, $55 per term part-time. *Payment plan:* installment. *Waivers:* senior citizens and employees or children of employees.

Applying *Options:* electronic application. *Required:* high school transcript. *Application deadlines:* rolling (freshmen), rolling (transfers). *Notification:* continuous (freshmen), continuous (transfers).

Freshman Application Contact NorthWest Arkansas Community College, One College Drive, Bentonville, AR 72712. *Phone:* 479-636-9222. *Toll-free phone:* 800-995-6922. *Fax:* 479-619-4116. *E-mail:* admissions@nwacc.edu. *Website:* http://www.nwacc.edu/.

Ozarka College
Melbourne, Arkansas

Freshman Application Contact Ms. Dylan Mowery, Director of Admissions, Ozarka College, PO Box 10, Melbourne, AR 72556. *Phone:* 870-368-7371 Ext. 2013. *Toll-free phone:* 800-821-4335. *E-mail:* dmmowery@ozarka.edu. *Website:* http://www.ozarka.edu/.

Phillips Community College of the University of Arkansas
Helena, Arkansas

Director of Admissions Mr. Lynn Boone, Registrar, Phillips Community College of the University of Arkansas, PO Box 785, Helena, AR 72342-0785. *Phone:* 870-338-6474. *Website:* http://www.pccua.edu/.

Pulaski Technical College

North Little Rock, Arkansas

Freshman Application Contact Mr. Clark Atkins, Director of Admissions, Pulaski Technical College, 3000 West Scenic Drive, North Little Rock, AR 72118. *Phone:* 501-812-2734. *Fax:* 501-812-2316.
E-mail: catkins@pulaskitech.edu. *Website:* http://www.pulaskitech.edu/.

Remington College–Little Rock Campus

Little Rock, Arkansas

Director of Admissions Brian Maggio, Director of Recruitment, Remington College–Little Rock Campus, 10600 Colonel Glenn Road, Suite 100, Little Rock, AR 72204. *Phone:* 501-312-0007. *Toll-free phone:* 800-323-8122. *Fax:* 501-225-3819. *E-mail:* brian.maggio@remingtoncollege.edu. *Website:* http://www.remingtoncollege.edu/.

Rich Mountain Community College

Mena, Arkansas

Director of Admissions Dr. Steve Rook, Dean of Students, Rich Mountain Community College, 1100 College Drive, Mena, AR 71953. *Phone:* 479-394-7622 Ext. 1400. *Website:* http://www.rmcc.edu/.

Shorter College

North Little Rock, Arkansas

Director of Admissions Mr. Keith Hunter, Director of Admissions, Shorter College, 604 Locust Street, North Little Rock, AR 72114-4885. *Phone:* 501-374-6305. *Website:* http://www.shortercollege.edu/.

South Arkansas Community College

El Dorado, Arkansas

Freshman Application Contact Dr. Stephanie Tully-Dartez, Director of Enrollment Services, South Arkansas Community College, PO Box 7010, El Dorado, AR 71731-7010. *Phone:* 870-864-7142. *Toll-free phone:* 800-955-2289. *Fax:* 870-864-7109. *E-mail:* dinman@southark.edu. *Website:* http://www.southark.edu/.

Southeast Arkansas College

Pine Bluff, Arkansas

Freshman Application Contact Ms. Barbara Dunn, Director of Admissions, Southeast Arkansas College, 1900 Hazel Street, Pine Bluff, AR 71603. *Phone:* 870-543-5957. *Toll-free phone:* 888-SEARK TC (in-state); 888-SEARC TC (out-of-state). *Fax:* 870-543-5957. *E-mail:* bdunn@seark.edu. *Website:* http://www.seark.edu/.

Southern Arkansas University Tech

Camden, Arkansas

- **State-supported** 2-year, founded 1967, part of Southern Arkansas University System
- **Rural** 96-acre campus
- **Endowment** $1.7 million
- **Coed,** 1,650 undergraduate students, 30% full-time, 51% women, 49% men
- **100% of applicants were admitted**

Undergraduates 501 full-time, 1,149 part-time. Students come from 12 states and territories; 2 other countries; 10% are from out of state; 36% Black or African American, non-Hispanic/Latino; 3% Hispanic/Latino; 0.5% Asian, non-Hispanic/Latino; 0.1% Native Hawaiian or other Pacific Islander, non-Hispanic/Latino; 0.4% American Indian or Alaska Native, non-Hispanic/Latino; 3% Two or more races, non-Hispanic/Latino; 0.1% Race/ethnicity unknown; 0.1% international; 0.1% transferred in; 2% live on campus.
Freshmen *Admission:* 954 applied, 954 admitted, 174 enrolled. *Average high school GPA:* 2.7.
Faculty *Total:* 93, 34% full-time, 3% with terminal degrees. *Student/faculty ratio:* 17:1.
Majors Aircraft powerplant technology; business administration and management; child-care provision; computer and information sciences; computer science; computer software and media applications related; computer technology/computer systems technology; education (multiple levels); engineering technologies and engineering related; environmental engineering technology; fire science/firefighting; fire services administration;

general studies; heavy/industrial equipment maintenance technologies related; industrial technology; middle school education; multi/interdisciplinary studies related; office management.
Academics *Calendar:* semesters. *Degree:* certificates and associate. *Special study options:* academic remediation for entering students, accelerated degree program, adult/continuing education programs, advanced placement credit, cooperative education, distance learning, double majors, external degree program, freshman honors college, honors programs, independent study, internships, off-campus study, part-time degree program, services for LD students, summer session for credit.
Library Southern Arkansas University Tech Learning Resource Center. *Books:* 17,910 (physical), 17,020 (digital/electronic); *Serial titles:* 964 (physical), 176 (digital/electronic); *Databases:* 9. Weekly public service hours: 45; students can reserve study rooms.
Student Life *Housing Options:* coed. Campus housing is university owned and leased by the school. *Activities and Organizations:* drama/theater group, student-run radio and television station, Phi Beta Lambda, TEC@Tech, Allied Health Student Club, Aviation Club, Multimedia Club. *Campus security:* 24-hour emergency response devices and patrols, late-night transport/escort service. *Student services:* personal/psychological counseling, women's center.
Athletics *Intramural sports:* basketball M/W, football M/W, soccer M/W, softball M/W, table tennis M/W, tennis M/W, volleyball M/W, weight lifting M/W.
Costs (2017–18) *One-time required fee:* $75. *Tuition:* state resident $3240 full-time, $108 per credit hour part-time; nonresident $4680 full-time, $156 per credit hour part-time. *Required fees:* $1437 full-time, $41 per credit hour part-time, $75 per term part-time. *Room and board:* $5611; room only: $2800. Room and board charges vary according to housing facility and location. *Payment plan:* installment. *Waivers:* senior citizens and employees or children of employees.
Applying *Options:* electronic application, deferred entrance. *Application fee:* $50. *Required:* high school transcript. *Application deadlines:* 8/15 (freshmen), rolling (transfers). *Notification:* continuous (freshmen), continuous (transfers).
Freshman Application Contact Mrs. Lisa Smith, Admissions Analyst, Southern Arkansas University Tech, PO Box 3499, Camden, AR 71711-1599. *Phone:* 870-574-4558. *Fax:* 870-574-4442. *E-mail:* lsmith@sautech.edu. *Website:* http://www.sautech.edu/.

University of Arkansas Community College at Batesville

Batesville, Arkansas

Freshman Application Contact Ms. Amy Foree, Enrollment Specialist, University of Arkansas Community College at Batesville, PO Box 3350, Batesville, AR 72503. *Phone:* 870-612-2113. *Toll-free phone:* 800-508-7878. *Fax:* 870-612-2129. *E-mail:* amy.foree@uaccb.edu. *Website:* http://www.uaccb.edu/.

University of Arkansas Community College at Hope

Hope, Arkansas

Freshman Application Contact University of Arkansas Community College at Hope, PO Box 140, Hope, AR 71802. *Phone:* 870-772-8174. *Website:* http://www.uacch.edu/.

University of Arkansas Community College at Morrilton

Morrilton, Arkansas

- **State-supported** 2-year, founded 1961, part of University of Arkansas System
- **Rural** 79-acre campus
- **Coed,** 2,029 undergraduate students, 62% full-time, 60% women, 40% men

Undergraduates 1,255 full-time, 774 part-time. Students come from 9 states and territories; 8 other countries; 0.9% are from out of state; 9% Black or African American, non-Hispanic/Latino; 8% Hispanic/Latino; 0.6% Asian, non-Hispanic/Latino; 0.3% American Indian or Alaska Native, non-Hispanic/Latino; 5% Two or more races, non-Hispanic/Latino; 0.8% Race/ethnicity unknown; 2% international; 11% transferred in.
Freshmen *Admission:* 1,166 applied, 900 admitted, 560 enrolled. *Average high school GPA:* 2.95. *Test scores:* ACT scores over 18: 72%; ACT scores over 24: 15%; ACT scores over 30: 1%.
Faculty *Total:* 77, 74% full-time, 12% with terminal degrees. *Student/faculty ratio:* 24:1.

Majors Autobody/collision and repair technology; automobile/automotive mechanics technology; business/commerce; child development; computer technology/computer systems technology; criminal justice/law enforcement administration; drafting and design technology; forensic science and technology; general studies; heating, air conditioning, ventilation and refrigeration maintenance technology; industrial mechanics and maintenance technology; liberal arts and sciences/liberal studies; middle school education; petroleum technology; registered nursing/registered nurse; surveying technology.

Academics *Calendar:* semesters. *Degree:* certificates and associate. *Special study options:* academic remediation for entering students, advanced placement credit, cooperative education, distance learning, double majors, independent study, internships, part-time degree program, services for LD students, summer session for credit.

Library E. Allen Gordon Library. *Books:* 26,352 (physical), 150,568 (digital/electronic); *Serial titles:* 81 (physical); *Databases:* 24. Weekly public service hours: 66; students can reserve study rooms.

Student Life *Housing:* college housing not available. *Activities and Organizations:* Student Activities Board, Phi Theta Kappa, Petroleum Students Organization, Student Nursing Association, Computer Information Systems Club. *Campus security:* 24-hour emergency response devices, late-night transport/escort service, campus alert system through phone call, text message, and/or e-mail. *Student services:* personal/psychological counseling.

Athletics *Intramural sports:* basketball M/W, football M/W, table tennis M/W, ultimate Frisbee M/W, volleyball M/W.

Standardized Tests *Recommended:* SAT or ACT (for admission), ACT Compass, ACCUPLACER.

Costs (2016–17) *Tuition:* area resident $2610 full-time, $87 per credit hour part-time; state resident $2850 full-time, $95 per credit hour part-time; nonresident $3840 full-time, $128 per credit hour part-time. Full-time tuition and fees vary according to course load and program. Part-time tuition and fees vary according to course load and program. *Required fees:* $1130 full-time, $37 per credit hour part-time, $10 per term part-time. *Payment plan:* installment. *Waivers:* senior citizens and employees or children of employees.

Financial Aid Of all full-time matriculated undergraduates who enrolled in 2015, 1,178 applied for aid, 1,028 were judged to have need, 31 had their need fully met. In 2015, 45 non-need-based awards were made. *Average percent of need met:* 44%. *Average financial aid package:* $6082. *Average need-based loan:* $1686. *Average need-based gift aid:* $3161. *Average non-need-based aid:* $1033.

Applying *Options:* electronic application, early admission, deferred entrance. *Required:* high school transcript. *Required for some:* immunization records, prior college transcript(s). *Application deadlines:* rolling (freshmen), rolling (transfers). *Notification:* continuous (freshmen), continuous (transfers).

Freshman Application Contact Ms. Robin Jones, Administrative Specialist, University of Arkansas Community College at Morrilton, 1537 University Boulevard, Morrilton, AR 72110. *Phone:* 501-977-2053. *Toll-free phone:* 800-264-1094. *Fax:* 501-977-2123. *E-mail:* jonesr@uaccm.edu. *Website:* http://www.uaccm.edu/.

CALIFORNIA

Advanced College
South Gate, California
Admissions Office Contact Advanced College, 13180 Paramount Boulevard, South Gate, CA 90280. *Website:* http://www.advancedcollege.edu/.

Advanced Computing Institute
Los Angeles, California
Admissions Office Contact Advanced Computing Institute, 3470 Wilshire Boulevard 11th Floor, Los Angeles, CA 90010-3911. *Website:* http://www.advancedcomputinginstitute.edu/.

Advanced Training Associates
El Cajon, California
Admissions Office Contact Advanced Training Associates, 1810 Gillespie Way, Suite 104, El Cajon, CA 92020. *Toll-free phone:* 800-720-2125. *Website:* http://www.advancedtraining.edu/.

Allan Hancock College
Santa Maria, California
Freshman Application Contact Ms. Adela Esquivel Swinson, Director of Admissions and Records, Allan Hancock College, 800 South College Drive, Santa Maria, CA 93454-6399. *Phone:* 805-922-6966 Ext. 3272. *Toll-free phone:* 866-342-5242. *Fax:* 805-922-3477. *Website:* http://www.hancockcollege.edu/.

American Academy of Dramatic Arts–Los Angeles
Hollywood, California
Freshman Application Contact Steven Hong, Director of Admissions, American Academy of Dramatic Arts–Los Angeles, 1336 North La Brea Avenue, Hollywood, CA 90028. *Phone:* 323-464-2777 Ext. 103. *Toll-free phone:* 800-222-2867. *E-mail:* shong@aada.edu. *Website:* http://www.aada.edu/.

American Career College
Anaheim, California
Director of Admissions Susan Pailet, Senior Executive Director of Admission, American Career College, 1200 North Magnolia Avenue, Anaheim, CA 92801. *Phone:* 714-952-9066. *Toll-free phone:* 877-832-0790. *E-mail:* info@americancareer.com. *Website:* http://americancareercollege.edu/.

American Career College
Los Angeles, California
Director of Admissions Tamra Adams, Director of Admissions, American Career College, 4021 Rosewood Avenue, Los Angeles, CA 90004. *Phone:* 323-668-7555. *Toll-free phone:* 877-832-0790. *E-mail:* info@americancareer.com. *Website:* http://americancareercollege.edu/.

American Career College
Ontario, California
Director of Admissions Juan Tellez, Director of Admissions, American Career College, 3130 East Sedona Court, Ontario, CA 91764. *Phone:* 951-739-0788. *Toll-free phone:* 877-832-0790. *E-mail:* info@americancareer.com. *Website:* http://americancareercollege.edu/.

American Medical Sciences Center
Glendale, California
Admissions Office Contact American Medical Sciences Center, 225 West Broadway, Suite 115, Glendale, CA 91204-5108. *Website:* http://www.amsc.edu/.

American River College
Sacramento, California
- **District-supported** 2-year, founded 1955, part of Los Rios Community College District System
- **Suburban** 153-acre campus
- **Coed**

Academics *Calendar:* semesters. *Degree:* certificates and associate. *Special study options:* academic remediation for entering students, adult/continuing education programs, advanced placement credit, cooperative education, English as a second language, part-time degree program, services for LD students, summer session for credit.

Student Life *Campus security:* 24-hour emergency response devices and patrols, student patrols, late-night transport/escort service.

Applying *Options:* early admission, deferred entrance.

Freshman Application Contact American River College, 4700 College Oak Drive, Sacramento, CA 95841-4286. *Phone:* 916-484-8171. *Website:* http://www.arc.losrios.edu/.

Antelope Valley College
Lancaster, California

- **District-supported** 2-year, founded 1929, part of California Community College System
- **Suburban** 135-acre campus with easy access to Los Angeles
- **Endowment** $3.7 million
- **Coed**

Academics *Calendar:* semesters. *Degree:* certificates and associate. *Special study options:* academic remediation for entering students, adult/continuing education programs, advanced placement credit, cooperative education, distance learning, English as a second language, external degree program, honors programs, independent study, part-time degree program, services for LD students, student-designed majors, study abroad, summer session for credit. *ROTC:* Army (c), Navy (c), Air Force (c).

Library Antelope Valley College Library. *Books:* 51,894 (physical), 154,754 (digital/electronic); *Serial titles:* 10 (physical), 22,330 (digital/electronic); *Databases:* 52. Weekly public service hours: 152; students can reserve study rooms.

Student Life *Campus security:* 24-hour emergency response devices and patrols, late-night transport/escort service.

Costs (2016–17) *Tuition:* state resident $1104 full-time, $46 per credit part-time; nonresident $6768 full-time, $236 per credit part-time. *Required fees:* $40 full-time, $20 per term part-time.

Applying *Options:* electronic application, early admission. *Recommended:* high school transcript.

Freshman Application Contact Welcome Center, Antelope Valley College, 3041 West Avenue K, SSV Building, Lancaster, CA 93536. *Phone:* 661-722-6300 Ext. 6331. *Website:* http://www.avc.edu/.

APT College
Carlsbad, California

Director of Admissions Monica Hoffman, Director of Admissions/Registrar, APT College, 1939 Palomar Oaks Way, Suite A, Carlsbad, CA 92011. *Phone:* 800-431-8488. *Toll-free phone:* 800-431-8488. *Fax:* 888-431-8588. *E-mail:* aptc@aptc.com. *Website:* http://www.aptc.edu/.

Bakersfield College
Bakersfield, California

Freshman Application Contact Bakersfield College, 1801 Panorama Drive, Bakersfield, CA 93305-1299. *Phone:* 661-395-4301. *Website:* http://www.bakersfieldcollege.edu/.

Barstow Community College
Barstow, California

Freshman Application Contact Barstow Community College, 2700 Barstow Road, Barstow, CA 92311-6699. *Phone:* 760-252-2411 Ext. 7236. *Website:* http://www.barstow.edu/.

Berkeley City College
Berkeley, California

Freshman Application Contact Dr. May Kuang-chi Chen, Vice President of Student Services, Berkeley City College, 2050 Center Street, Berkeley, CA 94704. *Phone:* 510-981-2820. *Fax:* 510-841-7333. *E-mail:* mrivas@peralta.edu. *Website:* http://www.berkeleycitycollege.edu/.

Beverly Hills Design Institute
Beverly Hills, California

- **Proprietary** primarily 2-year
- **Urban** campus with easy access to Los Angeles
- **Coed**

Undergraduates *Retention:* 75% of full-time freshmen returned.

Academics *Degrees:* associate and bachelor's. *Special study options:* double majors, English as a second language.

Library Main Library plus 1 other.

Student Life *Campus security:* 24-hour emergency response devices and patrols.

Standardized Tests *Recommended:* SAT or ACT (for admission).

Costs (2016–17) *One-time required fee:* $100. *Tuition:* $19,998 full-time, $621 per credit part-time. Full-time tuition and fees vary according to class time, course level, course load, degree level, location, program, reciprocity agreements, and student level. Part-time tuition and fees vary according to class time, course level, course load, degree level, location, program, reciprocity agreements, and student level. No tuition increase for student's term of enrollment. *Required fees:* $2340 full-time. *Payment plans:* tuition prepayment, installment.

Applying *Options:* electronic application, early admission. *Application fee:* $40. *Required:* essay or personal statement, interview. *Required for some:* high school transcript.

Freshman Application Contact Beverly Hills Design Institute, 8484 Wilshire Boulevard, Suite 730, Beverly Hills, CA 90211. *Phone:* 310-360-8888. *Website:* http://www.bhdi.edu/.

Brightwood College, Bakersfield Campus
Bakersfield, California

Freshman Application Contact Brightwood College, Bakersfield Campus, 1914 Wible Road, Bakersfield, CA 93304. *Phone:* 661-836-6300. *Toll-free phone:* 866-543-0208. *Website:* http://www.brightwood.edu/.

Brightwood College, Chula Vista Campus
Chula Vista, California

Freshman Application Contact Brightwood College, Chula Vista Campus, 555 Broadway, Suite 144, Chula Vista, CA 91910. *Phone:* 877-473-3052. *Toll-free phone:* 866-543-0208. *Website:* http://www.brightwood.edu/.

Brightwood College, Fresno Campus
Fresno, California

Freshman Application Contact Brightwood College, Fresno Campus, 44 Shaw Avenue, Fresno, CA 93612. *Phone:* 559-325-5100. *Toll-free phone:* 866-543-0208. *Website:* http://www.brightwood.edu/.

Brightwood College, Modesto Campus
Salida, California

Freshman Application Contact Brightwood College, Modesto Campus, 5172 Kiernan Court, Salida, CA 95368. *Phone:* 209-543-7000. *Toll-free phone:* 866-543-0208. *Website:* http://www.brightwood.edu/.

Brightwood College, North Hollywood Campus
North Hollywood, California

Freshman Application Contact Ms. Renee Codner, Director of Admissions, Brightwood College, North Hollywood Campus, 6180 Laurel Canyon Boulevard, Suite 101, North Hollywood, CA 91606. *Phone:* 818-763-2563 Ext. 240. *Toll-free phone:* 866-543-0208. *E-mail:* rcodner@mariccollege.edu. *Website:* http://www.brightwood.edu/.

Brightwood College, Palm Springs Campus
Palm Springs, California

Freshman Application Contact Brightwood College, Palm Springs Campus, 2475 East Tahquitz Canyon Way, Palm Springs, CA 92262. *Phone:* 760-778-3540. *Toll-free phone:* 866-543-0208. *Website:* http://www.brightwood.edu/.

Brightwood College, Riverside Campus
Riverside, California

Freshman Application Contact Brightwood College, Riverside Campus, 4040 Vine Street, Riverside, CA 92507. *Phone:* 951-276-1704. *Toll-free phone:* 866-543-0208. *Website:* http://www.brightwood.edu/.

Brightwood College, Sacramento Campus
Sacramento, California

Freshman Application Contact Brightwood College, Sacramento Campus, 4330 Watt Avenue, Suite 400, Sacramento, CA 95821. *Phone:* 916-649-8168. *Toll-free phone:* 866-543-0208. *Website:* http://www.brightwood.edu/.

Brightwood College, San Diego Campus
San Diego, California

Freshman Application Contact Brightwood College, San Diego Campus, 9055 Balboa Avenue, San Diego, CA 92123. *Phone:* 858-279-4500. *Toll-free phone:* 866-543-0208. *Website:* http://www.brightwood.edu/.

Brightwood College, Vista Campus
Vista, California

Freshman Application Contact Brightwood College, Vista Campus, 2022 University Drive, Vista, CA 92083. *Phone:* 760-630-1555. *Toll-free phone:* 866-543-0208. *Website:* http://www.brightwood.edu/.

Bryan University
Los Angeles, California

Admissions Office Contact Bryan University, 3580 Wilshire Boulevard, Los Angeles, CA 90010. *Website:* http://losangeles.bryanuniversity.edu/.

Butte College
Oroville, California

Freshman Application Contact Mr. Brad Zuniga, Director of Recruitment, Outreach and New Student Orientation, Butte College, 3536 Butte Campus Drive, Oroville, CA 95965-8399. *Phone:* 530-895-2948. *Website:* http://www.butte.edu/.

Cabrillo College
Aptos, California

Freshman Application Contact Tama Bolton, Director of Admissions and Records, Cabrillo College, 6500 Soquel Drive, Aptos, CA 95003-3194. *Phone:* 831-477-3548. *Fax:* 831-479-5782. *E-mail:* tabolton@cabrillo.edu. *Website:* http://www.cabrillo.edu/.

Cambridge Junior College
Yuba City, California

Freshman Application Contact Admissions Office, Cambridge Junior College, 990-A Klamath Lane, Yuba City, CA 95993. *Phone:* 530-674-9199. *Fax:* 530-671-7319. *Website:* http://www.cambridge.edu/.

Cañada College
Redwood City, California

- **District-supported** 2-year, founded 1968, part of San Mateo County Community College District System
- **Suburban** 131-acre campus with easy access to San Francisco, San Jose
- **Endowment** $150,000
- **Coed,** 5,433 undergraduate students, 7% full-time, 63% women, 37% men

Undergraduates 406 full-time, 5,027 part-time. 2% are from out of state; 3% Black or African American, non-Hispanic/Latino; 36% Hispanic/Latino; 10% Asian, non-Hispanic/Latino; 2% Native Hawaiian or other Pacific Islander, non-Hispanic/Latino; 0.2% American Indian or Alaska Native, non-Hispanic/Latino; 17% Two or more races, non-Hispanic/Latino; 2% Race/ethnicity unknown; 5% international.
Freshmen *Admission:* 394 applied, 470 enrolled.
Faculty *Total:* 241, 34% full-time. *Student/faculty ratio:* 16:1.
Majors Accounting technology and bookkeeping; administrative assistant and secretarial science; animation, interactive technology, video graphics and special effects; anthropology; apparel and textile manufacturing; archeology; art; biological and physical sciences; biology/biological sciences; business administration and management; chemistry; child-care provision; computer science; computer systems networking and telecommunications; dramatic/theater arts; economics; education; engineering; English; fashion/apparel design; geography; health and physical education/fitness; history; humanities; human services; interior design; international relations and affairs; legal assistant/paralegal; liberal arts and sciences/liberal studies; linguistics; mathematics; medical/clinical assistant; music; network and system administration; philosophy; physics; political science and government; psychology; radiologic technology/science; retailing; small business administration; sociology; Spanish; speech communication and rhetoric; sport and fitness administration/management.
Academics *Calendar:* semesters. *Degree:* certificates and associate. *Special study options:* academic remediation for entering students, accelerated degree

program, adult/continuing education programs, advanced placement credit, cooperative education, distance learning, double majors, English as a second language, honors programs, independent study, internships, part-time degree program, services for LD students, study abroad, summer session for credit. *ROTC:* Army (c), Navy (c), Air Force (c).
Library *Books:* 25,000 (physical), 230,000 (digital/electronic); *Serial titles:* 40 (physical), 20,000 (digital/electronic); *Databases:* 45. Weekly public service hours: 64; students can reserve study rooms.
Student Life *Housing:* college housing not available. *Activities and Organizations:* drama/theater group, choral group, Phi Theta Kappa, DREAMers Club, Community First, Glee Club, Civil Liberties Club. *Campus security:* 24-hour emergency response devices and patrols, late-night transport/escort service, 12-hour patrols by trained security personnel. *Student services:* health clinic, personal/psychological counseling.
Athletics *Intercollegiate sports:* baseball M, basketball M, golf W, soccer M/W, tennis W.
Costs (2016–17) *Tuition:* state resident $1380 full-time, $46 per unit part-time; nonresident $8070 full-time, $269 per unit part-time. Full-time tuition and fees vary according to course load. Part-time tuition and fees vary according to course load. *Required fees:* $56 full-time, $19 per term part-time. *Payment plan:* installment.
Financial Aid Of all full-time matriculated undergraduates who enrolled in 2014, 40 Federal Work-Study jobs (averaging $2026).
Applying *Options:* electronic application. *Recommended:* high school transcript. *Application deadlines:* rolling (freshmen), rolling (transfers).
Freshman Application Contact Cañada College, 4200 Farm Hill Boulevard, Redwood City, CA 94061-1099. *Phone:* 650-306-3125. *Website:* http://www.canadacollege.edu/.

Carrington College–Citrus Heights
Citrus Heights, California

- **Proprietary** 2-year, part of Carrington Colleges Group, Inc.
- **Coed**

Undergraduates 521 full-time, 47 part-time. 6% Black or African American, non-Hispanic/Latino; 18% Hispanic/Latino; 4% Asian, non-Hispanic/Latino; 2% Native Hawaiian or other Pacific Islander, non-Hispanic/Latino; 2% American Indian or Alaska Native, non-Hispanic/Latino; 6% Two or more races, non-Hispanic/Latino; 1% Race/ethnicity unknown; 0.4% international; 13% transferred in.
Faculty *Student/faculty ratio:* 34:1.
Academics *Degree:* certificates and associate.
Applying *Required:* essay or personal statement, high school transcript, interview.
Freshman Application Contact Carrington College–Citrus Heights, 7301 Greenback Lane, Suite A, Citrus Heights, CA 95621. *Website:* http://carrington.edu/.

Carrington College–Pleasant Hill
Pleasant Hill, California

- **Proprietary** 2-year, founded 1997, part of Carrington Colleges Group, Inc.
- **Coed**

Undergraduates 519 full-time, 97 part-time. 1% are from out of state; 12% Black or African American, non-Hispanic/Latino; 28% Hispanic/Latino; 14% Asian, non-Hispanic/Latino; 2% Native Hawaiian or other Pacific Islander, non-Hispanic/Latino; 1% American Indian or Alaska Native, non-Hispanic/Latino; 2% Two or more races, non-Hispanic/Latino; 4% Race/ethnicity unknown; 0.5% international; 17% transferred in.
Faculty *Student/faculty ratio:* 22:1.
Academics *Calendar:* semesters. *Degree:* certificates and associate.
Costs (2016–17) *Tuition:* $34,166 per degree program part-time. Full-time tuition and fees vary according to program. Part-time tuition and fees vary according to program.
Applying *Required:* essay or personal statement, high school transcript, interview.
Freshman Application Contact Carrington College–Pleasant Hill, 380 Civic Drive, Suite 300, Pleasant Hill, CA 94523. *Website:* http://carrington.edu/.

Carrington College–Pomona
Pomona, California

- **Proprietary** 2-year
- **Coed**

Undergraduates 278 full-time, 128 part-time. 28% are from out of state; 4% Black or African American, non-Hispanic/Latino; 64% Hispanic/Latino; 3% Asian, non-Hispanic/Latino; 0.5% Native Hawaiian or other Pacific Islander, non-Hispanic/Latino; 0.5% American Indian or Alaska Native, non-

Hispanic/Latino; 0.7% Two or more races, non-Hispanic/Latino; 0.5% Race/ethnicity unknown; 14% transferred in.
Faculty *Student/faculty ratio:* 20:1.
Academics *Degree:* certificates and associate.
Costs (2016–17) *Tuition:* $34,166 per degree program part-time. Full-time tuition and fees vary according to program. Part-time tuition and fees vary according to program.
Freshman Application Contact Carrington College–Pomona, 901 Corporate Center Drive, Suite 300, Pomona, CA 91768. *Toll-free phone:* 877-206-2106. *Website:* http://carrington.edu/.

Carrington College–Sacramento
Sacramento, California

- **Proprietary** 2-year, founded 1967, part of Carrington Colleges Group, Inc.
- **Coed**

Undergraduates 1,048 full-time, 224 part-time. 6% are from out of state; 10% Black or African American, non-Hispanic/Latino; 26% Hispanic/Latino; 12% Asian, non-Hispanic/Latino; 2% Native Hawaiian or other Pacific Islander, non-Hispanic/Latino; 1% American Indian or Alaska Native, non-Hispanic/Latino; 4% Two or more races, non-Hispanic/Latino; 8% Race/ethnicity unknown; 10% transferred in.
Faculty *Student/faculty ratio:* 16:1.
Academics *Calendar:* semesters. *Degree:* certificates and associate.
Standardized Tests *Required:* entrance test administered by Carrington College California (for admission).
Costs (2016–17) *Tuition:* $44,490 per degree program part-time. Full-time tuition and fees vary according to program. Part-time tuition and fees vary according to program.
Applying *Required:* essay or personal statement, high school transcript, interview.
Freshman Application Contact Carrington College–Sacramento, 8909 Folsom Boulevard, Sacramento, CA 95826. *Website:* http://carrington.edu/.

Carrington College–San Jose
San Jose, California

- **Proprietary** 2-year, founded 1999, part of Carrington Colleges Group, Inc.
- **Coed**

Undergraduates 739 full-time, 52 part-time. 1% are from out of state; 3% Black or African American, non-Hispanic/Latino; 49% Hispanic/Latino; 18% Asian, non-Hispanic/Latino; 3% Native Hawaiian or other Pacific Islander, non-Hispanic/Latino; 0.4% American Indian or Alaska Native, non-Hispanic/Latino; 4% Two or more races, non-Hispanic/Latino; 0.3% Race/ethnicity unknown; 0.8% international; 11% transferred in.
Faculty *Student/faculty ratio:* 24:1.
Academics *Calendar:* semesters. *Degree:* certificates and associate.
Standardized Tests *Required:* institutional entrance test (for admission).
Applying *Required:* essay or personal statement, high school transcript, interview.
Freshman Application Contact Carrington College–San Jose, 5883 Rue Ferrari, Suite 125, San Jose, CA 95138. *Website:* http://carrington.edu/.

Carrington College–San Leandro
San Leandro, California

- **Proprietary** 2-year, founded 1986, part of Carrington Colleges Group, Inc.
- **Coed**

Undergraduates 436 full-time, 42 part-time. 1% are from out of state; 18% Black or African American, non-Hispanic/Latino; 47% Hispanic/Latino; 13% Asian, non-Hispanic/Latino; 2% Native Hawaiian or other Pacific Islander, non-Hispanic/Latino; 0.8% American Indian or Alaska Native, non-Hispanic/Latino; 3% Two or more races, non-Hispanic/Latino; 0.6% Race/ethnicity unknown; 0.8% international; 14% transferred in.
Faculty *Student/faculty ratio:* 28:1.
Academics *Calendar:* semesters. *Degree:* certificates and associate.
Standardized Tests *Required:* entrance test administered by Carrington Colleges California (for admission).
Applying *Required:* essay or personal statement, high school transcript, interview.
Freshman Application Contact Carrington College–San Leandro, 15555 East 14th Street, Suite 500, San Leandro, CA 94578.
Website: http://carrington.edu/.

Carrington College–Stockton
Stockton, California

- **Proprietary** 2-year
- **Coed**

Undergraduates 550 full-time, 33 part-time. 8% Black or African American, non-Hispanic/Latino; 51% Hispanic/Latino; 10% Asian, non-Hispanic/Latino; 2% Native Hawaiian or other Pacific Islander, non-Hispanic/Latino; 0.5% American Indian or Alaska Native, non-Hispanic/Latino; 3% Two or more races, non-Hispanic/Latino; 1% Race/ethnicity unknown; 15% transferred in.
Faculty *Student/faculty ratio:* 56:1.
Academics *Degree:* certificates and associate.
Freshman Application Contact Carrington College–Stockton, 1313 West Robinhood Drive, Suite B, Stockton, CA 95207.
Website: http://carrington.edu/.

Casa Loma College–Van Nuys
Los Angeles, California

Admissions Office Contact Casa Loma College–Van Nuys, 6725 Kester Avenue, Los Angeles, CA 91405. *Website:* http://www.casalomacollege.edu/.

Cerritos College
Norwalk, California

- **District-supported** 2-year, founded 1956, part of California Community College System
- **Suburban** 140-acre campus with easy access to Los Angeles
- **Coed,** 22,043 undergraduate students, 33% full-time, 55% women, 45% men

Undergraduates 7,209 full-time, 14,834 part-time. Students come from 32 other countries; 1% are from out of state; 3% Black or African American, non-Hispanic/Latino; 70% Hispanic/Latino; 8% Asian, non-Hispanic/Latino; 0.6% Native Hawaiian or other Pacific Islander, non-Hispanic/Latino; 5% American Indian or Alaska Native, non-Hispanic/Latino; 1% Two or more races, non-Hispanic/Latino; 7% Race/ethnicity unknown; 0.7% international; 2% transferred in.
Freshmen *Admission:* 38,002 applied, 24,736 admitted, 3,398 enrolled.
Faculty *Total:* 845, 32% full-time.
Majors Accounting; administrative assistant and secretarial science; alternative fuel vehicle technology; animation, interactive technology, video graphics and special effects; anthropology; architectural engineering technology; art; audiology and speech-language pathology; autobody/collision and repair technology; automobile/automotive mechanics technology; biological and physical sciences; biology/biological sciences; biomedical technology; broadcast journalism; business administration and management; cabinetmaking and millwork; chemistry; cinematography and film/video production; computer programming; computer science; computer systems analysis; computer systems networking and telecommunications; cooking and related culinary arts; cosmetology; court reporting; criminal justice/police science; dance; data entry/microcomputer applications; dental hygiene; drafting and design technology; dramatic/theater arts; economics; electrical, electronic and communications engineering technology; English; fashion/apparel design; food technology and processing; French; geography; geology/earth science; German; Hispanic-American, Puerto Rican, and Mexican-American/Chicano studies; history; human services; industrial technology; insurance; international relations and affairs; journalism; kindergarten/preschool education; kinesiology and exercise science; legal administrative assistant/secretary; legal assistant/paralegal; liberal arts and sciences/liberal studies; machine tool technology; manufacturing engineering technology; marketing/marketing management; mathematics; medical/clinical assistant; music; pharmacy; philosophy; photography; physical education teaching and coaching; physical sciences related; physical therapy; physics; plastics and polymer engineering technology; political science and government; pre-engineering; psychology; real estate; registered nursing/registered nurse; religious studies; small business administration; sociology; Spanish; speech communication and rhetoric; sport and fitness administration/management; technology/industrial arts teacher education; visual and performing arts; welding technology; women's studies; zoology/animal biology.
Academics *Calendar:* semesters. *Degree:* certificates and associate. *Special study options:* academic remediation for entering students, advanced placement credit, distance learning, double majors, English as a second language, honors programs, independent study, part-time degree program, services for LD students, study abroad, summer session for credit.
Library Wilford Michael Library. *Books:* 117,647 (physical), 13,466 (digital/electronic); *Databases:* 66. Weekly public service hours: 71; students can reserve study rooms.

Student Life *Housing:* college housing not available. *Activities and Organizations:* drama/theater group, student-run newspaper, radio station, choral group, WPMD Student Radio, Anxiety Gaming Club, Commercial Radio Club, Abilities Empowered, Student Athlete Captain's Club. *Campus security:* 24-hour emergency response devices and patrols, student patrols, late-night transport/escort service. *Student services:* health clinic, personal/psychological counseling.

Athletics Member NJCAA. *Intercollegiate sports:* baseball M, basketball M/W, cross-country running M/W, football M, golf M, soccer M/W, softball W, swimming and diving M/W, tennis M/W, track and field M/W, volleyball W, water polo M, wrestling M.

Costs (2017–18) *One-time required fee:* $29. *Tuition:* state resident $0 full-time; nonresident $263 per unit part-time. Full-time tuition and fees vary according to course load. Part-time tuition and fees vary according to course load. *Required fees:* $1346 full-time, $46 per unit part-time, $342 per term part-time.

Financial Aid Of all full-time matriculated undergraduates who enrolled in 2015, 180 Federal Work-Study jobs (averaging $3000). 89 state and other part-time jobs (averaging $2734).

Applying *Options:* electronic application, early admission, deferred entrance. *Application deadlines:* rolling (freshmen), rolling (transfers).

Freshman Application Contact Cerritos College, 11110 Alondra Boulevard, Norwalk, CA 90650-6298. *Phone:* 562-860-2451 Ext. 2102. *Website:* http://www.cerritos.edu/.

Cerro Coso Community College
Ridgecrest, California

Freshman Application Contact Mrs. Heather Ootash, Counseling/Matriculation Coordinator, Cerro Coso Community College, 3000 College Heights Boulevard, Ridgecrest, CA 93555. *Phone:* 760-384-6291. *Fax:* 760-375-4776. *E-mail:* hostash@cerrocoso.edu. *Website:* http://www.cerrocoso.edu/.

Chabot College
Hayward, California

Director of Admissions Paulette Lino, Director of Admissions and Records, Chabot College, 25555 Hesperian Boulevard, Hayward, CA 94545-5001. *Phone:* 510-723-6700. *Website:* http://www.chabotcollege.edu/.

Chaffey College
Rancho Cucamonga, California

Freshman Application Contact Erlinda Martinez, Coordinator of Admissions, Chaffey College, 5885 Haven Avenue, Rancho Cucamonga, CA 91737-3002. *Phone:* 909-652-6610. *E-mail:* erlinda.martinez@chaffey.edu. *Website:* http://www.chaffey.edu/.

Citrus College
Glendora, California

- **District-supported** 2-year, founded 1915, part of California Community College System
- **Small-town** 104-acre campus with easy access to Los Angeles
- **Coed,** 12,780 undergraduate students, 39% full-time, 53% women, 47% men

Undergraduates 4,921 full-time, 7,859 part-time. 4% Black or African American, non-Hispanic/Latino; 61% Hispanic/Latino; 8% Asian, non-Hispanic/Latino; 0.1% Native Hawaiian or other Pacific Islander, non-Hispanic/Latino; 0.2% American Indian or Alaska Native, non-Hispanic/Latino; 3% Two or more races, non-Hispanic/Latino; 0.7% Race/ethnicity unknown; 4% international.

Freshmen *Admission:* 11,388 applied, 11,388 admitted, 2,183 enrolled.

Faculty *Total:* 509, 30% full-time. *Student/faculty ratio:* 30:1.

Majors Administrative assistant and secretarial science; art; automobile/automotive mechanics technology; behavioral sciences; biological and physical sciences; biology/biological sciences; business administration and management; business/commerce; child development; computer and information sciences related; computer graphics; computer science; construction trades related; cosmetology; criminal justice/law enforcement administration; criminal justice/police science; dance; dance related; data processing and data processing technology; dental assisting; diesel mechanics technology; drafting and design technology; dramatic/theater arts; electrical, electronic and communications engineering technology; engineering; engineering technology; English; English language and literature related; French; German; health and physical education/fitness; history; hydrology and water resources science; Japanese; journalism; liberal arts and sciences/liberal

studies; library and archives assisting; library and information science; licensed practical/vocational nurse training; mathematics; mechanical engineering/mechanical technology; modern languages; music; natural sciences; photography; physical education teaching and coaching; physical sciences; psychology; public administration; real estate; recording arts technology; registered nursing/registered nurse; security and loss prevention; social sciences; sociology; Spanish; speech communication and rhetoric; visual and performing arts; water quality and wastewater treatment management and recycling technology.

Academics *Calendar:* semesters. *Degree:* certificates, diplomas, and associate. *Special study options:* academic remediation for entering students, advanced placement credit, cooperative education, distance learning, double majors, English as a second language, honors programs, part-time degree program, services for LD students, study abroad, summer session for credit.

Library Hayden Library. Students can reserve study rooms.

Student Life *Activities and Organizations:* drama/theater group, student-run newspaper, choral group, Student Government, Alpha Gamma Sigma (AGS), Veterans Network, International Friendship Club, Citrus Business Association (CBA). *Campus security:* 24-hour patrols, student patrols, late-night transport/escort service. *Student services:* health clinic, personal/psychological counseling, legal services.

Athletics *Intercollegiate sports:* baseball M, basketball M/W, cross-country running M/W, football M, golf M/W, soccer M/W, softball W, swimming and diving W, volleyball W, water polo M/W.

Costs (2016–17) *Tuition:* state resident $1380 full-time, $46 per unit part-time; nonresident $8610 full-time, $241 per unit part-time. Full-time tuition and fees vary according to course load. Part-time tuition and fees vary according to course load. *Required fees:* $87 full-time.

Financial Aid Of all full-time matriculated undergraduates who enrolled in 2015, 141 Federal Work-Study jobs (averaging $5500).

Applying *Options:* electronic application, early decision. *Required:* high school transcript. *Application deadline:* rolling (freshmen).

Freshman Application Contact Admissions and Records, Citrus College, Glendora, CA 91741-1899. *Phone:* 626-914-8511. *Fax:* 626-914-8613. *E-mail:* admissions@citruscollege.edu. *Website:* http://www.citruscollege.edu/.

City College of San Francisco
San Francisco, California

Freshman Application Contact Ms. Mary Lou Leyba-Frank, Dean of Admissions and Records, City College of San Francisco, 50 Phelan Avenue, San Francisco, CA 94112-1821. *Phone:* 415-239-3291. *Fax:* 415-239-3936. *E-mail:* mleyba@ccsf.edu. *Website:* http://www.ccsf.edu/.

Coastline Community College
Fountain Valley, California

- **District-supported** 2-year, founded 1976, part of Coast Community College District System
- **Urban** campus with easy access to Orange County
- **Coed,** 11,431 undergraduate students, 22% full-time, 41% women, 59% men

Undergraduates 2,488 full-time, 8,943 part-time. 12% Black or African American, non-Hispanic/Latino; 28% Hispanic/Latino; 22% Asian, non-Hispanic/Latino; 0.5% Native Hawaiian or other Pacific Islander, non-Hispanic/Latino; 0.8% American Indian or Alaska Native, non-Hispanic/Latino; 4% Two or more races, non-Hispanic/Latino; 2% Race/ethnicity unknown.

Freshmen *Admission:* 900 enrolled.

Faculty *Total:* 282, 15% full-time. *Student/faculty ratio:* 32:1.

Majors Liberal arts and sciences/liberal studies.

Academics *Calendar:* semesters. *Degree:* certificates and associate. *Special study options:* academic remediation for entering students, accelerated degree program, adult/continuing education programs, advanced placement credit, cooperative education, distance learning, double majors, English as a second language, external degree program, honors programs, independent study, internships, off-campus study, part-time degree program, services for LD students, study abroad, summer session for credit.

Library Coastline Virtual Library plus 1 other.

Student Life *Housing:* college housing not available. *Campus security:* 24-hour emergency response devices. *Student services:* health clinic, personal/psychological counseling.

Costs (2016–17) *Tuition:* state resident $1104 full-time, $46 per unit part-time; nonresident $6648 full-time, $231 per unit part-time. Full-time tuition and fees vary according to course load. Part-time tuition and fees vary according to course load. *Required fees:* $32 full-time. *Payment plans:* installment, deferred payment.

Financial Aid Of all full-time matriculated undergraduates who enrolled in 2015, 12,392 applied for aid, 11,568 were judged to have need, 12 had their need fully met. *Average percent of need met:* 15%. *Average financial aid package:* $3819. *Average need-based loan:* $3290. *Average need-based gift aid:* $3714. *Average indebtedness upon graduation:* $10,514. *Financial aid deadline:* 8/15.

Applying *Options:* electronic application, early admission. *Recommended:* high school transcript. *Application deadlines:* rolling (freshmen), rolling (transfers).

Freshman Application Contact Jennifer McDonald, Director of Admissions and Records, Coastline Community College, 11460 Warner Ave, Fountain Valley, CA 92708. *Phone:* 714-241-6163.
Website: http://www.coastline.edu/.

College of Alameda
Alameda, California

Freshman Application Contact College of Alameda, 555 Ralph Appezzato Memorial Parkway, Alameda, CA 94501-2109. *Phone:* 510-748-2204.
Website: http://alameda.peralta.edu/.

College of Marin
Kentfield, California

- **District-supported** 2-year, founded 1926, part of California Community College System
- **Suburban** 410-acre campus with easy access to San Francisco
- **Coed,** 5,621 undergraduate students, 24% full-time, 58% women, 42% men

Undergraduates 1,328 full-time, 4,293 part-time. 4% Black or African American, non-Hispanic/Latino; 29% Hispanic/Latino; 7% Asian, non-Hispanic/Latino; 0.2% Native Hawaiian or other Pacific Islander, non-Hispanic/Latino; 0.2% American Indian or Alaska Native, non-Hispanic/Latino; 5% Two or more races, non-Hispanic/Latino; 1% Race/ethnicity unknown; 1% international.

Faculty *Total:* 320, 38% full-time.

Majors Accounting technology and bookkeeping; animation, interactive technology, video graphics and special effects; architectural technology; art; autobody/collision and repair technology; automobile/automotive mechanics technology; biological and physical sciences; biology/biological sciences; business administration and management; business/commerce; chemistry; child-care provision; cinematography and film/video production; computer science; computer systems networking and telecommunications; court reporting; criminal justice/police science; dance; data modeling/warehousing and database administration; dental assisting; design and visual communications; dramatic/theater arts; engineering; engineering technology; English; ethnic, cultural minority, gender, and group studies related; film/cinema/video studies; foreign languages and literatures; French; geography; geology/earth science; health and physical education/fitness; history; humanities; interior design; international relations and affairs; landscaping and groundskeeping; liberal arts and sciences/liberal studies; machine tool technology; mass communication/media; mathematics; medical administrative assistant and medical secretary; medical/clinical assistant; music; office management; physical sciences; physics; plant nursery management; political science and government; psychology; real estate; registered nursing/registered nurse; social sciences; Spanish; speech communication and rhetoric.

Academics *Calendar:* semesters. *Degree:* certificates and associate. *Special study options:* academic remediation for entering students, advanced placement credit, cooperative education, distance learning, double majors, English as a second language, part-time degree program, services for LD students, summer session for credit.

Library Main Library plus 1 other.

Student Life *Housing:* college housing not available. *Activities and Organizations:* drama/theater group, student-run newspaper, choral group. *Campus security:* 24-hour emergency response devices and patrols, security cameras. *Student services:* health clinic, personal/psychological counseling.

Athletics *Intercollegiate sports:* baseball M, basketball M/W, soccer M/W, softball W, swimming and diving M/W, track and field M/W, volleyball W, water polo M/W.

Costs (2016–17) *Tuition:* state resident $1380 full-time, $46 per credit part-time; nonresident $9210 full-time, $307 per credit part-time. Full-time tuition and fees vary according to course load. Part-time tuition and fees vary according to course load. *Required fees:* $108 full-time. *Payment plan:* installment.

Applying *Options:* electronic application. *Application deadlines:* rolling (freshmen), rolling (transfers).

Freshman Application Contact College of Marin, 835 College Avenue, Kentfield, CA 94904. *Phone:* 415-485-9414.
Website: http://www.marin.edu/.

College of San Mateo
San Mateo, California

Director of Admissions Mr. Henry Villareal, Dean of Admissions and Records, College of San Mateo, 1700 West Hillsdale Boulevard, San Mateo, CA 94402-3784. *Phone:* 650-574-6590. *E-mail:* csmadmission@smccd.edu.
Website: http://www.collegeofsanmateo.edu/.

College of the Canyons
Santa Clarita, California

- **District-supported** 2-year, founded 1969, part of California Community College System
- **Suburban** 224-acre campus with easy access to Los Angeles
- **Coed,** 17,975 undergraduate students, 34% full-time, 49% women, 46% men

Undergraduates 6,056 full-time, 11,118 part-time. Students come from 46 other countries; 3% are from out of state; 4% Black or African American, non-Hispanic/Latino; 49% Hispanic/Latino; 10% Asian, non-Hispanic/Latino; 0.2% Native Hawaiian or other Pacific Islander, non-Hispanic/Latino; 0.3% American Indian or Alaska Native, non-Hispanic/Latino; 3% Two or more races, non-Hispanic/Latino; 0.4% Race/ethnicity unknown; 1% international; 41% transferred in.

Freshmen *Admission:* 3,346 applied, 3,346 admitted, 2,542 enrolled.

Faculty *Total:* 762, 26% full-time. *Student/faculty ratio:* 25:1.

Majors Accounting technology and bookkeeping; administrative assistant and secretarial science; animation, interactive technology, video graphics and special effects; architectural drafting and CAD/CADD; art; athletic training; automobile/automotive mechanics technology; biological and physical sciences; building/construction site management; business administration and management; child-care provision; cinematography and film/video production; clinical/medical laboratory technology; computer science; computer systems networking and telecommunications; criminal justice/police science; dramatic/theater arts; English; fire prevention and safety technology; French; geography; geology/earth science; graphic design; health and physical education/fitness; history; hospitality administration; hotel/motel administration; humanities; interior design; journalism; legal assistant/paralegal; liberal arts and sciences/liberal studies; mathematics; music; musical theater; parks, recreation and leisure; philosophy; photography; physics; political science and government; pre-engineering; psychology; real estate; registered nursing/registered nurse; restaurant, culinary, and catering management; sales, distribution, and marketing operations; sign language interpretation and translation; small business administration; social sciences; sociology; Spanish; speech communication and rhetoric; surveying technology; water quality and wastewater treatment management and recycling technology; welding technology.

Academics *Calendar:* semesters. *Degree:* certificates and associate. *Special study options:* academic remediation for entering students, accelerated degree program, adult/continuing education programs, advanced placement credit, cooperative education, distance learning, double majors, English as a second language, honors programs, internships, part-time degree program, services for LD students, study abroad, summer session for credit.

Library College of the Canyons Library. Students can reserve study rooms.

Student Life *Housing:* college housing not available. *Activities and Organizations:* drama/theater group, choral group, Gamma Beta Phi, Phi Theta Kappa, American Medical Students Association, National Student Nurses Association, COC Sports Medicine Club. *Campus security:* 24-hour emergency response devices, late-night transport/escort service. *Student services:* health clinic, personal/psychological counseling, women's center.

Athletics *Intercollegiate sports:* baseball M, basketball M/W, cross-country running M/W, football M, golf M/W, soccer M/W, softball W, swimming and diving M/W, track and field M/W, volleyball W.

Costs (2017–18) *Tuition:* state resident $1154 full-time, $46 per credit hour part-time; nonresident $6458 full-time, $267 per credit hour part-time. Full-time tuition and fees vary according to course load. Part-time tuition and fees vary according to course load. *Required fees:* $50 full-time.

Financial Aid Of all full-time matriculated undergraduates who enrolled in 2015, 17,088 applied for aid, 12,026 were judged to have need. 104 Federal Work-Study jobs (averaging $2894).

Applying *Options:* electronic application. *Recommended:* high school transcript. *Application deadlines:* rolling (freshmen), rolling (transfers). *Notification:* continuous (freshmen), continuous (transfers).
Freshman Application Contact Dr. Jasmine Ruys, Dean, Enrollment Services, College of the Canyons, 26455 Rockwell Canyon Road, Santa Clarita, CA 91355. *Phone:* 661-362-3280. *Fax:* 661-254-7996.
E-mail: jasmine.ruys@canyons.edu.
Website: http://www.canyons.edu/.

College of the Desert
Palm Desert, California

- **District-supported** 2-year, founded 1959, part of California Community College System
- **Small-town** 160-acre campus
- **Coed,** 10,285 undergraduate students, 39% full-time, 54% women, 46% men

Undergraduates 3,989 full-time, 6,296 part-time. 8% are from out of state; 3% Black or African American, non-Hispanic/Latino; 69% Hispanic/Latino; 3% Asian, non-Hispanic/Latino; 0.1% Native Hawaiian or other Pacific Islander, non-Hispanic/Latino; 0.3% American Indian or Alaska Native, non-Hispanic/Latino; 2% Two or more races, non-Hispanic/Latino; 0.6% Race/ethnicity unknown; 3% international; 4% transferred in. *Retention:* 75% of full-time freshmen returned.
Freshmen *Admission:* 2,252 applied, 2,252 admitted, 1,505 enrolled.
Faculty *Student/faculty ratio:* 29:1.
Majors Agribusiness; agriculture; anthropology; applied horticulture/horticulture operations; architectural technology; art; automobile/automotive mechanics technology; biological and physical sciences; biology/biological sciences; building/construction site management; business administration and management; business/commerce; chemistry; child-care and support services management; computer graphics; computer science; creative writing; criminal justice/police science; crop production; culinary arts; dietetic technology; drafting and design technology; dramatic/theater arts; economics; English; environmental science; environmental studies; fire science/firefighting; French; geography; geology/earth science; health and physical education/fitness; heating, air conditioning, ventilation and refrigeration maintenance technology; history; hospitality administration; humanities; information technology; Italian; journalism; liberal arts and sciences/liberal studies; licensed practical/vocational nurse training; mass communication/media; mathematics; multi/interdisciplinary studies related; music; natural resources/conservation; office management; parks, recreation and leisure facilities management; philosophy; physics; political science and government; psychology; registered nursing/registered nurse; resort management; social sciences; sociology; Spanish; speech communication and rhetoric; substance abuse/addiction counseling; turf and turfgrass management; vehicle maintenance and repair technologies.
Academics *Calendar:* semesters. *Degree:* certificates, diplomas, and associate. *Special study options:* academic remediation for entering students, adult/continuing education programs, cooperative education, distance learning, double majors, English as a second language, part-time degree program, services for LD students, summer session for credit.
Library College of the Desert Library.
Student Life *Housing:* college housing not available. *Activities and Organizations:* drama/theater group, student-run newspaper, radio station. *Campus security:* 24-hour emergency response devices and patrols. *Student services:* health clinic, personal/psychological counseling.
Athletics Member NJCAA. *Intercollegiate sports:* baseball M, basketball M/W, cross-country running M/W, fencing M/W, football M, golf M/W, soccer M/W, softball W, tennis M/W, track and field M/W, volleyball W.
Costs (2016–17) *Tuition:* state resident $1289 full-time, $461 per year part-time; nonresident $6888 full-time, $2361 per year part-time. Full-time tuition and fees vary according to course load and program. Part-time tuition and fees vary according to course load and program. *Required fees:* $38 full-time, $46 per unit part-time, $38 per year part-time. *Payment plan:* installment. *Waivers:* employees or children of employees.
Applying *Options:* electronic application. *Application deadlines:* rolling (freshmen), rolling (transfers). *Notification:* continuous (freshmen), continuous (transfers).
Freshman Application Contact College of the Desert, 43-500 Monterey Avenue, Palm Desert, CA 92260-9305. *Phone:* 760-346-7441 Ext. 7441.
Website: http://www.collegeofthedesert.edu/.

College of the Redwoods
Eureka, California

Freshman Application Contact Director of Enrollment Management, College of the Redwoods, 7351 Tompkins Hill Road, Eureka, CA 95501-9300.

Phone: 707-476-4100. *Toll-free phone:* 800-641-0400. *Fax:* 707-476-4400.
Website: http://www.redwoods.edu/.

College of the Sequoias
Visalia, California

Freshman Application Contact Ms. Lisa Hott, Director for Admissions, College of the Sequoias, 915 South Mooney Boulevard, Visalia, CA 93277-2234. *Phone:* 559-737-4844. *Fax:* 559-737-4820.
Website: http://www.cos.edu/.

College of the Siskiyous
Weed, California

Freshman Application Contact Recruitment and Admissions, College of the Siskiyous, 800 College Avenue, Weed, CA 96094-2899. *Phone:* 530-938-5555. *Toll-free phone:* 888-397-4339.
E-mail: admissions-weed@siskyous.edu. *Website:* http://www.siskiyous.edu/.

Columbia College
Sonora, California

- **District-supported** 2-year, founded 1968, part of Yosemite Community College District System
- **Rural** 200-acre campus
- **Endowment** $312,432
- **Coed**

Undergraduates 717 full-time, 1,707 part-time. Students come from 2 states and territories; 1% are from out of state; 2% Black or African American, non-Hispanic/Latino; 16% Hispanic/Latino; 2% Asian, non-Hispanic/Latino; 0.4% Native Hawaiian or other Pacific Islander, non-Hispanic/Latino; 2% American Indian or Alaska Native, non-Hispanic/Latino; 2% Two or more races, non-Hispanic/Latino; 1% Race/ethnicity unknown; 12% transferred in.
Faculty *Student/faculty ratio:* 19:1.
Academics *Calendar:* semesters. *Degree:* certificates, diplomas, and associate. *Special study options:* academic remediation for entering students, cooperative education, distance learning, English as a second language, independent study, off-campus study, part-time degree program, services for LD students, summer session for credit.
Library Columbia College Library plus 1 other. *Books:* 40,828 (physical), 19,501 (digital/electronic); *Serial titles:* 4,151 (physical); *Databases:* 75. Weekly public service hours: 50; students can reserve study rooms.
Student Life *Campus security:* 24-hour emergency response devices and patrols, late-night transport/escort service.
Athletics Member NJCAA.
Costs (2016–17) *Tuition:* state resident $0 full-time; nonresident $6406 full-time. Full-time tuition and fees vary according to course load. Part-time tuition and fees vary according to course load. *Required fees:* $1150 full-time.
Financial Aid Of all full-time matriculated undergraduates who enrolled in 2010, 2,616 applied for aid, 2,232 were judged to have need. 29 Federal Work-Study jobs (averaging $1672). In 2010, 30. *Average non-need-based aid:* $100.
Applying *Options:* electronic application, early admission. *Recommended:* high school transcript.
Freshman Application Contact Admissions Office, Columbia College, 11600 Columbia College Drive, Sonora, CA 95370. *Phone:* 209-588-5231. *Fax:* 209-588-5337. *E-mail:* ccadmissions@yosemite.edu.
Website: http://www.gocolumbia.edu/.

Community Christian College
Redlands, California

Freshman Application Contact Mr. Enrique D. Melendez, Assistant Director of Admissions, Community Christian College, 251 Tennessee Street, Redlands, CA 92373. *Phone:* 909-222-9556. *Fax:* 909-335-9101.
E-mail: emelendez@cccollege.edu. *Website:* http://www.cccollege.edu/.

Concorde Career College
Garden Grove, California

Freshman Application Contact Chris Becker, Director, Concorde Career College, 12951 South Euclid Street, Suite 101, Garden Grove, CA 92840. *Phone:* 714-703-1900. *Fax:* 714-530-4737. *E-mail:* cbecker@concorde.edu.
Website: http://www.concorde.edu/.

Concorde Career College
North Hollywood, California

Freshman Application Contact Madeline Volker, Director, Concorde Career College, 12412 Victory Boulevard, North Hollywood, CA 91606. *Phone:* 818-766-8151. *Fax:* 818-766-1587. *E-mail:* mvolker@concorde.edu. *Website:* http://www.concorde.edu/.

Concorde Career College
San Bernardino, California

Admissions Office Contact Concorde Career College, 201 East Airport Drive, San Bernardino, CA 92408. *Website:* http://www.concorde.edu/.

Concorde Career College
San Diego, California

Admissions Office Contact Concorde Career College, 4393 Imperial Avenue, Suite 100, San Diego, CA 92113. *Website:* http://www.concorde.edu/.

Contra Costa College
San Pablo, California

Freshman Application Contact Admissions and Records Office, Contra Costa College, San Pablo, CA 94806. *Phone:* 510-235-7800 Ext. 7500. *Fax:* 510-412-0769. *E-mail:* a&r@contracosta.edu. *Website:* http://www.contracosta.edu/.

Copper Mountain College
Joshua Tree, California

Freshman Application Contact Greg Brown, Executive Vice President for Academic and Student Affairs, Copper Mountain College, 6162 Rotary Way, Joshua Tree, CA 92252. *Phone:* 760-366-3791. *Toll-free phone:* 866-366-3791. *Fax:* 760-366-5257. *E-mail:* gbrown@cmccd.edu. *Website:* http://www.cmccd.edu/.

Cosumnes River College
Sacramento, California

Freshman Application Contact Admissions and Records, Cosumnes River College, 8401 Center Parkway, Sacramento, CA 95823-5799. *Phone:* 916-691-7411. *Website:* http://www.crc.losrios.edu/.

Crafton Hills College
Yucaipa, California

Director of Admissions Larry Aycock, Admissions and Records Coordinator, Crafton Hills College, 11711 Sand Canyon Road, Yucaipa, CA 92399-1799. *Phone:* 909-389-3663. *E-mail:* laycock@craftonhills.edu. *Website:* http://www.craftonhills.edu/.

Cuesta College
San Luis Obispo, California

Freshman Application Contact Cuesta College, PO Box 8106, San Luis Obispo, CA 93403-8106. *Phone:* 805-546-3130 Ext. 2262. *Website:* http://www.cuesta.edu/.

Cuyamaca College
El Cajon, California

Freshman Application Contact Ms. Susan Topham, Dean of Admissions and Records, Cuyamaca College, 900 Rancho San Diego Parkway, El Cajon, CA 92019-4304. *Phone:* 619-660-4302. *Fax:* 619-660-4575. *E-mail:* susan.topham@gcccd.edu. *Website:* http://www.cuyamaca.net/.

Cypress College
Cypress, California

Freshman Application Contact Admissions Office, Cypress College, 9200 Valley View, Cypress, CA 90630-5897. *Phone:* 714-484-7346. *Fax:* 714-484-7446. *E-mail:* admissions@cypresscollege.edu. *Website:* http://www.cypresscollege.edu/.

De Anza College
Cupertino, California

- **District-supported** 2-year, founded 1967, part of California Community College System
- **Suburban** 112-acre campus with easy access to San Francisco, San Jose
- **Coed,** 21,099 undergraduate students, 48% full-time, 49% women, 51% men

Undergraduates 10,222 full-time, 10,877 part-time. 4% Black or African American, non-Hispanic/Latino; 28% Hispanic/Latino; 45% Asian, non-Hispanic/Latino; 0.8% Native Hawaiian or other Pacific Islander, non-Hispanic/Latino; 0.4% American Indian or Alaska Native, non-Hispanic/Latino; 2% Race/ethnicity unknown.

Freshmen *Admission:* 2,986 enrolled.

Faculty *Total:* 788, 35% full-time. *Student/faculty ratio:* 27:1.

Majors Accounting; administrative assistant and secretarial science; art; art history, criticism and conservation; automobile/automotive mechanics technology; behavioral sciences; biology/biological sciences; business administration and management; business machine repair; ceramic arts and ceramics; child development; commercial and advertising art; computer graphics; computer programming; computer science; construction engineering technology; corrections; criminal justice/law enforcement administration; criminal justice/police science; developmental and child psychology; drafting/design engineering technologies related; dramatic/theater arts; drawing; economics; engineering; engineering technology; English; environmental studies; film/cinema/video studies; history; humanities; industrial technology; information science/studies; international relations and affairs; journalism; legal assistant/paralegal; liberal arts and sciences/liberal studies; licensed practical/vocational nurse training; machine tool technology; marketing/marketing management; mass communication/media; mathematics; medical/clinical assistant; music; philosophy; photography; physical education teaching and coaching; physical therapy; physics; political science and government; pre-engineering; printmaking; professional, technical, business, and scientific writing; psychology; purchasing, procurement/acquisitions and contracts management; radio and television; real estate; registered nursing/registered nurse; rhetoric and composition; sculpture; social sciences; sociology; Spanish.

Academics *Calendar:* quarters. *Degree:* certificates, diplomas, and associate. *Special study options:* academic remediation for entering students, adult/continuing education programs, distance learning, English as a second language, honors programs, independent study, internships, part-time degree program, services for LD students, student-designed majors, study abroad, summer session for credit. *ROTC:* Army (c), Air Force (c).

Library A. Robert DeHart Learning Center. Study areas open 24 hours, 5&-7 days a week; students can reserve study rooms.

Student Life *Housing:* college housing not available. *Activities and Organizations:* drama/theater group, student-run newspaper, choral group, Student Nurses Association, Phi Theta Kappa, Automotive Club, Vietnamese Club, Filipino Club. *Campus security:* 24-hour emergency response devices, student patrols, late-night transport/escort service. *Student services:* health clinic, personal/psychological counseling, legal services.

Athletics Member NCAA. All Division II. *Intercollegiate sports:* baseball M, basketball M/W, cross-country running M/W, football M, golf M/W, soccer M/W, softball W, swimming and diving M/W, tennis M/W, track and field M/W, volleyball M/W, water polo M. *Intramural sports:* badminton M/W, basketball M, soccer M/W, swimming and diving M/W, volleyball M/W.

Costs (2016–17) *Tuition:* state resident $0 full-time; nonresident $5616 full-time, $156 per credit hour part-time. Full-time tuition and fees vary according to course load. Part-time tuition and fees vary according to course load. *Required fees:* $1270 full-time, $31 per credit hour part-time, $51 per term part-time. *Payment plan:* installment. *Waivers:* minority students and adult students.

Freshman Application Contact De Anza College, 21250 Stevens Creek Boulevard, Cupertino, CA 95014-5793. *Phone:* 408-864-8292. *Website:* http://www.deanza.fhda.edu/.

Deep Springs College
Deep Springs, California

Freshman Application Contact Jack Davis, Chair, Applications Committee, Deep Springs College, HC 72, Box 45001, Dyer, NV 89010-9803. *Phone:* 760-872-2000. *Fax:* 760-874-0314. *E-mail:* apcom@deepsprings.edu. *Website:* http://www.deepsprings.edu/.

Diablo Valley College
Pleasant Hill, California

Freshman Application Contact Ileana Dorn, Director of Admissions and Records, Diablo Valley College, Pleasant Hill, CA 94523-1529. *Phone:* 925-

685-1230 Ext. 2330. *Fax:* 925-609-8085. *E-mail:* idorn@dvc.edu.
Website: http://www.dvc.edu/.

East Los Angeles College
Monterey Park, California

Freshman Application Contact Mr. Jeremy Allred, Associate Dean of
Admissions, East Los Angeles College, 1301 Avenida Cesar Chavez,
Monterey Park, CA 91754. *Phone:* 323-265-8801. *Fax:* 323-265-8688.
E-mail: allredjp@elac.edu. *Website:* http://www.elac.edu/.

East San Gabriel Valley Regional Occupational Program & Technical Center
West Covina, California

Admissions Office Contact East San Gabriel Valley Regional Occupational
Program & Technical Center, 1501 West Del Norte Avenue, West Covina, CA
91790. *Website:* http://www.esgvrop.org/.

El Camino College
Torrance, California

Director of Admissions Mr. William Mulrooney, Director of Admissions, El
Camino College, 16007 Crenshaw Boulevard, Torrance, CA 90506-0001.
Phone: 310-660-3418. *Toll-free phone:* 866-ELCAMINO.
Fax: 310-660-6779. *E-mail:* wmulrooney@elcamino.edu.
Website: http://www.elcamino.edu/.

Empire College
Santa Rosa, California

Freshman Application Contact Ms. Dahnja Barker, Admissions Officer,
Empire College, 3035 Cleveland Avenue, Santa Rosa, CA 95403. *Phone:* 707-
546-4000. *Toll-free phone:* 877-395-8535. *Website:* http://www.empcol.edu/.

Evergreen Valley College
San Jose, California

Freshman Application Contact Evergreen Valley College, 3095 Yerba Buena
Road, San Jose, CA 95135-1598. *Phone:* 408-270-6423.
Website: http://www.evc.edu/.

Feather River College
Quincy, California

- **District-supported** primarily 2-year, founded 1968, part of California
  Community College System
- **Rural** 240-acre campus
- **Endowment** $48,148
- **Coed,** 1,663 undergraduate students, 29% full-time, 47% women, 53%
  men

Undergraduates 481 full-time, 1,182 part-time. Students come from 28 states
and territories; 6 other countries; 10% are from out of state; 12% Black or
African American, non-Hispanic/Latino; 25% Hispanic/Latino; 4% Asian,
non-Hispanic/Latino; 1% Native Hawaiian or other Pacific Islander, non-
Hispanic/Latino; 3% American Indian or Alaska Native, non-Hispanic/Latino;
6% Race/ethnicity unknown; 1% international; 14% transferred in; 42% live
on campus.
Freshmen *Admission:* 528 enrolled.
Faculty *Total:* 105, 24% full-time, 10% with terminal degrees. *Student/faculty
ratio:* 17:1.
Majors Accounting technology and bookkeeping; administrative assistant and
secretarial science; agriculture; anthropology; biology/biological sciences;
business/commerce; child-care provision; computer programming; cooking
and related culinary arts; corrections and criminal justice related; English;
environmental studies; health and physical education/fitness; history; horse
husbandry/equine science and management; humanities; kinesiology and
exercise science; liberal arts and sciences/liberal studies; licensed
practical/vocational nurse training; mathematics; natural
resources/conservation; parks, recreation and leisure; physical sciences;
political science and government; social sciences; sociology; visual and
performing arts; wildlife, fish and wildlands science and management.
Academics *Calendar:* semesters plus summer and winter terms. *Degrees:*
certificates, diplomas, associate, and bachelor's. *Special study options:*
academic remediation for entering students, adult/continuing education

programs, advanced placement credit, cooperative education, distance
learning, double majors, English as a second language, independent study,
part-time degree program, services for LD students, summer session for credit.
Library Feather River College Library. *Books:* 23,852 (physical), 130,000
(digital/electronic); *Serial titles:* 98 (physical), 28,376 (digital/electronic);
Databases: 35. Weekly public service hours: 61; students can reserve study
rooms.
Student Life *Housing Options:* coed. Campus housing is provided by a third
party. *Activities and Organizations:* drama/theater group, Phi Theta Kappa
Honor Society, International Cultural Club, Horse Show Team, Student
Environmental Association, Student Alliance for Equity. *Campus security:*
student patrols, part-time private security company patrols. *Student services:*
health clinic, personal/psychological counseling.
Athletics *Intercollegiate sports:* baseball M, basketball M/W, cross-country
running W, equestrian sports M(s)/W(s), football M, sand volleyball W, soccer
M/W, softball W, track and field W, volleyball W.
Standardized Tests *Recommended:* ACCUPLACER.
Costs (2016–17) *Tuition:* state resident $1380 full-time, $46 per credit part-
time; nonresident $7740 full-time, $258 per credit part-time. Full-time tuition
and fees vary according to course load. Part-time tuition and fees vary
according to course load. *Required fees:* $81 full-time, $2 per credit part-time,
$18 per term part-time. *Room and board:* room only: $5350. Room and board
charges vary according to housing facility. *Payment plan:* installment.
Financial Aid Of all full-time matriculated undergraduates who enrolled in
2015, 22 Federal Work-Study jobs (averaging $750). 103 state and other part-
time jobs (averaging $1504).
Applying *Options:* electronic application.
Freshman Application Contact Mrs. Leslie Mikesell, Director of Admissions
and Records, Feather River College, 570 Golden Eagle Avenue, Quincy, CA
95971. *Phone:* 530-283-0202 Ext. 285. *Toll-free phone:* 800-442-9799.
E-mail: info@frc.edu.
Website: http://www.frc.edu/.

FIDM/Fashion Institute of Design & Merchandising, Orange County Campus
Irvine, California

- **Proprietary** 2-year, founded 1981, part of FIDM/Fashion Institute of
  Design & Merchandising
- **Urban** campus with easy access to Los Angeles
- **Coed, primarily women,** 92 undergraduate students, 93% full-time, 96%
  women, 4% men

Undergraduates 86 full-time, 6 part-time. Students come from 11 states and
territories; 5 other countries; 12% are from out of state; 5% Black or African
American, non-Hispanic/Latino; 20% Hispanic/Latino; 14% Asian, non-
Hispanic/Latino; 2% Native Hawaiian or other Pacific Islander, non-
Hispanic/Latino; 2% Two or more races, non-Hispanic/Latino; 10%
Race/ethnicity unknown; 9% international; 38% transferred in.
Freshmen *Admission:* 164 applied, 95 admitted, 54 enrolled. *Average high
school GPA:* 2.9.
Faculty *Total:* 19, 21% full-time. *Student/faculty ratio:* 10:1.
Majors Apparel and textile marketing management; design and visual
communications; fashion/apparel design; fashion merchandising; graphic
design; interior design.
Academics *Calendar:* quarters. *Degree:* associate. *Special study options:*
academic remediation for entering students, accelerated degree program,
adult/continuing education programs, advanced placement credit, cooperative
education, distance learning, English as a second language, independent study,
internships, part-time degree program, services for LD students, study abroad,
summer session for credit.
Library FIDM Orange County Campus Library. Students can reserve study
rooms.
Student Life *Housing:* college housing not available. *Activities and
Organizations:* Cross-Cultural Student Alliance, Fashion Industry Club, Phi
Theta Kappa (national honor society), Student Council, FIDM MODE
Magazine. *Campus security:* 24-hour emergency response devices, late-night
transport/escort service, security guard escort.
Student services: personal/psychological counseling.
Standardized Tests *Recommended:* SAT or ACT (for admission).
Applying *Options:* electronic application, deferred entrance. *Application fee:*
$225. *Required:* essay or personal statement, high school transcript, minimum
2.5 GPA, 3 letters of recommendation, interview, entrance project. *Application
deadlines:* rolling (freshmen), rolling (transfers).
Freshman Application Contact Mr. Michael Mirabella, Admissions,
FIDM/Fashion Institute of Design & Merchandising, Orange County Campus,
17590 Gillette Avenue, Irvine, CA 92614-5610. *Phone:* 949-851-6200 Ext.
1750. *Toll-free phone:* 888-974-3436.
Website: http://www.fidm.edu/.

FIDM/Fashion Institute of Design & Merchandising, San Diego Campus
San Diego, California

- **Proprietary** 2-year, founded 1985, part of FIDM/Fashion Institute of Design & Merchandising
- **Urban** campus with easy access to San Diego
- **Coed, primarily women,** 75 undergraduate students, 92% full-time, 88% women, 12% men

Undergraduates 69 full-time, 6 part-time. Students come from 17 states and territories; 4 other countries; 23% are from out of state; 5% Black or African American, non-Hispanic/Latino; 35% Hispanic/Latino; 7% Asian, non-Hispanic/Latino; 1% American Indian or Alaska Native, non-Hispanic/Latino; 3% Two or more races, non-Hispanic/Latino; 3% Race/ethnicity unknown; 1% international; 44% transferred in. *Retention:* 82% of full-time freshmen returned.

Freshmen *Admission:* 149 applied, 58 admitted, 33 enrolled. *Average high school GPA:* 2.9. *Test scores:* ACT scores over 18: 100%; ACT scores over 24: 40%; ACT scores over 30: 10%.

Faculty *Total:* 27, 4% full-time.

Majors Design and visual communications; fashion/apparel design; fashion merchandising.

Academics *Calendar:* quarters. *Degree:* associate. *Special study options:* academic remediation for entering students, accelerated degree program, adult/continuing education programs, advanced placement credit, cooperative education, distance learning, English as a second language, independent study, internships, part-time degree program, services for LD students, study abroad, summer session for credit.

Library FIDM San Diego Campus Library. Students can reserve study rooms.

Student Life *Housing:* college housing not available. *Activities and Organizations:* Cross-Cultural Student Alliance, Fashion Industry Club, Phi Theta Kappa (national honor society), Student Council, FIDM MODE Magazine. *Campus security:* 24-hour emergency response devices and patrols. *Student services:* personal/psychological counseling.

Standardized Tests *Recommended:* SAT or ACT (for admission).

Costs (2017–18) *Tuition:* $30,575 full-time, $680 per unit part-time. Full-time tuition and fees vary according to program. Part-time tuition and fees vary according to program. *Payment plan:* installment. *Waivers:* employees or children of employees.

Applying *Options:* electronic application, deferred entrance. *Application fee:* $225. *Required:* essay or personal statement, high school transcript, minimum 2.5 GPA, 3 letters of recommendation, interview, major-determined project. *Application deadlines:* rolling (freshmen), rolling (transfers).

Freshman Application Contact Ms. Denise Baca, Campus Director, FIDM/Fashion Institute of Design & Merchandising, San Diego Campus, 350 Tenth Avenue, San Diego, CA 92101. *Phone:* 619-235-2049. *Toll-free phone:* 800-243-3436. *E-mail:* dbaca@fidm.edu. *Website:* http://www.fidm.edu/.

Folsom Lake College
Folsom, California

Freshman Application Contact Admissions Office, Folsom Lake College, 10 College Parkway, Folsom, CA 95630. *Phone:* 916-608-6500. *Website:* http://www.flc.losrios.edu/.

Foothill College
Los Altos Hills, California

Freshman Application Contact Ms. Shawna Aced, Registrar, Foothill College, Admissions and Records, 12345 El Monte Road, Los Altos Hills, CA 94022. *Phone:* 650-949-7771. *E-mail:* acedshawna@hda.edu. *Website:* http://www.foothill.edu/.

Fremont College
Cerritos, California

Freshman Application Contact Natasha Dawson, Director of Admissions, Fremont College, 18000 Studebaker Road, Suite 900A, Cerritos, CA 90703. *Phone:* 562-809-5100. *Toll-free phone:* 800-373-6668. *Fax:* 562-809-5100. *E-mail:* info@fremont.edu. *Website:* http://www.fremont.edu/.

Fresno City College
Fresno, California

Freshman Application Contact Office Assistant, Fresno City College, 1101 East University Avenue, Fresno, CA 93741-0002. *Phone:* 559-442-4600 Ext.

8604. *Fax:* 559-237-4232. *E-mail:* fcc.admissions@fresnocitycollege.edu. *Website:* http://www.fresnocitycollege.edu/.

Fullerton College
Fullerton, California

- **District-supported** 2-year, founded 1913, part of California Community College System
- **Suburban** 79-acre campus with easy access to Los Angeles
- **Coed,** 24,986 undergraduate students, 30% full-time, 47% women, 44% men

Undergraduates 7,547 full-time, 15,022 part-time. Students come from 22 states and territories; 1% are from out of state; 3% Black or African American, non-Hispanic/Latino; 53% Hispanic/Latino; 15% Asian, non-Hispanic/Latino; 0.6% American Indian or Alaska Native, non-Hispanic/Latino; 8% Race/ethnicity unknown. *Retention:* 59% of full-time freshmen returned.

Freshmen *Admission:* 3,424 enrolled.

Faculty *Total:* 1,017, 30% full-time. *Student/faculty ratio:* 25:1.

Majors Accounting technology and bookkeeping; administrative assistant and secretarial science; anthropology; apparel and textile marketing management; apparel and textiles; applied horticulture/horticulture operations; architectural technology; area studies related; art; astronomy; automobile/automotive mechanics technology; biological and physical sciences; biology/biological sciences; biomedical technology; building/construction site management; building/home/construction inspection; business administration and management; carpentry; chemical technology; chemistry; child-care provision; computer science; construction trades related; cosmetology; criminal justice/police science; dance; drafting and design technology; dramatic/theater arts; economics; electrical/electronics equipment installation and repair; engineering; English; environmental studies; ethnic, cultural minority, gender, and group studies related; fashion/apparel design; foods, nutrition, and wellness; foreign languages and literatures; geography; geology/earth science; graphic and printing equipment operation/production; graphic design; hazardous materials management and waste technology; health and physical education/fitness; health/medical preparatory programs related; history; humanities; information technology; interior design; international business/trade/commerce; journalism; landscaping and groundskeeping; legal administrative assistant/secretary; legal assistant/paralegal; liberal arts and sciences/liberal studies; mass communication/media; mathematics; mechanical engineering/mechanical technology; microbiology; music; parks, recreation and leisure; philosophy; physics; plant nursery management; political science and government; psychology; radio and television; real estate; recording arts technology; religious studies; sales, distribution, and marketing operations; small business administration; sociology; speech communication and rhetoric; sport and fitness administration/management; technology/industrial arts teacher education.

Academics *Calendar:* semesters. *Degree:* certificates and associate. *Special study options:* academic remediation for entering students, adult/continuing education programs, advanced placement credit, cooperative education, English as a second language, honors programs, part-time degree program, services for LD students, study abroad, summer session for credit. *ROTC:* Army (c), Navy (c), Air Force (c).

Library William T. Boyce Library.

Student Life *Housing:* college housing not available. *Activities and Organizations:* drama/theater group, student-run newspaper, radio station. *Student services:* health clinic, personal/psychological counseling, women's center, legal services.

Athletics *Intercollegiate sports:* badminton W, baseball M, basketball M/W, cross-country running M/W, football M, golf W, soccer M/W, softball W, swimming and diving M/W, tennis M/W, track and field M/W, volleyball W, water polo M/W.

Costs (2017–18) *Tuition:* state resident $1104 full-time, $46 per unit part-time; nonresident $5664 full-time, $109 per unit part-time. Full-time tuition and fees vary according to course load. Part-time tuition and fees vary according to course load. *Required fees:* $34 full-time, $34 per year part-time.

Financial Aid *Financial aid deadline:* 6/30.

Applying *Options:* electronic application, early admission. *Application deadlines:* rolling (freshmen), rolling (transfers).

Freshman Application Contact Fullerton College, 321 East Chapman Avenue, Fullerton, CA 92832-2095. *Phone:* 714-992-7076. *Website:* http://www.fullcoll.edu/.

Gavilan College
Gilroy, California

Freshman Application Contact Gavilan College, 5055 Santa Teresa Boulevard, Gilroy, CA 95020-9599. *Phone:* 408-848-4754. *Website:* http://www.gavilan.edu/.

Glendale Career College
Glendale, California

Admissions Office Contact Glendale Career College, 240 North Brand Boulevard, Lower Level, Glendale, CA 91203.
Website: http://www.glendalecareer.com/.

Glendale Community College
Glendale, California

Freshman Application Contact Ms. Sharon Combs, Dean, Admissions, and Records, Glendale Community College, 1500 North Verdugo Road, Glendale, CA 91208. *Phone:* 818-240-1000 Ext. 5910. *E-mail:* scombs@glendale.edu. *Website:* http://www.glendale.edu/.

Golden West College
Huntington Beach, California

- **District-supported** 2-year, founded 1966, part of Coast Community College District System
- **Suburban** 122-acre campus with easy access to Los Angeles
- **Endowment** $7.6 million
- **Coed,** 12,394 undergraduate students, 35% full-time, 53% women, 47% men

Undergraduates 4,394 full-time, 8,000 part-time. 1% are from out of state; 2% Black or African American, non-Hispanic/Latino; 32% Hispanic/Latino; 28% Asian, non-Hispanic/Latino; 0.5% Native Hawaiian or other Pacific Islander, non-Hispanic/Latino; 0.3% American Indian or Alaska Native, non-Hispanic/Latino; 4% Two or more races, non-Hispanic/Latino; 1% Race/ethnicity unknown; 2% international. *Retention:* 71% of full-time freshmen returned.
Freshmen *Admission:* 11,210 applied, 11,210 admitted, 2,298 enrolled.
Faculty *Total:* 534, 24% full-time. *Student/faculty ratio:* 33:1.
Majors Accounting; administrative assistant and secretarial science; architectural engineering technology; art; automobile/automotive mechanics technology; biological and physical sciences; biology/biological sciences; business administration and management; commercial and advertising art; consumer merchandising/retailing management; cosmetology; criminal justice/law enforcement administration; criminal justice/police science; drafting and design technology; electrical, electronic and communications engineering technology; engineering technology; graphic and printing equipment operation/production; humanities; journalism; legal administrative assistant/secretary; liberal arts and sciences/liberal studies; marketing/marketing management; mathematics; music; natural sciences; ornamental horticulture; physical sciences; radio and television; real estate; registered nursing/registered nurse; sign language interpretation and translation.
Academics *Calendar:* semesters plus summer session. *Degree:* certificates and associate. *Special study options:* academic remediation for entering students, adult/continuing education programs, advanced placement credit, cooperative education, distance learning, English as a second language, external degree program, honors programs, independent study, internships, part-time degree program, services for LD students, student-designed majors, study abroad, summer session for credit. *ROTC:* Air Force (c).
Library Golden West College Library plus 1 other. Weekly public service hours: 48; students can reserve study rooms.
Student Life *Housing:* college housing not available. *Activities and Organizations:* drama/theater group, student-run newspaper, choral group. *Campus security:* 24-hour emergency response devices and patrols, late-night transport/escort service. *Student services:* health clinic, personal/psychological counseling, legal services.
Athletics Member NJCAA. *Intercollegiate sports:* baseball M, cross-country running M/W, football M, soccer M/W, softball W, swimming and diving M/W, track and field M/W, volleyball M/W, water polo M/W.
Costs (2016–17) *Tuition:* state resident $1104 full-time, $46 per unit part-time; nonresident $7248 full-time, $302 per unit part-time. Full-time tuition and fees vary according to course load and program. Part-time tuition and fees vary according to course load and program. *Required fees:* $72 full-time, $36 per term part-time.
Applying *Options:* electronic application, early admission. *Required for some:* essay or personal statement. *Recommended:* high school transcript. *Application deadlines:* rolling (freshmen), rolling (transfers). *Notification:* continuous (freshmen), continuous (transfers).
Freshman Application Contact Golden West College, PO Box 2748, 15744 Golden West Street, Huntington Beach, CA 92647-2748. *Phone:* 714-892-7711 Ext. 58965.
Website: http://www.goldenwestcollege.edu/.

Golf Academy of America
Carlsbad, California

Director of Admissions Ms. Deborah Wells, Admissions Coordinator, Golf Academy of America, 1950 Camino Vida Roble, Suite 125, Carlsbad, CA 92008. *Phone:* 760-414-1501. *Toll-free phone:* 800-342-7342.
E-mail: sdga@sdgagolf.com. *Website:* http://www.golfacademy.edu/.

Grossmont College
El Cajon, California

Freshman Application Contact Admissions Office, Grossmont College, 8800 Grossmont College Drive, El Cajon, CA 92020-1799. *Phone:* 619-644-7186. *Website:* http://www.grossmont.edu/.

Gurnick Academy of Medical Arts
San Mateo, California

Admissions Office Contact Gurnick Academy of Medical Arts, 2121 South El Camino Real, Building C 2000, San Mateo, CA 94403.
Website: http://www.gurnick.edu/.

Hartnell College
Salinas, California

Director of Admissions Director of Admissions, Hartnell College, 411 Central Avenue, Salinas, CA 93901. *Phone:* 831-755-6711.
Fax: 831-759-6014. *Website:* http://www.hartnell.edu/.

Imperial Valley College
Imperial, California

- **District-supported** 2-year, founded 1922, part of California Community College System
- **Rural** 160-acre campus
- **Coed,** 7,828 undergraduate students
- **100%** of applicants were admitted

Undergraduates 1% Black or African American, non-Hispanic/Latino; 91% Hispanic/Latino; 0.6% Asian, non-Hispanic/Latino; 0.1% American Indian or Alaska Native, non-Hispanic/Latino; 0.4% Two or more races, non-Hispanic/Latino; 3% Race/ethnicity unknown.
Freshmen *Admission:* 1,724 applied, 1,724 admitted.
Faculty *Total:* 283. *Student/faculty ratio:* 28:1.
Majors Accounting; administrative assistant and secretarial science; agricultural business and management; agricultural mechanization; agriculture; anthropology; art; automobile/automotive mechanics technology; behavioral sciences; biological and physical sciences; business administration and management; criminal justice/law enforcement administration; English; fire science/firefighting; French; human development and family studies; humanities; hydrology and water resources science; information science/studies; journalism; kindergarten/preschool education; liberal arts and sciences/liberal studies; licensed practical/vocational nurse training; marketing/marketing management; mathematics; modern languages; music; physical education teaching and coaching; physical sciences; pre-engineering; psychology; registered nursing/registered nurse; social sciences; Spanish; welding technology.
Academics *Calendar:* semesters. *Degree:* certificates and associate. *Special study options:* academic remediation for entering students, accelerated degree program, adult/continuing education programs, advanced placement credit, distance learning, double majors, English as a second language, part-time degree program, services for LD students, student-designed majors, summer session for credit.
Library Spencer Library. *Databases:* 45. Weekly public service hours: 57; students can reserve study rooms.
Student Life *Housing:* college housing not available. *Activities and Organizations:* drama/theater group, student-run newspaper, choral group, Student Support Services Club, Pre-School Mothers, Care Club, Christian Club, Nursing Club. *Campus security:* student patrols, emergency phone poles on campus. *Student services:* health clinic, personal/psychological counseling.
Athletics Member NJCAA. *Intercollegiate sports:* baseball M, basketball M/W, cross-country running M/W, soccer M/W, softball W, tennis M/W, volleyball W.
Costs (2017–18) *Tuition:* state resident $1365 full-time, $46 per unit part-time; nonresident $7525 full-time, $209 per unit part-time. *Required fees:* $45 full-time.
Applying *Options:* electronic application. *Required for some:* high school transcript. *Recommended:* high school transcript. *Application deadlines:*

rolling (freshmen), rolling (transfers). *Notification:* continuous (freshmen), continuous (transfers).
Freshman Application Contact Imperial Valley College, 380 East Aten Road, PO Box 158, Imperial, CA 92251-0158. *Phone:* 760-355-6244. *Website:* http://www.imperial.edu/.

Institute of Technology
Clovis, California

Admissions Office Contact Institute of Technology, 564 West Herndon Avenue, Clovis, CA 93612. *Website:* http://www.iot.edu/.

Irvine Valley College
Irvine, California

Director of Admissions Mr. John Edwards, Director of Admissions, Records, and Enrollment Services, Irvine Valley College, 5500 Irvine Center Drive, Irvine, CA 92618. *Phone:* 949-451-5416. *Website:* http://www.ivc.edu/.

Lake Tahoe Community College
South Lake Tahoe, California

Freshman Application Contact Office of Admissions and Records, Lake Tahoe Community College, One College Drive, South Lake Tahoe, CA 96150. *Phone:* 530-541-4660 Ext. 211. *Fax:* 530-541-7852. *E-mail:* admissions@ltcc.edu. *Website:* http://www.ltcc.edu/.

Laney College
Oakland, California

Freshman Application Contact Mrs. Barbara Simmons, District Admissions Officer, Laney College, 900 Fallon Street, Oakland, CA 94607-4893. *Phone:* 510-466-7369. *Website:* http://www.laney.edu/.

Las Positas College
Livermore, California

Director of Admissions Mrs. Sylvia R. Rodriguez, Director of Admissions and Records, Las Positas College, 3000 Campus Hill Drive, Livermore, CA 94551. *Phone:* 925-373-4942. *Website:* http://www.laspositascollege.edu/.

Lassen Community College
Susanville, California

Freshman Application Contact Mr. Chris J. Alberico, Registrar, Lassen Community College, Highway 139, PO Box 3000, Susanville, CA 96130. *Phone:* 530-257-6181. *Website:* http://www.lassencollege.edu/.

Laurus College
San Luis Obispo, California

Admissions Office Contact Laurus College, 81 Higuera Street, Suite 110, San Luis Obispo, CA 93401. *Website:* http://www.lauruscollege.edu/.

Learnet Academy
Los Angeles, California

Admissions Office Contact Learnet Academy, 3251 West 6th Street, 2nd Floor, Los Angeles, CA 90020. *Website:* http://www.learnet.edu/.

Long Beach City College
Long Beach, California

Director of Admissions Mr. Ross Miyashiro, Dean of Admissions and Records, Long Beach City College, 4901 East Carson Street, Long Beach, CA 90808-1780. *Phone:* 562-938-4130. *Website:* http://www.lbcc.edu/.

Los Angeles City College
Los Angeles, California

- **District-supported** 2-year, founded 1929, part of Los Angeles Community College District (LACCD)
- **Urban** 42-acre campus
- **Coed**, 16,556 undergraduate students, 28% full-time, 56% women, 44% men
- 76% of applicants were admitted

Undergraduates 4,671 full-time, 11,885 part-time. 9% Black or African American, non-Hispanic/Latino; 50% Hispanic/Latino; 15% Asian, non-Hispanic/Latino; 2% American Indian or Alaska Native, non-Hispanic/Latino; 3% Race/ethnicity unknown; 4% international; 6% transferred in.
Freshmen *Admission:* 33,147 applied, 25,210 admitted, 1,002 enrolled.
Faculty *Total:* 572, 44% full-time.
Majors Accounting; administrative assistant and secretarial science; art; business administration and management; chemistry; child development; computer and information sciences and support services related; computer and information sciences related; computer engineering technology; criminal justice/law enforcement administration; dietetics; engineering; English; finance; French; German; human services; industrial radiologic technology; journalism; legal administrative assistant/secretary; marketing/marketing management; mathematics; music; photography; physics; radio and television; real estate; Spanish.
Academics *Calendar:* semesters. *Degree:* certificates, diplomas, and associate. *Special study options:* academic remediation for entering students, adult/continuing education programs, advanced placement credit, cooperative education, distance learning, double majors, English as a second language, freshman honors college, honors programs, internships, part-time degree program, services for LD students, study abroad, summer session for credit. *ROTC:* Army (c), Navy (c), Air Force (c).
Library Martin Luther King Jr.. *Books:* 155,954 (physical), 195,000 (digital/electronic); *Serial titles:* 87 (physical); *Databases:* 60. Weekly public service hours: 77; students can reserve study rooms.
Student Life *Housing:* college housing not available. *Activities and Organizations:* drama/theater group, student-run newspaper, choral group. *Campus security:* 24-hour emergency response devices and patrols, student patrols, late-night transport/escort service. *Student services:* health clinic, personal/psychological counseling.
Costs (2016–17) *Tuition:* state resident $1104 full-time, $46 per unit part-time; nonresident $5328 full-time, $222 per unit part-time. *Required fees:* $24 full-time, $12 per term part-time. *Room and board:* $4968.
Applying *Options:* electronic application. *Application deadlines:* 9/5 (freshmen), 9/5 (transfers). *Notification:* continuous until 9/5 (freshmen), continuous until 9/5 (transfers).
Freshman Application Contact Dr. Terri Anderson, Office of Outreach & Recruitment, Los Angeles City College, 855 North Vermont Avenue, Los Angeles, CA 90029-3590. *Phone:* 323-953-4000. *Website:* http://www.lacitycollege.edu/.

Los Angeles County College of Nursing and Allied Health
Los Angeles, California

Freshman Application Contact Admissions Office, Los Angeles County College of Nursing and Allied Health, 1237 North Mission Road, Los Angeles, CA 90033. *Phone:* 323-226-4911. *Website:* http://www.ladhs.org/wps/portal/CollegeOfNursing.

Los Angeles Harbor College
Wilmington, California

Freshman Application Contact Los Angeles Harbor College, 1111 Figueroa Place, Wilmington, CA 90744-2397. *Phone:* 310-233-4091. *Website:* http://www.lahc.edu/.

Los Angeles Mission College
Sylmar, California

Freshman Application Contact Los Angeles Mission College, 13356 Eldridge Avenue, Sylmar, CA 91342-3245. *Website:* http://www.lamission.edu/.

Los Angeles Pierce College
Woodland Hills, California

Director of Admissions Ms. Shelley L. Gerstl, Dean of Admissions and Records, Los Angeles Pierce College, 6201 Winnetka Avenue, Woodland Hills, CA 91371-0001. *Phone:* 818-719-6448.
Website: http://www.piercecollege.edu/.

Los Angeles Southwest College
Los Angeles, California

Director of Admissions Dan W. Walden, Dean of Academic Affairs, Los Angeles Southwest College, 1600 West Imperial Highway, Los Angeles, CA 90047-4810. *Phone:* 323-242-5511. *Website:* http://www.lasc.edu/.

Los Angeles Trade-Technical College
Los Angeles, California

- **District-supported** 2-year, founded 1925, part of Los Angeles Community College District System
- **Urban** 25-acre campus
- **Coed**

Undergraduates 4,160 full-time, 9,034 part-time.
Academics *Calendar:* semesters. *Degree:* certificates, diplomas, and associate. *Special study options:* academic remediation for entering students, adult/continuing education programs, advanced placement credit, cooperative education, English as a second language, part-time degree program, services for LD students, summer session for credit.
Library Los Angeles Trade-Technical College Library. *Books:* 2,640 (physical), 6,799 (digital/electronic); *Serial titles:* 93 (physical), 41 (digital/electronic); *Databases:* 48. Weekly public service hours: 52.
Student Life *Campus security:* 24-hour patrols, student patrols, late-night transport/escort service.
Costs (2016–17) *Tuition:* state resident $1220 full-time, $46 per unit part-time; nonresident $5832 full-time, $243 per unit part-time. *Required fees:* $42 full-time, $12 per term part-time.
Applying *Options:* electronic application. *Recommended:* high school transcript.
Freshman Application Contact Los Angeles Trade-Technical College, 400 West Washington Boulevard, Los Angeles, CA 90015-4108. *Phone:* 213-763-7127. *Website:* http://www.lattc.edu/.

Los Angeles Valley College
Valley Glen, California

- **District-supported** 2-year, founded 1949, part of Los Angeles Community College District System
- **Suburban** 105-acre campus with easy access to Los Angeles
- **Coed**

Undergraduates Students come from 20 states and territories; 21 other countries; 5% Black or African American, non-Hispanic/Latino; 50% Hispanic/Latino; 8% Asian, non-Hispanic/Latino; 0.2% Native Hawaiian or other Pacific Islander, non-Hispanic/Latino; 2% Two or more races, non-Hispanic/Latino; 4% Race/ethnicity unknown; 0.7% international. *Retention:* 84% of full-time freshmen returned.
Academics *Calendar:* semesters. *Degree:* certificates and associate. *Special study options:* academic remediation for entering students, adult/continuing education programs, cooperative education, distance learning, double majors, English as a second language, honors programs, independent study, internships, part-time degree program, services for LD students, student-designed majors, summer session for credit.
Library Los Angeles Valley Library.
Student Life *Campus security:* 24-hour emergency response devices and patrols, student patrols, late-night transport/escort service.
Athletics Member NJCAA.
Costs (2016–17) *Tuition:* state resident $1220 full-time, $610 per term part-time; nonresident $7538 full-time, $3804 per term part-time. Full-time tuition and fees vary according to course load and program. Part-time tuition and fees vary according to course load and program. *Required fees:* $22 full-time, $11 per term part-time. *Room and board:* Room and board charges vary according to housing facility.
Financial Aid Of all full-time matriculated undergraduates who enrolled in 2015, 65 Federal Work-Study jobs (averaging $4000).
Applying *Options:* electronic application, early admission. *Recommended:* high school transcript.
Freshman Application Contact Los Angeles Valley College, 5800 Fulton Avenue, Valley Glen, CA 91401. *Phone:* 818-947-5518. *Website:* http://www.lavc.edu/.

Los Medanos College
Pittsburg, California

Freshman Application Contact Ms. Gail Newman, Director of Admissions and Records, Los Medanos College, 2700 East Leland Road, Pittsburg, CA 94565-5197. *Phone:* 925-439-2181 Ext. 7500.
Website: http://www.losmedanos.net/.

Mendocino College
Ukiah, California

Freshman Application Contact Mendocino College, 1000 Hensley Creek Road, Ukiah, CA 95482-0300. *Phone:* 707-468-3103.
Website: http://www.mendocino.edu/.

Merced College
Merced, California

- **District-supported** 2-year, founded 1962, part of California Community College System
- **Small-town** 269-acre campus
- **Coed**, 12,525 undergraduate students, 37% full-time, 69% women, 31% men

Undergraduates 4,598 full-time, 7,927 part-time. 2% are from out of state.
Freshmen *Admission:* 2,593 applied, 2,593 admitted.
Faculty *Total:* 421, 34% full-time.
Majors Accounting technology and bookkeeping; administrative assistant and secretarial science; agribusiness; agricultural mechanics and equipment technology; agriculture; agronomy and crop science; animal/livestock husbandry and production; anthropology; applied horticulture/horticulture operations; architectural drafting and CAD/CADD; art; autobody/collision and repair technology; automobile/automotive mechanics technology; biology/biological sciences; biomedical technology; business administration and management; business/commerce; chemistry; child-care provision; computer installation and repair technology; computer science; cooking and related culinary arts; criminal justice/police science; crop production; diagnostic medical sonography and ultrasound technology; dramatic/theater arts; electrical/electronics equipment installation and repair; electrician; emergency medical technology (EMT paramedic); engineering technology; English; family and community services; fire prevention and safety technology; French; geography; geology/earth science; German; health and physical education/fitness; health/medical preparatory programs related; heating, ventilation, air conditioning and refrigeration engineering technology; history; horse husbandry/equine science and management; humanities; human services; information technology; instrumentation technology; international relations and affairs; kinesiology and exercise science; liberal arts and sciences/liberal studies; mathematics; mechanical drafting and CAD/CADD; mechanical engineering/mechanical technology; medical administrative assistant and medical secretary; music; office management; philosophy; photography; physics; pre-engineering; psychology; radiologic technology/science; real estate; registered nursing/registered nurse; sales, distribution, and marketing operations; small business administration; social sciences; sociology; Spanish; special education–early childhood; speech communication and rhetoric; welding technology.
Academics *Calendar:* semesters. *Degree:* certificates and associate. *Special study options:* academic remediation for entering students, adult/continuing education programs, advanced placement credit, cooperative education, English as a second language, honors programs, internships, off-campus study, part-time degree program, student-designed majors, study abroad, summer session for credit. *ROTC:* Army (c).
Library Lesher Library.
Student Life *Housing:* college housing not available. *Activities and Organizations:* drama/theater group, student-run newspaper, choral group. *Campus security:* 24-hour patrols, late-night transport/escort service. *Student services:* health clinic, personal/psychological counseling, women's center, legal services.
Athletics *Intercollegiate sports:* baseball M, basketball M/W, bowling M/W, cross-country running M, equestrian sports M/W, football M, golf M/W, soccer M, softball W, swimming and diving M/W, tennis M/W, track and field M/W, volleyball W, water polo M.
Financial Aid Of all full-time matriculated undergraduates who enrolled in 2014, 319 Federal Work-Study jobs (averaging $3456). 131 state and other part-time jobs (averaging $3456). *Financial aid deadline:* 7/15.

Applying *Options:* early admission. *Recommended:* high school transcript. *Application deadlines:* rolling (freshmen), rolling (transfers). *Notification:* continuous (freshmen), continuous (transfers).
Freshman Application Contact Dr. Anne DiCarlo, Director of Office of Relations with Schools, Merced College, 3600 M Street, Merced, CA 95348-2898. *Phone:* 209-386-6608.
Website: http://www.mccd.edu/.

Merritt College
Oakland, California

Freshman Application Contact Ms. Barbara Simmons, District Admissions Officer, Merritt College, 12500 Campus Drive, Oakland, CA 94619-3196. *Phone:* 510-466-7369. *E-mail:* hperdue@peralta.cc.ca.us. *Website:* http://www.merritt.edu/.

MiraCosta College
Oceanside, California

Freshman Application Contact Jane Sparks, Interim Director of Admissions and Records, MiraCosta College, One Barnard Drive, Oceanside, CA 92057. *Phone:* 760-795-6620. *Toll-free phone:* 888-201-8480.
E-mail: admissions@miracosta.edu. *Website:* http://www.miracosta.edu/.

See this page for display ad and page 340 for the College Close-Up.

Mission College
Santa Clara, California

Director of Admissions Daniel Sanidad, Dean of Student Services, Mission College, 3000 Mission College Boulevard, Santa Clara, CA 95054-1897. *Phone:* 408-855-5139. *Website:* http://www.missioncollege.edu/.

Modesto Junior College
Modesto, California

Freshman Application Contact Ms. Martha Robles, Dean of Student Services and Support, Modesto Junior College, 435 College Avenue, Modesto, CA 95350. *Phone:* 209-575-6470. *Fax:* 209-575-6859. *E-mail:* mjcadmissions@mail.yosemite.cc.ca.us. *Website:* http://www.mjc.edu/.

Monterey Peninsula College
Monterey, California

Director of Admissions Ms. Vera Coleman, Registrar, Monterey Peninsula College, 980 Fremont Street, Monterey, CA 93940-4799. *Phone:* 831-646-4007. *E-mail:* vcoleman@mpc.edu. *Website:* http://www.mpc.edu/.

Moorpark College
Moorpark, California

Freshman Application Contact Ms. Katherine Colborn, Registrar, Moorpark College, 7075 Campus Road, Moorpark, CA 93021-2899. *Phone:* 805-378-1415. *Website:* http://www.moorparkcollege.edu/.

Moreno Valley College
Moreno Valley, California

Freshman Application Contact Jamie Clifton, Director, Enrollment Services, Moreno Valley College, 16130 Lasselle Street, Moreno Valley, CA 92551. *Phone:* 951-571-6293. *E-mail:* admissions@mvc.edu. *Website:* http://www.mvc.edu/.

Mt. San Antonio College
Walnut, California

- **District-supported** 2-year, founded 1946, part of California Community College System
- **Suburban** 421-acre campus with easy access to Los Angeles
- **Coed,** 28,991 undergraduate students, 9% full-time, 8% women, 8% men
Undergraduates 2,577 full-time, 2,113 part-time. 4% Black or African American, non-Hispanic/Latino; 62% Hispanic/Latino; 17% Asian, non-Hispanic/Latino; 0.3% Native Hawaiian or other Pacific Islander, non-Hispanic/Latino; 0.2% American Indian or Alaska Native, non-Hispanic/Latino; 3% Two or more races, non-Hispanic/Latino; 0.7% Race/ethnicity unknown; 2% international. *Retention:* 79% of full-time freshmen returned.

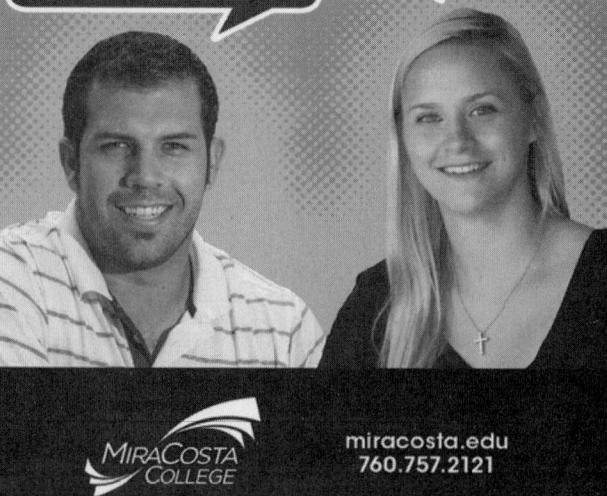

Freshmen *Admission:* 4,690 enrolled.

Faculty *Total:* 1,247, 31% full-time. *Student/faculty ratio:* 26:1.

Majors Accounting; administrative assistant and secretarial science; advertising; agricultural business and management; agriculture; airframe mechanics and aircraft maintenance technology; airline pilot and flight crew; air traffic control; animal/livestock husbandry and production; animal sciences; apparel and textiles; applied horticulture/horticulture operations; architectural engineering technology; avionics maintenance technology; biological and physical sciences; building/construction finishing, management, and inspection related; business administration and management; business teacher education; child development; civil engineering technology; commercial and advertising art; computer and information sciences; computer engineering technology; computer graphics; computer science; corrections; criminal justice/police science; dairy science; data processing and data processing technology; drafting and design technology; drafting/design engineering technologies related; electrical, electronic and communications engineering technology; emergency medical technology (EMT paramedic); engineering technology; English language and literature related; environmental studies; family and consumer sciences/human sciences; fashion merchandising; finance; fire science/firefighting; forest technology; health and physical education/fitness; heating, air conditioning, ventilation and refrigeration maintenance technology; horse husbandry/equine science and management; horticultural science; hotel/motel administration; humanities; industrial and product design; industrial radiologic technology; interior design; journalism; kindergarten/preschool education; landscape architecture; legal administrative assistant/secretary; legal assistant/paralegal; machine tool technology; marketing/marketing management; materials science; mathematics; medical administrative assistant and medical secretary; mental health counseling; music; occupational safety and health technology; ornamental horticulture; parks, recreation and leisure; parks, recreation and leisure facilities management; photography; physical sciences related; pre-engineering; quality control technology; radio and television; real estate; registered nursing/registered nurse; respiratory care therapy; sign language interpretation and translation; social sciences; surveying technology; transportation and materials moving related; visual and performing arts; welding technology; wildlife, fish and wildlands science and management.

Academics *Calendar:* semesters. *Degree:* certificates, diplomas, and associate. *Special study options:* academic remediation for entering students, adult/continuing education programs, advanced placement credit, cooperative education, distance learning, double majors, English as a second language, honors programs, independent study, part-time degree program, services for LD students, study abroad, summer session for credit. *ROTC:* Army (b), Air Force (b).

Library Learning Resources Center. *Books:* 75,587 (physical), 82,336 (digital/electronic); *Databases:* 113. Students can reserve study rooms.

Student Life *Housing:* college housing not available. *Activities and Organizations:* drama/theater group, student-run radio station, choral group, Alpha Gamma Sigma, Muslim Student Association, Student Government, Asian Student Association, Kasama-Filipino Student Organization. *Campus security:* 24-hour emergency response devices and patrols, late-night transport/escort service. *Student services:* health clinic, personal/psychological counseling, women's center.

Athletics *Intercollegiate sports:* badminton W, baseball M, basketball M/W, cheerleading M/W, cross-country running M/W, football M, golf M/W, soccer M/W, softball W, swimming and diving M/W, tennis M/W, track and field M/W, volleyball M/W, water polo M/W, wrestling M.

Costs (2016–17) *Tuition:* state resident $1288 full-time, $46 per unit part-time; nonresident $7364 full-time, $273 per unit part-time. Full-time tuition and fees vary according to course load and program. Part-time tuition and fees vary according to course load and program. *Required fees:* $60 full-time, $60 per term part-time.

Applying *Options:* electronic application, early admission, deferred entrance. *Required for some:* high school transcript. *Notification:* continuous (freshmen), continuous (transfers).

Freshman Application Contact Dr. George Bradshaw, Dean of Enrollment Management, Mt. San Antonio College, Walnut, CA 91789. *Phone:* 909-274-5570 Ext. 4505.

Website: http://www.mtsac.edu/.

Mt. San Jacinto College
San Jacinto, California

Freshman Application Contact Mt. San Jacinto College, 1499 North State Street, San Jacinto, CA 92583-2399. *Phone:* 951-639-5212.

Website: http://www.msjc.edu/.

MTI College
Sacramento, California

Freshman Application Contact Director of Admissions, MTI College, 5221 Madison Avenue, Sacramento, CA 95841. *Phone:* 916-339-1500. *Fax:* 916-339-0305. *Website:* http://www.mticollege.edu/.

Napa Valley College
Napa, California

Director of Admissions Mr. Oscar De Haro, Vice President of Student Services, Napa Valley College, 2277 Napa-Vallejo Highway, Napa, CA 94558-6236. *Phone:* 707-253-3000. *Toll-free phone:* 800-826-1077.

E-mail: odeharo@napavalley.edu. *Website:* http://www.napavalley.edu/.

National Career College
Panorama City, California

Admissions Office Contact National Career College, 14355 Roscoe Boulevard, Panorama City, CA 91402. *Website:* http://www.nccusa.edu/.

National Polytechnic College
Commerce, California

Admissions Office Contact National Polytechnic College, 6630 Telegraph Road, Commerce, CA 90040. *Website:* http://www.npcollege.edu/.

Norco College
Norco, California

- **District-supported** 2-year, founded 2010
- **Urban** 141-acre campus with easy access to Los Angeles
- **Coed**

Undergraduates 6% Black or African American, non-Hispanic/Latino; 57% Hispanic/Latino; 6% Asian, non-Hispanic/Latino; 3% Native Hawaiian or other Pacific Islander, non-Hispanic/Latino; 0.3% American Indian or Alaska Native, non-Hispanic/Latino; 3% Two or more races, non-Hispanic/Latino; 0.5% Race/ethnicity unknown.

Academics *Degree:* certificates and associate. *Special study options:* academic remediation for entering students, distance learning, English as a second language, honors programs, services for LD students, summer session for credit.

Applying *Options:* electronic application.

Freshman Application Contact Mark DeAsis, Director, Enrollment Services, Norco College, 2001 Third Street, Norco, CA 92860.

E-mail: admissionsnorco@norcocollege.edu.

Website: http://www.norcocollege.edu/.

North-West College
West Covina, California

Admissions Office Contact North-West College, 2121 West Garvey Avenue, West Covina, CA 91790. *Toll-free phone:* 888-408-4211.

Website: http://www.nw.edu/.

Ohlone College
Fremont, California

Freshman Application Contact Ohlone College, 43600 Mission Boulevard, Fremont, CA 94539-5884. *Phone:* 510-659-6107.

Website: http://www.ohlone.edu/.

Orange Coast College
Costa Mesa, California

- **District-supported** 2-year, founded 1947, part of Coast Community College District System
- **Suburban** 164-acre campus with easy access to Los Angeles
- **Endowment** $14.8 million
- **Coed,** 41,616 undergraduate students, 41% full-time, 48% women, 52% men

Undergraduates 17,244 full-time, 24,372 part-time. Students come from 75 other countries; 2% are from out of state; 2% Black or African American, non-Hispanic/Latino; 33% Hispanic/Latino; 20% Asian, non-Hispanic/Latino; 0.2% Native Hawaiian or other Pacific Islander, non-Hispanic/Latino; 0.2% American Indian or Alaska Native, non-Hispanic/Latino; 4% Two or more races, non-Hispanic/Latino; 1% Race/ethnicity unknown; 5% international; 5% transferred in.

Freshmen *Admission:* 4,257 enrolled.

Faculty *Total:* 715, 34% full-time. *Student/faculty ratio:* 32:1.

Majors Accounting; accounting technology and bookkeeping; aircraft powerplant technology; airframe mechanics and aircraft maintenance technology; airline flight attendant; animation, interactive technology, video graphics and special effects; anthropology; apparel and textile manufacturing; apparel and textile marketing management; applied horticulture/horticulture operations; architectural technology; art; audiology and speech-language pathology; aviation/airway management; biology/biological sciences; business administration and management; business/commerce; cardiovascular technology; chemistry; child-care and support services management; child-care provision; cinematography and film/video production; clinical/medical laboratory technology; commercial and advertising art; computer graphics; computer installation and repair technology; computer programming; computer science; construction trades; cooking and related culinary arts; culinary arts; dance; dance related; dental assisting; diagnostic medical sonography and ultrasound technology; dietetic technology; dramatic/theater arts; economics; electrical/electronics equipment installation and repair; electrocardiograph technology; electroneurodiagnostic/electroencephalographic technology; elementary education; engineering technologies and engineering related; family and consumer sciences/human sciences; fashion/apparel design; foods, nutrition, and wellness; foreign languages and literatures; geography; geology/earth science; health and physical education/fitness; health services/allied health/health sciences; history; hotel/motel administration; humanities; interior design; international business/trade/commerce; journalism; kinesiology and exercise science; liberal arts and sciences/liberal studies; machine tool technology; marine transportation related; mass communication/media; mathematics; medical/clinical assistant; mental health counseling; merchandising, sales, and marketing operations related (general); music; philosophy; photographic and film/video technology; photography; physical fitness technician; physics; political science and government; pre-engineering; psychology; real estate; recording arts technology; religious studies; respiratory care therapy; restaurant, culinary, and catering management; retail management; sales, distribution, and marketing operations; social sciences; sociology; Spanish; special education–early childhood; speech communication and rhetoric; tourism and travel services marketing; welding technology.

Academics *Calendar:* semesters plus summer session. *Degree:* certificates and associate. *Special study options:* academic remediation for entering students, adult/continuing education programs, advanced placement credit, cooperative education, distance learning, double majors, English as a second language, external degree program, freshman honors college, honors programs, internships, off-campus study, part-time degree program, services for LD students, student-designed majors, study abroad, summer session for credit. *ROTC:* Army (c), Air Force (c).

Library Main Library plus 1 other. *Books:* 108,078 (physical), 24,666 (digital/electronic); *Serial titles:* 91 (physical), 4 (digital/electronic); *Databases:* 59. Weekly public service hours: 64; students can reserve study rooms.

Student Life *Housing:* college housing not available. *Activities and Organizations:* drama/theater group, student-run newspaper, choral group, Architecture Club, Circle K, Doctors of Tomorrow, Speech, Theater, and Debate, Vietnamese Student Association. *Campus security:* 24-hour emergency response devices and patrols, student patrols, late-night transport/escort service. *Student services:* health clinic, personal/psychological counseling, legal services.

Athletics *Intercollegiate sports:* baseball M, basketball M/W, cheerleading M/W, crew M/W, cross-country running M/W, football M, golf M/W, soccer M/W, softball W, swimming and diving M/W, tennis M/W, track and field M/W, volleyball M/W, water polo M/W.

Costs (2017–18) *Tuition:* state resident $1380 full-time, $46 per unit part-time; nonresident $7680 full-time, $219 per unit part-time. Full-time tuition and fees vary according to program. Part-time tuition and fees vary according to program. *Required fees:* $900 full-time, $140 per term part-time. *Payment plan:* installment.

Financial Aid Of all full-time matriculated undergraduates who enrolled in 2015, 108 Federal Work-Study jobs (averaging $3000). *Financial aid deadline:* 5/28.

Applying *Options:* electronic application. *Application deadlines:* rolling (freshmen), rolling (transfers). *Notification:* continuous (freshmen), continuous (transfers).

Freshman Application Contact Efren Galvan, Director of Admissions, Records and Enrollment Technology, Orange Coast College, 2701 Fairview Road, Costa Mesa, CA 92926. *Phone:* 714-432-5774. *E-mail:* egalvan@occ.cccd.edu. *Website:* http://www.orangecoastcollege.edu/.

Oxnard College
Oxnard, California

- **District-supported** 2-year, founded 1975, part of Ventura County Community College District System
- **Urban** 119-acre campus
- **Endowment** $5.8 million
- **Coed**

Undergraduates 1,958 full-time, 5,048 part-time. Students come from 3 states and territories; 13% transferred in. *Retention:* 73% of full-time freshmen returned.

Faculty *Student/faculty ratio:* 30:1.

Academics *Calendar:* semesters. *Degree:* certificates, diplomas, and associate. *Special study options:* academic remediation for entering students, accelerated degree program, advanced placement credit, distance learning, double majors, English as a second language, honors programs, independent study, part-time degree program, services for LD students, summer session for credit.

Library Oxnard College Library. *Books:* 47,874 (physical), 141,577 (digital/electronic); *Serial titles:* 422 (physical), 9 (digital/electronic); *Databases:* 12. Students can reserve study rooms.

Student Life *Campus security:* 24-hour patrols, late-night transport/escort service.

Costs (2016–17) *Tuition:* state resident $1104 full-time, $46 per unit part-time; nonresident $6580 full-time, $235 per unit part-time. *Required fees:* $468 full-time, $15 per unit part-time, $19 per term part-time.

Financial Aid Of all full-time matriculated undergraduates who enrolled in 2015, 80 Federal Work-Study jobs (averaging $3000).

Applying *Options:* electronic application, early admission. *Recommended:* high school transcript.

Freshman Application Contact Mr. Joel Diaz, Registrar, Oxnard College, 4000 South Rose Avenue, Oxnard, CA 93033-6699. *Phone:* 805-986-5843. *Fax:* 805-986-5943. *E-mail:* jdiaz@vcccd.edu. *Website:* http://www.oxnardcollege.edu/.

Palomar College
San Marcos, California

- **District-supported** 2-year, founded 1946, part of California Community College System
- **Suburban** 156-acre campus with easy access to San Diego
- **Coed**, 25,244 undergraduate students, 100% full-time, 47% women, 53% men

Undergraduates 25,244 full-time.

Faculty *Total:* 1,305, 21% full-time. *Student/faculty ratio:* 21:1.

Majors Accounting technology and bookkeeping; administrative assistant and secretarial science; advertising; animation, interactive technology, video graphics and special effects; apparel and textile marketing management; archeology; architectural drafting and CAD/CADD; architectural technology; art; astronomy; autobody/collision and repair technology; automobile/automotive mechanics technology; biological and physical sciences; biology/biological sciences; broadcast journalism; building/home/construction inspection; business administration and management; business/commerce; cabinetmaking and millwork; carpentry; ceramic arts and ceramics; chemistry; child-care and support services management; child-care provision; commercial and advertising art; computer graphics; computer programming; computer systems networking and telecommunications; construction trades related; dance; dental assisting; design and visual communications; desktop publishing and digital imaging design; diesel mechanics technology; drafting and design technology; dramatic/theater arts; drawing; drywall installation; economics; education; electrical/electronics drafting and CAD/CADD; electrician; emergency medical technology (EMT paramedic); English; family and community services; family and consumer sciences/human sciences; fashion/apparel design; film/cinema/video studies; fire prevention and safety technology; foreign languages and literatures; forensic science and technology; French; geography; geography related; geology/earth science; graphic and printing equipment operation/production; graphic design; homeland security; humanities; information technology; insurance; interior design; international business/trade/commerce; journalism; kinesiology and exercise science; legal studies; liberal arts and sciences/liberal studies; library and archives assisting; masonry; mathematics; medical administrative assistant and medical secretary; metal and jewelry arts; music; parks, recreation and leisure; photographic and film/video technology; pre-engineering; psychology; public administration; radio and television; real estate; registered nursing/registered nurse; sculpture; sheet metal technology; sign language interpretation and translation; social sciences; sociology; special education–early childhood; speech communication and rhetoric; substance abuse/addiction counseling; water quality and wastewater treatment management and recycling technology; web page, digital/multimedia and information resources design; welding technology; women's studies.

Academics *Calendar:* semesters. *Degree:* certificates and associate. *Special study options:* academic remediation for entering students, advanced placement credit, cooperative education, distance learning, English as a second language, internships, part-time degree program, services for LD students, summer session for credit. *ROTC:* Air Force (c).

Library Palomar College Library.

Student Life *Housing:* college housing not available. *Activities and Organizations:* drama/theater group, student-run newspaper, radio and television station, choral group, SNAP (Student Nursing Association of Palomar College), Alpha Omega Rho Chapter of Phi Theta Kappa (international honor society), Active Minds, Student Veterans Organization, MEChA (Chicano organization). *Campus security:* 24-hour emergency response devices and patrols, late-night transport/escort service. *Student services:* health clinic, personal/psychological counseling.

Athletics *Intercollegiate sports:* baseball M, basketball M/W, football M, golf M, soccer M/W, softball W, swimming and diving M/W, tennis M/W, track and field M/W, volleyball M/W, water polo M/W, wrestling M. *Intramural sports:* basketball M/W, bowling M, golf M, skiing (downhill) M/W, soccer M, softball W, tennis M, volleyball M, water polo M, wrestling M.

Costs (2017–18) *Tuition:* state resident $1338 full-time, $46 per unit part-time; nonresident $8030 full-time, $285 per unit part-time. *Required fees:* $60 full-time.

Applying *Options:* electronic application. *Application deadlines:* rolling (freshmen), rolling (transfers). *Notification:* continuous (freshmen), continuous (transfers).

Freshman Application Contact Dr. Kendyl Magnuson, Senior Director of Enrollment Services, Palomar College, 1140 W Mission Road, San Marcos, CA 92069. *Phone:* 760-744-1150 Ext. 2171. *Fax:* 760-744-2932. *E-mail:* kmagnuson@palomar.edu. *Website:* http://www.palomar.edu/.

Palo Verde College
Blythe, California

Freshman Application Contact Diana Rodriguez, Vice President of Student Services, Palo Verde College, 1 College Drive, Blythe, CA 92225. *Phone:* 760-921-5428. *Fax:* 760-921-3608. *E-mail:* diana.rodriguez@paloverde.edu. *Website:* http://www.paloverde.edu/.

Pasadena City College
Pasadena, California

- **District-supported** 2-year, founded 1924, part of California Community College System
- **Urban** 55-acre campus with easy access to Los Angeles
- **Coed**

Undergraduates 11,068 full-time, 15,982 part-time. Students come from 20 states and territories; 150 other countries; 1% are from out of state; 4% Black or African American, non-Hispanic/Latino; 50% Hispanic/Latino; 24% Asian, non-Hispanic/Latino; 0.1% Native Hawaiian or other Pacific Islander, non-Hispanic/Latino; 0.1% American Indian or Alaska Native, non-Hispanic/Latino; 11% Two or more races, non-Hispanic/Latino; 0.7% Race/ethnicity unknown; 4% international; 9% transferred in. *Retention:* 78% of full-time freshmen returned.

Faculty *Student/faculty ratio:* 25:1.

Academics *Calendar:* semesters. *Degree:* certificates, diplomas, and associate. *Special study options:* academic remediation for entering students, adult/continuing education programs, advanced placement credit, distance learning, double majors, English as a second language, honors programs, independent study, internships, part-time degree program, services for LD students, study abroad, summer session for credit.

Library Pasadena City College Library plus 1 other. *Books:* 133,975 (physical), 35,619 (digital/electronic); *Databases:* 56. Weekly public service hours: 54; students can reserve study rooms.

Student Life *Campus security:* 24-hour emergency response devices and patrols, late-night transport/escort service, cadet patrols.

Costs (2016–17) *Tuition:* state resident $1152 full-time, $46 per unit part-time; nonresident $6180 full-time, $262 per unit part-time. *Required fees:* $48 full-time, $24 per hour part-time.

Applying *Options:* electronic application.

Freshman Application Contact Pasadena City College, 1570 East Colorado Boulevard, Pasadena, CA 91106-2041. *Phone:* 626-585-7614. *Fax:* 626-585-7915. *Website:* http://www.pasadena.edu/.

Pima Medical Institute
Chula Vista, California

Freshman Application Contact Admissions Office, Pima Medical Institute, 780 Bay Boulevard, Chula Vista, CA 91910. *Phone:* 619-425-3200. *Toll-free phone:* 800-477-PIMA. *Website:* http://www.pmi.edu/.

Platt College
Alhambra, California

Director of Admissions Mr. Detroit Whiteside, Director of Admissions, Platt College, 1000 South Fremont A9W, Alhambra, CA 91803. *Phone:* 323-258-8050. *Toll-free phone:* 888-866-6697 (in-state); 888-80-PLATT (out-of-state). *Website:* http://www.plattcollege.edu/.

Platt College
Ontario, California

Director of Admissions Ms. Jennifer Abandonato, Director of Admissions, Platt College, 3700 Inland Empire Boulevard, Ontario, CA 91764. *Phone:* 909-941-9410. *Toll-free phone:* 888-80-PLATT. *Website:* http://www.plattcollege.edu/.

Porterville College
Porterville, California

Director of Admissions Ms. Judy Pope, Director of Admissions and Records/Registrar, Porterville College, 100 East College Avenue, Porterville, CA 93257-6058. *Phone:* 559-791-2222. *Website:* http://www.pc.cc.ca.us/.

Professional Golfers Career College
Temecula, California

Freshman Application Contact Mr. Gary Gilleon, Professional Golfers Career College, 26109 Ynez Road, Temecula, CA 92591. *Phone:* 951-719-2994 Ext. 1021. *Toll-free phone:* 800-877-4380. *Fax:* 951-719-1643. *E-mail:* garygilleon@golfcollege.edu. *Website:* http://www.golfcollege.edu/.

Reedley College
Reedley, California

Freshman Application Contact Admissions and Records Office, Reedley College, 995 North Reed Avenue, Reedley, CA 93654. *Phone:* 559-638-0323. *Fax:* 559-637-2523. *Website:* http://www.reedleycollege.edu/.

Rio Hondo College
Whittier, California

- **District-supported** 2-year, founded 1960, part of California Community College System
- **Suburban** 128-acre campus with easy access to Los Angeles
- **Coed**, 18,367 undergraduate students, 22% full-time, 44% women, 56% men

Undergraduates 3,989 full-time, 14,378 part-time. Students come from 5 states and territories; 0.2% are from out of state; 2% Black or African American, non-Hispanic/Latino; 77% Hispanic/Latino; 6% Asian, non-Hispanic/Latino; 0.1% Native Hawaiian or other Pacific Islander, non-Hispanic/Latino; 0.2% American Indian or Alaska Native, non-Hispanic/Latino; 0.9% Two or more races, non-Hispanic/Latino; 5% Race/ethnicity unknown; 0.3% international; 8% transferred in.

Freshmen *Admission:* 17,882 enrolled.

Faculty *Total:* 560, 34% full-time. *Student/faculty ratio:* 34:1.

Majors Business teacher education; criminal justice/law enforcement administration; liberal arts and sciences/liberal studies; registered nursing/registered nurse.

Academics *Calendar:* semesters. *Degree:* certificates and associate. *Special study options:* academic remediation for entering students, adult/continuing education programs, advanced placement credit, distance learning, English as a second language, honors programs, part-time degree program, services for LD students, study abroad, summer session for credit. *ROTC:* Army (c), Navy (c), Air Force (c).

Library Library and Learning Resource Center plus 1 other. *Books:* 88,245 (physical); *Serial titles:* 104 (physical); *Databases:* 12. Weekly public service hours: 68; students can reserve study rooms.

Student Life *Housing:* college housing not available. *Activities and Organizations:* drama/theater group, student-run newspaper, radio station, choral group. *Campus security:* 24-hour patrols, late-night transport/escort service. *Student services:* health clinic, personal/psychological counseling, women's center, legal services.

Athletics *Intercollegiate sports:* baseball M, basketball M/W, cross-country running M/W, soccer M/W, softball W, swimming and diving M/W, tennis M/W, track and field M/W, volleyball W, water polo M/W, wrestling M.

Costs (2016–17) *Tuition:* state resident $1380 full-time, $46 per credit part-time; nonresident $7380 full-time, $200 per credit part-time. Full-time tuition and fees vary according to course load. Part-time tuition and fees vary according to course load. *Required fees:* $72 full-time.

Financial Aid Of all full-time matriculated undergraduates who enrolled in 2015, 150 Federal Work-Study jobs (averaging $3200). 35 state and other part-time jobs (averaging $3200). *Financial aid deadline:* 5/1.

Applying *Application deadlines:* rolling (freshmen), rolling (transfers). *Notification:* continuous (freshmen), continuous (transfers).

Freshman Application Contact Rio Hondo College, 3600 Workman Mill Road, Whittier, CA 90601-1699. *Phone:* 562-692-0921 Ext. 3415. *Website:* http://www.riohondo.edu/.

Riverside City College
Riverside, California

Freshman Application Contact Joy Chambers, Dean of Enrollment Services, Riverside City College, Riverside, CA 92506. *Phone:* 951-222-8600. *Fax:* 951-222-8037. *E-mail:* admissionsriverside@rcc.edu. *Website:* http://www.rcc.edu/.

Sacramento City College
Sacramento, California

Director of Admissions Mr. Sam T. Sandusky, Dean, Student Services, Sacramento City College, 3835 Freeport Boulevard, Sacramento, CA 95822-1386. *Phone:* 916-558-2438. *Website:* http://www.scc.losrios.edu/.

Saddleback College
Mission Viejo, California

Freshman Application Contact Admissions Office, Saddleback College, 28000 Marguerite Parkway, Mission Viejo, CA 92692. *Phone:* 949-582-4555. *Fax:* 949-347-8315. *E-mail:* earaiza@saddleback.edu. *Website:* http://www.saddleback.edu/.

Sage College
Moreno Valley, California

Admissions Office Contact Sage College, 12125 Day Street, Building L, Moreno Valley, CA 92557-6720. *Toll-free phone:* 888-755-SAGE. *Website:* http://www.sagecollege.edu/.

The Salvation Army College for Officer Training at Crestmont
Rancho Palos Verdes, California

Freshman Application Contact Capt. Brian Jones, Director of Curriculum, The Salvation Army College for Officer Training at Crestmont, 30840 Hawthorne Boulevard, Rancho Palos Verdes, CA 90275. *Phone:* 310-544-6442. *Fax:* 310-265-6520. *Website:* http://www.crestmont.edu/.

San Bernardino Valley College
San Bernardino, California

Director of Admissions Ms. Helena Johnson, Director of Admissions and Records, San Bernardino Valley College, 701 South Mount Vernon Avenue, San Bernardino, CA 92410-2748. *Phone:* 909-384-4401. *Website:* http://www.valleycollege.edu/.

San Diego City College
San Diego, California

Freshman Application Contact Ms. Lou Humphries, Registrar/Supervisor of Admissions, Records, Evaluations and Veterans, San Diego City College, 1313 Park Boulevard, San Diego, CA 92101-4787. *Phone:* 619-388-3474. *Fax:* 619-388-3505. *E-mail:* lhumphri@sdccd.edu. *Website:* http://www.sdcity.edu/.

San Diego Mesa College
San Diego, California

Freshman Application Contact Ms. Cheri Sawyer, Admissions Supervisor, San Diego Mesa College, 7250 Mesa College Drive, San Diego, CA 92111. *Phone:* 619-388-2686. *Fax:* 619-388-2960. *E-mail:* csawyer@sdccd.edu. *Website:* http://www.sdmesa.edu/.

San Diego Miramar College
San Diego, California

Freshman Application Contact Ms. Dana Stack, Admissions Supervisor, San Diego Miramar College, 10440 Black Mountain Road, San Diego, CA 92126-2999. *Phone:* 619-536-7854. *E-mail:* dstack@sdccd.edu. *Website:* http://www.sdmiramar.edu/.

San Joaquin Delta College
Stockton, California

- **District-supported** 2-year, founded 1935, part of California Community College System
- **Urban** 165-acre campus with easy access to Sacramento
- **Coed**, 17,213 undergraduate students, 38% full-time, 56% women, 34% men

Undergraduates 6,524 full-time, 9,042 part-time. Students come from 20 states and territories; 0.2% are from out of state; 10% Black or African American, non-Hispanic/Latino; 44% Hispanic/Latino; 17% Asian, non-Hispanic/Latino; 0.5% Native Hawaiian or other Pacific Islander, non-Hispanic/Latino; 0.4% American Indian or Alaska Native, non-Hispanic/Latino; 5% Two or more races, non-Hispanic/Latino; 0.6% Race/ethnicity unknown; 0.2% international. *Retention:* 77% of full-time freshmen returned.

Faculty *Total:* 544, 41% full-time. *Student/faculty ratio:* 27:1.

Majors Accounting; agricultural business and management; agricultural mechanization; agriculture; animal sciences; anthropology; art; automobile/automotive mechanics technology; biology/biological sciences; broadcast journalism; business administration and management; chemistry; civil engineering technology; commercial and advertising art; comparative literature; computer science; construction engineering technology; corrections; criminal justice/police science; crop production; culinary arts; dance; dramatic/theater arts; economics; electrical, electronic and communications engineering technology; engineering; engineering related; engineering technology; English; family and consumer sciences/human sciences; fashion merchandising; fire science/firefighting; geology/earth science; heating, air conditioning, ventilation and refrigeration maintenance technology; history; humanities; journalism; liberal arts and sciences/liberal studies; licensed practical/vocational nurse training; machine tool technology; mathematics; mechanical engineering/mechanical technology; music; natural resources management and policy; natural sciences; ornamental horticulture; philosophy; photography; physical education teaching and coaching; physical sciences; political science and government; psychology; registered nursing/registered nurse; religious studies; rhetoric and composition; social sciences; sociology.

Academics *Calendar:* semesters. *Degree:* certificates and associate. *Special study options:* academic remediation for entering students, adult/continuing education programs, advanced placement credit, cooperative education, distance learning, English as a second language, honors programs, independent study, part-time degree program, services for LD students, summer session for credit.

Library Goleman Library plus 1 other.

Student Life *Housing:* college housing not available. *Activities and Organizations:* drama/theater group, student-run newspaper, radio station, choral group. *Campus security:* 24-hour emergency response devices and patrols, late-night transport/escort service. *Student services:* personal/psychological counseling, legal services.

Athletics Member NJCAA. *Intercollegiate sports:* baseball M, basketball M/W, cross-country running M/W, fencing M/W, football M, golf M/W, soccer M/W, softball W, swimming and diving M/W, tennis M/W, track and field M/W, volleyball W, water polo M/W, wrestling M. *Intramural sports:* badminton M/W, basketball M/W, bowling M/W, soccer M/W, swimming and diving M/W, tennis M/W, ultimate Frisbee M/W, volleyball M/W, weight lifting M/W.

Costs (2016–17) *Tuition:* state resident $1380 full-time, $46 per unit part-time; nonresident $7950 full-time, $263 per unit part-time. *Waivers:* minority students and employees or children of employees.

Financial Aid Of all full-time matriculated undergraduates who enrolled in 2015, 11,810 applied for aid, 10,671 were judged to have need, 54 had their need fully met. 160 Federal Work-Study jobs (averaging $2671). *Average percent of need met:* 31%. *Average financial aid package:* $5230. *Average need-based loan:* $2921. *Average need-based gift aid:* $4991.

Applying *Options:* electronic application, early admission. *Application deadlines:* rolling (freshmen), rolling (transfers). *Notification:* continuous (freshmen), continuous (transfers).

Freshman Application Contact Ms. Karen Sea, Registrar, San Joaquin Delta College, 5151 Pacific Avenue, Stockton, CA 95207. *Phone:* 209-954-6127. *E-mail:* ksea@deltacollege.edu.

Website: http://www.deltacollege.edu/.

San Joaquin Valley College
Bakersfield, California

- **Proprietary** 2-year, founded 1977, part of San Joaquin Valley College
- **Suburban** campus with easy access to Bakersfield
- **Coed**

Undergraduates 864 full-time. 5% Black or African American, non-Hispanic/Latino; 57% Hispanic/Latino; 3% Asian, non-Hispanic/Latino; 0.2% Native Hawaiian or other Pacific Islander, non-Hispanic/Latino; 1% American Indian or Alaska Native, non-Hispanic/Latino; 0.9% Two or more races, non-Hispanic/Latino; 3% Race/ethnicity unknown; 3% international.

Faculty *Student/faculty ratio:* 25:1.

Academics *Calendar:* continuous. *Degree:* certificates and associate.

Applying *Required for some:* essay or personal statement, high school transcript, interview.

Freshman Application Contact Enrollment Services Director, San Joaquin Valley College, 201 New Stine Road, Bakersfield, CA 93309. *Phone:* 661-834-0126. *Toll-free phone:* 866-544-7898. *Fax:* 661-834-8124. *E-mail:* admissions@sjvc.edu.

Website: http://www.sjvc.edu/campuses/central-california/bakersfield.

San Joaquin Valley College
Fresno, California

- **Proprietary** 2-year, part of San Joaquin Valley College
- **Urban** campus with easy access to Fresno
- **Coed**

Undergraduates 1,019 full-time. 4% Black or African American, non-Hispanic/Latino; 57% Hispanic/Latino; 5% Asian, non-Hispanic/Latino; 0.7% Native Hawaiian or other Pacific Islander, non-Hispanic/Latino; 1% American Indian or Alaska Native, non-Hispanic/Latino; 5% Two or more races, non-Hispanic/Latino; 2% Race/ethnicity unknown; 2% international.

Faculty *Student/faculty ratio:* 33:1.

Academics *Calendar:* continuous. *Degree:* certificates and associate.

Applying *Required for some:* essay or personal statement, 1 letter of recommendation, interview.

Freshman Application Contact Enrollment Services Director, San Joaquin Valley College, 295 East Sierra Avenue, Fresno, CA 93710. *Phone:* 559-448-8282. *Toll-free phone:* 866-544-7898. *Fax:* 559-448-8250. *E-mail:* admissions@sjvc.edu.

Website: http://www.sjvc.edu/campuses/central-california/fresno/.

San Joaquin Valley College
Hanford, California

- **Proprietary** 2-year
- **Small-town** campus with easy access to Fresno
- **Coed**

Undergraduates 275 full-time. 4% Black or African American, non-Hispanic/Latino; 62% Hispanic/Latino; 1% Asian, non-Hispanic/Latino; 1% American Indian or Alaska Native, non-Hispanic/Latino; 4% Two or more races, non-Hispanic/Latino; 2% Race/ethnicity unknown; 4% international.

Faculty *Student/faculty ratio:* 59:1.

Academics *Calendar:* continuous. *Degree:* certificates and associate.

Freshman Application Contact San Joaquin Valley College, 215 West 7th Street, Hanford, CA 93230. *Toll-free phone:* 866-544-7898. *Website:* http://www.sjvc.edu/campuses/central-california/hanford/.

San Joaquin Valley College
Hesperia, California

- **Proprietary** 2-year, part of San Joaquin Valley College
- **Suburban** campus with easy access to San Bernadino
- **Coed**

Undergraduates 804 full-time. 12% Black or African American, non-Hispanic/Latino; 53% Hispanic/Latino; 1% Asian, non-Hispanic/Latino; 0.7% Native Hawaiian or other Pacific Islander, non-Hispanic/Latino; 1% American Indian or Alaska Native, non-Hispanic/Latino; 6% Two or more races, non-Hispanic/Latino; 2% Race/ethnicity unknown; 1% international.

Faculty *Student/faculty ratio:* 34:1.

Academics *Calendar:* continuous. *Degree:* certificates and associate.

Freshman Application Contact San Joaquin Valley College, 9331 Mariposa Road, Hesperia, CA 92344. *Toll-free phone:* 866-544-7898. *Website:* http://www.sjvc.edu/campuses/southern-california/victor-valley/.

San Joaquin Valley College
Lancaster, California

- **Proprietary** 2-year, founded 2012, part of San Joaquin Valley College
- **Suburban** campus
- **Coed**

Undergraduates 328 full-time. 21% Black or African American, non-Hispanic/Latino; 52% Hispanic/Latino; 1% Asian, non-Hispanic/Latino; 2% Native Hawaiian or other Pacific Islander, non-Hispanic/Latino; 0.6% American Indian or Alaska Native, non-Hispanic/Latino; 9% Two or more races, non-Hispanic/Latino; 2% Race/ethnicity unknown; 2% international.

Faculty *Student/faculty ratio:* 45:1.

Academics *Calendar:* continuous. *Degree:* certificates and associate.

Freshman Application Contact San Joaquin Valley College, 42135 10th Street West, Suite 147, Lancaster, CA 93534. *Toll-free phone:* 866-544-7898. *Website:* http://www.sjvc.edu/campuses/southern-california/antelope-valley/.

San Joaquin Valley College
Ontario, California

- **Proprietary** 2-year, part of San Joaquin Valley College
- **Urban** campus with easy access to Los Angeles
- **Coed**

Undergraduates 994 full-time. 6% Black or African American, non-Hispanic/Latino; 61% Hispanic/Latino; 6% Asian, non-Hispanic/Latino; 2% Native Hawaiian or other Pacific Islander, non-Hispanic/Latino; 0.3% American Indian or Alaska Native, non-Hispanic/Latino; 5% Two or more races, non-Hispanic/Latino; 2% Race/ethnicity unknown; 2% international.

Faculty *Student/faculty ratio:* 18:1.

Academics *Calendar:* continuous. *Degree:* certificates and associate.

Applying *Required for some:* essay or personal statement, interview.

Freshman Application Contact Enrollment Services Director, San Joaquin Valley College, 4580 Ontario Mills Parkway, Ontario, CA 91764. *Phone:* 909-948-7582. *Toll-free phone:* 866-544-7898. *Fax:* 909-948-3860. *E-mail:* admissions@sjvc.edu.

Website: http://www.sjvc.edu/campuses/southern-california/ontario/.

San Joaquin Valley College
Rancho Cordova, California

- **Proprietary** 2-year, part of San Joaquin Valley College
- **Suburban** campus with easy access to Sacramento
- **Coed**

Undergraduates 158 full-time. 2% Black or African American, non-Hispanic/Latino; 10% Hispanic/Latino; 18% Asian, non-Hispanic/Latino; 4% Native Hawaiian or other Pacific Islander, non-Hispanic/Latino; 6% Two or more races, non-Hispanic/Latino; 4% Race/ethnicity unknown; 4% international.

Faculty *Student/faculty ratio:* 22:1.

Academics *Calendar:* continuous. *Degree:* certificates and associate.

Applying *Required for some:* essay or personal statement, interview.

Freshman Application Contact Enrollment Services Director, San Joaquin Valley College, 11050 Olson Drive, Suite 210, Rancho Cordova, CA 95670. *Phone:* 916-638-7582. *Toll-free phone:* 866-544-7898. *Fax:* 916-638-7553. *E-mail:* admissions@sjvc.edu.

Website: http://www.sjvc.edu/campuses/northern-california/rancho-cordova/.

San Joaquin Valley College
Salida, California

- **Proprietary** 2-year, part of San Joaquin Valley College
- **Suburban** campus
- **Coed**

Undergraduates 465 full-time. Students come from 1 other state; 3% Black or African American, non-Hispanic/Latino; 47% Hispanic/Latino; 6% Asian, non-Hispanic/Latino; 2% Native Hawaiian or other Pacific Islander, non-Hispanic/Latino; 0.2% American Indian or Alaska Native, non-Hispanic/Latino; 6% Two or more races, non-Hispanic/Latino; 2% Race/ethnicity unknown; 3% international.

Faculty *Student/faculty ratio:* 31:1.

Academics *Calendar:* continuous. *Degree:* certificates and associate.

Applying *Required for some:* essay or personal statement, interview.
Freshman Application Contact Enrollment Services Director, San Joaquin Valley College, 5380 Pirrone Road, Salida, CA 95368. *Phone:* 209-543-8800. *Toll-free phone:* 866-544-7898. *Fax:* 209-543-8320.
E-mail: admissions@sjvc.edu.
Website: http://www.sjvc.edu/campuses/northern-california/modesto/.

San Joaquin Valley College
Temecula, California

- **Proprietary** 2-year, part of San Joaquin Valley College
- **Urban** campus with easy access to Los Angeles
- **Coed**

Undergraduates 728 full-time. 7% Black or African American, non-Hispanic/Latino; 40% Hispanic/Latino; 6% Asian, non-Hispanic/Latino; 2% Native Hawaiian or other Pacific Islander, non-Hispanic/Latino; 1% American Indian or Alaska Native, non-Hispanic/Latino; 6% Two or more races, non-Hispanic/Latino; 2% Race/ethnicity unknown; 5% international.
Faculty *Student/faculty ratio:* 32:1.
Academics *Calendar:* continuous. *Degree:* certificates and associate.
Freshman Application Contact Ms. Robyn Whiles, Enrollment Services Director, San Joaquin Valley College, 27270 Madison Avenue, Suite 103, Temecula, CA 92590. *Phone:* 559-651-2500. *Toll-free phone:* 866-544-7898.
E-mail: admissions@sjvc.edu.
Website: http://www.sjvc.edu/campuses/southern-california/temecula/.

San Joaquin Valley College
Visalia, California

- **Proprietary** 2-year, founded 1977, part of San Joaquin Valley College
- **Suburban** campus with easy access to Fresno
- **Coed**

Undergraduates 1,294 full-time. 2% Black or African American, non-Hispanic/Latino; 54% Hispanic/Latino; 6% Asian, non-Hispanic/Latino; 0.5% Native Hawaiian or other Pacific Islander, non-Hispanic/Latino; 0.9% American Indian or Alaska Native, non-Hispanic/Latino; 4% Two or more races, non-Hispanic/Latino; 2% Race/ethnicity unknown; 3% international.
Faculty *Student/faculty ratio:* 21:1.
Academics *Calendar:* continuous. *Degree:* certificates and associate. *Special study options:* academic remediation for entering students.
Library SJVC Visalia Campus Library.
Student Life *Campus security:* late-night transport/escort service, full-time security personnel.
Applying *Required for some:* essay or personal statement, high school transcript, interview.
Freshman Application Contact Susie Topjian, Enrollment Services Director, San Joaquin Valley College, 8400 West Mineral King Boulevard, Visalia, CA 93291. *Phone:* 559-651-2500. *Toll-free phone:* 866-544-7898. *Fax:* 559-734-9048. *E-mail:* admissions@sjvc.edu.
Website: http://www.sjvc.edu/campuses/central-california/visalia/.

San Joaquin Valley College–Fresno Aviation Campus
Fresno, California

- **Proprietary** 2-year, part of San Joaquin Valley College
- **Urban** campus with easy access to Fresno
- **Coed, primarily men**

Undergraduates 130 full-time. 2% Black or African American, non-Hispanic/Latino; 34% Hispanic/Latino; 11% Asian, non-Hispanic/Latino; 0.8% Native Hawaiian or other Pacific Islander, non-Hispanic/Latino; 0.8% American Indian or Alaska Native, non-Hispanic/Latino; 6% Two or more races, non-Hispanic/Latino; 2% Race/ethnicity unknown; 4% international.
Faculty *Student/faculty ratio:* 26:1.
Academics *Calendar:* semesters. *Degree:* associate.
Applying *Required for some:* essay or personal statement, high school transcript, interview.
Freshman Application Contact Enrollment Services Coordinator, San Joaquin Valley College–Fresno Aviation Campus, 4985 East Anderson Avenue, Fresno, CA 93727. *Phone:* 559-453-0123. *Toll-free phone:* 866-544-7898. *Fax:* 599-453-0133. *E-mail:* admissions@sjvc.edu.
Website: http://www.sjvc.edu/campuses/central-california/fresno-aviation/.

San Joaquin Valley College–Online
Visalia, California

- **Proprietary** 2-year, part of San Joaquin Valley College
- **Suburban** campus
- **Coed**

Undergraduates 1,005 full-time. 32% Black or African American, non-Hispanic/Latino; 17% Hispanic/Latino; 2% Asian, non-Hispanic/Latino; 0.1% Native Hawaiian or other Pacific Islander, non-Hispanic/Latino; 0.9% American Indian or Alaska Native, non-Hispanic/Latino; 5% Two or more races, non-Hispanic/Latino; 5% Race/ethnicity unknown; 0.6% international.
Faculty *Student/faculty ratio:* 42:1.
Academics *Calendar:* continuous. *Degree:* certificates and associate.
Applying *Options:* electronic application. *Required for some:* essay or personal statement, interview.
Freshman Application Contact Enrollment Services Director, San Joaquin Valley College–Online, 8344 West Mineral King Avenue, Visalia, CA 93291. *Toll-free phone:* 866-544-7898. *E-mail:* admissions@sjvc.edu.
Website: http://www.sjvc.edu/online-programs/.

San Jose City College
San Jose, California

Freshman Application Contact Mr. Carlo Santos, Director of Admissions/Registrar, San Jose City College, 2100 Moorpark Avenue, San Jose, CA 95128-2799. *Phone:* 408-288-3707. *Fax:* 408-298-1935. *Website:* http://www.sjcc.edu/.

Santa Ana College
Santa Ana, California

Freshman Application Contact Mrs. Christie Steward, Admissions Clerk, Santa Ana College, 1530 West 17th Street, Santa Ana, CA 92706-3398. *Phone:* 714-564-6053. *Website:* http://www.sac.edu/.

Santa Barbara Business College
Bakersfield, California

Admissions Office Contact Santa Barbara Business College, 5300 California Avenue, Bakersfield, CA 93309. *Website:* http://www.sbbcollege.edu/.

Santa Barbara Business College
Santa Maria, California

Admissions Office Contact Santa Barbara Business College, 303 East Plaza Drive, Santa Maria, CA 93454. *Website:* http://www.sbbcollege.edu/.

Santa Barbara City College
Santa Barbara, California

Freshman Application Contact Ms. Allison Curtis, Director of Admissions and Records, Santa Barbara City College, Santa Barbara, CA 93109. *Phone:* 805-965-0581 Ext. 2352. *Fax:* 805-962-0497. *E-mail:* admissions@sbcc.edu. *Website:* http://www.sbcc.edu/.

Santa Monica College
Santa Monica, California

- **District-supported** 2-year, founded 1929, part of California Community College System
- **Urban** 40-acre campus with easy access to Los Angeles
- **Coed**, 30,830 undergraduate students, 14% full-time, 53% women, 47% men

Undergraduates 4,346 full-time, 26,484 part-time. 8% are from out of state; 10% Black or African American, non-Hispanic/Latino; 46% Hispanic/Latino; 7% Asian, non-Hispanic/Latino; 0.2% Native Hawaiian or other Pacific Islander, non-Hispanic/Latino; 0.1% American Indian or Alaska Native, non-Hispanic/Latino; 4% Two or more races, non-Hispanic/Latino; 0.8% Race/ethnicity unknown; 11% international; 96% transferred in.
Freshmen *Admission:* 4,018 enrolled.
Majors Accounting; accounting technology and bookkeeping; administrative assistant and secretarial science; advertising; animation, interactive technology, video graphics and special effects; anthropology; apparel and textile marketing management; art; biological and physical sciences; business administration and management; child-care provision; child development; cinematography and film/video production; clinical/medical laboratory technology; commercial photography; computer programming; computer

science; cosmetology; dance; data entry/microcomputer applications; data modeling/warehousing and database administration; digital communication and media/multimedia; dramatic/theater arts; economics; energy management and systems technology; environmental science; environmental studies; ethnic studies; fashion/apparel design; film/cinema/video studies; geography; graphic design; hazardous materials management and waste technology; health and physical education/fitness; history; humanities; insurance; interior design; international relations and affairs; journalism; kinesiology and exercise science; legal administrative assistant/secretary; liberal arts and sciences/liberal studies; linguistics; logistics, materials, and supply chain management; mathematics; medical administrative assistant and medical secretary; medical/clinical assistant; music; office management; photographic and film/video technology; political science and government; radio and television; registered nursing/registered nurse; respiratory care therapy; rhetoric and composition; sales, distribution, and marketing operations; selling skills and sales; Spanish; special education–early childhood; speech communication and rhetoric; sport and fitness administration/management; theater design and technology; visual and performing arts; women's studies.

Academics *Calendar:* semester plus optional winter and summer terms. *Degree:* certificates and associate. *Special study options:* academic remediation for entering students, adult/continuing education programs, advanced placement credit, cooperative education, distance learning, English as a second language, honors programs, independent study, internships, part-time degree program, services for LD students, study abroad, summer session for credit. *ROTC:* Army (c).

Library Santa Monica College Library.

Student Life *Housing:* college housing not available. *Activities and Organizations:* drama/theater group, student-run newspaper, choral group. *Campus security:* 24-hour emergency response devices and patrols, student patrols, late-night transport/escort service. *Student services:* health clinic, personal/psychological counseling, women's center, legal services.

Athletics Member NJCAA. *Intercollegiate sports:* basketball M/W, cheerleading M/W, cross-country running M/W, football M, soccer M/W, swimming and diving M/W, tennis W, track and field M/W, volleyball M/W, water polo M/W.

Financial Aid Of all full-time matriculated undergraduates who enrolled in 2015, 450 Federal Work-Study jobs (averaging $3000).

Applying *Options:* early admission. *Required:* high school transcript. *Application deadlines:* 8/30 (freshmen), 8/30 (transfers). *Notification:* continuous until 8/30 (freshmen), continuous until 8/30 (transfers).

Freshman Application Contact Santa Monica College, 1900 Pico Boulevard, Santa Monica, CA 90405-1628. *Phone:* 310-434-4774.

Website: http://www.smc.edu/.

Santa Rosa Junior College
Santa Rosa, California

- **District-supported** 2-year, founded 1918, part of California Community College System
- **Urban** 100-acre campus with easy access to San Francisco
- **Endowment** $41.3 million
- **Coed,** 26,800 undergraduate students, 25% full-time, 45% women, 37% men

Undergraduates 6,830 full-time, 15,178 part-time. Students come from 36 other countries; 3% are from out of state; 2% Black or African American, non-Hispanic/Latino; 34% Hispanic/Latino; 5% Asian, non-Hispanic/Latino; 0.3% Native Hawaiian or other Pacific Islander, non-Hispanic/Latino; 0.7% American Indian or Alaska Native, non-Hispanic/Latino; 4% Two or more races, non-Hispanic/Latino; 7% Race/ethnicity unknown.

Freshmen *Admission:* 5,889 applied, 5,889 admitted.

Faculty *Total:* 1,323, 20% full-time, 13% with terminal degrees. *Student/faculty ratio:* 22:1.

Majors Agricultural business and management; agricultural communication/journalism; agroecology and sustainable agriculture; American Sign Language (ASL); animal sciences; anthropology; art; art history, criticism and conservation; automobile/automotive mechanics technology; behavioral sciences; biology/biological sciences; business administration and management; chemistry; child development; civil engineering technology; communication; community health services counseling; computer science; criminal justice/law enforcement administration; culinary arts; dance; dental hygiene; diesel mechanics technology; dietetic technology; digital communication and media/multimedia; dramatic/theater arts; early childhood education; economics; electrical, electronic and communications engineering technology; emergency medical technology (EMT paramedic); engineering; English; environmental studies; fashion/apparel design; fashion merchandising; fire science/firefighting; floriculture/floristry management; French; graphic design; health and physical education/fitness; history; horse husbandry/equine science and management; humanities; human resources management; human services; interior design; jazz/jazz studies; kinesiology and exercise science;

landscaping and groundskeeping; Latin American studies; legal assistant/paralegal; liberal arts and sciences/liberal studies; licensed practical/vocational nurse training; mathematics; medical/clinical assistant; music related; natural resources/conservation; natural sciences; nutrition sciences; parks, recreation and leisure facilities management; pharmacy technician; philosophy; physics; political science and government; psychology; radiologic technology/science; real estate; registered nursing/registered nurse; religious studies; restaurant/food services management; social sciences; sociology; Spanish; surveying technology; viticulture and enology; women's studies.

Academics *Calendar:* semesters. *Degree:* certificates and associate. *Special study options:* academic remediation for entering students, adult/continuing education programs, advanced placement credit, cooperative education, distance learning, English as a second language, independent study, internships, off-campus study, part-time degree program, services for LD students, study abroad, summer session for credit.

Library Doyle Library plus 1 other. Students can reserve study rooms.

Student Life *Housing:* college housing not available. *Activities and Organizations:* drama/theater group, student-run newspaper, choral group, AG Ambassadors, MECHA, Alpha Gamma Sigma, Phi Theta Kappa, Puente. *Campus security:* 24-hour emergency response devices and patrols, student patrols. *Student services:* health clinic, personal/psychological counseling.

Athletics Member NJCAA. *Intercollegiate sports:* baseball M, basketball M/W, cross-country running M/W, football M, golf M, ice hockey M(c), rugby M(c), soccer M/W, softball W, swimming and diving M/W, tennis M/W, track and field M/W, volleyball W, water polo M/W, wrestling M.

Costs (2017–18) *One-time required fee:* $40. *Tuition:* state resident $1280 full-time, $46 per unit part-time; nonresident $7328 full-time, $270 per unit part-time. Full-time tuition and fees vary according to course load. Part-time tuition and fees vary according to course load. *Payment plans:* installment, deferred payment.

Financial Aid Of all full-time matriculated undergraduates who enrolled in 2009, 135 Federal Work-Study jobs (averaging $2210). 43 state and other part-time jobs (averaging $7396).

Applying *Options:* electronic application, early admission. *Application deadlines:* rolling (freshmen), rolling (transfers). *Notification:* continuous (freshmen), continuous (transfers).

Freshman Application Contact Ms. Freyja Pereira, Dean, Admissions, Records and Enrollment Services, Santa Rosa Junior College, 1501 Mendocino Avenue, Santa Rosa, CA 95401. *Phone:* 707-527-4512. *Fax:* 707-527-4798. *E-mail:* fpereira@santarosa.edu.

Website: http://www.santarosa.edu/.

Santiago Canyon College
Orange, California

Freshman Application Contact Tuyen Nguyen, Admissions and Records, Santiago Canyon College, 8045 East Chapman Avenue, Orange, CA 92869. *Phone:* 714-628-4902. *Website:* http://www.sccollege.edu/.

Shasta College
Redding, California

Director of Admissions Dr. Kevin O'Rorke, Dean of Enrollment Services, Shasta College, PO Box 496006, 11555 Old Oregon Trail, Redding, CA 96049-6006. *Phone:* 530-242-7669. *Website:* http://www.shastacollege.edu/.

Sierra College
Rocklin, California

- **District-supported** 2-year, founded 1936, part of California Community College System
- **Suburban** 327-acre campus with easy access to Sacramento
- **Coed,** 18,758 undergraduate students, 26% full-time, 56% women, 44% men

Undergraduates 4,874 full-time, 13,884 part-time. Students come from 27 states and territories; 10 other countries; 0.7% are from out of state; 3% Black or African American, non-Hispanic/Latino; 17% Hispanic/Latino; 5% Asian, non-Hispanic/Latino; 2% Native Hawaiian or other Pacific Islander, non-Hispanic/Latino; 0.7% American Indian or Alaska Native, non-Hispanic/Latino; 6% Two or more races, non-Hispanic/Latino; 2% Race/ethnicity unknown; 0.9% international; 18% transferred in; 1% live on campus. *Retention:* 68% of full-time freshmen returned.

Freshmen *Admission:* 24,000 applied, 24,000 admitted, 4,444 enrolled.

Faculty *Total:* 870, 18% full-time. *Student/faculty ratio:* 25:1.

Majors Accounting; administrative assistant and secretarial science; agriculture; American Sign Language (ASL); animal/livestock husbandry and production; apparel and textile manufacturing; apparel and textile marketing management; applied horticulture/horticulture operations; architectural drafting and CAD/CADD; art; automobile/automotive mechanics technology; biological and physical sciences; biology/biological sciences; business administration and management; business/commerce; cabinetmaking and millwork; chemistry; child development; commercial photography; computer and information sciences and support services related; computer installation and repair technology; computer programming; computer systems networking and telecommunications; construction trades; corrections; criminal justice/police science; data entry/microcomputer applications; digital communication and media/multimedia; electrical/electronics equipment installation and repair; engineering; English; equestrian studies; fire science/firefighting; forestry; general studies; geology/earth science; graphic design; hazardous materials management and waste technology; health and physical education/fitness; industrial electronics technology; information technology; liberal arts and sciences/liberal studies; licensed practical/vocational nurse training; manufacturing engineering technology; mathematics; mechanical drafting and CAD/CADD; music; network and system administration; parks, recreation and leisure; philosophy; physics; psychology; real estate; registered nursing/registered nurse; rhetoric and composition; sales, distribution, and marketing operations; small business administration; social sciences; visual and performing arts; web page, digital/multimedia and information resources design; women's studies.

Academics *Calendar:* semesters. *Degree:* certificates and associate. *Special study options:* academic remediation for entering students, accelerated degree program, advanced placement credit, distance learning, double majors, English as a second language, honors programs, independent study, internships, off-campus study, part-time degree program, services for LD students, study abroad, summer session for credit.

Library Leary Resource Center plus 1 other.

Student Life *Housing Options:* coed. Campus housing is university owned. *Activities and Organizations:* drama/theater group, student-run newspaper, choral group, Drama Club, Student Government, Art Club, Band, Aggie Club. *Campus security:* 24-hour emergency response devices and patrols, late-night transport/escort service. *Student services:* health clinic, personal/psychological counseling.

Athletics *Intercollegiate sports:* baseball M, basketball M/W, football M, golf M/W, soccer W, softball W, swimming and diving M/W, tennis M/W, volleyball W, water polo M/W, wrestling M. *Intramural sports:* archery M/W, badminton M/W, basketball M/W, tennis M/W, volleyball M/W.

Costs (2016–17) *Tuition:* state resident $1380 full-time, $46 per credit hour part-time; nonresident $5790 full-time, $193 per credit hour part-time. Full-time tuition and fees vary according to course load. Part-time tuition and fees vary according to course load. *Required fees:* $46 full-time, $19 per term part-time. *Room and board:* $3700. *Payment plan:* installment.

Financial Aid Of all full-time matriculated undergraduates who enrolled in 2016, 5,508 applied for aid, 5,492 were judged to have need, 4 had their need fully met. In 2016, 76 non-need-based awards were made. *Average percent of need met:* 27%. *Average financial aid package:* $1962. *Average need-based gift aid:* $4384. *Average non-need-based aid:* $1022.

Applying *Options:* electronic application, early admission. *Application deadline:* rolling (freshmen). *Notification:* continuous (freshmen), continuous (transfers).

Freshman Application Contact Sierra College, 5000 Rocklin Road, Rocklin, CA 95677-3397. *Phone:* 916-660-7341. *Website:* http://www.sierracollege.edu/.

Skyline College
San Bruno, California

Freshman Application Contact Terry Stats, Admissions Office, Skyline College, 3300 College Drive, San Bruno, CA 94066-1698. *Phone:* 650-738-4251. *E-mail:* stats@smccd.net. *Website:* http://skylinecollege.edu/.

Solano Community College
Fairfield, California

Freshman Application Contact Solano Community College, 4000 Suisun Valley Road, Fairfield, CA 94534. *Phone:* 707-864-7000 Ext. 4313. *Website:* http://www.solano.edu/.

South Coast College
Orange, California

Director of Admissions South Coast College, 2011 West Chapman Avenue, Orange, CA 92868. *Toll-free phone:* 877-568-6130. *Website:* http://www.southcoastcollege.com/.

Southwestern College
Chula Vista, California

Freshman Application Contact Director of Admissions and Records, Southwestern College, 900 Otay Lakes Road, Chula Vista, CA 91910-7299. *Phone:* 619-421-6700 Ext. 5215. *Fax:* 619-482-6489. *Website:* http://www.swccd.edu/.

Spartan College of Aeronautics and Technology
Inglewood, California

Freshman Application Contact Admissions Office, Spartan College of Aeronautics and Technology, 8911 Aviation Boulevard, Inglewood, CA 90301. *Phone:* 866-451-0818. *Toll-free phone:* 800-879-0554. *Website:* http://www.spartan.edu/.

Taft College
Taft, California

Freshman Application Contact Nichole Cook, Admissions/Counseling Technician, Taft College, 29 Cougar Court, Taft, CA 93268. *Phone:* 661-763-7790. *Fax:* 661-763-7758. *E-mail:* ncook@taftcollege.edu. *Website:* http://www.taftcollege.edu/.

Unitek College
Fremont, California

Admissions Office Contact Unitek College, 4670 Auto Mall Parkway, Fremont, CA 94538. *Website:* http://www.unitekcollege.edu/.

Valley College of Medical Careers
West Hills, California

Admissions Office Contact Valley College of Medical Careers, 8399 Topanga Canyon Boulevard, Suite 200, West Hills, CA 91304. *Website:* http://www.vcmc.edu/.

Ventura College
Ventura, California

Freshman Application Contact Ms. Susan Bricker, Registrar, Ventura College, 4667 Telegraph Road, Ventura, CA 93003-3899. *Phone:* 805-654-6456. *Fax:* 805-654-6357. *E-mail:* sbricker@vcccd.net. *Website:* http://www.venturacollege.edu/.

Victor Valley College
Victorville, California

- **District-supported** 2-year, founded 1961, part of California Community College System
- **Small-town** 253-acre campus with easy access to Los Angeles
- **Coed**

Undergraduates 3% are from out of state. *Retention:* 61% of full-time freshmen returned.

Faculty *Student/faculty ratio:* 26:1.

Academics *Calendar:* semesters. *Degree:* certificates, diplomas, and associate. *Special study options:* academic remediation for entering students, accelerated degree program, advanced placement credit, cooperative education, distance learning, double majors, English as a second language, honors programs, independent study, internships, off-campus study, part-time degree program, services for LD students, study abroad, summer session for credit.

Library Learning Resource Center.

Student Life *Campus security:* 24-hour emergency response devices and patrols, late-night transport/escort service, part-time trained security personnel.

Athletics Member NCAA, NJCAA.

Financial Aid *Average need-based loan:* $6168. *Average need-based gift aid:* $3707.

Freshman Application Contact Ms. Greta Moon, Director of Admissions and Records (Interim), Victor Valley College, 18422 Bear Valley Road, Victorville, CA 92395. *Phone:* 760-245-4271. *Fax:* 760-843-7707. *E-mail:* moong@vvc.edu. *Website:* http://www.vvc.edu/.

West Coast Ultrasound Institute
Beverly Hills, California

Admissions Office Contact West Coast Ultrasound Institute, 291 S. La Cienega Boulevard, Suite 500, Beverly Hills, CA 90211. *Website:* http://wcui.edu/.

West Hills Community College
Coalinga, California

Freshman Application Contact Sandra Dagnino, West Hills Community College, 300 Cherry Lane, Coalinga, CA 93210-1399. *Phone:* 559-934-3203. *Toll-free phone:* 800-266-1114. *Fax:* 559-934-2830. *E-mail:* sandradagnino@ westhillscollege.com. *Website:* http://www.westhillscollege.com/.

West Hills Community College–Lemoore
Lemoore, California

Admissions Office Contact West Hills Community College–Lemoore, 555 College Avenue, Lemoore, CA 93245.
Website: http://www.westhillscollege.com/.

West Los Angeles College
Culver City, California

Director of Admissions Mr. Len Isaksen, Director of Admissions, West Los Angeles College, 9000 Overland Avenue, Culver City, CA 90230-3519. *Phone:* 310-287-4255. *Website:* http://www.lacolleges.net/.

West Valley College
Saratoga, California

Freshman Application Contact Ms. Barbara Ogilvie, Supervisor, Admissions and Records, West Valley College, 14000 Fruitvale Avenue, Saratoga, CA 95070-5698. *Phone:* 408-741-4630. *E-mail:* barbara_ogilvie@ westvalley.edu. *Website:* http://www.westvalley.edu/.

Woodland Community College
Woodland, California

Admissions Office Contact Woodland Community College, 2300 East Gibson Road, Woodland, CA 95776.
Website: http://www.yccd.edu/woodland/.

Yuba College
Marysville, California

Director of Admissions Dr. David Farrell, Dean of Student Development, Yuba College, 2088 North Beale Road, Marysville, CA 95901-7699. *Phone:* 530-741-6705. *Website:* http://www.yccd.edu/.

COLORADO

Aims Community College
Greeley, Colorado

Freshman Application Contact Ms. Susie Gallardo, Admissions Technician, Aims Community College, Box 69, 5401 West 20th Street, Greeley, CO 80632-0069. *Phone:* 970-330-8008 Ext. 6624.
E-mail: wgreen@chiron.aims.edu. *Website:* http://www.aims.edu/.

Arapahoe Community College
Littleton, Colorado

- **State-supported** 2-year, founded 1965, part of Colorado Community College and Occupational Education System
- **Suburban** 52-acre campus with easy access to Denver
- **Coed,** 9,383 undergraduate students, 18% full-time, 58% women, 42% men

Undergraduates 1,733 full-time, 7,650 part-time. 2% are from out of state; 3% Black or African American, non-Hispanic/Latino; 15% Hispanic/Latino; 4% Asian, non-Hispanic/Latino; 0.3% Native Hawaiian or other Pacific Islander, non-Hispanic/Latino; 0.7% American Indian or Alaska Native, non-Hispanic/Latino; 4% Two or more races, non-Hispanic/Latino; 6% Race/ethnicity unknown; 1% international. *Retention:* 47% of full-time freshmen returned.

Freshmen *Admission:* 1,792 applied, 1,792 admitted, 1,000 enrolled.
Faculty *Total:* 466, 22% full-time. *Student/faculty ratio:* 19:1.
Majors Accounting technology and bookkeeping; architectural engineering technology; automobile/automotive mechanics technology; building/construction site management; business administration and management; clinical/medical laboratory technology; computer and information sciences; computer systems networking and telecommunications; criminal justice/law enforcement administration; emergency medical technology (EMT paramedic); engineering technology; funeral service and mortuary science; game and interactive media design; general studies; graphic design; health and physical education/fitness; health information/medical records technology; interior design; journalism; legal assistant/paralegal; liberal arts and sciences and humanities related; liberal arts and sciences/liberal studies; music technology; physical therapy technology; registered nursing/registered nurse; retailing; science technologies related; telecommunications technology.
Academics *Calendar:* semesters. *Degree:* certificates, diplomas, and associate. *Special study options:* academic remediation for entering students, accelerated degree program, adult/continuing education programs, advanced placement credit, cooperative education, distance learning, double majors, English as a second language, external degree program, independent study, internships, off-campus study, part-time degree program, services for LD students, study abroad, summer session for credit. *ROTC:* Army (c), Air Force (c).
Library Weber Center for Learning Resources plus 1 other.
Student Life *Housing:* college housing not available. *Activities and Organizations:* drama/theater group, student-run newspaper, choral group, Student Veteran Association, Phi Theta Kappa, History Club, Jewelry Club, ASID (American Society of Interior Designers). *Campus security:* 24-hour emergency response devices and patrols, late-night transport/escort service. *Student services:* personal/psychological counseling.
Costs (2016–17) *Tuition:* state resident $4107 full-time, $137 per credit hour part-time; nonresident $16,850 full-time, $562 per credit hour part-time. Full-time tuition and fees vary according to program. Part-time tuition and fees vary according to program. *Required fees:* $243 full-time. *Payment plan:* installment. *Waivers:* employees or children of employees.
Applying *Options:* electronic application, early admission, deferred entrance. *Application deadlines:* rolling (freshmen), rolling (out-of-state freshmen), rolling (transfers). *Notification:* continuous (freshmen), continuous (out-of-state freshmen), continuous (transfers).
Freshman Application Contact Arapahoe Community College, 5900 South Santa Fe Drive, PO Box 9002, Littleton, CO 80160-9002.
Phone: 303-797-5623.
Website: http://www.arapahoe.edu/.

Bel–Rea Institute of Animal Technology
Denver, Colorado

- **Proprietary** 2-year, founded 1971
- **Suburban** 6-acre campus with easy access to Denver
- **Coed,** 400 undergraduate students

Undergraduates Students come from 20 states and territories; 40% are from out of state.
Freshmen *Admission:* 414 applied.
Majors Veterinary/animal health technology.
Academics *Calendar:* quarters. *Degree:* associate. *Special study options:* academic remediation for entering students, internships, off-campus study, part-time degree program, services for LD students, summer session for credit.
Library Bel-Rea Institute Library. Weekly public service hours: 38.
Student Life *Housing:* college housing not available.
Applying *Options:* electronic application, early admission, deferred entrance. *Required:* essay or personal statement, high school transcript, minimum 2.5 GPA, interview. *Application deadlines:* rolling (freshmen), rolling (transfers).
Freshman Application Contact Bel–Rea Institute of Animal Technology, 1681 South Dayton Street, Denver, CO 80247. *Phone:* 303-751-8700. *Toll-free phone:* 800-950-8001.
Website: http://www.belrea.edu/.

CollegeAmerica–Colorado Springs
Colorado Springs, Colorado

Freshman Application Contact CollegeAmerica–Colorado Springs, 2020 North Academy Boulevard, Colorado Springs, CO 80909. *Phone:* 719-637-0600. *Toll-free phone:* 800-622-2894.
Website: http://www.collegeamerica.edu/.

CollegeAmerica–Denver
Denver, Colorado
- **Independent** primarily 2-year, founded 1962
- **Urban** campus
- **Coed**

Faculty *Student/faculty ratio:* 15:1.
Academics *Calendar:* continuous. *Degrees:* associate and bachelor's. *Special study options:* academic remediation for entering students, accelerated degree program, cooperative education.
Freshman Application Contact Admissions Office, CollegeAmerica–Denver, 1385 South Colorado Boulevard, Denver, CO 80222. *Phone:* 303-300-8740 Ext. 7020. *Toll-free phone:* 800-622-2894.
Website: http://www.collegeamerica.edu/.

CollegeAmerica–Fort Collins
Fort Collins, Colorado
- **Independent** primarily 2-year, founded 1962
- **Suburban** campus
- **Coed**, 120 undergraduate students

Majors Accounting; allied health and medical assisting services related; business administration and management; computer science; health/health-care administration.
Academics *Calendar:* continuous. *Degrees:* associate and bachelor's. *Special study options:* cooperative education, distance learning, honors programs, independent study, internships.
Student Life *Housing:* college housing not available.
Applying *Required:* essay or personal statement, high school transcript, interview. *Recommended:* minimum 2.0 GPA. *Notification:* continuous (freshmen), continuous (transfers).
Freshman Application Contact CollegeAmerica–Fort Collins, 4601 South Mason Street, Fort Collins, CO 80525. *Phone:* 970-223-6060 Ext. 8002. *Toll-free phone:* 800-622-2894.
Website: http://www.collegeamerica.edu/.

Colorado Academy of Veterinary Technology
Colorado Springs, Colorado
Admissions Office Contact Colorado Academy of Veterinary Technology, 2766 Janitell Road, Colorado Springs, CO 80906.
Website: http://www.coloradovettech.com/.

Colorado Northwestern Community College
Rangely, Colorado
- **State-supported** 2-year, founded 1962, part of Colorado Community College and Occupational Education System
- **Rural** 150-acre campus
- **Coed**, 1,178 undergraduate students, 46% full-time, 59% women, 41% men

Undergraduates 538 full-time, 640 part-time. 18% are from out of state; 1% Black or African American, non-Hispanic/Latino; 6% Hispanic/Latino; 1% American Indian or Alaska Native, non-Hispanic/Latino; 7% Two or more races, non-Hispanic/Latino; 7% Race/ethnicity unknown; 1% international; 10% transferred in; 24% live on campus. *Retention:* 49% of full-time freshmen returned.
Freshmen *Admission:* 601 applied, 601 admitted, 177 enrolled.
Faculty *Total:* 100, 47% full-time. *Student/faculty ratio:* 12:1.
Majors Accounting; aircraft powerplant technology; airline pilot and flight crew; automobile/automotive mechanics technology; business/commerce; cosmetology; dental hygiene; early childhood education; emergency medical technology (EMT paramedic); equestrian studies; general studies; liberal arts and sciences/liberal studies; registered nursing/registered nurse; small business administration.
Academics *Calendar:* semesters. *Degree:* certificates and associate. *Special study options:* academic remediation for entering students, adult/continuing education programs, advanced placement credit, distance learning, double majors, independent study, internships, part-time degree program, services for LD students, student-designed majors, summer session for credit.
Library Colorado Northwestern Community College Library–Rangely plus 1 other. *Books:* 22,558 (physical), 8,100 (digital/electronic); *Serial titles:* 10,875 (physical); *Databases:* 42. Students can reserve study rooms.
Student Life *Housing:* on-campus residence required for freshman year. *Options:* coed. Campus housing is university owned. Freshman applicants given priority for college housing. *Activities and Organizations:* student-run newspaper. *Campus security:* student patrols, late-night transport/escort service, controlled dormitory access. *Student services:* health clinic, personal/psychological counseling.
Athletics Member NJCAA. *Intercollegiate sports:* baseball M(s), basketball M(s)/W(s), softball W(s), volleyball W(s). *Intramural sports:* basketball M/W, racquetball M/W, rock climbing M/W, skiing (cross-country) M/W, skiing (downhill) M/W, softball M/W, table tennis M/W, volleyball M/W.
Costs (2016–17) *Tuition:* state resident $4481 full-time, $137 per credit hour part-time; nonresident $6999 full-time, $234 per credit hour part-time. Full-time tuition and fees vary according to course load, location, and program. Part-time tuition and fees vary according to course load, location, and program. *Required fees:* $295 full-time, $9 per credit hour part-time, $13 per term part-time. *Room and board:* $6654; room only: $2356. Room and board charges vary according to board plan, housing facility, and location. *Payment plan:* installment. *Waivers:* employees or children of employees.
Applying *Options:* electronic application, early admission, deferred entrance. *Required:* high school transcript. *Required for some:* essay or personal statement, 3 letters of recommendation, interview. *Application deadlines:* rolling (freshmen), rolling (transfers). *Notification:* continuous (freshmen), continuous (transfers).
Freshman Application Contact Colorado Northwestern Community College, 500 Kennedy Drive, Rangely, CO 81648-3598. *Phone:* 970-824-1129.
Toll-free phone: 800-562-1105.
Website: http://www.cncc.edu/.

Colorado School of Healing Arts
Lakewood, Colorado
Freshman Application Contact Colorado School of Healing Arts, 7655 West Mississippi Avenue, Suite 100, Lakewood, CO 80220. *Phone:* 303-986-2320. *Toll-free phone:* 800-233-7114. *Fax:* 303-980-6594.
Website: http://www.csha.net/.

Colorado School of Trades
Lakewood, Colorado
Freshman Application Contact Colorado School of Trades, 1575 Hoyt Street, Lakewood, CO 80215-2996. *Phone:* 303-233-4697 Ext. 44. *Toll-free phone:* 800-234-4594. *Website:* http://www.schooloftrades.edu/.

Community College of Aurora
Aurora, Colorado
- **State-supported** 2-year, founded 1983, part of Colorado Community College System
- **Suburban** campus with easy access to Denver
- **Coed**, 7,386 undergraduate students, 20% full-time, 59% women, 41% men

Undergraduates 1,465 full-time, 5,914 part-time. 21% Black or African American, non-Hispanic/Latino; 28% Hispanic/Latino; 8% Asian, non-Hispanic/Latino; 2% American Indian or Alaska Native, non-Hispanic/Latino; 6% Race/ethnicity unknown; 3% international.
Freshmen *Admission:* 727 enrolled.
Faculty *Student/faculty ratio:* 20:1.
Majors Accounting technology and bookkeeping; child development; cinematography and film/video production; criminal justice/law enforcement administration; emergency medical technology (EMT paramedic); fire science/firefighting; general studies; heavy equipment maintenance technology; liberal arts and sciences and humanities related; liberal arts and sciences/liberal studies; management information systems; office management; science technologies related.
Academics *Calendar:* semesters. *Degree:* certificates and associate. *Special study options:* academic remediation for entering students, adult/continuing education programs, cooperative education, distance learning, English as a second language, external degree program, independent study, internships, off-campus study, part-time degree program, services for LD students, summer session for credit.
Library Community College of Aurora Learning Resource Center. *Books:* 2,885 (physical), 151,126 (digital/electronic); *Serial titles:* 11,719 (digital/electronic); *Databases:* 29. Weekly public service hours: 63.
Student Life *Housing:* college housing not available. *Activities and Organizations:* drama/theater group. *Campus security:* late-night transport/escort service. *Student services:* women's center.
Costs (2016–17) *Tuition:* state resident $3286 full-time, $199 per credit hour part-time; nonresident $13,480 full-time, $562 per credit hour part-time. Full-time tuition and fees vary according to course load, location, program, and reciprocity agreements. Part-time tuition and fees vary according to course load, location, program, and reciprocity agreements. *Required fees:* $416 full-

time, $12 per credit hour part-time, $57 per term part-time. *Payment plan:* installment. *Waivers:* employees or children of employees.
Applying *Required for some:* high school transcript.
Freshman Application Contact Community College of Aurora, 16000 East CentreTech Parkway, Aurora, CO 80011-9036. *Phone:* 303-360-4701. *Website:* http://www.ccaurora.edu/.

Community College of Denver
Denver, Colorado

Freshman Application Contact Mr. Michael Rusk, Dean of Students, Community College of Denver, PO Box 173363, Campus Box 201, Denver, CO 80127-3363. *Phone:* 303-556-6325. *Fax:* 303-556-2431. *E-mail:* enrollment_services@ccd.edu. *Website:* http://www.ccd.edu/.

Concorde Career College
Aurora, Colorado

Admissions Office Contact Concorde Career College, 111 North Havana Street, Aurora, CO 80010. *Website:* http://www.concorde.edu/.

Ecotech Institute
Aurora, Colorado

Admissions Office Contact Ecotech Institute, 1400 South Abilene Street, Aurora, CO 80012. *Website:* http://www.ecotechinstitute.com/.

Everest College
Colorado Springs, Colorado

Director of Admissions Director of Admissions, Everest College, 1815 Jet Wing Drive, Colorado Springs, CO 80916. *Phone:* 719-630-6580. *Toll-free phone:* 888-741-4270. *Fax:* 719-638-6818. *Website:* http://www.everest.edu/.

Everest College
Thornton, Colorado

Freshman Application Contact Admissions Office, Everest College, 9065 Grant Street, Thornton, CO 80229. *Phone:* 303-457-2757. *Toll-free phone:* 888-741-4270. *Fax:* 303-457-4030. *Website:* http://www.everest.edu/.

Front Range Community College
Westminster, Colorado

- **State-supported** 2-year, founded 1968, part of Community Colleges of Colorado System
- **Suburban** 90-acre campus with easy access to Denver
- **Endowment** $457,964
- **Coed,** 18,747 undergraduate students, 29% full-time, 57% women, 43% men

Undergraduates 5,514 full-time, 13,233 part-time. Students come from 49 states and territories; 87 other countries; 3% are from out of state; 2% Black or African American, non-Hispanic/Latino; 15% Hispanic/Latino; 4% Asian, non-Hispanic/Latino; 0.2% Native Hawaiian or other Pacific Islander, non-Hispanic/Latino; 0.8% American Indian or Alaska Native, non-Hispanic/Latino; 4% Two or more races, non-Hispanic/Latino; 4% Race/ethnicity unknown; 2% international; 12% transferred in. *Retention:* 56% of full-time freshmen returned.
Freshmen *Admission:* 6,061 applied, 6,061 admitted, 2,391 enrolled.
Faculty *Total:* 1,117, 22% full-time. *Student/faculty ratio:* 20:1.
Majors Accounting technology and bookkeeping; animation, interactive technology, video graphics and special effects; applied horticulture/horticulture operations; architectural engineering technology; automobile/automotive mechanics technology; business administration and management; CAD/CADD drafting/design technology; computer and information sciences; computer systems networking and telecommunications; early childhood education; energy management and systems technology; general studies; geographic information science and cartography; health information/medical records technology; heating, ventilation, air conditioning and refrigeration engineering technology; holistic health; hospitality administration; interior design; legal assistant/paralegal; liberal arts and sciences and humanities related; liberal arts and sciences/liberal studies; medical office assistant; recording arts technology; registered nursing/registered nurse; science technologies related; sign language interpretation and translation; surgical technology; veterinary/animal health technology; welding technology; wildlife, fish and wildlands science and management.

Academics *Calendar:* semesters. *Degree:* certificates and associate. *Special study options:* academic remediation for entering students, advanced placement credit, cooperative education, distance learning, double majors, English as a second language, freshman honors college, honors programs, independent study, internships, off-campus study, part-time degree program, services for LD students, student-designed majors, study abroad, summer session for credit. *ROTC:* Army (c), Air Force (c).
Library College Hill Library plus 2 others. *Books:* 57,957 (physical), 12,255 (digital/electronic); *Databases:* 33. Students can reserve study rooms.
Student Life *Housing:* college housing not available. *Activities and Organizations:* drama/theater group, student-run newspaper, Student Government Association, Student Colorado Registry of Interpreters for the Deaf, Students in Free Enterprise (SIFE), Gay-Straight Alliance, Recycling Club. *Campus security:* 24-hour emergency response devices and patrols, late-night transport/escort service. *Student services:* personal/psychological counseling.
Costs (2017–18) *Tuition:* state resident $3132 full-time; nonresident $12,849 full-time. Full-time tuition and fees vary according to program. Part-time tuition and fees vary according to program. *Required fees:* $395 full-time. *Payment plan:* installment. *Waivers:* employees or children of employees.
Applying *Options:* electronic application, early admission, deferred entrance.
Freshman Application Contact Ms. Miori Gidley, Registrar, Front Range Community College, Westminster, CO 80031. *Phone:* 303-404-5000. *Fax:* 303-439-2614. *E-mail:* miori.gidley@frontrange.edu. *Website:* http://www.frontrange.edu/.

IBMC College
Colorado Springs, Colorado

Director of Admissions Michelle Squibb, Admissions Representative, IBMC College, 6805 Corporate Drive, Suite 100, Colorado Springs, CO 80919. *Phone:* 719-596-7400. *Toll-free phone:* 800-748-2282. *Website:* http://www.ibmc.edu/.

IBMC College
Fort Collins, Colorado

- **Proprietary** 2-year, founded 1987
- **Suburban** campus with easy access to Denver
- **Coed,** 1,020 undergraduate students, 100% full-time, 85% women, 15% men
- **92%** of applicants were admitted

Undergraduates 1,020 full-time. 3% are from out of state; 1% Black or African American, non-Hispanic/Latino; 20% Hispanic/Latino; 0.5% Asian, non-Hispanic/Latino; 0.2% Native Hawaiian or other Pacific Islander, non-Hispanic/Latino; 0.6% American Indian or Alaska Native, non-Hispanic/Latino; 1% Two or more races, non-Hispanic/Latino. *Retention:* 69% of full-time freshmen returned.
Freshmen *Admission:* 1,064 applied, 977 admitted, 355 enrolled.
Faculty *Total:* 115, 40% full-time, 3% with terminal degrees. *Student/faculty ratio:* 8:1.
Majors Accounting technology and bookkeeping; business administration and management; dental assisting; legal assistant/paralegal; medical administrative assistant and medical secretary; medical/clinical assistant; office occupations and clerical services.
Academics *Calendar:* continuous. *Degree:* certificates, diplomas, and associate. *Special study options:* accelerated degree program, adult/continuing education programs, cooperative education, honors programs, internships, summer session for credit.
Library IBMC College plus 8 others. *Books:* 834 (physical), 124,000 (digital/electronic).
Student Life *Housing:* college housing not available. *Activities and Organizations:* Alpha Beta Kappa, Circle of Hope, Relay for Life, Peer Mentoring, Peer Tutor.
Costs (2017–18) *One-time required fee:* $50. *Tuition:* $12,600 full-time. Full-time tuition and fees vary according to course load and program. Part-time tuition and fees vary according to course load and program. No tuition increase for student's term of enrollment. *Payment plans:* tuition prepayment, installment. *Waivers:* children of alumni and employees or children of employees.
Financial Aid Of all full-time matriculated undergraduates who enrolled in 2015, 1,085 applied for aid, 944 were judged to have need, 701 had their need fully met. *Average percent of need met:* 72%. *Average financial aid package:* $7500. *Average need-based loan:* $4270. *Average need-based gift aid:* $3222. *Average indebtedness upon graduation:* $12,405.
Applying *Options:* electronic application. *Application fee:* $50. *Required:* high school transcript, interview. *Application deadline:* rolling (freshmen).
Freshman Application Contact Mr. Jeremy Shoup, Admissions and Marketing Coordinator, IBMC College, 3842 South Mason Street, Fort

Collins, CO 80525. *Phone:* 970-223-2669. *Toll-free phone:* 800-495-2669. *E-mail:* jshoup@ibmc.edu. *Website:* http://www.ibmc.edu/.

IntelliTec College
Colorado Springs, Colorado

Director of Admissions Director of Admissions, IntelliTec College, 2315 East Pikes Peak Avenue, Colorado Springs, CO 80909. *Phone:* 719-632-7626. *Toll-free phone:* 800-748-2282. *Website:* http://www.intelliteccollege.edu/.

IntelliTec College
Grand Junction, Colorado

Freshman Application Contact Admissions, IntelliTec College, 772 Horizon Drive, Grand Junction, CO 81506. *Phone:* 970-245-8101. *Toll-free phone:* 800-748-2282. *Fax:* 970-243-8074. *Website:* http://www.intelliteccollege.edu/.

IntelliTec College
Pueblo, Colorado

Admissions Office Contact IntelliTec College, 3673 Parker Boulevard, Pueblo, CO 81008. *Toll-free phone:* 800-748-2282. *Website:* http://www.intelliteccollege.edu/.

Lamar Community College
Lamar, Colorado

- **State-supported** 2-year, founded 1937, part of Colorado Community College and Occupational Education System
- **Small-town** 125-acre campus
- **Coed,** 777 undergraduate students, 52% full-time, 52% women, 48% men

Undergraduates 406 full-time, 371 part-time. Students come from 31 states and territories; 11 other countries; 11% are from out of state; 8% Black or African American, non-Hispanic/Latino; 21% Hispanic/Latino; 0.2% Asian, non-Hispanic/Latino; 0.2% Native Hawaiian or other Pacific Islander, non-Hispanic/Latino; 1% American Indian or Alaska Native, non-Hispanic/Latino; 4% Two or more races, non-Hispanic/Latino; 0.4% Race/ethnicity unknown; 3% international; 8% transferred in; 20% live on campus. *Retention:* 59% of full-time freshmen returned.

Freshmen *Admission:* 423 applied, 423 admitted, 142 enrolled.

Faculty *Total:* 43, 35% full-time. *Student/faculty ratio:* 22:1.

Majors Agricultural business and management; animal training; business automation/technology/data entry; construction trades; cosmetology; energy management and systems technology; executive assistant/executive secretary; liberal arts and sciences/liberal studies; marketing/marketing management; registered nursing/registered nurse; science technologies related; system, networking, and LAN/WAN management.

Academics *Calendar:* semesters. *Degree:* certificates, diplomas, and associate. *Special study options:* academic remediation for entering students, adult/continuing education programs, advanced placement credit, cooperative education, distance learning, double majors, English as a second language, independent study, internships, part-time degree program, services for LD students, student-designed majors, summer session for credit.

Library Learning Resources Center. *Books:* 10,144 (physical).

Student Life *Housing:* on-campus residence required for freshman year. *Options:* coed. Campus housing is university owned. *Campus security:* 24-hour emergency response devices and patrols, student patrols, late-night transport/escort service, controlled dormitory access. *Student services:* health clinic, personal/psychological counseling.

Athletics Member NJCAA. *Intercollegiate sports:* baseball M(s), basketball M(s)/W(s), equestrian sports M(s)/W(s), golf M(s), soccer M(c), softball W(s), volleyball W(s).

Costs (2017–18) *Tuition:* state resident $3132 full-time, $131 per credit hour part-time; nonresident $5352 full-time, $223 per credit hour part-time. Full-time tuition and fees vary according to course load, program, and reciprocity agreements. Part-time tuition and fees vary according to course load, program, and reciprocity agreements. *Required fees:* $414 full-time. *Room and board:* $6070; room only: $1950. Room and board charges vary according to housing facility. *Payment plan:* installment. *Waivers:* employees or children of employees.

Applying *Options:* electronic application, early admission. *Application deadlines:* 9/16 (freshmen), 9/16 (transfers).

Freshman Application Contact Director of Admissions, Lamar Community College, 2401 South Main Street, Lamar, CO 81052-3999. *Phone:* 719-336-1592. *Toll-free phone:* 800-968-6920. *E-mail:* admissions@lamarcc.edu. *Website:* http://www.lamarcc.edu/.

Lincoln College of Technology
Denver, Colorado

Freshman Application Contact Lincoln College of Technology, 11194 East 45th Avenue, Denver, CO 80239. *Phone:* 800-347-3232 Ext. 43032. *Toll-free phone:* 844-215-1513. *Website:* http://www.lincolntech.edu/.

Morgan Community College
Fort Morgan, Colorado

- **State-supported** 2-year, founded 1967, part of Colorado Community College and Occupational Education System
- **Small-town** 20-acre campus with easy access to Denver
- **Endowment** $2.7 million
- **Coed,** 1,474 undergraduate students, 22% full-time, 66% women, 34% men

Undergraduates 327 full-time, 1,147 part-time. Students come from 8 states and territories; 1% are from out of state; 3% Black or African American, non-Hispanic/Latino; 23% Hispanic/Latino; 0.5% Asian, non-Hispanic/Latino; 0.1% Native Hawaiian or other Pacific Islander, non-Hispanic/Latino; 0.7% American Indian or Alaska Native, non-Hispanic/Latino; 1% Two or more races, non-Hispanic/Latino; 6% Race/ethnicity unknown; 2% international; 2% transferred in. *Retention:* 62% of full-time freshmen returned.

Freshmen *Admission:* 189 enrolled.

Faculty *Total:* 93, 33% full-time. *Student/faculty ratio:* 14:1.

Majors Agribusiness; agricultural business technology; agricultural/farm supplies retailing and wholesaling; airline pilot and flight crew; animation, interactive technology, video graphics and special effects; autobody/collision and repair technology; automobile/automotive mechanics technology; business administration and management; child-care provision; emergency medical technology (EMT paramedic); farm and ranch management; general studies; health aide; liberal arts and sciences and humanities related; liberal arts and sciences/liberal studies; licensed practical/vocational nurse training; manufacturing engineering technology; massage therapy; medical/clinical assistant; medical office assistant; nursing assistant/aide and patient care assistant/aide; phlebotomy technology; physical therapy technology; registered nursing/registered nurse; science technologies related; welding technology.

Academics *Calendar:* semesters. *Degree:* certificates and associate. *Special study options:* academic remediation for entering students, adult/continuing education programs, advanced placement credit, distance learning, double majors, honors programs, independent study, internships, part-time degree program, services for LD students, summer session for credit.

Library Learning Resource Center. *Books:* 6,205 (physical), 205,240 (digital/electronic); *Serial titles:* 15 (physical), 18,964 (digital/electronic); *Databases:* 23.

Student Life *Housing:* college housing not available. *Activities and Organizations:* student-run newspaper. *Campus security:* security cameras, local police patrols, free public phones.

Costs (2017–18) *Tuition:* state resident $3286 full-time, $137 per credit hour part-time; nonresident $13,480 full-time, $562 per credit hour part-time. Full-time tuition and fees vary according to course load, program, and reciprocity agreements. Part-time tuition and fees vary according to course load, program, and reciprocity agreements. *Required fees:* $416 full-time, $13 per credit hour part-time, $13 per term part-time. *Payment plan:* installment. *Waivers:* employees or children of employees.

Applying *Options:* electronic application, early admission, deferred entrance. *Recommended:* high school transcript. *Application deadlines:* rolling (freshmen), rolling (out-of-state freshmen), rolling (transfers). *Notification:* continuous (freshmen), continuous (out-of-state freshmen), continuous (transfers).

Freshman Application Contact Ms. Kim Maxwell, Morgan Community College, 920 Barlow Road, Fort Morgan, CO 80701-4399. *Phone:* 970-542-3111. *Toll-free phone:* 800-622-0216. *Fax:* 970-867-6608. *E-mail:* kim.maxwell@morgancc.edu. *Website:* http://www.morgancc.edu/.

Northeastern Junior College
Sterling, Colorado

- **State-supported** 2-year, founded 1941, part of Colorado Community College and Occupational Education System
- **Small-town** 65-acre campus
- **Coed,** 1,469 undergraduate students, 63% full-time, 56% women, 44% men

Undergraduates 930 full-time, 539 part-time. Students come from 25 states and territories; 9 other countries; 10% are from out of state; 4% Black or African American, non-Hispanic/Latino; 6% Hispanic/Latino; 0.9% Asian, non-Hispanic/Latino; 0.3% Native Hawaiian or other Pacific Islander, non-Hispanic/Latino; 1% American Indian or Alaska Native, non-Hispanic/Latino;

12% Two or more races, non-Hispanic/Latino; 4% Race/ethnicity unknown; 3% international; 7% transferred in; 40% live on campus. *Retention:* 80% of full-time freshmen returned.

Freshmen *Admission:* 1,221 applied, 1,221 admitted, 466 enrolled. *Average high school GPA:* 2.95.

Faculty *Total:* 87, 59% full-time. *Student/faculty ratio:* 18:1.

Majors Accounting; agricultural business and management; agricultural teacher education; agriculture; agronomy and crop science; animal sciences; anthropology; art; art history, criticism and conservation; automobile/automotive mechanics technology; biology/biological sciences; business administration and management; chemistry; child development; communication; cosmetology; criminal justice/police science; dramatic/theater arts; economics; elementary education; emergency medical technology (EMT paramedic); English; equestrian studies; farm and ranch management; fine/studio arts; geography; geology/earth science; history; journalism; liberal arts and sciences/liberal studies; licensed practical/vocational nurse training; marketing/marketing management; mathematics; music; natural sciences; philosophy; physical education teaching and coaching; physical sciences; political science and government; pre-engineering; psychology; registered nursing/registered nurse; social sciences; sociology.

Academics *Calendar:* semesters. *Degree:* certificates and associate. *Special study options:* academic remediation for entering students, accelerated degree program, adult/continuing education programs, advanced placement credit, cooperative education, distance learning, double majors, English as a second language, honors programs, internships, part-time degree program, services for LD students, summer session for credit.

Library Monahan Library. *Books:* 27,055 (physical), 90,990 (digital/electronic); *Serial titles:* 109 (physical); *Databases:* 8. Weekly public service hours: 66.

Student Life *Housing:* on-campus residence required for freshman year. *Options:* coed, women-only. Campus housing is university owned. Freshman applicants given priority for college housing. *Activities and Organizations:* drama/theater group, choral group, Associated Student Government, Post Secondary Agriculture (PAS), Crossroads, NJC Ambassadors, Business Club. *Campus security:* 24-hour emergency response devices, late-night transport/escort service, controlled dormitory access. *Student services:* health clinic, personal/psychological counseling.

Athletics Member NJCAA. *Intercollegiate sports:* baseball M(s), basketball M(s)/W(s), equestrian sports M(s)/W(s), golf M(s)/W(s), soccer M(s)/W(s), softball W(s), volleyball W(s), wrestling M(s). *Intramural sports:* basketball M/W, volleyball M/W.

Costs (2016–17) *Tuition:* state resident $4107 full-time, $137 per credit hour part-time; nonresident $6161 full-time, $205 per credit hour part-time. Full-time tuition and fees vary according to course load and reciprocity agreements. Part-time tuition and fees vary according to course load and reciprocity agreements. *Required fees:* $603 full-time, $23 per credit hour part-time, $13 per term part-time. *Room and board:* $6760; room only: $3074. Room and board charges vary according to board plan and housing facility. *Payment plan:* installment. *Waivers:* senior citizens and employees or children of employees.

Financial Aid Of all full-time matriculated undergraduates who enrolled in 2015, 69 Federal Work-Study jobs (averaging $2650). 123 state and other part-time jobs (averaging $2650).

Applying *Options:* electronic application. *Recommended:* high school transcript. *Application deadlines:* rolling (freshmen), rolling (transfers). *Notification:* continuous (freshmen), continuous (transfers).

Freshman Application Contact Adam Kunkel, Director of Admission, Northeastern Junior College, Sterling, CO 80751. *Phone:* 970-521-7000. *Toll-free phone:* 800-626-4637. *Fax:* 970-521-6715. *E-mail:* adam.kunkel@njc.edu. *Website:* http://www.njc.edu/.

Otero Junior College
La Junta, Colorado

- **State-supported** 2-year, founded 1941, part of Colorado Community College System
- **Rural** 40-acre campus
- **Endowment** $1.5 million
- **Coed**, 1,449 undergraduate students

Undergraduates Students come from 20 states and territories; 10 other countries; 9% are from out of state; 3% Black or African American, non-Hispanic/Latino; 32% Hispanic/Latino; 0.8% Asian, non-Hispanic/Latino; 0.5% Native Hawaiian or other Pacific Islander, non-Hispanic/Latino; 1% American Indian or Alaska Native, non-Hispanic/Latino; 6% Race/ethnicity unknown; 3% international. *Retention:* 53% of full-time freshmen returned.

Faculty *Total:* 75, 47% full-time. *Student/faculty ratio:* 19:1.

Majors Administrative assistant and secretarial science; agricultural business and management; automobile/automotive mechanics technology; biological and physical sciences; biology/biological sciences; business administration and management; child development; comparative literature; data processing and data processing technology; dramatic/theater arts; elementary education; history; humanities; kindergarten/preschool education; legal administrative assistant/secretary; liberal arts and sciences/liberal studies; mathematics; medical administrative assistant and medical secretary; modern languages; political science and government; pre-engineering; psychology; registered nursing/registered nurse; social sciences.

Academics *Calendar:* semesters. *Degree:* certificates and associate. *Special study options:* academic remediation for entering students, adult/continuing education programs, advanced placement credit, distance learning, external degree program, honors programs, internships, part-time degree program, summer session for credit.

Library Wheeler Library.

Student Life *Housing:* on-campus residence required for freshman year. *Options:* men-only, women-only. Campus housing is university owned. *Activities and Organizations:* drama/theater group, choral group. *Campus security:* 24-hour patrols, late-night transport/escort service.

Athletics Member NJCAA. *Intercollegiate sports:* baseball M(s), basketball M(s)/W(s), golf M(s)/W(s), soccer M(s)/W(s), softball W(s), volleyball W(s), wrestling M(s). *Intramural sports:* basketball M/W, volleyball M/W.

Costs (2016–17) *Tuition:* state resident $3284 full-time, $137 per credit hour part-time; nonresident $5624 full-time, $234 per credit hour part-time. Full-time tuition and fees vary according to course load. Part-time tuition and fees vary according to course load. *Required fees:* $284 full-time, $9 per credit hour part-time. *Room and board:* $6330. Room and board charges vary according to board plan and housing facility. *Payment plans:* installment, deferred payment. *Waivers:* senior citizens.

Financial Aid Of all full-time matriculated undergraduates who enrolled in 2015, 30 Federal Work-Study jobs (averaging $2000). 100 state and other part-time jobs (averaging $2000).

Applying *Options:* electronic application, early admission. *Recommended:* high school transcript. *Application deadlines:* 8/15 (freshmen), 8/15 (transfers). *Notification:* continuous (freshmen), continuous (transfers).

Freshman Application Contact Mrs. Lauren Berg, Registrar, Otero Junior College, 1802 Colorado Avenue, La Junta, CO 81050. *Phone:* 719-384-6831. *Fax:* 719-384-6933. *E-mail:* lauren.berg@ojc.edu. *Website:* http://www.ojc.edu/.

Pikes Peak Community College
Colorado Springs, Colorado

Freshman Application Contact Pikes Peak Community College, 5675 South Academy Boulevard, Colorado Springs, CO 80906-5498. *Phone:* 719-540-7041. *Toll-free phone:* 866-411-7722. *Website:* http://www.ppcc.edu/.

Pima Medical Institute
Aurora, Colorado

Admissions Office Contact Pima Medical Institute, 13750 East Mississippi Avenue, Aurora, CO 80012. *Toll-free phone:* 800-477-PIMA. *Website:* http://www.pmi.edu/.

Pima Medical Institute
Colorado Springs, Colorado

Freshman Application Contact Pima Medical Institute, 3770 Citadel Drive North, Colorado Springs, CO 80909. *Phone:* 719-482-7462. *Toll-free phone:* 800-477-PIMA. *Website:* http://www.pmi.edu/.

Pima Medical Institute
Denver, Colorado

Freshman Application Contact Admissions Office, Pima Medical Institute, 7475 Dakin Street, Denver, CO 80221. *Phone:* 303-426-1800. *Toll-free phone:* 800-477-PIMA. *Website:* http://www.pmi.edu/.

Pueblo Community College
Pueblo, Colorado

- **State-supported** primarily 2-year, founded 1933, part of Colorado Community College System
- **Urban** 35-acre campus
- **Endowment** $1.1 million
- **Coed,** 5,562 undergraduate students, 65% full-time, 59% women, 41% men

Undergraduates 3,634 full-time, 1,928 part-time. Students come from 20 states and territories; 1 other country; 1% are from out of state; 3% Black or African American, non-Hispanic/Latino; 15% Hispanic/Latino; 0.8% Asian, non-Hispanic/Latino; 0.1% Native Hawaiian or other Pacific Islander, non-Hispanic/Latino; 2% American Indian or Alaska Native, non-Hispanic/Latino; 19% Two or more races, non-Hispanic/Latino; 0.5% Race/ethnicity unknown; 0.6% international; 6% transferred in. *Retention:* 55% of full-time freshmen returned.

Freshmen *Admission:* 1,685 applied, 1,685 admitted, 1,387 enrolled.

Faculty *Total:* 427, 26% full-time. *Student/faculty ratio:* 16:1.

Majors Accounting technology and bookkeeping; animation, interactive technology, video graphics and special effects; autobody/collision and repair technology; automobile/automotive mechanics technology; business administration and management; business automation/technology/data entry; communications technology; computer and information sciences; cooking and related culinary arts; cosmetology; criminal justice/law enforcement administration; dental assisting; dental hygiene; early childhood education; electrical, electronic and communications engineering technology; electromechanical and instrumentation and maintenance technologies related; emergency medical technology (EMT paramedic); engineering technology; fire science/firefighting; general studies; liberal arts and sciences and humanities related; liberal arts and sciences/liberal studies; library and archives assisting; machine shop technology; manufacturing engineering technology; medical office management; occupational therapist assistant; physical therapy technology; psychiatric/mental health services technology; radiologic technology/science; registered nursing/registered nurse; respiratory care therapy; science technologies related; surgical technology; web page, digital/multimedia and information resources design; welding technology.

Academics *Calendar:* semesters. *Degrees:* certificates, associate, and bachelor's. *Special study options:* academic remediation for entering students, accelerated degree program, advanced placement credit, cooperative education, distance learning, double majors, English as a second language, honors programs, independent study, internships, part-time degree program, services for LD students, summer session for credit.

Library PCC Library. *Books:* 19,162 (physical), 33,004 (digital/electronic); *Serial titles:* 695 (physical), 7,707 (digital/electronic); *Databases:* 12. Weekly public service hours: 60.

Student Life *Housing:* college housing not available. *Activities and Organizations:* drama/theater group, choral group, Phi Theta Kappa, Welding Club, Culinary Arts Club, Performing Arts Club, Art Club. *Campus security:* 24-hour emergency response devices and patrols, late-night transport/escort service. *Student services:* health clinic, personal/psychological counseling.

Costs (2017–18) *Tuition:* state resident $6216 full-time, $164 per credit hour part-time; nonresident $14,585 full-time, $569 per credit hour part-time. Full-time tuition and fees vary according to degree level, location, program, and reciprocity agreements. Part-time tuition and fees vary according to degree level, location, program, and reciprocity agreements. *Required fees:* $905 full-time, $20 per credit hour part-time, $57 per term part-time. *Payment plans:* installment, deferred payment. *Waivers:* employees or children of employees.

Applying *Options:* electronic application, early admission, deferred entrance. *Application deadlines:* rolling (freshmen), rolling (transfers). *Notification:* continuous until 9/1 (freshmen), continuous until 9/1 (transfers).

Freshman Application Contact Mrs. Barbara Benedict, Director of Admissions and Records, Pueblo Community College, 900 West Orman Avenue, Pueblo, CO 81004. *Phone:* 719-549-3039. *Toll-free phone:* 888-642-6017. *Fax:* 719-549-3012. *E-mail:* barbara.benedict@pueblocc.edu. *Website:* http://www.pueblocc.edu/.

Red Rocks Community College
Lakewood, Colorado

Freshman Application Contact Admissions Office, Red Rocks Community College, 13300 West 6th Avenue, Lakewood, CO 80228-1255. *Phone:* 303-914-6360. *Fax:* 303-914-6919. *E-mail:* admissions@rrcc.edu. *Website:* http://www.rrcc.edu/.

Spartan College of Aeronautics and Technology
Broomfield, Colorado

Freshman Application Contact Spartan College of Aeronautics and Technology, 10851 West 120th Avenue, Broomfield, CO 80021. *Phone:* 303-466-7383. *Toll-free phone:* 800-510-3216. *Website:* http://www.spartan.edu/.

Trinidad State Junior College
Trinidad, Colorado

Freshman Application Contact Bernadine DeGarbo, Student Services Administrative Assistant, Trinidad State Junior College, 600 Prospect Street, Trinidad, CO 81082. *Phone:* 719-846-5621. *Toll-free phone:* 800-621-8752.

Fax: 719-846-5620. *E-mail:* bernadine.degarbo@trinidadstate.edu. *Website:* http://www.trinidadstate.edu/.

CONNECTICUT

Asnuntuck Community College
Enfield, Connecticut

- **State-supported** 2-year, founded 1972, part of Connecticut State Colleges & Universities (CSCU)
- **Suburban** 36-acre campus
- **Endowment** $137,046
- **Coed,** 1,945 undergraduate students, 34% full-time, 43% women, 57% men

Undergraduates 652 full-time, 1,293 part-time. 8% are from out of state; 16% Black or African American, non-Hispanic/Latino; 13% Hispanic/Latino; 3% Asian, non-Hispanic/Latino; 0.3% American Indian or Alaska Native, non-Hispanic/Latino; 3% Two or more races, non-Hispanic/Latino; 2% Race/ethnicity unknown; 16% transferred in. *Retention:* 68% of full-time freshmen returned.

Freshmen *Admission:* 398 applied, 498 admitted, 510 enrolled.

Faculty *Total:* 141, 22% full-time. *Student/faculty ratio:* 17:1.

Majors Accounting technology and bookkeeping; banking and financial support services; business/commerce; communication; criminal justice/police science; early childhood education; engineering science; engineering technology; general studies; liberal arts and sciences/liberal studies; management information systems; psychiatric/mental health services technology.

Academics *Calendar:* semesters. *Degree:* certificates and associate. *Special study options:* academic remediation for entering students, adult/continuing education programs, advanced placement credit, cooperative education, distance learning, double majors, English as a second language, independent study, internships, part-time degree program, services for LD students, student-designed majors, summer session for credit.

Library ACC Library plus 1 other.

Student Life *Housing:* college housing not available. *Activities and Organizations:* student-run radio station. *Campus security:* 24-hour emergency response devices, late-night transport/escort service.

Costs (2016–17) *Tuition:* state resident $3600 full-time, $150 per credit hour part-time; nonresident $10,800 full-time, $450 per credit hour part-time. *Required fees:* $432 full-time. *Payment plan:* installment.

Applying *Options:* deferred entrance. *Application fee:* $20. *Required:* high school transcript, interview. *Application deadlines:* rolling (freshmen), rolling (transfers). *Notification:* continuous (freshmen), continuous (transfers).

Freshman Application Contact Jennifer Anilowski, Interim Director of Admissions, Asnuntuck Community College, 170 Elm Street, Enfield, CT 06082. *Phone:* 860-253-3090. *Fax:* 860-253-3014. *E-mail:* janilowski@asnuntuck.edu. *Website:* http://www.asnuntuck.edu/.

Capital Community College
Hartford, Connecticut

Freshman Application Contact Ms. Jackie Phillips, Director of the Welcome and Advising Center, Capital Community College, 950 Main Street, Hartford, CT 06103. *Phone:* 860-906-5078. *Toll-free phone:* 800-894-6126. *E-mail:* jphillips@ccc.commnet.edu. *Website:* http://www.ccc.commnet.edu/.

Gateway Community College
New Haven, Connecticut

Freshman Application Contact Mr. Joseph Carberry, Director of Enrollment Management, Gateway Community College, 20 Church Street, New Haven, CT 06510. *Phone:* 203-285-2011. *Toll-free phone:* 800-390-7723. *Fax:* 203-285-2018. *E-mail:* jcarberry@gatewayct.edu. *Website:* http://www.gwcc.commnet.edu/.

Goodwin College
East Hartford, Connecticut

Freshman Application Contact Mr. Nicholas Lentino, Assistant Vice President for Admissions, Goodwin College, One Riverside Drive, East Hartford, CT 06118. *Phone:* 860-727-6765. *Toll-free phone:* 800-889-3282. *Fax:* 860-291-9550. *E-mail:* nlentino@goodwin.edu. *Website:* http://www.goodwin.edu/.

Housatonic Community College

Bridgeport, Connecticut

- **State-supported** 2-year, founded 1965, part of Connecticut State Colleges & Universities (CSCU)
- **Urban** 4-acre campus with easy access to New York City
- **Coed,** 5,369 undergraduate students

Undergraduates 31% Black or African American, non-Hispanic/Latino; 33% Hispanic/Latino; 3% Asian, non-Hispanic/Latino; 0.2% Native Hawaiian or other Pacific Islander, non-Hispanic/Latino; 0.1% American Indian or Alaska Native, non-Hispanic/Latino; 2% Two or more races, non-Hispanic/Latino; 1% Race/ethnicity unknown.

Faculty *Total:* 308, 27% full-time, 14% with terminal degrees. *Student/faculty ratio:* 18:1.

Majors Accounting; administrative assistant and secretarial science; art; avionics maintenance technology; business administration and management; child development; clinical/medical laboratory technology; commercial and advertising art; computer typography and composition equipment operation; criminal justice/law enforcement administration; data processing and data processing technology; environmental studies; humanities; human services; journalism; liberal arts and sciences/liberal studies; mathematics; mental health counseling; physical therapy; pre-engineering; public administration; social sciences; substance abuse/addiction counseling.

Academics *Calendar:* semesters. *Degree:* certificates and associate. *Special study options:* academic remediation for entering students, adult/continuing education programs, advanced placement credit, cooperative education, distance learning, double majors, English as a second language, honors programs, independent study, internships, off-campus study, part-time degree program, services for LD students, summer session for credit.

Library Housatonic Community College Library. *Books:* 53,000 (physical), 29,000 (digital/electronic); *Databases:* 60. Students can reserve study rooms.

Student Life *Activities and Organizations:* drama/theater group, student-run newspaper, Student Senate, Association of Latin American Students, Community Action Network, Drama Club, Phi Theta Kappa. *Campus security:* 24-hour emergency response devices, late-night transport/escort service. *Student services:* health clinic, personal/psychological counseling, women's center.

Costs (2016–17) *Tuition:* state resident $4052 full-time, $155 per semester hour part-time; nonresident $10,800 full-time, $465 per semester hour part-time. *Required fees:* $452 full-time, $79 per credit hour part-time. *Payment plan:* installment. *Waivers:* senior citizens and employees or children of employees.

Financial Aid Of all full-time matriculated undergraduates who enrolled in 2015, 70 Federal Work-Study jobs (averaging $2850).

Applying *Options:* electronic application, deferred entrance. *Application fee:* $20. *Required:* high school transcript. *Required for some:* interview. *Application deadlines:* rolling (freshmen), rolling (transfers). *Notification:* continuous (freshmen), continuous (transfers).

Freshman Application Contact Mr. Earl Graham, Director of Admissions, Housatonic Community College, 900 Lafayette Boulevard, Bridgeport, CT 06604-4704. *Phone:* 203-332-5102. *E-mail:* egraham@hcc.commnet.edu. *Website:* http://www.housatonic.edu/.

Manchester Community College

Manchester, Connecticut

- **State-supported** 2-year, founded 1963, part of Connecticut State Colleges & Universities (CSCU)
- **Small-town** campus
- **Coed,** 6,780 undergraduate students, 32% full-time, 54% women, 46% men

Undergraduates 2,169 full-time, 4,611 part-time. 14% Black or African American, non-Hispanic/Latino; 19% Hispanic/Latino; 5% Asian, non-Hispanic/Latino; 0.2% American Indian or Alaska Native, non-Hispanic/Latino; 3% Two or more races, non-Hispanic/Latino; 6% Race/ethnicity unknown; 0.2% international; 16% transferred in.

Freshmen *Admission:* 2,824 applied, 2,801 admitted, 1,158 enrolled.

Faculty *Total:* 495, 23% full-time. *Student/faculty ratio:* 17:1.

Majors Accounting; administrative assistant and secretarial science; business administration and management; clinical/medical laboratory technology; commercial and advertising art; criminal justice/law enforcement administration; dramatic/theater arts; engineering science; fine/studio arts; general studies; hotel/motel administration; human services; industrial engineering; industrial technology; information science/studies; journalism; kindergarten/preschool education; legal administrative assistant/secretary; legal assistant/paralegal; liberal arts and sciences/liberal studies; management information systems; marketing/marketing management; medical administrative assistant and medical secretary; music; occupational therapist assistant; physical therapy technology; respiratory care therapy; social work;

speech communication and rhetoric; surgical technology; teacher assistant/aide.

Academics *Calendar:* semesters. *Degree:* certificates and associate. *Special study options:* adult/continuing education programs, part-time degree program.

Student Life *Housing:* college housing not available.

Athletics Member NJCAA. *Intercollegiate sports:* baseball M, basketball M/W, soccer M/W, softball W.

Costs (2017–18) *Tuition:* state resident $4208 full-time; nonresident $12,544 full-time. *Required fees:* $488 full-time. *Payment plan:* installment. *Waivers:* senior citizens and employees or children of employees.

Financial Aid *Financial aid deadline:* 8/13.

Applying *Options:* electronic application. *Required:* high school transcript.

Freshman Application Contact Director of Admissions, Manchester Community College, PO Box 1046, Manchester, CT 06045-1046. *Phone:* 860-512-3210. *Fax:* 860-512-3221. *Website:* http://www.manchestercc.edu/.

Middlesex Community College

Middletown, Connecticut

Freshman Application Contact Mensimah Shabazz, Director of Admissions, Middlesex Community College, Middletown, CT 06457-4889. *Phone:* 860-343-5742. *Fax:* 860-344-3055. *E-mail:* mshabazz@mxcc.commnet.edu. *Website:* http://www.mxcc.commnet.edu/.

Naugatuck Valley Community College

Waterbury, Connecticut

- **State-supported** 2-year, founded 1992, part of Connecticut State Colleges & Universities (CSCU)
- **Urban** 110-acre campus
- **Coed,** 6,651 undergraduate students, 34% full-time, 57% women, 43% men

Undergraduates 2,231 full-time, 4,420 part-time. Students come from 5 states and territories; 2 other countries; 0.4% are from out of state; 10% Black or African American, non-Hispanic/Latino; 28% Hispanic/Latino; 3% Asian, non-Hispanic/Latino; 0.2% Native Hawaiian or other Pacific Islander, non-Hispanic/Latino; 0.3% American Indian or Alaska Native, non-Hispanic/Latino; 2% Two or more races, non-Hispanic/Latino; 4% Race/ethnicity unknown; 0.3% international; 13% transferred in. *Retention:* 60% of full-time freshmen returned.

Freshmen *Admission:* 1,279 enrolled.

Faculty *Total:* 461, 21% full-time. *Student/faculty ratio:* 15:1.

Majors Accounting technology and bookkeeping; aeronautics/aviation/aerospace science and technology; art; automobile/automotive mechanics technology; behavioral sciences; business administration and management; business/commerce; computer engineering technology; criminal justice/police science; digital communication and media/multimedia; early childhood education; electrical, electronic and communications engineering technology; engineering science; engineering technology; environmental engineering technology; finance; fire services administration; general studies; horticultural science; hospitality administration; hotel/motel administration; legal assistant/paralegal; liberal arts and sciences/liberal studies; marketing/marketing management; medical radiologic technology; physical sciences related; physical therapy technology; psychiatric/mental health services technology; registered nursing/registered nurse; respiratory care therapy; restaurant/food services management; substance abuse/addiction counseling.

Academics *Calendar:* semesters. *Degree:* certificates and associate. *Special study options:* academic remediation for entering students, accelerated degree program, adult/continuing education programs, advanced placement credit, cooperative education, distance learning, English as a second language, external degree program, honors programs, independent study, internships, off-campus study, part-time degree program, services for LD students, summer session for credit.

Library Max R. Traurig Learning Resource Center. *Books:* 38,400 (physical); *Serial titles:* 108 (physical); *Databases:* 12. Weekly public service hours: 65; students can reserve study rooms.

Student Life *Housing:* college housing not available. *Activities and Organizations:* drama/theater group, student-run newspaper, choral group, Student Senate, Choral Society, Automotive Technician Club, Human Service Club, Legal Assistant Club. *Campus security:* 24-hour emergency response devices and patrols, late-night transport/escort service, security escort service. *Student services:* personal/psychological counseling, women's center.

Standardized Tests *Required:* ACCUPLACER (for admission).

Costs (2016–17) *Tuition:* state resident $4208 full-time, $155 per credit hour part-time; nonresident $12,544 full-time, $465 per credit hour part-time. Part-time tuition and fees vary according to course load. *Required fees:* $488 full-time, $92 per credit hour part-time. *Payment plan:* installment. *Waivers:* senior citizens and employees or children of employees.

Financial Aid Of all full-time matriculated undergraduates who enrolled in 2015, 70 Federal Work-Study jobs (averaging $1942). 16 state and other part-time jobs (averaging $1660).

Applying *Options:* electronic application, deferred entrance. *Application fee:* $20. *Required:* high school transcript. *Required for some:* interview. *Application deadlines:* rolling (freshmen), rolling (transfers). *Notification:* continuous (freshmen), continuous (transfers).

Freshman Application Contact Linda Stango, Director of Admissions, Naugatuck Valley Community College, Waterbury, CT 06708. *Phone:* 203-575-8016. *Fax:* 203-596-8766. *E-mail:* lstango@nvcc.commnet.edu. *Website:* http://www.nvcc.commnet.edu/.

Northwestern Connecticut Community College
Winsted, Connecticut

Freshman Application Contact Admissions Office, Northwestern Connecticut Community College, Park Place East, Winsted, CT 06098-1798. *Phone:* 860-738-6330. *Fax:* 860-738-6437. *E-mail:* admissions@nwcc.commnet.edu. *Website:* http://www.nwcc.commnet.edu/.

Norwalk Community College
Norwalk, Connecticut

- **State-supported** 2-year, founded 1961, part of Connecticut State Colleges & Universities (CSCU)
- **Suburban** 30-acre campus with easy access to New York City
- **Coed**, 5,869 undergraduate students, 35% full-time, 59% women, 41% men

Undergraduates 2,047 full-time, 3,822 part-time. 1% are from out of state; 17% Black or African American, non-Hispanic/Latino; 37% Hispanic/Latino; 5% Asian, non-Hispanic/Latino; 0.2% Native Hawaiian or other Pacific Islander, non-Hispanic/Latino; 0.2% American Indian or Alaska Native, non-Hispanic/Latino; 1% Two or more races, non-Hispanic/Latino; 5% Race/ethnicity unknown; 2% international; 7% transferred in. *Retention:* 61% of full-time freshmen returned.

Freshmen *Admission:* 851 enrolled.

Faculty *Total:* 397, 26% full-time. *Student/faculty ratio:* 18:1.

Majors Accounting; administrative assistant and secretarial science; architectural engineering technology; art; business administration and management; commercial and advertising art; computer and information systems security; computer systems networking and telecommunications; construction engineering technology; criminal justice/law enforcement administration; early childhood education; engineering science; finance; fine/studio arts; fire science/firefighting; general studies; graphic design; hotel/motel administration; human services; information science/studies; information technology; interior design; kinesiology and exercise science; legal assistant/paralegal; liberal arts and sciences/liberal studies; marketing/marketing management; medical office management; parks, recreation and leisure; psychology; registered nursing/registered nurse; respiratory care therapy; restaurant/food services management; speech communication and rhetoric; web page, digital/multimedia and information resources design.

Academics *Calendar:* semesters. *Degree:* certificates and associate. *Special study options:* academic remediation for entering students, advanced placement credit, cooperative education, distance learning, English as a second language, independent study, internships, part-time degree program, services for LD students, summer session for credit.

Library Everett I. L. Baker Library.

Student Life *Housing:* college housing not available. *Activities and Organizations:* drama/theater group, student-run newspaper, choral group, Student World Assembly, Accounting Club, Literature Club, Art Club, Phi Theta Kappa. *Campus security:* late-night transport/escort service, all buildings secured each evening, foot patrols and vehicle patrols by security from 7 am to 11 pm. *Student services:* personal/psychological counseling, women's center.

Costs (2016–17) *Tuition:* state resident $3720 full-time, $155 per credit hour part-time; nonresident $11,160 full-time, $465 per credit hour part-time. *Required fees:* $468 full-time. *Payment plan:* installment. *Waivers:* senior citizens and employees or children of employees.

Applying *Options:* electronic application, deferred entrance. *Required:* high school transcript, 4 math courses, 3 science courses, 2 labs, immunization form.

Freshman Application Contact Mr. Curtis Antrum, Admissions Counselor, Norwalk Community College, 188 Richards Avenue, Norwalk, CT 06854-

1655. *Phone:* 203-857-7060. *Fax:* 203-857-3335. *E-mail:* admissions@ncc.commnet.edu. *Website:* http://www.ncc.commnet.edu/.

Quinebaug Valley Community College
Danielson, Connecticut

Freshman Application Contact Dr. Toni Moumouris, Director of Admissions, Quinebaug Valley Community College, 742 Upper Maple Street, Danielson, CT 06239. *Phone:* 860-774-1130 Ext. 318. *Fax:* 860-774-7768. *E-mail:* qu_isd@commnet.edu. *Website:* http://www.qvcc.commnet.edu/.

St. Vincent's College
Bridgeport, Connecticut

- **Independent** primarily 2-year, founded 1991, affiliated with Roman Catholic Church
- **Urban** campus with easy access to New York City
- **Endowment** $4.1 million
- **Coed**, 763 undergraduate students, 9% full-time, 85% women, 15% men

Undergraduates 65 full-time, 698 part-time. Students come from 12 states and territories; 2% are from out of state; 15% Black or African American, non-Hispanic/Latino; 15% Hispanic/Latino; 2% Asian, non-Hispanic/Latino; 0.3% American Indian or Alaska Native, non-Hispanic/Latino; 21% Race/ethnicity unknown; 28% transferred in.

Freshmen *Admission:* 33 enrolled.

Faculty *Total:* 67, 27% full-time. *Student/faculty ratio:* 14:1.

Majors General studies; health/health-care administration; radiologic technology/science; registered nursing/registered nurse.

Academics *Calendar:* semesters. *Degrees:* certificates, associate, and bachelor's. *Special study options:* academic remediation for entering students, adult/continuing education programs, advanced placement credit, distance learning, internships, part-time degree program, summer session for credit.

Library Daniel T. Banks Health Science Library. *Books:* 1,500 (physical), 84,000 (digital/electronic); *Serial titles:* 81 (physical); *Databases:* 5. Weekly public service hours: 40; students can reserve study rooms.

Student Life *Housing:* college housing not available. *Activities and Organizations:* Radiography Club, Student Nurses Association, SALUTE (veterans national honor society), Phi Theta Kappa (honor society). *Campus security:* 24-hour emergency response devices and patrols, late-night transport/escort service.

Standardized Tests *Recommended:* SAT or ACT (for admission).

Costs (2016–17) *Tuition:* $14,520 full-time, $605 per credit hour part-time. Full-time tuition and fees vary according to course load. Part-time tuition and fees vary according to course load. *Required fees:* $350 full-time, $350 per year part-time. *Payment plan:* installment. *Waivers:* employees or children of employees.

Financial Aid Of all full-time matriculated undergraduates who enrolled in 2015, 45 applied for aid, 45 were judged to have need. *Average percent of need met:* 34%. *Average financial aid package:* $8755. *Average need-based loan:* $4070. *Average need-based gift aid:* $5754. *Average indebtedness upon graduation:* $35,263.

Applying *Required:* high school transcript. *Recommended:* minimum 2.0 GPA.

Freshman Application Contact St. Vincent's College, 2800 Main Street, Bridgeport, CT 06606-4292. *Toll-free phone:* 800-873-1013. *Website:* http://www.stvincentscollege.edu/.

Three Rivers Community College
Norwich, Connecticut

- **State-supported** 2-year, founded 1963, part of Connecticut State Colleges & Universities (CSCU)
- **Suburban** 40-acre campus with easy access to Hartford
- **Coed**, 4,259 undergraduate students, 33% full-time, 58% women, 42% men

Undergraduates 1,407 full-time, 2,852 part-time. Students come from 5 states and territories; 1% are from out of state; 8% Black or African American, non-Hispanic/Latino; 15% Hispanic/Latino; 4% Asian, non-Hispanic/Latino; 0.3% Native Hawaiian or other Pacific Islander, non-Hispanic/Latino; 0.6% American Indian or Alaska Native, non-Hispanic/Latino; 4% Two or more races, non-Hispanic/Latino; 4% Race/ethnicity unknown; 0.2% international; 7% transferred in. *Retention:* 56% of full-time freshmen returned.

Freshmen *Admission:* 860 enrolled.

Faculty *Total:* 277, 25% full-time. *Student/faculty ratio:* 17:1.

Majors Accounting; accounting technology and bookkeeping; architectural drafting and CAD/CADD; architectural engineering technology; banking and financial support services; business/commerce; child-care and support services management; computer engineering technology; construction management; criminal justice/police science; education; electrical, electronic and communications engineering technology; engineering science; engineering technology; environmental engineering technology; fine/studio arts; general studies; graphic design; hospitality administration; kinesiology and exercise science; laser and optical technology; liberal arts and sciences/liberal studies; management information systems; manufacturing engineering technology; marketing/marketing management; mechanical engineering/mechanical technology; nuclear/nuclear power technology; psychiatric/mental health services technology; registered nursing/registered nurse; sport and fitness administration/management.

Academics *Calendar:* semesters. *Degrees:* certificates and associate (engineering technology programs are offered on the Thames Valley Campus; liberal arts, transfer and career programs are offered on the Mohegan Campus). *Special study options:* adult/continuing education programs, part-time degree program.

Library Three Rivers Community College Learning Resource Center plus 1 other.

Student Life *Housing:* college housing not available. *Activities and Organizations:* student-run newspaper. *Campus security:* 24-hour emergency response devices, late-night transport/escort service, 14-hour patrols by trained security personnel.

Athletics *Intramural sports:* baseball M(c)/W(c), golf M(c)/W(c).

Costs (2016–17) *One-time required fee:* $40. *Tuition:* state resident $3720 full-time, $155 per credit hour part-time; nonresident $10,800 full-time, $450 per credit hour part-time. Full-time tuition and fees vary according to course load and reciprocity agreements. Part-time tuition and fees vary according to course load and reciprocity agreements. *Required fees:* $448 full-time. *Payment plan:* installment. *Waivers:* senior citizens and employees or children of employees.

Financial Aid Of all full-time matriculated undergraduates who enrolled in 2010, 1,135 applied for aid, 967 were judged to have need, 266 had their need fully met. *Average percent of need met:* 48%. *Average financial aid package:* $2631. *Average need-based loan:* $3308. *Average need-based gift aid:* $2409.

Applying *Options:* electronic application, early admission, deferred entrance. *Recommended:* high school transcript. *Application deadlines:* rolling (freshmen), rolling (transfers). *Notification:* continuous (freshmen), continuous (transfers).

Freshman Application Contact Admissions Office, Three Rivers Community College, CT. *Phone:* 860-215-9296. *E-mail:* admissions@trcc.commnet.edu. *Website:* http://www.threerivers.edu/.

Tunxis Community College
Farmington, Connecticut

- **State-supported** 2-year, founded 1969, part of Connecticut State Colleges & Universities (CSCU)
- **Suburban** 12-acre campus with easy access to Hartford
- **Coed**

Undergraduates 1,594 full-time, 2,485 part-time. Students come from 6 states and territories; 2% are from out of state; 7% Black or African American, non-Hispanic/Latino; 19% Hispanic/Latino; 4% Asian, non-Hispanic/Latino; 0.0% Native Hawaiian or other Pacific Islander, non-Hispanic/Latino; 0.2% American Indian or Alaska Native, non-Hispanic/Latino; 5% Race/ethnicity unknown; 0.1% international. *Retention:* 61% of full-time freshmen returned.

Faculty *Student/faculty ratio:* 17:1.

Academics *Calendar:* semesters. *Degree:* certificates and associate. *Special study options:* academic remediation for entering students, adult/continuing education programs, cooperative education, distance learning, double majors, English as a second language, honors programs, independent study, internships, part-time degree program, services for LD students, summer session for credit.

Library Tunxis Community College Library. Students can reserve study rooms.

Student Life *Campus security:* 24-hour emergency response devices.

Applying *Options:* deferred entrance. *Application fee:* $20. *Required:* high school transcript.

Freshman Application Contact Ms. Tamika Davis, Director of Admissions, Tunxis Community College, 271 Scott Swamp Road, Farmington, CT 06032. *Phone:* 860-773-1494. *Fax:* 860-606-9501. *E-mail:* pmccluskey@tunxis.edu. *Website:* http://www.tunxis.edu/.

DELAWARE

Delaware College of Art and Design
Wilmington, Delaware

Freshman Application Contact Ms. Allison Gullo, Delaware College of Art and Design, 600 North Market Street, Wilmington, DE 19801. *Phone:* 302-622-8867 Ext. 111. *Fax:* 302-622-8870. *E-mail:* agullo@dcad.edu. *Website:* http://www.dcad.edu/.

Delaware Technical & Community College, Jack F. Owens Campus
Georgetown, Delaware

Freshman Application Contact Ms. Claire McDonald, Admissions Counselor, Delaware Technical & Community College, Jack F. Owens Campus, PO Box 610, Georgetown, DE 19947. *Phone:* 302-856-5400. *Fax:* 302-856-9461. *Website:* http://www.dtcc.edu/.

Delaware Technical & Community College, Stanton/Wilmington Campus
Newark, Delaware

Freshman Application Contact Ms. Rebecca Bailey, Admissions Coordinator, Wilmington, Delaware Technical & Community College, Stanton/Wilmington Campus, 333 Shipley Street, Wilmington, DE 19713. *Phone:* 302-571-5343. *Fax:* 302-577-2548. *Website:* http://www.dtcc.edu/.

Delaware Technical & Community College, Terry Campus
Dover, Delaware

Freshman Application Contact Mrs. Maria Harris, Admissions Officer, Delaware Technical & Community College, Terry Campus, 100 Campus Drive, Dover, DE 19904. *Phone:* 302-857-1020. *Fax:* 302-857-1296. *E-mail:* terry-info@dtcc.edu. *Website:* http://www.dtcc.edu/.

FLORIDA

Academy for Nursing and Health Occupations
West Palm Beach, Florida

Admissions Office Contact Academy for Nursing and Health Occupations, 5154 Okeechobee Boulevard, Suite 201, West Palm Beach, FL 33417. *Website:* http://www.apnho.com/.

Advance Science Institute
Hialeah, Florida

Admissions Office Contact Advance Science Institute, 3750 W. 12 Avenue, Hialeah, FL 33012. *Website:* http://www.asimedschool.com/.

American Medical Academy
Miami, Florida

Admissions Office Contact American Medical Academy, 12215 SW 112 Street, Miami, FL 33186-4830. *Website:* http://www.ama.edu/.

ATA Career Education
Spring Hill, Florida

Admissions Office Contact ATA Career Education, 7351 Spring Hill Drive, Suite 11, Spring Hill, FL 34606. *Website:* http://www.atafl.edu/.

Aviator College of Aeronautical Science & Technology

Fort Pierce, Florida

Admissions Office Contact Aviator College of Aeronautical Science & Technology, 3800 St. Lucie Boulevard, Fort Pierce, FL 34946. *Website:* http://aviator.edu/FlightSchool/.

Broward College

Fort Lauderdale, Florida

Freshman Application Contact Mr. Willie J. Alexander, Associate Vice President for Student Affairs/College Registrar, Broward College, 225 East Las Olas Boulevard, Fort Lauderdale, FL 33301. *Phone:* 954-201-7471. *Fax:* 954-201-7466. *E-mail:* walexand@broward.edu. *Website:* http://www.broward.edu/.

Burnett International College

Boynton Beach, Florida

Admissions Office Contact Burnett International College, 1903 South Congress Avenue, Boynton Beach, FL 33426-6591. *Website:* http://www.burnett.edu/.

Cambridge College of Healthcare & Technology

Delray Beach, Florida

Admissions Office Contact Cambridge College of Healthcare & Technology, 5150 Linton Boulevard, Suite 340, Delray Beach, FL 33484. *Website:* http://www.cambridgehealth.edu/.

Chipola College

Marianna, Florida

- **State-supported** primarily 2-year, founded 1947
- **Rural** 105-acre campus
- **Coed**

Undergraduates 863 full-time, 1,284 part-time. Students come from 7 states and territories; 6 other countries; 8% are from out of state; 14% Black or African American, non-Hispanic/Latino; 0.7% Hispanic/Latino; 0.7% Asian, non-Hispanic/Latino; 0.1% Native Hawaiian or other Pacific Islander, non-Hispanic/Latino; 1% American Indian or Alaska Native, non-Hispanic/Latino; 4% Two or more races, non-Hispanic/Latino; 1% Race/ethnicity unknown; 7% transferred in.
Faculty *Student/faculty ratio:* 24:1.
Academics *Calendar:* semesters. *Degrees:* certificates, associate, and bachelor's. *Special study options:* academic remediation for entering students, adult/continuing education programs, advanced placement credit, distance learning, honors programs, independent study, part-time degree program, services for LD students, summer session for credit.
Library Chipola Library.
Student Life *Campus security:* night security personnel.
Athletics Member NJCAA.
Applying *Options:* early admission. *Required:* high school transcript.
Freshman Application Contact Mrs. Kathy L. Rehberg, Registrar, Chipola College, 3094 Indian Circle, Marianna, FL 32446-3065. *Phone:* 850-718-2233. *Fax:* 850-718-2287. *E-mail:* rehbergk@chipola.edu. *Website:* http://www.chipola.edu/.

City College

Altamonte Springs, Florida

Director of Admissions Ms. Kimberly Bowden, Director of Admissions, City College, 177 Montgomery Road, Altamonte Springs, FL 32714. *Phone:* 352-335-4000. *Fax:* 352-335-4303. *E-mail:* kbowden@citycollege.edu. *Website:* http://www.citycollege.edu/.

City College

Fort Lauderdale, Florida

Freshman Application Contact City College, 2000 West Commercial Boulevard, Suite 200, Fort Lauderdale, FL 33309. *Phone:* 954-492-5353. *Toll-free phone:* 866-314-5681. *Website:* http://www.citycollege.edu/.

City College

Gainesville, Florida

Freshman Application Contact Admissions Office, City College, 7001 Northwest 4th Boulevard, Gainesville, FL 32607. *Phone:* 352-335-4000. *Website:* http://www.citycollege.edu/.

City College

Hollywood, Florida

Admissions Office Contact City College, 6565 Taft Street, Hollywood, FL 33024. *Toll-free phone:* 866-314-5681. *Website:* http://www.citycollege.edu/.

City College

Miami, Florida

Freshman Application Contact Admissions Office, City College, 9300 South Dadeland Boulevard, Suite PH, Miami, FL 33156. *Phone:* 305-666-9242. *Fax:* 305-666-9243. *Website:* http://www.citycollege.edu/.

College of Business and Technology–Cutler Bay Campus

Cutler Bay, Florida

- **Proprietary** 2-year, founded 2009
- **Urban** campus with easy access to Miami
- **Coed,** 117 undergraduate students, 100% full-time, 70% women, 30% men

Undergraduates 117 full-time. Students come from 1 other state; 20% Black or African American, non-Hispanic/Latino; 69% Hispanic/Latino; 2% Asian, non-Hispanic/Latino; 0.9% Native Hawaiian or other Pacific Islander, non-Hispanic/Latino; 0.9% Two or more races, non-Hispanic/Latino; 0.9% Race/ethnicity unknown.
Freshmen *Admission:* 9 enrolled.
Faculty *Total:* 16, 19% full-time, 25% with terminal degrees. *Student/faculty ratio:* 16:1.
Majors Business administration and management; electrician; health information/medical records technology; medical/clinical assistant.
Academics *Calendar:* semesters. *Degree:* certificates, diplomas, and associate. *Special study options:* academic remediation for entering students, adult/continuing education programs, cooperative education, independent study, services for LD students.
Library CBT College–Cutler Bay Library. *Books:* 2,258 (physical); *Serial titles:* 28 (physical); *Databases:* 60.
Student Life *Housing:* college housing not available. *Campus security:* security guard patrol, local police department patrol.
Costs (2017–18) *Tuition:* $11,952 full-time. *Required fees:* $1400 full-time. *Payment plan:* installment.
Applying *Options:* electronic application. *Application fee:* $25. *Required:* high school transcript, interview.
Freshman Application Contact College of Business and Technology–Cutler Bay Campus, 19151 South Dixie Highway, Cutler Bay, FL 33157. *Phone:* 305-273-4499 Ext. 1100. *Website:* http://www.cbt.edu/.

College of Business and Technology–Flagler Campus

Miami, Florida

- **Proprietary** 2-year, founded 1988
- **Urban** campus
- **Coed,** 300 undergraduate students, 100% full-time, 5% women, 95% men

Undergraduates 300 full-time. Students come from 1 other state; 2 other countries; 1% Black or African American, non-Hispanic/Latino; 96% Hispanic/Latino; 0.3% American Indian or Alaska Native, non-Hispanic/Latino; 1% international.
Freshmen *Admission:* 94 enrolled.
Faculty *Total:* 26, 31% full-time. *Student/faculty ratio:* 21:1.
Majors Business administration and management; computer systems networking and telecommunications; electrician; heating, ventilation, air conditioning and refrigeration engineering technology.
Academics *Calendar:* semesters. *Degree:* certificates, diplomas, and associate. *Special study options:* academic remediation for entering students, adult/continuing education programs, cooperative education, English as a second language, independent study, services for LD students.
Library CBT College–Flagler Library. *Books:* 1,432 (physical); *Serial titles:* 16 (physical); *Databases:* 60.

Student Life *Housing:* college housing not available. *Campus security:* security guard patrol, local police department patrol.
Costs (2017–18) *Tuition:* $11,952 full-time. *Required fees:* $1400 full-time. *Payment plan:* installment.
Applying *Options:* electronic application. *Application fee:* $25. *Required:* high school transcript, interview.
Freshman Application Contact College of Business and Technology–Flagler Campus, 8230 West Flagler Street, Miami, FL 33144. *Phone:* 305-273-4499 Ext. 1100.
Website: http://www.cbt.edu/.

College of Business and Technology–Hialeah Campus
Hialeah, Florida

- **Proprietary** 2-year, founded 1988
- **Urban** campus with easy access to Miami
- **Coed, primarily men,** 238 undergraduate students, 100% full-time, 8% women, 92% men

Undergraduates 238 full-time. Students come from 1 other state; 0.4% Black or African American, non-Hispanic/Latino; 99% Hispanic/Latino; 0.4% Asian, non-Hispanic/Latino.
Freshmen *Admission:* 80 enrolled.
Faculty *Total:* 25, 16% full-time, 12% with terminal degrees. *Student/faculty ratio:* 21:1.
Majors Electrician; heating, ventilation, air conditioning and refrigeration engineering technology.
Academics *Calendar:* semesters. *Degree:* certificates, diplomas, and associate. *Special study options:* academic remediation for entering students, adult/continuing education programs, cooperative education, English as a second language, independent study, services for LD students.
Library CBT College–Hialeah Library. *Books:* 1,032 (physical); *Serial titles:* 5 (physical); *Databases:* 60.
Student Life *Housing:* college housing not available. *Campus security:* local police department patrols.
Costs (2017–18) *Tuition:* $11,952 full-time. *Required fees:* $1400 full-time. *Payment plan:* installment.
Applying *Options:* electronic application. *Application fee:* $25. *Required:* high school transcript, interview.
Freshman Application Contact College of Business and Technology–Hialeah Campus, 935 West 49 Street, Hialeah, FL 33012. *Phone:* 305-273-4499 Ext. 1100.
Website: http://www.cbt.edu/.

College of Business and Technology–Main Campus
Miami, Florida

- **Proprietary** primarily 2-year, founded 1988
- **Urban** campus
- **Coed,** 10 undergraduate students, 100% full-time, 80% women, 20% men

Undergraduates 10 full-time. Students come from 1 other state; 100% Hispanic/Latino.
Freshmen *Admission:* 10 enrolled.
Faculty *Total:* 1, 100% full-time. *Student/faculty ratio:* 10:1.
Majors Business administration and management.
Academics *Calendar:* semesters. *Degrees:* certificates, diplomas, associate, and bachelor's. *Special study options:* academic remediation for entering students, adult/continuing education programs, cooperative education, English as a second language, independent study.
Library CBT College-Miami Branch Library (Use Flagler). *Books:* 1,520 (physical); *Serial titles:* 10 (physical); *Databases:* 60.
Student Life *Housing:* college housing not available. *Campus security:* security guard posted at main entrance, local police department.
Costs (2017–18) *Tuition:* $11,952 full-time. *Required fees:* $1400 full-time. *Payment plan:* installment.
Applying *Options:* electronic application. *Application fee:* $25. *Required:* high school transcript, interview.
Freshman Application Contact College of Business and Technology–Main Campus, 8700 West Flagler Street, Suite 420, Miami, FL 33174. *Phone:* 305-273-4499 Ext. 1100.
Website: http://www.cbt.edu/.

College of Business and Technology–Miami Gardens
Miami Gardens, Florida

- **Proprietary** primarily 2-year, founded 2012
- **Urban** campus with easy access to Miami
- **Coed,** 113 undergraduate students, 100% full-time, 48% women, 52% men

Undergraduates 113 full-time. Students come from 1 other state; 1 other country; 27% Black or African American, non-Hispanic/Latino; 65% Hispanic/Latino; 3% Race/ethnicity unknown; 2% international.
Freshmen *Admission:* 11 enrolled.
Faculty *Total:* 19, 16% full-time, 37% with terminal degrees. *Student/faculty ratio:* 18:1.
Majors Business administration and management; computer systems networking and telecommunications; electrician; graphic design; health information/medical records technology.
Academics *Calendar:* semesters. *Degrees:* certificates, diplomas, associate, and bachelor's. *Special study options:* academic remediation for entering students, adult/continuing education programs, cooperative education, independent study, services for LD students.
Library CBT College–Miami Gardens Library. *Books:* 1,034 (physical); *Serial titles:* 15 (physical); *Databases:* 60.
Student Life *Housing:* college housing not available. *Campus security:* security guard posted at main entrance, local police department.
Costs (2017–18) *Tuition:* $11,952 full-time. *Required fees:* $1400 full-time. *Payment plan:* installment.
Applying *Options:* electronic application. *Application fee:* $25. *Required:* high school transcript, interview.
Freshman Application Contact College of Business and Technology–Miami Gardens, 5190 NW 167 Street, Miami Gardens, FL 33014. *Phone:* 305-273-4499 Ext. 1100.
Website: http://www.cbt.edu/.

College of Central Florida
Ocala, Florida

- **State and locally supported** primarily 2-year, founded 1957, part of Florida Community College System
- **Small-town** 139-acre campus
- **Endowment** $65.4 million
- **Coed,** 7,931 undergraduate students, 38% full-time, 63% women, 37% men

Undergraduates 3,036 full-time, 4,895 part-time. 16% are from out of state.
Freshmen *Admission:* 4,416 applied, 2,430 admitted, 1,503 enrolled.
Faculty *Total:* 374, 37% full-time, 10% with terminal degrees.
Majors Accounting technology and bookkeeping; advertising; agribusiness; agriculture; animal sciences; architecture; art; biology/biological sciences; business administration and management; business administration, management and operations related; business/commerce; chemistry; clinical laboratory science/medical technology; computer and information sciences; construction engineering technology; criminal justice/law enforcement administration; criminology; dental assisting; drafting and design technology; dramatic/theater arts; early childhood education; economics; elementary education; emergency medical technology (EMT paramedic); engineering; engineering technology; English; environmental studies; equestrian studies; family and consumer sciences/human sciences; fire science/firefighting; foreign languages and literatures; forestry; health information/medical records technology; health/medical preparatory programs related; health services/allied health/health sciences; history; humanities; human services; information technology; interior architecture; journalism; landscaping and groundskeeping; legal assistant/paralegal; liberal arts and sciences and humanities related; liberal arts and sciences/liberal studies; library and information science; marketing/marketing management; mathematics; medical radiologic technology; music; music teacher education; occupational therapy; office management; parks, recreation and leisure; philosophy; physical education teaching and coaching; physical therapy; physical therapy technology; physics; pre-law studies; premedical studies; pre-pharmacy studies; pre-veterinary studies; psychology; registered nursing/registered nurse; religious studies; restaurant, culinary, and catering management; secondary education; social sciences; social work; sociology; special education; statistics; veterinary/animal health technology.
Academics *Calendar:* semesters. *Degrees:* certificates, diplomas, associate, and bachelor's. *Special study options:* academic remediation for entering students, adult/continuing education programs, advanced placement credit, cooperative education, distance learning, English as a second language, freshman honors college, honors programs, independent study, internships, part-time degree program, services for LD students, summer session for credit.

Library Clifford B. Stearns Learning Resources Center. *Books:* 75,935 (physical), 43,910 (digital/electronic); *Databases:* 152. Students can reserve study rooms.

Student Life *Housing:* college housing not available. *Activities and Organizations:* drama/theater group, student-run newspaper, choral group, Inspirational Choir, Model United Nations, Performing Arts, Phi Theta Kappa (PTK), Student Nurses Association. *Campus security:* 24-hour emergency response devices and patrols, student patrols, late-night transport/escort service. *Student services:* personal/psychological counseling.

Athletics Member NJCAA. *Intercollegiate sports:* baseball M(s), basketball M(s)/W(s), softball W(s), volleyball W(s). *Intramural sports:* bowling M/W.

Costs (2016–17) *Tuition:* state resident $107 per credit hour part-time; nonresident $422 per credit hour part-time. Full-time tuition and fees vary according to course level, degree level, program, and student level. Part-time tuition and fees vary according to course level, degree level, program, and student level. *Waivers:* employees or children of employees.

Financial Aid *Average indebtedness upon graduation:* $2164.

Applying *Options:* electronic application, early admission. *Application fee:* $30. *Required:* high school transcript. *Application deadlines:* rolling (freshmen), rolling (transfers). *Notification:* continuous (freshmen), continuous (transfers).

Freshman Application Contact Ms. Devona Sewell, Registrar, Admission and Records, College of Central Florida, 3001 SW College Road, Ocala, FL 34474. *Phone:* 352-237-2111 Ext. 1398. *Fax:* 352-873-5882. *E-mail:* sewelld@cf.edu. *Website:* http://www.cf.edu/.

Concorde Career Institute
Jacksonville, Florida

Admissions Office Contact Concorde Career Institute, 7259 Salisbury Road, Jacksonville, FL 32256. *Website:* http://www.concorde.edu/.

Concorde Career Institute
Miramar, Florida

Admissions Office Contact Concorde Career Institute, 10933 Marks Way, Miramar, FL 33025. *Website:* http://www.concorde.edu/.

Concorde Career Institute
Orlando, Florida

Admissions Office Contact Concorde Career Institute, 3444 McCrory Place, Orlando, FL 32803. *Website:* http://www.concorde.edu/.

Concorde Career Institute
Tampa, Florida

Admissions Office Contact Concorde Career Institute, 4202 West Spruce Street, Tampa, FL 33607. *Website:* http://www.concorde.edu/.

Daytona College
Ormond Beach, Florida

Admissions Office Contact Daytona College, 469 South Nova Road, Ormond Beach, FL 32174-8445. *Website:* http://www.daytonacollege.edu/.

Daytona State College
Daytona Beach, Florida

- **State-supported** primarily 2-year, founded 1958, part of Florida Community College System
- **Suburban** 100-acre campus with easy access to Orlando
- **Endowment** $11.4 million
- **Coed,** 12,807 undergraduate students, 38% full-time, 61% women, 39% men

Undergraduates 4,830 full-time, 7,977 part-time. 3% are from out of state; 13% Black or African American, non-Hispanic/Latino; 17% Hispanic/Latino; 2% Asian, non-Hispanic/Latino; 0.2% Native Hawaiian or other Pacific Islander, non-Hispanic/Latino; 0.2% American Indian or Alaska Native, non-Hispanic/Latino; 3% Two or more races, non-Hispanic/Latino; 0.7% Race/ethnicity unknown; 0.7% international; 4% transferred in.

Freshmen *Admission:* 1,340 admitted, 1,340 enrolled.

Faculty *Total:* 853, 34% full-time, 17% with terminal degrees.

Majors Accounting; administrative assistant and secretarial science; architectural engineering technology; automobile/automotive mechanics technology; biology teacher education; business administration and management; child development; communications technology; computer and information sciences related; computer engineering; computer engineering related; computer graphics; computer/information technology services administration related; computer programming; computer programming (specific applications); computer science; computer systems networking and telecommunications; computer technology/computer systems technology; criminal justice/law enforcement administration; criminal justice/police science; culinary arts; dental hygiene; drafting and design technology; electrical, electronic and communications engineering technology; elementary education; emergency medical technology (EMT paramedic); engineering; fire science/firefighting; health information/medical records administration; hospitality administration; hotel/motel administration; human services; industrial radiologic technology; industrial technology; information technology; interior design; kindergarten/preschool education; legal assistant/paralegal; machine shop technology; mathematics teacher education; medical administrative assistant and medical secretary; occupational therapist assistant; photographic and film/video technology; physical therapy; plastics and polymer engineering technology; radio and television; registered nursing/registered nurse; respiratory care therapy; robotics technology; secondary education; special education–early childhood; tourism and travel services management.

Academics *Calendar:* semesters. *Degrees:* certificates, diplomas, associate, bachelor's, and postbachelor's certificates. *Special study options:* academic remediation for entering students, adult/continuing education programs, advanced placement credit, cooperative education, distance learning, double majors, English as a second language, external degree program, freshman honors college, honors programs, independent study, internships, off-campus study, part-time degree program, services for LD students, study abroad, summer session for credit. *ROTC:* Army (c), Air Force (c).

Library Mary Karl Memorial Learning Resources Center plus 1 other. *Books:* 35,000 (physical), 170,000 (digital/electronic); *Serial titles:* 250 (physical); *Databases:* 100. Weekly public service hours: 68; students can reserve study rooms.

Student Life *Housing:* college housing not available. *Activities and Organizations:* drama/theater group, student-run newspaper, choral group, Phi Theta Kappa International Honors Society, Student Government Association, Student Occupational Therapy Club, Massage Therapy Club, Student Paralegal Club, national fraternities, national sororities. *Campus security:* 24-hour emergency response devices and patrols, late-night transport/escort service. *Student services:* personal/psychological counseling, women's center.

Athletics Member NJCAA. *Intercollegiate sports:* baseball M(s), basketball M(s)/W(s), golf W(s), soccer M/W, softball W(s), volleyball W(s). *Intramural sports:* basketball M/W, football M/W, soccer M/W, table tennis M/W, tennis M/W.

Financial Aid *Average need-based gift aid:* $1813.

Applying *Options:* electronic application, early admission, deferred entrance. *Required:* high school transcript. *Application deadlines:* rolling (freshmen), rolling (transfers). *Notification:* continuous (freshmen), continuous (transfers).

Freshman Application Contact Dr. Karen Sanders, Director of Admissions and Recruitment, Daytona State College, 1200 International Speedway Boulevard, Daytona Beach, FL 32114. *Phone:* 386-506-3050. *E-mail:* sanderk@daytonastate.edu. *Website:* http://www.daytonastate.edu/.

Eastern Florida State College
Cocoa, Florida

Freshman Application Contact Ms. Stephanie Burnette, Registrar, Eastern Florida State College, 1519 Clearlake Road, Cocoa, FL 32922-6597. *Phone:* 321-433-7271. *Fax:* 321-433-7172. *E-mail:* cocoaadmissions@ brevardcc.edu. *Website:* http://www.easternflorida.edu/.

Everest University
Orange Park, Florida

Freshman Application Contact Admissions Office, Everest University, 805 Wells Road, Orange Park, FL 32073. *Phone:* 904-264-9122. *Website:* http://www.everest.edu/.

Florida Career College
Miami, Florida

Director of Admissions Mr. David Knobel, President, Florida Career College, 1321 Southwest 107th Avenue, Suite 201B, Miami, FL 33174. *Phone:* 305-553-6065. *Toll-free phone:* 888-852-7272. *Website:* http://www.anthem.edu/miami/.

Florida College of Natural Health

Maitland, Florida

Freshman Application Contact Admissions Office, Florida College of Natural Health, 2600 Lake Lucien Drive, Suite 140, Maitland, FL 32751. *Phone:* 407-261-0319. *Toll-free phone:* 800-393-7337. *Website:* http://www.fcnh.com/.

Florida College of Natural Health

Miami, Florida

Director of Admissions Admissions Coordinator, Florida College of Natural Health, 7925 Northwest 12th Street, Suite 201, Miami, FL 33126. *Phone:* 305-597-9599. *Toll-free phone:* 800-599-9599. *Fax:* 305-597-9110. *Website:* http://www.fcnh.com/.

Florida College of Natural Health

Pompano Beach, Florida

Freshman Application Contact Admissions Office, Florida College of Natural Health, 2001 West Sample Road, Suite 100, Pompano Beach, FL 33064. *Phone:* 954-975-6400. *Toll-free phone:* 800-541-9299. *Website:* http://www.fcnh.com/.

Florida Gateway College

Lake City, Florida

Freshman Application Contact Admissions, Florida Gateway College, 149 SE College Place, Lake City, FL 32025-8703. *Phone:* 386-755-4236. *E-mail:* admissions@fgc.edu. *Website:* http://www.fgc.edu/.

Florida Keys Community College

Key West, Florida

- **State-supported** primarily 2-year, founded 1965, part of Florida College System
- **Small-town** 20-acre campus
- **Coed,** 1,023 undergraduate students, 37% full-time, 58% women, 42% men

Undergraduates 377 full-time, 646 part-time. 8% Black or African American, non-Hispanic/Latino; 25% Hispanic/Latino; 1% Asian, non-Hispanic/Latino; 0.3% Native Hawaiian or other Pacific Islander, non-Hispanic/Latino; 0.1% American Indian or Alaska Native, non-Hispanic/Latino; 2% Two or more races, non-Hispanic/Latino; 8% Race/ethnicity unknown; 0.6% international.
Freshmen *Admission:* 195 enrolled.
Majors Business administration and management; business administration, management and operations related; computer programming; computer systems analysis; fishing and fisheries sciences and management; liberal arts and sciences/liberal studies; mechanical engineering technologies related; parks, recreation and leisure; registered nursing/registered nurse.
Academics *Calendar:* semesters. *Degrees:* certificates, associate, and bachelor's. *Special study options:* academic remediation for entering students, adult/continuing education programs, advanced placement credit, cooperative education, distance learning, double majors, English as a second language, independent study, internships, part-time degree program, services for LD students, student-designed majors, summer session for credit.
Library Florida Keys Community College Library. Students can reserve study rooms.
Student Life *Housing Options:* coed. *Activities and Organizations:* choral group. *Campus security:* 24-hour patrols. *Student services:* personal/psychological counseling.
Costs (2016–17) *Tuition:* state resident $2483 full-time, $109 per credit hour part-time; nonresident $9933 full-time, $439 per credit hour part-time. Full-time tuition and fees vary according to course load. Part-time tuition and fees vary according to course load. *Required fees:* $793 full-time. *Room and board:* $11,650; room only: $9620. *Payment plan:* installment. *Waivers:* employees or children of employees.
Financial Aid Of all full-time matriculated undergraduates who enrolled in 2015, 30 Federal Work-Study jobs (averaging $2000).
Applying *Options:* electronic application, early admission, deferred entrance. *Application fee:* $20. *Required for some:* high school transcript. *Application deadlines:* rolling (freshmen), rolling (transfers). *Notification:* continuous (freshmen), continuous (transfers).
Freshman Application Contact Florida Keys Community College, 5901 College Road, Key West, FL 33040-4397. *Phone:* 305-296-9081 Ext. 237. *Website:* http://www.fkcc.edu/.

The Florida School of Traditional Midwifery

Gainesville, Florida

Freshman Application Contact Admissions Office, The Florida School of Traditional Midwifery, 810 East University Avenue, 2nd Floor, Gainseville, FL 32601. *Phone:* 352-338-0766. *Fax:* 352-338-2013. *E-mail:* info@midwiferyschool.org. *Website:* http://www.midwiferyschool.org/.

Florida SouthWestern State College

Fort Myers, Florida

- **State and locally supported** primarily 2-year, founded 1962, part of Florida College System
- **Urban** 413-acre campus
- **Endowment** $731,365
- **Coed,** 16,616 undergraduate students, 34% full-time, 61% women, 39% men

Undergraduates 5,708 full-time, 10,908 part-time. Students come from 46 states and territories; 27 other countries; 4% are from out of state; 10% Black or African American, non-Hispanic/Latino; 28% Hispanic/Latino; 2% Asian, non-Hispanic/Latino; 0.2% Native Hawaiian or other Pacific Islander, non-Hispanic/Latino; 0.4% American Indian or Alaska Native, non-Hispanic/Latino; 2% Two or more races, non-Hispanic/Latino; 6% Race/ethnicity unknown; 2% international; 4% transferred in; 2% live on campus. *Retention:* 66% of full-time freshmen returned.
Freshmen *Admission:* 5,769 applied, 4,663 admitted, 3,257 enrolled. *Average high school GPA:* 2.96.
Faculty *Total:* 536, 35% full-time, 24% with terminal degrees. *Student/faculty ratio:* 31:1.
Majors Accounting technology and bookkeeping; architectural technology; biology/biotechnology laboratory technician; biology teacher education; business administration and management; business administration, management and operations related; cardiovascular technology; child-care provision; civil engineering technology; community health services counseling; computer programming; computer systems networking and telecommunications; criminal justice/law enforcement administration; dental hygiene; drafting and design technology; early childhood education; elementary education; emergency medical technology (EMT paramedic); English/language arts teacher education; fire prevention and safety technology; forensic science and technology; health information/medical records technology; homeland security, law enforcement, firefighting and protective services related; information technology; legal assistant/paralegal; liberal arts and sciences/liberal studies; management information systems; mathematics teacher education; medical radiologic technology; network and system administration; operations management; optician; physical therapy technology; registered nursing/registered nurse; respiratory care therapy; respiratory therapy technician; science teacher education; substance abuse/addiction counseling; turf and turfgrass management; web page, digital/multimedia and information resources design.
Academics *Calendar:* semesters. *Degrees:* certificates, associate, and bachelor's. *Special study options:* academic remediation for entering students, accelerated degree program, advanced placement credit, cooperative education, distance learning, double majors, English as a second language, honors programs, independent study, internships, off-campus study, part-time degree program, services for LD students, study abroad, summer session for credit.
Library Richard H. Rush Library. *Books:* 45,355 (physical), 28,410 (digital/electronic); *Databases:* 128. Weekly public service hours: 79.
Student Life *Housing Options:* coed. Campus housing is university owned. *Activities and Organizations:* drama/theater group, choral group. *Campus security:* 24-hour emergency response devices and patrols, late-night transport/escort service, controlled dormitory access, Rave Guardian app for students, faculty, and staff.
Athletics Member NJCAA. *Intercollegiate sports:* baseball M, softball W. *Intramural sports:* basketball M/W, soccer M/W, volleyball M/W.
Costs (2016–17) *Tuition:* state resident $2436 full-time, $81 per credit hour part-time; nonresident $9750 full-time, $325 per credit hour part-time. Full-time tuition and fees vary according to degree level. Part-time tuition and fees vary according to degree level. *Required fees:* $965 full-time. *Room and board:* $8860. Room and board charges vary according to board plan. *Payment plan:* installment. *Waivers:* employees or children of employees.
Financial Aid Of all full-time matriculated undergraduates who enrolled in 2014, 3,887 applied for aid, 3,311 were judged to have need, 68 had their need fully met. In 2014, 166 non-need-based awards were made. *Average percent of need met:* 47%. *Average financial aid package:* $6172. *Average need-based loan:* $3461. *Average need-based gift aid:* $5119. *Average non-need-based aid:* $2588.

Applying *Options:* electronic application, early admission, deferred entrance. *Application fee:* $30. *Required:* high school transcript. *Application deadlines:* 8/17 (freshmen), 8/17 (transfers). *Notification:* continuous (freshmen), continuous (transfers).

Freshman Application Contact FSW Admissions, Florida SouthWestern State College, 8099 College Parkway, Fort Myers, FL 33919. *Phone:* 239-489-9054. *Fax:* 239-489-9094. *E-mail:* admissions@fsw.edu. *Website:* http://www.fsw.edu/.

Florida State College at Jacksonville
Jacksonville, Florida

Freshman Application Contact Dr. Peter Biegel, Registrar, Florida State College at Jacksonville, 501 West State Street, Jacksonville, FL 32202. *Phone:* 904-632-5112. *Toll-free phone:* 888-873-1145. *E-mail:* pbiegel@fscj.edu. *Website:* http://www.fscj.edu/.

Florida Technical College
Orlando, Florida

Director of Admissions Ms. Jeanette E. Muschlitz, Director of Admissions, Florida Technical College, 12900 Challenger Parkway, Orlando, FL 32826. *Phone:* 407-678-5600. *Toll-free phone:* 888-574-2082. *Website:* http://www.ftccollege.edu/.

Fortis College
Cutler Bay, Florida

Admissions Office Contact Fortis College, 19600 South Dixie Highway, Suite B, Cutler Bay, FL 33157. *Toll-free phone:* 855-4-FORTIS. *Website:* http://www.fortis.edu/.

Fortis College
Orange Park, Florida

Admissions Office Contact Fortis College, 700 Blanding Boulevard, Suite 16, Orange Park, FL 32065. *Toll-free phone:* 855-4-FORTIS. *Website:* http://www.fortis.edu/.

Fortis Institute
Pensacola, Florida

Admissions Office Contact Fortis Institute, 4081 East Olive Road, Suite B, Pensacola, FL 32514. *Toll-free phone:* 855-4-FORTIS. *Website:* http://www.fortis.edu/.

Fortis Institute
Port St. Lucie, Florida

Admissions Office Contact Fortis Institute, 9022 South US Highway 1, Port St. Lucie, FL 34952. *Toll-free phone:* 855-4-FORTIS. *Website:* http://www.fortis.edu/.

Galen College of Nursing
St. Petersburg, Florida

Admissions Office Contact Galen College of Nursing, 11101 Roosevelt Boulevard North, St. Petersburg, FL 33716. *Toll-free phone:* 877-223-7040. *Website:* http://www.galencollege.edu/.

Golf Academy of America
Apopka, Florida

Admissions Office Contact Golf Academy of America, 510 South Hunt Club Boulevard, Apopka, FL 32703. *Website:* http://www.golfacademy.edu/.

Gulf Coast State College
Panama City, Florida

- **State-supported** primarily 2-year, founded 1957, part of Florida College System
- **Urban** 80-acre campus
- **Endowment** $30.5 million
- **Coed,** 5,483 undergraduate students, 34% full-time, 61% women, 39% men

Undergraduates 1,850 full-time, 3,633 part-time. Students come from 17 states and territories; 3% are from out of state; 12% Black or African American, non-Hispanic/Latino; 6% Hispanic/Latino; 3% Asian, non-Hispanic/Latino; 1% American Indian or Alaska Native, non-Hispanic/Latino; 4% Two or more races, non-Hispanic/Latino; 3% Race/ethnicity unknown; 0.4% international; 3% transferred in.

Freshmen *Admission:* 913 enrolled.

Faculty *Total:* 320, 47% full-time. *Student/faculty ratio:* 19:1.

Majors Accounting technology and bookkeeping; animation, interactive technology, video graphics and special effects; automation engineer technology; business administration and management; business administration, management and operations related; CAD/CADD drafting/design technology; child-care provision; civil engineering technology; communications technology; computer/information technology services administration related; computer programming; computer programming (vendor/product certification); computer systems networking and telecommunications; construction engineering technology; criminal justice/law enforcement administration; dental hygiene; diagnostic medical sonography and ultrasound technology; digital arts; digital communication and media/multimedia; early childhood education; electrical, electronic and communications engineering technology; emergency medical technology (EMT paramedic); engineering technology; fire prevention and safety technology; forensic science and technology; health services/allied health/health sciences; hospitality administration; liberal arts and sciences/liberal studies; management information systems; manufacturing engineering technology; medical administrative assistant and medical secretary; medical radiologic technology; music technology; network and system administration; nuclear medical technology; office management; physical therapy technology; registered nursing/registered nurse; respiratory care therapy; restaurant, culinary, and catering management; surgical technology; transportation/mobility management; web page, digital/multimedia and information resources design.

Academics *Calendar:* semesters. *Degrees:* certificates, associate, and bachelor's. *Special study options:* academic remediation for entering students, accelerated degree program, adult/continuing education programs, advanced placement credit, cooperative education, distance learning, double majors, English as a second language, external degree program, honors programs, independent study, off-campus study, part-time degree program, services for LD students, study abroad, summer session for credit.

Library Gulf Coast State College Library. *Books:* 44,254 (physical), 58,468 (digital/electronic); *Databases:* 152.

Student Life *Housing:* college housing not available. *Activities and Organizations:* drama/theater group, student-run newspaper, radio and television station, choral group. *Campus security:* 24-hour patrols, late-night transport/escort service, patrols by trained security personnel during campus hours. *Student services:* personal/psychological counseling.

Athletics Member NJCAA. *Intercollegiate sports:* baseball M(s), basketball M(s)/W(s), softball W(s), volleyball W(s).

Costs (2016–17) *Tuition:* state resident $2370 full-time, $99 per credit hour part-time; nonresident $8635 full-time, $360 per credit hour part-time. Full-time tuition and fees vary according to degree level. Part-time tuition and fees vary according to degree level. *Required fees:* $620 full-time, $26 per credit hour part-time.

Financial Aid Of all full-time matriculated undergraduates who enrolled in 2015, 145 Federal Work-Study jobs (averaging $3200). 60 state and other part-time jobs (averaging $2600).

Applying *Options:* electronic application, early admission, deferred entrance. *Application fee:* $20. *Required:* high school transcript. *Application deadlines:* rolling (freshmen), rolling (transfers). *Notification:* continuous (freshmen).

Freshman Application Contact Mrs. Sam Wagner, Application Process Specialist, Gulf Coast State College, 5230 West U.S. Highway 98, Panama City, FL 32401. *Phone:* 850-769-1551 Ext. 2936. *Fax:* 850-913-3308. *E-mail:* swagner1@gulfcoast.edu. *Website:* http://www.gulfcoast.edu/.

Gwinnett Institute
Orlando, Florida

Admissions Office Contact Gwinnett Institute, 1900 North Alafaya Trail, Orlando, FL 32826. *Website:* http://www.gwinnettcollege.com/Orlando/.

Hillsborough Community College
Tampa, Florida

- **State-supported** 2-year, founded 1968, part of Florida College System
- **Urban** campus with easy access to Tampa, Clearwater, St. Petersburg
- **Coed,** 27,061 undergraduate students, 40% full-time, 57% women, 43% men

Undergraduates 10,924 full-time, 16,137 part-time. Students come from 42 states and territories; 128 other countries; 1% are from out of state; 18% Black or African American, non-Hispanic/Latino; 29% Hispanic/Latino; 3% Asian, non-Hispanic/Latino; 0.2% Native Hawaiian or other Pacific Islander, non-Hispanic/Latino; 0.4% American Indian or Alaska Native, non-Hispanic/Latino; 3% Two or more races, non-Hispanic/Latino; 7% Race/ethnicity unknown; 3% international; 26% transferred in.
Freshmen *Admission:* 5,194 enrolled.
Faculty *Total:* 1,410, 22% full-time, 16% with terminal degrees. *Student/faculty ratio:* 24:1.
Majors Aquaculture; architectural engineering technology; biology/biotechnology laboratory technician; business administration and management; child-care and support services management; cinematography and film/video production; computer programming (specific applications); computer systems analysis; computer technology/computer systems technology; criminal justice/law enforcement administration; dental hygiene; diagnostic medical sonography and ultrasound technology; dietitian assistant; electrical, electronic and communications engineering technology; emergency medical technology (EMT paramedic); environmental control technologies related; executive assistant/executive secretary; fire prevention and safety technology; hospitality administration; legal assistant/paralegal; liberal arts and sciences/liberal studies; management information systems and services related; medical radiologic technology; network and system administration; nuclear medical technology; operations management; opticianry; optometric technician; psychiatric/mental health services technology; registered nursing/registered nurse; respiratory care therapy; restaurant, culinary, and catering management; restaurant/food services management; veterinary/animal health technology.
Academics *Calendar:* semesters. *Degree:* certificates and associate. *Special study options:* academic remediation for entering students, advanced placement credit, cooperative education, distance learning, English as a second language, honors programs, independent study, internships, off-campus study, part-time degree program, services for LD students, study abroad, summer session for credit. *ROTC:* Army (c), Air Force (c).
Library Dale Mabry Library plus 4 others. *Books:* 109,428 (physical), 44,898 (digital/electronic); *Serial titles:* 578 (physical), 47,889 (digital/electronic); *Databases:* 124.
Student Life *Housing Options:* Campus housing is provided by a third party. *Activities and Organizations:* drama/theater group, student-run newspaper, radio station, choral group. *Campus security:* 24-hour emergency response devices and patrols, late-night transport/escort service. *Student services:* personal/psychological counseling.
Athletics Member NJCAA. *Intercollegiate sports:* baseball M(s), basketball M(s)/W(s), softball W(s), tennis W(s), volleyball W(s).
Costs (2016–17) *Tuition:* state resident $2505 full-time, $104 per credit hour part-time; nonresident $9111 full-time, $380 per credit hour part-time. *Payment plan:* installment. *Waivers:* employees or children of employees.
Applying *Options:* electronic application, early admission. *Required:* high school transcript. *Application deadlines:* rolling (freshmen), rolling (transfers).
Freshman Application Contact Ms. Jennifer Young, College Registrar, Hillsborough Community College, PO Box 31127, Tampa, FL 33631-3127. *Phone:* 813-259-6565. *E-mail:* jyoung92@hccfl.edu.
Website: http://www.hccfl.edu/.

Key College
Dania Beach, Florida

Director of Admissions Mr. Ronald H. Dooley, President and Director of Admissions, Key College, 225 East Dania Beach Boulevard, Dania Beach, FL 33004. *Phone:* 954-581-2223 Ext. 23. *Toll-free phone:* 877-421-6149. *Website:* http://www.keycollege.edu/.

Lake-Sumter State College
Leesburg, Florida

Freshman Application Contact Ms. Bonnie Yanick, Enrollment Specialist, Lake-Sumter State College, 9501 U.S. Highway 441, Leesburg, FL 34788-8751. *Phone:* 352-365-3561. *Fax:* 352-365-3553. *E-mail:* admissinquiry@lscc.edu. *Website:* http://www.lssc.edu/.

Meridian College
Sarasota, Florida

Admissions Office Contact Meridian College, 7020 Professional Parkway East, Sarasota, FL 34240. *Website:* http://www.meridian.edu/.

★ Miami Dade College
Miami, Florida

- **State and locally supported** primarily 2-year, founded 1960, part of Florida College System
- **Urban** campus
- **Endowment** $137.1 million
- **Coed,** 55,206 undergraduate students, 38% full-time, 57% women, 43% men

Undergraduates 21,075 full-time, 34,131 part-time. Students come from 42 states and territories; 164 other countries; 0.4% are from out of state; 14% Black or African American, non-Hispanic/Latino; 69% Hispanic/Latino; 1% Asian, non-Hispanic/Latino; 0.1% Native Hawaiian or other Pacific Islander, non-Hispanic/Latino; 0.1% American Indian or Alaska Native, non-Hispanic/Latino; 0.5% Two or more races, non-Hispanic/Latino; 3% Race/ethnicity unknown; 6% international; 0.5% transferred in.
Freshmen *Admission:* 44,910 applied, 44,910 admitted, 11,610 enrolled.
Faculty *Total:* 2,453, 30% full-time, 25% with terminal degrees. *Student/faculty ratio:* 24:1.
Majors Accounting technology and bookkeeping; administrative assistant and secretarial science; aeronautics/aviation/aerospace science and technology; agriculture; airline pilot and flight crew; air traffic control; American studies; animation, interactive technology, video graphics and special effects; anthropology; architectural drafting and CAD/CADD; architectural engineering technology; architectural technology; art; Asian studies; audiology and speech-language pathology; automation engineer technology; aviation/airway management; banking and financial support services; behavioral sciences; biology/biological sciences; biology teacher education; biomedical technology; biotechnology; business administration and management; business administration, management and operations related; business automation/technology/data entry; CAD/CADD drafting/design technology; chemistry; chemistry teacher education; child-care provision; child development; cinematography and film/video production; civil engineering technology; clinical/medical laboratory technology; commercial and advertising art; community health services counseling; comparative literature; computer and information sciences; computer engineering technology; computer graphics; computer installation and repair technology; computer programming; computer programming (specific applications); computer programming (vendor/product certification); computer science; computer software technology; computer support specialist; computer systems networking and telecommunications; computer technology/computer systems technology; construction engineering technology; cooking and related culinary arts; corrections; corrections and criminal justice related; court reporting; criminal justice/law enforcement administration; criminal justice/police science; culinary arts; customer service support/call center/teleservice operation; dance; dental hygiene; diagnostic medical sonography and ultrasound technology; dietetics; dietetic technology; drafting and design technology; dramatic/theater arts; early childhood education; economics; education; education related; education (specific levels and methods) related; electrical and electronic engineering technologies related; electrical, electronic and communications engineering technology; electrician; elementary education; emergency medical technology (EMT paramedic); engineering; engineering related; engineering technology; English; entrepreneurship; environmental engineering technology; environmental science; finance; fire prevention and safety technology; fire science/firefighting; food science; forensic science and technology; forestry; French; funeral service and mortuary science; game and interactive media design; general studies; geology/earth science; German; health information/medical records administration; health information/medical records technology; health/medical preparatory programs related; health professions related; health services/allied health/health sciences; heating, air conditioning, ventilation and refrigeration maintenance technology; heating, ventilation, air conditioning and refrigeration engineering technology; histologic technician; histologic technology/histotechnologist; history; homeland security, law enforcement, firefighting and protective services related; horticultural science; hospitality administration; hotel/motel administration; humanities; human services; industrial technology; information science/studies; information technology; interior design; international relations and affairs; Italian; journalism; kindergarten/preschool education; landscaping and groundskeeping; Latin American studies; legal administrative assistant/secretary; legal assistant/paralegal; liberal arts and sciences/liberal studies; logistics, materials, and supply chain management; management information systems; manufacturing engineering technology; marketing/marketing management; massage therapy; mass communication/media; mathematics; mathematics

teacher education; medical/clinical assistant; medical radiologic technology; middle school education; music; music performance; music teacher education; music technology; natural sciences; network and system administration; nonprofit management; nuclear medical technology; office management; operations management; ophthalmic technology; opticianry; ornamental horticulture; parks, recreation and leisure; pharmacy technician; philosophy; phlebotomy technology; photographic and film/video technology; photography; physical education teaching and coaching; physical sciences; physical therapy technology; physician assistant; physics; physics teacher education; pipefitting and sprinkler fitting; plant nursery management; plumbing technology; political science and government; Portuguese; pre-engineering; psychology; public administration; radio and television; radio and television broadcasting technology; radiologic technology/science; real estate; recording arts technology; registered nursing/registered nurse; respiratory care therapy; respiratory therapy technician; restaurant, culinary, and catering management; restaurant/food services management; science teacher education; security and loss prevention; sheet metal technology; sign language interpretation and translation; social sciences; social work; sociology; Spanish; special education; special education–individuals with hearing impairments; substance abuse/addiction counseling; teacher assistant/aide; telecommunications technology; theater design and technology; tourism and travel services management; veterinary/animal health technology; web page, digital/multimedia and information resources design.

Academics *Calendar:* 16-16-6-6. *Degrees:* certificates, associate, bachelor's, and postbachelor's certificates. *Special study options:* academic remediation for entering students, accelerated degree program, adult/continuing education programs, advanced placement credit, cooperative education, distance learning, English as a second language, freshman honors college, honors programs, independent study, internships, off-campus study, part-time degree program, services for LD students, study abroad, summer session for credit. *ROTC:* Army (b), Air Force (c).

Library Miami Dade College Learning Resources plus 9 others. *Books:* 187,729 (physical), 59,920 (digital/electronic); *Serial titles:* 68,309 (physical), 40,849 (digital/electronic); *Databases:* 125. Weekly public service hours: 69; students can reserve study rooms.

Student Life *Housing:* college housing not available. *Activities and Organizations:* drama/theater group, student-run newspaper, radio and television station, choral group, Student Government Association, Phi Theta Kappa, Phi Beta Lambda (business), Future Educators of America Professional, Kappa Delta Pi Honor Society (education), national fraternities. *Campus security:* 24-hour emergency response devices and patrols, student patrols, late-night transport/escort service, Emergency Mass Notification System (EMNS), campus public address systems, LiveSafe mobile safety App for students/employees. *Student services:* health clinic, personal/psychological counseling.

Athletics Member NCAA, NJCAA. All NCAA Division I. *Intercollegiate sports:* baseball M(s), basketball M(s)/W(s), softball W(s), volleyball W(s).

Costs (2016–17) *One-time required fee:* $30. *Tuition:* state resident $1987 full-time, $83 per credit hour part-time; nonresident $7947 full-time, $331 per credit hour part-time. Full-time tuition and fees vary according to course load, degree level, and program. Part-time tuition and fees vary according to course load, degree level, and program. *Required fees:* $851 full-time, $35 per credit hour part-time. *Waivers:* employees or children of employees.

Financial Aid Of all full-time matriculated undergraduates who enrolled in 2015, 800 Federal Work-Study jobs (averaging $5000). 125 state and other part-time jobs (averaging $5000).

Applying *Options:* electronic application, early admission. *Application fee:* $30. *Required:* high school transcript. *Application deadlines:* rolling (freshmen), rolling (transfers). *Notification:* continuous (freshmen), continuous (transfers).

Freshman Application Contact Ms. Ferne Creary, Interim College Registrar, Miami Dade College, 11011 SW 104th Street, Miami, FL 33176. *Phone:* 305-237-2206. *Fax:* 305-237-2532. *E-mail:* fcreary@mdc.edu. *Website:* http://www.mdc.edu/.

See below for display ad and page 338 for the College Close-Up.

North Florida Community College
Madison, Florida

Freshman Application Contact Mr. Bobby Scott, North Florida Community College, 325 Northwest Turner Davis Drive, Madison, FL 32340. *Phone:* 850-973-9450. *Toll-free phone:* 866-937-6322. *Fax:* 850-973-1697. *Website:* http://www.nfcc.edu/.

Northwest Florida State College
Niceville, Florida

Freshman Application Contact Ms. Karen Cooper, Director of Admissions, Northwest Florida State College, 100 College Boulevard, Niceville, FL 32578. *Phone:* 850-729-4901. *Fax:* 850-729-5206. *E-mail:* cooperk@nwfsc.edu. *Website:* http://www.nwfsc.edu/.

Orion College
Plantation, Florida

Admissions Office Contact Orion College, 51 North State Road 7, Plantation, FL 33317. *Toll-free phone:* 888-331-9957.
Website: http://www.orioncollege.org/.

Pasco-Hernando State College
New Port Richey, Florida

Freshman Application Contact Ms. Estela Carrion, Director of Admissions and Student Records, Pasco-Hernando State College, 10230 Ridge Road, New Port Richey, FL 34654-5199. *Phone:* 727-816-3261. *Toll-free phone:* 877-TRY-PHSC. *Fax:* 727-816-3389. *E-mail:* carrioe@phsc.edu. *Website:* http://www.phsc.edu/.

Pensacola State College
Pensacola, Florida

- **State-supported** primarily 2-year, founded 1948, part of Florida College System
- **Urban** 130-acre campus
- **Coed,** 9,643 undergraduate students, 37% full-time, 61% women, 39% men

Undergraduates 3,576 full-time, 6,067 part-time. 15% Black or African American, non-Hispanic/Latino; 7% Hispanic/Latino; 3% Asian, non-Hispanic/Latino; 0.5% Native Hawaiian or other Pacific Islander, non-Hispanic/Latino; 0.8% American Indian or Alaska Native, non-Hispanic/Latino; 5% Two or more races, non-Hispanic/Latino; 2% Race/ethnicity unknown; 0.3% international.
Freshmen *Admission:* 3,608 applied, 3,608 admitted, 1,544 enrolled.
Faculty *Total:* 573, 30% full-time, 12% with terminal degrees. *Student/faculty ratio:* 18:1.
Majors Accounting; accounting technology and bookkeeping; administrative assistant and secretarial science; agricultural business and management; agriculture; art; art teacher education; biochemistry; biology/biological sciences; botany/plant biology; building/property maintenance; business administration and management; business administration, management and operations related; business/commerce; chemical technology; chemistry; child-care and support services management; child-care provision; civil engineering technology; commercial and advertising art; communications technology; computer and information sciences; computer and information sciences related; computer and information systems security; computer engineering; computer programming; computer programming (specific applications); computer programming (vendor/product certification); computer science; computer systems analysis; construction engineering technology; consumer services and advocacy; cooking and related culinary arts; criminal justice/law enforcement administration; cyber/computer forensics and counterterrorism; dental hygiene; diagnostic medical sonography and ultrasound technology; dietetics; drafting and design technology; dramatic/theater arts; early childhood education; education; electrical, electronic and communications engineering technology; elementary education; emergency medical technology (EMT paramedic); engineering; engineering technology; English; food service systems administration; foods, nutrition, and wellness; forensic science and technology; geology/earth science; graphic design; hazardous materials management and waste technology; health/health-care administration; health information/medical records administration; health information/medical records technology; history; homeland security related; hospitality administration; hotel/motel administration; hotel, motel, and restaurant management; information science/studies; journalism; landscaping and groundskeeping; legal administrative assistant/secretary; legal assistant/paralegal; liberal arts and sciences/liberal studies; management information systems; management information systems and services related; management science; mathematics; medical radiologic technology; music; music teacher education; natural resources management and policy; nursing assistant/aide and patient care assistant/aide; nursing science; ornamental horticulture; pharmacy technician; philosophy; photography; physical therapy technology; physics; pre-dentistry studies; pre-law studies; premedical studies; prenursing studies; pre-pharmacy studies; pre-veterinary studies; psychology; registered nursing/registered nurse; restaurant, culinary, and catering management; sociology; special education; telecommunications technology; veterinary/animal health technology.
Academics *Calendar:* semesters. *Degrees:* certificates, diplomas, associate, and bachelor's. *Special study options:* academic remediation for entering students, adult/continuing education programs, advanced placement credit, cooperative education, distance learning, double majors, English as a second language, external degree program, honors programs, independent study, part-time degree program, services for LD students, summer session for credit. *ROTC:* Army (b).

Library Edward M. Chadbourne Library plus 3 others.
Student Life *Housing:* college housing not available. *Activities and Organizations:* drama/theater group, student-run newspaper, choral group, Student Government Association, Health Occupations Students of America (HOSA), SkillsUSA, African-American Student Association, Forestry Club. *Campus security:* 24-hour emergency response devices and patrols, late-night transport/escort service. *Student services:* health clinic, personal/psychological counseling.
Athletics Member NJCAA. *Intercollegiate sports:* baseball M(s), basketball M(s)/W(s), softball W(s), volleyball W. *Intramural sports:* archery M/W, badminton M/W, basketball M/W, bowling M/W, cross-country running M/W, gymnastics M/W, racquetball M/W, sailing M/W, swimming and diving M/W, tennis M/W, track and field M/W, volleyball M/W, weight lifting M/W, wrestling M.
Costs (2016–17) *One-time required fee:* $30. *Tuition:* $105 per credit hour part-time; state resident $2510 full-time, $105 per credit hour part-time; nonresident $10,075 full-time, $420 per credit hour part-time. Full-time tuition and fees vary according to course level and degree level. Part-time tuition and fees vary according to course level and degree level. *Payment plan:* deferred payment. *Waivers:* senior citizens and employees or children of employees.
Financial Aid Of all full-time matriculated undergraduates who enrolled in 2015, 120 Federal Work-Study jobs (averaging $3000).
Applying *Options:* electronic application, early admission. *Application fee:* $30. *Required:* high school transcript. *Application deadlines:* 8/30 (freshmen), 8/30 (transfers). *Notification:* continuous until 8/30 (freshmen), continuous until 8/30 (transfers).
Freshman Application Contact Ms. Susan Desbrow, Registrar, Pensacola State College, 1000 College Boulevard, Pensacola, FL 32504. *Phone:* 850-484-1605. *Fax:* 850-484-1020. *E-mail:* kdutremble@pensacolastate.edu. *Website:* http://www.pensacolastate.edu/.

Praxis Institute
Miami, Florida

Admissions Office Contact Praxis Institute, 1850 SW 8th Street, 4th Floor, Miami, FL 33135. *Website:* http://the-praxisinstitute.com/.

Professional Hands Institute
Miami, Florida

Admissions Office Contact Professional Hands Institute, 10 NW 42 Avenue, Suite 200, Miami, FL 33126. *Website:* http://prohands.edu/.

Remington College–Heathrow Campus
Lake Mary, Florida

Admissions Office Contact Remington College–Heathrow Campus, 7131 Business Park Lane, Lake Mary, FL 32746. *Toll-free phone:* 800-323-8122. *Website:* http://www.remingtoncollege.edu/.

SABER College
Miami, Florida

Admissions Office Contact SABER College, 3990 W. Flagler Street, Suite 103, Miami, FL 33134. *Website:* http://www.sabercollege.com/.

St. Johns River State College
Palatka, Florida

Director of Admissions Dean of Admissions and Records, St. Johns River State College, 5001 Saint Johns Avenue, Palatka, FL 32177-3897. *Phone:* 386-312-4032. *Fax:* 386-312-4289. *Website:* http://www.sjrstate.edu/.

Seminole State College of Florida
Sanford, Florida

- **State and locally supported** primarily 2-year, founded 1966
- **Small-town** 200-acre campus with easy access to Orlando
- **Endowment** $24.6 million
- **Coed,** 17,706 undergraduate students, 35% full-time, 55% women, 45% men

Undergraduates 6,137 full-time, 11,569 part-time. Students come from 21 states and territories; 68 other countries; 3% are from out of state; 16% Black or African American, non-Hispanic/Latino; 24% Hispanic/Latino; 3% Asian, non-Hispanic/Latino; 0.3% Native Hawaiian or other Pacific Islander, non-Hispanic/Latino; 0.3% American Indian or Alaska Native, non-Hispanic/Latino; 3% Two or more races, non-Hispanic/Latino; 3%

Race/ethnicity unknown; 2% international; 7% transferred in. *Retention:* 52% of full-time freshmen returned.

Freshmen *Admission:* 4,587 applied, 2,941 admitted, 2,670 enrolled.

Faculty *Total:* 798, 26% full-time, 22% with terminal degrees. *Student/faculty ratio:* 26:1.

Majors Accounting; administrative assistant and secretarial science; architectural engineering technology; automobile/automotive mechanics technology; banking and financial support services; building/construction finishing, management, and inspection related; business administration and management; child development; civil engineering technology; computer and information sciences and support services related; computer and information sciences related; computer and information systems security; computer engineering related; computer engineering technology; computer graphics; computer hardware engineering; computer/information technology services administration related; computer programming; computer programming related; computer programming (specific applications); computer programming (vendor/product certification); computer software and media applications related; computer software engineering; computer systems networking and telecommunications; construction engineering technology; criminal justice/law enforcement administration; data entry/microcomputer applications; data entry/microcomputer applications related; data modeling/warehousing and database administration; data processing and data processing technology; drafting and design technology; electrical, electronic and communications engineering technology; emergency medical technology (EMT paramedic); finance; fire science/firefighting; industrial technology; information science/studies; information technology; interior design; legal assistant/paralegal; liberal arts and sciences/liberal studies; marketing/marketing management; network and system administration; physical therapy; registered nursing/registered nurse; respiratory care therapy; telecommunications technology; web/multimedia management and webmaster; web page, digital/multimedia and information resources design; word processing.

Academics *Calendar:* semesters. *Degrees:* certificates, diplomas, associate, bachelor's, and postbachelor's certificates. *Special study options:* academic remediation for entering students, accelerated degree program, adult/continuing education programs, advanced placement credit, cooperative education, distance learning, double majors, English as a second language, external degree program, honors programs, independent study, internships, part-time degree program, services for LD students, study abroad, summer session for credit. *ROTC:* Army (b).

Library Seminole State Library at Sanford Lake Mary plus 3 others. *Books:* 67,023 (physical), 145,374 (digital/electronic); *Serial titles:* 520 (physical), 18,003 (digital/electronic); *Databases:* 130. Weekly public service hours: 60; students can reserve study rooms.

Student Life *Housing:* college housing not available. *Activities and Organizations:* drama/theater group, student-run newspaper, choral group, Phi Beta Lambda, Phi Theta Kappa, Student Government Association, Sigma Phi Gamma, Hispanic Student Association. *Campus security:* 24-hour emergency response devices and patrols, late-night transport/escort service. *Student services:* personal/psychological counseling.

Athletics Member NJCAA. *Intercollegiate sports:* baseball M(s), golf W(s), softball W(s).

Costs (2017–18) *Tuition:* state resident $3597 full-time, $104 per credit hour part-time; nonresident $12,739 full-time, $382 per credit hour part-time. Full-time tuition and fees vary according to course level, course load, degree level, and program. Part-time tuition and fees vary according to course level, course load, degree level, and program. *Payment plan:* deferred payment. *Waivers:* senior citizens and employees or children of employees.

Applying *Options:* electronic application, early admission, deferred entrance. *Required:* high school transcript, minimum 2.0 GPA. *Application deadlines:* rolling (freshmen), rolling (transfers). *Notification:* continuous (freshmen), continuous (transfers).

Freshman Application Contact Ms. Pamela Mennechey, Associate Vice President - Student Recruitment and Enrollment, Seminole State College of Florida, Sanford, FL 32773-6199. *Phone:* 407-708-2050. *Fax:* 407-708-2395. *E-mail:* admissions@scc-fl.edu.
Website: http://www.seminolestate.edu/.

Southeastern College–West Palm Beach
West Palm Beach, Florida

- **Proprietary** 2-year, founded 1988
- **Urban** campus
- **Coed,** 1,063 undergraduate students

Undergraduates Students come from 6 states and territories; 2% are from out of state; 35% Black or African American, non-Hispanic/Latino; 41% Hispanic/Latino; 2% Asian, non-Hispanic/Latino; 0.2% American Indian or Alaska Native, non-Hispanic/Latino; 0.7% Two or more races, non-Hispanic/Latino; 3% Race/ethnicity unknown.

Majors Aesthetician/esthetician and skin care; business, management, and marketing related; computer and information sciences and support services related; computer systems networking and telecommunications; emergency medical technology (EMT paramedic); health professions related; licensed practical/vocational nurse training; massage therapy; medical/clinical assistant; medical insurance coding; medical insurance/medical billing; pharmacy technician; surgical technology.

Academics *Degree:* certificates, diplomas, and associate. *Special study options:* accelerated degree program, adult/continuing education programs, advanced placement credit, cooperative education, distance learning, English as a second language, internships, off-campus study, part-time degree program, services for LD students, summer session for credit.

Library Southeastern College Library. *Books:* 1,728 (physical); *Serial titles:* 26 (physical); *Databases:* 5. Weekly public service hours: 50.

Standardized Tests *Required:* Wonderlic Asssessment, TEAS (for admission).

Costs (2016–17) *One-time required fee:* $200. *Tuition:* $17,496 full-time, $729 per credit hour part-time. Full-time tuition and fees vary according to course load and program. Part-time tuition and fees vary according to course load and program. *Required fees:* $1763 full-time.

Applying *Application fee:* $55. *Required:* high school transcript, interview. *Required for some:* essay or personal statement, letters of recommendation. *Application deadlines:* rolling (freshmen), rolling (transfers), rolling (early action). *Early decision deadline:* rolling (for plan 1), rolling (for plan 2). *Notification:* continuous (freshmen), continuous (transfers), rolling (early decision plan 1), rolling (early decision plan 2), rolling (early action).

Freshman Application Contact Admissions Office, Southeastern College–West Palm Beach, 2081 Vista Parkway, Suite 100B, West Palm Beach, FL 33411.
Website: http://www.sec.edu/.

Southern Technical College
Orlando, Florida

Freshman Application Contact Mr. Robinson Elie, Director of Admissions, Southern Technical College, 1485 Florida Mall Avenue, Orlando, FL 32809. *Phone:* 407-438-6000. *Toll-free phone:* 877-347-5492.
E-mail: relie@southerntech.edu. *Website:* http://www.southerntech.edu/.

Southern Technical College
Tampa, Florida

Director of Admissions Admissions, Southern Technical College, 3910 Riga Boulevard, Tampa, FL 33619. *Phone:* 813-630-4401. *Toll-free phone:* 877-347-5492. *Website:* http://www.southerntech.edu/locations/tampa/.

South Florida State College
Avon Park, Florida

- **State-supported** primarily 2-year, founded 1965, part of Florida State College System
- **Rural** 228-acre campus with easy access to Tampa, St. Petersburg, Orlando
- **Endowment** $6.1 million
- **Coed,** 2,722 undergraduate students, 35% full-time, 62% women, 38% men

Undergraduates 945 full-time, 1,777 part-time. 3% are from out of state; 11% Black or African American, non-Hispanic/Latino; 35% Hispanic/Latino; 2% Asian, non-Hispanic/Latino; 0.3% Native Hawaiian or other Pacific Islander, non-Hispanic/Latino; 0.4% American Indian or Alaska Native, non-Hispanic/Latino; 3% Two or more races, non-Hispanic/Latino; 2% Race/ethnicity unknown; 1% international; 4% transferred in.

Freshmen *Admission:* 485 applied, 440 enrolled. *Average high school GPA:* 3.

Faculty *Total:* 148, 41% full-time, 18% with terminal degrees. *Student/faculty ratio:* 16:1.

Majors Accounting; accounting technology and bookkeeping; actuarial science; advertising; aerospace, aeronautical and astronautical/space engineering; agribusiness; agricultural economics; agricultural engineering; agricultural teacher education; agriculture; American studies; animal sciences; anthropology; applied mathematics; architecture; art; art history, criticism and conservation; art teacher education; astronomy; atmospheric sciences and meteorology; audiology and speech-language pathology; banking and financial support services; biochemistry; biological and physical sciences; biology/biological sciences; biomedical technology; botany/plant biology; business administration and management; business administration, management and operations related; business/commerce; business/managerial economics; business teacher education; chemical engineering; chemistry; chemistry related; city/urban, community and regional planning; civil engineering; civil engineering technology; clinical laboratory science/medical technology; computer and information sciences; computer engineering; computer engineering technology; computer programming; construction engineering technology; criminal justice/law enforcement administration; criminal justice/safety; dental hygiene; dietetics; dramatic/theater arts; early childhood education; economics; electrical and electronics engineering; electrical, electronic and communications engineering technology; elementary education; emergency medical technology (EMT paramedic); engineering; engineering science; engineering technology; English; English/language arts teacher education; entomology; environmental/environmental health engineering; environmental science; family and consumer sciences/home economics teacher education; finance; fine/studio arts; fire prevention and safety technology; food science; foreign languages and literatures; foreign language teacher education; forensic science and technology; forestry; French; general studies; geography; geology/earth science; gerontology; graphic design; health/health-care administration; health information/medical records administration; health services/allied health/health sciences; health teacher education; history; horticultural science; hospitality administration; humanities; human resources management; industrial engineering; information science/studies; insurance; international business/trade/commerce; international relations and affairs; jazz/jazz studies; journalism; kinesiology and exercise science; landscaping and groundskeeping; legal assistant/paralegal; liberal arts and sciences and humanities related; liberal arts and sciences/liberal studies; linguistics; management information systems; management science; manufacturing engineering technology; marine biology and biological oceanography; marketing/marketing management; materials engineering; mathematics; mathematics teacher education; mechanical engineering; medical microbiology and bacteriology; medical radiologic technology; middle school education; multi/interdisciplinary studies related; music; music history, literature, and theory; music performance; music teacher education; music theory and composition; music therapy; network and system administration; nuclear engineering; occupational therapy; ocean engineering; office management; operations management; parks, recreation and leisure facilities management; pharmacy; philosophy; philosophy and religious studies related; physics; physics related; plant sciences; political science and government; psychology; public administration; public relations/image management; radio and television; real estate; registered nursing/registered nurse; religious studies; respiratory care therapy; rhetoric and composition; science teacher education; secondary education; social psychology; social sciences; social science teacher education; social work; sociology; soil science and agronomy; Spanish; special education; special education–individuals with emotional disturbances; special education–individuals with intellectual disabilities; special education–individuals with specific learning disabilities; special education–individuals with vision impairments; speech communication and rhetoric; statistics; surveying technology; systems engineering; trade and industrial teacher education; transportation/mobility management; vocational rehabilitation counseling; water, wetlands, and marine resources management; zoology/animal biology.

Academics *Calendar:* semesters. *Degrees:* certificates, diplomas, associate, and bachelor's. *Special study options:* academic remediation for entering students, adult/continuing education programs, advanced placement credit, cooperative education, distance learning, English as a second language, independent study, internships, part-time degree program, services for LD students, summer session for credit.

Library Library Services.

Student Life *Housing Options:* Campus housing is provided by a third party. *Activities and Organizations:* Phi Theta Kappa, Phi Beta Lambda, Art Club, Anime and Gaming Club, Basketball Club. *Campus security:* 24-hour emergency response devices and patrols, late-night transport/escort service. *Student services:* personal/psychological counseling.

Athletics Member NJCAA. *Intercollegiate sports:* baseball M(s), cross-country running W(s), softball W(s), volleyball W(s). *Intramural sports:* basketball M(c)/W(c), soccer M(c)/W(c).

Costs (2017–18) *One-time required fee:* $15. *Tuition:* state resident $2593 full-time, $105 per credit hour part-time; nonresident $11,087 full-time, $394 per credit hour part-time. Full-time tuition and fees vary according to course level, course load, degree level, and program. Part-time tuition and fees vary according to course level, course load, degree level, and program. *Room and board:* $5920; room only: $2000. *Payment plan:* installment. *Waivers:* employees or children of employees.

Applying *Options:* electronic application, early admission, deferred entrance. *Application fee:* $15. *Required:* high school transcript. *Application deadline:* rolling (freshmen). *Notification:* continuous (freshmen).

Freshman Application Contact Ms. Mary Puckorius, Admissions Coordinator, South Florida State College, 600 West College Drive, Avon Park, FL 33825. *Phone:* 863-784-7416. *Website:* http://www.southflorida.edu/.

Sullivan and Cogliano Training Center
Miami Gardens, Florida

Admissions Office Contact Sullivan and Cogliano Training Center, 4760 North West 167th Street, Miami Gardens, FL 33014. *Website:* http://www.sctrain.edu/.

Tallahassee Community College
Tallahassee, Florida

- **State and locally supported** primarily 2-year, founded 1966, part of Florida College System
- **Suburban** 214-acre campus
- **Endowment** $10.0 million
- **Coed,** 12,200 undergraduate students, 47% full-time, 53% women, 47% men

Undergraduates 5,744 full-time, 6,456 part-time. Students come from 24 states and territories; 79 other countries; 3% are from out of state; 30% Black or African American, non-Hispanic/Latino; 12% Hispanic/Latino; 1% Asian, non-Hispanic/Latino; 0.1% Native Hawaiian or other Pacific Islander, non-Hispanic/Latino; 0.2% American Indian or Alaska Native, non-Hispanic/Latino; 4% Two or more races, non-Hispanic/Latino; 2% Race/ethnicity unknown; 1% international; 8% transferred in. *Retention:* 58% of full-time freshmen returned.

Freshmen *Admission:* 2,270 admitted, 2,270 enrolled.

Faculty *Total:* 568, 33% full-time, 72% with terminal degrees. *Student/faculty ratio:* 21:1.

Majors Accounting technology and bookkeeping; CAD/CADD drafting/design technology; commercial and advertising art; computer graphics; computer programming; computer programming (specific applications); computer systems networking and telecommunications; construction engineering technology; corrections; criminal justice/law enforcement administration; criminal justice/police science; dental assisting; dental hygiene; diagnostic medical sonography and ultrasound technology; drafting and design technology; early childhood education; emergency medical technology (EMT paramedic); entrepreneurship; environmental science; fire science/firefighting; health information/medical records technology; homeland security related; information technology; legal assistant/paralegal; liberal arts and sciences/liberal studies; manufacturing engineering technology; masonry; medical radiologic technology; nursing assistant/aide and patient care assistant/aide; office management; pharmacy technician; physical fitness technician; registered nursing/registered nurse; respiratory care therapy; security and loss prevention; surgical technology; web page, digital/multimedia and information resources design; welding technology.

Academics *Calendar:* semesters. *Degrees:* certificates, associate, and bachelor's. *Special study options:* academic remediation for entering students, accelerated degree program, adult/continuing education programs, advanced placement credit, distance learning, English as a second language, external degree program, honors programs, independent study, off-campus study, part-time degree program, services for LD students, study abroad, summer session for credit. *ROTC:* Army (c), Navy (c), Air Force (c).

Library Tallahassee Community College Library. Weekly public service hours: 68; students can reserve study rooms.

Student Life *Housing:* college housing not available. *Activities and Organizations:* drama/theater group, student-run newspaper, choral group, Student Government Association, International Student Organization, Phi Theta Kappa, Model United Nations, Honors Council. *Campus security:* 24-hour emergency response devices and patrols, late-night transport/escort service. *Student services:* personal/psychological counseling.

Athletics Member NJCAA. *Intercollegiate sports:* baseball M(s), basketball M(s)/W(s), softball W(s). *Intramural sports:* basketball M/W, football M/W, soccer M/W, softball M/W, volleyball M/W.

Costs (2016–17) *Tuition:* state resident $3025 full-time, $101 per credit hour part-time; nonresident $11,288 full-time, $387 per credit hour part-time. Full-time tuition and fees vary according to course load. Part-time tuition and fees vary according to course load. *Payment plans:* installment, deferred payment. *Waivers:* employees or children of employees.

Financial Aid Of all full-time matriculated undergraduates who enrolled in 2015, 4,359 applied for aid, 3,384 were judged to have need. 110 Federal Work-Study jobs (averaging $2172). *Average financial aid package:* $3507. *Average need-based gift aid:* $3733.

Applying *Options:* electronic application, early admission, deferred entrance. *Required:* high school transcript. *Application deadlines:* 8/1 (freshmen), 8/1 (transfers).

Freshman Application Contact Student Success Center, Tallahassee Community College, 444 Appleyard Drive, Tallahassee, FL 32304-2895. *Phone:* 850-201-8555. *E-mail:* admissions@tcc.fl.edu. *Website:* http://www.tcc.fl.edu/.

Ultimate Medical Academy Clearwater
Clearwater, Florida

- **Independent** 2-year, founded 1994
- **Urban** campus with easy access to Tampa
- **Coed,** 274 undergraduate students, 90% full-time, 83% women, 7% men

Undergraduates 247 full-time. 44% Black or African American, non-Hispanic/Latino; 11% Hispanic/Latino; 0.7% Asian, non-Hispanic/Latino; 1% American Indian or Alaska Native, non-Hispanic/Latino; 3% Two or more races, non-Hispanic/Latino; 9% Race/ethnicity unknown.
Freshmen *Admission:* 78 enrolled.
Majors Health services/allied health/health sciences.
Academics *Calendar:* continuous. *Degree:* diplomas and associate. *Special study options:* distance learning, part-time degree program, services for LD students.
Student Life *Housing:* college housing not available.
Applying *Required:* high school transcript. *Application deadline:* rolling (transfers).
Freshman Application Contact Ultimate Medical Academy Clearwater, 1255 Cleveland Street, Clearwater, FL 33755. *Toll-free phone:* 888-205-2510. *Website:* http://www.ultimatemedical.edu/.

Ultimate Medical Academy Online
Tampa, Florida

- **Independent** 2-year
- **Urban** campus
- **Coed,** 16,411 undergraduate students, 79% full-time, 94% women, 6% men

Undergraduates 13,017 full-time, 3,394 part-time. Students come from 50 states and territories; 54% Black or African American, non-Hispanic/Latino; 8% Hispanic/Latino; 0.5% Asian, non-Hispanic/Latino; 0.4% Native Hawaiian or other Pacific Islander, non-Hispanic/Latino; 1% American Indian or Alaska Native, non-Hispanic/Latino; 2% Two or more races, non-Hispanic/Latino; 1% Race/ethnicity unknown. *Retention:* 80% of full-time freshmen returned.
Freshmen *Admission:* 4,373 enrolled.
Majors Health/health-care administration; health information/medical records technology; health services/allied health/health sciences; human services; medical administrative assistant and medical secretary; medical insurance/medical billing; pharmacy technician.
Academics *Calendar:* continuous. *Degree:* diplomas and associate. *Special study options:* distance learning, part-time degree program, services for LD students.
Student Life *Housing:* college housing not available.
Applying *Options:* electronic application. *Required:* high school transcript. *Application deadline:* rolling (transfers).
Freshman Application Contact Online Admissions Department, Ultimate Medical Academy Online, 3101 West Dr. Martin Luther King Jr. Boulevard, Tampa, FL 33607. *Phone:* 888-209-8848. *Toll-free phone:* 888-205-2510. *E-mail:* onlineadmissions@ultimatemedical.edu. *Website:* http://www.ultimatemedical.edu/.

Universal Career School
Sweetwater, Florida

Admissions Office Contact Universal Career School, 10720 W. Flagler Street, Suite 21, Sweetwater, FL 33174. *Website:* http://www.ucs.edu/.

Virginia College in Fort Pierce
Fort Pierce, Florida

Admissions Office Contact Virginia College in Fort Pierce, 2810 South Federal Highway, Fort Pierce, FL 34982-6331. *Website:* http://www.vc.edu/.

Virginia College in Jacksonville
Jacksonville, Florida

Admissions Office Contact Virginia College in Jacksonville, 5940 Beach Boulevard, Jacksonville, FL 32207. *Website:* http://www.vc.edu/.

Virginia College in Pensacola
Pensacola, Florida

Admissions Office Contact Virginia College in Pensacola, 312 East Nine Mile Road, Suite 34, Pensacola, FL 32514. *Website:* http://www.vc.edu/.

WyoTech Daytona
Ormond Beach, Florida

Admissions Office Contact WyoTech Daytona, 470 Destination Daytona Lane, Ormond Beach, FL 32174. *Toll-free phone:* 800-881-2AMI. *Website:* http://www.wyotech.edu/.

GEORGIA

Albany Technical College
Albany, Georgia

- **State-supported** 2-year, founded 1961, part of Technical College System of Georgia
- **Coed,** 3,251 undergraduate students, 43% full-time, 62% women, 38% men

Undergraduates 1,401 full-time, 1,850 part-time. 0.7% are from out of state; 79% Black or African American, non-Hispanic/Latino; 1% Hispanic/Latino; 0.4% Asian, non-Hispanic/Latino; 0.1% American Indian or Alaska Native, non-Hispanic/Latino; 0.9% Two or more races, non-Hispanic/Latino. *Retention:* 52% of full-time freshmen returned.
Freshmen *Admission:* 613 enrolled.
Majors Accounting; adult development and aging; child development; computer and information sciences; corrections and criminal justice related; culinary arts; drafting and design technology; electrical and electronic engineering technologies related; forest technology; hotel/motel administration; human development and family studies related; industrial technology; manufacturing engineering technology; marketing/marketing management; medical radiologic technology; pharmacy technician; tourism and travel services management.
Academics *Calendar:* quarters. *Degree:* certificates, diplomas, and associate. *Special study options:* distance learning.
Library Albany Technical College Library and Media Center.
Student Life *Housing:* college housing not available.
Costs (2017–18) *Tuition:* state resident $89 per credit hour part-time; nonresident $178 per credit hour part-time.
Applying *Options:* early admission. *Application fee:* $25. *Required:* high school transcript.
Freshman Application Contact Albany Technical College, 1704 South Slappey Boulevard, Albany, GA 31701. *Phone:* 229-430-3520. *Toll-free phone:* 877-261-3113.
Website: http://www.albanytech.edu/.

Andrew College
Cuthbert, Georgia

Freshman Application Contact Ms. Bridget Kurkowski, Director of Admission, Andrew College, 413 College Street, Cuthbert, GA 39840. *Phone:* 229-732-5986. *Toll-free phone:* 800-664-9250. *Fax:* 229-732-2176. *E-mail:* admissions@andrewcollege.edu. *Website:* http://www.andrewcollege.edu/.

Athens Technical College
Athens, Georgia

- **State-supported** 2-year, founded 1958, part of Technical College System of Georgia
- **Suburban** campus
- **Coed,** 4,210 undergraduate students, 25% full-time, 63% women, 37% men

Undergraduates 1,036 full-time, 3,174 part-time. 0.4% are from out of state; 20% Black or African American, non-Hispanic/Latino; 7% Hispanic/Latino; 3% Asian, non-Hispanic/Latino; 0.1% Native Hawaiian or other Pacific Islander, non-Hispanic/Latino; 0.1% American Indian or Alaska Native, non-Hispanic/Latino; 0.4% Two or more races, non-Hispanic/Latino; 5% Race/ethnicity unknown. *Retention:* 63% of full-time freshmen returned.
Freshmen *Admission:* 701 enrolled.
Majors Accounting; administrative assistant and secretarial science; biology/biotechnology laboratory technician; child development; clinical laboratory science/medical technology; communications technology; computer programming; computer systems networking and telecommunications; criminal justice/law enforcement administration; dental assisting; dental hygiene; diagnostic medical sonography and ultrasound technology; electrical, electronic and communications engineering technology; emergency medical technology (EMT paramedic); hotel/motel administration; information science/studies; legal assistant/paralegal; licensed practical/vocational nurse training; logistics, materials, and supply chain management;

marketing/marketing management; medical radiologic technology; physical therapy; registered nursing/registered nurse; respiratory care therapy; surgical technology; tourism and travel services management; veterinary/animal health technology.
Academics *Calendar:* quarters. *Degree:* certificates, diplomas, and associate. *Special study options:* distance learning.
Student Life *Housing:* college housing not available.
Costs (2017–18) *Tuition:* state resident $89 per credit hour part-time; nonresident $178 per credit hour part-time.
Financial Aid Of all full-time matriculated undergraduates who enrolled in 2015, 34 Federal Work-Study jobs (averaging $3090).
Applying *Options:* early admission. *Application fee:* $25. *Required:* high school transcript.
Freshman Application Contact Athens Technical College, 800 US Highway 29 North, Athens, GA 30601-1500. *Phone:* 706-355-5008.
Website: http://www.athenstech.edu/.

Atlanta Metropolitan State College
Atlanta, Georgia

Freshman Application Contact Ms. Audrey Reid, Director, Office of Admissions, Atlanta Metropolitan State College, 1630 Metropolitan Parkway, SW, Atlanta, GA 30310-4498. *Phone:* 404-756-4004. *Fax:* 404-756-4407. *E-mail:* admissions@atlm.edu. *Website:* http://www.atlm.edu/.

Atlanta Technical College
Atlanta, Georgia

- **State-supported** 2-year, founded 1945, part of Technical College System of Georgia
- **Coed**, 3,775 undergraduate students, 37% full-time, 68% women, 32% men

Undergraduates 1,406 full-time, 2,369 part-time. 0.2% are from out of state; 91% Black or African American, non-Hispanic/Latino; 3% Hispanic/Latino; 1% Asian, non-Hispanic/Latino; 0.1% Native Hawaiian or other Pacific Islander, non-Hispanic/Latino; 0.1% American Indian or Alaska Native, non-Hispanic/Latino; 2% Two or more races, non-Hispanic/Latino; 0.2% Race/ethnicity unknown. *Retention:* 55% of full-time freshmen returned.
Freshmen *Admission:* 706 enrolled.
Majors Accounting; child development; computer programming; culinary arts; dental hygiene; health information/medical records technology; hotel/motel administration; information technology; legal assistant/paralegal; marketing/marketing management; tourism and travel services management.
Academics *Calendar:* quarters. *Degree:* certificates, diplomas, and associate. *Special study options:* distance learning, study abroad.
Student Life *Housing:* college housing not available.
Costs (2017–18) *Tuition:* state resident $89 per credit hour part-time; nonresident $178 per credit hour part-time.
Applying *Options:* early admission. *Application fee:* $25. *Required:* high school transcript.
Freshman Application Contact Atlanta Technical College, 1560 Metropolitan Parkway, SW, Atlanta, GA 30310. *Phone:* 404-225-4455. *Website:* http://www.atlantatech.edu/.

Augusta Technical College
Augusta, Georgia

- **State-supported** 2-year, founded 1961, part of Technical College System of Georgia
- **Urban** campus
- **Coed**, 4,370 undergraduate students, 39% full-time, 56% women, 44% men

Undergraduates 1,721 full-time, 2,649 part-time. 5% are from out of state; 48% Black or African American, non-Hispanic/Latino; 4% Hispanic/Latino; 1% Asian, non-Hispanic/Latino; 0.1% Native Hawaiian or other Pacific Islander, non-Hispanic/Latino; 0.4% American Indian or Alaska Native, non-Hispanic/Latino; 3% Two or more races, non-Hispanic/Latino; 2% Race/ethnicity unknown. *Retention:* 57% of full-time freshmen returned.
Freshmen *Admission:* 807 enrolled.
Majors Accounting; administrative assistant and secretarial science; biotechnology; business administration and management; cardiovascular technology; child development; computer programming; computer systems networking and telecommunications; criminal justice/safety; culinary arts; e-commerce; electrical, electronic and communications engineering technology; emergency medical technology (EMT paramedic); fire science/firefighting; information science/studies; marketing/marketing management; mechanical engineering/mechanical technology; medical radiologic technology;

occupational therapist assistant; parks, recreation and leisure facilities management; pharmacy technician; respiratory care therapy; respiratory therapy technician; surgical technology.
Academics *Calendar:* quarters. *Degree:* certificates, diplomas, and associate. *Special study options:* distance learning.
Library Information Technology Center.
Student Life *Housing:* college housing not available.
Costs (2017–18) *Tuition:* state resident $89 per credit hour part-time; nonresident $176 per credit hour part-time.
Applying *Options:* early admission. *Application fee:* $25. *Required:* high school transcript.
Freshman Application Contact Augusta Technical College, 3200 Augusta Tech Drive, Augusta, GA 30906. *Phone:* 706-771-4150.
Website: http://www.augustatech.edu/.

Bainbridge State College
Bainbridge, Georgia

- **State-supported** primarily 2-year, founded 1972, part of University System of Georgia
- **Small-town** 160-acre campus
- **Coed**, 2,459 undergraduate students, 32% full-time, 70% women, 30% men

Undergraduates 792 full-time, 1,667 part-time. Students come from 6 states and territories; 5 other countries; 4% are from out of state; 47% Black or African American, non-Hispanic/Latino; 2% Hispanic/Latino; 1% Asian, non-Hispanic/Latino; 0.2% American Indian or Alaska Native, non-Hispanic/Latino; 0.6% Two or more races, non-Hispanic/Latino; 0.5% Race/ethnicity unknown; 0.3% international.
Freshmen *Admission:* 616 admitted.
Faculty *Total:* 123, 48% full-time, 28% with terminal degrees.
Majors Accounting; administrative assistant and secretarial science; agribusiness; agriculture; art; biology/biological sciences; business administration and management; business teacher education; chemistry; criminal justice/law enforcement administration; data processing and data processing technology; drafting and design technology; dramatic/theater arts; education; electrical, electronic and communications engineering technology; elementary education; English; family and consumer sciences/human sciences; health information/medical records technology; health teacher education; history; information science/studies; kindergarten/preschool education; liberal arts and sciences/liberal studies; licensed practical/vocational nurse training; marketing/marketing management; mathematics; political science and government; psychology; registered nursing/registered nurse; rhetoric and composition; sociology; welding technology.
Academics *Calendar:* semesters. *Degrees:* certificates, diplomas, associate, and bachelor's. *Special study options:* academic remediation for entering students, advanced placement credit, distance learning, double majors, honors programs, independent study, part-time degree program, services for LD students, study abroad, summer session for credit.
Library Bainbridge State College Library. *Books:* 44,125 (physical), 31,917 (digital/electronic); *Serial titles:* 179 (physical), 2,052 (digital/electronic); *Databases:* 282. Weekly public service hours: 50; students can reserve study rooms.
Student Life *Housing:* college housing not available. *Activities and Organizations:* student-run newspaper, choral group, Adult Learners Student Organization, BANS, LPN Club, Honors, Student Government Association. *Campus security:* 24-hour emergency response devices and patrols, late-night transport/escort service, police patrols and electronically-controlled building access. *Student services:* personal/psychological counseling.
Standardized Tests *Required for some:* SAT or ACT (for admission), ACT Compass.
Costs (2016–17) *Tuition:* state resident $2181 full-time, $91 per credit hour part-time; nonresident $8256 full-time, $344 per credit hour part-time. Full-time tuition and fees vary according to course load and program. Part-time tuition and fees vary according to course load and program. *Required fees:* $1046 full-time, $523 per term part-time. *Waivers:* senior citizens and employees or children of employees.
Applying *Options:* electronic application, early admission. *Required for some:* high school transcript, minimum 1.8 GPA, 3 letters of recommendation, interview, immunizations/waivers, medical records, criminal background check. *Application deadlines:* rolling (freshmen), rolling (transfers). *Notification:* continuous (freshmen), continuous (transfers).
Freshman Application Contact Mr. Spencer Stewart, Associate Dean of Student Affairs, Bainbridge State College, 2500 East Shotwell Street, Bainbridge, GA 39819. *Phone:* 229-243-6030. *Toll-free phone:* 866-825-1715 (in-state); 888-825-1715 (out-of-state). *Fax:* 229-248-2848.
E-mail: sstewart@bainbridge.edu.
Website: http://www.bainbridge.edu/.

Brown College of Court Reporting
Atlanta, Georgia

Admissions Office Contact Brown College of Court Reporting, 1900 Emery Street NW, Suite 200, Atlanta, GA 30318. *Website:* http://www.bccr.edu/.

Central Georgia Technical College
Warner Robins, Georgia

- **State-supported** 2-year, founded 1966, part of Technical College System of Georgia
- **Suburban** campus
- **Coed,** 7,762 undergraduate students, 31% full-time, 64% women, 36% men

Undergraduates 2,380 full-time, 5,382 part-time. 1% are from out of state; 52% Black or African American, non-Hispanic/Latino; 3% Hispanic/Latino; 1% Asian, non-Hispanic/Latino; 0.1% Native Hawaiian or other Pacific Islander, non-Hispanic/Latino; 0.3% American Indian or Alaska Native, non-Hispanic/Latino; 1% Two or more races, non-Hispanic/Latino; 0.8% Race/ethnicity unknown. *Retention:* 51% of full-time freshmen returned.
Freshmen *Admission:* 1,583 enrolled.
Majors Accounting; administrative assistant and secretarial science; adult development and aging; banking and financial support services; business administration and management; cabinetmaking and millwork; cardiovascular technology; carpentry; child-care and support services management; child development; clinical/medical laboratory technology; computer programming; computer systems networking and telecommunications; criminal justice/safety; dental hygiene; drafting and design technology; e-commerce; electrical, electronic and communications engineering technology; hotel/motel administration; industrial technology; information science/studies; legal assistant/paralegal; marketing/marketing management; medical radiologic technology; tourism and travel services management; veterinary/animal health technology; web page, digital/multimedia and information resources design.
Academics *Calendar:* quarters. *Degree:* certificates, diplomas, and associate. *Special study options:* distance learning.
Student Life *Housing:* college housing not available.
Costs (2017–18) *Tuition:* state resident $89 per credit hour part-time; nonresident $178 per credit hour part-time.
Financial Aid Of all full-time matriculated undergraduates who enrolled in 2015, 175 Federal Work-Study jobs (averaging $2000). *Financial aid deadline:* 9/1.
Applying *Options:* early admission. *Application fee:* $25. *Required:* high school transcript.
Freshman Application Contact Central Georgia Technical College, 80 Cohen Walker Drive, Warner Robins, GA 31088. *Phone:* 770-531-6332. *Toll-free phone:* 866-430-0135.
Website: http://www.centralgatech.edu/.

Chattahoochee Technical College
Marietta, Georgia

- **State-supported** 2-year, founded 1961, part of Technical College System of Georgia
- **Suburban** campus
- **Coed,** 9,999 undergraduate students, 28% full-time, 56% women, 44% men

Undergraduates 2,813 full-time, 7,186 part-time. 0.2% are from out of state; 30% Black or African American, non-Hispanic/Latino; 12% Hispanic/Latino; 3% Asian, non-Hispanic/Latino; 0.1% Native Hawaiian or other Pacific Islander, non-Hispanic/Latino; 0.5% American Indian or Alaska Native, non-Hispanic/Latino; 2% Two or more races, non-Hispanic/Latino; 1% Race/ethnicity unknown. *Retention:* 52% of full-time freshmen returned.
Freshmen *Admission:* 1,980 enrolled.
Majors Accounting; administrative assistant and secretarial science; automobile/automotive mechanics technology; biomedical technology; business administration and management; child development; civil engineering technology; computer and information systems security; computer programming; computer systems networking and telecommunications; criminal justice/safety; culinary arts; drafting and design technology; electrical, electronic and communications engineering technology; fire science/firefighting; horticultural science; information science/studies; logistics, materials, and supply chain management; marketing/marketing management; medical radiologic technology; parks, recreation and leisure facilities management; web page, digital/multimedia and information resources design.
Academics *Calendar:* quarters. *Degree:* certificates, diplomas, and associate. *Special study options:* distance learning.
Student Life *Housing:* college housing not available.

Costs (2017–18) *Tuition:* state resident $89 per credit hour part-time; nonresident $178 per credit hour part-time.
Financial Aid Of all full-time matriculated undergraduates who enrolled in 2015, 40 Federal Work-Study jobs (averaging $2500).
Applying *Options:* early admission. *Application fee:* $25. *Required:* high school transcript.
Freshman Application Contact Chattahoochee Technical College, 980 South Cobb Drive, SE, Marietta, GA 30060. *Phone:* 770-757-3408.
Website: http://www.chattahoocheetech.edu/.

Coastal Pines Technical College
Waycross, Georgia

- **State-supported** 2-year, part of Technical College System of Georgia
- **Small-town** campus
- **Coed,** 2,775 undergraduate students, 22% full-time, 60% women, 40% men

Undergraduates 615 full-time, 2,160 part-time. 0.3% are from out of state; 27% Black or African American, non-Hispanic/Latino; 4% Hispanic/Latino; 1% Asian, non-Hispanic/Latino; 0.1% Native Hawaiian or other Pacific Islander, non-Hispanic/Latino; 0.3% American Indian or Alaska Native, non-Hispanic/Latino; 1% Two or more races, non-Hispanic/Latino; 0.3% Race/ethnicity unknown. *Retention:* 68% of full-time freshmen returned.
Freshmen *Admission:* 370 enrolled.
Majors Administrative assistant and secretarial science; child development; clinical/medical laboratory technology; computer systems networking and telecommunications; computer technology/computer systems technology; criminal justice/police science; forest technology; information science/studies; occupational safety and health technology; respiratory therapy technician; surgical technology.
Academics *Calendar:* quarters. *Degree:* certificates, diplomas, and associate. *Special study options:* distance learning.
Student Life *Housing:* college housing not available.
Costs (2017–18) *Tuition:* state resident $89 per credit hour part-time; nonresident $178 per credit hour part-time.
Applying *Options:* early admission. *Application fee:* $25. *Required:* high school transcript.
Freshman Application Contact Coastal Pines Technical College, 1701 Carswell Avenue, Waycross, GA 31503. *Phone:* 912-338-5251. *Toll-free phone:* 877-ED-AT-OTC.
Website: http://www.coastalpines.edu/.

Columbus Technical College
Columbus, Georgia

- **State-supported** 2-year, founded 1961, part of Technical College System of Georgia
- **Urban** campus
- **Coed,** 3,228 undergraduate students, 28% full-time, 65% women, 35% men

Undergraduates 910 full-time, 2,318 part-time. 13% are from out of state; 44% Black or African American, non-Hispanic/Latino; 6% Hispanic/Latino; 2% Asian, non-Hispanic/Latino; 0.3% Native Hawaiian or other Pacific Islander, non-Hispanic/Latino; 0.3% American Indian or Alaska Native, non-Hispanic/Latino; 3% Two or more races, non-Hispanic/Latino; 2% Race/ethnicity unknown. *Retention:* 53% of full-time freshmen returned.
Freshmen *Admission:* 558 enrolled.
Majors Accounting; administrative assistant and secretarial science; automobile/automotive mechanics technology; child development; computer engineering related; computer systems networking and telecommunications; dental hygiene; diagnostic medical sonography and ultrasound technology; drafting and design technology; electrical, electronic and communications engineering technology; emergency medical technology (EMT paramedic); health information/medical records technology; horticultural science; industrial technology; information science/studies; machine tool technology; mechanical engineering/mechanical technology; medical office management; medical radiologic technology; pharmacy technician; registered nursing/registered nurse; respiratory therapy technician; surgical technology; web page, digital/multimedia and information resources design.
Academics *Calendar:* quarters. *Degree:* certificates, diplomas, and associate. *Special study options:* distance learning.
Library Columbus Technical College Library.
Student Life *Housing:* college housing not available.
Costs (2017–18) *Tuition:* state resident $89 per credit hour part-time; nonresident $178 per credit hour part-time.
Financial Aid Of all full-time matriculated undergraduates who enrolled in 2015, 6 Federal Work-Study jobs (averaging $2000).

Applying *Options:* early admission. *Application fee:* $25. *Required:* high school transcript.
Freshman Application Contact Columbus Technical College, 928 Manchester Expressway, Columbus, GA 31904-6572. *Phone:* 706-649-1901. *Website:* http://www.columbustech.edu/.

East Georgia State College
Swainsboro, Georgia

- **State-supported** primarily 2-year, founded 1973, part of University System of Georgia
- **Rural** 207-acre campus
- **Coed,** 3,001 undergraduate students, 77% full-time, 59% women, 41% men

Undergraduates 2,308 full-time, 693 part-time. Students come from 5 states and territories; 1 other country; 0.2% are from out of state; 44% Black or African American, non-Hispanic/Latino; 4% Hispanic/Latino; 0.9% Asian, non-Hispanic/Latino; 0.1% Native Hawaiian or other Pacific Islander, non-Hispanic/Latino; 0.2% American Indian or Alaska Native, non-Hispanic/Latino; 3% Two or more races, non-Hispanic/Latino; 0.9% Race/ethnicity unknown; 0.3% international; 9% transferred in; 12% live on campus. *Retention:* 1% of full-time freshmen returned.
Freshmen *Admission:* 1,148 enrolled.
Faculty *Student/faculty ratio:* 26:1.
Majors Biology/biological sciences; fire services administration; liberal arts and sciences/liberal studies; medical/clinical assistant.
Academics *Calendar:* semesters. *Degrees:* certificates, associate, and bachelor's. *Special study options:* academic remediation for entering students, adult/continuing education programs, advanced placement credit, distance learning, honors programs, independent study, off-campus study, part-time degree program, services for LD students, study abroad, summer session for credit.
Library East Georgia College Library. Students can reserve study rooms.
Student Life *Housing Options:* coed. Campus housing is provided by a third party. *Activities and Organizations:* drama/theater group, student-run newspaper, choral group. *Campus security:* 24-hour patrols, late-night transport/escort service, controlled dormitory access. *Student services:* health clinic, personal/psychological counseling.
Athletics Member NJCAA. *Intercollegiate sports:* baseball M(s), basketball M(s)/W(s), softball W. *Intramural sports:* basketball M/W, cheerleading M(c)/W(c), football M/W, softball M/W.
Costs (2017–18) *One-time required fee:* $35. *Tuition:* state resident $2726 full-time, $91 per credit hour part-time; nonresident $10,320 full-time, $344 per credit hour part-time. Full-time tuition and fees vary according to class time, course load, location, and student level. Part-time tuition and fees vary according to class time, course load, location, and student level. *Required fees:* $886 full-time, $443 per term part-time. *Room and board:* $8504; room only: $5960. Room and board charges vary according to location. *Payment plan:* installment. *Waivers:* senior citizens.
Financial Aid Of all full-time matriculated undergraduates who enrolled in 2015, 43 Federal Work-Study jobs (averaging $1560).
Applying *Options:* early admission, deferred entrance. *Application fee:* $20. *Required:* high school transcript. *Application deadlines:* rolling (freshmen), rolling (transfers). *Notification:* continuous (freshmen), continuous (transfers).
Freshman Application Contact East Georgia State College, 131 College Circle, Swainsboro, GA 30401-2699. *Phone:* 478-289-2112. *Website:* http://www.ega.edu/.

Emory University, Oxford College
Oxford, Georgia

- **Independent Methodist** 2-year, founded 1836
- **Small-town** 150-acre campus with easy access to Atlanta
- **Endowment** $48.7 million
- **Coed**

Undergraduates 932 full-time, 4 part-time. Students come from 46 states and territories; 20 other countries; 75% are from out of state; 8% Black or African American, non-Hispanic/Latino; 7% Hispanic/Latino; 27% Asian, non-Hispanic/Latino; 0.1% Native Hawaiian or other Pacific Islander, non-Hispanic/Latino; 4% Two or more races, non-Hispanic/Latino; 3% Race/ethnicity unknown; 16% international; 99% live on campus. *Retention:* 93% of full-time freshmen returned.
Faculty *Student/faculty ratio:* 12:1.
Academics *Calendar:* semesters. *Degree:* associate. *Special study options:* advanced placement credit, independent study, internships, off-campus study, services for LD students, study abroad, summer session for credit. *ROTC:* Army (c), Navy (c), Air Force (c).
Library Hoke O'Kelly Library. *Books:* 84,104 (physical), 704,535 (digital/electronic).

Student Life *Campus security:* 24-hour emergency response devices and patrols, student patrols, late-night transport/escort service, controlled dormitory access.
Athletics Member NJCAA.
Standardized Tests *Required:* SAT or ACT (for admission).
Costs (2016–17) *Comprehensive fee:* $55,260 includes full-time tuition ($42,600), mandatory fees ($654), and room and board ($12,006). Part-time tuition: $1775 per credit hour. *Room and board:* college room only: $7788. Room and board charges vary according to board plan and housing facility.
Financial Aid Of all full-time matriculated undergraduates who enrolled in 2015, 225 Federal Work-Study jobs (averaging $1600).
Applying *Options:* electronic application, early admission, early decision, deferred entrance. *Application fee:* $75. *Required:* essay or personal statement, high school transcript, 1 letter of recommendation. *Recommended:* minimum 3.0 GPA, 2 letters of recommendation.
Freshman Application Contact Emory University, Oxford College, 100 Hamill Street, PO Box 1328, Oxford, GA 30054. *Phone:* 770-784-8328. *Toll-free phone:* 800-723-8328. *Website:* http://oxford.emory.edu/.

Fortis College
Smyrna, Georgia

Admissions Office Contact Fortis College, 2140 South Cobb Drive, Smyrna, GA 30080. *Toll-free phone:* 855-4-FORTIS. *Website:* http://www.fortis.edu/.

Georgia Highlands College
Rome, Georgia

- **State-supported** primarily 2-year, founded 1970, part of University System of Georgia
- **Suburban** 226-acre campus with easy access to Atlanta
- **Endowment** $37,568
- **Coed,** 5,994 undergraduate students, 47% full-time, 64% women, 36% men

Undergraduates 2,789 full-time, 3,205 part-time. Students come from 27 states and territories; 49 other countries; 1% are from out of state; 17% Black or African American, non-Hispanic/Latino; 13% Hispanic/Latino; 2% Asian, non-Hispanic/Latino; 0.1% Native Hawaiian or other Pacific Islander, non-Hispanic/Latino; 0.2% American Indian or Alaska Native, non-Hispanic/Latino; 3% Two or more races, non-Hispanic/Latino; 0.4% Race/ethnicity unknown; 7% transferred in. *Retention:* 69% of full-time freshmen returned.
Freshmen *Admission:* 4,467 applied, 3,095 admitted, 1,415 enrolled. *Average high school GPA:* 3.
Faculty *Total:* 287, 43% full-time, 12% with terminal degrees. *Student/faculty ratio:* 21:1.
Majors Agriculture; art; biology/biological sciences; business administration and management; chemistry; computer and information sciences; criminal justice/police science; dental hygiene; education; engineering; English; foreign languages and literatures; general studies; geology/earth science; health information/medical records administration; health services/allied health/health sciences; history; human services; information science/studies; journalism; mathematics; music; music management; philosophy; physics; political science and government; psychology; registered nursing/registered nurse; sociology; speech communication and rhetoric.
Academics *Calendar:* semesters. *Degrees:* associate and bachelor's. *Special study options:* academic remediation for entering students, advanced placement credit, cooperative education, distance learning, double majors, honors programs, independent study, part-time degree program, services for LD students, study abroad, summer session for credit.
Library Georgia Highlands College Library–Floyd Campus plus 4 others. *Books:* 72,257 (physical), 136,290 (digital/electronic); *Serial titles:* 54 (physical), 20 (digital/electronic); *Databases:* 349. Weekly public service hours: 58; students can reserve study rooms.
Student Life *Housing:* college housing not available. *Activities and Organizations:* student-run newspaper, Association of Nursing Students, Green Highlands, Brother 2 Brother, Student Government Association, Phi Theta Kappa. *Campus security:* 24-hour emergency response devices and patrols, emergency phone/email alert system. *Student services:* personal/psychological counseling.
Athletics Member NJCAA. *Intercollegiate sports:* baseball M(s), basketball M(s)/W(s), softball W(s). *Intramural sports:* basketball M/W, cheerleading M/W, football M/W, golf M/W, skiing (downhill) M/W, table tennis M/W, tennis M/W, ultimate Frisbee M/W, volleyball M/W, weight lifting M/W.
Costs (2017–18) *One-time required fee:* $30. *Tuition:* state resident $2181 full-time, $91 per credit hour part-time; nonresident $8256 full-time, $344 per credit hour part-time. Full-time tuition and fees vary according to course load. Part-time tuition and fees vary according to course load. *Required fees:* $1064

full-time, $412 per term part-time. *Payment plan:* installment. *Waivers:* senior citizens.

Financial Aid Of all full-time matriculated undergraduates who enrolled in 2015, 50 Federal Work-Study jobs (averaging $3500).

Applying *Options:* electronic application, deferred entrance. *Application fee:* $30. *Required:* high school transcript, minimum 2.0 GPA. *Application deadlines:* 7/15 (freshmen), 7/15 (transfers). *Notification:* continuous (freshmen), continuous (transfers).

Freshman Application Contact Charlene Graham, Assistant Director of Admissions, Georgia Highlands College, 3175 Cedartown Highway, Rome, GA 30161. *Phone:* 706-295-6339. *Toll-free phone:* 800-332-2406. *Fax:* 706-295-6341. *E-mail:* cgraham@highlands.edu.
Website: http://www.highlands.edu/.

Georgia Military College
Milledgeville, Georgia

- **Public** primarily 2-year, founded 1879
- **Small-town** campus
- **Endowment** $1.5 million
- **Coed,** 8,234 undergraduate students, 56% full-time, 60% women, 40% men

Undergraduates 4,587 full-time, 3,647 part-time. Students come from 35 states and territories; 5 other countries; 4% are from out of state; 44% Black or African American, non-Hispanic/Latino; 7% Hispanic/Latino; 2% Asian, non-Hispanic/Latino; 0.4% Native Hawaiian or other Pacific Islander, non-Hispanic/Latino; 2% American Indian or Alaska Native, non-Hispanic/Latino; 0.4% Two or more races, non-Hispanic/Latino; 3% Race/ethnicity unknown; 0.3% international; 8% transferred in; 3% live on campus. *Retention:* 53% of full-time freshmen returned.

Freshmen *Admission:* 1,700 enrolled.

Faculty *Total:* 564, 23% full-time. *Student/faculty ratio:* 21:1.

Majors Biology/biological sciences; business administration and management; business/commerce; computer and information systems security; computer science; criminal justice/law enforcement administration; early childhood education; English; general studies; health services/allied health/health sciences; health teacher education; history; homeland security; information technology; legal assistant/paralegal; logistics, materials, and supply chain management; management information systems; mass communication/media; mathematics; middle school education; political science and government; prenursing studies; psychology; secondary education; social work; sociology.

Academics *Calendar:* quarters. *Degrees:* associate and bachelor's. *Special study options:* academic remediation for entering students, advanced placement credit, cooperative education, distance learning, double majors, independent study, off-campus study, part-time degree program, services for LD students, student-designed majors, study abroad, summer session for credit. *ROTC:* Army (b).

Library Sibley Cone Library plus 1 other. *Books:* 38,125 (physical), 57,769 (digital/electronic); *Serial titles:* 52 (physical); *Databases:* 331. Weekly public service hours: 68.

Student Life *Housing:* on-campus residence required through sophomore year. *Options:* coed. Campus housing is university owned. Freshman campus housing is guaranteed. *Activities and Organizations:* drama/theater group, student-run newspaper, choral group, Student Government Association, Alpha Phi Omega National Service Fraternity, Phi Theta Kappa, Drama Club, Biology Club. *Campus security:* 24-hour emergency response devices and patrols, controlled dormitory access. *Student services:* health clinic.

Athletics Member NJCAA. *Intercollegiate sports:* cross-country running M/W, football M(s), golf M/W, riflery M/W, soccer M(s)/W(s), softball W(s). *Intramural sports:* badminton M/W, basketball M/W, golf M/W, softball M/W, tennis M/W, volleyball M/W.

Costs (2017–18) *Tuition:* state resident $5445 full-time, $122 per credit hour part-time; nonresident $5445 full-time, $122 per credit hour part-time. Full-time tuition and fees vary according to location. Part-time tuition and fees vary according to location. *Required fees:* $683 full-time, $30 per credit hour part-time. *Room and board:* $7500; room only: $3150. Room and board charges vary according to location. *Waivers:* employees or children of employees.

Financial Aid Of all full-time matriculated undergraduates who enrolled in 2012, 6,554 applied for aid, 6,132 were judged to have need, 282 had their need fully met. 121 Federal Work-Study jobs (averaging $1614). In 2012, 61 non-need-based awards were made. *Average percent of need met:* 47%. *Average financial aid package:* $9567. *Average need-based loan:* $3189. *Average need-based gift aid:* $4626. *Average non-need-based aid:* $2226.

Applying *Options:* electronic application, early admission, deferred entrance. *Application fee:* $35. *Required for some:* high school transcript, interview. *Application deadlines:* rolling (freshmen), rolling (transfers).

Freshman Application Contact Georgia Military College, 201 East Greene Street, Old Capitol Building, Milledgeville, GA 31061-3398. *Phone:* 478-387-4890. *Toll-free phone:* 800-342-0413.
Website: http://www.gmc.edu/.

Georgia Northwestern Technical College
Rome, Georgia

- **State-supported** 2-year, founded 1962, part of Technical College System of Georgia
- **Small-town** campus with easy access to Atlanta
- **Coed,** 6,016 undergraduate students, 30% full-time, 62% women, 38% men

Undergraduates 1,809 full-time, 4,207 part-time. 1% are from out of state; 10% Black or African American, non-Hispanic/Latino; 13% Hispanic/Latino; 0.6% Asian, non-Hispanic/Latino; 0.2% American Indian or Alaska Native, non-Hispanic/Latino; 2% Two or more races, non-Hispanic/Latino. *Retention:* 64% of full-time freshmen returned.

Freshmen *Admission:* 840 enrolled.

Majors Accounting; child development; computer programming; criminal justice/safety; environmental engineering technology; fire science/firefighting; information science/studies; legal assistant/paralegal; marketing/marketing management; medical office management; respiratory therapy technician; surgical technology; web page, digital/multimedia and information resources design.

Academics *Calendar:* quarters. *Degree:* certificates, diplomas, and associate. *Special study options:* distance learning.

Student Life *Housing:* college housing not available.

Costs (2017–18) *Tuition:* state resident $89 per credit hour part-time; nonresident $178 per credit hour part-time.

Applying *Options:* early admission. *Application fee:* $25. *Required:* high school transcript.

Freshman Application Contact Georgia Northwestern Technical College, One Maurice Culberson Drive, Rome, GA 30161. *Phone:* 706-295-6933. *Toll-free phone:* 866-983-GNTC.
Website: http://www.gntc.edu/.

Georgia Piedmont Technical College
Clarkston, Georgia

- **State-supported** 2-year, founded 1961, part of Technical College System of Georgia
- **Suburban** campus
- **Coed,** 4,103 undergraduate students, 22% full-time, 64% women, 36% men

Undergraduates 897 full-time, 3,206 part-time. 0.1% are from out of state; 82% Black or African American, non-Hispanic/Latino; 3% Hispanic/Latino; 2% Asian, non-Hispanic/Latino; 0.1% Native Hawaiian or other Pacific Islander, non-Hispanic/Latino; 0.1% American Indian or Alaska Native, non-Hispanic/Latino; 2% Two or more races, non-Hispanic/Latino; 0.5% Race/ethnicity unknown. *Retention:* 59% of full-time freshmen returned.

Freshmen *Admission:* 619 enrolled.

Majors Accounting; administrative assistant and secretarial science; automobile/automotive mechanics technology; business/commerce; clinical/medical laboratory technology; computer engineering technology; computer programming; computer systems networking and telecommunications; criminal justice/safety; drafting and design technology; electrical, electronic and communications engineering technology; electromechanical technology; engineering technology; heating, ventilation, air conditioning and refrigeration engineering technology; industrial technology; information science/studies; instrumentation technology; legal administrative assistant/secretary; legal assistant/paralegal; machine tool technology; marketing/marketing management; medical/clinical assistant; operations management; ophthalmic laboratory technology; opticianry; surgical technology; telecommunications technology.

Academics *Calendar:* quarters. *Degree:* certificates, diplomas, and associate. *Special study options:* distance learning.

Student Life *Housing:* college housing not available.

Costs (2017–18) *Tuition:* state resident $89 per credit hour part-time; nonresident $178 per credit hour part-time.

Financial Aid Of all full-time matriculated undergraduates who enrolled in 2010, 7,200 applied for aid, 7,100 were judged to have need. 145 Federal Work-Study jobs (averaging $4000). *Average financial aid package:* $4500. *Average need-based gift aid:* $4500.

Applying *Options:* early admission. *Application fee:* $25. *Required:* high school transcript.
Freshman Application Contact Georgia Piedmont Technical College, 495 North Indian Creek Drive, Clarkston, GA 30021-2397. *Phone:* 404-297-9522 Ext. 1229.
Website: http://www.gptc.edu/.

Gordon State College
Barnesville, Georgia

- **State-supported** primarily 2-year, founded 1852, part of University System of Georgia
- **Small-town** 235-acre campus with easy access to Atlanta
- **Coed,** 3,901 undergraduate students, 64% full-time, 66% women, 34% men
- 41% of applicants were admitted

Undergraduates 2,492 full-time, 1,409 part-time. 0.7% are from out of state; 37% Black or African American, non-Hispanic/Latino; 3% Hispanic/Latino; 0.9% Asian, non-Hispanic/Latino; 0.1% Native Hawaiian or other Pacific Islander, non-Hispanic/Latino; 3% Two or more races, non-Hispanic/Latino; 0.4% Race/ethnicity unknown; 0.2% international; 6% transferred in.
Freshmen *Admission:* 2,718 applied, 1,122 admitted, 881 enrolled.
Faculty *Total:* 199, 60% full-time, 52% with terminal degrees. *Student/faculty ratio:* 21:1.
Majors Art; astronomy; biological and biomedical sciences related; biology teacher education; business administration and management; chemistry; computer science; criminal justice/safety; dental services and allied professions related; dramatic/theater arts; early childhood education; elementary education; engineering; English; English as a second/foreign language (teaching); English/language arts teacher education; environmental science; foreign languages and literatures; forestry; general studies; health and physical education/fitness; health information/medical records administration; health/medical preparatory programs related; history; history teacher education; human services; information technology; liberal arts and sciences/liberal studies; mathematics; mathematics teacher education; middle school education; music; physics; political science and government; pre-engineering; pre-occupational therapy; pre-pharmacy studies; pre-physical therapy; psychology; radiologic technology/science; registered nursing/registered nurse; secondary education; social work; sociology; visual and performing arts.
Academics *Calendar:* semesters. *Degrees:* associate and bachelor's. *Special study options:* academic remediation for entering students, accelerated degree program, adult/continuing education programs, advanced placement credit, cooperative education, distance learning, double majors, honors programs, internships, off-campus study, part-time degree program, services for LD students, study abroad, summer session for credit.
Library Dorothy W. Hightower Collaborative Learning Center and Library. *Books:* 103,423 (physical), 35,999 (digital/electronic); *Serial titles:* 401 (physical), 87,985 (digital/electronic); *Databases:* 325. Weekly public service hours: 73.
Student Life *Housing:* on-campus residence required for freshman year. *Options:* coed. Campus housing is university owned. Freshman applicants given priority for college housing. *Activities and Organizations:* drama/theater group, student-run newspaper, choral group, Campus Activity Board, Student Government Association, Earth Wind Fire (science club), Student African American Brotherhood (SAAB), Swazi Step Team. *Campus security:* 24-hour emergency response devices and patrols, student patrols, controlled dormitory access, Resident Assistants and Resident Directors in housing, parking patrol. *Student services:* health clinic, personal/psychological counseling.
Athletics Member NJCAA. *Intercollegiate sports:* baseball M, basketball M, soccer M/W, softball W.
Standardized Tests *Required:* SAT or ACT (for admission).
Costs (2017–18) *Tuition:* state resident $3064 full-time, $103 per credit hour part-time; nonresident $11,322 full-time, $378 per credit hour part-time. *Required fees:* $1100 full-time, $550 per term part-time. *Room and board:* $8101. Room and board charges vary according to board plan and housing facility. *Payment plan:* installment.
Financial Aid Of all full-time matriculated undergraduates who enrolled in 2015, 75 Federal Work-Study jobs (averaging $1850).
Applying *Options:* electronic application, early admission, deferred entrance. *Application fee:* $30. *Required:* high school transcript. *Application deadlines:* rolling (freshmen), rolling (transfers).
Freshman Application Contact Gordon State College, 419 College Drive, Barnesville, GA 30204-1762. *Phone:* 678-359-5021. *Toll-free phone:* 800-282-6504.
Website: http://www.gordonstate.edu/.

Gupton-Jones College of Funeral Service
Decatur, Georgia

- **Independent** 2-year, founded 1920, part of Pierce Mortuary Colleges, Inc.
- **Suburban** 3-acre campus with easy access to Atlanta
- **Coed,** 220 undergraduate students, 100% full-time, 60% women, 40% men

Undergraduates 220 full-time. Students come from 15 states and territories; 2 other countries; 88% are from out of state; 72% Black or African American, non-Hispanic/Latino; 20% transferred in. *Retention:* 75% of full-time freshmen returned.
Freshmen *Admission:* 220 admitted, 220 enrolled. *Average high school GPA:* 2.01.
Faculty *Total:* 9, 78% full-time. *Student/faculty ratio:* 24:1.
Majors Mortuary science and embalming.
Academics *Calendar:* quarters. *Degree:* associate. *Special study options:* accelerated degree program, services for LD students.
Library Russell Millison Library. *Books:* 4,000 (physical).
Student Life *Housing:* college housing not available. *Activities and Organizations:* Student Council, national fraternities. *Campus security:* 24-hour emergency response devices.
Costs (2017–18) *Tuition:* $250 per quarter hour part-time. Full-time tuition and fees vary according to course load and program. Part-time tuition and fees vary according to course load and program. No tuition increase for student's term of enrollment. *Payment plan:* installment.
Applying *Options:* electronic application. *Application fee:* $50. *Required:* high school transcript, health questionnaire. *Application deadline:* rolling (freshmen).
Freshman Application Contact Gupton-Jones College of Funeral Service, 5141 Snapfinger Woods Drive, Decatur, GA 30035-4022. *Phone:* 770-593-2257. *Toll-free phone:* 800-848-5352.
Website: http://www.gupton-jones.edu/.

Gwinnett College
Lilburn, Georgia

Admissions Office Contact Gwinnett College, 4230 Lawrenceville Highway, Suite 11, Lilburn, GA 30047. *Website:* http://www.gwinnettcollege.edu/.

Gwinnett Technical College
Lawrenceville, Georgia

- **State-supported** 2-year, founded 1984, part of Technical College System of Georgia
- **Suburban** 88-acre campus
- **Coed,** 7,479 undergraduate students, 22% full-time, 59% women, 41% men

Undergraduates 1,636 full-time, 5,843 part-time. 0.2% are from out of state; 33% Black or African American, non-Hispanic/Latino; 15% Hispanic/Latino; 8% Asian, non-Hispanic/Latino; 0.2% Native Hawaiian or other Pacific Islander, non-Hispanic/Latino; 0.2% American Indian or Alaska Native, non-Hispanic/Latino; 4% Two or more races, non-Hispanic/Latino; 6% Race/ethnicity unknown. *Retention:* 56% of full-time freshmen returned.
Freshmen *Admission:* 1,062 enrolled.
Majors Accounting; administrative assistant and secretarial science; automobile/automotive mechanics technology; building/construction finishing, management, and inspection related; business administration and management; computer programming; computer science; computer systems networking and telecommunications; drafting and design technology; electrical, electronic and communications engineering technology; emergency medical technology (EMT paramedic); horticultural science; hotel/motel administration; information science/studies; interior design; machine tool technology; management information systems; marketing/marketing management; medical/clinical assistant; medical radiologic technology; ornamental horticulture; photography; physical therapy; physical therapy technology; respiratory care therapy; tourism and travel services management; veterinary/animal health technology.
Academics *Calendar:* semesters. *Degree:* certificates, diplomas, and associate. *Special study options:* distance learning, English as a second language, part-time degree program, services for LD students, summer session for credit.
Library Gwinnett Technical College Library plus 1 other.
Student Life *Housing:* college housing not available. *Campus security:* 24-hour emergency response devices and patrols. *Student services:* personal/psychological counseling.

Costs (2017–18) *Tuition:* state resident $89 per credit hour part-time; nonresident $178 per credit hour part-time.
Financial Aid Of all full-time matriculated undergraduates who enrolled in 2015, 20 Federal Work-Study jobs (averaging $2100).
Applying *Options:* electronic application, early admission. *Application fee:* $25. *Required:* high school transcript.
Freshman Application Contact Gwinnett Technical College, 5150 Sugarloaf Parkway, Lawrenceville, GA 30043-5702. *Phone:* 678-762-7580 Ext. 434. *Website:* http://www.gwinnetttech.edu/.

Interactive College of Technology
Chamblee, Georgia

- **Proprietary** 2-year, part of Interactive Learning Systems
- **Suburban** 14-acre campus
- **Coed**

Faculty *Student/faculty ratio:* 25:1.
Academics *Calendar:* semesters. *Degree:* certificates, diplomas, and associate. *Special study options:* academic remediation for entering students, accelerated degree program, adult/continuing education programs, advanced placement credit, double majors, English as a second language, independent study, internships, part-time degree program.
Applying *Application fee:* $50. *Required:* high school transcript, interview.
Freshman Application Contact Director of Admissions, Interactive College of Technology, 5303 New Peachtree Road, Chamblee, GA 30341. *Phone:* 770-216-2960. *Toll-free phone:* 800-447-2011. *Fax:* 770-216-2988. *Website:* http://ict.edu/.

Interactive College of Technology
Gainesville, Georgia

- **Proprietary** 2-year
- **Small-town** campus
- **Coed**

Academics *Calendar:* semesters. *Degree:* certificates, diplomas, and associate. *Special study options:* academic remediation for entering students, cooperative education, distance learning, English as a second language, internships.
Applying *Required:* high school transcript, interview.
Freshman Application Contact Interactive College of Technology, 2323 Browns Bridge Road, Gainesville, GA 30504. *Website:* http://ict.edu/.

Interactive College of Technology
Morrow, Georgia

Admissions Office Contact Interactive College of Technology, 1580 Southlake Parkway, Suite C, Morrow, GA 30260. *Website:* http://ict.edu/.

Lanier Technical College
Oakwood, Georgia

- **State-supported** 2-year, founded 1964, part of Technical College System of Georgia
- **Coed**, 3,636 undergraduate students, 28% full-time, 58% women, 42% men

Undergraduates 1,034 full-time, 2,602 part-time. 0.1% are from out of state; 9% Black or African American, non-Hispanic/Latino; 16% Hispanic/Latino; 3% Asian, non-Hispanic/Latino; 0.3% Native Hawaiian or other Pacific Islander, non-Hispanic/Latino; 0.5% American Indian or Alaska Native, non-Hispanic/Latino; 2% Two or more races, non-Hispanic/Latino; 0.1% Race/ethnicity unknown. *Retention:* 60% of full-time freshmen returned.
Freshmen *Admission:* 699 enrolled.
Majors Accounting; administrative assistant and secretarial science; banking and financial support services; child development; computer and information systems security; computer programming; computer science; computer systems networking and telecommunications; criminal justice/safety; drafting and design technology; electrical, electronic and communications engineering technology; fire science/firefighting; health professions related; industrial technology; information science/studies; interior design; marketing/marketing management; medical radiologic technology; occupational safety and health technology; surgical technology; web page, digital/multimedia and information resources design.
Academics *Calendar:* quarters. *Degree:* certificates, diplomas, and associate. *Special study options:* distance learning.
Student Life *Housing:* college housing not available.

Costs (2017–18) *Tuition:* state resident $89 per credit hour part-time; nonresident $178 per credit hour part-time.
Applying *Options:* early admission. *Application fee:* $25. *Required:* high school transcript.
Freshman Application Contact Lanier Technical College, 2990 Landrum Education Drive, PO Box 58, Oakwood, GA 30566. *Phone:* 770-531-6332. *Website:* http://www.laniertech.edu/.

Lincoln College of Technology
Marietta, Georgia

Admissions Office Contact Lincoln College of Technology, 2359 Windy Hill Road, Marietta, GA 30067. *Toll-free phone:* 844-215-1513. *Website:* http://www.lincolntech.edu/.

Medtech College
Marietta, Georgia

Admissions Office Contact Medtech College, 1130 Northchase Parkway, Suite 100, Marietta, GA 30067. *Website:* http://www.medtech-atlanta.com/atlanta-marietta-ga/.

Miller-Motte Technical College
Augusta, Georgia

Admissions Office Contact Miller-Motte Technical College, 621 Frontage Road NW, Augusta, GA 30907. *Toll-free phone:* 800-705-9182. *Website:* http://www.miller-motte.edu/.

Miller-Motte Technical College
Columbus, Georgia

Admissions Office Contact Miller-Motte Technical College, 1800 Box Road, Columbus, GA 31907. *Toll-free phone:* 800-705-9182. *Website:* http://www.miller-motte.edu/.

Miller-Motte Technical College
Macon, Georgia

Admissions Office Contact Miller-Motte Technical College, 175 Tom Hill Sr. Boulevard, Macon, GA 31210. *Toll-free phone:* 800-705-9182. *Website:* http://www.miller-motte.edu/.

North Georgia Technical College
Clarkesville, Georgia

- **State-supported** 2-year, founded 1943, part of Technical College System of Georgia
- **Coed**, 2,838 undergraduate students, 32% full-time, 60% women, 40% men

Undergraduates 918 full-time, 1,920 part-time. 0.7% are from out of state; 8% Black or African American, non-Hispanic/Latino; 5% Hispanic/Latino; 1% Asian, non-Hispanic/Latino; 0.1% Native Hawaiian or other Pacific Islander, non-Hispanic/Latino; 0.5% American Indian or Alaska Native, non-Hispanic/Latino; 2% Two or more races, non-Hispanic/Latino; 1% Race/ethnicity unknown. *Retention:* 61% of full-time freshmen returned.
Freshmen *Admission:* 628 enrolled.
Majors Administrative assistant and secretarial science; computer systems networking and telecommunications; criminal justice/safety; culinary arts; heating, ventilation, air conditioning and refrigeration engineering technology; horticultural science; industrial technology; parks, recreation and leisure facilities management; turf and turfgrass management; web page, digital/multimedia and information resources design.
Academics *Calendar:* quarters. *Degree:* certificates, diplomas, and associate. *Special study options:* distance learning.
Costs (2017–18) *Tuition:* state resident $89 per credit hour part-time; nonresident $178 per credit hour part-time.
Applying *Options:* early admission. *Application fee:* $25. *Required:* high school transcript.
Freshman Application Contact North Georgia Technical College, 1500 Georgia Highway 197, North, PO Box 65, Clarkesville, GA 30523. *Phone:* 706-754-7724.
Website: http://www.northgatech.edu/.

Oconee Fall Line Technical College
Sandersville, Georgia

- **State-supported** 2-year, part of Technical College System of Georgia
- **Coed,** 1,404 undergraduate students, 26% full-time, 63% women, 37% men

Undergraduates 362 full-time, 1,042 part-time. 45% Black or African American, non-Hispanic/Latino; 2% Hispanic/Latino; 0.5% Asian, non-Hispanic/Latino; 0.1% American Indian or Alaska Native, non-Hispanic/Latino; 2% Two or more races, non-Hispanic/Latino; 0.4% Race/ethnicity unknown. *Retention:* 52% of full-time freshmen returned.
Freshmen *Admission:* 261 enrolled.
Majors Accounting; administrative assistant and secretarial science; child development; computer systems networking and telecommunications; information science/studies.
Academics *Calendar:* quarters. *Degree:* certificates, diplomas, and associate. *Special study options:* distance learning.
Student Life *Housing:* college housing not available.
Costs (2017–18) *Tuition:* state resident $89 per credit hour part-time; nonresident $178 per credit hour part-time.
Applying *Options:* early admission. *Application fee:* $25. *Required:* high school transcript.
Freshman Application Contact Oconee Fall Line Technical College, 1189 Deepstep Road, Sandersville, GA 31082. *Phone:* 478-553-2050. *Toll-free phone:* 877-399-8324.
Website: http://www.oftc.edu/.

Ogeechee Technical College
Statesboro, Georgia

- **State-supported** 2-year, founded 1989, part of Technical College System of Georgia
- **Small-town** campus
- **Coed,** 1,904 undergraduate students, 38% full-time, 68% women, 32% men

Undergraduates 732 full-time, 1,172 part-time. 0.9% are from out of state; 33% Black or African American, non-Hispanic/Latino; 4% Hispanic/Latino; 0.5% Asian, non-Hispanic/Latino; 0.2% Native Hawaiian or other Pacific Islander, non-Hispanic/Latino; 0.2% American Indian or Alaska Native, non-Hispanic/Latino; 2% Two or more races, non-Hispanic/Latino. *Retention:* 58% of full-time freshmen returned.
Freshmen *Admission:* 335 enrolled.
Majors Accounting; administrative assistant and secretarial science; agribusiness; automobile/automotive mechanics technology; banking and financial support services; child development; computer systems networking and telecommunications; construction trades; culinary arts; dental hygiene; forest technology; funeral service and mortuary science; health information/medical records technology; hotel/motel administration; information science/studies; interior design; legal assistant/paralegal; marketing/marketing management; opticianry; tourism and travel services management; veterinary/animal health technology; water quality and wastewater treatment management and recycling technology; wildlife, fish and wildlands science and management; wood science and wood products/pulp and paper technology.
Academics *Calendar:* quarters. *Degree:* certificates, diplomas, and associate. *Special study options:* distance learning.
Student Life *Housing:* college housing not available.
Costs (2017–18) *Tuition:* state resident $89 per credit hour part-time; nonresident $178 per credit hour part-time.
Applying *Options:* early admission. *Application fee:* $25. *Required:* high school transcript.
Freshman Application Contact Ogeechee Technical College, One Joe Kennedy Boulevard, Statesboro, GA 30458. *Phone:* 912-871-1600. *Toll-free phone:* 800-646-1316.
Website: http://www.ogeecheetech.edu/.

SAE Institute Atlanta
Atlanta, Georgia

Admissions Office Contact SAE Institute Atlanta, 215 Peachtree Street NE, Atlanta, GA 30303. *Website:* http://www.sae.edu/.

Savannah Technical College
Savannah, Georgia

- **State-supported** 2-year, founded 1929, part of Technical College System of Georgia
- **Urban** campus
- **Coed,** 3,938 undergraduate students, 35% full-time, 60% women, 40% men

Undergraduates 1,393 full-time, 2,545 part-time. 2% are from out of state; 45% Black or African American, non-Hispanic/Latino; 7% Hispanic/Latino; 3% Asian, non-Hispanic/Latino; 0.2% Native Hawaiian or other Pacific Islander, non-Hispanic/Latino; 0.5% American Indian or Alaska Native, non-Hispanic/Latino; 3% Two or more races, non-Hispanic/Latino. *Retention:* 60% of full-time freshmen returned.
Freshmen *Admission:* 616 enrolled.
Majors Accounting; administrative assistant and secretarial science; automobile/automotive mechanics technology; child development; computer systems networking and telecommunications; criminal justice/safety; culinary arts; electrical, electronic and communications engineering technology; fire science/firefighting; heating, ventilation, air conditioning and refrigeration engineering technology; hotel/motel administration; industrial technology; information technology; marketing/marketing management; surgical technology; tourism and travel services management.
Academics *Calendar:* quarters. *Degree:* certificates, diplomas, and associate. *Special study options:* distance learning.
Student Life *Housing:* college housing not available.
Costs (2017–18) *Tuition:* state resident $89 per credit hour part-time; nonresident $178 per credit hour part-time.
Applying *Options:* early admission. *Application fee:* $25. *Required:* high school transcript.
Freshman Application Contact Savannah Technical College, 5717 White Bluff Road, Savannah, GA 31405. *Phone:* 912-443-5711. *Toll-free phone:* 800-769-6362.
Website: http://www.savannahtech.edu/.

Southeastern Technical College
Vidalia, Georgia

- **State-supported** 2-year, founded 1989, part of Technical College System of Georgia
- **Coed,** 1,563 undergraduate students, 28% full-time, 72% women, 28% men

Undergraduates 435 full-time, 1,128 part-time. 0.1% are from out of state; 27% Black or African American, non-Hispanic/Latino; 8% Hispanic/Latino; 0.2% Asian, non-Hispanic/Latino; 0.6% Two or more races, non-Hispanic/Latino. *Retention:* 53% of full-time freshmen returned.
Freshmen *Admission:* 295 enrolled.
Majors Accounting; administrative assistant and secretarial science; child development; computer systems networking and telecommunications; criminal justice/safety; dental hygiene; design and visual communications; electrical, electronic and communications engineering technology; information science/studies; marketing/marketing management; medical radiologic technology; respiratory therapy technician; web page, digital/multimedia and information resources design.
Academics *Calendar:* quarters. *Degree:* certificates, diplomas, and associate. *Special study options:* distance learning.
Student Life *Housing:* college housing not available.
Costs (2017–18) *Tuition:* state resident $89 per credit hour part-time; nonresident $178 per credit hour part-time.
Applying *Options:* early admission. *Application fee:* $25. *Required:* high school transcript.
Freshman Application Contact Southeastern Technical College, 3001 East First Street, Vidalia, GA 30474. *Phone:* 912-538-3121.
Website: http://www.southeasterntech.edu/.

Southern Crescent Technical College
Griffin, Georgia

- **State-supported** 2-year, founded 1965, part of Technical College System of Georgia
- **Small-town** campus
- **Coed,** 4,703 undergraduate students, 34% full-time, 66% women, 34% men

Undergraduates 1,601 full-time, 3,102 part-time. 0.1% are from out of state; 44% Black or African American, non-Hispanic/Latino; 5% Hispanic/Latino; 1% Asian, non-Hispanic/Latino; 0.2% American Indian or Alaska Native, non-Hispanic/Latino; 1% Two or more races, non-Hispanic/Latino; 0.9% Race/ethnicity unknown. *Retention:* 58% of full-time freshmen returned.
Freshmen *Admission:* 894 enrolled.

Majors Accounting; administrative assistant and secretarial science; automobile/automotive mechanics technology; business administration and management; child development; computer and information systems security; computer programming; computer systems networking and telecommunications; criminal justice/safety; drafting and design technology; electrical, electronic and communications engineering technology; emergency medical technology (EMT paramedic); heating, ventilation, air conditioning and refrigeration engineering technology; horticultural science; industrial technology; legal assistant/paralegal; manufacturing engineering technology; marketing/marketing management; medical radiologic technology; pharmacy technician; respiratory therapy technician; surgical technology; web page, digital/multimedia and information resources design.
Academics *Calendar:* quarters. *Degree:* certificates, diplomas, and associate. *Special study options:* distance learning.
Library Griffin Technical College Library.
Costs (2017–18) *Tuition:* state resident $89 per credit hour part-time; nonresident $178 per credit hour part-time.
Applying *Options:* early admission. *Application fee:* $25. *Required:* high school transcript.
Freshman Application Contact Southern Crescent Technical College, 501 Varsity Road, Griffin, GA 30223. *Phone:* 770-646-6160.
Website: http://www.sctech.edu/.

Southern Regional Technical College
Thomasville, Georgia

- **State-supported** 2-year, founded 1963, part of Technical College System of Georgia
- **Coed,** 3,521 undergraduate students, 33% full-time, 65% women, 35% men

Undergraduates 1,164 full-time, 2,357 part-time. 1% are from out of state; 33% Black or African American, non-Hispanic/Latino; 6% Hispanic/Latino; 0.4% Asian, non-Hispanic/Latino; 0.3% American Indian or Alaska Native, non-Hispanic/Latino; 0.6% Two or more races, non-Hispanic/Latino; 1% Race/ethnicity unknown. *Retention:* 61% of full-time freshmen returned.
Freshmen *Admission:* 521 enrolled.
Majors Accounting; administrative assistant and secretarial science; agricultural mechanization; child development; computer systems networking and telecommunications; criminal justice/safety; information science/studies; medical radiologic technology; registered nursing/registered nurse; respiratory care therapy; surgical technology.
Academics *Calendar:* quarters. *Degree:* certificates, diplomas, and associate. *Special study options:* distance learning.
Student Life *Housing:* college housing not available.
Costs (2017–18) *Tuition:* state resident $89 per credit hour part-time; nonresident $178 per credit hour part-time.
Applying *Options:* electronic application, early admission. *Application fee:* $25. *Required:* high school transcript.
Freshman Application Contact Southern Regional Technical College, 15689 US 19 North, Thomasville, GA 31792. *Phone:* 229-225-5089.
Website: http://www.southwestgatech.edu/.

South Georgia State College
Douglas, Georgia

Freshman Application Contact South Georgia State College, 100 West College Park Drive, Douglas, GA 31533-5098. *Phone:* 912-260-4409. *Toll-free phone:* 800-342-6364. *Website:* http://www.sgc.edu/.

South Georgia Technical College
Americus, Georgia

- **State-supported** 2-year, founded 1948, part of Technical College System of Georgia
- **Coed,** 1,829 undergraduate students, 50% full-time, 53% women, 47% men

Undergraduates 917 full-time, 912 part-time. 4% are from out of state; 54% Black or African American, non-Hispanic/Latino; 3% Hispanic/Latino; 0.5% Asian, non-Hispanic/Latino; 0.1% American Indian or Alaska Native, non-Hispanic/Latino; 0.5% Race/ethnicity unknown. *Retention:* 64% of full-time freshmen returned.
Freshmen *Admission:* 493 enrolled.
Majors Accounting; administrative assistant and secretarial science; child development; computer systems networking and telecommunications; criminal justice/safety; culinary arts; drafting and design technology; electrical,

electronic and communications engineering technology; heating, ventilation, air conditioning and refrigeration engineering technology; horticultural science; industrial technology; information science/studies; legal assistant/paralegal; manufacturing engineering technology; marketing/marketing management.
Academics *Calendar:* quarters. *Degree:* certificates, diplomas, and associate. *Special study options:* distance learning.
Costs (2017–18) *Tuition:* state resident $89 per credit hour part-time; nonresident $178 per credit hour part-time.
Applying *Options:* early admission. *Application fee:* $25. *Required:* high school transcript.
Freshman Application Contact South Georgia Technical College, 900 South Georgia Tech Parkway, Americus, GA 31709. *Phone:* 229-931-2299.
Website: http://www.southgatech.edu/.

Virginia College in Augusta
Augusta, Georgia

Admissions Office Contact Virginia College in Augusta, 2807 Wylds Road Extension, Suite B, Augusta, GA 30909. *Website:* http://www.vc.edu/.

Virginia College in Columbus
Columbus, Georgia

Admissions Office Contact Virginia College in Columbus, 5601 Veterans Parkway, Columbus, GA 31904. *Website:* http://www.vc.edu/.

Virginia College in Macon
Macon, Georgia

Admissions Office Contact Virginia College in Macon, 1901 Paul Walsh Drive, Macon, GA 31206. *Website:* http://www.vc.edu/.

Virginia College in Savannah
Savannah, Georgia

Admissions Office Contact Virginia College in Savannah, 14045 Abercorn Street, Suite 1503, Savannah, GA 31419. *Website:* http://www.vc.edu/.

West Georgia Technical College
Waco, Georgia

- **State-supported** 2-year, founded 1966, part of Technical College System of Georgia
- **Coed,** 6,743 undergraduate students, 29% full-time, 65% women, 35% men

Undergraduates 1,931 full-time, 4,812 part-time. 2% are from out of state; 32% Black or African American, non-Hispanic/Latino; 5% Hispanic/Latino; 1% Asian, non-Hispanic/Latino; 0.1% Native Hawaiian or other Pacific Islander, non-Hispanic/Latino; 0.4% American Indian or Alaska Native, non-Hispanic/Latino; 2% Two or more races, non-Hispanic/Latino; 0.6% Race/ethnicity unknown. *Retention:* 59% of full-time freshmen returned.
Freshmen *Admission:* 1,302 enrolled.
Majors Accounting; administrative assistant and secretarial science; automobile/automotive mechanics technology; child development; computer systems networking and telecommunications; criminal justice/safety; electrical, electronic and communications engineering technology; fire science/firefighting; health information/medical records technology; industrial technology; information science/studies; marketing/marketing management; medical radiologic technology; pharmacy technician; plastics and polymer engineering technology; social work; web page, digital/multimedia and information resources design.
Academics *Calendar:* quarters. *Degree:* certificates, diplomas, and associate. *Special study options:* distance learning.
Student Life *Housing:* college housing not available.
Costs (2017–18) *Tuition:* state resident $89 per credit hour part-time; nonresident $178 per credit hour part-time.
Financial Aid Of all full-time matriculated undergraduates who enrolled in 2015, 68 Federal Work-Study jobs (averaging $800).
Applying *Options:* early admission. *Application fee:* $25. *Required:* high school transcript.
Freshman Application Contact West Georgia Technical College, 176 Murphy Campus Boulevard, Waco, GA 30182. *Phone:* 770-537-5719.
Website: http://www.westgatech.edu/.

Wiregrass Georgia Technical College
Valdosta, Georgia

- **State-supported** 2-year, founded 1963, part of Technical College System of Georgia
- **Suburban** campus
- **Coed,** 3,940 undergraduate students, 24% full-time, 63% women, 37% men

Undergraduates 947 full-time, 2,993 part-time. 0.7% are from out of state; 32% Black or African American, non-Hispanic/Latino; 5% Hispanic/Latino; 0.8% Asian, non-Hispanic/Latino; 0.2% Native Hawaiian or other Pacific Islander, non-Hispanic/Latino; 0.4% American Indian or Alaska Native, non-Hispanic/Latino; 2% Two or more races, non-Hispanic/Latino; 0.2% Race/ethnicity unknown. *Retention:* 59% of full-time freshmen returned.
Freshmen *Admission:* 498 enrolled.
Majors Accounting; administrative assistant and secretarial science; banking and financial support services; child development; computer and information systems security; computer programming; computer systems networking and telecommunications; criminal justice/safety; drafting and design technology; e-commerce; fire science/firefighting; machine tool technology; marketing/marketing management; medical radiologic technology; web page, digital/multimedia and information resources design.
Academics *Calendar:* quarters. *Degree:* certificates, diplomas, and associate. *Special study options:* distance learning.
Student Life *Housing:* college housing not available.
Costs (2017–18) *Tuition:* state resident $89 per credit hour part-time; nonresident $178 per credit hour part-time.
Applying *Options:* early admission. *Application fee:* $25. *Required:* high school transcript.
Freshman Application Contact Wiregrass Georgia Technical College, 4089 Val Tech Road, Valdosta, GA 31602. *Phone:* 229-468-2278.
Website: http://www.wiregrass.edu/.

GUAM

Guam Community College
Mangilao, Guam

- **Territory-supported** 2-year, founded 1977
- **Small-town** 33-acre campus
- **Endowment** $8.8 million
- **Coed,** 2,428 undergraduate students, 43% full-time, 56% women, 44% men

Undergraduates 1,038 full-time, 1,390 part-time. 1% Black or African American, non-Hispanic/Latino; 0.5% Hispanic/Latino; 41% Asian, non-Hispanic/Latino; 54% Native Hawaiian or other Pacific Islander, non-Hispanic/Latino; 0.5% Race/ethnicity unknown; 1% international; 1% transferred in. *Retention:* 62% of full-time freshmen returned.
Freshmen *Admission:* 289 applied, 289 admitted, 485 enrolled.
Faculty *Total:* 194, 59% full-time. *Student/faculty ratio:* 15:1.
Majors Accounting; architectural drafting and CAD/CADD; automobile/automotive mechanics technology; business automation/technology/data entry; computer science; computer systems networking and telecommunications; criminal justice/law enforcement administration; crisis/emergency/disaster management; culinary arts related; design and visual communications; early childhood education; education; hotel/motel administration; human services; liberal arts and sciences/liberal studies; marketing/marketing management; medical/clinical assistant; office management; restaurant, culinary, and catering management; sales, distribution, and marketing operations; surveying technology; tourism and travel services management.
Academics *Calendar:* semesters. *Degree:* certificates, diplomas, and associate. *Special study options:* academic remediation for entering students, adult/continuing education programs, advanced placement credit, cooperative education, double majors, English as a second language, honors programs, independent study, internships, off-campus study, part-time degree program, services for LD students, summer session for credit. *ROTC:* Army (c).
Library Learning Resource Center. *Books:* 21,379 (physical), 157,000 (digital/electronic); *Databases:* 40. Weekly public service hours: 60; students can reserve study rooms.
Student Life *Housing:* college housing not available. *Campus security:* 12-hour patrols by trained security personnel. *Student services:* health clinic, personal/psychological counseling.
Costs (2016–17) *Tuition:* territory resident $3120 full-time, $130 per credit hour part-time; nonresident $3720 full-time, $155 per credit hour part-time.

Required fees: $294 full-time, $147 per term part-time. *Payment plans:* installment, deferred payment. *Waivers:* senior citizens and employees or children of employees.
Financial Aid Of all full-time matriculated undergraduates who enrolled in 2015, 83 Federal Work-Study jobs (averaging $940).
Applying *Options:* early admission. *Required:* high school transcript. *Application deadline:* rolling (freshmen). *Notification:* continuous (freshmen).
Freshman Application Contact Dr. Julie Ulloa-Heath, Registrar, Guam Community College, PO Box 23069 GMF, Barrigada, GU 96921. *Phone:* 671-735-5561. *Fax:* 671-735-5531. *E-mail:* julie.ulloaheath@guamcc.edu. *Website:* http://www.guamcc.edu/.

HAWAII

Hawaii Community College
Hilo, Hawaii

Director of Admissions Mrs. Tammy M. Tanaka, Admissions Specialist, Hawaii Community College, 1175 Manono Street, Hilo, HI 96720-5096. *Phone:* 808-974-7661. *Website:* http://www.hawcc.hawaii.edu/.

Hawaii Tokai International College
Kapolei, Hawaii

- **Independent** 2-year, founded 1992, part of Tokai University Educational System
- **Suburban** 7-acre campus with easy access to Honolulu
- **Coed,** 80 undergraduate students, 100% full-time, 50% women, 50% men

Undergraduates 80 full-time. Students come from 3 states and territories; 3 other countries; 23% are from out of state; 1% Hispanic/Latino; 8% Asian, non-Hispanic/Latino; 86% international; 34% live on campus. *Retention:* 91% of full-time freshmen returned.
Freshmen *Admission:* 50 applied, 43 admitted, 19 enrolled. *Average high school GPA:* 2.95.
Faculty *Total:* 19, 32% full-time, 42% with terminal degrees. *Student/faculty ratio:* 7:1.
Majors Liberal arts and sciences/liberal studies.
Academics *Calendar:* quarters. *Degree:* certificates, diplomas, and associate. *Special study options:* academic remediation for entering students, advanced placement credit, English as a second language, internships, part-time degree program, study abroad, summer session for credit.
Library Library and Learning Center plus 1 other. *Books:* 7,133 (physical); *Serial titles:* 29 (physical); *Databases:* 48. Weekly public service hours: 68; students can reserve study rooms.
Student Life *Housing Options:* men-only, women-only, special housing for students with disabilities. Campus housing is university owned. Freshman applicants given priority for college housing. *Activities and Organizations:* International Coffee Hour, King and Queen Club, Hula Club, Basketball Club, Phi Theta Kappa International Honor Society. *Campus security:* 24-hour emergency response devices and patrols, controlled dormitory access. *Student services:* health clinic, personal/psychological counseling.
Costs (2017–18) *One-time required fee:* $20. *Comprehensive fee:* $22,185 includes full-time tuition ($12,150), mandatory fees ($735), and room and board ($9300). Part-time tuition: $475 per credit hour. Part-time tuition and fees vary according to course load. *Room and board:* Room and board charges vary according to board plan.
Applying *Options:* electronic application, deferred entrance. *Application fee:* $50. *Required:* essay or personal statement, high school transcript, minimum 2.5 GPA. *Required for some:* interview. *Recommended:* 1 letter of recommendation. *Application deadlines:* rolling (freshmen), rolling (transfers). *Notification:* continuous (freshmen), continuous (transfers).
Freshman Application Contact Mr. Darrell Kicker, Director of Student Services, Hawaii Tokai International College, 91-971 Farrington Highway, Kapolei, HI 96707. *Phone:* 808-983-4202. *Fax:* 808-983-4107. *E-mail:* admissions@tokai.edu.
Website: http://www.htic.edu/.

Honolulu Community College
Honolulu, Hawaii

Freshman Application Contact Admissions Office, Honolulu Community College, 874 Dillingham Boulevard, Honolulu, HI 96817. *Phone:* 808-845-9129. *E-mail:* honcc@hawaii.edu. *Website:* http://www.honolulu.hawaii.edu/.

Kapiolani Community College
Honolulu, Hawaii

Freshman Application Contact Kapiolani Community College, 4303 Diamond Head Road, Honolulu, HI 96816-4421. *Phone:* 808-734-9555. *Website:* http://www.kapiolani.hawaii.edu/.

Kauai Community College
Lihue, Hawaii

Freshman Application Contact Mr. Leighton Oride, Admissions Officer and Registrar, Kauai Community College, 3-1901 Kaumualii Highway, Lihue, HI 96766. *Phone:* 808-245-8225. *Fax:* 808-245-8297. *E-mail:* arkauai@hawaii.edu. *Website:* http://kauai.hawaii.edu/.

Leeward Community College
Pearl City, Hawaii

- **State-supported** 2-year, founded 1968, part of University of Hawaii System
- **Suburban** 49-acre campus with easy access to Honolulu
- **Coed**

Undergraduates 3,296 full-time, 4,646 part-time. Students come from 13 other countries; 0.8% are from out of state; 2% Black or African American, non-Hispanic/Latino; 11% Hispanic/Latino; 37% Asian, non-Hispanic/Latino; 12% Native Hawaiian or other Pacific Islander, non-Hispanic/Latino; 0.3% American Indian or Alaska Native, non-Hispanic/Latino; 26% Two or more races, non-Hispanic/Latino; 1% Race/ethnicity unknown; 0.5% international; 7% transferred in. *Retention:* 65% of full-time freshmen returned.
Faculty *Student/faculty ratio:* 23:1.
Academics *Calendar:* semesters. *Degree:* certificates and associate. *Special study options:* academic remediation for entering students, advanced placement credit, cooperative education, distance learning, English as a second language, honors programs, independent study, internships, off-campus study, part-time degree program, services for LD students, study abroad, summer session for credit. *ROTC:* Air Force (c).
Student Life *Campus security:* 24-hour emergency response devices and patrols, late-night transport/escort service.
Applying *Options:* electronic application, early admission. *Application fee:* $25. *Required for some:* high school transcript.
Freshman Application Contact Ms. Sheryl Higa, Assistant Registrar, Leeward Community College, 96-045 Ala Ike, Pearl City, HI 96782-3393. *Phone:* 808-455-0643. *Website:* http://www.leeward.hawaii.edu/.

Remington College–Honolulu Campus
Honolulu, Hawaii

Director of Admissions Louis LaMair, Director of Recruitment, Remington College–Honolulu Campus, 1111 Bishop Street, Suite 400, Honolulu, HI 96813. *Phone:* 808-942-1000. *Toll-free phone:* 800-323-8122. *Fax:* 808-533-3064. *E-mail:* louis.lamair@remingtoncollege.edu. *Website:* http://www.remingtoncollege.edu/.

University of Hawaii Maui College
Kahului, Hawaii

Freshman Application Contact Mr. Stephen Kameda, Director of Admissions and Records, University of Hawaii Maui College, 310 Kaahumanu Avenue, Kahului, HI 96732. *Phone:* 808-984-3267. *Toll-free phone:* 800-479-6692. *Fax:* 808-984-3872. *E-mail:* skameda@hawaii.edu. *Website:* http://maui.hawaii.edu/.

Windward Community College
Kaneohe, Hawaii

Director of Admissions Geri Imai, Registrar, Windward Community College, 45-720 Keaahala Road, Kaneohe, HI 96744-3528. *Phone:* 808-235-7430. *E-mail:* gerii@hawaii.edu. *Website:* http://www.windward.hawaii.edu/.

IDAHO

Carrington College–Boise
Boise, Idaho

- **Proprietary** 2-year, founded 1980, part of Carrington Colleges Group, Inc.
- **Coed**

Undergraduates 380 full-time, 40 part-time. 15% are from out of state; 2% Black or African American, non-Hispanic/Latino; 15% Hispanic/Latino; 8% Asian, non-Hispanic/Latino; 0.2% Native Hawaiian or other Pacific Islander, non-Hispanic/Latino; 2% American Indian or Alaska Native, non-Hispanic/Latino; 2% Two or more races, non-Hispanic/Latino; 0.2% Race/ethnicity unknown; 19% transferred in.
Faculty *Student/faculty ratio:* 12:1.
Academics *Calendar:* semesters. *Degree:* certificates and associate.
Costs (2016–17) *Tuition:* $58,183 per degree program part-time. Full-time tuition and fees vary according to program. Part-time tuition and fees vary according to program.
Applying *Required:* essay or personal statement, high school transcript, interview, institutional entrance test.
Freshman Application Contact Carrington College–Boise, 1122 North Liberty Street, Boise, ID 83704. *Website:* http://carrington.edu/.

College of Southern Idaho
Twin Falls, Idaho

Freshman Application Contact Director of Admissions, Registration, and Records, College of Southern Idaho, PO Box 1238, Twin Falls, ID 83303-1238. *Phone:* 208-732-6232. *Toll-free phone:* 800-680-0274. *Fax:* 208-736-3014. *Website:* http://www.csi.edu/.

College of Western Idaho
Nampa, Idaho

Freshman Application Contact College of Western Idaho, 6056 Birch Lane, Nampa, ID 83687. *Website:* http://cwidaho.cc/.

Eastern Idaho Technical College
Idaho Falls, Idaho

- **State-supported** 2-year, founded 1969
- **Small-town** 40-acre campus
- **Coed,** 676 undergraduate students, 47% full-time, 63% women, 37% men

Undergraduates 321 full-time, 355 part-time. Students come from 1 other state; 0.3% Black or African American, non-Hispanic/Latino; 13% Hispanic/Latino; 0.9% Asian, non-Hispanic/Latino; 0.1% Native Hawaiian or other Pacific Islander, non-Hispanic/Latino; 0.6% American Indian or Alaska Native, non-Hispanic/Latino; 4% Two or more races, non-Hispanic/Latino; 2% Race/ethnicity unknown; 45% transferred in. *Retention:* 36% of full-time freshmen returned.
Freshmen *Admission:* 94 enrolled.
Faculty *Student/faculty ratio:* 8:1.
Majors Accounting; administrative assistant and secretarial science; automobile/automotive mechanics technology; computer systems networking and telecommunications; diesel mechanics technology; electrician; fire science/firefighting; legal assistant/paralegal; marketing/marketing management; medical/clinical assistant; registered nursing/registered nurse; surgical technology; web page, digital/multimedia and information resources design; welding technology.
Academics *Calendar:* semesters. *Degree:* certificates and associate. *Special study options:* academic remediation for entering students, adult/continuing education programs, advanced placement credit, English as a second language, part-time degree program, services for LD students, summer session for credit.
Library Richard and Lila Jordan Library plus 1 other.
Student Life *Housing:* college housing not available. *Campus security:* 24-hour emergency response devices and patrols.
Standardized Tests *Required for some:* ACT Compass, ACT ASSET, or CPT.
Costs (2016–17) *Tuition:* state resident $2404 full-time, $106 per credit part-time; nonresident $8806 full-time, $211 per credit part-time. Full-time tuition and fees vary according to course load and program. Part-time tuition and fees vary according to course load and program. *Required fees:* $30 full-time, $30 per year part-time. *Waivers:* employees or children of employees.
Financial Aid Of all full-time matriculated undergraduates who enrolled in 2015, 37 Federal Work-Study jobs (averaging $1176). 11 state and other part-time jobs (averaging $1619).

Applying *Options:* electronic application, deferred entrance. *Required:* high school transcript. *Required for some:* essay or personal statement, interview. *Application deadline:* rolling (freshmen).

Freshman Application Contact Hailey Mack, Career Placement and Recruiting Coordinator, Eastern Idaho Technical College, 1600 South 25th East, Idaho Falls, ID 83404. *Phone:* 208-524-5337 Ext. 35337. *Toll-free phone:* 800-662-0261. *Fax:* 208-524-0429. *E-mail:* hailey.mack@my.eitc.edu. *Website:* http://www.eitc.edu/.

North Idaho College
Coeur d'Alene, Idaho

Freshman Application Contact North Idaho College, 1000 West Garden Avenue, Coeur d Alene, ID 83814-2199. *Phone:* 208-769-3303. *Toll-free phone:* 877-404-4536 Ext. 3311. *E-mail:* admit@nic.edu. *Website:* http://www.nic.edu/.

ILLINOIS

Ambria College of Nursing
Hoffman Estates, Illinois

Admissions Office Contact Ambria College of Nursing, 5210 Trillium Boulevard, Hoffman Estates, IL 60192. *Website:* http://www.ambria.edu/.

Black Hawk College
Moline, Illinois

Freshman Application Contact Ms. Gabriella Hurtado, Recruitment Coordinator/Admissions Advisor, Black Hawk College, 6600-34th Avenue, Moline, IL 61265. *Phone:* 309-796-5341. *Toll-free phone:* 800-334-1311. *E-mail:* ghurtado@bhc.edu. *Website:* http://www.bhc.edu/.

Carl Sandburg College
Galesburg, Illinois

Director of Admissions Ms. Carol Kreider, Dean of Student Support Services, Carl Sandburg College, 2400 Tom L. Wilson Boulevard, Galesburg, IL 61401-9576. *Phone:* 309-341-5234. *Website:* http://www.sandburg.edu/.

City Colleges of Chicago, Harold Washington College
Chicago, Illinois

Freshman Application Contact Admissions Office, City Colleges of Chicago, Harold Washington College, 30 East Lake Street, Chicago, IL 60601-2449. *Phone:* 312-553-6010. *Website:* http://hwashington.ccc.edu/.

City Colleges of Chicago, Harry S. Truman College
Chicago, Illinois

Freshman Application Contact City Colleges of Chicago, Harry S. Truman College, 1145 West Wilson Avenue, Chicago, IL 60640-5616. *Phone:* 773-907-4000 Ext. 1112. *Website:* http://www.trumancollege.edu/.

City Colleges of Chicago, Kennedy-King College
Chicago, Illinois

- **State and locally supported** 2-year, founded 1935, part of City Colleges of Chicago
- **Urban** 40-acre campus with easy access to Chicago
- **Coed,** 2,825 undergraduate students, 56% full-time, 60% women, 40% men

Undergraduates 1,584 full-time, 1,234 part-time. Students come from 20 states and territories; 8 other countries; 1% are from out of state; 78% Black or African American, non-Hispanic/Latino; 14% Hispanic/Latino; 1% Asian, non-Hispanic/Latino; 0.1% American Indian or Alaska Native, non-Hispanic/Latino; 3% Two or more races, non-Hispanic/Latino; 0.6% Race/ethnicity unknown; 1% transferred in. *Retention:* 34% of full-time freshmen returned.

Freshmen *Admission:* 943 enrolled.

Faculty *Student/faculty ratio:* 30:1.

Majors Automobile/automotive mechanics technology; biological and physical sciences; business administration and management; child-care provision; criminal justice/safety; culinary arts; data processing and data processing technology; general studies; heating, air conditioning, ventilation and refrigeration maintenance technology; information technology; liberal arts and sciences/liberal studies; radio and television; social work; substance abuse/addiction counseling.

Academics *Calendar:* semesters. *Degree:* certificates and associate. *Special study options:* academic remediation for entering students, adult/continuing education programs, advanced placement credit, cooperative education, distance learning, English as a second language, honors programs, internships, part-time degree program, summer session for credit.

Library Harold Washington College Library.

Student Life *Housing:* college housing not available. *Activities and Organizations:* Dynamic Movement Dance Club, African American Studies Club, Access Ability Alliance Club, Phi Theta Kappa, Student Government Association. *Campus security:* late-night transport/escort service. *Student services:* personal/psychological counseling.

Athletics Member NJCAA. *Intercollegiate sports:* basketball M(s)/W(s), soccer M(s).

Financial Aid Of all full-time matriculated undergraduates who enrolled in 2015, 148 Federal Work-Study jobs (averaging $1539).

Applying *Options:* electronic application. *Required:* high school transcript. *Application deadlines:* rolling (freshmen), rolling (transfers).

Freshman Application Contact Nicholas Ambrose, Assistant Registrar, City Colleges of Chicago, Kennedy-King College, 6301 South Halsted Street, W-110, Chicago, IL 60621. *Phone:* 773-602-5090. *Fax:* 773-602-5055. *E-mail:* nambrose1@ccc.edu. *Website:* http://www.ccc.edu/colleges/kennedy/.

City Colleges of Chicago, Malcolm X College
Chicago, Illinois

Freshman Application Contact Ms. Kimberly Hollingsworth, Dean of Student Services, City Colleges of Chicago, Malcolm X College, 1900 West Van Buren Street, Chicago, IL 60612-3145. *Phone:* 312-850-7120. *Fax:* 312-850-7119. *E-mail:* khollingsworth@ccc.edu. *Website:* http://malcolmx.ccc.edu/.

City Colleges of Chicago, Olive-Harvey College
Chicago, Illinois

- **State and locally supported** 2-year, founded 1970, part of City Colleges of Chicago
- **Urban** 67-acre campus
- **Coed,** 2,979 undergraduate students, 37% full-time, 63% women, 37% men

Undergraduates 1,114 full-time, 1,865 part-time. 73% Black or African American, non-Hispanic/Latino; 16% Hispanic/Latino; 8% Asian, non-Hispanic/Latino; 0.1% American Indian or Alaska Native, non-Hispanic/Latino; 3% Two or more races, non-Hispanic/Latino; 4% Race/ethnicity unknown; 0.3% international; 7% transferred in. *Retention:* 49% of full-time freshmen returned.

Freshmen *Admission:* 329 enrolled.

Faculty *Total:* 124, 40% full-time. *Student/faculty ratio:* 23:1.

Majors Automobile/automotive mechanics technology; biological and physical sciences; business administration and management; child-care provision; criminal justice/safety; diesel mechanics technology; general studies; information technology; liberal arts and sciences/liberal studies; logistics, materials, and supply chain management; web/multimedia management and webmaster.

Academics *Calendar:* semesters. *Degree:* certificates and associate. *Special study options:* academic remediation for entering students, accelerated degree program, adult/continuing education programs, advanced placement credit, cooperative education, distance learning, English as a second language, independent study, internships, part-time degree program, services for LD students, summer session for credit.

Library Olga-Haley Library-Learning Resource Center. *Books:* 75,000 (physical), 26,571 (digital/electronic); *Serial titles:* 130 (physical), 2,049 (digital/electronic); *Databases:* 80.

Student Life *Housing:* college housing not available. *Activities and Organizations:* drama/theater group. *Campus security:* 24-hour emergency response devices and patrols. *Student services:* personal/psychological counseling, women's center.

Athletics Member NJCAA. *Intercollegiate sports:* baseball M, basketball M/W, volleyball W.

Costs (2016–17) *Tuition:* area resident $3506 full-time, $137 per credit hour part-time; state resident $9206 full-time, $436 per credit hour part-time; nonresident $11,906 full-time, $554 per credit hour part-time. Full-time tuition and fees vary according to program. Part-time tuition and fees vary according to course load and program. *Payment plan:* installment. *Waivers:* senior citizens and employees or children of employees.

Financial Aid Of all full-time matriculated undergraduates who enrolled in 2015, 150 Federal Work-Study jobs (averaging $3900).

Applying *Options:* electronic application, early admission, deferred entrance. *Required for some:* high school transcript. *Application deadlines:* rolling (freshmen), rolling (out-of-state freshmen), rolling (transfers). *Notification:* continuous (freshmen), continuous (out-of-state freshmen), continuous (transfers).

Freshman Application Contact Mr. Dorian Thomas, Registrar, City Colleges of Chicago, Olive-Harvey College, 10001 South Woodlawn Avenue, Room 1405, Chicago, IL 60628. *Phone:* 773-291-6384.
E-mail: dthomas236@ccc.edu.
Website: http://oliveharvey.ccc.edu/.

City Colleges of Chicago, Richard J. Daley College
Chicago, Illinois

Freshman Application Contact City Colleges of Chicago, Richard J. Daley College, 7500 South Pulaski Road, Chicago, IL 60652-1242. *Phone:* 773-838-7606. *Website:* http://daley.ccc.edu/.

City Colleges of Chicago, Wilbur Wright College
Chicago, Illinois

Freshman Application Contact Ms. Amy Aiello, Assistant Dean of Student Services, City Colleges of Chicago, Wilbur Wright College, Chicago, IL 60634. *Phone:* 773-481-8207. *Fax:* 773-481-8185. *E-mail:* aaiello@ccc.edu. *Website:* http://wright.ccc.edu/.

College of DuPage
Glen Ellyn, Illinois

Freshman Application Contact College of DuPage, IL.
E-mail: admissions@cod.edu. *Website:* http://www.cod.edu/.

College of Lake County
Grayslake, Illinois

Freshman Application Contact Director, Student Recruitment, College of Lake County, Grayslake, IL 60030-1198. *Phone:* 847-543-2383. *Fax:* 847-543-3061. *Website:* http://www.clcillinois.edu/.

Coyne College
Chicago, Illinois

- **Proprietary** 2-year
- **Urban** campus
- **Coed**

Undergraduates 522 full-time. Students come from 2 states and territories; 2% are from out of state; 36% Black or African American, non-Hispanic/Latino; 44% Hispanic/Latino; 0.8% Asian, non-Hispanic/Latino; 0.8% American Indian or Alaska Native, non-Hispanic/Latino; 4% Two or more races, non-Hispanic/Latino.

Academics *Calendar:* continuous. *Degree:* certificates, diplomas, and associate. *Special study options:* academic remediation for entering students, accelerated degree program, cooperative education, internships, off-campus study.

Library Coyne College Resource Center plus 1 other. *Books:* 2,500 (physical), 200 (digital/electronic).

Student Life *Campus security:* security guard during class times.

Standardized Tests *Required for some:* SAT or ACT (for admission), Wonderlic aptitude test.

Applying *Required:* interview, minimum Wonderlic Assessement score of 13, ACT score of 15, SAT score of 1800, or a degree from an accredited institution. *Required for some:* essay or personal statement, high school transcript, 1 letter of recommendation.

Freshman Application Contact Coyne College, 1 North State Street, Suite 400, Chicago, IL 60602. *Phone:* 773-577-8100 Ext. 8102. *Toll-free phone:* 800-707-1922. *Website:* http://www.coynecollege.edu/.

Danville Area Community College
Danville, Illinois

- **State and locally supported** 2-year, founded 1946, part of Illinois Community College Board
- **Small-town** 50-acre campus
- **Endowment** $14.0 million
- **Coed,** 2,704 undergraduate students, 39% full-time, 57% women, 43% men

Undergraduates 1,057 full-time, 1,647 part-time. Students come from 11 states and territories; 1 other country; 11% are from out of state; 13% Black or African American, non-Hispanic/Latino; 5% Hispanic/Latino; 1% Asian, non-Hispanic/Latino; 0.2% Native Hawaiian or other Pacific Islander, non-Hispanic/Latino; 0.3% American Indian or Alaska Native, non-Hispanic/Latino; 1% Two or more races, non-Hispanic/Latino; 7% Race/ethnicity unknown; 26% transferred in. *Retention:* 53% of full-time freshmen returned.

Freshmen *Admission:* 407 enrolled.

Faculty *Total:* 193, 34% full-time, 8% with terminal degrees. *Student/faculty ratio:* 16:1.

Majors Accounting technology and bookkeeping; agricultural business and management; automobile/automotive mechanics technology; business automation/technology/data entry; CAD/CADD drafting/design technology; child-care provision; computer programming (specific applications); computer systems networking and telecommunications; corrections; criminal justice/police science; electrician; energy management and systems technology; engineering; executive assistant/executive secretary; fire science/firefighting; floriculture/floristry management; general studies; health information/medical records technology; industrial electronics technology; industrial mechanics and maintenance technology; juvenile corrections; landscaping and groundskeeping; liberal arts and sciences/liberal studies; manufacturing engineering technology; medical administrative assistant and medical secretary; radiologic technology/science; registered nursing/registered nurse; selling skills and sales; teacher assistant/aide; turf and turfgrass management.

Academics *Calendar:* semesters. *Degree:* certificates and associate. *Special study options:* academic remediation for entering students, adult/continuing education programs, advanced placement credit, cooperative education, distance learning, double majors, English as a second language, independent study, internships, off-campus study, part-time degree program, services for LD students, summer session for credit.

Student Life *Housing:* college housing not available. *Activities and Organizations:* drama/theater group, choral group, Phi Theta Kappa International Honor Society, The Guild, Powerhouse Campus Ministry, Rad Tech Club, Ag Club. *Campus security:* 24-hour emergency response devices and patrols. *Student services:* personal/psychological counseling.

Athletics Member NJCAA. *Intercollegiate sports:* baseball M(s), basketball M(s)/W(s), cheerleading W, cross-country running M(s)/W(s), softball W(s).

Costs (2017–18) *Tuition:* area resident $4425 full-time, $140 per credit hour part-time; state resident $7275 full-time, $235 per credit hour part-time; nonresident $7275 full-time, $235 per credit hour part-time. Full-time tuition and fees vary according to program. Part-time tuition and fees vary according to program. *Required fees:* $700 full-time, $30 per credit hour part-time. *Payment plan:* installment. *Waivers:* senior citizens and employees or children of employees.

Financial Aid Of all full-time matriculated undergraduates who enrolled in 2016, 52 Federal Work-Study jobs (averaging $3000). 60 state and other part-time jobs (averaging $3000).

Applying *Options:* early admission, deferred entrance. *Required:* high school transcript. *Application deadlines:* rolling (freshmen), rolling (transfers).

Freshman Application Contact Mr. Nick Catlett, Coordinator of Recruitment, Danville Area Community College, 2000 East Main Street, Danville, IL 61832-5199. *Phone:* 217-443-8864. *Fax:* 217-443-8337. *E-mail:* ncatlett@dacc.edu.
Website: http://www.dacc.edu/.

Elgin Community College

Elgin, Illinois

- **State and locally supported** 2-year, founded 1949, part of Illinois Community College Board
- **Suburban** 145-acre campus with easy access to Chicago
- **Coed,** 9,949 undergraduate students, 32% full-time, 54% women, 46% men

Undergraduates 3,209 full-time, 6,740 part-time. Students come from 4 states and territories; 15 other countries; 0.2% are from out of state; 4% Black or African American, non-Hispanic/Latino; 42% Hispanic/Latino; 7% Asian, non-Hispanic/Latino; 0.1% Native Hawaiian or other Pacific Islander, non-Hispanic/Latino; 0.8% American Indian or Alaska Native, non-Hispanic/Latino; 3% Race/ethnicity unknown; 0.5% international; 4% transferred in. *Retention:* 77% of full-time freshmen returned.

Freshmen *Admission:* 1,380 enrolled.

Majors Accounting; administrative assistant and secretarial science; animation, interactive technology, video graphics and special effects; automobile/automotive mechanics technology; baking and pastry arts; biological and physical sciences; biology/biotechnology laboratory technician; business administration and management; CAD/CADD drafting/design technology; clinical/medical laboratory technology; computer and information systems security; criminal justice/police science; culinary arts; data entry/microcomputer applications; design and visual communications; engineering; entrepreneurship; executive assistant/executive secretary; fine/studio arts; fire science/firefighting; graphic design; health and physical education/fitness; heating, air conditioning, ventilation and refrigeration maintenance technology; industrial mechanics and maintenance technology; legal assistant/paralegal; liberal arts and sciences/liberal studies; machine tool technology; marketing/marketing management; music; physical therapy technology; radiologic technology/science; registered nursing/registered nurse; restaurant, culinary, and catering management; retailing; social work.

Academics *Calendar:* semesters. *Degree:* certificates, diplomas, and associate. *Special study options:* academic remediation for entering students, accelerated degree program, advanced placement credit, cooperative education, distance learning, double majors, English as a second language, honors programs, independent study, internships, off-campus study, part-time degree program, services for LD students, study abroad, summer session for credit.

Library Renner Academic Library & Learning Resources.

Student Life *Housing:* college housing not available. *Activities and Organizations:* drama/theater group, student-run newspaper, choral group, Phi Theta Kappa Honor Society, Organization of Latin American Students, Asian Filipino Club, Amnesty International, Student Government. *Campus security:* grounds patrolled daily 7 am-11 pm during the academic year. *Student services:* personal/psychological counseling, legal services.

Athletics Member NJCAA. *Intercollegiate sports:* baseball M(s), basketball M(s)/W(s), cross-country running M(s)/W(s), golf M(s), soccer M(s)/W(s), softball W(s), tennis M(s)/W(s), volleyball W(s).

Costs (2016–17) *Tuition:* area resident $3750 full-time, $125 per credit hour part-time; state resident $13,035 full-time, $434 per credit hour part-time; nonresident $14,934 full-time, $498 per credit hour part-time. *Required fees:* $6 per term part-time. *Payment plan:* installment. *Waivers:* senior citizens.

Applying *Options:* electronic application. *Required for some:* high school transcript, specific departmental requirements. *Application deadlines:* rolling (freshmen), rolling (transfers). *Notification:* continuous (freshmen), continuous (transfers).

Freshman Application Contact Admissions, Recruitment, and Student Life, Elgin Community College, 1700 Spartan Drive, Elgin, IL 60123. *Phone:* 847-214-7414. *E-mail:* admissions@elgin.edu. *Website:* http://www.elgin.edu/.

Fox College

Bedford Park, Illinois

- **Private** 2-year, founded 1932
- **Suburban** campus
- **Coed**
- 68% of applicants were admitted

Academics *Calendar:* semesters. *Degree:* diplomas and associate. *Special study options:* accelerated degree program, internships.

Freshman Application Contact Admissions Office, Fox College, 6640 South Cicero, Bedford Park, IL 60638. *Phone:* 708-444-4500. *Website:* http://www.foxcollege.edu/.

Harper College

Palatine, Illinois

- **State and locally supported** 2-year, founded 1965, part of Illinois Community College Board
- **Suburban** 200-acre campus with easy access to Chicago
- **Coed,** 14,142 undergraduate students, 45% full-time, 66% women, 34% men

Undergraduates 6,403 full-time, 7,739 part-time. Students come from 1 other state; 4% Black or African American, non-Hispanic/Latino; 27% Hispanic/Latino; 11% Asian, non-Hispanic/Latino; 0.2% Native Hawaiian or other Pacific Islander, non-Hispanic/Latino; 0.1% American Indian or Alaska Native, non-Hispanic/Latino; 3% Two or more races, non-Hispanic/Latino; 2% Race/ethnicity unknown; 0.8% international.

Freshmen *Admission:* 2,442 enrolled.

Faculty *Total:* 695, 30% full-time, 16% with terminal degrees. *Student/faculty ratio:* 24:1.

Majors Accounting; administrative assistant and secretarial science; architectural drafting and CAD/CADD; architectural engineering technology; art; banking and financial support services; biology/biological sciences; business administration and management; cardiovascular technology; chemistry; child-care provision; computer and information sciences; computer programming; computer programming (specific applications); computer science; criminal justice/law enforcement administration; cyber/computer forensics and counterterrorism; dental hygiene; diagnostic medical sonography and ultrasound technology; dietetics; dietetic technology; early childhood education; electrical, electronic and communications engineering technology; elementary education; emergency medical technology (EMT paramedic); engineering; English; environmental studies; fashion and fabric consulting; fashion/apparel design; fashion merchandising; finance; fine/studio arts; fire science/firefighting; food service systems administration; health teacher education; heating, air conditioning, ventilation and refrigeration maintenance technology; history; homeland security; hospitality administration; humanities; human services; interior design; international business/trade/commerce; legal administrative assistant/secretary; legal assistant/paralegal; liberal arts and sciences/liberal studies; marketing/marketing management; mathematics; medical administrative assistant and medical secretary; medical/clinical assistant; music; nanotechnology; philosophy; physical education teaching and coaching; physical sciences; psychology; public relations, advertising, and applied communication related; radiologic technology/science; registered nursing/registered nurse; sales, distribution, and marketing operations; small business administration; sociology and anthropology; speech communication and rhetoric; theater/theater arts management; web page, digital/multimedia and information resources design.

Academics *Calendar:* semesters. *Degree:* certificates and associate. *Special study options:* academic remediation for entering students, accelerated degree program, adult/continuing education programs, advanced placement credit, cooperative education, distance learning, English as a second language, freshman honors college, honors programs, independent study, internships, part-time degree program, services for LD students, study abroad, summer session for credit.

Library Harper College Library.

Student Life *Housing:* college housing not available. *Activities and Organizations:* drama/theater group, student-run newspaper, radio station, choral group, Student Radio Station, Program Board, Student Senate, Nursing Club, Phi Theta Kappa. *Campus security:* 24-hour emergency response devices and patrols, late-night transport/escort service. *Student services:* health clinic, personal/psychological counseling, women's center, legal services.

Athletics Member NJCAA. *Intercollegiate sports:* baseball M, basketball M/W, cross-country running M/W, soccer M/W, softball W, track and field M/W, volleyball W, wrestling M. *Intramural sports:* baseball M, basketball M, football M, racquetball M/W, softball M/W, table tennis M/W, tennis M/W, volleyball M/W.

Costs (2016–17) *Tuition:* area resident $3578 full-time, $119 per credit hour part-time; state resident $11,288 full-time, $376 per credit hour part-time; nonresident $13,553 full-time, $452 per credit hour part-time. Full-time tuition and fees vary according to course load and program. Part-time tuition and fees vary according to course load and program. No tuition increase for student's term of enrollment. *Required fees:* $619 full-time, $16 per credit hour part-time. *Payment plans:* installment, deferred payment. *Waivers:* senior citizens and employees or children of employees.

Financial Aid Of all full-time matriculated undergraduates who enrolled in 2015, 2,612 applied for aid, 2,155 were judged to have need, 59 had their need fully met. In 2015, 54 non-need-based awards were made. *Average percent of need met:* 42%. *Average financial aid package:* $5120. *Average need-based loan:* $3128. *Average need-based gift aid:* $4791. *Average non-need-based aid:* $2508.

Applying *Options:* electronic application. *Application fee:* $25. *Required:* high school transcript. *Application deadlines:* rolling (freshmen), rolling (transfers). *Notification:* continuous (freshmen), continuous (transfers).
Freshman Application Contact Admissions Office, Harper College, 1200 West Algonquin Road, Palatine, IL 60067. *Phone:* 847-925-6700. *Fax:* 847-925-6044. *E-mail:* admissions@harpercollege.edu.
Website: http://goforward.harpercollege.edu/.

Heartland Community College
Normal, Illinois

Freshman Application Contact Ms. Candace Brownlee, Director of Student Recruitment, Heartland Community College, 1500 West Raab Road, Normal, IL 61761. *Phone:* 309-268-8041. *Fax:* 309-268-7992.
E-mail: candace.brownlee@heartland.edu.
Website: http://www.heartland.edu/.

Highland Community College
Freeport, Illinois

- **State and locally supported** 2-year, founded 1962, part of Illinois Community College Board
- **Rural** 240-acre campus
- **Coed,** 1,857 undergraduate students, 48% full-time, 59% women, 41% men

Undergraduates 891 full-time, 966 part-time. 3% are from out of state; 8% Black or African American, non-Hispanic/Latino; 3% Hispanic/Latino; 1% Asian, non-Hispanic/Latino; 0.1% Native Hawaiian or other Pacific Islander, non-Hispanic/Latino; 2% American Indian or Alaska Native, non-Hispanic/Latino; 4% Two or more races, non-Hispanic/Latino; 2% Race/ethnicity unknown; 0.4% international; 3% transferred in.
Freshmen *Admission:* 824 applied, 824 admitted, 377 enrolled.
Faculty *Total:* 129, 36% full-time, 6% with terminal degrees. *Student/faculty ratio:* 16:1.
Majors Accounting; administrative assistant and secretarial science; autobody/collision and repair technology; automobile/automotive mechanics technology; biological and physical sciences; business administration and management; child-care provision; early childhood education; emergency medical technology (EMT paramedic); engineering; equestrian studies; general studies; graphic design; health information/medical records technology; heavy equipment maintenance technology; hospitality administration; industrial technology; information technology; liberal arts and sciences/liberal studies; mathematics teacher education; medical/clinical assistant; registered nursing/registered nurse; special education; teacher assistant/aide; web page, digital/multimedia and information resources design; welding technology.
Academics *Calendar:* semesters. *Degree:* certificates and associate. *Special study options:* academic remediation for entering students, adult/continuing education programs, advanced placement credit, cooperative education, distance learning, English as a second language, external degree program, honors programs, independent study, internships, part-time degree program, services for LD students, student-designed majors, summer session for credit.
Library Clarence Mitchell Library.
Student Life *Housing:* college housing not available. *Activities and Organizations:* drama/theater group, student-run newspaper, radio and television station, choral group, Phi Theta Kappa, Royal Scots, Prairie Wind, Intramurals, Collegiate Choir. *Campus security:* 24-hour emergency response devices and patrols. *Student services:* personal/psychological counseling.
Athletics Member NJCAA. *Intercollegiate sports:* baseball M(s), basketball M(s)/W(s), bowling M(s)/W(s), golf M(s)/W(s), softball W(s), volleyball W(s). *Intramural sports:* basketball M/W, volleyball M/W.
Costs (2017–18) *Tuition:* area resident $4230 full-time, $141 per credit hour part-time; state resident $7020 full-time, $234 per credit hour part-time; nonresident $7080 full-time, $236 per credit hour part-time. Full-time tuition and fees vary according to program and reciprocity agreements. Part-time tuition and fees vary according to program and reciprocity agreements. *Required fees:* $780 full-time, $25 per credit hour part-time, $15 per term part-time. *Payment plans:* installment, deferred payment. *Waivers:* minority students, senior citizens, and employees or children of employees.
Financial Aid Of all full-time matriculated undergraduates who enrolled in 2015, 740 applied for aid, 623 were judged to have need. 50 Federal Work-Study jobs (averaging $1739). 63 state and other part-time jobs (averaging $1564). In 2015, 47 non-need-based awards were made. *Average percent of need met:* 20%. *Average financial aid package:* $6088. *Average need-based loan:* $3061. *Average need-based gift aid:* $5552. *Average non-need-based aid:* $3516.
Applying *Options:* electronic application, early admission, deferred entrance. *Required for some:* high school transcript, 1 letter of recommendation.

Recommended: high school transcript. *Application deadlines:* rolling (freshmen), rolling (transfers).
Freshman Application Contact Mr. Jeremy Bradt, Director, Enrollment and Records, Highland Community College, 2998 West Pearl City Road, Freeport, IL 61032. *Phone:* 815-235-6121 Ext. 3500. *Fax:* 815-235-6130.
E-mail: jeremy.bradt@highland.edu.
Website: http://www.highland.edu/.

Illinois Central College
East Peoria, Illinois

- **State and locally supported** 2-year, founded 1967, part of Illinois Community College Board
- **Suburban** 430-acre campus
- **Coed,** 9,704 undergraduate students, 36% full-time, 55% women, 45% men

Undergraduates 3,475 full-time, 6,229 part-time. Students come from 22 states and territories; 4 other countries; 1% are from out of state; 11% Black or African American, non-Hispanic/Latino; 5% Hispanic/Latino; 2% Asian, non-Hispanic/Latino; 0.2% Native Hawaiian or other Pacific Islander, non-Hispanic/Latino; 0.3% American Indian or Alaska Native, non-Hispanic/Latino; 3% Two or more races, non-Hispanic/Latino; 0.2% Race/ethnicity unknown; 4% transferred in. *Retention:* 68% of full-time freshmen returned.
Freshmen *Admission:* 4,829 applied, 1,961 admitted, 1,052 enrolled.
Faculty *Total:* 548, 32% full-time, 11% with terminal degrees. *Student/faculty ratio:* 18:1.
Majors Accounting; administrative assistant and secretarial science; agricultural business and management; agricultural/farm supplies retailing and wholesaling; agricultural mechanics and equipment technology; animal/livestock husbandry and production; applied horticulture/horticulture operations; automobile/automotive mechanics technology; banking and financial support services; business administration and management; child-care provision; clinical/medical laboratory technology; community health services counseling; computer programming; computer systems networking and telecommunications; construction engineering technology; criminal justice/police science; crop production; culinary arts; dental hygiene; diesel mechanics technology; electrical, electronic and communications engineering technology; emergency medical technology (EMT paramedic); energy management and systems technology; engineering; fire science/firefighting; general studies; graphic design; health and physical education/fitness; heating, air conditioning, ventilation and refrigeration maintenance technology; industrial technology; legal assistant/paralegal; liberal arts and sciences/liberal studies; library and archives assisting; manufacturing engineering technology; mechanical engineering/mechanical technology; occupational therapist assistant; physical therapy technology; platemaking/imaging; radiologic technology/science; registered nursing/registered nurse; respiratory care therapy; retailing; robotics technology; sign language interpretation and translation; substance abuse/addiction counseling; surgical technology; teacher assistant/aide; web/multimedia management and webmaster; web page, digital/multimedia and information resources design; welding technology.
Academics *Calendar:* semesters. *Degree:* certificates and associate. *Special study options:* academic remediation for entering students, adult/continuing education programs, advanced placement credit, English as a second language, honors programs, independent study, internships, part-time degree program, services for LD students, summer session for credit.
Library Illinois Central College Library plus 2 others.
Student Life *Housing Options:* Campus housing is provided by a third party. *Activities and Organizations:* drama/theater group, student-run newspaper, radio station, choral group. *Campus security:* 24-hour emergency response devices and patrols, late-night transport/escort service. *Student services:* health clinic, personal/psychological counseling.
Athletics Member NJCAA. *Intercollegiate sports:* baseball M(s), basketball M(s)/W(s), cross-country running M(s)/W(s), golf M(s), soccer M(s)/W(s), softball W(s), volleyball W(s), weight lifting M/W. *Intramural sports:* basketball M/W, bowling M/W, football M/W, softball M/W, ultimate Frisbee M/W, volleyball M/W.
Financial Aid Of all full-time matriculated undergraduates who enrolled in 2011, 6,521 applied for aid, 5,525 were judged to have need.
Applying *Options:* electronic application, early admission. *Required:* high school transcript. *Application deadlines:* rolling (freshmen), rolling (out-of-state freshmen), rolling (transfers). *Notification:* continuous (freshmen), continuous (out-of-state freshmen), continuous (transfers).
Freshman Application Contact Angela Dreessen, Dean of Student Success, Illinois Central College, 1 College Drive, East Peoria, IL 61635-0001.
Phone: 309-694-5323.
Website: http://www.icc.edu/.

Illinois Eastern Community Colleges, Frontier Community College
Fairfield, Illinois

- **State and locally supported** 2-year, founded 1976, part of Illinois Eastern Community Colleges System
- **Rural** 8-acre campus
- **Coed,** 1,930 undergraduate students, 16% full-time, 61% women, 39% men

Undergraduates 318 full-time, 1,612 part-time. 2% are from out of state; 0.9% Black or African American, non-Hispanic/Latino; 0.7% Hispanic/Latino; 0.6% Asian, non-Hispanic/Latino; 0.3% American Indian or Alaska Native, non-Hispanic/Latino; 0.4% Race/ethnicity unknown.

Freshmen *Admission:* 110 enrolled.

Faculty *Total:* 95, 6% full-time. *Student/faculty ratio:* 23:1.

Majors Automobile/automotive mechanics technology; biological and physical sciences; business automation/technology/data entry; construction trades; corrections; emergency care attendant (EMT ambulance); engineering; executive assistant/executive secretary; fire science/firefighting; general studies; health information/medical records technology; information technology; liberal arts and sciences/liberal studies; registered nursing/registered nurse; sport and fitness administration/management; web page, digital/multimedia and information resources design.

Academics *Calendar:* semesters. *Degree:* certificates and associate. *Special study options:* academic remediation for entering students, adult/continuing education programs, advanced placement credit, cooperative education, distance learning, double majors, English as a second language, external degree program, independent study, part-time degree program, services for LD students, student-designed majors, summer session for credit.

Library Learning Resource Center plus 1 other.

Student Life *Housing:* college housing not available.

Athletics Member NJCAA. *Intercollegiate sports:* baseball M, golf M/W, softball W, volleyball W.

Costs (2017–18) *Tuition:* area resident $2656 full-time, $83 per semester hour part-time; state resident $8589 full-time, $268 per semester hour part-time; nonresident $10,580 full-time, $331 per semester hour part-time. *Required fees:* $810 full-time, $25 per semester hour part-time, $5 per term part-time. *Payment plan:* installment. *Waivers:* senior citizens and employees or children of employees.

Applying *Options:* electronic application, early admission, deferred entrance. *Required:* high school transcript. *Application deadlines:* rolling (freshmen), rolling (transfers). *Notification:* continuous (freshmen), continuous (transfers).

Freshman Application Contact Ms. Amy Loss, Coordinator of Registration and Records, Illinois Eastern Community Colleges, Frontier Community College, 2 Frontier Drive, Fairfield, IL 62837. *Phone:* 618-842-3711 Ext. 4114. *Toll-free phone:* 877-464-3687. *Fax:* 618-842-6340. *E-mail:* lossa@iecc.edu.

Website: http://www.iecc.edu/fcc/.

Illinois Eastern Community Colleges, Lincoln Trail College
Robinson, Illinois

- **State and locally supported** 2-year, founded 1969, part of Illinois Eastern Community Colleges System
- **Rural** 120-acre campus
- **Coed,** 938 undergraduate students, 43% full-time, 58% women, 42% men

Undergraduates 401 full-time, 537 part-time. 5% are from out of state; 4% Black or African American, non-Hispanic/Latino; 1% Hispanic/Latino; 2% Asian, non-Hispanic/Latino; 0.6% American Indian or Alaska Native, non-Hispanic/Latino; 0.2% Race/ethnicity unknown.

Freshmen *Admission:* 147 enrolled.

Faculty *Total:* 63, 25% full-time. *Student/faculty ratio:* 18:1.

Majors Biological and physical sciences; business automation/technology/data entry; computer systems networking and telecommunications; construction trades; corrections; general studies; health information/medical records administration; liberal arts and sciences/liberal studies; mechanical engineering/mechanical technology; medical/clinical assistant; quality control technology; sport and fitness administration/management; teacher assistant/aide; telecommunications technology.

Academics *Calendar:* semesters. *Degree:* certificates and associate. *Special study options:* academic remediation for entering students, adult/continuing education programs, advanced placement credit, cooperative education, distance learning, double majors, English as a second language, external degree program, independent study, internships, part-time degree program, services for LD students, student-designed majors, summer session for credit.

Library Eagleton Learning Resource Center plus 1 other.

Student Life *Housing:* college housing not available. *Activities and Organizations:* drama/theater group, choral group, national fraternities.

Athletics Member NJCAA. *Intercollegiate sports:* baseball M(s), basketball M(s)/W(s), softball W(s). *Intramural sports:* baseball M, basketball M, softball W.

Costs (2017–18) *Tuition:* area resident $2656 full-time, $83 per semester hour part-time; state resident $8589 full-time, $268 per semester hour part-time; nonresident $10,580 full-time, $331 per semester hour part-time. *Required fees:* $810 full-time, $25 per semester hour part-time, $5 per term part-time. *Payment plan:* installment. *Waivers:* senior citizens and employees or children of employees.

Applying *Options:* electronic application, early admission, deferred entrance. *Required:* high school transcript. *Application deadlines:* rolling (freshmen), rolling (transfers). *Notification:* continuous (freshmen), continuous (transfers).

Freshman Application Contact Ms. Megan Scott, Director of Admissions, Illinois Eastern Community Colleges, Lincoln Trail College, 11220 State Highway 1, Robinson, IL 62454. *Phone:* 618-544-8657 Ext. 1137. *Toll-free phone:* 866-582-4322. *Fax:* 618-544-7423. *E-mail:* scottm@iecc.edu. *Website:* http://www.iecc.edu/ltc/.

Illinois Eastern Community Colleges, Olney Central College
Olney, Illinois

- **State and locally supported** 2-year, founded 1962, part of Illinois Eastern Community Colleges System
- **Rural** 128-acre campus
- **Coed,** 1,219 undergraduate students, 41% full-time, 58% women, 42% men

Undergraduates 500 full-time, 719 part-time. 1% are from out of state; 2% Black or African American, non-Hispanic/Latino; 0.6% Hispanic/Latino; 1% Asian, non-Hispanic/Latino; 0.2% Race/ethnicity unknown.

Freshmen *Admission:* 164 enrolled.

Faculty *Total:* 93, 45% full-time. *Student/faculty ratio:* 13:1.

Majors Accounting; autobody/collision and repair technology; automobile/automotive mechanics technology; biological and physical sciences; business administration and management; business automation/technology/data entry; culinary arts; engineering; general studies; human resources management; industrial mechanics and maintenance technology; information technology; liberal arts and sciences/liberal studies; medical administrative assistant and medical secretary; medical radiologic technology; registered nursing/registered nurse.

Academics *Calendar:* semesters. *Degree:* certificates and associate. *Special study options:* academic remediation for entering students, adult/continuing education programs, advanced placement credit, cooperative education, distance learning, double majors, English as a second language, external degree program, independent study, internships, part-time degree program, services for LD students, student-designed majors, summer session for credit.

Library Anderson Learning Resources Center plus 1 other.

Student Life *Housing:* college housing not available. *Activities and Organizations:* drama/theater group, student-run newspaper, choral group.

Athletics Member NJCAA. *Intercollegiate sports:* baseball M(s), basketball M(s)/W(s), softball W(s). *Intramural sports:* baseball M, basketball M/W, softball W.

Costs (2017–18) *Tuition:* area resident $2656 full-time, $83 per semester hour part-time; state resident $8589 full-time, $268 per semester hour part-time; nonresident $10,580 full-time, $331 per semester hour part-time. *Required fees:* $810 full-time, $25 per semester hour part-time, $5 per term part-time. *Payment plan:* installment. *Waivers:* senior citizens and employees or children of employees.

Applying *Options:* electronic application, early admission, deferred entrance. *Required:* high school transcript. *Application deadlines:* rolling (freshmen), rolling (transfers). *Notification:* continuous (freshmen), continuous (transfers).

Freshman Application Contact Ms. Andrea Pampe, Assistant Dean for Student Services, Illinois Eastern Community Colleges, Olney Central College, 305 North West Street, Olney, IL 62450. *Phone:* 618-395-7777 Ext. 2005. *Toll-free phone:* 866-622-4322. *Fax:* 618-392-5212. *E-mail:* pampea@iecc.edu. *Website:* http://www.iecc.edu/occ/.

Illinois Eastern Community Colleges, Wabash Valley College
Mount Carmel, Illinois

- **State and locally supported** 2-year, founded 1960, part of Illinois Eastern Community Colleges System
- **Rural** 40-acre campus
- **Coed,** 4,175 undergraduate students, 12% full-time, 39% women, 61% men

Undergraduates 503 full-time, 3,672 part-time. 8% are from out of state; 3% Black or African American, non-Hispanic/Latino; 0.7% Hispanic/Latino; 0.8% Asian, non-Hispanic/Latino; 0.3% American Indian or Alaska Native, non-Hispanic/Latino; 0.1% Race/ethnicity unknown.
Freshmen *Admission:* 162 enrolled.
Faculty *Total:* 80, 44% full-time. *Student/faculty ratio:* 32:1.
Majors Agricultural business and management; agricultural production; biological and physical sciences; business administration and management; business automation/technology/data entry; child development; diesel mechanics technology; energy management and systems technology; engineering; executive assistant/executive secretary; general studies; industrial technology; legal assistant/paralegal; liberal arts and sciences/liberal studies; machine tool technology; manufacturing engineering technology; mining technology; radio and television; social work; sport and fitness administration/management; sports communication.
Academics *Calendar:* semesters. *Degree:* certificates and associate. *Special study options:* academic remediation for entering students, adult/continuing education programs, advanced placement credit, cooperative education, distance learning, double majors, English as a second language, external degree program, independent study, internships, part-time degree program, services for LD students, student-designed majors, summer session for credit.
Library Bauer Media Center plus 1 other.
Student Life *Housing:* college housing not available. *Activities and Organizations:* drama/theater group, student-run newspaper, radio and television station, choral group.
Athletics Member NJCAA. *Intercollegiate sports:* baseball M(s), basketball M(s)/W(s), softball W(s). *Intramural sports:* baseball M, basketball M/W, softball W.
Costs (2017–18) *Tuition:* area resident $2656 full-time, $83 per semester hour part-time; state resident $8589 full-time, $268 per semester hour part-time; nonresident $10,580 full-time, $331 per semester hour part-time. *Required fees:* $810 full-time, $25 per semester hour part-time, $5 per term part-time. *Payment plan:* installment. *Waivers:* senior citizens and employees or children of employees.
Applying *Options:* electronic application, early admission, deferred entrance. *Required:* high school transcript. *Application deadlines:* rolling (freshmen), rolling (transfers). *Notification:* continuous (freshmen), continuous (transfers).
Freshman Application Contact Mrs. Tiffany Cowger, Assistant Dean for Student Services, Illinois Eastern Community Colleges, Wabash Valley College, 2200 College Drive, Mt. Carmel, IL 62863. *Phone:* 618-262-8641 Ext. 3101. *Toll-free phone:* 866-982-4322. *Fax:* 618-262-8647.
E-mail: cowgert@iecc.edu.
Website: http://www.iecc.edu/wvc/.

Illinois Valley Community College
Oglesby, Illinois

- **District-supported** 2-year, founded 1924, part of Illinois Community College Board
- **Rural** 410-acre campus with easy access to Chicago
- **Endowment** $3.7 million
- **Coed,** 3,306 undergraduate students, 43% full-time, 59% women, 41% men

Undergraduates 1,420 full-time, 1,886 part-time. Students come from 2 states and territories; 1% are from out of state; 2% Black or African American, non-Hispanic/Latino; 9% Hispanic/Latino; 1% Asian, non-Hispanic/Latino; 0.1% Native Hawaiian or other Pacific Islander, non-Hispanic/Latino; 0.4% American Indian or Alaska Native, non-Hispanic/Latino; 3% Race/ethnicity unknown; 2% transferred in. *Retention:* 62% of full-time freshmen returned.
Freshmen *Admission:* 1,435 applied, 672 admitted, 384 enrolled.
Faculty *Total:* 270, 34% full-time. *Student/faculty ratio:* 16:1.
Majors Accounting; automobile/automotive mechanics technology; biological and physical sciences; business administration and management; business automation/technology/data entry; CAD/CADD drafting/design technology; child-care provision; child development; computer programming; computer systems networking and telecommunications; corrections; criminal justice/law enforcement administration; criminal justice/police science; data processing and data processing technology; drafting and design technology; drafting/design engineering technologies related; early childhood education; education; electrical, electronic and communications engineering technology;

electrician; elementary education; engineering; English; floriculture/floristry management; forensic science and technology; general studies; graphic design; industrial technology; information technology; journalism; juvenile corrections; landscaping and groundskeeping; liberal arts and sciences/liberal studies; marketing/marketing management; massage therapy; mechanical engineering/mechanical technology; network and system administration; pre-engineering; registered nursing/registered nurse; selling skills and sales; social work; teacher assistant/aide.
Academics *Calendar:* semesters. *Degree:* certificates and associate. *Special study options:* academic remediation for entering students, advanced placement credit, distance learning, English as a second language, honors programs, independent study, internships, off-campus study, part-time degree program, services for LD students, student-designed majors, study abroad, summer session for credit.
Library Jacobs Library.
Student Life *Housing:* college housing not available. *Activities and Organizations:* drama/theater group, student-run newspaper, choral group, Chemistry Club, Student Embassadors, Phi Theta Kappa, Illinois Valley Leaders for Service, Student Veterans Association. *Campus security:* 24-hour emergency response devices and patrols, late-night transport/escort service. *Student services:* personal/psychological counseling.
Athletics Member NJCAA. *Intercollegiate sports:* baseball M, basketball M/W, golf M, soccer M/W, softball W, tennis M/W. *Intramural sports:* basketball M, volleyball W.
Standardized Tests *Recommended:* ACT (for admission).
Costs (2016–17) *One-time required fee:* $10. *Tuition:* area resident $3498 full-time, $117 per credit hour part-time; state resident $10,286 full-time, $343 per credit hour part-time; nonresident $11,094 full-time, $370 per credit hour part-time. Full-time tuition and fees vary according to course load and reciprocity agreements. Part-time tuition and fees vary according to course load and reciprocity agreements. *Required fees:* $222 full-time, $7 per credit hour part-time, $5 per term part-time. *Payment plan:* deferred payment. *Waivers:* senior citizens and employees or children of employees.
Financial Aid Of all full-time matriculated undergraduates who enrolled in 2015, 81 Federal Work-Study jobs (averaging $955).
Applying *Options:* electronic application, early admission, deferred entrance. *Required:* high school transcript. *Application deadlines:* rolling (freshmen), rolling (transfers). *Notification:* continuous (freshmen), continuous (transfers).
Freshman Application Contact Mr. Quintin Overocker, Director of Admissions and Records, Illinois Valley Community College, Oglesby, IL 61348. *Phone:* 815-224-0437. *Fax:* 815-224-3033.
E-mail: quintin_overocker@ivcc.edu.
Website: http://www.ivcc.edu/.

John A. Logan College
Carterville, Illinois

Director of Admissions Mr. Terry Crain, Dean of Student Services, John A. Logan College, 700 Logan College Road, Carterville, IL 62918-9900. *Phone:* 618-985-3741 Ext. 8382. *Fax:* 618-985-4433.
E-mail: terrycrain@jalc.edu. *Website:* http://www.jalc.edu/.

John Wood Community College
Quincy, Illinois

Freshman Application Contact Mr. Lee Wibbell, Director of Admissions, John Wood Community College, Quincy, IL 62305-8736. *Phone:* 217-641-4339. *Fax:* 217-224-4208. *E-mail:* admissions@jwcc.edu.
Website: http://www.jwcc.edu/.

Joliet Junior College
Joliet, Illinois

Freshman Application Contact Ms. Jennifer Kloberdanz, Director of Admissions and Recruitment, Joliet Junior College, 1215 Houbolt Road, Joliet, IL 60431. *Phone:* 815-729-9020 Ext. 2414.
E-mail: admission@jjc.edu. *Website:* http://www.jjc.edu/.

Kankakee Community College
Kankakee, Illinois

- **State and locally supported** 2-year, founded 1966, part of Illinois Community College Board
- **Small-town** 185-acre campus with easy access to Chicago
- **Endowment** $6.5 million
- **Coed**

Undergraduates 1,222 full-time, 2,084 part-time. Students come from 17 states and territories; 7 other countries; 1% are from out of state; 14% Black or

African American, non-Hispanic/Latino; 12% Hispanic/Latino; 1% Asian, non-Hispanic/Latino; 0.1% Native Hawaiian or other Pacific Islander, non-Hispanic/Latino; 0.5% American Indian or Alaska Native, non-Hispanic/Latino; 1% Two or more races, non-Hispanic/Latino; 4% Race/ethnicity unknown; 0.2% international; 2% transferred in. *Retention:* 68% of full-time freshmen returned.

Faculty *Student/faculty ratio:* 14:1.

Academics *Calendar:* semesters. *Degrees:* certificates, diplomas, and associate (also offers continuing education program with significant enrollment not reflected in profile). *Special study options:* academic remediation for entering students, advanced placement credit, distance learning, English as a second language, honors programs, independent study, internships, off-campus study, part-time degree program, services for LD students, student-designed majors, study abroad, summer session for credit. *ROTC:* Army (c).

Library Kankakee Community College Learning Resource Center.

Student Life *Campus security:* 24-hour patrols, late-night transport/escort service.

Athletics Member NJCAA.

Financial Aid Of all full-time matriculated undergraduates who enrolled in 2015, 70 Federal Work-Study jobs (averaging $1100). *Financial aid deadline:* 10/1.

Applying *Options:* electronic application, early admission. *Required:* high school transcript.

Freshman Application Contact Ms. Kim Harpin, Director of Support Services, Kankakee Community College, 100 College Drive, Kankakee, IL 60901. *Phone:* 815-802-8472. *Fax:* 815-802-8472. *E-mail:* kharpin@kcc.edu. *Website:* http://www.kcc.edu/.

Kaskaskia College
Centralia, Illinois

- **State and locally supported** 2-year, founded 1966, part of Illinois Community College Board
- **Rural** 195-acre campus with easy access to St. Louis
- **Endowment** $7.4 million
- **Coed,** 3,665 undergraduate students, 36% full-time, 59% women, 41% men

Undergraduates 1,320 full-time, 2,345 part-time. Students come from 6 states and territories; 1 other country; 1% are from out of state; 4% Black or African American, non-Hispanic/Latino; 1% Hispanic/Latino; 1% Asian, non-Hispanic/Latino; 0.5% American Indian or Alaska Native, non-Hispanic/Latino; 2% Two or more races, non-Hispanic/Latino; 0.3% Race/ethnicity unknown; 19% transferred in.

Freshmen *Admission:* 201 applied, 201 admitted, 201 enrolled.

Faculty *Total:* 150, 43% full-time, 7% with terminal degrees. *Student/faculty ratio:* 23:1.

Majors Accounting; agriculture; animal sciences; applied horticulture/horticulture operations; architectural drafting and CAD/CADD; automobile/automotive mechanics technology; biological and physical sciences; business automation/technology/data entry; business/commerce; carpentry; child-care provision; clinical/medical laboratory technology; construction management; cosmetology; criminal justice/law enforcement administration; culinary arts; dental assisting; electrical, electronic and communications engineering technology; emergency medical technology (EMT paramedic); engineering; executive assistant/executive secretary; food service and dining room management; general studies; health information/medical records technology; heating, air conditioning, ventilation and refrigeration maintenance technology; industrial mechanics and maintenance technology; juvenile corrections; liberal arts and sciences/liberal studies; library and archives assisting; music; network and system administration; occupational therapist assistant; physical therapy technology; radiologic technology/science; registered nursing/registered nurse; respiratory care therapy; robotics technology; teacher assistant/aide; veterinary/animal health technology; web/multimedia management and webmaster; welding technology.

Academics *Calendar:* semesters. *Degree:* certificates and associate. *Special study options:* academic remediation for entering students, accelerated degree program, adult/continuing education programs, cooperative education, distance learning, double majors, English as a second language, honors programs, independent study, internships, off-campus study, part-time degree program, services for LD students, summer session for credit. *ROTC:* Army (c).

Library Kaskaskia College Library. *Books:* 17,285 (physical), 24,433 (digital/electronic); *Serial titles:* 24 (physical); *Databases:* 86. Weekly public service hours: 47.

Student Life *Housing:* college housing not available. *Activities and Organizations:* drama/theater group, choral group, Phi Theta Kappa, Student Radiography Club, LPN Club, Physical Therapy Club, Fellowship of Christian Athletes. *Campus security:* 24-hour emergency response devices and patrols,

late-night transport/escort service. *Student services:* personal/psychological counseling.

Athletics Member NJCAA. *Intercollegiate sports:* baseball M(s), basketball M(s)/W(s), cheerleading M(s)/W(s), cross-country running M(s)/W(s), golf M(s)/W(s), soccer W(s), softball W(s), tennis M(s), volleyball W(s).

Standardized Tests *Recommended:* SAT or ACT (for admission).

Costs (2016–17) *Tuition:* area resident $3990 full-time, $133 per credit hour part-time; state resident $7050 full-time, $235 per credit hour part-time; nonresident $11,850 full-time, $395 per credit hour part-time. Full-time tuition and fees vary according to program. Part-time tuition and fees vary according to program. *Required fees:* $480 full-time, $16 per credit hour part-time. *Payment plan:* installment. *Waivers:* senior citizens and employees or children of employees.

Financial Aid Of all full-time matriculated undergraduates who enrolled in 2015, 993 applied for aid, 859 were judged to have need, 44 had their need fully met. 62 Federal Work-Study jobs (averaging $2324). 30 state and other part-time jobs (averaging $1545). In 2015, 34 non-need-based awards were made. *Average percent of need met:* 37%. *Average financial aid package:* $5714. *Average need-based gift aid:* $4590. *Average non-need-based aid:* $3929.

Applying *Options:* electronic application, early admission, deferred entrance. *Required:* high school transcript. *Required for some:* interview. *Application deadlines:* rolling (freshmen), rolling (transfers). *Notification:* continuous (freshmen), continuous (transfers).

Freshman Application Contact Jenna Lammers, Registrar, Kaskaskia College, 27210 College Road, Centralia, IL 62801. *Phone:* 618-545-3044. *Toll-free phone:* 800-642-0859. *Fax:* 618-532-1990. *E-mail:* jlammers@kaskaskia.edu. *Website:* http://www.kaskaskia.edu/.

Kishwaukee College
Malta, Illinois

- **State and locally supported** 2-year, founded 1967, part of Illinois Community College Board
- **Rural** 120-acre campus with easy access to Chicago
- **Coed,** 3,775 undergraduate students, 43% full-time, 53% women, 47% men

Undergraduates 1,634 full-time, 2,141 part-time. 15% Black or African American, non-Hispanic/Latino; 15% Hispanic/Latino; 2% Asian, non-Hispanic/Latino; 0.1% Native Hawaiian or other Pacific Islander, non-Hispanic/Latino; 0.5% American Indian or Alaska Native, non-Hispanic/Latino; 3% Two or more races, non-Hispanic/Latino; 2% Race/ethnicity unknown. *Retention:* 59% of full-time freshmen returned.

Freshmen *Admission:* 614 enrolled.

Faculty *Total:* 236, 32% full-time, 6% with terminal degrees. *Student/faculty ratio:* 17:1.

Majors Administrative assistant and secretarial science; agricultural mechanization; airline pilot and flight crew; applied horticulture/horticulture operations; art; autobody/collision and repair technology; automobile/automotive mechanics technology; biological and physical sciences; business administration and management; CAD/CADD drafting/design technology; child-care and support services management; child-care provision; criminal justice/police science; criminal justice/safety; diesel mechanics technology; education (multiple levels); electrical, electronic and communications engineering technology; emergency medical technology (EMT paramedic); engineering; fine/studio arts; forensic science and technology; information technology; landscaping and groundskeeping; liberal arts and sciences/liberal studies; network and system administration; ornamental horticulture; radiologic technology/science; registered nursing/registered nurse; teacher assistant/aide.

Academics *Calendar:* semesters. *Degree:* certificates, diplomas, and associate. *Special study options:* academic remediation for entering students, adult/continuing education programs, advanced placement credit, cooperative education, distance learning, double majors, English as a second language, external degree program, freshman honors college, honors programs, independent study, internships, off-campus study, part-time degree program, services for LD students, study abroad, summer session for credit.

Library Kishwaukee College Library. Students can reserve study rooms.

Student Life *Housing:* college housing not available. *Activities and Organizations:* drama/theater group, student-run newspaper, choral group. *Campus security:* 24-hour emergency response devices and patrols. *Student services:* health clinic, personal/psychological counseling.

Athletics Member NJCAA. *Intercollegiate sports:* baseball M(s), basketball M(s)/W(s), softball W(s), volleyball W(s).

Costs (2016–17) *Tuition:* area resident $3870 full-time, $129 per credit hour part-time; state resident $7740 full-time, $258 per credit hour part-time; nonresident $11,610 full-time, $387 per credit hour part-time. Full-time tuition and fees vary according to program and reciprocity agreements. Part-time tuition and fees vary according to program and reciprocity agreements.

Required fees: $420 full-time, $12 per credit hour part-time. *Payment plans:* installment, deferred payment. *Waivers:* senior citizens and employees or children of employees.

Financial Aid *Average indebtedness upon graduation:* $4375.

Applying *Options:* electronic application, early admission, deferred entrance. *Required for some:* high school transcript. *Recommended:* high school transcript, transcripts from all other colleges or universities previously attended. *Application deadlines:* rolling (freshmen), rolling (transfers). *Notification:* continuous (freshmen), continuous (transfers).

Freshman Application Contact Ms. Graciela Horta, Coordinator-Student Outreach, Kishwaukee College, 21193 Malta Road, Malta, IL 60150. *Phone:* 815-825-1711. *E-mail:* graciela.horta@kishwaukeecollege.edu.

Website: http://www.kishwaukeecollege.edu/.

Lake Land College
Mattoon, Illinois

- **State and locally supported** 2-year, founded 1966, part of Illinois Community College Board
- **Rural** 308-acre campus
- **Endowment** $2.7 million
- **Coed**

Undergraduates 2,809 full-time, 3,542 part-time. 1% are from out of state; 0.6% transferred in. *Retention:* 89% of full-time freshmen returned.

Faculty *Student/faculty ratio:* 21:1.

Academics *Calendar:* semesters. *Degree:* certificates and associate. *Special study options:* academic remediation for entering students, accelerated degree program, adult/continuing education programs, cooperative education, distance learning, English as a second language, external degree program, honors programs, internships, part-time degree program, services for LD students, summer session for credit.

Library Virgil H. Judge Learning Resource Center plus 1 other.

Student Life *Campus security:* 24-hour patrols.

Athletics Member NJCAA.

Standardized Tests *Recommended:* ACT (for admission).

Financial Aid Of all full-time undergraduates who enrolled in 2015, 120 Federal Work-Study jobs (averaging $1400).

Applying *Options:* electronic application, early admission. *Recommended:* high school transcript.

Freshman Application Contact Mr. Jon VanDyke, Dean of Admissions Services, Lake Land College, Mattoon, IL 61938-9366. *Phone:* 217-234-5378. *E-mail:* admissions@lakeland.cc.il.us.

Website: http://www.lakelandcollege.edu/.

Lewis and Clark Community College
Godfrey, Illinois

- **District-supported** 2-year, founded 1970, part of Illinois Community College Board
- **Small-town** 275-acre campus with easy access to St. Louis
- **Coed**

Academics *Calendar:* semesters. *Degree:* certificates and associate. *Special study options:* academic remediation for entering students, adult/continuing education programs, advanced placement credit, cooperative education, distance learning, double majors, English as a second language, independent study, internships, off-campus study, part-time degree program, services for LD students, summer session for credit. *ROTC:* Army (b).

Library Reid Memorial Library. *Books:* 50,000 (physical), 123 (digital/electronic); *Serial titles:* 65 (physical), 12,000 (digital/electronic); *Databases:* 44. Weekly public service hours: 56; students can reserve study rooms.

Student Life *Campus security:* 24-hour emergency response devices and patrols.

Athletics Member NJCAA.

Financial Aid Of all full-time matriculated undergraduates who enrolled in 2014, 69 Federal Work-Study jobs (averaging $5700). 84 state and other part-time jobs (averaging $5700).

Applying *Options:* early admission, deferred entrance. *Required for some:* interview. *Recommended:* high school transcript.

Freshman Application Contact Lewis and Clark Community College, 5800 Godfrey Road, Godfrey, IL 62035-2466. *Phone:* 618-468-5100. *Toll-free phone:* 800-YES-LCCC. *Website:* http://www.lc.edu/.

Lincoln College
Lincoln, Illinois

- **Independent** primarily 2-year, founded 1865
- **Small-town** 42-acre campus
- **Coed,** 1,304 undergraduate students

Undergraduates 4% are from out of state.

Freshmen *Admission:* 1,537 applied, 1,045 admitted.

Faculty *Student/faculty ratio:* 15:1.

Majors Business administration and management; criminal justice/law enforcement administration; dramatic/theater arts; English; entrepreneurship; environmental science; general studies; health and physical education/fitness; history; human services; jazz/jazz studies; kinesiology and exercise science; logistics, materials, and supply chain management; mathematics; music; organizational leadership; prenursing studies; radio and television broadcasting technology; sport and fitness administration/management; voice and opera.

Academics *Calendar:* semesters. *Degrees:* associate and bachelor's. *Special study options:* academic remediation for entering students, accelerated degree program, freshman honors college, honors programs, independent study, part-time degree program, summer session for credit.

Library McKinstry Library.

Student Life *Housing:* on-campus residence required through sophomore year. *Options:* men-only, women-only. Campus housing is university owned. Freshman campus housing is guaranteed. *Activities and Organizations:* drama/theater group, student-run radio and television station, choral group, Black Student Union, Phi Theta Kappa, Purple Pulse, Student Activities Board, Woment of Worth. *Campus security:* 24-hour emergency response devices and patrols, controlled dormitory access. *Student services:* health clinic, personal/psychological counseling.

Athletics Member NJCAA. *Intercollegiate sports:* baseball M(s), basketball M(s)/W(s), cheerleading M(s)(c)/W(s)(c), cross-country running M(s)/W(s), golf M(s)/W(s), soccer M(s)/W(s), softball W(s), swimming and diving M(s)/W(s), track and field M(s)/W(s), volleyball M(s)(c)/W(s), wrestling M(s). *Intramural sports:* basketball M/W, football M/W, sand volleyball M/W, softball M/W, table tennis M/W.

Standardized Tests *Required:* SAT or ACT (for admission).

Costs (2017–18) *One-time required fee:* $50. *Tuition:* No tuition increase for student's term of enrollment. *Room and board:* $7400; room only: $2900. Room and board charges vary according to housing facility. *Payment plan:* installment.

Financial Aid Of all full-time matriculated undergraduates who enrolled in 2015, 200 Federal Work-Study jobs (averaging $900).

Applying *Options:* electronic application, early admission, deferred entrance. *Required:* high school transcript, minimum 2.0 GPA. *Required for some:* essay or personal statement, 2 letters of recommendation, interview. *Application deadlines:* rolling (freshmen), rolling (out-of-state freshmen), rolling (transfers).

Freshman Application Contact Lincoln College, 300 Keokuk Street, Lincoln, IL 62656-1699. *Phone:* 217-735-7251 Ext. 7251. *Toll-free phone:* 800-569-0558.

Website: http://www.lincolncollege.edu/.

Lincoln College of Technology
Melrose Park, Illinois

Admissions Office Contact Lincoln College of Technology, 8317 West North Avenue, Melrose Park, IL 60160. *Toll-free phone:* 844-215-1513. *Website:* http://www.lincolntech.edu/.

Lincoln Land Community College
Springfield, Illinois

Freshman Application Contact Mr. Ron Gregoire, Executive Director of Admissions and Records, Lincoln Land Community College, 5250 Shepherd Road, PO Box 19256, Springfield, IL 62794-9256. *Phone:* 217-786-2243. *Toll-free phone:* 800-727-4161. *Fax:* 217-786-2492. *E-mail:* ron.gregoire@llcc.edu. *Website:* http://www.llcc.edu/.

MacCormac College
Chicago, Illinois

Director of Admissions Mr. David Grassi, Director of Admissions, MacCormac College, 506 South Wabash Avenue, Chicago, IL 60605-1667. *Phone:* 312-922-1884 Ext. 102. *Website:* http://www.maccormac.edu/.

McHenry County College
Crystal Lake, Illinois

- **State and locally supported** 2-year, founded 1967, part of Illinois Community College Board
- **Suburban** 168-acre campus with easy access to Chicago
- **Coed,** 6,561 undergraduate students, 34% full-time, 53% women, 47% men

Undergraduates 2,243 full-time, 4,318 part-time. 0.4% are from out of state; 1% Black or African American, non-Hispanic/Latino; 16% Hispanic/Latino; 2% Asian, non-Hispanic/Latino; 0.2% Native Hawaiian or other Pacific Islander, non-Hispanic/Latino; 0.1% American Indian or Alaska Native, non-Hispanic/Latino; 2% Two or more races, non-Hispanic/Latino; 9% Race/ethnicity unknown; 0.2% international; 9% transferred in.

Freshmen *Admission:* 1,666 applied, 1,666 admitted, 1,011 enrolled. *Average high school GPA:* 2.25.

Faculty *Total:* 344, 29% full-time, 69% with terminal degrees. *Student/faculty ratio:* 19:1.

Majors Accounting; administrative assistant and secretarial science; animation, interactive technology, video graphics and special effects; applied horticulture/horticulture operations; biological and physical sciences; business administration and management; child-care provision; commercial photography; computer systems networking and telecommunications; construction management; criminal justice/police science; emergency medical technology (EMT paramedic); engineering; fine/studio arts; fire science/firefighting; general studies; health and physical education/fitness; information technology; liberal arts and sciences/liberal studies; music; occupational therapist assistant; operations management; registered nursing/registered nurse; restaurant, culinary, and catering management; robotics technology; selling skills and sales; special education.

Academics *Calendar:* semesters. *Degree:* certificates and associate. *Special study options:* academic remediation for entering students, accelerated degree program, adult/continuing education programs, advanced placement credit, cooperative education, distance learning, English as a second language, independent study, internships, part-time degree program, services for LD students, study abroad, summer session for credit.

Library McHenry County College Library. *Books:* 44,706 (physical), 1,272 (digital/electronic); *Serial titles:* 132 (physical), 16,018 (digital/electronic); *Databases:* 62.

Student Life *Housing:* college housing not available. *Activities and Organizations:* drama/theater group, student-run newspaper, radio station, choral group, Phi Theta Kappa, Student Senate, Equality Club, Writer's Block, Latinos Unidos. *Campus security:* 24-hour emergency response devices and patrols, late-night transport/escort service. *Student services:* personal/psychological counseling.

Athletics Member NJCAA. *Intercollegiate sports:* baseball M(s), basketball M(s)/W(s), soccer M(s), softball W(s), tennis M(s)/W(s), volleyball W(s).

Costs (2017–18) *Tuition:* area resident $3120 full-time, $104 per credit hour part-time; state resident $11,331 full-time, $378 per credit hour part-time; nonresident $13,718 full-time, $457 per credit hour part-time. Full-time tuition and fees vary according to course load. Part-time tuition and fees vary according to course load. *Required fees:* $284 full-time, $9 per credit hour part-time, $7 per term part-time. *Payment plan:* installment. *Waivers:* senior citizens and employees or children of employees.

Financial Aid Of all full-time matriculated undergraduates who enrolled in 2015, 200 Federal Work-Study jobs (averaging $3700). 130 state and other part-time jobs (averaging $2000).

Applying *Options:* electronic application, early admission, deferred entrance. *Application fee:* $15. *Recommended:* high school transcript. *Application deadlines:* rolling (freshmen), rolling (transfers). *Notification:* continuous (freshmen), continuous (transfers).

Freshman Application Contact Kellie Carper-Sowiak, Manager of New Student Transitions, McHenry County College, 8900 US Highway 14, Crystal Lake, IL 60012-2761. *Phone:* 815-455-8670.
E-mail: admissions@mchenry.edu.
Website: http://www.mchenry.edu/.

Midwestern Career College
Chicago, Illinois

Admissions Office Contact Midwestern Career College, 20 North Wacker Drive #3800, Chicago, IL 60606. *Website:* http://www.mccollege.edu/.

Moraine Valley Community College
Palos Hills, Illinois

- **State and locally supported** 2-year, founded 1967, part of Illinois Community College Board
- **Suburban** 294-acre campus with easy access to Chicago
- **Endowment** $13.3 million
- **Coed**

Undergraduates 6,393 full-time, 8,623 part-time. 0.2% are from out of state; 9% Black or African American, non-Hispanic/Latino; 23% Hispanic/Latino; 3% Asian, non-Hispanic/Latino; 0.1% Native Hawaiian or other Pacific Islander, non-Hispanic/Latino; 0.3% American Indian or Alaska Native, non-Hispanic/Latino; 2% Two or more races, non-Hispanic/Latino; 9% Race/ethnicity unknown; 2% international; 3% transferred in. *Retention:* 66% of full-time freshmen returned.

Faculty *Student/faculty ratio:* 21:1.

Academics *Calendar:* semesters. *Degree:* certificates and associate. *Special study options:* academic remediation for entering students, accelerated degree program, adult/continuing education programs, advanced placement credit, cooperative education, distance learning, double majors, English as a second language, honors programs, independent study, internships, off-campus study, part-time degree program, services for LD students, study abroad, summer session for credit.

Library *Books:* 64,610 (physical), 493 (digital/electronic); *Serial titles:* 314 (physical), 55 (digital/electronic); *Databases:* 63.

Student Life *Campus security:* 24-hour emergency response devices and patrols, late-night transport/escort service, campus police department, safety and security programs.

Athletics Member NJCAA.

Applying *Options:* electronic application, early admission, deferred entrance. *Recommended:* high school transcript.

Freshman Application Contact Mr. Andrew Sarata, Director, Admissions and Recruitment, Moraine Valley Community College, 9000 West College Parkway, Palos Hills, IL 60465-0937. *Phone:* 708-974-5357. *Fax:* 708-974-0681. *E-mail:* sarataa@morainevalley.edu.
Website: http://www.morainevalley.edu/.

Morrison Institute of Technology
Morrison, Illinois

Freshman Application Contact Mrs. Tammy Pruis, Admission Secretary, Morrison Institute of Technology, 701 Portland Avenue, Morrison, IL 61270. *Phone:* 815-772-7218. *Fax:* 815-772-7584.
E-mail: admissions@morrison.tec.il.us. *Website:* http://www.morrisontech.edu/.

Morton College
Cicero, Illinois

- **State and locally supported** 2-year, founded 1924, part of Illinois Community College Board
- **Suburban** 25-acre campus with easy access to Chicago
- **Coed,** 4,397 undergraduate students, 31% full-time, 58% women, 42% men

Undergraduates 1,347 full-time, 3,050 part-time. Students come from 10 states and territories; 0.7% are from out of state; 3% Black or African American, non-Hispanic/Latino; 84% Hispanic/Latino; 1% Asian, non-Hispanic/Latino; 0.5% Two or more races, non-Hispanic/Latino; 4% Race/ethnicity unknown; 4% transferred in. *Retention:* 64% of full-time freshmen returned.

Freshmen *Admission:* 658 applied, 658 admitted, 658 enrolled.

Faculty *Total:* 227, 24% full-time, 11% with terminal degrees. *Student/faculty ratio:* 20:1.

Majors Accounting; administrative assistant and secretarial science; art; automobile/automotive mechanics technology; biological and physical sciences; business administration and management; CAD/CADD drafting/design technology; child-care provision; computer support specialist; criminal justice/police science; data processing and data processing technology; drafting and design technology; early childhood education; finance; fine/studio arts; fire science/firefighting; health information/medical records technology; heating, air conditioning, ventilation and refrigeration maintenance technology; information technology; legal administrative assistant/secretary; liberal arts and sciences/liberal studies; marketing/marketing management; massage therapy; medical administrative assistant and medical secretary; music; physical therapy; physical therapy technology; registered nursing/registered nurse; web/multimedia management and webmaster.

Academics *Calendar:* semesters. *Degree:* certificates and associate. *Special study options:* academic remediation for entering students, adult/continuing

education programs, advanced placement credit, distance learning, English as a second language, internships, part-time degree program, services for LD students, student-designed majors, summer session for credit.

Library Learning Resource Center. Students can reserve study rooms.

Student Life *Housing:* college housing not available. *Activities and Organizations:* drama/theater group, student-run newspaper, radio station, Morton Ambassador Program, Campus Activities Board, Student Government Association, Nursing Club. *Campus security:* 24-hour patrols, security cameras.

Athletics Member NJCAA. *Intercollegiate sports:* baseball M(s), basketball M(s)/W(s), cross-country running M(s)/W(s), soccer M/W(s), softball W(s), volleyball W(s).

Costs (2016–17) *Tuition:* area resident $2816 full-time, $88 per credit hour part-time; state resident $6912 full-time, $216 per credit hour part-time; nonresident $8960 full-time, $280 per credit hour part-time. *Required fees:* $1076 full-time, $43 per credit hour part-time, $10 per term part-time. *Payment plan:* installment. *Waivers:* senior citizens and employees or children of employees.

Applying *Options:* electronic application. *Application fee:* $10. *Required:* high school transcript. *Application deadlines:* rolling (freshmen), rolling (transfers).

Freshman Application Contact Morton College, 3801 South Central Avenue, Cicero, IL 60804-4398. *Phone:* 708-656-8000 Ext. 2245. *Website:* http://www.morton.edu/.

Northwestern College–Bridgeview Campus
Bridgeview, Illinois

Admissions Office Contact Northwestern College–Bridgeview Campus, 7725 South Harlem Avenue, Bridgeview, IL 60645. *Toll-free phone:* 888-205-2283. *Website:* http://www.nc.edu/locations/bridgeview-campus/.

Northwestern College–Chicago Campus
Chicago, Illinois

Freshman Application Contact Northwestern College–Chicago Campus, 4829 North Lipps Avenue, Chicago, IL 60630. *Phone:* 708-233-5000. *Toll-free phone:* 888-205-2283. *Website:* http://www.nc.edu/locations/chicago-campus/.

Oakton Community College
Des Plaines, Illinois

- **District-supported** 2-year, founded 1969, part of Illinois Community College Board
- **Suburban** 193-acre campus with easy access to Chicago
- **Coed,** 8,934 undergraduate students

Majors Accounting technology and bookkeeping; administrative assistant and secretarial science; architectural drafting and CAD/CADD; automobile/automotive mechanics technology; banking and financial support services; biological and physical sciences; building/construction finishing, management, and inspection related; child-care provision; clinical/medical laboratory technology; computer programming; criminal justice/police science; electrical, electronic and communications engineering technology; engineering; fire science/firefighting; graphic design; health information/medical records administration; heating, ventilation, air conditioning and refrigeration engineering technology; information technology; liberal arts and sciences/liberal studies; manufacturing engineering technology; marketing/marketing management; mechanical engineering/mechanical technology; music; operations management; physical therapy technology; real estate; registered nursing/registered nurse; sales, distribution, and marketing operations; social work; substance abuse/addiction counseling.

Academics *Calendar:* semesters. *Degree:* certificates and associate. *Special study options:* academic remediation for entering students, adult/continuing education programs, advanced placement credit, distance learning, English as a second language, honors programs, independent study, internships, off-campus study, part-time degree program, services for LD students, study abroad, summer session for credit.

Library Oakton Community College Library plus 1 other.

Student Life *Housing:* college housing not available. *Activities and Organizations:* drama/theater group, student-run newspaper, choral group. *Campus security:* 24-hour emergency response devices and patrols, student patrols, late-night transport/escort service. *Student services:* health clinic, personal/psychological counseling.

Athletics Member NJCAA. *Intercollegiate sports:* baseball M, basketball M/W, cross-country running M/W, soccer M/W, softball W, tennis M/W, track

and field M/W, volleyball W. *Intramural sports:* basketball M/W, cheerleading W, soccer M, table tennis M/W, volleyball M/W.

Costs (2017–18) *Tuition:* area resident $2958 full-time; state resident $8208 full-time; nonresident $9960 full-time. Full-time tuition and fees vary according to course load. Part-time tuition and fees vary according to course load. *Required fees:* $188 full-time. *Payment plans:* installment, deferred payment. *Waivers:* senior citizens and employees or children of employees.

Applying *Options:* electronic application. *Application fee:* $25. *Required for some:* interview. *Recommended:* high school transcript. *Application deadlines:* rolling (freshmen), rolling (transfers). *Notification:* continuous (freshmen), continuous (transfers).

Freshman Application Contact Ms. Nicci Cisarik, Admissions Specialist, Oakton Community College, 1600 East Golf Road, Des Plaines, IL 60016-1268. *Phone:* 847-635-1913. *Fax:* 847-635-1890.
E-mail: ncisarik@oakton.edu.
Website: http://www.oakton.edu/.

Parkland College
Champaign, Illinois

Freshman Application Contact Mr. Tim Wendt, Director of Enrollment Services, Parkland College, Champaign, IL 61821-1899. *Phone:* 217-351-2482. *Toll-free phone:* 800-346-8089. *Fax:* 217-353-2640.
E-mail: admissions@parkland.edu. *Website:* http://www.parkland.edu/.

Prairie State College
Chicago Heights, Illinois

Freshman Application Contact Jaime Miller, Director of Admissions, Prairie State College, 202 South Halsted Street, Chicago Heights, IL 60411.
Phone: 708-709-3513. *E-mail:* jmmiller@prairiestate.edu.
Website: http://www.prairiestate.edu/.

Rend Lake College
Ina, Illinois

- **State-supported** 2-year, founded 1967, part of Illinois Community College Board
- **Rural** 350-acre campus
- **Coed,** 2,489 undergraduate students, 48% full-time, 56% women, 44% men

Undergraduates 1,205 full-time, 1,284 part-time. Students come from 4 states and territories; 2 other countries; 0.3% are from out of state; 4% Black or African American, non-Hispanic/Latino; 0.8% Hispanic/Latino; 0.6% Asian, non-Hispanic/Latino; 0.1% Native Hawaiian or other Pacific Islander, non-Hispanic/Latino; 0.3% American Indian or Alaska Native, non-Hispanic/Latino; 0.2% Race/ethnicity unknown; 4% transferred in.

Freshmen *Admission:* 560 admitted, 560 enrolled.

Faculty *Total:* 143, 43% full-time, 6% with terminal degrees. *Student/faculty ratio:* 18:1.

Majors Administrative assistant and secretarial science; agricultural business and management; agricultural mechanics and equipment technology; agricultural mechanization; agricultural production; architectural drafting and CAD/CADD; automobile/automotive mechanics technology; barbering; biological and physical sciences; biomedical technology; business/commerce; child-care provision; clinical/medical laboratory technology; computer programming; computer technology/computer systems technology; cosmetology; criminal justice/police science; culinary arts; electrical, electronic and communications engineering technology; electrician; emergency medical technology (EMT paramedic); engineering; fine/studio arts; graphic design; health information/medical records technology; heavy equipment maintenance technology; industrial mechanics and maintenance technology; liberal arts and sciences/liberal studies; manufacturing engineering technology; medical/clinical assistant; medical radiologic technology; medical staff services technology; mining technology; music; occupational therapist assistant; petroleum technology; registered nursing/registered nurse; surveying technology; veterinary/animal health technology; welding technology.

Academics *Calendar:* semesters. *Degree:* certificates and associate. *Special study options:* academic remediation for entering students, adult/continuing education programs, advanced placement credit, cooperative education, distance learning, double majors, English as a second language, honors programs, independent study, internships, off-campus study, part-time degree program, services for LD students, study abroad, summer session for credit.

Library Learning Resource Center. *Books:* 12,998 (physical), 32,346 (digital/electronic); *Serial titles:* 117 (physical), 24,174 (digital/electronic); *Databases:* 34. Weekly public service hours: 54; students can reserve study rooms.

Student Life *Housing:* college housing not available. *Activities and Organizations:* drama/theater group, choral group, Agriculture Club, Automotive Club, Art League, College Bowl, Musical Notes Society. *Campus security:* 24-hour emergency response devices and patrols, late-night transport/escort service. *Student services:* personal/psychological counseling.
Athletics Member NJCAA. *Intercollegiate sports:* baseball M(s), basketball M(s)/W(s), golf M(s)/W(s), softball W(s), tennis W(s), volleyball W(s).
Costs (2017–18) *Tuition:* area resident $3300 full-time, $110 per credit hour part-time; state resident $5250 full-time, $175 per credit hour part-time; nonresident $6000 full-time, $200 per credit hour part-time. Full-time tuition and fees vary according to course level, course load, program, and reciprocity agreements. Part-time tuition and fees vary according to course level, course load, program, and reciprocity agreements. *Required fees:* $600 full-time, $20 per credit hour part-time. *Payment plan:* installment. *Waivers:* senior citizens and employees or children of employees.
Financial Aid Of all full-time matriculated undergraduates who enrolled in 2015, 133 Federal Work-Study jobs (averaging $1000). 174 state and other part-time jobs (averaging $940).
Applying *Options:* electronic application, deferred entrance. *Required:* high school transcript. *Application deadlines:* 8/18 (freshmen), 8/18 (transfers).
Freshman Application Contact Mrs. Jena Jensik, Director of Advisement, Rend Lake College, 468 North Ken Gray Parkway, Ina, IL 62846-9801. *Phone:* 618-437-5321 Ext. 1293. *Toll-free phone:* 800-369-5321. *Fax:* 618-437-5677. *E-mail:* jensikj@rlc.edu. *Website:* http://www.rlc.edu/.

Richland Community College
Decatur, Illinois

- **District-supported** 2-year, founded 1971, part of Illinois Community College Board
- **Small-town** 117-acre campus
- **Coed**

Undergraduates 951 full-time, 2,054 part-time. Students come from 25 states and territories; 2% are from out of state; 16% Black or African American, non-Hispanic/Latino; 1% Hispanic/Latino; 1% Asian, non-Hispanic/Latino; 0.2% Native Hawaiian or other Pacific Islander, non-Hispanic/Latino; 0.6% American Indian or Alaska Native, non-Hispanic/Latino; 4% Race/ethnicity unknown; 0.8% transferred in. *Retention:* 57% of full-time freshmen returned.
Faculty *Student/faculty ratio:* 15:1.
Academics *Calendar:* semesters. *Degree:* certificates and associate. *Special study options:* academic remediation for entering students, adult/continuing education programs, advanced placement credit, distance learning, English as a second language, freshman honors college, honors programs, part-time degree program, services for LD students, student-designed majors, summer session for credit.
Library Kitty Lindsay Library. *Books:* 29,388 (physical), 15 (digital/electronic); *Serial titles:* 975 (physical); *Databases:* 28. Students can reserve study rooms.
Student Life *Campus security:* 24-hour emergency response devices and patrols.
Standardized Tests *Recommended:* ACT (for admission).
Costs (2016–17) *Tuition:* area resident $3744 full-time, $119 per credit hour part-time; state resident $5445 full-time, $201 per credit hour part-time; nonresident $462 per credit part-time. Full-time tuition and fees vary according to program and reciprocity agreements. Part-time tuition and fees vary according to program and reciprocity agreements. *Required fees:* $324 full-time, $2 per credit part-time.
Financial Aid Of all full-time matriculated undergraduates who enrolled in 2015, 43 Federal Work-Study jobs (averaging $1339). 129 state and other part-time jobs (averaging $578).
Applying *Options:* early admission. *Required:* high school transcript.
Freshman Application Contact Ms. Catherine Sebok, Director of Admissions and Records, Richland Community College, Decatur, IL 62521. *Phone:* 217-875-7200 Ext. 558. *Fax:* 217-875-7783. *E-mail:* csebok@richland.edu. *Website:* http://www.richland.edu/.

Rockford Career College
Rockford, Illinois

Director of Admissions Ms. Barbara Holliman, Director of Admissions, Rockford Career College, 1130 South Alpine Road, Suite 100, Rockford, IL 61108. *Phone:* 815-965-8616 Ext. 16.
Website: http://www.rockfordcareercollege.edu/.

Rock Valley College
Rockford, Illinois

- **District-supported** 2-year, founded 1964, part of Illinois Community College Board
- **Suburban** 217-acre campus with easy access to Chicago
- **Coed**, 6,937 undergraduate students, 45% full-time, 56% women, 44% men

Undergraduates 3,138 full-time, 3,799 part-time. 9% Black or African American, non-Hispanic/Latino; 15% Hispanic/Latino; 2% Asian, non-Hispanic/Latino; 0.1% Native Hawaiian or other Pacific Islander, non-Hispanic/Latino; 0.4% American Indian or Alaska Native, non-Hispanic/Latino; 2% Two or more races, non-Hispanic/Latino; 1% Race/ethnicity unknown; 0.3% international; 3% transferred in. *Retention:* 68% of full-time freshmen returned.
Freshmen *Admission:* 957 enrolled.
Faculty *Total:* 461, 34% full-time.
Majors Accounting; administrative assistant and secretarial science; automobile/automotive mechanics technology; avionics maintenance technology; business administration and management; child development; computer engineering technology; computer science; computer systems networking and telecommunications; construction engineering technology; criminal justice/law enforcement administration; dental hygiene; drafting/design engineering technologies related; electrical, electronic and communications engineering technology; electrician; energy management and systems technology; fire science/firefighting; graphic and printing equipment operation/production; human services; industrial and product design; industrial technology; liberal arts and sciences/liberal studies; marketing/marketing management; pre-engineering; quality control technology; registered nursing/registered nurse; respiratory care therapy; sheet metal technology; sport and fitness administration/management; surgical technology; tool and die technology; welding technology.
Academics *Calendar:* semesters. *Degree:* certificates and associate. *Special study options:* academic remediation for entering students, adult/continuing education programs, advanced placement credit, cooperative education, distance learning, English as a second language, honors programs, independent study, internships, part-time degree program, services for LD students, student-designed majors, study abroad, summer session for credit.
Library Educational Resource Center.
Student Life *Housing:* college housing not available. *Activities and Organizations:* drama/theater group, student-run newspaper, choral group, Black Student Alliance, Phi Theta Kappa, Adults on Campus, Inter-Varsity Club, Christian Fellowship. *Campus security:* 24-hour emergency response devices and patrols, late-night transport/escort service. *Student services:* personal/psychological counseling.
Athletics Member NJCAA. *Intercollegiate sports:* baseball M, basketball M/W, golf M, soccer M/W, softball W, squash W, tennis M/W, volleyball W. *Intramural sports:* skiing (downhill) M/W.
Costs (2016–17) *Tuition:* area resident $3000 full-time, $100 per credit hour part-time; state resident $8310 full-time, $277 per credit hour part-time; nonresident $15,270 full-time, $509 per credit hour part-time. Full-time tuition and fees vary according to course load. Part-time tuition and fees vary according to course load. *Required fees:* $314 full-time. *Payment plans:* installment, deferred payment. *Waivers:* employees or children of employees.
Financial Aid Of all full-time matriculated undergraduates who enrolled in 2015, 120 Federal Work-Study jobs (averaging $1800).
Applying *Required:* high school transcript.
Freshman Application Contact Mr. Melvin Allen, Executive Director of Recruitment & Admissions, Rock Valley College, 3301 North Mulford Road, Rockford, IL 61008. *Toll-free phone:* 800-973-7821. *E-mail:* m.allen@rockvalleycollege.edu. *Website:* http://www.rockvalleycollege.edu/.

SAE Institute Chicago
Chicago, Illinois

Admissions Office Contact SAE Institute Chicago, 820 North Orleans Street #125, Chicago, IL 60610. *Website:* http://www.sae.edu/.

Sauk Valley Community College
Dixon, Illinois

Freshman Application Contact Sauk Valley Community College, 173 Illinois Route 2, Dixon, IL 61021. *Phone:* 815-288-5511 Ext. 378. *Website:* http://www.svcc.edu/.

Shawnee Community College
Ullin, Illinois

- **State and locally supported** 2-year, founded 1967, part of Illinois Community College Board
- **Rural** 163-acre campus
- **Coed,** 1,819 undergraduate students, 44% full-time, 61% women, 39% men

Undergraduates 801 full-time, 1,018 part-time. Students come from 3 states and territories; 2% are from out of state; 15% Black or African American, non-Hispanic/Latino; 2% Hispanic/Latino; 0.6% Asian, non-Hispanic/Latino; 0.1% American Indian or Alaska Native, non-Hispanic/Latino; 2% Race/ethnicity unknown; 12% transferred in. *Retention:* 55% of full-time freshmen returned.
Freshmen *Admission:* 633 applied, 633 admitted, 115 enrolled.
Faculty *Total:* 169, 24% full-time, 4% with terminal degrees. *Student/faculty ratio:* 13:1.
Majors Accounting; administrative assistant and secretarial science; agricultural business and management; agriculture; agronomy and crop science; animal sciences; automobile/automotive mechanics technology; biological and physical sciences; business administration and management; business automation/technology/data entry; child development; clinical/medical laboratory technology; computer graphics; computer systems networking and telecommunications; cosmetology; criminal justice/police science; electrical, electronic and communications engineering technology; health information/medical records technology; human services; information science/studies; legal administrative assistant/secretary; liberal arts and sciences/liberal studies; medical administrative assistant and medical secretary; occupational therapist assistant; registered nursing/registered nurse; sheet metal technology; social work; veterinary/animal health technology; welding technology; wildlife, fish and wildlands science and management.
Academics *Calendar:* semesters. *Degree:* certificates, diplomas, and associate. *Special study options:* academic remediation for entering students, accelerated degree program, adult/continuing education programs, advanced placement credit, cooperative education, distance learning, double majors, English as a second language, external degree program, independent study, internships, off-campus study, part-time degree program, services for LD students, summer session for credit.
Library Shawnee Community College Library.
Student Life *Housing:* college housing not available. *Activities and Organizations:* drama/theater group, choral group, Phi Theta Kappa, Phi Beta Lambda, Music Club, Student Senate, Future Teachers Organization. *Campus security:* 24-hour patrols. *Student services:* personal/psychological counseling.
Athletics Member NJCAA. *Intercollegiate sports:* baseball M(s), basketball M(s)/W(s), softball W(s). *Intramural sports:* weight lifting M/W.
Standardized Tests *Required for some:* ACT (for admission). *Recommended:* ACT (for admission).
Costs (2016–17) *Tuition:* area resident $2616 full-time, $109 per credit hour part-time; state resident $4080 full-time, $170 per credit hour part-time; nonresident $4368 full-time, $182 per credit hour part-time. *Required fees:* $60 full-time. *Payment plans:* installment, deferred payment. *Waivers:* senior citizens and employees or children of employees.
Financial Aid Of all full-time matriculated undergraduates who enrolled in 2015, 60 Federal Work-Study jobs (averaging $2000). 50 state and other part-time jobs (averaging $2000).
Applying *Options:* electronic application, early admission, deferred entrance. *Required:* high school transcript. *Application deadlines:* rolling (freshmen), rolling (transfers). *Notification:* continuous (freshmen), continuous (transfers).
Freshman Application Contact Mrs. Erin King, Recruiter/Advisor, Shawnee Community College, 8364 Shawnee College Road, Ullin, IL 62992. *Phone:* 618-634-3200. *Toll-free phone:* 800-481-2242. *Fax:* 618-634-3300. *E-mail:* erink@shawneecc.edu.
Website: http://www.shawneecc.edu/.

Solex College
Wheeling, Illinois

Freshman Application Contact Solex College, 350 East Dundee Road, Wheeling, IL 60090. *Website:* http://www.solex.edu/.

Southeastern Illinois College
Harrisburg, Illinois

Freshman Application Contact Dr. David Nudo, Director of Counseling, Southeastern Illinois College, 3575 College Road, Harrisburg, IL 62946-4925.

Phone: 618-252-5400 Ext. 2430. *Toll-free phone:* 866-338-2742.
Website: http://www.sic.edu/.

South Suburban College
South Holland, Illinois

- **State and locally supported** 2-year, founded 1927, part of Illinois Community College Board
- **Suburban** 5-acre campus with easy access to Chicago
- **Coed,** 3,867 undergraduate students, 35% full-time, 66% women, 34% men

Undergraduates 1,348 full-time, 2,519 part-time. 3% are from out of state; 60% Black or African American, non-Hispanic/Latino; 18% Hispanic/Latino; 0.2% Asian, non-Hispanic/Latino; 1% American Indian or Alaska Native, non-Hispanic/Latino; 2% Two or more races, non-Hispanic/Latino; 1% Race/ethnicity unknown; 0.2% international. *Retention:* 20% of full-time freshmen returned.
Freshmen *Average high school GPA:* 2.33.
Faculty *Total:* 513, 22% full-time. *Student/faculty ratio:* 13:1.
Majors Accounting; accounting technology and bookkeeping; architectural drafting and CAD/CADD; biological and physical sciences; building/home/construction inspection; CAD/CADD drafting/design technology; child-care provision; construction engineering technology; court reporting; criminal justice/safety; electrical, electronic and communications engineering technology; executive assistant/executive secretary; fine/studio arts; information technology; kinesiology and exercise science; legal assistant/paralegal; liberal arts and sciences/liberal studies; nursing administration; occupational therapist assistant; office management; radiologic technology/science; small business administration; social work.
Academics *Calendar:* semesters. *Degree:* certificates and associate. *Special study options:* academic remediation for entering students, adult/continuing education programs, advanced placement credit, cooperative education, distance learning, English as a second language, honors programs, internships, off-campus study, part-time degree program, services for LD students, study abroad, summer session for credit.
Library South Suburban College Library plus 1 other. *Books:* 25,087 (physical); *Serial titles:* 58 (physical); *Databases:* 15. Weekly public service hours: 60; students can reserve study rooms.
Student Life *Housing:* college housing not available. *Activities and Organizations:* drama/theater group, choral group. *Campus security:* 24-hour emergency response devices and patrols.
Athletics Member NJCAA. *Intercollegiate sports:* baseball M, basketball M/W, soccer M/W, softball W, volleyball W.
Costs (2017–18) *Tuition:* area resident $4050 full-time, $135 per credit hour part-time; state resident $9990 full-time, $333 per credit hour part-time; nonresident $11,640 full-time, $388 per credit hour part-time. Full-time tuition and fees vary according to course load and reciprocity agreements. Part-time tuition and fees vary according to course load and reciprocity agreements. *Required fees:* $533 full-time. *Payment plan:* installment. *Waivers:* senior citizens and employees or children of employees.
Financial Aid Of all full-time matriculated undergraduates who enrolled in 2015, 4,111 applied for aid, 3,901 were judged to have need. 128 Federal Work-Study jobs (averaging $1678). In 2015, 59 non-need-based awards were made. *Average percent of need met:* 59%. *Average financial aid package:* $4850. *Average need-based gift aid:* $2350. *Average non-need-based aid:* $611.
Applying *Options:* early admission, deferred entrance. *Required:* high school transcript. *Required for some:* essay or personal statement. *Recommended:* essay or personal statement, minimum 2.0 GPA. *Application deadlines:* rolling (freshmen), rolling (transfers). *Notification:* continuous (freshmen), continuous (transfers).
Freshman Application Contact Ms. Tiffane Jones, Admissions, South Suburban College, 15800 South State Street, South Holland, IL 60473. *Phone:* 708-596-2000 Ext. 2158. *E-mail:* admissionsquestions@ssc.edu. *Website:* http://www.ssc.edu/.

Southwestern Illinois College
Belleville, Illinois

Freshman Application Contact Ms. Michelle Birk, Dean of Enrollment Services, Southwestern Illinois College, 2500 Carlyle Ave, Belleville, IL 62221. *Phone:* 618-235-2700 Ext. 5400. *Toll-free phone:* 866-942-SWIC. *Fax:* 618-222-9768. *E-mail:* michelle.birk@swic.edu. *Website:* http://www.swic.edu/.

Spoon River College
Canton, Illinois

- **State-supported** 2-year, founded 1959, part of Illinois Community College Board
- **Rural** 160-acre campus
- **Endowment** $2.4 million
- **Coed,** 1,560 undergraduate students, 48% full-time, 60% women, 40% men

Undergraduates 751 full-time, 809 part-time. Students come from 10 states and territories; 0.6% are from out of state; 11% Black or African American, non-Hispanic/Latino; 2% Hispanic/Latino; 0.8% Asian, non-Hispanic/Latino; 1% American Indian or Alaska Native, non-Hispanic/Latino; 0.5% Two or more races, non-Hispanic/Latino; 0.6% Race/ethnicity unknown; 0.1% international; 4% transferred in. *Retention:* 47% of full-time freshmen returned.
Freshmen *Admission:* 914 applied, 321 admitted, 259 enrolled.
Faculty *Total:* 121, 27% full-time. *Student/faculty ratio:* 13:1.
Majors Agricultural business and management; agricultural mechanics and equipment technology; agricultural mechanization; biological and physical sciences; entrepreneurship; general studies; health information/medical records administration; liberal arts and sciences/liberal studies; medical administrative assistant and medical secretary; natural resources management and policy; registered nursing/registered nurse; truck and bus driver/commercial vehicle operation/instruction.
Academics *Calendar:* semesters. *Degree:* certificates and associate. *Special study options:* academic remediation for entering students, accelerated degree program, adult/continuing education programs, advanced placement credit, distance learning, English as a second language, independent study, internships, part-time degree program, services for LD students, summer session for credit. *ROTC:* Army (c).
Library Library/Learning Resource Center. *Books:* 12,647 (physical), 135,000 (digital/electronic); *Serial titles:* 4,560 (digital/electronic); *Databases:* 31. Weekly public service hours: 40.
Student Life *Housing:* college housing not available. *Activities and Organizations:* drama/theater group, student-run newspaper, Student Government Association, PEEPS, Intramural Athletics, Habitat for Humanity, Drama Club. *Campus security:* 24-hour emergency response devices, night patrol by trained security personnel. *Student services:* personal/psychological counseling.
Athletics Member NJCAA. *Intercollegiate sports:* baseball M(s), softball W(s).
Costs (2017–18) *Tuition:* area resident $4160 full-time; state resident $9856 full-time; nonresident $10,688 full-time. Full-time tuition and fees vary according to location. Part-time tuition and fees vary according to location. *Required fees:* $640 full-time. *Payment plan:* installment. *Waivers:* senior citizens and employees or children of employees.
Financial Aid Of all full-time matriculated undergraduates who enrolled in 2013, 44 Federal Work-Study jobs (averaging $1735).
Applying *Options:* electronic application, early admission, deferred entrance. *Required:* high school transcript. *Application deadlines:* rolling (freshmen), rolling (transfers). *Notification:* continuous (freshmen), continuous (transfers).
Freshman Application Contact Ms. Missy Wilkinson, Dean of Student Services, Spoon River College, 23235 North County 22, Canton, IL 61520-9801. *Phone:* 309-649-6305. *Toll-free phone:* 800-334-7337. *Fax:* 309-649-6235. *E-mail:* info@src.edu.
Website: http://www.src.edu/.

Taylor Business Institute
Chicago, Illinois

Director of Admissions Mr. Rashed Jahangir, Taylor Business Institute, 318 West Adams, Chicago, IL 60606. *Website:* http://www.tbiil.edu/.

Tribeca Flashpoint College
Chicago, Illinois

Admissions Office Contact Tribeca Flashpoint College, 28 North Clark Street, Chicago, IL 60602. *Website:* http://www.tribecaflashpoint.edu/.

Triton College
River Grove, Illinois

Freshman Application Contact Ms. Mary-Rita Moore, Dean of Admissions, Triton College, 2000 Fifth Avenue, River Grove, IL 60171. *Phone:* 708-456-0300 Ext. 3679. *Fax:* 708-583-3162. *E-mail:* mpatrice@triton.edu. *Website:* http://www.triton.edu/.

Vatterott College
Fairview Heights, Illinois

Admissions Office Contact Vatterott College, 110 Commerce Lane, Fairview Heights, IL 62208. *Toll-free phone:* 888-202-2636.
Website: http://www.vatterott.edu/.

Vatterott College
Quincy, Illinois

Admissions Office Contact Vatterott College, 3609 North Marx Drive, Quincy, IL 62305. *Website:* http://www.vatterott.edu/.

Vet Tech Institute at Fox College
Tinley Park, Illinois

- **Private** 2-year, founded 2006
- **Suburban** campus
- **Coed**
- 65% of applicants were admitted

Academics *Calendar:* semesters. *Degree:* associate. *Special study options:* accelerated degree program, internships.
Freshman Application Contact Admissions Office, Vet Tech Institute at Fox College, 18020 South Oak Park Avenue, Tinley Park, IL 60477. *Phone:* 888-884-3694. *Toll-free phone:* 888-884-3694.
Website: http://chicago.vettechinstitute.edu/.

Waubonsee Community College
Sugar Grove, Illinois

Freshman Application Contact Joy Sanders, Admissions Manager, Waubonsee Community College, Route 47 at Waubonsee Drive, Sugar Grove, IL 60554. *Phone:* 630-466-7900 Ext. 5756. *Fax:* 630-466-6663. *E-mail:* admissions@waubonsee.edu. *Website:* http://www.waubonsee.edu/.

Worsham College of Mortuary Science
Wheeling, Illinois

Director of Admissions President, Worsham College of Mortuary Science, 495 Northgate Parkway, Wheeling, IL 60090-2646. *Phone:* 847-808-8444. *Website:* http://www.worshamcollege.com/.

INDIANA

Ancilla College
Donaldson, Indiana

- **Independent Roman Catholic** 2-year, founded 1937
- **Rural** 63-acre campus
- **Endowment** $5.7 million
- **Coed,** 504 undergraduate students, 76% full-time, 55% women, 45% men

Undergraduates 382 full-time, 122 part-time. Students come from 19 states and territories; 8 other countries; 6% are from out of state; 13% Black or African American, non-Hispanic/Latino; 11% Hispanic/Latino; 0.6% Asian, non-Hispanic/Latino; 5% Two or more races, non-Hispanic/Latino; 4% international; 13% transferred in; 35% live on campus. *Retention:* 41% of full-time freshmen returned.
Freshmen *Admission:* 1,305 applied, 798 admitted, 213 enrolled. *Average high school GPA:* 2.59.
Faculty *Total:* 58, 31% full-time, 10% with terminal degrees. *Student/faculty ratio:* 28:1.
Majors Agriculture; behavioral sciences; biological and physical sciences; business administration and management; business administration, management and operations related; computer and information sciences; criminal justice/safety; culinary arts related; early childhood education; elementary education; English; environmental studies; general studies; health/medical preparatory programs related; health services/allied health/health sciences; history; hospitality administration related; kinesiology and exercise science; liberal arts and sciences/liberal studies; logistics, materials, and supply chain management; mass communication/media; registered nursing/registered nurse; religious studies related; secondary education; speech communication and rhetoric; theology and religious vocations related.
Academics *Calendar:* semesters. *Degree:* certificates and associate. *Special study options:* academic remediation for entering students, adult/continuing

education programs, advanced placement credit, cooperative education, distance learning, double majors, independent study, internships, part-time degree program, services for LD students, student-designed majors, summer session for credit.

Library Gerald J. Ball Library. *Books:* 20,963 (physical), 3,767 (digital/electronic); *Serial titles:* 51 (physical); *Databases:* 71. Weekly public service hours: 64; students can reserve study rooms.

Student Life *Housing Options:* coed. Campus housing is university owned. Freshman applicants given priority for college housing. *Activities and Organizations:* Student Government Association, Ancilla Student Ambassadors, FFA, Phi Theta Kappa, Leaders for Life. *Campus security:* 24-hour emergency response devices and patrols, late-night transport/escort service, controlled dormitory access. *Student services:* personal/psychological counseling.

Athletics Member NJCAA. *Intercollegiate sports:* baseball M(s), basketball M(s)/W(s), bowling M(s)/W(s), cheerleading M(s)/W(s), cross-country running M(s)/W(s), golf M(s)/W(s), lacrosse M(s), soccer M(s)/W(s), softball W(s), volleyball W(s), wrestling M(s). *Intramural sports:* football M/W, sand volleyball M/W, soccer M/W, softball M/W, tennis M/W.

Costs (2017–18) *Comprehensive fee:* $25,030 includes full-time tuition ($15,600), mandatory fees ($230), and room and board ($9200). Full-time tuition and fees vary according to course load and program. Part-time tuition: $520 per credit hour. Part-time tuition and fees vary according to course load and program. *Required fees:* $55 per term part-time. *Payment plan:* installment. *Waivers:* employees or children of employees.

Financial Aid Of all full-time matriculated undergraduates who enrolled in 2016, 477 applied for aid, 433 were judged to have need. 11 Federal Work-Study jobs (averaging $2531). *Average need-based loan:* $2658. *Average need-based gift aid:* $2190. *Financial aid deadline:* 2/28.

Applying *Options:* electronic application. *Required:* high school transcript. *Application deadlines:* rolling (freshmen), rolling (transfers).

Freshman Application Contact Mr. Eric Wignall, Vice President of Enrollment Management, Ancilla College, PO Box 1, 9601 Union Road, Donaldson, IN 46513. *Phone:* 574-936-8898 Ext. 339. *Toll-free phone:* 866-ANCILLA. *Fax:* 574-935-1773. *E-mail:* admissions@ancilla.edu. *Website:* http://www.ancilla.edu/.

Brightwood College, Indianapolis Campus
Indianapolis, Indiana

Freshman Application Contact Director of Admissions, Brightwood College, Indianapolis Campus, 4200 South East Street, Indianapolis, IN 46227. *Phone:* 317-782-0315. *Toll-free phone:* 866-543-0208. *Website:* http://www.brightwood.edu/.

College of Court Reporting
Valparaiso, Indiana

Freshman Application Contact Ms. Nicky Rodriquez, Director of Admissions, College of Court Reporting, 455 West Lincolnway, Valparaiso, IN 46385. *Phone:* 219-942-1459 Ext. 222. *Toll-free phone:* 866-294-3974. *Fax:* 219-942-1631. *E-mail:* nrodriquez@ccr.edu. *Website:* http://www.ccr.edu/.

Fortis College
Indianapolis, Indiana

Freshman Application Contact Mr. Alex Teitelbaum, Vice President Systems and Administration, Fortis College, 9001 North Wesleyan Road, Suite 101, Indianapolis, IN 46268. *Phone:* 410-633-2929. *Toll-free phone:* 855-4-FORTIS. *E-mail:* kbennett@edaff.com. *Website:* http://www.fortis.edu/.

International Business College
Indianapolis, Indiana

- **Proprietary** 2-year, founded 1889
- **Suburban** campus
- **Coed**
- **71%** of applicants were admitted

Academics *Calendar:* semesters. *Degree:* diplomas and associate. *Special study options:* accelerated degree program, internships.

Freshman Application Contact Admissions Office, International Business College, 7205 Shadeland Station, Indianapolis, IN 46256. *Phone:* 317-813-2300. *Toll-free phone:* 800-589-6500. *Website:* http://www.ibcindianapolis.edu/.

Ivy Tech Community College–Bloomington
Bloomington, Indiana

- **State-supported** 2-year, founded 2001, part of Ivy Tech Community College System
- **Coed,** 5,885 undergraduate students, 32% full-time, 63% women, 37% men

Undergraduates 1,882 full-time, 4,003 part-time. 1% are from out of state; 3% Black or African American, non-Hispanic/Latino; 1% Hispanic/Latino; 2% Asian, non-Hispanic/Latino; 0.1% Native Hawaiian or other Pacific Islander, non-Hispanic/Latino; 0.4% American Indian or Alaska Native, non-Hispanic/Latino; 2% Two or more races, non-Hispanic/Latino; 21% Race/ethnicity unknown; 5% transferred in. *Retention:* 50% of full-time freshmen returned.

Freshmen *Admission:* 2,141 applied, 2,141 admitted, 882 enrolled.

Faculty *Total:* 318, 31% full-time. *Student/faculty ratio:* 19:1.

Majors Accounting technology and bookkeeping; administrative assistant and secretarial science; biotechnology; building/property maintenance; business administration and management; business automation/technology/data entry; cabinetmaking and millwork; computer and information sciences; computer science; computer systems networking and telecommunications; criminal justice/safety; data modeling/warehousing and database administration; drafting and design technology; early childhood education; education; electrical, electronic and communications engineering technology; electrician; emergency medical technology (EMT paramedic); engineering technology; executive assistant/executive secretary; fine/studio arts; general studies; heating, air conditioning, ventilation and refrigeration maintenance technology; hospitality administration; human services; industrial technology; informatics; information science/studies; information technology; legal assistant/paralegal; liberal arts and sciences/liberal studies; library and archives assisting; logistics, materials, and supply chain management; machine tool technology; manufacturing engineering technology; mechanic and repair technologies related; mechanics and repair; medical/health management and clinical assistant; medical radiologic technology; network and system administration; pipefitting and sprinkler fitting; psychiatric/mental health services technology; registered nursing/registered nurse; tool and die technology.

Academics *Calendar:* semesters. *Degree:* certificates and associate. *Special study options:* academic remediation for entering students, adult/continuing education programs, advanced placement credit, distance learning, external degree program, internships, part-time degree program, services for LD students, summer session for credit.

Student Life *Activities and Organizations:* Student Government, Phi Theta Kappa. *Campus security:* late-night transport/escort service.

Costs (2016–17) *Tuition:* state resident $4055 full-time, $135 per credit hour part-time; nonresident $7932 full-time, $264 per credit hour part-time. *Required fees:* $120 full-time, $60 per term part-time. *Payment plans:* installment, deferred payment. *Waivers:* senior citizens and employees or children of employees.

Financial Aid Of all full-time matriculated undergraduates who enrolled in 2015, 51 Federal Work-Study jobs (averaging $3259).

Applying *Options:* electronic application, deferred entrance. *Required:* high school transcript. *Required for some:* interview. *Application deadlines:* rolling (freshmen), rolling (transfers). *Notification:* continuous (freshmen), continuous (transfers).

Freshman Application Contact Mr. Neil Frederick, Assistant Director of Admissions, Ivy Tech Community College–Bloomington, 200 Daniels Way, Bloomington, IN 47404. *Phone:* 812-330-6026. *Toll-free phone:* 888-IVY-LINE. *Fax:* 812-332-8147. *E-mail:* nfrederi@ivytech.edu. *Website:* http://www.ivytech.edu/.

Ivy Tech Community College–Central Indiana
Indianapolis, Indiana

- **State-supported** 2-year, founded 1963, part of Ivy Tech Community College System
- **Urban** 10-acre campus
- **Coed,** 18,355 undergraduate students, 27% full-time, 54% women, 46% men

Undergraduates 4,919 full-time, 13,436 part-time. 1% are from out of state; 23% Black or African American, non-Hispanic/Latino; 5% Hispanic/Latino; 3% Asian, non-Hispanic/Latino; 0.2% Native Hawaiian or other Pacific Islander, non-Hispanic/Latino; 0.3% American Indian or Alaska Native, non-Hispanic/Latino; 4% Two or more races, non-Hispanic/Latino; 4% Race/ethnicity unknown; 6% transferred in. *Retention:* 46% of full-time freshmen returned.

Freshmen *Admission:* 3,453 enrolled.

Faculty *Total:* 946, 20% full-time. *Student/faculty ratio:* 23:1.

Majors Accounting technology and bookkeeping; automobile/automotive mechanics technology; biotechnology; business administration and management; business automation/technology/data entry; cabinetmaking and millwork; carpentry; child development; computer and information sciences; computer science; criminal justice/safety; data modeling/warehousing and database administration; design and visual communications; drafting and design technology; early childhood education; education; electrical, electronic and communications engineering technology; electrician; executive assistant/executive secretary; general studies; health information/medical records technology; heating, air conditioning, ventilation and refrigeration maintenance technology; hospitality administration related; human services; industrial production technologies related; industrial technology; informatics; information science/studies; information technology; legal assistant/paralegal; liberal arts and sciences/liberal studies; logistics, materials, and supply chain management; machine shop technology; machine tool technology; manufacturing engineering technology; masonry; mechanics and repair; medical/clinical assistant; medical/health management and clinical assistant; medical radiologic technology; network and system administration; occupational safety and health technology; painting and wall covering; pipefitting and sprinkler fitting; psychiatric/mental health services technology; registered nursing/registered nurse; respiratory care therapy; sheet metal technology; surgical technology; tool and die technology; transportation/mobility management.

Academics *Calendar:* semesters. *Degree:* certificates and associate. *Special study options:* academic remediation for entering students, adult/continuing education programs, advanced placement credit, cooperative education, distance learning, English as a second language, internships, off-campus study, part-time degree program, services for LD students, summer session for credit.

Student Life *Housing:* college housing not available. *Activities and Organizations:* student-run newspaper, Student Government, Phi Theta Kappa, Human Services Club, Administrative Office Assistants Club, Radiology Club. *Campus security:* 24-hour emergency response devices and patrols, late-night transport/escort service. *Student services:* personal/psychological counseling.

Athletics *Intramural sports:* baseball M, basketball M/W, cheerleading W, golf M/W, softball W, volleyball M/W.

Costs (2016–17) *Tuition:* state resident $4055 full-time, $135 per credit hour part-time; nonresident $7932 full-time, $264 per credit hour part-time. *Required fees:* $120 full-time, $60 per term part-time. *Payment plans:* installment, deferred payment. *Waivers:* senior citizens and employees or children of employees.

Financial Aid Of all full-time matriculated undergraduates who enrolled in 2015, 92 Federal Work-Study jobs (averaging $3766).

Applying *Options:* electronic application, early admission, deferred entrance. *Required:* high school transcript. *Required for some:* interview. *Application deadlines:* rolling (freshmen), rolling (transfers). *Notification:* continuous (freshmen), continuous (transfers).

Freshman Application Contact Ms. Tracy Funk, Director of Admissions, Ivy Tech Community College–Central Indiana, 50 West Fall Creek Parkway North Drive, Indianapolis, IN 46208-4777. *Phone:* 317-921-4371. *Toll-free phone:* 888-IVYLINE. *Fax:* 317-917-5919. *E-mail:* tfunk@ivytech.edu.

Website: http://www.ivytech.edu/.

Ivy Tech Community College–Columbus
Columbus, Indiana

- **State-supported** 2-year, founded 1963, part of Ivy Tech Community College System
- **Small-town** campus with easy access to Indianapolis
- **Coed,** 2,988 undergraduate students, 24% full-time, 60% women, 40% men

Undergraduates 715 full-time, 2,273 part-time. 1% are from out of state; 2% Black or African American, non-Hispanic/Latino; 3% Hispanic/Latino; 2% Asian, non-Hispanic/Latino; 0.1% Native Hawaiian or other Pacific Islander, non-Hispanic/Latino; 0.2% American Indian or Alaska Native, non-Hispanic/Latino; 2% Two or more races, non-Hispanic/Latino; 9% Race/ethnicity unknown; 4% transferred in. *Retention:* 58% of full-time freshmen returned.

Freshmen *Admission:* 407 enrolled.

Faculty *Total:* 196, 27% full-time. *Student/faculty ratio:* 15:1.

Majors Accounting technology and bookkeeping; administrative assistant and secretarial science; agriculture; automobile/automotive mechanics technology; business administration and management; business automation/technology/data entry; cabinetmaking and millwork; computer and information sciences; computer science; criminal justice/safety; data modeling/warehousing and database administration; dental assisting; design and visual communications; drafting and design technology; early childhood education; education; electrical and power transmission installation; electrical, electronic and communications engineering technology; emergency medical technology (EMT paramedic); engineering technology; executive assistant/executive secretary; general studies; heating, air conditioning, ventilation and refrigeration maintenance technology; hospitality administration; human services; industrial technology; informatics; information science/studies; information technology; interior design; legal assistant/paralegal; liberal arts and sciences/liberal studies; library and archives assisting; logistics, materials, and supply chain management; machine tool technology; manufacturing engineering technology; masonry; mechanic and repair technologies related; mechanics and repair; medical/clinical assistant; medical radiologic technology; pipefitting and sprinkler fitting; pre-engineering; psychiatric/mental health services technology; surgical technology; tool and die technology.

Academics *Calendar:* semesters. *Degree:* certificates and associate. *Special study options:* academic remediation for entering students, adult/continuing education programs, advanced placement credit, distance learning, internships, part-time degree program, services for LD students, summer session for credit.

Student Life *Housing:* college housing not available. *Activities and Organizations:* Student Government, Phi Theta Kappa, LPN Club. *Campus security:* late-night transport/escort service, trained evening security personnel, escort service.

Costs (2016–17) *Tuition:* state resident $4055 full-time, $135 per credit hour part-time; nonresident $7932 full-time, $264 per credit hour part-time. *Required fees:* $120 full-time, $60 per term part-time. *Payment plans:* installment, deferred payment. *Waivers:* senior citizens and employees or children of employees.

Financial Aid Of all full-time matriculated undergraduates who enrolled in 2015, 26 Federal Work-Study jobs (averaging $1694).

Applying *Options:* electronic application, early admission, deferred entrance. *Required:* high school transcript. *Required for some:* interview. *Application deadlines:* rolling (freshmen), rolling (transfers). *Notification:* continuous (freshmen), continuous (transfers).

Freshman Application Contact Alisa Deck, Director of Admissions, Ivy Tech Community College–Columbus, 4475 Central Avenue, Columbus, IN 47203-1868. *Phone:* 812-374-5129. *Toll-free phone:* 888-IVY-LINE. *Fax:* 812-372-0331. *E-mail:* adeck@ivytech.edu.

Website: http://www.ivytech.edu/.

Ivy Tech Community College–East Central
Muncie, Indiana

- **State-supported** 2-year, founded 1968, part of Ivy Tech Community College System
- **Suburban** 15-acre campus with easy access to Indianapolis
- **Coed,** 6,327 undergraduate students, 36% full-time, 60% women, 40% men

Undergraduates 2,253 full-time, 4,074 part-time. 1% are from out of state; 7% Black or African American, non-Hispanic/Latino; 2% Hispanic/Latino; 0.8% Asian, non-Hispanic/Latino; 0.1% Native Hawaiian or other Pacific Islander, non-Hispanic/Latino; 0.2% American Indian or Alaska Native, non-Hispanic/Latino; 4% Two or more races, non-Hispanic/Latino; 5% Race/ethnicity unknown; 5% transferred in. *Retention:* 48% of full-time freshmen returned.

Freshmen *Admission:* 1,114 enrolled.

Faculty *Total:* 468, 25% full-time. *Student/faculty ratio:* 15:1.

Majors Accounting technology and bookkeeping; administrative assistant and secretarial science; agriculture; automobile/automotive mechanics technology; building/property maintenance; business administration and management; carpentry; computer and information sciences; computer science; computer systems networking and telecommunications; construction trades; construction trades related; criminal justice/safety; data modeling/warehousing and database administration; dental assisting; dental hygiene; drafting and design technology; early childhood education; education; electrical, electronic and communications engineering technology; electrician; energy management and systems technology; engineering technology; executive assistant/executive secretary; general studies; health information/medical records technology; hospitality administration; hospitality administration related; human services; industrial mechanics and maintenance technology; industrial production technologies related; industrial technology; informatics; information science/studies; information technology; interior design; kinesiology and exercise science; legal assistant/paralegal; liberal arts and sciences/liberal studies; library and archives assisting; logistics, materials, and supply chain management; machine shop technology; machine tool technology; manufacturing engineering technology; masonry; medical/clinical assistant; medical/health management and clinical assistant; medical radiologic technology; network and system administration; painting and wall covering; physical therapy technology; pipefitting and sprinkler fitting; registered nursing/registered nurse; surgical technology; tool and die technology.

Academics *Calendar:* semesters. *Degree:* certificates and associate. *Special study options:* academic remediation for entering students, adult/continuing education programs, advanced placement credit, distance learning, internships, part-time degree program, services for LD students.

Student Life *Housing:* college housing not available. *Activities and Organizations:* Business Professionals of America, SkillsUSA–VICA, Student Government, Phi Theta Kappa, Human Services Club.

Costs (2016–17) *Tuition:* state resident $4055 full-time, $135 per credit hour part-time; nonresident $7932 full-time, $264 per credit hour part-time. *Required fees:* $120 full-time, $60 per term part-time. *Payment plans:* installment, deferred payment. *Waivers:* senior citizens and employees or children of employees.

Financial Aid Of all full-time matriculated undergraduates who enrolled in 2015, 65 Federal Work-Study jobs (averaging $2666).

Applying *Options:* electronic application, early admission, deferred entrance. *Required:* high school transcript. *Required for some:* interview. *Application deadlines:* rolling (freshmen), rolling (transfers). *Notification:* continuous (freshmen), continuous (transfers).

Freshman Application Contact Ms. Mary Lewellen, Ivy Tech Community College–East Central, 4301 South Cowan Road, Muncie, IN 47302-9448. *Phone:* 765-289-2291 Ext. 1391. *Toll-free phone:* 888-IVY-LINE. *Fax:* 765-289-2292. *E-mail:* mlewelle@ivytech.edu. *Website:* http://www.ivytech.edu/.

Ivy Tech Community College–Kokomo
Kokomo, Indiana

- **State-supported** 2-year, founded 1968, part of Ivy Tech Community College System
- **Small-town** 20-acre campus with easy access to Indianapolis
- **Coed,** 2,502 undergraduate students, 33% full-time, 58% women, 42% men

Undergraduates 821 full-time, 1,681 part-time. 6% Black or African American, non-Hispanic/Latino; 4% Hispanic/Latino; 2% Asian, non-Hispanic/Latino; 0.1% Native Hawaiian or other Pacific Islander, non-Hispanic/Latino; 0.4% American Indian or Alaska Native, non-Hispanic/Latino; 3% Two or more races, non-Hispanic/Latino; 3% Race/ethnicity unknown; 4% transferred in. *Retention:* 55% of full-time freshmen returned.

Freshmen *Admission:* 340 enrolled.

Faculty *Total:* 221, 27% full-time. *Student/faculty ratio:* 12:1.

Majors Accounting technology and bookkeeping; administrative assistant and secretarial science; agriculture; automobile/automotive mechanics technology; building/construction site management; building/property maintenance; business administration and management; communication and journalism related; computer and information sciences; computer science; computer systems networking and telecommunications; construction trades related; criminal justice/safety; data modeling/warehousing and database administration; dental assisting; dental hygiene; design and visual communications; drafting and design technology; early childhood education; education; electrical, electronic and communications engineering technology; electrician; emergency medical technology (EMT paramedic); engineering technology; executive assistant/executive secretary; general studies; health aide; health information/medical records technology; heating, air conditioning, ventilation and refrigeration maintenance technology; human services; industrial production technologies related; industrial technology; informatics; information science/studies; information technology; legal assistant/paralegal; liberal arts and sciences/liberal studies; library and archives assisting; machine shop technology; machine tool technology; manufacturing engineering technology; mechanic and repair technologies related; mechanics and repair; medical/clinical assistant; network and system administration; physical therapy technology; registered nursing/registered nurse; surgical technology; tool and die technology.

Academics *Calendar:* semesters. *Degree:* certificates and associate. *Special study options:* academic remediation for entering students, adult/continuing education programs, advanced placement credit, distance learning, internships, part-time degree program, services for LD students, summer session for credit.

Student Life *Housing:* college housing not available. *Activities and Organizations:* student-run newspaper, Student Government, Collegiate Secretaries International, Licensed Practical Nursing Club, Phi Theta Kappa. *Campus security:* 24-hour emergency response devices, late-night transport/escort service. *Student services:* personal/psychological counseling.

Costs (2016–17) *Tuition:* state resident $4055 full-time, $135 per credit hour part-time; nonresident $7932 full-time, $264 per credit hour part-time. *Required fees:* $120 full-time, $60 per term part-time. *Payment plans:* installment, deferred payment. *Waivers:* senior citizens and employees or children of employees.

Financial Aid Of all full-time matriculated undergraduates who enrolled in 2015, 45 Federal Work-Study jobs (averaging $1829).

Applying *Options:* electronic application, early admission. *Required:* high school transcript. *Required for some:* interview. *Application deadlines:* rolling (freshmen), rolling (transfers). *Notification:* continuous (freshmen), continuous (transfers).

Freshman Application Contact Mr. Mike Federspill, Director of Admissions, Ivy Tech Community College–Kokomo, 1815 East Morgan Street, Kokomo, IN 46903-1373. *Phone:* 765-459-0561 Ext. 233. *Toll-free phone:* 888-IVY-LINE. *Fax:* 765-454-5111. *E-mail:* mfedersp@ivytech.edu. *Website:* http://www.ivytech.edu/.

Ivy Tech Community College–Lafayette
Lafayette, Indiana

- **State-supported** 2-year, founded 1968, part of Ivy Tech Community College System
- **Suburban** campus with easy access to Indianapolis
- **Coed,** 4,862 undergraduate students, 39% full-time, 56% women, 44% men

Undergraduates 1,885 full-time, 2,977 part-time. 1% are from out of state; 5% Black or African American, non-Hispanic/Latino; 6% Hispanic/Latino; 2% Asian, non-Hispanic/Latino; 0.1% Native Hawaiian or other Pacific Islander, non-Hispanic/Latino; 0.2% American Indian or Alaska Native, non-Hispanic/Latino; 3% Two or more races, non-Hispanic/Latino; 10% Race/ethnicity unknown; 7% transferred in. *Retention:* 53% of full-time freshmen returned.

Freshmen *Admission:* 825 enrolled.

Faculty *Total:* 397, 22% full-time. *Student/faculty ratio:* 15:1.

Majors Accounting technology and bookkeeping; agriculture; automobile/automotive mechanics technology; biotechnology; building/property maintenance; business administration and management; business automation/technology/data entry; cabinetmaking and millwork; carpentry; chemical technology; clinical/medical laboratory technology; computer and information sciences; computer science; computer systems networking and telecommunications; criminal justice/safety; data modeling/warehousing and database administration; dental assisting; drafting and design technology; early childhood education; education; electrical, electronic and communications engineering technology; electrician; executive assistant/executive secretary; general studies; health aide; health information/medical records technology; heating, air conditioning, ventilation and refrigeration maintenance technology; human services; industrial production technologies related; industrial technology; informatics; information science/studies; information technology; legal assistant/paralegal; liberal arts and sciences/liberal studies; library and archives assisting; lineworker; machine tool technology; manufacturing engineering technology; masonry; mechanical engineering/mechanical technology; mechanic and repair technologies related; mechanics and repair; medical/clinical assistant; medical/health management and clinical assistant; painting and wall covering; pipefitting and sprinkler fitting; pre-engineering; psychiatric/mental health services technology; quality control and safety technologies related; registered nursing/registered nurse; respiratory care therapy; sheet metal technology; surgical technology; telecommunications technology.

Academics *Calendar:* semesters. *Degree:* certificates and associate. *Special study options:* academic remediation for entering students, advanced placement credit, distance learning, internships, part-time degree program, services for LD students, summer session for credit.

Student Life *Housing:* college housing not available. *Activities and Organizations:* student-run newspaper, Student Government, Phi Theta Kappa, LPN Club, Accounting Club, Student Computer Technology Association. *Student services:* personal/psychological counseling.

Costs (2016–17) *Tuition:* state resident $4055 full-time, $135 per credit hour part-time; nonresident $7932 full-time, $264 per credit hour part-time. *Required fees:* $120 full-time, $60 per term part-time. *Payment plans:* installment, deferred payment. *Waivers:* senior citizens and employees or children of employees.

Financial Aid Of all full-time matriculated undergraduates who enrolled in 2015, 65 Federal Work-Study jobs (averaging $2222). 1 state and other part-time job (averaging $2436).

Applying *Options:* electronic application. *Required:* high school transcript. *Required for some:* interview. *Application deadlines:* rolling (freshmen), rolling (transfers). *Notification:* continuous (freshmen), continuous (transfers).

Freshman Application Contact Mr. Ivan Hernanadez, Director of Admissions, Ivy Tech Community College–Lafayette, 3101 South Creasy Lane, PO Box 6299, Lafayette, IN 47903. *Phone:* 765-269-5116. *Toll-free phone:* 888-IVY-LINE. *Fax:* 765-772-9293. *E-mail:* ihernand@ivytech.edu. *Website:* http://www.ivytech.edu/.

Ivy Tech Community College–North Central

South Bend, Indiana

- **State-supported** 2-year, founded 1968, part of Ivy Tech Community College System
- **Suburban** 4-acre campus
- **Coed,** 4,984 undergraduate students, 30% full-time, 63% women, 37% men

Undergraduates 1,481 full-time, 3,503 part-time. 2% are from out of state; 14% Black or African American, non-Hispanic/Latino; 12% Hispanic/Latino; 2% Asian, non-Hispanic/Latino; 0.1% Native Hawaiian or other Pacific Islander, non-Hispanic/Latino; 0.5% American Indian or Alaska Native, non-Hispanic/Latino; 4% Two or more races, non-Hispanic/Latino; 4% Race/ethnicity unknown; 7% transferred in. *Retention:* 47% of full-time freshmen returned.

Freshmen *Admission:* 811 enrolled.

Faculty *Total:* 374, 28% full-time. *Student/faculty ratio:* 14:1.

Majors Accounting technology and bookkeeping; biotechnology; building/property maintenance; business administration and management; business automation/technology/data entry; cabinetmaking and millwork; carpentry; child-care and support services management; clinical/medical laboratory technology; computer and information sciences; criminal justice/safety; design and visual communications; early childhood education; educational/instructional technology; electrical, electronic and communications engineering technology; electrician; emergency medical technology (EMT paramedic); executive assistant/executive secretary; general studies; heating, air conditioning, ventilation and refrigeration maintenance technology; hospitality administration; human services; industrial production technologies related; industrial technology; interior design; ironworking; legal assistant/paralegal; liberal arts and sciences/liberal studies; library and archives assisting; machine tool technology; mechanic and repair technologies related; mechanics and repair; medical/clinical assistant; painting and wall covering; pipefitting and sprinkler fitting; registered nursing/registered nurse; sheet metal technology; telecommunications technology; tool and die technology.

Academics *Calendar:* semesters. *Degree:* certificates and associate. *Special study options:* academic remediation for entering students, adult/continuing education programs, advanced placement credit, distance learning, English as a second language, internships, off-campus study, part-time degree program, services for LD students, summer session for credit.

Student Life *Housing:* college housing not available. *Activities and Organizations:* Phi Theta Kappa, Student Government, LPN Club. *Campus security:* 24-hour emergency response devices and patrols, late-night transport/escort service, security during hours of operation. *Student services:* personal/psychological counseling, women's center.

Costs (2016–17) *Tuition:* state resident $4055 full-time, $135 per credit hour part-time; nonresident $7932 full-time, $264 per credit hour part-time. *Required fees:* $120 full-time, $60 per term part-time. *Payment plans:* installment, deferred payment. *Waivers:* senior citizens and employees or children of employees.

Financial Aid Of all full-time matriculated undergraduates who enrolled in 2015, 100 Federal Work-Study jobs (averaging $1538).

Applying *Options:* electronic application, early admission, deferred entrance. *Required:* high school transcript. *Required for some:* interview. *Application deadlines:* rolling (freshmen), rolling (transfers). *Notification:* continuous (freshmen), continuous (transfers).

Freshman Application Contact Darryl Williams, Bi-Regional Director of Admissions, Ivy Tech Community College–North Central, 220 Dean Johnson Boulevard, South Bend, IN 46601-3415. *Toll-free phone:* 888-IVY-LINE. *E-mail:* dwilliams770@ivytech.edu.
Website: http://www.ivytech.edu/.

Ivy Tech Community College–Northeast

Fort Wayne, Indiana

- **State-supported** 2-year, founded 1969, part of Ivy Tech Community College System
- **Urban** 22-acre campus
- **Coed,** 7,376 undergraduate students, 27% full-time, 53% women, 47% men

Undergraduates 2,017 full-time, 5,359 part-time. 1% are from out of state; 12% Black or African American, non-Hispanic/Latino; 5% Hispanic/Latino; 3% Asian, non-Hispanic/Latino; 0.2% Native Hawaiian or other Pacific Islander, non-Hispanic/Latino; 0.5% American Indian or Alaska Native, non-Hispanic/Latino; 4% Two or more races, non-Hispanic/Latino; 5% Race/ethnicity unknown; 7% transferred in. *Retention:* 50% of full-time freshmen returned.

Freshmen *Admission:* 1,612 enrolled.

Faculty *Total:* 449, 31% full-time. *Student/faculty ratio:* 16:1.

Majors Accounting technology and bookkeeping; agriculture; automobile/automotive mechanics technology; building/property maintenance; business administration and management; business automation/technology/data entry; cabinetmaking and millwork; computer and information sciences; computer science; construction trades; construction trades related; criminal justice/safety; data modeling/warehousing and database administration; drafting and design technology; early childhood education; electrical, electronic and communications engineering technology; electrician; executive assistant/executive secretary; heating, air conditioning, ventilation and refrigeration maintenance technology; hospitality administration; hospitality administration related; human services; industrial production technologies related; industrial technology; ironworking; legal assistant/paralegal; liberal arts and sciences/liberal studies; library and archives assisting; masonry; massage therapy; mechanics and repair; medical/clinical assistant; painting and wall covering; pipefitting and sprinkler fitting; psychiatric/mental health services technology; registered nursing/registered nurse; respiratory care therapy; sheet metal technology; tool and die technology.

Academics *Calendar:* semesters. *Degree:* certificates and associate. *Special study options:* adult/continuing education programs, advanced placement credit, distance learning, English as a second language, internships, part-time degree program, services for LD students, summer session for credit.

Student Life *Housing:* college housing not available. *Activities and Organizations:* student-run newspaper, Student Government, LPN Club, Phi Theta Kappa. *Campus security:* 24-hour emergency response devices and patrols, late-night transport/escort service.

Costs (2016–17) *Tuition:* state resident $4055 full-time, $135 per credit hour part-time; nonresident $7932 full-time, $264 per credit hour part-time. *Required fees:* $120 full-time, $60 per term part-time. *Payment plans:* installment, deferred payment. *Waivers:* senior citizens and employees or children of employees.

Financial Aid Of all full-time matriculated undergraduates who enrolled in 2015, 40 Federal Work-Study jobs (averaging $4041).

Applying *Options:* early admission. *Required:* high school transcript. *Required for some:* interview. *Application deadlines:* rolling (freshmen), rolling (transfers). *Notification:* continuous (freshmen), continuous (transfers).

Freshman Application Contact Robyn Boss, Director of Admissions, Ivy Tech Community College–Northeast, 3800 North Anthony Boulevard, Ft. Wayne, IN 46805-1489. *Phone:* 260-480-4211. *Toll-free phone:* 888-IVY-LINE. *Fax:* 260-480-2053. *E-mail:* rboss1@ivytech.edu.
Website: http://www.ivytech.edu/.

Ivy Tech Community College–Northwest

Gary, Indiana

- **State-supported** 2-year, founded 1963, part of Ivy Tech Community College System
- **Urban** 13-acre campus with easy access to Chicago
- **Coed,** 7,845 undergraduate students, 35% full-time, 59% women, 41% men

Undergraduates 2,735 full-time, 5,110 part-time. 1% are from out of state; 22% Black or African American, non-Hispanic/Latino; 10% Hispanic/Latino; 0.9% Asian, non-Hispanic/Latino; 0.1% Native Hawaiian or other Pacific Islander, non-Hispanic/Latino; 0.4% American Indian or Alaska Native, non-Hispanic/Latino; 4% Two or more races, non-Hispanic/Latino; 5% Race/ethnicity unknown; 8% transferred in. *Retention:* 51% of full-time freshmen returned.

Freshmen *Admission:* 1,447 enrolled.

Faculty *Total:* 495, 26% full-time. *Student/faculty ratio:* 18:1.

Majors Accounting technology and bookkeeping; automobile/automotive mechanics technology; building/property maintenance; business administration and management; business automation/technology/data entry; cabinetmaking and millwork; carpentry; child-care and support services management; computer and information sciences; construction trades; criminal justice/safety; drafting and design technology; early childhood education; electrical, electronic and communications engineering technology; electrician; executive assistant/executive secretary; funeral service and mortuary science; general studies; heating, air conditioning, ventilation and refrigeration maintenance technology; hospitality administration; human services; industrial technology; ironworking; legal assistant/paralegal; liberal arts and sciences/liberal studies; library and archives assisting; machine tool technology; masonry; mechanic and repair technologies related; mechanics and repair; medical/clinical assistant; occupational safety and health technology; painting and wall covering; pipefitting and sprinkler fitting; psychiatric/mental health services technology; registered nursing/registered nurse; respiratory care therapy; sheet metal technology; surgical technology; telecommunications technology; tool and die technology.

Academics *Calendar:* semesters. *Degree:* certificates and associate. *Special study options:* academic remediation for entering students, adult/continuing

education programs, advanced placement credit, distance learning, internships, part-time degree program, services for LD students, summer session for credit.

Student Life *Housing:* college housing not available. *Activities and Organizations:* Phi Theta Kappa, LPN Club, Computer Club, Student Government, Business Club. *Campus security:* 24-hour emergency response devices, late-night transport/escort service.

Costs (2016–17) *Tuition:* state resident $4055 full-time, $135 per credit hour part-time; nonresident $7932 full-time, $264 per credit hour part-time. *Required fees:* $120 full-time, $60 per term part-time. *Payment plans:* installment, deferred payment. *Waivers:* senior citizens and employees or children of employees.

Financial Aid Of all full-time matriculated undergraduates who enrolled in 2015, 74 Federal Work-Study jobs (averaging $2131).

Applying *Options:* electronic application, deferred entrance. *Required:* high school transcript. *Required for some:* interview. *Application deadlines:* rolling (freshmen), rolling (transfers). *Notification:* continuous (freshmen), continuous (transfers).

Freshman Application Contact Darryl Williams, Bi-Regional Director of Admissions, Ivy Tech Community College–Northwest, 1440 East 35th Avenue, Gary, IN 46409-499. *Phone:* 219-981-1111. *Toll-free phone:* 888-IVY-LINE. *E-mail:* dwilliams770@ivytech.edu.
Website: http://www.ivytech.edu/.

Ivy Tech Community College–Richmond
Richmond, Indiana

- **State-supported** 2-year, founded 1963, part of Ivy Tech Community College System
- **Small-town** 23-acre campus with easy access to Indianapolis
- **Coed,** 1,778 undergraduate students, 26% full-time, 63% women, 37% men

Undergraduates 455 full-time, 1,323 part-time. 1% are from out of state; 6% Black or African American, non-Hispanic/Latino; 1% Hispanic/Latino; 0.3% Asian, non-Hispanic/Latino; 0.1% Native Hawaiian or other Pacific Islander, non-Hispanic/Latino; 0.4% American Indian or Alaska Native, non-Hispanic/Latino; 2% Two or more races, non-Hispanic/Latino; 3% Race/ethnicity unknown; 6% transferred in. *Retention:* 50% of full-time freshmen returned.

Freshmen *Admission:* 297 enrolled.

Faculty *Total:* 127, 31% full-time. *Student/faculty ratio:* 13:1.

Majors Accounting technology and bookkeeping; agriculture; automobile/automotive mechanics technology; building/property maintenance; business administration and management; business automation/technology/data entry; cabinetmaking and millwork; computer and information sciences; computer science; construction trades; construction trades related; criminal justice/safety; data modeling/warehousing and database administration; early childhood education; education; electrical, electronic and communications engineering technology; electrician; emergency medical technology (EMT paramedic); engineering technology; executive assistant/executive secretary; general studies; heating, air conditioning, ventilation and refrigeration maintenance technology; human services; industrial production technologies related; industrial technology; informatics; information science/studies; information technology; legal assistant/paralegal; liberal arts and sciences and humanities related; liberal arts and sciences/liberal studies; library and archives assisting; logistics, materials, and supply chain management; machine shop technology; machine tool technology; manufacturing engineering technology; mechanics and repair; medical/clinical assistant; medical/health management and clinical assistant; medical radiologic technology; network and system administration; pipefitting and sprinkler fitting; psychiatric/mental health services technology; registered nursing/registered nurse; respiratory care therapy; tool and die technology.

Academics *Calendar:* semesters. *Degree:* certificates and associate. *Special study options:* academic remediation for entering students, adult/continuing education programs, advanced placement credit, distance learning, independent study, internships, off-campus study, part-time degree program, services for LD students, summer session for credit.

Student Life *Housing:* college housing not available. *Activities and Organizations:* student-run newspaper, Student Government, Phi Theta Kappa, LPN Club, CATS 2000, Business Professionals of America. *Campus security:* 24-hour emergency response devices, late-night transport/escort service. *Student services:* personal/psychological counseling.

Athletics *Intramural sports:* softball M/W.

Costs (2016–17) *Tuition:* state resident $4055 full-time, $135 per credit hour part-time; nonresident $7932 full-time, $264 per credit hour part-time. *Required fees:* $120 full-time, $60 per term part-time. *Payment plans:* installment, deferred payment. *Waivers:* senior citizens and employees or children of employees.

Financial Aid Of all full-time matriculated undergraduates who enrolled in 2015, 14 Federal Work-Study jobs (averaging $3106). 1 state and other part-time job (averaging $3380).

Applying *Options:* electronic application, early admission. *Required:* high school transcript. *Required for some:* interview. *Application deadlines:* rolling (freshmen), rolling (transfers). *Notification:* continuous (freshmen), continuous (transfers).

Freshman Application Contact Linda Przybysz, Director of Admissions, Ivy Tech Community College–Richmond, 2325 Chester Boulevard, Richmond, IN 47374-1298. *Phone:* 765-966-2656 Ext. 1246. *Toll-free phone:* 888-IVY-LINE. *E-mail:* lprzybys@ivytech.edu.
Website: http://www.ivytech.edu/.

Ivy Tech Community College–Sellersburg
Sellersburg, Indiana

- **State-supported** 2-year, founded 1968, part of Ivy Tech Community College System
- **Small-town** 63-acre campus with easy access to Louisville
- **Coed,** 4,585 undergraduate students, 18% full-time, 50% women, 50% men

Undergraduates 833 full-time, 3,752 part-time. 9% are from out of state; 7% Black or African American, non-Hispanic/Latino; 2% Hispanic/Latino; 0.7% Asian, non-Hispanic/Latino; 0.1% Native Hawaiian or other Pacific Islander, non-Hispanic/Latino; 0.2% American Indian or Alaska Native, non-Hispanic/Latino; 3% Two or more races, non-Hispanic/Latino; 15% Race/ethnicity unknown; 6% transferred in. *Retention:* 55% of full-time freshmen returned.

Freshmen *Admission:* 916 enrolled.

Faculty *Total:* 203, 27% full-time. *Student/faculty ratio:* 20:1.

Majors Accounting technology and bookkeeping; administrative assistant and secretarial science; automobile/automotive mechanics technology; building/property maintenance; business administration and management; business automation/technology/data entry; cabinetmaking and millwork; carpentry; clinical/medical laboratory technology; computer and information sciences; computer science; computer systems networking and telecommunications; data modeling/warehousing and database administration; design and visual communications; drafting and design technology; early childhood education; education; electrical, electronic and communications engineering technology; electrician; energy management and systems technology; engineering technology; executive assistant/executive secretary; general studies; heating, air conditioning, ventilation and refrigeration maintenance technology; human services; industrial technology; informatics; information science/studies; information technology; kinesiology and exercise science; legal assistant/paralegal; liberal arts and sciences/liberal studies; library and archives assisting; logistics, materials, and supply chain management; machine tool technology; mechanics and repair; medical/clinical assistant; medical/health management and clinical assistant; network and system administration; physical therapy technology; pipefitting and sprinkler fitting; psychiatric/mental health services technology; registered nursing/registered nurse; respiratory care therapy; sheet metal technology; telecommunications technology; tool and die technology.

Academics *Calendar:* semesters. *Degree:* certificates and associate. *Special study options:* academic remediation for entering students, adult/continuing education programs, advanced placement credit, cooperative education, distance learning, internships, part-time degree program, services for LD students, summer session for credit.

Student Life *Housing:* college housing not available. *Activities and Organizations:* Phi Theta Kappa, Practical Nursing Club, Medical Assistant Club, Accounting Club, Student Government. *Campus security:* late-night transport/escort service.

Costs (2016–17) *Tuition:* state resident $4055 full-time, $135 per credit hour part-time; nonresident $7932 full-time, $264 per credit hour part-time. *Required fees:* $120 full-time, $60 per term part-time. *Payment plans:* installment, deferred payment. *Waivers:* senior citizens and employees or children of employees.

Financial Aid Of all full-time matriculated undergraduates who enrolled in 2015, 20 Federal Work-Study jobs (averaging $5007). 1 state and other part-time job (averaging $6080).

Applying *Options:* electronic application, early admission, deferred entrance. *Required:* high school transcript. *Required for some:* interview. *Application deadlines:* rolling (freshmen), rolling (transfers). *Notification:* continuous (freshmen), continuous (transfers).

Freshman Application Contact Ben Harris, Director of Admissions, Ivy Tech Community College–Sellersburg, 8204 Highway 311, Sellersburg, IN 47172-1897. *Phone:* 812-246-3301 Ext. 4137. *Toll-free phone:* 888-IVY-LINE. *Fax:* 812-246-9905. *E-mail:* bharris88@ivytech.edu.
Website: http://www.ivytech.edu/.

Ivy Tech Community College–Southeast
Madison, Indiana

- **State-supported** 2-year, founded 1963, part of Ivy Tech Community College System
- **Small-town** 5-acre campus with easy access to Louisville
- **Coed,** 2,408 undergraduate students, 29% full-time, 67% women, 33% men

Undergraduates 692 full-time, 1,716 part-time. 1% are from out of state; 1% Black or African American, non-Hispanic/Latino; 0.6% Hispanic/Latino; 0.5% Asian, non-Hispanic/Latino; 0.2% American Indian or Alaska Native, non-Hispanic/Latino; 2% Two or more races, non-Hispanic/Latino; 9% Race/ethnicity unknown; 4% transferred in. *Retention:* 63% of full-time freshmen returned.

Freshmen *Admission:* 400 enrolled.

Faculty *Total:* 183, 30% full-time. *Student/faculty ratio:* 13:1.

Majors Accounting technology and bookkeeping; administrative assistant and secretarial science; business administration and management; business automation/technology/data entry; computer and information sciences; computer science; criminal justice/safety; data modeling/warehousing and database administration; drafting and design technology; early childhood education; education; electrical, electronic and communications engineering technology; executive assistant/executive secretary; general studies; human services; industrial technology; informatics; information science/studies; information technology; legal assistant/paralegal; liberal arts and sciences/liberal studies; logistics, materials, and supply chain management; manufacturing engineering technology; medical/clinical assistant; medical/health management and clinical assistant; medical radiologic technology; network and system administration; psychiatric/mental health services technology; registered nursing/registered nurse.

Academics *Calendar:* semesters. *Degree:* certificates and associate. *Special study options:* academic remediation for entering students, advanced placement credit, distance learning, internships, part-time degree program, services for LD students, summer session for credit.

Student Life *Housing:* college housing not available. *Activities and Organizations:* Student Government, Phi Theta Kappa, LPN Club. *Campus security:* 24-hour emergency response devices.

Costs (2016–17) *Tuition:* state resident $4055 full-time, $135 per credit hour part-time; nonresident $7932 full-time, $264 per credit hour part-time. *Required fees:* $120 full-time, $60 per term part-time. *Payment plans:* installment, deferred payment. *Waivers:* senior citizens and employees or children of employees.

Financial Aid Of all full-time matriculated undergraduates who enrolled in 2015, 26 Federal Work-Study jobs (averaging $1696).

Applying *Options:* electronic application. *Required:* high school transcript. *Required for some:* interview. *Application deadlines:* rolling (freshmen), rolling (transfers). *Notification:* continuous (freshmen), continuous (transfers).

Freshman Application Contact Shakira Grubbs, Director Express Enrollment Center, Ivy Tech Community College–Southeast, 590 Ivy Tech Drive, Madison, IN 47250-1881. *Phone:* 812-537-4010. *Toll-free phone:* 888-IVY-LINE. *E-mail:* sgrubbs5@ivytech.edu.
Website: http://www.ivytech.edu/.

Ivy Tech Community College–Southwest
Evansville, Indiana

- **State-supported** 2-year, founded 1963, part of Ivy Tech Community College System
- **Suburban** 15-acre campus
- **Coed,** 4,991 undergraduate students, 24% full-time, 55% women, 45% men

Undergraduates 1,181 full-time, 3,810 part-time. 1% are from out of state; 7% Black or African American, non-Hispanic/Latino; 1% Hispanic/Latino; 1% Asian, non-Hispanic/Latino; 0.2% Native Hawaiian or other Pacific Islander, non-Hispanic/Latino; 0.3% American Indian or Alaska Native, non-Hispanic/Latino; 3% Two or more races, non-Hispanic/Latino; 6% Race/ethnicity unknown; 5% transferred in. *Retention:* 52% of full-time freshmen returned.

Freshmen *Admission:* 639 enrolled.

Faculty *Total:* 290, 27% full-time. *Student/faculty ratio:* 17:1.

Majors Accounting technology and bookkeeping; administrative assistant and secretarial science; agriculture; automobile/automotive mechanics technology; biotechnology; boilermaking; building/property maintenance; business administration and management; business automation/technology/data entry; cabinetmaking and millwork; carpentry; computer and information sciences; computer science; construction/heavy equipment/earthmoving equipment operation; criminal justice/safety; data modeling/warehousing and database administration; design and visual communications; drafting and design technology; early childhood education; education; electrical, electronic and

communications engineering technology; electrician; emergency medical technology (EMT paramedic); energy management and systems technology; engineering technology; executive assistant/executive secretary; general studies; heating, air conditioning, ventilation and refrigeration maintenance technology; hospitality administration; human services; industrial production technologies related; industrial technology; informatics; information science/studies; information technology; interior design; ironworking; legal assistant/paralegal; library and archives assisting; logistics, materials, and supply chain management; machine tool technology; manufacturing engineering technology; masonry; mechanic and repair technologies related; mechanics and repair; medical/clinical assistant; medical/health management and clinical assistant; network and system administration; painting and wall covering; pre-engineering; psychiatric/mental health services technology; registered nursing/registered nurse; sheet metal technology; surgical technology; telecommunications technology; tool and die technology.

Academics *Calendar:* semesters. *Degree:* certificates and associate. *Special study options:* academic remediation for entering students, advanced placement credit, cooperative education, distance learning, independent study, internships, part-time degree program, services for LD students, summer session for credit.

Student Life *Housing:* college housing not available. *Activities and Organizations:* Student Government, Phi Theta Kappa, LPN Club, National Association of Industrial Technology, Design Club. *Campus security:* late-night transport/escort service.

Costs (2016–17) *Tuition:* state resident $4055 full-time, $135 per credit hour part-time; nonresident $7932 full-time, $264 per credit hour part-time. *Required fees:* $120 full-time, $60 per term part-time. *Payment plans:* installment, deferred payment. *Waivers:* senior citizens and employees or children of employees.

Financial Aid Of all full-time matriculated undergraduates who enrolled in 2015, 65 Federal Work-Study jobs (averaging $2264).

Applying *Options:* electronic application, early admission, deferred entrance. *Required:* high school transcript. *Required for some:* interview. *Application deadlines:* rolling (freshmen), rolling (transfers). *Notification:* continuous (freshmen), continuous (transfers).

Freshman Application Contact Ms. Denise Johnson-Kincade, Director of Admissions, Ivy Tech Community College–Southwest, 3501 First Avenue, Evansville, IN 47710-3398. *Phone:* 812-429-1430. *Toll-free phone:* 888-IVY-LINE. *Fax:* 812-429-9878. *E-mail:* ajohnson@ivytech.edu.
Website: http://www.ivytech.edu/.

Ivy Tech Community College–Wabash Valley
Terre Haute, Indiana

- **State-supported** 2-year, founded 1966, part of Ivy Tech Community College System
- **Suburban** 55-acre campus with easy access to Indianapolis
- **Coed,** 4,060 undergraduate students, 34% full-time, 55% women, 45% men

Undergraduates 1,372 full-time, 2,688 part-time. 1% are from out of state; 4% Black or African American, non-Hispanic/Latino; 0.6% Hispanic/Latino; 0.5% Asian, non-Hispanic/Latino; 0.1% Native Hawaiian or other Pacific Islander, non-Hispanic/Latino; 0.2% American Indian or Alaska Native, non-Hispanic/Latino; 3% Two or more races, non-Hispanic/Latino; 4% Race/ethnicity unknown; 6% transferred in. *Retention:* 55% of full-time freshmen returned.

Freshmen *Admission:* 638 enrolled.

Faculty *Total:* 287, 34% full-time. *Student/faculty ratio:* 19:1.

Majors Accounting technology and bookkeeping; agricultural mechanization; agriculture; airframe mechanics and aircraft maintenance technology; automobile/automotive mechanics technology; building/property maintenance; business administration and management; cabinetmaking and millwork; carpentry; chemical technology; clinical/medical laboratory technology; computer and information sciences; computer science; computer systems networking and telecommunications; construction/heavy equipment/earthmoving equipment operation; criminal justice/safety; data modeling/warehousing and database administration; design and visual communications; drafting and design technology; early childhood education; education; electrical, electronic and communications engineering technology; electrician; emergency medical technology (EMT paramedic); energy management and systems technology; engineering technology; executive assistant/executive secretary; general studies; health aide; health information/medical records technology; heating, air conditioning, ventilation and refrigeration maintenance technology; human services; industrial production technologies related; industrial technology; informatics; information science/studies; information technology; ironworking; legal assistant/paralegal; liberal arts and sciences/liberal studies; library and archives assisting; logistics, materials, and supply chain management; machine shop technology; machine tool technology; manufacturing engineering technology; masonry; mechanics and repair; medical/clinical assistant; medical/health management and clinical assistant; medical radiologic technology; network and system administration; occupational safety and health technology; painting and wall covering; pipefitting and sprinkler fitting; quality control and safety technologies related; registered nursing/registered nurse; respiratory care therapy; sheet metal technology; surgical technology; tool and die technology.

Academics *Calendar:* semesters. *Degree:* certificates and associate. *Special study options:* academic remediation for entering students, adult/continuing education programs, advanced placement credit, distance learning, internships, part-time degree program, services for LD students, summer session for credit.

Student Life *Housing:* college housing not available. *Activities and Organizations:* Student Government, Phi Theta Kappa, LPN Club, National Association of Industrial Technology. *Campus security:* 24-hour emergency response devices. *Student services:* personal/psychological counseling, women's center.

Athletics *Intramural sports:* basketball M/W, volleyball M/W.

Costs (2016–17) *Tuition:* state resident $4055 full-time, $135 per credit hour part-time; nonresident $7932 full-time, $264 per credit hour part-time. *Required fees:* $120 full-time, $60 per term part-time. *Payment plans:* installment, deferred payment. *Waivers:* senior citizens and employees or children of employees.

Financial Aid Of all full-time matriculated undergraduates who enrolled in 2015, 51 Federal Work-Study jobs (averaging $2110). 1 state and other part-time job (averaging $2963).

Applying *Options:* electronic application, early admission, deferred entrance. *Required:* high school transcript. *Required for some:* interview. *Application deadlines:* rolling (freshmen), rolling (transfers). *Notification:* continuous (freshmen), continuous (transfers).

Freshman Application Contact Nina Storey, Director of Admissions, Ivy Tech Community College–Wabash Valley, 7999 U.S. Highway 41 South, Terre Haute, IN 47802-4898. *Phone:* 812-298-2288. *Toll-free phone:* 888-IVY-LINE. *E-mail:* nstorey@ivytech.edu. *Website:* http://www.ivytech.edu/.

Lincoln College of Technology
Indianapolis, Indiana

Director of Admissions Ms. Cindy Ryan, Director of Admissions, Lincoln College of Technology, 7225 Winton Drive, Building 128, Indianapolis, IN 46268. *Phone:* 317-632-5553. *Toll-free phone:* 844-215-1513. *Website:* http://www.lincolntech.edu/.

Mid-America College of Funeral Service
Jeffersonville, Indiana

Freshman Application Contact Mr. Richard Nelson, Dean of Students, Mid-America College of Funeral Service, 3111 Hamburg Pike, Jeffersonville, IN 47130-9630. *Phone:* 812-288-8878. *Toll-free phone:* 800-221-6158. *Fax:* 812-288-5942. *E-mail:* macfs@mindspring.com. *Website:* http://www.mid-america.edu/.

Vet Tech Institute at International Business College
Fort Wayne, Indiana

- **Private** 2-year, founded 2005
- **Suburban** campus
- **Coed**
- 54% of applicants were admitted

Academics *Calendar:* semesters. *Degree:* associate. *Special study options:* accelerated degree program, internships.

Freshman Application Contact Admissions Office, Vet Tech Institute at International Business College, 5699 Coventry Lane, Fort Wayne, IN 46804. *Phone:* 800-589-6363. *Toll-free phone:* 800-589-6363. *Website:* http://ftwayne.vettechinstitute.edu/.

Vet Tech Institute at International Business College
Indianapolis, Indiana

- **Private** 2-year, founded 2007
- **Suburban** campus
- **Coed**
- 51% of applicants were admitted

Academics *Calendar:* semesters. *Degree:* associate. *Special study options:* accelerated degree program, internships.

Freshman Application Contact Admissions Office, Vet Tech Institute at International Business College, 7205 Shadeland Station, Indianapolis, IN 46256. *Phone:* 800-589-6500. *Toll-free phone:* 800-589-6500. *Website:* http://indianapolis.vettechinstitute.edu/.

Vincennes University
Vincennes, Indiana

- **State-supported** primarily 2-year, founded 1801
- **Small-town** 160-acre campus
- **Coed,** 18,897 undergraduate students, 30% full-time, 46% women, 54% men

Undergraduates 5,630 full-time, 13,267 part-time. Students come from 40 states and territories; 15 other countries; 19% are from out of state; 10% Black or African American, non-Hispanic/Latino; 8% Hispanic/Latino; 0.7% Asian, non-Hispanic/Latino; 0.3% Native Hawaiian or other Pacific Islander, non-Hispanic/Latino; 0.3% American Indian or Alaska Native, non-Hispanic/Latino; 2% Two or more races, non-Hispanic/Latino; 5% Race/ethnicity unknown; 0.7% international; 0.9% transferred in; 40% live on campus. *Retention:* 54% of full-time freshmen returned.

Freshmen *Admission:* 5,486 applied, 4,346 admitted, 2,620 enrolled.

Faculty *Total:* 1,344, 16% full-time. *Student/faculty ratio:* 16:1.

Majors Accounting technology and bookkeeping; administrative assistant and secretarial science; agricultural business and management; agricultural engineering; agriculture; aircraft powerplant technology; airline pilot and flight crew; American Sign Language (ASL); anthropology; applied horticulture/horticulture operations; architectural drafting and CAD/CADD; art; art teacher education; art therapy; autobody/collision and repair technology; automobile/automotive mechanics technology; behavioral sciences; biochemistry; biological and biomedical sciences related; biological and physical sciences; biology/biological sciences; biotechnology; building/home/construction inspection; business administration and management; business/commerce; chemistry; chemistry related; chemistry teacher education; child-care and support services management; child-care provision; civil engineering; commercial and advertising art; communications technology; computer and information sciences; computer/information technology services administration related; computer programming; computer science; computer systems networking and telecommunications; construction trades; corrections and criminal justice related; cosmetology; criminal justice/police science; culinary arts; design and applied arts related; diesel mechanics technology; dietetics; dramatic/theater arts; early childhood education; economics; education; electrical, electronic and communications engineering technology; elementary education; emergency medical technology (EMT paramedic); engineering technology; English; English/language arts teacher education; family and consumer sciences/home economics teacher education; family and consumer sciences/human sciences; fashion merchandising; finance; fire science/firefighting; food science; foreign languages and literatures; foreign languages related; funeral service and mortuary science; geology/earth science; graphic and printing equipment operation/production; health and physical education/fitness; health information/medical records technology; history; hospitality administration; hotel/motel administration; industrial technology; journalism; legal assistant/paralegal; liberal arts and sciences/liberal studies; manufacturing engineering technology; marketing/marketing management; massage therapy; mathematics; mathematics teacher education; mechanical drafting and CAD/CADD; mechanical engineering/mechanical technology; medical radiologic technology; music; music teacher education; natural resources/conservation; nuclear medical technology; ophthalmic and optometric support services and allied professions related; parks, recreation and leisure; pharmacy technician; philosophy; photojournalism; physical education teaching and coaching; physical sciences; physical therapy technology; political science and government; pre-dentistry studies; premedical studies; pre-pharmacy studies; pre-veterinary studies; psychology; public relations/image management; radio and television broadcasting technology; recording arts technology; registered nursing/registered nurse; restaurant, culinary, and catering management; robotics technology; science teacher education; secondary education; securities services administration; security and loss prevention; sheet metal technology; social work; sociology; special education; sport and fitness administration/management; surgical technology; surveying technology; teacher assistant/aide; theater design and technology; tool and die technology; web/multimedia management and webmaster; woodworking.

Academics *Calendar:* semesters. *Degrees:* certificates, associate, and bachelor's. *Special study options:* academic remediation for entering students, accelerated degree program, adult/continuing education programs, advanced placement credit, distance learning, double majors, English as a second language, external degree program, freshman honors college, honors programs, independent study, internships, off-campus study, part-time degree program, services for LD students, student-designed majors, summer session for credit. *ROTC:* Army (b), Air Force (c).

Library Shake Learning Resource Center.

Student Life *Housing:* on-campus residence required for freshman year. *Options:* coed, men-only, women-only. Campus housing is university owned. Freshman campus housing is guaranteed. *Activities and Organizations:* drama/theater group, student-run newspaper, radio and television station, choral group, national fraternities, national sororities. *Campus security:* 24-hour emergency response devices and patrols, student patrols, late-night transport/escort service, controlled dormitory access, surveillance cameras. *Student services:* health clinic, personal/psychological counseling.

Athletics Member NJCAA. *Intercollegiate sports:* baseball M, basketball M/W, bowling M, cross-country running M/W, golf M, track and field M/W, volleyball W.

Costs (2016–17) *Tuition:* state resident $5122 full-time; nonresident $12,731 full-time. Full-time tuition and fees vary according to course level, course load, location, program, reciprocity agreements, and student level. Part-time tuition and fees vary according to course level, course load, location, program, reciprocity agreements, and student level. *Required fees:* $453 full-time. *Room and board:* $9332. Room and board charges vary according to board plan, gender, and housing facility. *Payment plan:* installment. *Waivers:* senior citizens and employees or children of employees.

Applying *Options:* electronic application, deferred entrance. *Application fee:* $20. *Required:* high school transcript. *Required for some:* interview. *Application deadlines:* rolling (freshmen), rolling (transfers). *Notification:* continuous until 8/1 (freshmen), continuous (transfers).

Freshman Application Contact Vincennes University, 1002 North First Street, Vincennes, IN 47591. *Phone:* 812-888-4313.

Toll-free phone: 800-742-9198.

Website: http://www.vinu.edu/.

IOWA

Clinton Community College
Clinton, Iowa

Freshman Application Contact Mr. Gary Mohr, Executive Director of Enrollment Management and Marketing, Clinton Community College, 1000 Lincoln Boulevard, Clinton, IA 52732-6299. *Phone:* 563-336-3322. *Toll-free phone:* 800-462-3255. *Fax:* 563-336-3350. *E-mail:* gmohr@eicc.edu. *Website:* http://www.eicc.edu/ccc/.

Des Moines Area Community College
Ankeny, Iowa

- **State and locally supported** 2-year, founded 1966, part of Iowa Area Community Colleges System
- **Small-town** 362-acre campus
- **Endowment** $6.2 million
- **Coed,** 22,446 undergraduate students, 30% full-time, 54% women, 46% men

Undergraduates 6,644 full-time, 15,802 part-time. Students come from 38 states and territories; 9 other countries; 2% are from out of state; 5% Black or African American, non-Hispanic/Latino; 7% Hispanic/Latino; 4% Asian, non-Hispanic/Latino; 0.1% Native Hawaiian or other Pacific Islander, non-Hispanic/Latino; 0.3% American Indian or Alaska Native, non-Hispanic/Latino; 2% Two or more races, non-Hispanic/Latino; 9% Race/ethnicity unknown; 0.9% international; 5% transferred in. *Retention:* 60% of full-time freshmen returned.

Freshmen *Admission:* 2,946 enrolled.

Faculty *Total:* 848, 38% full-time. *Student/faculty ratio:* 14:1.

Majors Accounting; accounting and business/management; accounting technology and bookkeeping; agricultural/farm supplies retailing and wholesaling; apparel and accessories marketing; applied horticulture/horticultural business services related; architectural drafting and CAD/CADD; autobody/collision and repair technology; automobile/automotive mechanics technology; biomedical technology;

business administration and management; child-care provision; civil engineering technology; clinical/medical laboratory technology; commercial and advertising art; communications systems installation and repair technology; computer and information sciences and support services related; computer engineering technology; computer programming (specific applications); criminal justice/law enforcement administration; culinary arts; dental hygiene; desktop publishing and digital imaging design; diesel mechanics technology; electrical, electronic and communications engineering technology; fire prevention and safety technology; funeral service and mortuary science; health/health-care administration; heating, air conditioning, ventilation and refrigeration maintenance technology; hospitality administration; industrial electronics technology; industrial mechanics and maintenance technology; information technology; language interpretation and translation; legal assistant/paralegal; liberal arts and sciences/liberal studies; licensed practical/vocational nurse training; machine tool technology; marketing/marketing management; mechanical drafting and CAD/CADD; medical administrative assistant and medical secretary; medical/clinical assistant; office management; registered nursing/registered nurse; respiratory care therapy; sales, distribution, and marketing operations; sport and fitness administration/management; surveying engineering; tool and die technology; veterinary/animal health technology.

Academics *Calendar:* semesters. *Degrees:* certificates, diplomas, and associate (profile also includes information from the Boone, Carroll, Des Moines, and Newton campuses). *Special study options:* academic remediation for entering students, adult/continuing education programs, advanced placement credit, cooperative education, distance learning, English as a second language, honors programs, off-campus study, part-time degree program, services for LD students, student-designed majors, summer session for credit.

Library DMACC District Library plus 4 others.

Student Life *Housing Options:* coed. Campus housing is university owned. *Activities and Organizations:* drama/theater group, student-run newspaper, choral group, Agri-Business Club, Horticulture Club, Hospitality Arts Club, Iowa Delta Epsilon Chi, Dental Hygienist Club. *Campus security:* 24-hour emergency response devices and patrols, late-night transport/escort service. *Student services:* health clinic, personal/psychological counseling.

Athletics Member NJCAA. *Intercollegiate sports:* baseball M(s), basketball M(s)/W(s), cross-country running W(s), golf M(s)/W(s), volleyball W(s). *Intramural sports:* badminton M/W, basketball M/W, football M/W, golf M/W, soccer M/W, volleyball M/W.

Standardized Tests *Required for some:* SAT or ACT (for admission), ACT Compass.

Financial Aid Of all full-time matriculated undergraduates who enrolled in 2015, 377 Federal Work-Study jobs (averaging $1055).

Applying *Options:* electronic application, early admission, deferred entrance. *Required for some:* high school transcript, interview. *Application deadlines:* rolling (freshmen), rolling (transfers).

Freshman Application Contact Mr. Michael Lentsch, Director of Program Development, Des Moines Area Community College, 2006 South Ankeny Boulevard, Ankeny, IA 50021-8995. *Phone:* 515-965-7086.

Toll-free phone: 800-362-2127. *E-mail:* mjleutsch@dmacc.edu.

Website: http://www.dmacc.edu/.

Ellsworth Community College
Iowa Falls, Iowa

Director of Admissions Mrs. Nancy Walters, Registrar, Ellsworth Community College, 1100 College Avenue, Iowa Falls, IA 50126-1199. *Phone:* 641-648-4611. *Toll-free phone:* 800-ECC-9235.

Website: http://www.iavalley.cc.ia.us/ecc/.

Hawkeye Community College
Waterloo, Iowa

- **State and locally supported** 2-year, founded 1966
- **Rural** 320-acre campus
- **Endowment** $2.2 million
- **Coed,** 5,532 undergraduate students, 47% full-time, 55% women, 45% men

Undergraduates 2,620 full-time, 2,912 part-time. Students come from 12 states and territories; 9 other countries; 1% are from out of state; 10% Black or African American, non-Hispanic/Latino; 4% Hispanic/Latino; 1% Asian, non-Hispanic/Latino; 0.1% Native Hawaiian or other Pacific Islander, non-Hispanic/Latino; 0.2% American Indian or Alaska Native, non-Hispanic/Latino; 3% Two or more races, non-Hispanic/Latino; 0.9% international; 29% transferred in.

Freshmen *Admission:* 2,827 applied, 2,498 admitted, 1,046 enrolled. *Test scores:* ACT scores over 18: 49%; ACT scores over 24: 16%; ACT scores over 30: 3%.

Faculty *Total:* 288, 40% full-time, 10% with terminal degrees. *Student/faculty ratio:* 21:1.

Majors Accounting; agricultural/farm supplies retailing and wholesaling; agricultural power machinery operation; animal/livestock husbandry and production; autobody/collision and repair technology; automation engineer technology; automobile/automotive mechanics technology; carpentry; child-care provision; civil engineering technology; clinical/medical laboratory technology; commercial photography; computer/information technology services administration related; computer systems networking and telecommunications; criminal justice/police science; dental hygiene; desktop publishing and digital imaging design; diesel mechanics technology; digital communication and media/multimedia; electrical, electronic and communications engineering technology; electromechanical technology; emergency medical technology (EMT paramedic); energy management and systems technology; executive assistant/executive secretary; fire science/firefighting; golf course operation and grounds management; hospitality administration; human resources management; landscaping and groundskeeping; liberal arts and sciences/liberal studies; machine tool technology; medical administrative assistant and medical secretary; medical insurance coding; multi/interdisciplinary studies related; natural resources management and policy; occupational therapist assistant; physical therapy technology; registered nursing/registered nurse; respiratory care therapy; sales, distribution, and marketing operations; web page, digital/multimedia and information resources design.

Academics *Calendar:* semesters. *Degree:* certificates, diplomas, and associate. *Special study options:* academic remediation for entering students, accelerated degree program, adult/continuing education programs, advanced placement credit, cooperative education, distance learning, English as a second language, external degree program, part-time degree program, services for LD students, study abroad, summer session for credit. *ROTC:* Army (c).

Library Hawkeye Community College Library. *Books:* 29,615 (physical), 162,828 (digital/electronic); *Serial titles:* 156 (physical), 44 (digital/electronic); *Databases:* 28. Weekly public service hours: 70; students can reserve study rooms.

Student Life *Housing:* college housing not available. *Activities and Organizations:* drama/theater group, choral group, Student Leadership, Phi Theta Kappa, Student Ambassadors, Physical Therapy Asst, Natural Resources. *Campus security:* 24-hour patrols. *Student services:* health clinic, personal/psychological counseling, women's center.

Athletics Member NJCAA. *Intercollegiate sports:* riflery M/W, soccer M/W. *Intramural sports:* badminton M/W, basketball M/W, bowling M/W, football M/W, golf M/W, soccer M/W, softball M/W, table tennis M/W, volleyball M/W.

Standardized Tests *Required:* ACT Compass or the equivalent from ACT or accredited college course(s) (for admission). *Required for some:* ACT (for admission).

Costs (2016–17) *Tuition:* state resident $4508 full-time, $161 per credit hour part-time; nonresident $5208 full-time, $186 per credit hour part-time. *Required fees:* $210 full-time, $8 per credit hour part-time. *Payment plan:* installment.

Applying *Options:* electronic application, deferred entrance. *Required:* high school transcript. *Application deadlines:* rolling (freshmen), rolling (transfers). *Notification:* continuous (freshmen), continuous (transfers).

Freshman Application Contact Ms. Holly Grimm-See, Associate Director, Admissions and Recruitment, Hawkeye Community College, PO Box 8015, Waterloo, IA 50704-8015. *Phone:* 319-296-4277. *Toll-free phone:* 800-670-4769. *Fax:* 319-296-2505. *E-mail:* holly.grimm-see@hawkeyecollege.edu. *Website:* http://www.hawkeyecollege.edu/.

Indian Hills Community College
Ottumwa, Iowa

Freshman Application Contact Mrs. Jane Sapp, Admissions Officer, Indian Hills Community College, 525 Grandview Avenue, Building #1, Ottumwa, IA 52501-1398. *Phone:* 641-683-5155. *Toll-free phone:* 800-726-2585. *Website:* http://www.ihcc.cc.ia.us/.

Iowa Central Community College
Fort Dodge, Iowa

- **State and locally supported** 2-year, founded 1966
- **Small-town** 110-acre campus
- **Coed,** 5,634 undergraduate students, 52% full-time, 50% women, 50% men

Undergraduates 2,956 full-time, 2,678 part-time. Students come from 38 states and territories; 28 other countries; 9% are from out of state; 9% Black or African American, non-Hispanic/Latino; 8% Hispanic/Latino; 1% Asian, non-Hispanic/Latino; 0.2% Native Hawaiian or other Pacific Islander, non-Hispanic/Latino; 0.6% American Indian or Alaska Native, non-Hispanic/Latino; 1% Two or more races, non-Hispanic/Latino; 6% Race/ethnicity unknown; 1% international; 3% transferred in; 18% live on campus.

Freshmen *Admission:* 1,092 applied, 1,247 enrolled.

Faculty *Total:* 416, 21% full-time. *Student/faculty ratio:* 19:1.

Majors Accounting; administrative assistant and secretarial science; airline pilot and flight crew; automobile/automotive mechanics technology; aviation/airway management; biological and physical sciences; broadcast journalism; business administration and management; business teacher education; carpentry; clinical/medical laboratory technology; community organization and advocacy; computer engineering technology; criminal justice/police science; data processing and data processing technology; drafting and design technology; education; electrical, electronic and communications engineering technology; hospitality and recreation marketing; industrial radiologic technology; journalism; liberal arts and sciences/liberal studies; licensed practical/vocational nurse training; machine tool technology; mass communication/media; medical/clinical assistant; occupational therapy; physical therapy; radio and television; registered nursing/registered nurse; science teacher education; social work; sociology; telecommunications technology; welding technology.

Academics *Calendar:* semesters. *Degree:* certificates, diplomas, and associate. *Special study options:* academic remediation for entering students, adult/continuing education programs, advanced placement credit, cooperative education, distance learning, English as a second language, independent study, internships, part-time degree program, services for LD students, study abroad, summer session for credit.

Library Iowa Central Community College Library plus 1 other. Students can reserve study rooms.

Student Life *Housing Options:* men-only, women-only. Campus housing is university owned. *Activities and Organizations:* drama/theater group, student-run newspaper, radio station, choral group, marching band, Student Senate, BPA, Phi Beta Lambda. *Campus security:* 24-hour emergency response devices and patrols, student patrols, late-night transport/escort service, controlled dormitory access. *Student services:* health clinic, personal/psychological counseling.

Athletics Member NJCAA. *Intercollegiate sports:* baseball M(s), basketball M(s)/W(s), bowling M(s)/W(s), cheerleading M(s)/W(s), cross-country running M/W, football M(s), golf M(s)/W(s), rugby M(c), soccer M(s)/W(s), softball W(s), swimming and diving M/W, tennis M(s)/W(s), volleyball W(s), wrestling M(s). *Intramural sports:* basketball M/W, football M, golf M/W, softball W, table tennis M/W, tennis M/W, volleyball M/W, weight lifting M, wrestling M.

Costs (2016–17) *Tuition:* state resident $172 per credit hour part-time; nonresident $247 per credit hour part-time. Full-time tuition and fees vary according to course load and program. Part-time tuition and fees vary according to course load and program. *Payment plan:* installment.

Applying *Options:* electronic application, early admission, deferred entrance. *Required for some:* high school transcript, letters of recommendation, interview. *Recommended:* high school transcript. *Application deadlines:* rolling (freshmen), rolling (transfers). *Notification:* continuous (freshmen), continuous (transfers).

Freshman Application Contact Mrs. Sue Flattery, Enrollment Management Secretary, Iowa Central Community College, One Triton Circle, Fort Dodge, IA 50501. *Phone:* 515-574-1010 Ext. 2402. *Toll-free phone:* 800-362-2793. *Fax:* 515-576-7207. *E-mail:* flattery@iowacentral.com. *Website:* http://www.iccc.cc.ia.us/.

Iowa Lakes Community College
Estherville, Iowa

Freshman Application Contact Iowa Lakes Community College, IA. *Phone:* 712-362-7923 Ext. 7923. *Toll-free phone:* 800-521-5054. *E-mail:* info@iowalakes.edu. *Website:* http://www.iowalakes.edu/.

Iowa Western Community College
Council Bluffs, Iowa

Freshman Application Contact Ms. Tori Christie, Director of Admissions, Iowa Western Community College, 2700 College Road, Box 4-C, Council Bluffs, IA 51502. *Phone:* 712-325-3288. *Toll-free phone:* 800-432-5852. *E-mail:* admissions@iwcc.edu. *Website:* http://www.iwcc.edu/.

Kaplan University, Cedar Falls
Cedar Falls, Iowa

Freshman Application Contact Kaplan University, Cedar Falls, 7009 Nordic Drive, Cedar Falls, IA 50613. *Phone:* 319-277-0220. *Toll-free phone:* 800-987-7734. *Website:* http://www.kaplanuniversity.edu/.

Kaplan University, Cedar Rapids
Cedar Rapids, Iowa

Freshman Application Contact Kaplan University, Cedar Rapids, 3165 Edgewood Parkway, SW, Cedar Rapids, IA 52404. *Phone:* 319-363-0481. *Toll-free phone:* 800-987-7734. *Website:* http://www.kaplanuniversity.edu/.

Kaplan University, Des Moines
Urbandale, Iowa

Freshman Application Contact Kaplan University, Des Moines, 4655 121st Street, Urbandale, IA 50323. *Phone:* 515-727-2100. *Toll-free phone:* 800-987-7734. *Website:* http://www.kaplanuniversity.edu/.

Kirkwood Community College
Cedar Rapids, Iowa

Freshman Application Contact Kirkwood Community College, PO Box 2068, Cedar Rapids, IA 52406-2068. *Phone:* 319-398-5517. *Toll-free phone:* 800-332-2055. *Website:* http://www.kirkwood.edu/.

Marshalltown Community College
Marshalltown, Iowa

Freshman Application Contact Ms. Deana Inman, Director of Admissions, Marshalltown Community College, 3700 South Center Street, Marshalltown, IA 50158-4760. *Phone:* 641-752-7106. *Toll-free phone:* 866-622-4748. *Fax:* 641-752-8149. *Website:* http://www.marshalltowncommunitycollege.com/.

Muscatine Community College
Muscatine, Iowa

Freshman Application Contact Gary Mohr, Executive Director of Enrollment Management and Marketing, Muscatine Community College, 152 Colorado Street, Muscatine, IA 52761-5396. *Phone:* 563-336-3322. *Toll-free phone:* 800-351-4669. *Fax:* 563-336-3350. *E-mail:* gmohr@eicc.edu. *Website:* http://www.eicc.edu/general/muscatine/.

Northeast Iowa Community College
Calmar, Iowa

- **State and locally supported** 2-year, founded 1966, part of Iowa Area Community Colleges System
- **Rural** 210-acre campus
- **Coed,** 4,786 undergraduate students, 28% full-time, 55% women, 45% men

Undergraduates 1,326 full-time, 3,460 part-time. 15% are from out of state; 4% Black or African American, non-Hispanic/Latino; 2% Hispanic/Latino; 0.4% Asian, non-Hispanic/Latino; 0.3% Native Hawaiian or other Pacific Islander, non-Hispanic/Latino; 0.5% American Indian or Alaska Native, non-Hispanic/Latino; 1% Two or more races, non-Hispanic/Latino; 3% Race/ethnicity unknown; 0.3% international; 4% transferred in. *Retention:* 63% of full-time freshmen returned.
Freshmen *Admission:* 1,720 applied, 784 admitted, 537 enrolled.
Faculty *Total:* 331, 38% full-time, 6% with terminal degrees. *Student/faculty ratio:* 13:1.
Majors Accounting; administrative assistant and secretarial science; agribusiness; agricultural and food products processing; agricultural power machinery operation; agricultural production; automobile/automotive mechanics technology; business administration and management; business automation/technology/data entry; clinical/medical laboratory technology; computer programming (specific applications); construction trades; cosmetology; crop production; dairy husbandry and production; desktop publishing and digital imaging design; electrical, electronic and communications engineering technology; electrician; emergency medical technology (EMT paramedic); energy management and systems technology; fire science/firefighting; health information/medical records technology; liberal arts and sciences/liberal studies; plumbing technology; radiologic technology/science; registered nursing/registered nurse; respiratory care therapy; sales, distribution, and marketing operations; social work.
Academics *Calendar:* semesters. *Degree:* certificates, diplomas, and associate. *Special study options:* academic remediation for entering students, adult/continuing education programs, advanced placement credit, cooperative education, distance learning, double majors, external degree program, honors programs, internships, off-campus study, part-time degree program, services for LD students, summer session for credit.
Library Wilder Resource Center and Burton Payne Library plus 2 others.

Student Life *Housing:* college housing not available. *Activities and Organizations:* student-run newspaper, choral group, national fraternities, national sororities. *Campus security:* security personnel on weeknights. *Student services:* personal/psychological counseling.
Athletics *Intramural sports:* basketball M/W, bowling M/W, football M, golf M/W, skiing (downhill) M/W, softball M/W, volleyball M/W.
Costs (2016–17) *Tuition:* state resident $4480 full-time, $160 per credit hour part-time; nonresident $4620 full-time, $165 per credit hour part-time. Full-time tuition and fees vary according to course load and program. Part-time tuition and fees vary according to course load and program. *Required fees:* $532 full-time, $19 per credit hour part-time. *Payment plan:* installment. *Waivers:* employees or children of employees.
Applying *Options:* electronic application. *Recommended:* high school transcript.
Freshman Application Contact Ms. Brynn McConnell, Admissions Representative, Northeast Iowa Community College, Calmar, IA 52132. *Phone:* 563-562-3263 Ext. 307. *Toll-free phone:* 800-728-CALMAR. *Fax:* 563-562-4369. *E-mail:* mcconnellb@nicc.edu. *Website:* http://www.nicc.edu/.

North Iowa Area Community College
Mason City, Iowa

Freshman Application Contact Ms. Rachel McGuire, Director of Enrollment Services, North Iowa Area Community College, 500 College Drive, Mason City, IA 50401. *Phone:* 641-422-4104. *Toll-free phone:* 888-GO NIACC Ext. 4245. *Fax:* 641-422-4385. *E-mail:* request@niacc.edu. *Website:* http://www.niacc.edu/.

Northwest Iowa Community College
Sheldon, Iowa

Director of Admissions Ms. Lisa Story, Director of Enrollment Management, Northwest Iowa Community College, 603 West Park Street, Sheldon, IA 51201-1046. *Phone:* 712-324-5061 Ext. 115. *Toll-free phone:* 800-352-4907. *E-mail:* lstory@nwicc.edu. *Website:* http://www.nwicc.edu/.

Ross College
Bettendorf, Iowa

Freshman Application Contact Ross College, 2119 East Kimberly Road, Bettendorf, IA 52722. *Phone:* 563-344-1500. *Toll-free phone:* 866-815-5578. *Website:* http://www.rosseducation.edu/.

St. Luke's College
Sioux City, Iowa

- **Independent** primarily 2-year, founded 1967, part of UnityPoint Health
- **Rural** 3-acre campus with easy access to Omaha
- **Endowment** $1.0 million
- **Coed,** 259 undergraduate students, 46% full-time, 90% women, 10% men

Undergraduates 118 full-time, 141 part-time. Students come from 13 states and territories; 1 other country; 35% are from out of state; 2% Black or African American, non-Hispanic/Latino; 8% Hispanic/Latino; 2% Asian, non-Hispanic/Latino; 0.4% American Indian or Alaska Native, non-Hispanic/Latino; 2% Race/ethnicity unknown; 8% transferred in. *Retention:* 86% of full-time freshmen returned.
Freshmen *Admission:* 15 applied, 10 admitted, 10 enrolled. *Average high school GPA:* 3.37.
Faculty *Total:* 48, 52% full-time, 8% with terminal degrees. *Student/faculty ratio:* 5:1.
Majors Health services/allied health/health sciences; radiologic technology/science; registered nursing/registered nurse; respiratory care therapy.
Academics *Calendar:* semesters. *Degrees:* certificates, associate, and bachelor's. *Special study options:* advanced placement credit, distance learning, services for LD students, summer session for credit.
Library St. Luke's College. *Books:* 2,705 (physical); *Serial titles:* 63 (physical); *Databases:* 31. Weekly public service hours: 65.
Student Life *Housing:* college housing not available. *Campus security:* 24-hour emergency response devices and patrols, late-night transport/escort service. *Student services:* health clinic, personal/psychological counseling.
Standardized Tests *Required:* SAT or ACT (for admission).
Costs (2017–18) *Tuition:* $18,900 full-time, $525 per credit part-time. Full-time tuition and fees vary according to course load, degree level, and program. Part-time tuition and fees vary according to course load, degree level, and program. *Required fees:* $1560 full-time. *Payment plans:* installment, deferred payment. *Waivers:* employees or children of employees.

Financial Aid Of all full-time matriculated undergraduates who enrolled in 2016, 78 applied for aid, 78 were judged to have need. 6 Federal Work-Study jobs (averaging $750). 1 state and other part-time job (averaging $500). *Average percent of need met:* 80%. *Average financial aid package:* $14,964. *Average need-based loan:* $6000. *Average need-based gift aid:* $5123. *Average indebtedness upon graduation:* $18,665.

Applying *Options:* electronic application. *Application fee:* $50. *Required:* essay or personal statement, high school transcript, minimum 2.5 GPA, interview. *Application deadline:* 8/1 (freshmen). *Notification:* continuous (transfers).

Freshman Application Contact Ms. Sherry McCarthy, Admissions Coordinator, St. Luke's College, 2720 Stone Park Boulevard, Sioux City, IA 51104. *Phone:* 712-279-3149. *Toll-free phone:* 800-352-4660 Ext. 3149. *Fax:* 712-233-8017. *E-mail:* sherry.mccarthy@stlukescollege.edu. *Website:* http://stlukescollege.edu/.

Scott Community College

Bettendorf, Iowa

Freshman Application Contact Mr. Gary Mohr, Executive Director of Enrollment Management and Marketing, Scott Community College, 500 Belmont Road, Bettendorf, IA 52722-6804. *Phone:* 563-336-3322. *Toll-free phone:* 800-895-0811. *Fax:* 563-336-3350. *E-mail:* gmohr@eicc.edu. *Website:* http://www.eicc.edu/scc/.

Southeastern Community College

West Burlington, Iowa

- **State and locally supported** 2-year, founded 1968, part of Iowa Department of Education Division of Community Colleges
- **Small-town** 160-acre campus
- **Coed,** 3,167 undergraduate students, 41% full-time, 51% women, 39% men

Undergraduates 1,312 full-time, 1,532 part-time. 12% are from out of state; 5% Black or African American, non-Hispanic/Latino; 5% Hispanic/Latino; 1% Asian, non-Hispanic/Latino; 0.1% Native Hawaiian or other Pacific Islander, non-Hispanic/Latino; 0.7% American Indian or Alaska Native, non-Hispanic/Latino; 4% Two or more races, non-Hispanic/Latino; 6% Race/ethnicity unknown; 0.9% international; 2% transferred in; 2% live on campus.

Freshmen *Admission:* 1,008 applied, 780 admitted, 494 enrolled. *Average high school GPA:* 2.93.

Faculty *Total:* 120, 56% full-time, 11% with terminal degrees. *Student/faculty ratio:* 17:1.

Majors Accounting; administrative assistant and secretarial science; agricultural business and management; agronomy and crop science; artificial intelligence; automobile/automotive mechanics technology; biomedical technology; business administration and management; child development; computer programming; construction engineering technology; cosmetology; criminal justice/law enforcement administration; drafting and design technology; electrical, electronic and communications engineering technology; emergency medical technology (EMT paramedic); engineering related; industrial radiologic technology; information science/studies; liberal arts and sciences/liberal studies; licensed practical/vocational nurse training; machine tool technology; mechanical engineering/mechanical technology; medical/clinical assistant; registered nursing/registered nurse; respiratory care therapy; substance abuse/addiction counseling; trade and industrial teacher education; welding technology.

Academics *Calendar:* semesters. *Degree:* certificates, diplomas, and associate. *Special study options:* adult/continuing education programs, part-time degree program.

Library Yohe Memorial Library.

Student Life *Housing Options:* coed, men-only, special housing for students with disabilities. Campus housing is university owned. *Campus security:* controlled dormitory access, night patrols by trained security personnel.

Athletics Member NJCAA. *Intercollegiate sports:* baseball M(s), basketball M(s), softball W(s), volleyball W(s). *Intramural sports:* basketball M, bowling M/W, softball M/W, volleyball M/W, weight lifting M/W.

Financial Aid Of all full-time matriculated undergraduates who enrolled in 2015, 1,027 applied for aid, 810 were judged to have need. In 2015, 30 non-need-based awards were made. *Average financial aid package:* $6405. *Average need-based loan:* $3008. *Average need-based gift aid:* $4506. *Average non-need-based aid:* $3698.

Applying *Options:* early admission, deferred entrance.

Freshman Application Contact Ms. Stacy White, Admissions, Southeastern Community College, 1500 West Agency Road, West Burlington, IA 52655-0180. *Phone:* 319-752-2731 Ext. 8137. *Toll-free phone:* 866-722-4692. *E-mail:* admoff@scciowa.edu. *Website:* http://www.scciowa.edu/.

Southwestern Community College

Creston, Iowa

Freshman Application Contact Ms. Lisa Carstens, Admissions Coordinator, Southwestern Community College, 1501 West Townline Street, Creston, IA 50801. *Phone:* 641-782-7081 Ext. 453. *Toll-free phone:* 800-247-4023. *Fax:* 641-782-3312. *E-mail:* carstens@swcciowa.edu. *Website:* http://www.swcciowa.edu/.

Vatterott College

Des Moines, Iowa

Freshman Application Contact Mr. Dana Smith, Co-Director, Vatterott College, 7000 Fleur Drive, Suite 290, Des Moines, IA 50321. *Phone:* 515-309-9000. *Toll-free phone:* 888-553-6627. *Fax:* 515-309-0366. *Website:* http://www.vatterott.edu/.

Western Iowa Tech Community College

Sioux City, Iowa

- **State-supported** 2-year, founded 1966, part of Iowa Department of Education Division of Community Colleges
- **Suburban** 143-acre campus
- **Endowment** $1.7 million
- **Coed**

Undergraduates 2,292 full-time, 3,860 part-time. Students come from 30 states and territories; 8 other countries; 10% are from out of state; 3% Black or African American, non-Hispanic/Latino; 15% Hispanic/Latino; 2% Asian, non-Hispanic/Latino; 0.2% Native Hawaiian or other Pacific Islander, non-Hispanic/Latino; 2% American Indian or Alaska Native, non-Hispanic/Latino; 2% Two or more races, non-Hispanic/Latino; 11% Race/ethnicity unknown; 0.7% international; 4% transferred in; 5% live on campus. *Retention:* 52% of full-time freshmen returned.

Faculty *Student/faculty ratio:* 16:1.

Academics *Calendar:* semesters. *Degree:* certificates, diplomas, and associate. *Special study options:* academic remediation for entering students, accelerated degree program, advanced placement credit, cooperative education, distance learning, double majors, English as a second language, honors programs, independent study, internships, off-campus study, part-time degree program, services for LD students, student-designed majors, study abroad, summer session for credit.

Library Western Iowa Tech Community College Library Services plus 1 other. *Books:* 17,232 (physical), 12,438 (digital/electronic). Weekly public service hours: 60.

Student Life *Campus security:* 24-hour emergency response devices and patrols, controlled dormitory access.

Standardized Tests *Recommended:* ACT (for admission), SAT or ACT (for admission).

Financial Aid Of all full-time matriculated undergraduates who enrolled in 2015, 148 Federal Work-Study jobs (averaging $1000). 2 state and other part-time jobs (averaging $2500).

Applying *Options:* electronic application, early admission, deferred entrance. *Recommended:* high school transcript.

Freshman Application Contact Ms. Lora Vander Zwaag, Registrar, Western Iowa Tech Community College, 4647 Stone Avenue, Sioux City, IA 51106. *Phone:* 712-274-6400. *Toll-free phone:* 800-352-4649 Ext. 6403. *Fax:* 712-274-6441. *E-mail:* lora.vanderzwaag@witcc.edu. *Website:* http://www.witcc.edu/.

KANSAS

Allen Community College

Iola, Kansas

- **State and locally supported** 2-year, founded 1923, part of Kansas State Board of Regents
- **Small-town** 88-acre campus
- **Coed,** 2,379 undergraduate students

Faculty *Student/faculty ratio:* 18:1.

Majors Accounting; administrative assistant and secretarial science; agricultural production; architecture; art; athletic training; banking and financial support services; biology/biological sciences; business administration and management; business/commerce; business teacher education; chemistry; child development; computer science; computer systems networking and telecommunications; criminal justice/law enforcement administration; data processing and data processing technology; drafting and design technology;

dramatic/theater arts; economics; electrical and electronics engineering; electrical, electronic and communications engineering technology; elementary education; emergency medical technology (EMT paramedic); engineering; engineering technology; equestrian studies; family and consumer sciences/human sciences; farm and ranch management; forestry; general studies; geography; health aide; health and physical education/fitness; history; home health aide/home attendant; hospital and health-care facilities administration; humanities; industrial technology; information science/studies; journalism; language interpretation and translation; library and information science; mathematics; music; nuclear/nuclear power technology; nursing assistant/aide and patient care assistant/aide; parks, recreation and leisure facilities management; philosophy; physical therapy; physics; political science and government; pre-dentistry studies; pre-law studies; premedical studies; pre-pharmacy studies; pre-veterinary studies; psychology; religious studies; rhetoric and composition; secondary education; social work; sociology; technology/industrial arts teacher education; writing.

Academics *Calendar:* semesters. *Degree:* certificates and associate. *Special study options:* academic remediation for entering students, adult/continuing education programs, cooperative education, distance learning, English as a second language, independent study, internships, part-time degree program, services for LD students, student-designed majors, summer session for credit.

Library Learning Resource Center plus 1 other.

Student Life *Housing Options:* men-only, women-only. Campus housing is university owned. *Activities and Organizations:* drama/theater group, student-run newspaper, choral group, Intramurals, Student Senate, Theatre, Phi Theta Kappa. *Student services:* personal/psychological counseling.

Athletics Member NJCAA. *Intercollegiate sports:* baseball M(s), basketball M(s)/W(s), cheerleading M(s)/W(s), cross-country running M(s)/W(s), golf M(s), soccer M(s)/W(s), softball W(s), track and field M(s)/W(s), volleyball W(s). *Intramural sports:* basketball M/W, football M/W, soccer M/W, softball M/W, table tennis M/W, tennis M/W, volleyball M/W.

Costs (2017–18) *Tuition:* state resident $1920 full-time; nonresident $1920 full-time. *Required fees:* $1280 full-time. *Room and board:* $4950. *Payment plan:* installment. *Waivers:* senior citizens and employees or children of employees.

Financial Aid Of all full-time matriculated undergraduates who enrolled in 2008, 510 applied for aid, 411 were judged to have need, 384 had their need fully met. 40 Federal Work-Study jobs (averaging $2600). 112 state and other part-time jobs (averaging $2600). In 2008, 22 non-need-based awards were made. *Average percent of need met:* 80%. *Average financial aid package:* $4738. *Average need-based loan:* $2482. *Average need-based gift aid:* $3257. *Average non-need-based aid:* $1241.

Applying *Options:* electronic application, early admission, deferred entrance. *Required:* high school transcript. *Application deadlines:* 8/24 (freshmen), 8/24 (transfers). *Notification:* continuous (freshmen), continuous (transfers).

Freshman Application Contact Rebecca Bilderback, Director of Admissions, Allen Community College, 1801 North Cottonwood, Iola, KS 66749. *Phone:* 620-365-5116 Ext. 267. *Fax:* 620-365-7406.
E-mail: bilderback@allencc.edu.
Website: http://www.allencc.edu/.

Barton County Community College
Great Bend, Kansas

- **State and locally supported** 2-year, founded 1969, part of Kansas Board of Regents
- **Rural** 140-acre campus
- **Coed**

Undergraduates 1,978 full-time, 3,314 part-time. 13% Black or African American, non-Hispanic/Latino; 10% Hispanic/Latino; 4% Asian, non-Hispanic/Latino; 0.9% Native Hawaiian or other Pacific Islander, non-Hispanic/Latino; 0.7% American Indian or Alaska Native, non-Hispanic/Latino; 2% Two or more races, non-Hispanic/Latino; 2% Race/ethnicity unknown; 0.5% international; 8% live on campus.

Faculty *Student/faculty ratio:* 25:1.

Academics *Calendar:* semesters. *Degree:* certificates and associate. *Special study options:* academic remediation for entering students, accelerated degree program, adult/continuing education programs, advanced placement credit, cooperative education, distance learning, double majors, English as a second language, external degree program, honors programs, independent study, internships, part-time degree program, services for LD students, summer session for credit. *ROTC:* Army (b).

Library Barton County Community College Library.

Student Life *Campus security:* 24-hour emergency response devices and patrols.

Athletics Member NJCAA.

Costs (2016–17) *Tuition:* state resident $2304 full-time, $72 per credit hour part-time; nonresident $3296 full-time, $103 per credit hour part-time. Full-time tuition and fees vary according to course load. Part-time tuition and fees vary according to course load. *Required fees:* $1024 full-time, $32 per credit

hour part-time. *Room and board:* $8003. Room and board charges vary according to board plan. *Payment plans:* installment, deferred payment.

Applying *Options:* electronic application, early admission. *Recommended:* high school transcript.

Freshman Application Contact Ms. Tana Cooper, Director of Admissions and Promotions, Barton County Community College, 245 Northeast 30th Road, Great Bend, KS 67530. *Phone:* 620-792-9241. *Toll-free phone:* 800-722-6842. *Fax:* 620-786-1160. *E-mail:* admissions@bartonccc.edu. *Website:* http://www.bartonccc.edu/.

Bryan University
Topeka, Kansas

Admissions Office Contact Bryan University, 1527 SW Fairlawn Road, Topeka, KS 66604. *Website:* http://www.bryanu.edu/.

Butler Community College
El Dorado, Kansas

Freshman Application Contact Mr. Glenn Lygrisse, Interim Director of Enrollment Management, Butler Community College, 901 South Haverhill Road, El Dorado, KS 67042. *Phone:* 316-321-2222. *Fax:* 316-322-3109. *E-mail:* admissions@butlercc.edu. *Website:* http://www.butlercc.edu/.

Cloud County Community College
Concordia, Kansas

- **State and locally supported** 2-year, founded 1965, part of Kansas Community College System
- **Rural** 35-acre campus
- **Coed,** 2,038 undergraduate students, 40% full-time, 59% women, 41% men

Undergraduates 811 full-time, 1,227 part-time. Students come from 22 states and territories; 38 other countries; 8% are from out of state; 7% Black or African American, non-Hispanic/Latino; 6% Hispanic/Latino; 1% Asian, non-Hispanic/Latino; 0.6% American Indian or Alaska Native, non-Hispanic/Latino; 4% Two or more races, non-Hispanic/Latino; 4% Race/ethnicity unknown; 4% international; 6% transferred in. *Retention:* 63% of full-time freshmen returned.

Freshmen *Admission:* 332 enrolled.

Faculty *Total:* 306, 13% full-time. *Student/faculty ratio:* 11:1.

Majors Administrative assistant and secretarial science; agricultural business and management; agricultural/farm supplies retailing and wholesaling; business administration and management; business, management, and marketing related; child-care and support services management; child development; criminal justice/police science; graphic design; journalism; legal assistant/paralegal; liberal arts and sciences/liberal studies; mechanic and repair technologies related; office occupations and clerical services; radio and television broadcasting technology; registered nursing/registered nurse; system, networking, and LAN/WAN management; teacher assistant/aide; web page, digital/multimedia and information resources design.

Academics *Calendar:* semesters. *Degree:* certificates, diplomas, and associate. *Special study options:* academic remediation for entering students, adult/continuing education programs, advanced placement credit, cooperative education, distance learning, English as a second language, freshman honors college, honors programs, internships, part-time degree program, services for LD students, summer session for credit.

Library Cloud County Community College Library. *Books:* 16,807 (physical), 9,784 (digital/electronic); *Databases:* 45. Weekly public service hours: 40.

Student Life *Housing Options:* Campus housing is university owned. *Activities and Organizations:* drama/theater group, student-run newspaper, radio station, choral group. *Campus security:* 24-hour emergency response devices. *Student services:* health clinic.

Athletics Member NJCAA. *Intercollegiate sports:* baseball M(s), basketball M(s)/W(s), cheerleading M(s)/W(s), cross-country running M(s)/W(s), soccer M(s), softball W(s), tennis M(s)/W(s), track and field M(s)/W(s), volleyball W(s), wrestling M(s). *Intramural sports:* baseball M, basketball M/W, equestrian sports M/W, softball W, volleyball M/W.

Costs (2017–18) *Tuition:* area resident $2070 full-time, $69 per credit hour part-time; state resident $2220 full-time, $74 per credit hour part-time; nonresident $2370 full-time, $79 per credit hour part-time. Full-time tuition and fees vary according to course level, course load, location, program, reciprocity agreements, and student level. Part-time tuition and fees vary according to course level, course load, location, program, reciprocity agreements, and student level. *Required fees:* $750 full-time, $25 per credit hour part-time. *Room and board:* $5800. Room and board charges vary according to board plan and housing facility. *Payment plan:* installment. *Waivers:* senior citizens and employees or children of employees.

Financial Aid Of all full-time matriculated undergraduates who enrolled in 2015, 122 Federal Work-Study jobs (averaging $800).
Applying *Options:* early admission, deferred entrance. *Required:* high school transcript. *Application deadlines:* 9/11 (freshmen), 9/11 (transfers). *Notification:* continuous (freshmen), continuous (transfers).
Freshman Application Contact Shane Olson, Director of Admissions, Cloud County Community College, 2221 Campus Drive, PO Box 1002, Concordia, KS 66901-1002. *Phone:* 785-243-1435 Ext. 213. *Toll-free phone:* 800-729-5101. *E-mail:* solson@cloud.edu.
Website: http://www.cloud.edu/.

Coffeyville Community College
Coffeyville, Kansas

Freshman Application Contact Stacia Meek, Admissions Counselor/Marketing Event Coordinator, Coffeyville Community College, 400 West 11th Street, Coffeyville, KS 67337-5063. *Phone:* 620-252-7100. *Toll-free phone:* 877-51-RAVEN. *E-mail:* staciam@coffeyville.edu. *Website:* http://www.coffeyville.edu/.

Colby Community College
Colby, Kansas

Freshman Application Contact Ms. Nikol Nolan, Admissions Director, Colby Community College, Colby, KS 67701-4099. *Phone:* 785-462-3984 Ext. 5496. *Toll-free phone:* 888-634-9350. *Fax:* 785-460-4691. *E-mail:* admissions@colbycc.edu. *Website:* http://www.colbycc.edu/.

Cowley County Community College and Area Vocational–Technical School
Arkansas City, Kansas

Freshman Application Contact Ms. Lory West, Director of Admissions, Cowley County Community College and Area Vocational–Technical School, PO Box 1147, Arkansas City, KS 67005. *Phone:* 620-441-5594. *Toll-free phone:* 800-593-CCCC. *Fax:* 620-441-5350. *E-mail:* admissions@cowley.edu. *Website:* http://www.cowley.edu/.

Dodge City Community College
Dodge City, Kansas

- **State and locally supported** 2-year, founded 1935, part of Kansas State Board of Regents
- **Small-town** 143-acre campus
- **Coed,** 1,804 undergraduate students, 53% full-time, 47% women, 53% men

Undergraduates 951 full-time, 853 part-time. 9% Black or African American, non-Hispanic/Latino; 40% Hispanic/Latino; 1% Asian, non-Hispanic/Latino; 0.2% Native Hawaiian or other Pacific Islander, non-Hispanic/Latino; 1% American Indian or Alaska Native, non-Hispanic/Latino; 2% Two or more races, non-Hispanic/Latino.
Faculty *Total:* 195, 27% full-time. *Student/faculty ratio:* 12:1.
Majors Accounting; administrative assistant and secretarial science; agricultural business and management; agricultural economics; agricultural mechanization; agronomy and crop science; animal sciences; art; athletic training; automobile/automotive mechanics technology; behavioral sciences; biological and physical sciences; biology/biological sciences; broadcast journalism; business administration and management; chemistry; child development; clinical laboratory science/medical technology; communications technology; computer programming; computer science; construction engineering technology; cosmetology; criminal justice/law enforcement administration; data processing and data processing technology; dramatic/theater arts; education; electrical, electronic and communications engineering technology; elementary education; engineering; engineering technology; English; equestrian studies; farm and ranch management; finance; fire science/firefighting; forestry; health information/medical records administration; history; humanities; hydrology and water resources science; industrial technology; information science/studies; journalism; legal administrative assistant/secretary; liberal arts and sciences/liberal studies; licensed practical/vocational nurse training; marketing/marketing management; mass communication/media; mathematics; medical administrative assistant and medical secretary; music; music teacher education; physical education teaching and coaching; physical sciences; physical therapy; physics; political science and government; pre-engineering; pre-pharmacy studies; psychology; radio and television; real estate; registered nursing/registered nurse; respiratory care therapy; rhetoric and composition; social sciences; social work; welding technology; wildlife biology.

Academics *Calendar:* semesters. *Degree:* certificates and associate. *Special study options:* academic remediation for entering students, adult/continuing education programs, advanced placement credit, cooperative education, distance learning, English as a second language, external degree program, internships, off-campus study, part-time degree program, services for LD students, summer session for credit.
Library Learning Resource Center. Students can reserve study rooms.
Student Life *Housing:* on-campus residence required for freshman year. *Options:* men-only, women-only. Campus housing is university owned. Freshman applicants given priority for college housing. *Activities and Organizations:* student-run radio and television station, choral group. *Campus security:* 24-hour emergency response devices and patrols, late-night transport/escort service, controlled dormitory access. *Student services:* personal/psychological counseling.
Athletics Member NJCAA. *Intercollegiate sports:* baseball M(s), basketball M(s)/W(s), cheerleading M(s)/W(s), cross-country running M(s)/W(s), football M(s), golf M(s)/W(s), soccer M(s)/W(s), softball W(s), track and field M(s)/W(s), volleyball W(s). *Intramural sports:* basketball M/W, bowling M/W, racquetball M/W, volleyball M/W, weight lifting M/W.
Costs (2017–18) *One-time required fee:* $50. *Tuition:* area resident $930 full-time, $31 per credit hour part-time; state resident $1470 full-time, $49 per credit hour part-time; nonresident $1710 full-time, $57 per credit hour part-time. *Required fees:* $1800 full-time, $40 per credit hour part-time, $25 per credit hour part-time. *Room and board:* $6400. Room and board charges vary according to board plan and housing facility. *Payment plans:* installment, deferred payment. *Waivers:* senior citizens and employees or children of employees.
Applying *Options:* electronic application, early admission, deferred entrance. *Required:* high school transcript. *Application deadlines:* rolling (freshmen), rolling (transfers). *Notification:* continuous (freshmen), continuous (transfers).
Freshman Application Contact Dodge City Community College, 2501 North 14th Avenue, Dodge City, KS 67801-2399. *Phone:* 620-225-1321. *Website:* http://www.dc3.edu/.

Donnelly College
Kansas City, Kansas

- **Independent Roman Catholic** primarily 2-year, founded 1949
- **Urban** 4-acre campus
- **Coed,** 318 undergraduate students, 74% full-time, 73% women, 27% men

Undergraduates 236 full-time, 82 part-time. Students come from 2 states and territories; 24 other countries; 32% are from out of state; 33% Black or African American, non-Hispanic/Latino; 45% Hispanic/Latino; 5% Asian, non-Hispanic/Latino; 0.9% Native Hawaiian or other Pacific Islander, non-Hispanic/Latino; 0.6% American Indian or Alaska Native, non-Hispanic/Latino; 3% Two or more races, non-Hispanic/Latino; 0.3% Race/ethnicity unknown; 2% international; 14% transferred in. *Retention:* 55% of full-time freshmen returned.
Freshmen *Admission:* 408 applied, 408 admitted, 97 enrolled.
Faculty *Total:* 49, 45% full-time. *Student/faculty ratio:* 10:1.
Majors Computer and information systems security; elementary education; liberal arts and sciences/liberal studies; nonprofit management.
Academics *Calendar:* semesters. *Degrees:* certificates, associate, and bachelor's. *Special study options:* academic remediation for entering students, advanced placement credit, distance learning, English as a second language, external degree program, honors programs, independent study, part-time degree program, services for LD students, summer session for credit.
Library Trant Memorial Library plus 1 other.
Student Life *Housing Options:* men-only, women-only. Campus housing is university owned. *Activities and Organizations:* Organization of Student Leadership, Student Ambassadors, Healthy Student Task Force, Men's Soccer Club, Women's Soccer Club. *Campus security:* 24-hour emergency response devices. *Student services:* personal/psychological counseling.
Athletics *Intramural sports:* basketball M/W, soccer M/W, volleyball M/W.
Costs (2016–17) *Comprehensive fee:* $13,702 includes full-time tuition ($6720), mandatory fees ($132), and room and board ($6850). Full-time tuition and fees vary according to course level, degree level, and program. Part-time tuition: $278 per credit hour. Part-time tuition and fees vary according to course level. *Required fees:* $3 per credit hour part-time, $60 per term part-time. *Room and board:* college room only: $4000. Room and board charges vary according to housing facility. *Payment plan:* installment. *Waivers:* senior citizens and employees or children of employees.
Applying *Options:* electronic application, early admission, deferred entrance. *Recommended:* high school transcript. *Application deadlines:* rolling (freshmen), rolling (transfers).
Freshman Application Contact Ms. Kimkisha Stevenson, Director of Admissions, Donnelly College, 608 North 18th Street, Kansas City, KS 66102. *Phone:* 913-621-8762. *Fax:* 913-621-8719.
E-mail: admissions@donnelly.edu.
Website: http://www.donnelly.edu/.

Flint Hills Technical College
Emporia, Kansas

Freshman Application Contact Admissions Office, Flint Hills Technical College, 3301 West 18th Avenue, Emporia, KS 66801. *Phone:* 620-341-1325. *Toll-free phone:* 800-711-6947. *Website:* http://www.fhtc.edu/.

Fort Scott Community College
Fort Scott, Kansas

Director of Admissions Mrs. Mert Barrows, Director of Admissions, Fort Scott Community College, 2108 South Horton, Fort Scott, KS 66701. *Phone:* 620-223-2700 Ext. 353. *Toll-free phone:* 800-874-3722. *Website:* http://www.fortscott.edu/.

Garden City Community College
Garden City, Kansas

Freshman Application Contact Office of Admissions, Garden City Community College, 801 Campus Drive, Garden City, KS 67846. *Phone:* 620-276-9531. *Toll-free phone:* 800-658-1696. *Fax:* 620-276-9650. *E-mail:* admissions@gccks.edu. *Website:* http://www.gccks.edu/.

Hesston College
Hesston, Kansas

- **Independent Mennonite** primarily 2-year, founded 1909
- **Small-town** 50-acre campus with easy access to Wichita
- **Endowment** $12.0 million
- **Coed,** 401 undergraduate students, 95% full-time, 58% women, 42% men

Undergraduates 382 full-time, 19 part-time. Students come from 30 states and territories; 14 other countries; 49% are from out of state; 5% Black or African American, non-Hispanic/Latino; 12% Hispanic/Latino; 2% Asian, non-Hispanic/Latino; 0.5% American Indian or Alaska Native, non-Hispanic/Latino; 4% Two or more races, non-Hispanic/Latino; 0.5% Race/ethnicity unknown; 9% international; 16% transferred in; 71% live on campus. *Retention:* 77% of full-time freshmen returned.
Freshmen *Admission:* 475 applied, 280 admitted, 139 enrolled. *Average high school GPA:* 3.41. *Test scores:* SAT critical reading scores over 500: 39%; SAT math scores over 500: 50%; SAT writing scores over 500: 36%; ACT scores over 18: 78%; SAT critical reading scores over 600: 14%; SAT math scores over 600: 17%; SAT writing scores over 600: 11%; ACT scores over 24: 27%; SAT math scores over 700: 3%; ACT scores over 30: 7%.
Faculty *Total:* 51, 75% full-time, 27% with terminal degrees. *Student/faculty ratio:* 8:1.
Majors Aeronautics/aviation/aerospace science and technology; airline pilot and flight crew; air traffic control; biblical studies; business administration and management; computer/information technology services administration related; early childhood education; general studies; kindergarten/preschool education; liberal arts and sciences/liberal studies; pastoral studies/counseling; registered nursing/registered nurse; youth ministry.
Academics *Calendar:* semesters. *Degrees:* associate and bachelor's. *Special study options:* academic remediation for entering students, adult/continuing education programs, advanced placement credit, cooperative education, double majors, English as a second language, independent study, internships, part-time degree program, services for LD students, summer session for credit.
Library Mary Miller Library. Students can reserve study rooms.
Student Life *Housing:* on-campus residence required through sophomore year. *Options:* men-only, women-only. Campus housing is university owned. Freshman campus housing is guaranteed. *Activities and Organizations:* drama/theater group, student-run newspaper, choral group, Peace and Service Club, Intramural Sports, Ministry Assistants. *Campus security:* 24-hour emergency response devices, controlled dormitory access. *Student services:* health clinic, personal/psychological counseling, women's center.
Athletics Member NJCAA. *Intercollegiate sports:* baseball M(s), basketball M(s)/W(s), cross-country running M(s)/W(s), golf M(s), soccer M(s)/W(s), softball W(s), tennis M(s)/W(s), track and field M(s)/W(s), volleyball W(s). *Intramural sports:* basketball M/W, golf M(c)/W(c), sand volleyball M/W, soccer M/W, ultimate Frisbee M/W, volleyball M/W.
Standardized Tests *Required:* SAT or ACT (for admission).
Costs (2017–18) *Comprehensive fee:* $34,996 includes full-time tuition ($25,988), mandatory fees ($430), and room and board ($8578). Full-time tuition and fees vary according to course load and program. Part-time tuition: $1079 per credit hour. Part-time tuition and fees vary according to course load. *Required fees:* $108 per term part-time. *Payment plans:* installment, deferred payment. *Waivers:* employees or children of employees.
Financial Aid Of all full-time matriculated undergraduates who enrolled in 2015, 120 Federal Work-Study jobs (averaging $800).

Applying *Options:* electronic application, early admission, deferred entrance. *Required:* high school transcript. *Required for some:* 2 letters of recommendation, interview. *Application deadlines:* rolling (freshmen), rolling (out-of-state freshmen), rolling (transfers).
Freshman Application Contact Rachel Swartzendruber-Miller, Vice President of Admissions, Hesston College, Hesston, KS 67062. *Phone:* 620-327-8206. *Toll-free phone:* 800-995-2757. *Fax:* 620-327-8300. *E-mail:* admissions@hesston.edu. *Website:* http://www.hesston.edu/.

Highland Community College
Highland, Kansas

Director of Admissions Ms. Cheryl Rasmussen, Vice President of Student Services, Highland Community College, 606 West Main Street, Highland, KS 66035. *Phone:* 785-442-6020. *Fax:* 785-442-6106. *Website:* http://www.highlandcc.edu/.

Hutchinson Community College
Hutchinson, Kansas

- **State and locally supported** 2-year, founded 1928, part of Kansas Board of Regents
- **Small-town** 47-acre campus with easy access to Wichita
- **Coed,** 5,868 undergraduate students, 40% full-time, 53% women, 47% men

Undergraduates 2,322 full-time, 3,546 part-time. Students come from 43 states and territories; 8 other countries; 7% are from out of state; 7% Black or African American, non-Hispanic/Latino; 11% Hispanic/Latino; 0.8% Asian, non-Hispanic/Latino; 0.1% Native Hawaiian or other Pacific Islander, non-Hispanic/Latino; 1% American Indian or Alaska Native, non-Hispanic/Latino; 4% Two or more races, non-Hispanic/Latino; 7% Race/ethnicity unknown; 0.7% international; 7% transferred in; 8% live on campus.
Freshmen *Admission:* 1,190 applied, 1,190 admitted, 1,117 enrolled. *Average high school GPA:* 3.13.
Faculty *Total:* 384, 28% full-time. *Student/faculty ratio:* 17:1.
Majors Administrative assistant and secretarial science; agricultural mechanics and equipment technology; agriculture; architectural drafting and CAD/CADD; autobody/collision and repair technology; automation engineer technology; automobile/automotive mechanics technology; biology/biological sciences; biology/biotechnology laboratory technician; business and personal/financial services marketing; business/commerce; carpentry; childcare and support services management; clinical/medical laboratory technology; communications technology; computer and information sciences; computer systems analysis; computer systems networking and telecommunications; criminal justice/police science; design and visual communications; drafting and design technology; drama and dance teacher education; education; electrical, electronic and communications engineering technology; electrical/electronics equipment installation and repair; emergency medical technology (EMT paramedic); engineering; English; family and consumer sciences/human sciences; farm and ranch management; fire science/firefighting; foreign languages and literatures; graphic communications; health information/medical records technology; legal assistant/paralegal; liberal arts and sciences/liberal studies; machine tool technology; manufacturing engineering technology; mathematics; mechanical drafting and CAD/CADD; medical radiologic technology; natural resources management and policy; pharmacy technician; physical sciences; physical therapy technology; psychology; radio and television broadcasting technology; radiologic technology/science; registered nursing/registered nurse; respiratory care therapy; respiratory therapy technician; retailing; social sciences; speech communication and rhetoric; sport and fitness administration/management; surgical technology; visual and performing arts; web page, digital/multimedia and information resources design; welding technology.
Academics *Calendar:* semesters. *Degree:* certificates and associate. *Special study options:* academic remediation for entering students, advanced placement credit, cooperative education, distance learning, double majors, English as a second language, honors programs, independent study, internships, part-time degree program, services for LD students, summer session for credit.
Library John F. Kennedy Library plus 1 other. *Books:* 41,545 (physical), 14,112 (digital/electronic); *Serial titles:* 203 (physical); *Databases:* 28. Weekly public service hours: 69.
Student Life *Housing Options:* men-only, women-only. Campus housing is university owned. *Activities and Organizations:* drama/theater group, student-run newspaper, choral group, CKI (Circle K), Social Dance Club, SPARK (non-denominational religious group), DragonLAN, Chess Club. *Campus security:* 24-hour emergency response devices and patrols, student patrols, late-night transport/escort service, controlled dormitory access. *Student services:* health clinic, personal/psychological counseling.

Athletics Member NJCAA. *Intercollegiate sports:* baseball M(s), basketball M(s)/W(s), cheerleading M(s)/W(s), cross-country running M(s)/W(s), football M(s), golf M(s), soccer W(s), softball W(s), track and field M(s)/W(s), volleyball W(s). *Intramural sports:* basketball M/W, football M/W, soccer M/W, table tennis M/W, tennis M/W, volleyball M/W.

Costs (2017–18) *Tuition:* area resident $2464 full-time, $77 per credit hour part-time; state resident $2787 full-time, $87 per credit hour part-time; nonresident $3776 full-time, $118 per credit hour part-time. *Required fees:* $608 full-time, $19 per credit hour part-time. *Room and board:* $5728. Room and board charges vary according to board plan and housing facility. *Payment plan:* installment. *Waivers:* employees or children of employees.

Applying *Options:* electronic application, early admission, deferred entrance. *Required:* high school transcript. *Required for some:* interview. *Application deadlines:* rolling (freshmen), rolling (transfers). *Notification:* continuous (freshmen), continuous (transfers).

Freshman Application Contact Mr. Corbin Strobel, Director of Admissions, Hutchinson Community College, 1300 North Plum, Hutchinson, KS 67501. *Phone:* 620-665-3536. *Toll-free phone:* 888-GO-HUTCH. *Fax:* 620-665-3301. *E-mail:* strobelc@hutchcc.edu.
Website: http://www.hutchcc.edu/.

Independence Community College
Independence, Kansas

Freshman Application Contact Ms. Brittany Thornton, Admissions Coordinator, Independence Community College, PO Box 708, 1057 W. College Avenue, Independence, KS 673001. *Phone:* 620-332-5495. *Toll-free phone:* 800-842-6063. *Fax:* 620-331-0946. *E-mail:* bthornton@indycc.edu. *Website:* http://www.indycc.edu/.

Johnson County Community College
Overland Park, Kansas

- **State and locally supported** 2-year, founded 1967, part of Kansas State Board of Education
- **Suburban** 220-acre campus with easy access to Kansas City
- **Endowment** $20.0 million
- **Coed,** 19,139 undergraduate students, 32% full-time, 53% women, 47% men

Undergraduates 6,059 full-time, 13,051 part-time. Students come from 40 states and territories; 88 other countries; 9% are from out of state; 6% Black or African American, non-Hispanic/Latino; 9% Hispanic/Latino; 4% Asian, non-Hispanic/Latino; 0.2% Native Hawaiian or other Pacific Islander, non-Hispanic/Latino; 0.6% American Indian or Alaska Native, non-Hispanic/Latino; 3% Two or more races, non-Hispanic/Latino; 5% Race/ethnicity unknown; 3% international; 5% transferred in. *Retention:* 64% of full-time freshmen returned.

Freshmen *Admission:* 2,149 enrolled.

Faculty *Total:* 871, 36% full-time. *Student/faculty ratio:* 20:1.

Majors Accounting technology and bookkeeping; administrative assistant and secretarial science; automobile/automotive mechanics technology; biology/biotechnology laboratory technician; business administration and management; CAD/CADD drafting/design technology; child-care and support services management; civil engineering technology; computer programming; computer programming (specific applications); computer systems networking and telecommunications; cosmetology; criminal justice/police science; culinary arts; dental hygiene; electrical/electronics equipment installation and repair; electrician; emergency medical technology (EMT paramedic); entrepreneurship; fashion/apparel design; fashion merchandising; fire science/firefighting; graphic design; ground transportation related; heating, ventilation, air conditioning and refrigeration engineering technology; hotel/motel administration; industrial mechanics and maintenance technology; interior design; legal administrative assistant/secretary; legal assistant/paralegal; liberal arts and sciences/liberal studies; marketing/marketing management; mechanic and repair technologies related; medical office assistant; registered nursing/registered nurse; respiratory care therapy; restaurant, culinary, and catering management; sales, distribution, and marketing operations; sign language interpretation and translation; web page, digital/multimedia and information resources design; welding technology.

Academics *Calendar:* semesters. *Degree:* certificates and associate. *Special study options:* academic remediation for entering students, adult/continuing education programs, advanced placement credit, cooperative education, distance learning, double majors, English as a second language, honors programs, independent study, internships, off-campus study, part-time degree program, services for LD students, student-designed majors, study abroad, summer session for credit.

Library Johnson County Community College Library. *Books:* 75,947 (physical); *Databases:* 137.

Student Life *Housing:* college housing not available. *Activities and Organizations:* drama/theater group, student-run newspaper, radio station. *Campus security:* 24-hour emergency response devices and patrols, late-night transport/escort service. *Student services:* personal/psychological counseling.

Athletics Member NJCAA. *Intercollegiate sports:* baseball M(s), basketball M(s)/W(s), cross-country running M(s)/W(s), soccer M(s)/W(s), softball W(s), track and field M(s)/W(s), volleyball W(s). *Intramural sports:* basketball M/W, soccer M, volleyball M/W.

Costs (2017–18) *Tuition:* area resident $2310 full-time, $77 per credit hour part-time; state resident $2820 full-time, $94 per credit hour part-time; nonresident $6120 full-time, $204 per credit hour part-time. Full-time tuition and fees vary according to course load. Part-time tuition and fees vary according to course load. *Required fees:* $480 full-time, $16 per credit hour part-time. *Waivers:* senior citizens and employees or children of employees.

Financial Aid Of all full-time matriculated undergraduates who enrolled in 2015, 85 Federal Work-Study jobs (averaging $4000).

Applying *Options:* electronic application, early admission. *Required for some:* high school transcript. *Application deadlines:* rolling (freshmen), rolling (transfers). *Notification:* continuous (freshmen), continuous (transfers).

Freshman Application Contact Johnson County Community College, 12345 College Boulevard, Overland Park, KS 66210-1299. *Phone:* 913-469-8500 Ext. 3865.
Website: http://www.johnco.cc.ks.us/.

Kansas City Kansas Community College
Kansas City, Kansas

Freshman Application Contact Dr. Denise McDowell, Dean of Enrollment Management/Registrar, Kansas City Kansas Community College, Admissions Office, 7250 State Avenue, Kansas City, KS 66112. *Phone:* 913-288-7694. *Fax:* 913-288-7648. *E-mail:* dmcdowell@kckcc.edu.
Website: http://www.kckcc.edu/.

Labette Community College
Parsons, Kansas

Freshman Application Contact Ms. Tammy Fuentez, Director of Admission, Labette Community College, 200 South 14th Street, Parsons, KS 67357-4299. *Phone:* 620-421-6700. *Toll-free phone:* 888-522-3883. *Fax:* 620-421-0180. *Website:* http://www.labette.edu/.

Manhattan Area Technical College
Manhattan, Kansas

- **State and locally supported** 2-year, founded 1965
- **Rural** 18-acre campus
- **Coed,** 825 undergraduate students, 42% full-time, 50% women, 50% men

Undergraduates 349 full-time, 476 part-time. Students come from 10 states and territories; 1% are from out of state; 6% Black or African American, non-Hispanic/Latino; 8% Hispanic/Latino; 2% Asian, non-Hispanic/Latino; 0.1% Native Hawaiian or other Pacific Islander, non-Hispanic/Latino; 0.6% American Indian or Alaska Native, non-Hispanic/Latino; 3% Two or more races, non-Hispanic/Latino; 1% Race/ethnicity unknown; 0.1% international; 16% transferred in. *Retention:* 26% of full-time freshmen returned.

Freshmen *Admission:* 87 admitted, 87 enrolled.

Faculty *Total:* 80, 36% full-time, 5% with terminal degrees. *Student/faculty ratio:* 11:1.

Majors Accounting technology and bookkeeping; administrative assistant and secretarial science; autobody/collision and repair technology; automobile/automotive mechanics technology; biology/biotechnology laboratory technician; building/construction finishing, management, and inspection related; building/property maintenance; CAD/CADD drafting/design technology; carpentry; clinical/medical laboratory technology; computer systems networking and telecommunications; computer technology/computer systems technology; drafting and design technology; electrical and power transmission installation; electrical and power transmission installation related; heating, air conditioning, ventilation and refrigeration maintenance technology; heating, ventilation, air conditioning and refrigeration engineering technology; licensed practical/vocational nurse training; management information systems; medical office assistant; multi/interdisciplinary studies related; network and system administration; registered nursing/registered nurse; welding technology.

Academics *Calendar:* semesters. *Degree:* certificates and associate. *Special study options:* academic remediation for entering students, adult/continuing education programs, advanced placement credit, cooperative education, distance learning, double majors, honors programs, internships, part-time degree program, services for LD students, student-designed majors, summer session for credit.

Library MATC Library. *Books:* 2,031 (physical), 3,665 (digital/electronic); *Databases:* 42. Weekly public service hours: 50.
Student Life *Housing:* college housing not available. *Campus security:* late-night transport/escort service, evening security guards.
Costs (2017–18) *Tuition:* state resident $4350 full-time, $175 per credit hour part-time; nonresident $4350 full-time, $175 per credit hour part-time. Full-time tuition and fees vary according to course load and program. Part-time tuition and fees vary according to course load and program. *Required fees:* $1500 full-time, $50 per credit hour part-time. *Payment plan:* installment. *Waivers:* employees or children of employees.
Applying *Options:* electronic application. *Application fee:* $40. *Required:* high school transcript. *Required for some:* essay or personal statement, 3 letters of recommendation, interview, specific admission criteria for pre-allied health programs, Class A CDL for electric power and distribution program. *Application deadlines:* rolling (freshmen), rolling (transfers).
Freshman Application Contact Mr. Neil Ross, Director of Admissions, Manhattan Area Technical College, 3136 Dickens Avenue, Manhattan, KS 66503. *Phone:* 785-320-4554. *Toll-free phone:* 800-352-7575. *Fax:* 785-587-2804. *E-mail:* neilross@manhattantech.edu.
Website: http://www.manhattantech.edu/.

Neosho County Community College
Chanute, Kansas

Freshman Application Contact Ms. Lisa Last, Dean of Student Development, Neosho County Community College, 800 West 14th Street, Chanute, KS 66720. *Phone:* 620-431-2820 Ext. 213. *Toll-free phone:* 800-729-6222. *Fax:* 620-431-0082. *E-mail:* llast@neosho.edu.
Website: http://www.neosho.edu/.

North Central Kansas Technical College
Beloit, Kansas

Freshman Application Contact Ms. Judy Heidrick, Director of Admissions, North Central Kansas Technical College, PO Box 507, 3033 US Highway 24, Beloit, KS 67420. *Toll-free phone:* 800-658-4655. *E-mail:* jheidrick@ncktc.tec.ks.us. *Website:* http://www.ncktc.edu/.

Northwest Kansas Technical College
Goodland, Kansas

Admissions Office Contact Northwest Kansas Technical College, PO Box 668, 1209 Harrison Street, Goodland, KS 67735. *Toll-free phone:* 800-316-4127. *Website:* http://www.nwktc.edu/.

Pinnacle Career Institute
Lawrence, Kansas

Admissions Office Contact Pinnacle Career Institute, 1601 West 23rd Street, Suite 200, Lawrence, KS 66046. *Toll-free phone:* 877-241-3097. *Website:* http://www.pcitraining.edu/.

Pratt Community College
Pratt, Kansas

Freshman Application Contact Ms. Theresa Ziehr, Office Assistant, Student Services, Pratt Community College, 348 Northeast State Road 61, Pratt, KS 67124. *Phone:* 620-450-2217. *Toll-free phone:* 800-794-3091. *Fax:* 620-672-5288. *E-mail:* theresaz@prattcc.edu. *Website:* http://www.prattcc.edu/.

Salina Area Technical College
Salina, Kansas

- **State and locally supported** 2-year, founded 1965
- **Small-town** campus
- **Coed,** 582 undergraduate students, 37% full-time, 47% women, 53% men
Undergraduates 216 full-time, 366 part-time. 2% Black or African American, non-Hispanic/Latino; 7% Hispanic/Latino; 0.9% Asian, non-Hispanic/Latino; 0.2% Native Hawaiian or other Pacific Islander, non-Hispanic/Latino; 1% American Indian or Alaska Native, non-Hispanic/Latino; 4% Two or more races, non-Hispanic/Latino; 0.2% international.
Freshmen *Admission:* 103 enrolled.
Majors Administrative assistant and secretarial science; autobody/collision and repair technology; automobile/automotive mechanics technology; CAD/CADD drafting/design technology; carpentry; dental assisting; electrician; emergency care attendant (EMT ambulance); graphic design; heating, air conditioning, ventilation and refrigeration maintenance technology; machine tool technology; medical/clinical assistant; medication aide; medium/heavy vehicle and truck technology; nursing assistant/aide and patient care assistant/aide; rehabilitation aide; truck and bus driver/commercial vehicle operation/instruction; welding technology.
Academics *Degree:* certificates and associate. *Special study options:* academic remediation for entering students, adult/continuing education programs, advanced placement credit, cooperative education, distance learning, independent study, internships, part-time degree program, services for LD students, student-designed majors, summer session for credit.
Student Life *Housing:* college housing not available. *Activities and Organizations:* Student Government Association.
Standardized Tests *Required:* ACCUPLACER (for admission).
Costs (2016–17) *Tuition:* state resident $4531 full-time, $130 per credit hour part-time; nonresident $4531 full-time, $130 per credit hour part-time. Full-time tuition and fees vary according to program. Part-time tuition and fees vary according to program. *Required fees:* $1962 full-time, $18 per credit hour part-time. *Payment plan:* installment. *Waivers:* employees or children of employees.
Applying *Options:* electronic application. *Required:* high school transcript. *Required for some:* essay or personal statement, 1 letter of recommendation. *Application deadlines:* rolling (freshmen), rolling (transfers). *Notification:* continuous (freshmen), continuous (transfers).
Freshman Application Contact Mrs. Rebekah Ohlde, Dir. of Academic Advising, Salina Area Technical College, 2562 Centennial Road, Salina, KS 67401. *Phone:* 785-309-3119. *Fax:* 785-309-3101.
E-mail: rebekah.ohlde@salinatech.edu.
Website: http://www.salinatech.edu/.

Seward County Community College and Area Technical School
Liberal, Kansas

Director of Admissions Dr. Gerald Harris, Dean of Student Services, Seward County Community College and Area Technical School, PO Box 1137, Liberal, KS 67905-1137. *Phone:* 620-624-1951 Ext. 617. *Toll-free phone:* 800-373-9951. *Website:* http://www.sccc.edu/.

Vatterott College
Wichita, Kansas

Admissions Office Contact Vatterott College, 8853 37th Street North, Wichita, KS 67226. *Website:* http://www.vatterott.edu/.

Wichita Area Technical College
Wichita, Kansas

Freshman Application Contact Mr. Andy McFayden, Director, Admissions, Wichita Area Technical College, 4004 N. Webb Road, Suite 100, Wichita, KS 67226 . *Phone:* 316-677-9400. *Fax:* 316-677-9555. *E-mail:* info@watc.edu. *Website:* http://www.watc.edu/.

Wichita Technical Institute
Wichita, Kansas

Admissions Office Contact Wichita Technical Institute, 2051 S. Meridian Avenue, Wichita, KS 67213. *Website:* http://www.wti.edu/.

KENTUCKY

American National University
Danville, Kentucky

Director of Admissions James McGuire, Campus Director, American National University, 115 East Lexington Avenue, Danville, KY 40422. *Phone:* 859-236-6991. *Toll-free phone:* 888-9-JOBREADY.
Website: http://www.an.edu/.

American National University
Florence, Kentucky

Director of Admissions Mr. Terry Kovacs, Campus Director, American National University, 8095 Connector Drive, Florence, KY 41042. *Phone:* 859-525-6510. *Toll-free phone:* 888-9-JOBREADY. *Website:* http://www.an.edu/.

American National University
Lexington, Kentucky

Director of Admissions Kim Thomasson, Campus Director, American National University, 2376 Sir Barton Way, Lexington, KY 40509. *Phone:* 859-253-0621. *Toll-free phone:* 888-9-JOBREADY. *Website:* http://www.an.edu/.

American National University
Louisville, Kentucky

Director of Admissions Vincent C. Tinebra, Campus Director, American National University, 4205 Dixie Highway, Louisville, KY 40216. *Phone:* 502-447-7634. *Toll-free phone:* 888-9-JOBREADY. *Website:* http://www.an.edu/.

American National University
Pikeville, Kentucky

Director of Admissions Tammy Riley, Campus Director, American National University, 50 National College Boulevard, Pikeville, KY 41501. *Phone:* 606-478-7200. *Toll-free phone:* 888-9-JOBREADY. *Website:* http://www.an.edu/.

American National University
Richmond, Kentucky

Director of Admissions Ms. Keeley Gadd, Campus Director, American National University, 125 South Killarney Lane, Richmond, KY 40475. *Phone:* 859-623-8956. *Toll-free phone:* 888-9-JOBREADY. *Website:* http://www.an.edu/.

Ashland Community and Technical College
Ashland, Kentucky

Freshman Application Contact Ashland Community and Technical College, 1400 College Drive, Ashland, KY 41101-3683. *Phone:* 606-326-2008. *Toll-free phone:* 800-928-4256. *Website:* http://www.ashland.kctcs.edu/.

ATA College
Louisville, Kentucky

Freshman Application Contact Admissions Office, ATA College, 10180 Linn Station Road, Suite A200, Louisville, KY 40223. *Phone:* 502-371-8330. *Fax:* 502-371-8598. *Website:* http://www.ata.edu/.

Beckfield College
Florence, Kentucky

- **Proprietary** primarily 2-year, founded 1984
- **Suburban** campus
- **Coed**

Academics *Calendar:* quarters. *Degrees:* certificates, diplomas, associate, bachelor's, and postbachelor's certificates.
Applying *Application fee:* $150.
Freshman Application Contact Mrs. Leah Boerger, Director of Admissions, Beckfield College, 16 Spiral Drive, Florence, KY 41042. *Phone:* 859-371-9393. *E-mail:* lboerger@beckfield.edu. *Website:* http://www.beckfield.edu/.

Big Sandy Community and Technical College
Prestonsburg, Kentucky

Director of Admissions Jimmy Wright, Director of Admissions, Big Sandy Community and Technical College, One Bert T. Combs Drive, Prestonsburg, KY 41653-1815. *Phone:* 606-886-3863. *Toll-free phone:* 888-641-4132. *E-mail:* jimmy.wright@kctcs.edu. *Website:* http://www.bigsandy.kctcs.edu/.

Bluegrass Community and Technical College
Lexington, Kentucky

Freshman Application Contact Mrs. Shelbie Hugle, Director of Admission Services, Bluegrass Community and Technical College, 470 Cooper Drive, Lexington, KY 40506. *Phone:* 859-246-6216. *Toll-free phone:* 800-744-4872 (in-state); 866-744-4872 (out-of-state). *E-mail:* shelbie.hugle@kctcs.edu. *Website:* http://www.bluegrass.kctcs.edu/.

Daymar College
Bellevue, Kentucky

Freshman Application Contact Ms. Cathy Baird, Director of Admissions, Daymar College, 119 Fairfield Avenue, Bellevue, KY 41073. *Phone:* 859-291-0800. *Toll-free phone:* 877-258-7796. *Fax:* 859-491-7500. *Website:* http://www.daymarcollege.edu/.

Daymar College
Bowling Green, Kentucky

Freshman Application Contact Mrs. Traci Henderson, Admissions Director, Daymar College, 2421 Fitzgerald Industrial Drive, Bowling Green, KY 42101. *Phone:* 270-843-6750. *Toll-free phone:* 877-258-7796. *E-mail:* thenderson@daymarcollege.edu. *Website:* http://www.daymarcollege.edu/.

Elizabethtown Community and Technical College
Elizabethtown, Kentucky

- **State-supported** 2-year, founded 1966, part of Kentucky Community and Technical College System
- **Small-town** 80-acre campus
- **Endowment** $655,000
- **Coed**

Undergraduates 2,822 full-time, 4,531 part-time. Students come from 17 states and territories; 0.5% are from out of state; 7% Black or African American, non-Hispanic/Latino; 3% Hispanic/Latino; 0.9% Asian, non-Hispanic/Latino; 0.2% Native Hawaiian or other Pacific Islander, non-Hispanic/Latino; 0.4% American Indian or Alaska Native, non-Hispanic/Latino; 3% Two or more races, non-Hispanic/Latino; 3% Race/ethnicity unknown; 3% transferred in.
Faculty *Student/faculty ratio:* 22:1.
Academics *Calendar:* semesters. *Degree:* certificates, diplomas, and associate. *Special study options:* academic remediation for entering students, advanced placement credit, cooperative education, distance learning, internships, off-campus study, part-time degree program, services for LD students, summer session for credit.
Library ECTC Media Center.
Student Life *Campus security:* late-night transport/escort service.
Standardized Tests *Recommended:* ACT (for admission).
Applying *Options:* electronic application. *Required for some:* high school transcript.
Freshman Application Contact Elizabethtown Community and Technical College, 620 College Street Road, Elizabethtown, KY 42701. *Phone:* 270-706-8800. *Toll-free phone:* 877-246-2322. *Website:* http://www.elizabethtown.kctcs.edu/.

Galen College of Nursing
Louisville, Kentucky

Admissions Office Contact Galen College of Nursing, 1031 Zorn Avenue, Suite 400, Louisville, KY 40207. *Toll-free phone:* 877-223-7040. *Website:* http://www.galencollege.edu/.

Gateway Community and Technical College
Florence, Kentucky

- **State-supported** 2-year, founded 1961, part of Kentucky Community and Technical College System
- **Suburban** campus with easy access to Cincinnati
- **Coed**, 4,429 undergraduate students, 30% full-time, 51% women, 49% men

Undergraduates 1,314 full-time, 3,078 part-time. 6% are from out of state; 7% Black or African American, non-Hispanic/Latino; 3% Hispanic/Latino; 0.7% Asian, non-Hispanic/Latino; 0.1% Native Hawaiian or other Pacific Islander, non-Hispanic/Latino; 0.2% American Indian or Alaska Native, non-Hispanic/Latino; 2% Two or more races, non-Hispanic/Latino; 3% Race/ethnicity unknown; 1% transferred in.
Freshmen *Admission:* 1,384 applied, 1,366 admitted, 420 enrolled.
Faculty *Total:* 239, 35% full-time. *Student/faculty ratio:* 19:1.

Majors Business administration and management; computer and information sciences; criminal justice/law enforcement administration; early childhood education; educational/instructional technology; engineering technology; fire science/firefighting; general studies; health professions related; industrial technology; manufacturing engineering technology; office occupations and clerical services; registered nursing/registered nurse; teacher assistant/aide.
Academics *Calendar:* semesters. *Degree:* certificates, diplomas, and associate. *Special study options:* academic remediation for entering students, cooperative education, distance learning, internships, part-time degree program, services for LD students, summer session for credit.
Library Main Library plus 3 others.
Student Life *Housing:* college housing not available. *Activities and Organizations:* National Technical Honor Society, Student Government Association, Speech Team, American Criminal Justice Association, Phi Theta Kappa. *Campus security:* 24-hour emergency response devices, campus security during hours of operation. *Student services:* personal/psychological counseling.
Standardized Tests *Required:* ACT or SAT; KYOTE (Math); TABE-Advanced (Reading and Writing) (for admission).
Costs (2016–17) *Tuition:* state resident $3744 full-time, $156 per credit hour part-time; nonresident $13,104 full-time, $546 per credit hour part-time. Full-time tuition and fees vary according to course load. Part-time tuition and fees vary according to course load. *Required fees:* $40 per term part-time. *Payment plan:* installment. *Waivers:* senior citizens and employees or children of employees.
Applying *Options:* electronic application, early admission, deferred entrance. *Required:* high school transcript. *Application deadlines:* rolling (freshmen), rolling (transfers). *Notification:* continuous (freshmen), continuous (transfers).
Freshman Application Contact Gateway Community and Technical College, 500 Technology Way, Florence, KY 41042. *Phone:* 859-442-4176. *E-mail:* andre.washington@kctcs.edu. *Website:* http://www.gateway.kctcs.edu/.

Hazard Community and Technical College
Hazard, Kentucky

Freshman Application Contact Director of Admissions, Hazard Community and Technical College, 1 Community College Drive, Hazard, KY 41701-2403. *Phone:* 606-487-3102. *Toll-free phone:* 800-246-7521. *Website:* http://www.hazard.kctcs.edu/.

Henderson Community College
Henderson, Kentucky

Freshman Application Contact Ms. Teresa Hamiton, Admissions Counselor, Henderson Community College, 2660 South Green Street, Henderson, KY 42420-4623. *Phone:* 270-827-1867 Ext. 354. *Toll-free phone:* 800-696-9958. *Website:* http://www.henderson.kctcs.edu/.

Hopkinsville Community College
Hopkinsville, Kentucky

- **State-supported** 2-year, founded 1965, part of Kentucky Community and Technical College System
- **Small-town** 69-acre campus with easy access to Nashville
- **Coed**

Undergraduates 1,245 full-time, 1,875 part-time. 22% Black or African American, non-Hispanic/Latino; 9% Hispanic/Latino; 1% Asian, non-Hispanic/Latino; 0.8% Native Hawaiian or other Pacific Islander, non-Hispanic/Latino; 0.5% American Indian or Alaska Native, non-Hispanic/Latino; 4% Two or more races, non-Hispanic/Latino; 2% Race/ethnicity unknown; 0.2% international; 7% transferred in. *Retention:* 43% of full-time freshmen returned.
Faculty *Student/faculty ratio:* 12:1.
Academics *Calendar:* semesters. *Degree:* certificates, diplomas, and associate. *Special study options:* academic remediation for entering students, advanced placement credit, cooperative education, distance learning, honors programs, independent study, part-time degree program, services for LD students, summer session for credit.
Library Learning Resource Center.
Student Life *Campus security:* 24-hour emergency response devices, late-night transport/escort service, security provided by trained security personnel during hours of normal operation.
Financial Aid Of all full-time matriculated undergraduates who enrolled in 2015, 30 Federal Work-Study jobs (averaging $1500). *Financial aid deadline:* 6/30.

Applying *Options:* electronic application, deferred entrance. *Recommended:* high school transcript.
Freshman Application Contact Hopkinsville Community College, KY. *Phone:* 270-707-3811. *Toll-free phone:* 866-534-2224. *Website:* http://hopkinsville.kctcs.edu/.

Interactive College of Technology
Newport, Kentucky

- **Proprietary** 2-year, founded 1980, part of Interactive Learning Systems
- **Small-town** campus with easy access to Cincinnati
- **Coed**

Academics *Calendar:* semesters. *Degree:* certificates, diplomas, and associate. *Special study options:* academic remediation for entering students, distance learning, internships, part-time degree program.
Freshman Application Contact Diana Mamas, Interactive College of Technology, 76 Carothers Road, Newport, KY 41071. *Phone:* 859-282-8989. *Fax:* 859-282-8475. *E-mail:* dmamas@ict.edu. *Website:* http://ict.edu/.

Jefferson Community and Technical College
Louisville, Kentucky

Freshman Application Contact Ms. Melanie Vaughan-Cooke, Admissions Coordinator, Jefferson Community and Technical College, Louisville, KY 40202. *Phone:* 502-213-4000. *Fax:* 502-213-2540. *Website:* http://www.jefferson.kctcs.edu/.

Madisonville Community College
Madisonville, Kentucky

Director of Admissions Mr. Jay Parent, Registrar, Madisonville Community College, 2000 College Drive, Madisonville, KY 42431-9185. *Phone:* 270-821-2250. *Website:* http://www.madisonville.kctcs.edu/.

Maysville Community and Technical College
Maysville, Kentucky

- **State-supported** 2-year, founded 1967, part of Kentucky Community and Technical College System
- **Rural** 12-acre campus
- **Coed,** 3,525 undergraduate students

Undergraduates 3% Black or African American, non-Hispanic/Latino; 2% Hispanic/Latino; 0.3% Asian, non-Hispanic/Latino; 0.1% Native Hawaiian or other Pacific Islander, non-Hispanic/Latino; 0.1% American Indian or Alaska Native, non-Hispanic/Latino; 2% Two or more races, non-Hispanic/Latino; 0.9% Race/ethnicity unknown; 0.1% international.
Majors Business administration and management; computer and information sciences; electromechanical technology; engineering technology; executive assistant/executive secretary; family systems; interdisciplinary studies; liberal arts and sciences/liberal studies; machine shop technology; registered nursing/registered nurse; respiratory care therapy; welding technology.
Academics *Calendar:* semesters. *Degree:* certificates, diplomas, and associate. *Special study options:* academic remediation for entering students, adult/continuing education programs, advanced placement credit, cooperative education, distance learning, English as a second language, external degree program, honors programs, independent study, internships, off-campus study, part-time degree program, services for LD students, summer session for credit.
Library Finch Library.
Student Life *Housing:* college housing not available. *Activities and Organizations:* student-run television station. *Campus security:* student patrols, evening parking lot security. *Student services:* personal/psychological counseling.
Financial Aid Of all full-time matriculated undergraduates who enrolled in 2015, 30 Federal Work-Study jobs (averaging $1960).
Applying *Options:* electronic application, early admission. *Required:* high school transcript. *Application deadlines:* rolling (freshmen), rolling (transfers). *Notification:* continuous (freshmen), continuous (transfers).
Freshman Application Contact Maysville Community and Technical College, 1755 US 68, Maysville, KY 41056. *Phone:* 606-759-7141 Ext. 66271. *Website:* http://www.maysville.kctcs.edu/.

Maysville Community and Technical College
Morehead, Kentucky

Director of Admissions Patee Massie, Registrar, Maysville Community and Technical College, 609 Viking Drive, Morehead, KY 40351. *Phone:* 606-759-7141 Ext. 66184. *Website:* http://www.maysville.kctcs.edu/.

Owensboro Community and Technical College
Owensboro, Kentucky

- **State-supported** 2-year, founded 1986, part of Kentucky Community and Technical College System
- **Suburban** 102-acre campus
- **Coed,** 4,001 undergraduate students, 38% full-time, 50% women, 50% men

Undergraduates 1,515 full-time, 2,486 part-time. Students come from 24 states and territories; 1 other country; 4% are from out of state; 4% Black or African American, non-Hispanic/Latino; 2% Hispanic/Latino; 0.6% Asian, non-Hispanic/Latino; 0.2% American Indian or Alaska Native, non-Hispanic/Latino; 3% Two or more races, non-Hispanic/Latino; 0.2% Race/ethnicity unknown. *Retention:* 59% of full-time freshmen returned.
Freshmen *Admission:* 537 enrolled.
Faculty *Total:* 141, 57% full-time, 11% with terminal degrees. *Student/faculty ratio:* 23:1.
Majors Agricultural production; automobile/automotive mechanics technology; business administration and management; child-care provision; computer and information sciences; criminal justice/law enforcement administration; diesel mechanics technology; dramatic/theater arts; electrical and electronic engineering technologies related; emergency medical technology (EMT paramedic); executive assistant/executive secretary; fine/studio arts; fire science/firefighting; health and medical administrative services related; human services; industrial mechanics and maintenance technology; liberal arts and sciences/liberal studies; machine shop technology; medical administrative assistant and medical secretary; multi/interdisciplinary studies related; radiologic technology/science; registered nursing/registered nurse; surgical technology; veterinary/animal health technology; welding technology.
Academics *Calendar:* semesters. *Degree:* certificates, diplomas, and associate. *Special study options:* academic remediation for entering students, adult/continuing education programs, advanced placement credit, cooperative education, distance learning, English as a second language, external degree program, honors programs, independent study, off-campus study, part-time degree program, services for LD students, student-designed majors, study abroad, summer session for credit. *ROTC:* Army (b).
Library Main Campus Library. *Books:* 24,422 (physical), 331,446 (digital/electronic); *Serial titles:* 19 (physical); *Databases:* 52. Weekly public service hours: 48.
Student Life *Housing:* college housing not available. *Activities and Organizations:* drama/theater group, choral group, Student Government Association. *Campus security:* 24-hour emergency response devices, late-night transport/escort service.
Standardized Tests *Recommended:* SAT or ACT (for admission).
Costs (2016–17) *Tuition:* state resident $4680 full-time, $156 per credit hour part-time; nonresident $16,380 full-time, $546 per credit hour part-time. Full-time tuition and fees vary according to course load and reciprocity agreements. Part-time tuition and fees vary according to course load and reciprocity agreements. *Required fees:* $240 full-time, $8 per credit hour part-time. *Payment plan:* installment. *Waivers:* senior citizens and employees or children of employees.
Financial Aid Of all full-time matriculated undergraduates who enrolled in 2015, 2,165 applied for aid, 1,897 were judged to have need, 365 had their need fully met. 28 Federal Work-Study jobs (averaging $5357). In 2015, 23 non-need-based awards were made. *Average percent of need met:* 50%. *Average financial aid package:* $5800. *Average need-based loan:* $2200. *Average need-based gift aid:* $3600. *Average non-need-based aid:* $1000. *Financial aid deadline:* 7/1.
Applying *Options:* electronic application. *Required:* high school transcript. *Application deadlines:* rolling (freshmen), rolling (transfers). *Notification:* continuous (freshmen), continuous (transfers).
Freshman Application Contact Ms. Barbara Tipmore, Director of Counseling Services, Owensboro Community and Technical College, 4800 New Hartford Road, Owensboro, KY 42303. *Phone:* 270-686-4530. *Toll-free phone:* 866-755-6282. *E-mail:* barb.tipmore@kctcs.edu. *Website:* http://www.owensboro.kctcs.edu/.

Ross College
Hopkinsville, Kentucky

Freshman Application Contact Ross College, 4001 Fort Cambell Boulevard, Hopkinsville, KY 42240. *Phone:* 270-886-1302. *Toll-free phone:* 866-815-5578. *Website:* http://www.rosseducation.edu/.

Somerset Community College
Somerset, Kentucky

- **State-supported** 2-year, founded 1965, part of Kentucky Community and Technical College System
- **Small-town** 70-acre campus
- **Coed,** 6,639 undergraduate students

Undergraduates *Retention:* 60% of full-time freshmen returned.
Freshmen *Admission:* 5,075 applied, 2,824 admitted.
Faculty *Total:* 340, 54% full-time. *Student/faculty ratio:* 24:1.
Majors Aircraft powerplant technology; business administration and management; child-care provision; clinical/medical laboratory assistant; computer and information sciences; criminal justice/law enforcement administration; engineering technology; executive assistant/executive secretary; industrial mechanics and maintenance technology; liberal arts and sciences/liberal studies; medical administrative assistant and medical secretary; medical radiologic technology; multi/interdisciplinary studies related; physical therapy technology; registered nursing/registered nurse; respiratory care therapy; surgical technology; teacher assistant/aide.
Academics *Calendar:* semesters. *Degree:* certificates, diplomas, and associate. *Special study options:* academic remediation for entering students, adult/continuing education programs, advanced placement credit, distance learning, part-time degree program, summer session for credit.
Library Somerset Community College Library.
Student Life *Housing:* college housing not available. *Activities and Organizations:* drama/theater group, student-run newspaper.
Costs (2016–17) *Tuition:* state resident $4680 full-time, $156 per credit hour part-time; nonresident $16,380 full-time, $546 per credit hour part-time. Full-time tuition and fees vary according to course load. Part-time tuition and fees vary according to course load. *Required fees:* $240 full-time. *Payment plan:* installment. *Waivers:* senior citizens and employees or children of employees.
Applying *Options:* electronic application, early admission. *Required:* high school transcript. *Application deadlines:* 8/14 (freshmen), 8/14 (transfers). *Notification:* continuous (freshmen), continuous (transfers).
Freshman Application Contact Director of Admission, Somerset Community College, 808 Monticello Street, Somerset, KY 42501-2973. *Phone:* 606-451-6630. *Toll-free phone:* 877-629-9722. *E-mail:* somerset-admissions@kctcs.edu. *Website:* http://www.somerset.kctcs.edu/.

Southcentral Kentucky Community and Technical College
Bowling Green, Kentucky

Director of Admissions Mark Garrett, Chief Student Affairs Officer, Southcentral Kentucky Community and Technical College, 1845 Loop Drive, Bowling Green, KY 42101. *Phone:* 270-901-1114. *Toll-free phone:* 800-790-0990. *Website:* http://www.bowlinggreen.kctcs.edu/.

Southeast Kentucky Community and Technical College
Cumberland, Kentucky

Freshman Application Contact Southeast Kentucky Community and Technical College, 700 College Road, Cumberland, KY 40823-1099. *Phone:* 606-589-2145 Ext. 13018. *Toll-free phone:* 888-274-SECC. *Website:* http://www.southeast.kctcs.edu/.

Spencerian College
Louisville, Kentucky

- **Proprietary** primarily 2-year, founded 1892
- **Urban** 10-acre campus
- **Coed,** 416 undergraduate students, 56% full-time, 86% women, 14% men

Undergraduates 231 full-time, 185 part-time. Students come from 4 states and territories; 19% are from out of state; 19% Black or African American, non-Hispanic/Latino; 2% Hispanic/Latino; 1% Asian, non-Hispanic/Latino; 0.2% American Indian or Alaska Native, non-Hispanic/Latino; 12% Two or more races, non-Hispanic/Latino; 9% Race/ethnicity unknown; 13% transferred in; 1% live on campus.

Freshmen *Admission:* 99 enrolled.
Faculty *Total:* 90, 38% full-time. *Student/faculty ratio:* 6:1.
Majors Clinical laboratory science/medical technology; clinical/medical laboratory technology; massage therapy; medical insurance coding; radiologic technology/science; registered nursing/registered nurse; respiratory care therapy; surgical technology.
Academics *Calendar:* quarters. *Degrees:* certificates, diplomas, associate, and bachelor's. *Special study options:* distance learning, internships, summer session for credit.
Library Spencerian College Learning Resource Center.
Student Life *Housing Options:* coed. Campus housing is university owned. *Campus security:* security on campus during school hours.
Costs (2017–18) *Tuition:* $19,800 full-time. Full-time tuition and fees vary according to class time, degree level, and program. Part-time tuition and fees vary according to class time, degree level, and program. *Room only:* Room and board charges vary according to housing facility. *Waivers:* children of alumni and employees or children of employees.
Applying *Application fee:* $50. *Required:* high school transcript. *Required for some:* essay or personal statement, interview, specific selective admission criteria for some medical programs. *Notification:* continuous (freshmen), continuous (transfers).
Freshman Application Contact Spencerian College, 4627 Dixie Highway, Louisville, KY 40216. *Phone:* 502-447-1000 Ext. 7808. *Toll-free phone:* 800-264-1799.
Website: http://www.spencerian.edu/.

Spencerian College–Lexington
Lexington, Kentucky

- **Proprietary** 2-year, founded 1997, part of The Sullivan University System, Inc.
- **Urban** campus with easy access to Louisville
- **Coed,** 74 undergraduate students, 88% full-time, 81% women, 19% men

Undergraduates 65 full-time, 9 part-time. Students come from 1 other state.
Freshmen *Average high school GPA:* 2.5.
Faculty *Total:* 29, 69% full-time. *Student/faculty ratio:* 3:1.
Majors Clinical/medical laboratory technology; medical office management; radiologic technology/science.
Academics *Calendar:* quarters. *Degree:* certificates, diplomas, and associate. *Special study options:* academic remediation for entering students, cooperative education, independent study, part-time degree program, services for LD students, summer session for credit.
Library Spencerian College Library.
Student Life *Housing Options:* men-only, women-only. Campus housing is leased by the school. *Activities and Organizations:* student-run newspaper. *Campus security:* 24-hour emergency response devices.
Standardized Tests *Required for some:* ACT ASSET.
Costs (2017–18) *Tuition:* $19,800 full-time, $395 per credit hour part-time. Full-time tuition and fees vary according to class time, course load, program, and student level. Part-time tuition and fees vary according to class time, course load, program, and student level. *Payment plans:* tuition prepayment, installment, deferred payment. *Waivers:* employees or children of employees.
Applying *Application fee:* $50. *Required:* high school transcript, interview. *Application deadline:* rolling (freshmen).
Freshman Application Contact Spencerian College–Lexington, 2355 Harrodsburg Road, Lexington, KY 40504. *Phone:* 859-223-9608 Ext. 5430. *Toll-free phone:* 800-456-3253.
Website: http://www.spencerian.edu/.

Sullivan College of Technology and Design
Louisville, Kentucky

Freshman Application Contact Ms. Heather Wilson, Director of Admissions, Sullivan College of Technology and Design, 3901 Atkinson Square Drive, Louisville, KY 40218. *Phone:* 502-456-6509 Ext. 8220. *Toll-free phone:* 800-884-6528. *Fax:* 502-456-2341. *E-mail:* hwilson@sctd.edu.
Website: http://www.sctd.edu/.

West Kentucky Community and Technical College
Paducah, Kentucky

Freshman Application Contact Ms. Debbie Smith, Admissions Counselor, West Kentucky Community and Technical College, 4810 Alben Barkley Drive, Paducah, KY 42001. *Phone:* 270-554-3266. *E-mail:* debbie.smith@kctcs.edu. *Website:* http://www.westkentucky.kctcs.edu/.

LOUISIANA

Baton Rouge Community College
Baton Rouge, Louisiana

Director of Admissions Nancy Clay, Interim Executive Director for Enrollment Services, Baton Rouge Community College, 201 Community College Drive, Baton Rouge, LA 70806. *Phone:* 225-216-8700. *Toll-free phone:* 800-601-4558. *Website:* http://www.mybrcc.edu/.

Baton Rouge School of Computers
Baton Rouge, Louisiana

Freshman Application Contact Admissions Office, Baton Rouge School of Computers, 9352 Interline Avenue, Baton Rouge, LA 70809. *Phone:* 225-923-2524. *Toll-free phone:* 888-920-2772. *Fax:* 225-923-2979. *E-mail:* admissions@brsc.net. *Website:* http://www.brsc.edu/.

Bossier Parish Community College
Bossier City, Louisiana

- **State-supported** 2-year, founded 1967, part of Louisiana Community and Technical College System
- **Urban** 64-acre campus with easy access to Shreveport
- **Coed,** 6,043 undergraduate students, 58% full-time, 63% women, 37% men

Undergraduates 3,475 full-time, 2,568 part-time. 2% are from out of state; 40% Black or African American, non-Hispanic/Latino; 4% Hispanic/Latino; 0.6% Asian, non-Hispanic/Latino; 0.2% Native Hawaiian or other Pacific Islander, non-Hispanic/Latino; 1% American Indian or Alaska Native, non-Hispanic/Latino; 3% Two or more races, non-Hispanic/Latino; 3% Race/ethnicity unknown; 0.3% international; 12% transferred in. *Retention:* 42% of full-time freshmen returned.
Freshmen *Admission:* 3,782 applied, 3,768 admitted, 1,120 enrolled. *Average high school GPA:* 2.73.
Faculty *Total:* 240, 51% full-time, 8% with terminal degrees. *Student/faculty ratio:* 27:1.
Majors Administrative assistant and secretarial science; audiovisual communications technologies related; business/commerce; child-care provision; computer/information technology services administration related; construction engineering; construction engineering technology; criminal justice/safety; culinary arts; drafting and design technology; dramatic/theater arts; education; educational/instructional technology; emergency medical technology (EMT paramedic); engineering; foods, nutrition, and wellness; general studies; hospital and health-care facilities administration; industrial mechanics and maintenance technology; industrial technology; information science/studies; liberal arts and sciences and humanities related; liberal arts and sciences/liberal studies; medical/clinical assistant; music; natural sciences; occupational therapist assistant; petroleum technology; pharmacy technician; physical therapy; physical therapy technology; recording arts technology; registered nursing/registered nurse; respiratory care therapy; visual and performing arts related.
Academics *Calendar:* semesters. *Degree:* certificates, diplomas, and associate. *Special study options:* academic remediation for entering students, adult/continuing education programs, advanced placement credit, distance learning, double majors, part-time degree program, services for LD students, summer session for credit.
Library Bossier Parish Community College Library.
Student Life *Housing:* college housing not available. *Activities and Organizations:* drama/theater group, student-run newspaper, choral group. *Campus security:* student patrols. *Student services:* personal/psychological counseling.
Athletics Member NJCAA. *Intercollegiate sports:* baseball M(s), basketball M(s), soccer W, softball W(s). *Intramural sports:* badminton M/W, bowling M/W, football M, racquetball M, softball M, table tennis M/W, volleyball M/W.
Costs (2016–17) *Tuition:* state resident $3335 full-time, $139 per credit hour part-time; nonresident $8012 full-time, $334 per credit hour part-time. Full-time tuition and fees vary according to course load, location, and program. Part-time tuition and fees vary according to course load, location, and program. *Required fees:* $804 full-time, $31 per credit hour part-time, $30 per term part-time. *Payment plan:* deferred payment. *Waivers:* employees or children of employees.
Financial Aid Of all full-time matriculated undergraduates who enrolled in 2015, 2,969 applied for aid, 2,718 were judged to have need, 71 had their need fully met. In 2015, 1 non-need-based awards were made. *Average percent of need met:* 33%. *Average financial aid package:* $8324. *Average need-based*

loan: $2121. *Average need-based gift aid:* $1728. *Average non-need-based aid:* $500.
Applying *Options:* early admission.
Freshman Application Contact Mr. Richard Cockerham, Registrar, Bossier Parish Community College, 6220 East Texas Street, Bossier City, LA 71111. *Phone:* 318-678-6093. *Fax:* 318-678-6390.
Website: http://www.bpcc.edu/.

Cameron College
New Orleans, Louisiana

Admissions Office Contact Cameron College, 2740 Canal Street, New Orleans, LA 70119. *Website:* http://www.cameroncollege.com/.

Central Louisiana Technical Community College
Alexandria, Louisiana

Director of Admissions Ms. Janice Bolden, Vice Chancellor of Student Services, Enrollment Management and College Registrar, Central Louisiana Technical Community College, 4311 South MacArthur Drive, Alexandria, LA 71302. *Phone:* 800-351-7611. *Website:* http://www.cltcc.edu/.

Delgado Community College
New Orleans, Louisiana

Freshman Application Contact Ms. Gwen Boute, Director of Admissions, Delgado Community College, 615 City Park Avenue, New Orleans, LA 70119. *Phone:* 504-671-5010. *Fax:* 504-483-1895. *E-mail:* enroll@dcc.edu. *Website:* http://www.dcc.edu/.

Delta School of Business and Technology
Lake Charles, Louisiana

Freshman Application Contact Jeffery Tibodeaux, Director of Admissions, Delta School of Business and Technology, 517 Broad Street, Lake Charles, LA 70601. *Phone:* 337-439-5765. *Website:* http://www.deltatech.edu/.

Fletcher Technical Community College
Schriever, Louisiana

Director of Admissions Admissions Office, Fletcher Technical Community College, 1407 Highway 311, Schriever, LA 70395. *Phone:* 985-857-3659. *Website:* http://www.fletcher.edu/.

Fortis College
Baton Rouge, Louisiana

Director of Admissions Ms. Sheri Kirley, Associate Director of Admissions, Fortis College, 9255 Interline Avenue, Baton Rouge, LA 70809. *Phone:* 225-248-1015. *Toll-free phone:* 855-4-FORTIS. *Website:* http://www.fortis.edu/.

ITI Technical College
Baton Rouge, Louisiana

- **Proprietary** 2-year, founded 1973
- **Suburban** 10-acre campus
- **Coed**

Majors Computer technology/computer systems technology; drafting and design technology; electrical, electronic and communications engineering technology; information science/studies; information technology; instrumentation technology; manufacturing engineering technology; office occupations and clerical services.
Academics *Calendar:* quarters. *Degree:* certificates and associate. *Special study options:* internships.
Library ITI Technical College Library.
Student Life *Housing:* college housing not available. *Campus security:* electronic alarm devices during non-business hours, security cameras 24-hours.
Applying *Required:* high school transcript, interview.
Freshman Application Contact Mr. Shawn Norris, Admissions Director, ITI Technical College, 13944 Airline Highway, Baton Rouge, LA 70817. *Phone:* 225-752-4230 Ext. 261. *Toll-free phone:* 888-211-7165. *Fax:* 225-756-0903. *E-mail:* snorris@iticollege.edu.
Website: http://www.iticollege.edu/.

Louisiana Culinary Institute
Baton Rouge, Louisiana

Admissions Office Contact Louisiana Culinary Institute, 10550 Airline Highway, Baton Rouge, LA 70816. *Toll-free phone:* 877-533-3198.
Website: http://www.lci.edu/.

Louisiana Delta Community College
Monroe, Louisiana

Freshman Application Contact Ms. Kathy Gardner, Interim Dean of Enrollment Services, Louisiana Delta Community College, 7500 Millhaven Drive, Monroe, LA 71203. *Phone:* 318-345-9261. *Toll-free phone:* 866-500-LDCC. *Website:* http://www.ladelta.edu/.

Louisiana State University at Eunice
Eunice, Louisiana

- **State-supported** 2-year, founded 1967, part of Louisiana State University System
- **Small-town** 199-acre campus
- **Coed,** 2,906 undergraduate students, 48% full-time, 70% women, 30% men

Undergraduates 1,388 full-time, 1,518 part-time. Students come from 16 states and territories; 6 other countries; 2% are from out of state; 25% Black or African American, non-Hispanic/Latino; 2% Hispanic/Latino; 0.7% Asian, non-Hispanic/Latino; 0.5% American Indian or Alaska Native, non-Hispanic/Latino; 2% Two or more races, non-Hispanic/Latino; 1% Race/ethnicity unknown; 0.3% international; 25% transferred in.
Freshmen *Admission:* 1,483 applied, 1,482 admitted, 869 enrolled.
Faculty *Total:* 140, 54% full-time, 16% with terminal degrees.
Majors Business administration and management; child-care provision; computer programming; criminal justice/police science; data processing and data processing technology; fire science/firefighting; general studies; liberal arts and sciences and humanities related; radiologic technology/science; registered nursing/registered nurse; respiratory care therapy.
Academics *Calendar:* semesters. *Degree:* certificates and associate. *Special study options:* academic remediation for entering students, adult/continuing education programs, advanced placement credit, cooperative education, distance learning, honors programs, off-campus study, part-time degree program, services for LD students, summer session for credit.
Library Arnold LeDoux Library. *Books:* 67,183 (physical), 90 (digital/electronic). Weekly public service hours: 90.
Student Life *Housing:* college housing not available. *Activities and Organizations:* Student Government Association, Students in Free Enterprise (SIFE), Criminal Justice Society, Student Nurses Association, Phi Theta Kappa. *Campus security:* 24-hour emergency response devices and patrols.
Athletics Member NJCAA. *Intercollegiate sports:* baseball M, basketball W, softball W. *Intramural sports:* basketball M/W, football M, softball M/W, tennis M/W, volleyball M/W.
Costs (2017–18) *Tuition:* state resident $2868 full-time, $177 per credit hour part-time; nonresident $8232 full-time, $401 per credit hour part-time. Full-time tuition and fees vary according to class time, course level, course load, degree level, location, program, reciprocity agreements, and student level. Part-time tuition and fees vary according to class time, course level, degree level, location, program, reciprocity agreements, and student level. *Required fees:* $1390 full-time, $30 per credit hour part-time. *Payment plan:* deferred payment. *Waivers:* senior citizens and employees or children of employees.
Financial Aid Of all full-time matriculated undergraduates who enrolled in 2015, 78 Federal Work-Study jobs (averaging $1525).
Applying *Options:* electronic application, early admission. *Application fee:* $25. *Required:* high school transcript. *Application deadlines:* 8/7 (freshmen), 8/7 (transfers).
Freshman Application Contact Ms. Tasha Naquin, Admissions Counselor, Louisiana State University at Eunice, PO Box 1129, Eunice, LA 70535. *Phone:* 337-550-1329. *Toll-free phone:* 888-367-5783.
E-mail: admissions@lsue.edu.
Website: http://www.lsue.edu/.

McCann School of Business & Technology
Monroe, Louisiana

Freshman Application Contact Mrs. Susan Boudreaux, Admissions Office, McCann School of Business & Technology, 2319 Louisville Avenue, Monroe, LA 71201. *Phone:* 318-323-2889. *Toll-free phone:* 866-865-8065. *Fax:* 318-324-9883. *E-mail:* susan.boudreaux@careertc.edu. *Website:* http://www.mccann.edu/.

McCann School of Business & Technology
Shreveport, Louisiana

Admissions Office Contact McCann School of Business & Technology, 1227 Shreveport-Barksdale Highway, Shreveport, LA 71105. *Toll-free phone:* 866-865-8065. *Website:* http://www.mccann.edu/.

Northshore Technical Community College
Bogalusa, Louisiana

Director of Admissions Admissions Office, Northshore Technical Community College, 1710 Sullivan Drive, Bogalusa, LA 70427. *Phone:* 985-732-6640. *Website:* http://www.northshorecollege.edu/.

Northwest Louisiana Technical College
Minden, Louisiana

Director of Admissions Ms. Helen Deville, Admissions Office, Northwest Louisiana Technical College, 9500 Industrial Drive, Minden, LA 71055. *Phone:* 318-371-3035. *Toll-free phone:* 800-529-1387. *Fax:* 318-371-3155. *Website:* http://www.nwltc.edu/.

Nunez Community College
Chalmette, Louisiana

- **State-supported** 2-year, founded 1992, part of Louisiana Community and Technical College System
- **Suburban** 20-acre campus with easy access to New Orleans
- **Endowment** $1.2 million
- **Coed,** 2,586 undergraduate students, 31% full-time, 62% women, 38% men

Undergraduates 803 full-time, 1,783 part-time. Students come from 7 states and territories; 4 other countries; 1% are from out of state; 37% Black or African American, non-Hispanic/Latino; 7% Hispanic/Latino; 2% Asian, non-Hispanic/Latino; 0.2% Native Hawaiian or other Pacific Islander, non-Hispanic/Latino; 0.6% American Indian or Alaska Native, non-Hispanic/Latino; 2% Two or more races, non-Hispanic/Latino; 4% Race/ethnicity unknown; 0.5% international; 13% transferred in.
Freshmen *Admission:* 232 admitted, 232 enrolled. *Average high school GPA:* 2.38.
Faculty *Total:* 101, 44% full-time. *Student/faculty ratio:* 22:1.
Majors Business/commerce; child-care provision; education; general studies; industrial technology; kindergarten/preschool education; legal assistant/paralegal; liberal arts and sciences and humanities related.
Academics *Calendar:* semesters. *Degree:* certificates, diplomas, and associate. *Special study options:* academic remediation for entering students, adult/continuing education programs, advanced placement credit, cooperative education, distance learning, double majors, independent study, internships, off-campus study, part-time degree program, services for LD students, student-designed majors, summer session for credit.
Library Nunez Community College Library.
Student Life *Housing:* college housing not available. *Campus security:* late-night transport/escort service, security cameras. *Student services:* health clinic, personal/psychological counseling.
Financial Aid Of all full-time matriculated undergraduates who enrolled in 2015, 70 Federal Work-Study jobs (averaging $1452).
Applying *Options:* electronic application, early admission, deferred entrance. *Application fee:* $20. *Required for some:* high school transcript. *Application deadlines:* rolling (freshmen), rolling (transfers).
Freshman Application Contact Mrs. Becky Maillet, Nunez Community College, 3710 Paris Road, Chalmette, LA 70043. *Phone:* 504-278-6477. *E-mail:* bmaillet@nunez.edu. *Website:* http://www.nunez.edu/.

Remington College–Baton Rouge Campus
Baton Rouge, Louisiana

Director of Admissions Monica Butler-Johnson, Director of Recruitment, Remington College–Baton Rouge Campus, 4520 South Sherwood Forrest Boulevard, Baton Rouge, LA 70816. *Phone:* 225-236-3200. *Toll-free phone:* 800-323-8122. *Fax:* 225-922-3250. *E-mail:* monica.johnson@remingtoncollege.edu. *Website:* http://www.remingtoncollege.edu/.

Remington College–Lafayette Campus
Lafayette, Louisiana

Freshman Application Contact Remington College–Lafayette Campus, 303 Rue Louis XIV, Lafayette, LA 70508. *Phone:* 337-981-4010. *Toll-free phone:* 800-323-8122. *Website:* http://www.remingtoncollege.edu/.

Remington College–Shreveport
Shreveport, Louisiana

Freshman Application Contact Mr. Marc Wright, Remington College–Shreveport, 2106 West Bert Kouns Industrial Loop, Shreveport, LA 71118. *Phone:* 318-671-4000. *Toll-free phone:* 800-323-8122. *Website:* http://www.remingtoncollege.edu/.

River Parishes Community College
Gonzales, Louisiana

Director of Admissions Ms. Allison Dauzat, Dean of Students and Enrollment Management, River Parishes Community College, 925 West Edenborne Parkway, Gonzales, LA 70737. *Phone:* 225-675-8270. *Fax:* 225-675-5478. *E-mail:* adauzat@rpcc.cc.la.us. *Website:* http://www.rpcc.edu/.

South Central Louisiana Technical College
Morgan City, Louisiana

Director of Admissions Ms. Melanie Henry, Admissions Office, South Central Louisiana Technical College, 900 Youngs Road, Morgan City, LA 70380. *Phone:* 504-380-2436. *Fax:* 504-380-2440. *Website:* http://www.scl.edu/.

Southern University at Shreveport
Shreveport, Louisiana

- **State-supported** 2-year, founded 1964, part of Southern University System
- **Urban** 103-acre campus
- **Endowment** $619,644
- **Coed,** 3,240 undergraduate students, 54% full-time, 65% women, 35% men

Undergraduates 1,762 full-time, 1,478 part-time. Students come from 24 states and territories; 5 other countries; 5% are from out of state; 88% Black or African American, non-Hispanic/Latino; 0.3% Hispanic/Latino; 0.3% Asian, non-Hispanic/Latino; 0.1% American Indian or Alaska Native, non-Hispanic/Latino; 0.3% Two or more races, non-Hispanic/Latino; 7% international; 6% transferred in; 7% live on campus. *Retention:* 45% of full-time freshmen returned.
Freshmen *Admission:* 694 enrolled. *Average high school GPA:* 2. *Test scores:* ACT scores over 18: 8%.
Faculty *Total:* 166, 45% full-time, 7% with terminal degrees. *Student/faculty ratio:* 21:1.
Majors Accounting; accounting technology and bookkeeping; avionics maintenance technology; banking and financial support services; biology/biological sciences; business/commerce; cardiovascular technology; chemistry; clinical/medical laboratory technology; computer science; criminal justice/law enforcement administration; dental hygiene; electrical, electronic and communications engineering technology; general studies; health information/medical records administration; health information/medical records technology; hospitality administration; hotel/motel administration; human services; kindergarten/preschool education; legal assistant/paralegal; liberal arts and sciences and humanities related; mathematics; mechanical engineering/mechanical technology; medical radiologic technology; mental health counseling; physical therapy technology; public administration; radiologic technology/science; registered nursing/registered nurse; respiratory care therapy; robotics technology; sociology; surgical technology; teacher assistant/aide; tourism and travel services management.
Academics *Calendar:* semesters. *Degree:* certificates and associate. *Special study options:* academic remediation for entering students, adult/continuing education programs, advanced placement credit, cooperative education, distance learning, double majors, English as a second language, honors programs, internships, part-time degree program, services for LD students, student-designed majors, summer session for credit. *ROTC:* Army (c).
Library Library/Learning Resources Center plus 1 other. *Books:* 56,174 (physical), 11,097 (digital/electronic); *Serial titles:* 164 (physical); *Databases:* 76. Students can reserve study rooms.

Student Life *Housing Options:* coed. Campus housing is provided by a third party. *Activities and Organizations:* student-run newspaper, choral group, marching band, Afro-American Society, SUSLA Gospel Choir, Student Center Board, Allied Health, Engineering Club. *Campus security:* 24-hour emergency response devices and patrols, controlled dormitory access. *Student services:* personal/psychological counseling.

Athletics Member NJCAA. *Intercollegiate sports:* basketball M(s)/W(s). *Intramural sports:* basketball M/W, cheerleading M/W, soccer M.

Standardized Tests *Required for some:* SAT or ACT (for admission). *Recommended:* ACT (for admission).

Costs (2017–18) *Tuition:* state resident $2618 full-time; nonresident $5918 full-time. Full-time tuition and fees vary according to program. Part-time tuition and fees vary according to program. *Required fees:* $1378 full-time. *Room and board:* Room and board charges vary according to board plan and housing facility. *Payment plan:* deferred payment. *Waivers:* employees or children of employees.

Applying *Required:* high school transcript.

Freshman Application Contact Ms. Danielle Anderson, Admissions Advisor, Southern University at Shreveport, 3050 Martin Luther King Jr. Drive, Shreveport, LA 71107. *Phone:* 318-670-9211. *Toll-free phone:* 800-458-1472. *Fax:* 318-670-6483. *E-mail:* danderson@susla.edu. *Website:* http://www.susla.edu/.

South Louisiana Community College
Lafayette, Louisiana

Freshman Application Contact Director of Admissions, South Louisiana Community College, 1101 Bertrand Drive, Lafayette, LA 70506. *Phone:* 337-521-8953. *E-mail:* admissions@solacc.edu. *Website:* http://www.solacc.edu/.

Sowela Technical Community College
Lake Charles, Louisiana

- **State-supported** 2-year, founded 1938, part of Louisiana Community and Technical College System
- **Urban** 84-acre campus
- **Endowment** $383,426
- **Coed,** 3,241 undergraduate students, 57% full-time, 46% women, 54% men
- 100% of applicants were admitted

Undergraduates 1,848 full-time, 1,393 part-time. Students come from 11 states and territories; 7 other countries; 1% are from out of state; 24% Black or African American, non-Hispanic/Latino; 3% Hispanic/Latino; 0.7% Asian, non-Hispanic/Latino; 0.7% American Indian or Alaska Native, non-Hispanic/Latino; 3% Two or more races, non-Hispanic/Latino; 5% Race/ethnicity unknown; 0.3% international; 2% transferred in. *Retention:* 55% of full-time freshmen returned.

Freshmen *Admission:* 687 applied, 685 admitted, 687 enrolled. *Average high school GPA:* 2.8.

Faculty *Total:* 152, 49% full-time, 8% with terminal degrees. *Student/faculty ratio:* 24:1.

Majors Accounting technology and bookkeeping; administrative assistant and secretarial science; aircraft powerplant technology; business/commerce; chemical technology; commercial and advertising art; computer programming; computer systems networking and telecommunications; criminal justice/safety; culinary arts; drafting and design technology; general studies; instrumentation technology; liberal arts and sciences and humanities related.

Academics *Calendar:* semesters. *Degree:* certificates, diplomas, and associate. *Special study options:* academic remediation for entering students, accelerated degree program, adult/continuing education programs, advanced placement credit, distance learning, double majors, external degree program, internships, off-campus study, part-time degree program, services for LD students, summer session for credit.

Library Library and Learning Resource Center plus 2 others. *Books:* 8,318 (physical), 11,838 (digital/electronic). Weekly public service hours: 50; students can reserve study rooms.

Student Life *Housing:* college housing not available. *Activities and Organizations:* student-run newspaper, choral group, SkillsUSA, Student Government Association (SGA), Phi Theta Kappa, Criminal Justice Club, Astronomy Club. *Campus security:* security guard on duty. *Student services:* personal/psychological counseling.

Applying *Options:* electronic application, early admission. *Required:* high school transcript, proof of immunization, proof of Selective Service status. *Application deadlines:* rolling (freshmen), rolling (transfers). *Notification:* continuous (freshmen), continuous (transfers).

Freshman Application Contact Office of Admissions, Sowela Technical Community College, 3820 Senator J. Bennett Johnston Avenue, Lake Charles, LA 70616. *Phone:* 337-421-6550. *Toll-free phone:* 800-256-0483. *Fax:* 337-491-2663. *Website:* http://www.sowela.edu/.

Virginia College in Baton Rouge
Baton Rouge, Louisiana

Admissions Office Contact Virginia College in Baton Rouge, 9501 Cortana Place, Baton Rouge, LA 70815. *Website:* http://www.vc.cdu/.

Virginia College in Shreveport/Bossier City
Bossier City, Louisiana

Admissions Office Contact Virginia College in Shreveport/Bossier City, 2950 East Texas Street, Suite C, Bossier City, LA 71111. *Website:* http://www.vc.edu/.

MAINE

Beal College
Bangor, Maine

- **Proprietary** 2-year, founded 1891
- **Small-town** 4-acre campus
- **Coed**

Undergraduates 363 full-time, 101 part-time. Students come from 1 other state; 0.9% Black or African American, non-Hispanic/Latino; 1% Hispanic/Latino; 0.6% Asian, non-Hispanic/Latino; 0.2% Native Hawaiian or other Pacific Islander, non-Hispanic/Latino; 2% American Indian or Alaska Native, non-Hispanic/Latino; 4% Race/ethnicity unknown; 10% transferred in. *Retention:* 60% of full-time freshmen returned.

Faculty *Student/faculty ratio:* 30:1.

Academics *Calendar:* modular. *Degree:* certificates, diplomas, and associate. *Special study options:* accelerated degree program, adult/continuing education programs, advanced placement credit, internships, part-time degree program, summer session for credit.

Library Beal College Library.

Applying *Options:* deferred entrance. *Application fee:* $30. *Required:* essay or personal statement, high school transcript, 1 letter of recommendation, interview, entrance exam, immunizations.

Freshman Application Contact Sierra Kennedy, Admissions Assistant, Beal College, 99 Farm Road, Bangor, ME 04401. *Phone:* 207-947-4591. *Toll-free phone:* 800-660-7351. *Fax:* 207-947-0208. *E-mail:* admissions@bealcollege.edu. *Website:* http://www.bealcollege.edu/.

Central Maine Community College
Auburn, Maine

- **State-supported** 2-year, founded 1964, part of Maine Community College System
- **Small-town** 135-acre campus
- **Endowment** $800,000
- **Coed,** 3,025 undergraduate students, 40% full-time, 53% women, 47% men

Undergraduates 1,205 full-time, 1,820 part-time. Students come from 12 states and territories; 3 other countries; 5% are from out of state; 7% Black or African American, non-Hispanic/Latino; 2% Hispanic/Latino; 0.9% Asian, non-Hispanic/Latino; 0.1% Native Hawaiian or other Pacific Islander, non-Hispanic/Latino; 0.8% American Indian or Alaska Native, non-Hispanic/Latino; 4% Two or more races, non-Hispanic/Latino; 9% Race/ethnicity unknown; 0.7% international; 7% transferred in; 8% live on campus.

Freshmen *Admission:* 2,593 applied, 1,077 admitted, 693 enrolled.

Faculty *Total:* 203, 27% full-time, 1% with terminal degrees. *Student/faculty ratio:* 17:1.

Majors Accounting; administrative assistant and secretarial science; automobile/automotive mechanics technology; biology/biological sciences; building construction technology; business administration and management; civil engineering technology; construction trades related; criminal justice/law enforcement administration; criminal justice/safety; early childhood education; electromechanical technology; graphic and printing equipment operation/production; graphic communications; human services; liberal arts and sciences/liberal studies; licensed practical/vocational nurse training; machine tool technology; medical/clinical assistant; multi/interdisciplinary studies related; network and system administration; physical fitness technician; registered nursing/registered nurse.

Academics *Calendar:* semesters. *Degree:* certificates and associate. *Special study options:* academic remediation for entering students, accelerated degree program, adult/continuing education programs, advanced placement credit,

cooperative education, distance learning, English as a second language, independent study, internships, part-time degree program, services for LD students, summer session for credit.
Library Central Maine Community College Library. *Books:* 18,068 (physical); *Serial titles:* 117 (physical); *Databases:* 129. Weekly public service hours: 60; students can reserve study rooms.
Student Life *Housing Options:* coed, men-only, women-only. Campus housing is university owned. Freshman applicants given priority for college housing. *Activities and Organizations:* drama/theater group. *Campus security:* 24-hour emergency response devices, student patrols, controlled dormitory access, night patrols by police.
Athletics Member USCAA. *Intercollegiate sports:* baseball M, basketball M/W, golf M/W, ice hockey M(c), soccer M/W, softball W. *Intramural sports:* volleyball M/W.
Standardized Tests *Recommended:* SAT (for admission), SAT and SAT Subject Tests or ACT (for admission), SAT Subject Tests (for admission).
Costs (2017–18) *Tuition:* state resident $2760 full-time, $1380 per year part-time; nonresident $5520 full-time, $2760 per year part-time. Full-time tuition and fees vary according to course load and program. Part-time tuition and fees vary according to course load and program. *Required fees:* $1080 full-time, $35 per credit hour part-time. *Room and board:* $9340. Room and board charges vary according to housing facility. *Payment plan:* installment. *Waivers:* employees or children of employees.
Financial Aid Of all full-time matriculated undergraduates who enrolled in 2015, 89 Federal Work-Study jobs (averaging $1200). *Financial aid deadline:* 8/1.
Applying *Options:* electronic application, deferred entrance. *Application fee:* $20. *Required:* high school transcript. *Recommended:* essay or personal statement. *Application deadlines:* rolling (freshmen), rolling (transfers). *Notification:* continuous (freshmen), continuous (transfers).
Freshman Application Contact Ms. Joan Nichols, Admissions Assistant, Central Maine Community College, 1250 Turner Street, Auburn, ME 04210. *Phone:* 207-755-5273. *Toll-free phone:* 800-891-2002. *Fax:* 207-755-5493. *E-mail:* enroll@cmcc.edu.
Website: http://www.cmcc.edu/.

Eastern Maine Community College
Bangor, Maine

Freshman Application Contact Mr. W. Gregory Swett, Director of Admissions, Eastern Maine Community College, 354 Hogan Road, Bangor, ME 04401. *Phone:* 207-974-4680. *Toll-free phone:* 800-286-9357. *Fax:* 207-974-4683. *E-mail:* admissions@emcc.edu. *Website:* http://www.emcc.edu/.

Kaplan University, Lewiston
Lewiston, Maine

Freshman Application Contact Kaplan University, Lewiston, 475 Lisbon Street, Lewiston, ME 04240. *Phone:* 207-333-3300. *Toll-free phone:* 800-987-7734. *Website:* http://www.kaplanuniversity.edu/.

Kaplan University, South Portland
South Portland, Maine

Freshman Application Contact Kaplan University, South Portland, 265 Western Avenue, South Portland, ME 04106. *Phone:* 207-774-6126. *Toll-free phone:* 800-987-7734. *Website:* http://www.kaplanuniversity.edu/.

Kennebec Valley Community College
Fairfield, Maine

- **State-supported** 2-year, founded 1970, part of Maine Community College System
- **Small-town** campus
- **Endowment** $2.8 million
- **Coed**

Undergraduates 724 full-time, 1,727 part-time. Students come from 15 states and territories; 2% are from out of state; 0.8% Black or African American, non-Hispanic/Latino; 1% Hispanic/Latino; 0.6% Asian, non-Hispanic/Latino; 0.8% American Indian or Alaska Native, non-Hispanic/Latino; 1% Two or more races, non-Hispanic/Latino; 7% Race/ethnicity unknown; 8% transferred in.
Academics *Calendar:* semesters. *Degree:* certificates, diplomas, and associate. *Special study options:* academic remediation for entering students,

accelerated degree program, adult/continuing education programs, advanced placement credit, distance learning, external degree program, independent study, internships, part-time degree program, services for LD students, summer session for credit.
Library Lunder Library plus 2 others.
Student Life *Campus security:* evening security patrol.
Standardized Tests *Required for some:* HESI nursing exam, HOBET for allied health programs, ACCUPLACER. *Recommended:* SAT or ACT (for admission).
Costs (2016–17) *One-time required fee:* $30. *Tuition:* state resident $2760 full-time, $92 per credit hour part-time; nonresident $5520 full-time, $184 per credit hour part-time. *Required fees:* $1284 full-time.
Financial Aid Of all full-time matriculated undergraduates who enrolled in 2015, 1,875 applied for aid, 1,627 were judged to have need, 14 had their need fully met. 27 Federal Work-Study jobs (averaging $1338). In 2015, 12. *Average percent of need met:* 52. *Average financial aid package:* $7483. *Average need-based loan:* $3217. *Average need-based gift aid:* $6087. *Average non-need-based aid:* $1214.
Applying *Options:* electronic application, deferred entrance. *Application fee:* $20. *Required:* essay or personal statement, high school transcript. *Required for some:* interview.
Freshman Application Contact Mr. Crichton McKenna, Assistant Director of Admissions, Kennebec Valley Community College, 92 Western Avenue, Fairfield, ME 04937-1367. *Phone:* 207-453-5155. *Toll-free phone:* 800-528-5882. *Fax:* 207-453-5011. *E-mail:* admissions@kvcc.me.edu. *Website:* http://www.kvcc.me.edu/.

The Landing School
Arundel, Maine

Freshman Application Contact Kristin Potter, Admissions Representative, The Landing School, 286 River Road, Arundel, ME 04046. *Phone:* 207-985-7976. *E-mail:* info@landingschool.edu.
Website: http://www.landingschool.edu/.

Maine College of Health Professions
Lewiston, Maine

- **Independent** 2-year, founded 1891
- **Urban** campus
- **Coed**, 169 undergraduate students, 34% full-time, 89% women, 11% men

Undergraduates 58 full-time, 111 part-time. Students come from 4 states and territories; 1% are from out of state; 0.6% Black or African American, non-Hispanic/Latino; 1% Hispanic/Latino; 2% Asian, non-Hispanic/Latino; 4% live on campus.
Freshmen *Admission:* 13 applied, 6 admitted, 6 enrolled. *Average high school GPA:* 3.63.
Faculty *Total:* 19, 89% full-time, 16% with terminal degrees. *Student/faculty ratio:* 5:1.
Majors Nuclear medical technology; radiologic technology/science; registered nursing/registered nurse.
Academics *Calendar:* semesters. *Degree:* associate. *Special study options:* advanced placement credit, off-campus study, services for LD students, summer session for credit.
Library Gerrish True Health Sciences Library plus 1 other. *Books:* 2,816 (physical), 172 (digital/electronic); *Databases:* 17. Study areas open 24 hours, 5&-7 days a week.
Student Life *Housing Options:* coed. Campus housing is university owned. *Activities and Organizations:* Student Government. *Campus security:* 24-hour emergency response devices and patrols, late-night transport/escort service, controlled dormitory access. *Student services:* health clinic, personal/psychological counseling.
Standardized Tests *Required:* SAT or ACT (for admission). *Required for some:* HESI Entrance Exam for nursing, ACCUPLACER.
Costs (2016–17) *Tuition:* $9380 full-time. *Required fees:* $1670 full-time. *Room only:* $2350. *Waivers:* employees or children of employees.
Applying *Options:* electronic application. *Application fee:* $50. *Required:* essay or personal statement, high school transcript, high school or college-level algebra, second math, biology, chemistry. *Application deadline:* 4/14 (freshmen). *Notification:* 5/1 (freshmen).
Freshman Application Contact Ms. Erica Watson, Admissions Director, Maine College of Health Professions, 70 Middle Street, Lewiston, ME 04240. *Phone:* 207-795-2843. *Fax:* 207-795-2849. *E-mail:* watsoner@mchp.edu. *Website:* http://www.mchp.edu/.

Northern Maine Community College
Presque Isle, Maine

- **State-supported** 2-year, founded 1963, part of Maine Community College System
- **Small-town** 86-acre campus
- **Coed,** 955 undergraduate students, 60% full-time, 40% women, 38% men

Undergraduates 573 full-time, 177 part-time. Students come from 4 states and territories; 4% are from out of state; 9% transferred in; 63% live on campus. *Retention:* 57% of full-time freshmen returned.

Freshmen *Admission:* 761 applied, 404 admitted, 196 enrolled.

Faculty *Total:* 77, 58% full-time.

Majors Accounting; automobile/automotive mechanics technology; business administration and management; carpentry; computer systems networking and telecommunications; construction trades related; drafting and design technology; electrical, electronic and communications engineering technology; emergency medical technology (EMT paramedic); general studies; heating, air conditioning, ventilation and refrigeration maintenance technology; kindergarten/preschool education; liberal arts and sciences and humanities related; machine tool technology; pipefitting and sprinkler fitting; registered nursing/registered nurse.

Academics *Calendar:* semesters. *Degree:* certificates and associate. *Special study options:* academic remediation for entering students, adult/continuing education programs, advanced placement credit, cooperative education, double majors, independent study, internships, off-campus study, part-time degree program, services for LD students, summer session for credit.

Library Northern Maine Technical College Library.

Student Life *Housing Options:* coed. Campus housing is university owned. *Activities and Organizations:* Student Senate, Alpha Beta Gamma, Phi Theta Kappa, Student Nurses Association. *Campus security:* 24-hour emergency response devices and patrols, controlled dormitory access. *Student services:* health clinic.

Athletics *Intercollegiate sports:* golf M/W, soccer M/W. *Intramural sports:* basketball M(c)/W(c), ice hockey M(c)/W(c), racquetball M(c)/W(c), skiing (cross-country) M(c)/W(c), volleyball M(c)/W(c).

Costs (2016–17) *One-time required fee:* $66. *Tuition:* state resident $2760 full-time, $92 per credit hour part-time; nonresident $5520 full-time, $184 per credit hour part-time. Full-time tuition and fees vary according to course load, program, and reciprocity agreements. Part-time tuition and fees vary according to course load, program, and reciprocity agreements. *Required fees:* $739 full-time, $9 per credit hour part-time, $15 per term part-time. *Room and board:* $6426; room only: $2832. Room and board charges vary according to board plan and housing facility. *Payment plan:* installment. *Waivers:* senior citizens and employees or children of employees.

Financial Aid Of all full-time matriculated undergraduates who enrolled in 2012, 664 applied for aid, 612 were judged to have need, 17 had their need fully met. In 2012, 10 non-need-based awards were made. *Average percent of need met:* 48%. *Average financial aid package:* $6588. *Average need-based loan:* $3072. *Average need-based gift aid:* $4815. *Average non-need-based aid:* $890.

Applying *Options:* electronic application, early admission, deferred entrance. *Application fee:* $20. *Required:* high school transcript, interview. *Recommended:* essay or personal statement, minimum 2.0 GPA. *Application deadline:* rolling (freshmen). *Notification:* continuous (freshmen).

Freshman Application Contact Ms. Nancy Gagnon, Admissions Secretary, Northern Maine Community College, 33 Edgemont Drive, Presque Isle, ME 04769-2016. *Phone:* 207-768-2785. *Toll-free phone:* 800-535-6682. *Fax:* 207-768-2848. *E-mail:* ngagnon@nmcc.edu. *Website:* http://www.nmcc.edu/.

Southern Maine Community College
South Portland, Maine

- **State-supported** 2-year, founded 1946, part of Maine Community College System
- **Suburban** 80-acre campus
- **Coed**

Undergraduates 2,618 full-time, 3,427 part-time. Students come from 25 states and territories; 19 other countries; 4% are from out of state; 6% Black or African American, non-Hispanic/Latino; 3% Hispanic/Latino; 2% Asian, non-Hispanic/Latino; 0.1% Native Hawaiian or other Pacific Islander, non-Hispanic/Latino; 0.6% American Indian or Alaska Native, non-Hispanic/Latino; 2% Two or more races, non-Hispanic/Latino; 4% Race/ethnicity unknown; 0.4% international; 8% transferred in; 5% live on campus. *Retention:* 55% of full-time freshmen returned.

Faculty *Student/faculty ratio:* 18:1.

Academics *Calendar:* semesters. *Degree:* certificates and associate. *Special study options:* academic remediation for entering students, advanced placement credit, distance learning, double majors, English as a second language, honors programs, independent study, internships, off-campus study, part-time degree program, services for LD students, study abroad, summer session for credit.

Library Southern Maine Community College Library. *Books:* 20,586 (physical), 30,783 (digital/electronic); *Serial titles:* 1,026 (physical), 23,074 (digital/electronic); *Databases:* 34. Weekly public service hours: 68; students can reserve study rooms.

Student Life *Campus security:* 24-hour emergency response devices and patrols, student patrols, late-night transport/escort service, controlled dormitory access.

Athletics Member USCAA.

Standardized Tests *Recommended:* SAT or ACT (for admission).

Financial Aid Of all full-time matriculated undergraduates who enrolled in 2015, 130 Federal Work-Study jobs (averaging $1500).

Applying *Options:* electronic application. *Application fee:* $20. *Required:* high school transcript.

Freshman Application Contact Amy Lee, Director of Enrollment Services, Southern Maine Community College, 2 Fort Road, South, Portland, ME 04106. *Phone:* 207-741-5800. *Toll-free phone:* 877-282-2182. *Fax:* 207-741-5760. *E-mail:* alee@smccme.edu. *Website:* http://www.smccme.edu/.

Washington County Community College
Calais, Maine

- **State-supported** 2-year, founded 1969, part of Maine Community College System
- **Rural** 40-acre campus
- **Coed**

Undergraduates Students come from 4 states and territories; 1 other country; 3% are from out of state. *Retention:* 63% of full-time freshmen returned.

Faculty *Student/faculty ratio:* 11:1.

Academics *Calendar:* semesters. *Degree:* certificates, diplomas, and associate. *Special study options:* academic remediation for entering students, adult/continuing education programs, advanced placement credit, cooperative education, distance learning, double majors, external degree program, independent study, internships, off-campus study, part-time degree program, services for LD students, study abroad.

Library Washington County Technical College Library.

Student Life *Campus security:* 24-hour emergency response devices.

Financial Aid Of all full-time matriculated undergraduates who enrolled in 2014, 269 applied for aid, 269 were judged to have need.

Applying *Options:* deferred entrance. *Application fee:* $20. *Required:* essay or personal statement, high school transcript, interview. *Recommended:* minimum 2.0 GPA.

Freshman Application Contact Washington County Community College, One College Drive, Calais, ME 04619. *Phone:* 207-454-1000. *Toll-free phone:* 800-210-6932. *Website:* http://www.wccc.me.edu/.

York County Community College
Wells, Maine

- **State-supported** 2-year, founded 1994, part of Maine Community College System
- **Small-town** 84-acre campus with easy access to Boston
- **Coed,** 1,827 undergraduate students, 23% full-time, 64% women, 36% men

Undergraduates 427 full-time, 1,400 part-time. Students come from 10 states and territories; 3% are from out of state; 1% Black or African American, non-Hispanic/Latino; 2% Hispanic/Latino; 1% Asian, non-Hispanic/Latino; 0.1% Native Hawaiian or other Pacific Islander, non-Hispanic/Latino; 0.4% American Indian or Alaska Native, non-Hispanic/Latino; 2% Two or more races, non-Hispanic/Latino; 17% Race/ethnicity unknown; 0.2% international; 14% transferred in. *Retention:* 51% of full-time freshmen returned.

Freshmen *Admission:* 569 applied, 329 admitted, 262 enrolled.

Faculty *Total:* 149, 15% full-time, 12% with terminal degrees. *Student/faculty ratio:* 14:1.

Majors Accounting; animation, interactive technology, video graphics and special effects; architectural drafting and CAD/CADD; business administration and management; computer science; construction trades related; criminal justice/safety; culinary arts; drafting and design technology; early childhood education; education; gerontology; health information/medical records technology; health services/allied health/health sciences; hospitality administration; human services; liberal arts and sciences/liberal studies; machine tool technology; medical/clinical assistant; multi/interdisciplinary studies related; network and system administration; veterinary/animal health technology.

Academics *Calendar:* semesters. *Degree:* certificates and associate. *Special study options:* academic remediation for entering students, adult/continuing education programs, advanced placement credit, cooperative education, distance learning, internships, off-campus study, part-time degree program, services for LD students, summer session for credit.

Library Library and Learning Resource Center plus 1 other. *Books:* 12,399 (physical); *Serial titles:* 1,625 (physical); *Databases:* 28. Weekly public service hours: 57; students can reserve study rooms.

Student Life *Housing:* college housing not available. *Activities and Organizations:* Student Senate, Phi Theta Kappa, Criminal Justice Club. *Student services:* personal/psychological counseling.

Athletics *Intramural sports:* basketball M/W, ice hockey M/W, soccer M/W, softball M/W, ultimate Frisbee M/W, volleyball M/W.

Costs (2017–18) *Tuition:* state resident $2760 full-time, $92 per credit part-time; nonresident $5520 full-time, $184 per credit part-time. Full-time tuition and fees vary according to course level and course load. Part-time tuition and fees vary according to course level and course load. *Required fees:* $780 full-time. *Payment plan:* installment. *Waivers:* senior citizens and employees or children of employees.

Financial Aid Of all full-time matriculated undergraduates who enrolled in 2015, 453 applied for aid, 388 were judged to have need, 24 had their need fully met. In 2015, 28 non-need-based awards were made. *Average percent of need met:* 37%. *Average financial aid package:* $6029. *Average need-based loan:* $2947. *Average need-based gift aid:* $4946. *Average non-need-based aid:* $799. *Average indebtedness upon graduation:* $6500.

Applying *Options:* electronic application, deferred entrance. *Application fee:* $20. *Required:* high school transcript. *Recommended:* interview. *Application deadlines:* rolling (freshmen), rolling (transfers). *Notification:* continuous (freshmen), continuous (transfers).

Freshman Application Contact Fred Quistgard, Director of Admissions, York County Community College, 112 College Drive, Wells, ME 04090. *Phone:* 207-216-4406 Ext. 311. *Toll-free phone:* 800-580-3820. *Fax:* 207-641-0837.

Website: http://www.yccc.edu/.

MARSHALL ISLANDS

College of the Marshall Islands
Majuro, Marshall Islands, Marshall Islands

- **State-supported** 2-year
- **Rural** campus
- **Endowment** $1.2 million
- **Coed,** 995 undergraduate students, 70% full-time, 47% women, 53% men

Undergraduates 693 full-time, 302 part-time. 100% Native Hawaiian or other Pacific Islander, non-Hispanic/Latino; 0.3% American Indian or Alaska Native, non-Hispanic/Latino; 0.4% international; 0.3% transferred in.

Freshmen *Admission:* 333 admitted, 333 enrolled.

Faculty *Total:* 64, 75% full-time. *Student/faculty ratio:* 14:1.

Majors Business administration and management; elementary education; health professions related; liberal arts and sciences/liberal studies; registered nursing/registered nurse.

Academics *Degree:* associate.

Student Life *Housing Options:* Campus housing is university owned and leased by the school.

Financial Aid Of all full-time matriculated undergraduates who enrolled in 2015, 984 applied for aid, 984 were judged to have need. *Average financial aid package:* $4372. *Average need-based gift aid:* $4372. *Financial aid deadline:* 7/15.

Applying *Application fee:* $5. *Required:* high school transcript, minimum 2.0 GPA, health examination form. *Application deadlines:* 6/29 (freshmen), 6/29 (transfers). *Notification:* continuous (freshmen), continuous (transfers).

Freshman Application Contact Ms. Jomi Monica Capelle, Director of Admissions and Records, College of the Marshall Islands, PO Box 1258, Majuro, MH 96960, Marshall Islands. *Phone:* 692-625-6823. *Fax:* 692-625-7203. *E-mail:* cmiadmissions@cmi.edu.

Website: http://www.cmi.edu/.

MARYLAND

Allegany College of Maryland
Cumberland, Maryland

Freshman Application Contact Ms. Cathy Nolan, Director of Admissions and Registration, Allegany College of Maryland, Cumberland, MD 21502.

Phone: 301-784-5000 Ext. 5202. *Fax:* 301-784-5220. *E-mail:* cnolan@allegany.edu. *Website:* http://www.allegany.edu/.

Anne Arundel Community College
Arnold, Maryland

- **State and locally supported** 2-year, founded 1961
- **Suburban** 230-acre campus with easy access to Baltimore and Washington, DC
- **Coed,** 13,904 undergraduate students, 28% full-time, 59% women, 41% men

Undergraduates 3,907 full-time, 9,997 part-time. Students come from 21 states and territories; 94 other countries; 0.8% are from out of state; 18% Black or African American, non-Hispanic/Latino; 7% Hispanic/Latino; 4% Asian, non-Hispanic/Latino; 0.3% Native Hawaiian or other Pacific Islander, non-Hispanic/Latino; 0.4% American Indian or Alaska Native, non-Hispanic/Latino; 4% Two or more races, non-Hispanic/Latino; 6% Race/ethnicity unknown; 1% international; 29% transferred in.

Freshmen *Admission:* 2,939 applied, 2,939 admitted, 2,114 enrolled.

Faculty *Total:* 1,280, 20% full-time, 25% with terminal degrees. *Student/faculty ratio:* 12:1.

Majors Accounting technology and bookkeeping; architectural drafting and CAD/CADD; business administration and management; business administration, management and operations related; business/commerce; chemistry teacher education; child-care and support services management; clinical/medical laboratory technology; communications technologies and support services related; computer and information sciences; computer and information systems security; computer systems networking and telecommunications; criminal justice/law enforcement administration; criminal justice/police science; early childhood education; electrical and electronics engineering; electrical, electronic and communications engineering technology; engineering; English/language arts teacher education; entrepreneurship; fire prevention and safety technology; gerontology; graphic design; health and physical education/fitness; health information/medical records technology; hotel/motel administration; legal assistant/paralegal; liberal arts and sciences and humanities related; liberal arts and sciences/liberal studies; management information systems; management information systems and services related; mathematics; mathematics teacher education; mechatronics, robotics, and automation engineering; medical administrative assistant and medical secretary; medical radiologic technology; multi/interdisciplinary studies related; occupational safety and health technology; physical therapy technology; physics teacher education; pre-law studies; psychiatric/mental health services technology; public health; registered nursing/registered nurse; Spanish language teacher education; substance abuse/addiction counseling; surgical technology.

Academics *Calendar:* semesters. *Degree:* certificates and associate. *Special study options:* academic remediation for entering students, advanced placement credit, cooperative education, distance learning, English as a second language, honors programs, independent study, internships, part-time degree program, services for LD students, summer session for credit. *ROTC:* Army (c), Air Force (c).

Library Andrew G. Truxal Library plus 1 other. *Books:* 152,186 (physical), 114,000 (digital/electronic); *Serial titles:* 135 (physical), 15,000 (digital/electronic); *Databases:* 60. Weekly public service hours: 77.

Student Life *Housing:* college housing not available. *Activities and Organizations:* drama/theater group, student-run newspaper, choral group, Adventure Society, Entrepreneurs Club, Christian Coalition Organization, Gay/Straight Alliance, History Club. *Campus security:* 24-hour emergency response devices and patrols, student patrols, late-night transport/escort service. *Student services:* health clinic, personal/psychological counseling.

Athletics Member NJCAA. *Intercollegiate sports:* baseball M, basketball M/W, cross-country running W, golf M, lacrosse M/W, soccer M/W, softball W, volleyball W.

Costs (2016–17) *Tuition:* area resident $3240 full-time, $108 per credit hour part-time; state resident $6240 full-time, $208 per credit hour part-time; nonresident $11,010 full-time, $367 per credit hour part-time. Full-time tuition and fees vary according to program. Part-time tuition and fees vary according to program. *Required fees:* $770 full-time, $26 per credit hour part-time. *Payment plans:* installment, deferred payment. *Waivers:* adult students, senior citizens, and employees or children of employees.

Applying *Options:* electronic application, early admission. *Required:* high school transcript. *Required for some:* letters of recommendation. *Application deadlines:* rolling (freshmen), rolling (transfers). *Notification:* continuous (freshmen), continuous (transfers).

Freshman Application Contact Mr. Thomas McGinn, Director of Enrollment Development and Admissions, Anne Arundel Community College, 101 College Parkway, Arnold, MD 21012-1895. *Phone:* 410-777-2240. *Fax:* 410-777-2246. *E-mail:* 4info@aacc.edu.

Website: http://www.aacc.edu/.

Baltimore City Community College
Baltimore, Maryland

Freshman Application Contact Baltimore City Community College, 2901 Liberty Heights Avenue, Baltimore, MD 21215-7893. *Phone:* 410-462-8311. *Toll-free phone:* 888-203-1261. *Website:* http://www.bccc.edu/.

Brightwood College, Baltimore Campus
Baltimore, Maryland

Freshman Application Contact Brightwood College, Baltimore Campus, 1520 South Caton Avenue, Baltimore, MD 21227. *Phone:* 410-644-6400. *Toll-free phone:* 866-543-0208. *Website:* http://www.brightwood.edu/.

Brightwood College, Beltsville Campus
Beltsville, Maryland

Freshman Application Contact Brightwood College, Beltsville Campus, 4600 Powder Mill Road, Beltsville, MD 20705. *Phone:* 301-937-8448. *Toll-free phone:* 866-543-0208. *Website:* http://www.brightwood.edu/.

Brightwood College, Towson Campus
Towson, Maryland

Freshman Application Contact Brightwood College, Towson Campus, 803 Glen Eagles Court, Towson, MD 21286. *Phone:* 410-296-5350. *Toll-free phone:* 866-543-0208. *Website:* http://www.brightwood.edu/.

Carroll Community College
Westminster, Maryland

- **State and locally supported** 2-year, founded 1993, part of Maryland Higher Education Commission
- **Suburban** 80-acre campus with easy access to Baltimore
- **Endowment** $6.1 million
- **Coed,** 3,362 undergraduate students, 35% full-time, 60% women, 40% men

Undergraduates 1,164 full-time, 2,198 part-time. Students come from 7 states and territories; 21 other countries; 2% are from out of state; 4% Black or African American, non-Hispanic/Latino; 4% Hispanic/Latino; 2% Asian, non-Hispanic/Latino; 0.1% Native Hawaiian or other Pacific Islander, non-Hispanic/Latino; 0.3% American Indian or Alaska Native, non-Hispanic/Latino; 3% Two or more races, non-Hispanic/Latino; 2% Race/ethnicity unknown; 0.1% international; 5% transferred in.
Freshmen *Admission:* 693 applied, 693 admitted, 676 enrolled.
Faculty *Total:* 250, 30% full-time, 6% with terminal degrees. *Student/faculty ratio:* 14:1.
Majors Accounting technology and bookkeeping; administrative assistant and secretarial science; architectural drafting and CAD/CADD; art; business administration and management; chemistry teacher education; child-care and support services management; computer engineering; computer graphics; criminal justice/police science; early childhood education; education; electrical and electronics engineering; elementary education; emergency medical technology (EMT paramedic); English/language arts teacher education; forensic science and technology; general studies; health information/medical records technology; health professions related; kinesiology and exercise science; legal studies; liberal arts and sciences/liberal studies; licensed practical/vocational nurse training; management information systems; mathematics teacher education; multi/interdisciplinary studies related; music; physical therapy technology; psychology; registered nursing/registered nurse; Spanish language teacher education; theater design and technology.
Academics *Calendar:* semesters plus winter and summer sessions. *Degree:* certificates and associate. *Special study options:* academic remediation for entering students, advanced placement credit, distance learning, English as a second language, honors programs, independent study, internships, part-time degree program, services for LD students, summer session for credit.
Library Carroll Community College Library plus 1 other. *Books:* 41,599 (physical), 695 (digital/electronic); *Serial titles:* 2,491 (physical), 18,070 (digital/electronic); *Databases:* 44.
Student Life *Housing:* college housing not available. *Activities and Organizations:* drama/theater group, choral group, Student Government Organization, S.T.E.M. Club, Campus Activities Board, Service Learning Club, Early Childhood Education Club. *Campus security:* 24-hour emergency response devices, late night security escort to vehicle in parking lot.

Costs (2016–17) *Tuition:* area resident $4812 full-time, $160 per credit hour part-time; state resident $6972 full-time, $232 per credit hour part-time; nonresident $9744 full-time, $325 per credit hour part-time. *Payment plan:* deferred payment. *Waivers:* senior citizens and employees or children of employees.
Financial Aid Of all full-time matriculated undergraduates who enrolled in 2015, 48 Federal Work-Study jobs (averaging $1935).
Applying *Options:* electronic application. *Required:* high school transcript. *Application deadlines:* rolling (freshmen), rolling (out-of-state freshmen), rolling (transfers). *Notification:* continuous (freshmen), continuous (out-of-state freshmen), continuous (transfers).
Freshman Application Contact Ms. Candace Edwards, Director of Admissions, Carroll Community College, 1601 Washington Road, Westminster, MD 21157. *Phone:* 410-386-8405. *Toll-free phone:* 888-221-9748. *Fax:* 410-386-8446. *E-mail:* cedwards@carrollcc.edu. *Website:* http://www.carrollcc.edu/.

Cecil College
North East, Maryland

- **County-supported** primarily 2-year, founded 1968
- **Small-town** 159-acre campus with easy access to Baltimore
- **Coed,** 2,612 undergraduate students, 36% full-time, 63% women, 37% men

Undergraduates 947 full-time, 1,665 part-time. Students come from 10 states and territories; 21 other countries; 11% are from out of state; 11% Black or African American, non-Hispanic/Latino; 6% Hispanic/Latino; 1% Asian, non-Hispanic/Latino; 0.1% Native Hawaiian or other Pacific Islander, non-Hispanic/Latino; 0.2% American Indian or Alaska Native, non-Hispanic/Latino; 4% Two or more races, non-Hispanic/Latino; 0.5% Race/ethnicity unknown; 0.7% international; 4% transferred in. *Retention:* 60% of full-time freshmen returned.
Freshmen *Admission:* 448 enrolled.
Faculty *Total:* 294, 17% full-time, 5% with terminal degrees. *Student/faculty ratio:* 11:1.
Majors Administrative assistant and secretarial science; aeronautics/aviation/aerospace science and technology; air traffic control; animation, interactive technology, video graphics and special effects; applied horticulture/horticulture operations; biology/biological sciences; biotechnology; business administration and management; business/commerce; business/corporate communications; chemistry; child-care and support services management; commercial photography; criminal justice/police science; design and visual communications; drawing; education; electrical, electronic and communications engineering technology; elementary education; emergency medical technology (EMT paramedic); English/language arts teacher education; financial planning and services; fine/studio arts; fire science/firefighting; general studies; health services/allied health/health sciences; horse husbandry/equine science and management; human resources management; liberal arts and sciences/liberal studies; logistics, materials, and supply chain management; management information systems; marketing/marketing management; mathematics; office management; photography; physics; purchasing, procurement/acquisitions and contracts management; registered nursing/registered nurse; secondary education; transportation and materials moving related; transportation/mobility management; web page, digital/multimedia and information resources design.
Academics *Calendar:* semesters. *Degrees:* certificates, associate, and bachelor's. *Special study options:* academic remediation for entering students, accelerated degree program, adult/continuing education programs, advanced placement credit, cooperative education, distance learning, double majors, English as a second language, independent study, internships, off-campus study, part-time degree program, services for LD students, summer session for credit.
Library Cecil County Veterans Memorial Library.
Student Life *Activities and Organizations:* drama/theater group, Student Government, Non-Traditional Student Organization, Student Nurses Association, national fraternities. *Campus security:* 24-hour emergency response devices, late-night transport/escort service, armed patrols from 6:30 am until 7:00 pm. *Student services:* personal/psychological counseling, women's center.
Athletics Member NJCAA. *Intercollegiate sports:* baseball M(s), basketball M(s)/W(s), cheerleading W, lacrosse M(c), soccer M(s)/W(s), softball W(s), tennis W(s), volleyball W(s).
Costs (2017–18) *Tuition:* area resident $3210 full-time, $107 per credit hour part-time; state resident $5910 full-time, $197 per credit hour part-time; nonresident $7260 full-time, $242 per credit hour part-time. *Required fees:* $420 full-time. *Payment plan:* deferred payment. *Waivers:* senior citizens and employees or children of employees.

Applying *Options:* electronic application, early admission, deferred entrance. *Required:* high school transcript. *Application deadlines:* rolling (freshmen), rolling (transfers). *Notification:* continuous (freshmen), continuous (transfers). **Freshman Application Contact** Dr. Diane Lane, Cecil College, One Seahawk Drive, North East, MD 21901-1999. *Phone:* 410-287-1002. *Fax:* 410-287-1001. *E-mail:* dlane@cecil.edu. *Website:* http://www.cecil.edu/.

Chesapeake College
Wye Mills, Maryland

- **State and locally supported** 2-year, founded 1965
- **Rural** 170-acre campus with easy access to Baltimore and Washington, DC
- **Endowment** $2.3 million
- **Coed,** 2,112 undergraduate students, 30% full-time, 65% women, 35% men

Undergraduates 641 full-time, 1,471 part-time. 16% Black or African American, non-Hispanic/Latino; 6% Hispanic/Latino; 1% Asian, non-Hispanic/Latino; 0.9% American Indian or Alaska Native, non-Hispanic/Latino; 3% Two or more races, non-Hispanic/Latino; 4% Race/ethnicity unknown; 1% international; 42% transferred in. *Retention:* 53% of full-time freshmen returned.
Freshmen *Admission:* 505 enrolled.
Faculty *Total:* 113, 50% full-time, 20% with terminal degrees. *Student/faculty ratio:* 15:1.
Majors Accounting technology and bookkeeping; agricultural production; biology/biological sciences; business administration and management; business/commerce; chemistry teacher education; child-care and support services management; computer and information sciences and support services related; computer and information systems security; computer science; corrections and criminal justice related; early childhood education; education; elementary education; emergency medical technology (EMT paramedic); engineering-related technologies; engineering technologies and engineering related; English/language arts teacher education; environmental science; general studies; health and physical education related; hospitality administration; hospitality administration related; landscape architecture; legal assistant/paralegal; liberal arts and sciences and humanities related; liberal arts and sciences/liberal studies; mathematics teacher education; medical radiologic technology; mental and social health services and allied professions related; physical therapy; physical therapy technology; physics teacher education; registered nursing/registered nurse.
Academics *Calendar:* semesters. *Degree:* certificates and associate. *Special study options:* academic remediation for entering students, adult/continuing education programs, advanced placement credit, distance learning, English as a second language, honors programs, independent study, internships, part-time degree program, services for LD students, summer session for credit.
Library Learning Resource Center. *Books:* 44,000 (physical), 300,000 (digital/electronic); *Serial titles:* 38 (physical), 25,500 (digital/electronic); *Databases:* 56. Weekly public service hours: 56.
Student Life *Housing:* college housing not available. *Activities and Organizations:* drama/theater group, Student Senate, Geek club, Green Team, Phi Theta Kappa, UHURU. *Campus security:* 24-hour emergency response devices.
Athletics Member NJCAA. *Intercollegiate sports:* baseball M, basketball M/W, soccer M, softball W, volleyball W.
Costs (2016–17) *Tuition:* area resident $3600 full-time, $120 per credit hour part-time; state resident $5640 full-time, $188 per credit hour part-time; nonresident $7950 full-time, $265 per credit hour part-time. *Required fees:* $1100 full-time, $35 per credit hour part-time, $25 per term part-time. *Payment plan:* installment. *Waivers:* senior citizens and employees or children of employees.
Financial Aid Of all full-time matriculated undergraduates who enrolled in 2015, 32 Federal Work-Study jobs (averaging $1482).
Applying *Options:* electronic application. *Required:* high school transcript. *Application deadlines:* rolling (freshmen), rolling (transfers). *Notification:* continuous (freshmen), continuous (transfers).
Freshman Application Contact Ms. Angela Denherder, Director of Student Recruitment and Outreach, Chesapeake College, PO Box 8, Wye Mills, MD 21679-0008. *Phone:* 410-827-5856. *E-mail:* adenherder@chesapeake.edu. *Website:* http://www.chesapeake.edu/.

College of Southern Maryland
La Plata, Maryland

Freshman Application Contact Admissions Department, College of Southern Maryland, PO Box 910, La Plata, MD 20646-0910. *Phone:* 301-934-2251. *Toll-free phone:* 800-933-9177. *Fax:* 301-934-7698. *E-mail:* askme@csmd.edu. *Website:* http://www.csmd.edu/.

Community College of Baltimore County
Baltimore, Maryland

- **County-supported** 2-year, founded 1957
- **Suburban** 350-acre campus with easy access to Baltimore
- **Coed,** 21,416 undergraduate students, 29% full-time, 61% women, 39% men

Undergraduates 6,105 full-time, 15,311 part-time. 39% Black or African American, non-Hispanic/Latino; 5% Hispanic/Latino; 6% Asian, non-Hispanic/Latino; 0.2% Native Hawaiian or other Pacific Islander, non-Hispanic/Latino; 0.3% American Indian or Alaska Native, non-Hispanic/Latino; 3% Two or more races, non-Hispanic/Latino; 0.6% Race/ethnicity unknown; 5% international.
Freshmen *Admission:* 3,969 enrolled.
Faculty *Total:* 1,203, 36% full-time, 10% with terminal degrees.
Majors Accounting technology and bookkeeping; administrative assistant and secretarial science; aeronautics/aviation/aerospace science and technology; airline pilot and flight crew; air traffic control; applied horticulture/horticulture operations; architectural drafting and CAD/CADD; automobile/automotive mechanics technology; aviation/airway management; biological and physical sciences; building/construction finishing, management, and inspection related; building/construction site management; business administration and management; business/commerce; chemistry teacher education; child-care and support services management; clinical/medical laboratory technology; commercial and advertising art; communications technologies and support services related; computer and information sciences; computer and information systems security; computer engineering; computer systems networking and telecommunications; criminal justice/police science; dental hygiene; early childhood education; education; electrical and electronics engineering; elementary education; emergency medical technology (EMT paramedic); engineering; engineering technologies and engineering related; funeral service and mortuary science; geography; heating, ventilation, air conditioning and refrigeration engineering technology; hotel/motel administration; hydraulics and fluid power technology; legal assistant/paralegal; liberal arts and sciences and humanities related; liberal arts and sciences/liberal studies; management information systems; manufacturing engineering technology; massage therapy; mathematics teacher education; medical administrative assistant and medical secretary; medical informatics; medical radiologic technology; occupational safety and health technology; occupational therapy; parks, recreation, leisure, and fitness studies related; physics teacher education; psychiatric/mental health services technology; registered nursing/registered nurse; respiratory care therapy; sign language interpretation and translation; Spanish language teacher education; substance abuse/addiction counseling; surveying technology; veterinary/animal health technology; visual and performing arts.
Academics *Calendar:* semesters. *Degree:* certificates and associate. *Special study options:* academic remediation for entering students, advanced placement credit, cooperative education, distance learning, English as a second language, honors programs, independent study, internships, off-campus study, part-time degree program, services for LD students, study abroad, summer session for credit.
Student Life *Housing:* college housing not available. *Activities and Organizations:* drama/theater group, student-run newspaper, choral group. *Campus security:* 24-hour emergency response devices and patrols, late-night transport/escort service.
Athletics Member NJCAA. *Intercollegiate sports:* baseball M(s), basketball M(s)/W(s), cross-country running M(s)/W(s), lacrosse M(s)/W(s), soccer M(s)/W(s), softball W(s), volleyball W(s).
Costs (2016–17) *Tuition:* area resident $3540 full-time, $118 per credit hour part-time; state resident $6660 full-time, $222 per credit hour part-time; nonresident $10,110 full-time, $337 per credit hour part-time. Full-time tuition and fees vary according to course load. Part-time tuition and fees vary according to course load. *Required fees:* $892 full-time. *Payment plan:* installment. *Waivers:* minority students, senior citizens, and employees or children of employees.
Applying *Options:* electronic application. *Required:* high school transcript. *Application deadlines:* rolling (freshmen), rolling (transfers).
Freshman Application Contact Ms. Diane Drake, Director of Admissions, Community College of Baltimore County, 7201 Rossville Boulevard, Baltimore, MD 21237-3899. *Phone:* 443-840-4392. *E-mail:* ddrake@ccbcmd.edu. *Website:* http://www.ccbcmd.edu/.

Fortis College
Landover, Maryland

Admissions Office Contact Fortis College, 4351 Garden City Drive, Landover, MD 20785. *Toll-free phone:* 855-4-FORTIS. *Website:* http://www.fortis.edu/.

Frederick Community College
Frederick, Maryland

- **State and locally supported** 2-year, founded 1957
- **Small-town** 100-acre campus with easy access to Baltimore and Washington, DC
- **Endowment** $9.6 million
- **Coed,** 6,252 undergraduate students, 32% full-time, 56% women, 44% men

Undergraduates 1,996 full-time, 4,256 part-time. 2% are from out of state; 15% Black or African American, non-Hispanic/Latino; 12% Hispanic/Latino; 4% Asian, non-Hispanic/Latino; 0.1% Native Hawaiian or other Pacific Islander, non-Hispanic/Latino; 0.3% American Indian or Alaska Native, non-Hispanic/Latino; 5% Two or more races, non-Hispanic/Latino; 0.2% Race/ethnicity unknown; 0.7% international; 3% transferred in. *Retention:* 44% of full-time freshmen returned.

Freshmen *Admission:* 1,369 enrolled.

Faculty *Total:* 475, 21% full-time, 16% with terminal degrees. *Student/faculty ratio:* 13:1.

Majors Accounting; art; biology/biological sciences; building/construction finishing, management, and inspection related; business administration and management; chemistry; child development; computer science; criminal justice/law enforcement administration; drafting and design technology; early childhood education; education; elementary education; emergency medical technology (EMT paramedic); engineering; fire science/firefighting; general studies; human services; information technology; legal assistant/paralegal; liberal arts and sciences/liberal studies; mathematics; mathematics teacher education; medical administrative assistant and medical secretary; medical/clinical assistant; nuclear medical technology; political science and government; psychology; registered nursing/registered nurse; respiratory care therapy; Spanish language teacher education; surgical technology.

Academics *Calendar:* semesters. *Degree:* certificates and associate. *Special study options:* academic remediation for entering students, adult/continuing education programs, advanced placement credit, cooperative education, distance learning, English as a second language, external degree program, freshman honors college, honors programs, independent study, internships, off-campus study, part-time degree program, services for LD students, study abroad, summer session for credit.

Library FCC Library. *Books:* 11,831 (physical), 47,478 (digital/electronic); *Serial titles:* 19 (physical); *Databases:* 25. Students can reserve study rooms.

Student Life *Housing:* college housing not available. *Activities and Organizations:* drama/theater group, student-run newspaper. *Campus security:* 24-hour emergency response devices and patrols, late-night transport/escort service. *Student services:* personal/psychological counseling, women's center.

Athletics Member NJCAA. *Intercollegiate sports:* baseball M, basketball M/W, golf M/W, lacrosse M/W, soccer M/W, softball W, volleyball W.

Costs (2016–17) *Tuition:* area resident $4255 full-time, $119 per credit hour part-time; state resident $8455 full-time, $259 per credit hour part-time; nonresident $11,215 full-time, $351 per credit hour part-time. Full-time tuition and fees vary according to course load. Part-time tuition and fees vary according to course load. *Required fees:* $685 full-time, $25 per credit hour part-time, $274 per semester part-time. *Payment plans:* installment, deferred payment. *Waivers:* senior citizens.

Financial Aid Of all full-time matriculated undergraduates who enrolled in 2015, 25 Federal Work-Study jobs (averaging $1368). 14 state and other part-time jobs (averaging $2715).

Applying *Options:* electronic application. *Recommended:* high school transcript. *Application deadlines:* rolling (freshmen), rolling (transfers). *Notification:* continuous (freshmen), continuous (transfers).

Freshman Application Contact Ms. Lisa A. Freel, Director of Admissions, Frederick Community College, 7932 Opossumtown Pike, Frederick, MD 21702. *Phone:* 301-846-2468. *Fax:* 301-624-2799.
E-mail: admissions@frederick.edu.
Website: http://www.frederick.edu/.

Garrett College
McHenry, Maryland

- **State and locally supported** 2-year, founded 1966
- **Rural** 62-acre campus
- **Coed,** 754 undergraduate students, 69% full-time, 51% women, 49% men

Undergraduates 523 full-time, 231 part-time. Students come from 12 states and territories; 6 other countries; 19% are from out of state; 25% Black or African American, non-Hispanic/Latino; 1% Hispanic/Latino; 0.3% American Indian or Alaska Native, non-Hispanic/Latino; 3% Two or more races, non-Hispanic/Latino; 0.3% Race/ethnicity unknown; 1% international; 4% transferred in; 24% live on campus.

Freshmen *Admission:* 1,159 applied, 820 admitted, 192 enrolled. *Average high school GPA:* 2.52.

Faculty *Total:* 55, 36% full-time, 7% with terminal degrees. *Student/faculty ratio:* 19:1.

Majors Business administration and management; business automation/technology/data entry; business/commerce; corrections; early childhood education; education; electrical and electronics engineering; elementary education; liberal arts and sciences and humanities related; liberal arts and sciences/liberal studies; management information systems; sport and fitness administration/management; wildlife, fish and wildlands science and management.

Academics *Calendar:* semesters. *Degree:* certificates and associate. *Special study options:* academic remediation for entering students, adult/continuing education programs, advanced placement credit, cooperative education, distance learning, double majors, external degree program, honors programs, independent study, internships, part-time degree program, services for LD students, summer session for credit.

Library Learning Resource Center. *Books:* 31,225 (physical), 35,243 (digital/electronic); *Serial titles:* 119 (physical); *Databases:* 21. Weekly public service hours: 64.

Student Life *Housing Options:* coed, special housing for students with disabilities. Campus housing is university owned and leased by the school. *Activities and Organizations:* SGA, International Students Club, CRU, SING (Students in Need Group), Rock Climbing Wall (open sessions). *Campus security:* 24-hour emergency response devices and patrols, controlled dormitory access. *Student services:* health clinic, personal/psychological counseling.

Athletics Member NJCAA. *Intercollegiate sports:* baseball M(s), basketball M(s)/W(s), golf M, softball W(s), volleyball W(s). *Intramural sports:* basketball M/W, cheerleading M(c)/W(c), football M/W, ultimate Frisbee M/W.

Costs (2017–18) *Tuition:* area resident $2884 full-time, $103 per credit hour part-time; state resident $6300 full-time, $225 per credit hour part-time; nonresident $7420 full-time, $265 per credit hour part-time. Full-time tuition and fees vary according to program and reciprocity agreements. Part-time tuition and fees vary according to program and reciprocity agreements. *Required fees:* $896 full-time, $32 per credit hour part-time, $25 per term part-time. *Room and board:* $7400; room only: $5400. Room and board charges vary according to board plan and housing facility. *Payment plans:* installment, deferred payment. *Waivers:* senior citizens and employees or children of employees.

Financial Aid Of all full-time matriculated undergraduates who enrolled in 2015, 432 applied for aid, 432 were judged to have need. 55 Federal Work-Study jobs (averaging $743). 4 state and other part-time jobs (averaging $625). *Average percent of need met:* 63%. *Average financial aid package:* $8350. *Average need-based loan:* $1918. *Average need-based gift aid:* $4525. *Average non-need-based aid:* $2814. *Average indebtedness upon graduation:* $3960.

Applying *Options:* electronic application, early admission, deferred entrance. *Required:* high school transcript. *Application deadlines:* rolling (freshmen), rolling (transfers). *Notification:* continuous (freshmen), continuous (transfers).

Freshman Application Contact Mrs. Shauna McQuade, Director of Enrollment Management, Garrett College, 687 Mosser Road, McHenry, MD 21541. *Phone:* 301-387-3739. *Toll-free phone:* 866-55-GARRETT.
E-mail: admissions@garrettcollege.edu.
Website: http://www.garrettcollege.edu/.

Hagerstown Community College
Hagerstown, Maryland

- **State and locally supported** 2-year, founded 1946
- **Suburban** 319-acre campus with easy access to Baltimore and Washington, DC
- **Coed,** 4,276 undergraduate students, 25% full-time, 62% women, 38% men

Undergraduates 1,090 full-time, 3,186 part-time. 9% Black or African American, non-Hispanic/Latino; 6% Hispanic/Latino; 2% Asian, non-Hispanic/Latino; 0.2% Native Hawaiian or other Pacific Islander, non-Hispanic/Latino; 0.2% American Indian or Alaska Native, non-Hispanic/Latino; 4% Two or more races, non-Hispanic/Latino; 2% Race/ethnicity unknown; 1% international; 8% transferred in.

Freshmen *Admission:* 793 enrolled.

Faculty *Total:* 232, 34% full-time, 6% with terminal degrees. *Student/faculty ratio:* 16:1.

Majors Accounting technology and bookkeeping; animation, interactive technology, video graphics and special effects; biology/biotechnology laboratory technician; business administration and management; business/commerce; child-care and support services management; commercial and advertising art; computer and information sciences; computer and information systems security; criminal justice/police science; dental hygiene; early childhood education; education; elementary education; emergency medical technology (EMT paramedic); engineering; engineering technologies and engineering related; English/language arts teacher education; industrial technology; instrumentation technology; liberal arts and sciences and humanities related; liberal arts and sciences/liberal studies; management information systems; mechanical engineering/mechanical technology; medical radiologic technology; psychiatric/mental health services technology; registered nursing/registered nurse; transportation/mobility management; web page, digital/multimedia and information resources design.

Academics *Calendar:* semesters. *Degree:* certificates and associate. *Special study options:* academic remediation for entering students, accelerated degree program, adult/continuing education programs, advanced placement credit, cooperative education, distance learning, English as a second language, honors programs, independent study, internships, off-campus study, part-time degree program, services for LD students, summer session for credit.

Library William Brish Library.

Student Life *Activities and Organizations:* drama/theater group, student-run newspaper, choral group, Phi Theta Kappa, Robinwood Players Theater Club, Association of Nursing Students, Radiography Club, Art and Design Club. *Campus security:* 24-hour patrols, student patrols. *Student services:* personal/psychological counseling.

Athletics Member NJCAA. *Intercollegiate sports:* baseball M(s), basketball M(s)/W(s), cross-country running M(s)/W(s), golf M/W, soccer M(s)/W, softball W(s), track and field M(s)/W(s), volleyball W(s). *Intramural sports:* cheerleading M/W, golf M/W, lacrosse M/W, table tennis M/W, tennis M/W.

Costs (2016–17) *Tuition:* area resident $3042 full-time, $117 per credit hour part-time; state resident $4758 full-time, $183 per credit hour part-time; nonresident $6266 full-time, $241 per credit hour part-time. Full-time tuition and fees vary according to course load, program, and reciprocity agreements. Part-time tuition and fees vary according to course load, program, and reciprocity agreements. *Required fees:* $522 full-time, $12 per credit hour part-time, $30 per term part-time. *Payment plan:* installment. *Waivers:* senior citizens and employees or children of employees.

Financial Aid Of all full-time matriculated undergraduates who enrolled in 2016, 823 applied for aid, 688 were judged to have need, 32 had their need fully met. 43 Federal Work-Study jobs (averaging $2054). 170 state and other part-time jobs (averaging $2500). In 2016, 27 non-need-based awards were made. *Average percent of need met:* 47%. *Average financial aid package:* $5815. *Average need-based loan:* $3149. *Average need-based gift aid:* $4705. *Average non-need-based aid:* $834.

Applying *Options:* electronic application, early admission, deferred entrance. *Required for some:* high school transcript. *Application deadlines:* rolling (freshmen), rolling (out-of-state freshmen), rolling (transfers). *Notification:* continuous (freshmen), continuous (out-of-state freshmen), continuous (transfers).

Freshman Application Contact Mr. Kevin L. Crawford, Director, Admissions & Enrollment Management, Hagerstown Community College, 11400 Robinwood Drive, Hagerstown, MD 21742-6514. *Phone:* 240-500-2412. *Fax:* 301-791-9165. *E-mail:* klcrawford@hagerstowncc.edu. *Website:* http://www.hagerstowncc.edu/.

Harford Community College
Bel Air, Maryland

- **State and locally supported** 2-year, founded 1957
- **Small-town** 352-acre campus with easy access to Baltimore
- **Coed,** 10,310 undergraduate students, 40% full-time, 58% women, 42% men

Undergraduates 4,174 full-time, 6,136 part-time. Students come from 25 states and territories; 64 other countries; 3% are from out of state; 16% Black or African American, non-Hispanic/Latino; 5% Hispanic/Latino; 3% Asian, non-Hispanic/Latino; 0.2% Native Hawaiian or other Pacific Islander, non-Hispanic/Latino; 0.4% American Indian or Alaska Native, non-Hispanic/Latino; 3% Two or more races, non-Hispanic/Latino; 0.9% Race/ethnicity unknown; 1% international; 2% transferred in.

Freshmen *Admission:* 1,240 applied, 1,240 admitted, 1,240 enrolled.

Faculty *Total:* 339, 30% full-time, 11% with terminal degrees. *Student/faculty ratio:* 20:1.

Majors Accounting; administrative assistant and secretarial science; advertising; agribusiness; agriculture; anthropology; biology/biological sciences; business administration and management; chemistry; chemistry teacher education; civil drafting and CAD/CADD; computer and information sciences; computer science; criminal justice/police science; digital arts; early childhood education; education; education (specific levels and methods) related; education (specific subject areas) related; electroneurodiagnostic/electroencephalographic technology; elementary education; engineering; engineering technology; English; English/language arts teacher education; entrepreneurship; environmental engineering technology; environmental science; fine/studio arts; general studies; graphic design; history; human resources management; information science/studies; interior design; international relations and affairs; legal assistant/paralegal; marketing/marketing management; mass communication/media; mathematics;

mathematics teacher education; medical office assistant; music; philosophy; photography; physics; physics teacher education; political science and government; psychology; registered nursing, nursing administration, nursing research and clinical nursing related; social work; sociology; Spanish language teacher education; special education; special education–early childhood; special education–elementary school; teacher assistant/aide; theater design and technology.

Academics *Calendar:* semesters. *Degree:* certificates, diplomas, and associate. *Special study options:* academic remediation for entering students, adult/continuing education programs, advanced placement credit, cooperative education, distance learning, double majors, English as a second language, honors programs, independent study, internships, part-time degree program, services for LD students, student-designed majors, study abroad, summer session for credit.

Library Harford Community College Library.

Student Life *Housing:* college housing not available. *Activities and Organizations:* drama/theater group, student-run newspaper, radio station, choral group, Phi Theta Kappa, Student Nurses Association, Gamers Guild, Actor's Guild, Future Educators of America. *Campus security:* 24-hour patrols, late-night transport/escort service. *Student services:* personal/psychological counseling.

Athletics Member NJCAA. *Intercollegiate sports:* baseball M(s), basketball M(s)/W(s), cross-country running M(s)/W(s), golf M(s), lacrosse M(s)/W(s), soccer M(s)/W(s), softball W(s), tennis M(s)/W(s), volleyball W(s). *Intramural sports:* badminton M/W, basketball M/W, cheerleading M(c)/W(c), football M/W, soccer M/W, softball M/W, swimming and diving M/W, tennis M/W, volleyball M/W.

Costs (2016–17) *Tuition:* area resident $3720 full-time, $124 per credit hour part-time; state resident $6330 full-time, $211 per credit hour part-time; nonresident $8940 full-time, $298 per credit hour part-time. *Required fees:* $744 full-time, $25 per credit hour part-time. *Payment plan:* installment. *Waivers:* senior citizens and employees or children of employees.

Financial Aid Of all full-time matriculated undergraduates who enrolled in 2015, 1,417 applied for aid, 974 were judged to have need. 61 Federal Work-Study jobs (averaging $2136).

Applying *Options:* electronic application. *Application deadlines:* rolling (freshmen), rolling (transfers). *Notification:* continuous (freshmen), continuous (out-of-state freshmen), continuous (transfers).

Freshman Application Contact Jennifer Starkey, Enrollment Services Associate - Admissions, Harford Community College, 401 Thomas Run Road, Bel Air, MD 21015-1698. *Phone:* 443-412-2311. *Fax:* 443-412-2169. *E-mail:* jestarkey@harford.edu. *Website:* http://www.harford.edu/.

Howard Community College
Columbia, Maryland

- **State and locally supported** 2-year, founded 1966
- **Suburban** 122-acre campus with easy access to Baltimore and Washington, DC
- **Coed,** 9,741 undergraduate students, 35% full-time, 53% women, 41% men

Undergraduates 3,448 full-time, 5,715 part-time. Students come from 13 states and territories; 111 other countries; 0.3% are from out of state; 29% Black or African American, non-Hispanic/Latino; 11% Hispanic/Latino; 13% Asian, non-Hispanic/Latino; 0.3% Native Hawaiian or other Pacific Islander, non-Hispanic/Latino; 0.3% American Indian or Alaska Native, non-Hispanic/Latino; 5% Two or more races, non-Hispanic/Latino; 3% Race/ethnicity unknown; 5% international; 85% transferred in.

Freshmen *Admission:* 1,373 applied, 1,363 admitted, 789 enrolled.

Faculty *Total:* 819, 24% full-time, 7% with terminal degrees. *Student/faculty ratio:* 15:1.

Majors Accounting; art; biological and physical sciences; biomedical technology; biotechnology; business administration and management; cardiovascular technology; child development; clinical laboratory science/medical technology; computer and information sciences related; computer graphics; computer/information technology services administration related; computer science; computer systems networking and telecommunications; criminal justice/law enforcement administration; design and applied arts related; diagnostic medical sonography and ultrasound technology; dramatic/theater arts; electrical, electronic and communications engineering technology; elementary education; emergency medical technology (EMT paramedic); engineering; environmental studies; financial planning and services; general studies; health teacher education; information science/studies; information technology; kindergarten/preschool education; legal administrative assistant/secretary; liberal arts and sciences/liberal studies; licensed practical/vocational nurse training; medical administrative assistant and medical secretary; music; nuclear medical technology; office management; photography; physical sciences; physical therapy technology; premedical studies; pre-pharmacy studies; registered nursing/registered nurse; secondary education; social sciences; sport and fitness administration/management; substance abuse/addiction counseling; telecommunications technology; theater design and technology.

Academics *Calendar:* semesters. *Degree:* certificates and associate. *Special study options:* academic remediation for entering students, adult/continuing education programs, advanced placement credit, cooperative education, distance learning, double majors, English as a second language, external degree program, freshman honors college, honors programs, internships, off-campus study, part-time degree program, services for LD students, study abroad, summer session for credit.

Library Howard Community College Library. Students can reserve study rooms.

Student Life *Housing:* college housing not available. *Activities and Organizations:* drama/theater group, student-run newspaper, radio station, choral group, Phi Theta Kappa, Nursing Club, Black Leadership Organization, Student Newspaper, Student Government Association. *Campus security:* 24-hour emergency response devices and patrols, late-night transport/escort service. *Student services:* personal/psychological counseling.

Athletics Member NJCAA. *Intercollegiate sports:* basketball M/W, cross-country running M/W, lacrosse M/W, soccer M/W, track and field M/W, volleyball W. *Intramural sports:* basketball M/W.

Standardized Tests *Required for some:* SAT or ACT (for admission).

Costs (2016–17) *Tuition:* area resident $4020 full-time, $134 per semester hour part-time; state resident $6510 full-time, $217 per semester hour part-time; nonresident $7860 full-time, $262 per semester hour part-time. Full-time tuition and fees vary according to course load. Part-time tuition and fees vary according to course load. *Required fees:* $674 full-time, $22 per semester hour part-time. *Payment plan:* installment. *Waivers:* senior citizens and employees or children of employees.

Financial Aid Of all full-time matriculated undergraduates who enrolled in 2013, 571 applied for aid, 477 were judged to have need. In 2013, 31 non-need-based awards were made. *Average percent of need met:* 22%. *Average financial aid package:* $3871. *Average need-based loan:* $2525. *Average need-based gift aid:* $4032. *Average non-need-based aid:* $1288.

Applying *Options:* electronic application, early admission, deferred entrance. *Application fee:* $25. *Required for some:* essay or personal statement, high school transcript, minimum 3.2 GPA, 2 letters of recommendation. *Application deadlines:* rolling (freshmen), rolling (transfers). *Notification:* continuous (freshmen), continuous (transfers).

Freshman Application Contact Ms. Christine Palmer, Assistant Director of Admissions, Howard Community College, 10901 Little Patuxent Parkway, Columbia, MD 21044-3197. *Phone:* 443-518-4599. *Fax:* 443-518-4589. *E-mail:* admissions@howardcc.edu.
Website: http://www.howardcc.edu/.

Kaplan University, Hagerstown Campus
Hagerstown, Maryland

Freshman Application Contact Kaplan University, Hagerstown Campus, 18618 Crestwood Drive, Hagerstown, MD 21742. *Phone:* 301-739-2680 Ext. 217. *Toll-free phone:* 800-987-7734.
Website: http://www.kaplanuniversity.edu/.

Lincoln College of Technology
Columbia, Maryland

Admissions Office Contact Lincoln College of Technology, 9325 Snowden River Parkway, Columbia, MD 21046. *Toll-free phone:* 844-215-1513.
Website: http://www.lincolntech.edu/.

Montgomery College
Rockville, Maryland

- **State and locally supported** 2-year, founded 1946
- **Suburban** 333-acre campus with easy access to Washington, DC
- **Endowment** $23.8 million
- **Coed,** 23,916 undergraduate students, 36% full-time, 53% women, 47% men

Undergraduates 8,493 full-time, 15,423 part-time. Students come from 26 states and territories; 159 other countries; 3% are from out of state; 26% Black or African American, non-Hispanic/Latino; 24% Hispanic/Latino; 12% Asian, non-Hispanic/Latino; 0.2% Native Hawaiian or other Pacific Islander, non-Hispanic/Latino; 0.2% American Indian or Alaska Native, non-Hispanic/Latino; 3% Two or more races, non-Hispanic/Latino; 0.1% Race/ethnicity unknown; 9% international; 63% transferred in.
Freshmen *Admission:* 10,707 applied, 10,707 admitted, 3,648 enrolled.
Faculty *Total:* 1,404, 35% full-time, 34% with terminal degrees. *Student/faculty ratio:* 17:1.

Majors Accounting technology and bookkeeping; American Sign Language (ASL); animation, interactive technology, video graphics and special effects; applied horticulture/horticulture operations; architectural drafting and CAD/CADD; art; automobile/automotive mechanics technology; biology/biotechnology laboratory technician; building/construction finishing, management, and inspection related; business/commerce; chemistry teacher education; child-care provision; commercial and advertising art; commercial photography; communications technologies and support services related; computer and information sciences; computer and information systems security; computer technology/computer systems technology; criminal justice/police science; crisis/emergency/disaster management; data entry/microcomputer applications; diagnostic medical sonography and ultrasound technology; early childhood education; elementary education; engineering; English/language arts teacher education; fire prevention and safety technology; geography; health information/medical records technology; hotel/motel administration; interior design; legal assistant/paralegal; liberal arts and sciences and humanities related; liberal arts and sciences/liberal studies; mathematics teacher education; medical radiologic technology; physical therapy technology; physics teacher education; psychiatric/mental health services technology; registered nursing/registered nurse; Spanish language teacher education; speech communication and rhetoric; surgical technology; web page, digital/multimedia and information resources design.

Academics *Calendar:* semesters. *Degree:* certificates and associate. *Special study options:* academic remediation for entering students, adult/continuing education programs, advanced placement credit, cooperative education, distance learning, double majors, English as a second language, external degree program, honors programs, independent study, internships, off-campus study, part-time degree program, services for LD students, study abroad, summer session for credit. *ROTC:* Air Force (c).

Library Montgomery College Library plus 2 others. *Books:* 282,902 (physical), 21,883 (digital/electronic); *Serial titles:* 847 (physical), 109,125 (digital/electronic); *Databases:* 128. Weekly public service hours: 71; students can reserve study rooms.

Student Life *Activities and Organizations:* drama/theater group, student-run newspaper, choral group, marching band, Math Club, Engineers without Borders (EWB), STEM Education Community Club, Anime Club, Green Tech Clubs. *Campus security:* 24-hour emergency response devices and patrols, controlled dormitory access. *Student services:* personal/psychological counseling, women's center.

Athletics Member NJCAA. *Intercollegiate sports:* baseball M, basketball M/W, soccer M/W, softball W, tennis M/W, track and field M/W, volleyball W. *Intramural sports:* baseball M, basketball M/W, cheerleading W, cross-country running M, soccer M/W, softball W, tennis M/W, track and field M/W, volleyball W.

Costs (2016–17) *Tuition:* area resident $3416 full-time, $122 per credit hour part-time; state resident $6972 full-time, $249 per credit hour part-time; nonresident $9632 full-time, $344 per credit hour part-time. Full-time tuition and fees vary according to course load. Part-time tuition and fees vary according to course load. *Required fees:* $1159 full-time, $41 per credit hour part-time. *Room and board:* $13,430; room only: $5310. *Payment plan:* installment. *Waivers:* senior citizens and employees or children of employees.

Financial Aid Of all full-time matriculated undergraduates who enrolled in 2014, 217 Federal Work-Study jobs (averaging $3469).

Applying *Options:* electronic application, early admission, deferred entrance. *Application fee:* $25. *Recommended:* high school transcript. *Application deadlines:* rolling (freshmen), rolling (transfers). *Notification:* continuous (freshmen), continuous (transfers).

Freshman Application Contact Montgomery College, 51 Mannakee Street, Rockville, MD 20850. *Phone:* 240-567-5036.
Website: http://www.montgomerycollege.edu/.

Prince George's Community College
Largo, Maryland

Freshman Application Contact Ms. Vera Bagley, Director of Admissions and Records, Prince George's Community College, 301 Largo Road, Largo, MD 20774-2199. *Phone:* 301-322-0801. *Fax:* 301-322-0119. *E-mail:* enrollmentservices@pgcc.edu. *Website:* http://www.pgcc.edu/.

Wor-Wic Community College
Salisbury, Maryland

- **State and locally supported** 2-year, founded 1976
- **Small-town** 202-acre campus
- **Endowment** $15.2 million
- **Coed,** 3,098 undergraduate students, 27% full-time, 65% women, 35% men

Undergraduates 833 full-time, 2,265 part-time. Students come from 8 states and territories; 4 other countries; 2% are from out of state; 27% Black or

African American, non-Hispanic/Latino; 5% Hispanic/Latino; 2% Asian, non-Hispanic/Latino; 0.1% Native Hawaiian or other Pacific Islander, non-Hispanic/Latino; 0.3% American Indian or Alaska Native, non-Hispanic/Latino; 4% Two or more races, non-Hispanic/Latino; 1% Race/ethnicity unknown; 0.6% international; 6% transferred in.

Freshmen *Admission:* 1,011 applied, 1,011 admitted, 596 enrolled.

Faculty *Total:* 157, 45% full-time, 20% with terminal degrees. *Student/faculty ratio:* 16:1.

Majors Administrative assistant and secretarial science; biological and physical sciences; business administration and management; business/commerce; child-care and support services management; computer and information sciences; computer systems analysis; criminal justice/police science; early childhood education; education; elementary education; emergency medical technology (EMT paramedic); hospitality administration; liberal arts and sciences and humanities related; liberal arts and sciences/liberal studies; medical radiologic technology; occupational therapist assistant; physical therapy technology; registered nursing/registered nurse; substance abuse/addiction counseling.

Academics *Calendar:* semesters. *Degree:* certificates and associate. *Special study options:* academic remediation for entering students, accelerated degree program, adult/continuing education programs, advanced placement credit, distance learning, double majors, English as a second language, honors programs, independent study, internships, part-time degree program, services for LD students, summer session for credit.

Library Patricia M. Hazel Media Center plus 4 others. *Databases:* 75.

Student Life *Housing:* college housing not available. *Activities and Organizations:* drama/theater group, Anime Club, Criminal Justice Club, Role Playing Game Association, Veterans and Military Association, Alpha Nu Omicron (PTK). *Campus security:* 24-hour emergency response devices, late-night transport/escort service, patrols by trained security personnel 9 am to midnight. *Student services:* personal/psychological counseling.

Costs (2016–17) *Tuition:* area resident $3180 full-time, $106 per credit part-time; state resident $7110 full-time, $237 per credit part-time; nonresident $8760 full-time, $292 per credit part-time. *Required fees:* $510 full-time, $17 per credit part-time. *Payment plan:* installment. *Waivers:* senior citizens and employees or children of employees.

Applying *Options:* electronic application, early admission. *Recommended:* high school transcript. *Application deadlines:* rolling (freshmen), rolling (transfers).

Freshman Application Contact Mr. Richard Webster, Director of Admissions, Wor-Wic Community College, 32000 Campus Drive, Salisbury, MD 21804. *Phone:* 410-334-2895. *Fax:* 410-334-2954. *E-mail:* admissions@worwic.edu. *Website:* http://www.worwic.edu/.

MASSACHUSETTS

Bay State College
Boston, Massachusetts

Freshman Application Contact Kimberly Odusami, Director of Admissions, Bay State College, 122 Commonwealth Avenue, Boston, MA 02116. *Phone:* 617-217-9186. *Toll-free phone:* 800-81-LEARN. *E-mail:* admissions@baystate.edu. *Website:* http://www.baystate.edu/.

See below for display ad and page 334 for the College Close-Up.

Benjamin Franklin Institute of Technology
Boston, Massachusetts

Freshman Application Contact Ms. Brittainy Johnson, Associate Director of Admissions, Benjamin Franklin Institute of Technology, Boston, MA 02116. *Phone:* 617-423-4630 Ext. 122. *Toll-free phone:* 877-400-BFIT. *Fax:* 617-482-3706. *E-mail:* bjohnson@bfit.edu. *Website:* http://www.bfit.edu/.

Berkshire Community College
Pittsfield, Massachusetts

- **State-supported** 2-year, founded 1960, part of Massachusetts Public Higher Education System
- **Rural** 180-acre campus with easy access to Hartford, CT; Albany, NY
- **Coed,** 1,959 undergraduate students, 32% full-time, 62% women, 38% men

Undergraduates 635 full-time, 1,324 part-time. 8% are from out of state; 7% Black or African American, non-Hispanic/Latino; 9% Hispanic/Latino; 2% Asian, non-Hispanic/Latino; 0.2% Native Hawaiian or other Pacific Islander, non-Hispanic/Latino; 0.6% American Indian or Alaska Native, non-

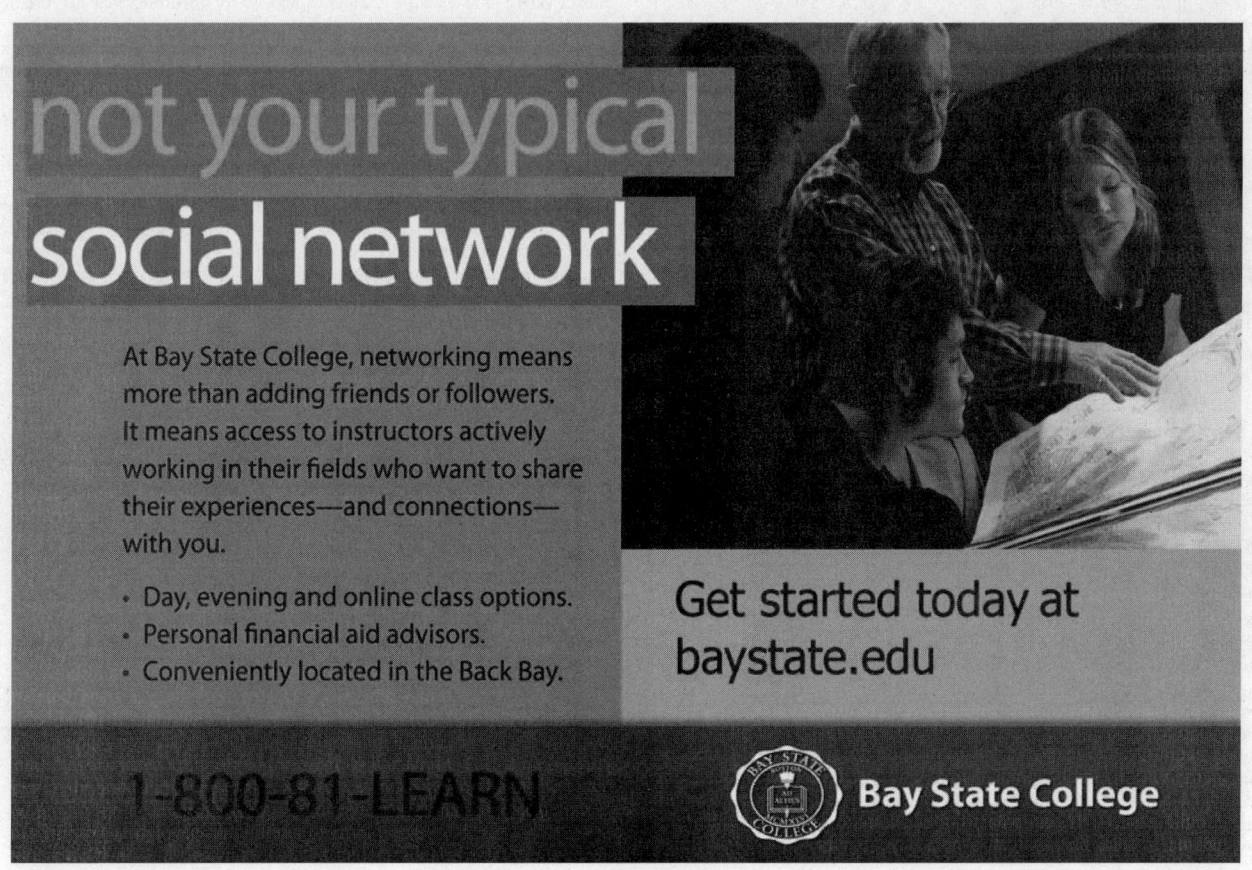

Hispanic/Latino; 2% Two or more races, non-Hispanic/Latino; 4% Race/ethnicity unknown; 0.2% international; 4% transferred in.
Freshmen *Admission:* 752 applied, 745 admitted, 338 enrolled.
Faculty *Total:* 176, 32% full-time. *Student/faculty ratio:* 10:1.
Majors Business administration and management; business automation/technology/data entry; business/commerce; community organization and advocacy; computer and information sciences; criminal justice/safety; electrical, electronic and communications engineering technology; engineering; environmental studies; fire science/firefighting; health professions related; hospitality administration; human services; international/global studies; liberal arts and sciences/liberal studies; medical insurance coding; physical therapy technology; registered nursing/registered nurse; respiratory care therapy; visual and performing arts.
Academics *Calendar:* semesters. *Degree:* certificates and associate. *Special study options:* academic remediation for entering students, accelerated degree program, adult/continuing education programs, advanced placement credit, cooperative education, distance learning, English as a second language, freshman honors college, honors programs, independent study, internships, off-campus study, part-time degree program, services for LD students, summer session for credit.
Library Jonathan Edwards Library. *Books:* 52,501 (physical), 45,753 (digital/electronic); *Serial titles:* 983 (physical), 88 (digital/electronic); *Databases:* 88. Weekly public service hours: 52; students can reserve study rooms.
Student Life *Housing:* college housing not available. *Activities and Organizations:* drama/theater group, choral group, Mass PIRG, Student Nurse Organization, Student Senate, Diversity Club, LPN Organization. *Campus security:* 24-hour emergency response devices and patrols, late-night transport/escort service. *Student services:* personal/psychological counseling.
Athletics *Intramural sports:* basketball M/W, cross-country running M/W, soccer M/W, track and field M/W, weight lifting M/W, wrestling M/W.
Costs (2016–17) *Tuition:* state resident $1248 full-time; nonresident $12,480 full-time. Full-time tuition and fees vary according to class time, course load, and reciprocity agreements. Part-time tuition and fees vary according to class time, course load, and reciprocity agreements. *Required fees:* $8772 full-time. *Payment plan:* installment. *Waivers:* senior citizens and employees or children of employees.
Financial Aid Of all full-time matriculated undergraduates who enrolled in 2015, 1,537 applied for aid, 1,365 were judged to have need. 157 Federal Work-Study jobs (averaging $531). 169 state and other part-time jobs (averaging $556). In 2015, 5 non-need-based awards were made. *Average financial aid package:* $4632. *Average need-based loan:* $1382. *Average need-based gift aid:* $4076. *Average non-need-based aid:* $500.
Applying *Options:* electronic application, deferred entrance. *Required:* high school transcript. *Application deadlines:* rolling (freshmen), rolling (transfers). *Notification:* continuous (freshmen), continuous (transfers).
Freshman Application Contact Ms. Tina Schettini, Senior Admissions Counselor, Berkshire Community College, 1350 West Street, Pittsfield, MA 01201-5786. *Phone:* 413-236-1635. *Toll-free phone:* 800-816-1233. *Fax:* 413-496-9511. *E-mail:* tschetti@berkshirecc.edu.
Website: http://www.berkshirecc.edu/.

Bristol Community College
Fall River, Massachusetts

Freshman Application Contact Ms. Shilo Henriques, Dean of Admissions, Bristol Community College, 777 Elsbree Street, Fall River, MA 02720. *Phone:* 508-678-2811 Ext. 2947. *Fax:* 508-730-3265. *E-mail:* shilo.henriques@bristolcc.edu. *Website:* http://www.bristolcc.edu/.

Bunker Hill Community College
Boston, Massachusetts

- **State-supported** 2-year, founded 1973
- **Urban** 21-acre campus
- **Endowment** $4.3 million
- **Coed**, 13,324 undergraduate students, 32% full-time, 56% women, 44% men
- **83%** of applicants were admitted

Undergraduates 4,327 full-time, 8,997 part-time. 24% Black or African American, non-Hispanic/Latino; 23% Hispanic/Latino; 10% Asian, non-Hispanic/Latino; 0.1% Native Hawaiian or other Pacific Islander, non-Hispanic/Latino; 0.4% American Indian or Alaska Native, non-Hispanic/Latino; 3% Two or more races, non-Hispanic/Latino; 10% Race/ethnicity unknown; 6% international.
Freshmen *Admission:* 5,777 applied, 4,785 admitted, 2,036 enrolled.
Faculty *Total:* 697, 22% full-time. *Student/faculty ratio:* 20:1.
Majors Accounting; art; bioengineering and biomedical engineering; biology/biological sciences; biotechnology; business administration and

management; business administration, management and operations related; business operations support and secretarial services related; cardiovascular technology; chemistry; clinical/medical laboratory technology; computer and information sciences and support services related; computer and information systems security; computer/information technology services administration related; computer programming; computer programming (specific applications); computer science; computer systems networking and telecommunications; criminal justice/law enforcement administration; criminal justice/police science; culinary arts; data entry/microcomputer applications; design and visual communications; diagnostic medical sonography and ultrasound technology; dramatic/theater arts; early childhood education; education; electrical/electronics maintenance and repair technology related; emergency medical technology (EMT paramedic); engineering; English; entrepreneurship; finance; fine arts related; fire prevention and safety technology; foreign languages and literatures; general studies; health information/medical records administration; history; hospitality administration; hospitality administration related; human services; international business/trade/commerce; legal assistant/paralegal; mass communication/media; mathematics; medical administrative assistant and medical secretary; medical radiologic technology; music; operations management; physics; psychology; registered nursing/registered nurse; respiratory therapy technician; sociology; speech communication and rhetoric; sport and fitness administration/management; tourism and travel services management; web page, digital/multimedia and information resources design.
Academics *Calendar:* semesters. *Degree:* certificates and associate. *Special study options:* academic remediation for entering students, accelerated degree program, advanced placement credit, cooperative education, distance learning, English as a second language, external degree program, honors programs, independent study, internships, part-time degree program, services for LD students, study abroad, summer session for credit.
Library Bunker Hill Community College Library. *Books:* 43,885 (physical), 74,811 (digital/electronic); *Serial titles:* 92 (physical), 42 (digital/electronic); *Databases:* 110. Weekly public service hours: 86.
Student Life *Housing:* college housing not available. *Activities and Organizations:* drama/theater group, student-run radio station, choral group, Alpha Kappa Mu Honor Society, Asian-Pacific Students Association, Music Club, Latinos Unidos Club, Haitian Students Club. *Campus security:* 24-hour emergency response devices and patrols, late-night transport/escort service. *Student services:* health clinic, personal/psychological counseling.
Athletics Member NJCAA. *Intercollegiate sports:* baseball M, basketball M/W, soccer M/W, volleyball W. *Intramural sports:* basketball M/W, soccer M/W, volleyball M/W.
Costs (2016–17) *Tuition:* state resident $576 full-time, $24 per credit hour part-time; nonresident $5520 full-time, $230 per credit hour part-time. Full-time tuition and fees vary according to course load, program, and reciprocity agreements. Part-time tuition and fees vary according to course load, program, and reciprocity agreements. *Required fees:* $3312 full-time, $138 per credit hour part-time. *Payment plan:* installment. *Waivers:* minority students, senior citizens, and employees or children of employees.
Financial Aid Of all full-time matriculated undergraduates who enrolled in 2016, 166 Federal Work-Study jobs (averaging $2707).
Applying *Options:* electronic application. *Required:* high school transcript. *Application deadlines:* rolling (freshmen), rolling (transfers). *Notification:* continuous (freshmen), continuous (transfers).
Freshman Application Contact Bunker Hill Community College, 250 New Rutherford Avenue, Boston, MA 02129. *Phone:* 617-228 Ext. 3398.
Website: http://www.bhcc.mass.edu/.

Cape Cod Community College
West Barnstable, Massachusetts

Freshman Application Contact Director of Admissions, Cape Cod Community College, 2240 Iyannough Road, West Barnstable, MA 02668-1599. *Phone:* 508-362-2131 Ext. 4311. *Toll-free phone:* 877-846-3672. *Fax:* 508-375-4089. *E-mail:* admiss@capecod.edu.
Website: http://www.capecod.edu/.

FINE Mortuary College, LLC
Norwood, Massachusetts

- **Proprietary** 2-year, founded 1996
- **Suburban** campus with easy access to Boston
- **Coed,** 91 undergraduate students, 10% full-time, 60% women, 40% men

Undergraduates 9 full-time, 82 part-time. Students come from 5 states and territories; 78% are from out of state; 4% Black or African American, non-Hispanic/Latino; 7% Hispanic/Latino; 1% Two or more races, non-Hispanic/Latino.
Freshmen *Admission:* 21 applied, 19 admitted, 17 enrolled.

Faculty *Total:* 17, 12% full-time, 59% with terminal degrees. *Student/faculty ratio:* 6:1.
Majors Funeral service and mortuary science.
Academics *Calendar:* continuous. *Degree:* associate. *Special study options:* academic remediation for entering students, distance learning, internships, off-campus study, part-time degree program, summer session for credit.
Library FINE Multimedia Center.
Student Life *Housing:* college housing not available.
Costs (2017–18) *Tuition:* $19,980 full-time. *Payment plan:* installment. *Waivers:* employees or children of employees.
Applying *Application fee:* $75. *Required:* essay or personal statement, high school transcript, 1 letter of recommendation. *Recommended:* interview. *Application deadlines:* rolling (freshmen), rolling (transfers), rolling (early action). *Early decision deadline:* rolling (for plan 1), rolling (for plan 2). *Notification:* continuous (freshmen), continuous (transfers), rolling (early decision plan 1), rolling (early decision plan 2), rolling (early action).
Freshman Application Contact FINE Mortuary College, LLC, 150 Kerry Place, Norwood, MA 02062.
Website: http://www.fmc.edu/.

Greenfield Community College
Greenfield, Massachusetts

Freshman Application Contact Ms. Colleen Kucinski, Assistant Director of Admission, Greenfield Community College, 1 College Drive, Greenfield, MA 01301-9739. *Phone:* 413-775-1000. *Fax:* 413-773-5129. *E-mail:* admission@gcc.mass.edu. *Website:* http://www.gcc.mass.edu/.

Holyoke Community College
Holyoke, Massachusetts

- **State-supported** 2-year, founded 1946, part of Massachusetts Public Higher Education System
- **Small-town** 135-acre campus
- **Endowment** $12.8 million
- **Coed,** 5,890 undergraduate students, 44% full-time, 62% women, 38% men

Undergraduates 2,573 full-time, 3,317 part-time. Students come from 22 states and territories; 2% are from out of state; 6% Black or African American, non-Hispanic/Latino; 26% Hispanic/Latino; 2% Asian, non-Hispanic/Latino; 0.1% Native Hawaiian or other Pacific Islander, non-Hispanic/Latino; 0.4% American Indian or Alaska Native, non-Hispanic/Latino; 3% Two or more races, non-Hispanic/Latino; 3% Race/ethnicity unknown; 0.8% international; 7% transferred in.
Freshmen *Admission:* 1,414 enrolled.
Faculty *Total:* 458, 28% full-time, 25% with terminal degrees. *Student/faculty ratio:* 15:1.
Majors Accounting technology and bookkeeping; administrative assistant and secretarial science; art; biology/biological sciences; biotechnology; business administration and management; chemistry; child-care and support services management; computer programming (specific applications); criminal justice/safety; engineering; environmental control technologies related; health and physical education/fitness; health services/allied health/health sciences; hospitality administration related; liberal arts and sciences and humanities related; liberal arts and sciences/liberal studies; mathematics; medical radiologic technology; music; physics; registered nursing/registered nurse; retailing; social work; sport and fitness administration/management; veterinary/animal health technology.
Academics *Calendar:* semesters. *Degree:* certificates and associate. *Special study options:* academic remediation for entering students, adult/continuing education programs, advanced placement credit, cooperative education, distance learning, double majors, English as a second language, external degree program, honors programs, independent study, internships, off-campus study, part-time degree program, services for LD students, student-designed majors, study abroad, summer session for credit. *ROTC:* Army (c), Air Force (c).
Library Holyoke Community College Library plus 1 other. *Books:* 51,746 (physical), 141,786 (digital/electronic); *Serial titles:* 26 (physical), 32,539 (digital/electronic); *Databases:* 125. Weekly public service hours: 65; students can reserve study rooms.
Student Life *Housing:* college housing not available. *Activities and Organizations:* drama/theater group, student-run newspaper, radio station, Drama Club, Japanese Anime Club, Student Senate, LISA Club, STRIVE. *Campus security:* 24-hour emergency response devices and patrols, late-night transport/escort service. *Student services:* health clinic, personal/psychological counseling, women's center.
Athletics Member NJCAA. *Intercollegiate sports:* baseball M, basketball M/W, cross-country running M/W, golf M/W, soccer M/W, softball W, track and field M/W, volleyball W.

Costs (2016–17) *One-time required fee:* $65. *Tuition:* state resident $576 full-time, $178 per credit hour part-time; nonresident $5520 full-time, $384 per credit hour part-time. Full-time tuition and fees vary according to course load. Part-time tuition and fees vary according to course load. *Required fees:* $3830 full-time, $115 per term part-time. *Payment plan:* installment. *Waivers:* senior citizens and employees or children of employees.
Applying *Options:* electronic application, early admission, deferred entrance. *Required:* high school transcript. *Recommended:* interview. *Application deadlines:* rolling (freshmen), rolling (transfers). *Notification:* continuous (freshmen), continuous (transfers).
Freshman Application Contact Ms. Renee Tastad, Director of Admissions and Transfer Affairs, Holyoke Community College, Admission Office, Holyoke, MA 01040. *Phone:* 413-552-2321. *Fax:* 413-552-2045.
E-mail: admissions@hcc.edu.
Website: http://www.hcc.edu/.

Labouré College
Milton, Massachusetts

Director of Admissions Ms. Gina M. Morrissette, Director of Admissions, Labouré College, 303 Adams Street, Milton, MA 02186. *Phone:* 617-296-8300. *Website:* http://www.laboure.edu/.

Massachusetts Bay Community College
Wellesley Hills, Massachusetts

- **State-supported** 2-year, founded 1961
- **Suburban** 84-acre campus with easy access to Boston
- **Coed,** 4,855 undergraduate students, 33% full-time, 53% women, 47% men

Undergraduates 1,625 full-time, 3,230 part-time. Students come from 11 states and territories; 94 other countries; 2% are from out of state; 16% Black or African American, non-Hispanic/Latino; 18% Hispanic/Latino; 5% Asian, non-Hispanic/Latino; 0.1% Native Hawaiian or other Pacific Islander, non-Hispanic/Latino; 0.7% American Indian or Alaska Native, non-Hispanic/Latino; 8% Race/ethnicity unknown; 2% international; 6% transferred in. *Retention:* 59% of full-time freshmen returned.
Freshmen *Admission:* 1,952 applied, 1,944 admitted, 1,020 enrolled.
Faculty *Total:* 302, 25% full-time. *Student/faculty ratio:* 18:1.
Majors Accounting; animal physiology; automobile/automotive mechanics technology; bioinformatics; biological and biomedical sciences related; biology/biotechnology laboratory technician; business administration and management; business/commerce; community health and preventive medicine; computer and information sciences and support services related; computer and information systems security; computer/information technology services administration related; computer science; criminal justice/law enforcement administration; early childhood education; electrical and electronic engineering technologies related; electrical, electronic and communications engineering technology; elementary education; engineering technologies and engineering related; engineering technology; English; environmental control technologies related; general studies; hospitality administration; human services; international business/trade/commerce; international/global studies; legal assistant/paralegal; liberal arts and sciences/liberal studies; mathematics; mechanical engineering/mechanical technology; network and system administration; radiologic technology/science; registered nursing/registered nurse; social sciences.
Academics *Calendar:* semesters. *Degree:* certificates and associate. *Special study options:* academic remediation for entering students, adult/continuing education programs, advanced placement credit, cooperative education, distance learning, double majors, English as a second language, honors programs, independent study, internships, part-time degree program, services for LD students, study abroad, summer session for credit.
Library Perkins Library plus 2 others. *Books:* 42,097 (physical), 7,584 (digital/electronic); *Serial titles:* 30 (physical), 26,704 (digital/electronic); *Databases:* 83. Weekly public service hours: 78.
Student Life *Housing:* college housing not available. *Activities and Organizations:* drama/theater group, choral group, Student Government Association, Business Club, Veterans Club, Legal Studies and Criminal Justice Club, Gamer's Guild. *Campus security:* 24-hour emergency response devices and patrols. *Student services:* personal/psychological counseling.
Athletics Member NJCAA. *Intercollegiate sports:* baseball M, basketball M/W, golf M/W, soccer M/W, softball W, volleyball W. *Intramural sports:* soccer M/W.
Costs (2016–17) *Tuition:* state resident $576 full-time, $24 per credit part-time; nonresident $5520 full-time, $230 per credit part-time. Full-time tuition and fees vary according to class time, program, and reciprocity agreements. Part-time tuition and fees vary according to class time, program, and reciprocity agreements. *Required fees:* $3920 full-time, $173 per credit part-

time, $40 per term part-time. *Payment plan:* installment. *Waivers:* senior citizens and employees or children of employees.

Financial Aid Of all full-time matriculated undergraduates who enrolled in 2015, 59 Federal Work-Study jobs (averaging $1840).

Applying *Options:* electronic application, deferred entrance. *Required for some:* high school transcript. *Application deadlines:* rolling (freshmen), rolling (transfers). *Notification:* continuous (freshmen), continuous (transfers).

Freshman Application Contact Ms. Alison McCarty, Director of Admissions, Massachusetts Bay Community College, 50 Oakland Street, Wellesley Hills, MA 02481. *Phone:* 781-239-2506.
E-mail: amccarty1@massbay.edu.
Website: http://www.massbay.edu/.

Massasoit Community College

Brockton, Massachusetts

Freshman Application Contact Michelle Hughes, Director of Admissions, Massasoit Community College, 1 Massasoit Boulevard, Brockton, MA 02302-3996. *Phone:* 508-588-9100. *Toll-free phone:* 800-CAREERS. *Website:* http://www.massasoit.mass.edu/.

Middlesex Community College

Bedford, Massachusetts

- **State-supported** 2-year, founded 1970, part of Massachusetts Public Higher Education System
- **Suburban** 200-acre campus with easy access to Boston
- **Coed,** 8,745 undergraduate students, 36% full-time, 59% women, 41% men

Undergraduates 3,155 full-time, 5,590 part-time. 7% Black or African American, non-Hispanic/Latino; 19% Hispanic/Latino; 13% Asian, non-Hispanic/Latino; 0.2% American Indian or Alaska Native, non-Hispanic/Latino; 2% Two or more races, non-Hispanic/Latino; 0.4% Race/ethnicity unknown; 2% international.

Freshmen *Admission:* 1,621 enrolled.

Majors Aircraft powerplant technology; art; automobile/automotive mechanics technology; biology/biological sciences; biology/biotechnology laboratory technician; business administration and management; clinical/medical laboratory technology; commercial and advertising art; computer and information sciences; computer and information sciences and support services related; computer engineering technology; computer programming; construction management; criminal justice/law enforcement administration; criminal justice/safety; dental assisting; dental hygiene; dental laboratory technology; diagnostic medical sonography and ultrasound technology; electrical, electronic and communications engineering technology; electrical/electronics drafting and CAD/CADD; elementary education; engineering technologies and engineering related; fashion merchandising; fine/studio arts; fire prevention and safety technology; fire science/firefighting; forensic science and technology; general studies; hotel/motel administration; kindergarten/preschool education; legal assistant/paralegal; liberal arts and sciences/liberal studies; mathematics related; medical/clinical assistant; medical radiologic technology; office occupations and clerical services; physical sciences; psychiatric/mental health services technology; registered nursing/registered nurse; social sciences; web page, digital/multimedia and information resources design.

Academics *Calendar:* semesters. *Degree:* certificates and associate. *Special study options:* academic remediation for entering students, accelerated degree program, adult/continuing education programs, advanced placement credit, cooperative education, distance learning, English as a second language, honors programs, independent study, internships, off-campus study, part-time degree program, services for LD students, study abroad, summer session for credit. *ROTC:* Air Force (c).

Library Main Library plus 1 other.

Student Life *Housing:* college housing not available. *Activities and Organizations:* drama/theater group. *Campus security:* 24-hour emergency response devices and patrols. *Student services:* health clinic, personal/psychological counseling, legal services.

Athletics *Intercollegiate sports:* ice hockey M. *Intramural sports:* basketball M/W, soccer M, softball M/W, volleyball M/W.

Standardized Tests *Required for some:* ACCUPLACER, TEAS.

Financial Aid Of all full-time matriculated undergraduates who enrolled in 2015, 68 Federal Work-Study jobs (averaging $2200).

Applying *Options:* electronic application, early admission. *Required for some:* high school transcript, 3 letters of recommendation, interview.

Application deadlines: rolling (freshmen), rolling (transfers). *Notification:* continuous (freshmen), continuous (transfers).

Freshman Application Contact Middlesex Community College, 591 Springs Road, Bedford, MA 01730-1655. *Phone:* 978-656-3211.
Toll-free phone: 800-818-3434.
Website: http://www.middlesex.mass.edu/.

Mount Wachusett Community College

Gardner, Massachusetts

- **State-supported** 2-year, founded 1963, part of Massachusetts Public Higher Education System
- **Small-town** 270-acre campus with easy access to Boston
- **Endowment** $358,277
- **Coed,** 3,961 undergraduate students, 39% full-time, 65% women, 35% men

Undergraduates 1,537 full-time, 2,424 part-time. 7% Black or African American, non-Hispanic/Latino; 16% Hispanic/Latino; 3% Asian, non-Hispanic/Latino; 0.1% Native Hawaiian or other Pacific Islander, non-Hispanic/Latino; 0.5% American Indian or Alaska Native, non-Hispanic/Latino; 3% Two or more races, non-Hispanic/Latino; 2% Race/ethnicity unknown; 0.3% international; 7% transferred in.

Freshmen *Admission:* 1,932 applied, 1,932 admitted, 813 enrolled. *Average high school GPA:* 2.67.

Faculty *Total:* 393, 19% full-time, 15% with terminal degrees. *Student/faculty ratio:* 12:1.

Majors Allied health and medical assisting services related; alternative and complementary medical support services related; art; automobile/automotive mechanics technology; biotechnology; business administration and management; business/commerce; child-care and support services management; child development; clinical/medical laboratory technology; computer and information sciences; computer graphics; corrections; criminal justice/law enforcement administration; dental hygiene; energy management and systems technology; environmental studies; fire prevention and safety technology; general studies; health information/medical records administration; human services; legal assistant/paralegal; liberal arts and sciences/liberal studies; medical/clinical assistant; physical therapy technology; plastics and polymer engineering technology; quality control and safety technologies related; radio and television broadcasting technology; registered nursing/registered nurse; web page, digital/multimedia and information resources design.

Academics *Calendar:* semesters. *Degree:* certificates, diplomas, and associate. *Special study options:* academic remediation for entering students, accelerated degree program, adult/continuing education programs, advanced placement credit, cooperative education, distance learning, double majors, English as a second language, honors programs, independent study, internships, part-time degree program, services for LD students, study abroad, summer session for credit. *ROTC:* Army (c).

Library LaChance Library. *Books:* 36,000 (physical), 45,753 (digital/electronic); *Serial titles:* 26 (physical); *Databases:* 96. Weekly public service hours: 57; students can reserve study rooms.

Student Life *Housing:* college housing not available. *Activities and Organizations:* drama/theater group, student-run newspaper, Otaku Anime Club, Dental Hygienist Club, Parent Support Group, Student Government Association, Student Nurses Association. *Campus security:* 24-hour emergency response devices and patrols, late-night transport/escort service, security cameras, access cards for laboratory access. *Student services:* health clinic, personal/psychological counseling.

Athletics *Intramural sports:* badminton M/W, basketball M/W, football M/W, soccer M/W, softball M/W, table tennis M/W, volleyball M/W, water polo M/W.

Costs (2016–17) *Tuition:* state resident $600 full-time, $25 per credit hour part-time; nonresident $5520 full-time, $230 per credit hour part-time. Full-time tuition and fees vary according to program and reciprocity agreements. Part-time tuition and fees vary according to program and reciprocity agreements. *Required fees:* $4708 full-time, $182 per credit hour part-time, $125 per term part-time. *Payment plan:* installment. *Waivers:* senior citizens and employees or children of employees.

Financial Aid Of all full-time matriculated undergraduates who enrolled in 2015, 1,350 applied for aid, 1,084 were judged to have need, 94 had their need fully met. In 2015, 28 non-need-based awards were made. *Average percent of need met:* 96%. *Average financial aid package:* $5863. *Average need-based loan:* $1758. *Average need-based gift aid:* $5218. *Average non-need-based aid:* $707.

Applying *Options:* electronic application, early admission. *Required:* high school transcript. *Required for some:* 2 letters of recommendation. *Recommended:* interview. *Application deadlines:* rolling (freshmen), rolling (transfers). *Notification:* continuous (freshmen), continuous (transfers).

Freshman Application Contact Ms. Marcia Rosbury-Henne, Dean of Admissions and Enrollment, Mount Wachusett Community College, 444

Green Street, Gardner, MA 01440-1378. *Phone:* 978-632-6600 Ext. 337. *Fax:* 978-630-9558. *E-mail:* admissions@mwcc.mass.edu. *Website:* http://www.mwcc.mass.edu/.

Northern Essex Community College
Haverhill, Massachusetts

- **State-supported** 2-year, founded 1960
- **Suburban** 106-acre campus with easy access to Boston
- **Endowment** $3.8 million
- **Coed,** 5,976 undergraduate students, 35% full-time, 60% women, 40% men

Undergraduates 2,069 full-time, 3,907 part-time. Students come from 7 states and territories; 13% are from out of state; 4% Black or African American, non-Hispanic/Latino; 39% Hispanic/Latino; 2% Asian, non-Hispanic/Latino; 0.4% Native Hawaiian or other Pacific Islander, non-Hispanic/Latino; 0.2% American Indian or Alaska Native, non-Hispanic/Latino; 1% Two or more races, non-Hispanic/Latino; 4% Race/ethnicity unknown; 0.6% international; 6% transferred in. *Retention:* 61% of full-time freshmen returned.
Freshmen *Admission:* 2,166 applied, 2,137 admitted, 1,258 enrolled.
Faculty *Total:* 517, 22% full-time.
Majors Accounting; biology/biological sciences; business administration and management; business/commerce; business teacher education; civil engineering technology; commercial and advertising art; computer and information sciences; computer engineering technology; computer graphics; computer programming; computer programming related; computer programming (specific applications); computer science; computer systems networking and telecommunications; computer typography and composition equipment operation; criminal justice/law enforcement administration; dance; data processing and data processing technology; dental assisting; dramatic/theater arts; education; electrical, electronic and communications engineering technology; elementary education; emergency medical technology (EMT paramedic); engineering science; finance; general studies; health information/medical records administration; history; hotel/motel administration; human services; industrial radiologic technology; international relations and affairs; journalism; kindergarten/preschool education; legal assistant/paralegal; liberal arts and sciences/liberal studies; logistics, materials, and supply chain management; machine tool technology; marketing/marketing management; materials science; medical administrative assistant and medical secretary; medical transcription; mental health counseling; music; parks, recreation and leisure; physical education teaching and coaching; political science and government; psychology; public health; radiologic technology/science; registered nursing/registered nurse; respiratory care therapy; respiratory therapy technician; science technologies; sign language interpretation and translation; sport and fitness administration/management; telecommunications technology; web/multimedia management and webmaster; web page, digital/multimedia and information resources design.
Academics *Calendar:* semesters. *Degree:* certificates and associate. *Special study options:* academic remediation for entering students, adult/continuing education programs, advanced placement credit, cooperative education, distance learning, double majors, English as a second language, freshman honors college, honors programs, independent study, internships, off-campus study, part-time degree program, services for LD students, study abroad, summer session for credit. *ROTC:* Air Force (c).
Library Bentley Library. *Books:* 41,604 (physical), 11,287 (digital/electronic); *Serial titles:* 3,440 (physical), 27,741 (digital/electronic); *Databases:* 68.
Student Life *Housing:* college housing not available. *Activities and Organizations:* drama/theater group, student-run newspaper, choral group. *Campus security:* 24-hour emergency response devices and patrols.
Athletics Member NJCAA. *Intercollegiate sports:* baseball M, basketball M/W, cross-country running M/W, softball W, track and field M/W, volleyball M/W. *Intramural sports:* basketball M/W, cross-country running M/W, football M/W, soccer M/W, volleyball M/W, weight lifting M/W.
Standardized Tests *Required for some:* Psychological Corporation Aptitude Test for practical nursing.
Costs (2017–18) *Tuition:* state resident $600 full-time, $25 per credit hour part-time; nonresident $6384 full-time, $266 per credit hour part-time. Full-time tuition and fees vary according to program and reciprocity agreements. Part-time tuition and fees vary according to program and reciprocity agreements. *Required fees:* $4176 full-time, $174 per credit hour part-time. *Payment plan:* installment. *Waivers:* employees or children of employees.
Financial Aid Of all full-time matriculated undergraduates who enrolled in 2015, 74 Federal Work-Study jobs (averaging $1759).

Applying *Options:* early admission. *Required:* high school transcript. *Application deadlines:* rolling (freshmen), rolling (transfers). *Notification:* continuous (freshmen), continuous (transfers).
Freshman Application Contact Northern Essex Community College, 100 Elliott Street, Haverhill, MA 01830. *Phone:* 978-556-3616.
Website: http://www.necc.mass.edu/.

North Shore Community College
Danvers, Massachusetts

- **State-supported** 2-year, founded 1965
- **Suburban** campus with easy access to Boston
- **Endowment** $7.4 million
- **Coed,** 6,315 undergraduate students, 34% full-time, 61% women, 39% men

Undergraduates 2,142 full-time, 4,173 part-time. Students come from 12 states and territories; 8 other countries; 2% are from out of state; 9% Black or African American, non-Hispanic/Latino; 24% Hispanic/Latino; 5% Asian, non-Hispanic/Latino; 0.1% Native Hawaiian or other Pacific Islander, non-Hispanic/Latino; 0.2% American Indian or Alaska Native, non-Hispanic/Latino; 2% Two or more races, non-Hispanic/Latino; 2% Race/ethnicity unknown; 0.1% international; 8% transferred in.
Freshmen *Admission:* 3,884 applied, 3,550 admitted, 1,198 enrolled.
Faculty *Total:* 486, 28% full-time, 18% with terminal degrees. *Student/faculty ratio:* 17:1.
Majors Accounting; administrative assistant and secretarial science; airline pilot and flight crew; biology/biotechnology laboratory technician; business administration and management; child development; computer and information sciences related; computer engineering technology; computer graphics; computer programming; computer programming (specific applications); computer science; criminal justice/law enforcement administration; culinary arts; data entry/microcomputer applications; engineering science; fire science/firefighting; foods, nutrition, and wellness; gerontology; health professions related; hospitality administration; information science/studies; interdisciplinary studies; kindergarten/preschool education; legal administrative assistant/secretary; legal assistant/paralegal; liberal arts and sciences/liberal studies; marketing/marketing management; medical administrative assistant and medical secretary; medical radiologic technology; mental health counseling; occupational therapy; physical therapy technology; pre-engineering; registered nursing/registered nurse; respiratory care therapy; substance abuse/addiction counseling; tourism and travel services management; veterinary/animal health technology; web page, digital/multimedia and information resources design.
Academics *Calendar:* semesters. *Degree:* certificates and associate. *Special study options:* academic remediation for entering students, accelerated degree program, adult/continuing education programs, advanced placement credit, cooperative education, distance learning, English as a second language, honors programs, independent study, internships, part-time degree program, services for LD students, summer session for credit.
Library Learning Resource Center plus 2 others.
Student Life *Housing:* college housing not available. *Activities and Organizations:* drama/theater group, student-run newspaper, Program Council, Student Government, Performing Arts, Student Newspaper, Phi Theta Kappa, national fraternities. *Campus security:* 24-hour emergency response devices and patrols, late-night transport/escort service. *Student services:* health clinic, personal/psychological counseling, women's center.
Athletics *Intramural sports:* basketball M/W, soccer M/W.
Costs (2017–18) *One-time required fee:* $300. *Tuition:* state resident $600 full-time, $25 per credit part-time; nonresident $6168 full-time, $257 per credit part-time. Full-time tuition and fees vary according to program. Part-time tuition and fees vary according to program. *Required fees:* $4848 full-time, $177 per credit part-time. *Payment plan:* installment. *Waivers:* senior citizens and employees or children of employees.
Financial Aid Of all full-time matriculated undergraduates who enrolled in 2009, 1,658 applied for aid, 1,438 were judged to have need, 23 had their need fully met. 123 Federal Work-Study jobs (averaging $1359). In 2009, 11 non-need-based awards were made. *Average percent of need met:* 18%. *Average financial aid package:* $6856. *Average need-based loan:* $1639. *Average need-based gift aid:* $2522. *Average non-need-based aid:* $614.
Applying *Options:* electronic application, early admission, deferred entrance. *Required for some:* essay or personal statement, high school transcript, interview. *Application deadlines:* rolling (freshmen), rolling (transfers). *Notification:* continuous (freshmen), continuous (transfers).
Freshman Application Contact Mrs. Gissel Lopez, Academic Counselor, North Shore Community College, Danvers, MA 01923. *Phone:* 978-762-4000 Ext. 2108. *Fax:* 978-762-4015. *E-mail:* gilopez@northshore.edu.
Website: http://www.northshore.edu/.

Quincy College
Quincy, Massachusetts

- **City-supported** 2-year, founded 1958
- **Suburban** 2-acre campus with easy access to Boston
- **Endowment** $112,021
- **Coed**

Undergraduates 1,844 full-time, 2,888 part-time. Students come from 18 states and territories; 1% are from out of state; 25% Black or African American, non-Hispanic/Latino; 7% Hispanic/Latino; 6% Asian, non-Hispanic/Latino; 0.1% Native Hawaiian or other Pacific Islander, non-Hispanic/Latino; 0.3% American Indian or Alaska Native, non-Hispanic/Latino; 2% Two or more races, non-Hispanic/Latino; 9% Race/ethnicity unknown; 8% international; 0.3% transferred in. *Retention:* 53% of full-time freshmen returned.

Faculty *Student/faculty ratio:* 18:1.

Academics *Calendar:* semesters. *Degree:* certificates and associate. *Special study options:* academic remediation for entering students, adult/continuing education programs, advanced placement credit, distance learning, English as a second language, external degree program, independent study, internships, part-time degree program, services for LD students, summer session for credit.

Library Anselmo Library plus 1 other. *Books:* 10,543 (physical), 240,593 (digital/electronic); *Serial titles:* 12 (physical), 1,922 (digital/electronic); *Databases:* 52.

Student Life *Campus security:* 24-hour emergency response devices.

Applying *Options:* electronic application, early admission, deferred entrance. *Application fee:* $30. *Required:* high school transcript.

Freshman Application Contact Quincy College, 1250 Hancock Street, Quincy, MA 02169. *Phone:* 617-984-1710. *Toll-free phone:* 800-698-1700. *Website:* http://www.quincycollege.edu/.

Quinsigamond Community College
Worcester, Massachusetts

- **State-supported** 2-year, founded 1963, part of Massachusetts System of Higher Education
- **Urban** 57-acre campus with easy access to Boston
- **Endowment** $438,122
- **Coed,** 7,699 undergraduate students, 38% full-time, 57% women, 43% men

Undergraduates 2,938 full-time, 4,761 part-time. Students come from 10 states and territories; 31 other countries; 0.7% are from out of state; 13% Black or African American, non-Hispanic/Latino; 18% Hispanic/Latino; 4% Asian, non-Hispanic/Latino; 0.1% Native Hawaiian or other Pacific Islander, non-Hispanic/Latino; 0.4% American Indian or Alaska Native, non-Hispanic/Latino; 2% Two or more races, non-Hispanic/Latino; 5% Race/ethnicity unknown; 0.6% international; 6% transferred in.

Freshmen *Admission:* 3,989 applied, 2,375 admitted, 1,577 enrolled.

Faculty *Total:* 550, 26% full-time, 15% with terminal degrees. *Student/faculty ratio:* 16:1.

Majors Alternative and complementary medicine related; automobile/automotive mechanics technology; bioengineering and biomedical engineering; biology/biological sciences; biomedical technology; biotechnology; business administration and management; business/commerce; chemistry; community health and preventive medicine; computer and information sciences; computer and information systems security; computer engineering technology; computer graphics; computer programming (specific applications); computer science; computer systems analysis; criminal justice/police science; data modeling/warehousing and database administration; deaf studies; dental hygiene; dental services and allied professions related; directing and theatrical production; electrical, electronic and communications engineering technology; electromechanical technology; elementary education; emergency medical technology (EMT paramedic); energy management and systems technology; engineering technologies and engineering related; environmental science; executive assistant/executive secretary; fire services administration; game and interactive media design; general studies; health information/medical records technology; health services/allied health/health sciences; hospitality administration; human services; kindergarten/preschool education; laser and optical technology; liberal arts and sciences/liberal studies; manufacturing engineering technology; medical administrative assistant and medical secretary; music; occupational therapist assistant; pre-pharmacy studies; psychology; radiologic technology/science; registered nursing/registered nurse; respiratory care therapy; restaurant/food services management; telecommunications technology; trade and industrial teacher education; web page, digital/multimedia and information resources design.

Academics *Calendar:* semesters. *Degree:* certificates and associate. *Special study options:* academic remediation for entering students, accelerated degree program, advanced placement credit, cooperative education, distance learning,

double majors, English as a second language, honors programs, independent study, internships, off-campus study, part-time degree program, services for LD students, summer session for credit. *ROTC:* Army (c).

Library Alden Library plus 1 other. *Books:* 56,229 (physical), 92,140 (digital/electronic); *Serial titles:* 40 (physical), 64,200 (digital/electronic); *Databases:* 73. Weekly public service hours: 67; students can reserve study rooms.

Student Life *Housing:* college housing not available. *Activities and Organizations:* drama/theater group, student-run newspaper, Academic-Related Clubs, Phi Theta Kappa, Student Senate, Anime Club, Psi Beta Club. *Campus security:* 24-hour emergency response devices and patrols, late-night transport/escort service. *Student services:* personal/psychological counseling.

Athletics Member NJCAA. *Intercollegiate sports:* baseball M, basketball M/W, softball W. *Intramural sports:* basketball M/W, cheerleading W(c), soccer M/W, table tennis M/W, ultimate Frisbee M/W, volleyball M/W.

Costs (2017–18) *Tuition:* state resident $576 full-time, $24 per credit part-time; nonresident $5520 full-time, $230 per credit part-time. Full-time tuition and fees vary according to course load and program. Part-time tuition and fees vary according to course load and program. *Required fees:* $5820 full-time, $167 per credit part-time, $455 per term part-time. *Payment plan:* installment. *Waivers:* senior citizens and employees or children of employees.

Applying *Options:* electronic application. *Application fee:* $20. *Required:* high school transcript. *Required for some:* interview. *Application deadlines:* rolling (freshmen), rolling (transfers). *Notification:* continuous (freshmen), continuous (transfers).

Freshman Application Contact Quinsigamond Community College, 670 West Boylston Street, Worcester, MA 01606-2092. *Phone:* 508-854-4576. *Website:* http://www.qcc.edu/.

Roxbury Community College
Roxbury Crossing, Massachusetts

Director of Admissions Nancy Santos, Director, Admissions, Roxbury Community College, 1234 Columbus Avenue, Roxbury Crossing, MA 02120-3400. *Phone:* 617-541-5310. *Website:* http://www.rcc.mass.edu/.

Salter College
Chicopee, Massachusetts

Admissions Office Contact Salter College, 645 Shawinigan Drive, Chicopee, MA 01020. *Website:* http://www.saltercollege.com/.

Salter College
West Boylston, Massachusetts

Admissions Office Contact Salter College, 184 West Boylston Street, West Boylston, MA 01583. *Website:* http://www.saltercollege-us.com/.

Springfield Technical Community College
Springfield, Massachusetts

- **State-supported** 2-year, founded 1967
- **Urban** 34-acre campus
- **Coed,** 5,622 undergraduate students, 42% full-time, 57% women, 43% men

Undergraduates 2,348 full-time, 3,274 part-time. Students come from 7 states and territories; 37 other countries; 3% are from out of state; 16% Black or African American, non-Hispanic/Latino; 29% Hispanic/Latino; 3% Asian, non-Hispanic/Latino; 0.1% Native Hawaiian or other Pacific Islander, non-Hispanic/Latino; 0.4% American Indian or Alaska Native, non-Hispanic/Latino; 2% Two or more races, non-Hispanic/Latino; 0.1% Race/ethnicity unknown; 0.8% international; 6% transferred in.

Freshmen *Admission:* 3,111 applied, 2,563 admitted, 1,040 enrolled.

Faculty *Total:* 333, 43% full-time. *Student/faculty ratio:* 17:1.

Majors Accounting; administrative assistant and secretarial science; animation, interactive technology, video graphics and special effects; architectural and building sciences; automobile/automotive mechanics technology; biology/biological sciences; biotechnology; building/construction finishing, management, and inspection related; business administration and management; business/commerce; chemistry; civil engineering technology; clinical/medical laboratory technology; commercial and advertising art; commercial photography; computer and information systems security; computer engineering technology; computer programming (specific applications); computer science; criminal justice/police science; dental hygiene; diagnostic medical sonography and ultrasound technology; early childhood education; electrical, electronic and communications engineering technology; electromechanical technology; elementary education; engineering;

fine/studio arts; fire prevention and safety technology; heating, air conditioning, ventilation and refrigeration maintenance technology; landscaping and groundskeeping; laser and optical technology; liberal arts and sciences/liberal studies; marketing/marketing management; mathematics; mechanical engineering/mechanical technology; medical administrative assistant and medical secretary; medical/clinical assistant; medical insurance coding; occupational therapist assistant; physical therapy technology; physics; premedical studies; radio and television broadcasting technology; radiologic technology/science; recording arts technology; registered nursing/registered nurse; respiratory care therapy; secondary education; small business administration; sport and fitness administration/management; surgical technology; telecommunications technology.

Academics *Calendar:* semesters. *Degree:* certificates and associate. *Special study options:* academic remediation for entering students, adult/continuing education programs, advanced placement credit, cooperative education, distance learning, English as a second language, honors programs, independent study, internships, off-campus study, part-time degree program, services for LD students, summer session for credit.

Library Springfield Technical Community College Library. *Books:* 45,975 (physical), 9,270 (digital/electronic); *Serial titles:* 159 (physical), 12 (digital/electronic); *Databases:* 93. Weekly public service hours: 61.

Student Life *Housing:* college housing not available. *Activities and Organizations:* drama/theater group, student-run newspaper, Phi Theta Kappa, Campus Civitian Club, Tech Times (student newspaper), Dental Hygiene Club, Landscape Design Club. *Campus security:* 24-hour emergency response devices and patrols, late-night transport/escort service. *Student services:* health clinic, personal/psychological counseling, legal services.

Athletics Member NJCAA. *Intercollegiate sports:* basketball M/W, golf M, soccer M/W, wrestling M. *Intramural sports:* basketball M/W, cross-country running M/W, golf M/W, skiing (cross-country) M/W, volleyball M/W, weight lifting M/W.

Standardized Tests *Required for some:* SAT (for admission).

Costs (2017–18) *Tuition:* state resident $750 full-time, $25 per credit part-time; nonresident $7260 full-time, $242 per credit part-time. Full-time tuition and fees vary according to course load and reciprocity agreements. Part-time tuition and fees vary according to course load and reciprocity agreements. No tuition increase for student's term of enrollment. *Required fees:* $4986 full-time, $159 per credit part-time, $108 per term part-time. *Payment plan:* installment. *Waivers:* senior citizens and employees or children of employees.

Applying *Options:* electronic application. *Required:* high school transcript. *Required for some:* interview. *Application deadlines:* rolling (freshmen), rolling (transfers). *Notification:* continuous (freshmen), continuous (transfers). **Freshman Application Contact** Mr. LaRue Pierce, Dean of Students, Springfield Technical Community College, Springfield, MA 01105. *Phone:* 413-781-7822 Ext. 4078. *E-mail:* lapierce@stcc.edu. *Website:* http://www.stcc.edu/.

Urban College of Boston
Boston, Massachusetts

Director of Admissions Dr. Henry J. Johnson, Director of Enrollment Services/Registrar, Urban College of Boston, 178 Tremont Street, Boston, MA 02111. *Phone:* 617-348-6353. *Website:* http://www.urbancollege.edu/.

MICHIGAN

Alpena Community College
Alpena, Michigan

Freshman Application Contact Mr. Mike Kollien, Director of Admissions, Alpena Community College, 665 Johnson, Alpena, MI 49707. *Phone:* 989-358-7339. *Toll-free phone:* 888-468-6222. *Fax:* 989-358-7540. *E-mail:* kollienm@alpenacc.edu. *Website:* http://www.alpenacc.edu/.

Bay de Noc Community College
Escanaba, Michigan

Freshman Application Contact Ms. Jessica LeMarch, Director of Admissions, Bay de Noc Community College, 2001 North Lincoln Road, Escanaba, MI 49829. *Phone:* 906-217-4010. *Toll-free phone:* 800-221-2001. *Fax:* 906-217-1714. *E-mail:* jessica.lamarch@baycollege.edu. *Website:* http://www.baycollege.edu/.

Bay Mills Community College
Brimley, Michigan

Freshman Application Contact Ms. Elaine Lehre, Admissions Officer, Bay Mills Community College, 12214 West Lakeshore Drive, Brimley, MI 49715. *Phone:* 906-248-3354. *Toll-free phone:* 800-844-BMCC. *Fax:* 906-248-3351. *Website:* http://www.bmcc.edu/.

Delta College
University Center, Michigan

- **District-supported** 2-year, founded 1961
- **Rural** 640-acre campus
- **Endowment** $20.1 million
- **Coed,** 9,132 undergraduate students, 36% full-time, 55% women, 45% men

Undergraduates 3,312 full-time, 5,820 part-time. Students come from 5 states and territories; 1 other country; 8% Black or African American, non-Hispanic/Latino; 6% Hispanic/Latino; 0.7% Asian, non-Hispanic/Latino; 0.5% American Indian or Alaska Native, non-Hispanic/Latino; 2% Two or more races, non-Hispanic/Latino; 2% Race/ethnicity unknown; 0.6% international; 3% transferred in.

Freshmen *Admission:* 1,692 applied, 1,692 admitted, 1,692 enrolled.

Faculty *Total:* 539, 38% full-time. *Student/faculty ratio:* 16:1.

Majors Accounting technology and bookkeeping; administrative assistant and secretarial science; architectural engineering technology; automobile/automotive mechanics technology; building/construction finishing, management, and inspection related; building/property maintenance; business administration and management; carpentry; chemical technology; child-care provision; computer and information sciences related; computer and information systems security; computer installation and repair technology; computer programming; computer systems networking and telecommunications; construction engineering technology; corrections; criminal justice/police science; dental assisting; dental hygiene; diagnostic medical sonography and ultrasound technology; diesel mechanics technology; electrical and power transmission installation; electrician; energy management and systems technology; environmental engineering technology; fine/studio arts; fire prevention and safety technology; fire science/firefighting; fire services administration; general studies; heating, air conditioning, ventilation and refrigeration maintenance technology; industrial mechanics and maintenance technology; journalism; legal assistant/paralegal; liberal arts and sciences/liberal studies; machine shop technology; manufacturing engineering technology; marketing/marketing management; mechanical engineering/mechanical technology; mechatronics, robotics, and automation engineering; medical administrative assistant and medical secretary; medical radiologic technology; merchandising; peace studies and conflict resolution; physical therapy technology; pipefitting and sprinkler fitting; plumbing technology; precision metal working related; precision production related; radio and television; registered nursing/registered nurse; respiratory care therapy; retailing; salon/beauty salon management; security and loss prevention; sheet metal technology; small business administration; sport and fitness administration/management; surgical technology; technology/industrial arts teacher education; tool and die technology; water quality and wastewater treatment management and recycling technology; web/multimedia management and webmaster; welding technology.

Academics *Calendar:* semesters. *Degree:* certificates and associate. *Special study options:* academic remediation for entering students, adult/continuing education programs, advanced placement credit, cooperative education, distance learning, double majors, freshman honors college, honors programs, independent study, internships, off-campus study, part-time degree program, services for LD students, study abroad, summer session for credit.

Library Library Learning Information Center. *Books:* 55,653 (physical); *Serial titles:* 292 (physical); *Databases:* 35. Weekly public service hours: 71.

Student Life *Housing:* college housing not available. *Activities and Organizations:* drama/theater group, student-run newspaper, choral group, DECA, Phi Theta Kappa, DCSNA (student nursing association), Physical Therapy Assistant (PTA) Club, Honors. *Campus security:* 24-hour emergency response devices, student patrols, late-night transport/escort service. *Student services:* personal/psychological counseling.

Athletics Member NJCAA. *Intercollegiate sports:* baseball M, basketball M(s)/W(s), golf M, soccer W, softball W(s). *Intramural sports:* basketball M/W, cross-country running M/W, soccer M/W.

Costs (2016–17) *Tuition:* area resident $2587 full-time, $100 per credit hour part-time; state resident $4420 full-time, $170 per credit hour part-time; nonresident $8320 full-time, $320 per credit hour part-time. Full-time tuition and fees vary according to course load. Part-time tuition and fees vary according to course load. *Required fees:* $80 full-time, $40 per term part-time. *Payment plan:* installment. *Waivers:* senior citizens and employees or children of employees.

Financial Aid Of all full-time matriculated undergraduates who enrolled in 2015, 115 Federal Work-Study jobs (averaging $2307). 67 state and other part-time jobs (averaging $2214).

Applying *Options:* electronic application, early admission, deferred entrance. *Required for some:* essay or personal statement. *Recommended:* high school transcript. *Application deadlines:* rolling (freshmen), rolling (transfers). *Notification:* continuous (freshmen), continuous (transfers).

Freshman Application Contact Mr. Zachary Ward, Director of Admissions and Recruitment, Delta College, 1961 Delta Road, University Center, MI 48710. *Phone:* 989-686-9590. *Fax:* 989-667-2202.
E-mail: admit@delta.edu.
Website: http://www.delta.edu/.

Glen Oaks Community College
Centreville, Michigan

Freshman Application Contact Ms. Beverly M. Andrews, Director of Admissions/Registrar, Glen Oaks Community College, 62249 Shimmel Road, Centreville, MI 49032-9719. *Phone:* 269-294-4249. *Toll-free phone:* 888-994-7818. *Fax:* 269-467-4114. *E-mail:* thowden@glenoaks.edu. *Website:* http://www.glenoaks.edu/.

Gogebic Community College
Ironwood, Michigan

Freshman Application Contact Ms. Kim Zeckovich, Director of Admissions, Marketing, and Public Relations, Gogebic Community College, E. 4946 Jackson Road, Ironwood, MI 49938. *Phone:* 906-932-4231 Ext. 347. *Toll-free phone:* 800-682-5910. *Fax:* 906-932-2339. *E-mail:* jeanneg@gogebic.edu. *Website:* http://www.gogebic.edu/.

Grand Rapids Community College
Grand Rapids, Michigan

- **District-supported** 2-year, founded 1914, part of Michigan Department of Education
- **Urban** 35-acre campus
- **Endowment** $30.8 million
- **Coed,** 14,464 undergraduate students, 30% full-time, 50% women, 50% men

Undergraduates 4,321 full-time, 10,143 part-time. Students come from 10 states and territories; 23 other countries; 1% are from out of state; 9% Black or African American, non-Hispanic/Latino; 12% Hispanic/Latino; 4% Asian, non-Hispanic/Latino; 0.1% Native Hawaiian or other Pacific Islander, non-Hispanic/Latino; 0.6% American Indian or Alaska Native, non-Hispanic/Latino; 3% Two or more races, non-Hispanic/Latino; 3% Race/ethnicity unknown; 0.4% international; 8% transferred in. *Retention:* 53% of full-time freshmen returned.

Freshmen *Admission:* 5,365 applied, 2,956 enrolled. *Average high school GPA:* 2.9.

Faculty *Total:* 914, 27% full-time. *Student/faculty ratio:* 21:1.

Majors Architectural technology; architecture; art; automobile/automotive mechanics technology; business administration and management; chemistry; child-care and support services management; computer and information sciences; computer and information systems security; computer programming; computer programming (specific applications); computer support specialist; computer systems networking and telecommunications; corrections; criminal justice/law enforcement administration; criminal justice/police science; culinary arts; dental hygiene; electrical, electronic and communications engineering technology; elementary education; engineering; English; fashion merchandising; foreign languages and literatures; forestry; geology/earth science; heating, air conditioning, ventilation and refrigeration maintenance technology; industrial technology; journalism; landscaping and groundskeeping; liberal arts and sciences/liberal studies; library and information science; licensed practical/vocational nurse training; medical administrative assistant and medical secretary; music; music teacher education; physical education teaching and coaching; plastics and polymer engineering technology; quality control technology; recording arts technology; registered nursing/registered nurse; restaurant, culinary, and catering management; secondary education; welding technology.

Academics *Calendar:* semesters. *Degree:* certificates and associate. *Special study options:* academic remediation for entering students, adult/continuing education programs, advanced placement credit, cooperative education, distance learning, English as a second language, honors programs, independent study, internships, off-campus study, part-time degree program, services for LD students, study abroad, summer session for credit.

Library Arthur Andrews Memorial Library.

Student Life *Housing:* college housing not available. *Activities and Organizations:* drama/theater group, student-run newspaper, choral group,

Student Congress, Phi Theta Kappa, Hispanic Student Organization, Student Gamers Association, Foreign Affairs Club. *Campus security:* 24-hour emergency response devices, late-night transport/escort service. *Student services:* personal/psychological counseling.

Athletics Member NJCAA. *Intercollegiate sports:* baseball M(s), basketball M(s)/W(s), cross-country running M/W, golf M(s), softball W(s), volleyball W(s).

Costs (2016–17) *Tuition:* area resident $3330 full-time, $111 per contact hour part-time; state resident $7140 full-time, $238 per contact hour part-time; nonresident $10,590 full-time, $353 per contact hour part-time. Full-time tuition and fees vary according to course load and program. Part-time tuition and fees vary according to course load and program. *Required fees:* $459 full-time, $15 per contact hour part-time, $90 per term part-time. *Payment plan:* installment. *Waivers:* employees or children of employees.

Financial Aid Of all full-time matriculated undergraduates who enrolled in 2008, 6,142 applied for aid, 4,896 were judged to have need, 1,012 had their need fully met. In 2008, 96 non-need-based awards were made. *Average financial aid package:* $4850. *Average need-based loan:* $2764. *Average need-based gift aid:* $3984. *Average non-need-based aid:* $1051.

Applying *Options:* electronic application, early admission, deferred entrance. *Required:* high school transcript. *Application deadline:* 8/30 (freshmen). *Notification:* continuous (freshmen), continuous (transfers).

Freshman Application Contact Ms. Diane Patrick, Director of Admissions, Grand Rapids Community College, Grand Rapids, MI 49503-3201. *Phone:* 616-234-4100. *Fax:* 616-234-4005. *E-mail:* dpatrick@grcc.edu. *Website:* http://www.grcc.edu/.

Henry Ford College
Dearborn, Michigan

Freshman Application Contact Admissions Office, Henry Ford College, 5101 Evergreen Road, Dearborn, MI 48128-1495. *Phone:* 313-845-6403. *Toll-free phone:* 800-585-HFCC. *Fax:* 313-845-6464.
E-mail: enroll@hfcc.edu. *Website:* http://www.hfcc.edu/.

Jackson College
Jackson, Michigan

Freshman Application Contact Mr. Daniel Vainner, Registrar, Jackson College, 2111 Emmons Road, Jackson, MI 49201. *Phone:* 517-796-8425. *Toll-free phone:* 888-522-7344. *Fax:* 517-796-8446.
E-mail: admissions@jccmi.edu. *Website:* http://www.jccmi.edu/.

Kalamazoo Valley Community College
Kalamazoo, Michigan

Freshman Application Contact Kalamazoo Valley Community College, PO Box 4070, Kalamazoo, MI 49003-4070. *Phone:* 269-488-4207. *Website:* http://www.kvcc.edu/.

Kellogg Community College
Battle Creek, Michigan

- **State and locally supported** 2-year, founded 1956, part of Michigan Department of Education
- **Urban** 120-acre campus
- **Coed,** 4,815 undergraduate students, 25% full-time, 67% women, 33% men

Undergraduates 1,180 full-time, 3,635 part-time. Students come from 2 states and territories; 8 other countries; 9% Black or African American, non-Hispanic/Latino; 5% Hispanic/Latino; 2% Asian, non-Hispanic/Latino; 0.1% Native Hawaiian or other Pacific Islander, non-Hispanic/Latino; 0.7% American Indian or Alaska Native, non-Hispanic/Latino; 4% Two or more races, non-Hispanic/Latino; 7% Race/ethnicity unknown; 0.3% international; 4% transferred in.

Freshmen *Admission:* 454 applied, 454 admitted, 454 enrolled.

Faculty *Total:* 265, 32% full-time, 8% with terminal degrees. *Student/faculty ratio:* 16:1.

Majors Accounting technology and bookkeeping; administrative assistant and secretarial science; animation, interactive technology, video graphics and special effects; business administration and management; CAD/CADD drafting/design technology; child-care and support services management; community organization and advocacy; computer graphics; computer programming; computer programming (specific applications); computer technology/computer systems technology; corrections; criminal justice/safety; dental hygiene; drafting and design technology; electrician; elementary education; emergency medical technology (EMT paramedic); general studies; graphic design; heating, air conditioning, ventilation and refrigeration maintenance technology; industrial production technologies related; industrial technology; legal administrative assistant/secretary; liberal arts and sciences and humanities related; liberal arts and sciences/liberal studies; machine tool technology; medical administrative assistant and medical secretary; medical radiologic technology; physical therapy technology; pipefitting and sprinkler fitting; registered nursing/registered nurse; welding technology.

Academics *Calendar:* semesters. *Degree:* certificates and associate. *Special study options:* academic remediation for entering students, accelerated degree program, adult/continuing education programs, advanced placement credit, cooperative education, distance learning, double majors, English as a second language, freshman honors college, honors programs, independent study, internships, off-campus study, part-time degree program, services for LD students, summer session for credit.

Library Emory W. Morris Learning Resource Center. *Books:* 51,350 (physical), 30,935 (digital/electronic); *Serial titles:* 1,870 (physical); *Databases:* 80. Weekly public service hours: 81; students can reserve study rooms.

Student Life *Housing:* college housing not available. *Activities and Organizations:* drama/theater group, student-run newspaper, choral group, Tech Club, Phi Theta Kappa, Student Nurses Association, Crude Arts Club, Art League. *Campus security:* 24-hour emergency response devices and patrols, late-night transport/escort service.

Athletics Member NJCAA. *Intercollegiate sports:* baseball M(s), basketball M(s)/W(s), soccer W, softball W(s), volleyball W(s).

Costs (2017–18) *Tuition:* area resident $2532 full-time, $106 per credit hour part-time; state resident $4104 full-time, $171 per credit hour part-time; nonresident $5874 full-time, $245 per credit hour part-time. *Required fees:* $360 full-time, $15 per credit hour part-time. *Payment plan:* installment. *Waivers:* senior citizens and employees or children of employees.

Financial Aid Of all full-time matriculated undergraduates who enrolled in 2015, 41 Federal Work-Study jobs (averaging $2251). 43 state and other part-time jobs (averaging $2058).

Applying *Options:* electronic application, early admission. *Required for some:* high school transcript, minimum 2.0 GPA. *Application deadlines:* rolling (freshmen), rolling (transfers). *Notification:* continuous (freshmen), continuous (transfers).

Freshman Application Contact Ms. Meredith Stravers, Director of Admissions, Kellogg Community College, 450 North Avenue, Battle Creek, MI 49017. *Phone:* 269-965-3931 Ext. 2644. *Fax:* 269-965-4133. *E-mail:* straversm@kellogg.edu. *Website:* http://www.kellogg.edu/.

Keweenaw Bay Ojibwa Community College
Baraga, Michigan

- **County-supported** 2-year
- **Rural** campus
- **Coed**

Undergraduates 43 full-time, 34 part-time. Students come from 1 other state.
Academics *Calendar:* semesters. *Degree:* associate.
Applying *Application fee:* $20. *Required:* high school transcript.
Freshman Application Contact Ms. Megan Shanahan, Admissions Officer, Keweenaw Bay Ojibwa Community College, 111 Beartown Road, Baraga, MI 49908. *Phone:* 909-353-4600. *E-mail:* megan@kbocc.org. *Website:* http://www.kbocc.edu/.

Kirtland Community College
Roscommon, Michigan

- **District-supported** 2-year, founded 1966
- **Rural** 180-acre campus
- **Coed**, 1,529 undergraduate students, 31% full-time, 61% women, 39% men

Undergraduates 469 full-time, 1,060 part-time. Students come from 4 states and territories; 0.9% Black or African American, non-Hispanic/Latino; 2% Hispanic/Latino; 0.7% Asian, non-Hispanic/Latino; 0.9% American Indian or Alaska Native, non-Hispanic/Latino; 1% Two or more races, non-Hispanic/Latino; 1% Race/ethnicity unknown; 0.1% international.
Freshmen *Admission:* 601 applied, 601 admitted, 180 enrolled. *Test scores:* ACT scores over 18: 57%; ACT scores over 24: 7%; ACT scores over 30: 1%.
Faculty *Total:* 121, 26% full-time. *Student/faculty ratio:* 18:1.
Majors Automobile/automotive mechanics technology; business administration and management; cardiovascular technology; cosmetology; criminal justice/law enforcement administration; criminal justice/police science; electrical, electronic and communications engineering technology; electromechanical technology; emergency medical technology (EMT paramedic); general studies; graphic design; health information/medical

records technology; heating, air conditioning, ventilation and refrigeration maintenance technology; liberal arts and sciences/liberal studies; medical/clinical assistant; registered nursing/registered nurse; robotics technology; surgical technology; welding technology.

Academics *Calendar:* semesters. *Degree:* certificates and associate. *Special study options:* academic remediation for entering students, adult/continuing education programs, advanced placement credit, cooperative education, distance learning, honors programs, independent study, internships, part-time degree program, services for LD students, summer session for credit.

Library Kirtland Community College Library plus 1 other. *Books:* 27,253 (physical), 168,414 (digital/electronic); *Databases:* 51. Weekly public service hours: 48; students can reserve study rooms.

Student Life *Housing:* college housing not available. *Campus security:* 24-hour emergency response devices, student patrols, late-night transport/escort service, campus warning siren, uniformed armed police officers, RAVE alert system (text, email, voice).

Athletics Member NJCAA. *Intercollegiate sports:* bowling M(s)/W(s), cross-country running M(s)/W(s), golf M(s)/W(s).

Standardized Tests *Recommended:* SAT or ACT (for admission).

Costs (2016–17) *Tuition:* area resident $3270 full-time, $109 per contact hour part-time; state resident $4740 full-time, $158 per contact hour part-time; nonresident $7350 full-time, $245 per contact hour part-time. *Required fees:* $630 full-time, $21 per contact hour part-time. *Payment plan:* installment. *Waivers:* senior citizens and employees or children of employees.

Financial Aid Of all full-time matriculated undergraduates who enrolled in 2015, 50 Federal Work-Study jobs (averaging $1253). 28 state and other part-time jobs (averaging $1647).

Applying *Options:* electronic application. *Application deadlines:* rolling (freshmen), rolling (transfers). *Notification:* continuous until 8/15 (freshmen), continuous until 8/15 (transfers).

Freshman Application Contact Ms. Michelle Vyskocil, Dean of Student Services, Kirtland Community College, 10775 North Saint Helen Road, Roscommon, MI 48653. *Phone:* 989-275-5000 Ext. 248. *Fax:* 989-275-6789. *E-mail:* registrar@kirtland.edu. *Website:* http://www.kirtland.edu/.

Lake Michigan College
Benton Harbor, Michigan

Freshman Application Contact Mr. Louis Thomas, Lead Admissions Specialist, Lake Michigan College, 2755 East Napier Avenue, Benton Harbor, MI 49022-1899. *Phone:* 269-927-6584. *Toll-free phone:* 800-252-1LMC. *Fax:* 269-927-6718. *E-mail:* thomas@lakemichigancollege.edu. *Website:* http://www.lakemichigancollege.edu/.

Lansing Community College
Lansing, Michigan

- **State and locally supported** 2-year, founded 1957, part of Michigan Department of Education
- **Urban** 28-acre campus
- **Endowment** $7.3 million
- **Coed**, 13,583 undergraduate students, 37% full-time, 54% women, 46% men

Undergraduates 5,088 full-time, 8,495 part-time. 10% Black or African American, non-Hispanic/Latino; 8% Hispanic/Latino; 3% Asian, non-Hispanic/Latino; 0.2% Native Hawaiian or other Pacific Islander, non-Hispanic/Latino; 0.5% American Indian or Alaska Native, non-Hispanic/Latino; 3% Two or more races, non-Hispanic/Latino; 5% Race/ethnicity unknown; 1% international.
Freshmen *Admission:* 2,329 enrolled.
Majors Accounting related; accounting technology and bookkeeping; administrative assistant and secretarial science; African American/Black studies; agricultural business and management; aircraft powerplant technology; airframe mechanics and aircraft maintenance technology; airline pilot and flight crew; American studies; animation, interactive technology, video graphics and special effects; anthropology; architectural engineering technology; architectural technology; art; art history, criticism and conservation; autobody/collision and repair technology; automobile/automotive mechanics technology; avionics maintenance technology; banking and financial support services; biology/biological sciences; biotechnology; business administration and management; business/commerce; carpentry; chemical technology; chemistry; child-care provision; cinematography and film/video production; civil engineering technology; community organization and advocacy; computer and information sciences; computer programming (specific applications); computer systems networking and telecommunications; computer technology/computer systems technology; construction/heavy equipment/earthmoving equipment operation; construction management; corrections; criminal justice/police science;

customer service support/call center/teleservice operation; data modeling/warehousing and database administration; dental hygiene; diagnostic medical sonography and ultrasound technology; dramatic/theater arts; e-commerce; economics; electrical and power transmission installation; electrician; electromechanical technology; elementary education; emergency medical technology (EMT paramedic); energy management and systems technology; engineering; engineering physics/applied physics; English; environmental engineering technology; fashion merchandising; fine/studio arts; fire science/firefighting; foreign languages and literatures; French; geography; Germanic languages; graphic design; health and physical education/fitness; heating, air conditioning, ventilation and refrigeration maintenance technology; higher education/higher education administration; histologic technician; history; hotel/motel administration; humanities; human resources management; industrial production technologies related; interior design; international business/trade/commerce; international relations and affairs; Japanese; juvenile corrections; legal assistant/paralegal; liberal arts and sciences/liberal studies; licensed practical/vocational nurse training; machine tool technology; magnetic resonance imaging (MRI) technology; management information systems; mathematics; mechanical drafting and CAD/CADD; music; music performance; office management; philosophy; photography; political science and government; premedical studies; psychology; radio and television broadcasting technology; radiologic technology/science; real estate; registered nursing/registered nurse; religious studies; sales, distribution, and marketing operations; secondary education; selling skills and sales; sign language interpretation and translation; social sciences; sociology; Spanish; speech communication and rhetoric; surgical technology; surveying technology; teacher assistant/aide; theater design and technology; tourism and travel services management; veterinary/animal health technology; web page, digital/multimedia and information resources design; welding technology.

Academics *Calendar:* semesters. *Degree:* certificates and associate. *Special study options:* academic remediation for entering students, adult/continuing education programs, advanced placement credit, cooperative education, distance learning, double majors, English as a second language, external degree program, honors programs, independent study, internships, part-time degree program, services for LD students, study abroad, summer session for credit. *ROTC:* Army (c), Air Force (c).

Library Lansing Community College Library.

Student Life *Housing:* college housing not available. *Activities and Organizations:* drama/theater group, student-run newspaper, choral group, American Marketing Association, Phi Theta Kappa, Future Teachers' Club, Health Career Related Clubs (Dental Hygiene, Nurses), Gay-Straight Alliance, national fraternities, national sororities. *Campus security:* 24-hour emergency response devices and patrols, student patrols, late-night transport/escort service. *Student services:* personal/psychological counseling, women's center.

Athletics Member NJCAA. *Intercollegiate sports:* baseball M(s), basketball M(s)/W(s), cross-country running M(s)/W(s), softball W(s), track and field M/W, volleyball W(s).

Costs (2017–18) *Tuition:* area resident $2640 full-time; state resident $5280 full-time; nonresident $7920 full-time. *Required fees:* $380 full-time.

Applying *Options:* electronic application, early admission, deferred entrance. *Required for some:* essay or personal statement, high school transcript, 2 letters of recommendation, interview, specific additional requirements for health, aviation, music, police academy, and fire academy program admissions. *Application deadlines:* 8/7 (freshmen), 8/7 (transfers).

Freshman Application Contact Ms. Tammy Grossbauer, Director of Admissions/Registrar, Lansing Community College, 1121 Enrollment Services, PO BOX 40010, Lansing, MI 48901. *Phone:* 517-483-1200. *Toll-free phone:* 800-644-4LCC. *Fax:* 517-483-1170. *E-mail:* grossbt@lcc.edu. *Website:* http://www.lcc.edu/.

Macomb Community College
Warren, Michigan

- **District-supported** 2-year, founded 1954, part of Michigan Public Community College System
- **Suburban** 384-acre campus with easy access to Detroit
- **Endowment** $20.4 million
- **Coed**, 21,734 undergraduate students, 30% full-time, 53% women, 47% men

Undergraduates 6,468 full-time, 15,266 part-time. Students come from 4 states and territories; 11% Black or African American, non-Hispanic/Latino; 3% Hispanic/Latino; 5% Asian, non-Hispanic/Latino; 0.1% Native Hawaiian or other Pacific Islander, non-Hispanic/Latino; 0.5% American Indian or Alaska Native, non-Hispanic/Latino; 2% Two or more races, non-Hispanic/Latino; 8% Race/ethnicity unknown; 2% international. *Retention:* 56% of full-time freshmen returned.

Freshmen *Admission:* 3,336 enrolled.

Faculty *Total:* 971, 21% full-time. *Student/faculty ratio:* 25:1.

Majors Accounting; administrative assistant and secretarial science; agriculture; architectural drafting and CAD/CADD; automobile/automotive mechanics technology; automotive engineering technology; biology/biological sciences; business administration and management; business automation/technology/data entry; business/commerce; cabinetmaking and millwork; chemistry; child-care and support services management; civil engineering technology; commercial and advertising art; computer programming; computer programming (specific applications); construction engineering technology; criminal justice/law enforcement administration; criminal justice/police science; culinary arts; drafting and design technology; drafting/design engineering technologies related; electrical, electronic and communications engineering technology; electrical/electronics equipment installation and repair; electromechanical technology; emergency medical technology (EMT paramedic); energy management and systems technology; engineering related; finance; fire prevention and safety technology; forensic science and technology; general studies; graphic and printing equipment operation/production; heating, air conditioning, ventilation and refrigeration maintenance technology; heating, ventilation, air conditioning and refrigeration engineering technology; industrial mechanics and maintenance technology; industrial technology; international/global studies; legal assistant/paralegal; legal studies; liberal arts and sciences/liberal studies; machine tool technology; manufacturing engineering technology; marketing/marketing management; mathematics; mechanical drafting and CAD/CADD; mechanical engineering/mechanical technology; mechanic and repair technologies related; medical/clinical assistant; mental health counseling; metallurgical technology; music performance; occupational therapist assistant; operations management; physical therapy technology; plastics and polymer engineering technology; plumbing technology; pre-engineering; quality control and safety technologies related; quality control technology; registered nursing/registered nurse; respiratory care therapy; robotics technology; sheet metal technology; social psychology; speech communication and rhetoric; surgical technology; surveying technology; tool and die technology; veterinary/animal health technology; welding technology.

Academics *Calendar:* semesters. *Degree:* certificates and associate. *Special study options:* academic remediation for entering students, adult/continuing education programs, advanced placement credit, cooperative education, English as a second language, honors programs, internships, off-campus study, part-time degree program, services for LD students, student-designed majors, summer session for credit.

Library Library of South Campus.

Student Life *Housing:* college housing not available. *Activities and Organizations:* drama/theater group, Phi Beta Kappa, Adventure Unlimited, Alpha Rho Rho, SADD. *Campus security:* 24-hour emergency response devices and patrols, late-night transport/escort service, security phones in parking lots, surveillance cameras. *Student services:* health clinic, personal/psychological counseling.

Athletics Member NJCAA. *Intercollegiate sports:* baseball M(s), basketball M(s), cross-country running M(s)/W(s), soccer M(s), softball W(s), track and field M(s)/W(s), volleyball W(s). *Intramural sports:* baseball M, basketball M, bowling M/W, cross-country running M/W, football M/W, skiing (cross-country) M/W, skiing (downhill) M/W, volleyball M/W.

Costs (2016–17) *Tuition:* area resident $3007 full-time, $97 per credit hour part-time; state resident $4960 full-time, $160 per credit hour part-time; nonresident $7130 full-time, $230 per credit hour part-time. Full-time tuition and fees vary according to course load. Part-time tuition and fees vary according to course load. *Required fees:* $275 full-time, $5 per credit hour part-time, $60 per term part-time. *Waivers:* employees or children of employees.

Applying *Options:* early admission, deferred entrance. *Application deadlines:* rolling (freshmen), rolling (transfers).

Freshman Application Contact Mr. Brian Bouwman, Coordinator of Admissions and Transfer Credit, Macomb Community College, 14500 East 12 Mile Road, Warren, MI 48088-3896. *Phone:* 586-445-7246. *Toll-free phone:* 866-MACOMB1. *Fax:* 586-445-7140. *E-mail:* stevensr@macomb.edu. *Website:* http://www.macomb.edu/.

MIAT College of Technology
Canton, Michigan

Admissions Office Contact MIAT College of Technology, 2955 South Haggerty Road, Canton, MI 48188. *Website:* http://www.miat.edu/.

Mid Michigan Community College
Harrison, Michigan

Freshman Application Contact Jennifer Casebeer, Admissions Specialist, Mid Michigan Community College, 1375 South Clare Avenue, Harrison, MI 48625-9447. *Phone:* 989-386-6661. *E-mail:* apply@midmich.edu. *Website:* http://www.midmich.edu/.

Monroe County Community College
Monroe, Michigan

- **County-supported** 2-year, founded 1964, part of Michigan Department of Education
- **Small-town** 150-acre campus with easy access to Detroit, Toledo
- **Coed**, 3,144 undergraduate students, 30% full-time, 57% women, 43% men

Undergraduates 954 full-time, 2,190 part-time. Students come from 2 other countries; 4% are from out of state; 3% Black or African American, non-Hispanic/Latino; 3% Hispanic/Latino; 0.8% Asian, non-Hispanic/Latino; 0.1% Native Hawaiian or other Pacific Islander, non-Hispanic/Latino; 0.3% American Indian or Alaska Native, non-Hispanic/Latino; 0.7% Two or more races, non-Hispanic/Latino; 8% Race/ethnicity unknown; 0.1% international.

Freshmen *Admission:* 2,500 applied, 2,500 admitted. *Average high school GPA:* 2.5.

Faculty *Total:* 180, 25% full-time.

Majors Accounting; administrative assistant and secretarial science; architectural engineering technology; art; biology/biological sciences; business administration and management; child development; clinical laboratory science/medical technology; computer and information sciences related; computer engineering technology; computer graphics; computer programming (specific applications); criminal justice/police science; criminal justice/safety; culinary arts; data processing and data processing technology; drafting and design technology; electrical, electronic and communications engineering technology; elementary education; English; finance; funeral service and mortuary science; industrial technology; information technology; journalism; legal administrative assistant/secretary; liberal arts and sciences/liberal studies; marketing/marketing management; mass communication/media; mathematics; medical administrative assistant and medical secretary; physical therapy; pre-engineering; psychology; registered nursing/registered nurse; respiratory care therapy; rhetoric and composition; social work; web/multimedia management and webmaster; web page, digital/multimedia and information resources design; welding technology; word processing.

Academics *Calendar:* semesters. *Degree:* certificates and associate. *Special study options:* academic remediation for entering students, advanced placement credit, distance learning, honors programs, independent study, part-time degree program, services for LD students, study abroad, summer session for credit.

Library Campbell Learning Resource Center.

Student Life *Housing:* college housing not available. *Activities and Organizations:* drama/theater group, student-run newspaper, choral group, Student Government, Society of Auto Engineers, Oasis, Nursing Students Organization, Respiratory Therapy. *Campus security:* police patrols during open hours.

Standardized Tests *Required:* ACT, ACT Compass, SAT, ACCUPLACER (for admission). *Required for some:* ACT (for admission). *Recommended:* ACT (for admission).

Costs (2017–18) *Tuition:* area resident $3118 full-time; state resident $5014 full-time; nonresident $5518 full-time. Full-time tuition and fees vary according to reciprocity agreements. Part-time tuition and fees vary according to reciprocity agreements. *Required fees:* $70 full-time. *Payment plan:* installment. *Waivers:* senior citizens and employees or children of employees.

Applying *Options:* early admission, deferred entrance. *Required:* high school transcript. *Application deadline:* rolling (transfers). *Notification:* continuous (freshmen), continuous (transfers).

Freshman Application Contact Mr. Mark V. Hall, Director of Admissions and Guidance Services, Monroe County Community College, 1555 South Raisinville Road, Monroe, MI 48161. *Phone:* 734-384-4261. *Toll-free phone:* 877-YES-MCCC. *Fax:* 734-242-9711. *E-mail:* mhall@monroeccc.edu. *Website:* http://www.monroeccc.edu/.

Montcalm Community College
Sidney, Michigan

Freshman Application Contact Ms. Debra Alexander, Associate Dean of Student Services, Montcalm Community College, 2800 College Drive, SW, Sidney, MI 48885. *Phone:* 989-328-1276. *Toll-free phone:* 877-328-2111. *E-mail:* admissions@montcalm.edu. *Website:* http://www.montcalm.edu/.

Mott Community College
Flint, Michigan

- **District-supported** 2-year, founded 1923
- **Urban** 32-acre campus with easy access to Detroit
- **Endowment** $40.1 million
- **Coed**, 8,013 undergraduate students, 27% full-time, 58% women, 42% men

Undergraduates 2,186 full-time, 5,827 part-time. 17% Black or African American, non-Hispanic/Latino; 5% Hispanic/Latino; 0.7% Asian, non-Hispanic/Latino; 0.1% Native Hawaiian or other Pacific Islander, non-Hispanic/Latino; 0.7% American Indian or Alaska Native, non-Hispanic/Latino; 4% Two or more races, non-Hispanic/Latino; 3% Race/ethnicity unknown; 0.3% international; 2% transferred in.

Freshmen *Admission:* 1,498 enrolled.

Faculty *Total:* 429, 35% full-time, 12% with terminal degrees. *Student/faculty ratio:* 17:1.

Majors Accounting technology and bookkeeping; architectural engineering technology; automation engineer technology; automobile/automotive mechanics technology; baking and pastry arts; biology/biological sciences; business administration and management; business/commerce; child-care provision; cinematography and film/video production; communications technology; community health services counseling; computer programming; computer programming (specific applications); computer systems networking and telecommunications; corrections; criminal justice/police science; culinary arts; dental assisting; dental hygiene; drafting and design technology; early childhood education; electrical, electronic and communications engineering technology; emergency medical technology (EMT paramedic); engineering technologies and engineering related; entrepreneurship; fire prevention and safety technology; food service systems administration; general studies; graphic design; heating, ventilation, air conditioning and refrigeration engineering technology; histologic technician; liberal arts and sciences/liberal studies; marketing/marketing management; mechanical engineering/mechanical technology; medical radiologic technology; music technology; occupational therapist assistant; photography; physical therapy technology; precision production related; registered nursing/registered nurse; respiratory care therapy; salon/beauty salon management; sign language interpretation and translation; visual and performing arts.

Academics *Calendar:* semesters. *Degree:* certificates and associate. *Special study options:* academic remediation for entering students, accelerated degree program, adult/continuing education programs, advanced placement credit, cooperative education, distance learning, double majors, English as a second language, honors programs, independent study, internships, part-time degree program, services for LD students, summer session for credit.

Library Charles Stewart Mott Library.

Student Life *Housing:* college housing not available. *Activities and Organizations:* choral group, Otaku Club, Respiratory Care Student Society, Physical Therapist Assistants, Occupational Therapist Assistants, Transitions Cosmetology, national fraternities, national sororities. *Campus security:* 24-hour emergency response devices and patrols, student patrols, late-night transport/escort service, closed-circuit TV surveillance, whistle alert program, 3P Campaign: Prevent, Protect, and Prosecute Violence Against Women. *Student services:* health clinic, personal/psychological counseling.

Athletics Member NJCAA. *Intercollegiate sports:* baseball M(s), basketball M(s)/W(s), cross-country running M(s)/W(s), golf M(s), softball W(s), volleyball W(s). *Intramural sports:* cheerleading W(c).

Costs (2017–18) *Tuition:* $135 per credit hour part-time; state resident $183 per credit hour part-time; nonresident $261 per credit hour part-time. Full-time tuition and fees vary according to course load. Part-time tuition and fees vary according to course load. *Required fees:* $17 per credit hour part-time, $138 per credit hour part-time. *Payment plan:* installment. *Waivers:* senior citizens and employees or children of employees.

Applying *Options:* electronic application, early admission, deferred entrance. *Required:* high school transcript. *Application deadline:* 8/31 (freshmen). *Notification:* continuous (transfers).

Freshman Application Contact Ms. Regina Broomfield, Supervisor of Admissions Operations - Outreach and Recruitment, Mott Community College, 1401 East Court Street, Flint, MI 48503. *Phone:* 810-762-0358. *Toll-free phone:* 800-852-8614. *Fax:* 810-232-9442. *E-mail:* regina.broomfield@mcc.edu. *Website:* http://www.mcc.edu/.

Muskegon Community College
Muskegon, Michigan

- **State and locally supported** 2-year, founded 1926, part of Michigan Department of Education
- **Small-town** 112-acre campus with easy access to Grand Rapids
- **Coed**

Undergraduates 1,488 full-time, 3,018 part-time. Students come from 4 states and territories; 9% Black or African American, non-Hispanic/Latino; 3% Hispanic/Latino; 0.8% Asian, non-Hispanic/Latino; 0.1% Native Hawaiian or other Pacific Islander, non-Hispanic/Latino; 0.9% American Indian or Alaska Native, non-Hispanic/Latino; 4% Two or more races, non-Hispanic/Latino; 5% Race/ethnicity unknown; 0.4% international. *Retention:* 59% of full-time freshmen returned.
Faculty *Student/faculty ratio:* 19:1.
Academics *Calendar:* semesters. *Degree:* associate. *Special study options:* academic remediation for entering students, adult/continuing education programs, cooperative education, honors programs, part-time degree program, student-designed majors, summer session for credit.
Library Hendrik Meijer and Technology Center.
Student Life *Campus security:* 24-hour emergency response devices, on-campus security officer.
Athletics Member NJCAA.
Financial Aid Of all full-time matriculated undergraduates who enrolled in 2015, 250 Federal Work-Study jobs (averaging $2500). 50 state and other part-time jobs (averaging $2500).
Applying *Options:* electronic application, early admission, deferred entrance. *Required:* high school transcript.
Freshman Application Contact Mr. Johnathon Skidmore, Senior Clerk 1 Admissions, Muskegon Community College, 221 South Quarterline Road, Muskegon, MI 49442-1493. *Phone:* 231-777-0366. *Toll-free phone:* 866-711-4622. *E-mail:* johnathon.skidmore@muskegoncc.edu.
Website: http://www.muskegoncc.edu/.

North Central Michigan College
Petoskey, Michigan

Director of Admissions Ms. Julieanne Tobin, Director of Enrollment Management, North Central Michigan College, 1515 Howard Street, Petoskey, MI 49770-8717. *Phone:* 231-439-6511. *Toll-free phone:* 888-298-6605. *E-mail:* jtobin@ncmich.edu. *Website:* http://www.ncmich.edu/.

Northwestern Michigan College
Traverse City, Michigan

Freshman Application Contact Catheryn Claerhout, Director of Admissions, Northwestern Michigan College, 1701 E. Front Street, Traverse City, MI 49686. *Phone:* 231-995-1034. *Toll-free phone:* 800-748-0566. *E-mail:* c.claerhout@nmc.edu. *Website:* http://www.nmc.edu/.

Oakland Community College
Bloomfield Hills, Michigan

Freshman Application Contact Stephan M. Linden, Registrar, Oakland Community College, 2480 Opdyke Road, Bloomfield Hills, MI 48304-2266. *Phone:* 248-341-2192. *Fax:* 248-341-2099. *E-mail:* smlinden@oaklandcc.edu. *Website:* http://www.oaklandcc.edu/.

Saginaw Chippewa Tribal College
Mount Pleasant, Michigan

- **Independent** 2-year, founded 1998
- **Small-town** campus
- **Coed,** 141 undergraduate students, 40% full-time, 65% women, 35% men

Undergraduates 57 full-time, 84 part-time. 1% Black or African American, non-Hispanic/Latino; 4% Hispanic/Latino; 0.7% Native Hawaiian or other Pacific Islander, non-Hispanic/Latino; 80% American Indian or Alaska Native, non-Hispanic/Latino; 0.7% Two or more races, non-Hispanic/Latino; 0.7% transferred in.
Freshmen *Admission:* 22 enrolled.
Faculty *Total:* 21, 33% full-time, 14% with terminal degrees. *Student/faculty ratio:* 7:1.

Majors American Indian/Native American studies; business/commerce; liberal arts and sciences/liberal studies.
Academics *Calendar:* semesters. *Degree:* associate. *Special study options:* part-time degree program, summer session for credit.
Library Saginaw Chippewa Tribal College Library. *Books:* 2,134 (physical), 12,155 (digital/electronic); *Serial titles:* 4 (physical). Students can reserve study rooms.
Student Life *Housing:* college housing not available.
Costs (2016–17) *Tuition:* $1560 full-time, $60 per contact hour part-time. Full-time tuition and fees vary according to class time, course level, course load, degree level, location, program, and student level. Part-time tuition and fees vary according to class time, course level, course load, degree level, location, program, and student level. *Required fees:* $650 full-time, $25 per credit hour part-time. *Payment plans:* installment, deferred payment.
Applying *Required:* high school transcript.
Freshman Application Contact Ms. Amanda Flaugher, Admissions Officer/Registrar/Financial Aid, Saginaw Chippewa Tribal College, 2274 Enterprise Drive, Mount Pleasant, MI 48858. *Phone:* 989-775-4123. *Fax:* 989-775-4528. *E-mail:* aflaugher@sagchip.edu. *Website:* http://www.sagchip.edu/.

St. Clair County Community College
Port Huron, Michigan

- **State and locally supported** 2-year, founded 1923, part of Michigan Department of Education
- **Small-town** 25-acre campus with easy access to Detroit
- **Coed,** 3,625 undergraduate students, 39% full-time, 61% women, 39% men

Undergraduates 1,415 full-time, 2,210 part-time. *Retention:* 58% of full-time freshmen returned.
Freshmen *Admission:* 585 enrolled.
Faculty *Total:* 254, 29% full-time. *Student/faculty ratio:* 19:1.
Majors Accounting technology and bookkeeping; automation engineer technology; business/commerce; commercial and advertising art; computer programming; computer systems networking and telecommunications; corrections; criminal justice/law enforcement administration; data processing and data processing technology; drafting and design technology; electrical, electronic and communications engineering technology; emergency medical technology (EMT paramedic); energy management and systems technology; engineering; executive assistant/executive secretary; fire science/firefighting; health information/medical records technology; liberal arts and sciences/liberal studies; manufacturing engineering technology; marketing/marketing management; massage therapy; medical radiologic technology; office management; registered nursing/registered nurse; web/multimedia management and webmaster; welding engineering technology.
Academics *Calendar:* semesters. *Degree:* certificates and associate. *Special study options:* academic remediation for entering students, adult/continuing education programs, advanced placement credit, cooperative education, distance learning, honors programs, independent study, part-time degree program, services for LD students, summer session for credit.
Library Main Library plus 1 other.
Student Life *Housing:* college housing not available. *Activities and Organizations:* drama/theater group, student-run newspaper, radio station, Phi Theta Kappa, Business Club, Gay-Straight Alliance, Criminal Justice Club. *Campus security:* 24-hour emergency response devices, late-night transport/escort service, patrols by security until 10 pm. *Student services:* personal/psychological counseling.
Athletics Member NJCAA. *Intercollegiate sports:* baseball M(s), basketball M(s)/W(s), cross-country running M/W, golf M, softball W(s), volleyball W(s).
Costs (2016–17) *Tuition:* area resident $3689 full-time, $105 per contact hour part-time; state resident $6758 full-time, $204 per contact hour part-time; nonresident $9672 full-time, $298 per contact hour part-time. Full-time tuition and fees vary according to course load and location. Part-time tuition and fees vary according to course load and location. *Required fees:* $154 full-time, $14 per contact hour part-time. *Payment plan:* deferred payment. *Waivers:* senior citizens and employees or children of employees.
Applying *Options:* electronic application, early admission. *Required:* high school transcript. *Application deadlines:* rolling (freshmen), rolling (transfers).
Freshman Application Contact St. Clair County Community College, 323 Erie Street, PO Box 5015, Port Huron, MI 48061-5015. *Phone:* 810-989-5501. *Toll-free phone:* 800-553-2427. *Website:* http://www.sc4.edu/.

Schoolcraft College
Livonia, Michigan

- **District-supported** primarily 2-year, founded 1961, part of Michigan Department of Education
- **Suburban** campus with easy access to Detroit
- **Coed,** 11,339 undergraduate students, 28% full-time, 54% women, 46% men

Undergraduates 3,134 full-time, 8,205 part-time. 14% Black or African American, non-Hispanic/Latino; 4% Hispanic/Latino; 4% Asian, non-Hispanic/Latino; 0.1% Native Hawaiian or other Pacific Islander, non-Hispanic/Latino; 0.7% American Indian or Alaska Native, non-Hispanic/Latino; 3% Two or more races, non-Hispanic/Latino; 7% Race/ethnicity unknown; 1% international; 24% transferred in. *Retention:* 62% of full-time freshmen returned.

Freshmen *Admission:* 2,118 enrolled.

Faculty *Total:* 524, 19% full-time. *Student/faculty ratio:* 24:1.

Majors Accounting technology and bookkeeping; biomedical technology; business administration and management; business automation/technology/data entry; business/commerce; child development; computer graphics; computer programming; computer programming (specific applications); criminal justice/police science; culinary arts; drafting and design technology; education; electrical, electronic and communications engineering technology; emergency medical technology (EMT paramedic); engineering; environmental engineering technology; executive assistant/executive secretary; fine arts related; fire science/firefighting; foods and nutrition related; general studies; health information/medical records technology; health services/allied health/health sciences; homeland security, law enforcement, firefighting and protective services related; manufacturing engineering technology; marketing/marketing management; massage therapy; mechatronics, robotics, and automation engineering; metallurgical technology; physical fitness technician; pre-pharmacy studies; radio and television broadcasting technology; recording arts technology; registered nursing/registered nurse; salon/beauty salon management; small business administration; web page, digital/multimedia and information resources design; welding technology.

Academics *Calendar:* semesters. *Degrees:* certificates, associate, and bachelor's. *Special study options:* academic remediation for entering students, accelerated degree program, adult/continuing education programs, advanced placement credit, distance learning, English as a second language, honors programs, independent study, internships, part-time degree program, services for LD students, study abroad, summer session for credit.

Library Bradner Library. Students can reserve study rooms.

Student Life *Housing:* college housing not available. *Activities and Organizations:* drama/theater group, student-run newspaper, choral group, Phi Theta Kappa, The Schoolcraft Connection Newspaper, Student Activities Board, Project Playhem Gaming Club, Otaku Anime Japanese Animation Club. *Campus security:* 24-hour emergency response devices and patrols, late-night transport/escort service. *Student services:* personal/psychological counseling, women's center.

Athletics Member NJCAA. *Intercollegiate sports:* baseball M, basketball M(s)/W(s), bowling M/W, cross-country running M/W, golf M, soccer M(s)/W(s), softball W, volleyball W(s).

Costs (2016–17) *Tuition:* area resident $3060 full-time, $102 per credit hour part-time; state resident $4440 full-time, $148 per credit hour part-time; nonresident $6540 full-time, $218 per credit hour part-time. *Required fees:* $776 full-time, $23 per credit hour part-time, $43 per term part-time. *Payment plans:* installment, deferred payment. *Waivers:* senior citizens and employees or children of employees.

Financial Aid Of all full-time matriculated undergraduates who enrolled in 2015, 42 Federal Work-Study jobs (averaging $1722).

Applying *Options:* electronic application, early admission, deferred entrance. *Required for some:* high school transcript. *Recommended:* high school transcript. *Application deadlines:* rolling (freshmen), rolling (transfers).

Freshman Application Contact Ms. Lisa Bushaw, Director of Admissions, Schoolcraft College, 18600 Haggerty Road, Livonia, MI 48152-2696. *Phone:* 734-462-4683. *E-mail:* admissions@schoolcraft.edu. *Website:* http://www.schoolcraft.edu/.

Southwestern Michigan College
Dowagiac, Michigan

- **State and locally supported** 2-year, founded 1964
- **Rural** 240-acre campus
- **Coed,** 2,262 undergraduate students, 47% full-time, 58% women, 42% men

Undergraduates 1,059 full-time, 1,203 part-time. Students come from 10 states and territories; 1 other country; 14% are from out of state; 10% Black or African American, non-Hispanic/Latino; 7% Hispanic/Latino; 1% Asian, non-Hispanic/Latino; 0.2% Native Hawaiian or other Pacific Islander, non-Hispanic/Latino; 2% American Indian or Alaska Native, non-Hispanic/Latino; 4% Two or more races, non-Hispanic/Latino; 3% Race/ethnicity unknown; 0.1% international; 5% transferred in; 22% live on campus. *Retention:* 57% of full-time freshmen returned.

Freshmen *Admission:* 2,241 applied, 2,232 admitted, 568 enrolled.

Faculty *Total:* 140, 41% full-time, 27% with terminal degrees. *Student/faculty ratio:* 17:1.

Majors Accounting technology and bookkeeping; agricultural production; automation engineer technology; automobile/automotive mechanics technology; business administration and management; carpentry; computer programming; computer systems networking and telecommunications; criminal justice/safety; early childhood education; engineering technology; fire science/firefighting; general studies; graphic design; health information/medical records technology; industrial mechanics and maintenance technology; liberal arts and sciences/liberal studies; machine tool technology; medical/clinical assistant; prenursing studies; professional, technical, business, and scientific writing; registered nursing/registered nurse; social work; sport and fitness administration/management.

Academics *Calendar:* semesters. *Degree:* certificates and associate. *Special study options:* academic remediation for entering students, accelerated degree program, adult/continuing education programs, advanced placement credit, cooperative education, English as a second language, honors programs, independent study, internships, part-time degree program, services for LD students, summer session for credit.

Library Fred L. Mathews Library. *Books:* 22,164 (physical), 621 (digital/electronic); *Serial titles:* 12 (physical); *Databases:* 17. Weekly public service hours: 61; students can reserve study rooms.

Student Life *Housing Options:* coed. Campus housing is university owned. *Activities and Organizations:* drama/theater group, choral group, Advocates for All, Business Club, Criminal Justice Club, Rock Climbing Club, STEM Club. *Campus security:* 24-hour emergency response devices and patrols, controlled dormitory access, day and evening police patrols. *Student services:* personal/psychological counseling.

Athletics *Intramural sports:* basketball M/W, football M/W, rock climbing M/W, soccer M/W, softball M/W, volleyball M/W.

Costs (2016–17) *Tuition:* area resident $2997 full-time, $115 per contact hour part-time; state resident $3907 full-time, $150 per contact hour part-time; nonresident $4264 full-time, $164 per contact hour part-time. *Required fees:* $1242 full-time, $48 per contact hour part-time. *Room and board:* $8860; room only: $6160. *Payment plan:* installment. *Waivers:* employees or children of employees.

Financial Aid Of all full-time matriculated undergraduates who enrolled in 2015, 125 Federal Work-Study jobs (averaging $1000). 75 state and other part-time jobs (averaging $1000).

Applying *Options:* electronic application, deferred entrance. *Required:* high school transcript. *Required for some:* interview. *Application deadlines:* rolling (freshmen), rolling (transfers). *Notification:* continuous (freshmen), continuous (transfers).

Freshman Application Contact Ms. Angela Palsak, Executive Director of Student Services, Southwestern Michigan College, Dowagiac, MI 49047. *Phone:* 269-782-1000 Ext. 1310. *Toll-free phone:* 800-456-8675. *Fax:* 269-782-1331. *E-mail:* apalsak@swmich.edu. *Website:* http://www.swmich.edu/.

Washtenaw Community College
Ann Arbor, Michigan

Freshman Application Contact Washtenaw Community College, 4800 East Huron River Drive, PO Box D-1, Ann Arbor, MI 48106. *Phone:* 734-973-3315. *Website:* http://www.wccnet.edu/.

Wayne County Community College District
Detroit, Michigan

- **State and locally supported** 2-year, founded 1967
- **Urban** campus
- **Coed,** 16,822 undergraduate students, 15% full-time, 65% women, 35% men

Undergraduates 2,531 full-time, 14,291 part-time. 78% Black or African American, non-Hispanic/Latino; 1% Hispanic/Latino; 0.8% Asian, non-Hispanic/Latino; 0.1% Native Hawaiian or other Pacific Islander, non-Hispanic/Latino; 0.4% American Indian or Alaska Native, non-Hispanic/Latino; 6% Two or more races, non-Hispanic/Latino; 7% Race/ethnicity unknown; 1% international; 14% transferred in.

Freshmen *Admission:* 3,171 enrolled.

Faculty *Student/faculty ratio:* 24:1.

Majors Accounting technology and bookkeeping; adult development and aging; agricultural business and management related; aircraft powerplant technology; airframe mechanics and aircraft maintenance technology; American Sign Language (ASL); anesthesiologist assistant; autobody/collision and repair technology; automobile/automotive mechanics technology; biomedical technology; building/property maintenance; business administration and management; CAD/CADD drafting/design technology; child-care and support services management; computer numerically controlled (CNC) machinist technology; computer programming; corrections; criminal justice/police science; data modeling/warehousing and database administration; dental assisting; dental hygiene; digital communication and media/multimedia; e-commerce; electrical and electronic engineering technologies related; electrical, electronic and communications engineering technology; elementary education; emergency medical technology (EMT paramedic); entrepreneurship; fire prevention and safety technology; food service systems administration; game and interactive media design; heating, air conditioning, ventilation and refrigeration maintenance technology; homeland security, law enforcement, firefighting and protective services related; hotel, motel, and restaurant management; legal assistant/paralegal; liberal arts and sciences/liberal studies; logistics, materials, and supply chain management; manufacturing engineering technology; mortuary science and embalming; office management; pharmacy technician; phlebotomy technology; physician assistant; pre-engineering; psychiatric/mental health services technology; registered nursing/registered nurse; security and loss prevention; social work; substance abuse/addiction counseling; surgical technology; system, networking, and LAN/WAN management; web/multimedia management and webmaster; welding technology.
Academics *Calendar:* semesters. *Degree:* certificates and associate. *Special study options:* academic remediation for entering students, adult/continuing education programs, advanced placement credit, cooperative education, distance learning, English as a second language, honors programs, internships, part-time degree program, services for LD students, study abroad, summer session for credit.
Library Learning Resource Center plus 5 others.
Student Life *Housing:* college housing not available. *Campus security:* 24-hour emergency response devices.
Athletics Member NJCAA. *Intercollegiate sports:* basketball M/W, bowling M/W, cross-country running M/W, golf M, volleyball W.
Financial Aid Of all full-time matriculated undergraduates who enrolled in 2015, 239 Federal Work-Study jobs (averaging $2360). 147 state and other part-time jobs (averaging $1200).
Applying *Options:* electronic application, early admission, deferred entrance. *Required:* high school transcript. *Application deadlines:* rolling (freshmen), rolling (transfers).
Freshman Application Contact Mr. Adrian Phillips, District Associate Vice Chancellor of Student Services, Wayne County Community College District, 801 West Fort Street, Detroit, MI 48226-9975. *Phone:* 313-496-2820. *Fax:* 313-962-1643. *E-mail:* aphilli1@wcccd.edu.
Website: http://www.wcccd.edu/.

West Shore Community College
Scottville, Michigan

Freshman Application Contact Wendy Fought, Director of Admissions, West Shore Community College, PO Box 277, 3000 North Stiles Road, Scottville, MI 49454-0277. *Phone:* 231-843-5503. *Fax:* 231-845-3944. *E-mail:* admissions@westshore.edu. *Website:* http://www.westshore.edu/.

MICRONESIA

College of Micronesia–FSM
Kolonia Pohnpei, Federated States of Micronesia, Micronesia

Freshman Application Contact Rita Hinga, Student Services Specialist, College of Micronesia–FSM, PO Box 159, Kolonia Pohnpei, FM 96941-0159, Micronesia. *Phone:* 691-320-3795 Ext. 15. *E-mail:* rhinga@comfsm.fm. *Website:* http://www.comfsm.fm/.

MINNESOTA

Alexandria Technical and Community College
Alexandria, Minnesota

- **State-supported** 2-year, founded 1961, part of Minnesota State Colleges and Universities System
- **Small-town** 98-acre campus
- **Coed,** 2,577 undergraduate students

Undergraduates Students come from 20 states and territories; 3% are from out of state; 2% Black or African American, non-Hispanic/Latino; 2% Hispanic/Latino; 0.6% Asian, non-Hispanic/Latino; 0.3% Native Hawaiian or other Pacific Islander, non-Hispanic/Latino; 1% American Indian or Alaska Native, non-Hispanic/Latino; 9% Race/ethnicity unknown.
Faculty *Total:* 96, 68% full-time, 5% with terminal degrees. *Student/faculty ratio:* 21:1.
Majors Accounting; automation engineer technology; business administration and management; clinical/medical laboratory technology; commercial and advertising art; computer systems networking and telecommunications; criminal justice/police science; diesel mechanics technology; early childhood education; fashion merchandising; human services; information science/studies; interior design; legal administrative assistant/secretary; legal assistant/paralegal; liberal arts and sciences/liberal studies; mechanical drafting and CAD/CADD; medical administrative assistant and medical secretary; multi/interdisciplinary studies related; office management; physical fitness technician; pre-engineering; registered nursing/registered nurse; sales, distribution, and marketing operations; speech-language pathology assistant.
Academics *Calendar:* semesters. *Degree:* certificates, diplomas, and associate. *Special study options:* academic remediation for entering students, advanced placement credit, distance learning, double majors, independent study, internships, part-time degree program, services for LD students, student-designed majors, summer session for credit.
Library Learning Resource Center. *Books:* 7,582 (physical), 13,367 (digital/electronic); *Serial titles:* 24 (physical); *Databases:* 14. Weekly public service hours: 51; students can reserve study rooms.
Student Life *Activities and Organizations:* Student Senate, Intercultural Club, Trapshooting League, GAT (Gamers of Alex Tech), Book Club. *Campus security:* student patrols, late-night transport/escort service, security cameras inside and outside. *Student services:* personal/psychological counseling.
Athletics *Intramural sports:* basketball M/W, football M/W, softball M/W, volleyball M/W.
Costs (2016–17) *Tuition:* state resident $4768 full-time, $159 per credit part-time; nonresident $4768 full-time, $159 per credit part-time. *Required fees:* $590 full-time, $20 per credit part-time. *Room and board:* $5200. *Payment plan:* deferred payment. *Waivers:* senior citizens and employees or children of employees.
Financial Aid Of all full-time matriculated undergraduates who enrolled in 2015, 94 Federal Work-Study jobs (averaging $1871).
Applying *Options:* electronic application, early admission, deferred entrance. *Application fee:* $20. *Required:* high school transcript. *Required for some:* interview. *Recommended:* interview. *Application deadlines:* rolling (freshmen), rolling (transfers). *Notification:* continuous (freshmen), continuous (transfers).
Freshman Application Contact Vicki Sward, Information Center Manager, Alexandria Technical and Community College, 1601 Jefferson Street, Alexandria, MN 56308. *Phone:* 320-762-4600. *Toll-free phone:* 888-234-1222. *Fax:* 320-762-4501. *E-mail:* info@alextech.edu. *Website:* http://www.alextech.edu/.

Anoka-Ramsey Community College
Coon Rapids, Minnesota

- **State-supported** 2-year, founded 1965, part of Minnesota State Colleges and Universities System
- **Suburban** 230-acre campus with easy access to Minneapolis-St. Paul
- **Coed,** 9,015 undergraduate students, 38% full-time, 60% women, 39% men

Undergraduates 3,386 full-time, 5,488 part-time. 9% Black or African American, non-Hispanic/Latino; 5% Hispanic/Latino; 4% Asian, non-Hispanic/Latino; 0.1% Native Hawaiian or other Pacific Islander, non-Hispanic/Latino; 0.5% American Indian or Alaska Native, non-Hispanic/Latino; 4% Two or more races, non-Hispanic/Latino; 0.8% Race/ethnicity unknown; 0.5% international; 25% transferred in. *Retention:* 54% of full-time freshmen returned.
Freshmen *Admission:* 995 enrolled.
Faculty *Total:* 248, 51% full-time. *Student/faculty ratio:* 32:1.

Majors Accounting; accounting technology and bookkeeping; biology/biological sciences; biomedical technology; business administration and management; business/commerce; community health and preventive medicine; computer science; computer systems networking and telecommunications; creative writing; dramatic/theater arts; environmental science; fine/studio arts; health services/allied health/health sciences; holistic health; human resources management; interdisciplinary studies; liberal arts and sciences/liberal studies; music; pharmacy technician; physical fitness technician; physical therapy technology; pre-engineering; registered nursing/registered nurse; sales, distribution, and marketing operations.

Academics *Calendar:* semesters. *Degree:* certificates and associate. *Special study options:* academic remediation for entering students, accelerated degree program, advanced placement credit, cooperative education, distance learning, double majors, English as a second language, honors programs, independent study, internships, off-campus study, part-time degree program, services for LD students, study abroad, summer session for credit. *ROTC:* Air Force (c).

Library Coon Rapids Campus Library plus 1 other. *Books:* 56,573 (physical), 15,450 (digital/electronic); *Serial titles:* 176 (physical), 71 (digital/electronic); *Databases:* 30. Weekly public service hours: 63.

Student Life *Housing:* college housing not available. *Activities and Organizations:* drama/theater group, student-run newspaper, choral group, Student Senate, Swing Dance Club, Concert Choir, Anime Association, Concert Band. *Campus security:* 24-hour emergency response devices, late-night transport/escort service. *Student services:* health clinic, personal/psychological counseling.

Athletics Member NJCAA. *Intercollegiate sports:* baseball M, basketball M/W, soccer M/W, softball W, volleyball W. *Intramural sports:* badminton M/W, basketball M/W, bowling M/W, football M/W, golf M/W, ice hockey M/W, soccer M/W, softball M/W, tennis M/W, volleyball M/W.

Costs (2017–18) *Tuition:* state resident $4305 full-time, $144 per credit part-time; nonresident $4305 full-time, $144 per credit part-time. Full-time tuition and fees vary according to course load and program. Part-time tuition and fees vary according to course load and program. *Required fees:* $665 full-time, $22 per credit part-time. *Payment plans:* installment, deferred payment. *Waivers:* senior citizens and employees or children of employees.

Applying *Options:* electronic application, early admission, deferred entrance. *Required for some:* high school transcript. *Application deadlines:* rolling (freshmen), rolling (transfers). *Notification:* continuous (freshmen), continuous (transfers).

Freshman Application Contact Admissions Department, Anoka-Ramsey Community College, 11200 Mississippi Boulevard NW, Coon Rapids, MN 55433-3470. *Phone:* 763-433-1300. *Fax:* 763-433-1521.
E-mail: admissions@anokaramsey.edu.
Website: http://www.anokaramsey.edu/.

Anoka Technical College
Anoka, Minnesota

- **State-supported** 2-year, founded 1967, part of Minnesota State Colleges and Universities System
- **Small-town** 23-acre campus with easy access to Minneapolis-St. Paul
- **Coed,** 1,814 undergraduate students, 46% full-time, 57% women, 43% men

Undergraduates 832 full-time, 977 part-time. 9% Black or African American, non-Hispanic/Latino; 4% Hispanic/Latino; 4% Asian, non-Hispanic/Latino; 0.1% Native Hawaiian or other Pacific Islander, non-Hispanic/Latino; 0.4% American Indian or Alaska Native, non-Hispanic/Latino; 4% Two or more races, non-Hispanic/Latino; 1% Race/ethnicity unknown; 0.1% international; 55% transferred in. *Retention:* 49% of full-time freshmen returned.

Freshmen *Admission:* 241 enrolled.

Faculty *Total:* 88, 60% full-time. *Student/faculty ratio:* 18:1.

Majors Accounting; administrative assistant and secretarial science; architectural drafting and CAD/CADD; automobile/automotive mechanics technology; biomedical technology; computer numerically controlled (CNC) machinist technology; computer technology/computer systems technology; court reporting; data processing and data processing technology; developmental services worker; electrical, electronic and communications engineering technology; golf course operation and grounds management; health information/medical records technology; landscaping and groundskeeping; legal administrative assistant/secretary; mechanical drafting and CAD/CADD; medical administrative assistant and medical secretary; medical/clinical assistant; occupational therapist assistant; office management; surgical technology; welding technology.

Academics *Calendar:* semesters. *Degree:* certificates, diplomas, and associate. *Special study options:* academic remediation for entering students, advanced placement credit, cooperative education, distance learning, double majors, English as a second language, internships, part-time degree program, services for LD students.

Library Anoka Technical College Library. *Books:* 7,402 (physical), 8,635 (digital/electronic); *Serial titles:* 17 (physical), 2 (digital/electronic);

Databases: 41. Weekly public service hours: 59; students can reserve study rooms.

Student Life *Housing:* college housing not available. *Campus security:* 24-hour emergency response devices, late-night transport/escort service. *Student services:* personal/psychological counseling.

Costs (2017–18) *Tuition:* state resident $4960 full-time, $165 per credit part-time; nonresident $4960 full-time, $165 per credit part-time. Full-time tuition and fees vary according to course load, program, and reciprocity agreements. Part-time tuition and fees vary according to course load, program, and reciprocity agreements. *Required fees:* $575 full-time, $19 per credit part-time. *Payment plan:* installment. *Waivers:* senior citizens and employees or children of employees.

Applying *Options:* electronic application, deferred entrance. *Required:* high school transcript. *Required for some:* interview.

Freshman Application Contact Enrollment Services, Anoka Technical College, 1355 West Highway 10, Anoka, MN 55303. *Phone:* 763-576-7710. *E-mail:* enrollmentservices@anokatech.edu.
Website: http://www.anokatech.edu/.

Central Lakes College
Brainerd, Minnesota

- **State-supported** 2-year, founded 1938, part of Minnesota State Colleges and Universities System
- **Small-town** campus
- **Endowment** $7.3 million
- **Coed**

Undergraduates 1,680 full-time, 2,594 part-time. Students come from 32 states and territories; 0.3% are from out of state; 3% Black or African American, non-Hispanic/Latino; 2% Hispanic/Latino; 0.7% Asian, non-Hispanic/Latino; 0.1% Native Hawaiian or other Pacific Islander, non-Hispanic/Latino; 1% American Indian or Alaska Native, non-Hispanic/Latino; 3% Two or more races, non-Hispanic/Latino; 4% Race/ethnicity unknown; 0.1% international. *Retention:* 58% of full-time freshmen returned.

Faculty *Student/faculty ratio:* 20:1.

Academics *Calendar:* semesters. *Degree:* certificates, diplomas, and associate. *Special study options:* academic remediation for entering students, advanced placement credit, distance learning, English as a second language, external degree program, independent study, internships, off-campus study, part-time degree program, services for LD students, summer session for credit.

Library Learning Resource Center.

Student Life *Campus security:* 24-hour emergency response devices and patrols, student patrols, late-night transport/escort service.

Athletics Member NJCAA.

Costs (2016–17) *Tuition:* state resident $4773 full-time, $159 per credit hour part-time; nonresident $4773 full-time, $159 per credit hour part-time. Full-time tuition and fees vary according to course load and program. Part-time tuition and fees vary according to course load and program. *Required fees:* $611 full-time, $21 per credit hour part-time.

Applying *Options:* electronic application, deferred entrance. *Application fee:* $20. *Required:* high school transcript.

Freshman Application Contact Ms. Rose Tretter, Central Lakes College, 501 West College Drive, Brainerd, MN 56401-3904. *Phone:* 218-855-8036. *Toll-free phone:* 800-933-0346. *Fax:* 218-855-8220. *E-mail:* cdaniels@clcmn.edu.
Website: http://www.clcmn.edu/.

Century College
White Bear Lake, Minnesota

- **State-supported** 2-year, founded 1970, part of Minnesota State Colleges and Universities System
- **Suburban** 170-acre campus with easy access to Minneapolis-St. Paul
- **Coed,** 8,597 undergraduate students, 42% full-time, 55% women, 45% men

Undergraduates 3,578 full-time, 5,019 part-time. Students come from 33 states and territories; 55 other countries; 6% are from out of state; 10% Black or African American, non-Hispanic/Latino; 8% Hispanic/Latino; 18% Asian, non-Hispanic/Latino; 0.2% Native Hawaiian or other Pacific Islander, non-Hispanic/Latino; 0.4% American Indian or Alaska Native, non-Hispanic/Latino; 4% Two or more races, non-Hispanic/Latino; 0.7% Race/ethnicity unknown; 2% international; 42% transferred in.

Freshmen *Admission:* 2,844 applied, 2,844 admitted, 1,185 enrolled.

Faculty *Total:* 360, 53% full-time, 18% with terminal degrees. *Student/faculty ratio:* 21:1.

Majors Accounting; administrative assistant and secretarial science; animation, interactive technology, video graphics and special effects; applied horticulture/horticulture operations; building/property maintenance; business administration and management; CAD/CADD drafting/design technology; cinematography and film/video production; commercial photography;

computer and information systems security; computer science; computer systems networking and telecommunications; computer technology/computer systems technology; cosmetology; criminal justice/police science; criminal justice/safety; cyber/computer forensics and counterterrorism; dental assisting; dental hygiene; e-commerce; education; emergency medical technology (EMT paramedic); energy management and systems technology; engineering technology; fine/studio arts; graphic design; health services/allied health/health sciences; heating, air conditioning, ventilation and refrigeration maintenance technology; homeland security, law enforcement, firefighting and protective services related; horticultural science; human services; information science/studies; interior design; language interpretation and translation; liberal arts and sciences/liberal studies; marketing/marketing management; medical administrative assistant and medical secretary; multi/interdisciplinary studies related; music; orthotics/prosthetics; pre-engineering; radiologic technology/science; registered nursing/registered nurse; substance abuse/addiction counseling; teacher assistant/aide; web page, digital/multimedia and information resources design.

Academics *Calendar:* semesters. *Degree:* certificates, diplomas, and associate. *Special study options:* academic remediation for entering students, advanced placement credit, distance learning, double majors, English as a second language, honors programs, independent study, internships, part-time degree program, services for LD students, student-designed majors, summer session for credit. *ROTC:* Air Force (c).

Library Century College Library. *Books:* 58,064 (physical), 182,603 (digital/electronic); *Serial titles:* 407 (physical), 36,841 (digital/electronic); *Databases:* 63. Weekly public service hours: 65; students can reserve study rooms.

Student Life *Housing:* college housing not available. *Activities and Organizations:* drama/theater group, student-run newspaper, choral group, Anime Club, Phi Theta Kappa, Planning Activities Committee, Spanish Club, Speech. *Campus security:* late-night transport/escort service, day patrols. *Student services:* health clinic, personal/psychological counseling.

Athletics Member NJCAA. *Intercollegiate sports:* baseball M, soccer M/W, softball W. *Intramural sports:* badminton M/W, basketball M/W, bowling M/W, football M/W, golf M/W, ice hockey M/W, skiing (downhill) M/W, soccer M/W, softball M/W, table tennis M/W, ultimate Frisbee M/W, volleyball M/W.

Costs (2016–17) *Tuition:* state resident $4770 full-time, $159 per semester hour part-time; nonresident $4770 full-time, $159 per semester hour part-time. Full-time tuition and fees vary according to class time, program, and reciprocity agreements. Part-time tuition and fees vary according to class time, program, and reciprocity agreements. *Required fees:* $590 full-time, $20 per semester hour part-time. *Payment plan:* installment. *Waivers:* senior citizens and employees or children of employees.

Financial Aid Of all full-time matriculated undergraduates who enrolled in 2015, 81 Federal Work-Study jobs (averaging $2763). 85 state and other part-time jobs (averaging $2646).

Applying *Options:* electronic application, deferred entrance. *Application fee:* $20. *Required:* high school transcript. *Application deadlines:* rolling (freshmen), rolling (transfers).

Freshman Application Contact Robert Beaver, Assistant Admissions Director, Century College, 3300 Century Avenue North, White Bear Lake, MN 55110. *Phone:* 651-779-5744. *Toll-free phone:* 800-228-1978. *Fax:* 651-773-1796. *E-mail:* admissions@century.edu.
Website: http://www.century.edu/.

Dakota County Technical College
Rosemount, Minnesota

Freshman Application Contact Mr. Patrick Lair, Admissions Director, Dakota County Technical College, 1300 East 145th Street, Rosemount, MN 55068. *Phone:* 651-423-8399. *Toll-free phone:* 877-YES-DCTC. *Fax:* 651-423-8775. *E-mail:* admissions@dctc.mnscu.edu.
Website: http://www.dctc.edu/.

Duluth Business University
Duluth, Minnesota

- **Proprietary** primarily 2-year, founded 1891
- **Small-town** 2-acre campus
- **Coed, primarily women,** 111 undergraduate students, 59% full-time, 95% women, 5% men

Undergraduates 65 full-time, 46 part-time. Students come from 6 states and territories; 21% are from out of state; 2% Black or African American, non-Hispanic/Latino; 0.9% Hispanic/Latino; 4% American Indian or Alaska Native, non-Hispanic/Latino.

Freshmen *Admission:* 12 enrolled.

Majors Business administration and management; health information/medical records technology; veterinary/animal health technology.

Academics *Calendar:* quarters. *Degrees:* diplomas, associate, and bachelor's. *Special study options:* part-time degree program.

Student Life *Housing:* college housing not available.

Standardized Tests *Required:* ACT (for admission).

Applying *Application fee:* $35. *Required:* high school transcript, interview.

Freshman Application Contact Mrs. Teri Linder, Admissions Representative, Duluth Business University, 4724 Mike Colalillo Drive, Duluth, MN 55807. *Phone:* 218-722-4000. *Toll-free phone:* 800-777-8406. *Fax:* 218-628-2127. *E-mail:* teri@dbumn.edu.
Website: http://www.dbumn.edu/.

Dunwoody College of Technology
Minneapolis, Minnesota

- **Independent** primarily 2-year, founded 1914
- **Urban** 12-acre campus with easy access to Minneapolis-St. Paul
- **Endowment** $25.0 million
- **Coed, primarily men,** 1,264 undergraduate students, 84% full-time, 16% women, 84% men

Undergraduates 1,062 full-time, 202 part-time. 3% are from out of state; 5% Black or African American, non-Hispanic/Latino; 3% Hispanic/Latino; 7% Asian, non-Hispanic/Latino; 0.2% Native Hawaiian or other Pacific Islander, non-Hispanic/Latino; 0.2% American Indian or Alaska Native, non-Hispanic/Latino; 4% Two or more races, non-Hispanic/Latino; 4% Race/ethnicity unknown; 20% transferred in. *Retention:* 50% of full-time freshmen returned.

Freshmen *Admission:* 1,168 applied, 763 admitted, 209 enrolled. *Average high school GPA:* 2.62.

Faculty *Total:* 142, 61% full-time, 13% with terminal degrees. *Student/faculty ratio:* 11:1.

Majors Architectural drafting and CAD/CADD; architectural technology; architecture; autobody/collision and repair technology; automobile/automotive mechanics technology; building/construction site management; business administration and management; CAD/CADD drafting/design technology; civil engineering technology; computer numerically controlled (CNC) machinist technology; computer science; computer systems networking and telecommunications; construction management; desktop publishing and digital imaging design; electrical, electronic and communications engineering technology; electrical/electronics drafting and CAD/CADD; electrician; graphic design; heating, air conditioning, ventilation and refrigeration maintenance technology; heating, ventilation, air conditioning and refrigeration engineering technology; industrial technology; interior design; manufacturing engineering; medical radiologic technology; printing press operation; robotics technology; tool and die technology; web page, digital/multimedia and information resources design; welding technology.

Academics *Calendar:* semesters. *Degrees:* certificates, associate, and bachelor's. *Special study options:* academic remediation for entering students, adult/continuing education programs, cooperative education, distance learning, independent study, internships, study abroad, summer session for credit.

Library Learning Resource Center plus 1 other. *Books:* 2,500 (physical), 162,865 (digital/electronic); *Serial titles:* 131 (physical); *Databases:* 24. Weekly public service hours: 55.

Student Life *Housing:* college housing not available. *Activities and Organizations:* Phi Theta Kappa, Historic Green, Dunwoody Motorsports Club, Architectural Institute of America Student Chapter, Professional Association for Design. *Campus security:* 24-hour emergency response devices, late-night transport/escort service. *Student services:* women's center.

Standardized Tests *Required for some:* ACT (for admission).

Costs (2017–18) *Tuition:* $18,826 full-time, $654 per credit part-time. Full-time tuition and fees vary according to course load, degree level, and program. Part-time tuition and fees vary according to course load, degree level, and program. *Required fees:* $1652 full-time, $1458 per term part-time. *Payment plan:* installment. *Waivers:* employees or children of employees.

Financial Aid Of all full-time matriculated undergraduates who enrolled in 2015, 859 applied for aid, 769 were judged to have need, 34 had their need fully met. 26 Federal Work-Study jobs (averaging $2376). 29 state and other part-time jobs (averaging $3546). In 2015, 46 non-need-based awards were made. *Average percent of need met:* 33%. *Average financial aid package:* $8555. *Average need-based loan:* $3599. *Average need-based gift aid:* $6254. *Average non-need-based aid:* $2119.

Applying *Options:* electronic application. *Application fee:* $50. *Required:* essay or personal statement, high school transcript. *Required for some:* minimum 3.0 GPA, letters of recommendation, resumé. *Recommended:* minimum 2.5 GPA, interview. *Application deadlines:* rolling (freshmen), rolling (transfers). *Notification:* continuous (freshmen), continuous (transfers).

Freshman Application Contact Kelly OBrien, Director of Admissions, Dunwoody College of Technology, 818 Dunwoody Boulevard, Minneapolis, MN 55403. *Phone:* 612-381-3302. *Toll-free phone:* 800-292-4625. *Fax:* 612-677-3131. *E-mail:* kobrien@dunwoody.edu.
Website: http://www.dunwoody.edu/.

Fond du Lac Tribal and Community College
Cloquet, Minnesota

Freshman Application Contact Kathie Jubie, Admissions Representative, Fond du Lac Tribal and Community College, 2101 14th Street, Cloquet, MN 55720. *Phone:* 218-879-0808. *Toll-free phone:* 800-657-3712. *E-mail:* admissions@fdltcc.edu. *Website:* http://www.fdltcc.edu/.

Hennepin Technical College
Brooklyn Park, Minnesota

- **State-supported** 2-year, founded 1972, part of Minnesota State Colleges and Universities System
- **Suburban** 100-acre campus with easy access to Minneapolis-St. Paul
- **Endowment** $942,735
- **Coed,** 5,299 undergraduate students

Undergraduates 4% are from out of state; 23% Black or African American, non-Hispanic/Latino; 8% Hispanic/Latino; 10% Asian, non-Hispanic/Latino; 0.1% Native Hawaiian or other Pacific Islander, non-Hispanic/Latino; 0.5% American Indian or Alaska Native, non-Hispanic/Latino; 2% Two or more races, non-Hispanic/Latino; 2% Race/ethnicity unknown; 0.3% international. **Freshmen** *Admission:* 1,987 applied, 1,987 admitted. **Faculty** *Total:* 235, 49% full-time. *Student/faculty ratio:* 21:1. **Majors** Accounting; administrative assistant and secretarial science; architectural drafting and CAD/CADD; autobody/collision and repair technology; automation engineer technology; automobile/automotive mechanics technology; business administration and management; CAD/CADD drafting/design technology; carpentry; child development; computer numerically controlled (CNC) machinist technology; computer programming; computer systems networking and telecommunications; dental assisting; desktop publishing and digital imaging design; drafting/design engineering technologies related; electrical, electronic and communications engineering technology; fire science/firefighting; graphic design; greenhouse management; heating, air conditioning, ventilation and refrigeration maintenance technology; hydraulics and fluid power technology; landscaping and groundskeeping; licensed practical/vocational nurse training; machine tool technology; management information systems; manufacturing engineering technology; medical administrative assistant and medical secretary; medium/heavy vehicle and truck technology; plastics and polymer engineering technology; recording arts technology; tool and die technology; urban forestry; web page, digital/multimedia and information resources design. **Academics** *Calendar:* semesters. *Degree:* certificates, diplomas, and associate. *Special study options:* academic remediation for entering students, adult/continuing education programs, advanced placement credit, cooperative education, distance learning, double majors, English as a second language, independent study, internships, part-time degree program, services for LD students, student-designed majors, summer session for credit. **Library** Hennepin Technical College Library plus 1 other. *Books:* 10,784 (physical), 215,854 (digital/electronic); *Serial titles:* 30 (physical); *Databases:* 48. Weekly public service hours: 60. **Student Life** *Housing:* college housing not available. *Activities and Organizations:* Student Senate, SkillsUSA, Student Nurses Who Care, Veterans. *Campus security:* late-night transport/escort service, security service. *Student services:* personal/psychological counseling. **Costs (2016–17)** *Tuition:* state resident $5150 full-time, $155 per credit part-time; nonresident $5150 full-time, $155 per credit part-time. Full-time tuition and fees vary according to program. Part-time tuition and fees vary according to program. *Required fees:* $498 full-time, $17 per credit part-time. *Payment plan:* installment. *Waivers:* senior citizens and employees or children of employees. **Financial Aid** Of all full-time matriculated undergraduates who enrolled in 2015, 72 Federal Work-Study jobs (averaging $3000). **Applying** *Options:* electronic application. *Recommended:* high school transcript. *Application deadlines:* rolling (freshmen), rolling (transfers). *Notification:* continuous (freshmen), continuous (transfers). **Freshman Application Contact** Admissions, Hennepin Technical College, 9000 Brooklyn Boulevard, Brooklyn Park, MN 55445. *Phone:* 763-488-2580. *Toll-free phone:* 800-345-4655 (in-state); 800-645-4655 (out-of-state). *Fax:* 763-550-2113. *E-mail:* info@hennepintech.edu. *Website:* http://www.hennepintech.edu/.

Herzing University
Minneapolis, Minnesota

Freshman Application Contact Ms. Shelly Larson, Director of Admissions, Herzing University, 5700 West Broadway, Minneapolis, MN 55428. *Phone:* 763-231-3155. *Toll-free phone:* 800-596-0724. *Fax:* 763-535-9205. *E-mail:* info@mpls.herzing.edu. *Website:* http://www.herzing.edu/minneapolis.

Hibbing Community College
Hibbing, Minnesota

Freshman Application Contact Admissions, Hibbing Community College, 1515 East 25th Street, Hibbing, MN 55746. *Phone:* 218-262-7200. *Toll-free phone:* 800-224-4HCC. *Fax:* 218-262-6717. *E-mail:* admissions@hibbing.edu. *Website:* http://www.hcc.mnscu.edu/.

The Institute of Production and Recording
Minneapolis, Minnesota

Freshman Application Contact The Institute of Production and Recording, 300 North 1st Avenue, Suite 500, Minneapolis, MN 55401. *Website:* http://www.ipr.edu/.

Inver Hills Community College
Inver Grove Heights, Minnesota

Freshman Application Contact Mr. Casey Carmody, Admissions Representative, Inver Hills Community College, 2500 East 80th Street, Inver Grove Heights, MN 55076-3224. *Phone:* 651-450-3589. *Fax:* 651-450-3677. *E-mail:* admissions@inverhills.edu. *Website:* http://www.inverhills.edu/.

Itasca Community College
Grand Rapids, Minnesota

Freshman Application Contact Ms. Candace Perry, Director of Enrollment Services, Itasca Community College, Grand Rapids, MN 55744. *Phone:* 218-322-2340. *Toll-free phone:* 800-996-6422. *Fax:* 218-327-4350. *E-mail:* iccinfo@itascacc.edu. *Website:* http://www.itascacc.edu/.

Lake Superior College
Duluth, Minnesota

- **State-supported** 2-year, founded 1995, part of Minnesota State Colleges and Universities System
- **Urban** 105-acre campus
- **Coed,** 5,050 undergraduate students, 42% full-time, 58% women, 42% men

Undergraduates 2,108 full-time, 2,942 part-time. Students come from 28 states and territories; 6 other countries; 15% are from out of state; 4% Black or African American, non-Hispanic/Latino; 3% Hispanic/Latino; 1% Asian, non-Hispanic/Latino; 0.1% Native Hawaiian or other Pacific Islander, non-Hispanic/Latino; 2% American Indian or Alaska Native, non-Hispanic/Latino; 4% Two or more races, non-Hispanic/Latino; 1% Race/ethnicity unknown; 0.1% international; 39% transferred in. **Freshmen** *Admission:* 1,062 applied, 1,062 admitted, 700 enrolled. **Faculty** *Total:* 251, 39% full-time, 6% with terminal degrees. *Student/faculty ratio:* 21:1. **Majors** Accounting; accounting technology and bookkeeping; airframe mechanics and aircraft maintenance technology; airline pilot and flight crew; architectural drafting and CAD/CADD; autobody/collision and repair technology; automation engineer technology; automobile/automotive mechanics technology; aviation/airway management; building construction technology; business administration and management; business automation/technology/data entry; CAD/CADD drafting/design technology; carpentry; civil engineering technology; clinical/medical laboratory technology; computer numerically controlled (CNC) machinist technology; computer support specialist; computer systems networking and telecommunications; computer technology/computer systems technology; dental hygiene; electrical, electronic and communications engineering technology; electrician; fine/studio arts; fire prevention and safety technology; fire science/firefighting; fire services administration; health services/allied health/health sciences; legal administrative assistant/secretary; legal assistant/paralegal; liberal arts and sciences/liberal studies; licensed practical/vocational nurse training; machine tool technology; management information systems; massage therapy; mechanical drafting and CAD/CADD; medical administrative assistant and medical secretary; medical/clinical assistant; medical insurance coding; medical office assistant; medical reception; medical transcription; multi/interdisciplinary studies related; network and system administration; nursing assistant/aide and patient care assistant/aide; office management; office occupations and clerical services; organizational leadership; phlebotomy technology; physical therapy technology; quality control and safety technologies related; radio and television broadcasting technology; radiologic technology/science; registered nursing/registered nurse; renal/dialysis technology; respiratory care therapy; sheet metal technology; surgical technology; teacher assistant/aide; truck and bus driver/commercial vehicle operation/instruction; web page, digital/multimedia and information resources design; welding technology.

Academics *Calendar:* semesters. *Degree:* certificates, diplomas, and associate. *Special study options:* academic remediation for entering students, advanced placement credit, distance learning, double majors, independent study, internships, part-time degree program, services for LD students, study abroad, summer session for credit.

Library Harold P. Erickson Library. Students can reserve study rooms.

Student Life *Housing:* college housing not available. *Activities and Organizations:* choral group. *Campus security:* 24-hour emergency response devices, late-night transport/escort service.

Student services: personal/psychological counseling.

Athletics Member NJCAA. *Intercollegiate sports:* soccer M/W.

Costs (2016–17) *Tuition:* state resident $4373 full-time; nonresident $8747 full-time. Full-time tuition and fees vary according to course load, program, and reciprocity agreements. Part-time tuition and fees vary according to course load, program, and reciprocity agreements. *Required fees:* $736 full-time. *Payment plans:* installment, deferred payment. *Waivers:* senior citizens and employees or children of employees.

Applying *Options:* electronic application. *Application fee:* $20. *Required:* high school transcript. *Application deadlines:* rolling (freshmen), rolling (transfers). *Notification:* continuous (freshmen), continuous (transfers).

Freshman Application Contact Ms. Melissa Leno, Director of Admissions, Lake Superior College, 2101 Trinity Road, Duluth, MN 55811. *Phone:* 218-733-5903. *Toll-free phone:* 800-432-2884. *E-mail:* enroll@lsc.edu. *Website:* http://www.lsc.edu/.

Leech Lake Tribal College
Cass Lake, Minnesota

Freshman Application Contact Ms. Shelly Braford, Recruiter, Leech Lake Tribal College, PO Box 180, 6945 Littlewolf Road NW, Cass Lake, MN 56633. *Phone:* 218-335-4200 Ext. 4270. *Fax:* 218-335-4217. *E-mail:* shelly.braford@lltc.edu. *Website:* http://www.lltc.edu/.

Mesabi Range College
Virginia, Minnesota

- **State-supported** 2-year, founded 1918, part of Minnesota State Colleges and Universities System
- **Small-town** 30-acre campus
- **Coed,** 1,151 undergraduate students, 56% full-time, 48% women, 52% men

Undergraduates 648 full-time, 502 part-time. Students come from 6 states and territories; 2 other countries; 4% are from out of state; 7% Black or African American, non-Hispanic/Latino; 1% Hispanic/Latino; 0.3% Asian, non-Hispanic/Latino; 3% American Indian or Alaska Native, non-Hispanic/Latino; 8% Race/ethnicity unknown; 10% live on campus.

Freshmen *Admission:* 1,150 enrolled.

Faculty *Total:* 165. *Student/faculty ratio:* 24:1.

Majors Administrative assistant and secretarial science; business/commerce; computer graphics; computer/information technology services administration related; computer programming related; computer programming (specific applications); computer software and media applications related; computer systems networking and telecommunications; electrical/electronics equipment installation and repair; human services; information technology; instrumentation technology; liberal arts and sciences/liberal studies; pre-engineering; substance abuse/addiction counseling; web page, digital/multimedia and information resources design.

Academics *Calendar:* semesters. *Degree:* certificates, diplomas, and associate. *Special study options:* academic remediation for entering students, adult/continuing education programs, advanced placement credit, cooperative education, distance learning, independent study, internships, off-campus study, part-time degree program, services for LD students, student-designed majors, study abroad, summer session for credit.

Library Mesabi Library.

Student Life *Housing Options:* coed. Campus housing is provided by a third party. *Activities and Organizations:* drama/theater group, Student Senate, Human Services Club, Career Program Clubs, Student Life Club, Gaming Club. *Student services:* personal/psychological counseling.

Athletics Member NJCAA. *Intercollegiate sports:* baseball M, basketball M/W, football M, golf M/W, softball W, volleyball W. *Intramural sports:* basketball M/W, ice hockey M/W, volleyball M/W.

Costs (2017–18) *Tuition:* state resident $4680 full-time, $156 per credit hour part-time; nonresident $5850 full-time, $195 per credit hour part-time.

Required fees: $582 full-time, $19 per credit hour part-time. *Room and board:* room only: $2100.

Financial Aid Of all full-time matriculated undergraduates who enrolled in 2011, 168 Federal Work-Study jobs (averaging $1227). 82 state and other part-time jobs (averaging $1380).

Applying *Options:* electronic application, early admission, deferred entrance. *Application fee:* $20. *Required:* high school transcript. *Application deadlines:* rolling (freshmen), rolling (transfers). *Notification:* continuous (freshmen), continuous (transfers).

Freshman Application Contact Ms. Brenda Kochevar, Enrollment Services Director, Mesabi Range College, Virginia, MN 55792. *Phone:* 218-749-0314. *Toll-free phone:* 800-657-3860. *Fax:* 218-749-0318. *E-mail:* b.kochevar@mesabirange.edu. *Website:* http://www.mesabirange.edu/.

Minneapolis Business College
Roseville, Minnesota

- **Proprietary** 2-year, founded 1874
- **Suburban** campus with easy access to Minneapolis-St. Paul
- **Coed**
- 87% of applicants were admitted

Academics *Calendar:* semesters. *Degree:* diplomas and associate. *Special study options:* accelerated degree program, internships.

Freshman Application Contact Admissions Office, Minneapolis Business College, 1711 West County Road B, Roseville, MN 55113. *Phone:* 651-636-7406. *Toll-free phone:* 800-279-5200. *Website:* http://www.minneapolisbusinesscollege.edu/.

Minneapolis Community and Technical College
Minneapolis, Minnesota

Freshman Application Contact Minneapolis Community and Technical College, 1501 Hennepin Avenue, Minneapolis, MN 55403. *Phone:* 612-659-6200. *Toll-free phone:* 800-247-0911. *E-mail:* admissions.office@minneapolis.edu. *Website:* http://www.minneapolis.edu/.

Minnesota State College–Southeast Technical
Winona, Minnesota

- **State-supported** 2-year, founded 1992, part of Minnesota State Colleges and Universities System
- **Small-town** 132-acre campus with easy access to Minneapolis-St. Paul
- **Coed,** 1,961 undergraduate students, 41% full-time, 60% women, 40% men

Undergraduates 800 full-time, 1,161 part-time. 27% are from out of state; 5% Black or African American, non-Hispanic/Latino; 4% Hispanic/Latino; 2% Asian, non-Hispanic/Latino; 0.3% American Indian or Alaska Native, non-Hispanic/Latino; 2% Two or more races, non-Hispanic/Latino; 0.1% Race/ethnicity unknown; 0.5% international; 12% transferred in. *Retention:* 35% of full-time freshmen returned.

Freshmen *Admission:* 673 admitted, 242 enrolled. *Average high school GPA:* 2.7.

Faculty *Total:* 119, 52% full-time, 4% with terminal degrees. *Student/faculty ratio:* 15:1.

Majors Accounting; accounting technology and bookkeeping; administrative assistant and secretarial science; autobody/collision and repair technology; biomedical technology; business administration and management; CAD/CADD drafting/design technology; carpentry; computer programming; computer systems networking and telecommunications; computer technology/computer systems technology; cosmetology; criminal justice/safety; early childhood education; electrical, electronic and communications engineering technology; heating, air conditioning, ventilation and refrigeration maintenance technology; industrial mechanics and maintenance technology; legal administrative assistant/secretary; massage therapy; medical administrative assistant and medical secretary; multi/interdisciplinary studies related; radiologic technology/science; registered nursing/registered nurse; retailing; sales, distribution, and marketing operations; selling skills and sales; web page, digital/multimedia and information resources design.

Academics *Calendar:* semesters. *Degree:* certificates, diplomas, and associate. *Special study options:* distance learning, double majors, internships.

Library Learning Resource Center.

Student Life *Housing:* college housing not available. *Activities and Organizations:* student-run newspaper. *Campus security:* 24-hour emergency response devices, late-night transport/escort service.

Costs (2017–18) *Tuition:* state resident $4969 full-time, $166 per credit hour part-time; nonresident $4969 full-time, $166 per credit hour part-time. Full-time tuition and fees vary according to program. Part-time tuition and fees vary according to program. *Required fees:* $648 full-time, $22 per credit hour part-time. *Payment plan:* installment. *Waivers:* senior citizens and employees or children of employees.

Financial Aid Of all full-time matriculated undergraduates who enrolled in 2015, 728 applied for aid, 650 were judged to have need, 12 had their need fully met. 32 Federal Work-Study jobs (averaging $2381). In 2015, 31 non-need-based awards were made. *Average percent of need met:* 37%. *Average financial aid package:* $6615. *Average need-based loan:* $3208. *Average need-based gift aid:* $4658. *Average non-need-based aid:* $2796. *Average indebtedness upon graduation:* $18,236.

Applying *Options:* electronic application. *Application fee:* $20. *Required:* high school transcript. *Recommended:* interview. *Application deadlines:* rolling (freshmen), rolling (transfers). *Notification:* continuous (freshmen), continuous (transfers).

Freshman Application Contact Admissions, SE Technical, Minnesota State College–Southeast Technical, 1250 Homer Road, PO Box 409, Winona, MN 55987. *Phone:* 877-853-8324. *Toll-free phone:* 800-372-8164. *Fax:* 507-453-2715. *E-mail:* enrollmentservices@southeastmn.edu. *Website:* http://www.southeastmn.edu/.

Minnesota State Community and Technical College

Fergus Falls, Minnesota

- **State-supported** 2-year, founded 1960, part of Minnesota State Colleges and Universities System
- **Rural** campus
- **Coed,** 6,303 undergraduate students, 41% full-time, 60% women, 40% men

Undergraduates 2,581 full-time, 3,722 part-time. 7% Black or African American, non-Hispanic/Latino; 4% Hispanic/Latino; 2% Asian, non-Hispanic/Latino; 0.1% Native Hawaiian or other Pacific Islander, non-Hispanic/Latino; 1% American Indian or Alaska Native, non-Hispanic/Latino; 3% Two or more races, non-Hispanic/Latino; 11% Race/ethnicity unknown; 2% live on campus.

Freshmen *Admission:* 1,012 enrolled.

Faculty *Total:* 456, 42% full-time, 5% with terminal degrees. *Student/faculty ratio:* 18:1.

Majors Accounting; administrative assistant and secretarial science; agricultural and food products processing; architectural drafting and CAD/CADD; art; autobody/collision and repair technology; automobile/automotive mechanics technology; banking and financial support services; biochemistry and molecular biology; biology/biological sciences; building/construction site management; business administration and management; business automation/technology/data entry; business/commerce; cardiovascular technology; carpentry; chemistry; civil engineering technology; clinical/medical laboratory technology; computer and information systems security; computer engineering technology; computer programming; computer systems networking and telecommunications; computer technology/computer systems technology; construction management; cooking and related culinary arts; cosmetology; criminal justice/safety; dental assisting; dental hygiene; diesel mechanics technology; electrical and electronic engineering technologies related; electrical, electronic and communications engineering technology; environmental studies; equestrian studies; fashion merchandising; financial planning and services; fire services administration; graphic design; health information/medical records technology; heating, ventilation, air conditioning and refrigeration engineering technology; horse husbandry/equine science and management; human resources management; industrial mechanics and maintenance technology; information technology; legal administrative assistant/secretary; legal assistant/paralegal; liberal arts and sciences/liberal studies; licensed practical/vocational nurse training; lineworker; manufacturing engineering technology; marine maintenance and ship repair technology; marketing/marketing management; mechanical drafting and CAD/CADD; medical administrative assistant and medical secretary; merchandising, sales, and marketing operations related (general); multi/interdisciplinary studies related; music; office management; pharmacy technician; plumbing technology; pre-engineering; radiologic technology/science; registered nursing/registered nurse; sales, distribution, and marketing operations; sign language interpretation and translation; surgical technology; teacher assistant/aide; telecommunications technology; web page, digital/multimedia and information resources design.

Academics *Calendar:* semesters. *Degree:* certificates, diplomas, and associate. *Special study options:* academic remediation for entering students, accelerated degree program, advanced placement credit, cooperative education, distance learning, double majors, English as a second language, freshman honors college, honors programs, independent study, internships, off-campus study, part-time degree program, services for LD students, study abroad, summer session for credit.

Library Minnesota State Community and Technical College - Fergus Falls Library plus 4 others.

Student Life *Housing Options:* coed. Campus housing is university owned. *Activities and Organizations:* drama/theater group, choral group, Student Senate, Students In Free Enterprise (SIFE), Phi Theta Kappa, Business Professionals of America, SkillsUSA–VICA. *Campus security:* 24-hour emergency response devices, late-night transport/escort service, security for special events. *Student services:* personal/psychological counseling, women's center.

Athletics Member NJCAA. *Intercollegiate sports:* baseball M, basketball M/W, football M, golf M/W, softball W, volleyball W. *Intramural sports:* badminton M/W, basketball M, bowling M/W, football M/W, golf M/W, skiing (cross-country) M/W, skiing (downhill) M/W, soccer M/W, softball M/W, table tennis M/W, tennis M/W, volleyball M/W, weight lifting M/W.

Costs (2017–18) *Tuition:* state resident $4774 full-time, $159 per credit part-time; nonresident $4774 full-time, $159 per credit part-time. Full-time tuition and fees vary according to location and program. Part-time tuition and fees vary according to location and program. *Room and board:* Room and board charges vary according to board plan and housing facility. *Waivers:* senior citizens and employees or children of employees.

Financial Aid *Financial aid deadline:* 7/1.

Applying *Options:* electronic application, early admission, deferred entrance. *Application fee:* $20. *Required:* high school transcript. *Application deadlines:* rolling (freshmen), rolling (transfers). *Notification:* continuous (freshmen), continuous (transfers).

Freshman Application Contact Minnesota State Community and Technical College, 1414 College Way, Fergus Falls, MN 56537-1009. *Phone:* 218-736-1544. *Toll-free phone:* 877-450-3322. *Website:* http://www.minnesota.edu/.

Minnesota State Community and Technical College–Detroit Lakes

Detroit Lakes, Minnesota

- **State-supported** 2-year, founded 1966, part of Minnesota State Colleges and Universities System
- **Small-town** campus
- **Coed,** 6,391 undergraduate students, 42% full-time, 59% women, 41% men

Undergraduates 2,658 full-time, 3,733 part-time. 18% Black or African American, non-Hispanic/Latino; 7% Hispanic/Latino; 4% Asian, non-Hispanic/Latino; 0.2% Native Hawaiian or other Pacific Islander, non-Hispanic/Latino; 1% American Indian or Alaska Native, non-Hispanic/Latino; 2% Two or more races, non-Hispanic/Latino; 0.3% international.

Freshmen *Admission:* 1,071 enrolled.

Faculty *Total:* 276, 56% full-time.

Majors Accounting; administrative assistant and secretarial science; architectural drafting and CAD/CADD; architectural technology; civil engineering technology; computer and information systems security; early childhood education; engineering technology; entrepreneurship; legal assistant/paralegal; liberal arts and sciences/liberal studies; licensed practical/vocational nurse training; marine maintenance and ship repair technology; marketing/marketing management; multi/interdisciplinary studies related; nursing practice; office management; radiologic technology/science; registered nursing/registered nurse; sales, distribution, and marketing operations; teacher assistant/aide.

Academics *Calendar:* semesters. *Degree:* certificates and associate.

Student Life *Housing:* college housing not available.

Athletics Member NJCAA.

Costs (2016–17) *Tuition:* state resident $4824 full-time, $161 per credit hour part-time; nonresident $4824 full-time, $161 per credit hour part-time. Full-time tuition and fees vary according to location and program. Part-time tuition and fees vary according to location and program. *Required fees:* $514 full-time. *Waivers:* senior citizens and employees or children of employees.

Applying *Application fee:* $20. *Required:* high school transcript, immunization record.

Freshman Application Contact Minnesota State Community and Technical College–Detroit Lakes, 900 Highway 34, E, Detroit Lakes, MN 56501. *Phone:* 218-846-3777. *Toll-free phone:* 800-492-4836. *Website:* http://www.minnesota.edu/.

Minnesota State Community and Technical College–Moorhead
Moorhead, Minnesota

- **State-supported** 2-year, part of Minnesota State Colleges and Universities System
- **Rural** campus
- **Coed,** 6,303 undergraduate students, 41% full-time, 60% women, 40% men

Undergraduates 2,581 full-time, 3,722 part-time.
Freshmen *Admission:* 1,012 enrolled.
Faculty *Total:* 276, 56% full-time.
Majors Accounting; administrative assistant and secretarial science; automobile/automotive mechanics technology; automotive engineering technology; biology/biological sciences; business administration and management; business/commerce; cardiovascular technology; chemistry; computer programming; computer systems networking and telecommunications; construction management; criminal justice/law enforcement administration; criminal justice/safety; dental assisting; dental hygiene; diesel mechanics technology; engineering; environmental studies; graphic design; human resources development; human resources management; information technology; liberal arts and sciences/liberal studies; licensed practical/vocational nurse training; mechanical drafting and CAD/CADD; medical administrative assistant and medical secretary; multi/interdisciplinary studies related; nursing practice; office management; plumbing technology; pre-engineering; registered nursing/registered nurse; sales, distribution, and marketing operations; sign language interpretation and translation; surgical technology.
Academics *Calendar:* semesters. *Degree:* certificates, diplomas, and associate.
Student Life *Housing:* college housing not available.
Costs (2016–17) *Tuition:* state resident $4824 full-time, $161 per credit hour part-time; nonresident $4824 full-time, $161 per credit hour part-time. Full-time tuition and fees vary according to location and program. Part-time tuition and fees vary according to location and program. *Required fees:* $514 full-time. *Waivers:* senior citizens and employees or children of employees.
Applying *Application fee:* $20. *Required:* high school transcript, immunization record.
Freshman Application Contact Minnesota State Community and Technical College–Moorhead, 1900 28th Avenue, South, Moorhead, MN 56560. *Phone:* 218-299-6824. *Toll-free phone:* 800-426-5603.
Website: http://www.minnesota.edu/.

Minnesota State Community and Technical College–Wadena
Wadena, Minnesota

- **State-supported** 2-year
- **Small-town** campus
- **Coed,** 6,303 undergraduate students, 41% full-time, 60% women, 40% men

Undergraduates 2,581 full-time, 3,722 part-time. 0.5% Black or African American, non-Hispanic/Latino; 3% Hispanic/Latino; 0.3% American Indian or Alaska Native, non-Hispanic/Latino; 3% Two or more races, non-Hispanic/Latino.
Freshmen *Admission:* 1,009 enrolled.
Faculty *Total:* 276, 56% full-time.
Majors Electrical and power transmission installation related; industrial mechanics and maintenance technology; liberal arts and sciences/liberal studies; licensed practical/vocational nurse training; lineworker; medical administrative assistant and medical secretary; multi/interdisciplinary studies related; network and system administration; nursing practice; office management; registered nursing/registered nurse.
Academics *Calendar:* semesters. *Degree:* certificates and associate.
Student Life *Housing:* college housing not available.
Costs (2016–17) *Tuition:* state resident $4824 full-time, $161 per credit hour part-time; nonresident $4824 full-time, $161 per credit hour part-time. Full-time tuition and fees vary according to location and program. Part-time tuition and fees vary according to location and program. *Required fees:* $514 full-time. *Waivers:* senior citizens and employees or children of employees.
Applying *Application fee:* $20. *Required:* high school transcript, immunization record.
Freshman Application Contact Minnesota State Community and Technical College–Wadena, 405 Colfax Avenue, SW, PO Box 566, Wadena, MN 56482. *Phone:* 218-631-7818. *Toll-free phone:* 800-247-2007.
Website: http://www.minnesota.edu/.

Minnesota West Community and Technical College
Pipestone, Minnesota

- **State-supported** 2-year, founded 1967, part of Minnesota State Colleges and Universities System
- **Rural** campus
- **Coed,** 3,182 undergraduate students, 36% full-time, 57% women, 43% men

Undergraduates 1,153 full-time, 2,029 part-time. 11% are from out of state; 5% Black or African American, non-Hispanic/Latino; 6% Hispanic/Latino; 3% Asian, non-Hispanic/Latino; 0.1% Native Hawaiian or other Pacific Islander, non-Hispanic/Latino; 0.9% American Indian or Alaska Native, non-Hispanic/Latino; 2% Two or more races, non-Hispanic/Latino; 5% Race/ethnicity unknown. *Retention:* 60% of full-time freshmen returned.
Freshmen *Average high school GPA:* 2.62.
Faculty *Total:* 146, 66% full-time. *Student/faculty ratio:* 21:1.
Majors Accounting; administrative assistant and secretarial science; agribusiness; agricultural and food products processing; agricultural/farm supplies retailing and wholesaling; agricultural production; agriculture; agronomy and crop science; automobile/automotive mechanics technology; biology/biotechnology laboratory technician; business administration and management; business/commerce; child-care and support services management; clinical/medical laboratory technology; computer and information systems security; computer engineering technology; computer science; computer systems networking and telecommunications; computer technology/computer systems technology; criminal justice/police science; dental assisting; diesel mechanics technology; electrical and power transmission installation; electrical and power transmission installation related; electrician; energy management and systems technology; hospital and health-care facilities administration; human services; hydraulics and fluid power technology; information technology; liberal arts and sciences and humanities related; liberal arts and sciences/liberal studies; lineworker; manufacturing engineering technology; medical administrative assistant and medical secretary; medical/clinical assistant; medical insurance coding; plumbing technology; radiologic technology/science; registered nursing/registered nurse; robotics technology; surgical technology.
Academics *Calendar:* semesters. *Degrees:* certificates, diplomas, and associate (profile contains information from Canby, Granite Falls, Jackson, and Worthington campuses). *Special study options:* academic remediation for entering students, advanced placement credit, cooperative education, distance learning, double majors, external degree program, honors programs, independent study, internships, part-time degree program, services for LD students, summer session for credit.
Library Library and Academic Resource Center plus 4 others.
Student Life *Activities and Organizations:* choral group.
Athletics Member NJCAA. *Intercollegiate sports:* baseball M, basketball M/W, cheerleading W, football M, softball W, volleyball W, wrestling M.
Costs (2016–17) *One-time required fee:* $20. *Tuition:* state resident $5435 full-time, $170 per credit part-time; nonresident $5435 full-time, $170 per credit part-time. Full-time tuition and fees vary according to program and reciprocity agreements. Part-time tuition and fees vary according to program and reciprocity agreements. *Required fees:* $582 full-time, $18 per credit part-time. *Payment plan:* installment. *Waivers:* senior citizens and employees or children of employees.
Financial Aid Of all full-time matriculated undergraduates who enrolled in 2015, 1,717 applied for aid. 124 Federal Work-Study jobs (averaging $1822). 95 state and other part-time jobs (averaging $1534).
Applying *Options:* electronic application. *Application fee:* $20. *Required:* high school transcript. *Application deadlines:* rolling (freshmen), rolling (transfers). *Notification:* continuous (freshmen), continuous (transfers).
Freshman Application Contact Ms. Crystal Strouth, College Registrar, Minnesota West Community and Technical College, 1450 Collegeway, Worthington, MN 56187. *Phone:* 507-372-3451. *Toll-free phone:* 800-658-2330. *Fax:* 507-372-5803. *E-mail:* crystal.strouth@mnwest.edu.
Website: http://www.mnwest.edu/.

Normandale Community College
Bloomington, Minnesota

Freshman Application Contact Admissions Office, Normandale Community College, 9700 France Avenue South, Bloomington, MN 55431. *Phone:* 952-358-8201. *Toll-free phone:* 800-481-5412. *Fax:* 952-358-8230. *E-mail:* information@normandale.edu. *Website:* http://www.normandale.edu/.

North Hennepin Community College
Brooklyn Park, Minnesota

- **State-supported** 2-year, founded 1966, part of Minnesota State Colleges and Universities System
- **Suburban** 80-acre campus with easy access to Minneapolis-St. Paul
- **Endowment** $952,413
- **Coed**

Undergraduates 2,055 full-time, 4,792 part-time. Students come from 26 states and territories; 36 other countries; 26% Black or African American, non-Hispanic/Latino; 4% Hispanic/Latino; 15% Asian, non-Hispanic/Latino; 0.3% Native Hawaiian or other Pacific Islander, non-Hispanic/Latino; 0.9% American Indian or Alaska Native, non-Hispanic/Latino; 4% Race/ethnicity unknown; 1% international.
Academics *Calendar:* semesters. *Degree:* certificates and associate. *Special study options:* academic remediation for entering students, accelerated degree program, adult/continuing education programs, advanced placement credit, distance learning, double majors, English as a second language, external degree program, honors programs, independent study, internships, off-campus study, part-time degree program, services for LD students, student-designed majors, study abroad, summer session for credit. *ROTC:* Army (c), Navy (c), Air Force (c).
Library Learning Resource Center.
Student Life *Campus security:* 24-hour emergency response devices, student patrols, late-night transport/escort service.
Costs (2016–17) *Tuition:* state resident $3922 full-time, $163 per credit part-time; nonresident $3922 full-time, $163 per credit part-time. Full-time tuition and fees vary according to location and program. Part-time tuition and fees vary according to location and program. *Required fees:* $445 full-time, $19 per credit part-time.
Applying *Options:* electronic application, early admission, deferred entrance. *Application fee:* $20. *Recommended:* high school transcript.
Freshman Application Contact Mr. Sean Olson, Associate Director of Admissions and Outreach, North Hennepin Community College, 7411 85th Avenue North, Brooklyn Park, MN 55445. *Phone:* 763-424-0724. *Toll-free phone:* 800-818-0395. *Fax:* 763-493-0563. *E-mail:* solson2@nhcc.edu. *Website:* http://www.nhcc.edu/.

Northland Community and Technical College
Thief River Falls, Minnesota

- **State-supported** 2-year, founded 1949, part of Minnesota State Colleges and Universities System
- **Small-town** 239-acre campus
- **Coed**, 3,599 undergraduate students, 38% full-time, 56% women, 44% men

Undergraduates 1,375 full-time, 2,224 part-time. Students come from 24 states and territories; 1 other country; 7% are from out of state; 7% Black or African American, non-Hispanic/Latino; 4% Hispanic/Latino; 3% Asian, non-Hispanic/Latino; 0.1% Native Hawaiian or other Pacific Islander, non-Hispanic/Latino; 2% American Indian or Alaska Native, non-Hispanic/Latino; 4% Two or more races, non-Hispanic/Latino; 5% Race/ethnicity unknown; 0.5% international; 11% transferred in. *Retention:* 56% of full-time freshmen returned.
Freshmen *Admission:* 1,200 applied, 1,200 admitted, 527 enrolled.
Faculty *Total:* 150, 61% full-time, 7% with terminal degrees. *Student/faculty ratio:* 19:1.
Majors Accounting technology and bookkeeping; administrative assistant and secretarial science; agricultural mechanics and equipment technology; agriculture; airframe mechanics and aircraft maintenance technology; architectural drafting and CAD/CADD; autobody/collision and repair technology; automation engineer technology; automobile/automotive mechanics technology; business administration and management; computer support specialist; computer systems networking and telecommunications; criminal justice/police science; dietetic technology; emergency medical technology (EMT paramedic); fire prevention and safety technology; health services/allied health/health sciences; heating, air conditioning, ventilation and refrigeration maintenance technology; liberal arts and sciences/liberal studies; manufacturing engineering technology; medical administrative assistant and medical secretary; medical insurance coding; occupational therapist assistant; pharmacy technician; physical therapy technology; radiologic technology/science; registered nursing/registered nurse; respiratory care therapy; sales, distribution, and marketing operations; signal/geospatial intelligence; special products marketing; surgical technology; teacher assistant/aide.

Academics *Calendar:* semesters. *Degree:* certificates, diplomas, and associate. *Special study options:* academic remediation for entering students, adult/continuing education programs, advanced placement credit, cooperative education, distance learning, double majors, internships, off-campus study, part-time degree program, services for LD students, summer session for credit.
Library Northland Community and Technical College Library plus 1 other. *Books:* 24,000 (physical), 19,000 (digital/electronic); *Serial titles:* 55 (physical); *Databases:* 47. Weekly public service hours: 82; students can reserve study rooms.
Student Life *Housing:* college housing not available. *Activities and Organizations:* student-run radio station, choral group, Student Senate, PAMA, AD Nursing, PN Nursing, Fire Tech. *Campus security:* student patrols, late-night transport/escort service. *Student services:* personal/psychological counseling, women's center.
Athletics Member NJCAA. *Intercollegiate sports:* baseball M, basketball M/W, football M, softball W, volleyball W, wrestling M. *Intramural sports:* basketball M/W, bowling M/W, golf M/W, ice hockey M/W, racquetball M/W, rock climbing M/W, soccer M/W, softball M/W, volleyball M/W, weight lifting M/W.
Costs (2017–18) *Tuition:* state resident $4901 full-time, $163 per credit hour part-time; nonresident $4901 full-time, $163 per credit hour part-time. Full-time tuition and fees vary according to course load, program, and reciprocity agreements. Part-time tuition and fees vary according to course load, program, and reciprocity agreements. *Required fees:* $584 full-time, $19 per credit hour part-time. *Waivers:* senior citizens and employees or children of employees.
Financial Aid Of all full-time matriculated undergraduates who enrolled in 2011, 98 Federal Work-Study jobs (averaging $2701). 68 state and other part-time jobs (averaging $2839).
Applying *Options:* electronic application, early admission, deferred entrance. *Application fee:* $20. *Required:* high school transcript. *Application deadlines:* 8/24 (freshmen), 8/24 (transfers). *Notification:* continuous (freshmen), continuous (transfers).
Freshman Application Contact Mrs. Nicki Carlson, Director of Enrollment Management, Northland Community and Technical College, 1101 Highway One East, Thief River Falls, MN 56701. *Phone:* 218-683-8546. *Toll-free phone:* 800-959-6282. *Fax:* 218-683-8980. *E-mail:* nicki.carlson@northlandcollege.edu. *Website:* http://www.northlandcollege.edu/.

Northwest Technical College
Bemidji, Minnesota

- **State-supported** 2-year, founded 1993, part of Minnesota State Colleges and Universities System
- **Small-town** campus
- **Coed**

Undergraduates 336 full-time, 778 part-time. 7% are from out of state; 2% Black or African American, non-Hispanic/Latino; 2% Hispanic/Latino; 0.4% Asian, non-Hispanic/Latino; 0.3% Native Hawaiian or other Pacific Islander, non-Hispanic/Latino; 8% American Indian or Alaska Native, non-Hispanic/Latino; 7% Two or more races, non-Hispanic/Latino; 2% Race/ethnicity unknown; 0.3% international; 13% transferred in; 4% live on campus. *Retention:* 49% of full-time freshmen returned.
Faculty *Student/faculty ratio:* 14:1.
Academics *Calendar:* semesters. *Degree:* certificates, diplomas, and associate. *Special study options:* part-time degree program.
Library Northwest Technical College Learning Enrichment Center.
Costs (2016–17) *Tuition:* state resident $5138 full-time, $171 per credit hour part-time; nonresident $5138 full-time, $171 per credit hour part-time. Full-time tuition and fees vary according to location, program, and reciprocity agreements. Part-time tuition and fees vary according to location, program, and reciprocity agreements. *Required fees:* $290 full-time, $10 per credit hour part-time. *Room and board:* $7924. Room and board charges vary according to board plan and housing facility.
Applying *Options:* electronic application. *Application fee:* $20. *Required:* high school transcript.
Freshman Application Contact Ms. Kari Kantack-Miller, Diversity and Enrollment Representative, Northwest Technical College, 905 Grant Avenue, Southeast, Bemidji, MN 56601. *Phone:* 218-333-6645. *Toll-free phone:* 800-942-8324. *Fax:* 218-333-6694. *E-mail:* kari.kantack@ntcmn.edu. *Website:* http://www.ntcmn.edu/.

Pine Technical and Community College
Pine City, Minnesota

Freshman Application Contact Pine Technical and Community College, 900 4th Street SE, Pine City, MN 55063. *Phone:* 320-629-5100. *Toll-free phone:* 800-521-7463. *Website:* http://www.pine.edu/.

Rainy River Community College
International Falls, Minnesota

- **State-supported** 2-year, founded 1967, part of Minnesota State Colleges and Universities System
- **Small-town** 80-acre campus
- **Coed,** 268 undergraduate students, 80% full-time, 59% women, 41% men

Undergraduates 215 full-time, 53 part-time. Students come from 19 states and territories; 1 other country; 16% Black or African American, non-Hispanic/Latino; 6% Hispanic/Latino; 0.7% Asian, non-Hispanic/Latino; 5% American Indian or Alaska Native, non-Hispanic/Latino; 2% international.
Faculty *Total:* 25, 40% full-time. *Student/faculty ratio:* 15:1.
Majors Administrative assistant and secretarial science; biological and physical sciences; business administration and management; liberal arts and sciences/liberal studies; pre-engineering.
Academics *Calendar:* semesters. *Degree:* certificates, diplomas, and associate. *Special study options:* academic remediation for entering students, adult/continuing education programs, advanced placement credit, cooperative education, honors programs, independent study, internships, part-time degree program, services for LD students, summer session for credit.
Library Rainy River Community College Library.
Student Life *Housing Options:* special housing for students with disabilities. Campus housing is university owned. *Activities and Organizations:* drama/theater group, Anishinaabe Student Coalition, Student Senate, Black Student Association. *Campus security:* 24-hour emergency response devices, late-night transport/escort service, controlled dormitory access. *Student services:* personal/psychological counseling.
Athletics Member NJCAA. *Intercollegiate sports:* basketball M/W, ice hockey W, softball W, volleyball W. *Intramural sports:* archery M/W, badminton M/W, baseball M, bowling M/W, cheerleading M/W, cross-country running M/W, ice hockey M, skiing (cross-country) M/W, skiing (downhill) M/W, swimming and diving M/W, table tennis M/W, tennis M/W, volleyball M/W, weight lifting M/W.
Costs (2016–17) *Tuition:* state resident $4681 full-time; nonresident $5851 full-time. Full-time tuition and fees vary according to course load and reciprocity agreements. Part-time tuition and fees vary according to course load and reciprocity agreements. *Required fees:* $595 full-time. *Room and board:* $3930; room only: $3130. *Waivers:* employees or children of employees.
Financial Aid Of all full-time matriculated undergraduates who enrolled in 2016, 75 Federal Work-Study jobs (averaging $3200). 10 state and other part-time jobs (averaging $2500).
Applying *Options:* electronic application, early admission, deferred entrance. *Application fee:* $20. *Recommended:* high school transcript. *Application deadlines:* rolling (freshmen), rolling (transfers). *Notification:* continuous (freshmen), continuous (transfers).
Freshman Application Contact Ms. Berta Wilcox, Registrar, Rainy River Community College, 1501 Highway 71, International Falls, MN 56649. *Phone:* 218-285-2207. *Toll-free phone:* 800-456-3996. *Fax:* 218-285-2314. *E-mail:* berta.wilcox@rainyriver.edu.
Website: http://www.rainyriver.edu/.

Ridgewater College
Willmar, Minnesota

- **State-supported** 2-year, founded 1961, part of Minnesota State Colleges and Universities System
- **Small-town** 83-acre campus
- **Coed**

Undergraduates 2,002 full-time, 1,561 part-time.
Academics *Calendar:* semesters. *Degree:* certificates, diplomas, and associate. *Special study options:* academic remediation for entering students, advanced placement credit, cooperative education, distance learning, internships, off-campus study, part-time degree program, services for LD students, student-designed majors, study abroad, summer session for credit.
Student Life *Campus security:* 24-hour emergency response devices.
Athletics Member NJCAA.
Costs (2016–17) *Tuition:* state resident $4791 full-time, $160 per credit part-time; nonresident $4791 full-time, $160 per credit part-time. Full-time tuition and fees vary according to course load and reciprocity agreements. Part-time tuition and fees vary according to course load and reciprocity agreements. *Required fees:* $582 full-time, $19 per credit part-time.
Financial Aid Of all full-time matriculated undergraduates who enrolled in 2015, 350 Federal Work-Study jobs (averaging $3000). 133 state and other part-time jobs (averaging $2400).
Applying *Options:* electronic application. *Application fee:* $20. *Required:* high school transcript. *Required for some:* interview.
Freshman Application Contact Ms. Linda Duering, Admissions Assistant, Ridgewater College, 2101 15th Avenue NW, Willmar, MN 56201. *Phone:* 320-222-5976. *Toll-free phone:* 800-722-1151.
E-mail: linda.duering@ridgewater.edu. *Website:* http://www.ridgewater.edu/.

Riverland Community College
Austin, Minnesota

Freshman Application Contact Riverland Community College, 1900 8th Avenue, NW, Austin, MN 55912. *Phone:* 507-433-0600. *Toll-free phone:* 800-247-5039. *Website:* http://www.riverland.edu/.

Rochester Community and Technical College
Rochester, Minnesota

Director of Admissions Mr. Troy Tynsky, Director of Admissions, Rochester Community and Technical College, 851 30th Avenue, SE, Rochester, MN 55904-4999. *Phone:* 507-280-3509. *Website:* http://www.rctc.edu/.

St. Cloud Technical & Community College
St. Cloud, Minnesota

Freshman Application Contact Ms. Jodi Elness, Admissions Office, St. Cloud Technical & Community College, 1540 Northway Drive, St. Cloud, MN 56303. *Phone:* 320-308-5089. *Toll-free phone:* 800-222-1009. *Fax:* 320-308-5981. *E-mail:* jelness@sctcc.edu. *Website:* http://www.sctcc.edu/.

Saint Paul College–A Community & Technical College
St. Paul, Minnesota

Freshman Application Contact Ms. Sarah Carrico, Saint Paul College–A Community & Technical College, 235 Marshall Avenue, Saint Paul, MN 55102. *Phone:* 651-846-1424. *Toll-free phone:* 800-227-6029. *Fax:* 651-846-1703. *E-mail:* admissions@saintpaul.edu.
Website: http://www.saintpaul.edu/.

South Central College
North Mankato, Minnesota

Freshman Application Contact Ms. Beverly Herda, Director of Admissions, South Central College, 1920 Lee Boulevard, North Mankato, MN 56003. *Phone:* 507-389-7334. *Fax:* 507-388-9951. *Website:* http://southcentral.edu/.

Vermilion Community College
Ely, Minnesota

Freshman Application Contact Mr. Todd Heiman, Director of Enrollment Services, Vermilion Community College, 1900 East Camp Street, Ely, MN 55731-1996. *Phone:* 218-365-7224. *Toll-free phone:* 800-657-3608. *Website:* http://www.vcc.edu/.

White Earth Tribal and Community College
Mahnomen, Minnesota

Admissions Office Contact White Earth Tribal and Community College, 102 3rd Street NE, Mahnomen, MN 56557. *Website:* http://www.wetcc.edu/.

MISSISSIPPI

Antonelli College
Hattiesburg, Mississippi

Freshman Application Contact Mrs. Karen Gautreau, Director, Antonelli College, 1500 North 31st Avenue, Hattiesburg, MS 39401. *Phone:* 601-583-4100. *Fax:* 601-583-0839. *E-mail:* admissionsh@antonellicollege.edu. *Website:* http://www.antonellicollege.edu/.

Antonelli College
Jackson, Mississippi

Freshman Application Contact Antonelli College, 2323 Lakeland Drive, Jackson, MS 39232. *Phone:* 601-362-9991. *Website:* http://www.antonellicollege.edu/.

Blue Cliff College–Gulfport
Gulfport, Mississippi

Admissions Office Contact Blue Cliff College–Gulfport, 12251 Bernard Parkway, Gulfport, MS 39503. *Website:* http://www.bluecliffcollege.edu/.

Coahoma Community College
Clarksdale, Mississippi

Freshman Application Contact Mrs. Wanda Holmes, Director of Admissions and Records, Coahoma Community College, Clarksdale, MS 38614-9799. *Phone:* 662-621-4205. *Toll-free phone:* 866-470-1CCC. *Website:* http://www.ccc.cc.ms.us/.

Copiah-Lincoln Community College
Wesson, Mississippi

- **State and locally supported** 2-year, founded 1928, part of Mississippi Community College Board
- **Rural** 525-acre campus with easy access to Jackson
- **Endowment** $2.5 million
- **Coed**

Undergraduates 2,509 full-time, 648 part-time. Students come from 6 states and territories; 1% are from out of state; 42% Black or African American, non-Hispanic/Latino; 1% Hispanic/Latino; 0.3% Asian, non-Hispanic/Latino; 0.3% American Indian or Alaska Native, non-Hispanic/Latino; 0.2% Two or more races, non-Hispanic/Latino; 1% Race/ethnicity unknown; 6% transferred in; 30% live on campus.

Academics *Calendar:* semesters. *Degree:* certificates and associate. *Special study options:* academic remediation for entering students, adult/continuing education programs, advanced placement credit, honors programs, part-time degree program, student-designed majors, summer session for credit.

Library Oswalt Memorial Library.

Student Life *Campus security:* 24-hour patrols.

Athletics Member NJCAA.

Financial Aid Of all full-time matriculated undergraduates who enrolled in 2015, 125 Federal Work-Study jobs (averaging $1000).

Applying *Options:* early admission. *Required:* high school transcript.

Freshman Application Contact Ms. Gay Langham, Student Records Manager, Copiah-Lincoln Community College, PO Box 649, Wesson, MS 39191-0457. *Phone:* 601-643-8307. *E-mail:* gay.langham@colin.edu. *Website:* http://www.colin.edu/.

East Central Community College
Decatur, Mississippi

Director of Admissions Ms. Donna Luke, Director of Admissions, Records, and Research, East Central Community College, PO Box 129, Decatur, MS 39327-0129. *Phone:* 601-635-2111 Ext. 206. *Toll-free phone:* 877-462-3222. *Website:* http://www.eccc.edu/.

East Mississippi Community College
Scooba, Mississippi

Director of Admissions Ms. Melinda Sciple, Admissions Officer, East Mississippi Community College, PO Box 158, Scooba, MS 39358-0158. *Phone:* 662-476-5041. *Website:* http://www.eastms.edu/.

Hinds Community College
Raymond, Mississippi

- **State and locally supported** 2-year, founded 1917, part of Mississippi Community College Board
- **Small-town** 671-acre campus with easy access to Jackson
- **Coed**, 11,469 undergraduate students, 67% full-time, 61% women, 39% men

Undergraduates 7,695 full-time, 3,774 part-time. Students come from 32 states and territories; 24 other countries; 3% are from out of state; 55% Black or African American, non-Hispanic/Latino; 2% Hispanic/Latino; 0.8% Asian, non-Hispanic/Latino; 0.2% American Indian or Alaska Native, non-Hispanic/Latino; 3% Two or more races, non-Hispanic/Latino; 1% Race/ethnicity unknown.

Freshmen *Admission:* 2,783 enrolled.

Majors Accounting technology and bookkeeping; administrative assistant and secretarial science; aeronautics/aviation/aerospace science and technology; agribusiness; agricultural mechanization related; airframe mechanics and aircraft maintenance technology; applied horticulture/horticultural business services related; architectural engineering technology; arts, entertainment, and media management related; aviation/airway management; banking and financial support services; child-care provision; clinical/medical laboratory technology; computer and information systems security; computer installation and repair technology; computer programming; computer systems networking and telecommunications; cooking and related culinary arts; corrections and criminal justice related; court reporting; dental assisting; diagnostic medical sonography and ultrasound technology; diesel mechanics technology; drafting and design technology; electrical, electronic and communications engineering technology; electrical/electronics equipment installation and repair; electrician; emergency medical technology (EMT paramedic); fashion merchandising; game and interactive media design; general studies; geographic information science and cartography; graphic design; health and medical administrative services related; health information/medical records technology; heating, air conditioning, ventilation and refrigeration maintenance technology; hospitality administration; landscaping and groundskeeping; legal assistant/paralegal; logistics, materials, and supply chain management; marketing/marketing management; medical/clinical assistant; multi/interdisciplinary studies related; photographic and film/video technology; physical therapy technology; plant protection and integrated pest management; plumbing technology; poultry science; radio and television broadcasting technology; radiologic technology/science; real estate; registered nursing/registered nurse; respiratory care therapy; sign language interpretation and translation; surgical technology; telecommunications technology; tourism and travel services management; veterinary/animal health technology.

Academics *Calendar:* semesters. *Degrees:* certificates and associate (profile includes Raymond, Jackson Academic and Technical Center, Jackson Nursing-Allied Health Center, Rankin, Utica, and Vicksburg campus locations). *Special study options:* academic remediation for entering students, accelerated degree program, adult/continuing education programs, advanced placement credit, cooperative education, distance learning, double majors, honors programs, independent study, internships, part-time degree program, services for LD students, study abroad, summer session for credit. *ROTC:* Army (b).

Library McLendon Library plus 5 others. Students can reserve study rooms.

Student Life *Housing Options:* coed, men-only, women-only, special housing for students with disabilities. Campus housing is university owned. *Activities and Organizations:* drama/theater group, student-run newspaper, choral group, marching band. *Campus security:* 24-hour emergency response devices and patrols, late-night transport/escort service, controlled dormitory access. *Student services:* personal/psychological counseling.

Athletics Member NJCAA. *Intercollegiate sports:* baseball M(s), basketball M(s)/W(s), cheerleading M(s)/W(s), football M(s), golf M(s), soccer M(s)/W(s), softball W(s), tennis M(s)/W(s), track and field M(s)/W(s). *Intramural sports:* basketball M/W, bowling M/W, cross-country running M/W, football M/W, golf M/W, softball M/W, swimming and diving M/W, tennis M/W, ultimate Frisbee M/W, volleyball M/W.

Costs (2016–17) *Tuition:* state resident $2640 full-time, $110 per semester hour part-time; nonresident $5440 full-time, $210 per semester hour part-time. Part-time tuition and fees vary according to course load. *Required fees:* $200 full-time, $100 per term part-time. *Room and board:* $4000. Room and board charges vary according to housing facility. *Payment plan:* installment. *Waivers:* senior citizens and employees or children of employees.

Financial Aid Of all full-time matriculated undergraduates who enrolled in 2015, 300 Federal Work-Study jobs (averaging $1250). 200 state and other part-time jobs (averaging $1000).

Freshman Application Contact Hinds Community College, PO Box 1100, Raymond, MS 39154-1100. *Phone:* 601-857-3280. *Toll-free phone:* 800-HINDSCC. *Website:* http://www.hindscc.edu/.

Holmes Community College
Goodman, Mississippi

Director of Admissions Dr. Lynn Wright, Dean of Admissions and Records, Holmes Community College, PO Box 369, Goodman, MS 39079-0369. *Phone:* 601-472-2312 Ext. 1023. *Toll-free phone:* 800-HOLMES-4. *Website:* http://www.holmescc.edu/.

Itawamba Community College

Fulton, Mississippi

- **State and locally supported** 2-year, founded 1947, part of Mississippi State Board for Community and Junior Colleges
- **Small-town** 300-acre campus
- **Coed**

Undergraduates 3,605 full-time, 2,006 part-time. *Retention:* 70% of full-time freshmen returned.

Faculty *Student/faculty ratio:* 19:1.

Academics *Calendar:* semesters. *Degree:* certificates and associate. *Special study options:* academic remediation for entering students, adult/continuing education programs, cooperative education, distance learning, English as a second language, honors programs, part-time degree program, services for LD students, summer session for credit. *ROTC:* Army (b).

Athletics Member NJCAA.

Costs (2016–17) *Tuition:* state resident $2500 full-time, $120 per semester hour part-time; nonresident $4700 full-time, $120 per semester hour part-time. *Required fees:* $120 full-time, $120 per semester part-time. *Room and board:* $3510; room only: $1500. Room and board charges vary according to board plan and housing facility.

Financial Aid Of all full-time matriculated undergraduates who enrolled in 2013, 230 Federal Work-Study jobs (averaging $2500).

Applying *Options:* electronic application, early admission. *Required:* high school transcript.

Freshman Application Contact Mr. Larry Boggs, Director of Student Recruitment and Scholarships, Itawamba Community College, 602 West Hill Street, Fulton, MS 38843. *Phone:* 601-862-8252. *E-mail:* laboggs@iccms.edu. *Website:* http://www.iccms.edu/.

Jones County Junior College

Ellisville, Mississippi

Director of Admissions Mrs. Dianne Speed, Director of Admissions and Records, Jones County Junior College, 900 South Court Street, Ellisville, MS 39437-3901. *Phone:* 601-477-4025. *Website:* http://www.jcjc.edu/.

Meridian Community College

Meridian, Mississippi

- **State and locally supported** 2-year, founded 1937, part of Mississippi Community College Board
- **Small-town** 91-acre campus
- **Endowment** $12.7 million
- **Coed,** 3,598 undergraduate students, 69% full-time, 69% women, 31% men

Undergraduates 2,473 full-time, 1,125 part-time. Students come from 8 states and territories; 1 other country; 3% are from out of state; 42% Black or African American, non-Hispanic/Latino; 1% Hispanic/Latino; 0.6% Asian, non-Hispanic/Latino; 2% American Indian or Alaska Native, non-Hispanic/Latino; 4% Race/ethnicity unknown; 0.6% international; 12% live on campus. *Retention:* 54% of full-time freshmen returned.

Freshmen *Admission:* 362 enrolled.

Faculty *Total:* 209, 74% full-time, 4% with terminal degrees. *Student/faculty ratio:* 18:1.

Majors Administrative assistant and secretarial science; child-care provision; clinical/medical laboratory technology; dental hygiene; drafting and design technology; electrical, electronic and communications engineering technology; emergency medical technology (EMT paramedic); fire science/firefighting; machine tool technology; marketing/marketing management; registered nursing/registered nurse; respiratory care therapy; telecommunications technology.

Academics *Calendar:* semesters. *Degree:* certificates and associate. *Special study options:* academic remediation for entering students, accelerated degree program, adult/continuing education programs, advanced placement credit, cooperative education, distance learning, double majors, English as a second language, freshman honors college, honors programs, independent study, internships, part-time degree program, services for LD students, summer session for credit.

Library L. O. Todd Library. *Books:* 49,345 (physical), 63,815 (digital/electronic); *Databases:* 13.

Student Life *Housing Options:* coed, men-only, women-only. Campus housing is university owned. *Activities and Organizations:* drama/theater group, student-run radio station, choral group, Phi Theta Kappa, VICA (Vocational Industrial Clubs of America), Health Occupations Students of America, Organization of Student Nurses, Distributive Education Clubs of America. *Campus security:* 24-hour patrols by law enforcement officers. *Student services:* personal/psychological counseling.

Athletics Member NJCAA. *Intercollegiate sports:* baseball M(s), basketball M(s)/W(s), cross-country running M(s)/W(s), golf M(s), soccer M(s)/W(s), softball W(s), tennis M(s)/W(s), track and field M(s)/W(s). *Intramural sports:* basketball M/W, cross-country running M/W, swimming and diving M/W, tennis M/W, volleyball M/W.

Standardized Tests *Recommended:* ACT (for admission).

Costs (2017–18) *Tuition:* state resident $2300 full-time, $150 per credit hour part-time; nonresident $3380 full-time, $157 per credit hour part-time. Full-time tuition and fees vary according to program. Part-time tuition and fees vary according to program. *Required fees:* $240 full-time, $6 per credit hour part-time, $25 per term part-time. *Room and board:* Room and board charges vary according to housing facility. *Waivers:* employees or children of employees.

Applying *Options:* early admission. *Required:* high school transcript, minimum 2.0 GPA. *Application deadlines:* rolling (freshmen), rolling (out-of-state freshmen), rolling (transfers). *Notification:* continuous (freshmen), continuous (out-of-state freshmen), continuous (transfers).

Freshman Application Contact Ms. Angela Payne, Director of Admissions, Meridian Community College, 910 Highway 19 North, Meridian, MS 39307. *Phone:* 601-484-8357. *Toll-free phone:* 800-MCC-THE-1. *E-mail:* apayne@meridiancc.edu. *Website:* http://www.meridiancc.edu/.

Miller-Motte Technical College

Gulfport, Mississippi

Admissions Office Contact Miller-Motte Technical College, 12121 Highway 49 North, Gulfport, MS 39503. *Toll-free phone:* 800-705-9182. *Website:* http://www.miller-motte.edu/.

Mississippi Delta Community College

Moorhead, Mississippi

Freshman Application Contact Mississippi Delta Community College, PO Box 668, Highway 3 and Cherry Street, Moorhead, MS 38761-0668. *Phone:* 662-246-6302. *Website:* http://www.msdelta.edu/.

Mississippi Gulf Coast Community College

Perkinston, Mississippi

Freshman Application Contact Mrs. Nichol Green, Director of Admissions, Mississippi Gulf Coast Community College, PO Box 548, Perkinston, MS 39573. *Phone:* 601-928-6264. *Fax:* 601-928-6345. *Website:* http://www.mgccc.edu/.

Northeast Mississippi Community College

Booneville, Mississippi

Freshman Application Contact Office of Enrollment Services, Northeast Mississippi Community College, 101 Cunningham Boulevard, Booneville, MS 38829. *Phone:* 662-720-7239. *Toll-free phone:* 800-555-2154. *E-mail:* admitme@nemcc.edu. *Website:* http://www.nemcc.edu/.

Northwest Mississippi Community College

Senatobia, Mississippi

Freshman Application Contact Northwest Mississippi Community College, 4975 Highway 51 North, Senatobia, MS 38668-1701. *Phone:* 662-562-3222. *Website:* http://www.northwestms.edu/.

Pearl River Community College

Poplarville, Mississippi

Freshman Application Contact Mr. J. Dow Ford, Director of Admissions, Pearl River Community College, 101 Highway 11 North, Poplarville, MS 39470. *Phone:* 601-403-1000. *E-mail:* dford@prcc.edu. *Website:* http://www.prcc.edu/.

Southwest Mississippi Community College
Summit, Mississippi

Freshman Application Contact Mr. Matthew Calhoun, Vice President of Admissions and Records, Southwest Mississippi Community College, 1156 College Drive, Summit, MS 39666. *Phone:* 601-276-2001. *Fax:* 601-276-3888. *E-mail:* mattc@smcc.edu. *Website:* http://www.smcc.cc.ms.us/.

Virginia College in Biloxi
Biloxi, Mississippi

Admissions Office Contact Virginia College in Biloxi, 920 Cedar Lake Road, Biloxi, MS 39532. *Website:* http://www.vc.edu/.

Virginia College in Jackson
Jackson, Mississippi

Director of Admissions Director of Admissions, Virginia College in Jackson, 5841 Ridgewood Road, Jackson, MS 39211. *Phone:* 601-977-0960. *Website:* http://www.vc.edu/.

MISSOURI

American Trade School
Saint Ann, Missouri

Admissions Office Contact American Trade School, 3925 Industrial Drive, Saint Ann, MO 63074. *Website:* http://www.americantradeschool.edu/.

Bryan University
Columbia, Missouri

Admissions Office Contact Bryan University, 3215 LeMone Industrial Boulevard, Columbia, MO 65201. *Toll-free phone:* 855-566-0650. *Website:* http://www.bryanu.edu/.

Concorde Career College
Kansas City, Missouri

Freshman Application Contact Deborah Crow, Director, Concorde Career College, 3239 Broadway Street, Kansas City, MO 64111. *Phone:* 816-531-5223. *Fax:* 816-756-3231. *E-mail:* dcrow@concorde.edu. *Website:* http://www.concorde.edu/.

Cottey College
Nevada, Missouri

- **Independent** primarily 2-year, founded 1884
- **Small-town** 51-acre campus
- **Endowment** $108.8 million
- **Women only**
- 74% of applicants were admitted

Undergraduates Students come from 43 states and territories; 25 other countries; 80% are from out of state; 8% Black or African American, non-Hispanic/Latino; 10% Hispanic/Latino; 2% Asian, non-Hispanic/Latino; 0.6% Native Hawaiian or other Pacific Islander, non-Hispanic/Latino; 2% American Indian or Alaska Native, non-Hispanic/Latino; 5% Two or more races, non-Hispanic/Latino; 14% international; 98% live on campus. *Retention:* 79% of full-time freshmen returned.
Faculty *Student/faculty ratio:* 10:1.
Academics *Calendar:* semesters. *Degrees:* associate and bachelor's. *Special study options:* advanced placement credit, distance learning, independent study, internships, part-time degree program, services for LD students, study abroad.
Library Blanche Skiff Ross Memorial Library plus 1 other.
Student Life *Campus security:* 24-hour emergency response devices and patrols, late-night transport/escort service, controlled dormitory access.
Athletics Member NJCAA.
Standardized Tests *Required:* SAT or ACT (for admission). *Required for some:* TOEFL, IELTS.
Costs (2016–17) *Comprehensive fee:* $27,200 includes full-time tuition ($19,300), mandatory fees ($900), and room and board ($7000). Part-time tuition: $125 per credit hour. Part-time tuition and fees vary according to course load and program. *Required fees:* $21 per credit hour part-time, $63 per term part-time. *Room and board:* college room only: $4000. Room and board charges vary according to housing facility.
Financial Aid Of all full-time matriculated undergraduates who enrolled in 2015, 255 applied for aid, 238 were judged to have need, 79 had their need fully met. 21 Federal Work-Study jobs (averaging $2099). 159 state and other part-time jobs (averaging $2056). In 2015, 73. *Average percent of need met:* 86. *Average financial aid package:* $20,584. *Average need-based loan:* $3087. *Average need-based gift aid:* $17,312. *Average non-need-based aid:* $14,919. *Average indebtedness upon graduation:* $26,427.
Applying *Options:* early decision, early action. *Required:* essay or personal statement, high school transcript, 1 letter of recommendation. *Recommended:* minimum 2.6 GPA, interview.
Freshman Application Contact Enrollment Office, Cottey College, 1000 West Austin Boulevard, Nevada, MO 64772. *Phone:* 417-667-8181. *Toll-free phone:* 888-526-8839. *Fax:* 417-667-8103. *E-mail:* enrollmgt@cottey.edu. *Website:* http://www.cottey.edu/.

Court Reporting Institute of St. Louis
Clayton, Missouri

Freshman Application Contact Admissions Office, Court Reporting Institute of St. Louis, 7730 Carondelet Avenue, Suite 400, Clayton, MO 63105. *Phone:* 713-996-8300. *Toll-free phone:* 888-208-6780. *Website:* http://www.cri.edu/st-louis-court-reporting-school.asp.

Crowder College
Neosho, Missouri

- **State and locally supported** 2-year, founded 1963, part of Missouri Coordinating Board for Higher Education
- **Rural** 608-acre campus
- **Coed,** 5,710 undergraduate students, 46% full-time, 64% women, 36% men

Undergraduates 2,638 full-time, 3,072 part-time. Students come from 12 states and territories; 6% are from out of state; 1% Black or African American, non-Hispanic/Latino; 8% Hispanic/Latino; 1% Asian, non-Hispanic/Latino; 0.4% Native Hawaiian or other Pacific Islander, non-Hispanic/Latino; 2% American Indian or Alaska Native, non-Hispanic/Latino; 2% Two or more races, non-Hispanic/Latino; 1% Race/ethnicity unknown; 1% international; 5% transferred in; 10% live on campus. *Retention:* 64% of full-time freshmen returned.
Freshmen *Admission:* 1,320 enrolled.
Faculty *Total:* 449, 21% full-time, 7% with terminal degrees. *Student/faculty ratio:* 12:1.
Majors Administrative assistant and secretarial science; agribusiness; agricultural mechanization; agriculture; art; autobody/collision and repair technology; automobile/automotive mechanics technology; biology/biological sciences; business administration and management; business automation/technology/data entry; computer systems analysis; computer systems networking and telecommunications; construction engineering technology; construction trades; drafting and design technology; dramatic/theater arts; education; electrical, electronic and communications engineering technology; elementary education; emergency medical technology (EMT paramedic); energy management and systems technology; environmental engineering technology; executive assistant/executive secretary; farm and ranch management; fire science/firefighting; general studies; health information/medical records technology; industrial technology; legal administrative assistant/secretary; liberal arts and sciences/liberal studies; manufacturing engineering technology; mass communication/media; mathematics; mathematics and computer science; medical administrative assistant and medical secretary; music; occupational therapist assistant; physical education teaching and coaching; physical sciences; pre-engineering; psychology; public relations/image management; registered nursing/registered nurse; solar energy technology; veterinary/animal health technology; welding technology.
Academics *Calendar:* semesters. *Degree:* certificates and associate. *Special study options:* academic remediation for entering students, adult/continuing education programs, advanced placement credit, cooperative education, English as a second language, freshman honors college, honors programs, independent study, part-time degree program, student-designed majors, study abroad, summer session for credit.
Library Bill & Margot Lee Library.
Student Life *Housing Options:* men-only, women-only. Campus housing is university owned. *Activities and Organizations:* drama/theater group, student-run newspaper, choral group, Phi Theta Kappa, Students in Free Enterprise (SIFE), Baptist Student Union, Student Senate, Student Ambassadors. *Campus security:* 24-hour patrols.

Athletics Member NJCAA. *Intercollegiate sports:* baseball M(s), basketball W(s), soccer M(s).

Costs (2016–17) *Tuition:* area resident $2460 full-time, $82 per credit hour part-time; state resident $3840 full-time, $128 per credit hour part-time; nonresident $3840 full-time, $128 per credit hour part-time. *Required fees:* $600 full-time, $20 per credit hour part-time. *Room and board:* $3300; room only: $2300. Room and board charges vary according to board plan and housing facility. *Payment plan:* installment. *Waivers:* senior citizens and employees or children of employees.

Financial Aid Of all full-time matriculated undergraduates who enrolled in 2015, 150 Federal Work-Study jobs (averaging $1000).

Applying *Application fee:* $25. *Required:* high school transcript. *Application deadlines:* rolling (freshmen), rolling (transfers). *Notification:* continuous (freshmen).

Freshman Application Contact Mr. James P. Dickey, Admissions Coordinator, Crowder College, Neosho, MO 64850. *Phone:* 417-451-3223 Ext. 5466. *Toll-free phone:* 866-238-7788. *Fax:* 417-455-5731. *E-mail:* jamesdickey@crowder.edu. *Website:* http://www.crowder.edu/.

Culinary Institute of St. Louis at Hickey College

St. Louis, Missouri

- **Private** 2-year, founded 2009
- **Suburban** campus
- **Coed**
- 81% of applicants were admitted

Academics *Calendar:* semesters. *Degree:* associate.

Freshman Application Contact Admissions Office, Culinary Institute of St. Louis at Hickey College, 2700 North Lindbergh Boulevard, St. Louis, MO 63114. *Phone:* 314-434-2212. *Website:* http://www.ci-stl.com/.

East Central College

Union, Missouri

- **District-supported** 2-year, founded 1959
- **Rural** 207-acre campus with easy access to St. Louis
- **Endowment** $3.1 million
- **Coed**, 2,966 undergraduate students, 47% full-time, 62% women, 38% men

Undergraduates 1,385 full-time, 1,581 part-time. Students come from 1 other state; 0.9% Black or African American, non-Hispanic/Latino; 2% Hispanic/Latino; 0.6% Asian, non-Hispanic/Latino; 0.2% Native Hawaiian or other Pacific Islander, non-Hispanic/Latino; 0.5% American Indian or Alaska Native, non-Hispanic/Latino; 0.5% Two or more races, non-Hispanic/Latino; 0.8% Race/ethnicity unknown; 4% transferred in.

Freshmen *Admission:* 683 admitted, 654 enrolled.

Faculty *Total:* 220, 31% full-time, 5% with terminal degrees. *Student/faculty ratio:* 16:1.

Majors Accounting technology and bookkeeping; automobile/automotive mechanics technology; biology/biotechnology laboratory technician; business/commerce; child-care and support services management; commercial and advertising art; computer systems networking and telecommunications; construction trades; construction trades related; culinary arts; education; emergency medical technology (EMT paramedic); engineering; fine/studio arts; fire science/firefighting; general studies; health information/medical records technology; heating, air conditioning, ventilation and refrigeration maintenance technology; heavy/industrial equipment maintenance technologies related; machine tool technology; medical/clinical assistant; medical radiologic technology; music; occupational therapist assistant; precision production related; registered nursing/registered nurse; respiratory care therapy; technical teacher education; welding technology.

Academics *Calendar:* semesters. *Degree:* certificates and associate. *Special study options:* academic remediation for entering students, adult/continuing education programs, advanced placement credit, distance learning, English as a second language, honors programs, independent study, internships, off-campus study, part-time degree program, services for LD students, study abroad, summer session for credit.

Library East Central College Library. *Books:* 23,635 (physical), 202,752 (digital/electronic); *Serial titles:* 61 (physical), 8 (digital/electronic); *Databases:* 32. Weekly public service hours: 55; students can reserve study rooms.

Student Life *Housing:* college housing not available. *Activities and Organizations:* drama/theater group, student-run newspaper, choral group, Phi Theta Kappa, Students-Missouri State Teachers Association, R&R Club.

Campus security: 24-hour emergency response devices, late-night transport/escort service. *Student services:* personal/psychological counseling.

Athletics Member NJCAA. *Intercollegiate sports:* soccer M(s), softball W(s), volleyball W(s).

Costs (2016–17) *Tuition:* area resident $1824 full-time; state resident $2664 full-time; nonresident $4032 full-time. Full-time tuition and fees vary according to program. Part-time tuition and fees vary according to program. *Required fees:* $552 full-time. *Waivers:* senior citizens and employees or children of employees.

Applying *Options:* electronic application, early admission, deferred entrance. *Required:* high school transcript. *Application deadlines:* rolling (freshmen), rolling (transfers).

Freshman Application Contact Mr. Nathaniel Mitchell, Director, Admissions, East Central College, 1964 Prairie Dell Road, Union, MO 63084. *Phone:* 636-584-6552. *E-mail:* nathaniel.mitchell@eastcentral.edu. *Website:* http://www.eastcentral.edu/.

Jefferson College

Hillsboro, Missouri

- **District-supported** 2-year, founded 1963
- **Rural** 455-acre campus with easy access to St. Louis
- **Endowment** $689,969
- **Coed**

Undergraduates 2,287 full-time, 2,418 part-time. 2% Black or African American, non-Hispanic/Latino; 0.4% Hispanic/Latino; 0.8% Asian, non-Hispanic/Latino; 0.1% Native Hawaiian or other Pacific Islander, non-Hispanic/Latino; 0.6% American Indian or Alaska Native, non-Hispanic/Latino; 5% Race/ethnicity unknown; 0.3% international.

Faculty *Student/faculty ratio:* 17:1.

Academics *Calendar:* semesters. *Degree:* certificates, diplomas, and associate. *Special study options:* academic remediation for entering students, adult/continuing education programs, advanced placement credit, distance learning, English as a second language, freshman honors college, honors programs, internships, off-campus study, part-time degree program, services for LD students, summer session for credit.

Library Jefferson College Library plus 1 other. *Books:* 75,216 (physical), 183,744 (digital/electronic); *Serial titles:* 54 (physical), 31,939 (digital/electronic); *Databases:* 62. Weekly public service hours: 66; students can reserve study rooms.

Student Life *Campus security:* 24-hour patrols, campus police department.

Athletics Member NJCAA.

Costs (2016–17) *One-time required fee:* $25. *Tuition:* area resident $2910 full-time, $97 per credit hour part-time; state resident $4380 full-time, $146 per credit hour part-time; nonresident $5820 full-time, $194 per credit hour part-time. Full-time tuition and fees vary according to course load and program. Part-time tuition and fees vary according to course load and program. *Required fees:* $90 full-time, $3 per credit hour part-time, $10 per term part-time. *Room and board:* $5644. Room and board charges vary according to housing facility.

Financial Aid Of all full-time matriculated undergraduates who enrolled in 2015, 2,013 applied for aid, 1,528 were judged to have need, 70 had their need fully met. 81 Federal Work-Study jobs (averaging $1339). 92 state and other part-time jobs (averaging $1431). In 2015, 168. *Average percent of need met:* 56. *Average financial aid package:* $5062. *Average need-based loan:* $3075. *Average need-based gift aid:* $2484. *Average non-need-based aid:* $2126.

Applying *Options:* electronic application, early admission. *Application fee:* $25. *Required:* high school transcript.

Freshman Application Contact Dr. Kimberly Harvey, Director of Student Records and Admissions Services, Jefferson College, 1000 Viking Drive, Hillsboro, MO 63050-2441. *Phone:* 636-481-3205 Ext. 3205. *Fax:* 636-789-5103. *E-mail:* admissions@jeffco.edu. *Website:* http://www.jeffco.edu/.

L'Ecole Culinaire–Kansas City

Kansas City, Missouri

Admissions Office Contact L'Ecole Culinaire–Kansas City, 310 Ward Parkway, Kansas City, MO 64112. *Toll-free phone:* 855-549-7577. *Website:* http://www.lecole.edu/kansas-city/.

L'Ecole Culinaire–St. Louis

St. Louis, Missouri

Admissions Office Contact L'Ecole Culinaire–St. Louis, 9811 South Forty Drive, St. Louis, MO 63124. *Toll-free phone:* 855-764-0043. *Website:* http://www.lecole.edu/st-louis/.

Metro Business College
Cape Girardeau, Missouri

Director of Admissions Ms. Kyla Evans, Admissions Director, Metro Business College, 1732 North Kingshighway, Cape Girardeau, MO 63701. *Phone:* 573-334-9181. *Toll-free phone:* 888-206-4545. *Fax:* 573-334-0617. *Website:* http://www.metrobusinesscollege.edu/.

Metro Business College
Jefferson City, Missouri

- **Proprietary** 2-year, founded 1979
- **Suburban** campus
- **Coed, primarily women**

Undergraduates Students come from 1 other state; 18% Black or African American, non-Hispanic/Latino; 2% Asian, non-Hispanic/Latino; 0.7% American Indian or Alaska Native, non-Hispanic/Latino; 4% Race/ethnicity unknown.
Faculty *Student/faculty ratio:* 11:1.
Academics *Calendar:* continuous. *Degree:* certificates and associate. *Special study options:* academic remediation for entering students, adult/continuing education programs, advanced placement credit, independent study, internships, part-time degree program, services for LD students, summer session for credit.
Standardized Tests *Required:* Wonderlic aptitude test (for admission).
Costs (2016–17) *One-time required fee:* $100. *Tuition:* $11,250 full-time, $278 per quarter hour part-time. Full-time tuition and fees vary according to program. Part-time tuition and fees vary according to program. No tuition increase for student's term of enrollment. *Required fees:* $125 full-time. *Payment plans:* tuition prepayment, installment, deferred payment.
Applying *Required:* essay or personal statement, high school transcript, interview.
Freshman Application Contact Ms. Cheri Chockley, Campus Director, Metro Business College, 210 El Mercado Plaza, Jefferson City, MO 65109. *Phone:* 573-635-6600. *Toll-free phone:* 888-206-4545. *Fax:* 573-635-6999. *E-mail:* cheri@metrobusinesscollege.edu.
Website: http://www.metrobusinesscollege.edu/.

Metro Business College
Rolla, Missouri

Freshman Application Contact Admissions Office, Metro Business College, 1202 East Highway 72, Rolla, MO 65401. *Phone:* 573-364-8464. *Toll-free phone:* 888-206-4545. *Fax:* 573-364-8077. *E-mail:* inforolla@metrobusinesscollege.edu.
Website: http://www.metrobusinesscollege.edu/.

Metropolitan Community College–Kansas City
Kansas City, Missouri

Freshman Application Contact Dr. Tuesday Stanley, Vice Chancellor of Student Development and Enrollment Services, Metropolitan Community College–Kansas City, 3200 Broadway, Kansas City, MO 64111-2429. *Phone:* 816-604-1253. *E-mail:* tuesday.stanley@mcckc.edu. *Website:* http://www.mcckc.edu/.

Midwest Institute
Fenton, Missouri

Freshman Application Contact Admissions Office, Midwest Institute, 964 South Highway Drive, Fenton, MO 63026. *Toll-free phone:* 800-695-5550. *Website:* http://www.midwestinstitute.com/.

Midwest Institute
St. Louis, Missouri

Freshman Application Contact Admissions Office, Midwest Institute, 4260 Shoreline Drive, St. Louis, MO 63045. *Phone:* 314-344-4440. *Toll-free phone:* 800-695-5550. *Fax:* 314-344-0495. *Website:* http://www.midwestinstitute.com/.

Mineral Area College
Park Hills, Missouri

Freshman Application Contact Pam Reeder, Registrar, Mineral Area College, PO Box 1000, Park Hills, MO 63601-1000. *Phone:* 573-518-2204. *Fax:* 573-518-2166. *E-mail:* preeder@mineralarea.edu.
Website: http://www.mineralarea.edu/.

Missouri State University–West Plains
West Plains, Missouri

- **State-supported** 2-year, founded 1963, part of Missouri State University
- **Small-town** 20-acre campus
- **Endowment** $7.4 million
- **Coed,** 2,123 undergraduate students, 46% full-time, 57% women, 34% men

Undergraduates 987 full-time, 957 part-time. Students come from 19 states and territories; 9 other countries; 4% are from out of state; 5% Black or African American, non-Hispanic/Latino; 3% Hispanic/Latino; 0.4% Asian, non-Hispanic/Latino; 0.2% Native Hawaiian or other Pacific Islander, non-Hispanic/Latino; 1% American Indian or Alaska Native, non-Hispanic/Latino; 3% Two or more races, non-Hispanic/Latino; 3% Race/ethnicity unknown; 0.8% international; 4% transferred in; 4% live on campus. *Retention:* 54% of full-time freshmen returned.
Freshmen *Admission:* 1,037 applied, 398 admitted, 458 enrolled. *Average high school GPA:* 3.16.
Faculty *Total:* 125, 31% full-time, 12% with terminal degrees. *Student/faculty ratio:* 18:1.
Majors Agriculture; animation, interactive technology, video graphics and special effects; business/commerce; criminal justice/police science; elementary education; engineering; food science; general studies; health/medical preparatory programs related; health services/allied health/health sciences; human development and family studies; industrial production technologies related; registered nursing/registered nurse; respiratory care therapy; restaurant, culinary, and catering management; viticulture and enology.
Academics *Calendar:* semesters. *Degree:* certificates and associate. *Special study options:* academic remediation for entering students, adult/continuing education programs, advanced placement credit, cooperative education, distance learning, honors programs, internships, off-campus study, part-time degree program, services for LD students, study abroad, summer session for credit.
Library Garnett Library. *Books:* 43,135 (physical), 261,723 (digital/electronic); *Serial titles:* 121 (physical), 2,889 (digital/electronic). Weekly public service hours: 49.
Student Life *Housing Options:* coed, special housing for students with disabilities. Campus housing is university owned and is provided by a third party. *Activities and Organizations:* Student Government Association, Student Nurses Association, Student Ambassadors, TRIO Club, Phi Beta Lambda. *Campus security:* 24-hour patrols, student patrols, late-night transport/escort service, access only with key; agreement with city police for patrols. *Student services:* personal/psychological counseling, legal services.
Athletics Member NJCAA. *Intercollegiate sports:* basketball M(s), volleyball W(s).
Costs (2017–18) *Tuition:* state resident $3720 full-time; nonresident $7440 full-time. Full-time tuition and fees vary according to program. Part-time tuition and fees vary according to program. *Required fees:* $510 full-time. *Room and board:* $5910. *Payment plan:* deferred payment. *Waivers:* senior citizens and employees or children of employees.
Financial Aid Of all full-time matriculated undergraduates who enrolled in 2015, 63 Federal Work-Study jobs (averaging $2000).
Applying *Options:* electronic application. *Application fee:* $15. *Required for some:* high school transcript. *Application deadlines:* rolling (freshmen), rolling (out-of-state freshmen), rolling (transfers). *Notification:* continuous (freshmen), continuous (out-of-state freshmen), continuous (transfers).
Freshman Application Contact Ms. Melissa Jett, Coordinator of Admissions, Missouri State University–West Plains, 128 Garfield, West Plains, MO 65775. *Phone:* 417-255-7955. *Toll-free phone:* 888-466-7897. *Fax:* 417-255-7959. *E-mail:* melissajett@missouristate.edu.
Website: http://wp.missouristate.edu/.

Moberly Area Community College
Moberly, Missouri

Freshman Application Contact Dr. James Grant, Dean of Student Services, Moberly Area Community College, Moberly, MO 65270-1304. *Phone:* 660-263-4110 Ext. 235. *Toll-free phone:* 800-622-2070. *Fax:* 660-263-2406. *E-mail:* info@macc.edu. *Website:* http://www.macc.edu/.

North Central Missouri College
Trenton, Missouri

- **District-supported** 2-year, founded 1925
- **Small-town** 2-acre campus
- **Coed,** 1,505 undergraduate students, 53% full-time, 71% women, 29% men

Undergraduates 796 full-time, 709 part-time. Students come from 10 states and territories; 1% are from out of state; 6% transferred in. *Retention:* 69% of full-time freshmen returned.
Freshmen *Admission:* 708 applied, 626 admitted, 339 enrolled.
Faculty *Total:* 94, 35% full-time, 6% with terminal degrees. *Student/faculty ratio:* 16:1.
Majors Accounting; administrative assistant and secretarial science; agricultural business and management; automobile/automotive mechanics technology; business administration and management; carpentry; computer engineering technology; construction engineering technology; criminal justice/law enforcement administration; data processing and data processing technology; drafting and design technology; early childhood education; e-commerce; electrical, electronic and communications engineering technology; emergency medical technology (EMT paramedic); farm and ranch management; human services; liberal arts and sciences/liberal studies; marketing/marketing management; medical/clinical assistant; registered nursing/registered nurse.
Academics *Calendar:* semesters. *Degree:* certificates and associate. *Special study options:* academic remediation for entering students, accelerated degree program, adult/continuing education programs, advanced placement credit, cooperative education, distance learning, internships, part-time degree program, services for LD students, summer session for credit.
Library North Central Missouri College Library.
Student Life *Housing Options:* men-only, women-only. Campus housing is university owned. *Activities and Organizations:* drama/theater group, Student Nurses Association, Student Practical Nurses Association, Delta Epsilon Chi (business), Pre-med Club, Postsecondary Agriculture Students. *Campus security:* controlled dormitory access. *Student services:* personal/psychological counseling.
Athletics Member NJCAA. *Intercollegiate sports:* baseball M(s), basketball M(s)/W(s), softball W(s).
Standardized Tests *Recommended:* SAT or ACT (for admission).
Financial Aid Of all full-time matriculated undergraduates who enrolled in 2015, 40 Federal Work-Study jobs (averaging $1500). 25 state and other part-time jobs (averaging $1200).
Applying *Application fee:* $15. *Required:* high school transcript. *Application deadlines:* rolling (freshmen), rolling (transfers).
Freshman Application Contact Jamie Cunningham, Admissions Recruiter, North Central Missouri College, Trenton, MO 64683. *Phone:* 660-359-3948 Ext. 1414. *E-mail:* jcunningham@Mail.Ncmissouri.edu.
Website: http://www.ncmissouri.edu/.

Ozarks Technical Community College
Springfield, Missouri

- **District-supported** 2-year, founded 1990, part of Missouri Coordinating Board for Higher Education
- **Urban** campus
- **Endowment** $2.8 million
- **Coed,** 13,260 undergraduate students, 44% full-time, 59% women, 41% men

Undergraduates 5,826 full-time, 7,434 part-time. Students come from 31 states and territories; 2% are from out of state; 3% Black or African American, non-Hispanic/Latino; 5% Hispanic/Latino; 1% Asian, non-Hispanic/Latino; 0.2% Native Hawaiian or other Pacific Islander, non-Hispanic/Latino; 0.5% American Indian or Alaska Native, non-Hispanic/Latino; 5% Two or more races, non-Hispanic/Latino; 2% Race/ethnicity unknown.
Faculty *Total:* 994, 21% full-time. *Student/faculty ratio:* 21:1.
Majors Accounting; administrative assistant and secretarial science; autobody/collision and repair technology; automobile/automotive mechanics technology; business administration and management; business machine repair; computer systems networking and telecommunications; construction engineering technology; culinary arts; diesel mechanics technology; electrical, electronic and communications engineering technology; emergency medical technology (EMT paramedic); fire science/firefighting; graphic and printing equipment operation/production; health information/medical records technology; heating, air conditioning, ventilation and refrigeration maintenance technology; heavy equipment maintenance technology; hotel/motel administration; industrial technology; information science/studies; instrumentation technology; kindergarten/preschool education; liberal arts and sciences/liberal studies; machine tool technology; management information systems; mechanical drafting and CAD/CADD; occupational therapist assistant; occupational therapy; physical sciences; physical therapy technology; radio and television broadcasting technology; respiratory care therapy; turf and turfgrass management; welding technology.
Academics *Calendar:* semesters. *Degree:* certificates, diplomas, and associate. *Special study options:* academic remediation for entering students, adult/continuing education programs, cooperative education, distance learning, double majors, English as a second language, honors programs, internships, off-campus study, part-time degree program, services for LD students, summer session for credit.
Library Main Library plus 1 other.
Student Life *Housing:* college housing not available. *Activities and Organizations:* student-run newspaper, choral group, Phi Theta Kappa. *Campus security:* 24-hour emergency response devices. *Student services:* personal/psychological counseling.
Costs (2017–18) *Tuition:* area resident $2352 full-time, $98 per credit hour part-time; state resident $3564 full-time, $149 per credit hour part-time; nonresident $4752 full-time, $198 per credit hour part-time. Full-time tuition and fees vary according to program. Part-time tuition and fees vary according to program. *Required fees:* $500 full-time, $22 per credit hour part-time, $50 per term part-time. *Payment plans:* installment, deferred payment. *Waivers:* employees or children of employees.
Financial Aid Of all full-time matriculated undergraduates who enrolled in 2015, 201 Federal Work-Study jobs.
Applying *Options:* electronic application. *Required:* high school transcript. *Application deadlines:* rolling (freshmen), rolling (transfers). *Notification:* continuous (freshmen), continuous (transfers).
Freshman Application Contact Ozarks Technical Community College, 1001 E. Chestnut Expressway, Springfield, MO 65802.
Website: http://www.otc.edu/.

Pinnacle Career Institute
Kansas City, Missouri

Director of Admissions Ms. Ruth Matous, Director of Admissions, Pinnacle Career Institute, 10301 Hickman Mills Drive, Kansas City, MO 64137. *Phone:* 816-331-5700 Ext. 212. *Toll-free phone:* 877-241-3097.
Website: http://www.pcitraining.edu/.

Pinnacle Career Institute
Kansas City, Missouri

Freshman Application Contact Pinnacle Career Institute, 11500 NW Ambassador Drive, Suite 221, Kansas City, MO 64153. *Phone:* 816-331-5700. *Toll-free phone:* 877-241-3097. *Website:* http://www.pcitraining.edu/.

Ranken Technical College
St. Louis, Missouri

- **Independent** primarily 2-year, founded 1907
- **Urban** 10-acre campus
- **Coed, primarily men**

Academics *Calendar:* semesters. *Degrees:* certificates, associate, and bachelor's. *Special study options:* academic remediation for entering students, adult/continuing education programs, advanced placement credit, cooperative education, distance learning, independent study, internships, part-time degree program, services for LD students, summer session for credit.
Library Ashley Gray, Jr. Learning Center.
Student Life *Campus security:* 24-hour emergency response devices and patrols.
Financial Aid Of all full-time matriculated undergraduates who enrolled in 2015, 30 Federal Work-Study jobs (averaging $2000).
Applying *Options:* electronic application. *Application fee:* $25. *Required:* essay or personal statement, high school transcript, interview.
Freshman Application Contact Ranken Technical College, 4431 Finney Avenue, St. Louis, MO 63113. *Phone:* 314-371-0233 Ext. 4811.
Toll-free phone: 866-4-RANKEN. *Website:* http://www.ranken.edu/.

St. Charles Community College
Cottleville, Missouri

- **State-supported** 2-year, founded 1986, part of Missouri Coordinating Board for Higher Education
- **Suburban** 228-acre campus with easy access to St. Louis
- **Coed,** 6,756 undergraduate students, 49% full-time, 56% women, 44% men

Undergraduates 3,286 full-time, 3,470 part-time. Students come from 23 states and territories; 41 other countries; 6% Black or African American, non-Hispanic/Latino; 5% Hispanic/Latino; 2% Asian, non-Hispanic/Latino; 0.1%

Native Hawaiian or other Pacific Islander, non-Hispanic/Latino; 0.2% American Indian or Alaska Native, non-Hispanic/Latino; 4% Two or more races, non-Hispanic/Latino; 3% Race/ethnicity unknown; 2% international; 8% transferred in.
Freshmen *Admission:* 2,479 applied, 2,479 admitted, 1,397 enrolled.
Faculty *Total:* 391, 28% full-time, 20% with terminal degrees. *Student/faculty ratio:* 20:1.
Majors Accounting technology and bookkeeping; biology/biological sciences; chemistry; child-care and support services management; child-care provision; civil engineering; commercial and advertising art; computer programming; criminal justice/police science; drafting and design technology; education (specific subject areas) related; emergency medical technology (EMT paramedic); engineering; environmental health; general studies; health information/medical records technology; human services; liberal arts and sciences/liberal studies; marketing/marketing management; occupational therapist assistant; office management; precision production related; pre-engineering; pre-pharmacy studies; registered nursing/registered nurse; teacher assistant/aide; welding technology.
Academics *Calendar:* semesters. *Degree:* certificates and associate. *Special study options:* academic remediation for entering students, adult/continuing education programs, advanced placement credit, cooperative education, distance learning, double majors, English as a second language, honors programs, independent study, internships, part-time degree program, services for LD students, study abroad, summer session for credit.
Library Paul and Helen Schnare Library. *Books:* 68,244 (physical), 30,170 (digital/electronic); *Serial titles:* 348 (physical), 266,814 (digital/electronic); *Databases:* 43. Weekly public service hours: 72.
Student Life *Activities and Organizations:* drama/theater group, student-run newspaper, choral group, Phi Theta Kappa, Student Nurse Organization, GAMES Club, SAGE (Straights and Gays for Equality), Student Veterans Organization. *Campus security:* 24-hour emergency response devices and patrols, late-night transport/escort service, campus police officers on duty during normal operating hours. *Student services:* personal/psychological counseling.
Athletics Member NJCAA. *Intercollegiate sports:* baseball M(s), soccer M(s)/W(s), softball W(s).
Costs (2017–18) *Tuition:* area resident $2532 full-time; state resident $3576 full-time; nonresident $5160 full-time. Full-time tuition and fees vary according to course load and program. Part-time tuition and fees vary according to course load and program. *Required fees:* $192 full-time. *Payment plan:* installment. *Waivers:* senior citizens and employees or children of employees.
Financial Aid Of all full-time matriculated undergraduates who enrolled in 2015, 26 Federal Work-Study jobs.
Applying *Options:* electronic application, early admission, deferred entrance. *Application fee:* $10. *Required for some:* high school transcript, minimum 2.5 GPA. *Recommended:* high school transcript. *Application deadlines:* rolling (freshmen), rolling (out-of-state freshmen), rolling (transfers). *Notification:* continuous (freshmen), continuous (out-of-state freshmen), continuous (transfers).
Freshman Application Contact Ms. Kathy Brockgreitens-Gober, Dean of Enrollment Services, St. Charles Community College, 4601 Mid Rivers Mall Drive, Cottleville, MO 63376-0975. *Phone:* 636-922-8229. *Fax:* 636-922-8236. *E-mail:* regist@stchas.edu.
Website: http://www.stchas.edu/.

St. Louis College of Health Careers
Fenton, Missouri

Admissions Office Contact St. Louis College of Health Careers, 1297 North Highway Drive, Fenton, MO 63026. *Website:* http://www.slchc.com/.

St. Louis College of Health Careers
St. Louis, Missouri

Freshman Application Contact Admissions Office, St. Louis College of Health Careers, 909 South Taylor Avenue, St. Louis, MO 63110-1511. *Phone:* 314-652-0300. *Toll-free phone:* 888-789-4820. *Fax:* 314-652-4825. *Website:* http://www.slchc.com/.

St. Louis Community College
St. Louis, Missouri

- **Public** 2-year, founded 1962, part of St. Louis Community College System
- **Suburban** campus with easy access to St. Louis
- **Coed**, 19,052 undergraduate students, 38% full-time, 60% women, 40% men

Undergraduates 7,209 full-time, 11,843 part-time. Students come from 25 states and territories; 112 other countries; 1% are from out of state; 34% Black or African American, non-Hispanic/Latino; 3% Hispanic/Latino; 4% Asian, non-Hispanic/Latino; 0.2% Native Hawaiian or other Pacific Islander, non-Hispanic/Latino; 0.3% American Indian or Alaska Native, non-Hispanic/Latino; 4% Two or more races, non-Hispanic/Latino; 1% Race/ethnicity unknown; 1% international; 6% transferred in. *Retention:* 62% of full-time freshmen returned.
Freshmen *Admission:* 3,320 enrolled.
Faculty *Total:* 1,422, 28% full-time. *Student/faculty ratio:* 17:1.
Academics *Calendar:* semesters. *Degree:* certificates and associate. *Special study options:* academic remediation for entering students, accelerated degree program, adult/continuing education programs, advanced placement credit, distance learning, English as a second language, honors programs, independent study, internships, part-time degree program, services for LD students, study abroad, summer session for credit.
Student Life *Housing:* college housing not available. *Activities and Organizations:* drama/theater group, student-run newspaper. *Campus security:* 24-hour emergency response devices, late-night transport/escort service. *Student services:* personal/psychological counseling.
Athletics Member NJCAA. *Intercollegiate sports:* baseball M(s), basketball M(s)/W(s), soccer M(s)/W(s), softball W(s), volleyball W(s).
Costs (2017–18) *Tuition:* area resident $2700 full-time, $90 per credit hour part-time; state resident $4080 full-time, $136 per credit hour part-time; nonresident $5760 full-time, $192 per credit hour part-time. Full-time tuition and fees vary according to course load. Part-time tuition and fees vary according to course load. *Required fees:* $480 full-time, $16 per credit hour part-time. *Payment plan:* installment. *Waivers:* senior citizens and employees or children of employees.
Applying *Options:* electronic application. *Required for some:* high school transcript, interview. *Application deadlines:* rolling (freshmen), rolling (transfers). *Notification:* continuous (freshmen), continuous (transfers).
Freshman Application Contact St. Louis Community College, 300 South Broadway, St. Louis, MO 63102.
Website: http://www.stlcc.edu/.

Southeast Missouri Hospital College of Nursing and Health Sciences
Cape Girardeau, Missouri

Freshman Application Contact Southeast Missouri Hospital College of Nursing and Health Sciences, 2001 William Street, Cape Girardeau, MO 63701. *Phone:* 573-334-6825 Ext. 12. *Website:* http://www.sehcollege.edu/.

State Fair Community College
Sedalia, Missouri

Freshman Application Contact State Fair Community College, 3201 West 16th Street, Sedalia, MO 65301-2199. *Phone:* 660-596-7379. *Toll-free phone:* 877-311-7322. *Website:* http://www.sfccmo.edu/.

State Technical College of Missouri
Linn, Missouri

Freshman Application Contact State Technical College of Missouri, One Technology Drive, Linn, MO 65051-9606. *Phone:* 573-897-5196. *Toll-free phone:* 800-743-TECH. *Website:* http://www.statetechmo.edu/.

Texas County Technical College
Houston, Missouri

Admissions Office Contact Texas County Technical College, 6915 S. Hwy 63, Houston, MO 65483. *Website:* http://www.texascountytech.edu/.

Three Rivers Community College
Poplar Bluff, Missouri

- **State and locally supported** 2-year, founded 1966, part of Missouri Coordinating Board for Higher Education
- **Rural** 80-acre campus
- **Coed**, 3,505 undergraduate students, 56% full-time, 65% women, 35% men

Undergraduates 1,959 full-time, 1,546 part-time. Students come from 11 states and territories; 2 other countries; 4% are from out of state; 10% Black or African American, non-Hispanic/Latino; 1% Hispanic/Latino; 0.5% Asian, non-Hispanic/Latino; 0.1% Native Hawaiian or other Pacific Islander, non-Hispanic/Latino; 0.7% American Indian or Alaska Native, non-Hispanic/Latino; 5% Race/ethnicity unknown; 0.3% international; 3% transferred in; 5% live on campus.

Freshmen *Admission:* 902 applied, 902 admitted, 902 enrolled.

Faculty *Total:* 293, 24% full-time, 5% with terminal degrees.

Majors Accounting technology and bookkeeping; administrative assistant and secretarial science; agricultural mechanization; agricultural production; child-care and support services management; clinical/medical laboratory technology; computer systems networking and telecommunications; criminal justice/police science; diesel mechanics technology; education (multiple levels); education (specific subject areas) related; electrical, electronic and communications engineering technology; electrician; emergency medical technology (EMT paramedic); environmental health; fire science/firefighting; forest/forest resources management; forest technology; general studies; geographic information science and cartography; health/medical preparatory programs related; heating, air conditioning, ventilation and refrigeration maintenance technology; hospitality administration; industrial mechanics and maintenance technology; international/global studies; liberal arts and sciences/liberal studies; licensed practical/vocational nurse training; marketing/marketing management; mechanic and repair technologies related; occupational safety and health technology; occupational therapist assistant; office management; physical therapy technology; plumbing technology; pre-engineering; prenursing studies; pre-optometry; pre-pharmacy studies; quality control technology; registered nursing/registered nurse; sociology; surveying technology; welding technology.

Academics *Calendar:* semesters. *Degree:* certificates and associate. *Special study options:* academic remediation for entering students, accelerated degree program, adult/continuing education programs, advanced placement credit, distance learning, double majors, English as a second language, external degree program, honors programs, independent study, internships, part-time degree program, services for LD students, summer session for credit.

Library Rutland Library. *Books:* 13,598 (physical), 179,481 (digital/electronic); *Serial titles:* 27 (physical); *Databases:* 52. Weekly public service hours: 61; students can reserve study rooms.

Student Life *Housing Options:* coed. Campus housing is university owned. *Activities and Organizations:* drama/theater group, choral group, Marketing Management Association, Phi Theta Kappa, Phi Beta Lambda, GO FAR, TRCC Aggies. *Student services:* personal/psychological counseling.

Athletics Member NJCAA. *Intercollegiate sports:* baseball M(s), basketball M(s)/W(s), softball W(s).

Costs (2017–18) *Tuition:* area resident $2760 full-time, $92 per credit hour part-time; state resident $4200 full-time, $140 per credit hour part-time; nonresident $5340 full-time, $178 per credit hour part-time. *Required fees:* $1050 full-time, $35 per credit hour part-time. *Room and board:* room only: $3440. *Payment plan:* installment.

Applying *Options:* electronic application, early admission. *Required for some:* high school transcript. *Recommended:* high school transcript. *Application deadlines:* rolling (freshmen), rolling (transfers). *Notification:* continuous (freshmen), continuous (transfers).

Freshman Application Contact Three Rivers Community College, 2080 Three Rivers Boulevard, Poplar Bluff, MO 63901-2393. *Toll-free phone:* 877-TRY-TRCC.

Website: http://www.trcc.edu/.

Vatterott College
Berkeley, Missouri

Director of Admissions Ann Farajallah, Director of Admissions, Vatterott College, 8580 Evans Avenue, Berkeley, MO 63134. *Phone:* 314-264-1020. *Toll-free phone:* 888-553-6627. *Website:* http://www.vatterott.edu/.

Vatterott College
Joplin, Missouri

Admissions Office Contact Vatterott College, 809 Illinois Avenue, Joplin, MO 64801. *Toll-free phone:* 800-934-6975. *Website:* http://www.vatterott.edu/.

Vatterott College
Kansas City, Missouri

Admissions Office Contact Vatterott College, 4131 N. Corrington Avenue, Kansas City, MO 64117. *Toll-free phone:* 888-553-6627. *Website:* http://www.vatterott.edu/.

Vatterott College
St. Charles, Missouri

Director of Admissions Gertrude Bogan-Jones, Director of Admissions, Vatterott College, 3550 West Clay Street, St. Charles, MO 63301. *Phone:* 636-978-7488. *Toll-free phone:* 888-553-6627. *Fax:* 636-978-5121. *E-mail:* ofallon@vatterott-college.edu. *Website:* http://www.vatterott.edu/.

Vatterott College
St. Joseph, Missouri

Director of Admissions Director of Admissions, Vatterott College, 3709 Belt Highway, St. Joseph, MO 64506. *Phone:* 816-364-5399. *Toll-free phone:* 888-553-6627. *Fax:* 816-364-1593. *Website:* http://www.vatterott.edu/.

Vatterott College
Springfield, Missouri

Freshman Application Contact Mr. Scott Lester, Director of Admissions, Vatterott College, 3850 South Campbell Avenue, Springfield, MO 65807. *Phone:* 417-831-8116. *Toll-free phone:* 888-553-6627. *Fax:* 417-831-5099. *E-mail:* springfield@vatterott-college.edu. *Website:* http://www.vatterott.edu/.

Vatterott College
Sunset Hills, Missouri

Director of Admissions Director of Admission, Vatterott College, 12900 Maurer Industrial Drive, Sunset Hills, MO 63127. *Phone:* 314-843-4200. *Toll-free phone:* 888-553-6627. *Fax:* 314-843-1709. *Website:* http://www.vatterott.edu/.

Vet Tech Institute at Hickey College
St. Louis, Missouri

- **Private** 2-year, founded 2007
- **Suburban** campus
- **Coed**
- 58% of applicants were admitted

Academics *Calendar:* semesters. *Degree:* associate. *Special study options:* accelerated degree program, internships.

Freshman Application Contact Admissions Office, Vet Tech Institute at Hickey College, 2780 North Lindbergh Boulevard, St. Louis, MO 63114. *Phone:* 888-884-1459. *Toll-free phone:* 888-884-1459. *Website:* http://stlouis.vettechinstitute.edu/.

WellSpring School of Allied Health
Kansas City, Missouri

Admissions Office Contact WellSpring School of Allied Health, 9140 Ward Parkway, Suite 100, Kansas City, MO 64114. *Website:* http://www.wellspring.edu/.

Wentworth Military Academy and College
Lexington, Missouri

Freshman Application Contact Capt. Mike Bellis, College Admissions Director, Wentworth Military Academy and College, 1880 Washington Avenue, Lexington, MO 64067. *Phone:* 660-259-2221 Ext. 1351. *Fax:* 660-259-2677. *E-mail:* admissions@wma.edu. *Website:* http://www.wma.edu/.

MONTANA

Aaniiih Nakoda College
Harlem, Montana
- **Federally supported** 2-year, founded 1984
- **Rural** 3-acre campus
- **Coed,** 236 undergraduate students

Faculty *Student/faculty ratio:* 11:1.
Majors American Indian/Native American studies; business/commerce; computer and information sciences; computer technology/computer systems technology; early childhood education; elementary education; health services/allied health/health sciences; human services; kindergarten/preschool education; liberal arts and sciences/liberal studies; natural resources management and policy; psychology.
Academics *Calendar:* quarters. *Degree:* certificates and associate. *Special study options:* academic remediation for entering students, cooperative education, part-time degree program.
Library Fort Belknap College Library.
Student Life *Housing:* college housing not available. *Activities and Organizations:* student-run radio station. *Campus security:* 24-hour patrols.
Applying *Options:* early admission, deferred entrance. *Application fee:* $10. *Required:* high school transcript. *Application deadlines:* rolling (freshmen), rolling (transfers). *Notification:* continuous (freshmen), continuous (transfers).
Freshman Application Contact Aaniiih Nakoda College, PO Box 159, Harlem, MT 59526-0159. *Phone:* 406-353-2607 Ext. 233. *Website:* http://www.ancollege.edu/.

Blackfeet Community College
Browning, Montana
Freshman Application Contact Ms. Deana M. McNabb, Registrar and Admissions Officer, Blackfeet Community College, PO Box 819, Browning, MT 59417-0819. *Phone:* 406-338-5421. *Toll-free phone:* 800-549-7457. *Fax:* 406-338-3272. *Website:* http://www.bfcc.edu/.

Chief Dull Knife College
Lame Deer, Montana
Freshman Application Contact Director of Admissions, Chief Dull Knife College, PO Box 98, 1 College Drive, Lame Deer, MT 59043-0098. *Phone:* 406-477-6215. *Website:* http://www.cdkc.edu/.

Dawson Community College
Glendive, Montana
- **State and locally supported** 2-year, founded 1940
- **Rural** 300-acre campus
- **Endowment** $3.5 million
- **Coed**

Undergraduates 162 full-time, 142 part-time. Students come from 20 states and territories; 5 other countries; 35% are from out of state; 4% Black or African American, non-Hispanic/Latino; 6% Hispanic/Latino; 2% Asian, non-Hispanic/Latino; 1% American Indian or Alaska Native, non-Hispanic/Latino; 2% Two or more races, non-Hispanic/Latino; 2% Race/ethnicity unknown; 3% international; 17% transferred in.
Faculty *Student/faculty ratio:* 16:1.
Academics *Calendar:* semesters. *Degree:* certificates and associate. *Special study options:* academic remediation for entering students, adult/continuing education programs, distance learning, independent study, internships, part-time degree program, services for LD students, summer session for credit.
Library Jane Carey Memorial Library plus 1 other. *Books:* 33,477 (physical), 13,359 (digital/electronic); *Serial titles:* 81 (physical); *Databases:* 118. Weekly public service hours: 40; students can reserve study rooms.
Student Life *Campus security:* 24-hour emergency response devices.
Athletics Member NJCAA.
Financial Aid Of all full-time matriculated undergraduates who enrolled in 2015, 153 applied for aid, 153 were judged to have need. 24 Federal Work-Study jobs (averaging $2136). 13 state and other part-time jobs (averaging $2136). *Average percent of need met:* 92.
Applying *Options:* electronic application, deferred entrance. *Application fee:* $30. *Required:* high school transcript.
Freshman Application Contact Mrs. Daneen Peterson, Admissions Specialist, Dawson Community College, 300 College Drive, Glendive, MT 59330. *Phone:* 406-377-9411. *Toll-free phone:* 800-821-8320. *Fax:* 406-377-8132. *E-mail:* dpeterson@dawson.edu. *Website:* http://www.dawson.edu/.

Flathead Valley Community College
Kalispell, Montana
Freshman Application Contact Ms. Marlene C. Stoltz, Admissions/Graduation Coordinator, Flathead Valley Community College, 777 Grandview Drive, Kalispell, MT 59901-2622. *Phone:* 406-756-3846. *Toll-free phone:* 800-313-3822. *E-mail:* mstoltz@fvcc.cc.mt.us. *Website:* http://www.fvcc.edu/.

Fort Peck Community College
Poplar, Montana
Director of Admissions Mr. Robert McAnally, Vice President for Student Services, Fort Peck Community College, PO Box 398, Poplar, MT 59255-0398. *Phone:* 406-768-6329. *Website:* http://www.fpcc.edu/.

Great Falls College Montana State University
Great Falls, Montana
- **State-supported** 2-year, founded 1969, part of Montana University System
- **Small-town** 40-acre campus
- **Endowment** $11,300
- **Coed,** 1,674 undergraduate students, 39% full-time, 71% women, 29% men

Undergraduates 658 full-time, 1,016 part-time. Students come from 30 states and territories; 1 other country; 5% are from out of state; 2% Black or African American, non-Hispanic/Latino; 5% Hispanic/Latino; 1% Asian, non-Hispanic/Latino; 0.3% Native Hawaiian or other Pacific Islander, non-Hispanic/Latino; 5% American Indian or Alaska Native, non-Hispanic/Latino; 6% Two or more races, non-Hispanic/Latino; 3% Race/ethnicity unknown; 10% transferred in.
Freshmen *Admission:* 427 applied, 379 admitted, 232 enrolled.
Faculty *Total:* 108, 43% full-time, 14% with terminal degrees. *Student/faculty ratio:* 15:1.
Majors Accounting technology and bookkeeping; computer systems networking and telecommunications; dental hygiene; emergency medical technology (EMT paramedic); entrepreneurship; health information/medical records technology; information technology; liberal arts and sciences and humanities related; licensed practical/vocational nurse training; medical/clinical assistant; physical therapy technology; radiologic technology/science; respiratory care therapy; surgical technology; welding technology.
Academics *Calendar:* semesters. *Degree:* certificates and associate. *Special study options:* academic remediation for entering students, advanced placement credit, distance learning, double majors, independent study, internships, off-campus study, part-time degree program, services for LD students, summer session for credit.
Library Weaver Library plus 1 other. *Books:* 9,239 (physical), 266,102 (digital/electronic); *Databases:* 69. Students can reserve study rooms.
Student Life *Activities and Organizations:* choral group, The Associated Students of Great Falls College Montana State University, Phi Theta Kappa, Physical Therapy Assistant Club, Dental Hygiene Assistant Club, Nursing Club. *Campus security:* 24-hour emergency response devices.
Costs (2017–18) *Tuition:* state resident $2496 full-time; nonresident $8748 full-time. Full-time tuition and fees vary according to course load, location, and program. Part-time tuition and fees vary according to course load, location, and program. *Required fees:* $634 full-time. *Payment plan:* deferred payment. *Waivers:* minority students, senior citizens, and employees or children of employees.
Financial Aid Of all full-time matriculated undergraduates who enrolled in 2015, 658 applied for aid, 656 were judged to have need, 170 had their need fully met. In 2015, 12 non-need-based awards were made. *Average percent of need met:* 75%. *Average financial aid package:* $8997. *Average need-based loan:* $5841. *Average need-based gift aid:* $4807. *Average non-need-based aid:* $684.
Applying *Options:* electronic application, early admission. *Application fee:* $30. *Required:* high school transcript, proof of immunization. *Application deadlines:* rolling (freshmen), rolling (transfers). *Notification:* continuous (freshmen), continuous (transfers).
Freshman Application Contact Mr. Joe Simonsen, Admissions, Great Falls College Montana State University, 2100 16th Avenue South, Great Falls, MT 59405. *Phone:* 406-771-4309. *Toll-free phone:* 800-446-2698. *Fax:* 406-771-2267. *E-mail:* joe.simonsen@gfcmsu.edu. *Website:* http://www.gfcmsu.edu/.

Helena College University of Montana
Helena, Montana

Freshman Application Contact Mr. Ryan Loomis, Admissions Representative/Recruiter, Helena College University of Montana, 1115 North Roberts Street, Helena, MT 59601. *Phone:* 406-447-6904. *Toll-free phone:* 800-241-4882. *Website:* http://www.umhelena.edu/.

Highlands College of Montana Tech
Butte, Montana

Admissions Office Contact Highlands College of Montana Tech, 25 Basin Creek Road, Butte, MT 59701.
Website: http://www.mtech.edu/academics/highlands/.

Little Big Horn College
Crow Agency, Montana

Freshman Application Contact Ms. Ann Bullis, Dean of Student Services, Little Big Horn College, Box 370, 1 Forest Lane, Crow Agency, MT 59022-0370. *Phone:* 406-638-2228 Ext. 50. *Website:* http://www.lbhc.edu/.

Miles Community College
Miles City, Montana

Freshman Application Contact Mr. Haley Anderson, Admissions Representative, Miles Community College, 2715 Dickinson Street, Miles City, MT 59301. *Phone:* 406-874-6178. *Toll-free phone:* 800-541-9281. *E-mail:* andersonh@milescc.edu. *Website:* http://www.milescc.edu/.

Salish Kootenai College
Pablo, Montana

Freshman Application Contact Ms. Jackie Moran, Admissions Officer, Salish Kootenai College, PO Box 70, Pablo, MT 59855-0117. *Phone:* 406-275-4866. *Fax:* 406-275-4810. *E-mail:* jackie_moran@skc.edu. *Website:* http://www.skc.edu/.

Stone Child College
Box Elder, Montana

Director of Admissions Mr. Ted Whitford, Director of Admissions/Registrar, Stone Child College, RR1, Box 1082, Box Elder, MT 59521. *Phone:* 406-395-4313 Ext. 110. *E-mail:* uanet337@quest.ocsc.montana.edu. *Website:* http://www.stonechild.edu/.

NEBRASKA

Central Community College–Columbus Campus
Columbus, Nebraska

Freshman Application Contact Ms. Erica Leffler, Admissions/Recruiting Coordinator, Central Community College–Columbus Campus, PO Box 1027, Columbus, NE 68602-1027. *Phone:* 402-562-1296. *Toll-free phone:* 877-CCC-0780. *Fax:* 402-562-1201. *E-mail:* eleffler@ccneb.edu. *Website:* http://www.ccneb.edu/.

Central Community College–Grand Island Campus
Grand Island, Nebraska

Freshman Application Contact Michelle Lubken, Admissions Director, Central Community College–Grand Island Campus, PO Box 4903, Grand Island, NE 68802-4903. *Phone:* 308-398-7406 Ext. 406. *Toll-free phone:* 877-CCC-0780. *Fax:* 308-398-7398. *E-mail:* mlubken@ccneb.edu. *Website:* http://www.ccneb.edu/.

Central Community College–Hastings Campus
Hastings, Nebraska

Freshman Application Contact Mr. Robert Glenn, Admissions and Recruiting Director, Central Community College–Hastings Campus, PO Box 1024, East Highway 6, Hastings, NE 68902-1024. *Phone:* 402-461-2428. *Toll-free phone:* 877-CCC-0780. *E-mail:* rglenn@ccneb.edu. *Website:* http://www.ccneb.edu/.

CHI Health School of Radiologic Technology
Omaha, Nebraska

Admissions Office Contact CHI Health School of Radiologic Technology, 7500 Mercy Road, Omaha, NE 68124-9832.
Website: http://www.chihealth.com/school-of-radiologic-technology.

Kaplan University, Lincoln
Lincoln, Nebraska

Freshman Application Contact Kaplan University, Lincoln, 1821 K Street, Lincoln, NE 68508. *Phone:* 402-474-5315. *Toll-free phone:* 800-987-7734. *Website:* http://www.kaplanuniversity.edu/.

Kaplan University, Omaha
Omaha, Nebraska

Freshman Application Contact Kaplan University, Omaha, 5425 North 103rd Street, Omaha, NE 68134. *Phone:* 402-572-8500. *Toll-free phone:* 800-987-7734. *Website:* http://www.kaplanuniversity.edu/.

Little Priest Tribal College
Winnebago, Nebraska

Freshman Application Contact Little Priest Tribal College, PO Box 270, Winnebago, NE 68071. *Phone:* 402-878-2380 Ext. 112. *Website:* http://www.littlepriest.edu/.

Metropolitan Community College
Omaha, Nebraska

- **State and locally supported** 2-year, founded 1974, part of Nebraska Coordinating Commission for Postsecondary Education
- **Urban** 172-acre campus
- **Endowment** $1.4 million
- **Coed,** 17,003 undergraduate students, 42% full-time, 57% women, 43% men

Undergraduates 7,095 full-time, 9,908 part-time. 3% are from out of state; 17% transferred in. *Retention:* 50% of full-time freshmen returned.
Freshmen *Admission:* 4,141 applied, 4,141 admitted, 1,663 enrolled.
Faculty *Total:* 877, 23% full-time, 6% with terminal degrees. *Student/faculty ratio:* 16:1.
Majors Accounting; administrative assistant and secretarial science; architectural engineering technology; automobile/automotive mechanics technology; business administration and management; child development; civil engineering technology; commercial and advertising art; computer programming; construction engineering technology; criminal justice/police science; culinary arts; drafting and design technology; electrical, electronic and communications engineering technology; graphic and printing equipment operation/production; heating, air conditioning, ventilation and refrigeration maintenance technology; heavy equipment maintenance technology; human services; interior design; kindergarten/preschool education; legal administrative assistant/secretary; legal assistant/paralegal; legal studies; liberal arts and sciences/liberal studies; licensed practical/vocational nurse training; mental health counseling; ornamental horticulture; photography; pre-engineering; registered nursing/registered nurse; respiratory care therapy; surgical technology; welding technology.
Academics *Calendar:* quarters. *Degree:* certificates, diplomas, and associate. *Special study options:* academic remediation for entering students, adult/continuing education programs, advanced placement credit, cooperative education, distance learning, English as a second language, independent study, internships, part-time degree program, services for LD students, summer session for credit. *ROTC:* Army (c).
Library Metropolitan Community College plus 2 others.

Student Life *Housing Options:* coed, men-only, women-only, special housing for students with disabilities. Campus housing is university owned. *Campus security:* 24-hour emergency response devices and patrols, late-night transport/escort service, controlled dormitory access, security on duty 9 pm to 6 am. *Student services:* personal/psychological counseling.

Costs (2016–17) *Tuition:* state resident $2655 full-time, $59 per credit hour part-time; nonresident $3983 full-time, $89 per credit hour part-time. Full-time tuition and fees vary according to course load and program. Part-time tuition and fees vary according to course load and program. *Required fees:* $225 full-time, $5 per credit hour part-time. *Room and board:* $2850. *Payment plans:* installment, deferred payment. *Waivers:* senior citizens and employees or children of employees.

Applying *Options:* early admission. *Recommended:* high school transcript. *Application deadlines:* rolling (freshmen), rolling (transfers). *Notification:* continuous (freshmen), continuous (transfers).

Freshman Application Contact Ms. Maria Vazquez, Associate Vice President for Student Affairs, Metropolitan Community College, PO Box 3777, Omaha, NE 69103-0777. *Phone:* 402-457-2430. *Toll-free phone:* 800-228-9553. *Fax:* 402-457-2238. *E-mail:* mvazquez@mccneb.edu. *Website:* http://www.mccneb.edu/.

Mid-Plains Community College
North Platte, Nebraska

- **District-supported** 2-year, founded 1973
- **Small-town** campus
- **Endowment** $5.9 million
- **Coed,** 2,276 undergraduate students, 35% full-time, 60% women, 40% men

Undergraduates 806 full-time, 1,470 part-time. Students come from 31 states and territories; 5 other countries; 13% are from out of state; 2% Black or African American, non-Hispanic/Latino; 8% Hispanic/Latino; 0.7% Asian, non-Hispanic/Latino; 0.2% Native Hawaiian or other Pacific Islander, non-Hispanic/Latino; 0.7% American Indian or Alaska Native, non-Hispanic/Latino; 1% Two or more races, non-Hispanic/Latino; 3% Race/ethnicity unknown; 1% international; 4% transferred in; 20% live on campus.

Freshmen *Admission:* 402 applied, 402 admitted, 497 enrolled.

Faculty *Total:* 305, 22% full-time, 3% with terminal degrees. *Student/faculty ratio:* 9:1.

Majors Administrative assistant and secretarial science; autobody/collision and repair technology; automobile/automotive mechanics technology; building/construction finishing, management, and inspection related; business administration and management; clinical/medical laboratory technology; commercial and advertising art; computer and information sciences; construction engineering technology; dental assisting; diesel mechanics technology; fine arts related; fire science/firefighting; heating, air conditioning, ventilation and refrigeration maintenance technology; liberal arts and sciences/liberal studies; licensed practical/vocational nurse training; registered nursing/registered nurse; transportation and materials moving related; welding technology.

Academics *Calendar:* semesters. *Degree:* certificates, diplomas, and associate. *Special study options:* academic remediation for entering students, accelerated degree program, adult/continuing education programs, advanced placement credit, cooperative education, distance learning, double majors, English as a second language, external degree program, independent study, internships, part-time degree program, services for LD students, summer session for credit.

Library von Riesen Library plus 1 other. *Books:* 17,993 (physical), 51,889 (digital/electronic); *Serial titles:* 50 (physical); *Databases:* 37. Weekly public service hours: 70; students can reserve study rooms.

Student Life *Housing Options:* coed, special housing for students with disabilities. Campus housing is university owned. *Activities and Organizations:* drama/theater group, student-run newspaper, choral group, Student Senate, Phi Theta Kappa, Phi Beta Lambda, Intercollegiate Athletics, MPCC Student Nurses Association, national fraternities, national sororities. *Campus security:* controlled dormitory access, patrols by trained security personnel. *Student services:* personal/psychological counseling.

Athletics Member NJCAA. *Intercollegiate sports:* baseball M(s), basketball M(s)/W(s), golf M(s), softball W(s), volleyball W(s). *Intramural sports:* baseball M, basketball M/W, softball W, volleyball W.

Standardized Tests *Required for some:* ACCUPLACER. *Recommended:* ACT (for admission).

Costs (2016–17) *Tuition:* state resident $2520 full-time, $84 per credit hour part-time; nonresident $3270 full-time, $109 per credit hour part-time. Full-

time tuition and fees vary according to course load, program, and reciprocity agreements. Part-time tuition and fees vary according to course load, program, and reciprocity agreements. *Required fees:* $450 full-time, $15 per credit hour part-time. *Room and board:* $6100. Room and board charges vary according to board plan, housing facility, and location. *Payment plan:* installment. *Waivers:* senior citizens and employees or children of employees.

Financial Aid Of all full-time matriculated undergraduates who enrolled in 2015, 593 applied for aid, 457 were judged to have need, 147 had their need fully met. 30 Federal Work-Study jobs (averaging $1798). In 2015, 71 non-need-based awards were made. *Average percent of need met:* 78%. *Average financial aid package:* $7936. *Average need-based loan:* $2762. *Average need-based gift aid:* $3757. *Average non-need-based aid:* $1205. *Average indebtedness upon graduation:* $12,013.

Applying *Options:* electronic application, deferred entrance. *Required:* high school transcript. *Required for some:* 2 letters of recommendation, interview. *Application deadlines:* rolling (freshmen), rolling (transfers). *Notification:* continuous (freshmen), continuous (transfers).

Freshman Application Contact Sandy Ablard, Admissions Specialist, Mid-Plains Community College, 1101 Halligan Drive, North Platte, NE 69101. *Phone:* 308-535-3609. *Toll-free phone:* 800-658-4308 (in-state); 800-658-4348 (out-of-state). *Fax:* 308-534-5767. *E-mail:* ablards@mpcc.edu. *Website:* http://www.mpcc.edu/.

Myotherapy Institute
Lincoln, Nebraska

Freshman Application Contact Admissions Office, Myotherapy Institute, 4001 Pioneers Woods Drive, Lincoln, NE 68506. *Phone:* 402-421-7410. *Website:* http://www.myotherapy.edu/.

Nebraska College of Technical Agriculture
Curtis, Nebraska

Freshman Application Contact Kevin Martin, Assistant Admissions Coordinator, Nebraska College of Technical Agriculture, 404 East 7th Street, Curtis, NE 69025. *Phone:* 308-367-4124. *Toll-free phone:* 800-3CURTIS. *Website:* http://www.ncta.unl.edu/.

Nebraska Indian Community College
Macy, Nebraska

- **Federally supported** 2-year, founded 1979
- **Rural** 22-acre campus with easy access to Omaha
- **Coed,** 175 undergraduate students, 21% full-time, 67% women, 33% men

Undergraduates 36 full-time, 139 part-time. Students come from 3 states and territories; 11% are from out of state; 6% transferred in.

Freshmen *Admission:* 37 enrolled.

Faculty *Total:* 21, 29% full-time. *Student/faculty ratio:* 7:1.

Majors American Indian/Native American studies; building/construction finishing, management, and inspection related; business administration and management; child-care and support services management; clinical/medical social work.

Academics *Calendar:* semesters. *Degree:* certificates and associate. *Special study options:* academic remediation for entering students, adult/continuing education programs, distance learning, double majors, independent study, internships, part-time degree program, study abroad, summer session for credit.

Library Macy Library plus 1 other. *Books:* 17,555 (physical), 370 (digital/electronic).

Student Life *Housing:* college housing not available. *Activities and Organizations:* Student Senate.

Costs (2016–17) *One-time required fee:* $50. *Tuition:* state resident $4080 full-time, $170 per credit hour part-time; nonresident $4080 full-time, $170 per credit hour part-time. *Payment plan:* installment. *Waivers:* children of alumni, senior citizens, and employees or children of employees.

Applying *Required:* high school transcript, certificate of tribal enrollment if applicable.

Freshman Application Contact Troy Munhofen, Registrar, Nebraska Indian Community College, PO Box 428, Macy, NE 68039. *Phone:* 402-241-5922. *Toll-free phone:* 844-440-NICC. *Fax:* 402-837-4183. *E-mail:* tmunhofen@thenicc.edu. *Website:* http://www.thenicc.edu/.

Northeast Community College
Norfolk, Nebraska

- **State and locally supported** 2-year, founded 1973, part of Nebraska Coordinating Commission for Postsecondary Education
- **Small-town** 202-acre campus
- **Coed,** 5,075 undergraduate students, 42% full-time, 46% women, 54% men

Undergraduates 2,121 full-time, 2,954 part-time. Students come from 12 states and territories; 5% are from out of state; 1% Black or African American, non-Hispanic/Latino; 10% Hispanic/Latino; 0.4% Asian, non-Hispanic/Latino; 1% American Indian or Alaska Native, non-Hispanic/Latino; 2% Two or more races, non-Hispanic/Latino; 4% Race/ethnicity unknown; 1% international; 5% transferred in; 13% live on campus. *Retention:* 70% of full-time freshmen returned.

Freshmen *Admission:* 951 enrolled.

Faculty *Total:* 294, 40% full-time. *Student/faculty ratio:* 17:1.

Majors Accounting; administrative assistant and secretarial science; agribusiness; agriculture; agronomy and crop science; animal sciences; applied horticulture/horticultural business services related; architectural drafting and CAD/CADD; art; athletic training; audiovisual communications technologies related; autobody/collision and repair technology; automobile/automotive mechanics technology; biology/biological sciences; building/construction finishing, management, and inspection related; business administration and management; business/commerce; chemistry; computer and information sciences; computer science; corrections; criminal justice/police science; diesel mechanics technology; dietetics; dramatic/theater arts; early childhood education; education; electrician; electromechanical technology; elementary education; emergency medical technology (EMT paramedic); energy management and systems technology; engineering; English; farm and ranch management; finance; funeral service and mortuary science; general studies; graphic design; health and physical education/fitness; health information/medical records technology; health/medical preparatory programs related; heating, air conditioning, ventilation and refrigeration maintenance technology; human services; kinesiology and exercise science; liberal arts and sciences/liberal studies; library and archives assisting; library and information science; lineworker; mass communication/media; mathematics; medical administrative assistant and medical secretary; medical radiologic technology; music management; music performance; music teacher education; office occupations and clerical services; physical therapy technology; physics; predentistry studies; pre-law studies; premedical studies; prenursing studies; prepharmacy studies; pre-veterinary studies; psychology; registered nursing/registered nurse; respiratory care therapy; secondary education; social sciences; speech communication and rhetoric; surgical technology; veterinary/animal health technology.

Academics *Calendar:* semesters. *Degree:* certificates, diplomas, and associate. *Special study options:* academic remediation for entering students, adult/continuing education programs, advanced placement credit, cooperative education, distance learning, double majors, English as a second language, independent study, internships, off-campus study, part-time degree program, services for LD students, study abroad, summer session for credit.

Library Library Resource Center. *Books:* 20,648 (physical); *Serial titles:* 411 (physical); *Databases:* 70. Weekly public service hours: 78.

Student Life *Housing Options:* coed, special housing for students with disabilities. Campus housing is university owned. *Activities and Organizations:* drama/theater group, student-run newspaper, radio and television station, choral group, Phi Theta Kappa, Farm Bureau Club, Enactus, Christian Student Fellowship, Love Your Melon. *Campus security:* 24-hour emergency response devices and patrols, controlled dormitory access, building walk-throughs and parking lot patrols, door and dorm checks, armed security. *Student services:* health clinic, personal/psychological counseling.

Athletics Member NJCAA. *Intercollegiate sports:* baseball M(s), basketball M(s)/W(s), golf M(s), soccer M(s)/W(s), softball W(s), volleyball W(s). *Intramural sports:* basketball M/W, bowling M/W, football M/W, sand volleyball M/W, softball M/W, table tennis M/W, volleyball M/W.

Costs (2016–17) *Tuition:* state resident $2700 full-time, $90 per credit hour part-time; nonresident $3780 full-time, $126 per credit hour part-time. *Required fees:* $585 full-time, $20 per credit hour part-time. *Room and board:* $8002; room only: $5100. Room and board charges vary according to board plan and housing facility. *Payment plan:* installment. *Waivers:* employees or children of employees.

Financial Aid Of all full-time matriculated undergraduates who enrolled in 2015, 1,658 applied for aid, 1,349 were judged to have need, 193 had their need fully met. 67 Federal Work-Study jobs (averaging $1116). In 2015, 22 non-need-based awards were made. *Average percent of need met:* 67%. *Average financial aid package:* $6470. *Average need-based loan:* $3099. *Average need-based gift aid:* $5086. *Average non-need-based aid:* $743. *Average indebtedness upon graduation:* $11,285.

Applying *Options:* electronic application, early admission. *Required for some:* essay or personal statement, high school transcript, 3 letters of recommendation, interview. *Recommended:* high school transcript. *Application deadlines:* rolling (freshmen), rolling (transfers). *Notification:* continuous (freshmen), continuous (transfers).

Freshmen Application Contact Tiffany Hopper, Admissions Specialist, Northeast Community College, 801 East Benjamin Avenue, PO Box 469, Norfolk, NE 68702-0469. *Phone:* 402-844-7260. *Toll-free phone:* 800-348-9033 Ext. 7260. *E-mail:* admission@northeast.edu. *Website:* http://www.northeast.edu/.

Omaha School of Massage and Healthcare of Herzing University
Omaha, Nebraska

Admissions Office Contact Omaha School of Massage and Healthcare of Herzing University, 9748 Park Drive, Omaha, NE 68127.
Website: http://www.osmhc.com/.

Southeast Community College, Beatrice Campus
Beatrice, Nebraska

Freshman Application Contact Admissions Office, Southeast Community College, Beatrice Campus, 4771 West Scott Road, Beatrice, NE 68310. *Phone:* 402-228-3468. *Toll-free phone:* 800-233-5027. *Fax:* 402-228-2218. *Website:* http://www.southeast.edu/.

Southeast Community College, Lincoln Campus
Lincoln, Nebraska

- **District-supported** 2-year, founded 1973, part of Southeast Community College Area
- **Suburban** 115-acre campus with easy access to Omaha
- **Coed,** 9,262 undergraduate students, 43% full-time, 52% women, 48% men

Undergraduates 3,942 full-time, 5,320 part-time. 7% are from out of state; 6% Black or African American, non-Hispanic/Latino; 8% Hispanic/Latino; 3% Asian, non-Hispanic/Latino; 0.1% Native Hawaiian or other Pacific Islander, non-Hispanic/Latino; 0.7% American Indian or Alaska Native, non-Hispanic/Latino; 4% Two or more races, non-Hispanic/Latino; 0.5% Race/ethnicity unknown.

Freshmen *Admission:* 1,348 enrolled.

Faculty *Total:* 742, 50% full-time. *Student/faculty ratio:* 12:1.

Majors Administrative assistant and secretarial science; automobile/automotive mechanics technology; business administration and management; child-care and support services management; clinical laboratory science/medical technology; clinical/medical laboratory technology; clinical/medical social work; commercial and advertising art; computer and information sciences; criminal justice/safety; drafting and design technology; electrical, electronic and communications engineering technology; emergency medical technology (EMT paramedic); fire science/firefighting; health/healthcare administration; liberal arts and sciences/liberal studies; medical radiologic technology; network and system administration; physical therapy technology; registered nursing/registered nurse; respiratory care therapy; restaurant, culinary, and catering management; surgical technology; welding technology.

Academics *Calendar:* quarters. *Degree:* certificates, diplomas, and associate. *Special study options:* academic remediation for entering students, advanced placement credit, cooperative education, distance learning, English as a second language, independent study, internships, off-campus study, part-time degree program, services for LD students, summer session for credit.

Library Lincoln Campus Learning Resource Center. *Books:* 26,473 (physical), 37,630 (digital/electronic); *Serial titles:* 338 (physical), 97 (digital/electronic); *Databases:* 67. Weekly public service hours: 68.

Student Life *Housing:* college housing not available. *Campus security:* late-night transport/escort service.

Athletics *Intercollegiate sports:* baseball M, basketball M/W, golf M, softball W, volleyball W. *Intramural sports:* basketball M/W, football M, sand volleyball M/W, softball M/W, volleyball M/W.

Standardized Tests *Recommended:* ACT (for admission).

Costs (2017–18) *Tuition:* state resident $2948 full-time, $66 per quarter hour part-time; nonresident $3578 full-time, $80 per quarter hour part-time. Full-time tuition and fees vary according to course load. Part-time tuition and fees vary according to course load. *Required fees:* $90 full-time, $2 per quarter hour part-time. *Waivers:* employees or children of employees.

Applying *Options:* electronic application, early admission, deferred entrance. *Required:* high school transcript. *Application deadlines:* rolling (freshmen), rolling (transfers).
Freshman Application Contact Admissions Office, Southeast Community College, Lincoln Campus, 8800 O Street, Lincoln, NE 68520. *Phone:* 402-471-3333. *Toll-free phone:* 800-642-4075. *Fax:* 402-437-2404.
E-mail: admissions@southeast.edu.
Website: http://www.southeast.edu/.

Southeast Community College, Milford Campus
Milford, Nebraska

- **District-supported** 2-year, founded 1941, part of Southeast Community College System
- **Small-town** 50-acre campus with easy access to Omaha
- **Coed, primarily men,** 9,262 undergraduate students, 43% full-time, 52% women, 48% men

Undergraduates 3,942 full-time, 5,320 part-time. 7% are from out of state; 6% Black or African American, non-Hispanic/Latino; 8% Hispanic/Latino; 3% Asian, non-Hispanic/Latino; 0.1% Native Hawaiian or other Pacific Islander, non-Hispanic/Latino; 0.7% American Indian or Alaska Native, non-Hispanic/Latino; 4% Two or more races, non-Hispanic/Latino; 0.5% Race/ethnicity unknown.
Freshmen *Admission:* 1,348 enrolled.
Faculty *Total:* 742, 50% full-time. *Student/faculty ratio:* 12:1.
Majors Architectural engineering technology; autobody/collision and repair technology; automobile/automotive mechanics technology; building/construction finishing, management, and inspection related; business administration and management; civil engineering technology; diesel mechanics technology; electrical, electronic and communications engineering technology; energy management and systems technology; heating, air conditioning, ventilation and refrigeration maintenance technology; machine tool technology; manufacturing engineering; network and system administration; quality control technology.
Academics *Calendar:* quarters. *Degree:* diplomas and associate. *Special study options:* academic remediation for entering students, advanced placement credit, cooperative education, distance learning, internships, part-time degree program, services for LD students, summer session for credit.
Library Milford Campus Learning Resource Center. *Books:* 26,473 (physical), 37,630 (digital/electronic); *Serial titles:* 338 (physical), 97 (digital/electronic); *Databases:* 67. Weekly public service hours: 51; students can reserve study rooms.
Student Life *Housing Options:* men-only, women-only, special housing for students with disabilities. Campus housing is university owned. *Campus security:* late-night transport/escort service, controlled dormitory access.
Athletics Member NJCAA. *Intercollegiate sports:* baseball M, basketball M/W, golf M, softball W, volleyball W. *Intramural sports:* basketball M/W, football M, sand volleyball M/W, softball M/W, volleyball M/W.
Standardized Tests *Recommended:* ACT (for admission).
Costs (2017–18) *Tuition:* state resident $2948 full-time, $66 per quarter hour part-time; nonresident $3578 full-time, $80 per quarter hour part-time. Full-time tuition and fees vary according to course load. Part-time tuition and fees vary according to course load. *Required fees:* $90 full-time, $2 per quarter hour part-time. *Room and board:* $6150. Room and board charges vary according to board plan, gender, housing facility, location, and student level. *Waivers:* employees or children of employees.
Applying *Options:* electronic application, early admission, deferred entrance. *Required:* high school transcript. *Application deadlines:* rolling (freshmen), rolling (transfers). *Notification:* continuous (freshmen), continuous (transfers).
Freshman Application Contact Admissions Office, Southeast Community College, Milford Campus, 600 State Street, Milford, NE 68405. *Phone:* 402-761-2131. *Toll-free phone:* 800-933-7223. *Fax:* 402-761-2324.
E-mail: admissions@southeast.edu.
Website: http://www.southeast.edu/.

Universal College of Healing Arts
Omaha, Nebraska

Admissions Office Contact Universal College of Healing Arts, 8702 North 30th Street, Omaha, NE 68112-1810. *Website:* http://www.ucha.edu/.

Western Nebraska Community College
Sidney, Nebraska

Director of Admissions Mr. Troy Archuleta, Admissions and Recruitment Director, Western Nebraska Community College, 371 College Drive, Sidney,

NE 69162. *Phone:* 308-635-6015. *Toll-free phone:* 800-222-9682.
E-mail: rhovey@wncc.net. *Website:* http://www.wncc.net/.

NEVADA

Brightwood College, Las Vegas Campus
Las Vegas, Nevada

Freshman Application Contact Admissions Office, Brightwood College, Las Vegas Campus, 3535 West Sahara Avenue, Las Vegas, NV 89102. *Phone:* 702-368-2338. *Toll-free phone:* 866-543-0208.
Website: http://www.brightwood.edu/.

Career College of Northern Nevada
Sparks, Nevada

Freshman Application Contact Ms. Laura Goldhammer, Director of Admissions, Career College of Northern Nevada, 1421 Pullman Drive, Sparks, NV 89434. *Phone:* 775-856-2266 Ext. 11. *Fax:* 775-856-0935.
E-mail: lgoldhammer@ccnn4u.com. *Website:* http://www.ccnn.edu/.

Carrington College–Las Vegas
Las Vegas, Nevada

- **Proprietary** 2-year, part of Carrington Colleges Group, Inc.
- **Coed**

Undergraduates 298 full-time, 72 part-time. 2% are from out of state; 18% Black or African American, non-Hispanic/Latino; 24% Hispanic/Latino; 21% Asian, non-Hispanic/Latino; 5% Native Hawaiian or other Pacific Islander, non-Hispanic/Latino; 0.8% American Indian or Alaska Native, non-Hispanic/Latino; 2% Two or more races, non-Hispanic/Latino; 3% Race/ethnicity unknown; 22% transferred in.
Faculty *Student/faculty ratio:* 32:1.
Academics *Degree:* certificates and associate.
Costs (2016–17) *Tuition:* $44,582 per degree program part-time.
Applying *Required:* essay or personal statement, high school transcript, interview, institutional entrance test.
Freshman Application Contact Carrington College–Las Vegas, 5740 South Eastern Avenue, Suite 140, Las Vegas, NV 89119.
Website: http://carrington.edu/.

Carrington College–Reno
Reno, Nevada

- **Proprietary** 2-year, part of Carrington Colleges Group, Inc.
- **Coed**

Undergraduates 257 full-time, 70 part-time. 11% are from out of state; 0.6% Black or African American, non-Hispanic/Latino; 18% Hispanic/Latino; 8% Asian, non-Hispanic/Latino; 1% Native Hawaiian or other Pacific Islander, non-Hispanic/Latino; 0.3% American Indian or Alaska Native, non-Hispanic/Latino; 1% Two or more races, non-Hispanic/Latino; 0.9% Race/ethnicity unknown; 19% transferred in.
Faculty *Student/faculty ratio:* 15:1.
Academics *Degree:* certificates and associate.
Costs (2016–17) *Tuition:* $50,599 per degree program part-time. Full-time tuition and fees vary according to program. Part-time tuition and fees vary according to program.
Applying *Required:* essay or personal statement, high school transcript, interview, institutional entrance test.
Freshman Application Contact Carrington College–Reno, 5580 Kietzke Lane, Reno, NV 89511. *Phone:* 775-335-2900.
Website: http://carrington.edu/.

College of Southern Nevada
Las Vegas, Nevada

Freshman Application Contact Admissions and Records, College of Southern Nevada, 6375 West Charleston Boulevard, Las Vegas, NV 89146. *Phone:* 702-651-4060. *Website:* http://www.csn.edu/.

Everest College
Henderson, Nevada

Admissions Office Contact Everest College, 170 North Stephanie Street, Henderson, NV 89074. *Toll-free phone:* 888-741-4270. *Website:* http://www.everest.edu/.

Great Basin College
Elko, Nevada

- **State-supported** primarily 2-year, founded 1967, part of Nevada System of Higher Education
- **Small-town** 45-acre campus
- **Endowment** $6.7 million
- **Coed**, 3,362 undergraduate students, 27% full-time, 65% women, 35% men

Undergraduates 903 full-time, 2,459 part-time. Students come from 28 states and territories; 26 other countries; 6% are from out of state; 2% Black or African American, non-Hispanic/Latino; 19% Hispanic/Latino; 2% Asian, non-Hispanic/Latino; 0.6% Native Hawaiian or other Pacific Islander, non-Hispanic/Latino; 3% American Indian or Alaska Native, non-Hispanic/Latino; 3% Two or more races, non-Hispanic/Latino; 6% Race/ethnicity unknown; 7% transferred in; 4% live on campus. *Retention:* 65% of full-time freshmen returned.

Freshmen *Admission:* 804 applied, 490 admitted, 411 enrolled.

Majors Accounting technology and bookkeeping; biology/biological sciences; business administration and management; business/commerce; computer and information sciences; computer graphics; computer/information technology services administration related; computer systems networking and telecommunications; criminal justice/safety; data processing and data processing technology; diesel mechanics technology; early childhood education; electrical, electronic and communications engineering technology; elementary education; emergency medical technology (EMT paramedic); English; general studies; geological and earth sciences/geosciences related; human services; industrial technology; instrumentation technology; interdisciplinary studies; liberal arts and sciences/liberal studies; management science; natural resources management and policy related; office occupations and clerical services; operations management; radiologic technology/science; registered nursing/registered nurse; science technologies; secondary education; social sciences; social work; surveying technology; welding technology.

Academics *Calendar:* semesters. *Degrees:* certificates, associate, bachelor's, and postbachelor's certificates. *Special study options:* academic remediation for entering students, accelerated degree program, adult/continuing education programs, cooperative education, distance learning, double majors, English as a second language, external degree program, independent study, off-campus study, part-time degree program, services for LD students, summer session for credit.

Library Learning Resource Center. *Books:* 94,193 (physical), 250,157 (digital/electronic); *Serial titles:* 2,946 (physical), 230,872 (digital/electronic); *Databases:* 80. Weekly public service hours: 46; students can reserve study rooms.

Student Life *Housing Options:* coed, special housing for students with disabilities. Campus housing is university owned. *Campus security:* late-night transport/escort service, evening patrols by trained security personnel. *Student services:* personal/psychological counseling.

Costs (2017–18) *Tuition:* state resident $2850 full-time, $1330 per year part-time; nonresident $9628 full-time, $2383 per year part-time. *Required fees:* $165 full-time, $6 per unit part-time. *Room and board:* room only: $3150. Room and board charges vary according to housing facility. *Payment plan:* installment. *Waivers:* employees or children of employees.

Financial Aid Of all full-time matriculated undergraduates who enrolled in 2016, 425 applied for aid, 383 were judged to have need, 17 had their need fully met. In 2016, 90 non-need-based awards were made. *Average financial aid package:* $2220. *Average need-based loan:* $3201. *Average need-based gift aid:* $2885. *Average non-need-based aid:* $992.

Applying *Options:* electronic application, early admission, deferred entrance. *Application fee:* $10. *Application deadlines:* rolling (freshmen), rolling (transfers). *Notification:* continuous (freshmen), continuous (transfers).

Freshman Application Contact Ms. Jan King, Director of Admissions and Registrar, Great Basin College, 1500 College Parkway, Elko, NV 89801. *Phone:* 775-753-2102. *E-mail:* jan.king@gbcnv.edu. *Website:* http://www.gbcnv.edu/.

Northwest Career College
Las Vegas, Nevada

Admissions Office Contact Northwest Career College, 7398 Smoke Ranch Road, Suite 100, Las Vegas, NV 89128. *Website:* http://www.northwestcareercollege.edu/.

Pima Medical Institute
Las Vegas, Nevada

Freshman Application Contact Admissions Office, Pima Medical Institute, 3333 East Flamingo Road, Las Vegas, NV 89121. *Phone:* 702-458-9650 Ext. 202. *Toll-free phone:* 800-477-PIMA. *Website:* http://www.pmi.edu/.

Truckee Meadows Community College
Reno, Nevada

- **State-supported** primarily 2-year, founded 1971, part of Nevada System of Higher Education
- **Suburban** 63-acre campus
- **Endowment** $9.4 million
- **Coed**, 10,873 undergraduate students, 26% full-time, 54% women, 46% men

Undergraduates 2,843 full-time, 8,030 part-time. Students come from 24 states and territories; 19 other countries; 7% are from out of state; 2% Black or African American, non-Hispanic/Latino; 27% Hispanic/Latino; 6% Asian, non-Hispanic/Latino; 0.1% Native Hawaiian or other Pacific Islander, non-Hispanic/Latino; 1% American Indian or Alaska Native, non-Hispanic/Latino; 4% Two or more races, non-Hispanic/Latino; 2% Race/ethnicity unknown; 0.4% international; 6% transferred in. *Retention:* 63% of full-time freshmen returned.

Freshmen *Admission:* 2,012 applied, 2,012 admitted, 1,485 enrolled.

Faculty *Total:* 530, 29% full-time. *Student/faculty ratio:* 21:1.

Majors Anthropology; architectural drafting and CAD/CADD; architecture; automobile/automotive mechanics technology; biology/biological sciences; business/commerce; chemistry; civil engineering; commercial and advertising art; computer programming (specific applications); computer systems networking and telecommunications; cooking and related culinary arts; criminal justice/police science; criminal justice/safety; crisis/emergency/disaster management; dental assisting; dental hygiene; diesel mechanics technology; dietetics; drafting and design technology; elementary education; energy management and systems technology; engineering; engineering technologies and engineering related; English; entrepreneurial and small business operations; environmental science; fine arts related; fire prevention and safety technology; foods, nutrition, and wellness; general studies; geology/earth science; heating, air conditioning, ventilation and refrigeration maintenance technology; history; kindergarten/preschool education; landscape architecture; legal assistant/paralegal; liberal arts and sciences/liberal studies; logistics, materials, and supply chain management; management information systems and services related; manufacturing engineering technology; mathematics; medical radiologic technology; mental health counseling; music; music performance; natural resources/conservation; philosophy; physics; psychology; registered nursing/registered nurse; science, technology and society; veterinary/animal health technology; welding technology.

Academics *Calendar:* semesters. *Degrees:* certificates, associate, and bachelor's. *Special study options:* academic remediation for entering students, accelerated degree program, adult/continuing education programs, advanced placement credit, cooperative education, distance learning, double majors, English as a second language, independent study, internships, part-time degree program, services for LD students, summer session for credit. *ROTC:* Army (c).

Library Elizabeth Sturm Library.

Student Life *Housing:* college housing not available. *Activities and Organizations:* drama/theater group, student-run newspaper, Entrepreneurship Club, International Club, Phi Theta Kappa, Student Government Association, Student Media and Broadcasting Club. *Campus security:* 24-hour emergency response devices and patrols, late-night transport/escort service. *Student services:* personal/psychological counseling.

Costs (2016–17) *Tuition:* state resident $3030 full-time, $92 per credit hour part-time; nonresident $9675 full-time, $192 per credit hour part-time. Full-time tuition and fees vary according to course load, degree level, and program. Part-time tuition and fees vary according to course load, degree level, and program. *Required fees:* $165 full-time, $9 per credit hour part-time. *Payment plan:* installment. *Waivers:* employees or children of employees.

Financial Aid Of all full-time matriculated undergraduates who enrolled in 2015, 126 Federal Work-Study jobs (averaging $5000). 368 state and other part-time jobs (averaging $5000).

Applying *Options:* electronic application, early admission, early decision. *Application fee:* $10. *Application deadlines:* rolling (freshmen), rolling (out-of-state freshmen), rolling (transfers). *Notification:* continuous (freshmen), continuous (out-of-state freshmen), continuous (transfers).

Freshman Application Contact Truckee Meadows Community College, 7000 Dandini Boulevard, Reno, NV 89512-3901. *Phone:* 775-673-7240. *Website:* http://www.tmcc.edu/.

Western Nevada College
Carson City, Nevada

- **State-supported** primarily 2-year, founded 1971, part of Nevada System of Higher Education
- **Small-town** 200-acre campus
- **Endowment** $250,000
- **Coed,** 3,567 undergraduate students, 35% full-time, 55% women, 45% men

Undergraduates 1,231 full-time, 2,336 part-time. Students come from 6 states and territories; 21 other countries; 3% are from out of state; 2% Black or African American, non-Hispanic/Latino; 22% Hispanic/Latino; 2% Asian, non-Hispanic/Latino; 0.8% Native Hawaiian or other Pacific Islander, non-Hispanic/Latino; 2% American Indian or Alaska Native, non-Hispanic/Latino; 3% Two or more races, non-Hispanic/Latino; 4% Race/ethnicity unknown; 0.3% international; 6% transferred in. *Retention:* 55% of full-time freshmen returned.
Freshmen *Admission:* 804 applied, 652 admitted, 652 enrolled.
Faculty *Total:* 241, 22% full-time. *Student/faculty ratio:* 18:1.
Majors Accounting; automobile/automotive mechanics technology; building construction technology; business administration and management; business/commerce; commercial and advertising art; computer and information sciences; construction management; criminal justice/law enforcement administration; deaf studies; general studies; industrial technology; liberal arts and sciences/liberal studies; machine tool technology; management information systems; manufacturing engineering technology; physical sciences; registered nursing/registered nurse; welding technology.
Academics *Calendar:* semesters. *Degrees:* certificates, associate, and bachelor's. *Special study options:* academic remediation for entering students, adult/continuing education programs, advanced placement credit, cooperative education, distance learning, double majors, English as a second language, honors programs, independent study, internships, part-time degree program, services for LD students, summer session for credit.
Library Western Nevada College Library and Media Services plus 1 other. *Books:* 35,923 (physical), 4,544 (digital/electronic); *Serial titles:* 2,725 (physical); *Databases:* 33. Weekly public service hours: 61; students can reserve study rooms.
Student Life *Housing:* college housing not available. *Activities and Organizations:* drama/theater group, choral group, Associated Students of Western Nevada, Soccer Club, Veterans Club, National Student Nurses Association, American Sign Language Club. *Campus security:* late-night transport/escort service. *Student services:* personal/psychological counseling.
Athletics *Intramural sports:* soccer M(c)/W(c).
Costs (2017–18) *Tuition:* state resident $3015 full-time, $1407 per credit part-time; nonresident $9793 full-time, $2460 per credit part-time. Full-time tuition and fees vary according to degree level. Part-time tuition and fees vary according to degree level. *Payment plans:* tuition prepayment, installment. *Waivers:* employees or children of employees.
Financial Aid Of all full-time matriculated undergraduates who enrolled in 2016, 445 applied for aid, 413 were judged to have need, 8 had their need fully met. In 2016, 52 non-need-based awards were made. *Average financial aid package:* $2308. *Average need-based loan:* $2450. *Average need-based gift aid:* $2607. *Average non-need-based aid:* $627.
Applying *Options:* electronic application, early admission. *Application fee:* $15. *Required for some:* high school transcript. *Recommended:* high school transcript. *Application deadlines:* rolling (freshmen), rolling (transfers).
Freshman Application Contact Admissions and Records, Western Nevada College, 2201 West College Parkway, Carson City, NV 89703. *Phone:* 775-445-2377. *Fax:* 775-445-3147. *E-mail:* wncc_aro@wncc.edu. *Website:* http://www.wnc.edu/.

NEW HAMPSHIRE

Great Bay Community College
Portsmouth, New Hampshire

Freshman Application Contact Mr. Matt Thornton, Admissions Coordinator, Great Bay Community College, 320 Corporate Drive, Portsmouth, NH 03801. *Phone:* 603-427-7605. *Toll-free phone:* 800-522-1194. *E-mail:* askgreatbay@ccsnh.edu. *Website:* http://www.greatbay.edu/.

Lakes Region Community College
Laconia, New Hampshire

Freshman Application Contact Ms. Kathy Plummer, Admissions, Lakes Region Community College, Admissions Office, 379 Belmont Road, Laconia, NH 03246. *Phone:* 603-524-3207 Ext. 6410. *Toll-free phone:* 800-357-2992. *E-mail:* lrccinfo@ccsnh.edu. *Website:* http://www.lrcc.edu/.

Manchester Community College
Manchester, New Hampshire

Freshman Application Contact Ms. Jacquie Poirier, Coordinator of Admissions, Manchester Community College, 1066 Front Street, Manchester, NH 03102-8518. *Phone:* 603-668-6706 Ext. 283. *Toll-free phone:* 800-924-3445. *E-mail:* jpoirier@nhctc.edu. *Website:* http://www.mccnh.edu/.

Nashua Community College
Nashua, New Hampshire

Freshman Application Contact Ms. Patricia Goodman, Vice President of Student Services, Nashua Community College, Nashua, NH 03063. *Phone:* 603-882-6923 Ext. 1529. *Fax:* 603-882-8690. *E-mail:* pgoodman@ccsnh.edu. *Website:* http://www.nashuacc.edu/.

NHTI, Concord's Community College
Concord, New Hampshire

- **State-supported** 2-year, founded 1964, part of Community College System of New Hampshire
- **Small-town** 225-acre campus with easy access to Boston
- **Coed,** 3,700 undergraduate students

Undergraduates 23% live on campus.
Freshmen *Average high school GPA:* 2.5.
Faculty *Total:* 109, 9% with terminal degrees. *Student/faculty ratio:* 15:1.
Majors Accounting; animation, interactive technology, video graphics and special effects; architectural engineering technology; business administration and management; computer and information sciences; computer engineering technology; computer programming (specific applications); computer systems networking and telecommunications; criminal justice/law enforcement administration; dental assisting; dental hygiene; diagnostic medical sonography and ultrasound technology; electrical, electronic and communications engineering technology; emergency medical technology (EMT paramedic); engineering technology; general studies; hotel/motel administration; human resources management; human services; kindergarten/preschool education; legal assistant/paralegal; liberal arts and sciences/liberal studies; marketing/marketing management; mechanical engineering/mechanical technology; mental health counseling; real estate; registered nursing/registered nurse; sport and fitness administration/management; substance abuse/addiction counseling; teacher assistant/aide; tourism and travel services management; visual and performing arts.
Academics *Calendar:* semesters. *Degree:* certificates, diplomas, and associate. *Special study options:* academic remediation for entering students, adult/continuing education programs, advanced placement credit, distance learning, double majors, English as a second language, external degree program, part-time degree program, services for LD students, summer session for credit.
Library Main Library plus 1 other.
Student Life *Housing Options:* coed. Campus housing is university owned. *Activities and Organizations:* drama/theater group, Phi Theta Kappa, Student Senate, Student Nurses Association, Criminal Justice Club, Outing Club. *Campus security:* 24-hour emergency response devices and patrols, late-night transport/escort service, controlled dormitory access, cameras in vital locations. *Student services:* health clinic, personal/psychological counseling.
Athletics *Intercollegiate sports:* baseball M, basketball M/W, gymnastics M/W, soccer M/W, softball W, volleyball M/W. *Intramural sports:* softball W, volleyball M/W.
Standardized Tests *Required for some:* National League of Nursing Exam. *Recommended:* SAT or ACT (for admission).
Applying *Options:* electronic application. *Application fee:* $20. *Required:* high school transcript. *Required for some:* essay or personal statement, interview. *Recommended:* minimum 2.0 GPA. *Application deadlines:* rolling (freshmen), rolling (transfers). *Notification:* continuous (freshmen), continuous (transfers).
Freshman Application Contact NHTI, Concord's Community College, 31 College Drive, Concord, NH 03301-7412. *Toll-free phone:* 800-247-0179. *Website:* http://www.nhti.edu/.

River Valley Community College

Claremont, New Hampshire

- **State-supported** 2-year, part of Community College System of New Hampshire
- **Rural** 80-acre campus
- **Coed**
- 77% of applicants were admitted

Undergraduates 236 full-time, 773 part-time. 6% are from out of state; 0.7% Black or African American, non-Hispanic/Latino; 2% Hispanic/Latino; 2% Asian, non-Hispanic/Latino; 1% American Indian or Alaska Native, non-Hispanic/Latino; 0.8% Two or more races, non-Hispanic/Latino; 9% Race/ethnicity unknown.

Faculty *Student/faculty ratio:* 6:1.

Academics *Calendar:* semesters. *Degree:* certificates, diplomas, and associate. *Special study options:* academic remediation for entering students, distance learning, double majors, independent study, part-time degree program, services for LD students, summer session for credit.

Library Charles Puksta Library plus 1 other.

Student Life *Campus security:* 24-hour emergency response devices, security personnel on campus 6:30 am to 10 pm.

Financial Aid Of all full-time matriculated undergraduates who enrolled in 2014, 18 Federal Work-Study jobs (averaging $1450).

Applying *Options:* electronic application. *Application fee:* $20. *Required:* high school transcript. *Required for some:* 2 letters of recommendation, interview.

Freshman Application Contact River Valley Community College, 1 College Place, Claremont, NH 03743. *Phone:* 603-542-7744 Ext. 5323. *Toll-free phone:* 800-837-0658. *Website:* http://www.rivervalley.edu/.

St. Joseph School of Nursing

Nashua, New Hampshire

- **Independent** 2-year, founded 1964, affiliated with Roman Catholic Church
- **Urban** campus with easy access to Boston, Portland
- **Coed**

Undergraduates 63 full-time, 81 part-time. Students come from 3 states and territories; 9 other countries; 27% are from out of state; 24% transferred in.

Academics *Calendar:* semesters. *Degree:* associate. *Special study options:* academic remediation for entering students, advanced placement credit, services for LD students, summer session for credit.

Student Life *Campus security:* 24-hour emergency response devices and patrols, late-night transport/escort service.

Costs (2016–17) *Tuition:* $10,770 full-time, $870 per course part-time. Full-time tuition and fees vary according to course load and program. Part-time tuition and fees vary according to course load and program. *Required fees:* $759 full-time, $33 per credit part-time.

Applying *Options:* electronic application. *Application fee:* $50. *Required:* essay or personal statement, high school transcript, minimum 2.5 GPA, 3 letters of recommendation, interview.

Freshman Application Contact Mrs. L. Nadeau, Admissions, St. Joseph School of Nursing, 5 Woodward Avenue, Nashua, NH 03060. *Toll-free phone:* 800-370-3169. *Website:* http://www.sjhacademiccenter.org/.

White Mountains Community College

Berlin, New Hampshire

- **State-supported** 2-year, founded 1966, part of Community College System of New Hampshire
- **Rural** 325-acre campus
- **Coed,** 762 undergraduate students, 40% full-time, 65% women, 35% men

Undergraduates 306 full-time, 456 part-time. Students come from 5 states and territories; 5% are from out of state; 0.3% Black or African American, non-Hispanic/Latino; 1% Hispanic/Latino; 0.4% Asian, non-Hispanic/Latino; 0.8% Two or more races, non-Hispanic/Latino; 11% Race/ethnicity unknown; 9% transferred in.

Freshmen *Admission:* 206 enrolled.

Faculty *Total:* 129, 16% full-time, 8% with terminal degrees.

Majors Accounting; automobile/automotive mechanics technology; baking and pastry arts; business administration and management; computer and information sciences; criminal justice/safety; culinary arts; diesel mechanics technology; early childhood education; education; environmental studies; general studies; health services/allied health/health sciences; human services; liberal arts and sciences/liberal studies; medical/clinical assistant; medical office assistant; office management; registered nursing/registered nurse; resort management; welding technology.

Academics *Calendar:* semesters. *Degree:* certificates, diplomas, and associate. *Special study options:* academic remediation for entering students, adult/continuing education programs, advanced placement credit, cooperative education, distance learning, double majors, external degree program, independent study, internships, part-time degree program, services for LD students, student-designed majors, summer session for credit.

Library Fortier Library. *Books:* 17,808 (physical); *Serial titles:* 35 (physical); *Databases:* 48. Weekly public service hours: 55; students can reserve study rooms.

Student Life *Housing:* college housing not available. *Activities and Organizations:* Student Senate. *Campus security:* 24-hour emergency response devices, late-night transport/escort service. *Student services:* personal/psychological counseling.

Standardized Tests *Required for some:* TEAS for associate's degree nursing program.

Costs (2016–17) *One-time required fee:* $65. *Tuition:* state resident $6000 full-time, $200 per credit part-time; nonresident $13,650 full-time, $455 per credit part-time. Full-time tuition and fees vary according to class time, location, and program. Part-time tuition and fees vary according to class time, location, and program. *Required fees:* $510 full-time, $17 per credit part-time. *Payment plans:* installment, deferred payment. *Waivers:* senior citizens and employees or children of employees.

Applying *Required:* high school transcript.

Freshman Application Contact Ms. Kristen Miller, Admissions Counselor, White Mountains Community College, 2020 Riverside Drive, Berlin, NH 03570. *Phone:* 603-342-3002. *Toll-free phone:* 800-445-4525. *Fax:* 603-752-6335. *E-mail:* kmiller@ccsnh.edu. *Website:* http://www.wmcc.edu/.

NEW JERSEY

Assumption College for Sisters

Denville, New Jersey

Freshman Application Contact Sr. Gerardine Tantsits, Academic Dean/Registrar, Assumption College for Sisters, 350 Bernardsville Road, Mendham, NJ 07945-2923. *Phone:* 973-543-6528 Ext. 228. *Fax:* 973-543-1738. *E-mail:* deanregistrar@acs350.org. *Website:* http://www.acs350.org/.

Atlantic Cape Community College

Mays Landing, New Jersey

Freshman Application Contact Mrs. Linda McLeod, Assistant Director, Admissions and College Recruitment, Atlantic Cape Community College, 5100 Black Horse Pike, Mays Landing, NJ 08330-2699. *Phone:* 609-343-5009. *Fax:* 609-343-4921. *E-mail:* accadmit@atlantic.edu. *Website:* http://www.atlantic.edu/.

Bergen Community College

Paramus, New Jersey

Freshman Application Contact Admissions Office, Bergen Community College, 400 Paramus Road, Paramus, NJ 07652-1595. *Phone:* 201-447-7195. *E-mail:* admsoffice@bergen.edu. *Website:* http://www.bergen.edu/.

Brookdale Community College

Lincroft, New Jersey

Director of Admissions Ms. Kim Toomey, Registrar, Brookdale Community College, 765 Newman Springs Road, Lincroft, NJ 07738-1597. *Phone:* 732-224-2268. *Website:* http://www.brookdalecc.edu/.

Camden County College

Blackwood, New Jersey

- **State and locally supported** 2-year, founded 1967, part of New Jersey Office of the Secretary of Higher Education
- **Suburban** 320-acre campus with easy access to Philadelphia
- **Coed,** 11,263 undergraduate students, 50% full-time, 57% women, 43% men

Undergraduates 5,646 full-time, 5,617 part-time. 20% Black or African American, non-Hispanic/Latino; 16% Hispanic/Latino; 5% Asian, non-Hispanic/Latino; 0.2% Native Hawaiian or other Pacific Islander, non-Hispanic/Latino; 1% American Indian or Alaska Native, non-Hispanic/Latino; 0.9% Two or more races, non-Hispanic/Latino; 5% Race/ethnicity unknown; 2% international; 11% transferred in.

Freshmen *Admission:* 9,430 applied, 2,073 enrolled.

Faculty *Total:* 678, 19% full-time.

Majors Accounting technology and bookkeeping; administrative assistant and secretarial science; automotive engineering technology; biology/biotechnology laboratory technician; business administration and management; cinematography and film/video production; clinical/medical laboratory technology; computer and information sciences; criminal justice/police science; dental assisting; dental hygiene; desktop publishing and digital imaging design; dietetics; dietetic technology; drafting and design technology; early childhood education; education (multiple levels); electrical, electronic and communications engineering technology; electromechanical technology; emergency medical technology (EMT paramedic); engineering science; engineering technologies and engineering related; fine/studio arts; fire prevention and safety technology; fire services administration; health information/medical records administration; health services/allied health/health sciences; industrial production technologies related; legal assistant/paralegal; liberal arts and sciences/liberal studies; management information systems; marketing/marketing management; massage therapy; mechanical engineering/mechanical technology; mechanical engineering technologies related; opticianry; radio and television broadcasting technology; registered nursing/registered nurse; rehabilitation and therapeutic professions related; sign language interpretation and translation; social work; speech communication and rhetoric; sport and fitness administration/management; substance abuse/addiction counseling; veterinary/animal health technology.

Academics *Calendar:* semesters. *Degree:* certificates and associate. *Special study options:* academic remediation for entering students, adult/continuing education programs, advanced placement credit, cooperative education, distance learning, double majors, English as a second language, external degree program, freshman honors college, honors programs, independent study, internships, off-campus study, part-time degree program, services for LD students, study abroad, summer session for credit.

Library Learning Resource Center.

Student Life *Housing:* college housing not available. *Activities and Organizations:* drama/theater group, student-run newspaper, radio station, choral group. *Campus security:* 24-hour emergency response devices, late-night transport/escort service. *Student services:* health clinic.

Athletics Member NJCAA. *Intercollegiate sports:* baseball M, basketball M/W, golf M, soccer M/W, softball W. *Intramural sports:* baseball M, basketball M/W, soccer M/W, softball W.

Costs (2017–18) *Tuition:* area resident $3210 full-time, $107 per credit part-time; state resident $3330 full-time, $111 per credit part-time; nonresident $3330 full-time, $111 per credit part-time. Full-time tuition and fees vary according to course load and program. Part-time tuition and fees vary according to course load and program. *Required fees:* $1110 full-time, $37 per credit part-time. *Payment plans:* installment, deferred payment. *Waivers:* employees or children of employees.

Financial Aid Of all full-time matriculated undergraduates who enrolled in 2015, 117 Federal Work-Study jobs (averaging $1126).

Applying *Options:* electronic application, early admission. *Required for some:* high school transcript. *Application deadlines:* rolling (freshmen), rolling (transfers).

Freshman Application Contact Donald Delaney, Director of Program Outreach, Camden County College, PO Box 200, Blackwood, NJ 08012-0200. *Phone:* 856-227-7200 Ext. 4660. *Fax:* 856-374-4916. *E-mail:* ddelaney@camdencc.edu. *Website:* http://www.camdencc.edu/.

County College of Morris
Randolph, New Jersey

- **County-supported** 2-year, founded 1966
- **Suburban** 218-acre campus with easy access to New York City
- **Endowment** $4.4 million
- **Coed,** 8,067 undergraduate students, 47% full-time, 49% women, 51% men

Undergraduates 3,821 full-time, 4,246 part-time. Students come from 9 states and territories; 0.2% are from out of state; 5% Black or African American, non-Hispanic/Latino; 20% Hispanic/Latino; 5% Asian, non-Hispanic/Latino; 0.1% Native Hawaiian or other Pacific Islander, non-Hispanic/Latino; 0.3% American Indian or Alaska Native, non-Hispanic/Latino; 2% Two or more races, non-Hispanic/Latino; 7% Race/ethnicity unknown; 3% international; 6% transferred in. *Retention:* 74% of full-time freshmen returned.

Freshmen *Admission:* 4,170 applied, 2,562 admitted, 1,703 enrolled.

Majors Agricultural business and management; biology/biotechnology laboratory technician; business administration and management; business, management, and marketing related; chemical technology; communication and media related; computer science; criminal justice/police science; culinary arts; design and applied arts related; electrical, electronic and communications engineering technology; engineering science; engineering technologies and engineering related; fine arts related; fire prevention and safety technology; graphic design; hospitality administration; information technology; kindergarten/preschool education; kinesiology and exercise science; liberal arts and sciences/liberal studies; management information systems; mechanical engineering/mechanical technology; multi/interdisciplinary studies related; music related; occupational therapist assistant; photography; public administration; public health; radiologic technology/science; registered nursing/registered nurse; respiratory care therapy; telecommunications technology; web page, digital/multimedia and information resources design.

Academics *Calendar:* semesters. *Degree:* certificates and associate. *Special study options:* academic remediation for entering students, accelerated degree program, advanced placement credit, cooperative education, distance learning, double majors, English as a second language, independent study, internships, services for LD students, study abroad, summer session for credit.

Library Learning Resource Center plus 1 other. *Books:* 40,675 (physical), 3,527 (digital/electronic); *Serial titles:* 83 (physical), 3 (digital/electronic); *Databases:* 78. Weekly public service hours: 68.

Student Life *Housing:* college housing not available. *Activities and Organizations:* drama/theater group, student-run newspaper, choral group, Phi Theta Kappa Honor Society, EOF Student Alliance, Student Nurses Association, New Social Engine, Volunteer Club. *Campus security:* 24-hour emergency response devices and patrols, late-night transport/escort service. *Student services:* health clinic, personal/psychological counseling, women's center.

Athletics Member NJCAA. *Intercollegiate sports:* baseball M(s), basketball M(s)/W(s), golf M, lacrosse M, soccer M/W(s), softball W(s), volleyball W. *Intramural sports:* badminton M, basketball M/W, bowling M/W, soccer M/W, table tennis M/W, tennis M/W, volleyball M/W.

Costs (2017–18) *Tuition:* area resident $3750 full-time, $125 per credit hour part-time; state resident $7500 full-time, $250 per credit hour part-time; nonresident $10,710 full-time, $357 per credit hour part-time. Full-time tuition and fees vary according to course load, location, and program. Part-time tuition and fees vary according to course load, location, and program. *Required fees:* $1080 full-time, $29 per credit hour part-time, $21 per course part-time. *Waivers:* senior citizens and employees or children of employees.

Financial Aid Of all full-time matriculated undergraduates who enrolled in 2015, 588 Federal Work-Study jobs (averaging $1947).

Applying *Options:* electronic application. *Application fee:* $30. *Required:* high school transcript. *Application deadlines:* rolling (freshmen), rolling (transfers). *Notification:* continuous (freshmen), continuous (transfers).

Freshman Application Contact County College of Morris, 214 Center Grove Road, Randolph, NJ 07869-2086. *Phone:* 973-328-5096. *Website:* http://www.ccm.edu/.

Cumberland County College
Vineland, New Jersey

Freshman Application Contact Ms. Anne Daly-Eimer, Director of Admissions and Registration, Cumberland County College, 3322 College Drive, Vineland, NJ 08360. *Phone:* 856-691-8600. *Website:* http://www.cccnj.edu/.

Eastern International College
Belleville, New Jersey

Admissions Office Contact Eastern International College, 251 Washington Avenue, Belleville, NJ 07109. *Website:* http://www.eicollege.edu/.

Eastern International College
Jersey City, New Jersey

Admissions Office Contact Eastern International College, 684 Newark Avenue, Jersey City, NJ 07306. *Website:* http://www.eicollege.edu/.

Eastwick College
Hackensack, New Jersey

Admissions Office Contact Eastwick College, 250 Moore Street, Hackensack, NJ 07601. *Website:* http://www.eastwickcollege.edu/.

Eastwick College
Nutley, New Jersey

Admissions Office Contact Eastwick College, 103 Park Avenue, Nutley, NJ 07110. *Website:* http://www.eastwickcollege.edu/.

Eastwick College
Ramsey, New Jersey

Admissions Office Contact Eastwick College, 10 South Franklin Turnpike, Ramsey, NJ 07446. *Website:* http://www.eastwickcollege.edu/.

Essex County College
Newark, New Jersey

Freshman Application Contact Ms. Marva Mack, Director of Admissions, Essex County College, 303 University Avenue, Newark, NJ 07102. *Phone:* 973-877-3119. *Fax:* 973-623-6449. *Website:* http://www.essex.edu/.

Hudson County Community College
Jersey City, New Jersey

- **State and locally supported** 2-year, founded 1974
- **Urban** campus with easy access to New York City
- **Coed,** 8,449 undergraduate students, 61% full-time, 60% women, 40% men

Undergraduates 5,146 full-time, 3,303 part-time. 14% Black or African American, non-Hispanic/Latino; 56% Hispanic/Latino; 8% Asian, non-Hispanic/Latino; 0.6% Native Hawaiian or other Pacific Islander, non-Hispanic/Latino; 0.4% American Indian or Alaska Native, non-Hispanic/Latino; 2% Two or more races, non-Hispanic/Latino; 8% Race/ethnicity unknown; 0.5% international; 4% transferred in. *Retention:* 56% of full-time freshmen returned.
Freshmen *Admission:* 2,001 enrolled.
Faculty *Total:* 661, 13% full-time.
Majors Accounting; accounting technology and bookkeeping; baking and pastry arts; biological and physical sciences; business administration and management; child-care provision; computer and information sciences; computer engineering technology; computer graphics; criminal justice/police science; culinary arts; dietetic technology; electrical, electronic and communications engineering technology; emergency medical technology (EMT paramedic); engineering science; engineering technologies and engineering related; environmental studies; fine/studio arts; geographic information science and cartography; health information/medical records technology; health services/allied health/health sciences; hospitality administration; legal assistant/paralegal; liberal arts and sciences/liberal studies; licensed practical/vocational nurse training; medical/clinical assistant; medical transcription; radiologic technology/science; registered nursing/registered nurse; respiratory care therapy; social work.
Academics *Calendar:* semesters. *Degree:* certificates and associate. *Special study options:* academic remediation for entering students, advanced placement credit, distance learning, English as a second language, honors programs, independent study, internships, part-time degree program, services for LD students, summer session for credit.
Library Hudson County Community College Library plus 1 other. *Books:* 49,853 (physical), 2,881 (digital/electronic); *Serial titles:* 1,269 (physical), 750 (digital/electronic); *Databases:* 74.
Student Life *Housing:* college housing not available. *Activities and Organizations:* drama/theater group, student-run newspaper. *Campus security:* 24-hour emergency response devices, late-night transport/escort service. *Student services:* personal/psychological counseling.
Costs (2017–18) *Tuition:* area resident $3870 full-time, $129 per credit hour part-time; state resident $7740 full-time, $258 per credit hour part-time; nonresident $11,610 full-time, $387 per credit hour part-time. Full-time tuition and fees vary according to course load and program. Part-time tuition and fees vary according to course load and program. *Required fees:* $1433 full-time, $46 per credit hour part-time, $25 per term part-time. *Payment plan:* installment. *Waivers:* senior citizens and employees or children of employees.
Financial Aid Of all full-time matriculated undergraduates who enrolled in 2015, 102 Federal Work-Study jobs (averaging $3000).
Applying *Options:* electronic application. *Application fee:* $20. *Application deadlines:* 9/1 (freshmen), 9/1 (transfers). *Notification:* continuous until 9/1 (freshmen), continuous until 9/1 (transfers).
Freshman Application Contact Hudson County Community College, 70 Sip Avenue, Jersey City, NJ 07306. *Phone:* 201-360-4111. *Website:* http://www.hccc.edu/.

Jersey College
Teterboro, New Jersey

- **Proprietary** 2-year, founded 2003
- **Urban** 1-acre campus with easy access to New York City
- **Coed, primarily women,** 2,743 undergraduate students, 100% full-time, 91% women, 9% men
- **71%** of applicants were admitted

Undergraduates 2,743 full-time. Students come from 14 states and territories; 28% are from out of state; 63% Black or African American, non-Hispanic/Latino; 10% Hispanic/Latino; 4% Asian, non-Hispanic/Latino; 0.5% Native Hawaiian or other Pacific Islander, non-Hispanic/Latino; 0.3% American Indian or Alaska Native, non-Hispanic/Latino; 1% Two or more races, non-Hispanic/Latino; 7% Race/ethnicity unknown; 15% transferred in.
Freshmen *Admission:* 204 applied, 145 admitted, 50 enrolled.
Faculty *Total:* 217, 42% full-time, 7% with terminal degrees. *Student/faculty ratio:* 16:1.
Majors Registered nursing/registered nurse.
Academics *Degree:* diplomas and associate. *Special study options:* academic remediation for entering students, accelerated degree program, adult/continuing education programs.
Library Main Library. *Books:* 14,981 (physical), 145,557 (digital/electronic); *Serial titles:* 555 (physical); *Databases:* 3. Students can reserve study rooms.
Standardized Tests *Required for some:* math and reading entrance exams. *Recommended:* SAT or ACT (for admission).
Applying *Required:* essay or personal statement, high school transcript, 2 letters of recommendation, interview, proof of U.S. citizenship or Permanent Resident Card. *Application deadlines:* rolling (freshmen), rolling (transfers). *Notification:* continuous (freshmen), continuous (transfers).
Freshman Application Contact Jersey College, 546 US Highway 46, Teterboro, NJ 07608.
Website: http://www.jerseycollege.edu/.

Mercer County Community College
Trenton, New Jersey

- **State and locally supported** 2-year, founded 1966
- **Suburban** 292-acre campus with easy access to New York City, Philadelphia
- **Coed,** 7,979 undergraduate students, 39% full-time, 51% women, 49% men

Undergraduates 3,077 full-time, 4,902 part-time. Students come from 7 states and territories; 89 other countries; 1% are from out of state; 22% Black or African American, non-Hispanic/Latino; 18% Hispanic/Latino; 6% Asian, non-Hispanic/Latino; 0.2% Native Hawaiian or other Pacific Islander, non-Hispanic/Latino; 0.2% American Indian or Alaska Native, non-Hispanic/Latino; 2% Two or more races, non-Hispanic/Latino; 9% Race/ethnicity unknown; 4% international; 3% transferred in. *Retention:* 71% of full-time freshmen returned.
Freshmen *Admission:* 1,748 enrolled.
Faculty *Total:* 797. *Student/faculty ratio:* 18:1.
Majors Accounting; administrative assistant and secretarial science; airline flight attendant; airline pilot and flight crew; architectural engineering technology; art; art history, criticism and conservation; automotive engineering technology; aviation/airway management; biology/biological sciences; biology/biotechnology laboratory technician; business administration and management; ceramic arts and ceramics; chemistry; civil engineering technology; clinical/medical laboratory technology; commercial and advertising art; community organization and advocacy; computer graphics; computer science; computer systems networking and telecommunications; corrections; criminal justice/police science; culinary arts; dance; dramatic/theater arts; electrical, electronic and communications engineering technology; engineering science; fire science/firefighting; funeral service and mortuary science; health professions related; heating, ventilation, air conditioning and refrigeration engineering technology; hotel/motel administration; humanities; legal assistant/paralegal; liberal arts and sciences/liberal studies; management information systems; mass communication/media; mathematics; medical radiologic technology; music; ornamental horticulture; photography; physical therapy technology; physics; plant sciences; radio and television broadcasting technology; registered nursing/registered nurse; respiratory care therapy; sculpture; teacher assistant/aide.
Academics *Calendar:* semesters. *Degree:* certificates and associate. *Special study options:* academic remediation for entering students, accelerated degree program, adult/continuing education programs, advanced placement credit, cooperative education, distance learning, double majors, English as a second language, external degree program, independent study, internships, part-time degree program, services for LD students, student-designed majors, summer session for credit. *ROTC:* Army (c), Air Force (c).

Library Mercer County Community College Library plus 1 other.
Student Life *Housing:* college housing not available. *Activities and Organizations:* drama/theater group, student-run newspaper, radio station, choral group, Student Government Association, Student Radio Station, African-American Student Organization, Student Activities Board, Phi Theta Kappa. *Campus security:* 24-hour emergency response devices and patrols. *Student services:* personal/psychological counseling.
Athletics Member NJCAA. *Intercollegiate sports:* baseball M, basketball M(s)/W(s), golf M/W, soccer M(s)/W(s), softball W, tennis M/W, track and field M/W. *Intramural sports:* basketball M/W, skiing (downhill) M/W, softball M/W, volleyball M/W.
Costs (2016–17) *Tuition:* area resident $2916 full-time, $122 per credit hour part-time; state resident $4080 full-time, $170 per credit hour part-time; nonresident $6216 full-time, $259 per credit hour part-time. Full-time tuition and fees vary according to program and reciprocity agreements. Part-time tuition and fees vary according to program and reciprocity agreements. *Required fees:* $852 full-time, $36 per credit hour part-time. *Payment plan:* installment. *Waivers:* senior citizens and employees or children of employees.
Financial Aid Of all full-time matriculated undergraduates who enrolled in 2016, 76 Federal Work-Study jobs (averaging $2348). 10 state and other part-time jobs (averaging $1952).
Applying *Options:* electronic application, deferred entrance. *Required:* high school transcript. *Recommended:* interview. *Application deadlines:* rolling (freshmen), rolling (transfers). *Notification:* continuous (freshmen), continuous (transfers).
Freshman Application Contact Dr. L. Campbell, Dean for Student and Academic Services, Mercer County Community College, 1200 Old Trenton Road, PO Box B, Trenton, NJ 08690-1004. *Phone:* 609-586-4800 Ext. 3222. *Toll-free phone:* 800-392-MCCC. *Fax:* 609-586-6944.
E-mail: admiss@mccc.edu.
Website: http://www.mccc.edu/.

Middlesex County College

Edison, New Jersey

- **County-supported** 2-year, founded 1964
- **Suburban** 200-acre campus with easy access to New York City
- **Coed,** 11,673 undergraduate students

Undergraduates 11% Black or African American, non-Hispanic/Latino; 30% Hispanic/Latino; 14% Asian, non-Hispanic/Latino; 0.5% Native Hawaiian or other Pacific Islander, non-Hispanic/Latino; 0.4% American Indian or Alaska Native, non-Hispanic/Latino; 3% Two or more races, non-Hispanic/Latino; 7% Race/ethnicity unknown; 2% international. *Retention:* 62% of full-time freshmen returned.
Faculty *Student/faculty ratio:* 24:1.
Majors Accounting; administrative assistant and secretarial science; automotive engineering technology; biology/biotechnology laboratory technician; biotechnology; business administration and management; civil engineering technology; clinical/medical laboratory technology; communications technologies and support services related; computer and information sciences; criminal justice/police science; dental hygiene; dietitian assistant; electrical, electronic and communications engineering technology; energy management and systems technology; engineering science; engineering technologies and engineering related; environmental control technologies related; fire prevention and safety technology; geology/earth science; graphic communications related; health professions related; health services/allied health/health sciences; hotel/motel administration; industrial production technologies related; legal assistant/paralegal; liberal arts and sciences/liberal studies; marketing/marketing management; mechanical engineering/mechanical technology; mechanical engineering technologies related; medical radiologic technology; merchandising, sales, and marketing operations related (specialized); physical sciences; registered nursing/registered nurse; rehabilitation and therapeutic professions related; respiratory care therapy; small business administration; surveying technology; teacher assistant/aide; visual and performing arts.
Academics *Calendar:* semesters. *Degree:* certificates and associate. *Special study options:* academic remediation for entering students, adult/continuing education programs, advanced placement credit, cooperative education, distance learning, English as a second language, independent study, internships, off-campus study, part-time degree program, services for LD students, study abroad, summer session for credit. *ROTC:* Army (c).
Library Middlesex County College Library plus 1 other.
Student Life *Housing:* college housing not available. *Activities and Organizations:* drama/theater group, student-run newspaper, radio station, choral group. *Campus security:* 24-hour emergency response devices and patrols. *Student services:* health clinic, personal/psychological counseling.
Athletics Member NJCAA. *Intercollegiate sports:* baseball M, basketball M/W, cross-country running M/W, soccer M/W, softball W, track and field M/W, wrestling M.

Costs (2016–17) *One-time required fee:* $86. *Tuition:* area resident $4275 full-time, $108 per credit part-time; state resident $8550 full-time, $216 per credit part-time; nonresident $8550 full-time, $216 per credit part-time. *Required fees:* $35 per credit part-time. *Payment plan:* installment. *Waivers:* employees or children of employees.
Financial Aid Of all full-time matriculated undergraduates who enrolled in 2015, 69 Federal Work-Study jobs (averaging $3350).
Applying *Options:* early admission, deferred entrance. *Application fee:* $25. *Required:* high school transcript. *Application deadlines:* rolling (freshmen), rolling (transfers). *Notification:* continuous (freshmen), continuous (transfers).
Freshman Application Contact Middlesex County College, 2600 Woodbridge Avenue, PO Box 3050, Edison, NJ 08818-3050.
Website: http://www.middlesexcc.edu/.

Ocean County College

Toms River, New Jersey

- **County-supported** 2-year, founded 1964
- **Suburban** 275-acre campus with easy access to Philadelphia
- **Coed**

Undergraduates 4,611 full-time, 4,052 part-time. Students come from 36 states and territories; 0.9% are from out of state; 5% Black or African American, non-Hispanic/Latino; 11% Hispanic/Latino; 2% Asian, non-Hispanic/Latino; 0.2% Native Hawaiian or other Pacific Islander, non-Hispanic/Latino; 0.3% American Indian or Alaska Native, non-Hispanic/Latino; 2% Two or more races, non-Hispanic/Latino; 4% Race/ethnicity unknown; 1% international; 4% transferred in. *Retention:* 69% of full-time freshmen returned.
Faculty *Student/faculty ratio:* 25:1.
Academics *Calendar:* semesters. *Degree:* certificates, diplomas, and associate. *Special study options:* academic remediation for entering students, accelerated degree program, adult/continuing education programs, advanced placement credit, cooperative education, distance learning, English as a second language, honors programs, internships, part-time degree program, services for LD students, study abroad, summer session for credit.
Library Ocean County College Library. *Books:* 69,761 (physical), 170,000 (digital/electronic); *Serial titles:* 290 (physical); *Databases:* 42. Weekly public service hours: 68; students can reserve study rooms.
Student Life *Campus security:* 24-hour emergency response devices and patrols, late-night transport/escort service, security cameras in hallways and parking lots.
Athletics Member NJCAA.
Standardized Tests *Required for some:* ACCUPLACER or waiver for degree-seeking students.
Costs (2016–17) *Tuition:* area resident $3360 full-time, $112 per credit part-time; state resident $4050 full-time, $135 per credit part-time; nonresident $6750 full-time, $225 per credit part-time. Full-time tuition and fees vary according to program. Part-time tuition and fees vary according to program. *Required fees:* $985 full-time, $32 per credit part-time, $20 per term part-time.
Financial Aid Of all full-time matriculated undergraduates who enrolled in 2015, 76 Federal Work-Study jobs (averaging $1300). 45 state and other part-time jobs (averaging $850).
Applying *Options:* electronic application. *Required for some:* high school transcript.
Freshman Application Contact Ms. Sheenah Hartigan, CRM Communications Administrator, Ocean County College, College Drive, PO Box 2001, Toms River, NJ 08754-2001. *Phone:* 732-255-0400 Ext. 2189. *E-mail:* shartigan@ocean.edu. *Website:* http://www.ocean.edu/.

Passaic County Community College

Paterson, New Jersey

Freshman Application Contact Mr. Patrick Noonan, Director of Admissions, Passaic County Community College, One College Boulevard, Paterson, NJ 07505-1179. *Phone:* 973-684-6304. *Website:* http://www.pccc.cc.nj.us/.

Raritan Valley Community College

Branchburg, New Jersey

- **State and locally supported** 2-year, founded 1965
- **Suburban** 225-acre campus with easy access to New York City, Philadelphia
- **Endowment** $989,044
- **Coed,** 8,226 undergraduate students, 41% full-time, 47% women, 53% men

Undergraduates 3,363 full-time, 4,863 part-time. Students come from 11 states and territories; 1% are from out of state; 12% Black or African American, non-Hispanic/Latino; 21% Hispanic/Latino; 5% Asian, non-

Hispanic/Latino; 0.3% Native Hawaiian or other Pacific Islander, non-Hispanic/Latino; 0.2% American Indian or Alaska Native, non-Hispanic/Latino; 2% Two or more races, non-Hispanic/Latino; 7% Race/ethnicity unknown; 2% international; 5% transferred in. *Retention:* 68% of full-time freshmen returned.
Freshmen *Admission:* 1,664 enrolled.
Faculty *Total:* 469, 27% full-time. *Student/faculty ratio:* 21:1.
Majors Accounting related; accounting technology and bookkeeping; administrative assistant and secretarial science; animation, interactive technology, video graphics and special effects; automotive engineering technology; business administration and management; business/commerce; child-care provision; cinematography and film/video production; communication and media related; computer and information sciences and support services related; computer programming (vendor/product certification); computer systems networking and telecommunications; construction engineering technology; corrections; criminal justice/law enforcement administration; criminal justice/police science; critical incident response/special police operations; dance; dental assisting; dental hygiene; design and applied arts related; diesel mechanics technology; digital communication and media/multimedia; engineering science; engineering technologies and engineering related; English; financial planning and services; fine/studio arts; health and physical education/fitness; health information/medical records technology; health services/allied health/health sciences; heating, ventilation, air conditioning and refrigeration engineering technology; information technology; interior design; international business/trade/commerce; kindergarten/preschool education; kinesiology and exercise science; legal assistant/paralegal; liberal arts and sciences/liberal studies; lineworker; management information systems; manufacturing engineering technology; marketing/marketing management; medical/clinical assistant; meeting and event planning; multi/interdisciplinary studies related; music; opticianry; optometric technician; registered nursing/registered nurse; respiratory care therapy; restaurant, culinary, and catering management; small business administration; web page, digital/multimedia and information resources design.
Academics *Calendar:* semesters. *Degree:* certificates and associate. *Special study options:* academic remediation for entering students, adult/continuing education programs, advanced placement credit, cooperative education, distance learning, double majors, English as a second language, freshman honors college, honors programs, independent study, internships, off-campus study, part-time degree program, services for LD students, summer session for credit.
Library Evelyn S. Field Library. *Books:* 76,075 (physical), 109,201 (digital/electronic); *Databases:* 81.
Student Life *Housing:* college housing not available. *Activities and Organizations:* drama/theater group, student-run newspaper, radio station, choral group, Phi Theta Kappa, Orgullo Latino, Student Nurses Association, Business Club/SIFE, Environmental Club. *Campus security:* 24-hour emergency response devices and patrols, late-night transport/escort service, 24-hour outdoor and indoor surveillance cameras, 24-hour communication center. *Student services:* personal/psychological counseling.
Athletics Member NJCAA. *Intercollegiate sports:* baseball M(s), basketball M(s)/W(s), cross-country running M/W, golf M/W, soccer M/W, volleyball W. *Intramural sports:* basketball M/W, soccer M/W, softball W, volleyball W.
Costs (2016–17) *Tuition:* area resident $4290 full-time, $143 per credit hour part-time; state resident $5340 full-time, $178 per credit hour part-time; nonresident $5340 full-time, $178 per credit hour part-time. *Required fees:* $924 full-time, $22 per credit hour part-time, $132 per term part-time. *Payment plan:* installment. *Waivers:* employees or children of employees.
Financial Aid Of all full-time matriculated undergraduates who enrolled in 2015, 12 Federal Work-Study jobs (averaging $2500).
Applying *Required:* high school transcript.
Freshman Application Contact Mr. Daniel Palubniak, Registrar, Enrollment Services, Raritan Valley Community College, 118 Lamington Road, Branchburg, NJ 08876. *Phone:* 908-526-1200 Ext. 8206. *Fax:* 908-704-3442. *E-mail:* dpalubni@raritanval.edu.
Website: http://www.raritanval.edu/.

Rowan College at Burlington County
Pemberton, New Jersey

- **County-supported** 2-year, founded 1966
- **Suburban** 225-acre campus with easy access to Philadelphia
- **Coed**

Undergraduates 4,289 full-time, 4,473 part-time. Students come from 23 states and territories; 0.9% are from out of state; 20% Black or African American, non-Hispanic/Latino; 10% Hispanic/Latino; 4% Asian, non-Hispanic/Latino; 0.2% Native Hawaiian or other Pacific Islander, non-Hispanic/Latino; 0.2% American Indian or Alaska Native, non-Hispanic/Latino; 3% Two or more races, non-Hispanic/Latino; 5% Race/ethnicity unknown; 2% international.

Faculty *Student/faculty ratio:* 26:1.
Academics *Calendar:* semesters plus 2 summer terms. *Degree:* certificates and associate. *Special study options:* academic remediation for entering students, accelerated degree program, adult/continuing education programs, advanced placement credit, cooperative education, distance learning, double majors, English as a second language, honors programs, independent study, internships, part-time degree program, services for LD students, study abroad, summer session for credit.
Library William K. McDaniel Integrated Learning Resource Center plus 1 other.
Student Life *Campus security:* 24-hour emergency response devices and patrols, late-night transport/escort service, electronic entrances to buildings and rooms, surveillance cameras.
Athletics Member NJCAA.
Costs (2016–17) *Tuition:* area resident $3000 full-time, $100 per credit hour part-time; state resident $3480 full-time, $116 per credit hour part-time; nonresident $5430 full-time, $181 per credit hour part-time. Full-time tuition and fees vary according to program. Part-time tuition and fees vary according to program. *Required fees:* $1065 full-time, $36 per credit hour part-time. *Payment plans:* installment, deferred payment.
Financial Aid Of all full-time matriculated undergraduates who enrolled in 2015, 100 Federal Work-Study jobs (averaging $1200). 100 state and other part-time jobs (averaging $2000).
Applying *Options:* electronic application, early admission, deferred entrance. *Application fee:* $20. *Recommended:* high school transcript.
Freshman Application Contact Rowan College at Burlington County, 601 Pemberton Browns Mills Road, Pemberton, NJ 08068. *Phone:* 609-894-9311 Ext. 1200. *Website:* http://www.rcbc.edu/.

Rowan College at Gloucester County
Sewell, New Jersey

Freshman Application Contact Ms. Judy Atkinson, Registrar/Admissions, Rowan College at Gloucester County, 1400 Tanyard Road, Sewell, NJ 08080. *Phone:* 856-415-2209. *E-mail:* jatkinso@gccnj.edu.
Website: http://www.rcgc.edu/.

Salem Community College
Carneys Point, New Jersey

Freshman Application Contact Kelly McShay, Director of Retention and Admissions, Salem Community College, 460 Hollywood Avenue, Carneys Point, NJ 08069. *Phone:* 856-351-2919. *E-mail:* kmcshay@salemcc.edu. *Website:* http://www.salemcc.edu/.

Sussex County Community College
Newton, New Jersey

- **State and locally supported** 2-year, founded 1981, part of New Jersey Commission on Higher Education
- **Small-town** 160-acre campus with easy access to New York City
- **Coed,** 2,589 undergraduate students, 55% full-time, 51% women, 47% men

Undergraduates 1,412 full-time, 1,127 part-time. Students come from 3 states and territories; 2% Black or African American, non-Hispanic/Latino; 4% Hispanic/Latino; 1% Asian, non-Hispanic/Latino; 0.1% Native Hawaiian or other Pacific Islander, non-Hispanic/Latino; 0.4% American Indian or Alaska Native, non-Hispanic/Latino; 7% Two or more races, non-Hispanic/Latino; 0.7% Race/ethnicity unknown.
Freshmen *Admission:* 613 enrolled.
Majors Accounting; automotive engineering technology; biological and physical sciences; broadcast journalism; business administration and management; commercial and advertising art; computer and information sciences; corrections and criminal justice related; English; environmental studies; fine/studio arts; fire protection related; health professions related; human services; journalism; legal assistant/paralegal; liberal arts and sciences/liberal studies.
Academics *Calendar:* semesters. *Degree:* certificates and associate. *Special study options:* academic remediation for entering students, advanced placement credit, distance learning, double majors, English as a second language, internships, part-time degree program, services for LD students, summer session for credit.
Library Sussex County Community College Library. Students can reserve study rooms.
Student Life *Housing:* college housing not available. *Activities and Organizations:* drama/theater group, student-run newspaper, choral group. *Campus security:* late-night transport/escort service, trained security personnel. *Student services:* personal/psychological counseling.

Athletics Member NJCAA. *Intercollegiate sports:* baseball M, basketball M/W, soccer M/W, softball W.

Financial Aid Of all full-time matriculated undergraduates who enrolled in 2015, 29 Federal Work-Study jobs (averaging $1500).

Applying *Options:* electronic application. *Application deadlines:* rolling (freshmen), rolling (transfers). *Notification:* continuous (freshmen), continuous (transfers).

Freshman Application Contact Mr. Todd Poltersdorf, Director of Admissions, Sussex County Community College, 1 College Hill Road, Newton, NJ 07860. *Phone:* 973-300-2253. *E-mail:* tpoltersdorf@sussex.edu. *Website:* http://www.sussex.edu/.

Union County College
Cranford, New Jersey

Freshman Application Contact Ms. Nina Hernandez, Director of Admissions, Records, and Registration, Union County College, Cranford, NJ 07016. *Phone:* 908-709-7127. *Fax:* 908-709-7125. *E-mail:* hernandez@ucc.edu. *Website:* http://www.ucc.edu/.

Warren County Community College
Washington, New Jersey

Freshman Application Contact Shannon Horwath, Associate Director of Admissions, Warren County Community College, 475 Route 57 West, Washington, NJ 07882-9605. *Phone:* 908-835-2300. *E-mail:* shorwath@warren.edu. *Website:* http://www.warren.edu/.

NEW MEXICO

Carrington College–Albuquerque
Albuquerque, New Mexico

- **Proprietary** 2-year, part of Carrington Colleges Group, Inc.
- **Coed**

Undergraduates 399 full-time, 43 part-time. 2% are from out of state; 3% Black or African American, non-Hispanic/Latino; 56% Hispanic/Latino; 2% Asian, non-Hispanic/Latino; 0.2% Native Hawaiian or other Pacific Islander, non-Hispanic/Latino; 21% American Indian or Alaska Native, non-Hispanic/Latino; 0.5% Two or more races, non-Hispanic/Latino; 1% Race/ethnicity unknown; 24% transferred in.

Faculty *Student/faculty ratio:* 28:1.

Academics *Degree:* certificates and associate.

Applying *Required:* essay or personal statement, high school transcript, interview, institutional entrance test.

Freshman Application Contact Carrington College–Albuquerque, 1001 Menaul Boulevard NE, Albuquerque, NM 87107. *Website:* http://carrington.edu/.

Central New Mexico Community College
Albuquerque, New Mexico

- **State-supported** 2-year, founded 1965
- **Urban** 304-acre campus
- **Endowment** $1.8 million
- **Coed**, 24,781 undergraduate students, 29% full-time, 57% women, 43% men

Undergraduates 7,105 full-time, 17,676 part-time. 0.4% are from out of state; 2% Black or African American, non-Hispanic/Latino; 50% Hispanic/Latino; 2% Asian, non-Hispanic/Latino; 0.2% Native Hawaiian or other Pacific Islander, non-Hispanic/Latino; 6% American Indian or Alaska Native, non-Hispanic/Latino; 2% Two or more races, non-Hispanic/Latino; 7% Race/ethnicity unknown; 0.1% international; 4% transferred in.

Freshmen *Admission:* 5,147 applied, 5,147 admitted, 3,719 enrolled.

Faculty *Total:* 986, 34% full-time. *Student/faculty ratio:* 24:1.

Majors Accounting; administrative assistant and secretarial science; airframe mechanics and aircraft maintenance technology; anthropology; architectural drafting and CAD/CADD; art; biology/biological sciences; biotechnology; building construction technology; business administration and management; chemistry; cinematography and film/video production; clinical/medical laboratory technology; communication; computer and information sciences; computer science; construction management; cosmetology; criminal justice/law enforcement administration; criminology; culinary arts; diagnostic medical sonography and ultrasound technology; dramatic/theater arts; early childhood education; education (multiple levels); electrician; emergency medical technology (EMT paramedic); English; environmental design/architecture; fire science/firefighting; foods, nutrition, and wellness; foreign languages and literatures; general studies; geographic information science and cartography; geography; geology/earth science; health and physical education/fitness; health information/medical records administration; health information/medical records technology; health services/allied health/health sciences; heating, air conditioning, ventilation and refrigeration maintenance technology; history; hospitality administration; human development and family studies; Latin American studies; legal assistant/paralegal; liberal arts and sciences/liberal studies; machine tool technology; mathematics; nursing assistant/aide and patient care assistant/aide; opticianry; physical therapy technology; physics; pre-engineering; pre-law studies; psychology; radiologic technology/science; registered nursing/registered nurse; respiratory care therapy; restaurant, culinary, and catering management; sociology; surgical technology; surveying engineering; technology/industrial arts teacher education; vehicle maintenance and repair technologies related; veterinary/animal health technology; welding technology.

Academics *Calendar:* trimesters. *Degree:* certificates and associate. *Special study options:* academic remediation for entering students, accelerated degree program, adult/continuing education programs, advanced placement credit, cooperative education, distance learning, English as a second language, honors programs, independent study, internships, off-campus study, part-time degree program, services for LD students, summer session for credit. *ROTC:* Army (c), Navy (c), Air Force (c).

Library Main Campus Library plus 5 others.

Student Life *Housing:* college housing not available. *Activities and Organizations:* student-run newspaper. *Campus security:* 24-hour emergency response devices and patrols, late-night transport/escort service.

Costs (2016–17) *Tuition:* state resident $1248 full-time, $52 per credit hour part-time; nonresident $6624 full-time, $276 per credit hour part-time. *Required fees:* $224 full-time, $6 per credit hour part-time, $40 per term part-time. *Payment plan:* installment. *Waivers:* senior citizens and employees or children of employees.

Financial Aid Of all full-time matriculated undergraduates who enrolled in 2015, 5,879 applied for aid, 5,326 were judged to have need. 147 Federal Work-Study jobs (averaging $3690). 253 state and other part-time jobs (averaging $3096). In 2015, 132 non-need-based awards were made. *Average need-based loan:* $3035. *Average need-based gift aid:* $2303. *Average non-need-based aid:* $940.

Applying *Options:* electronic application. *Application deadlines:* rolling (freshmen), rolling (transfers). *Notification:* continuous (freshmen), continuous (transfers).

Freshman Application Contact Glenn Damiani, Sr. Director, Enrollment Services, Central New Mexico Community College, Albuquerque, NM 87106. *Phone:* 505-224-3223. *E-mail:* gdamiani@cnm.edu. *Website:* http://www.cnm.edu/.

Clovis Community College
Clovis, New Mexico

Freshman Application Contact Ms. Rosie Corrie, Director of Admissions and Records/Registrar, Clovis Community College, Clovis, NM 88101-8381. *Phone:* 575-769-4962. *Toll-free phone:* 800-769-1409. *Fax:* 575-769-4190. *E-mail:* admissions@clovis.edu. *Website:* http://www.clovis.edu/.

Doña Ana Community College
Las Cruces, New Mexico

Freshman Application Contact Mrs. Ricci Montes, Admissions Advisor, Doña Ana Community College, MSC-3DA, Box 30001, 3400 South Espina Street, Las Cruces, NM 88003-8001. *Phone:* 575-527-7683. *Toll-free phone:* 800-903-7503. *Fax:* 575-527-7515. *Website:* http://dacc.nmsu.edu/.

Eastern New Mexico University–Roswell
Roswell, New Mexico

Freshman Application Contact Eastern New Mexico University–Roswell, PO Box 6000, Roswell, NM 88202-6000. *Phone:* 505-624-7142. *Toll-free phone:* 800-243-6687 (in-state); 800-624-7000 (out-of-state). *Website:* http://www.roswell.enmu.edu/.

IntelliTec College
Albuquerque, New Mexico

Admissions Office Contact IntelliTec College, 5001 Montgomery Boulevard NE, Suite A24, Albuquerque, NM 87109. *Website:* http://www.intelliteccollege.edu/.

Luna Community College
Las Vegas, New Mexico

Freshman Application Contact Ms. Henrietta Griego, Director of Admissions, Recruitment, and Retention, Luna Community College, PO Box 1510, Las Vegas, NM 87701. *Phone:* 505-454-2020. *Toll-free phone:* 800-588-7232. *Fax:* 505-454-2588. *E-mail:* hgriego@luna.cc.nm.us. *Website:* http://www.luna.edu/.

Mesalands Community College
Tucumcari, New Mexico

Director of Admissions Mr. Ken Brashear, Director of Enrollment Management, Mesalands Community College, 911 South Tenth Street, Tucumcari, NM 88401. *Phone:* 505-461-4413. *Website:* http://www.mesalands.edu/.

New Mexico Junior College
Hobbs, New Mexico

- **State and locally supported** 2-year, founded 1965, part of New Mexico Commission on Higher Education
- **Small-town** 185-acre campus
- **Coed,** 3,222 undergraduate students

Undergraduates Students come from 17 states and territories; 7 other countries; 10% are from out of state; 15% live on campus.
Freshmen *Average high school GPA:* 2.75.
Faculty *Total:* 120, 54% full-time. *Student/faculty ratio:* 19:1.
Majors Accounting; administrative assistant and secretarial science; agriculture; art; automobile/automotive mechanics technology; biological and physical sciences; biology/biological sciences; business administration and management; chemistry; clinical/medical laboratory technology; commercial and advertising art; computer graphics; computer programming; computer science; cosmetology; criminal justice/police science; education; elementary education; engineering; English; environmental studies; finance; health professions related; history; liberal arts and sciences/liberal studies; licensed practical/vocational nurse training; marketing/marketing management; mathematics; medical administrative assistant and medical secretary; medical/clinical assistant; music; petroleum technology; physical education teaching and coaching; registered nursing/registered nurse; welding technology.
Academics *Calendar:* semesters. *Degree:* certificates and associate. *Special study options:* academic remediation for entering students, advanced placement credit, cooperative education, distance learning, internships, part-time degree program, services for LD students, summer session for credit.
Library Pannell Library.
Student Life *Housing:* on-campus residence required for freshman year. *Options:* Campus housing is university owned. *Activities and Organizations:* choral group, Student Nurses Association, Phi Theta Kappa, Fellowship of Christian Athletes. *Campus security:* 24-hour emergency response devices and patrols, late-night transport/escort service, controlled dormitory access. *Student services:* health clinic, personal/psychological counseling.
Athletics Member NJCAA. *Intercollegiate sports:* baseball M(s), basketball M(s)/W(s), golf M(s). *Intramural sports:* badminton M/W, basketball M/W, cross-country running M/W, football M, racquetball M/W, table tennis M/W, volleyball M/W, weight lifting M/W.
Costs (2017–18) *Tuition:* $37 per credit hour part-time; state resident $57 per credit hour part-time; nonresident $64 per credit hour part-time. Full-time tuition and fees vary according to course load. Part-time tuition and fees vary according to course load. *Required fees:* $19 per credit hour part-time. *Room and board:* Room and board charges vary according to board plan and housing facility. *Payment plan:* deferred payment. *Waivers:* senior citizens and employees or children of employees.
Applying *Options:* electronic application, early admission, deferred entrance. *Application deadlines:* rolling (freshmen), rolling (out-of-state freshmen), rolling (transfers), rolling (early action). *Early decision deadline:* rolling (for plan 1), rolling (for plan 2). *Notification:* continuous (freshmen), continuous (out-of-state freshmen), continuous (transfers), rolling (early decision plan 1), rolling (early decision plan 2), rolling (early action).
Freshman Application Contact New Mexico Junior College, 5317 Lovington Highway, Hobbs, NM 88240-9123. *Phone:* 575-492-2587. *Toll-free phone:* 800-657-6260.
Website: http://www.nmjc.edu/.

New Mexico Military Institute
Roswell, New Mexico

Freshman Application Contact New Mexico Military Institute, Roswell, NM 88201-5173. *Phone:* 505-624-8050. *Toll-free phone:* 800-421-5376. *Fax:*

505-624-8058. *E-mail:* admissions@nmmi.edu. *Website:* http://www.nmmi.edu/.

New Mexico State University–Alamogordo
Alamogordo, New Mexico

Freshman Application Contact Ms. Elma Hernandez, Coordinator of Admissions and Records, New Mexico State University–Alamogordo, 2400 North Scenic Drive, Alamogordo, NM 88311-0477. *Phone:* 575-439-3700. *E-mail:* advisor@nmsua.nmsu.edu. *Website:* http://nmsua.edu/.

New Mexico State University–Carlsbad
Carlsbad, New Mexico

Freshman Application Contact Ms. Everal Shannon, Records Specialist, New Mexico State University–Carlsbad, 1500 University Drive, Carlsbad, NM 88220. *Phone:* 575-234-9222. *Fax:* 575-885-4951. *E-mail:* eshannon@nmsu.edu. *Website:* http://www.cavern.nmsu.edu/.

New Mexico State University–Grants
Grants, New Mexico

Director of Admissions Ms. Irene Lutz, Campus Student Services Officer, New Mexico State University–Grants, 1500 3rd Street, Grants, NM 87020-2025. *Phone:* 505-287-7981. *Website:* http://grants.nmsu.edu/.

Pima Medical Institute
Albuquerque, New Mexico

Freshman Application Contact Admissions Office, Pima Medical Institute, 4400 Cutler Avenue NE, Albuquerque, NM 87110. *Phone:* 505-881-1234. *Toll-free phone:* 800-477-PIMA. *Fax:* 505-881-5329. *Website:* http://www.pmi.edu/.

San Juan College
Farmington, New Mexico

- **State-supported** 2-year, founded 1958, part of New Mexico Higher Education Department
- **Small-town** 698-acre campus
- **Endowment** $13.4 million
- **Coed,** 5,479 undergraduate students, 49% full-time, 66% women, 34% men

Undergraduates 2,693 full-time, 2,786 part-time. Students come from 52 states and territories; 31 other countries; 28% are from out of state; 1% Black or African American, non-Hispanic/Latino; 16% Hispanic/Latino; 0.7% Asian, non-Hispanic/Latino; 0.1% Native Hawaiian or other Pacific Islander, non-Hispanic/Latino; 35% American Indian or Alaska Native, non-Hispanic/Latino; 2% Two or more races, non-Hispanic/Latino; 4% Race/ethnicity unknown; 1% international; 11% transferred in.
Freshmen *Admission:* 818 applied, 818 admitted, 818 enrolled.
Faculty *Total:* 315, 50% full-time, 7% with terminal degrees. *Student/faculty ratio:* 20:1.
Majors Accounting technology and bookkeeping; American Indian/Native American studies; autobody/collision and repair technology; automobile/automotive mechanics technology; biology/biological sciences; business administration and management; carpentry; chemistry; child-care provision; clinical/medical laboratory technology; commercial and advertising art; cosmetology; criminal justice/police science; data processing and data processing technology; dental hygiene; diesel mechanics technology; drafting and design technology; electrical, electronic and communications engineering technology; elementary education; emergency medical technology (EMT paramedic); engineering; engineering technology; fire science/firefighting; general studies; geology/earth science; health and physical education/fitness; health information/medical records technology; industrial mechanics and maintenance technology; industrial technology; instrumentation technology; landscaping and groundskeeping; legal assistant/paralegal; liberal arts and sciences/liberal studies; mathematics; occupational safety and health technology; occupational therapist assistant; parks, recreation and leisure; physical sciences; physical therapy technology; physics; premedical studies; psychology; registered nursing/registered nurse; respiratory care therapy; secondary education; social work; special education; surgical technology; theater design and technology; veterinary/animal health technology; welding technology.
Academics *Calendar:* semesters. *Degree:* certificates, diplomas, and associate. *Special study options:* academic remediation for entering students,

adult/continuing education programs, advanced placement credit, cooperative education, distance learning, double majors, English as a second language, freshman honors college, honors programs, independent study, internships, part-time degree program, services for LD students, summer session for credit. **Library** San Juan College Library. *Books:* 76,509 (physical), 184,032 (digital/electronic); *Serial titles:* 237 (physical), 18,076 (digital/electronic); *Databases:* 63. Weekly public service hours: 69.

Student Life *Housing:* college housing not available. *Activities and Organizations:* drama/theater group, student-run newspaper, choral group, AGAVE, SJC National Society of Leadership and Success, Psychology/PSI Beta, National Honor Society of Leadership and Success (NSLS), American Indian Science and Leadership Society (AISES), national fraternities, national sororities. *Campus security:* 24-hour emergency response devices and patrols, late-night transport/escort service. *Student services:* personal/psychological counseling.

Athletics *Intramural sports:* basketball M/W, soccer M/W, ultimate Frisbee M/W, volleyball M/W.

Costs (2017–18) *Tuition:* state resident $1104 full-time, $46 per credit hour part-time; nonresident $3504 full-time, $146 per credit hour part-time. Full-time tuition and fees vary according to reciprocity agreements. Part-time tuition and fees vary according to reciprocity agreements. *Required fees:* $388 full-time, $78 per term part-time. *Payment plans:* tuition prepayment, installment. *Waivers:* senior citizens and employees or children of employees.

Financial Aid Of all full-time matriculated undergraduates who enrolled in 2015, 150 Federal Work-Study jobs (averaging $2500). 175 state and other part-time jobs (averaging $2500).

Applying *Options:* electronic application, early admission, deferred entrance. *Application fee:* $10. *Required:* high school transcript. *Application deadlines:* rolling (freshmen), rolling (transfers). *Notification:* continuous (freshmen), continuous (transfers).

Freshman Application Contact Mrs. Abby Calcote, Coordinator of Enrollment Services, San Juan College, 4601 College Boulevard, Farmington, NM 87402. *Phone:* 505-566-3572. *Fax:* 505-566-3500. *E-mail:* calcotea@sanjuancollege.edu. *Website:* http://www.sanjuancollege.edu/.

Santa Fe Community College
Santa Fe, New Mexico

- **State and locally supported** 2-year, founded 1983
- **Rural** 366-acre campus with easy access to Albuquerque
- **Coed,** 9,619 undergraduate students, 23% full-time, 63% women, 37% men

Undergraduates 2,243 full-time, 7,376 part-time. Students come from 42 states and territories; 2% Black or African American, non-Hispanic/Latino; 44% Hispanic/Latino; 2% Asian, non-Hispanic/Latino; 0.1% Native Hawaiian or other Pacific Islander, non-Hispanic/Latino; 5% American Indian or Alaska Native, non-Hispanic/Latino; 1% Two or more races, non-Hispanic/Latino; 3% Race/ethnicity unknown; 0.1% international. *Retention:* 51% of full-time freshmen returned.

Freshmen *Admission:* 353 applied, 353 admitted, 619 enrolled. **Faculty** *Total:* 490, 17% full-time, 10% with terminal degrees. *Student/faculty ratio:* 13:1.

Majors Accounting; administrative assistant and secretarial science; architectural drafting and CAD/CADD; art; art history, criticism and conservation; automobile/automotive mechanics technology; behavioral sciences; biology/biological sciences; business administration and management; ceramic arts and ceramics; cinematography and film/video production; commercial photography; computer and information sciences; computer programming; construction engineering technology; criminal justice/police science; criminal justice/safety; culinary arts; dental assisting; design and visual communications; drafting and design technology; education; electrical, electronic and communications engineering technology; engineering; environmental studies; ethnic, cultural minority, gender, and group studies related; fashion/apparel design; film/cinema/video studies; fine and studio arts management; general studies; health and physical education/fitness; hospitality administration; humanities; interior design; intermedia/multimedia; kindergarten/preschool education; legal assistant/paralegal; metal and jewelry arts; parks, recreation and leisure; photography; physical sciences; printmaking; psychology; radio and television broadcasting technology; radiologic technology/science; registered nursing/registered nurse; respiratory care therapy; sculpture; sign language interpretation and translation; social work; Spanish; surveying technology; water quality and wastewater treatment management and recycling technology; woodworking.

Academics *Calendar:* semesters. *Degrees:* certificates, associate, and postbachelor's certificates. *Special study options:* academic remediation for entering students, adult/continuing education programs, advanced placement credit, cooperative education, distance learning, double majors, English as a second language, external degree program, honors programs, independent

study, internships, part-time degree program, services for LD students, summer session for credit.

Library Learning Resource Center.

Student Life *Housing:* college housing not available. *Activities and Organizations:* Student Ambassadors, Student Government Association, The Clay Club, Phi Theta Kappa. *Campus security:* 24-hour emergency response devices and patrols, late-night transport/escort service. *Student services:* personal/psychological counseling.

Applying *Options:* electronic application, early admission, deferred entrance. *Recommended:* high school transcript. *Application deadlines:* rolling (freshmen), rolling (transfers). *Notification:* continuous (freshmen), continuous (transfers).

Freshman Application Contact Marcos Maez, Student Recruitment & Outreach Administrator, Santa Fe Community College, 6401 Richards Ave, Santa Fe, NM 87508. *Phone:* 505-428-1779. *E-mail:* marcos.maez@sfcc.edu. *Website:* http://www.sfcc.edu/.

Southwestern Indian Polytechnic Institute
Albuquerque, New Mexico

- **Federally supported** 2-year, founded 1971
- **Suburban** 144-acre campus with easy access to Albuquerque
- **Coed,** 402 undergraduate students, 86% full-time, 55% women, 45% men

Undergraduates 346 full-time, 56 part-time. Students come from 18 states and territories; 60% live on campus.

Freshmen *Admission:* 183 applied, 157 admitted, 103 enrolled. *Average high school GPA:* 2.11.

Faculty *Total:* 41, 56% full-time, 12% with terminal degrees. *Student/faculty ratio:* 16:1.

Majors Accounting technology and bookkeeping; business administration and management; business/commerce; early childhood education; engineering; geographic information science and cartography; institutional food workers; liberal arts and sciences/liberal studies; natural resources and conservation related; opticianry; system, networking, and LAN/WAN management.

Academics *Calendar:* trimesters. *Degree:* certificates and associate. *Special study options:* academic remediation for entering students, advanced placement credit, cooperative education, distance learning, double majors, internships, part-time degree program, services for LD students, summer session for credit.

Library Southwestern Indian Polytechnic Institute Library.

Student Life *Housing Options:* men-only, women-only. Campus housing is university owned. *Activities and Organizations:* Dance Club, Student Senate, Culinary Arts, Natural Resources, Pow-Wow Club. *Campus security:* 24-hour emergency response devices and patrols, late-night transport/escort service. *Student services:* personal/psychological counseling.

Athletics *Intramural sports:* basketball M/W, softball M/W, volleyball M/W.

Costs (2016–17) *Tuition:* The Bureau of Indian Education (BIE) provides tuition, room board, and books to students at minimal charge. *Required fees:* $1095 full-time, $290 per term part-time. *Room and board:* $675. *Payment plan:* deferred payment.

Financial Aid Of all full-time matriculated undergraduates who enrolled in 2016, 202 applied for aid, 202 were judged to have need. 14 Federal Work-Study jobs (averaging $700). 15 state and other part-time jobs (averaging $800). *Average percent of need met:* 43%. *Average financial aid package:* $4592. *Average need-based gift aid:* $3550.

Applying *Required:* high school transcript, Certificate of Indian Blood, physical, immunization records. *Application deadlines:* 7/30 (freshmen), 7/30 (transfers). *Notification:* continuous (freshmen).

Freshman Application Contact Lamarita Vicenti, First Year Counselor, Southwestern Indian Polytechnic Institute, PO Box 10146, 9169 Coors Rd NW, Albuquerque, NM 87184. *Phone:* 505-922-6516. *Toll-free phone:* 800-586-7474. *E-mail:* lamarita.vicenti@bie.edu. *Website:* http://www.sipi.edu/.

University of New Mexico–Gallup
Gallup, New Mexico

- **State-supported** 2-year, founded 1968, part of New Mexico Commission on Higher Education
- **Small-town** 80-acre campus
- **Coed**

Undergraduates 1,163 full-time, 1,310 part-time. 11% are from out of state; 0.5% Black or African American, non-Hispanic/Latino; 13% Hispanic/Latino; 0.9% Asian, non-Hispanic/Latino; 76% American Indian or Alaska Native, non-Hispanic/Latino; 2% Two or more races, non-Hispanic/Latino; 0.8%

Race/ethnicity unknown; 0.4% international; 4% transferred in. *Retention:* 56% of full-time freshmen returned.

Faculty *Student/faculty ratio:* 20:1.

Academics *Calendar:* semesters. *Degree:* certificates, diplomas, and associate. *Special study options:* academic remediation for entering students, adult/continuing education programs, advanced placement credit, cooperative education, distance learning, double majors, honors programs, independent study, internships, off-campus study, part-time degree program, services for LD students, summer session for credit.

Library Zollinger Library plus 1 other. Study areas open 24 hours, 5&-7 days a week.

Student Life *Campus security:* late-night transport/escort service.

Costs (2016–17) *Tuition:* state resident $1932 full-time, $81 per credit hour part-time; nonresident $4708 full-time, $196 per credit hour part-time.

Applying *Options:* electronic application. *Application fee:* $15. *Required for some:* high school transcript.

Freshman Application Contact University of New Mexico–Gallup, 705 Gurley Avenue, Gallup, NM 87301. *Phone:* 505-863-7576. *Website:* http://www.gallup.unm.edu/.

University of New Mexico–Los Alamos Branch

Los Alamos, New Mexico

Freshman Application Contact Mrs. Irene K. Martinez, Enrollment Representative, University of New Mexico–Los Alamos Branch, 4000 University Drive, Los Alamos, NM 87544-2233. *Phone:* 505-662-0332. *E-mail:* l65130@unm.edu. *Website:* http://losalamos.unm.edu/.

University of New Mexico–Taos

Taos, New Mexico

Director of Admissions Vickie Alvarez, Student Enrollment Associate, University of New Mexico–Taos, 115 Civic Plaza Drive, Taos, NM 87571. *Phone:* 575-737-6425. *E-mail:* valvarez@unm.edu. *Website:* http://taos.unm.edu/.

University of New Mexico–Valencia Campus

Los Lunas, New Mexico

Director of Admissions Richard M. Hulett, Director of Admissions and Recruitment, University of New Mexico–Valencia Campus, 280 La Entrada, Los Lunas, NM 87031-7633. *Phone:* 505-277-2446. *E-mail:* mhulett@unm.edu. *Website:* http://www.unm.edu/~unmvc/.

NEW YORK

Adirondack Community College

Queensbury, New York

- **State and locally supported** 2-year, founded 1960, part of State University of New York System
- **Small-town** 141-acre campus
- **Endowment** $3.9 million
- **Coed,** 3,850 undergraduate students, 56% full-time, 58% women, 42% men

Undergraduates 2,156 full-time, 1,694 part-time. Students come from 10 states and territories; 11 other countries; 0.7% are from out of state; 3% Black or African American, non-Hispanic/Latino; 4% Hispanic/Latino; 0.9% Asian, non-Hispanic/Latino; 0.5% American Indian or Alaska Native, non-Hispanic/Latino; 2% Two or more races, non-Hispanic/Latino; 5% Race/ethnicity unknown; 0.4% international; 6% transferred in. *Retention:* 60% of full-time freshmen returned.

Freshmen *Admission:* 1,563 applied, 1,530 admitted, 927 enrolled.

Faculty *Total:* 260, 33% full-time. *Student/faculty ratio:* 23:1.

Majors Accounting; accounting technology and bookkeeping; business administration and management; computer science; computer systems networking and telecommunications; cooking and related culinary arts; creative writing; criminal justice/police science; design and visual communications; electrical, electronic and communications engineering technology; electrician; engineering; food technology and processing; hospitality administration; information technology; liberal arts and sciences/liberal studies; marketing/marketing management; music; music

performance; parks, recreation and leisure facilities management; radio and television broadcasting technology; registered nursing/registered nurse; sport and fitness administration/management; substance abuse/addiction counseling; tourism and travel services management.

Academics *Calendar:* semesters. *Degree:* certificates and associate. *Special study options:* academic remediation for entering students, accelerated degree program, adult/continuing education programs, advanced placement credit, cooperative education, distance learning, double majors, independent study, internships, part-time degree program, services for LD students, study abroad, summer session for credit.

Library SUNY Adirondack Library.

Student Life *Housing Options:* coed. *Activities and Organizations:* drama/theater group, student-run radio and television station, choral group. *Campus security:* late-night transport/escort service, patrols by trained security personnel 8 am to 10 pm. *Student services:* personal/psychological counseling.

Athletics Member NJCAA. *Intercollegiate sports:* baseball M, basketball M/W, bowling M/W, cross-country running M/W, golf M/W, soccer M/W, softball W, tennis M/W, volleyball W. *Intramural sports:* badminton M/W, basketball M/W, volleyball M/W.

Costs (2016–17) *Tuition:* state resident $4176 full-time, $174 per credit hour part-time; nonresident $8352 full-time, $348 per credit hour part-time. Full-time tuition and fees vary according to course load and program. Part-time tuition and fees vary according to course load and program. *Required fees:* $517 full-time, $18 per credit hour part-time, $2 per term part-time. *Room and board:* $10,790; room only: $7380. Room and board charges vary according to board plan. *Payment plan:* installment. *Waivers:* senior citizens and employees or children of employees.

Financial Aid Of all full-time matriculated undergraduates who enrolled in 2015, 98 Federal Work-Study jobs (averaging $462).

Applying *Options:* electronic application. *Application fee:* $35.

Freshman Application Contact Office of Admissions, Adirondack Community College, 640 Bay Road, Queensbury, NY 12804. *Phone:* 518-743-2264. *Toll-free phone:* 888-SUNY-ADK. *Fax:* 518-743-2200. *Website:* http://www.sunyacc.edu/.

American Academy McAllister Institute of Funeral Service

New York, New York

Freshman Application Contact Mr. Norman Provost, Registrar, American Academy McAllister Institute of Funeral Service, 450 West 56th Street, New York, NY 10019-3602. *Phone:* 212-757-1190. *Toll-free phone:* 866-932-2264. *Website:* http://www.funeraleducation.org/.

American Academy of Dramatic Arts–New York

New York, New York

- **Independent** 2-year, founded 1884
- **Urban** campus
- **Coed,** 310 undergraduate students, 100% full-time, 68% women, 32% men

Undergraduates 310 full-time. 53% live on campus.

Freshmen *Admission:* 440 applied, 359 admitted, 113 enrolled.

Faculty *Total:* 31, 32% full-time, 35% with terminal degrees. *Student/faculty ratio:* 8:1.

Majors Dramatic/theater arts.

Academics *Calendar:* semesters. *Degree:* certificates and associate. *Special study options:* academic remediation for entering students, honors programs.

Library Academy/CBS Library.

Student Life *Housing Options:* coed. Campus housing is leased by the school. Freshman applicants given priority for college housing. *Activities and Organizations:* national fraternities. *Campus security:* 24-hour emergency response devices and patrols, controlled dormitory access, trained security guard during hours of operation and for campus housing. *Student services:* personal/psychological counseling.

Costs (2017–18) *Comprehensive fee:* $34,740 includes full-time tuition ($33,420), mandatory fees ($750), and room and board ($570). *Room and board:* Room and board charges vary according to housing facility. *Payment plan:* installment. *Waivers:* employees or children of employees.

Financial Aid Of all full-time matriculated undergraduates who enrolled in 2012, 240 applied for aid, 231 were judged to have need. 50 Federal Work-Study jobs (averaging $900). 50 state and other part-time jobs (averaging $2000). In 2012, 59 non-need-based awards were made. *Average percent of need met:* 67%. *Average financial aid package:* $18,150. *Average need-based loan:* $4500. *Average need-based gift aid:* $7000. *Average non-need-based aid:* $7000. *Average indebtedness upon graduation:* $15,000. *Financial aid deadline:* 5/15.

Applying *Options:* electronic application, deferred entrance. *Application fee:* $50. *Required:* essay or personal statement, high school transcript, minimum 2.0 GPA, 2 letters of recommendation, interview, audition. *Application deadlines:* rolling (freshmen), rolling (transfers). *Notification:* continuous (freshmen), continuous (transfers).
Freshman Application Contact Kerin Reilly, Director of Admissions, American Academy of Dramatic Arts–New York, 120 Madison Avenue, New York, NY 10016. *Phone:* 212-686-9244 Ext. 333. *Toll-free phone:* 800-463-8990. *E-mail:* kreilly@aada.edu.
Website: http://www.aada.edu/.

ASA College
Brooklyn, New York

Freshman Application Contact Admissions Office, ASA College, 81 Willoughby Street, Brooklyn, NY 11201. *Phone:* 718-522-9073. *Toll-free phone:* 877-679-8772. *Website:* http://www.asa.edu/.

The Belanger School of Nursing
Schenectady, New York

- **Independent** 2-year, founded 1906
- **Urban** campus
- **Coed, primarily women,** 119 undergraduate students, 33% full-time, 85% women, 15% men

Undergraduates 39 full-time, 80 part-time. Students come from 1 other state; 8% Black or African American, non-Hispanic/Latino; 5% Hispanic/Latino; 10% Asian, non-Hispanic/Latino; 0.8% Two or more races, non-Hispanic/Latino.
Freshmen *Average high school GPA:* 3.5.
Faculty *Student/faculty ratio:* 4:1.
Majors Registered nursing/registered nurse.
Academics *Degree:* associate. *Special study options:* honors programs, part-time degree program, summer session for credit.
Library Ellis Medicine's Health Services Library. *Books:* 2,000 (physical). Weekly public service hours: 40.
Student Life *Housing:* college housing not available. *Activities and Organizations:* Student Government. *Campus security:* on-campus security department 24/7.
Standardized Tests *Required:* Kaplan Admission Test (for admission).
Costs (2016–17) *Tuition:* $9525 full-time, $8595 per year part-time. Full-time tuition and fees vary according to course level, course load, and student level. Part-time tuition and fees vary according to course level, course load, and student level. *Required fees:* $1700 full-time, $430 per credit part-time, $760 per year part-time. *Payment plan:* installment.
Applying *Required:* essay or personal statement, high school transcript, minimum 3.0 GPA, 2 letters of recommendation.
Freshman Application Contact Carolyn Lansing, Student Services Manager, The Belanger School of Nursing, 650 McClellan Street, Schenectady, NY 12304. *Phone:* 518-831-8810. *Fax:* 518-243-4470.
E-mail: lansingc@ellismedicine.org.
Website: http://www.ellismedicine.org/school-of-nursing/.

Bill and Sandra Pomeroy College of Nursing at Crouse Hospital
Syracuse, New York

Freshman Application Contact Ms. Amy Graham, Enrollment Management Supervisor, Bill and Sandra Pomeroy College of Nursing at Crouse Hospital, 765 Irving Avenue, Syracuse, NY 13210. *Phone:* 315-470-7481. *Fax:* 315-470-7925. *E-mail:* amygraham@crouse.org.
Website: http://www.crouse.org/nursing/.

Borough of Manhattan Community College of the City University of New York
New York, New York

- **State and locally supported** 2-year, founded 1963, part of City University of New York System
- **Urban** 5-acre campus
- **Coed,** 26,748 undergraduate students, 68% full-time, 57% women, 43% men

Undergraduates 18,189 full-time, 8,559 part-time. 3% are from out of state; 30% Black or African American, non-Hispanic/Latino; 40% Hispanic/Latino;

13% Asian, non-Hispanic/Latino; 0.4% American Indian or Alaska Native, non-Hispanic/Latino; 6% international; 6% transferred in.
Freshmen *Admission:* 24,209 applied, 23,637 admitted, 6,580 enrolled. *Test scores:* SAT critical reading scores over 500: 10%; SAT math scores over 500: 9%; SAT critical reading scores over 600: 1%; SAT math scores over 600: 2%.
Faculty *Total:* 1,582, 33% full-time, 32% with terminal degrees. *Student/faculty ratio:* 24:1.
Majors Accounting; accounting technology and bookkeeping; administrative assistant and secretarial science; animation, interactive technology, video graphics and special effects; art history, criticism and conservation; biotechnology; business administration and management; community organization and advocacy; computer and information sciences; computer science; criminal justice/police science; emergency medical technology (EMT paramedic); engineering; English; foreign languages and literatures; forensic science and technology; general studies; geographic information science and cartography; gerontology; health information/medical records technology; health services/allied health/health sciences; history; liberal arts and sciences/liberal studies; mathematics; medical informatics; physical sciences; psychology; public health education and promotion; radio and television broadcasting technology; registered nursing/registered nurse; respiratory therapy technician; small business administration; sociology; teacher assistant/aide; visual and performing arts; web page, digital/multimedia and information resources design.
Academics *Calendar:* semesters. *Degree:* certificates and associate. *Special study options:* academic remediation for entering students, accelerated degree program, adult/continuing education programs, advanced placement credit, cooperative education, distance learning, English as a second language, honors programs, independent study, internships, off-campus study, part-time degree program, services for LD students, study abroad, summer session for credit.
Library A. Philip Randolph Library plus 1 other. *Books:* 124,572 (physical), 488,639 (digital/electronic); *Serial titles:* 1,292 (physical), 94,735 (digital/electronic); *Databases:* 33,624. Weekly public service hours: 80; students can reserve study rooms.
Student Life *Activities and Organizations:* drama/theater group, student-run newspaper, choral group, Anime Club, Muslim Students Association, Psychology Club, Resurgence in Christ, Urban Mentors and Leaders Association. *Campus security:* 24-hour patrols. *Student services:* health clinic, personal/psychological counseling, women's center.
Athletics Member NJCAA. *Intercollegiate sports:* baseball M, basketball M/W, soccer M/W, volleyball W.
Standardized Tests *Recommended:* SAT or ACT (for admission).
Costs (2017–18) *Tuition:* state resident $4800 full-time, $210 per credit part-time; nonresident $7680 full-time, $320 per credit part-time. Part-time tuition and fees vary according to course load. *Required fees:* $369 full-time, $100 per term part-time. *Payment plans:* installment, deferred payment. *Waivers:* senior citizens and employees or children of employees.
Financial Aid Of all full-time matriculated undergraduates who enrolled in 2015, 15,714 applied for aid, 14,693 were judged to have need.
Applying *Options:* electronic application, deferred entrance. *Application fee:* $65. *Required:* high school transcript. *Application deadlines:* rolling (freshmen), rolling (transfers). *Notification:* continuous (freshmen), continuous (transfers).
Freshman Application Contact Dr. Eugenio Barrios, Director of Enrollment Management, Borough of Manhattan Community College of the City University of New York, 199 Chambers Street, Room S-310, New York, NY 10007. *Phone:* 212-220-1265. *Toll-free phone:* 866-583-5729. *Fax:* 212-220-2366. *E-mail:* admissions@bmcc.cuny.edu.
Website: http://www.bmcc.cuny.edu/.

Bronx Community College of the City University of New York
Bronx, New York

Freshman Application Contact Ms. Patricia A. Ramos, Admissions Officer, Bronx Community College of the City University of New York, 2155 University Avenue, Bronx, NY 10453. *Phone:* 718-289-5888.
E-mail: admission@bcc.cuny.edu. *Website:* http://www.bcc.cuny.edu/.

Broome Community College
Binghamton, New York

Freshman Application Contact Ms. Jenae Norris, Director of Admissions, Broome Community College, PO Box 1017, Upper Front Street, Binghamton, NY 13902. *Phone:* 607-778-5001. *Fax:* 607-778-5394. *E-mail:* admissions@sunybroome.edu. *Website:* http://www.sunybroome.edu/.

Bryant & Stratton College–Albany Campus

Albany, New York

Freshman Application Contact Mr. Robert Ferrell, Director of Admissions, Bryant & Stratton College–Albany Campus, 1259 Central Avenue, Albany, NY 12205. *Phone:* 518-437-1802 Ext. 205. *Fax:* 518-437-1048. *Website:* http://www.bryantstratton.edu/.

Bryant & Stratton College–Amherst Campus

Clarence, New York

Freshman Application Contact Mr. Brian K. Dioguardi, Director of Admissions, Bryant & Stratton College–Amherst Campus, Audubon Business Center, 40 Hazelwood Drive, Amherst, NY 14228. *Phone:* 716-691-0012. *Fax:* 716-691-0012. *E-mail:* bkdioguardi@bryantstratton.edu. *Website:* http://www.bryantstratton.edu/.

Bryant & Stratton College–Buffalo Campus

Buffalo, New York

Freshman Application Contact Mr. Philip J. Struebel, Director of Admissions, Bryant & Stratton College–Buffalo Campus, 465 Main Street, Suite 400, Buffalo, NY 14203. *Phone:* 716-884-9120. *Fax:* 716-884-0091. *E-mail:* pjstruebel@bryantstratton.edu. *Website:* http://www.bryantstratton.edu/.

Bryant & Stratton College–Greece Campus

Rochester, New York

Freshman Application Contact Bryant & Stratton College–Greece Campus, 854 Long Pond Road, Rochester, NY 14612. *Phone:* 585-720-0660. *Website:* http://www.bryantstratton.edu/.

Bryant & Stratton College–Henrietta Campus

Rochester, New York

Freshman Application Contact Bryant & Stratton College–Henrietta Campus, 1225 Jefferson Road, Rochester, NY 14623. *Phone:* 585-292-5627 Ext. 101. *Website:* http://www.bryantstratton.edu/.

Bryant & Stratton College–Orchard Park Campus

Orchard Park, New York

Freshman Application Contact Bryant & Stratton College–Orchard Park Campus, 200 Redtail Road, Orchard Park, NY 14127. *Phone:* 716-677-9500. *Website:* http://www.bryantstratton.edu/.

Bryant & Stratton College–Syracuse Campus

Syracuse, New York

Freshman Application Contact Ms. Dawn Rajkowski, Director of High School Enrollments, Bryant & Stratton College–Syracuse Campus, 953 James Street, Syracuse, NY 13203-2502. *Phone:* 315-472-6603 Ext. 248. *Fax:* 315-474-4383. *Website:* http://www.bryantstratton.edu/.

Bryant & Stratton College–Syracuse North Campus

Liverpool, New York

Freshman Application Contact Ms. Heather Macnik, Director of Admissions, Bryant & Stratton College–Syracuse North Campus, 8687 Carling Road, Liverpool, NY 13090. *Phone:* 315-652-6500. *Website:* http://www.bryantstratton.edu/.

Cayuga County Community College

Auburn, New York

- **State and locally supported** 2-year, founded 1953, part of State University of New York System
- **Small-town** 50-acre campus with easy access to Rochester, Syracuse
- **Endowment** $13.3 million
- **Coed,** 4,297 undergraduate students, 38% full-time, 58% women, 42% men

Undergraduates 1,616 full-time, 2,681 part-time. Students come from 11 states and territories; 11 other countries; 1% are from out of state; 5% Black or African American, non-Hispanic/Latino; 4% Hispanic/Latino; 1% Asian, non-Hispanic/Latino; 0.1% Native Hawaiian or other Pacific Islander, non-Hispanic/Latino; 0.5% American Indian or Alaska Native, non-Hispanic/Latino; 2% Two or more races, non-Hispanic/Latino; 5% Race/ethnicity unknown; 4% transferred in. *Retention:* 59% of full-time freshmen returned.

Freshmen *Admission:* 1,717 applied, 1,397 admitted, 589 enrolled.

Faculty *Total:* 229, 22% full-time. *Student/faculty ratio:* 23:1.

Majors Accounting technology and bookkeeping; art; business administration and management; child-care and support services management; communication and journalism related; communications systems installation and repair technology; computer and information sciences; computer and information sciences and support services related; corrections; criminal justice/police science; drafting and design technology; education (multiple levels); electrical, electronic and communications engineering technology; entrepreneurship; fine/studio arts; game and interactive media design; general studies; geography; graphic design; health services/allied health/health sciences; humanities; information science/studies; liberal arts and sciences/liberal studies; literature related; mathematics related; mechanical engineering; mechanical engineering/mechanical technology; music related; occupational therapist assistant; psychology related; radio, television, and digital communication related; registered nursing/registered nurse; science technologies related; sport and fitness administration/management; telecommunications technology; wine steward/sommelier; writing.

Academics *Calendar:* semesters. *Degree:* certificates and associate. *Special study options:* academic remediation for entering students, advanced placement credit, cooperative education, distance learning, honors programs, internships, off-campus study, part-time degree program, services for LD students, study abroad, summer session for credit.

Library Norman F. Bourke Memorial Library plus 2 others. *Books:* 87,056 (physical), 150,000 (digital/electronic); *Serial titles:* 292 (physical), 60,000 (digital/electronic); *Databases:* 100. Weekly public service hours: 61; students can reserve study rooms.

Student Life *Housing:* college housing not available. *Activities and Organizations:* drama/theater group, student-run newspaper, radio and television station, choral group, Student Activity Board, Student Government, Criminal Justice Club, Tutor Club, Early Childhood Club. *Campus security:* security from 8 am to 9 pm. *Student services:* health clinic, personal/psychological counseling.

Athletics Member NJCAA. *Intercollegiate sports:* basketball M/W, bowling M/W, golf M/W, soccer M/W, softball W, volleyball W. *Intramural sports:* basketball M/W, volleyball M/W.

Costs (2017–18) *Tuition:* state resident $4499 full-time, $187 per credit hour part-time; nonresident $8996 full-time, $374 per credit hour part-time. Full-time tuition and fees vary according to course load, location, and program. Part-time tuition and fees vary according to course load, location, and program. *Required fees:* $572 full-time, $21 per credit hour part-time. *Payment plan:* installment. *Waivers:* employees or children of employees.

Financial Aid Of all full-time matriculated undergraduates who enrolled in 2015, 150 Federal Work-Study jobs (averaging $2000). 200 state and other part-time jobs (averaging $1000).

Applying *Options:* electronic application. *Required:* high school transcript. *Required for some:* specific additional requirement for nursing and occupational therapy programs. *Application deadlines:* rolling (freshmen), rolling (transfers). *Notification:* continuous (freshmen), continuous (transfers).

Freshman Application Contact Cayuga County Community College, 197 Franklin Street, Auburn, NY 13021-3099. *Phone:* 315-255-1743 Ext. 2244. *Toll-free phone:* 866-598-8883. *Website:* http://www.cayuga-cc.edu/.

Clinton Community College
Plattsburgh, New York

- **State and locally supported** 2-year, founded 1969, part of State University of New York System
- **Small-town** 100-acre campus
- **Coed,** 1,913 undergraduate students, 50% full-time, 58% women, 42% men

Undergraduates 960 full-time, 953 part-time. Students come from 12 states and territories; 22 other countries; 3% are from out of state; 5% Black or African American, non-Hispanic/Latino; 2% Hispanic/Latino; 2% Asian, non-Hispanic/Latino; 0.3% Native Hawaiian or other Pacific Islander, non-Hispanic/Latino; 0.5% American Indian or Alaska Native, non-Hispanic/Latino; 3% Two or more races, non-Hispanic/Latino; 10% Race/ethnicity unknown; 2% international; 17% transferred in; 10% live on campus. *Retention:* 58% of full-time freshmen returned.
Freshmen *Admission:* 1,206 applied, 365 admitted, 333 enrolled.
Faculty *Total:* 111, 55% full-time. *Student/faculty ratio:* 11:1.
Majors Accounting; biological and physical sciences; business administration and management; community organization and advocacy; computer/information technology services administration related; consumer merchandising/retailing management; criminal justice/law enforcement administration; criminal justice/police science; electrical, electronic and communications engineering technology; energy management and systems technology; engineering technologies and engineering related; humanities; liberal arts and sciences/liberal studies; mechanical engineering/mechanical technology; physical education teaching and coaching; registered nursing/registered nurse; social sciences.
Academics *Calendar:* semesters. *Degree:* certificates and associate. *Special study options:* academic remediation for entering students, adult/continuing education programs, advanced placement credit, cooperative education, distance learning, English as a second language, external degree program, honors programs, independent study, internships, off-campus study, part-time degree program, services for LD students, student-designed majors, summer session for credit.
Library Clinton Community College Learning Resource Center plus 1 other. *Books:* 10,000 (physical); *Databases:* 100. Study areas open 24 hours, 5&-7 days a week; students can reserve study rooms.
Student Life *Housing Options:* coed, special housing for students with disabilities. Campus housing is provided by a third party. Freshman campus housing is guaranteed. *Activities and Organizations:* drama/theater group, student-run newspaper, choral group, Athletics, Future Human Services Professionals, PTK (honor society), Drama Club, Criminal Justice Club. *Campus security:* 24-hour emergency response devices and patrols, late-night transport/escort service, controlled dormitory access. *Student services:* health clinic, personal/psychological counseling.
Athletics Member NJCAA. *Intercollegiate sports:* baseball M, basketball M/W, soccer M/W. *Intramural sports:* volleyball M/W.
Costs (2017–18) *Tuition:* state resident $4300 full-time, $179 per credit hour part-time; nonresident $9300 full-time, $383 per credit hour part-time. Full-time tuition and fees vary according to course load and program. Part-time tuition and fees vary according to course load and program. *Required fees:* $1047 full-time, $33 per credit hour part-time. *Room and board:* $9692; room only: $5170. Room and board charges vary according to board plan. *Payment plan:* installment. *Waivers:* employees or children of employees.
Financial Aid *Average financial aid package:* $7160. *Average need-based loan:* $3027. *Average need-based gift aid:* $5654.
Applying *Options:* electronic application, deferred entrance. *Required:* high school transcript. *Required for some:* essay or personal statement, 3 letters of recommendation, interview. *Application deadlines:* 8/26 (freshmen), 9/3 (transfers). *Notification:* continuous (freshmen), continuous (out-of-state freshmen), continuous (transfers).
Freshman Application Contact Clinton Community College, 136 Clinton Point Drive, Plattsburgh, NY 12901-9573. *Phone:* 518-562-4171. *Toll-free phone:* 800-552-1160.
Website: http://www.clinton.edu/.

Cochran School of Nursing
Yonkers, New York

- **Independent** 2-year, founded 1894
- **Urban** campus with easy access to New York City
- **Coed, primarily women,** 96 undergraduate students, 14% full-time, 78% women, 22% men

Undergraduates 13 full-time, 83 part-time. 2% are from out of state; 14% Black or African American, non-Hispanic/Latino; 33% Hispanic/Latino; 4% Asian, non-Hispanic/Latino; 32% Race/ethnicity unknown; 33% transferred in.
Freshmen *Average high school GPA:* 3.
Faculty *Total:* 9, 89% full-time. *Student/faculty ratio:* 10:1.

Majors Registered nursing/registered nurse.
Academics *Calendar:* semesters. *Degree:* associate. *Special study options:* advanced placement credit, part-time degree program.
Library Cochran School of Nursing Library. *Books:* 2,340 (physical), 559 (digital/electronic); *Serial titles:* 29 (physical), 7 (digital/electronic); *Databases:* 13. Study areas open 24 hours, 5&-7 days a week.
Student Life *Housing:* college housing not available. *Campus security:* 24-hour emergency response devices and patrols, late-night transport/escort service. *Student services:* health clinic, personal/psychological counseling.
Costs (2016–17) *Tuition:* $9571 full-time, $563 per credit part-time. Full-time tuition and fees vary according to course load and student level. Part-time tuition and fees vary according to course load and student level. *Required fees:* $1571 full-time, $734 per term part-time. *Payment plan:* installment.
Applying *Options:* deferred entrance. *Application fee:* $35. *Required:* high school transcript. *Application deadline:* 5/15 (freshmen). *Notification:* 5/15 (freshmen), continuous (transfers).
Freshman Application Contact Brandy Haughton, Admissions Counselor, Cochran School of Nursing, 967 North Broadway, Yonkers, NY 10701. *Phone:* 914-964-4606. *Fax:* 914-964-4796.
E-mail: bhaughton@riversidehealth.org.
Website: http://www.cochranschoolofnursing.us/.

The College of Westchester
White Plains, New York

- **Proprietary** primarily 2-year, founded 1915
- **Suburban** campus with easy access to New York City
- **Coed,** 1,021 undergraduate students, 79% full-time, 65% women, 35% men

Undergraduates 808 full-time, 213 part-time. Students come from 5 states and territories; 3% are from out of state; 36% Black or African American, non-Hispanic/Latino; 46% Hispanic/Latino; 2% Asian, non-Hispanic/Latino; 0.2% American Indian or Alaska Native, non-Hispanic/Latino; 1% Two or more races, non-Hispanic/Latino; 4% Race/ethnicity unknown; 11% transferred in. *Retention:* 70% of full-time freshmen returned.
Freshmen *Admission:* 735 applied, 690 admitted, 192 enrolled.
Faculty *Total:* 69, 46% full-time. *Student/faculty ratio:* 18:1.
Majors Accounting; business administration and management; commercial and advertising art; computer software and media applications related; health/health-care administration; health information/medical records administration; medical/clinical assistant; network and system administration; web page, digital/multimedia and information resources design.
Academics *Calendar:* semesters. *Degrees:* certificates, associate, and bachelor's. *Special study options:* academic remediation for entering students, accelerated degree program, adult/continuing education programs, cooperative education, distance learning, double majors, honors programs, internships, part-time degree program, summer session for credit.
Library Dr. William R. Papallo Library.
Student Life *Housing:* college housing not available. *Activities and Organizations:* student-run newspaper.
Student services: personal/psychological counseling.
Standardized Tests *Recommended:* SAT (for admission).
Costs (2017–18) *Tuition:* $20,115 full-time, $745 per credit part-time. *Required fees:* $1000 full-time, $100 per course part-time. *Payment plan:* installment. *Waivers:* employees or children of employees.
Applying *Options:* electronic application, deferred entrance. *Application fee:* $40. *Required:* high school transcript, interview. *Required for some:* essay or personal statement. *Application deadlines:* rolling (freshmen), rolling (transfers).
Freshman Application Contact Mr. Matt Curtis, Vice President, Enrollment Management, The College of Westchester, 325 Central Avenue, PO Box 710, White Plains, NY 10602. *Phone:* 914-948-4442 Ext. 313. *Toll-free phone:* 855-403-7722. *Fax:* 914-948-5441. *E-mail:* admissions@cw.edu.
Website: http://www.cw.edu/.

Columbia-Greene Community College
Hudson, New York

- **State and locally supported** 2-year, founded 1966, part of State University of New York System
- **Rural** 143-acre campus
- **Coed,** 1,643 undergraduate students, 41% full-time, 63% women, 37% men

Undergraduates 678 full-time, 965 part-time. Students come from 5 states and territories; 1 other country; 0.5% are from out of state; 8% Black or African American, non-Hispanic/Latino; 6% Hispanic/Latino; 2% Asian, non-Hispanic/Latino; 0.2% Native Hawaiian or other Pacific Islander, non-Hispanic/Latino; 0.2% American Indian or Alaska Native, non-Hispanic/Latino; 4% Two or more races, non-Hispanic/Latino; 0.9%

Race/ethnicity unknown; 0.1% international; 7% transferred in. *Retention:* 61% of full-time freshmen returned.
Freshmen *Admission:* 325 enrolled.
Faculty *Total:* 85, 52% full-time. *Student/faculty ratio:* 17:1.
Majors Accounting technology and bookkeeping; administrative assistant and secretarial science; art; automobile/automotive mechanics technology; business administration and management; business/commerce; computer and information sciences; criminal justice/law enforcement administration; cyber/computer forensics and counterterrorism; environmental studies; general studies; humanities; human services; information technology; liberal arts and sciences/liberal studies; medical/clinical assistant; registered nursing/registered nurse.
Academics *Calendar:* semesters. *Degree:* certificates and associate. *Special study options:* academic remediation for entering students, advanced placement credit, cooperative education, distance learning, double majors, English as a second language, honors programs, independent study, internships, part-time degree program, services for LD students, summer session for credit.
Student Life *Housing:* college housing not available. *Activities and Organizations:* student-run radio station, Criminal Justice Club, Human Services Club, Psychology Club, Student Senate, Animal Advocates. *Campus security:* 24-hour emergency response devices and patrols, student patrols, late-night transport/escort service. *Student services:* personal/psychological counseling.
Athletics Member NCAA, NJCAA. All NCAA Division III. *Intercollegiate sports:* baseball M, basketball M, cross-country running M/W, golf M/W, softball W, track and field M/W. *Intramural sports:* badminton M/W, basketball M/W, golf M/W, table tennis M/W, volleyball M/W.
Costs (2016–17) *Tuition:* state resident $4392 full-time, $183 per semester hour part-time; nonresident $8784 full-time, $366 per semester hour part-time. Full-time tuition and fees vary according to course load and program. Part-time tuition and fees vary according to course load and program. *Required fees:* $352 full-time, $15 per semester hour part-time, $5 per term part-time. *Payment plan:* installment. *Waivers:* senior citizens and employees or children of employees.
Applying *Required for some:* interview. *Recommended:* high school transcript.
Freshman Application Contact Ms. Rachel Kappel, Director of Admissions, Columbia-Greene Community College, 4400 Route 23, Hudson, NY 12534. *Phone:* 518-828-4181 Ext. 3370. *Fax:* 518-822-2015.
E-mail: rachel.kappel@sunycgcc.edu.
Website: http://www.sunycgcc.edu/.

Corning Community College
Corning, New York

- **State and locally supported** 2-year, founded 1956, part of State University of New York System
- **Rural** 500-acre campus
- **Endowment** $521,628
- **Coed**

Undergraduates 1,929 full-time, 2,043 part-time. Students come from 9 states and territories; 14 other countries; 7% are from out of state; 4% Black or African American, non-Hispanic/Latino; 2% Hispanic/Latino; 1% Asian, non-Hispanic/Latino; 0.1% Native Hawaiian or other Pacific Islander, non-Hispanic/Latino; 0.5% American Indian or Alaska Native, non-Hispanic/Latino; 3% Two or more races, non-Hispanic/Latino; 5% Race/ethnicity unknown; 0.2% international; 3% transferred in; 6% live on campus. *Retention:* 56% of full-time freshmen returned.
Faculty *Student/faculty ratio:* 18:1.
Academics *Calendar:* semesters. *Degree:* certificates and associate. *Special study options:* academic remediation for entering students, accelerated degree program, adult/continuing education programs, advanced placement credit, cooperative education, distance learning, double majors, English as a second language, honors programs, independent study, internships, off-campus study, part-time degree program, services for LD students, student-designed majors, study abroad, summer session for credit.
Library Arthur A. Houghton, Jr. Library. *Books:* 28,518 (physical), 185,642 (digital/electronic); *Serial titles:* 571 (physical), 27,480 (digital/electronic); *Databases:* 190. Weekly public service hours: 63; students can reserve study rooms.
Student Life *Campus security:* 24-hour emergency response devices and patrols, late-night transport/escort service, controlled dormitory access.
Athletics Member NJCAA.
Costs (2016–17) *Tuition:* state resident $4314 full-time, $180 per credit hour part-time; nonresident $8628 full-time, $360 per credit hour part-time. Part-time tuition and fees vary according to course load. *Required fees:* $558 full-time, $28 per credit hour part-time. *Room and board:* $9224; room only: $6200. Room and board charges vary according to housing facility.

Financial Aid Of all full-time matriculated undergraduates who enrolled in 2015, 264 Federal Work-Study jobs (averaging $1128).
Applying *Options:* electronic application, early admission. *Required:* high school transcript. *Required for some:* interview.
Freshman Application Contact Corning Community College, One Academic Drive, Corning, NY 14830-3297. *Phone:* 607-962-9540. *Toll-free phone:* 800-358-7171. *Website:* http://www.corning-cc.edu/.

Dutchess Community College
Poughkeepsie, New York

- **State and locally supported** 2-year, founded 1957, part of State University of New York System
- **Suburban** 130-acre campus with easy access to New York City
- **Coed**, 9,348 undergraduate students, 44% full-time, 54% women, 46% men

Undergraduates 4,072 full-time, 5,276 part-time. 0.3% are from out of state; 11% Black or African American, non-Hispanic/Latino; 18% Hispanic/Latino; 3% Asian, non-Hispanic/Latino; 0.1% Native Hawaiian or other Pacific Islander, non-Hispanic/Latino; 0.2% American Indian or Alaska Native, non-Hispanic/Latino; 4% Two or more races, non-Hispanic/Latino; 3% Race/ethnicity unknown; 1% international; 3% transferred in; 5% live on campus.
Freshmen *Admission:* 5,732 applied, 4,040 admitted, 1,950 enrolled. *Average high school GPA:* 2.5.
Faculty *Total:* 554, 23% full-time, 6% with terminal degrees. *Student/faculty ratio:* 19:1.
Majors Accounting; accounting technology and bookkeeping; airline pilot and flight crew; architectural engineering technology; art; aviation/airway management; business administration and management; child-care and support services management; clinical/medical laboratory technology; commercial and advertising art; communications systems installation and repair technology; community health services counseling; computer/information technology services administration related; computer science; construction trades related; criminal justice/police science; electrical, electronic and communications engineering technology; emergency medical technology (EMT paramedic); engineering; fire services administration; general studies; humanities; human services; information science/studies; legal assistant/paralegal; liberal arts and sciences and humanities related; liberal arts and sciences/liberal studies; physical education teaching and coaching; registered nursing/registered nurse; speech communication and rhetoric; visual and performing arts.
Academics *Calendar:* semesters. *Degree:* certificates and associate. *Special study options:* academic remediation for entering students, adult/continuing education programs, advanced placement credit, distance learning, English as a second language, freshman honors college, honors programs, internships, off-campus study, part-time degree program, services for LD students, summer session for credit.
Library Dutchess Library plus 1 other. *Books:* 89,515 (physical), 159,235 (digital/electronic); *Serial titles:* 128 (physical), 336,174 (digital/electronic); *Databases:* 70. Weekly public service hours: 70.
Student Life *Housing Options:* coed, men-only, women-only, special housing for students with disabilities. Campus housing is provided by a third party. *Activities and Organizations:* drama/theater group, student-run newspaper, radio station, choral group, Rap, Poetry and Music, Outdoor Adventure, Student Government Association, Gamers Club, Masquer's Guild Theatre Club. *Campus security:* 24-hour emergency response devices and patrols, late-night transport/escort service, controlled dormitory access, Mass Notification System. *Student services:* health clinic, personal/psychological counseling.
Athletics Member NJCAA. *Intercollegiate sports:* baseball M, basketball M/W, cross-country running M/W, soccer M, softball W, volleyball W.
Costs (2016–17) *Tuition:* state resident $3528 full-time, $140 per credit hour part-time; nonresident $7056 full-time, $280 per credit hour part-time. *Required fees:* $432 full-time, $10 per hour part-time, $19 per term part-time. *Room and board:* $10,500. Room and board charges vary according to board plan. *Payment plan:* installment. *Waivers:* senior citizens and employees or children of employees.
Applying *Options:* electronic application, early admission, deferred entrance. *Required:* high school transcript. *Application deadlines:* rolling (freshmen), rolling (transfers). *Notification:* continuous (freshmen), continuous (transfers).
Freshman Application Contact Dutchess Community College, 53 Pendell Road, Poughkeepsie, NY 12601-1595. *Phone:* 845-431-8010.
Website: http://www.sunydutchess.edu/.

Elmira Business Institute
Elmira, New York

Freshman Application Contact Ms. Lindsay Dull, Director of Student services, Elmira Business Institute, Elmira, NY 14901. *Phone:* 607-733-7177.

Toll-free phone: 800-843-1812. *E-mail:* info@ebi-college.com. *Website:* http://www.ebi-college.com/.

Erie Community College
Buffalo, New York

- **State and locally supported** 2-year, founded 1971, part of State University of New York System
- **Urban** 1-acre campus
- **Coed,** 2,424 undergraduate students, 76% full-time, 60% women, 40% men

Undergraduates 1,840 full-time, 584 part-time. Students come from 15 states and territories; 7 other countries; 0.8% are from out of state; 32% Black or African American, non-Hispanic/Latino; 9% Hispanic/Latino; 6% Asian, non-Hispanic/Latino; 0.9% American Indian or Alaska Native, non-Hispanic/Latino; 3% Two or more races, non-Hispanic/Latino; 8% Race/ethnicity unknown; 4% international; 7% transferred in.
Freshmen *Admission:* 2,546 applied, 1,812 admitted, 584 enrolled.
Faculty *Student/faculty ratio:* 19:1.
Majors Building/property maintenance; business administration and management; child-care and support services management; criminal justice/law enforcement administration; crisis/emergency/disaster management; culinary arts; fine/studio arts; general studies; health and physical education/fitness; health and wellness; humanities; legal assistant/paralegal; liberal arts and sciences and humanities related; liberal arts and sciences/liberal studies; medical radiologic technology; registered nursing/registered nurse; substance abuse/addiction counseling.
Academics *Calendar:* semesters plus summer sessions, winter intersession. *Degree:* certificates, diplomas, and associate. *Special study options:* academic remediation for entering students, adult/continuing education programs, advanced placement credit, cooperative education, distance learning, double majors, English as a second language, honors programs, independent study, internships, part-time degree program, services for LD students, student-designed majors, study abroad, summer session for credit. *ROTC:* Army (c).
Library Leon E. Butler Library. *Books:* 21,834 (physical), 2,557 (digital/electronic); *Serial titles:* 98 (physical); *Databases:* 70. Weekly public service hours: 60; students can reserve study rooms.
Student Life *Housing:* college housing not available. *Activities and Organizations:* HPER, Art Club, ECC Cricket Club/Sharks, Spoken Word Poetry Club. *Campus security:* 24-hour emergency response devices and patrols, late-night transport/escort service. *Student services:* health clinic, personal/psychological counseling, women's center.
Athletics Member NJCAA. *Intercollegiate sports:* baseball M, basketball M/W, bowling M/W, cheerleading W, football M, ice hockey M, lacrosse W, soccer M/W, softball W, swimming and diving M/W, volleyball W.
Costs (2016–17) *One-time required fee:* $75. *Tuition:* state resident $4733 full-time, $198 per credit hour part-time; nonresident $9466 full-time, $396 per credit hour part-time. *Required fees:* $675 full-time, $19 per credit hour part-time, $75 per term part-time. *Payment plan:* installment. *Waivers:* senior citizens and employees or children of employees.
Applying *Options:* electronic application. *Application fee:* $25. *Required:* high school transcript. *Required for some:* interview. *Application deadlines:* rolling (freshmen), rolling (transfers). *Notification:* continuous (freshmen), continuous (transfers).
Freshman Application Contact Erie Community College, 121 Ellicott Street, Buffalo, NY 14203-2698. *Phone:* 716-851-1155. *Fax:* 716-270-2821. *E-mail:* admissions@ecc.edu.
Website: http://www.ecc.edu/.

Erie Community College, North Campus
Williamsville, New York

- **State and locally supported** 2-year, founded 1946, part of State University of New York System
- **Suburban** 120-acre campus with easy access to Buffalo
- **Coed,** 5,224 undergraduate students, 67% full-time, 49% women, 51% men

Undergraduates 3,518 full-time, 1,706 part-time. Students come from 21 states and territories; 28 other countries; 0.8% are from out of state; 12% Black or African American, non-Hispanic/Latino; 5% Hispanic/Latino; 4% Asian, non-Hispanic/Latino; 0.2% Native Hawaiian or other Pacific Islander, non-Hispanic/Latino; 0.3% American Indian or Alaska Native, non-Hispanic/Latino; 2% Two or more races, non-Hispanic/Latino; 9% Race/ethnicity unknown; 4% international; 8% transferred in.
Freshmen *Admission:* 4,244 applied, 2,870 admitted, 1,090 enrolled.
Faculty *Student/faculty ratio:* 19:1.
Majors Biology/biotechnology laboratory technician; building/construction site management; business administration and management; civil engineering technology; clinical/medical laboratory technology; computer and information

sciences; criminal justice/law enforcement administration; criminal justice/police science; culinary arts; dental hygiene; dietitian assistant; electrical, electronic and communications engineering technology; engineering; environmental engineering technology; environmental science; fine/studio arts; general studies; health and physical education/fitness; health and wellness; health information/medical records technology; humanities; industrial technology; liberal arts and sciences/liberal studies; mechanical engineering/mechanical technology; medical administrative assistant and medical secretary; nanotechnology; occupational therapist assistant; office management; opticianry; registered nursing/registered nurse; respiratory care therapy; restaurant/food services management.
Academics *Calendar:* semesters plus summer sessions, winter intersession. *Degree:* certificates, diplomas, and associate. *Special study options:* academic remediation for entering students, adult/continuing education programs, advanced placement credit, cooperative education, distance learning, double majors, English as a second language, honors programs, independent study, internships, part-time degree program, services for LD students, student-designed majors, study abroad, summer session for credit. *ROTC:* Army (c).
Library Richard R. Dry Memorial Library. *Books:* 48,977 (physical), 2,557 (digital/electronic); *Serial titles:* 166 (physical); *Databases:* 70. Weekly public service hours: 63.
Student Life *Housing:* college housing not available. *Activities and Organizations:* Dental Hygiene, American Public Works Association, Student Occupational Therapy Association, International Student Organization. *Campus security:* 24-hour emergency response devices and patrols, late-night transport/escort service. *Student services:* health clinic, personal/psychological counseling, women's center.
Athletics Member NJCAA. *Intercollegiate sports:* baseball M, basketball M/W, bowling M/W, cheerleading W, football M, ice hockey M, lacrosse W, soccer M/W, softball W, swimming and diving M/W, volleyball W.
Costs (2016–17) *One-time required fee:* $75. *Tuition:* state resident $4733 full-time, $198 per credit hour part-time; nonresident $9466 full-time, $396 per credit hour part-time. *Required fees:* $675 full-time, $19 per credit hour part-time, $75 per term part-time. *Payment plan:* installment. *Waivers:* senior citizens and employees or children of employees.
Applying *Options:* electronic application. *Application fee:* $25. *Required:* high school transcript. *Required for some:* interview. *Application deadlines:* rolling (freshmen), rolling (transfers). *Notification:* continuous (freshmen), continuous (transfers).
Freshman Application Contact Erie Community College, North Campus, 6205 Main Street, Williamsville, NY 14221-7095. *Phone:* 716-851-1455. *Fax:* 716-270-2961. *E-mail:* admissions@ecc.edu.
Website: http://www.ecc.edu/.

Erie Community College, South Campus
Orchard Park, New York

- **State and locally supported** 2-year, founded 1974, part of State University of New York System
- **Suburban** 110-acre campus with easy access to Buffalo
- **Coed,** 3,630 undergraduate students, 59% full-time, 44% women, 56% men

Undergraduates 2,132 full-time, 1,498 part-time. Students come from 20 states and territories; 9 other countries; 173% are from out of state; 9% Black or African American, non-Hispanic/Latino; 4% Hispanic/Latino; 2% Asian, non-Hispanic/Latino; 0.1% Native Hawaiian or other Pacific Islander, non-Hispanic/Latino; 1% American Indian or Alaska Native, non-Hispanic/Latino; 2% Two or more races, non-Hispanic/Latino; 12% Race/ethnicity unknown; 1% international; 7% transferred in.
Freshmen *Admission:* 2,561 applied, 2,121 admitted, 701 enrolled.
Faculty *Student/faculty ratio:* 19:1.
Majors Architectural engineering technology; autobody/collision and repair technology; automobile/automotive mechanics technology; business administration and management; CAD/CADD drafting/design technology; communications systems installation and repair technology; computer technology/computer systems technology; criminal justice/law enforcement administration; dental laboratory technology; emergency medical technology (EMT paramedic); fine/studio arts; fire services administration; general studies; graphic and printing equipment operation/production; health and physical education/fitness; health and wellness; humanities; information technology; liberal arts and sciences/liberal studies; speech communication and rhetoric.
Academics *Calendar:* semesters plus summer sessions, winter intersession. *Degree:* certificates, diplomas, and associate. *Special study options:* academic remediation for entering students, adult/continuing education programs, advanced placement credit, cooperative education, distance learning, double majors, English as a second language, honors programs, independent study, internships, part-time degree program, services for LD students, student-designed majors, study abroad, summer session for credit. *ROTC:* Army (c).

Library ECC South Campus Libarary. *Books:* 35,737 (physical), 2,557 (digital/electronic); *Serial titles:* 156 (physical); *Databases:* 70. Weekly public service hours: 63.

Student Life *Housing:* college housing not available. *Activities and Organizations:* Architecture Club, Criminal Justice Club, Sign Language Club. *Campus security:* 24-hour emergency response devices and patrols, late-night transport/escort service. *Student services:* health clinic, personal/psychological counseling, women's center.

Athletics Member NJCAA. *Intercollegiate sports:* baseball M, basketball M/W, bowling M/W, cheerleading W, football M, ice hockey M, lacrosse W, soccer M/W, softball W, swimming and diving M/W, volleyball W.

Costs (2016–17) *One-time required fee:* $75. *Tuition:* state resident $4733 full-time, $198 per credit hour part-time; nonresident $9466 full-time, $396 per credit hour part-time. *Required fees:* $675 full-time, $19 per credit hour part-time, $75 per term part-time. *Payment plan:* installment. *Waivers:* senior citizens and employees or children of employees.

Applying *Options:* electronic application. *Application fee:* $25. *Required:* high school transcript. *Required for some:* interview. *Application deadlines:* rolling (freshmen), rolling (transfers). *Notification:* continuous (freshmen), continuous (transfers).

Freshman Application Contact Erie Community College, South Campus, 4041 Southwestern Boulevard, Orchard Park, NY 14127-2199. *Phone:* 716-851-1655. *Fax:* 716-851-1687. *E-mail:* admissions@ecc.edu. *Website:* http://www.ecc.edu/.

Eugenio María de Hostos Community College of the City University of New York

Bronx, New York

Freshman Application Contact Mr. Roland Velez, Director of Admissions, Eugenio María de Hostos Community College of the City University of New York, 120 149th Street, Bronx, NY 10451. *Phone:* 718-319-7968. *Fax:* 718-319-7919. *E-mail:* admissions@hostos.cuny.edu. *Website:* http://www.hostos.cuny.edu/.

Fashion Institute of Technology

New York, New York

- **State and locally supported** comprehensive, founded 1944, part of State University of New York System
- **Urban** 5-acre campus with easy access to New York City
- **Coed, primarily women,** 9,096 undergraduate students, 81% full-time, 85% women, 15% men

Undergraduates 7,395 full-time, 1,701 part-time. 32% are from out of state; 9% Black or African American, non-Hispanic/Latino; 18% Hispanic/Latino; 11% Asian, non-Hispanic/Latino; 0.2% Native Hawaiian or other Pacific Islander, non-Hispanic/Latino; 0.2% American Indian or Alaska Native, non-Hispanic/Latino; 3% Two or more races, non-Hispanic/Latino; 0.8% Race/ethnicity unknown; 12% international; 8% transferred in; 21% live on campus. *Retention:* 89% of full-time freshmen returned.

Freshmen *Admission:* 4,632 applied, 1,872 admitted, 1,273 enrolled. *Average high school GPA:* 3.6.

Faculty *Total:* 931, 25% full-time. *Student/faculty ratio:* 17:1.

Majors Advertising; animation, interactive technology, video graphics and special effects; apparel and textile manufacturing; cinematography and film/video production; commercial and advertising art; commercial photography; design and applied arts related; entrepreneurial and small business related; fashion/apparel design; fashion merchandising; fashion modeling; film/cinema/video studies; fine and studio arts management; fine/studio arts; graphic design; illustration; industrial and product design; interior design; international marketing; marketing research; merchandising, sales, and marketing operations related (specialized); metal and jewelry arts; special products marketing.

Academics *Calendar:* semesters. *Degrees:* certificates, associate, bachelor's, and master's. *Special study options:* academic remediation for entering students, advanced placement credit, distance learning, English as a second language, honors programs, independent study, internships, part-time degree program, services for LD students, study abroad, summer session for credit.

Library Gladys Marcus Library.

Student Life *Housing Options:* coed, women-only, special housing for students with disabilities. Campus housing is university owned. Freshman applicants given priority for college housing. *Activities and Organizations:* drama/theater group, student-run newspaper, radio and television station, choral group. *Campus security:* 24-hour emergency response devices and patrols, late-night transport/escort service, controlled dormitory access. *Student services:* health clinic, personal/psychological counseling.

Athletics Member NJCAA. *Intercollegiate sports:* cross-country running M/W, soccer W, swimming and diving M/W, table tennis M/W, tennis M/W, track and field M/W, volleyball W.

Costs (2016–17) *Tuition:* state resident $6470 full-time, $270 per credit hour part-time; nonresident $19,592 full-time, $816 per credit hour part-time. Full-time tuition and fees vary according to degree level. Part-time tuition and fees vary according to degree level. *Required fees:* $745 full-time. *Room and board:* $13,386; room only: $8910. Room and board charges vary according to board plan and housing facility. *Waivers:* employees or children of employees.

Financial Aid Of all full-time matriculated undergraduates who enrolled in 2015, 4,591 applied for aid, 3,763 were judged to have need, 1,664 had their need fully met. In 2015, 230 non-need-based awards were made. *Average percent of need met:* 67%. *Average financial aid package:* $11,804. *Average need-based loan:* $3135. *Average need-based gift aid:* $6078. *Average non-need-based aid:* $773. *Average indebtedness upon graduation:* $24,850.

Applying *Options:* electronic application. *Application fee:* $50. *Required:* essay or personal statement, high school transcript. *Required for some:* portfolio for art and design programs. *Application deadlines:* 1/1 (freshmen), 1/1 (transfers). *Notification:* 4/1 (freshmen), 4/1 (transfers).

Freshman Application Contact Ms. Magda Francois, Director of Admissions and Strategic Recruitment, Fashion Institute of Technology, Seventh Avenue at 27th Street, New York, NY 10001-5992. *E-mail:* fitinfo@fitnyc.edu. *Website:* http://www.fitnyc.edu/.

See previous page for display ad and page 336 for the College Close-Up.

Finger Lakes Community College
Canandaigua, New York

- **State and locally supported** 2-year, founded 1965, part of State University of New York System
- **Small-town** 300-acre campus with easy access to Rochester
- **Coed,** 6,521 undergraduate students, 40% full-time, 57% women, 43% men

Undergraduates 2,587 full-time, 3,934 part-time. Students come from 15 states and territories; 2 other countries; 0.3% are from out of state; 5% Black or African American, non-Hispanic/Latino; 5% Hispanic/Latino; 1% Asian, non-Hispanic/Latino; 0.3% American Indian or Alaska Native, non-Hispanic/Latino; 3% Two or more races, non-Hispanic/Latino; 13% Race/ethnicity unknown; 3% transferred in.

Freshmen *Admission:* 2,493 applied, 2,211 admitted, 1,039 enrolled.

Faculty *Total:* 313, 37% full-time. *Student/faculty ratio:* 22:1.

Majors Accounting; administrative assistant and secretarial science; animation, interactive technology, video graphics and special effects; architectural engineering technology; biological and physical sciences; biology/biological sciences; biology/biotechnology laboratory technician; business administration and management; chemistry; commercial and advertising art; computer and information sciences; computer science; criminal justice/law enforcement administration; criminal justice/police science; culinary arts; data processing and data processing technology; digital communication and media/multimedia; drafting and design technology; dramatic/theater arts; early childhood education; e-commerce; emergency medical technology (EMT paramedic); engineering science; environmental studies; fine/studio arts; fishing and fisheries sciences and management; hotel/motel administration; humanities; human services; instrumentation technology; kindergarten/preschool education; legal assistant/paralegal; liberal arts and sciences/liberal studies; marketing/marketing management; mass communication/media; mathematics; mechanical engineering/mechanical technology; music; natural resources/conservation; natural resources law enforcement and protective services; natural resources management and policy; natural resources management and policy related; ornamental horticulture; physical education teaching and coaching; physics; political science and government; pre-engineering; psychology; recording arts technology; registered nursing/registered nurse; resort management; social sciences; sociology; sports studies; substance abuse/addiction counseling; tourism and travel services management; viticulture and enology.

Academics *Calendar:* semesters. *Degree:* certificates and associate. *Special study options:* academic remediation for entering students, accelerated degree program, advanced placement credit, distance learning, double majors, honors programs, independent study, internships, off-campus study, part-time degree program, services for LD students, study abroad, summer session for credit. *ROTC:* Air Force (c).

Library Charles Meder Library. Students can reserve study rooms.

Student Life *Housing Options:* Campus housing is provided by a third party. *Activities and Organizations:* drama/theater group, student-run radio station, choral group. *Campus security:* 24-hour emergency response devices and patrols, late-night transport/escort service. *Student services:* health clinic, personal/psychological counseling, legal services.

Athletics Member NJCAA. *Intercollegiate sports:* baseball M, basketball M/W, cross-country running M/W, lacrosse M, soccer M/W, softball W, track

and field M/W, volleyball W. *Intramural sports:* basketball M/W, tennis M/W, volleyball M/W.

Costs (2016–17) *Tuition:* state resident $4368 full-time, $183 per credit hour part-time; nonresident $8736 full-time, $366 per credit hour part-time. Full-time tuition and fees vary according to course load. Part-time tuition and fees vary according to course load. *Required fees:* $584 full-time, $19 per credit hour part-time. *Payment plan:* installment. *Waivers:* senior citizens and employees or children of employees.

Financial Aid Of all full-time matriculated undergraduates who enrolled in 2016, 2,122 applied for aid, 1,950 were judged to have need. In 2016, 8 non-need-based awards were made. *Average non-need-based aid:* $1050.

Applying *Options:* electronic application, early admission, deferred entrance. *Application fee:* $20. *Required:* high school transcript. *Application deadlines:* 8/25 (freshmen), 8/25 (transfers).

Freshman Application Contact Ms. Bonnie B. Ritts, Director of Admissions, Finger Lakes Community College, 3325 Marvin Sands Drive, Canandaigua, NY 14424-8395. *Phone:* 585-785-1279. *Fax:* 585-785- 1734. *E-mail:* admissions@flcc.edu. *Website:* http://www.flcc.edu/.

Finger Lakes Health College of Nursing
Geneva, New York

Admissions Office Contact Finger Lakes Health College of Nursing, 196 North Street, Geneva, NY 14456. *Website:* http://www.flhcon.com/.

Fiorello H. LaGuardia Community College of the City University of New York
Long Island City, New York

- **State and locally supported** 2-year, founded 1970, part of City University of New York System
- **Urban** 25-acre campus with easy access to New York City
- **Coed,** 19,332 undergraduate students, 55% full-time, 57% women, 43% men

Undergraduates 10,642 full-time, 8,690 part-time. Students come from 14 states and territories; 151 other countries; 0.2% are from out of state; 15% Black or African American, non-Hispanic/Latino; 42% Hispanic/Latino; 12% Asian, non-Hispanic/Latino; 0.3% Native Hawaiian or other Pacific Islander, non-Hispanic/Latino; 0.3% American Indian or Alaska Native, non-Hispanic/Latino; 1% Two or more races, non-Hispanic/Latino; 19% Race/ethnicity unknown; 4% international; 7% transferred in.

Freshmen *Admission:* 20,608 applied, 20,608 admitted, 2,950 enrolled.

Faculty *Total:* 1,126, 36% full-time, 30% with terminal degrees. *Student/faculty ratio:* 22:1.

Majors Accounting technology and bookkeeping; administrative assistant and secretarial science; adult development and aging; biology/biological sciences; business administration and management; civil engineering; commercial photography; computer and information sciences and support services related; computer installation and repair technology; computer programming; computer science; computer systems networking and telecommunications; criminal justice/safety; data entry/microcomputer applications; dietetic technology; digital arts; dramatic/theater arts; electrical and electronics engineering; emergency medical technology (EMT paramedic); energy management and systems technology; English; environmental science; fine/studio arts; industrial and product design; Japanese; legal assistant/paralegal; liberal arts and sciences/liberal studies; licensed practical/vocational nurse training; mechanical engineering; medical radiologic technology; occupational therapist assistant; philosophy; physical therapy technology; psychiatric/mental health services technology; psychology; recording arts technology; registered nursing/registered nurse; restaurant/food services management; Spanish; speech communication and rhetoric; teacher assistant/aide; tourism and travel services management; veterinary/animal health technology; visual and performing arts.

Academics *Calendar:* enhanced semester. *Degree:* certificates and associate. *Special study options:* academic remediation for entering students, accelerated degree program, adult/continuing education programs, advanced placement credit, cooperative education, distance learning, double majors, English as a second language, honors programs, independent study, internships, off-campus study, part-time degree program, services for LD students, student-designed majors, study abroad, summer session for credit.

Library Fiorello H. LaGuardia Community College Library Media Resources Center plus 1 other. *Books:* 97,308 (physical), 543,900 (digital/electronic); *Serial titles:* 529 (physical); *Databases:* 235,978. Weekly public service hours: 50; students can reserve study rooms.

Student Life *Housing:* college housing not available. *Activities and Organizations:* drama/theater group, student-run newspaper, radio station,

Bangladesh Student Association, Christian Club, Chinese Club, Web Radio, Black Student Union. *Campus security:* 24-hour emergency response devices and patrols, late-night transport/escort service. *Student services:* health clinic, personal/psychological counseling, women's center, legal services.

Athletics *Intercollegiate sports:* basketball M/W. *Intramural sports:* basketball M/W, bowling M/W, cheerleading M/W, soccer M/W, swimming and diving M/W, table tennis M/W, volleyball M/W.

Costs (2016–17) *Tuition:* state resident $4800 full-time, $210 per credit part-time; nonresident $7680 full-time, $320 per credit part-time. *Required fees:* $208 full-time, $105 per term part-time. *Payment plan:* installment. *Waivers:* senior citizens and employees or children of employees.

Financial Aid Of all full-time matriculated undergraduates who enrolled in 2012, 7,961 applied for aid, 7,741 were judged to have need, 286 had their need fully met. 352 Federal Work-Study jobs (averaging $1175). *Average percent of need met:* 45%. *Average financial aid package:* $5523. *Average need-based gift aid:* $5818.

Applying *Options:* electronic application, early admission, deferred entrance. *Application fee:* $65. *Required:* high school transcript. *Application deadlines:* rolling (freshmen), rolling (transfers). *Notification:* continuous (freshmen), continuous (transfers).

Freshman Application Contact Ms. LaVora Desvigne, Director of Admissions, Fiorello H. LaGuardia Community College of the City University of New York, RM-147, 31-10 Thomson Avenue, Long Island City, NY 11101. *Phone:* 718-482-5114. *Fax:* 718-482-5112. *E-mail:* admissions@lagcc.cuny.edu. *Website:* http://www.lagcc.cuny.edu/.

Fulton-Montgomery Community College
Johnstown, New York

Freshman Application Contact Fulton-Montgomery Community College, 2805 State Highway 67, Johnstown, NY 12095-3790. *Phone:* 518-762-4651 Ext. 8301. *Website:* http://www.fmcc.suny.edu/.

Genesee Community College
Batavia, New York

- **State and locally supported** 2-year, founded 1966, part of State University of New York System
- **Small-town** 256-acre campus with easy access to Buffalo, Rochester
- **Endowment** $4.6 million
- **Coed,** 6,141 undergraduate students, 41% full-time, 63% women, 37% men

Undergraduates 2,515 full-time, 3,626 part-time. Students come from 25 states and territories; 20 other countries; 2% are from out of state; 10% Black or African American, non-Hispanic/Latino; 5% Hispanic/Latino; 0.7% Asian, non-Hispanic/Latino; 1% American Indian or Alaska Native, non-Hispanic/Latino; 3% Two or more races, non-Hispanic/Latino; 3% Race/ethnicity unknown; 4% international; 5% transferred in.

Freshmen *Admission:* 2,916 applied, 2,079 admitted, 914 enrolled.

Faculty *Total:* 347, 26% full-time, 10% with terminal degrees. *Student/faculty ratio:* 17:1.

Majors Accounting; biology/biological sciences; biology/biotechnology laboratory technician; biotechnology; business administration and management; business administration, management and operations related; business, management, and marketing related; business operations support and secretarial services related; chemistry; civil drafting and CAD/CADD; clinical/medical laboratory technology; computer and information sciences related; computer graphics; computer installation and repair technology; computer programming related; computer science; computer software and media applications related; computer support specialist; computer systems networking and telecommunications; corrections and criminal justice related; criminal justice/law enforcement administration; criminal justice/police science; criminal justice/safety; criminology; digital arts; drafting and design technology; drafting/design engineering technologies related; dramatic/theater arts; dramatic/theater arts and stagecraft related; e-commerce; education; education (multiple levels); education related; elementary education; engineering; engineering science; entrepreneurship; fashion/apparel design; fashion merchandising; fine/studio arts; food technology and processing; foreign languages related; general studies; gerontology; graphic design; health and physical education/fitness; health and physical education related; health professions related; hospitality administration; hotel/motel administration; humanities; human services; information science/studies; kindergarten/preschool education; legal assistant/paralegal; liberal arts and sciences and humanities related; liberal arts and sciences/liberal studies; marketing/marketing management; mass communication/media; mathematics; mathematics related; medical administrative assistant and medical secretary; nanotechnology; network and system administration; nursing practice; parks,

recreation, leisure, and fitness studies related; physical education teaching and coaching; physical therapy; physical therapy technology; polysomnography; psychology; psychology related; radio and television; radio and television broadcasting technology; radio, television, and digital communication related; registered nursing, nursing administration, nursing research and clinical nursing related; registered nursing/registered nurse; respiratory care therapy; social sciences; social sciences related; social work; social work related; sports studies; substance abuse/addiction counseling; teacher assistant/aide; theater design and technology; theater/theater arts management; tourism and travel services management; tourism promotion; veterinary/animal health technology; web page, digital/multimedia and information resources design.

Academics *Calendar:* semesters. *Degree:* certificates and associate. *Special study options:* academic remediation for entering students, adult/continuing education programs, advanced placement credit, cooperative education, distance learning, double majors, English as a second language, honors programs, independent study, internships, part-time degree program, services for LD students, study abroad, summer session for credit. *ROTC:* Army (c).

Library Alfred C. OConnell Library. *Books:* 79,535 (physical), 17,645 (digital/electronic); *Serial titles:* 164 (physical), 67,604 (digital/electronic); *Databases:* 89. Weekly public service hours: 76.

Student Life *Housing Options:* special housing for students with disabilities. Campus housing is provided by a third party. *Activities and Organizations:* drama/theater group, student-run newspaper, radio station, choral group, DECA (Distributive Education Clubs of America), PTK Honor Society, Multi Cultural Communications Club, Education Club, FORUM Theater Group. *Campus security:* 24-hour emergency response devices and patrols, student patrols, late-night transport/escort service, controlled dormitory access. *Student services:* health clinic, personal/psychological counseling.

Athletics Member NJCAA. *Intercollegiate sports:* baseball M(s), basketball M(s)/W(s), cheerleading M/W, golf M/W, lacrosse M(s)/W(s), soccer M/W, softball W, swimming and diving M/W, volleyball W(s). *Intramural sports:* badminton M/W, basketball M/W, soccer M/W, tennis M/W, track and field M/W, volleyball M/W, water polo M/W.

Costs (2016–17) *Tuition:* state resident $3950 full-time, $160 per credit hour part-time; nonresident $4550 full-time, $185 per credit hour part-time. Full-time tuition and fees vary according to course load. Part-time tuition and fees vary according to course load. *Required fees:* $510 full-time, $18 per credit hour part-time. *Room and board:* $8350; room only: $6200. Room and board charges vary according to board plan and housing facility. *Payment plan:* installment. *Waivers:* senior citizens and employees or children of employees.

Financial Aid Of all full-time matriculated undergraduates who enrolled in 2015, 2,533 applied for aid, 2,135 were judged to have need, 1,102 had their need fully met. 140 Federal Work-Study jobs (averaging $1009). 106 state and other part-time jobs (averaging $1774). *Average percent of need met:* 83%. *Average financial aid package:* $5039. *Average need-based loan:* $3655. *Average need-based gift aid:* $3299.

Applying *Options:* electronic application. *Required:* high school transcript. *Required for some:* 1 letter of recommendation. *Application deadlines:* rolling (freshmen), rolling (transfers). *Notification:* continuous (freshmen), continuous (transfers).

Freshman Application Contact Mrs. Tanya Lane-Martin, Director of Admissions, Genesee Community College, Batavia, NY 14020. *Phone:* 585-343-0055 Ext. 6413. *Toll-free phone:* 866-CALL GCC. *Fax:* 585-345-6892. *E-mail:* tmlanemartin@genesee.edu. *Website:* http://www.genesee.edu/.

Helene Fuld College of Nursing
New York, New York

- **Independent** primarily 2-year, founded 1945
- **Urban** campus
- **Coed, primarily women**

Undergraduates 91 full-time, 263 part-time. Students come from 4 states and territories; 8% are from out of state; 74% Black or African American, non-Hispanic/Latino; 12% Hispanic/Latino; 6% Asian, non-Hispanic/Latino; 100% transferred in.

Faculty *Student/faculty ratio:* 11:1.

Academics *Calendar:* quarters semester for BS program. *Degrees:* associate and bachelor's (program only open to licensed practical nurses). *Special study options:* accelerated degree program, part-time degree program, summer session for credit.

Library Peggy Wines Memorial Library plus 1 other.

Student Life *Campus security:* security guard during hours of operation.

Standardized Tests *Required:* Nelson Denny Reading Test (for admission).

Costs (2016–17) *Tuition:* $341 per quarter hour part-time. Full-time tuition and fees vary according to course load, degree level, and program. Part-time tuition and fees vary according to course load, degree level, and program.

Applying *Options:* deferred entrance. *Application fee:* $110. *Required:* essay or personal statement, high school transcript, 2 letters of recommendation, must be Licensed Practical Nurse. *Required for some:* interview.

Freshman Application Contact Helene Fuld College of Nursing, 24 East 120th Street, New York, NY 10035. *Phone:* 212-616-7271.
Website: http://www.helenefuld.edu/.

Herkimer County Community College
Herkimer, New York

- **State and locally supported** 2-year, founded 1966, part of State University of New York System
- **Small-town** 500-acre campus with easy access to Syracuse
- **Coed**

Undergraduates 1,752 full-time, 1,267 part-time. Students come from 34 states and territories; 17 other countries; 4% are from out of state; 11% Black or African American, non-Hispanic/Latino; 5% Hispanic/Latino; 1% Asian, non-Hispanic/Latino; 0.5% American Indian or Alaska Native, non-Hispanic/Latino; 1% Two or more races, non-Hispanic/Latino; 1% Race/ethnicity unknown; 3% international; 7% transferred in; 19% live on campus.

Faculty *Student/faculty ratio:* 21:1.

Academics *Calendar:* semesters. *Degree:* certificates and associate. *Special study options:* academic remediation for entering students, adult/continuing education programs, advanced placement credit, distance learning, English as a second language, honors programs, independent study, internships, part-time degree program, services for LD students, summer session for credit. *ROTC:* Army (c).

Library Herkimer County Community College Library. *Books:* 73,618 (physical), 33,173 (digital/electronic); *Serial titles:* 218 (physical), 58,707 (digital/electronic); *Databases:* 96. Weekly public service hours: 65.

Student Life *Campus security:* 24-hour emergency response devices and patrols.

Athletics Member NJCAA.

Costs (2016–17) *Tuition:* state resident $4270 full-time, $159 per credit hour part-time; nonresident $7000 full-time, $278 per credit hour part-time. Full-time tuition and fees vary according to location and program. Part-time tuition and fees vary according to location and program. *Required fees:* $780 full-time, $14 per credit hour part-time, $70 per term part-time. *Room and board:* $9620; room only: $6400. Room and board charges vary according to board plan and housing facility.

Financial Aid Of all full-time matriculated undergraduates who enrolled in 2015, 150 Federal Work-Study jobs (averaging $700).

Applying *Required:* high school transcript.

Freshman Application Contact Herkimer County Community College, 100 Reservoir Road, Herkimer, NY 13350. *Phone:* 315-866-0300 Ext. 8278. *Toll-free phone:* 888-464-4222 Ext. 8278. *Website:* http://www.herkimer.edu/.

Hudson Valley Community College
Troy, New York

Freshman Application Contact Ms. Marie Claire Bauer, Director of Admissions, Hudson Valley Community College, 80 Vandenburgh Avenue, Troy, NY 12180-6096. *Phone:* 518-629-7309. *Toll-free phone:* 877-325-HVCC. *Website:* http://www.hvcc.edu/.

Island Drafting and Technical Institute
Amityville, New York

- **Proprietary** 2-year, founded 1957
- **Suburban** campus with easy access to New York City
- **Coed, primarily men**

Undergraduates 112 full-time. 11% Black or African American, non-Hispanic/Latino; 24% Hispanic/Latino; 0.9% Native Hawaiian or other Pacific Islander, non-Hispanic/Latino; 2% American Indian or Alaska Native, non-Hispanic/Latino; 6% Two or more races, non-Hispanic/Latino; 19% Race/ethnicity unknown. *Retention:* 91% of full-time freshmen returned.

Faculty *Student/faculty ratio:* 15:1.

Academics *Calendar:* semesters. *Degree:* certificates, diplomas, and associate. *Special study options:* accelerated degree program, adult/continuing education programs, summer session for credit.

Costs (2016–17) *Tuition:* $15,750 full-time, $525 per credit part-time. No tuition increase for student's term of enrollment. *Required fees:* $450 full-time.

Applying *Options:* early admission. *Application fee:* $40. *Required:* interview. *Recommended:* high school transcript.

Freshman Application Contact Larry Basile, Island Drafting and Technical Institute, 128 Broadway, Amityville, NY 11701. *Phone:* 631-691-8733 Ext.

114. *Fax:* 631-691-8738. *E-mail:* info@idti.edu.
Website: http://www.idti.edu/.

Jamestown Business College
Jamestown, New York

- **Proprietary** primarily 2-year, founded 1886
- **Small-town** 1-acre campus
- **Coed,** 311 undergraduate students, 98% full-time, 74% women, 26% men

Undergraduates 305 full-time, 6 part-time. Students come from 2 states and territories; 10% are from out of state; 2% Black or African American, non-Hispanic/Latino; 20% Hispanic/Latino; 0.3% Asian, non-Hispanic/Latino; 5% American Indian or Alaska Native, non-Hispanic/Latino; 4% Two or more races, non-Hispanic/Latino; 1% Race/ethnicity unknown; 14% transferred in.

Freshmen *Admission:* 159 applied, 131 admitted, 99 enrolled. *Average high school GPA:* 2.7.

Faculty *Total:* 25, 24% full-time, 8% with terminal degrees. *Student/faculty ratio:* 23:1.

Majors Administrative assistant and secretarial science; business administration and management; medical/clinical assistant; office management.

Academics *Calendar:* quarters. *Degrees:* certificates, associate, and bachelor's. *Special study options:* advanced placement credit, double majors, part-time degree program, summer session for credit.

Library James Prendergast Library. *Books:* 173,745 (physical), 12,508 (digital/electronic); *Serial titles:* 103 (physical), 70 (digital/electronic); *Databases:* 55. Weekly public service hours: 55; study areas open 24 hours, 5&-7 days a week.

Student Life *Housing:* college housing not available. *Campus security:* 24-hour emergency response devices, all students have a key card for building entrance.

Costs (2016–17) *One-time required fee:* $25. *Tuition:* $11,700 full-time, $325 per credit hour part-time. Full-time tuition and fees vary according to course load. Part-time tuition and fees vary according to course load. *Required fees:* $900 full-time, $150 per term part-time. *Waivers:* employees or children of employees.

Applying *Application fee:* $25. *Required:* essay or personal statement, high school transcript, interview. *Application deadlines:* rolling (freshmen), rolling (transfers).

Freshman Application Contact Mrs. Brenda Salemme, Director of Admissions, Jamestown Business College, 7 Fairmount Avenue, Box 429, Jamestown, NY 14702-0429. *Phone:* 716-664-5100. *Fax:* 716-664-3144.
E-mail: brendasalemme@jbc.edu.
Website: http://www.jbc.edu/.

Jamestown Community College
Jamestown, New York

- **State and locally supported** 2-year, founded 1950, part of State University of New York System
- **Small-town** 107-acre campus
- **Endowment** $13.8 million
- **Coed,** 4,617 undergraduate students, 47% full-time, 58% women, 42% men

Undergraduates 2,149 full-time, 2,468 part-time. Students come from 13 states and territories; 9 other countries; 9% are from out of state; 4% Black or African American, non-Hispanic/Latino; 7% Hispanic/Latino; 0.5% Asian, non-Hispanic/Latino; 0.2% Native Hawaiian or other Pacific Islander, non-Hispanic/Latino; 1% American Indian or Alaska Native, non-Hispanic/Latino; 3% Two or more races, non-Hispanic/Latino; 0.9% Race/ethnicity unknown; 0.6% international; 4% transferred in; 8% live on campus.

Freshmen *Admission:* 1,657 applied, 1,654 admitted, 824 enrolled. *Average high school GPA:* 3.25.

Faculty *Total:* 350, 25% full-time. *Student/faculty ratio:* 17:1.

Majors Accounting technology and bookkeeping; administrative assistant and secretarial science; airline pilot and flight crew; biology/biotechnology laboratory technician; business administration and management; computer and information sciences; criminal justice/law enforcement administration; criminal justice/police science; engineering; environmental science; fine/studio arts; general studies; health and physical education/fitness; health information/medical records technology; humanities; human services; information science/studies; information technology; international/global studies; liberal arts and sciences and humanities related; liberal arts and sciences/liberal studies; mechanical engineering/mechanical technology; music; occupational therapist assistant; registered nursing/registered nurse; speech communication and rhetoric; teacher assistant/aide; welding technology.

Academics *Calendar:* semesters. *Degree:* certificates and associate. *Special study options:* academic remediation for entering students, adult/continuing

education programs, advanced placement credit, distance learning, honors programs, independent study, internships, off-campus study, part-time degree program, services for LD students, study abroad, summer session for credit.

Library Hultquist Library plus 1 other. *Books:* 90,813 (physical), 2,360 (digital/electronic); *Serial titles:* 687 (physical), 14 (digital/electronic); *Databases:* 89. Weekly public service hours: 63.

Student Life *Housing Options:* coed. Campus housing is university owned. *Activities and Organizations:* drama/theater group, choral group, Nursing Club, SOTA (occupational therapy), Earth Awareness Club, JCC Pride, Impact (Interfaith Christian Club). *Campus security:* 24-hour emergency response devices, controlled dormitory access. *Student services:* health clinic, personal/psychological counseling.

Athletics Member NJCAA. *Intercollegiate sports:* baseball M, basketball M/W, golf M/W, soccer M/W, softball W, swimming and diving M/W, volleyball W, wrestling M. *Intramural sports:* basketball M/W, bowling M/W, cross-country running M/W, softball M/W, volleyball M/W.

Costs (2016–17) *One-time required fee:* $85. *Tuition:* state resident $4630 full-time, $193 per credit hour part-time; nonresident $9260 full-time, $386 per credit hour part-time. Full-time tuition and fees vary according to course load and program. Part-time tuition and fees vary according to course load and program. *Required fees:* $870 full-time, $25 per credit hour part-time. *Room and board:* $10,750; room only: $7500. Room and board charges vary according to board plan. *Payment plan:* installment. *Waivers:* employees or children of employees.

Financial Aid Of all full-time matriculated undergraduates who enrolled in 2015, 85 Federal Work-Study jobs (averaging $1500). 85 state and other part-time jobs (averaging $1300).

Applying *Options:* electronic application, deferred entrance. *Required:* high school transcript. *Application deadlines:* rolling (freshmen), rolling (transfers). *Notification:* continuous (freshmen), continuous (transfers).

Freshman Application Contact Ms. Wendy Present, Director of Admissions, Jamestown Community College, 525 Falconer Street, PO Box 20, Jamestown, NY 14702-0020. *Phone:* 716-338-1001. *Toll-free phone:* 800-388-8557. *Fax:* 716-338-1450. *E-mail:* admissions@mail.sunyjcc.edu. *Website:* http://www.sunyjcc.edu/.

Jefferson Community College
Watertown, New York

- **State and locally supported** 2-year, founded 1961, part of State University of New York System
- **Small-town** 90-acre campus with easy access to Syracuse
- **Coed**, 3,748 undergraduate students, 56% full-time, 58% women, 42% men

Undergraduates 2,095 full-time, 1,653 part-time. 7% Black or African American, non-Hispanic/Latino; 11% Hispanic/Latino; 2% Asian, non-Hispanic/Latino; 0.5% Native Hawaiian or other Pacific Islander, non-Hispanic/Latino; 0.6% American Indian or Alaska Native, non-Hispanic/Latino; 3% Two or more races, non-Hispanic/Latino; 3% Race/ethnicity unknown; 0.7% international; 6% transferred in.

Freshmen *Admission:* 873 enrolled.

Faculty *Total:* 77.

Majors Accounting; accounting technology and bookkeeping; administrative assistant and secretarial science; animal/livestock husbandry and production; business administration and management; child-care and support services management; child development; community organization and advocacy; computer and information sciences; computer and information sciences and support services related; computer/information technology services administration related; computer science; computer technology/computer systems technology; criminal justice/law enforcement administration; early childhood education; emergency medical technology (EMT paramedic); engineering; engineering science; fire prevention and safety technology; fire services administration; hospitality administration; humanities; human services; information science/studies; legal assistant/paralegal; liberal arts and sciences/liberal studies; mathematics; mechanical engineering technologies related; medical administrative assistant and medical secretary; office management; office occupations and clerical services; registered nursing/registered nurse; sport and fitness administration/management; teacher assistant/aide; tourism promotion.

Academics *Calendar:* semesters. *Degree:* certificates and associate. *Special study options:* academic remediation for entering students, advanced placement credit, cooperative education, distance learning, double majors, honors programs, independent study, internships, part-time degree program, services for LD students, student-designed majors, summer session for credit.

Library Melvil Dewey Library plus 1 other.

Student Life *Activities and Organizations:* student-run newspaper. *Campus security:* 24-hour emergency response devices and patrols. *Student services:* health clinic, personal/psychological counseling.

Athletics Member NJCAA. *Intercollegiate sports:* baseball M, basketball M/W, lacrosse M/W, soccer M/W, softball W, volleyball W.

Standardized Tests *Recommended:* SAT or ACT (for admission).

Costs (2016–17) *Tuition:* state resident $4392 full-time, $183 per credit hour part-time; nonresident $6888 full-time, $287 per credit hour part-time. Full-time tuition and fees vary according to course load, location, and program. Part-time tuition and fees vary according to course load, location, and program. *Required fees:* $431 full-time. *Room and board:* $11,900; room only: $8150. Room and board charges vary according to board plan. *Payment plan:* installment. *Waivers:* senior citizens and employees or children of employees.

Financial Aid Of all full-time matriculated undergraduates who enrolled in 2009, 1,748 applied for aid. 98 Federal Work-Study jobs (averaging $1093).

Applying *Options:* electronic application, early admission, deferred entrance. *Required:* high school transcript. *Required for some:* interview. *Application deadlines:* 9/6 (freshmen), rolling (transfers). *Notification:* continuous (freshmen), continuous (transfers).

Freshman Application Contact Ms. Rosanne N. Weir, Director of Admissions, Jefferson Community College, 1220 Coffeen Street, Watertown, NY 13601. *Phone:* 315-786-2277. *Toll-free phone:* 888-435-6522. *Fax:* 315-786-2459. *E-mail:* admissions@sunyjefferson.edu. *Website:* http://www.sunyjefferson.edu/.

Kingsborough Community College of the City University of New York
Brooklyn, New York

- **State and locally supported** 2-year, founded 1963, part of City University of New York System
- **Urban** 72-acre campus with easy access to New York City
- **Coed**, 16,195 undergraduate students, 55% full-time, 55% women, 45% men

Undergraduates 8,860 full-time, 7,335 part-time. Students come from 13 states and territories; 136 other countries; 1% are from out of state; 28% Black or African American, non-Hispanic/Latino; 16% Hispanic/Latino; 14% Asian, non-Hispanic/Latino; 0.2% American Indian or Alaska Native, non-Hispanic/Latino; 7% Race/ethnicity unknown; 3% international; 9% transferred in. *Retention:* 70% of full-time freshmen returned.

Freshmen *Admission:* 2,113 enrolled. *Average high school GPA:* 2.7.

Majors Accounting; administrative assistant and secretarial science; art; biology/biological sciences; broadcast journalism; business administration and management; chemistry; commercial and advertising art; community health services counseling; computer and information sciences; computer science; cooking and related culinary arts; criminal justice/law enforcement administration; data processing and data processing technology; design and applied arts related; dramatic/theater arts; early childhood education; education; elementary education; engineering science; fashion merchandising; health and physical education related; human services; journalism; labor and industrial relations; liberal arts and sciences/liberal studies; marine maintenance and ship repair technology; marketing/marketing management; mathematics; mental health counseling; music; parks, recreation and leisure; physical therapy; physical therapy technology; physics; psychiatric/mental health services technology; registered nursing/registered nurse; sport and fitness administration/management; teacher assistant/aide; tourism and travel services management.

Academics *Calendar:* semesters. *Degree:* associate. *Special study options:* academic remediation for entering students, adult/continuing education programs, advanced placement credit, distance learning, English as a second language, honors programs, independent study, internships, off-campus study, part-time degree program, services for LD students, summer session for credit.

Library Robert J. Kibbee Library.

Student Life *Housing:* college housing not available. *Activities and Organizations:* drama/theater group, student-run newspaper, radio station, choral group, Peer Advisors, Caribbean Club, DECA. *Campus security:* 24-hour emergency response devices and patrols. *Student services:* health clinic, personal/psychological counseling, women's center.

Athletics Member NJCAA. *Intercollegiate sports:* baseball M, basketball M/W, soccer M, softball W, tennis M/W, track and field M/W, volleyball W. *Intramural sports:* baseball M, basketball M/W, soccer M, softball W, tennis M/W, track and field M/W, volleyball W.

Costs (2017–18) *Tuition:* state resident $4800 full-time, $210 per credit hour part-time; nonresident $7680 full-time, $320 per credit hour part-time. *Required fees:* $456 full-time, $121 per term part-time. *Payment plan:* installment. *Waivers:* senior citizens.

Applying *Application fee:* $65. *Required:* high school transcript. *Application deadlines:* 8/15 (freshmen), rolling (transfers).

Freshman Application Contact Mr. Javier Morgades, Director of Admissions Information Center, Kingsborough Community College of the City University of New York, 2001 Oriental Boulevard, Brooklyn, NY 11235. *Phone:* 718-368-4600. *E-mail:* info@kbcc.cuny.edu. *Website:* http://www.kbcc.cuny.edu/.

Long Island Business Institute
Flushing, New York

- **Proprietary** 2-year, founded 1968
- **Urban** campus with easy access to New York City
- **Coed**, 1,118 undergraduate students, 88% full-time, 69% women, 31% men

Undergraduates 985 full-time, 133 part-time. Students come from 2 states and territories; 19 other countries; 12% Black or African American, non-Hispanic/Latino; 21% Hispanic/Latino; 52% Asian, non-Hispanic/Latino; 0.1% American Indian or Alaska Native, non-Hispanic/Latino; 0.1% Two or more races, non-Hispanic/Latino; 0.2% Race/ethnicity unknown; 7% international.

Freshmen *Admission:* 234 applied, 218 admitted, 796 enrolled.

Faculty *Total:* 129, 13% full-time, 5% with terminal degrees. *Student/faculty ratio:* 19:1.

Majors Accounting; business administration and management; business, management, and marketing related; court reporting; homeland security; hospitality administration related; medical office management.

Academics *Calendar:* semesters. *Degrees:* certificates and associate (information provided for Commack and Flushing campuses). *Special study options:* academic remediation for entering students, adult/continuing education programs, advanced placement credit, cooperative education, English as a second language, honors programs, independent study, part-time degree program, summer session for credit.

Library Flushing Main Campus Library plus 2 others. *Books:* 2,000 (physical), 250 (digital/electronic); *Serial titles:* 10 (physical), 3 (digital/electronic); *Databases:* 5.

Student Life *Housing:* college housing not available. *Activities and Organizations:* Small Business Club, Web Design Club, Investment Club, Court Reporting Alumni Association. *Campus security:* 24-hour emergency response devices.

Costs (2017–18) *Tuition:* $13,299 full-time, $375 per credit hour part-time. *Required fees:* $1470 full-time, $490 per term part-time. *Payment plans:* installment, deferred payment.

Applying *Options:* electronic application. *Required:* high school transcript, interview. *Application deadlines:* rolling (freshmen), rolling (transfers).

Freshman Application Contact Mr. Keith Robertson, Director of Admissions, Long Island Business Institute, 408 Broadway, 2nd Floor, New York, NY 10013. *Phone:* 212-226-7300. *E-mail:* krobertson@libi.edu. *Website:* http://www.libi.edu/.

Mandl School
New York, New York

Admissions Office Contact Mandl School, 254 West 54th Street, 9th Floor, New York, NY 10019. *Website:* http://www.mandlschool.com/.

Memorial College of Nursing
Albany, New York

Freshman Application Contact Admissions Office, Memorial College of Nursing, 600 Northern Boulevard, Albany, NY 12204. *Website:* http://www.nehealth.com/son/.

Mildred Elley–New York City
New York, New York

Admissions Office Contact Mildred Elley–New York City, 25 Broadway, 16th Floor, New York, NY 10004-1010. *Website:* http://www.mildred-elley.edu/.

Mildred Elley School
Albany, New York

Director of Admissions Mr. Michael Cahalan, Enrollment Manager, Mildred Elley School, 855 Central Avenue, Albany, NY 12206. *Phone:* 518-786-3171 Ext. 227. *Toll-free phone:* 800-622-6327. *Website:* http://www.mildred-elley.edu/.

Mohawk Valley Community College
Utica, New York

- **State and locally supported** 2-year, founded 1946, part of State University of New York System
- **Suburban** 80-acre campus
- **Endowment** $4.5 million
- **Coed**, 6,625 undergraduate students, 52% full-time, 54% women, 46% men

Undergraduates 3,412 full-time, 3,213 part-time. Students come from 14 states and territories; 22 other countries; 0.5% are from out of state; 10% Black or African American, non-Hispanic/Latino; 9% Hispanic/Latino; 5% Asian, non-Hispanic/Latino; 0.2% Native Hawaiian or other Pacific Islander, non-Hispanic/Latino; 0.6% American Indian or Alaska Native, non-Hispanic/Latino; 3% Two or more races, non-Hispanic/Latino; 0.3% Race/ethnicity unknown; 1% international; 5% transferred in; 7% live on campus.

Freshmen *Admission:* 2,726 applied, 2,720 admitted, 1,195 enrolled. *Average high school GPA:* 2.79.

Faculty *Total:* 487, 27% full-time, 13% with terminal degrees. *Student/faculty ratio:* 18:1.

Majors Accounting technology and bookkeeping; administrative assistant and secretarial science; advertising; aeronautical/aerospace engineering technology; airframe mechanics and aircraft maintenance technology; art; banking and financial support services; building/property maintenance; business administration and management; CAD/CADD drafting/design technology; chemical technology; civil engineering technology; commercial and advertising art; commercial photography; computer and information sciences; computer and information sciences and support services related; computer and information systems security; computer programming; criminal justice/law enforcement administration; dietetic technology; digital arts; electrical, electronic and communications engineering technology; electrical/electronics maintenance and repair technology related; emergency care attendant (EMT ambulance); engineering; fire services administration; general studies; health information/medical records technology; heating, air conditioning, ventilation and refrigeration maintenance technology; hotel/motel administration; humanities; human services; law enforcement investigation and interviewing; liberal arts and sciences and humanities related; liberal arts and sciences/liberal studies; mechanical engineering/mechanical technology; mechanical engineering technologies related; medical/clinical assistant; medical radiologic technology; operations management; parks, recreation and leisure facilities management; registered nursing/registered nurse; respiratory care therapy; restaurant, culinary, and catering management; semiconductor manufacturing technology; sign language interpretation and translation; substance abuse/addiction counseling; web page, digital/multimedia and information resources design; welding technology.

Academics *Calendar:* semesters. *Degree:* certificates and associate. *Special study options:* academic remediation for entering students, advanced placement credit, distance learning, double majors, English as a second language, honors programs, independent study, internships, off-campus study, part-time degree program, services for LD students, student-designed majors, summer session for credit.

Library Mohawk Valley Community College Library plus 1 other. *Books:* 101,206 (physical), 1,892 (digital/electronic); *Serial titles:* 450 (physical), 130,047 (digital/electronic); *Databases:* 110. Weekly public service hours: 126.

Student Life *Housing Options:* coed, men-only, women-only, special housing for students with disabilities. Campus housing is provided by a third party. Freshman applicants given priority for college housing. *Activities and Organizations:* drama/theater group, student-run newspaper, Student Congress, Phi Theta Kappa, Catalyst, Program Board, Kidz-n-Coaches. *Campus security:* 24-hour emergency response devices and patrols, late-night transport/escort service, controlled dormitory access. *Student services:* health clinic, personal/psychological counseling.

Athletics Member NJCAA. *Intercollegiate sports:* baseball M, basketball M/W, bowling M/W, cross-country running M/W, golf M/W, ice hockey M, lacrosse M/W, soccer M/W, softball W, tennis M/W, track and field M/W, volleyball W. *Intramural sports:* badminton M/W, basketball M/W, soccer M/W, volleyball M/W.

Costs (2017–18) *Tuition:* state resident $4284 full-time, $170 per credit hour part-time; nonresident $8568 full-time, $340 per credit hour part-time. *Required fees:* $776 full-time, $29 per credit hour part-time, $26 per term part-time. *Room and board:* Room and board charges vary according to board plan. *Payment plans:* installment, deferred payment. *Waivers:* senior citizens and employees or children of employees.

Financial Aid Of all full-time matriculated undergraduates who enrolled in 2015, 229 Federal Work-Study jobs (averaging $1750).

Applying *Options:* electronic application, deferred entrance. *Required for some:* high school transcript. *Recommended:* interview. *Application*

deadlines: rolling (freshmen), rolling (transfers). *Notification:* continuous (freshmen), continuous (transfers).
Freshman Application Contact Mr. Nolan Snyder, Technical Assistant, Admissions, Mohawk Valley Community College, 1101 Sherman Drive, Utica, NY 13501. *Phone:* 315-792-5640. *Toll-free phone:* 800-SEE-MVCC. *Fax:* 315-792-5527. *E-mail:* nsynder@mvcc.edu.
Website: http://www.mvcc.edu/.

Monroe Community College
Rochester, New York

- **State and locally supported** 2-year, founded 1961, part of State University of New York System
- **Suburban** 314-acre campus with easy access to Buffalo
- **Coed,** 13,587 undergraduate students, 60% full-time, 53% women, 47% men

Undergraduates 8,214 full-time, 5,373 part-time. Students come from 40 states and territories; 46 other countries; 1% are from out of state; 19% Black or African American, non-Hispanic/Latino; 9% Hispanic/Latino; 4% Asian, non-Hispanic/Latino; 0.2% Native Hawaiian or other Pacific Islander, non-Hispanic/Latino; 0.5% American Indian or Alaska Native, non-Hispanic/Latino; 4% Two or more races, non-Hispanic/Latino; 0.7% Race/ethnicity unknown; 1% international. *Retention:* 49% of full-time freshmen returned.
Freshmen *Admission:* 16,328 applied, 11,928 admitted, 3,014 enrolled.
Faculty *Total:* 754, 39% full-time, 15% with terminal degrees. *Student/faculty ratio:* 22:1.
Majors Accounting; administrative assistant and secretarial science; art; automobile/automotive mechanics technology; behavioral sciences; biological and physical sciences; biology/biological sciences; biology/biotechnology laboratory technician; business administration and management; chemical engineering; chemistry; civil engineering technology; commercial and advertising art; computer and information sciences and support services related; computer and information sciences related; computer engineering related; computer engineering technology; computer science; construction engineering technology; consumer merchandising/retailing management; corrections; criminal justice/law enforcement administration; criminal justice/police science; data processing and data processing technology; dental hygiene; electrical, electronic and communications engineering technology; engineering science; environmental studies; family and consumer sciences/human sciences; fashion/apparel design; fashion merchandising; fire science/firefighting; food technology and processing; forestry; graphic and printing equipment operation/production; health information/medical records administration; heating, air conditioning, ventilation and refrigeration maintenance technology; history; hotel/motel administration; human services; industrial radiologic technology; industrial technology; information science/studies; information technology; instrumentation technology; interior design; international business/trade/commerce; landscape architecture; laser and optical technology; legal administrative assistant/secretary; liberal arts and sciences/liberal studies; marketing/marketing management; mass communication/media; mathematics; mechanical engineering/mechanical technology; music; parks, recreation and leisure; physical education teaching and coaching; physics; political science and government; pre-pharmacy studies; quality control technology; registered nursing/registered nurse; social sciences; special products marketing; telecommunications technology; tourism and travel services management.
Academics *Calendar:* semesters. *Degree:* certificates and associate. *Special study options:* academic remediation for entering students, accelerated degree program, adult/continuing education programs, advanced placement credit, cooperative education, English as a second language, honors programs, internships, off-campus study, part-time degree program, services for LD students, summer session for credit. *ROTC:* Army (c), Navy (c), Air Force (c).
Library LeRoy V. Good Library. Weekly public service hours: 58; students can reserve study rooms.
Student Life *Housing Options:* coed, men-only, women-only. Campus housing is university owned. *Activities and Organizations:* drama/theater group, student-run newspaper, radio station, choral group, Student Newspaper, Phi Theta Kappa, Student Government. *Campus security:* 24-hour emergency response devices and patrols, late-night transport/escort service, controlled dormitory access. *Student services:* health clinic, personal/psychological counseling.
Athletics Member NCAA, NJCAA. All NCAA Division III. *Intercollegiate sports:* baseball M(s), basketball M(s)/W(s), golf M, ice hockey M(s), lacrosse M(s), soccer M(s)/W(s), softball W, swimming and diving M(s)/W(s), tennis M/W, volleyball W. *Intramural sports:* archery M/W, basketball M/W, bowling M/W, cheerleading W, cross-country running M/W, football M, lacrosse W, racquetball M/W, rugby M, skiing (cross-country) M/W, soccer M/W, softball M/W, swimming and diving M/W, tennis M/W, volleyball M/W.
Costs (2016–17) *Tuition:* state resident $4100 full-time, $171 per credit hour part-time; nonresident $8200 full-time, $342 per credit hour part-time. Full-

time tuition and fees vary according to program. Part-time tuition and fees vary according to course load and program. *Required fees:* $709 full-time, $76 per credit hour part-time. *Room and board:* room only: $6358. Room and board charges vary according to housing facility. *Payment plan:* installment. *Waivers:* senior citizens and employees or children of employees.
Applying *Options:* electronic application, early admission. *Required:* high school transcript. *Application deadlines:* rolling (freshmen), rolling (transfers). *Notification:* continuous (freshmen), continuous (transfers).
Freshman Application Contact Ms. Christine Casalinuovo-Adams, Director of Admissions, Monroe Community College, 1000 East Henrietta Road, Rochester, NY 14623. *Phone:* 585-292-2222. *Fax:* 585-292-3860.
E-mail: admissions@monroecc.edu.
Website: http://www.monroecc.edu/.

Montefiore School of Nursing
Mount Vernon, New York

Director of Admissions Sandra Farrior, Coordinator of Student Services, Montefiore School of Nursing, 53 Valentine Street, Mount Vernon, NY 10550. *Phone:* 914-361-6472. *E-mail:* hopferadmissions@sshsw.org.
Website: http://www.montefiorehealthsystem.org/landing.cfm?id=19.

Nassau Community College
Garden City, New York

- **State and locally supported** 2-year, founded 1959, part of State University of New York System
- **Suburban** 225-acre campus with easy access to New York City
- **Coed,** 36,408 undergraduate students, 62% full-time, 50% women, 50% men

Undergraduates 22,514 full-time, 13,894 part-time. Students come from 19 states and territories; 69 other countries; 0.3% are from out of state; 22% Black or African American, non-Hispanic/Latino; 26% Hispanic/Latino; 7% Asian, non-Hispanic/Latino; 0.3% Native Hawaiian or other Pacific Islander, non-Hispanic/Latino; 0.3% American Indian or Alaska Native, non-Hispanic/Latino; 0.9% Two or more races, non-Hispanic/Latino; 5% Race/ethnicity unknown; 0.9% international; 4% transferred in. *Retention:* 32% of full-time freshmen returned.
Freshmen *Admission:* 4,080 enrolled. *Average high school GPA:* 2.51.
Faculty *Total:* 1,368, 35% full-time, 30% with terminal degrees. *Student/faculty ratio:* 21:1.
Majors Accounting; accounting technology and bookkeeping; administrative assistant and secretarial science; African American/Black studies; art; business administration and management; civil engineering technology; clinical/medical laboratory technology; commercial and advertising art; computer and information sciences; computer and information sciences related; computer graphics; computer science; computer systems networking and telecommunications; criminal justice/law enforcement administration; criminal justice/safety; dance; data processing and data processing technology; design and visual communications; dramatic/theater arts; engineering; entrepreneurship; fashion/apparel design; fashion merchandising; funeral service and mortuary science; general studies; hotel/motel administration; instrumentation technology; insurance; interior design; kindergarten/preschool education; legal administrative assistant/secretary; legal assistant/paralegal; liberal arts and sciences/liberal studies; management information systems; marketing/marketing management; mass communication/media; mathematics; medical administrative assistant and medical secretary; medical radiologic technology; music performance; photography; physical therapy technology; real estate; registered nursing/registered nurse; rehabilitation and therapeutic professions related; respiratory care therapy; retailing; speech communication and rhetoric; surgical technology; theater design and technology; transportation and materials moving related; visual and performing arts.
Academics *Calendar:* semesters. *Degree:* certificates and associate. *Special study options:* academic remediation for entering students, adult/continuing education programs, advanced placement credit, cooperative education, distance learning, English as a second language, honors programs, internships, off-campus study, part-time degree program, services for LD students, summer session for credit.
Library A. Holly Patterson Library.
Student Life *Housing:* college housing not available. *Activities and Organizations:* drama/theater group, student-run newspaper, radio station, choral group, Muslim Student Association, Make a Difference Club, Interact Club, Political Science Club, Investment Club. *Campus security:* 24-hour emergency response devices and patrols, late-night transport/escort service. *Student services:* personal/psychological counseling, women's center.
Athletics Member NJCAA. *Intercollegiate sports:* baseball M, basketball M/W, bowling M/W, cheerleading M/W, cross-country running M/W, football M, golf M/W, lacrosse M/W, soccer M/W, softball W, tennis M/W, track and field M/W, volleyball W, wrestling M. *Intramural sports:* badminton M/W,

baseball M, basketball M/W, racquetball M/W, soccer M/W, softball M/W, swimming and diving M/W, table tennis M/W, tennis M/W, volleyball M/W.
Costs (2017–18) *Tuition:* state resident $2267 full-time, $189 per credit part-time; nonresident $4534 full-time, $378 per credit part-time. Full-time tuition and fees vary according to program. Part-time tuition and fees vary according to program. *Required fees:* $100 full-time.
Financial Aid Of all full-time matriculated undergraduates who enrolled in 2015, 400 Federal Work-Study jobs (averaging $3000).
Applying *Options:* electronic application, deferred entrance. *Application fee:* $40. *Required:* high school transcript. *Required for some:* minimum 3.0 GPA, interview. *Recommended:* minimum 2.0 GPA. *Application deadlines:* 8/7 (freshmen), 8/7 (transfers). *Notification:* continuous (freshmen), continuous (transfers).
Freshman Application Contact Nassau Community College, 1 Education Drive, Garden City, NY 11530-6793. *Phone:* 516-572-7345.
Website: http://www.ncc.edu/.

Niagara County Community College
Sanborn, New York

- **State and locally supported** 2-year, founded 1962, part of State University of New York System
- **Rural** 287-acre campus with easy access to Buffalo
- **Endowment** $9.1 million
- **Coed**, 5,892 undergraduate students, 58% full-time, 58% women, 42% men

Undergraduates 3,408 full-time, 2,484 part-time. Students come from 17 states and territories; 3 other countries; 1% are from out of state; 11% Black or African American, non-Hispanic/Latino; 4% Hispanic/Latino; 1% Asian, non-Hispanic/Latino; 1% American Indian or Alaska Native, non-Hispanic/Latino; 4% Race/ethnicity unknown; 8% transferred in; 4% live on campus.
Freshmen *Admission:* 2,643 applied, 2,250 admitted, 1,155 enrolled. *Average high school GPA:* 2.48.
Faculty *Total:* 337, 31% full-time, 11% with terminal degrees. *Student/faculty ratio:* 17:1.
Majors Accounting; administrative assistant and secretarial science; animal sciences; baking and pastry arts; biological and physical sciences; business administration and management; business, management, and marketing related; chemical technology; computer science; consumer merchandising/retailing management; criminal justice/law enforcement administration; culinary arts; design and applied arts related; drafting and design technology; drafting/design engineering technologies related; dramatic/theater arts; elementary education; fine/studio arts; general studies; hospitality administration; humanities; human services; information science/studies; liberal arts and sciences/liberal studies; massage therapy; mass communication/media; mathematics; medical/clinical assistant; medical radiologic technology; music; natural resources/conservation; occupational health and industrial hygiene; parks, recreation and leisure; physical education teaching and coaching; physical therapy technology; registered nursing/registered nurse; social sciences; sport and fitness administration/management; surgical technology; tourism and travel services management; web page, digital/multimedia and information resources design; wine steward/sommelier.
Academics *Calendar:* semesters. *Degree:* certificates and associate. *Special study options:* academic remediation for entering students, adult/continuing education programs, advanced placement credit, cooperative education, distance learning, double majors, honors programs, independent study, internships, off-campus study, part-time degree program, services for LD students, student-designed majors, study abroad, summer session for credit. *ROTC:* Army (c).
Library Henrietta G. Lewis Library. *Books:* 85,446 (physical); *Serial titles:* 290 (physical); *Databases:* 87. Weekly public service hours: 64.
Student Life *Housing Options:* coed. Campus housing is provided by a third party. *Activities and Organizations:* drama/theater group, student-run newspaper, radio station, choral group, Student Radio Station, Student Nurses Association, Phi Theta Kappa, Alpha Beta Gamma, Physical Education Club. *Campus security:* 24-hour emergency response devices and patrols, student patrols, late-night transport/escort service. *Student services:* health clinic, personal/psychological counseling.
Athletics Member NJCAA. *Intercollegiate sports:* baseball M, basketball M(s)/W(s), golf M/W, soccer M/W, softball W, volleyball W, wrestling M(s). *Intramural sports:* basketball M/W, ice hockey M, racquetball M/W, soccer M/W, tennis M/W.
Costs (2017–18) *Tuition:* state resident $4080 full-time, $170 per credit hour part-time; nonresident $10,200 full-time, $425 per credit part-time. Full-time tuition and fees vary according to course load and program. Part-time tuition and fees vary according to course load and program. *Required fees:* $438 full-time, $111 per term part-time. *Room and board:* $11,189; room only: $8698. Room and board charges vary according to housing facility. *Payment plan:* installment. *Waivers:* senior citizens and employees or children of employees.

Financial Aid Of all full-time matriculated undergraduates who enrolled in 2015, 5,916 applied for aid, 5,916 were judged to have need. 76 Federal Work-Study jobs (averaging $1302). 123 state and other part-time jobs (averaging $848). *Average percent of need met:* 85%. *Average financial aid package:* $5300. *Average need-based loan:* $3039. *Average need-based gift aid:* $947.
Applying *Options:* electronic application, early admission. *Required:* high school transcript. *Required for some:* minimum 2.0 GPA. *Notification:* continuous until 8/31 (freshmen), continuous until 8/31 (transfers).
Freshman Application Contact Ms. Julia Pitman, Interim Director of Enrollment Services, Niagara County Community College, 3111 Saunders Settlement Road, Sanborn, NY 14132. *Phone:* 716-614-6200. *Fax:* 716-614-6820. *E-mail:* admissions@niagaracc.suny.edu.
Website: http://www.niagaracc.suny.edu/.

North Country Community College
Saranac Lake, New York

Freshman Application Contact Enrollment Management Assistant, North Country Community College, 23 Santanoni Avenue, PO Box 89, Saranac Lake, NY 12983-0089. *Phone:* 518-891-2915 Ext. 686. *Toll-free phone:* 800-TRY-NCCC (in-state); 888-TRY-NCCC (out-of-state). *Fax:* 518-891-0898. *E-mail:* info@nccc.edu. *Website:* http://www.nccc.edu/.

Onondaga Community College
Syracuse, New York

- **State and locally supported** 2-year, founded 1962, part of State University of New York System
- **Suburban** 280-acre campus
- **Endowment** $10.5 million
- **Coed**

Undergraduates 5,895 full-time, 5,991 part-time. Students come from 25 states and territories; 19 other countries; 1% are from out of state; 13% Black or African American, non-Hispanic/Latino; 5% Hispanic/Latino; 3% Asian, non-Hispanic/Latino; 0.1% Native Hawaiian or other Pacific Islander, non-Hispanic/Latino; 1% American Indian or Alaska Native, non-Hispanic/Latino; 3% Two or more races, non-Hispanic/Latino; 27% Race/ethnicity unknown; 0.4% international; 49% transferred in; 6% live on campus.
Faculty *Student/faculty ratio:* 24:1.
Academics *Calendar:* semesters. *Degree:* certificates, diplomas, and associate. *Special study options:* academic remediation for entering students, accelerated degree program, adult/continuing education programs, advanced placement credit, cooperative education, distance learning, double majors, English as a second language, external degree program, honors programs, internships, part-time degree program, services for LD students, study abroad, summer session for credit. *ROTC:* Air Force (c).
Library Sidney B. Coulter Library plus 1 other. *Books:* 84,742 (physical), 542 (digital/electronic); *Serial titles:* 194 (physical), 10 (digital/electronic); *Databases:* 92. Weekly public service hours: 67; students can reserve study rooms.
Student Life *Campus security:* 24-hour emergency response devices and patrols, controlled dormitory access.
Athletics Member NJCAA.
Costs (2016–17) *Tuition:* state resident $4570 full-time, $190 per credit hour part-time; nonresident $9140 full-time, $380 per credit hour part-time. Full-time tuition and fees vary according to program. Part-time tuition and fees vary according to course load and program. *Required fees:* $584 full-time. *Room and board:* $7900; room only: $5470. Room and board charges vary according to board plan.
Financial Aid Of all full-time matriculated undergraduates who enrolled in 2014, 5,594 applied for aid, 5,025 were judged to have need, 227 had their need fully met. 99 Federal Work-Study jobs (averaging $3161). *Average percent of need met:* 1. *Average financial aid package:* $6747. *Average need-based loan:* $3000. *Average need-based gift aid:* $5539.
Applying *Options:* electronic application. *Required:* high school transcript. *Required for some:* minimum 2.0 GPA, interview.
Freshman Application Contact Mr. Denny Nicholson, Onondaga Community College, 4585 West Seneca Turnpike, Syracuse, NY 13215. *Phone:* 315-488-2912. *Fax:* 315-488-2107. *E-mail:* admissions@sunyocc.edu. *Website:* http://www.sunyocc.edu/.

Orange County Community College
Middletown, New York

Freshman Application Contact Michael Roe, Director of Admissions and Recruitment, Orange County Community College, 115 South Street, Middletown, NY 10940. *Phone:* 845-341-4205. *Fax:* 845-343-1228. *E-mail:* apply@sunyorange.edu. *Website:* http://www.sunyorange.edu/.

Phillips Beth Israel School of Nursing
New York, New York

- **Independent** primarily 2-year, founded 1904
- **Urban** campus
- **Endowment** $750,000
- **Coed**

Undergraduates 34 full-time, 220 part-time. Students come from 7 states and territories; 5 other countries; 15% are from out of state; 30% Black or African American, non-Hispanic/Latino; 14% Hispanic/Latino; 15% Asian, non-Hispanic/Latino; 7% Native Hawaiian or other Pacific Islander, non-Hispanic/Latino; 0.4% international; 35% transferred in. *Retention:* 84% of full-time freshmen returned.
Faculty *Student/faculty ratio:* 8:1.
Academics *Calendar:* semesters. *Degrees:* associate and bachelor's. *Special study options:* academic remediation for entering students, accelerated degree program, advanced placement credit, distance learning, honors programs, off-campus study, part-time degree program, services for LD students, study abroad, summer session for credit.
Library Phillips Health Science Library. *Books:* 400 (physical), 25 (digital/electronic); *Databases:* 10.
Student Life *Campus security:* 24-hour emergency response devices.
Standardized Tests *Recommended:* SAT (for admission).
Costs (2016–17) *Tuition:* $18,950 full-time, $575 per credit part-time. Full-time tuition and fees vary according to degree level. Part-time tuition and fees vary according to degree level. *Required fees:* $2775 full-time.
Financial Aid *Financial aid deadline:* 6/1.
Applying *Options:* deferred entrance. *Application fee:* $50. *Required:* essay or personal statement, high school transcript, minimum 2.5 GPA, 2 letters of recommendation, interview.
Freshman Application Contact Mrs. Bernice Pass-Stern, Assistant Dean, Phillips Beth Israel School of Nursing, 776 Sixth Avenue, 4th Floor, New York, NY 10010-6354. *Phone:* 212-614-6176. *Fax:* 212-614-6109. *E-mail:* bstern@chpnet.org. *Website:* http://www.pbisn.edu/.

Plaza College
Forest Hills, New York

Freshman Application Contact Dean Vanessa Lopez, Dean of Admissions, Plaza College, 118-33 Queens Boulevard, Forest Hills, NY 11375. *Phone:* 718-779-1430. *E-mail:* info@plazacollege.edu. *Website:* http://www.plazacollege.edu/.

Queensborough Community College of the City University of New York
Bayside, New York

- **State and locally supported** 2-year, founded 1958, part of City University of New York System
- **Urban** 37-acre campus with easy access to New York City
- **Coed**, 15,569 undergraduate students, 58% full-time, 54% women, 46% men

Undergraduates 9,105 full-time, 6,464 part-time. Students come from 130 other countries; 0.2% are from out of state; 22% Black or African American, non-Hispanic/Latino; 33% Hispanic/Latino; 24% Asian, non-Hispanic/Latino; 0.8% Native Hawaiian or other Pacific Islander, non-Hispanic/Latino; 0.8% American Indian or Alaska Native, non-Hispanic/Latino; 1% Two or more races, non-Hispanic/Latino; 4% international; 6% transferred in. *Retention:* 63% of full-time freshmen returned.
Freshmen *Admission:* 3,316 admitted, 3,316 enrolled.
Faculty *Total:* 909, 44% full-time, 59% with terminal degrees. *Student/faculty ratio:* 19:1.
Majors Accounting; accounting technology and bookkeeping; administrative assistant and secretarial science; biotechnology; business administration and management; business, management, and marketing related; chemistry; clinical/medical laboratory technology; communication and journalism related; computer engineering technology; computer installation and repair technology; criminal justice/law enforcement administration; data processing and data processing technology; digital arts; electrical, electronic and communications engineering technology; engineering; engineering science; environmental design/architecture; environmental engineering technology; environmental health; fine/studio arts; forensic science and technology; general studies; health professions related; health services/allied health/health sciences; information science/studies; information technology; laser and optical technology; liberal arts and sciences/liberal studies; massage therapy; mechanical drafting and CAD/CADD; mechanical engineering/mechanical technology; medical/clinical assistant; medical office management; museum studies; musical instrument fabrication and repair; physical sciences; recording arts technology; registered nursing/registered nurse; telecommunications technology; visual and performing arts.
Academics *Calendar:* semesters. *Degree:* certificates and associate. *Special study options:* academic remediation for entering students, accelerated degree program, advanced placement credit, cooperative education, distance learning, double majors, English as a second language, honors programs, independent study, internships, off-campus study, part-time degree program, services for LD students, student-designed majors, study abroad, summer session for credit. *ROTC:* Army (c).
Library The Kurt R. Schmeller Library.
Student Life *Housing:* college housing not available. *Activities and Organizations:* drama/theater group, student-run newspaper, choral group, Phi Theta kappa, Student Organization for Disability Awareness (SODA), ASAP Club, CSTEP Club, NYPIRG. *Campus security:* 24-hour patrols, late-night transport/escort service. *Student services:* health clinic, personal/psychological counseling, legal services.
Athletics Member NJCAA. *Intercollegiate sports:* baseball M, basketball M/W, cross-country running M/W, soccer M, softball W, swimming and diving M/W, track and field M/W, volleyball W. *Intramural sports:* badminton M/W, basketball M/W, football M/W, swimming and diving M/W, table tennis M/W, volleyball M/W.
Costs (2017–18) *Tuition:* state resident $4800 full-time, $210 per credit part-time; nonresident $9600 full-time, $320 per credit part-time. Full-time tuition and fees vary according to course load. Part-time tuition and fees vary according to course load. *Required fees:* $409 full-time, $106 per term part-time. *Payment plan:* installment. *Waivers:* senior citizens and employees or children of employees.
Applying *Options:* electronic application, deferred entrance. *Application fee:* $65. *Required:* high school transcript. *Application deadlines:* 2/1 (freshmen), 2/1 (transfers). *Notification:* continuous (freshmen), continuous (transfers).
Freshman Application Contact Mr. Anthony Davis, Director of Admissions and Recruitment, Queensborough Community College of the City University of New York, 222-05 56th Avenue, Bayside, NY 11364. *Phone:* 718-631-6262 Ext. 1. *Fax:* 718-281-5189. *Website:* http://www.qcc.cuny.edu/.

Rockland Community College
Suffern, New York

Freshman Application Contact Rockland Community College, 145 College Road, Suffern, NY 10901-3699. *Phone:* 845-574-4484. *Toll-free phone:* 800-722-7666. *Website:* http://www.sunyrockland.edu/.

St. Elizabeth College of Nursing
Utica, New York

Freshman Application Contact Donna Ernst, Director of Recruitment, St. Elizabeth College of Nursing, 2215 Genesee Street, Utica, NY 13501. *Phone:* 315-798-8189. *E-mail:* dernst@secon.edu. *Website:* http://www.secon.edu/.

St. Joseph's College of Nursing
Syracuse, New York

- **Independent Roman Catholic** 2-year, founded 1898
- **Urban** campus
- **Coed**

Undergraduates 166 full-time, 107 part-time. Students come from 2 states and territories; 20% live on campus.
Faculty *Student/faculty ratio:* 9:1.
Academics *Calendar:* semesters. *Degree:* associate. *Special study options:* academic remediation for entering students, adult/continuing education programs, advanced placement credit, cooperative education, internships, part-time degree program, services for LD students.
Library St. Joseph's Hospital Health Center School of Nursing Library.
Student Life *Campus security:* 24-hour patrols.
Standardized Tests *Required:* SAT or ACT (for admission).
Costs (2016–17) *Tuition:* $16,960 full-time, $530 per credit part-time. Full-time tuition and fees vary according to program. Part-time tuition and fees vary according to program. *Required fees:* $1340 full-time. *Room only:* $5500.
Applying *Options:* electronic application, deferred entrance. *Application fee:* $50. *Required:* essay or personal statement, high school transcript, minimum 3.0 GPA, 2 letters of recommendation, interview, high school or college algebra, biology and chemistry.
Freshman Application Contact Ms. Felicia Corp, Recruiter, St. Joseph's College of Nursing, 206 Prospect Avenue, Syracuse, NY 13203. *Phone:* 315-448-5040. *Fax:* 315-448-5745. *E-mail:* collegeofnursing@sjhsyr.org. *Website:* http://www.sjhsyr.org/nursing/.

St. Paul's School of Nursing
Rego Park, New York

Director of Admissions Nancy Wolinski, Chairperson of Admissions, St. Paul's School of Nursing, 97-77 Queens Boulevard, Rego Park, NY 11374. *Phone:* 718-357-0500 Ext. 131. *E-mail:* nwolinski@svcmcny.org. *Website:* http://www.stpaulsschoolofnursing.com/.

St. Paul's School of Nursing
Staten Island, New York

Admissions Office Contact St. Paul's School of Nursing, Corporate Commons Two, 2 Teleport Drive, Suite 203, Staten Island, NY 10311. *Website:* http://www.stpaulsschoolofnursing.com/.

Samaritan Hospital School of Nursing
Troy, New York

Director of Admissions Ms. Diane Dyer, Student Services Coordinator, Samaritan Hospital School of Nursing, 1300 Massachusetts Avenue, Troy, NY 12180. *Phone:* 518-271-3734. *Fax:* 518-271-3303. *E-mail:* marronej@nehealth.com. *Website:* http://www.nehealth.com/.

Schenectady County Community College
Schenectady, New York

- **State and locally supported** 2-year, founded 1969, part of State University of New York System
- **Urban** 50-acre campus
- **Coed**

Undergraduates 2,235 full-time, 3,916 part-time. 14% Black or African American, non-Hispanic/Latino; 6% Hispanic/Latino; 7% Asian, non-Hispanic/Latino; 0.8% Native Hawaiian or other Pacific Islander, non-Hispanic/Latino; 1% American Indian or Alaska Native, non-Hispanic/Latino; 2% Two or more races, non-Hispanic/Latino; 2% Race/ethnicity unknown; 6% transferred in.
Academics *Calendar:* semesters. *Degree:* certificates and associate. *Special study options:* academic remediation for entering students, adult/continuing education programs, advanced placement credit, distance learning, double majors, English as a second language, honors programs, internships, off-campus study, part-time degree program, services for LD students, summer session for credit.
Library Begley Library.
Student Life *Campus security:* 24-hour emergency response devices and patrols, late-night transport/escort service.
Athletics Member NJCAA.
Financial Aid Of all full-time matriculated undergraduates who enrolled in 2015, 50 Federal Work-Study jobs (averaging $2400).
Applying *Options:* electronic application, early admission, deferred entrance. *Required:* high school transcript.
Freshman Application Contact Mr. David Sampson, Director of Admissions, Schenectady County Community College, 78 Washington Avenue, Schenectady, NY 12305-2294. *Phone:* 518-381-1370. *E-mail:* sampsodg@gw.sunysccc.edu. *Website:* http://www.sunysccc.edu/.

State University of New York College of Technology at Alfred
Alfred, New York

- **State-supported** primarily 2-year, founded 1908, part of State University of New York System
- **Rural** 1084-acre campus with easy access to Rochester, Buffalo
- **Endowment** $4.5 million
- **Coed**, 3,699 undergraduate students, 91% full-time, 38% women, 62% men

Undergraduates 3,378 full-time, 321 part-time. Students come from 35 states and territories; 9 other countries; 4% are from out of state; 10% Black or African American, non-Hispanic/Latino; 7% Hispanic/Latino; 1% Asian, non-Hispanic/Latino; 0.1% Native Hawaiian or other Pacific Islander, non-Hispanic/Latino; 0.2% American Indian or Alaska Native, non-Hispanic/Latino; 2% Two or more races, non-Hispanic/Latino; 1% Race/ethnicity unknown; 2% international; 9% transferred in; 64% live on campus. *Retention:* 88% of full-time freshmen returned.
Freshmen *Admission:* 4,912 applied, 2,790 admitted, 1,058 enrolled. *Average high school GPA:* 3.04. *Test scores:* SAT critical reading scores over 500:

36%; SAT math scores over 500: 47%; SAT critical reading scores over 600: 8%; SAT math scores over 600: 12%; SAT critical reading scores over 700: 1%; SAT math scores over 700: 1%.
Faculty *Total:* 226, 77% full-time, 28% with terminal degrees. *Student/faculty ratio:* 18:1.
Majors Accounting technology and bookkeeping; agribusiness; agriculture; animation, interactive technology, video graphics and special effects; architectural engineering technology; architecture; autobody/collision and repair technology; automobile/automotive mechanics technology; biology/biological sciences; business administration and management; business, management, and marketing related; computer and information sciences; computer and information systems security; computer engineering technology; computer programming (specific applications); construction engineering technology; construction management; construction trades related; court reporting; criminology; culinary arts; diesel mechanics technology; drafting and design technology; electrical and power transmission installation; electrical, electronic and communications engineering technology; engineering; environmental engineering technology; environmental science; financial planning and services; forensic science and technology; general studies; graphic design; health information/medical records technology; heating, air conditioning, ventilation and refrigeration maintenance technology; heavy/industrial equipment maintenance technologies related; humanities; human resources management; human services; information science/studies; interior design; intermedia/multimedia; liberal arts and sciences and humanities related; liberal arts and sciences/liberal studies; machine shop technology; masonry; mechanical engineering/mechanical technology; radiologic technology/science; registered nursing/registered nurse; sales, distribution, and marketing operations; sport and fitness administration/management; surveying technology; system, networking, and LAN/WAN management; vehicle maintenance and repair technologies related; veterinary/animal health technology; web/multimedia management and webmaster; welding technology.
Academics *Calendar:* semesters. *Degrees:* certificates, associate, and bachelor's. *Special study options:* academic remediation for entering students, accelerated degree program, adult/continuing education programs, advanced placement credit, cooperative education, distance learning, double majors, English as a second language, honors programs, independent study, internships, off-campus study, part-time degree program, services for LD students, student-designed majors, study abroad, summer session for credit. *ROTC:* Army (c).
Library Walter C. Hinkle Memorial Library plus 1 other. *Books:* 54,671 (physical), 49,782 (digital/electronic); *Serial titles:* 253 (physical), 164,768 (digital/electronic); *Databases:* 193. Weekly public service hours: 88.
Student Life *Housing Options:* coed, men-only, women-only, special housing for students with disabilities. Campus housing is university owned. Freshman campus housing is guaranteed. *Activities and Organizations:* drama/theater group, student-run newspaper, radio station, choral group, Outdoor Recreation Club, Caribbean Student Association, Alfred Programming Board, Pioneer Woodsmen, Disaster Relief Team. *Campus security:* 24-hour emergency response devices and patrols, late-night transport/escort service, controlled dormitory access, residence hall entrance guards. *Student services:* health clinic, personal/psychological counseling.
Athletics Member NCAA, USCAA. All Division III. *Intercollegiate sports:* baseball M, basketball M/W, cross-country running M/W, football M, lacrosse M, soccer M/W, softball W, swimming and diving M/W, track and field M/W, volleyball W, wrestling M. *Intramural sports:* basketball M/W, equestrian sports M(c)/W(c), football M, golf M/W, ice hockey M(c), rock climbing M/W, soccer M/W, softball M/W, swimming and diving M/W, tennis M/W, ultimate Frisbee M/W, volleyball M/W.
Standardized Tests *Required for some:* SAT or ACT (for admission). *Recommended:* SAT or ACT (for admission).
Costs (2016–17) *One-time required fee:* $110. *Tuition:* state resident $6470 full-time, $270 per credit part-time; nonresident $9740 full-time, $406 per credit part-time. Full-time tuition and fees vary according to course load and degree level. Part-time tuition and fees vary according to course load and degree level. *Required fees:* $1605 full-time, $66 per credit part-time, $10 per credit part-time. *Room and board:* $11,820; room only: $7280. Room and board charges vary according to board plan and housing facility. *Payment plan:* installment. *Waivers:* employees or children of employees.
Financial Aid Of all full-time matriculated undergraduates who enrolled in 2015, 3,095 applied for aid, 2,712 were judged to have need, 330 had their need fully met. In 2015, 184 non-need-based awards were made. *Average percent of need met:* 57%. *Average financial aid package:* $11,156. *Average need-based loan:* $3939. *Average need-based gift aid:* $6852. *Average non-need-based aid:* $5680. *Average indebtedness upon graduation:* $30,796.
Applying *Options:* electronic application. *Application fee:* $50. *Required:* high school transcript, minimum 2.0 GPA, Common Application with essay on supplemental application. *Recommended:* essay or personal statement,

interview. *Application deadlines:* rolling (freshmen), rolling (transfers). *Notification:* continuous (freshmen), continuous (transfers).

Freshman Application Contact Mrs. Goodrich Deborah, Associate Vice President for Enrollment Management, State University of New York College of Technology at Alfred, Huntington Administration Building, 10 Upper College Drive, Alfred, NY 14802. *Phone:* 607-587-3945. *Toll-free phone:* 800-4-ALFRED. *Fax:* 607-587-4299. *E-mail:* admissions@alfredstate.edu. *Website:* http://www.alfredstate.edu/.

Stella and Charles Guttman Community College
New York, New York

Admissions Office Contact Stella and Charles Guttman Community College, 50 West 40th Street, New York, NY 10018. *Website:* http://guttman.cuny.edu/.

Suffolk County Community College
Selden, New York

Freshman Application Contact Suffolk County Community College, 533 College Road, Selden, NY 11784-2899. *Phone:* 631-451-4000. *Website:* http://www.sunysuffolk.edu/.

Sullivan County Community College
Loch Sheldrake, New York

- **State and locally supported** 2-year, founded 1962, part of State University of New York System
- **Rural** 405-acre campus
- **Endowment** $921,102
- **Coed,** 1,610 undergraduate students, 51% full-time, 52% women, 48% men

Undergraduates 820 full-time, 790 part-time. Students come from 4 states and territories; 3 other countries; 3% are from out of state; 18% Black or African American, non-Hispanic/Latino; 22% Hispanic/Latino; 2% Asian, non-Hispanic/Latino; 0.2% Native Hawaiian or other Pacific Islander, non-Hispanic/Latino; 0.1% American Indian or Alaska Native, non-Hispanic/Latino; 3% Two or more races, non-Hispanic/Latino; 4% Race/ethnicity unknown; 0.6% international; 6% transferred in; 22% live on campus.

Freshmen *Admission:* 1,433 applied, 1,371 admitted, 343 enrolled. *Average high school GPA:* 2.9.

Faculty *Total:* 101, 41% full-time, 16% with terminal degrees. *Student/faculty ratio:* 21:1.

Majors Accounting; administrative assistant and secretarial science; baking and pastry arts; business administration and management; commercial and advertising art; computer graphics; computer programming (specific applications); construction engineering technology; consumer merchandising/retailing management; criminal justice/police science; crisis/emergency/disaster management; culinary arts; data entry/microcomputer applications; electrical, electronic and communications engineering technology; elementary education; environmental studies; fire prevention and safety technology; forensic science and technology; hospitality administration; human services; information science/studies; kindergarten/preschool education; legal assistant/paralegal; liberal arts and sciences/liberal studies; marketing/marketing management; mathematics; medical/clinical assistant; parks, recreation and leisure; photography; psychology; radio and television; radio, television, and digital communication related; registered nursing/registered nurse; respiratory care therapy; science technologies related; sport and fitness administration/management; tourism and travel services management.

Academics *Calendar:* semesters. *Degree:* certificates and associate. *Special study options:* academic remediation for entering students, adult/continuing education programs, advanced placement credit, cooperative education, distance learning, double majors, honors programs, independent study, internships, off-campus study, part-time degree program, services for LD students, summer session for credit.

Library Hermann Memorial Library plus 1 other. *Books:* 55,406 (physical), 145,000 (digital/electronic); *Serial titles:* 109 (physical), 52,671 (digital/electronic); *Databases:* 118. Weekly public service hours: 62.

Student Life *Housing Options:* coed. Campus housing is provided by a third party. Freshman applicants given priority for college housing. *Activities and Organizations:* drama/theater group, Science Alliance, Black Student Union, Gay-Straight Alliance, Dance Club, Honor Society. *Campus security:* 24-hour emergency response devices and patrols, student patrols, controlled dormitory access. *Student services:* health clinic, personal/psychological counseling, legal services.

Athletics Member NJCAA. *Intercollegiate sports:* baseball M, basketball M/W, cross-country running M/W, softball W, volleyball W, wrestling M. *Intramural sports:* baseball M, basketball M/W, bowling M/W, cross-country running M/W, golf M/W, racquetball M/W, soccer M/W, softball M/W, table tennis M/W, tennis M/W, volleyball M/W, weight lifting M/W.

Costs (2017–18) *Tuition:* state resident $4674 full-time, $195 per credit hour part-time; nonresident $9348 full-time, $312 per credit hour part-time. Full-time tuition and fees vary according to program. Part-time tuition and fees vary according to program. *Required fees:* $876 full-time, $37 per credit hour part-time. *Room and board:* $9450; room only: $6050. Room and board charges vary according to board plan and housing facility. *Payment plans:* installment, deferred payment. *Waivers:* senior citizens and employees or children of employees.

Financial Aid Of all full-time matriculated undergraduates who enrolled in 2015, 711 applied for aid, 652 were judged to have need, 652 had their need fully met. 50 Federal Work-Study jobs (averaging $1055). 27 state and other part-time jobs (averaging $2580). *Average percent of need met:* 100%. *Average financial aid package:* $4466. *Average need-based loan:* $1625. *Average need-based gift aid:* $4466.

Applying *Options:* electronic application, early admission, deferred entrance. *Required:* high school transcript. *Application deadlines:* rolling (freshmen), rolling (transfers). *Notification:* continuous (freshmen), continuous (transfers). **Freshman Application Contact** Mr. Steven Alhona, Admissions Recruiter, Sullivan County Community College, 112 College Road, Loch Sheldrake, NY 12759. *Phone:* 845-434-5750 Ext. 4356. *Toll-free phone:* 800-577-5243. *Fax:* 845-434-4806. *E-mail:* salhona@sunysullivan.edu. *Website:* http://www.sullivan.suny.edu/.

TCI–College of Technology
New York, New York

Freshman Application Contact TCI–College of Technology, 320 West 31st Street, New York, NY 10001-2705. *Phone:* 212-594-4000. *Toll-free phone:* 800-878-8246. *Website:* http://www.tcicollege.edu/.

Tompkins Cortland Community College
Dryden, New York

- **State and locally supported** 2-year, founded 1968, part of State University of New York System
- **Rural** 300-acre campus
- **Coed,** 2,844 undergraduate students, 70% full-time, 57% women, 43% men

Undergraduates 1,981 full-time, 863 part-time. Students come from 17 states and territories; 23 other countries; 3% are from out of state; 13% Black or African American, non-Hispanic/Latino; 10% Hispanic/Latino; 2% Asian, non-Hispanic/Latino; 0.4% American Indian or Alaska Native, non-Hispanic/Latino; 4% Two or more races, non-Hispanic/Latino; 9% Race/ethnicity unknown; 3% international; 8% transferred in.

Freshmen *Admission:* 748 enrolled.

Faculty *Total:* 250, 25% full-time, 22% with terminal degrees. *Student/faculty ratio:* 18:1.

Majors Accounting technology and bookkeeping; agroecology and sustainable agriculture; biology/biotechnology laboratory technician; business administration and management; child-care and support services management; commercial and advertising art; computer and information sciences; computer support specialist; construction engineering technology; creative writing; criminal justice/law enforcement administration; criminal justice/police science; culinary arts; digital communication and media/multimedia; engineering; entrepreneurship; environmental studies; hotel, motel, and restaurant management; humanities; human services; information science/studies; international business/trade/commerce; international/global studies; legal assistant/paralegal; liberal arts and sciences and humanities related; liberal arts and sciences/liberal studies; parks, recreation and leisure; parks, recreation and leisure facilities management; photographic and film/video technology; radio and television broadcasting technology; registered nursing/registered nurse; special products marketing; speech communication and rhetoric; sport and fitness administration/management; substance abuse/addiction counseling.

Academics *Calendar:* semesters. *Degree:* certificates and associate. *Special study options:* academic remediation for entering students, adult/continuing education programs, advanced placement credit, cooperative education, distance learning, double majors, English as a second language, freshman honors college, honors programs, independent study, internships, off-campus study, part-time degree program, services for LD students, study abroad, summer session for credit.

Library Gerald A. Barry Memorial Library plus 1 other.

Student Life *Housing Options:* coed. Campus housing is provided by a third party. *Activities and Organizations:* drama/theater group, College

Entertainment Board, Sport Management Club, Nursing Club, Media Club, Writer's Guild. *Campus security:* 24-hour patrols, late-night transport/escort service, controlled dormitory access, armed peace officers. *Student services:* health clinic, personal/psychological counseling.

Athletics Member NJCAA. *Intercollegiate sports:* baseball M, basketball M/W, golf M/W, lacrosse M, soccer M/W, softball W, volleyball W. *Intramural sports:* archery M/W, badminton M/W, basketball M/W, bowling M/W, football M/W, golf M/W, lacrosse M/W, racquetball M/W, skiing (cross-country) M/W, skiing (downhill) M/W, soccer M/W, softball M/W, squash M/W, swimming and diving M/W, table tennis M/W, tennis M/W, ultimate Frisbee M/W, volleyball M/W, water polo M/W, weight lifting M/W, wrestling M/W.

Costs (2016–17) *Tuition:* state resident $4790 full-time, $172 per credit hour part-time; nonresident $9880 full-time, $354 per credit hour part-time. Part-time tuition and fees vary according to course load. *Required fees:* $1042 full-time, $37 per credit hour part-time, $17 per term part-time. *Room and board:* $10,540. Room and board charges vary according to board plan and housing facility. *Payment plans:* installment, deferred payment. *Waivers:* employees or children of employees.

Financial Aid Of all full-time matriculated undergraduates who enrolled in 2015, 150 Federal Work-Study jobs (averaging $1000). 150 state and other part-time jobs (averaging $1000).

Applying *Options:* electronic application, early admission, deferred entrance. *Required:* high school transcript. *Required for some:* essay or personal statement, interview. *Application deadlines:* rolling (freshmen), rolling (transfers). *Notification:* continuous (freshmen), continuous (transfers).

Freshman Application Contact Mr. Sandy Drumluk, Director of Admissions, Tompkins Cortland Community College, 170 North Street, PO Box 139, Dryden, NY 13053-0139. *Phone:* 607-844-6580. *Toll-free phone:* 888-567-8211. *Fax:* 607-844-6538. *E-mail:* admissions@tc3.edu.
Website: http://www.TC3.edu/.

Trocaire College
Buffalo, New York

- **Independent** primarily 2-year, founded 1958
- **Urban** 1-acre campus
- **Endowment** $7.3 million
- **Coed, primarily women**

Undergraduates 621 full-time, 748 part-time. Students come from 4 states and territories; 1 other country; 0.2% are from out of state; 13% Black or African American, non-Hispanic/Latino; 5% Hispanic/Latino; 1% Asian, non-Hispanic/Latino; 0.1% Native Hawaiian or other Pacific Islander, non-Hispanic/Latino; 1% American Indian or Alaska Native, non-Hispanic/Latino; 1% Two or more races, non-Hispanic/Latino; 9% Race/ethnicity unknown; 0.1% international; 16% transferred in.
Faculty *Student/faculty ratio:* 11:1.
Academics *Calendar:* semesters. *Degrees:* certificates, associate, and bachelor's. *Special study options:* academic remediation for entering students, adult/continuing education programs, advanced placement credit, cooperative education, distance learning, double majors, external degree program, independent study, internships, off-campus study, part-time degree program, services for LD students, study abroad, summer session for credit.
Library The Rachel R. Savarino Library plus 1 other. *Books:* 10,822 (physical), 1,308 (digital/electronic); *Databases:* 90.
Student Life *Campus security:* 24-hour emergency response devices and patrols, late-night transport/escort service.
Standardized Tests *Required:* ACCUPLACER (for admission).
Applying *Options:* electronic application, deferred entrance. *Required:* high school transcript. *Required for some:* essay or personal statement, 1 letter of recommendation. *Recommended:* minimum 1.9 GPA, interview.
Freshman Application Contact Trocaire College, 360 Choate Avenue, Buffalo, NY 14220-2094. *Phone:* 716-826-2558.
Website: http://www.trocaire.edu/.

Ulster County Community College
Stone Ridge, New York

- **State and locally supported** 2-year, founded 1961, part of State University of New York System
- **Rural** 165-acre campus
- **Endowment** $8.0 million
- **Coed,** 3,416 undergraduate students, 40% full-time, 54% women, 46% men

Undergraduates 1,380 full-time, 2,036 part-time. Students come from 8 states and territories; 2 other countries; 0.2% are from out of state; 7% Black or African American, non-Hispanic/Latino; 12% Hispanic/Latino; 1% Asian, non-Hispanic/Latino; 0.2% Native Hawaiian or other Pacific Islander, non-Hispanic/Latino; 0.2% American Indian or Alaska Native, non-Hispanic/Latino; 4% Two or more races, non-Hispanic/Latino; 4% Race/ethnicity unknown; 0.5% international; 5% transferred in.
Freshmen *Admission:* 459 applied, 459 admitted, 483 enrolled.
Faculty *Total:* 151, 42% full-time. *Student/faculty ratio:* 20:1.
Majors Accounting technology and bookkeeping; biology teacher education; business administration and management; chemistry teacher education; commercial and advertising art; community organization and advocacy; computer and information sciences; criminal justice/law enforcement administration; drafting/design engineering technologies related; dramatic/theater arts; engineering; environmental control technologies related; environmental studies; fashion/apparel design; humanities; human services; kindergarten/preschool education; liberal arts and sciences/liberal studies; management information systems and services related; mathematics teacher education; music; natural resources/conservation; parks, recreation and leisure facilities management; registered nursing/registered nurse; science teacher education; social studies teacher education; Spanish language teacher education; speech communication and rhetoric; system, networking, and LAN/WAN management; veterinary/animal health technology; visual and performing arts.
Academics *Calendar:* semesters. *Degree:* certificates, diplomas, and associate. *Special study options:* academic remediation for entering students, adult/continuing education programs, advanced placement credit, cooperative education, distance learning, double majors, English as a second language, honors programs, independent study, internships, off-campus study, part-time degree program, services for LD students, student-designed majors, study abroad, summer session for credit.
Library McDonald Dewitt Library. *Books:* 77,078 (physical), 164,597 (digital/electronic); *Serial titles:* 139 (physical), 135,595 (digital/electronic); *Databases:* 77. Weekly public service hours: 44.
Student Life *Housing:* college housing not available. *Activities and Organizations:* drama/theater group, choral group, Vet Tech, Biology Club, Nursing Club, Business Club, Visual Arts Club. *Campus security:* 24-hour emergency response devices. *Student services:* personal/psychological counseling.
Athletics Member NJCAA. *Intercollegiate sports:* baseball M, basketball M/W, golf M, soccer M, softball W, tennis M, volleyball W.
Costs (2016–17) *Tuition:* state resident $4330 full-time, $165 per credit hour part-time; nonresident $8660 full-time, $330 per credit hour part-time. *Required fees:* $867 full-time, $65 per course part-time, $38 per term part-time. *Payment plans:* installment, deferred payment. *Waivers:* senior citizens and employees or children of employees.
Financial Aid Of all full-time matriculated undergraduates who enrolled in 2015, 45 Federal Work-Study jobs (averaging $1000).
Applying *Options:* electronic application, early admission, deferred entrance. *Required:* high school transcript. *Application deadlines:* rolling (freshmen), rolling (transfers). *Notification:* continuous (freshmen), continuous (transfers).
Freshman Application Contact Admissions Office, Ulster County Community College, 491 Cottekill Road, Stone Ridge, NY 12484. *Phone:* 845-687-5022. *Toll-free phone:* 800-724-0833.
E-mail: admissionsoffice@sunyulster.edu.
Website: http://www.sunyulster.edu/.

Westchester Community College
Valhalla, New York

- **State and locally supported** 2-year, founded 1946, part of State University of New York System
- **Suburban** 218-acre campus with easy access to New York City
- **Coed,** 12,842 undergraduate students, 54% full-time, 52% women, 48% men

Undergraduates 6,973 full-time, 5,869 part-time. Students come from 14 states and territories; 53 other countries; 22% Black or African American, non-Hispanic/Latino; 34% Hispanic/Latino; 4% Asian, non-Hispanic/Latino; 0.3% Native Hawaiian or other Pacific Islander, non-Hispanic/Latino; 0.9% American Indian or Alaska Native, non-Hispanic/Latino; 2% Two or more races, non-Hispanic/Latino; 5% Race/ethnicity unknown; 6% transferred in.
Freshmen *Admission:* 4,596 applied, 4,596 admitted, 2,348 enrolled.
Faculty *Total:* 844, 20% full-time, 6% with terminal degrees.
Majors Accounting; accounting technology and bookkeeping; administrative assistant and secretarial science; animal sciences; art; athletic training; business administration and management; child-care and support services management; civil engineering technology; commercial and advertising art; community organization and advocacy; computer and information sciences; computer and information sciences and support services related; computer and information systems security; consumer merchandising/retailing management; corrections; design and applied arts related; dietitian assistant; digital arts; digital communication and media/multimedia; drafting and design technology; education (multiple levels); electrical, electronic and communications engineering technology; emergency medical technology (EMT paramedic); engineering; environmental control technologies related; environmental

science; environmental studies; food service systems administration; humanities; information science/studies; international business/trade/commerce; journalism; legal assistant/paralegal; liberal arts and sciences/liberal studies; marketing related; mechanical engineering/mechanical technology; medical administrative assistant and medical secretary; medical radiologic technology; practical nursing, vocational nursing and nursing assistants related; registered nursing/registered nurse; respiratory care therapy; restaurant, culinary, and catering management; retailing; small business administration; speech communication and rhetoric; substance abuse/addiction counseling; teacher assistant/aide; visual and performing arts.
Academics *Calendar:* semesters. *Degree:* certificates and associate. *Special study options:* academic remediation for entering students, adult/continuing education programs, advanced placement credit, cooperative education, distance learning, double majors, English as a second language, honors programs, independent study, internships, off-campus study, part-time degree program, services for LD students, study abroad, summer session for credit.
Library Harold L. Drimmer Library.
Student Life *Housing:* college housing not available. *Activities and Organizations:* student-run newspaper, radio station, choral group, Deca Fashion Retail, Future Educators, Respiratory Club, Black Student Union, Diversity Action. *Campus security:* 24-hour emergency response devices and patrols, late-night transport/escort service. *Student services:* health clinic, personal/psychological counseling, women's center.
Athletics Member NJCAA. *Intercollegiate sports:* baseball M, basketball M/W, bowling M/W, golf M, soccer M, softball W, volleyball W. *Intramural sports:* badminton M/W, basketball M/W, softball M/W, swimming and diving M/W, tennis M/W, volleyball M/W, weight lifting M/W.
Costs (2017–18) *Tuition:* state resident $4280 full-time, $179 per credit hour part-time; nonresident $11,770 full-time, $493 per credit hour part-time. Full-time tuition and fees vary according to location. Part-time tuition and fees vary according to location. *Required fees:* $443 full-time, $102 per term part-time. *Payment plan:* installment.
Financial Aid Of all full-time matriculated undergraduates who enrolled in 2015, 4,906 applied for aid, 4,168 were judged to have need. *Average financial aid package:* $3924. *Average need-based loan:* $1808. *Average need-based gift aid:* $3585.
Applying *Options:* electronic application. *Application fee:* $35. *Required:* high school transcript. *Required for some:* interview. *Application deadline:* rolling (freshmen).
Freshman Application Contact Ms. Gloria Leon, Director of Admissions, Westchester Community College, 75 Grasslands Road, Administration Building, Valhalla, NY 10595-1698. *Phone:* 914-606-6735. *Fax:* 914-606-6540. *E-mail:* admissions@sunywcc.edu.
Website: http://www.sunywcc.edu/.

See below for display ad and page 344 for the College Close-Up.

Wood Tobe–Coburn School
New York, New York
- **Proprietary** 2-year, founded 1879
- **Urban** campus
- **Coed**
- 89% of applicants were admitted

Academics *Calendar:* semesters. *Degree:* diplomas and associate. *Special study options:* accelerated degree program, internships.
Freshman Application Contact Admissions Office, Wood Tobe–Coburn School, 8 East 40th Street, New York, NY 10016. *Phone:* 212-686-9040. *Toll-free phone:* 800-394-9663. *Website:* http://www.woodtobecoburn.edu/.

NORTH CAROLINA

Alamance Community College
Graham, North Carolina
- **State-supported** 2-year, founded 1958, part of North Carolina Community College System
- **Small-town** 48-acre campus
- **Endowment** $2.9 million
- **Coed,** 4,459 undergraduate students, 60% full-time, 61% women, 39% men

Undergraduates 2,679 full-time, 1,780 part-time. Students come from 7 states and territories; 6 other countries; 1% are from out of state; 21% Black or African American, non-Hispanic/Latino; 10% Hispanic/Latino; 2% Asian, non-Hispanic/Latino; 0.7% American Indian or Alaska Native, non-Hispanic/Latino; 3% Two or more races, non-Hispanic/Latino; 0.7% international; 27% transferred in.
Freshmen *Admission:* 784 enrolled.
Faculty *Total:* 435, 26% full-time, 3% with terminal degrees. *Student/faculty ratio:* 12:1.

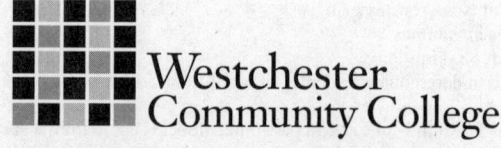

Majors Accounting technology and bookkeeping; animal sciences; applied horticulture/horticulture operations; automobile/automotive mechanics technology; banking and financial support services; biotechnology; business administration and management; carpentry; clinical/medical laboratory technology; commercial and advertising art; criminal justice/safety; culinary arts; electrical, electronic and communications engineering technology; executive assistant/executive secretary; heating, ventilation, air conditioning and refrigeration engineering technology; information science/studies; kindergarten/preschool education; legal administrative assistant/secretary; liberal arts and sciences/liberal studies; machine tool technology; mechanical engineering/mechanical technology; medical administrative assistant and medical secretary; medical/clinical assistant; office occupations and clerical services; registered nursing/registered nurse; retailing; teacher assistant/aide; welding technology.

Academics *Calendar:* semesters. *Degree:* certificates, diplomas, and associate. *Special study options:* academic remediation for entering students, adult/continuing education programs, cooperative education, distance learning, double majors, English as a second language, independent study, off-campus study, part-time degree program, services for LD students, summer session for credit.

Library Learning Resources Center. Weekly public service hours: 64; students can reserve study rooms.

Student Life *Housing:* college housing not available. *Campus security:* 24-hour emergency response devices and patrols, student patrols, late-night transport/escort service. *Student services:* personal/psychological counseling.

Costs (2016–17) *Tuition:* state resident $2432 full-time, $76 per credit hour part-time; nonresident $8576 full-time, $268 per credit hour part-time. Full-time tuition and fees vary according to course load. Part-time tuition and fees vary according to course load. *Required fees:* $30 full-time, $5 per credit hour part-time. *Payment plan:* installment.

Financial Aid Of all full-time matriculated undergraduates who enrolled in 2010, 4,000 applied for aid, 3,000 were judged to have need. 200 Federal Work-Study jobs. *Average percent of need met:* 30%. *Average financial aid package:* $4500. *Average need-based gift aid:* $4500. *Average indebtedness upon graduation:* $2500.

Applying *Options:* electronic application. *Required:* high school transcript. *Application deadlines:* rolling (freshmen), rolling (transfers). *Notification:* continuous (freshmen), continuous (transfers).

Freshman Application Contact Ms. Elizabeth Brehler, Director for Enrollment Management, Alamance Community College, Graham, NC 27253-8000. *Phone:* 336-506-4120. *Fax:* 336-506-4264.
E-mail: brehlere@alamancecc.edu.
Website: http://www.alamancecc.edu/.

Asheville-Buncombe Technical Community College
Asheville, North Carolina

Freshman Application Contact Asheville-Buncombe Technical Community College, 340 Victoria Road, Asheville, NC 28801-4897. *Phone:* 828-254-1921 Ext. 7520. *Website:* http://www.abtech.edu/.

Beaufort County Community College
Washington, North Carolina

Freshman Application Contact Mr. Gary Burbage, Director of Admissions, Beaufort County Community College, PO Box 1069, 5337 US Highway 264 East, Washington, NC 27889-1069. *Phone:* 252-940-6233. *Fax:* 252-940-6393. *E-mail:* garyb@beaufortccc.edu. *Website:* http://www.beaufortccc.edu/.

Bladen Community College
Dublin, North Carolina

Freshman Application Contact Ms. Andrea Fisher, Enrollment Specialist, Bladen Community College, PO Box 266, Dublin, NC 28332. *Phone:* 910-879-5593. *Fax:* 910-879-5564. *E-mail:* acarterfisher@bladencc.edu. *Website:* http://www.bladen.cc.nc.us/.

Blue Ridge Community College
Flat Rock, North Carolina

Freshman Application Contact Blue Ridge Community College, 180 West Campus Drive, Flat Rock, NC 28731. *Phone:* 828-694-1810. *Website:* http://www.blueridge.edu/.

Brightwood College, Charlotte Campus
Charlotte, North Carolina

Freshman Application Contact Director of Admissions, Brightwood College, Charlotte Campus, 6070 East Independence Boulevard, Charlotte, NC 28212. *Phone:* 704-567-3700. *Toll-free phone:* 866-543-0208.
Website: http://www.brightwood.edu/.

Brunswick Community College
Supply, North Carolina

Freshman Application Contact Admissions Counselor, Brunswick Community College, 50 College Road, PO Box 30, Supply, NC 28462-0030. *Phone:* 910-755-7300. *Toll-free phone:* 800-754-1050. *Fax:* 910-754-9609. *E-mail:* admissions@brunswickcc.edu.
Website: http://www.brunswickcc.edu/.

Caldwell Community College and Technical Institute
Hudson, North Carolina

- **State-supported** 2-year, founded 1964, part of North Carolina Community College System
- **Small-town** 50-acre campus
- **Coed,** 3,805 undergraduate students, 39% full-time, 56% women, 44% men

Undergraduates 1,472 full-time, 2,333 part-time.
Freshmen *Admission:* 530 enrolled.
Faculty *Total:* 420, 31% full-time, 9% with terminal degrees. *Student/faculty ratio:* 18:1.
Majors Accounting; automobile/automotive mechanics technology; biological and physical sciences; biomedical technology; business administration and management; computer programming; cosmetology; culinary arts; diagnostic medical sonography and ultrasound technology; early childhood education; education; electrical and electronics engineering; emergency medical technology (EMT paramedic); fine/studio arts; hotel, motel, and restaurant management; information technology; landscape architecture; legal assistant/paralegal; liberal arts and sciences/liberal studies; mechanical engineering/mechanical technology; medical/clinical assistant; medical office management; nuclear medical technology; office occupations and clerical services; physical therapy technology; radiologic technology/science; registered nursing/registered nurse; speech-language pathology assistant.
Academics *Calendar:* semesters. *Degree:* certificates, diplomas, and associate. *Special study options:* academic remediation for entering students, adult/continuing education programs, advanced placement credit, cooperative education, distance learning, double majors, independent study, part-time degree program, services for LD students, summer session for credit.
Library Broyhill Center for Learning Resources. Students can reserve study rooms.
Student Life *Housing:* college housing not available. *Activities and Organizations:* drama/theater group, choral group. *Campus security:* trained security personnel during hours of operation. *Student services:* personal/psychological counseling.
Athletics Member NJCAA. *Intercollegiate sports:* basketball M/W. *Intramural sports:* basketball M/W.
Costs (2017–18) *Tuition:* state resident $1872 full-time; nonresident $6864 full-time. Full-time tuition and fees vary according to course load and program. Part-time tuition and fees vary according to course load and program. *Required fees:* $38 full-time, $9 per course part-time. *Payment plan:* installment.
Financial Aid Of all full-time matriculated undergraduates who enrolled in 2015, 69 Federal Work-Study jobs (averaging $960).
Applying *Options:* early admission. *Required:* high school transcript. *Application deadlines:* rolling (freshmen), rolling (transfers). *Notification:* continuous (freshmen), continuous (transfers).
Freshman Application Contact Patricia Brinkley, Admissions Representative, Caldwell Community College and Technical Institute, 2855 Hickory Boulevard, Hudson, NC 28638. *Phone:* 828-726-2700.
Fax: 828-726-2709. *E-mail:* pbrinkley@cccti.edu.
Website: http://www.cccti.edu/.

Cape Fear Community College
Wilmington, North Carolina

- **State-supported** 2-year, founded 1959, part of North Carolina Community College System
- **Urban** 150-acre campus
- **Endowment** $8.8 million
- **Coed,** 9,067 undergraduate students, 43% full-time, 57% women, 43% men

Undergraduates 3,898 full-time, 5,169 part-time. Students come from 48 states and territories; 52 other countries; 6% are from out of state; 12% Black or African American, non-Hispanic/Latino; 8% Hispanic/Latino; 1% Asian, non-Hispanic/Latino; 0.2% Native Hawaiian or other Pacific Islander, non-Hispanic/Latino; 0.7% American Indian or Alaska Native, non-Hispanic/Latino; 3% Two or more races, non-Hispanic/Latino; 1% Race/ethnicity unknown; 0.1% international; 8% transferred in.
Freshmen *Admission:* 4,629 applied, 3,071 admitted, 1,860 enrolled.
Faculty *Total:* 773, 39% full-time. *Student/faculty ratio:* 12:1.
Majors Accounting technology and bookkeeping; architectural engineering technology; automobile/automotive mechanics technology; baking and pastry arts; building/property maintenance; business administration and management; chemical technology; cinematography and film/video production; computer systems networking and telecommunications; computer technology/computer systems technology; cosmetology; criminal justice/police science; culinary arts; dental hygiene; diagnostic medical sonography and ultrasound technology; early childhood education; electrical, electronic and communications engineering technology; electrical/electronics equipment installation and repair; electromechanical and instrumentation and maintenance technologies related; emergency medical technology (EMT paramedic); executive assistant/executive secretary; fire prevention and safety technology; hotel/motel administration; instrumentation technology; interior design; landscaping and groundskeeping; language interpretation and translation; liberal arts and sciences/liberal studies; machine shop technology; marine maintenance and ship repair technology; mechanical engineering/mechanical technology; medical office management; medical radiologic technology; nuclear/nuclear power technology; occupational therapist assistant; oceanography (chemical and physical); registered nursing/registered nurse; surgical technology.
Academics *Calendar:* semesters. *Degree:* certificates, diplomas, and associate. *Special study options:* academic remediation for entering students, adult/continuing education programs, advanced placement credit, cooperative education, distance learning, double majors, English as a second language, independent study, off-campus study, part-time degree program, services for LD students, summer session for credit.
Library Cape Fear Community College Library.
Student Life *Housing:* college housing not available. *Activities and Organizations:* student-run newspaper, choral group, Nursing Club, Dental Hygiene Club, Pineapple Guild, Phi Theta Kappa, Occupational Therapy. *Campus security:* 24-hour emergency response devices and patrols, late-night transport/escort service, armed police officers. *Student services:* personal/psychological counseling.
Athletics Member NJCAA. *Intercollegiate sports:* basketball M/W, cheerleading M/W, golf M, soccer M/W, volleyball W. *Intramural sports:* basketball M/W, table tennis M/W.
Costs (2016–17) *Tuition:* state resident $2432 full-time, $76 per credit hour part-time; nonresident $8576 full-time, $268 per credit hour part-time. Full-time tuition and fees vary according to course load. Part-time tuition and fees vary according to course load. *Required fees:* $316 full-time, $78 per credit hour part-time. *Payment plan:* installment.
Applying *Options:* electronic application, early admission. *Required for some:* high school transcript, interview. *Application deadlines:* 8/18 (freshmen), rolling (transfers). *Notification:* continuous (freshmen), continuous (transfers).
Freshman Application Contact Ms. Linda Kasyan, Director of Admissions, Cape Fear Community College, 411 North Front Street, Wilmington, NC 28401-3993. *Phone:* 910-362-7054. *Toll-free phone:* 877-799-2322. *Fax:* 910-362-7080. *E-mail:* admissions@cfcc.edu.
Website: http://www.cfcc.edu/.

Carolinas College of Health Sciences
Charlotte, North Carolina

- **Public** 2-year, founded 1990
- **Urban** 3-acre campus with easy access to Charlotte
- **Endowment** $2.4 million
- **Coed,** 433 undergraduate students, 11% full-time, 91% women, 9% men

Undergraduates 49 full-time, 384 part-time. Students come from 12 states and territories; 10% are from out of state; 10% Black or African American, non-Hispanic/Latino; 6% Hispanic/Latino; 3% Asian, non-Hispanic/Latino;

0.5% Native Hawaiian or other Pacific Islander, non-Hispanic/Latino; 0.2% American Indian or Alaska Native, non-Hispanic/Latino; 3% Two or more races, non-Hispanic/Latino; 4% Race/ethnicity unknown.
Freshmen *Admission:* 19 enrolled. *Average high school GPA:* 3.59.
Faculty *Total:* 51, 49% full-time, 24% with terminal degrees. *Student/faculty ratio:* 9:1.
Majors Medical radiologic technology; radiologic technology/science; registered nursing/registered nurse.
Academics *Calendar:* semesters. *Degree:* certificates, diplomas, and associate. *Special study options:* advanced placement credit, distance learning, independent study, off-campus study, part-time degree program, services for LD students, study abroad, summer session for credit.
Library AHEC Library. Study areas open 24 hours, 5&-7 days a week; students can reserve study rooms.
Student Life *Housing:* college housing not available. *Campus security:* 24-hour emergency response devices and patrols, late-night transport/escort service. *Student services:* health clinic, personal/psychological counseling.
Standardized Tests *Required for some:* SAT or ACT (for admission).
Costs (2017–18) *Tuition:* state resident $14,335 full-time, $333 per credit hour part-time; nonresident $14,335 full-time, $333 per credit hour part-time. Full-time tuition and fees vary according to course load and program. Part-time tuition and fees vary according to course load and program. *Required fees:* $1480 full-time, $175 per term part-time. *Payment plan:* installment. *Waivers:* employees or children of employees.
Financial Aid Of all full-time matriculated undergraduates who enrolled in 2014, 7 Federal Work-Study jobs (averaging $3569).
Applying *Options:* electronic application. *Application fee:* $50. *Required:* minimum 2.5 GPA. *Required for some:* high school transcript, 3 letters of recommendation, interview.
Freshman Application Contact Ms. Merritt Newman, Admissions Representative, Carolinas College of Health Sciences, 1200 Blythe Boulevard, Charlotte, NC 28203. *Phone:* 704-355-5583. *Fax:* 704-355-9336.
E-mail: merritt.newman@carolinascollege.edu.
Website: http://www.carolinascollege.edu/.

Carteret Community College
Morehead City, North Carolina

- **State-supported** 2-year, founded 1963, part of North Carolina Community College System
- **Small-town** 40-acre campus
- **Endowment** $4.1 million
- **Coed,** 1,363 undergraduate students, 42% full-time, 69% women, 31% men

Undergraduates 571 full-time, 792 part-time. Students come from 8 states and territories; 1% are from out of state; 9% Black or African American, non-Hispanic/Latino; 4% Hispanic/Latino; 1% Asian, non-Hispanic/Latino; 0.2% Native Hawaiian or other Pacific Islander, non-Hispanic/Latino; 0.7% American Indian or Alaska Native, non-Hispanic/Latino; 3% Two or more races, non-Hispanic/Latino; 2% Race/ethnicity unknown; 11% transferred in.
Freshmen *Admission:* 1,593 applied, 1,532 admitted, 207 enrolled.
Faculty *Total:* 161, 37% full-time, 5% with terminal degrees. *Student/faculty ratio:* 9:1.
Majors Aquaculture; baking and pastry arts; business administration and management; computer engineering technology; computer software and media applications related; computer systems networking and telecommunications; criminal justice/law enforcement administration; culinary arts; early childhood education; emergency medical technology (EMT paramedic); hotel, motel, and restaurant management; information technology; legal assistant/paralegal; liberal arts and sciences/liberal studies; massage therapy; medical administrative assistant and medical secretary; medical/clinical assistant; medical office computer specialist; mental and social health services and allied professions related; office management; photographic and film/video technology; radiologic technology/science; registered nursing/registered nurse; respiratory care therapy.
Academics *Calendar:* semesters. *Degrees:* certificates, diplomas, associate, and postbachelor's certificates. *Special study options:* academic remediation for entering students, adult/continuing education programs, cooperative education, distance learning, double majors, internships, part-time degree program, services for LD students, summer session for credit.
Library Michael J. Smith Learning Resource Center. *Books:* 18,182 (physical), 173,614 (digital/electronic); *Databases:* 74. Weekly public service hours: 63.
Student Life *Housing:* college housing not available. *Activities and Organizations:* drama/theater group, student-run newspaper, Student Government Association, Medical Assisting Club, Respiratory Therapy Club, Radiography Club, Chess Club. *Campus security:* late-night transport/escort service, security service from 7 am until 11:30 pm.

Costs (2017–18) *Tuition:* state resident $1800 full-time, $76 per credit hour part-time; nonresident $6522 full-time, $268 per credit hour part-time. *Required fees:* $90 full-time, $24 per term part-time.

Applying *Options:* electronic application. *Required for some:* high school transcript. *Application deadlines:* rolling (freshmen), rolling (transfers). *Notification:* continuous (freshmen), continuous (transfers).

Freshman Application Contact Gabriel Raynor, Admissions Officer, Carteret Community College, 3505 Arendell Street, Morehead City, NC 28557-2989. *Phone:* 252-222-6253. *Fax:* 252-222-6265. *E-mail:* admissions@carteret.edu. *Website:* http://www.carteret.edu/.

Catawba Valley Community College
Hickory, North Carolina

- **State-supported** 2-year, founded 1960, part of North Carolina Community College System
- **Small-town** 50-acre campus with easy access to Charlotte
- **Endowment** $3.2 million
- **Coed**

Undergraduates 1,870 full-time, 2,701 part-time. Students come from 3 states and territories; 9% Black or African American, non-Hispanic/Latino; 10% Hispanic/Latino; 9% Asian, non-Hispanic/Latino; 0.2% Native Hawaiian or other Pacific Islander, non-Hispanic/Latino; 0.8% American Indian or Alaska Native, non-Hispanic/Latino; 1% Two or more races, non-Hispanic/Latino; 2% Race/ethnicity unknown; 21% transferred in.

Faculty *Student/faculty ratio:* 12:1.

Academics *Calendar:* semesters. *Degree:* certificates, diplomas, and associate. *Special study options:* academic remediation for entering students, adult/continuing education programs, advanced placement credit, cooperative education, distance learning, double majors, English as a second language, independent study, part-time degree program, services for LD students, student-designed majors, summer session for credit.

Library CVCC Library. *Books:* 31,890 (physical), 61 (digital/electronic); *Serial titles:* 26 (physical), 11 (digital/electronic); *Databases:* 12. Weekly public service hours: 59; students can reserve study rooms.

Student Life *Campus security:* 24-hour emergency response devices, late-night transport/escort service.

Athletics Member NJCAA.

Standardized Tests *Required:* TABE for Basic Law Enforcement Training (BLET); PSB for nursing, dental hygiene, EMS, electroneurodiagnostic technology, health occupations, radiography, surgical technology; TEAS for surgical technology programs (for admission).

Costs (2016–17) *Tuition:* state resident $2128 full-time, $76 per credit hour part-time; nonresident $7504 full-time, $268 per contact hour part-time. Part-time tuition and fees vary according to course load. *Required fees:* $123 full-time, $61 per contact hour part-time, $61 per term part-time.

Applying *Options:* electronic application. *Required:* high school transcript. *Required for some:* 1 letter of recommendation.

Freshman Application Contact Catawba Valley Community College, 2550 Highway 70 SE, Hickory, NC 28602-9699. *Phone:* 828-327-7000 Ext. 4618. *Website:* http://www.cvcc.edu/.

Central Carolina Community College
Sanford, North Carolina

Freshman Application Contact Mrs. Jamie Tyson Childress, Dean of Enrollment/Registrar, Central Carolina Community College, 1105 Kelly Drive, Sanford, NC 27330-9000. *Phone:* 919-718-7239. *Toll-free phone:* 800-682-8353. *Fax:* 919-718-7380. *Website:* http://www.cccc.edu/.

Central Piedmont Community College
Charlotte, North Carolina

Freshman Application Contact Ms. Linda McComb, Associate Dean, Central Piedmont Community College, PO Box 35009, Charlotte, NC 28235-5009. *Phone:* 704-330-6784. *Fax:* 704-330-6136. *Website:* http://www.cpcc.edu/.

Cleveland Community College
Shelby, North Carolina

- **State-supported** 2-year, founded 1965, part of North Carolina Community College System
- **Small-town** 43-acre campus with easy access to Charlotte
- **Coed**

Undergraduates 1,029 full-time, 1,961 part-time. 22% Black or African American, non-Hispanic/Latino; 4% Hispanic/Latino; 1% Asian, non-Hispanic/Latino; 0.1% Native Hawaiian or other Pacific Islander, non-Hispanic/Latino; 0.3% American Indian or Alaska Native, non-Hispanic/Latino; 2% Two or more races, non-Hispanic/Latino; 2% Race/ethnicity unknown.

Faculty *Student/faculty ratio:* 10:1.

Academics *Calendar:* semesters. *Degree:* certificates, diplomas, and associate. *Special study options:* academic remediation for entering students, adult/continuing education programs, advanced placement credit, cooperative education, distance learning, double majors, English as a second language, independent study, off-campus study, part-time degree program, summer session for credit.

Library Jim & Patsy Rose Library.

Student Life *Campus security:* security personnel during hours of operation.

Costs (2016–17) *Tuition:* state resident $2432 full-time; nonresident $8576 full-time. Full-time tuition and fees vary according to course load. Part-time tuition and fees vary according to course load. *Required fees:* $94 full-time.

Financial Aid Of all full-time matriculated undergraduates who enrolled in 2015, 20 Federal Work-Study jobs.

Applying *Options:* electronic application, deferred entrance. *Required:* high school transcript.

Freshman Application Contact Cleveland Community College, 137 South Post Road, Shelby, NC 28152. *Phone:* 704-669-4139. *Website:* http://www.clevelandcc.edu/.

Coastal Carolina Community College
Jacksonville, North Carolina

Freshman Application Contact Ms. Heather Calihan, Counseling Coordinator, Coastal Carolina Community College, Jacksonville, NC 28546. *Phone:* 910-938-6241. *Fax:* 910-455-2767. *E-mail:* calihanh@coastal.cc.nc.us. *Website:* http://www.coastalcarolina.edu/.

College of The Albemarle
Elizabeth City, North Carolina

- **State-supported** 2-year, founded 1960, part of North Carolina Community College System
- **Small-town** 40-acre campus
- **Coed,** 2,052 undergraduate students, 35% full-time, 64% women, 36% men

Undergraduates 715 full-time, 1,337 part-time. Students come from 17 states and territories; 4 other countries.

Freshmen *Admission:* 411 enrolled.

Faculty *Total:* 122, 49% full-time.

Majors Administrative assistant and secretarial science; architectural engineering technology; art; biotechnology; business administration and management; computer engineering technology; computer programming; computer programming (specific applications); construction trades; crafts, folk art and artisanry; criminal justice/law enforcement administration; culinary arts; data entry/microcomputer applications; drafting/design engineering technologies related; dramatic/theater arts; education; information science/studies; information technology; liberal arts and sciences/liberal studies; licensed practical/vocational nurse training; marine maintenance and ship repair technology; medical administrative assistant and medical secretary; metal and jewelry arts; music; registered nursing/registered nurse; teacher assistant/aide.

Academics *Calendar:* semesters. *Degree:* certificates, diplomas, and associate. *Special study options:* academic remediation for entering students, adult/continuing education programs, advanced placement credit, cooperative education, English as a second language, part-time degree program, services for LD students, summer session for credit.

Library Learning Resources Center.

Student Life *Housing:* college housing not available. *Activities and Organizations:* drama/theater group, choral group, Phi Beta Lambda, Phi Theta Kappa. *Campus security:* 24-hour patrols. *Student services:* personal/psychological counseling.

Athletics *Intramural sports:* archery M/W, badminton M/W, baseball M/W, basketball M/W, football M/W, golf M/W, gymnastics M/W, sailing M/W, soccer M(c), softball M/W, swimming and diving M/W, table tennis M/W, tennis M/W, volleyball M/W.

Costs (2016–17) *One-time required fee:* $147. *Tuition:* state resident $2080 full-time, $76 per credit hour part-time; nonresident $6705 full-time, $268 per credit hour part-time. Full-time tuition and fees vary according to course load, location, and program. *Payment plans:* installment, deferred payment.

Applying *Options:* electronic application, early admission, deferred entrance. *Required:* high school transcript. *Application deadlines:* rolling (freshmen), rolling (transfers). *Notification:* continuous (freshmen), continuous (transfers).

Freshman Application Contact Angie Godfrey-Dawson, Director of Admissions/Financial Aid, College of The Albemarle, PO Box 2327, Elizabeth City, NC 27906-2327. *Phone:* 252-335-0821 Ext. 2360. *Fax:* 252-335-2011. *Website:* http://www.albemarle.edu/.

Craven Community College
New Bern, North Carolina

- **State-supported** 2-year, founded 1965, part of North Carolina Community College System
- **Suburban** 100-acre campus
- **Coed,** 2,883 undergraduate students, 37% full-time, 58% women, 42% men

Undergraduates 1,074 full-time, 1,809 part-time. 16% Black or African American, non-Hispanic/Latino; 8% Hispanic/Latino; 2% Asian, non-Hispanic/Latino; 0.3% Native Hawaiian or other Pacific Islander, non-Hispanic/Latino; 0.8% American Indian or Alaska Native, non-Hispanic/Latino; 4% Two or more races, non-Hispanic/Latino; 6% Race/ethnicity unknown; 2% international; 5% transferred in.

Freshmen *Admission:* 525 enrolled.

Faculty *Total:* 216, 34% full-time. *Student/faculty ratio:* 13:1.

Majors Accounting; airframe mechanics and aircraft maintenance technology; automobile/automotive mechanics technology; banking and financial support services; business administration and management; computer and information systems security; computer programming (specific applications); computer systems networking and telecommunications; criminal justice/law enforcement administration; criminal justice/safety; early childhood education; electrical, electronic and communications engineering technology; electromechanical technology; elementary education; entrepreneurship; general studies; health information/medical records technology; heating, air conditioning, ventilation and refrigeration maintenance technology; hotel, motel, and restaurant management; information technology; legal administrative assistant/secretary; liberal arts and sciences and humanities related; liberal arts and sciences/liberal studies; machine shop technology; mechanical engineering/mechanical technology; medical administrative assistant and medical secretary; medical/clinical assistant; medical office management; office management; physical therapy technology; pre-engineering; registered nursing/registered nurse; special education; system, networking, and LAN/WAN management; tool and die technology; welding technology.

Academics *Calendar:* semesters. *Degree:* certificates, diplomas, and associate. *Special study options:* academic remediation for entering students, adult/continuing education programs, advanced placement credit, cooperative education, distance learning, double majors, English as a second language, honors programs, independent study, internships, part-time degree program, services for LD students, study abroad, summer session for credit.

Library R. C. Godwin Memorial Library. *Books:* 25,333 (physical), 285,381 (digital/electronic); *Serial titles:* 45 (physical), 19,586 (digital/electronic); *Databases:* 86. Students can reserve study rooms.

Student Life *Housing:* college housing not available. *Activities and Organizations:* choral group. *Campus security:* 24-hour patrols. *Student services:* personal/psychological counseling.

Costs (2016–17) *Tuition:* state resident $1824 full-time, $76 per credit hour part-time; nonresident $6432 full-time, $268 per credit hour part-time. Full-time tuition and fees vary according to course load. Part-time tuition and fees vary according to course load. *Required fees:* $229 full-time, $114 per term part-time. *Payment plan:* installment. *Waivers:* senior citizens.

Applying *Options:* electronic application. *Required:* high school transcript. *Application deadlines:* rolling (freshmen), rolling (transfers).

Freshman Application Contact Craven Community College, 800 College Court, New Bern, NC 28562. *Phone:* 252-638-4597.

Website: http://www.cravencc.edu/.

Davidson County Community College
Lexington, North Carolina

Freshman Application Contact Davidson County Community College, PO Box 1287, Lexington, NC 27293-1287. *Phone:* 336-249-8186 Ext. 6715. *Fax:* 336-224-0240. *E-mail:* admissions@davidsonccc.edu. *Website:* http://www.davidsonccc.edu/.

Durham Technical Community College
Durham, North Carolina

Director of Admissions Ms. Penny Augustine, Director of Admissions and Testing, Durham Technical Community College, 1637 Lawson Street,

Durham, NC 27703-5023. *Phone:* 919-686-3619.
Website: http://www.durhamtech.edu/.

Edgecombe Community College
Tarboro, North Carolina

Freshman Application Contact Ms. Jackie Heath, Admissions Officer, Edgecombe Community College, 2009 West Wilson Street, Tarboro, NC 27886-9399. *Phone:* 252-823-5166 Ext. 254.
Website: http://www.edgecombe.edu/.

Fayetteville Technical Community College
Fayetteville, North Carolina

- **State-supported** 2-year, founded 1961, part of North Carolina Community College System
- **Suburban** 204-acre campus with easy access to Raleigh
- **Endowment** $39,050
- **Coed,** 11,380 undergraduate students, 37% full-time, 57% women, 43% men

Undergraduates 4,219 full-time, 7,161 part-time. Students come from 47 states and territories; 33 other countries; 22% are from out of state; 37% Black or African American, non-Hispanic/Latino; 11% Hispanic/Latino; 2% Asian, non-Hispanic/Latino; 0.6% Native Hawaiian or other Pacific Islander, non-Hispanic/Latino; 2% American Indian or Alaska Native, non-Hispanic/Latino; 4% Two or more races, non-Hispanic/Latino; 4% Race/ethnicity unknown; 0.5% international; 7% transferred in.

Freshmen *Admission:* 4,392 applied, 4,392 admitted, 2,232 enrolled. *Average high school GPA:* 2.9.

Faculty *Total:* 528, 51% full-time, 5% with terminal degrees. *Student/faculty ratio:* 19:1.

Majors Accounting; applied horticulture/horticulture operations; architectural engineering technology; autobody/collision and repair technology; automobile/automotive mechanics technology; banking and financial support services; building/construction finishing, management, and inspection related; business administration and management; civil engineering technology; commercial and advertising art; computer and information systems security; computer programming; computer systems networking and telecommunications; cosmetology; criminal justice/safety; crisis/emergency/disaster management; culinary arts; dental hygiene; early childhood education; electrical, electronic and communications engineering technology; electrician; elementary education; emergency medical technology (EMT paramedic); fire prevention and safety technology; forensic science and technology; funeral service and mortuary science; game and interactive media design; general studies; gunsmithing; health and physical education related; heating, air conditioning, ventilation and refrigeration maintenance technology; hotel, motel, and restaurant management; human resources management; information science/studies; information technology; legal assistant/paralegal; liberal arts and sciences and humanities related; liberal arts and sciences/liberal studies; logistics, materials, and supply chain management; machine shop technology; marketing/marketing management; medical office management; office management; operations management; pharmacy technician; physical therapy technology; pre-engineering; public administration; radiologic technology/science; registered nursing/registered nurse; respiratory care therapy; speech-language pathology assistant; surgical technology; surveying technology.

Academics *Calendar:* semesters. *Degree:* certificates, diplomas, and associate. *Special study options:* academic remediation for entering students, accelerated degree program, adult/continuing education programs, advanced placement credit, cooperative education, distance learning, double majors, English as a second language, honors programs, independent study, internships, off-campus study, part-time degree program, services for LD students, summer session for credit.

Library Paul H. Thompson Library plus 1 other. *Books:* 55,249 (physical), 250,000 (digital/electronic); *Serial titles:* 58 (physical), 2 (digital/electronic); *Databases:* 149.

Student Life *Housing:* college housing not available. *Activities and Organizations:* choral group, Parents for Higher Education, Phi Theta Kappa, Phi Beta Lambda, Surgical Technology Club, FTCC Game Club. *Campus security:* 24-hour emergency response devices and patrols, late-night transport/escort service, campus-wide emergency notification system. *Student services:* personal/psychological counseling.

Athletics Member NJCAA. *Intercollegiate sports:* basketball M/W, golf M/W. *Intramural sports:* basketball M/W, tennis M/W.

Costs (2016–17) *One-time required fee:* $25. *Tuition:* state resident $2432 full-time, $76 per credit hour part-time; nonresident $8576 full-time, $268 per credit hour part-time. Full-time tuition and fees vary according to course load.

Part-time tuition and fees vary according to course load. *Required fees:* $96 full-time, $48 per term part-time. *Payment plan:* installment. *Waivers:* employees or children of employees.

Financial Aid Of all full-time matriculated undergraduates who enrolled in 2015, 75 Federal Work-Study jobs (averaging $2000). *Financial aid deadline:* 6/1.

Applying *Options:* electronic application, deferred entrance. *Required for some:* essay or personal statement, high school transcript, interview. *Application deadlines:* rolling (freshmen), rolling (transfers). *Notification:* continuous (freshmen), continuous (transfers).

Freshman Application Contact Dr. Louanna Castleman, Director of Admissions, Fayetteville Technical Community College, 2201 Hull Road, PO Box 35236, Fayetteville, NC 28303. *Phone:* 910-678-0141. *Fax:* 910-678-0085. *E-mail:* castleml@faytechcc.edu. *Website:* http://www.faytechcc.edu/.

Forsyth Technical Community College
Winston-Salem, North Carolina

Freshman Application Contact Admissions Office, Forsyth Technical Community College, 2100 Silas Creek Parkway, Winston-Salem, NC 27103-5197. *Phone:* 336-734-7556. *E-mail:* admissions@forsythtech.edu. *Website:* http://www.forsythtech.edu/.

Gaston College
Dallas, North Carolina

Freshman Application Contact Terry Basier, Director of Enrollment Management and Admissions, Gaston College, 201 Highway 321 South, Dallas, NC 28034. *Phone:* 704-922-6214. *Fax:* 704-922-6443. *Website:* http://www.gaston.edu/.

Guilford Technical Community College
Jamestown, North Carolina

Freshman Application Contact Guilford Technical Community College, PO Box 309, Jamestown, NC 27282-0309. *Phone:* 336-334-4822 Ext. 50125. *Website:* http://www.gtcc.edu/.

Halifax Community College
Weldon, North Carolina

- **State and locally supported** 2-year, founded 1967, part of North Carolina Community College System
- **Rural** 109-acre campus
- **Endowment** $1.1 million
- **Coed,** 1,136 undergraduate students, 49% full-time, 62% women, 38% men

Undergraduates 560 full-time, 576 part-time. Students come from 3 states and territories; 5 other countries; 50% Black or African American, non-Hispanic/Latino; 2% Hispanic/Latino; 0.8% Asian, non-Hispanic/Latino; 2% American Indian or Alaska Native, non-Hispanic/Latino; 2% Two or more races, non-Hispanic/Latino; 2% Race/ethnicity unknown; 0.4% international; 5% transferred in. *Retention:* 65% of full-time freshmen returned.

Freshmen *Admission:* 226 enrolled. *Average high school GPA:* 2.5.

Faculty *Total:* 102, 52% full-time, 3% with terminal degrees. *Student/faculty ratio:* 11:1.

Majors Business administration and management; clinical/medical laboratory technology; commercial and advertising art; criminal justice/safety; dental hygiene; early childhood education; electromechanical and instrumentation and maintenance technologies related; information technology; legal assistant/paralegal; liberal arts and sciences and humanities related; liberal arts and sciences/liberal studies; medical administrative assistant and medical secretary; medical office management; mental and social health services and allied professions related; office management; registered nursing/registered nurse; welding technology.

Academics *Calendar:* semesters. *Degree:* certificates, diplomas, and associate. *Special study options:* academic remediation for entering students, cooperative education, distance learning, double majors, English as a second language, independent study, part-time degree program, services for LD students, summer session for credit.

Library Learning Resources Center plus 1 other. *Books:* 30,034 (physical), 193,780 (digital/electronic); *Serial titles:* 95 (physical), 22,186 (digital/electronic); *Databases:* 133. Weekly public service hours: 60; students can reserve study rooms.

Student Life *Housing:* college housing not available. *Activities and Organizations:* Phi Theta Kappa, PRIDE, Women of Excellence. *Campus security:* 24-hour emergency response devices, 12-hour patrols by trained security personnel. *Student services:* health clinic.

Costs (2017–18) *Tuition:* state resident $76 per credit hour part-time; nonresident $268 per credit hour part-time. Full-time tuition and fees vary according to course load. Part-time tuition and fees vary according to course load. *Payment plan:* installment.

Applying *Required:* high school transcript.

Freshman Application Contact Mrs. Chalisa Harrell, Director of Admissions, Halifax Community College, PO Drawer 809, Weldon, NC 27890-0809. *Phone:* 252-536-7220. *E-mail:* charrell821@halifaxcc.edu. *Website:* http://www.halifaxcc.edu/.

Harrison College
Morrisville, North Carolina

Freshman Application Contact Mr. Jason Howanec, Vice President of Enrollment, Harrison College, 500 N. Meridian Street, Indianapolis, IN 46204. *Phone:* 800-919-2500. *E-mail:* admissions@harrison.edu. *Website:* http://www.harrison.edu/.

Haywood Community College
Clyde, North Carolina

- **State and locally supported** 2-year, founded 1965, part of North Carolina Community College System
- **Rural** 85-acre campus
- **Coed,** 2,127 undergraduate students, 33% full-time, 51% women, 33% men

Undergraduates 695 full-time, 1,099 part-time. Students come from 4 states and territories; 8% Black or African American, non-Hispanic/Latino; 3% Hispanic/Latino; 0.4% Asian, non-Hispanic/Latino; 0.1% Native Hawaiian or other Pacific Islander, non-Hispanic/Latino; 2% American Indian or Alaska Native, non-Hispanic/Latino; 0.5% Two or more races, non-Hispanic/Latino; 1% Race/ethnicity unknown; 0.1% international. *Retention:* 73% of full-time freshmen returned.

Freshmen *Admission:* 223 enrolled.

Majors Accounting; accounting technology and bookkeeping; applied horticulture/horticulture operations; autobody/collision and repair technology; automobile/automotive mechanics technology; building/construction finishing, management, and inspection related; business administration and management; child-care and support services management; computer systems networking and telecommunications; cosmetology; crafts, folk art and artisanry; criminal justice/law enforcement administration; criminal justice/safety; early childhood education; electrical, electronic and communications engineering technology; electrician; electromechanical and instrumentation and maintenance technologies related; elementary education; entrepreneurship; fiber, textile and weaving arts; forest technology; information technology; liberal arts and sciences and humanities related; liberal arts and sciences/liberal studies; machine shop technology; medical/clinical assistant; medical office management; metal and jewelry arts; pre-engineering; registered nursing/registered nurse; welding technology; wildlife, fish and wildlands science and management.

Academics *Calendar:* semesters. *Degree:* certificates, diplomas, and associate. *Special study options:* academic remediation for entering students, adult/continuing education programs, advanced placement credit, cooperative education, distance learning, double majors, English as a second language, honors programs, independent study, internships, part-time degree program, services for LD students, study abroad, summer session for credit.

Library Freedlander Learning Resource Center. *Books:* 41,680 (physical), 405,792 (digital/electronic); *Serial titles:* 141 (physical), 22,186 (digital/electronic); *Databases:* 86. Weekly public service hours: 57; students can reserve study rooms.

Student Life *Housing:* college housing not available. *Campus security:* 24-hour emergency response devices and patrols.

Athletics *Intramural sports:* archery M(c)/W(c).

Costs (2017–18) *Tuition:* state resident $1216 full-time, $76 per credit hour part-time; nonresident $4288 full-time, $268 per credit hour part-time. Full-time tuition and fees vary according to program. Part-time tuition and fees vary according to program. *Required fees:* $106 full-time, $39 per credit hour part-time. *Payment plan:* deferred payment.

Financial Aid Of all full-time matriculated undergraduates who enrolled in 2015, 41 Federal Work-Study jobs (averaging $857).

Applying *Options:* electronic application. *Required:* high school transcript. *Required for some:* interview. *Application deadlines:* rolling (freshmen), rolling (transfers).

Freshman Application Contact Enrollment Technician, Haywood Community College, 185 Freedlander Drive, Clyde, NC 28721-9453.

Phone: 828-627-4669. *Toll-free phone:* 866-GOTOHCC.
E-mail: enrollment@haywood.edu.
Website: http://www.haywood.edu/.

Isothermal Community College
Spindale, North Carolina

Freshman Application Contact Ms. Vickie Searcy, Enrollment Management Office, Isothermal Community College, PO Box 804, Spindale, NC 28160-0804. *Phone:* 828-286-3636 Ext. 251. *Fax:* 828-286-8109. *E-mail:* vsearcy@isothermal.edu. *Website:* http://www.isothermal.edu/.

James Sprunt Community College
Kenansville, North Carolina

- **State-supported** 2-year, founded 1964, part of North Carolina Community College System
- **Rural** 51-acre campus with easy access to Raleigh, Wilmington
- **Endowment** $1.2 million
- **Coed,** 1,228 undergraduate students, 36% full-time, 67% women, 33% men

Undergraduates 440 full-time, 788 part-time. Students come from 4 states and territories; 3% are from out of state; 28% Black or African American, non-Hispanic/Latino; 21% Hispanic/Latino; 0.3% Asian, non-Hispanic/Latino; 0.5% American Indian or Alaska Native, non-Hispanic/Latino; 2% Two or more races, non-Hispanic/Latino; 0.2% Race/ethnicity unknown; 0.2% international; 4% transferred in.
Freshmen *Admission:* 973 applied, 972 admitted, 190 enrolled.
Faculty *Total:* 65, 48% full-time, 3% with terminal degrees. *Student/faculty ratio:* 15:1.
Majors Accounting; agribusiness; animal sciences; business administration and management; child development; commercial and advertising art; criminal justice/safety; early childhood education; elementary education; general studies; information technology; institutional food workers; liberal arts and sciences and humanities related; liberal arts and sciences/liberal studies; medical/clinical assistant; registered nursing/registered nurse; viticulture and enology.
Academics *Calendar:* semesters. *Degree:* certificates, diplomas, and associate. *Special study options:* academic remediation for entering students, accelerated degree program, advanced placement credit, cooperative education, distance learning, double majors, English as a second language, independent study, internships, part-time degree program, services for LD students, summer session for credit.
Library James Sprunt Community College Library. *Books:* 24,775 (physical), 193,780 (digital/electronic); *Serial titles:* 72 (physical), 22,188 (digital/electronic); *Databases:* 77. Weekly public service hours: 44.
Student Life *Housing:* college housing not available. *Activities and Organizations:* student-run newspaper, choral group, Student Nurses Association, Art Club, Alumni Association, National Technical-Vocational Honor Society, Phi Theta Kappa, national sororities. *Campus security:* day, evening, and Saturday trained security personnel. *Student services:* personal/psychological counseling.
Athletics *Intramural sports:* basketball M/W, soccer M/W.
Costs (2017–18) *Tuition:* state resident $2502 full-time, $76 per semester hour part-time; nonresident $8646 full-time, $268 per semester hour part-time. Full-time tuition and fees vary according to course load. Part-time tuition and fees vary according to course load. *Required fees:* $76 full-time, $35 per term part-time.
Financial Aid Of all full-time matriculated undergraduates who enrolled in 2015, 35 Federal Work-Study jobs (averaging $1057).
Applying *Options:* electronic application. *Required:* high school transcript. *Application deadlines:* rolling (freshmen), rolling (transfers). *Notification:* continuous (freshmen), continuous (transfers).
Freshman Application Contact Ms. Wanda Edwards, Admissions Specialist, James Sprunt Community College, PO Box 398, 133 James Sprunt Drive, Kenansville, NC 28349. *Phone:* 910-296-6078. *Fax:* 910-296-1222. *E-mail:* wedwards@jamessprunt.edu.
Website: http://www.jamessprunt.edu/.

Johnston Community College
Smithfield, North Carolina

- **State-supported** 2-year, founded 1969, part of North Carolina Community College System
- **Rural** 100-acre campus
- **Endowment** $5.1 million
- **Coed,** 3,903 undergraduate students, 40% full-time, 65% women, 35% men

Undergraduates 1,549 full-time, 2,354 part-time. 13% Black or African American, non-Hispanic/Latino; 13% Hispanic/Latino; 0.7% Asian, non-Hispanic/Latino; 0.1% Native Hawaiian or other Pacific Islander, non-Hispanic/Latino; 0.6% American Indian or Alaska Native, non-Hispanic/Latino; 2% Two or more races, non-Hispanic/Latino; 9% Race/ethnicity unknown; 1% international. *Retention:* 66% of full-time freshmen returned.
Freshmen *Admission:* 524 enrolled.
Majors Accounting; administrative assistant and secretarial science; business administration and management; criminal justice/police science; diesel mechanics technology; early childhood education; heating, air conditioning, ventilation and refrigeration maintenance technology; legal assistant/paralegal; liberal arts and sciences/liberal studies; medical/clinical assistant; medical office management; office management; registered nursing/registered nurse.
Academics *Calendar:* semesters. *Degree:* certificates, diplomas, and associate. *Special study options:* academic remediation for entering students, adult/continuing education programs, advanced placement credit, cooperative education, distance learning, double majors, honors programs, independent study, part-time degree program, services for LD students, summer session for credit.
Library Johnston Community College Library plus 1 other. *Books:* 38,090 (physical), 65 (digital/electronic); *Serial titles:* 69 (physical), 11 (digital/electronic); *Databases:* 10. Weekly public service hours: 57; students can reserve study rooms.
Student Life *Housing:* college housing not available. *Campus security:* 24-hour patrols. *Student services:* personal/psychological counseling.
Athletics Member NJCAA. *Intercollegiate sports:* basketball M/W, golf M/W.
Standardized Tests *Required:* NC DAP (for admission). *Recommended:* SAT or ACT (for admission).
Costs (2016–17) *Tuition:* state resident $2529 full-time, $76 per credit part-time; nonresident $8673 full-time, $268 per credit part-time. *Required fees:* $97 full-time. *Payment plan:* installment.
Financial Aid Of all full-time matriculated undergraduates who enrolled in 2015, 35 Federal Work-Study jobs (averaging $1853).
Applying *Options:* electronic application. *Required:* high school transcript, interview. *Application deadlines:* rolling (freshmen), rolling (transfers). *Notification:* continuous (freshmen), continuous (transfers).
Freshman Application Contact Mrs. Megan L. Shaner, Director of Enrollment and Student Success, Johnston Community College, Smithfield, NC 27577-2350. *Phone:* 919-209-2201. *Fax:* 919-989-7862.
E-mail: mlshaner@johnstoncc.edu.
Website: http://www.johnstoncc.edu/.

King's College
Charlotte, North Carolina

- **Proprietary** 2-year, founded 1901
- **Suburban** campus
- **Coed**
- 77% of applicants were admitted

Academics *Calendar:* semesters. *Degree:* diplomas and associate. *Special study options:* accelerated degree program, internships.
Freshman Application Contact Admissions Office, King's College, 322 Lamar Avenue, Charlotte, NC 28204-2436. *Phone:* 704-372-0266. *Toll-free phone:* 800-768-2255. *Website:* http://www.kingscollegecharlotte.edu/.

Lenoir Community College
Kinston, North Carolina

- **State-supported** 2-year, founded 1960, part of North Carolina Community College System
- **Small-town** 86-acre campus
- **Coed,** 2,674 undergraduate students, 39% full-time, 61% women, 39% men

Undergraduates 1,036 full-time, 1,638 part-time. Students come from 28 states and territories; 2 other countries; 2% are from out of state; 37% Black or African American, non-Hispanic/Latino; 6% Hispanic/Latino; 0.5% Asian, non-Hispanic/Latino; 0.1% Native Hawaiian or other Pacific Islander, non-Hispanic/Latino; 0.8% American Indian or Alaska Native, non-

Hispanic/Latino; 1% Two or more races, non-Hispanic/Latino; 1% international; 20% transferred in.

Freshmen *Admission:* 1,692 applied, 1,493 admitted, 345 enrolled.

Faculty *Total:* 128, 66% full-time, 8% with terminal degrees. *Student/faculty ratio:* 15:1.

Majors Accounting; aeronautical/aerospace engineering technology; agroecology and sustainable agriculture; airline pilot and flight crew; applied horticulture/horticulture operations; autobody/collision and repair technology; automobile/automotive mechanics technology; computer engineering technology; computer systems networking and telecommunications; cosmetology; criminal justice/safety; culinary arts; elementary education; emergency medical technology (EMT paramedic); energy management and systems technology; graphic design; gunsmithing; industrial electronics technology; information technology; liberal arts and sciences and humanities related; liberal arts and sciences/liberal studies; logistics, materials, and supply chain management; machine shop technology; marketing/marketing management; massage therapy; medical/clinical assistant; medical office management; mental and social health services and allied professions related; office management; operations management; polysomnography; public administration; radiologic technology/science; registered nursing/registered nurse; trade and industrial teacher education; welding technology.

Academics *Calendar:* semesters. *Degree:* certificates, diplomas, and associate. *Special study options:* academic remediation for entering students, adult/continuing education programs, advanced placement credit, cooperative education, distance learning, double majors, English as a second language, independent study, part-time degree program, summer session for credit.

Library Learning Resources Center plus 1 other. *Books:* 17,763 (physical), 193,845 (digital/electronic); *Serial titles:* 25 (physical), 22,186 (digital/electronic); *Databases:* 77. Students can reserve study rooms.

Student Life *Housing:* college housing not available. *Activities and Organizations:* choral group, Student Government Association, Surgical Technology, Computer Engineering, Nightingals, Transitional and Career Studies. *Campus security:* 24-hour emergency response devices and patrols, student patrols. *Student services:* personal/psychological counseling.

Athletics Member NJCAA. *Intercollegiate sports:* baseball M, basketball M/W, volleyball W.

Standardized Tests *Recommended:* SAT or ACT (for admission).

Costs (2017–18) *Tuition:* state resident $2280 full-time, $76 per credit part-time; nonresident $8040 full-time, $268 per credit part-time. Full-time tuition and fees vary according to course load. Part-time tuition and fees vary according to course load. *Required fees:* $119 full-time. *Waivers:* employees or children of employees.

Applying *Options:* electronic application, early admission. *Required:* high school transcript. *Application deadlines:* rolling (freshmen), rolling (transfers). *Notification:* continuous (freshmen), continuous (transfers).

Freshman Application Contact Mrs. Kim Hill, Director of Admissions, Lenoir Community College, PO Box 188, Kinston, NC 28502-0188. *Phone:* 252-527-6223 Ext. 301. *Fax:* 252-233-6895. *E-mail:* krhill01@lenoircc.edu. *Website:* http://www.lenoircc.edu/.

Living Arts College
Raleigh, North Carolina

- **Proprietary** primarily 2-year, founded 1992
- **Suburban** campus with easy access to Raleigh
- **Coed**

Undergraduates Students come from 8 states and territories; 1 other country; 1% are from out of state; 35% live on campus. *Retention:* 69% of full-time freshmen returned.

Faculty *Student/faculty ratio:* 10:1.

Academics *Calendar:* quarters. *Degrees:* certificates, diplomas, associate, and bachelor's. *Special study options:* cooperative education, summer session for credit.

Student Life *Campus security:* controlled dormitory access.

Standardized Tests *Required:* Wonderlic aptitude test (for admission).

Applying *Options:* electronic application, early admission, early decision, early action, deferred entrance. *Application fee:* $25. *Required:* essay or personal statement, high school transcript, interview. *Required for some:* portfolio.

Freshman Application Contact Julie Wenta, Director of Admissions, Living Arts College, 3000 Wakefield Crossing Drive, Raleigh, NC 27614. *Phone:* 919-488-5902. *Toll-free phone:* 800-288-7442. *Fax:* 919-488-8490. *E-mail:* jwenta@living-arts-college.edu. *Website:* http://www.living-arts-college.edu/.

Louisburg College
Louisburg, North Carolina

Freshman Application Contact Ms. Stephanie Tolbert, Vice President for Enrollment Management, Louisburg College, 501 North Main Street, Louisburg, NC 27549-2399. *Phone:* 919-497-3233. *Toll-free phone:* 800-775-0208. *Fax:* 919-496-1788. *E-mail:* admissions@louisburg.edu. *Website:* http://www.louisburg.edu/.

Martin Community College
Williamston, North Carolina

- **State-supported** 2-year, founded 1968, part of North Carolina Community College System
- **Rural** 65-acre campus
- **Coed**

Academics *Calendar:* semesters. *Degree:* certificates, diplomas, and associate. *Special study options:* academic remediation for entering students, advanced placement credit, cooperative education, distance learning, independent study, internships, off-campus study, part-time degree program, services for LD students, summer session for credit.

Library Martin Community College Learning Resources Center.

Student Life *Campus security:* 24-hour emergency response devices, part-time patrols by trained security personnel.

Financial Aid Of all full-time matriculated undergraduates who enrolled in 2015, 30 Federal Work-Study jobs (averaging $1200).

Applying *Options:* electronic application. *Required:* high school transcript.

Freshman Application Contact Martin Community College, 1161 Kehukee Park Road, Williamston, NC 27892. *Phone:* 252-792-1521 Ext. 244. *Website:* http://www.martincc.edu/.

Mayland Community College
Spruce Pine, North Carolina

Director of Admissions Ms. Cathy Morrison, Director of Admissions, Mayland Community College, PO Box 547, Spruce Pine, NC 28777-0547. *Phone:* 828-765-7351 Ext. 224. *Toll-free phone:* 800-462-9526. *Website:* http://www.mayland.edu/.

McDowell Technical Community College
Marion, North Carolina

Freshman Application Contact Mr. Rick L. Wilson, Director of Admissions, McDowell Technical Community College, 54 College Drive, Marion, NC 28752. *Phone:* 828-652-0632. *Fax:* 828-652-1014. *E-mail:* rickw@mcdowelltech.edu. *Website:* http://www.mcdowelltech.edu/.

Miller-Motte College
Cary, North Carolina

Admissions Office Contact Miller-Motte College, 2205 Walnut Street, Cary, NC 27518. *Toll-free phone:* 800-705-9182. *Website:* http://www.miller-motte.edu/.

Miller-Motte College
Fayetteville, North Carolina

Admissions Office Contact Miller-Motte College, 3725 Ramsey Street, Fayetteville, NC 28311. *Toll-free phone:* 800-705-9182. *Website:* http://www.miller-motte.edu/.

Miller-Motte College
Greenville, North Carolina

Admissions Office Contact Miller-Motte College, 1021 WH Smith Boulevard, Suite 102, Greenville, NC 27834. *Toll-free phone:* 800-705-9182. *Website:* http://www.miller-motte.edu/.

Miller-Motte College
Jacksonville, North Carolina

Admissions Office Contact Miller-Motte College, 1291 Hargett Street, Jacksonville, NC 28540. *Toll-free phone:* 800-705-9182. *Website:* http://www.miller-motte.edu/.

Miller-Motte College
Raleigh, North Carolina

Admissions Office Contact Miller-Motte College, 3901 Capital Boulevard, Suite 151, Raleigh, NC 27604. *Toll-free phone:* 800-705-9182. *Website:* http://www.miller-motte.edu/.

Miller-Motte College
Wilmington, North Carolina

Freshman Application Contact Admissions Office, Miller-Motte College, 5000 Market Street, Wilmington, NC 28405. *Toll-free phone:* 800-705-9182. *Website:* http://www.miller-motte.edu/.

Mitchell Community College
Statesville, North Carolina

- **State-supported** 2-year, founded 1852, part of North Carolina Community College System
- **Small-town** 8-acre campus with easy access to Charlotte
- **Endowment** $14.2 million
- **Coed,** 3,024 undergraduate students, 38% full-time, 62% women, 38% men

Undergraduates 1,151 full-time, 1,873 part-time. 14% Black or African American, non-Hispanic/Latino; 9% Hispanic/Latino; 3% Asian, non-Hispanic/Latino; 0.2% Native Hawaiian or other Pacific Islander, non-Hispanic/Latino; 0.6% American Indian or Alaska Native, non-Hispanic/Latino; 1% Two or more races, non-Hispanic/Latino; 1% Race/ethnicity unknown; 0.6% international; 3% transferred in. *Retention:* 54% of full-time freshmen returned.
Freshmen *Admission:* 474 enrolled.
Faculty *Total:* 198, 42% full-time. *Student/faculty ratio:* 17:1.
Majors Accounting; agribusiness; business administration and management; child-care and support services management; computer programming; computer programming (specific applications); computer systems analysis; cooking and related culinary arts; criminal justice/law enforcement administration; early childhood education; electrical, electronic and communications engineering technology; electrician; electromechanical and instrumentation and maintenance technologies related; elementary education; engineering/industrial management; executive assistant/executive secretary; general studies; health professions related; information science/studies; information technology; kindergarten/preschool education; liberal arts and sciences and humanities related; liberal arts and sciences/liberal studies; machine shop technology; manufacturing engineering; manufacturing engineering technology; mechanical drafting and CAD/CADD; mechanical engineering/mechanical technology; mechatronics, robotics, and automation engineering; medical/clinical assistant; office management; operations management; registered nursing/registered nurse; special education–early childhood; teacher assistant/aide.
Academics *Calendar:* semesters. *Degree:* certificates, diplomas, and associate. *Special study options:* academic remediation for entering students, adult/continuing education programs, advanced placement credit, cooperative education, distance learning, English as a second language, part-time degree program, services for LD students, summer session for credit.
Library Huskins Library. *Books:* 13,384 (physical), 490,992 (digital/electronic); *Databases:* 10. Students can reserve study rooms.
Student Life *Housing:* college housing not available. *Activities and Organizations:* choral group, Cosmetology Club, Early Childhood Association, Student Nurses Association, Phi Theta Kappa, Student Government Association. *Campus security:* late-night transport/escort service, day and evening security guards. *Student services:* personal/psychological counseling.
Costs (2017–18) *Tuition:* state resident $2280 full-time; nonresident $8040 full-time. Full-time tuition and fees vary according to course load. Part-time tuition and fees vary according to course load. *Required fees:* $199 full-time. *Payment plan:* installment.
Financial Aid Of all full-time matriculated undergraduates who enrolled in 2015, 30 Federal Work-Study jobs.
Applying *Options:* electronic application. *Required:* high school transcript. *Application deadlines:* rolling (freshmen), rolling (transfers). *Notification:* continuous (freshmen), continuous (transfers).
Freshman Application Contact Mitchell Community College, 500 West Broad Street, Statesville, NC 28677. *Phone:* 704-878-3281. *Website:* http://www.mitchellcc.edu/.

Montgomery Community College
Troy, North Carolina

- **State-supported** 2-year, founded 1967, part of North Carolina Community College System
- **Rural** 159-acre campus
- **Coed,** 818 undergraduate students, 34% full-time, 63% women, 37% men

Undergraduates 277 full-time, 541 part-time. Students come from 4 states and territories; 1% are from out of state; 18% Black or African American, non-Hispanic/Latino; 13% Hispanic/Latino; 1% Asian, non-Hispanic/Latino; 1%

American Indian or Alaska Native, non-Hispanic/Latino; 0.9% Two or more races, non-Hispanic/Latino; 0.1% international.
Freshmen *Admission:* 124 enrolled.
Faculty *Total:* 113, 32% full-time. *Student/faculty ratio:* 7:1.
Majors Business administration and management; criminal justice/safety; early childhood education; electrician; electromechanical and instrumentation and maintenance technologies related; forest technology; gunsmithing; heating, air conditioning, ventilation and refrigeration maintenance technology; information technology; liberal arts and sciences/liberal studies; medical/clinical assistant; mental and social health services and allied professions related; office management.
Academics *Calendar:* semesters. *Degree:* certificates, diplomas, and associate. *Special study options:* academic remediation for entering students, advanced placement credit, distance learning, English as a second language, part-time degree program, services for LD students, summer session for credit.
Library Montgomery Community College Learning Resource Center. *Books:* 18,791 (physical), 44,708 (digital/electronic); *Databases:* 71. Weekly public service hours: 55.
Student Life *Housing:* college housing not available. *Activities and Organizations:* Student Government Association, Nursing Club, Gunsmithing Society, Medical Assisting Club, Forestry Club. *Campus security:* 24-hour emergency response devices. *Student services:* personal/psychological counseling.
Costs (2017–18) *Tuition:* state resident $2432 full-time, $76 per credit hour part-time; nonresident $8576 full-time, $268 per credit hour part-time. Full-time tuition and fees vary according to course load. Part-time tuition and fees vary according to course load. *Required fees:* $105 full-time, $53 per term part-time. *Payment plan:* installment.
Financial Aid Of all full-time matriculated undergraduates who enrolled in 2015, 24 Federal Work-Study jobs (averaging $500).
Applying *Options:* electronic application, early admission, deferred entrance. *Required:* high school transcript. *Application deadlines:* rolling (freshmen), rolling (transfers). *Notification:* continuous (freshmen), continuous (transfers).
Freshman Application Contact Ms. Tavia Housley, Enrollment Specialist, Montgomery Community College, 1011 Page Street, Troy, NC 27371. *Phone:* 910-898-9612. *Toll-free phone:* 877-572-6222.
E-mail: housleyt@montgomery.edu.
Website: http://www.montgomery.edu/.

Nash Community College
Rocky Mount, North Carolina

Freshman Application Contact Ms. Dorothy Gardner, Admissions Officer, Nash Community College, PO Box 7488, Rocky Mount, NC 27804. *Phone:* 252-451-8300. *E-mail:* dgardner@nashcc.edu.
Website: http://www.nashcc.edu/.

Pamlico Community College
Grantsboro, North Carolina

Director of Admissions Mr. Floyd H. Hardison, Admissions Counselor, Pamlico Community College, PO Box 185, Grantsboro, NC 28529-0185. *Phone:* 252-249-1851 Ext. 28. *Website:* http://www.pamlicocc.edu/.

Piedmont Community College
Roxboro, North Carolina

- **State-supported** 2-year, founded 1970, part of North Carolina Community College System
- **Small-town** 178-acre campus
- **Coed,** 1,298 undergraduate students, 37% full-time, 60% women, 40% men

Undergraduates 479 full-time, 819 part-time.
Faculty *Student/faculty ratio:* 12:1.
Majors Accounting; business administration and management; child-care and support services management; cinematography and film/video production; criminal justice/safety; early childhood education; electrical and power transmission installation; electrician; electromechanical and instrumentation and maintenance technologies related; general studies; graphic communications; health professions related; historic preservation and conservation; industrial technology; information technology; liberal arts and sciences and humanities related; liberal arts and sciences/liberal studies; medical administrative assistant and medical secretary; medical/clinical assistant; medical office management; mental and social health services and allied professions related; office management; registered nursing/registered nurse.
Academics *Calendar:* semesters. *Degree:* certificates, diplomas, and associate. *Special study options:* academic remediation for entering students, adult/continuing education programs, advanced placement credit, cooperative

education, distance learning, double majors, English as a second language, off-campus study, part-time degree program, summer session for credit.
Library Learning Resource Center.
Student Life *Housing:* college housing not available. *Activities and Organizations:* drama/theater group, choral group. *Campus security:* routine patrols by the local sheriff's department.
Athletics *Intramural sports:* volleyball M/W.
Costs (2016–17) *Tuition:* state resident $1824 full-time, $76 per credit hour part-time; nonresident $6432 full-time, $268 per credit hour part-time. Full-time tuition and fees vary according to course load. Part-time tuition and fees vary according to course load. *Required fees:* $115 full-time, $57 per term part-time. *Payment plan:* installment.
Applying *Options:* electronic application, early admission, deferred entrance. *Required for some:* high school transcript. *Application deadlines:* rolling (freshmen), rolling (transfers). *Notification:* continuous (freshmen), continuous (transfers).
Freshman Application Contact Piedmont Community College, PO Box 1197, Roxboro, NC 27573-1197. *Phone:* 336-599-1181 Ext. 2163. *Website:* http://www.piedmontcc.edu/.

Pitt Community College
Winterville, North Carolina

Freshman Application Contact Dr. Kimberly Williamson, Interim Coordinator of Counseling, Pitt Community College, PO Drawer 7007, Greenville, NC 27835-7007. *Phone:* 252-493-7217. *Fax:* 252-321-4612. *E-mail:* pittadm@pcc.pitt.cc.nc.us. *Website:* http://www.pittcc.edu/.

Randolph Community College
Asheboro, North Carolina

- **State-supported** 2-year, founded 1962, part of North Carolina Community College System
- **Small-town** 40-acre campus with easy access to Greensboro, Winston-Salem, High Point
- **Endowment** $9.9 million
- **Coed,** 2,696 undergraduate students, 35% full-time, 63% women, 37% men

Undergraduates 936 full-time, 1,760 part-time. Students come from 2 states and territories; 15 other countries; 5% Black or African American, non-Hispanic/Latino; 16% Hispanic/Latino; 1% Asian, non-Hispanic/Latino; 0.2% Native Hawaiian or other Pacific Islander, non-Hispanic/Latino; 1% American Indian or Alaska Native, non-Hispanic/Latino; 13% Two or more races, non-Hispanic/Latino; 0.9% international; 32% transferred in. *Retention:* 66% of full-time freshmen returned.
Freshmen *Admission:* 2,772 applied, 2,772 admitted, 493 enrolled. *Average high school GPA:* 2.95.
Faculty *Total:* 286, 29% full-time. *Student/faculty ratio:* 10:1.
Majors Accounting; autobody/collision and repair technology; automobile/automotive mechanics technology; business administration and management; commercial and advertising art; commercial photography; computer systems networking and telecommunications; cosmetology; criminal justice/safety; early childhood education; electrician; electromechanical technology; funeral service and mortuary science; human services; information technology; interior design; liberal arts and sciences and humanities related; liberal arts and sciences/liberal studies; machine shop technology; mechatronics, robotics, and automation engineering; medical/clinical assistant; medical office management; photographic and film/video technology; photojournalism; physical therapy technology; radiologic technology/science; registered nursing/registered nurse.
Academics *Calendar:* semesters. *Degree:* certificates, diplomas, and associate. *Special study options:* academic remediation for entering students, adult/continuing education programs, advanced placement credit, cooperative education, distance learning, double majors, English as a second language, independent study, internships, off-campus study, part-time degree program, services for LD students, summer session for credit. *ROTC:* Air Force (c).
Library R. Alton Cox Learning Resources Center. *Books:* 25,000 (physical).
Student Life *Housing:* college housing not available. *Activities and Organizations:* Student Government Association, Phi Theta Kappa, Student Nurse Association, Phi Beta Lambda, Veterans Club. *Campus security:* 24-hour emergency response devices, security officer during hours of operation.
Costs (2017–18) *Tuition:* state resident $2432 full-time, $76 per credit hour part-time; nonresident $8576 full-time, $268 per credit hour part-time.

Required fees: $88 full-time, $3 per credit hour part-time. *Payment plan:* installment.
Applying *Options:* electronic application, deferred entrance. *Application deadlines:* rolling (freshmen), rolling (transfers). *Notification:* continuous (freshmen), continuous (transfers).
Freshman Application Contact Ms. Brandi F. Hagerman, Director of Enrollment Management/Registrar, Randolph Community College, 629 Industrial Park Avenue, Asheboro, NC 27205-7333. *Phone:* 336-633-0213. *Fax:* 336-629-9547. *E-mail:* bhagerman@randolph.edu. *Website:* http://www.randolph.edu/.

Richmond Community College
Hamlet, North Carolina

- **State-supported** 2-year, founded 1964, part of North Carolina Community College System
- **Rural** 163-acre campus
- **Coed,** 2,550 undergraduate students, 44% full-time, 65% women, 35% men

Undergraduates 1,114 full-time, 1,436 part-time. 0.5% are from out of state; 8% Black or African American, non-Hispanic/Latino; 3% Hispanic/Latino; 0.1% Asian, non-Hispanic/Latino; 40% Native Hawaiian or other Pacific Islander, non-Hispanic/Latino; 28% American Indian or Alaska Native, non-Hispanic/Latino; 2% Two or more races, non-Hispanic/Latino; 17% Race/ethnicity unknown; 0.3% international; 6% transferred in.
Freshmen *Admission:* 388 enrolled.
Faculty *Student/faculty ratio:* 15:1.
Majors Accounting; business administration and management; computer engineering technology; criminal justice/safety; early childhood education; electrical and power transmission installation; electrical, electronic and communications engineering technology; electromechanical and instrumentation and maintenance technologies related; electromechanical technology; elementary education; entrepreneurship; health information/medical records technology; health professions related; heating, air conditioning, ventilation and refrigeration maintenance technology; information technology; liberal arts and sciences/liberal studies; mechanical engineering/mechanical technology; medical/clinical assistant; medical office computer specialist; medical office management; mental and social health services and allied professions related; office management; registered nursing/registered nurse.
Academics *Calendar:* semesters. *Degree:* certificates, diplomas, and associate. *Special study options:* academic remediation for entering students, adult/continuing education programs, advanced placement credit, cooperative education, distance learning, double majors, English as a second language, independent study, internships, part-time degree program, student-designed majors, summer session for credit.
Library Richmond Community College Library.
Student Life *Housing:* college housing not available. *Campus security:* 24-hour emergency response devices, security guard during hours of operation. *Student services:* personal/psychological counseling.
Costs (2016–17) *Tuition:* state resident $2432 full-time, $76 per credit hour part-time; nonresident $8576 full-time, $268 per credit hour part-time. Full-time tuition and fees vary according to course load. Part-time tuition and fees vary according to course load. *Required fees:* $78 full-time, $32 per term part-time. *Payment plan:* installment. *Waivers:* employees or children of employees.
Financial Aid Of all full-time matriculated undergraduates who enrolled in 2015, 35 Federal Work-Study jobs (averaging $2000).
Applying *Options:* electronic application, deferred entrance. *Required:* high school transcript. *Application deadlines:* rolling (freshmen), rolling (transfers). *Notification:* continuous (freshmen), continuous (transfers).
Freshman Application Contact Cayce Holmes, Registrar, Richmond Community College, PO Box 1189, 1042 W. Hamlet Avenue, Hamlet, NC 28345. *Phone:* 910-410-1737. *Fax:* 910-582-7102. *E-mail:* ccholmes@richmondcc.edu. *Website:* http://www.richmondcc.edu/.

Roanoke-Chowan Community College
Ahoskie, North Carolina

Director of Admissions Miss Sandra Copeland, Director, Counseling Services, Roanoke-Chowan Community College, 109 Community College Road, Ahoskie, NC 27910. *Phone:* 252-862-1225. *Website:* http://www.roanokechowan.edu/.

Robeson Community College
Lumberton, North Carolina

Freshman Application Contact Ms. Patricia Locklear, College Recruiter, Robeson Community College, PO Box 1420, Lumberton, NC 28359. *Phone:* 910-272-3356 Ext. 251. *Fax:* 910-618-5686. *E-mail:* plocklear@robeson.edu. *Website:* http://www.robeson.edu/.

Rockingham Community College
Wentworth, North Carolina

- **State-supported** 2-year, founded 1964, part of North Carolina Community College System
- **Rural** 257-acre campus
- **Coed,** 1,779 undergraduate students, 38% full-time, 59% women, 41% men

Undergraduates 668 full-time, 1,111 part-time. Students come from 2 states and territories.
Freshmen *Admission:* 334 enrolled.
Faculty *Total:* 131, 48% full-time, 7% with terminal degrees. *Student/faculty ratio:* 18:1.
Majors Accounting; agricultural and food products processing; banking and financial support services; biology/biotechnology laboratory technician; business administration and management; corrections and criminal justice related; criminal justice/police science; early childhood education; electrical, electronic and communications engineering technology; electrician; general studies; health/health-care administration; information technology; liberal arts and sciences/liberal studies; logistics, materials, and supply chain management; machine shop technology; medical office management; office management; registered nursing/registered nurse; respiratory care therapy.
Academics *Calendar:* semesters. *Degree:* certificates, diplomas, and associate. *Special study options:* academic remediation for entering students, adult/continuing education programs, advanced placement credit, cooperative education, part-time degree program, student-designed majors, summer session for credit.
Library Gerald B. James Library.
Student Life *Housing:* college housing not available. *Campus security:* 24-hour emergency response devices and patrols. *Student services:* personal/psychological counseling.
Athletics Member NJCAA. *Intercollegiate sports:* baseball M, volleyball W. *Intramural sports:* table tennis M/W, tennis M/W, volleyball M/W.
Costs (2017–18) *Tuition:* state resident $1716 full-time, $76 per credit hour part-time; nonresident $6324 full-time, $268 per credit hour part-time. *Required fees:* $116 full-time, $44 per term part-time.
Financial Aid Of all full-time matriculated undergraduates who enrolled in 2015, 37 Federal Work-Study jobs (averaging $2300).
Applying *Options:* electronic application, early admission, deferred entrance. *Application deadlines:* rolling (freshmen), rolling (transfers). *Notification:* continuous (freshmen), continuous (transfers).
Freshman Application Contact Mr. Derrick Satterfield, Director of Enrollment Services, Rockingham Community College, PO Box 38, Wentworth, NC 27375-0038. *Phone:* 336-342-4261 Ext. 2114. *Fax:* 336-342-1809. *E-mail:* admissions@rockinghamcc.edu. *Website:* http://www.rockinghamcc.edu/.

Rowan-Cabarrus Community College
Salisbury, North Carolina

- **State-supported** 2-year, founded 1963, part of North Carolina Community College System
- **Small-town** 100-acre campus with easy access to Charlotte
- **Coed,** 5,180 undergraduate students

Majors Accounting; automobile/automotive mechanics technology; building/property maintenance; business administration and management; business administration, management and operations related; computer and information systems security; computer programming; cosmetology; criminal justice/law enforcement administration; early childhood education; electrical, electronic and communications engineering technology; electrician; elementary education; general studies; industrial technology; information science/studies; information technology; liberal arts and sciences/liberal studies; marketing/marketing management; medical office management; office management; radiologic technology/science; registered nursing/registered nurse; system, networking, and LAN/WAN management.
Academics *Calendar:* semesters. *Degree:* certificates, diplomas, and associate. *Special study options:* academic remediation for entering students, adult/continuing education programs, advanced placement credit, cooperative education, distance learning, English as a second language, internships, part-time degree program, services for LD students, summer session for credit.
Library Learning Resource Center. Students can reserve study rooms.

Student Life *Housing:* college housing not available. *Campus security:* on-campus security during hours of operation. *Student services:* personal/psychological counseling.
Costs (2017–18) *Tuition:* state resident $2432 full-time, $76 per credit hour part-time; nonresident $8576 full-time, $268 per credit hour part-time. Full-time tuition and fees vary according to course load. Part-time tuition and fees vary according to course load. *Required fees:* $194 full-time, $79 per term part-time. *Payment plan:* installment. *Waivers:* employees or children of employees.
Applying *Required:* high school transcript. *Application deadlines:* rolling (freshmen), rolling (transfers).
Freshman Application Contact Rowan-Cabarrus Community College, 1333 Jake Alexander Boulevard South, Salisbury, NC 28146. *Website:* http://www.rccc.edu/.

Sampson Community College
Clinton, North Carolina

Director of Admissions Mr. William R. Jordan, Director of Admissions, Sampson Community College, PO Box 318, 1801 Sunset Avenue, Highway 24 West, Clinton, NC 28329-0318. *Phone:* 910-592-8084 Ext. 2022. *Website:* http://www.sampsoncc.edu/.

Sandhills Community College
Pinehurst, North Carolina

Freshman Application Contact Mr. Isai Robledo, Recruiter, Sandhills Community College, 3395 Airport Road, Pinehurst, NC 28374-8299. *Phone:* 910-246-5365. *Toll-free phone:* 800-338-3944. *Fax:* 910-695-3981. *E-mail:* robledoi@sandhills.edu. *Website:* http://www.sandhills.edu/.

Southeastern Community College
Whiteville, North Carolina

Freshman Application Contact Ms. Sylvia McQueen, Registrar, Southeastern Community College, PO Box 151, Whiteville, NC 28472. *Phone:* 910-642-7141 Ext. 249. *Fax:* 910-642-5658. *Website:* http://www.sccnc.edu/.

South Piedmont Community College
Polkton, North Carolina

Freshman Application Contact Ms. Amanda Secrest, Assistant Director Admissions and Testing, South Piedmont Community College, PO Box 126, Polkton, NC 28135. *Phone:* 704-290-5847. *Toll-free phone:* 800-766-0319. *E-mail:* asecrest@spcc.edu. *Website:* http://www.spcc.edu/.

Southwestern Community College
Sylva, North Carolina

- **State-supported** 2-year, founded 1964, part of North Carolina Community College System
- **Small-town** 77-acre campus
- **Coed,** 2,566 undergraduate students, 35% full-time, 59% women, 41% men

Undergraduates 903 full-time, 1,663 part-time.
Freshmen *Admission:* 339 enrolled.
Faculty *Student/faculty ratio:* 16:1.
Majors Accounting; automobile/automotive mechanics technology; business administration and management; child development; clinical/medical laboratory technology; commercial and advertising art; computer engineering technology; cosmetology; criminal justice/police science; culinary arts; electrical, electronic and communications engineering technology; emergency medical technology (EMT paramedic); environmental studies; health information/medical records administration; health information/medical records technology; information science/studies; legal assistant/paralegal; liberal arts and sciences/liberal studies; massage therapy; medical radiologic technology; mental health counseling; parks, recreation, leisure, and fitness studies related; physical therapy technology; registered nursing/registered nurse; respiratory care therapy; substance abuse/addiction counseling; system, networking, and LAN/WAN management; trade and industrial teacher education.
Academics *Calendar:* semesters. *Degree:* certificates, diplomas, and associate. *Special study options:* academic remediation for entering students, adult/continuing education programs, advanced placement credit, cooperative education, distance learning, double majors, English as a second language, honors programs, independent study, off-campus study, part-time degree program, services for LD students, summer session for credit.

Library Holt Library.

Student Life *Housing:* college housing not available. *Campus security:* security during hours of operation. *Student services:* personal/psychological counseling.

Costs (2016–17) *Tuition:* state resident $2128 full-time, $76 per credit hour part-time; nonresident $7504 full-time, $268 per credit hour part-time. Full-time tuition and fees vary according to course load and program. Part-time tuition and fees vary according to course load and program. *Required fees:* $85 full-time, $3 per credit hour part-time, $1 per year part-time. *Payment plan:* installment.

Applying *Required:* high school transcript. *Required for some:* minimum 2.5 GPA, interview.

Freshman Application Contact Martin Aucoin, Director of Enrollment Management, Southwestern Community College, 447 College Drive, Sylva, NC 28779. *Phone:* 828-339-4217. *Toll-free phone:* 800-447-4091 (in-state); 800-447-7091 (out-of-state). *E-mail:* m_aucoin@southwesternccc.edu. *Website:* http://www.southwesternccc.edu/.

Stanly Community College
Albemarle, North Carolina

Freshman Application Contact Mrs. Denise B. Ross, Associate Dean, Admissions, Stanly Community College, 141 College Drive, Albemarle, NC 28001. *Phone:* 704-982-0121 Ext. 264. *Fax:* 704-982-0255. *E-mail:* dross7926@stanly.edu. *Website:* http://www.stanly.edu/.

Surry Community College
Dobson, North Carolina

Freshman Application Contact Renita Hazelwood, Director of Admissions, Surry Community College, 630 South Main Street, Dobson, NC 27017. *Phone:* 336-386-3392. *Fax:* 336-386-3690. *E-mail:* hazelwoodr@surry.edu. *Website:* http://www.surry.edu/.

Tri-County Community College
Murphy, North Carolina

Freshman Application Contact Dr. Jason Chambers, Director of Student Services and Admissions, Tri-County Community College, 21 Campus Circle, Murphy, NC 28906-7919. *Phone:* 828-837-6810. *Fax:* 828-837-3266. *E-mail:* jchambers@tricountyccc.edu. *Website:* http://www.tricountyccc.edu/.

Vance-Granville Community College
Henderson, North Carolina

Freshman Application Contact Ms. Kathy Kutl, Admissions Officer, Vance-Granville Community College, PO Box 917, State Road 1126, Henderson, NC 27536. *Phone:* 252-492-2061 Ext. 3265. *Fax:* 252-430-0460. *Website:* http://www.vgcc.edu/.

Virginia College in Greensboro
Greensboro, North Carolina

Admissions Office Contact Virginia College in Greensboro, 3740 South Holden Road, Greensboro, NC 27406. *Website:* http://www.vc.edu/.

Wake Technical Community College
Raleigh, North Carolina

Director of Admissions Ms. Susan Bloomfield, Director of Admissions, Wake Technical Community College, 9101 Fayetteville Road, Raleigh, NC 27603-5696. *Phone:* 919-866-5452. *E-mail:* srbloomfield@waketech.edu. *Website:* http://www.waketech.edu/.

Wayne Community College
Goldsboro, North Carolina

- **State and locally supported** 2-year, founded 1957, part of North Carolina Community College System
- **Small-town** 175-acre campus with easy access to Raleigh
- **Endowment** $92,408
- **Coed**

Undergraduates 1,813 full-time, 2,024 part-time. 4% are from out of state; 27% Black or African American, non-Hispanic/Latino; 8% Hispanic/Latino; 2% Asian, non-Hispanic/Latino; 0.3% Native Hawaiian or other Pacific Islander, non-Hispanic/Latino; 0.6% American Indian or Alaska Native, non-Hispanic/Latino; 0.8% Two or more races, non-Hispanic/Latino; 2% Race/ethnicity unknown; 0.3% international; 26% transferred in.

Faculty *Student/faculty ratio:* 20:1.

Academics *Calendar:* semesters. *Degree:* certificates, diplomas, and associate. *Special study options:* academic remediation for entering students, adult/continuing education programs, advanced placement credit, cooperative education, distance learning, double majors, English as a second language, external degree program, honors programs, part-time degree program, services for LD students, summer session for credit.

Library Dr. Clyde A. Erwin, Jr. Library.

Student Life *Campus security:* 24-hour emergency response devices and patrols.

Standardized Tests *Recommended:* SAT or ACT (for admission).

Costs (2016–17) *Tuition:* state resident $2280 full-time, $76 per credit hour part-time; nonresident $8040 full-time, $268 per credit hour part-time. Full-time tuition and fees vary according to course load. Part-time tuition and fees vary according to course load. *Required fees:* $108 full-time, $46 per term part-time.

Financial Aid Of all full-time matriculated undergraduates who enrolled in 2015, 100 Federal Work-Study jobs (averaging $2000).

Applying *Options:* electronic application. *Required:* high school transcript, interview.

Freshman Application Contact Mrs. Jennifer P. Mayo, Associate Director of Admissions and Records, Wayne Community College, PO Box 8002, Goldsboro, NC 27533. *Phone:* 919-735-5151 Ext. 6721. *Fax:* 919-736-9425. *E-mail:* jbmayo@waynecc.edu. *Website:* http://www.waynecc.edu/.

Western Piedmont Community College
Morgantown, North Carolina

- **State-supported** 2-year, founded 1964, part of North Carolina Community College System
- **Small-town** 130-acre campus
- **Coed**

Undergraduates 7% Black or African American, non-Hispanic/Latino; 5% Hispanic/Latino; 7% Asian, non-Hispanic/Latino; 0.2% Native Hawaiian or other Pacific Islander, non-Hispanic/Latino; 0.3% American Indian or Alaska Native, non-Hispanic/Latino; 0.5% Race/ethnicity unknown.

Academics *Calendar:* semesters. *Degree:* certificates, diplomas, and associate. *Special study options:* academic remediation for entering students, adult/continuing education programs, advanced placement credit, cooperative education, distance learning, double majors, English as a second language, part-time degree program, services for LD students, summer session for credit.

Costs (2016–17) *Tuition:* state resident $2432 full-time, $76 per credit hour part-time; nonresident $8576 full-time, $268 per credit hour part-time. *Required fees:* $145 full-time.

Applying *Options:* electronic application. *Required:* high school transcript.

Freshman Application Contact Susan Williams, Director of Admissions, Western Piedmont Community College, 1001 Burkemont Avenue, Morganton, NC 28655-4511. *Phone:* 828-438-6051. *Fax:* 828-438-6065. *E-mail:* swilliams@wpcc.edu. *Website:* http://www.wpcc.edu/.

Wilkes Community College
Wilkesboro, North Carolina

Freshman Application Contact Mr. Mac Warren, Director of Admissions, Wilkes Community College, PO Box 120, Wilkesboro, NC 28697. *Phone:* 336-838-6141. *Fax:* 336-838-6547. *E-mail:* mac.warren@wilkescc.edu. *Website:* http://www.wilkescc.edu/.

Wilson Community College
Wilson, North Carolina

Freshman Application Contact Mrs. Maegan Williams, Admissions Technician, Wilson Community College, Wilson, NC 27893-0305. *Phone:* 252-246-1275. *Fax:* 252-243-7148. *E-mail:* mwilliams@wilsoncc.edu. *Website:* http://www.wilsoncc.edu/.

NORTH DAKOTA

Bismarck State College
Bismarck, North Dakota

- **State-supported** primarily 2-year, founded 1939, part of North Dakota University System
- **Urban** 120-acre campus
- **Endowment** $16.3 million
- **Coed,** 3,976 undergraduate students, 56% full-time, 43% women, 57% men

Undergraduates 2,241 full-time, 1,735 part-time. Students come from 49 states and territories; 8 other countries; 22% are from out of state; 3% Black or African American, non-Hispanic/Latino; 3% Hispanic/Latino; 0.6% Asian, non-Hispanic/Latino; 0.2% Native Hawaiian or other Pacific Islander, non-Hispanic/Latino; 2% American Indian or Alaska Native, non-Hispanic/Latino; 3% Two or more races, non-Hispanic/Latino; 2% Race/ethnicity unknown; 0.3% international; 7% transferred in; 14% live on campus. *Retention:* 74% of full-time freshmen returned.

Freshmen *Admission:* 1,068 applied, 1,068 admitted, 878 enrolled. *Average high school GPA:* 3.03. *Test scores:* ACT scores over 18: 72%; ACT scores over 24: 13%.

Faculty *Total:* 348, 35% full-time, 11% with terminal degrees. *Student/faculty ratio:* 14:1.

Majors Administrative assistant and secretarial science; agricultural business and management; autobody/collision and repair technology; automobile/automotive mechanics technology; business automation/technology/data entry; business/commerce; carpentry; clinical/medical laboratory technology; commercial and advertising art; computer systems networking and telecommunications; criminal justice/safety; electrical, electronic and communications engineering technology; emergency medical technology (EMT paramedic); engineering technology; environmental control technologies related; farm and ranch management; heating, air conditioning, ventilation and refrigeration maintenance technology; human services; industrial mechanics and maintenance technology; industrial production technologies related; industrial technology; instrumentation technology; legal administrative assistant/secretary; liberal arts and sciences/liberal studies; lineworker; medical administrative assistant and medical secretary; multi/interdisciplinary studies related; nuclear engineering technology; operations management; petroleum technology; public relations/image management; recording arts technology; registered nursing/registered nurse; surgical technology; surveying technology; web page, digital/multimedia and information resources design; welding technology.

Academics *Calendar:* semesters. *Degrees:* certificates, diplomas, associate, and bachelor's. *Special study options:* academic remediation for entering students, adult/continuing education programs, advanced placement credit, cooperative education, distance learning, double majors, independent study, internships, part-time degree program, services for LD students, study abroad, summer session for credit.

Library Bismarck State College Library. *Books:* 61,059 (physical), 16,804 (digital/electronic); *Serial titles:* 121 (physical), 114 (digital/electronic); *Databases:* 88. Weekly public service hours: 67; students can reserve study rooms.

Student Life *Housing Options:* coed, men-only, women-only, special housing for students with disabilities. Campus housing is university owned. *Activities and Organizations:* drama/theater group, student-run newspaper, radio station, choral group, Intramural Sports, Campus Crusade, Student Government Association, Concert/Chamber Choir, Drama Club. *Campus security:* late-night transport/escort service, controlled dormitory access. *Student services:* personal/psychological counseling.

Athletics Member NJCAA. *Intercollegiate sports:* baseball M(s), basketball M(s)/W(s), golf M/W, softball W(s), volleyball W(s). *Intramural sports:* basketball M/W, football M/W, volleyball M/W.

Standardized Tests *Recommended:* ACT (for admission).

Costs (2016–17) *Tuition:* state resident $2916 full-time, $121 per credit hour part-time; nonresident $7785 full-time, $324 per credit hour part-time. Full-time tuition and fees vary according to course level, course load, degree level, location, program, and reciprocity agreements. Part-time tuition and fees vary according to course level, course load, degree level, location, program, and reciprocity agreements. *Required fees:* $743 full-time, $31 per credit hour part-time. *Room and board:* $7400; room only: $2600. Room and board charges vary according to board plan and housing facility. *Waivers:* minority students and employees or children of employees.

Financial Aid Of all full-time matriculated undergraduates who enrolled in 2015, 1,507 applied for aid, 906 were judged to have need, 341 had their need fully met. In 2015, 230 non-need-based awards were made. *Average percent of need met:* 67%. *Average financial aid package:* $8283. *Average need-based loan:* $4493. *Average need-based gift aid:* $4696. *Average non-need-based aid:* $1388.

Applying *Options:* electronic application, early admission, deferred entrance. *Application fee:* $35. *Required:* high school transcript. *Required for some:* interview. *Application deadlines:* rolling (freshmen), rolling (transfers). *Notification:* continuous (freshmen), continuous (transfers).

Freshman Application Contact Karen Erickson, Director of Admissions and Enrollment Services, Bismarck State College, PO Box 5587, Bismarck, ND 58506. *Phone:* 701-224-5424. *Toll-free phone:* 800-445-5073. *Fax:* 701-224-5643. *E-mail:* karen.erickson@bismarckstate.edu. *Website:* http://www.bismarckstate.edu/.

Cankdeska Cikana Community College
Fort Totten, North Dakota

Director of Admissions Mr. Ermen Brown Jr., Registrar, Cankdeska Cikana Community College, PO Box 269, Fort Totten, ND 58335-0269. *Phone:* 701-766-1342. *Toll-free phone:* 888-783-1463. *Website:* http://www.littlehoop.edu/.

Dakota College at Bottineau
Bottineau, North Dakota

- **State-supported** 2-year, founded 1906, part of North Dakota University System
- **Small-town** 35-acre campus
- **Coed,** 811 undergraduate students

Faculty *Student/faculty ratio:* 8:1.

Majors Accounting; accounting related; accounting technology and bookkeeping; administrative assistant and secretarial science; adult development and aging; advertising; agriculture; applied horticulture/horticultural business services related; applied horticulture/horticulture operations; biology/biological sciences; business administration and management; business automation/technology/data entry; chemistry; child-care and support services management; child-care provision; computer and information sciences; computer and information sciences and support services related; computer software and media applications related; computer technology/computer systems technology; crop production; education; entrepreneurial and small business related; environmental engineering technology; executive assistant/executive secretary; fishing and fisheries sciences and management; floriculture/floristry management; general studies; greenhouse management; health and physical education/fitness; health services/allied health/health sciences; history; horticultural science; hospitality and recreation marketing; humanities; information science/studies; information technology; landscaping and groundskeeping; land use planning and management; liberal arts and sciences and humanities related; liberal arts and sciences/liberal studies; licensed practical/vocational nurse training; marketing/marketing management; marketing related; mathematics; medical administrative assistant and medical secretary; medical/clinical assistant; medical insurance coding; medical office assistant; natural resources/conservation; network and system administration; office management; office occupations and clerical services; ornamental horticulture; parks, recreation and leisure; parks, recreation and leisure facilities management; parks, recreation, leisure, and fitness studies related; photography; physical sciences; physical sciences related; premedical studies; prenursing studies; pre-veterinary studies; psychology; receptionist; registered nursing/registered nurse; science technologies related; small business administration; social sciences; teacher assistant/aide; urban forestry; wildlife, fish and wildlands science and management; zoology/animal biology.

Academics *Calendar:* semesters. *Degree:* certificates, diplomas, and associate. *Special study options:* academic remediation for entering students, advanced placement credit, cooperative education, distance learning, double majors, off-campus study, part-time degree program, services for LD students, summer session for credit.

Library Dakota College at Bottineau Library plus 1 other.

Student Life *Housing:* on-campus residence required through sophomore year. *Options:* men-only, women-only. Campus housing is university owned. Freshman campus housing is guaranteed. *Activities and Organizations:* drama/theater group, Student Senate, Wildlife Club/Horticulture Club, Snowboarding Club, Phi Theta Kappa, Delta Epsilon Chi. *Campus security:* controlled dormitory access, security cameras. *Student services:* health clinic, personal/psychological counseling.

Athletics Member NJCAA. *Intercollegiate sports:* baseball M(s), basketball M(s)/W(s), football M, ice hockey M(s), softball W(s), volleyball W(s). *Intramural sports:* badminton M/W, basketball M/W, skiing (downhill) M/W, table tennis M/W, volleyball M/W.

Costs (2016–17) *Tuition:* $145 per credit hour part-time; state resident $4281 full-time, $145 per credit hour part-time; nonresident $6015 full-time, $217 per credit hour part-time. Full-time tuition and fees vary according to location, program, and reciprocity agreements. Part-time tuition and fees vary according to location, program, and reciprocity agreements. *Room and board:* $7775; room only: $3575. Room and board charges vary according to board plan and housing facility. *Payment plan:* installment.

Financial Aid Of all full-time matriculated undergraduates who enrolled in 2015, 296 applied for aid, 246 were judged to have need, 62 had their need fully met. 65 Federal Work-Study jobs (averaging $668). In 2015, 26 non-need-based awards were made. *Average percent of need met:* 70%. *Average financial aid package:* $10,004. *Average need-based loan:* $5400. *Average need-based gift aid:* $5196. *Average non-need-based aid:* $2012. *Average indebtedness upon graduation:* $12,305.

Applying *Options:* electronic application, early admission, deferred entrance. *Application fee:* $35. *Required:* high school transcript, immunization records, previous college official transcripts. *Application deadlines:* rolling (freshmen), rolling (transfers).

Freshman Application Contact Mrs. Robyn Poitra, Admissions Clerk, Dakota College at Bottineau, 105 Simrall Boulevard, Bottineau, ND 58318. *Phone:* 701-228-5487. *Toll-free phone:* 800-542-6866. *Fax:* 701-228-5499. *E-mail:* robyn.poitra@dakotacollege.edu. *Website:* http://www.dakotacollege.edu/.

Lake Region State College
Devils Lake, North Dakota

- **State-supported** 2-year, founded 1941, part of North Dakota University System
- **Small-town** 120-acre campus
- **Coed,** 1,947 undergraduate students, 26% full-time, 55% women, 45% men

Undergraduates 501 full-time, 1,446 part-time. Students come from 37 states and territories; 25 other countries; 16% are from out of state; 4% Black or African American, non-Hispanic/Latino; 4% Hispanic/Latino; 0.7% Asian, non-Hispanic/Latino; 0.3% Native Hawaiian or other Pacific Islander, non-Hispanic/Latino; 6% American Indian or Alaska Native, non-Hispanic/Latino; 4% Two or more races, non-Hispanic/Latino; 2% Race/ethnicity unknown; 5% international; 10% live on campus. *Retention:* 63% of full-time freshmen returned.

Freshmen *Admission:* 200 enrolled.

Faculty *Total:* 45.

Majors Administrative assistant and secretarial science; agricultural business and management; automobile/automotive mechanics technology; business administration and management; child-care provision; computer installation and repair technology; criminal justice/police science; electrical and electronic engineering technologies related; language interpretation and translation; liberal arts and sciences/liberal studies; management information systems; merchandising, sales, and marketing operations related (general); physical fitness technician; registered nursing/registered nurse; speech-language pathology.

Academics *Calendar:* semesters. *Degree:* certificates, diplomas, and associate. *Special study options:* academic remediation for entering students, cooperative education, distance learning, double majors, English as a second language, honors programs, internships, part-time degree program, services for LD students, summer session for credit.

Library Paul Hoghaug Library. *Books:* 48,000 (physical), 18,000 (digital/electronic); *Databases:* 7.

Student Life *Housing Options:* coed, men-only, women-only. Campus housing is university owned. *Activities and Organizations:* drama/theater group, Student Senate, Phi Theta Kappa, Delta Epsilon Chi, Phi Theta Lambda, Student Nurse Organization. *Campus security:* 24-hour emergency response devices, controlled dormitory access. *Student services:* personal/psychological counseling.

Athletics Member NJCAA. *Intercollegiate sports:* baseball M(s), basketball M(s)/W(s), softball W(s), volleyball W(s). *Intramural sports:* basketball M/W, riflery M/W, soccer M/W, volleyball M/W, weight lifting M/W.

Standardized Tests *Required for some:* SAT or ACT (for admission).

Costs (2016–17) *Tuition:* state resident $3326 full-time, $139 per credit part-time; nonresident $3326 full-time, $139 per credit part-time. Full-time tuition and fees vary according to course load, location, and program. Part-time tuition and fees vary according to course load, location, and program. *Required fees:* $877 full-time, $29 per credit part-time. *Room and board:* $6425. Room and board charges vary according to board plan and housing facility. *Payment plan:* installment. *Waivers:* minority students, senior citizens, and employees or children of employees.

Financial Aid Of all full-time matriculated undergraduates who enrolled in 2015, 364 applied for aid, 292 were judged to have need, 132 had their need fully met. In 2015, 88 non-need-based awards were made. *Average percent of need met:* 79%. *Average financial aid package:* $10,371. *Average need-based loan:* $4974. *Average need-based gift aid:* $5814. *Average non-need-based aid:* $1164. *Average indebtedness upon graduation:* $9405.

Applying *Options:* electronic application. *Application fee:* $35. *Required for some:* high school transcript, immunization records, college transcripts. *Application deadlines:* rolling (freshmen), rolling (transfers). *Notification:* continuous (freshmen), continuous (transfers).

Freshman Application Contact Lisa Howard, Administrative Assistant, Admissions Office, Lake Region State College, 1801 College Drive North, Devils Lake, ND 58301. *Phone:* 701-662-1519. *Toll-free phone:* 800-443-1313. *Fax:* 701-662-1581. *E-mail:* lisa.howard@lrsc.edu. *Website:* http://www.lrsc.edu/.

North Dakota State College of Science
Wahpeton, North Dakota

Freshman Application Contact Ms. Barb Mund, Director of Admissions and Records, North Dakota State College of Science, 800 North 6th Street, Wahpeton, ND 58076. *Phone:* 701-671-2204. *Toll-free phone:* 800-342-4325. *Fax:* 701-671-2201. *E-mail:* barb.mund@ndscs.edu. *Website:* http://www.ndscs.edu/.

Nueta Hidatsa Sahnish College
New Town, North Dakota

Freshman Application Contact Office of Admissions, Nueta Hidatsa Sahnish College, PO Box 490, 220 8th Avenue North, New Town, ND 58763-0490. *Phone:* 701-627-4738 Ext. 295. *Website:* http://www.nhsc.edu/.

Turtle Mountain Community College
Belcourt, North Dakota

Director of Admissions Ms. Joni LaFontaine, Admissions/Records Officer, Turtle Mountain Community College, Box 340, Belcourt, ND 58316-0340. *Phone:* 701-477-5605 Ext. 217. *E-mail:* jlafontaine@tm.edu. *Website:* http://my.tm.edu/.

United Tribes Technical College
Bismarck, North Dakota

Freshman Application Contact Ms. Vivian Gillette, Director of Admissions, United Tribes Technical College, Bismarck, ND 58504. *Phone:* 701-255-3285 Ext. 1334. *Fax:* 701-530-0640. *E-mail:* vgillette@uttc.edu. *Website:* http://www.uttc.edu/.

Williston State College
Williston, North Dakota

- **State-supported** 2-year, founded 1957, part of North Dakota University System
- **Small-town** 80-acre campus
- **Endowment** $52,200
- **Coed,** 1,039 undergraduate students, 60% full-time, 61% women, 39% men

Undergraduates 620 full-time, 419 part-time. Students come from 28 states and territories; 9 other countries; 15% are from out of state; 4% Black or African American, non-Hispanic/Latino; 8% Hispanic/Latino; 0.7% Asian, non-Hispanic/Latino; 0.2% Native Hawaiian or other Pacific Islander, non-Hispanic/Latino; 3% American Indian or Alaska Native, non-Hispanic/Latino; 5% Two or more races, non-Hispanic/Latino; 4% Race/ethnicity unknown; 4% international; 17% transferred in. *Retention:* 57% of full-time freshmen returned.

Freshmen *Admission:* 401 applied, 311 admitted, 255 enrolled.

Faculty *Total:* 33, 94% full-time, 3% with terminal degrees. *Student/faculty ratio:* 23:1.

Majors Accounting technology and bookkeeping; agriculture; business administration, management and operations related; diesel mechanics technology; liberal arts and sciences/liberal studies; licensed practical/vocational nurse training; massage therapy; medium/heavy vehicle and truck technology; multi/interdisciplinary studies related; petroleum technology; psychiatric/mental health services technology; registered nursing/registered nurse; speech-language pathology; system, networking, and LAN/WAN management; welding technology.

Academics *Calendar:* semesters. *Degree:* certificates and associate. *Special study options:* academic remediation for entering students, advanced placement credit, cooperative education, distance learning, double majors, English as a second language, independent study, part-time degree program, services for LD students, student-designed majors, study abroad, summer session for credit.

Library Williston State College Learning Commons. *Books:* 8,866 (physical), 6,910 (digital/electronic); *Databases:* 45. Students can reserve study rooms.

Student Life *Housing Options:* coed, special housing for students with disabilities. Campus housing is university owned. *Activities and Organizations:* student-run newspaper, choral group, Phi Theta Kappa, Student Senate, Teton Activity Board, Biz-Tech, Student Nurses Organization. *Campus security:* controlled dormitory access. *Student services:* personal/psychological counseling.

Athletics Member NJCAA. *Intercollegiate sports:* baseball M(s), basketball M(s)/W(s), ice hockey M(c), softball W(s), volleyball W(s).

Costs (2016–17) *One-time required fee:* $35. *Tuition:* state resident $2946 full-time, $113 per credit hour part-time; nonresident $2946 full-time, $113 per credit hour part-time. Full-time tuition and fees vary according to course load, location, program, and reciprocity agreements. Part-time tuition and fees vary according to course load, location, program, and reciprocity agreements. *Required fees:* $1465 full-time, $56 per credit hour part-time. *Room and board:* $9066; room only: $5200. Room and board charges vary according to board plan and housing facility. *Payment plan:* installment. *Waivers:* minority students, senior citizens, and employees or children of employees.

Applying *Options:* electronic application, deferred entrance. *Application fee:* $35. *Required:* high school transcript. *Application deadlines:* rolling (freshmen), rolling (transfers). *Notification:* continuous (freshmen), continuous (transfers).

Freshman Application Contact Ms. Jamee Robbins, Enrollment Services Associate, Williston State College, 1410 University Avenue, Williston, ND 58801. *Phone:* 701-774-4278. *Toll-free phone:* 888-863-9455. *E-mail:* jamee.robbins@willistonstate.edu. *Website:* http://www.willistonstate.edu/.

NORTHERN MARIANA ISLANDS

Northern Marianas College
Saipan, Northern Mariana Islands

Freshman Application Contact Ms. Leilani M. Basa-Alam, Admission Specialist, Northern Marianas College, PO Box 501250, Saipan, MP 96950-1250. *Phone:* 670-234-3690 Ext. 1539. *Fax:* 670-235-4967. *E-mail:* leilanib@nmcnet.edu. *Website:* http://www.marianas.edu/.

OHIO

AIC College of Design
Cincinnati, Ohio

Freshman Application Contact Megan Orsburn, Admissions Assistant, AIC College of Design, 1171 E. Kemper Road, Cincinnati, OH 45246. *Phone:* 513-751-1206. *Website:* http://www.aic-arts.edu/.

American Institute of Alternative Medicine
Columbus, Ohio

Admissions Office Contact American Institute of Alternative Medicine, 6685 Doubletree Avenue, Columbus, OH 43229. *Website:* http://www.aiam.edu/.

American National University
Kettering, Ohio

Director of Admissions Gregory J. Shields, Director, American National University, 1837 Woodman Center Drive, Kettering, OH 45420. *Phone:* 937-299-9450. *Website:* http://www.an.edu/.

American National University
Youngstown, Ohio

Admissions Office Contact American National University, 3487 Belmont Avenue, Youngstown, OH 44505. *Website:* http://www.an.edu/.

Antonelli College
Cincinnati, Ohio

Freshman Application Contact Antonelli College, 124 East Seventh Street, Cincinnati, OH 45202. *Phone:* 513-241-4338. *Toll-free phone:* 877-500-4304. *Website:* http://www.antonellicollege.edu/.

ATS Institute of Technology
Highland Heights, Ohio

Freshman Application Contact Admissions Office, ATS Institute of Technology, 325 Alpha Park, Highland Heights, OH 44143. *Phone:* 440-449-1700 Ext. 103. *E-mail:* info@atsinstitute.edu. *Website:* http://www.atsinstitute.edu/cleveland/.

Beckfield College
Cincinnati, Ohio

- **Proprietary** 2-year, founded 1984
- **Suburban** campus
- **Coed**

Academics *Calendar:* quarters. *Degree:* diplomas and associate.

Costs (2016–17) *Comprehensive fee:* $25,452 includes full-time tuition ($12,780), mandatory fees ($501), and room and board ($12,171). Full-time tuition and fees vary according to program. Part-time tuition: $355 per credit hour. Part-time tuition and fees vary according to program. *Payment plans:* tuition prepayment, installment, deferred payment.

Freshman Application Contact Beckfield College, 225 Pictoria Drive, Suite 200, Cincinnati, OH 45246. *Website:* http://www.beckfield.edu/.

Belmont College
St. Clairsville, Ohio

Director of Admissions Michael Sterling, Director of Recruitment, Belmont College, 120 Fox Shannon Place, St. Clairsville, OH 43950-9735. *Phone:* 740-695-9500 Ext. 1563. *Toll-free phone:* 800-423-1188. *E-mail:* msterling@btc.edu. *Website:* http://www.belmontcollege.edu/.

Bowling Green State University–Firelands College
Huron, Ohio

- **State-supported** primarily 2-year, founded 1968, part of Bowling Green State University System
- **Rural** 216-acre campus with easy access to Cleveland, Toledo
- **Coed,** 2,162 undergraduate students, 43% full-time, 64% women, 36% men

Undergraduates 940 full-time, 1,222 part-time. Students come from 6 states and territories; 1 other country; 1% are from out of state; 5% Black or African American, non-Hispanic/Latino; 5% Hispanic/Latino; 0.7% Asian, non-Hispanic/Latino; 0.4% American Indian or Alaska Native, non-Hispanic/Latino; 4% Two or more races, non-Hispanic/Latino; 4% Race/ethnicity unknown; 0.1% international. *Retention:* 52% of full-time freshmen returned.

Freshmen *Admission:* 378 enrolled. *Average high school GPA:* 2.95.

Faculty *Total:* 113, 44% full-time. *Student/faculty ratio:* 19:1.

Majors Allied health and medical assisting services related; business administration and management; communications technologies and support services related; computer and information sciences and support services related; computer systems networking and telecommunications; criminal justice/safety; design and visual communications; diagnostic medical sonography and ultrasound technology; education; health professions related; human services; industrial technology; interdisciplinary studies; liberal arts and sciences/liberal studies; management information systems and services related; mechanical engineering/mechanical technology; medical radiologic technology; registered nursing/registered nurse; respiratory care therapy; social work.

Academics *Calendar:* semesters. *Degrees:* certificates, associate, and bachelor's (also offers some upper-level and graduate courses). *Special study options:* academic remediation for entering students, adult/continuing education programs, advanced placement credit, cooperative education, distance learning, double majors, honors programs, independent study, internships, part-time degree program, services for LD students, student-designed majors, study abroad, summer session for credit. *ROTC:* Army (c), Air Force (c).

Library BGSU Firelands College Library.

Student Life *Housing:* college housing not available. *Activities and Organizations:* drama/theater group, choral group, Society of Fandom and Gaming, Student Government, Student Theater Guild, Safe Space, Society of Leadership and Success. *Campus security:* 24-hour emergency response devices, late-night transport/escort service, patrols by trained security personnel.

Athletics *Intramural sports:* basketball M/W, bowling M/W, football M, table tennis M/W, volleyball M/W.

Costs (2017–18) *Tuition:* state resident $4706 full-time, $196 per credit hour part-time; nonresident $12,014 full-time, $501 per credit hour part-time. Full-time tuition and fees vary according to location and reciprocity agreements. Part-time tuition and fees vary according to location and reciprocity agreements. *Required fees:* $240 full-time, $9 per credit hour part-time, $120 per term part-time. *Payment plan:* installment. *Waivers:* children of alumni, senior citizens, and employees or children of employees.

Applying *Options:* electronic application, early admission, deferred entrance. *Application fee:* $45. *Required:* high school transcript. *Application deadlines:* 8/6 (freshmen), 8/6 (transfers). *Notification:* continuous (freshmen), continuous (transfers).

Freshman Application Contact Cheryl Chafee, Assistant Director of Admissions and Financial Aid, Bowling Green State University–Firelands College, One University Drive, Huron, OH 44839-9791. *Phone:* 419-433-5560. *Toll-free phone:* 800-322-4787. *Fax:* 419-372-0604. *E-mail:* cchafee@bgsu.edu. *Website:* http://www.firelands.bgsu.edu/.

Bradford School
Columbus, Ohio

- **Proprietary** 2-year, founded 1911
- **Suburban** campus
- **Coed**

Academics *Calendar:* semesters. *Degree:* diplomas and associate. *Special study options:* accelerated degree program, internships.

Freshman Application Contact Admissions Office, Bradford School, 2469 Stelzer Road, Columbus, OH 43219. *Phone:* 614-416-6200. *Toll-free phone:* 800-678-7981. *Website:* http://www.bradfordschoolcolumbus.edu/.

Brightwood College, Dayton Campus
Dayton, Ohio

Freshman Application Contact Brightwood College, Dayton Campus, 2800 East River Road, Dayton, OH 45439. *Phone:* 937-294-6155. *Toll-free phone:* 866-543-0208. *Website:* http://www.brightwood.edu/.

Bryant & Stratton College–Eastlake Campus
Eastlake, Ohio

Freshman Application Contact Ms. Melanie Pettit, Director of Admissions, Bryant & Stratton College–Eastlake Campus, 35350 Curtis Boulevard, Eastlake, OH 44095. *Phone:* 440-510-1112. *Website:* http://www.bryantstratton.edu/.

Bryant & Stratton College–Parma Campus
Parma, Ohio

Freshman Application Contact Bryant & Stratton College–Parma Campus, 12955 Snow Road, Parma, OH 44130-1005. *Phone:* 216-265-3151. *Toll-free phone:* 866-948-0571. *Website:* http://www.bryantstratton.edu/.

Central Ohio Technical College
Newark, Ohio

- **State-supported** 2-year, founded 1971, part of Ohio Department of Higher Education
- **Small-town** 177-acre campus with easy access to Columbus
- **Endowment** $2.8 million
- **Coed**

Undergraduates 969 full-time, 2,597 part-time. 1% are from out of state; 10% Black or African American, non-Hispanic/Latino; 2% Hispanic/Latino; 0.9% Asian, non-Hispanic/Latino; 0.3% American Indian or Alaska Native, non-Hispanic/Latino; 3% Two or more races, non-Hispanic/Latino; 8% Race/ethnicity unknown; 12% transferred in. *Retention:* 46% of full-time freshmen returned.

Faculty *Student/faculty ratio:* 15:1.

Academics *Calendar:* semesters. *Degree:* certificates and associate. *Special study options:* academic remediation for entering students, accelerated degree program, adult/continuing education programs, advanced placement credit, cooperative education, distance learning, double majors, internships, off-campus study, part-time degree program, services for LD students, student-designed majors, summer session for credit.

Library Newark Campus Library.

Student Life *Campus security:* 24-hour emergency response devices and patrols, student patrols, late-night transport/escort service.

Costs (2016–17) *One-time required fee:* $80. *Tuition:* state resident $4296 full-time, $179 per semester hour part-time; nonresident $7056 full-time, $294 per semester hour part-time. Full-time tuition and fees vary according to course load. Part-time tuition and fees vary according to course load.

Financial Aid Of all full-time matriculated undergraduates who enrolled in 2015, 43 Federal Work-Study jobs (averaging $4000).

Applying *Options:* electronic application, early admission, deferred entrance. *Required for some:* high school transcript.

Freshman Application Contact Brad Pulcini, Director of Gateway Operations, Central Ohio Technical College, 1179 University Drive, Newark, OH 43055-1767. *Phone:* 740-755-7139. *Toll-free phone:* 800-9NEWARK. *E-mail:* bpulcini@cotc.edu. *Website:* http://www.cotc.edu/.

Chatfield College
St. Martin, Ohio

- **Independent** 2-year, founded 1970, affiliated with Roman Catholic Church
- **Rural** 200-acre campus with easy access to Cincinnati, Dayton
- **Endowment** $2.9 million
- **Coed**

Undergraduates 197 full-time, 199 part-time. Students come from 1 other state; 62% Black or African American, non-Hispanic/Latino; 0.4% Hispanic/Latino; 0.4% Asian, non-Hispanic/Latino; 0.8% Two or more races, non-Hispanic/Latino; 3% Race/ethnicity unknown; 0.4% international; 0.8% transferred in.

Faculty *Student/faculty ratio:* 8:1.

Academics *Calendar:* semesters. *Degree:* associate. *Special study options:* academic remediation for entering students, adult/continuing education programs, advanced placement credit, internships, off-campus study, part-time degree program, summer session for credit.

Library Chatfield College Library. *Books:* 20,284 (physical), 89,098 (digital/electronic); *Serial titles:* 8 (physical); *Databases:* 47. Students can reserve study rooms.

Student Life *Campus security:* 12-hour night patrols by security.

Costs (2016–17) *Tuition:* $10,523 full-time, $407 per credit hour part-time. *Required fees:* $348 full-time, $101 per term part-time. *Payment plans:* installment, deferred payment.

Financial Aid Of all full-time matriculated undergraduates who enrolled in 2015, 10 Federal Work-Study jobs (averaging $1500). 4 state and other part-time jobs (averaging $800). *Financial aid deadline:* 8/1.

Applying *Options:* early admission, deferred entrance. *Application fee:* $10.

Freshman Application Contact Chatfield College, 20918 State Route 251, St. Martin, OH 45118-9705. *Phone:* 513-875-3344 Ext. 138. *Website:* http://www.chatfield.edu/.

The Christ College of Nursing and Health Sciences
Cincinnati, Ohio

Freshman Application Contact Mr. Bradley Jackson, Admissions, The Christ College of Nursing and Health Sciences, 2139 Auburn Avenue, Cincinnati, OH 45219. *Phone:* 513-585-0016. *E-mail:* bradley.jackson@thechristcollege.edu. *Website:* http://www.thechristcollege.edu/.

Cincinnati State Technical and Community College
Cincinnati, Ohio

- **State-supported** 2-year, founded 1966, part of Ohio Board of Regents
- **Urban** 46-acre campus
- **Coed**

Undergraduates 2,873 full-time, 6,757 part-time. 9% are from out of state; 26% Black or African American, non-Hispanic/Latino; 2% Hispanic/Latino; 2% Asian, non-Hispanic/Latino; 0.1% Native Hawaiian or other Pacific Islander, non-Hispanic/Latino; 0.4% American Indian or Alaska Native, non-Hispanic/Latino; 3% Two or more races, non-Hispanic/Latino; 5% Race/ethnicity unknown; 2% international. *Retention:* 49% of full-time freshmen returned.

Faculty *Student/faculty ratio:* 11:1.

Academics *Calendar:* 5 10-week terms. *Degree:* certificates and associate. *Special study options:* academic remediation for entering students, advanced placement credit, cooperative education, distance learning, double majors, English as a second language, honors programs, independent study, internships, off-campus study, part-time degree program, services for LD students, student-designed majors, summer session for credit. *ROTC:* Army (c).

Library Johnnie Mae Berry Library.

Student Life *Campus security:* 24-hour emergency response devices and patrols, late-night transport/escort service.

Athletics Member NJCAA.

Costs (2016–17) *One-time required fee:* $15. *Tuition:* state resident $3567 full-time, $149 per credit hour part-time; nonresident $7135 full-time, $297 per credit hour part-time. *Required fees:* $258 full-time, $9 per credit hour part-time, $47 per term part-time.

Financial Aid Of all full-time matriculated undergraduates who enrolled in 2015, 100 Federal Work-Study jobs (averaging $3500).

Applying *Options:* electronic application, deferred entrance. *Required:* high school transcript.

Freshman Application Contact Ms. Gabriele Boeckermann, Director of Admission, Cincinnati State Technical and Community College, Office of Admissions, 3520 Central Parkway, Cincinnati, OH 45223-2690. *Phone:* 513-569-1550. *Toll-free phone:* 877-569-0115. *Fax:* 513-569-1562. *E-mail:* adm@cincinnatistate.edu. *Website:* http://www.cincinnatistate.edu/.

Clark State Community College
Springfield, Ohio

Freshman Application Contact Admissions Office, Clark State Community College, PO Box 570, Springfield, OH 45501-0570. *Phone:* 937-328-3858. *Fax:* 937-328-6133. *E-mail:* admissions@clarkstate.edu. *Website:* http://www.clarkstate.edu/.

Columbus Culinary Institute at Bradford School
Columbus, Ohio

- **Private** 2-year, founded 2006
- **Suburban** campus
- **Coed**
- 58% of applicants were admitted

Academics *Calendar:* semesters. *Degree:* associate.

Freshman Application Contact Admissions Office, Columbus Culinary Institute at Bradford School, 2435 Stelzer Road, Columbus, OH 43219. *Phone:* 614-944-4200. *Toll-free phone:* 877-506-5006. *Website:* http://www.columbusculinary.com/.

Columbus State Community College
Columbus, Ohio

- **State-supported** 2-year, founded 1963, part of Ohio Department of Higher Education
- **Urban** 188-acre campus with easy access to Columbus
- **Coed,** 27,109 undergraduate students, 26% full-time, 53% women, 47% men

Undergraduates 7,025 full-time, 20,084 part-time. Students come from 49 states and territories; 81 other countries; 2% are from out of state; 18% Black or African American, non-Hispanic/Latino; 5% Hispanic/Latino; 3% Asian, non-Hispanic/Latino; 0.1% Native Hawaiian or other Pacific Islander, non-Hispanic/Latino; 0.4% American Indian or Alaska Native, non-Hispanic/Latino; 3% Two or more races, non-Hispanic/Latino; 6% Race/ethnicity unknown; 1% international; 14% transferred in. *Retention:* 61% of full-time freshmen returned.

Freshmen *Admission:* 18,486 applied, 17,589 admitted, 4,055 enrolled.

Faculty *Student/faculty ratio:* 19:1.

Majors Accounting technology and bookkeeping; administrative assistant and secretarial science; aeronautical/aerospace engineering technology; architectural engineering technology; automotive engineering technology; building/property maintenance; business administration and management; cabinetmaking and millwork; carpentry; child-care and support services management; civil engineering technology; clinical/medical laboratory science and allied professions related; clinical/medical laboratory technology; commercial photography; computer and information sciences; computer programming (specific applications); construction engineering technology; construction trades; criminal justice/police science; culinary arts; dental hygiene; electrical and electronic engineering technologies related; electrical, electronic and communications engineering technology; electromechanical technology; emergency medical technology (EMT paramedic); entrepreneurship; environmental engineering technology; finance and financial management services related; fire science/firefighting; game and interactive media design; general studies; geographic information science and cartography; graphic and printing equipment operation/production; health and physical education/fitness; health information/medical records administration;

heating, ventilation, air conditioning and refrigeration engineering technology; hospitality administration; human resources management; international business/trade/commerce; kinesiology and exercise science; legal assistant/paralegal; liberal arts and sciences/liberal studies; logistics, materials, and supply chain management; management information systems; marketing/marketing management; marketing related; massage therapy; mechanical engineering/mechanical technology; medical/clinical assistant; medical radiologic technology; psychiatric/mental health services technology; quality control technology; real estate; registered nursing/registered nurse; respiratory care therapy; sheet metal technology; sign language interpretation and translation; sport and fitness administration/management; surgical technology; surveying technology; tourism and travel services management; veterinary/animal health technology; welding technology.

Academics *Calendar:* semesters. *Degree:* certificates and associate. *Special study options:* academic remediation for entering students, adult/continuing education programs, advanced placement credit, cooperative education, distance learning, double majors, English as a second language, honors programs, independent study, internships, off-campus study, part-time degree program, services for LD students, student-designed majors, study abroad, summer session for credit. *ROTC:* Army (c).

Library Columbus State Library plus 1 other. *Books:* 32,991 (physical), 52,921 (digital/electronic); *Databases:* 185. Weekly public service hours: 76.

Student Life *Housing:* college housing not available. *Activities and Organizations:* choral group, Phi Theta Kappa, Student Nurses Association, Student American Dental Hygiene Association, Landscaping Association. *Campus security:* 24-hour emergency response devices and patrols, late-night transport/escort service, Vehicle Assistance with lockouts and jump starts. *Student services:* personal/psychological counseling.

Athletics Member NCAA, NJCAA. All NCAA Division III. *Intercollegiate sports:* basketball M/W, cross-country running M/W, golf M/W, volleyball W. *Intramural sports:* basketball M/W, soccer M/W.

Costs (2016–17) *One-time required fee:* $50. *Tuition:* state resident $6117 full-time, $136 per credit hour part-time; nonresident $13,546 full-time, $301 per credit hour part-time. *Required fees:* $60 per term part-time. *Payment plans:* installment, deferred payment. *Waivers:* senior citizens and employees or children of employees.

Financial Aid Of all full-time matriculated undergraduates who enrolled in 2015, 133 Federal Work-Study jobs (averaging $1500).

Applying *Options:* electronic application, early admission, deferred entrance. *Application fee:* $50. *Required for some:* essay or personal statement, high school transcript, minimum 3.0 GPA, 1 letter of recommendation, interview. *Recommended:* high school transcript. *Application deadlines:* 8/21 (freshmen), 8/21 (out-of-state freshmen), 8/21 (transfers). *Notification:* continuous (freshmen), continuous (out-of-state freshmen), continuous (transfers).

Freshman Application Contact Director of Admissions, Columbus State Community College, 550 E. Spring Street, Columbus, OH 43215. *Phone:* 614-287-2669. *Toll-free phone:* 800-621-6407 Ext. 2669. *Fax:* 614-287-6019. *Website:* http://www.cscc.edu/.

Cuyahoga Community College
Cleveland, Ohio

Freshman Application Contact Mr. Kevin McDaniel, Director of Admissions and Records, Cuyahoga Community College, Cleveland, OH 44115. *Phone:* 216-987-4030. *Toll-free phone:* 800-954-8742. *Fax:* 216-696-2567. *Website:* http://www.tri-c.edu/.

Davis College
Toledo, Ohio

- **Proprietary** 2-year, founded 1858
- **Urban** 1-acre campus with easy access to Detroit
- **Coed**

Undergraduates 34 full-time, 125 part-time. Students come from 2 states and territories; 2% are from out of state; 40% Black or African American, non-Hispanic/Latino; 2% Hispanic/Latino; 0.6% American Indian or Alaska Native, non-Hispanic/Latino; 4% Race/ethnicity unknown.

Faculty *Student/faculty ratio:* 7:1.

Academics *Calendar:* quarters. *Degree:* certificates, diplomas, and associate. *Special study options:* academic remediation for entering students, adult/continuing education programs, advanced placement credit, distance learning, internships, part-time degree program, summer session for credit.

Library Davis College Resource Center. *Books:* 2,108 (physical); *Serial titles:* 109 (physical).

Student Life *Campus security:* interior and exterior security cameras.

Costs (2016–17) *Tuition:* $12,600 full-time, $350 per credit hour part-time. *Required fees:* $1050 full-time, $350 per term part-time.

Financial Aid Of all full-time matriculated undergraduates who enrolled in 2015, 10 Federal Work-Study jobs (averaging $3500).
Applying *Options:* electronic application, early admission, deferred entrance. *Application fee:* $30. *Required:* high school transcript, interview.
Freshman Application Contact Mr. Timothy Brunner, Davis College, 4747 Monroe Street, Toledo, OH 43623-4307. *Phone:* 419-473-2700. *Toll-free phone:* 800-477-7021. *Fax:* 419-473-2472. *E-mail:* tbrunner@daviscollege.edu. *Website:* http://www.daviscollege.edu/.

Daymar College
Columbus, Ohio

Freshman Application Contact Holly Hankinson, Admissions Office, Daymar College, 2745 Winchester Pike, Columbus, OH 43232. *Phone:* 740-687-6126. *Toll-free phone:* 877-258-7796. *E-mail:* hhankinson@daymarcollege.edu. *Website:* http://www.daymarcollege.edu/.

Eastern Gateway Community College
Steubenville, Ohio

- **State and locally supported** 2-year, founded 1966, part of Ohio Board of Regents
- **Small-town** 83-acre campus with easy access to Pittsburgh
- **Endowment** $448,293
- **Coed**

Undergraduates 1,199 full-time, 1,825 part-time. Students come from 5 states and territories; 1 other country; 21% Black or African American, non-Hispanic/Latino; 2% Hispanic/Latino; 0.5% Asian, non-Hispanic/Latino; 0.1% Native Hawaiian or other Pacific Islander, non-Hispanic/Latino; 0.4% American Indian or Alaska Native, non-Hispanic/Latino; 4% Two or more races, non-Hispanic/Latino; 1% Race/ethnicity unknown; 0.1% international.
Faculty *Student/faculty ratio:* 23:1.
Academics *Calendar:* semesters. *Degree:* certificates and associate. *Special study options:* academic remediation for entering students, accelerated degree program, adult/continuing education programs, cooperative education, distance learning, double majors, off-campus study, part-time degree program, services for LD students, summer session for credit.
Library Eastern Gateway Community College Library.
Student Life *Campus security:* 24-hour emergency response devices, day and evening security.
Standardized Tests *Required for some:* SAT or ACT (for admission).
Costs (2016–17) *Tuition:* area resident $3330 full-time, $111 per credit hour part-time; state resident $3510 full-time, $117 per credit hour part-time; nonresident $6750 full-time, $225 per credit hour part-time. Full-time tuition and fees vary according to program and reciprocity agreements. Part-time tuition and fees vary according to program and reciprocity agreements.
Financial Aid Of all full-time matriculated undergraduates who enrolled in 2015, 30 Federal Work-Study jobs (averaging $1500).
Applying *Options:* electronic application, early admission, deferred entrance. *Application fee:* $20. *Required for some:* high school transcript.
Freshman Application Contact Mr. Ryan Ogrodnik, Director of Admissions, Eastern Gateway Community College, 4000 Sunset Boulevard, Steubenville, OH 43952. *Phone:* 740-264-5591 Ext. 1656. *Toll-free phone:* 800-68-COLLEGE. *Fax:* 740-266-2944. *E-mail:* rogrodnik@egcc.edu. *Website:* http://www.egcc.edu/.

Edison State Community College
Piqua, Ohio

- **State-supported** 2-year, founded 1973, part of Ohio Board of Regents
- **Small-town** 131-acre campus with easy access to Dayton, Columbus, Cincinnati
- **Coed,** 3,367 undergraduate students, 24% full-time, 60% women, 40% men

Undergraduates 804 full-time, 2,563 part-time. Students come from 3 states and territories; 1 other country; 2% are from out of state; 5% Black or African American, non-Hispanic/Latino; 2% Hispanic/Latino; 2% Asian, non-Hispanic/Latino; 0.2% Native Hawaiian or other Pacific Islander, non-Hispanic/Latino; 0.5% American Indian or Alaska Native, non-Hispanic/Latino; 0.6% Two or more races, non-Hispanic/Latino; 3% Race/ethnicity unknown; 0.1% international; 3% transferred in. *Retention:* 57% of full-time freshmen returned.
Freshmen *Admission:* 306 applied, 305 admitted, 542 enrolled. *Average high school GPA:* 2.92.

Faculty *Total:* 192, 26% full-time, 9% with terminal degrees. *Student/faculty ratio:* 17:1.
Majors Accounting; art; biology/biological sciences; business administration and management; child development; clinical/medical laboratory technology; computer and information sciences; computer and information systems security; computer programming; computer systems networking and telecommunications; criminal justice/police science; dramatic/theater arts; economics; education; electrical, electronic and communications engineering technology; electromechanical technology; English; executive assistant/executive secretary; geology/earth science; health/medical preparatory programs related; history; human resources management; industrial technology; legal assistant/paralegal; liberal arts and sciences/liberal studies; logistics, materials, and supply chain management; manufacturing engineering technology; marketing/marketing management; mathematics; mechanical drafting and CAD/CADD; medical administrative assistant and medical secretary; medical/clinical assistant; medium/heavy vehicle and truck technology; philosophy and religious studies related; physical therapy technology; prenursing studies; psychology; registered nursing/registered nurse; social work; speech communication and rhetoric.
Academics *Calendar:* semesters. *Degrees:* certificates, associate, and postbachelor's certificates. *Special study options:* academic remediation for entering students, accelerated degree program, adult/continuing education programs, advanced placement credit, distance learning, double majors, English as a second language, honors programs, independent study, internships, off-campus study, part-time degree program, services for LD students, student-designed majors, summer session for credit.
Library Edison Community College Library. *Books:* 19,494 (physical), 104,398 (digital/electronic); *Serial titles:* 150 (physical), 10,845 (digital/electronic); *Databases:* 244. Weekly public service hours: 54; students can reserve study rooms.
Student Life *Housing:* college housing not available. *Activities and Organizations:* drama/theater group, student-run newspaper. *Campus security:* late-night transport/escort service, 18-hour patrols by trained security personnel. *Student services:* health clinic.
Athletics Member NJCAA. *Intercollegiate sports:* baseball M(s), basketball M(s)/W(s), softball W, volleyball W(s).
Financial Aid Of all full-time matriculated undergraduates who enrolled in 2015, 42 Federal Work-Study jobs (averaging $3000).
Applying *Options:* electronic application. *Required:* high school transcript. *Application deadlines:* rolling (freshmen), rolling (transfers).
Freshman Application Contact Ms. Loleta Collins, Director of Student Services, Edison State Community College, 1973 Edison Drive, Piqua, OH 45356. *Phone:* 937-778-7983. *E-mail:* lcollins@edisonohio.edu. *Website:* http://www.edisonohio.edu/.

ETI Technical College of Niles
Niles, Ohio

- **Proprietary** 2-year, founded 1989
- **Small-town** 1-acre campus with easy access to Cleveland, Pittsburgh
- **Coed**

Undergraduates 62 full-time, 62 part-time. Students come from 2 states and territories; 1% are from out of state; 23% Black or African American, non-Hispanic/Latino; 0.8% Hispanic/Latino; 0.8% Asian, non-Hispanic/Latino; 2% transferred in.
Faculty *Student/faculty ratio:* 5:1.
Academics *Calendar:* semesters. *Degree:* diplomas and associate. *Special study options:* academic remediation for entering students, adult/continuing education programs, double majors, internships, part-time degree program, services for LD students.
Library Main Library plus 1 other.
Student Life *Campus security:* 24-hour emergency response devices.
Costs (2016–17) *Tuition:* $11,000 full-time, $400 per credit part-time. Full-time tuition and fees vary according to course load, degree level, and program. Part-time tuition and fees vary according to course load, degree level, and program. No tuition increase for student's term of enrollment. *Required fees:* $500 full-time, $250 per term part-time.
Financial Aid Of all full-time matriculated undergraduates who enrolled in 2016, 44 applied for aid, 44 were judged to have need. In 2016, 44. *Average financial aid package:* $10,639. *Average need-based loan:* $3500. *Average need-based gift aid:* $7139.
Applying *Options:* early admission, deferred entrance. *Application fee:* $50. *Required:* high school transcript, interview.
Freshman Application Contact Ms. Diane Marsteller, Director of Admissions, ETI Technical College of Niles, 2076 Youngstown-Warren Road, Niles, OH 44446-4398. *Phone:* 330-652-9919 Ext. 16. *Fax:* 330-652-4399. *E-mail:* dianemarsteller@eticollege.edu. *Website:* http://eticollege.edu/.

Fortis College
Centerville, Ohio

Freshman Application Contact Fortis College, 555 East Alex Bell Road, Centerville, OH 45459. *Phone:* 937-433-3410. *Toll-free phone:* 855-4-FORTIS. *Website:* http://www.fortis.edu/.

Fortis College
Cincinnati, Ohio

Admissions Office Contact Fortis College, 11499 Chester Road, Suite 200, Cincinnati, OH 45246. *Toll-free phone:* 855-4-FORTIS. *Website:* http://www.fortis.edu/.

Fortis College
Cuyahoga Falls, Ohio

Freshman Application Contact Admissions Office, Fortis College, 2545 Bailey Road, Cuyahoga Falls, OH 44221. *Phone:* 330-923-9959. *Toll-free phone:* 855-4-FORTIS. *Fax:* 330-923-0886. *Website:* http://www.fortis.edu/.

Fortis College
Ravenna, Ohio

Freshman Application Contact Admissions Office, Fortis College, 653 Enterprise Parkway, Ravenna, OH 44266. *Toll-free phone:* 855-4-FORTIS. *Website:* http://www.fortis.edu/.

Fortis College
Westerville, Ohio

Admissions Office Contact Fortis College, 4151 Executive Parkway, Suite 120, Westerville, OH 43081. *Toll-free phone:* 855-4-FORTIS. *Website:* http://www.fortis.edu/.

Gallipolis Career College
Gallipolis, Ohio

Freshman Application Contact Mr. Jack Henson, Director of Admissions, Gallipolis Career College, 1176 Jackson Pike, Suite 312, Gallipolis, OH 45631. *Phone:* 740-446-4367. *Toll-free phone:* 800-214-0452. *Fax:* 740-446-4124. *E-mail:* admissions@gallipoliscareercollege.com. *Website:* http://gallipoliscareercollege.edu/.

Good Samaritan College of Nursing and Health Science
Cincinnati, Ohio

Freshman Application Contact Admissions Office, Good Samaritan College of Nursing and Health Science, 375 Dixmyth Avenue, Cincinnati, OH 45220. *Phone:* 513-862-2743. *Fax:* 513-862-3572. *Website:* http://www.gscollege.edu/.

Herzing University
Akron, Ohio

Admissions Office Contact Herzing University, 1600 South Arlington Street, Suite 100, Akron, OH 44306. *Toll-free phone:* 800-596-0724. *Website:* http://www.herzing.edu/akron.

Herzing University
Toledo, Ohio

Admissions Office Contact Herzing University, 5212 Hill Avenue, Toledo, OH 43615. *Toll-free phone:* 800-596-0724. *Website:* http://www.herzing.edu/toledo.

Hocking College
Nelsonville, Ohio

Freshman Application Contact Hocking College, 3301 Hocking Parkway, Nelsonville, OH 45764-9588. *Phone:* 740-753-3591 Ext. 7080. *Website:* http://www.hocking.edu/.

Hondros College
Westerville, Ohio

Director of Admissions Ms. Carol Thomas, Operations Manager, Hondros College, 4140 Executive Parkway, Westerville, OH 43081-3855. *Phone:* 614-508-7244. *Toll-free phone:* 888-HONDROS. *Website:* http://www.hondros.edu/.

International College of Broadcasting
Dayton, Ohio

- **Proprietary** 2-year, founded 1968
- **Urban** campus with easy access to Dayton
- **Coed**

Majors Audiovisual communications technologies related; radio and television broadcasting technology.

Academics *Calendar:* semesters. *Degree:* diplomas and associate. *Special study options:* academic remediation for entering students, internships, services for LD students.

Student Life *Housing:* college housing not available. *Activities and Organizations:* student-run radio station.

Costs (2016–17) *Tuition:* $30,485 full-time. Full-time tuition and fees vary according to program. Part-time tuition and fees vary according to program. No tuition increase for student's term of enrollment. *Required fees:* $100 full-time. *Payment plans:* tuition prepayment, installment.

Applying *Options:* early admission. *Required:* high school transcript, interview.

Freshman Application Contact International College of Broadcasting, 6 South Smithville Road, Dayton, OH 45431-1833. *Phone:* 937-258-8251. *Toll-free phone:* 800-517-7284. *Website:* http://www.icb.edu/.

James A. Rhodes State College
Lima, Ohio

Freshman Application Contact Traci Cox, Director, Office of Admissions, James A. Rhodes State College, Lima, OH 45804-3597. *Phone:* 419-995-8040. *E-mail:* cox.t@rhodesstate.edu. *Website:* http://www.rhodesstate.edu/.

Kent State University at Ashtabula
Ashtabula, Ohio

- **State-supported** primarily 2-year, founded 1958, part of Kent State University System
- **Small-town** 83-acre campus with easy access to Cleveland
- **Coed,** 2,074 undergraduate students, 57% full-time, 63% women, 37% men

Undergraduates 1,186 full-time, 888 part-time. Students come from 24 states and territories; 2 other countries; 5% are from out of state; 6% Black or African American, non-Hispanic/Latino; 4% Hispanic/Latino; 1% Asian, non-Hispanic/Latino; 0.2% Native Hawaiian or other Pacific Islander, non-Hispanic/Latino; 0.3% American Indian or Alaska Native, non-Hispanic/Latino; 3% Two or more races, non-Hispanic/Latino; 2% Race/ethnicity unknown; 0.6% international; 5% transferred in. *Retention:* 59% of full-time freshmen returned.

Freshmen *Admission:* 292 applied, 289 admitted, 183 enrolled. *Average high school GPA:* 2.92. *Test scores:* SAT critical reading scores over 500: 100%; SAT math scores over 500: 100%; SAT writing scores over 500: 100%; ACT scores over 18: 62%; SAT critical reading scores over 600: 33%; SAT math scores over 600: 83%; SAT writing scores over 600: 80%; ACT scores over 24: 12%; SAT writing scores over 700: 40%.

Faculty *Total:* 96, 51% full-time. *Student/faculty ratio:* 23:1.

Majors Accounting technology and bookkeeping; administrative assistant and secretarial science; aerospace, aeronautical and astronautical/space engineering; business administration and management; business/commerce; computer programming (specific applications); criminal justice/safety; English; general studies; health and medical administrative services related; health/medical preparatory programs related; hospitality administration; liberal arts and sciences and humanities related; medical radiologic technology; occupational therapist assistant; physical therapy technology; psychology; registered nursing/registered nurse; respiratory care therapy; sociology; speech communication and rhetoric; viticulture and enology.

Academics *Calendar:* semesters. *Degrees:* certificates, associate, and bachelor's (also offers some upper-level and graduate courses). *Special study options:* academic remediation for entering students, advanced placement credit, distance learning, double majors, independent study, internships, part-time degree program, services for LD students, student-designed majors, study abroad, summer session for credit.

Library Kent State at Ashtabula Library. *Books:* 66,090 (physical); *Serial titles:* 454 (physical). Weekly public service hours: 56.

Student Life *Housing:* college housing not available. *Activities and Organizations:* Student Government, Student Veterans Association, Student Nurses Association, Student Occupational Therapy Association, Media Club. *Campus security:* 24-hour emergency response devices.

Athletics *Intramural sports:* volleyball M(c)/W(c).

Standardized Tests *Recommended:* SAT or ACT (for admission).

Costs (2016–17) *One-time required fee:* $150. *Tuition:* state resident $5664 full-time, $258 per credit hour part-time; nonresident $14,028 full-time, $620 per credit hour part-time. Full-time tuition and fees vary according to course level and course load. Part-time tuition and fees vary according to course level and course load. *Payment plan:* installment. *Waivers:* senior citizens and employees or children of employees.

Financial Aid Of all full-time matriculated undergraduates who enrolled in 2016, 536 applied for aid, 479 were judged to have need, 12 had their need fully met. In 2016, 9 non-need-based awards were made. *Average percent of need met:* 53%. *Average financial aid package:* $7465. *Average need-based loan:* $3745. *Average need-based gift aid:* $4668. *Average non-need-based aid:* $1479.

Applying *Options:* electronic application, deferred entrance. *Application fee:* $40. *Required:* high school transcript. *Application deadlines:* 8/15 (freshmen), 8/15 (transfers). *Notification:* continuous (freshmen), continuous (transfers).

Freshman Application Contact Megan Krippel, Admissions Coordinator, Kent State University at Ashtabula, 3300 Lake Road West, Ashtabula, OH 44004. *Phone:* 440-964-4217. *Fax:* 440-964-4269.
E-mail: ashtabula_admissions@kent.edu.
Website: http://www.ashtabula.kent.edu/.

Kent State University at East Liverpool
East Liverpool, Ohio

- **State-supported** primarily 2-year, founded 1967, part of Kent State University System
- **Small-town** 3-acre campus with easy access to Pittsburgh, Youngstown
- **Coed,** 1,302 undergraduate students, 55% full-time, 69% women, 31% men

Undergraduates 710 full-time, 592 part-time. Students come from 3 states and territories; 7% are from out of state; 5% Black or African American, non-Hispanic/Latino; 2% Hispanic/Latino; 0.7% Asian, non-Hispanic/Latino; 0.1% Native Hawaiian or other Pacific Islander, non-Hispanic/Latino; 0.3% American Indian or Alaska Native, non-Hispanic/Latino; 3% Two or more races, non-Hispanic/Latino; 3% Race/ethnicity unknown; 0.4% international; 4% transferred in. *Retention:* 46% of full-time freshmen returned.

Freshmen *Admission:* 118 applied, 118 admitted, 83 enrolled. *Average high school GPA:* 3.01. *Test scores:* ACT scores over 18: 71%; ACT scores over 24: 11%.

Faculty *Total:* 54, 41% full-time. *Student/faculty ratio:* 28:1.

Majors Accounting technology and bookkeeping; business/commerce; computer programming (specific applications); criminal justice/safety; English; general studies; legal assistant/paralegal; liberal arts and sciences and humanities related; occupational therapist assistant; physical therapy technology; psychology; registered nursing/registered nurse; speech communication and rhetoric.

Academics *Calendar:* semesters. *Degrees:* certificates, associate, and bachelor's. *Special study options:* academic remediation for entering students, accelerated degree program, advanced placement credit, distance learning, double majors, freshman honors college, honors programs, independent study, internships, part-time degree program, services for LD students, student-designed majors, summer session for credit. *ROTC:* Army (c), Air Force (c).

Library Paul Blair Memorial Library. *Books:* 21,499 (physical); *Serial titles:* 238 (physical). Weekly public service hours: 46.

Student Life *Housing:* college housing not available. *Activities and Organizations:* Undergraduate Student Government, Student Nurses Association, Environmental Club, Student Occupational Therapist Assistants, Physical Therapist Assistant Club. *Campus security:* 24-hour emergency response devices, student patrols, late-night transport/escort service. *Student services:* personal/psychological counseling.

Standardized Tests *Recommended:* SAT or ACT (for admission).

Costs (2016–17) *One-time required fee:* $150. *Tuition:* state resident $5664 full-time, $258 per credit hour part-time; nonresident $14,028 full-time, $620 per credit hour part-time. Full-time tuition and fees vary according to course level and course load. Part-time tuition and fees vary according to course level and course load. *Payment plan:* installment. *Waivers:* senior citizens and employees or children of employees.

Financial Aid Of all full-time matriculated undergraduates who enrolled in 2016, 204 applied for aid, 170 were judged to have need, 16 had their need

fully met. In 2016, 7 non-need-based awards were made. *Average percent of need met:* 57%. *Average financial aid package:* $7200. *Average need-based loan:* $3566. *Average need-based gift aid:* $4692. *Average non-need-based aid:* $2250.

Applying *Options:* electronic application, deferred entrance. *Application fee:* $40. *Required:* high school transcript. *Application deadlines:* 8/15 (freshmen), 8/15 (transfers). *Notification:* continuous (freshmen), continuous (transfers).

Freshman Application Contact Office of Admissions, Kent State University at East Liverpool, 400 East 4th Street, East Liverpool, OH 43920-3497. *Phone:* 330-385-3805.
Website: http://www.eliv.kent.edu/.

Kent State University at Salem
Salem, Ohio

- **State-supported** primarily 2-year, founded 1966, part of Kent State University System
- **Rural** 100-acre campus with easy access to Youngstown
- **Coed,** 1,673 undergraduate students, 66% full-time, 69% women, 31% men

Undergraduates 1,098 full-time, 575 part-time. Students come from 4 states and territories; 1 other country; 2% are from out of state; 3% Black or African American, non-Hispanic/Latino; 2% Hispanic/Latino; 0.8% Asian, non-Hispanic/Latino; 0.2% American Indian or Alaska Native, non-Hispanic/Latino; 2% Two or more races, non-Hispanic/Latino; 3% Race/ethnicity unknown; 0.5% international; 5% transferred in. *Retention:* 59% of full-time freshmen returned.

Freshmen *Admission:* 282 applied, 282 admitted, 176 enrolled. *Average high school GPA:* 3.01. *Test scores:* SAT critical reading scores over 500: 50%; SAT math scores over 500: 50%; SAT writing scores over 500: 50%; ACT scores over 18: 69%; SAT critical reading scores over 600: 50%; SAT math scores over 600: 50%; ACT scores over 24: 15%; ACT scores over 30: 1%.

Faculty *Total:* 124, 31% full-time. *Student/faculty ratio:* 19:1.

Majors Accounting technology and bookkeeping; administrative assistant and secretarial science; applied horticulture/horticulture operations; business administration and management; business/commerce; computer programming (specific applications); criminal justice/safety; early childhood education; education related; English; general studies; health and medical administrative services related; human development and family studies; liberal arts and sciences and humanities related; medical radiologic technology; psychology; registered nursing/registered nurse; speech communication and rhetoric.

Academics *Calendar:* semesters. *Degrees:* certificates, associate, and bachelor's (also offers some upper-level and graduate courses). *Special study options:* academic remediation for entering students, accelerated degree program, adult/continuing education programs, advanced placement credit, cooperative education, distance learning, double majors, freshman honors college, honors programs, independent study, part-time degree program, services for LD students, student-designed majors, study abroad, summer session for credit. *ROTC:* Army (c), Air Force (c).

Library Kent State Salem Library. *Books:* 23,500 (physical); *Serial titles:* 4,500 (physical).

Student Life *Housing:* college housing not available. *Campus security:* 24-hour emergency response devices, late-night transport/escort service. *Student services:* personal/psychological counseling.

Standardized Tests *Required for some:* SAT or ACT (for admission). *Recommended:* SAT or ACT (for admission).

Costs (2016–17) *One-time required fee:* $150. *Tuition:* state resident $5664 full-time, $258 per credit hour part-time; nonresident $14,028 full-time, $620 per credit hour part-time. Full-time tuition and fees vary according to course level and course load. Part-time tuition and fees vary according to course level and course load. *Payment plan:* installment. *Waivers:* senior citizens and employees or children of employees.

Financial Aid Of all full-time matriculated undergraduates who enrolled in 2016, 619 applied for aid, 523 were judged to have need, 31 had their need fully met. In 2016, 31 non-need-based awards were made. *Average percent of need met:* 55%. *Average financial aid package:* $7059. *Average need-based loan:* $3896. *Average need-based gift aid:* $4665. *Average non-need-based aid:* $649.

Applying *Options:* electronic application, deferred entrance. *Application fee:* $40. *Required:* high school transcript. *Required for some:* essay or personal statement. *Application deadlines:* 12/15 (freshmen), 12/15 (transfers). *Notification:* continuous (freshmen), continuous (transfers).

Freshman Application Contact Office of Admissions, Kent State University at Salem, 2491 State Route 45 South, Salem, OH 44460-9412. *Phone:* 330-332-0361.
Website: http://www.salem.kent.edu/.

Kent State University at Trumbull
Warren, Ohio

- **State-supported** primarily 2-year, founded 1954, part of Kent State University System
- **Suburban** 438-acre campus with easy access to Akron, Youngstown
- **Coed,** 2,377 undergraduate students, 63% full-time, 61% women, 39% men

Undergraduates 1,501 full-time, 876 part-time. Students come from 7 states and territories; 6 other countries; 3% are from out of state; 8% Black or African American, non-Hispanic/Latino; 2% Hispanic/Latino; 0.9% Asian, non-Hispanic/Latino; 0.1% Native Hawaiian or other Pacific Islander, non-Hispanic/Latino; 0.2% American Indian or Alaska Native, non-Hispanic/Latino; 2% Two or more races, non-Hispanic/Latino; 3% Race/ethnicity unknown; 0.4% international; 7% transferred in. *Retention:* 54% of full-time freshmen returned.

Freshmen *Admission:* 429 applied, 427 admitted, 272 enrolled. *Average high school GPA:* 2.82. *Test scores:* ACT scores over 18: 63%; ACT scores over 24: 10%.

Faculty *Total:* 106, 49% full-time. *Student/faculty ratio:* 26:1.

Majors Accounting technology and bookkeeping; administrative assistant and secretarial science; business administration and management; business/commerce; computer programming (specific applications); criminal justice/safety; electrical and electronic engineering technologies related; emergency medical technology (EMT paramedic); English; environmental engineering technology; general studies; health/health-care administration; industrial production technologies related; industrial technology; legal assistant/paralegal; liberal arts and sciences and humanities related; mechanical engineering/mechanical technology; psychology; public health; registered nursing/registered nurse; speech communication and rhetoric; urban forestry.

Academics *Calendar:* semesters. *Degrees:* associate, bachelor's, and master's (also offers some upper-level and graduate courses). *Special study options:* academic remediation for entering students, adult/continuing education programs, advanced placement credit, distance learning, double majors, freshman honors college, honors programs, independent study, internships, part-time degree program, services for LD students, student-designed majors, summer session for credit. *ROTC:* Army (c), Air Force (c).

Library Gelbke Library at Kent State Trumbull. *Books:* 40,000 (physical), 100,000 (digital/electronic); *Serial titles:* 40 (physical); *Databases:* 459. Weekly public service hours: 56.

Student Life *Housing:* college housing not available. *Activities and Organizations:* drama/theater group, The National Society for Leadership and Success, Sigma Alpha Pi, Jurisprudence Organization, Student Nurses Association, Pride Alliance, S.E.E.D.S.. *Campus security:* 24-hour emergency response devices, late-night transport/escort service, patrols by trained security personnel during hours of operation. *Student services:* personal/psychological counseling.

Standardized Tests *Recommended:* SAT or ACT (for admission).

Costs (2016–17) *One-time required fee:* $150. *Tuition:* state resident $5664 full-time, $258 per credit hour part-time; nonresident $14,028 full-time, $620 per credit hour part-time. Full-time tuition and fees vary according to course level and course load. Part-time tuition and fees vary according to course level and course load. *Payment plan:* installment. *Waivers:* senior citizens and employees or children of employees.

Financial Aid Of all full-time matriculated undergraduates who enrolled in 2016, 758 applied for aid, 655 were judged to have need, 39 had their need fully met. In 2016, 46 non-need-based awards were made. *Average percent of need met:* 57%. *Average financial aid package:* $7387. *Average need-based loan:* $3851. *Average need-based gift aid:* $4655. *Average non-need-based aid:* $1468.

Applying *Options:* electronic application, deferred entrance. *Application fee:* $40. *Required:* high school transcript. *Application deadlines:* 8/15 (freshmen), 8/15 (transfers). *Notification:* continuous (freshmen), continuous (transfers).

Freshman Application Contact Office of Enrollment Management, Kent State University at Trumbull, 4314 Mahoning Avenue, NW, Warren, OH 44483-1998. *Phone:* 330-675-8860. *E-mail:* trumbullinfo@kent.edu. *Website:* http://www.trumbull.kent.edu/.

Kent State University at Tuscarawas
New Philadelphia, Ohio

- **State-supported** primarily 2-year, founded 1962, part of Kent State University System
- **Small-town** 180-acre campus with easy access to Akron, Canton
- **Coed,** 2,035 undergraduate students, 60% full-time, 58% women, 42% men

Undergraduates 1,226 full-time, 809 part-time. Students come from 5 states and territories; 3 other countries; 2% are from out of state; 3% Black or African American, non-Hispanic/Latino; 2% Hispanic/Latino; 1% Asian, non-Hispanic/Latino; 0.0% Native Hawaiian or other Pacific Islander, non-Hispanic/Latino; 0.2% American Indian or Alaska Native, non-Hispanic/Latino; 2% Two or more races, non-Hispanic/Latino; 3% Race/ethnicity unknown; 0.2% international; 6% transferred in. *Retention:* 69% of full-time freshmen returned.

Freshmen *Admission:* 390 applied, 388 admitted, 267 enrolled. *Average high school GPA:* 2.98. *Test scores:* SAT writing scores over 500: 50%; ACT scores over 18: 76%; ACT scores over 24: 17%; ACT scores over 30: 1%.

Faculty *Total:* 119, 39% full-time. *Student/faculty ratio:* 22:1.

Majors Accounting technology and bookkeeping; administrative assistant and secretarial science; agribusiness; business administration and management; business/commerce; CAD/CADD drafting/design technology; computer programming (specific applications); criminal justice/safety; early childhood education; education related; electrical and electronic engineering technologies related; engineering technology; English; general studies; industrial technology; liberal arts and sciences and humanities related; mechanical engineering/mechanical technology; psychology; registered nursing/registered nurse; speech communication and rhetoric; veterinary/animal health technology.

Academics *Calendar:* semesters. *Degrees:* certificates, diplomas, associate, and bachelor's (also offers some upper-level and graduate courses). *Special study options:* academic remediation for entering students, accelerated degree program, adult/continuing education programs, advanced placement credit, distance learning, double majors, freshman honors college, independent study, internships, part-time degree program, services for LD students, student-designed majors, study abroad, summer session for credit. *ROTC:* Army (c), Air Force (c).

Library Kent State Tuscarawas Library. *Books:* 52,500 (physical), 12 (digital/electronic); *Serial titles:* 540 (physical).

Student Life *Housing:* college housing not available. *Activities and Organizations:* choral group, Student Nurses Association, Technology Club, Vet Tech Student Chapter, Realms of Roleplay, Vision. *Campus security:* 24-hour emergency response devices.

Athletics Member USCAA. *Intercollegiate sports:* baseball M, basketball M/W, cross-country running M/W, golf M, soccer M/W, softball W, track and field M/W, volleyball W, wrestling M. *Intramural sports:* bowling M/W.

Standardized Tests *Recommended:* SAT or ACT (for admission).

Costs (2016–17) *One-time required fee:* $150. *Tuition:* state resident $5664 full-time, $258 per credit hour part-time; nonresident $14,028 full-time, $620 per credit hour part-time. Full-time tuition and fees vary according to course level and course load. Part-time tuition and fees vary according to course level and course load. *Payment plan:* installment. *Waivers:* senior citizens and employees or children of employees.

Financial Aid Of all full-time matriculated undergraduates who enrolled in 2016, 639 applied for aid, 538 were judged to have need, 52 had their need fully met. In 2016, 6 non-need-based awards were made. *Average percent of need met:* 59%. *Average financial aid package:* $6682. *Average need-based loan:* $3737. *Average need-based gift aid:* $4331. *Average non-need-based aid:* $2977.

Applying *Options:* electronic application, deferred entrance. *Application fee:* $40. *Required:* high school transcript. *Application deadlines:* 8/15 (freshmen), 8/15 (transfers). *Notification:* continuous (freshmen), continuous (transfers).

Freshman Application Contact Office of Admissions, Kent State University at Tuscarawas, 330 University Drive NE, New Philadelphia, OH 44663-9403. *Phone:* 330-339-3391. *E-mail:* infotusc@kent.edu. *Website:* http://www.tusc.kent.edu/.

Lakeland Community College
Kirtland, Ohio

- **State and locally supported** 2-year, founded 1967, part of Ohio Department of Higher Education
- **Suburban** 380-acre campus with easy access to Cleveland
- **Endowment** $35,367
- **Coed,** 7,997 undergraduate students, 32% full-time, 58% women, 42% men

Undergraduates 2,557 full-time, 5,440 part-time. Students come from 6 states and territories; 14% Black or African American, non-Hispanic/Latino; 3% Hispanic/Latino; 1% Asian, non-Hispanic/Latino; 0.1% Native Hawaiian or other Pacific Islander, non-Hispanic/Latino; 0.3% American Indian or Alaska Native, non-Hispanic/Latino; 2% Two or more races, non-Hispanic/Latino; 3% Race/ethnicity unknown; 0.1% international; 5% transferred in.

Freshmen *Admission:* 957 enrolled.

Faculty *Total:* 405, 25% full-time. *Student/faculty ratio:* 17:1.

Majors Accounting; administrative assistant and secretarial science; biotechnology; business administration and management; child-care provision; civil engineering technology; clinical/medical laboratory technology; commercial and advertising art; computer engineering technology; computer programming (specific applications); computer systems analysis; computer systems networking and telecommunications; computer technology/computer systems technology; corrections; criminal justice/police science; dental hygiene; electrical, electronic and communications engineering technology; energy management and systems technology; fire prevention and safety technology; health professions related; homeland security, law enforcement, firefighting and protective services related; hospitality administration; instrumentation technology; legal assistant/paralegal; liberal arts and sciences/liberal studies; management information systems; marketing/marketing management; mechanical engineering/mechanical technology; medical radiologic technology; nuclear medical technology; ophthalmic technology; quality control technology; registered nursing/registered nurse; respiratory care therapy; restaurant, culinary, and catering management; sign language interpretation and translation; social work; surgical technology; tourism and travel services management.

Academics *Calendar:* semesters. *Degree:* certificates and associate. *Special study options:* academic remediation for entering students, adult/continuing education programs, advanced placement credit, cooperative education, distance learning, English as a second language, external degree program, independent study, internships, off-campus study, part-time degree program, services for LD students, study abroad, summer session for credit.

Library Lakeland Community College Library.

Student Life *Housing:* college housing not available. *Activities and Organizations:* drama/theater group, student-run newspaper, radio station, choral group, Campus Activities Board, Lakeland Student Government, Lakeland Signers, Gamer's Guild. *Campus security:* 24-hour emergency response devices and patrols, student patrols, late-night transport/escort service. *Student services:* health clinic, personal/psychological counseling, women's center.

Athletics Member NJCAA. *Intercollegiate sports:* baseball M(s), basketball M(s)/W(s), golf M(s), soccer M(s), softball W(s), volleyball W(s).

Standardized Tests *Required:* ACT Compass (for admission).

Costs (2017–18) *Tuition:* area resident $3287 full-time, $110 per credit hour part-time; state resident $4136 full-time, $138 per credit hour part-time; nonresident $9176 full-time, $306 per credit hour part-time. Full-time tuition and fees vary according to course load. Part-time tuition and fees vary according to course load. *Required fees:* $29 full-time, $14 per term part-time. *Payment plan:* installment. *Waivers:* senior citizens and employees or children of employees.

Financial Aid Of all full-time matriculated undergraduates who enrolled in 2015, 3,430 applied for aid, 2,959 were judged to have need, 469 had their need fully met. 63 Federal Work-Study jobs (averaging $3489). *Average percent of need met:* 56%. *Average financial aid package:* $7024. *Average need-based loan:* $3232. *Average need-based gift aid:* $5250.

Applying *Options:* electronic application, early admission, deferred entrance. *Application fee:* $15. *Required:* high school transcript. *Application deadlines:* 9/1 (freshmen), 9/1 (transfers). *Notification:* continuous until 9/1 (freshmen), continuous until 9/1 (transfers).

Freshman Application Contact Lakeland Community College, 7700 Clocktower Drive, Kirtland, OH 44094-5198. *Phone:* 440-525-7230. *Toll-free phone:* 800-589-8520.

Website: http://www.lakelandcc.edu/.

Lorain County Community College
Elyria, Ohio

- **State and locally supported** 2-year, founded 1963, part of University System of Ohio
- **Suburban** 280-acre campus with easy access to Cleveland
- **Coed,** 11,548 undergraduate students, 28% full-time, 61% women, 39% men

Undergraduates 3,199 full-time, 8,349 part-time. Students come from 27 states and territories; 37 other countries; 1% are from out of state; 10% Black or African American, non-Hispanic/Latino; 10% Hispanic/Latino; 1% Asian, non-Hispanic/Latino; 0.1% Native Hawaiian or other Pacific Islander, non-Hispanic/Latino; 0.4% American Indian or Alaska Native, non-Hispanic/Latino; 4% Two or more races, non-Hispanic/Latino; 1% Race/ethnicity unknown; 0.8% international; 4% transferred in. *Retention:* 67% of full-time freshmen returned.

Freshmen *Admission:* 1,533 enrolled.

Majors Accounting; agroecology and sustainable agriculture; building/construction site management; business administration and management; clinical/medical laboratory technology; computer engineering technologies related; computer engineering technology; computer programming related; computer systems networking and telecommunications; computer technology/computer systems technology; construction engineering technology; corrections; criminal justice/police science; culinary arts; dental hygiene; diagnostic medical sonography and ultrasound technology; early childhood education; education (multiple levels); electrical and power transmission installation; electrical, electronic and communications engineering technology; emergency medical technology (EMT paramedic); energy management and systems technology; entrepreneurship; fire science/firefighting; human resources management; liberal arts and sciences/liberal studies; manufacturing engineering technology; mechatronics, robotics, and automation engineering; medical/clinical assistant; medical radiologic technology; occupational therapist assistant; physical therapy technology; public administration; registered nursing/registered nurse; social work; solar energy technology; sport and fitness administration/management; surgical technology; tourism and travel services management; web page, digital/multimedia and information resources design; welding technology.

Academics *Calendar:* semesters. *Degree:* certificates and associate. *Special study options:* academic remediation for entering students, adult/continuing education programs, advanced placement credit, cooperative education, distance learning, double majors, English as a second language, honors programs, independent study, internships, part-time degree program, services for LD students, student-designed majors, study abroad, summer session for credit.

Library Learning Resource Center. *Books:* 100,830 (physical), 527 (digital/electronic); *Serial titles:* 1,287 (physical). Weekly public service hours: 57; students can reserve study rooms.

Student Life *Housing:* college housing not available. *Activities and Organizations:* drama/theater group, student-run newspaper, radio and television station, choral group, Phi Theta Kappa, Black Progressives, Los Unidos, Student Nurses Association, Student Dental Hygienist Club. *Campus security:* 24-hour emergency response devices and patrols, late-night transport/escort service. *Student services:* health clinic, personal/psychological counseling, women's center, legal services.

Athletics Member NJCAA. *Intercollegiate sports:* baseball M, basketball M/W, cross-country running M/W, soccer M(c)/W(c), softball W, tennis M(c)/W(c), volleyball W. *Intramural sports:* bowling M/W, football M/W, golf M/W, table tennis M/W, weight lifting M/W.

Costs (2016–17) *Tuition:* area resident $2796 full-time, $108 per credit hour part-time; state resident $3398 full-time, $131 per credit hour part-time; nonresident $7021 full-time, $270 per credit hour part-time. No tuition increase for student's term of enrollment. *Required fees:* $281 full-time, $11 per credit hour part-time. *Payment plans:* installment, deferred payment. *Waivers:* senior citizens and employees or children of employees.

Financial Aid Of all full-time matriculated undergraduates who enrolled in 2015, 2,379 applied for aid, 1,937 were judged to have need, 81 had their need fully met. 96 Federal Work-Study jobs (averaging $1978). In 2015, 223 non-need-based awards were made. *Average percent of need met:* 55%. *Average financial aid package:* $5248. *Average need-based loan:* $3125. *Average need-based gift aid:* $4523. *Average non-need-based aid:* $3048.

Applying *Options:* electronic application. *Required for some:* high school transcript. *Application deadlines:* rolling (freshmen), rolling (transfers). *Notification:* continuous (freshmen), continuous (transfers).

Freshman Application Contact Lorain County Community College, 1005 Abbe Road, North, Elyria, OH 44035. *Phone:* 440-366-7622. *Toll-free phone:* 800-995-5222 Ext. 4032.

Website: http://www.lorainccc.edu/.

Marion Technical College
Marion, Ohio

Freshman Application Contact Mr. Joel Liles, Dean of Enrollment Services, Marion Technical College, 1467 Mount Vernon Avenue, Marion, OH 43302. *Phone:* 740-389-4636 Ext. 249. *Fax:* 740-389-6136. *E-mail:* enroll@mtc.edu. *Website:* http://www.mtc.edu/.

Miami University Middletown
Middletown, Ohio

Freshman Application Contact Diane Cantonwine, Assistant Director of Admission and Financial Aid, Miami University Middletown, 4200 East University Boulevard, Middletown, OH 45042-3497. *Phone:* 513-727-3346. *Toll-free phone:* 866-426-4643. *Fax:* 513-727-3223. *E-mail:* cantondm@muohio.edu. *Website:* http://regionals.miamioh.edu/.

North Central State College
Mansfield, Ohio

Freshman Application Contact Ms. Nikia L. Fletcher, Director of Admissions, North Central State College, 2441 Kenwood Circle, PO Box 698, Mansfield, OH 44901-0698. *Phone:* 419-755-4813. *Toll-free phone:* 888-755-4899. *E-mail:* nfletcher@ncstatecollege.edu. *Website:* http://www.ncstatecollege.edu/.

Northwest State Community College
Archbold, Ohio

Freshman Application Contact Mrs. Amanda Potts, Director of Admissions, Northwest State Community College, 22600 State Route 34, Archbold, OH 43502. *Phone:* 419-267-1364. *Toll-free phone:* 855-267-5511. *Fax:* 419-267-3688. *E-mail:* apotts@northweststate.edu. *Website:* http://www.northweststate.edu/.

Ohio Business College
Hilliard, Ohio

Freshman Application Contact Ohio Business College, 4525 Trueman Boulevard, Hilliard, OH 43026. *Toll-free phone:* 800-954-4274. *Website:* http://www.ohiobusinesscollege.edu/.

Ohio Business College
Sandusky, Ohio

Freshman Application Contact Ohio Business College, 5202 Timber Commons Drive, Sandusky, OH 44870. *Phone:* 419-627-8345. *Toll-free phone:* 888-627-8345. *Website:* http://www.ohiobusinesscollege.edu/.

Ohio Business College
Sheffield Village, Ohio

- **Proprietary** 2-year, founded 1903, part of Tri State Educational Systems
- **Suburban** campus with easy access to Cleveland
- **Coed**

Academics *Calendar:* quarters. *Degree:* diplomas and associate. *Special study options:* academic remediation for entering students, accelerated degree program, adult/continuing education programs, advanced placement credit, double majors, external degree program, independent study, internships, part-time degree program, summer session for credit.
Library Ohio Business College Library.
Applying *Options:* electronic application. *Application fee:* $25. *Required:* high school transcript, interview.
Freshman Application Contact Ohio Business College, 5095 Waterford Drive, Sheffield Village, OH 44035. *Toll-free phone:* 888-514-3126. *Website:* http://www.ohiobusinesscollege.edu/.

The Ohio State University Agricultural Technical Institute
Wooster, Ohio

- **State-supported** 2-year, founded 1971, part of The Ohio State University
- **Small-town** 1942-acre campus with easy access to Cleveland, Columbus, Akron, Canton
- **Coed,** 772 undergraduate students, 94% full-time, 51% women, 49% men

Undergraduates 722 full-time, 50 part-time. Students come from 9 states and territories; 2% are from out of state; 4% transferred in. *Retention:* 64% of full-time freshmen returned.
Freshmen *Admission:* 622 applied, 534 admitted, 359 enrolled. *Test scores:* ACT scores over 18: 57%; ACT scores over 24: 11%.
Faculty *Total:* 70, 47% full-time, 33% with terminal degrees. *Student/faculty ratio:* 17:1.
Majors Agribusiness; agricultural business and management; agricultural business technology; agricultural communication/journalism; agricultural economics; agricultural mechanization; agricultural power machinery operation; agricultural teacher education; agronomy and crop science; animal/livestock husbandry and production; animal sciences; biology/biotechnology laboratory technician; building/construction site management; construction engineering technology; construction management; crop production; dairy husbandry and production; dairy science; environmental science; equestrian studies; floriculture/floristry management; greenhouse management; heavy equipment maintenance technology; horse husbandry/equine science and management; horticultural science; hydraulics and fluid power technology; industrial technology; landscaping and groundskeeping; livestock management; natural resources management and policy; natural resources management and policy related; plant nursery management; soil science and agronomy; turf and turfgrass management.
Academics *Calendar:* semesters. *Degree:* certificates, diplomas, and associate. *Special study options:* academic remediation for entering students, accelerated degree program, adult/continuing education programs, advanced placement credit, cooperative education, distance learning, double majors, independent study, internships, off-campus study, part-time degree program, services for LD students, student-designed majors, study abroad. *ROTC:* Army (c), Navy (c), Air Force (c).
Library Agricultural Technical Institute Library plus 1 other.
Student Life *Housing:* on-campus residence required for freshman year. *Options:* coed, special housing for students with disabilities. Campus housing is university owned. *Activities and Organizations:* Hoof-n-Hide Club, Collegiate FFA, Campus Crusade for Christ, Phi Theta Kappa, Community Council. *Campus security:* 24-hour emergency response devices and patrols, controlled dormitory access. *Student services:* personal/psychological counseling.
Athletics *Intramural sports:* archery M/W, badminton M/W, basketball M/W, bowling M/W, football M/W, racquetball M/W, soccer M/W, softball M/W, volleyball M/W, weight lifting M/W.
Standardized Tests *Required for some:* SAT or ACT (for admission).
Costs (2016–17) *Tuition:* state resident $7104 full-time, $296 per credit hour part-time; nonresident $24,432 full-time, $1018 per credit hour part-time. Full-time tuition and fees vary according to course load, location, and program. Part-time tuition and fees vary according to course load, location, and program. *Room and board:* $7330; room only: $6530. Room and board charges vary according to board plan and location. *Payment plan:* installment. *Waivers:* senior citizens and employees or children of employees.
Financial Aid Of all full-time matriculated undergraduates who enrolled in 2010, 540 applied for aid, 474 were judged to have need, 25 had their need fully met. 64 Federal Work-Study jobs (averaging $2000). In 2010, 24 non-need-based awards were made. *Average percent of need met:* 44%. *Average financial aid package:* $6859. *Average need-based loan:* $3826. *Average need-based gift aid:* $4241. *Average non-need-based aid:* $2107.
Applying *Options:* electronic application. *Application fee:* $60. *Required:* high school transcript. *Application deadlines:* 6/1 (freshmen), 6/1 (transfers). *Notification:* continuous (freshmen).
Freshman Application Contact Ms. Julia Morris, Admissions Counselor, The Ohio State University Agricultural Technical Institute, 1328 Dover Road, Wooster, OH 44691. *Phone:* 330-287-1327. *Toll-free phone:* 800-647-8283 Ext. 1327. *Fax:* 330-287-1333. *E-mail:* morris.878@osu.edu. *Website:* http://www.ati.osu.edu/.

Ohio Technical College
Cleveland, Ohio

- **Proprietary** 2-year, founded 1969
- **Urban** 18-acre campus
- **Coed**, 1,072 undergraduate students, 100% full-time, 5% women, 95% men

Undergraduates 1,072 full-time. Students come from 34 states and territories; 5 other countries; 47% are from out of state; 16% Black or African American, non-Hispanic/Latino; 7% Hispanic/Latino; 0.8% Asian, non-Hispanic/Latino; 0.6% American Indian or Alaska Native, non-Hispanic/Latino; 3% Two or more races, non-Hispanic/Latino; 1% Race/ethnicity unknown; 0.8% international. *Retention:* 74% of full-time freshmen returned.

Freshmen *Admission:* 334 enrolled.

Faculty *Total:* 53, 79% full-time. *Student/faculty ratio:* 20:1.

Majors Autobody/collision and repair technology; automobile/automotive mechanics technology; diesel mechanics technology; high performance and custom engine technology; mechanic and repair technologies related; vehicle maintenance and repair technologies; welding technology.

Academics *Degree:* certificates, diplomas, and associate. *Special study options:* services for LD students.

Library Ohio Technical College Library Resource Center. *Books:* 1,522 (physical); *Databases:* 6. Weekly public service hours: 40.

Student Life *Housing Options:* Campus housing is provided by a third party. *Campus security:* late-night transport/escort service. *Student services:* personal/psychological counseling.

Costs (2016–17) *Comprehensive fee:* $25,350 includes full-time tuition ($24,154) and room and board ($1196). Full-time tuition and fees vary according to program. No tuition increase for student's term of enrollment. *Room and board:* college room only: $848. *Payment plans:* tuition prepayment, installment.

Applying *Required:* high school transcript, interview.

Freshman Application Contact Ohio Technical College, 1374 East 51st Street, Cleveland, OH 44103. *Phone:* 216-881-1700. *Toll-free phone:* 800-322-7000. *Website:* http://www.ohiotech.edu/.

Ohio Valley College of Technology
East Liverpool, Ohio

Freshman Application Contact Mr. Scott S. Rogers, Director, Ohio Valley College of Technology, 15258 State Route 170, East Liverpool, OH 43920. *Phone:* 330-385-1070. *Website:* http://www.ovct.edu/.

Owens Community College
Toledo, Ohio

Freshman Application Contact Ms. Meghan L. Schmidbauer, Director, Admissions, Owens Community College, PO Box 10000, Toledo, OH 43699. *Phone:* 567-661-2155. *Toll-free phone:* 800-GO-OWENS. *Fax:* 567-661-7734. *E-mail:* meghan_schmidbauer@owens.edu. *Website:* http://www.owens.edu/.

Professional Skills Institute
Maumee, Ohio

Director of Admissions Ms. Hope Finch, Director of Marketing, Professional Skills Institute, 1505 Holland Road, Maumee, OH 43537. *Phone:* 419-531-9610. *Website:* http://www.proskills.edu/.

Remington College–Cleveland Campus
Cleveland, Ohio

Director of Admissions Director of Recruitment, Remington College–Cleveland Campus, 14445 Broadway Avenue, Cleveland, OH 44125. *Phone:* 216-475-7520. *Toll-free phone:* 800-323-8122. *Fax:* 216-475-6055. *Website:* http://www.remingtoncollege.edu/.

Rosedale Bible College
Irwin, Ohio

- **Independent Mennonite** 2-year, founded 1952
- **Rural** campus with easy access to Columbus
- **Coed**, 89 undergraduate students

Freshmen *Admission:* 86 applied, 70 admitted.

Faculty *Total:* 2. *Student/faculty ratio:* 14:1.

Majors Biblical studies.

Academics *Calendar:* 4-1-4. *Degree:* associate. *Special study options:* adult/continuing education programs, cooperative education, independent study, internships, off-campus study, part-time degree program, services for LD students, study abroad. *ROTC:* Army (c), Navy (c), Air Force (c).

Student Life *Housing Options:* men-only, women-only. Campus housing is university owned. *Activities and Organizations:* drama/theater group, choral group. *Student services:* personal/psychological counseling.

Costs (2017–18) *One-time required fee:* $50. *Comprehensive fee:* $14,381 includes full-time tuition ($8400), mandatory fees ($331), and room and board ($5650). Full-time tuition and fees vary according to course load. Part-time tuition: $280 per credit hour. *Required fees:* $70 per year part-time. *Room and board:* Room and board charges vary according to housing facility. *Payment plan:* installment. *Waivers:* senior citizens and employees or children of employees.

Applying *Options:* electronic application, early admission. *Application fee:* $50. *Required:* essay or personal statement, high school transcript, 2 letters of recommendation. *Application deadline:* rolling (freshmen).

Freshman Application Contact Rosedale Bible College, 2270 Rosedale Road, Irwin, OH 43029-9501. *Phone:* 740-857-1311. *Website:* http://www.rosedale.edu/.

Ross College
Canton, Ohio

Freshman Application Contact Ross College, 4300 Munson Street NW, Canton, OH 44718. *Phone:* 330-494-1214. *Toll-free phone:* 866-815-5578. *Website:* http://www.rosseducation.edu/.

School of Advertising Art
Kettering, Ohio

- **Proprietary** 2-year, founded 1983
- **Suburban** 5-acre campus with easy access to Columbus
- **Coed**, 197 undergraduate students, 98% full-time, 71% women, 29% men

Undergraduates 194 full-time, 3 part-time. Students come from 4 states and territories; 17% are from out of state; 6% Black or African American, non-Hispanic/Latino; 4% Hispanic/Latino; 2% Asian, non-Hispanic/Latino; 1% American Indian or Alaska Native, non-Hispanic/Latino; 0.5% Two or more races, non-Hispanic/Latino; 0.5% Race/ethnicity unknown; 3% transferred in. *Retention:* 76% of full-time freshmen returned.

Freshmen *Admission:* 339 applied, 222 admitted, 100 enrolled. *Average high school GPA:* 3.06.

Faculty *Total:* 21, 48% full-time, 5% with terminal degrees. *Student/faculty ratio:* 14:1.

Majors Commercial and advertising art.

Academics *Calendar:* semesters. *Degree:* associate.

Library SAA Library.

Student Life *Housing:* college housing not available. *Activities and Organizations:* Fine Art Club, Photography Club, Yoga Club. *Student services:* personal/psychological counseling.

Costs (2017–18) *Tuition:* $26,714 full-time. Full-time tuition and fees vary according to class time, course level, course load, degree level, location, program, reciprocity agreements, and student level. *Required fees:* $1000 full-time. *Payment plan:* installment. *Waivers:* employees or children of employees.

Applying *Options:* electronic application. *Required:* high school transcript, minimum 2.0 GPA, interview. *Required for some:* essay or personal statement, 2 letters of recommendation.

Freshman Application Contact Ms. Abigail Heaney, Housing and Marketing Coordinator, School of Advertising Art, 1725 East David Road, Kettering, OH 45440. *Phone:* 937-294-0592. *Toll-free phone:* 877-300-9866. *Fax:* 937-294-5869. *E-mail:* abbie@saa.edu. *Website:* http://www.saa.edu/.

Sinclair Community College
Dayton, Ohio

Freshman Application Contact Ms. Sara Smith, Director and Systems Manager, Outreach Services, Sinclair Community College, 444 West Third Street, Dayton, OH 45402-1460. *Phone:* 937-512-3060. *Toll-free phone:* 800-315-3000. *Fax:* 937-512-2393. *E-mail:* ssmith@sinclair.edu. *Website:* http://www.sinclair.edu/.

Southern State Community College
Hillsboro, Ohio

Freshman Application Contact Ms. Wendy Johnson, Director of Admissions, Southern State Community College, Hillsboro, OH 45133.

Phone: 937-393-3431 Ext. 2720. *Toll-free phone:* 800-628-7722. *Fax:* 937-393-6682. *E-mail:* wjohnson@sscc.edu. *Website:* http://www.sscc.edu/.

Stark State College
North Canton, Ohio

- **State-related** 2-year, founded 1960, part of University System of Ohio
- **Suburban** 100-acre campus with easy access to Cleveland
- **Endowment** $5.2 million
- **Coed,** 12,370 undergraduate students, 27% full-time, 57% women, 43% men

Undergraduates 3,356 full-time, 9,014 part-time. Students come from 21 states and territories; 1 other country; 1% are from out of state; 13% Black or African American, non-Hispanic/Latino; 1% Hispanic/Latino; 2% Asian, non-Hispanic/Latino; 0.1% Native Hawaiian or other Pacific Islander, non-Hispanic/Latino; 0.4% American Indian or Alaska Native, non-Hispanic/Latino; 3% Two or more races, non-Hispanic/Latino; 7% Race/ethnicity unknown; 7% transferred in.
Freshmen *Admission:* 1,772 enrolled. *Average high school GPA:* 2.35.
Faculty *Total:* 521, 35% full-time. *Student/faculty ratio:* 22:1.
Majors Accounting; accounting and finance; administrative assistant and secretarial science; biomedical technology; business administration and management; civil engineering technology; clinical/medical laboratory technology; computer and information sciences; computer programming (specific applications); computer systems networking and telecommunications; court reporting; dental hygiene; finance; health information/medical records administration; human services; industrial technology; legal administrative assistant/secretary; marketing/marketing management; mechanical engineering/mechanical technology; medical/clinical assistant; occupational therapy; operations management; physical therapy; registered nursing/registered nurse; respiratory care therapy; substance abuse/addiction counseling; web page, digital/multimedia and information resources design.
Academics *Calendar:* semesters. *Degree:* certificates and associate. *Special study options:* academic remediation for entering students, adult/continuing education programs, cooperative education, distance learning, double majors, external degree program, independent study, internships, off-campus study, part-time degree program, services for LD students, student-designed majors, summer session for credit.
Library Learning Resource Center plus 1 other.
Student Life *Housing:* college housing not available. *Activities and Organizations:* student-run newspaper, Phi Theta Kappa, Business Student Club, Institute of Management Accountants, Stark State College Association of Medical Assistants, Student Health Information Management Association. *Campus security:* 24-hour emergency response devices and patrols, student patrols, late-night transport/escort service, patrols by trained security personnel during hours of operation. *Student services:* personal/psychological counseling.
Costs (2017–18) *One-time required fee:* $95. *Tuition:* state resident $2796 full-time, $117 per credit hour part-time; nonresident $4980 full-time, $208 per credit hour part-time. Full-time tuition and fees vary according to course load and program. Part-time tuition and fees vary according to program. *Required fees:* $890 full-time, $37 per credit hour part-time, $30 per term part-time. *Payment plan:* installment. *Waivers:* senior citizens and employees or children of employees.
Financial Aid Of all full-time matriculated undergraduates who enrolled in 2014, 1,939 applied for aid, 1,697 were judged to have need, 6 had their need fully met. 74 Federal Work-Study jobs (averaging $2306). *Average need-based loan:* $2537. *Average need-based gift aid:* $4317.
Applying *Required:* high school transcript.
Freshman Application Contact J. P. Cooney, Executive Director to Recruitment, Admissions and Marketing, Stark State College, 6200 Frank Road NE, Canton, OH 44720. *Phone:* 330-494-6170 Ext. 4401. *Toll-free phone:* 800-797-8275. *E-mail:* info@starkstate.edu. *Website:* http://www.starkstate.edu/.

Stautzenberger College
Brecksville, Ohio

Admissions Office Contact Stautzenberger College, 8001 Katherine Boulevard, Brecksville, OH 44141. *Toll-free phone:* 800-437-2997. *Website:* http://www.sctoday.edu/.

Stautzenberger College
Maumee, Ohio

Director of Admissions Ms. Karen Fitzgerald, Director of Admissions and Marketing, Stautzenberger College, 1796 Indian Wood Circle, Maumee, OH 43537. *Phone:* 419-866-0261. *Toll-free phone:* 800-552-5099. *Fax:* 419-867-

9821. *E-mail:* klfitzgerald@stautzenberger.com.
Website: http://www.sctoday.edu/maumee/.

Terra State Community College
Fremont, Ohio

Freshman Application Contact Mr. Heath Martin, Director of Admissions and Enrollment Services, Terra State Community College, 2830 Napoleon Road, Fremont, OH 43420. *Phone:* 419-559-2154. *Toll-free phone:* 866-AT-TERRA. *Fax:* 419-559-2352. *Website:* http://www.terra.edu/.

Trumbull Business College
Warren, Ohio

- **Proprietary** 2-year, founded 1972
- **Small-town** 6-acre campus with easy access to Cleveland and Youngstown, OH; Pittsburgh, PA
- **Coed**

Undergraduates 103 full-time, 56 part-time. Students come from 3 states and territories; 2% are from out of state; 23% Black or African American, non-Hispanic/Latino; 1% Hispanic/Latino; 3% Two or more races, non-Hispanic/Latino; 8% transferred in. *Retention:* 43% of full-time freshmen returned.
Faculty *Student/faculty ratio:* 10:1.
Academics *Calendar:* quarters. *Degree:* certificates, diplomas, and associate. *Special study options:* academic remediation for entering students, adult/continuing education programs, advanced placement credit, distance learning, part-time degree program, summer session for credit.
Financial Aid Of all full-time matriculated undergraduates who enrolled in 2015, 2 Federal Work-Study jobs. *Financial aid deadline:* 9/30.
Applying *Application fee:* $75. *Required:* high school transcript, interview.
Freshman Application Contact Trumbull Business College, 3200 Ridge Avenue SE, Warren, OH 44484. *Phone:* 330-369-6792. *Toll-free phone:* 888-766-1598. *Website:* http://www.trumbull.edu/.

The University of Akron Wayne College
Orrville, Ohio

Freshman Application Contact Ms. Alicia Broadus, Student Services Counselor, The University of Akron Wayne College, Orrville, OH 44667. *Phone:* 800-221-8308 Ext. 8901. *Toll-free phone:* 800-221-8308. *Fax:* 330-684-8989. *E-mail:* wayneadmissions@uakron.edu. *Website:* http://www.wayne.uakron.edu/.

University of Cincinnati Blue Ash College
Cincinnati, Ohio

- **State-supported** primarily 2-year, founded 1967, part of Ohio Department of Higher Education
- **Suburban** 120-acre campus with easy access to Cincinnati
- **Endowment** $457,000
- **Coed,** 5,065 undergraduate students, 64% full-time, 58% women, 42% men

Undergraduates 3,241 full-time, 1,824 part-time. Students come from 9 states and territories; 12 other countries; 3% are from out of state; 21% Black or African American, non-Hispanic/Latino; 3% Hispanic/Latino; 3% Asian, non-Hispanic/Latino; 0.1% Native Hawaiian or other Pacific Islander, non-Hispanic/Latino; 0.3% American Indian or Alaska Native, non-Hispanic/Latino; 3% Two or more races, non-Hispanic/Latino; 7% Race/ethnicity unknown; 2% international; 11% transferred in. *Retention:* 64% of full-time freshmen returned.
Freshmen *Admission:* 1,301 enrolled. *Average high school GPA:* 2.73.
Faculty *Total:* 339, 50% full-time. *Student/faculty ratio:* 16:1.
Majors Accounting technology and bookkeeping; business administration and management; business administration, management and operations related; business/commerce; chemical technology; commercial and advertising art; computer technology/computer systems technology; criminal justice/safety; dental hygiene; education; executive assistant/executive secretary; general studies; health/medical preparatory programs related; kindergarten/preschool education; liberal arts and sciences/liberal studies; library and information science; medical administrative assistant and medical secretary; medical/clinical assistant; medical radiologic technology; photographic and film/video technology; pre-law studies; pre-pharmacy studies; psychology; public health education and promotion; real estate; registered nursing/registered nurse; retailing; science technologies related; secondary

education; social work; speech communication and rhetoric; veterinary/animal health technology.

Academics *Calendar:* semesters. *Degrees:* certificates, associate, bachelor's, and postbachelor's certificates. *Special study options:* academic remediation for entering students, adult/continuing education programs, advanced placement credit, distance learning, double majors, off-campus study, part-time degree program, services for LD students, study abroad, summer session for credit. *ROTC:* Army (c), Air Force (c).

Library UC Blue Ash College Library. *Books:* 19,690 (physical). Weekly public service hours: 50; students can reserve study rooms.

Student Life *Housing:* college housing not available. *Campus security:* 24-hour emergency response devices and patrols, student patrols, late-night transport/escort service. *Student services:* personal/psychological counseling.

Costs (2017–18) *Tuition:* state resident $6010 full-time, $251 per credit hour part-time; nonresident $14,808 full-time, $617 per credit hour part-time. Full-time tuition and fees vary according to course load, degree level, location, program, and reciprocity agreements. Part-time tuition and fees vary according to course load, degree level, location, and reciprocity agreements. *Required fees:* $736 full-time. *Payment plan:* installment. *Waivers:* senior citizens and employees or children of employees.

Financial Aid Of all full-time matriculated undergraduates who enrolled in 2015, 285 Federal Work-Study jobs (averaging $2903).

Applying *Options:* electronic application, deferred entrance. *Application fee:* $50. *Required:* high school transcript. *Application deadlines:* rolling (freshmen), rolling (transfers). *Notification:* continuous (freshmen), continuous (transfers).

Freshman Application Contact University of Cincinnati Blue Ash College, 9555 Plainfield Road, Cincinnati, OH 45236-1007. *Phone:* 513-745-5700. *Website:* http://www.ucblueash.edu/.

University of Cincinnati Clermont College
Batavia, Ohio

- **State-supported** primarily 2-year, founded 1972, part of University of Cincinnati System
- **Rural** 91-acre campus with easy access to Cincinnati
- **Coed,** 2,883 undergraduate students, 55% full-time, 57% women, 43% men

Undergraduates 1,595 full-time, 1,288 part-time. 4% are from out of state; 2% Black or African American, non-Hispanic/Latino; 3% Hispanic/Latino; 1% Asian, non-Hispanic/Latino; 0.1% Native Hawaiian or other Pacific Islander, non-Hispanic/Latino; 0.2% American Indian or Alaska Native, non-Hispanic/Latino; 2% Two or more races, non-Hispanic/Latino; 9% Race/ethnicity unknown; 0.3% international. *Retention:* 61% of full-time freshmen returned.

Freshmen *Admission:* 1,255 applied, 606 admitted, 606 enrolled. *Average high school GPA:* 2.93.

Faculty *Total:* 293, 32% full-time. *Student/faculty ratio:* 13:1.

Majors Accounting; aeronautics/aviation/aerospace science and technology; audiology and speech-language pathology; biology/biological sciences; business administration and management; business/commerce; chemistry; computer technology/computer systems technology; computer typography and composition equipment operation; criminal justice/safety; data processing and data processing technology; elementary education; environmental studies; general studies; health information/medical records technology; health professions related; information science/studies; kindergarten/preschool education; legal assistant/paralegal; liberal arts and sciences/liberal studies; manufacturing engineering technology; middle school education; multi/interdisciplinary studies related; organizational behavior; physical therapy technology; pre-law studies; pre-pharmacy studies; psychology; respiratory care therapy; science technologies related; secondary education; social sciences; social work; special education; sport and fitness administration/management; surgical technology.

Academics *Calendar:* semesters. *Degrees:* certificates, associate, bachelor's, and postbachelor's certificates. *Special study options:* academic remediation for entering students, adult/continuing education programs, advanced placement credit, cooperative education, distance learning, double majors, independent study, internships, off-campus study, part-time degree program, services for LD students, student-designed majors, study abroad, summer session for credit. *ROTC:* Army (c).

Library UC Clermont College Library. Students can reserve study rooms.

Student Life *Housing:* college housing not available. *Activities and Organizations:* student-run newspaper, Active Minds, PACE (Professionalism Academics Character Experiences), Phi Theta Kappa, Association of Paralegal Students, Cheerleading. *Campus security:* 24-hour emergency response devices and patrols. *Student services:* personal/psychological counseling.

Athletics Member USCAA. *Intercollegiate sports:* baseball M, basketball M/W, cheerleading W, soccer M/W, softball W, volleyball W.

Costs (2016–17) *Tuition:* state resident $5316 full-time, $222 per credit part-time; nonresident $12,548 full-time, $523 per credit part-time. Full-time tuition and fees vary according to course level, degree level, program, and reciprocity agreements. Part-time tuition and fees vary according to course level, degree level, program, and reciprocity agreements. *Payment plan:* installment. *Waivers:* senior citizens and employees or children of employees.

Applying *Options:* electronic application, deferred entrance. *Application fee:* $50. *Required:* high school transcript. *Application deadlines:* 7/11 (freshmen), 7/11 (transfers). *Notification:* continuous (freshmen), continuous (transfers).

Freshman Application Contact Mrs. Jamie Adkins, University Services Associate, University of Cincinnati Clermont College, 4200 Clermont College Drive, Batavia, OH 45103. *Phone:* 513-732-5294. *Toll-free phone:* 866-446-2822. *Fax:* 513-732-5303. *E-mail:* jamie.adkins@uc.edu. *Website:* http://www.ucclermont.edu/.

Vatterott College
Broadview Heights, Ohio

Director of Admissions Mr. Jack Chalk, Director of Admissions, Vatterott College, 5025 East Royalton Road, Broadview Heights, OH 44147. *Phone:* 440-526-1660. *Toll-free phone:* 888-553-6627. *Website:* http://www.vatterott.edu/.

Vet Tech Institute at Bradford School
Columbus, Ohio

- **Private** 2-year, founded 2005
- **Suburban** campus
- **Coed**
- **33%** of applicants were admitted

Academics *Calendar:* semesters. *Degree:* associate. *Special study options:* accelerated degree program, internships.

Freshman Application Contact Admissions Office, Vet Tech Institute at Bradford School, 2469 Stelzer Road, Columbus, OH 43219. *Phone:* 800-678-7981. *Toll-free phone:* 800-678-7981. *Website:* http://columbus.vettechinstitute.edu/.

Virginia Marti College of Art and Design
Lakewood, Ohio

- **Proprietary** primarily 2-year, founded 1966
- **Urban** campus with easy access to Cleveland
- **Coed,** 108 undergraduate students

Undergraduates Students come from 1 other state. *Retention:* 62% of full-time freshmen returned.

Freshmen *Admission:* 88 applied.

Faculty *Student/faculty ratio:* 12:1.

Majors Commercial and advertising art; digital communication and media/multimedia; fashion/apparel design; fashion merchandising; interior design.

Academics *Calendar:* quarters. *Degrees:* certificates, associate, and bachelor's. *Special study options:* academic remediation for entering students, adult/continuing education programs, distance learning, independent study, internships, part-time degree program, services for LD students, summer session for credit.

Library VMCAD Library.

Student Life *Housing:* college housing not available. *Campus security:* 24-hour emergency response devices. *Student services:* personal/psychological counseling.

Standardized Tests *Required:* SAT or ACT (for admission). *Required for some:* Wonderlic.

Costs (2017–18) *Tuition:* $420 per credit hour part-time. *Waivers:* employees or children of employees.

Applying *Options:* electronic application, early admission, deferred entrance. *Required:* essay or personal statement, high school transcript, minimum 2.0 GPA. *Required for some:* entrance evaluation test. *Recommended:* 1 letter of recommendation, interview. *Application deadlines:* rolling (freshmen), rolling (out-of-state freshmen), rolling (transfers).

Freshman Application Contact Regina Reihard, Admissions Representative, Virginia Marti College of Art and Design, 11724 Detroit Ave, Lakewood, OH 44107. *Phone:* 216-221-8584 Ext. 113. *E-mail:* rreihard@vmcad.edu. *Website:* http://www.vmcad.edu/.

Washington State Community College
Marietta, Ohio

Freshman Application Contact Ms. Rebecca Peroni, Director of Admissions, Washington State Community College, 110 Colegate Drive, Marietta, OH 45750. *Phone:* 740-374-8716. *Fax:* 740-376-0257.
E-mail: rperoni@wscc.edu. *Website:* http://www.wscc.edu/.

Zane State College
Zanesville, Ohio

Director of Admissions Mr. Paul Young, Director of Admissions, Zane State College, 1555 Newark Road, Zanesville, OH 43701-2626. *Phone:* 740-454-2501 Ext. 1225. *Toll-free phone:* 800-686-8324.
E-mail: pyoung@zanestate.edu. *Website:* http://www.zanestate.edu/.

OKLAHOMA

Carl Albert State College
Poteau, Oklahoma

- **State-supported** 2-year, founded 1934, part of Oklahoma State Regents for Higher Education
- **Small-town** 78-acre campus
- **Endowment** $5.7 million
- **Coed,** 2,194 undergraduate students, 60% full-time, 63% women, 37% men

Undergraduates 1,320 full-time, 874 part-time. Students come from 9 states and territories; 3% Black or African American, non-Hispanic/Latino; 7% Hispanic/Latino; 0.3% Asian, non-Hispanic/Latino; 25% American Indian or Alaska Native, non-Hispanic/Latino; 6% Two or more races, non-Hispanic/Latino; 1% Race/ethnicity unknown; 1% international; 12% live on campus.
Freshmen *Admission:* 586 enrolled.
Faculty *Student/faculty ratio:* 16:1.
Majors Biology/biological sciences; business administration and management; business/commerce; child development; computer and information sciences; elementary education; engineering; engineering technologies and engineering related; English; foods, nutrition, and wellness; health professions related; health services/allied health/health sciences; hotel/motel administration; management information systems; mathematics; physical education teaching and coaching; physical sciences; physical therapy technology; pre-law studies; registered nursing/registered nurse; rhetoric and composition; secondary education; social sciences; telecommunications technology.
Academics *Calendar:* semesters. *Degree:* certificates and associate. *Special study options:* academic remediation for entering students, adult/continuing education programs, cooperative education, part-time degree program.
Library Joe E. White Library.
Student Life *Housing Options:* men-only, women-only. Campus housing is university owned. *Activities and Organizations:* drama/theater group, student-run newspaper, radio station, choral group, Student Government Association, Phi Theta Kappa, Baptist Student Union, BACCHUS, Student Physical Therapist Assistant Association. *Campus security:* security guards. *Student services:* health clinic, personal/psychological counseling.
Athletics Member NJCAA. *Intercollegiate sports:* baseball M, basketball M(s)/W(s), softball M. *Intramural sports:* tennis M/W, volleyball M/W, weight lifting M.
Costs (2016–17) *Tuition:* state resident $1815 full-time, $113 per credit hour part-time; nonresident $3286 full-time, $235 per credit hour part-time. Full-time tuition and fees vary according to course load. Part-time tuition and fees vary according to course load. *Required fees:* $1274 full-time, $500 per term part-time. *Room and board:* $2111; room only: $1600. Room and board charges vary according to board plan. *Payment plan:* installment. *Waivers:* employees or children of employees.
Financial Aid Of all full-time matriculated undergraduates who enrolled in 2015, 112 Federal Work-Study jobs (averaging $2100).
Applying *Required:* high school transcript. *Notification:* continuous (freshmen), continuous (transfers).
Freshman Application Contact Carl Albert State College, 1507 South McKenna, Poteau, OK 74953-5208. *Phone:* 918-647-1301.
Website: http://www.carlalbert.edu/.

Clary Sage College
Tulsa, Oklahoma

- **Proprietary** 2-year, founded 2006
- **Urban** 6-acre campus with easy access to Tulsa
- **Coed, primarily women,** 406 undergraduate students, 100% full-time, 89% women, 11% men

Undergraduates 406 full-time. Students come from 9 states and territories; 3% are from out of state; 20% Black or African American, non-Hispanic/Latino; 5% Hispanic/Latino; 3% Asian, non-Hispanic/Latino; 0.5% Native Hawaiian or other Pacific Islander, non-Hispanic/Latino; 17% American Indian or Alaska Native, non-Hispanic/Latino; 4% Two or more races, non-Hispanic/Latino; 4% Race/ethnicity unknown; 58% transferred in.
Freshmen *Admission:* 334 enrolled.
Faculty *Total:* 28, 100% full-time. *Student/faculty ratio:* 15:1.
Academics *Calendar:* continuous. *Degree:* diplomas and associate. *Special study options:* adult/continuing education programs, distance learning, internships.
Student Life *Housing:* college housing not available. *Activities and Organizations:* Student Ambassadors. *Campus security:* security guard during hours of operation.
Costs (2017–18) *Tuition:* $12,987 full-time. Full-time tuition and fees vary according to class time, course level, course load, degree level, location, program, reciprocity agreements, and student level. Part-time tuition and fees vary according to class time, course level, location, reciprocity agreements, and student level. *Required fees:* $1233 full-time. *Payment plans:* tuition prepayment, installment. *Waivers:* employees or children of employees.
Applying *Options:* electronic application. *Application fee:* $100. *Required:* essay or personal statement, high school transcript, interview. *Application deadlines:* rolling (freshmen), rolling (transfers). *Notification:* continuous (freshmen), continuous (transfers).
Freshman Application Contact Dr. Raye Mahlberg, Campus Director, Clary Sage College, 3131 South Sheridan, Tulsa, OK 74145. *Phone:* 918-298-8200 Ext. 1025. *E-mail:* rmahlberg@clarysagecollege.com.
Website: http://www.clarysagecollege.com/.

College of the Muscogee Nation
Okmulgee, Oklahoma

Admissions Office Contact College of the Muscogee Nation, 2170 Raven Circle, Okmulgee, OK 74447-0917. *Website:* http://www.mvsktc.org/.

Community Care College
Tulsa, Oklahoma

- **Independent** 2-year, founded 1995
- **Urban** 6-acre campus with easy access to Tulsa
- **Coed, primarily women,** 623 undergraduate students, 100% full-time, 92% women, 8% men

Undergraduates 623 full-time. Students come from 18 states and territories; 4% are from out of state; 17% Black or African American, non-Hispanic/Latino; 7% Hispanic/Latino; 2% Asian, non-Hispanic/Latino; 0.2% Native Hawaiian or other Pacific Islander, non-Hispanic/Latino; 19% American Indian or Alaska Native, non-Hispanic/Latino; 3% Two or more races, non-Hispanic/Latino; 2% Race/ethnicity unknown.
Freshmen *Admission:* 512 enrolled.
Faculty *Total:* 26, 92% full-time, 12% with terminal degrees. *Student/faculty ratio:* 25:1.
Majors Accounting technology and bookkeeping; business administration, management and operations related; dental assisting; early childhood education; health and physical education/fitness; health/health-care administration; legal assistant/paralegal; medical/clinical assistant; medical insurance coding; pharmacy technician; surgical technology; veterinary/animal health technology.
Academics *Calendar:* continuous. *Degree:* diplomas and associate. *Special study options:* adult/continuing education programs, distance learning, independent study, internships, services for LD students.
Student Life *Housing:* college housing not available. *Activities and Organizations:* Student Ambassadors. *Campus security:* campus security personnel during school hours.
Costs (2017–18) *Tuition:* $13,175 full-time. Full-time tuition and fees vary according to class time, course level, course load, degree level, location, program, and reciprocity agreements. Part-time tuition and fees vary according to class time, course level, location, and reciprocity agreements. *Required fees:* $1062 full-time. *Payment plans:* tuition prepayment, installment. *Waivers:* employees or children of employees.
Applying *Options:* electronic application. *Required:* essay or personal statement, high school transcript, interview. *Required for some:* 1 letter of

recommendation. *Application deadline:* rolling (freshmen). *Notification:* continuous (freshmen).
Freshman Application Contact Dr. Kevin Kirk, President, Community Care College, 4242 South Sheridan, Tulsa, OK 74145. *Phone:* 918-610-0027 Ext. 2003. *Fax:* 918-610-0029. *E-mail:* kkirk@communitycarecollege.edu. *Website:* http://www.communitycarecollege.edu/.

Connors State College
Warner, Oklahoma

Freshman Application Contact Ms. Sonya Baker, Registrar, Connors State College, Route 1 Box 1000, Warner, OK 74469-9700. *Phone:* 918-463-6233. *Website:* http://www.connorsstate.edu/.

Eastern Oklahoma State College
Wilburton, Oklahoma

Freshman Application Contact Ms. Leah McLaughlin, Director of Admissions, Eastern Oklahoma State College, 1301 West Main, Wilburton, OK 74578-4999. *Phone:* 918-465-1811. *Toll-free phone:* 855-534-3672. *Fax:* 918-465-2431. *E-mail:* lmiller@eosc.edu. *Website:* http://www.eosc.edu/.

Murray State College
Tishomingo, Oklahoma

- **State-supported** 2-year, founded 1908, part of Oklahoma State Regents for Higher Education
- **Rural** 120-acre campus
- **Coed,** 2,674 undergraduate students, 49% full-time, 70% women, 30% men

Undergraduates 1,317 full-time, 1,357 part-time. Students come from 19 states and territories; 9 other countries; 4% are from out of state; 5% Black or African American, non-Hispanic/Latino; 6% Hispanic/Latino; 0.3% Asian, non-Hispanic/Latino; 0.1% Native Hawaiian or other Pacific Islander, non-Hispanic/Latino; 13% American Indian or Alaska Native, non-Hispanic/Latino; 9% Two or more races, non-Hispanic/Latino; 2% Race/ethnicity unknown; 0.1% international; 11% live on campus. *Retention:* 49% of full-time freshmen returned.
Faculty *Total:* 152, 38% full-time. *Student/faculty ratio:* 20:1.
Majors Agricultural teacher education; agriculture; biological and biomedical sciences related; biology/biological sciences; chemistry; child-care provision; child development; computer and information sciences; corrections and criminal justice related; elementary education; fine arts related; general studies; gunsmithing; history; humanities; industrial production technologies related; information science/studies; management science; mathematics; natural resources and conservation related; occupational therapist assistant; physical education teaching and coaching; physical therapy technology; psychology related; registered nursing/registered nurse; veterinary/animal health technology.
Academics *Calendar:* semesters. *Degree:* associate. *Special study options:* academic remediation for entering students, advanced placement credit, distance learning, honors programs, internships, part-time degree program, services for LD students, summer session for credit.
Library Murray State College Library plus 1 other.
Student Life *Housing:* on-campus residence required for freshman year. *Options:* coed, men-only, special housing for students with disabilities. Campus housing is university owned. Freshman campus housing is guaranteed. *Activities and Organizations:* drama/theater group, choral group. *Campus security:* 24-hour patrols. *Student services:* personal/psychological counseling.
Athletics Member NJCAA. *Intercollegiate sports:* baseball M(s), basketball M(s)/W(s), cheerleading M/W, golf M(s)/W(s), soccer M/W, softball W(s). *Intramural sports:* basketball M/W.
Standardized Tests *Required:* SAT or ACT (for admission).
Financial Aid Of all full-time matriculated undergraduates who enrolled in 2015, 68 Federal Work-Study jobs (averaging $3354). 20 state and other part-time jobs (averaging $2516).
Applying *Options:* electronic application, early admission. *Required:* high school transcript. *Application deadlines:* rolling (freshmen), rolling (transfers). *Notification:* continuous (freshmen), continuous (transfers).
Freshman Application Contact Murray State College, One Murray Campus, Tishomingo, OK 73460. *Phone:* 580-371-2371 Ext. 171. *Website:* http://www.mscok.edu/.

Northeastern Oklahoma Agricultural and Mechanical College
Miami, Oklahoma

Freshman Application Contact Amy Ishmael, Vice President for Enrollment Management, Northeastern Oklahoma Agricultural and Mechanical College, 200 I Street, NE, Miami, OK 74354-6434. *Phone:* 918-540-6212. *Toll-free phone:* 800-464-6636. *Fax:* 918-540-6946. *E-mail:* neoadmission@neo.edu. *Website:* http://www.neo.edu/.

Northern Oklahoma College
Tonkawa, Oklahoma

Freshman Application Contact Ms. Sheri Snyder, Director of College Relations, Northern Oklahoma College, 1220 East Grand Avenue, PO Box 310, Tonkawa, OK 74653-0310. *Phone:* 580-628-6290. *Website:* http://www.noc.edu/.

Oklahoma City Community College
Oklahoma City, Oklahoma

- **State-supported** 2-year, founded 1969, part of Oklahoma State Regents for Higher Education
- **Urban** 143-acre campus with easy access to Oklahoma City
- **Endowment** $287,559
- **Coed,** 12,529 undergraduate students, 36% full-time, 59% women, 41% men

Undergraduates 4,547 full-time, 7,982 part-time. Students come from 22 states and territories; 52 other countries; 3% are from out of state; 8% Black or African American, non-Hispanic/Latino; 13% Hispanic/Latino; 4% Asian, non-Hispanic/Latino; 0.2% Native Hawaiian or other Pacific Islander, non-Hispanic/Latino; 4% American Indian or Alaska Native, non-Hispanic/Latino; 7% Two or more races, non-Hispanic/Latino; 4% Race/ethnicity unknown; 9% international; 37% transferred in.
Freshmen *Admission:* 5,877 applied, 3,561 admitted, 1,989 enrolled.
Faculty *Total:* 642, 22% full-time, 14% with terminal degrees. *Student/faculty ratio:* 20:1.
Majors Accounting and finance; administrative assistant and secretarial science; aeronautical/aerospace engineering technology; American government and politics; animation, interactive technology, video graphics and special effects; architectural drafting and CAD/CADD; art; automobile/automotive mechanics technology; banking and financial support services; biology/biological sciences; biotechnology; broadcast journalism; business administration and management; business/commerce; chemistry; child development; cinematography and film/video production; commercial and advertising art; computer engineering technology; computer science; computer systems analysis; computer systems networking and telecommunications; cyber/electronic operations and warfare; design and applied arts related; design and visual communications; diesel mechanics technology; digital communication and media/multimedia; drafting and design technology; dramatic/theater arts; elementary education; emergency medical technology (EMT paramedic); engineering technologies and engineering related; fine/studio arts; foreign languages and literatures; game and interactive media design; general studies; geographic information science and cartography; graphic communications; health information/medical records administration; history; humanities; legal administrative assistant/secretary; liberal arts and sciences/liberal studies; literature; mass communication/media; mathematics; medical/clinical assistant; multi/interdisciplinary studies related; music; occupational therapy; philosophy; photographic and film/video technology; physical therapy; physics; political science and government; pre-engineering; psychology; public relations, advertising, and applied communication; registered nursing/registered nurse; respiratory care therapy; sociology; speech-language pathology assistant; surgical technology; system, networking, and LAN/WAN management.
Academics *Calendar:* semesters. *Degree:* certificates and associate. *Special study options:* academic remediation for entering students, accelerated degree program, advanced placement credit, cooperative education, distance learning, double majors, English as a second language, honors programs, independent study, internships, part-time degree program, services for LD students, student-designed majors, summer session for credit.
Library Keith Leftwich Memorial Library. *Books:* 86,229 (physical), 12,108 (digital/electronic); *Serial titles:* 216 (physical), 25 (digital/electronic); *Databases:* 39. Weekly public service hours: 84.
Student Life *Housing:* college housing not available. *Activities and Organizations:* drama/theater group, student-run newspaper, choral group, Nursing Student Association, Health Professions Club, Hispanic Student Organization, Christians on Campus, Agnostics, Atheists and Free-Thinkers.

Campus security: 24-hour emergency response devices and patrols, late-night transport/escort service. *Student services:* personal/psychological counseling.

Athletics *Intramural sports:* badminton M/W, basketball M/W, football M/W, soccer M/W, table tennis M/W, ultimate Frisbee M/W, volleyball M/W, weight lifting M/W.

Costs (2016–17) *One-time required fee:* $25. *Tuition:* state resident $2753 full-time, $92 per credit hour part-time; nonresident $8285 full-time, $276 per credit hour part-time. Full-time tuition and fees vary according to class time and course level. Part-time tuition and fees vary according to class time and course level. *Required fees:* $974 full-time, $32 per credit hour part-time. *Payment plan:* installment. *Waivers:* senior citizens and employees or children of employees.

Financial Aid Of all full-time matriculated undergraduates who enrolled in 2015, 101 Federal Work-Study jobs (averaging $2383). 440 state and other part-time jobs (averaging $3211).

Applying *Options:* electronic application. *Application fee:* $30. *Required for some:* high school transcript, college and university transcripts. *Application deadlines:* rolling (freshmen), rolling (transfers). *Notification:* continuous (freshmen), continuous (transfers).

Freshman Application Contact Mrs. Mary Bodine Al-Sharif, Director of Recruitment and Admissions, Oklahoma City Community College, 7777 South May Avenue, Oklahoma City, OK 73159. *Phone:* 405-682-7743. *Fax:* 405-682-7817. *E-mail:* mary.bodineal-sharif@occc.edu.
Website: http://www.occc.edu/.

Oklahoma State University Institute of Technology
Okmulgee, Oklahoma

- **State-supported** primarily 2-year, founded 1946, part of Oklahoma State University
- **Small-town** 160-acre campus with easy access to Tulsa
- **Endowment** $7.6 million
- **Coed,** 2,397 undergraduate students, 71% full-time, 36% women, 64% men

Undergraduates 1,713 full-time, 684 part-time. Students come from 25 states and territories; 16 other countries; 13% are from out of state; 5% Black or African American, non-Hispanic/Latino; 6% Hispanic/Latino; 0.7% Asian, non-Hispanic/Latino; 13% American Indian or Alaska Native, non-Hispanic/Latino; 10% Two or more races, non-Hispanic/Latino; 14% Race/ethnicity unknown; 2% international; 9% transferred in; 30% live on campus. *Retention:* 56% of full-time freshmen returned.

Freshmen *Admission:* 1,849 applied, 1,849 admitted, 627 enrolled. *Average high school GPA:* 3. *Test scores:* ACT scores over 18: 61%; ACT scores over 24: 11%; ACT scores over 30: 1%.

Faculty *Total:* 164, 76% full-time, 5% with terminal degrees. *Student/faculty ratio:* 14:1.

Majors Autobody/collision and repair technology; automotive engineering technology; business/commerce; civil engineering technology; computer and information systems security; construction engineering technology; culinary arts related; diesel mechanics technology; education (multiple levels); engineering technology; graphic design; health services/allied health/health sciences; heating, air conditioning, ventilation and refrigeration maintenance technology; information technology; instrumentation technology; intermedia/multimedia; mechanical engineering/mechanical technology; mechanic and repair technologies related; multi/interdisciplinary studies related; orthotics/prosthetics; petroleum technology; photography; registered nursing/registered nurse.

Academics *Calendar:* trimesters. *Degrees:* associate and bachelor's. *Special study options:* academic remediation for entering students, adult/continuing education programs, advanced placement credit, distance learning, double majors, independent study, internships, part-time degree program, services for LD students, summer session for credit.

Library Oklahoma State University Institute of Technology Library. *Books:* 9,743 (physical), 130,437 (digital/electronic); *Serial titles:* 77,907 (digital/electronic); *Databases:* 31. Weekly public service hours: 66; students can reserve study rooms.

Student Life *Housing:* on-campus residence required for freshman year. *Options:* coed, men-only. Campus housing is university owned. Freshman applicants given priority for college housing. *Activities and Organizations:* Phi Theta Kappa, Visual Communications Collective, Air Conditioning and Refrigeration Club, Future Chefs Association, Association of Information Technology Professionals. *Campus security:* 24-hour emergency response devices and patrols, late-night transport/escort service, controlled dormitory access. *Student services:* health clinic, personal/psychological counseling.

Athletics *Intramural sports:* basketball M/W, football M/W, racquetball M/W, soccer M/W, softball M/W, table tennis M/W, volleyball M/W.

Standardized Tests *Required for some:* SAT or ACT (for admission). *Recommended:* ACT (for admission).

Costs (2017–18) *Tuition:* state resident $3900 full-time, $130 per credit hour part-time; nonresident $9510 full-time, $317 per credit hour part-time. Full-time tuition and fees vary according to course level, course load, location, program, and student level. Part-time tuition and fees vary according to course level, course load, location, program, and student level. *Required fees:* $1200 full-time, $40 per credit hour part-time. *Room and board:* $6724. Room and board charges vary according to board plan and housing facility. *Payment plan:* installment. *Waivers:* senior citizens and employees or children of employees.

Financial Aid Of all full-time matriculated undergraduates who enrolled in 2015, 1,857 applied for aid, 1,598 were judged to have need, 1,151 had their need fully met. In 2015, 217 non-need-based awards were made. *Average percent of need met:* 75%. *Average financial aid package:* $7600. *Average need-based loan:* $4500. *Average need-based gift aid:* $7600. *Average non-need-based aid:* $500. *Financial aid deadline:* 6/30.

Applying *Options:* deferred entrance. *Required:* high school transcript. *Application deadlines:* rolling (freshmen), rolling (transfers).

Freshman Application Contact Kyle Gregorio, Assistant Registrar, Oklahoma State University Institute of Technology, 1801 E. 4th Street, Okmulgee, OK 74447. *Phone:* 918-293-5274. *Toll-free phone:* 800-722-4471. *Fax:* 918-293-4643. *E-mail:* kyleg@okstate.edu.
Website: http://www.osuit.edu/.

Oklahoma State University–Oklahoma City
Oklahoma City, Oklahoma

- **State-supported** primarily 2-year, founded 1961, part of Oklahoma State University
- **Urban** 110-acre campus with easy access to Oklahoma City
- **Coed,** 5,963 undergraduate students, 31% full-time, 60% women, 40% men

Undergraduates 1,878 full-time, 4,085 part-time. Students come from 26 states and territories; 4% are from out of state; 13% Black or African American, non-Hispanic/Latino; 11% Hispanic/Latino; 3% Asian, non-Hispanic/Latino; 3% American Indian or Alaska Native, non-Hispanic/Latino; 12% Two or more races, non-Hispanic/Latino; 5% Race/ethnicity unknown.

Freshmen *Admission:* 2,412 applied, 795 admitted.

Faculty *Total:* 414, 21% full-time. *Student/faculty ratio:* 14:1.

Majors Accounting; American Sign Language (ASL); architectural drafting and CAD/CADD; architectural engineering technology; building/home/construction inspection; business administration and management; cardiovascular technology; construction engineering technology; construction management; construction trades; criminal justice/police science; dietetics and clinical nutrition services related; early childhood education; electrical and power transmission installation; electrical and power transmission installation related; electrical, electronic and communications engineering technology; electrocardiograph technology; emergency medical technology (EMT paramedic); energy management and systems technology; engineering technology; fire science/firefighting; general studies; health/health-care administration; homeland security, law enforcement, firefighting and protective services related; horticultural science; information science/studies; information technology; language interpretation and translation; management science; public administration and social service professions related; radiologic technology/science; registered nursing/registered nurse; sign language interpretation and translation; substance abuse/addiction counseling; surveying technology; veterinary/animal health technology.

Academics *Calendar:* semesters. *Degrees:* certificates, associate, and bachelor's. *Special study options:* academic remediation for entering students, advanced placement credit, distance learning, double majors, honors programs, independent study, internships, part-time degree program, services for LD students, study abroad, summer session for credit.

Library Oklahoma State University, Oklahoma City Library. *Books:* 47,903 (physical); *Serial titles:* 237 (physical); *Databases:* 72. Weekly public service hours: 73; students can reserve study rooms.

Student Life *Housing:* college housing not available. *Activities and Organizations:* OSU-OKC Chapter of the OK Student Nurse Association, Veterinary Technician Association, Hispanic Student Association, Student Leaders of Tomorrow, Student Government Association. *Campus security:* 24-hour patrols, late-night transport/escort service.

Costs (2017–18) *Tuition:* state resident $2938 full-time, $122 per credit hour part-time; nonresident $8171 full-time, $340 per credit hour part-time. Full-time tuition and fees vary according to class time, course level, and degree level. Part-time tuition and fees vary according to class time, course level, and degree level. No tuition increase for student's term of enrollment. *Required fees:* $70 full-time, $35 per term part-time. *Payment plans:* tuition prepayment, installment. *Waivers:* senior citizens and employees or children of employees.

Applying *Options:* electronic application. *Required for some:* high school transcript. *Application deadlines:* rolling (freshmen), rolling (transfers). *Notification:* continuous (freshmen), continuous (transfers).
Freshman Application Contact Mr. Kyle Williams, Senior Director of Enrollment Management, Oklahoma State University–Oklahoma City, 900 North Portland Avenue, AD202, Oklahoma City, OK 73107. *Phone:* 405-945-9152. *Toll-free phone:* 800-560-4099. *E-mail:* wilkylw@osuokc.edu. *Website:* http://www.osuokc.edu/.

Oklahoma Technical College
Tulsa, Oklahoma

- **Independent** 2-year, founded 2009
- **Urban** 9-acre campus with easy access to Tulsa
- **Coed,** 186 undergraduate students, 100% full-time, 4% women, 96% men

Undergraduates 186 full-time. Students come from 6 states and territories; 5% are from out of state; 11% Black or African American, non-Hispanic/Latino; 8% Hispanic/Latino; 1% Asian, non-Hispanic/Latino; 0.5% Native Hawaiian or other Pacific Islander, non-Hispanic/Latino; 18% American Indian or Alaska Native, non-Hispanic/Latino; 1% Two or more races, non-Hispanic/Latino; 6% Race/ethnicity unknown.
Freshmen *Admission:* 185 enrolled.
Faculty *Total:* 19, 100% full-time. *Student/faculty ratio:* 10:1.
Academics *Calendar:* continuous. *Degree:* diplomas and associate. *Special study options:* adult/continuing education programs, internships, services for LD students.
Student Life *Housing:* college housing not available. *Activities and Organizations:* Student Ambassadors. *Campus security:* campus security during school hours. *Student services:* personal/psychological counseling.
Costs (2017–18) *Tuition:* $17,325 full-time. Full-time tuition and fees vary according to class time, course level, course load, location, program, and student level. Part-time tuition and fees vary according to class time. *Required fees:* $1858 full-time. *Payment plans:* tuition prepayment, installment. *Waivers:* employees or children of employees.
Applying *Options:* electronic application. *Application fee:* $100. *Required:* essay or personal statement, high school transcript, interview. *Application deadlines:* rolling (freshmen), rolling (transfers). *Notification:* continuous (freshmen), continuous (transfers).
Freshman Application Contact Mr. Jeremy Cooper, Campus Director, Oklahoma Technical College, 4444 South Sheridan Road, Tulsa, OK 74145. *Phone:* 918-895-7500 Ext. 3007. *Fax:* 918-895-7885. *E-mail:* jcooper@oklahomatechnicalcollege.com. *Website:* http://www.oklahomatechnicalcollege.com/.

Platt College
Moore, Oklahoma

Admissions Office Contact Platt College, 201 North Eastern Avenue, Moore, OK 73160. *Toll-free phone:* 877-392-6616. *Website:* http://www.plattcolleges.edu/.

Platt College
Oklahoma City, Oklahoma

Admissions Office Contact Platt College, 2727 West Memorial Road, Oklahoma City, OK 73134. *Toll-free phone:* 877-392-6616. *Website:* http://www.plattcolleges.edu/.

Platt College
Oklahoma City, Oklahoma

Freshman Application Contact Ms. Kim Lamb, Director of Admissions, Platt College, 309 South Ann Arbor, Oklahoma City, OK 73128. *Phone:* 405-946-7799. *Toll-free phone:* 877-392-6616. *Fax:* 405-943-2150. *E-mail:* klamb@plattcollege.org. *Website:* http://www.plattcolleges.edu/.

Platt College
Tulsa, Oklahoma

Director of Admissions Mrs. Susan Rone, Director, Platt College, 3801 South Sheridan Road, Tulsa, OK 74145. *Phone:* 918-663-9000. *Toll-free phone:* 877-392-6616. *Fax:* 918-622-1240. *E-mail:* susanr@plattcollege.org. *Website:* http://www.plattcolleges.edu/.

Redlands Community College
El Reno, Oklahoma

Freshman Application Contact Redlands Community College, 1300 South Country Club Road, El Reno, OK 73036-5304. *Phone:* 405-262-2552 Ext. 1263. *Toll-free phone:* 866-415-6367. *Website:* http://www.redlandscc.edu/.

Rose State College
Midwest City, Oklahoma

Freshman Application Contact Ms. Mechelle Aitson-Roessler, Registrar and Director of Admissions, Rose State College, 6420 Southeast 15th Street, Midwest City, OK 73110-2799. *Phone:* 405-733-7308. *Toll-free phone:* 866-621-0987. *Fax:* 405-736-0203. *E-mail:* maitson@ms.rose.cc.ok.us. *Website:* http://www.rose.edu/.

Seminole State College
Seminole, Oklahoma

- **State-supported** 2-year, founded 1931, part of Oklahoma State Regents for Higher Education
- **Small-town** 40-acre campus with easy access to Oklahoma City
- **Endowment** $3.1 million
- **Coed,** 1,634 undergraduate students, 54% full-time, 66% women, 34% men

Undergraduates 878 full-time, 756 part-time. Students come from 16 states and territories; 9 other countries; 3% are from out of state; 6% Black or African American, non-Hispanic/Latino; 3% Hispanic/Latino; 0.4% Asian, non-Hispanic/Latino; 0.3% Native Hawaiian or other Pacific Islander, non-Hispanic/Latino; 26% American Indian or Alaska Native, non-Hispanic/Latino; 0.2% Race/ethnicity unknown; 1% international; 7% transferred in; 8% live on campus.
Freshmen *Admission:* 404 applied, 404 admitted, 404 enrolled.
Faculty *Total:* 87, 46% full-time, 3% with terminal degrees. *Student/faculty ratio:* 19:1.
Majors Accounting; art; behavioral sciences; biological and biomedical sciences related; biology/biological sciences; business administration and management; business/commerce; child development; clinical/medical laboratory technology; computer science; criminal justice/law enforcement administration; criminal justice/police science; elementary education; engineering; English; fine arts related; general studies; humanities; liberal arts and sciences/liberal studies; management information systems and services related; mathematics; physical education teaching and coaching; physical sciences; pre-engineering; psychology related; registered nursing/registered nurse; social sciences.
Academics *Calendar:* semesters. *Degree:* diplomas and associate. *Special study options:* academic remediation for entering students, adult/continuing education programs, advanced placement credit, cooperative education, distance learning, double majors, English as a second language, independent study, off-campus study, part-time degree program, services for LD students, study abroad, summer session for credit.
Library Boren Library plus 1 other. *Books:* 29,131 (physical); *Serial titles:* 35 (physical), 11 (digital/electronic); *Databases:* 8. Weekly public service hours: 48.
Student Life *Housing Options:* coed. Campus housing is university owned. *Activities and Organizations:* Student Government Association, Native American Student Association, Psi Beta Honor Society, Student Nurses Association, Phi Theta Kappa. *Campus security:* 24-hour emergency response devices and patrols, student patrols, late-night transport/escort service, controlled dormitory access.
Athletics Member NJCAA. *Intercollegiate sports:* baseball M(s), basketball M(s)/W(s), cheerleading W, golf M(s)/W(s), soccer W, softball W(s), tennis M(s)/W(s), volleyball W(s).
Costs (2016–17) *One-time required fee:* $15. *Tuition:* state resident $2504 full-time, $91 per credit hour part-time; nonresident $7664 full-time, $277 per credit hour part-time. Full-time tuition and fees vary according to location and program. Part-time tuition and fees vary according to location and program. *Required fees:* $1305 full-time, $48 per credit hour part-time. *Room and board:* $7070. *Payment plans:* installment, deferred payment. *Waivers:* senior citizens and employees or children of employees.
Financial Aid Of all full-time matriculated undergraduates who enrolled in 2015, 13 Federal Work-Study jobs (averaging $4455).
Applying *Options:* early admission, deferred entrance. *Application fee:* $15. *Recommended:* high school transcript. *Application deadlines:* rolling

(freshmen), rolling (transfers). *Notification:* continuous (freshmen), continuous (transfers).
Freshman Application Contact Mrs. Corey Quiett, Registrar, Seminole State College, PO Box 351, 2701 Boren Boulevard, Seminole, OK 74818-0351. *Phone:* 405-382-9501. *Fax:* 405-382-9524. *E-mail:* c.quiett@sscok.edu. *Website:* http://www.sscok.edu/.

Spartan College of Aeronautics and Technology
Tulsa, Oklahoma

Freshman Application Contact Mr. Mark Fowler, Vice President of Student Records and Finance, Spartan College of Aeronautics and Technology, 8820 East Pine Street, Tulsa, OK 74115. *Phone:* 918-836-6886. *Toll-free phone:* 800-331-1204. *Website:* http://www.spartan.edu/.

Tulsa Community College
Tulsa, Oklahoma

- **State-supported** 2-year, founded 1968, part of Oklahoma State Regents for Higher Education
- **Urban** 160-acre campus
- **Coed**

Undergraduates 5,713 full-time, 10,995 part-time. 9% Black or African American, non-Hispanic/Latino; 8% Hispanic/Latino; 4% Asian, non-Hispanic/Latino; 0.1% Native Hawaiian or other Pacific Islander, non-Hispanic/Latino; 8% American Indian or Alaska Native, non-Hispanic/Latino; 9% Two or more races, non-Hispanic/Latino; 3% Race/ethnicity unknown; 2% international; 3% transferred in.
Faculty *Student/faculty ratio:* 19:1.
Academics *Calendar:* semesters. *Degree:* certificates and associate. *Special study options:* academic remediation for entering students, accelerated degree program, adult/continuing education programs, advanced placement credit, cooperative education, distance learning, English as a second language, freshman honors college, honors programs, independent study, internships, off-campus study, part-time degree program, services for LD students, student-designed majors, study abroad, summer session for credit.
Student Life *Campus security:* 24-hour emergency response devices and patrols, student patrols, late-night transport/escort service.
Costs (2016–17) *Tuition:* state resident $3803 full-time, $97 per credit hour part-time; nonresident $9803 full-time, $297 per credit hour part-time. *Required fees:* $894 full-time, $29 per credit hour part-time, $5 per term part-time.
Financial Aid Of all full-time matriculated undergraduates who enrolled in 2016, 4,561 applied for aid, 3,342 were judged to have need, 233 had their need fully met. In 2016, 581. *Average percent of need met:* 71. *Average financial aid package:* $4003. *Average need-based loan:* $1725. *Average need-based gift aid:* $2924. *Average non-need-based aid:* $1675.
Applying *Options:* electronic application, early admission. *Application fee:* $20. *Required:* high school transcript.
Freshman Application Contact Ms. Traci Heck, Dean of Enrollment Management, Tulsa Community College, 6111 East Skelly Drive, Tulsa, OK 74135. *Phone:* 918-595-3411. *E-mail:* traci.heck@tulsacc.edu. *Website:* http://www.tulsacc.edu/.

Tulsa Welding School
Tulsa, Oklahoma

Freshman Application Contact Mrs. Debbie Renee Burke, Vice President/Executive Director, Tulsa Welding School, 2545 East 11th Street, Tulsa, OK 74104. *Phone:* 918-587-6789 Ext. 2258. *Toll-free phone:* 888-765-5555. *Fax:* 918-295-6812. *E-mail:* dburke@twsweld.com. *Website:* http://www.tulsaweldingschool.com/.

Vatterott College
Tulsa, Oklahoma

Freshman Application Contact Mr. Terry Queeno, Campus Director, Vatterott College, 4343 South 118th East Avenue, Suite A, Tulsa, OK 74146. *Phone:* 918-836-6656. *Toll-free phone:* 888-553-6627. *Fax:* 918-836-9698. *E-mail:* tulsa@vatterott-college.edu. *Website:* http://www.vatterott.edu/.

Vatterott College
Warr Acres, Oklahoma

Freshman Application Contact Mr. Mark Hybers, Director of Admissions, Vatterott College, Oklahoma City, OK 73127. *Phone:* 405-945-0088 Ext.

4416. *Toll-free phone:* 888-553-6627. *Fax:* 405-945-0788. *E-mail:* mark.hybers@vatterott-college.edu. *Website:* http://www.vatterott.edu/.

Virginia College in Tulsa
Tulsa, Oklahoma

Admissions Office Contact Virginia College in Tulsa, 5124 South Peoria Avenue, Tulsa, OK 74105. *Website:* http://www.vc.edu/.

Western Oklahoma State College
Altus, Oklahoma

Freshman Application Contact Dean Chad E. Wiginton, Dean of Student Support Services, Western Oklahoma State College, 2801 North Main, Altus, OK 73521. *Phone:* 580-477-7918. *Fax:* 580-477-7716. *E-mail:* chad.wiginton@wosc.edu. *Website:* http://www.wosc.edu/.

OREGON

American College of Healthcare Sciences
Portland, Oregon

Freshman Application Contact Admissions Office, American College of Healthcare Sciences, 5940 SW Hood Avenue, Portland, OR 97239. *Phone:* 503-244-0726. *Toll-free phone:* 800-487-8839. *Fax:* 503-244-0727. *E-mail:* achs@achs.edu. *Website:* http://www.achs.edu/.

Blue Mountain Community College
Pendleton, Oregon

Director of Admissions Ms. Theresa Bosworth, Director of Admissions, Blue Mountain Community College, 2411 Northwest Carden Avenue, PO Box 100, Pendleton, OR 97801-1000. *Phone:* 541-278-5774. *E-mail:* tbosworth@bluecc.edu. *Website:* http://www.bluecc.edu/.

Central Oregon Community College
Bend, Oregon

- **District-supported** 2-year, founded 1949, part of Oregon Community College Association
- **Small-town** 193-acre campus
- **Endowment** $16.7 million
- **Coed,** 5,711 undergraduate students, 44% full-time, 54% women, 46% men

Undergraduates 2,519 full-time, 3,192 part-time. 7% are from out of state; 0.5% Black or African American, non-Hispanic/Latino; 11% Hispanic/Latino; 1% Asian, non-Hispanic/Latino; 0.3% Native Hawaiian or other Pacific Islander, non-Hispanic/Latino; 2% American Indian or Alaska Native, non-Hispanic/Latino; 4% Two or more races, non-Hispanic/Latino; 9% Race/ethnicity unknown; 8% transferred in; 6% live on campus.
Freshmen *Admission:* 1,877 applied, 1,877 admitted, 1,190 enrolled.
Faculty *Total:* 319, 41% full-time. *Student/faculty ratio:* 19:1.
Majors Accounting; airline pilot and flight crew; art; automobile/automotive mechanics technology; biological and physical sciences; biology/biological sciences; business administration and management; CAD/CADD drafting/design technology; child-care and support services management; computer and information sciences related; computer science; computer systems networking and telecommunications; cooking and related culinary arts; customer service management; dental assisting; dietetics; drafting and design technology; early childhood education; education; electrical, electronic and communications engineering technology; emergency medical technology (EMT paramedic); engineering; entrepreneurship; fire science/firefighting; fishing and fisheries sciences and management; foreign languages and literatures; forestry; forest technology; health and physical education/fitness; health information/medical records technology; hotel/motel administration; humanities; industrial technology; kinesiology and exercise science; liberal arts and sciences/liberal studies; licensed practical/vocational nurse training; management information systems; manufacturing engineering technology; marketing/marketing management; massage therapy; mathematics; medical/clinical assistant; natural resources/conservation; physical sciences; physical therapy; polymer/plastics engineering; pre-law studies; premedical studies; pre-pharmacy studies; radiologic technology/science; registered

nursing/registered nurse; retailing; social sciences; speech communication and rhetoric; sport and fitness administration/management; substance abuse/addiction counseling.

Academics *Calendar:* quarters. *Degree:* certificates and associate. *Special study options:* academic remediation for entering students, cooperative education, distance learning, double majors, English as a second language, independent study, internships, part-time degree program, services for LD students, student-designed majors, study abroad, summer session for credit. *ROTC:* Army (c).

Library COCC Library plus 1 other.

Student Life *Housing Options:* coed. Campus housing is university owned. *Activities and Organizations:* drama/theater group, student-run newspaper, choral group, Club Sports, Student Newspaper, Criminal Justice Club, Aviation Club. *Campus security:* 24-hour emergency response devices and patrols, late-night transport/escort service, controlled dormitory access. *Student services:* personal/psychological counseling.

Athletics *Intercollegiate sports:* golf M/W. *Intramural sports:* baseball M, basketball M/W, cross-country running M/W, football M, rugby M, skiing (cross-country) M/W, skiing (downhill) M/W, soccer M/W, track and field M/W, volleyball M/W, weight lifting M/W.

Costs (2016–17) *Tuition:* area resident $3348 full-time, $93 per credit hour part-time; state resident $4500 full-time, $125 per credit hour part-time; nonresident $8192 full-time, $256 per credit hour part-time. *Required fees:* $349 full-time, $8 per credit hour part-time. *Room and board:* $10,551. Room and board charges vary according to board plan. *Payment plan:* installment. *Waivers:* employees or children of employees.

Financial Aid Of all full-time matriculated undergraduates who enrolled in 2015, 1,901 applied for aid, 1,651 were judged to have need, 133 had their need fully met. 347 Federal Work-Study jobs (averaging $3600). In 2015, 20 non-need-based awards were made. *Average percent of need met:* 71%. *Average financial aid package:* $11,607. *Average need-based loan:* $3550. *Average need-based gift aid:* $6689. *Average non-need-based aid:* $1690.

Applying *Options:* electronic application. *Application fee:* $25. *Application deadlines:* rolling (freshmen), rolling (transfers). *Notification:* continuous (freshmen), continuous (transfers).

Freshman Application Contact Central Oregon Community College, 2600 Northwest College Way, Bend, OR 97703. *Phone:* 541-383-7500. *Website:* http://www.cocc.edu/.

Chemeketa Community College
Salem, Oregon

Freshman Application Contact Admissions Office, Chemeketa Community College, PO Box 14009, Salem, OR 97309. *Phone:* 503-399-5001. *E-mail:* admissions@chemeketa.edu. *Website:* http://www.chemeketa.edu/.

Clackamas Community College
Oregon City, Oregon

Freshman Application Contact Ms. Tara Sprehe, Registrar, Clackamas Community College, 19600 South Molalla Avenue, Oregon City, OR 97045. *Phone:* 503-657-6958 Ext. 2742. *Fax:* 503-650-6654. *E-mail:* pattyw@clackamas.edu. *Website:* http://www.clackamas.edu/.

Clatsop Community College
Astoria, Oregon

Freshman Application Contact Ms. Monica Van Steenberg, Recruiting Coordinator, Clatsop Community College, 1651 Lexington Avenue, Astoria, OR 97103. *Phone:* 503-338-2417. *Toll-free phone:* 855-252-8767. *Fax:* 503-325-5738. *E-mail:* admissions@clatsopcc.edu. *Website:* http://www.clatsopcc.edu/.

Columbia Gorge Community College
The Dalles, Oregon

Freshman Application Contact Columbia Gorge Community College, 400 East Scenic Drive, The Dalles, OR 97058. *Phone:* 541-506-6025. *Website:* http://www.cgcc.cc.or.us/.

Concorde Career College
Portland, Oregon

Admissions Office Contact Concorde Career College, 1425 NE Irving Street, Portland, OR 97232. *Website:* http://www.concorde.edu/.

Klamath Community College
Klamath Falls, Oregon

Freshman Application Contact Tammi Garlock, Retention Coordinator, Klamath Community College, 7390 South 6th Street, Klamath Falls, OR 97603. *Phone:* 541-882-3521. *Fax:* 541-885-7758. *E-mail:* garlock@klamathcc.edu. *Website:* http://www.klamathcc.edu/.

Lane Community College
Eugene, Oregon

Freshman Application Contact Lane Community College, 4000 East 30th Avenue, Eugene, OR 97405-0640. *Phone:* 541-747-4501 Ext. 2686. *Website:* http://www.lanecc.edu/.

Linn-Benton Community College
Albany, Oregon

Freshman Application Contact Ms. Kim Sullivan, Outreach Coordinator, Linn-Benton Community College, 6500 Pacific Boulevard, SW, Albany, OR 97321. *Phone:* 541-917-4847. *Fax:* 541-917-4838. *E-mail:* admissions@linnbenton.edu. *Website:* http://www.linnbenton.edu/.

Mt. Hood Community College
Gresham, Oregon

Director of Admissions Dr. Craig Kolins, Associate Vice President of Enrollment Services, Mt. Hood Community College, 26000 Southeast Stark Street, Gresham, OR 97030-3300. *Phone:* 503-491-7265. *Website:* http://www.mhcc.edu/.

Oregon Coast Community College
Newport, Oregon

- **Public** 2-year, founded 1987
- **Small-town** 24-acre campus
- **Coed,** 486 undergraduate students, 47% full-time, 65% women, 35% men

Undergraduates 227 full-time, 259 part-time. Students come from 4 states and territories; 1% are from out of state; 0.2% Black or African American, non-Hispanic/Latino; 13% Hispanic/Latino; 1% Asian, non-Hispanic/Latino; 0.7% Native Hawaiian or other Pacific Islander, non-Hispanic/Latino; 2% American Indian or Alaska Native, non-Hispanic/Latino; 7% Two or more races, non-Hispanic/Latino; 3% Race/ethnicity unknown; 6% transferred in. *Retention:* 65% of full-time freshmen returned.

Freshmen *Admission:* 75 applied, 75 admitted, 75 enrolled.

Faculty *Total:* 67, 15% full-time, 15% with terminal degrees. *Student/faculty ratio:* 17:1.

Majors Accounting technology and bookkeeping; administrative assistant and secretarial science; criminal justice/safety; general studies; liberal arts and sciences/liberal studies; marine biology and biological oceanography; registered nursing/registered nurse.

Academics *Calendar:* quarters. *Degree:* certificates and associate. *Special study options:* academic remediation for entering students, cooperative education, distance learning, English as a second language, honors programs, internships, part-time degree program, services for LD students, summer session for credit.

Library Oregon Coast Community College Library. *Books:* 13,033 (physical), 110,699 (digital/electronic); *Serial titles:* 2,771 (physical); *Databases:* 53. Students can reserve study rooms.

Student Life *Housing:* college housing not available. *Activities and Organizations:* Psych Club, Triangle Club, Writing Club, ASG. *Campus security:* 24-hour emergency response devices.

Costs (2017–18) *Tuition:* state resident $3564 full-time, $99 per credit part-time; nonresident $7704 full-time, $214 per credit part-time. Full-time tuition and fees vary according to course load and program. Part-time tuition and fees vary according to course load and program. *Required fees:* $576 full-time, $16 per credit part-time. *Payment plan:* deferred payment. *Waivers:* senior citizens and employees or children of employees.

Applying *Options:* electronic application. *Required for some:* essay or personal statement, 2 letters of recommendation, interview.

Freshman Application Contact Student Services, Oregon Coast Community College, 400 SE College Way, Newport, OR 97366. *Phone:* 541-265-2283. *Fax:* 541-265-3820. *E-mail:* webinfo@occc.cc.or.us. *Website:* http://www.oregoncoastcc.org/.

★ Pioneer Pacific College
Wilsonville, Oregon

Freshman Application Contact Elizabeth Cox, Director of Admissions, Pioneer Pacific College, 27501 SW Parkway Avenue, Wilsonville, OR 97070. *Phone:* 503-688-2178. *Toll-free phone:* 866-PPC-INFO. *Fax:* 503-682-1514. *E-mail:* wil-info@pioneerpacific.edu. *Website:* http://www.pioneerpacific.edu/.

See this page for display ad and page 342 for the College Close-Up.

Portland Community College
Portland, Oregon

Freshman Application Contact Admissions and Registration Office, Portland Community College, PO Box 19000, Portland, OR 97280. *Phone:* 503-977-8888. *Toll-free phone:* 866-922-1010. *Website:* http://www.pcc.edu/.

Rogue Community College
Grants Pass, Oregon

- **State and locally supported** 2-year, founded 1970
- **Rural** 84-acre campus
- **Endowment** $9.3 million
- **Coed,** 4,901 undergraduate students, 39% full-time, 57% women, 43% men

Undergraduates 1,896 full-time, 3,005 part-time. Students come from 26 states and territories; 4 other countries; 3% are from out of state; 0.9% Black or African American, non-Hispanic/Latino; 17% Hispanic/Latino; 2% Asian, non-Hispanic/Latino; 0.5% Native Hawaiian or other Pacific Islander, non-Hispanic/Latino; 1% American Indian or Alaska Native, non-Hispanic/Latino; 4% Two or more races, non-Hispanic/Latino; 4% Race/ethnicity unknown; 0.1% international; 5% transferred in.

Freshmen *Admission:* 852 applied, 802 admitted, 919 enrolled. *Average high school GPA:* 3.06.

Faculty *Total:* 473, 15% full-time. *Student/faculty ratio:* 18:1.

Majors Accounting technology and bookkeeping; automobile/automotive mechanics technology; business administration and management; business/commerce; child-care and support services management; computer and information sciences; computer science; computer software technology; construction engineering technology; construction trades; criminal justice/police science; diesel mechanics technology; electrical and power transmission installation; electrical, electronic and communications engineering technology; emergency medical technology (EMT paramedic); family and community services; fire prevention and safety technology; general studies; liberal arts and sciences/liberal studies; manufacturing engineering technology; marketing/marketing management; mechanics and repair; medical office computer specialist; registered nursing/registered nurse; social work; visual and performing arts; welding technology.

Academics *Calendar:* quarters. *Degree:* certificates and associate. *Special study options:* academic remediation for entering students, adult/continuing education programs, advanced placement credit, cooperative education, distance learning, double majors, English as a second language, independent study, internships, part-time degree program, services for LD students, study abroad, summer session for credit.

Library Rogue Community College Library. *Books:* 26,630 (physical).

Student Life *Activities and Organizations:* drama/theater group, student-run newspaper, choral group. *Campus security:* 24-hour emergency response devices and patrols, late-night transport/escort service. *Student services:* personal/psychological counseling.

Athletics *Intercollegiate sports:* soccer M/W. *Intramural sports:* badminton M/W, basketball M/W, soccer M/W, softball M/W, volleyball M/W.

Costs (2016–17) *Tuition:* state resident $3564 full-time, $99 per credit hour part-time; nonresident $4356 full-time, $121 per credit hour part-time. Full-time tuition and fees vary according to reciprocity agreements. Part-time tuition and fees vary according to reciprocity agreements. *Required fees:* $600 full-time, $5 per credit hour part-time, $100 per term part-time. *Payment plan:* installment. *Waivers:* senior citizens and employees or children of employees.

Financial Aid Of all full-time matriculated undergraduates who enrolled in 2016, 1,490 applied for aid, 1,252 were judged to have need, 78 had their need fully met. 68 Federal Work-Study jobs (averaging $3011). In 2016, 41 non-need-based awards were made. *Average percent of need met:* 78%. *Average financial aid package:* $8375. *Average need-based loan:* $3194. *Average need-based gift aid:* $5840. *Average non-need-based aid:* $1710.

Applying *Options:* electronic application, early admission. *Application deadlines:* rolling (freshmen), rolling (out-of-state freshmen), rolling (transfers).

Freshman Application Contact Mr. John Duarte, Director of Enrollment Services, Rogue Community College, 3345 Redwood Highway, Grants Pass, OR 97527-9291. *Phone:* 541-956-7176. *Fax:* 541-471-3585. *E-mail:* jduarte@roguecc.edu. *Website:* http://www.roguecc.edu/.

Southwestern Oregon Community College
Coos Bay, Oregon

- **State and locally supported** 2-year, founded 1961
- **Small-town** 174-acre campus
- **Endowment** $851,280
- **Coed**

Undergraduates 1,129 full-time, 1,209 part-time. Students come from 24 states and territories; 6 other countries; 30% are from out of state; 1% Black or African American, non-Hispanic/Latino; 9% Hispanic/Latino; 1% Asian, non-Hispanic/Latino; 0.9% Native Hawaiian or other Pacific Islander, non-Hispanic/Latino; 3% American Indian or Alaska Native, non-Hispanic/Latino; 4% Two or more races, non-Hispanic/Latino; 17% Race/ethnicity unknown; 0.9% international; 17% live on campus.

Faculty *Student/faculty ratio:* 15:1.

Academics *Calendar:* quarters. *Degree:* certificates, diplomas, and associate. *Special study options:* academic remediation for entering students, adult/continuing education programs, advanced placement credit, cooperative education, distance learning, double majors, English as a second language, honors programs, independent study, internships, part-time degree program, services for LD students, summer session for credit.

Library Southwestern Oregon Community College Library. *Books:* 28,092 (physical), 857 (digital/electronic); *Serial titles:* 101 (physical); *Databases:* 58. Weekly public service hours: 43.

Student Life *Campus security:* 24-hour emergency response devices and patrols, late-night transport/escort service, controlled dormitory access.

Athletics Member NJCAA.

Costs (2016–17) *One-time required fee:* $40. *Tuition:* state resident $4095 full-time, $91 per credit part-time; nonresident $4095 full-time, $91 per credit part-time. Full-time tuition and fees vary according to program. Part-time tuition and fees vary according to program. *Required fees:* $1755 full-time, $29 per credit part-time, $30 per course part-time. *Room and board:* $7769. Room and board charges vary according to board plan. *Payment plans:* installment, deferred payment.

Applying *Options:* electronic application, early admission. *Application fee:* $40. *Required for some:* high school transcript.

Freshman Application Contact Miss Barb Shreckengost, Admissions, Southwestern Oregon Community College, 1988 Newmark Avenue, Coos Bay, OR 97420. *Phone:* 541-888-7636. *Toll-free phone:* 800-962-2838. *E-mail:* lwells@socc.edu. *Website:* http://www.socc.edu/.

Sumner College
Portland, Oregon

- **Proprietary** 2-year, founded 1974
- **Urban** campus with easy access to Portland
- **Coed, primarily women**

Undergraduates 261 full-time. 10% are from out of state; 15% Black or African American, non-Hispanic/Latino; 6% Hispanic/Latino; 7% Asian, non-Hispanic/Latino; 0.8% Race/ethnicity unknown.

Faculty *Student/faculty ratio:* 15:1.

Academics *Calendar:* quarters. *Degree:* diplomas and associate. *Special study options:* academic remediation for entering students, distance learning.

Library Main Library plus 2 others. *Books:* 800 (physical); *Serial titles:* 100 (digital/electronic); *Databases:* 2. Weekly public service hours: 50; students can reserve study rooms.

Applying *Required:* high school transcript, interview. *Required for some:* essay or personal statement, interview.

Freshman Application Contact Sumner College, 15115 SW Sequoia Parkway, Suite 200, Portland, OR 97224. *Website:* http://www.sumnercollege.edu/.

Tillamook Bay Community College
Tillamook, Oregon

Freshman Application Contact Lori Gates, Tillamook Bay Community College, 4301 Third Street, Tillamook, OR 97141. *Phone:* 503-842-8222. *Fax:* 503-842-2214. *E-mail:* gates@tillamookbay.cc. *Website:* http://www.tbcc.cc.or.us/.

Treasure Valley Community College
Ontario, Oregon

- **State and locally supported** 2-year, founded 1962
- **Rural** 90-acre campus with easy access to Boise
- **Coed,** 2,170 undergraduate students, 44% full-time, 57% women, 43% men

Undergraduates 958 full-time, 1,212 part-time. Students come from 15 states and territories; 2 other countries; 67% are from out of state; 2% Black or African American, non-Hispanic/Latino; 25% Hispanic/Latino; 0.7% Asian, non-Hispanic/Latino; 0.3% Native Hawaiian or other Pacific Islander, non-Hispanic/Latino; 1% American Indian or Alaska Native, non-Hispanic/Latino; 3% Two or more races, non-Hispanic/Latino; 4% Race/ethnicity unknown; 0.4% international; 5% transferred in; 6% live on campus. *Retention:* 40% of full-time freshmen returned.

Freshmen *Admission:* 2,447 applied, 2,447 admitted, 455 enrolled.

Faculty *Total:* 86, 55% full-time, 79% with terminal degrees. *Student/faculty ratio:* 21:1.

Majors Agricultural business and management; agricultural economics; agriculture; agronomy and crop science; airline pilot and flight crew; animal sciences; business/commerce; carpentry; computer and information sciences; criminal justice/police science; drafting and design technology; elementary education; farm and ranch management; fire prevention and safety technology; fire science/firefighting; horse husbandry/equine science and management; horticultural science; legal administrative assistant/secretary; management information systems; medical administrative assistant and medical secretary; medical transcription; natural resources/conservation; office management; range science and management; registered nursing/registered nurse; soil science and agronomy; solar energy technology; substance abuse/addiction counseling; welding technology; wildlife, fish and wildlands science and management.

Academics *Calendar:* quarters. *Degree:* certificates and associate. *Special study options:* academic remediation for entering students, accelerated degree program, adult/continuing education programs, advanced placement credit, cooperative education, distance learning, English as a second language, honors programs, independent study, internships, off-campus study, part-time degree program, services for LD students, summer session for credit.

Library Treasure Valley Community College Library. *Books:* 28,277 (physical), 276,342 (digital/electronic); *Serial titles:* 97 (physical), 15 (digital/electronic); *Databases:* 9. Weekly public service hours: 72; study areas open 24 hours, 5&-7 days a week; students can reserve study rooms.

Student Life *Housing Options:* coed. Campus housing is university owned. *Activities and Organizations:* choral group, Phi Theta Kappa, Natural Resources, International Business Club, Circle K International (service organization), Ag Ambassadors. *Campus security:* 24-hour emergency response devices, late-night transport/escort service, controlled dormitory access, emergency response phone and computer notifications.

Athletics *Intercollegiate sports:* baseball M(s), basketball M(s)/W(s), cross-country running M(s)/W(s), soccer M(s)/W(s), softball W(s), tennis M(s)/W(s), track and field M(s)/W(s), volleyball W(s). *Intramural sports:* basketball M/W, soccer M/W, softball M/W, table tennis M/W, volleyball M/W.

Costs (2017–18) *Tuition:* state resident $4410 full-time, $98 per credit part-time; nonresident $4860 full-time, $108 per credit part-time. Full-time tuition and fees vary according to location. Part-time tuition and fees vary according to location. *Required fees:* $990 full-time, $22 per credit part-time. *Room and board:* $7187; room only: $3926. Room and board charges vary according to board plan. *Payment plan:* installment. *Waivers:* employees or children of employees.

Financial Aid Of all full-time matriculated undergraduates who enrolled in 2015, 90 Federal Work-Study jobs (averaging $1500).

Applying *Options:* electronic application, early admission, deferred entrance. *Application deadlines:* rolling (freshmen), rolling (out-of-state freshmen), rolling (transfers). *Notification:* continuous (freshmen), continuous (out-of-state freshmen), continuous (transfers).

Freshman Application Contact Kelly Young, Office of Admissions and Student Services, Treasure Valley Community College, 650 College Boulevard, Ontario, OR 97914. *Phone:* 541-881-5822. *E-mail:* kmyoung@tvcc.cc. *Website:* http://www.tvcc.cc/.

Umpqua Community College
Roseburg, Oregon

Freshman Application Contact Admissions Office, Umpqua Community College, PO Box 967, Roseburg, OR 97470-0226. *Phone:* 541-440-7743. *Fax:* 541-440-4612. *Website:* http://www.umpqua.edu/.

PENNSYLVANIA

All-State Career School–Essington Campus
Essington, Pennsylvania

Admissions Office Contact All-State Career School–Essington Campus, 50 West Powhattan Ave, Essington, PA 19029.
Website: http://www.allstatecareer.edu/.

Antonelli Institute
Erdenheim, Pennsylvania
- **Proprietary** 2-year, founded 1938
- **Suburban** 15-acre campus with easy access to Philadelphia
- **Coed**
- 87% of applicants were admitted

Academics *Calendar:* semesters. *Degree:* associate.
Financial Aid Of all full-time matriculated undergraduates who enrolled in 2015, 5 Federal Work-Study jobs (averaging $2000).
Freshman Application Contact Admissions Office, Antonelli Institute, 300 Montgomery Avenue, Erdenheim, PA 19038. *Phone:* 800-722-7871. *Toll-free phone:* 800-722-7871. *Website:* http://www.antonelli.edu/.

Berks Technical Institute
Wyomissing, Pennsylvania

Freshman Application Contact Mr. Allan Brussolo, Academic Dean, Berks Technical Institute, 2205 Ridgewood Road, Wyomissing, PA 19610-1168. *Phone:* 610-372-1722. *Toll-free phone:* 866-591-8384. *Fax:* 610-376-4684. *E-mail:* abrussolo@berks.edu. *Website:* http://www.berks.edu/.

Bidwell Training Center
Pittsburgh, Pennsylvania

Freshman Application Contact Admissions Office, Bidwell Training Center, 1815 Metropolitan Street, Pittsburgh, PA 15233. *Phone:* 412-322-1773. *Toll-free phone:* 800-516-1800. *E-mail:* admissions@mcg-btc.org. *Website:* http://www.bidwell-training.org/.

Bradford School
Pittsburgh, Pennsylvania
- **Proprietary** 2-year, founded 1968
- **Urban** campus
- **Coed**
- 84% of applicants were admitted

Academics *Calendar:* semesters. *Degree:* diplomas and associate. *Special study options:* accelerated degree program, internships.
Freshman Application Contact Admissions Office, Bradford School, 125 West Station Square Drive, Pittsburgh, PA 15219. *Phone:* 412-391-6710. *Toll-free phone:* 800-391-6810. *Website:* http://www.bradfordpittsburgh.edu/.

Brightwood Career Institute, Broomall Campus
Broomall, Pennsylvania

Freshman Application Contact Brightwood Career Institute, Broomall Campus, 1991 Sproul Road, Suite 42, Broomall, PA 19008. *Phone:* 610-353-3300. *Toll-free phone:* 866-536-2023.
Website: http://www.brightwoodcareer.edu/.

Brightwood Career Institute, Harrisburg Campus
Harrisburg, Pennsylvania

Freshman Application Contact Brightwood Career Institute, Harrisburg Campus, 5650 Derry Street, Harrisburg, PA 17111. *Phone:* 717-558-1300. *Toll-free phone:* 866-536-2023. *Website:* http://www.brightwoodcareer.edu/.

Brightwood Career Institute, Philadelphia Campus
Philadelphia, Pennsylvania

Freshman Application Contact Admissions Director, Brightwood Career Institute, Philadelphia Campus, 3010 Market Street, Philadelphia, PA 19104. *Toll-free phone:* 866-536-2023. *Website:* http://www.brightwoodcareer.edu/.

Brightwood Career Institute, Philadelphia Mills Campus
Philadelphia, Pennsylvania

Freshman Application Contact Brightwood Career Institute, Philadelphia Mills Campus, 177 Franklin Mills Boulevard, Philadelphia, PA 19154. *Phone:* 215-612-6600. *Toll-free phone:* 866-536-2023.
Website: http://www.brightwoodcareer.edu/.

Brightwood Career Institute, Pittsburgh Campus
Pittsburgh, Pennsylvania

Freshman Application Contact Brightwood Career Institute, Pittsburgh Campus, 933 Penn Avenue, Pittsburgh, PA 15222. *Phone:* 412-261-2647. *Toll-free phone:* 866-536-2023. *Website:* http://www.brightwoodcareer.edu/.

Bucks County Community College
Newtown, Pennsylvania
- **County-supported** 2-year, founded 1964
- **Suburban** 200-acre campus with easy access to Philadelphia
- **Endowment** $6.0 million
- **Coed,** 8,232 undergraduate students, 34% full-time, 55% women, 45% men

Undergraduates 2,790 full-time, 5,442 part-time. Students come from 9 states and territories; 1% are from out of state; 5% Black or African American, non-Hispanic/Latino; 7% Hispanic/Latino; 4% Asian, non-Hispanic/Latino; 0.1% Native Hawaiian or other Pacific Islander, non-Hispanic/Latino; 0.7% American Indian or Alaska Native, non-Hispanic/Latino; 2% Two or more races, non-Hispanic/Latino; 15% Race/ethnicity unknown; 75% transferred in. *Retention:* 68% of full-time freshmen returned.
Freshmen *Admission:* 3,424 applied, 3,324 admitted, 1,906 enrolled.
Faculty *Total:* 644, 23% full-time, 24% with terminal degrees. *Student/faculty ratio:* 16:1.
Majors Accounting technology and bookkeeping; art history, criticism and conservation; baking and pastry arts; biology/biotechnology laboratory technician; biology teacher education; building/home/construction inspection; business administration and management; business, management, and marketing related; cabinetmaking and millwork; chemical technology; child-care provision; cinematography and film/video production; commercial and advertising art; commercial photography; computer and information sciences; computer systems networking and telecommunications; criminal justice/safety; culinary arts; early childhood education; engineering technology; English; environmental science; food service systems administration; health professions related; history; history teacher education; human development and family studies; humanities; industrial technology; information science/studies; journalism; kinesiology and exercise science; legal professions and studies related; liberal arts and sciences and humanities related; liberal arts and sciences/liberal studies; mathematics; mathematics teacher education; medical/clinical assistant; medical insurance coding; multi/interdisciplinary studies related; music; network and system administration; neuroscience; physical education teaching and coaching; psychology; radiologic technology/science; registered nursing/registered nurse; retailing; small business administration; speech communication and rhetoric; sport and fitness administration/management; tourism and travel services management; visual and performing arts; web page, digital/multimedia and information resources design.
Academics *Calendar:* semesters. *Degree:* certificates and associate. *Special study options:* academic remediation for entering students, adult/continuing

education programs, advanced placement credit, cooperative education, distance learning, English as a second language, external degree program, independent study, internships, part-time degree program, services for LD students, student-designed majors, summer session for credit.

Library Bucks County Community College Library. *Books:* 112,342 (physical), 8,471 (digital/electronic); *Serial titles:* 202 (physical), 53 (digital/electronic); *Databases:* 48. Weekly public service hours: 72; students can reserve study rooms.

Student Life *Housing:* college housing not available. *Activities and Organizations:* drama/theater group, student-run newspaper, radio and television station, choral group, Phi Theta Kappa, Intervarsity Christian Fellowship, Drama Club, Habitat for Humanity, Bucks Business Association. *Campus security:* 24-hour emergency response devices and patrols, late-night transport/escort service. *Student services:* personal/psychological counseling, women's center.

Athletics Member NJCAA. *Intercollegiate sports:* baseball M, basketball M/W, golf M, soccer M/W, softball W, tennis M/W, volleyball W. *Intramural sports:* baseball M, basketball M/W, equestrian sports W(c), football M, skiing (downhill) M(c)/W(c), soccer M/W, table tennis M, tennis M/W, ultimate Frisbee M/W, volleyball W.

Costs (2016–17) *Tuition:* area resident $4200 full-time, $140 per credit hour part-time; state resident $8400 full-time, $280 per credit hour part-time; nonresident $12,600 full-time, $420 per credit hour part-time. Full-time tuition and fees vary according to program. Part-time tuition and fees vary according to program. *Required fees:* $1160 full-time, $62 per credit hour part-time, $247 per term part-time. *Payment plans:* installment, deferred payment. *Waivers:* senior citizens and employees or children of employees.

Financial Aid Of all full-time matriculated undergraduates who enrolled in 2015, 139 Federal Work-Study jobs (averaging $1893).

Applying *Options:* electronic application, early admission. *Required:* high school transcript. *Required for some:* essay or personal statement, interview.

Freshman Application Contact Ms. Marlene Barlow, Director of Admissions, Bucks County Community College, Newtown, PA 18940. *Phone:* 215-968-8137. *Fax:* 215-968-8110. *E-mail:* marlene.barlow@bucks.edu. *Website:* http://www.bucks.edu/.

Butler County Community College
Butler, Pennsylvania

- **County-supported** 2-year, founded 1965
- **Rural** 300-acre campus with easy access to Pittsburgh
- **Coed**

Undergraduates 1,706 full-time, 1,867 part-time. 1% are from out of state; 3% Black or African American, non-Hispanic/Latino; 2% Hispanic/Latino; 0.3% Asian, non-Hispanic/Latino; 0.1% American Indian or Alaska Native, non-Hispanic/Latino; 1% Two or more races, non-Hispanic/Latino; 17% Race/ethnicity unknown; 0.2% international.

Faculty *Student/faculty ratio:* 18:1.

Academics *Calendar:* semesters. *Degree:* certificates and associate. *Special study options:* academic remediation for entering students, adult/continuing education programs, advanced placement credit, cooperative education, distance learning, English as a second language, internships, part-time degree program, services for LD students, summer session for credit.

Library John A. Beck, Jr. Library. *Books:* 60,000 (digital/electronic).

Student Life *Campus security:* 24-hour emergency response devices, late-night transport/escort service.

Athletics Member NJCAA.

Costs (2016–17) *Tuition:* area resident $3120 full-time, $104 per credit hour part-time; state resident $6240 full-time, $208 per credit hour part-time; nonresident $9360 full-time, $312 per credit hour part-time. *Required fees:* $1470 full-time, $49 per credit hour part-time.

Financial Aid Of all full-time matriculated undergraduates who enrolled in 2015, 77 Federal Work-Study jobs (averaging $1595).

Applying *Options:* electronic application. *Application fee:* $25. *Required:* high school transcript. *Required for some:* interview.

Freshman Application Contact Mr. Robert Morris, Director of Admissions, Butler County Community College, College Drive, PO Box 1205, Butler, PA 16003-1203. *Phone:* 724-287-8711 Ext. 344. *Toll-free phone:* 888-826-2829. *Fax:* 724-287-4961. *E-mail:* robert.morris@bc3.edu. *Website:* http://www.bc3.edu/.

Career Training Academy
Lower Burrell, Pennsylvania

- **Proprietary** 2-year, founded 1986
- **Coed, primarily women**

Faculty *Student/faculty ratio:* 20:1.

Academics *Calendar:* quarters. *Degrees:* diplomas and associate (profile includes branch campuses in Monroeville and Pittsburgh, PA).

Applying *Application fee:* $30. *Required:* essay or personal statement, high school transcript, minimum 1.5 GPA, interview.

Director of Admissions Ms. Tyna Pitignano, Career Training Academy, 179 Hillcrest Shopping Center, Lower Burrell, PA 15068. *Phone:* 724-337-1000. *Toll-free phone:* 866-673-7773. *E-mail:* admissions@careeta.edu. *Website:* http://www.careerta.edu/.

Career Training Academy
Monroeville, Pennsylvania

Freshman Application Contact Career Training Academy, 4314 Old William Penn Highway, Suite 103, Monroeville, PA 15146. *Phone:* 412-372-3900. *Toll-free phone:* 866-673-7773. *Website:* http://www.careerta.edu/.

Career Training Academy
Pittsburgh, Pennsylvania

Freshman Application Contact Jaimie Vignone, Career Training Academy, 1014 West View Park Drive, Pittsburgh, PA 15229. *Phone:* 412-367-4000. *Toll-free phone:* 866-673-7773. *Fax:* 412-369-7223. *E-mail:* admission3@careerta.edu. *Website:* http://www.careerta.edu/.

Commonwealth Technical Institute
Johnstown, Pennsylvania

Freshman Application Contact Mr. Jason Gies, Admissions Supervisor, Commonwealth Technical Institute, Hiram G. Andrews Center, 727 Goucher Street, Johnstown, PA 15905. *Phone:* 814-255-8200 Ext. 0564. *Toll-free phone:* 800-762-4211. *Fax:* 814-255-8283. *E-mail:* jgies@pa.gov. *Website:* http://www.portal.state.pa.us/portal/server.pt/community/commonwealth_technical_institute/10361.

Community College of Allegheny County
Pittsburgh, Pennsylvania

- **County-supported** 2-year, founded 1966
- **Urban** 242-acre campus
- **Coed,** 16,092 undergraduate students, 35% full-time, 55% women, 45% men

Undergraduates 5,687 full-time, 10,405 part-time.

Freshmen *Admission:* 3,822 enrolled.

Faculty *Student/faculty ratio:* 18:1.

Majors Accounting technology and bookkeeping; administrative assistant and secretarial science; airline pilot and flight crew; applied horticulture/horticulture operations; architectural drafting and CAD/CADD; art; athletic training; automotive engineering technology; aviation/airway management; banking and financial support services; biology/biological sciences; building/property maintenance; business administration and management; business automation/technology/data entry; business machine repair; carpentry; chemical technology; chemistry; child-care provision; child development; civil drafting and CAD/CADD; civil engineering technology; clinical/medical laboratory technology; commercial and advertising art; communications technologies and support services related; community health services counseling; computer engineering technology; computer systems networking and telecommunications; computer technology/computer systems technology; construction engineering technology; construction trades related; corrections; cosmetology and personal grooming arts related; court reporting; criminal justice/police science; culinary arts; diagnostic medical sonography and ultrasound technology; dietitian assistant; drafting and design technology; drafting/design engineering technologies related; dramatic/theater arts; education (specific levels and methods) related; education (specific subject areas) related; electrical, electronic and communications engineering technology; electroneurodiagnostic/electroencephalographic technology; energy management and systems technology; engineering technologies and engineering related; English; entrepreneurship; environmental engineering technology; fire prevention and safety technology; food service systems administration; foreign languages and literatures; general studies; greenhouse management; health and physical education/fitness; health information/medical records technology; health professions related; health unit coordinator/ward clerk; heating, air conditioning, ventilation and refrigeration maintenance technology; hotel/motel administration; housing and human environments related; human development and family studies related; humanities; human resources management; industrial technology; insurance; journalism; landscaping and groundskeeping; legal administrative assistant/secretary; legal assistant/paralegal; liberal arts and sciences/liberal studies; licensed practical/vocational nurse training; machine shop technology;

management information systems; marketing/marketing management; mathematics; mechanical drafting and CAD/CADD; medical administrative assistant and medical secretary; medical/clinical assistant; medical radiologic technology; music; nuclear medical technology; nursing assistant/aide and patient care assistant/aide; occupational therapist assistant; office management; ornamental horticulture; perioperative/operating room and surgical nursing; pharmacy technician; physical therapy technology; physics; plant nursery management; psychiatric/mental health services technology; psychology; quality control technology; real estate; registered nursing/registered nurse; respiratory care therapy; restaurant, culinary, and catering management; retailing; robotics technology; science technologies related; sheet metal technology; sign language interpretation and translation; social sciences; social work; sociology; solar energy technology; substance abuse/addiction counseling; surgical technology; therapeutic recreation; tourism promotion; turf and turfgrass management; visual and performing arts related; welding technology.

Academics *Calendar:* semesters. *Degree:* certificates, diplomas, and associate. *Special study options:* part-time degree program.
Library Community College of Allegheny County Library.
Student Life *Housing:* college housing not available. *Activities and Organizations:* drama/theater group, student-run radio and television station, choral group. *Campus security:* 24-hour emergency response devices and patrols, late-night transport/escort service. *Student services:* health clinic, personal/psychological counseling.
Athletics Member NJCAA. *Intercollegiate sports:* baseball M, basketball M/W, bowling M/W, golf M/W, ice hockey M, softball W, table tennis M/W, tennis M/W, volleyball W. *Intramural sports:* badminton M/W, basketball M/W, bowling M/W, cross-country running M/W, football M, golf M/W, lacrosse M, racquetball M/W, softball M/W, table tennis M/W, tennis M/W, volleyball M/W, weight lifting M/W.
Costs (2016–17) *Tuition:* area resident $3233 full-time, $108 per credit part-time; state resident $6465 full-time, $216 per credit part-time; nonresident $9698 full-time, $323 per credit part-time. Full-time tuition and fees vary according to program. Part-time tuition and fees vary according to program. *Payment plan:* installment. *Waivers:* senior citizens and employees or children of employees.
Applying *Options:* early decision, early action. *Recommended:* high school transcript.
Freshman Application Contact Admissions Office, Community College of Allegheny County, 808 Ridge Avenue, Pittsburgh, PA 15212.
Phone: 412-237-2511.
Website: http://www.ccac.edu/.

Community College of Beaver County
Monaca, Pennsylvania

Freshman Application Contact Enrollment Management, Community College of Beaver County, One Campus Drive, Monaca, PA 15061-2588. *Phone:* 724-480-3500. *Toll-free phone:* 800-335-0222. *E-mail:* admissions@ccbc.edu. *Website:* http://www.ccbc.edu/.

Community College of Philadelphia
Philadelphia, Pennsylvania

- **State and locally supported** 2-year, founded 1964
- **Urban** 14-acre campus with easy access to Philadelphia
- **Coed,** 30,194 undergraduate students

Undergraduates Students come from 50 other countries.
Faculty *Total:* 1,038, 42% full-time.
Majors Accounting; art; automobile/automotive mechanics technology; business administration and management; clinical/medical laboratory technology; computer science; construction engineering technology; criminal justice/law enforcement administration; culinary arts; dental hygiene; drafting and design technology; education; engineering; engineering technology; facilities planning and management; fire science/firefighting; health professions related; hotel/motel administration; human services; kindergarten/preschool education; liberal arts and sciences/liberal studies; medical radiologic technology; music; photography; psychology; recording arts technology; registered nursing/registered nurse; respiratory care therapy; sign language interpretation and translation.
Academics *Calendar:* semesters. *Degree:* certificates, diplomas, and associate. *Special study options:* academic remediation for entering students, accelerated degree program, adult/continuing education programs, advanced placement credit, cooperative education, distance learning, English as a second language, external degree program, honors programs, independent study, internships, off-campus study, part-time degree program, services for LD

students, student-designed majors, study abroad, summer session for credit. *ROTC:* Army (c).
Library Main Campus Library plus 2 others. *Books:* 84,000 (physical); *Databases:* 40. Weekly public service hours: 30; students can reserve study rooms.
Student Life *Housing:* college housing not available. *Activities and Organizations:* drama/theater group, student-run newspaper, choral group, Philadelphia L.E.A.D.S, Phi Theta Kappa, Student Government Association, Vanguard Student Newspaper, Fundraising Club. *Campus security:* 24-hour emergency response devices and patrols, phone/alert systems in classrooms/buildings, electronic messages/alerts, ID required to enter buildings. *Student services:* personal/psychological counseling, women's center, legal services.
Athletics Member NJCAA. *Intercollegiate sports:* basketball M/W, cheerleading M/W, cross-country running M/W, tennis M/W, track and field M/W, volleyball W. *Intramural sports:* soccer M/W, volleyball M/W.
Costs (2016–17) *Tuition:* area resident $4440 full-time, $153 per credit hour part-time; state resident $8880 full-time, $306 per credit hour part-time; nonresident $13,320 full-time, $459 per credit hour part-time. Full-time tuition and fees vary according to course load and program. Part-time tuition and fees vary according to course load and program. *Payment plan:* installment. *Waivers:* senior citizens and employees or children of employees.
Applying *Options:* electronic application, early admission, deferred entrance. *Required for some:* high school transcript, specific entry requirements for allied health and nursing programs. *Application deadlines:* rolling (freshmen), rolling (transfers). *Notification:* continuous (freshmen), continuous (transfers).
Freshman Application Contact Community College of Philadelphia, 1700 Spring Garden Street, Philadelphia, PA 19130-3991. *Phone:* 215-751-8010. *Website:* http://www.ccp.edu/.

Consolidated School of Business
Lancaster, Pennsylvania

Freshman Application Contact Ms. Libby Paul, Admissions Representative, Consolidated School of Business, 2124 Ambassador Circle, Lancaster, PA 17603. *Phone:* 717-394-6211. *Toll-free phone:* 800-541-8298. *Fax:* 717-394-6213. *E-mail:* lpaul@csb.edu. *Website:* http://www.csb.edu/.

Consolidated School of Business
York, Pennsylvania

Freshman Application Contact Ms. Sandra Swanger, Admissions Representative, Consolidated School of Business, 1605 Clugston Road, York, PA 17404. *Phone:* 717-764-9550. *Toll-free phone:* 800-520-0691. *Fax:* 717-764-9469. *E-mail:* sswanger@csb.edu. *Website:* http://www.csb.edu/.

Dean Institute of Technology
Pittsburgh, Pennsylvania

Director of Admissions Mr. Nicholas Ali, Admissions Director, Dean Institute of Technology, 1501 West Liberty Avenue, Pittsburgh, PA 15226-1103. *Phone:* 412-531-4433. *Website:* http://www.deantech.edu/.

Delaware County Community College
Media, Pennsylvania

Freshman Application Contact Ms. Hope Diehl, Director of Admissions and Enrollment Services, Delaware County Community College, 901 South Media Line Road, Media, PA 19063-1094. *Phone:* 610-359-5050. *Fax:* 610-723-1530. *E-mail:* admiss@dccc.edu. *Website:* http://www.dccc.edu/.

Douglas Education Center
Monessen, Pennsylvania

Freshman Application Contact Ms. Sherry Lee Walters, Director of Enrollment Services, Douglas Education Center, 130 Seventh Street, Monessen, PA 15062. *Phone:* 724-684-3684 Ext. 2181. *Toll-free phone:* 800-413-6013. *Website:* http://www.dec.edu/.

Erie Institute of Technology
Erie, Pennsylvania

Freshman Application Contact Erie Institute of Technology, 940 Millcreek Mall, Erie, PA 16565. *Phone:* 814-868-9900. *Toll-free phone:* 866-868-3743. *Website:* http://www.erieit.edu/.

Fortis Institute
Erie, Pennsylvania

Director of Admissions Guy M. Euliano, President, Fortis Institute, 5757 West 26th Street, Erie, PA 16506. *Phone:* 814-838-7673. *Toll-free phone:* 855-4-FORTIS. *Fax:* 814-838-8642. *E-mail:* geuliano@tsbi.org. *Website:* http://www.fortis.edu/.

Fortis Institute
Forty Fort, Pennsylvania

Freshman Application Contact Admissions Office, Fortis Institute, 166 Slocum Street, Forty Fort, PA 18704. *Phone:* 570-288-8400. *Toll-free phone:* 855-4-FORTIS. *Website:* http://www.fortis.edu/.

Fortis Institute
Scranton, Pennsylvania

Director of Admissions Ms. Heather Contardi, Director of Admissions, Fortis Institute, 517 Ash Street, Scranton, PA 18509. *Phone:* 570-558-1818. *Toll-free phone:* 855-4-FORTIS. *Fax:* 570-342-4537. *E-mail:* heatherp@markogroup.com. *Website:* http://www.fortis.edu/.

Great Lakes Institute of Technology
Erie, Pennsylvania

Admissions Office Contact Great Lakes Institute of Technology, 5100 Peach Street, Erie, PA 16509. *Website:* http://www.glit.edu/.

Harcum College
Bryn Mawr, Pennsylvania

Freshman Application Contact Office of Enrollment Management, Harcum College, 750 Montgomery Avenue, Bryn Mawr, PA 19010-3476. *Phone:* 610-526-6050. *E-mail:* enroll@harcum.edu. *Website:* http://www.harcum.edu/.

Harrisburg Area Community College
Harrisburg, Pennsylvania

- **State and locally supported** 2-year, founded 1964
- **Urban** 212-acre campus
- **Coed,** 18,837 undergraduate students, 29% full-time, 64% women, 36% men

Undergraduates 5,377 full-time, 13,460 part-time. Students come from 30 states and territories; 63 other countries; 2% are from out of state; 11% Black or African American, non-Hispanic/Latino; 10% Hispanic/Latino; 3% Asian, non-Hispanic/Latino; 0.1% Native Hawaiian or other Pacific Islander, non-Hispanic/Latino; 0.2% American Indian or Alaska Native, non-Hispanic/Latino; 3% Two or more races, non-Hispanic/Latino; 2% Race/ethnicity unknown; 2% international; 5% transferred in.

Freshmen *Admission:* 12,814 applied, 12,812 admitted, 2,434 enrolled.

Faculty *Total:* 1,057, 31% full-time, 47% with terminal degrees. *Student/faculty ratio:* 17:1.

Majors Accounting technology and bookkeeping; administrative assistant and secretarial science; architectural engineering technology; architecture; automobile/automotive mechanics technology; biology/biological sciences; business administration and management; business/commerce; cardiovascular technology; chemistry; civil engineering technology; clinical/medical laboratory technology; communication and journalism related; computer and information sciences; computer and information systems security; computer science; computer systems networking and telecommunications; construction engineering technology; construction trades; criminal justice/law enforcement administration; criminal justice/police science; culinary arts; dental hygiene; design and visual communications; diagnostic medical sonography and ultrasound technology; dietetics; dramatic/theater arts; early childhood education; electrical, electronic and communications engineering technology; electrician; emergency medical technology (EMT paramedic); engineering; engineering technologies and engineering related; environmental science; fire science/firefighting; general studies; geographic information science and cartography; graphic design; health and physical education/fitness; health/health-care administration; health professions related; health services administration; heating, air conditioning, ventilation and refrigeration maintenance technology; human services; international relations and affairs; legal assistant/paralegal; mathematics; mechanical engineering/mechanical

technology; mechatronics, robotics, and automation engineering; medical/clinical assistant; medical informatics; music management; nuclear medical technology; philosophy; photography; physical sciences; psychology; radiologic technology/science; registered nursing/registered nurse; respiratory care therapy; sales, distribution, and marketing operations; secondary education; social sciences; social work; structural engineering; surgical technology; visual and performing arts; viticulture and enology; web page, digital/multimedia and information resources design.

Academics *Calendar:* semesters. *Degree:* certificates, diplomas, and associate. *Special study options:* academic remediation for entering students, adult/continuing education programs, advanced placement credit, distance learning, double majors, English as a second language, honors programs, independent study, internships, part-time degree program, services for LD students, summer session for credit. *ROTC:* Army (b).

Library McCormick Library.

Student Life *Housing:* college housing not available. *Activities and Organizations:* drama/theater group, student-run newspaper, Student Government Association, Phi Theta Kappa, African-American Student Association, Mosiaco Club, Fourth Estate. *Campus security:* 24-hour emergency response devices and patrols, late-night transport/escort service.

Athletics *Intercollegiate sports:* basketball M/W, golf M/W, soccer M, volleyball M/W.

Costs (2016–17) *Tuition:* area resident $4224 full-time, $176 per credit hour part-time; state resident $5112 full-time, $213 per credit hour part-time; nonresident $6144 full-time, $256 per credit hour part-time. Full-time tuition and fees vary according to location and program. Part-time tuition and fees vary according to location and program. *Required fees:* $1152 full-time, $48 per credit hour part-time. *Payment plan:* installment. *Waivers:* employees or children of employees.

Financial Aid Of all full-time matriculated undergraduates who enrolled in 2016, 3,610 applied for aid, 2,741 were judged to have need.

Applying *Options:* electronic application, early admission, deferred entrance. *Application fee:* $35. *Required for some:* high school transcript, 1 letter of recommendation, interview.

Freshman Application Contact Harrisburg Area Community College, Harrisburg, PA 17110. *Toll-free phone:* 800-ABC-HACC. *E-mail:* admit@hacc.edu. *Website:* http://www.hacc.edu/.

JNA Institute of Culinary Arts
Philadelphia, Pennsylvania

- **Proprietary** 2-year, founded 1988
- **Urban** campus with easy access to Philadelphia
- **Coed,** 59 undergraduate students, 100% full-time, 51% women, 49% men

Undergraduates 59 full-time. Students come from 7 states and territories; 10% are from out of state; 57% Black or African American, non-Hispanic/Latino; 11% Hispanic/Latino; 3% Asian, non-Hispanic/Latino. *Retention:* 60% of full-time freshmen returned.

Freshmen *Admission:* 28 enrolled.

Majors Restaurant, culinary, and catering management.

Academics *Calendar:* continuous. *Degree:* associate.

Costs (2016–17) *Tuition:* $12,650 full-time, $375 per credit hour part-time. Full-time tuition and fees vary according to program. No tuition increase for student's term of enrollment. *Required fees:* $75 full-time. *Payment plan:* installment. *Waivers:* employees or children of employees.

Freshman Application Contact Admissions Office, JNA Institute of Culinary Arts, 1212 South Broad Street, Philadelphia, PA 19146. *Website:* http://www.culinaryarts.com/.

Johnson College
Scranton, Pennsylvania

Freshman Application Contact Ms. Melissa Ide, Director of Enrollment Management, Johnson College, 3427 North Main Avenue, Scranton, PA 18508. *Phone:* 570-702-8910. *Toll-free phone:* 800-2WE-WORK. *Fax:* 570-348-2181. *E-mail:* admit@johnson.edu. *Website:* http://www.johnson.edu/.

Keystone Technical Institute
Harrisburg, Pennsylvania

Freshman Application Contact Tom Bogush, Director of Admissions, Keystone Technical Institute, 2301 Academy Drive, Harrisburg, PA 17112. *Phone:* 717-545-4747. *Toll-free phone:* 800-400-3322. *Fax:* 717-901-9090. *E-mail:* info@acadcampus.com. *Website:* http://www.kti.edu/.

Lackawanna College
Scranton, Pennsylvania

- **Independent** 2-year, founded 1894
- **Urban** 4-acre campus
- **Coed,** 1,691 undergraduate students, 65% full-time, 42% women, 58% men

Undergraduates 1,104 full-time, 587 part-time. 14% are from out of state; 20% Black or African American, non-Hispanic/Latino; 9% Hispanic/Latino; 2% Asian, non-Hispanic/Latino; 0.2% American Indian or Alaska Native, non-Hispanic/Latino; 2% Two or more races, non-Hispanic/Latino; 4% Race/ethnicity unknown; 0.5% international; 20% live on campus. *Retention:* 53% of full-time freshmen returned.

Freshmen *Admission:* 349 enrolled. *Test scores:* SAT critical reading scores over 500: 19%; SAT math scores over 500: 23%; SAT writing scores over 500: 15%; SAT critical reading scores over 600: 2%; SAT math scores over 600: 3%; SAT writing scores over 600: 1%.

Faculty *Total:* 168, 16% full-time, 5% with terminal degrees. *Student/faculty ratio:* 16:1.

Majors Accounting; accounting technology and bookkeeping; administrative assistant and secretarial science; banking and financial support services; biology/biological sciences; biotechnology; business administration and management; business administration, management and operations related; business/commerce; cardiopulmonary technology; communications technology; computer and information sciences; criminal justice/safety; diagnostic medical sonography and ultrasound technology; early childhood education; education; emergency medical technology (EMT paramedic); environmental studies; general studies; humanities; human services; industrial electronics technology; industrial technology; legal assistant/paralegal; liberal arts and sciences/liberal studies; management information systems; mass communication/media; medical administrative assistant and medical secretary; mental health counseling; petroleum technology; speech communication and rhetoric; surgical technology.

Academics *Calendar:* semesters. *Degree:* certificates, diplomas, and associate. *Special study options:* academic remediation for entering students, adult/continuing education programs, cooperative education, double majors, English as a second language, internships, part-time degree program, services for LD students, summer session for credit. *ROTC:* Army (c), Air Force (c).

Library Albright Memorial Library plus 1 other. Students can reserve study rooms.

Student Life *Housing:* on-campus residence required through sophomore year. *Options:* coed, men-only. Campus housing is university owned. *Activities and Organizations:* Student Government, Student/Alumni Association, United Cultures Leadership Association, Green Falcons (sustainability action group), Sonography Club. *Campus security:* 24-hour emergency response devices and patrols, late-night transport/escort service, controlled dormitory access, patrols by college liaison staff. *Student services:* personal/psychological counseling.

Athletics Member NJCAA. *Intercollegiate sports:* baseball M(s), basketball M(s)/W(s), cheerleading W(s), cross-country running M(s)/W(s), football M(s), golf M(s)/W(s), soccer W(s), softball W(s), volleyball W(s).

Standardized Tests *Recommended:* SAT (for admission), ACT (for admission), SAT or ACT (for admission).

Costs (2016–17) *Comprehensive fee:* $23,380 includes full-time tuition ($13,870), mandatory fees ($710), and room and board ($8800). Full-time tuition and fees vary according to course load. Part-time tuition: $499 per credit. *Required fees:* $105 per term part-time. *Room and board:* college room only: $6000. *Payment plans:* installment, deferred payment. *Waivers:* employees or children of employees.

Financial Aid Of all full-time matriculated undergraduates who enrolled in 2015, 1,047 applied for aid, 984 were judged to have need, 42 had their need fully met. 82 Federal Work-Study jobs (averaging $961). 22 state and other part-time jobs (averaging $517). In 2015, 11 non-need-based awards were made. *Average percent of need met:* 50%. *Average financial aid package:* $9289. *Average need-based loan:* $3277. *Average need-based gift aid:* $6925. *Average non-need-based aid:* $2854. *Average indebtedness upon graduation:* $19,780.

Applying *Options:* electronic application, early admission, deferred entrance. *Application fee:* $35. *Required:* high school transcript, interview. *Application deadlines:* rolling (freshmen), rolling (transfers).

Freshman Application Contact Ms. Michelle Ketten, Associate Director of Admissions, Lackawanna College, 501 Vine Street, Scranton, PA 18509. *Phone:* 570-504-8094. *Toll-free phone:* 877-346-3552. *Fax:* 570-961-7843. *E-mail:* kettenm@lackawanna.edu. *Website:* http://www.lackawanna.edu/.

Lancaster County Career and Technology Center
Willow Street, Pennsylvania

Admissions Office Contact Lancaster County Career and Technology Center, 1730 Hans Herr Drive, Willow Street, PA 17584. *Website:* http://www.lcctc.org/.

Lansdale School of Business
North Wales, Pennsylvania

- **Proprietary** 2-year, founded 1918
- **Suburban** campus with easy access to Philadelphia
- **Coed,** 372 undergraduate students

Majors Accounting and business/management; business automation/technology/data entry; computer graphics; computer software and media applications related; computer systems networking and telecommunications; legal assistant/paralegal; marketing/marketing management; medical/clinical assistant; web/multimedia management and webmaster; web page, digital/multimedia and information resources design.

Academics *Calendar:* semesters. *Degree:* certificates, diplomas, and associate. *Special study options:* accelerated degree program, adult/continuing education programs, double majors, honors programs, independent study, internships, off-campus study, part-time degree program, summer session for credit.

Library Lansdale School of Business Library.

Student Life *Housing:* college housing not available. *Activities and Organizations:* student-run newspaper.

Applying *Application fee:* $30. *Required:* high school transcript, interview. *Application deadlines:* rolling (freshmen), rolling (transfers).

Freshman Application Contact Lansdale School of Business, 290 Wissahickon Avenue, North Wales, PA 19454. *Phone:* 215-699-5700 Ext. 112. *Toll-free phone:* 800-219-0486. *Website:* http://www.lsb.edu/.

Laurel Business Institute
Uniontown, Pennsylvania

Freshman Application Contact Mrs. Lisa Dolan, Laurel Business Institute, 11 East Penn Street, PO Box 877, Uniontown, PA 15401. *Phone:* 724-439-4900 Ext. 158. *Fax:* 724-439-3607. *E-mail:* ldolan@laurel.edu. *Website:* http://www.laurel.edu/locations/uniontown.

Laurel Technical Institute
Sharon, Pennsylvania

Freshman Application Contact Irene Lewis, Laurel Technical Institute, 200 Sterling Avenue, Sharon, PA 16146. *Phone:* 724-983-0700. *Fax:* 724-983-8355. *E-mail:* info@biop.edu. *Website:* http://www.laurel.edu/locations/sharon.

Lehigh Carbon Community College
Schnecksville, Pennsylvania

- **State and locally supported** 2-year, founded 1967
- **Suburban** 254-acre campus with easy access to Philadelphia
- **Endowment** $5.0 million
- **Coed,** 6,620 undergraduate students, 38% full-time, 61% women, 39% men

Undergraduates 2,502 full-time, 4,118 part-time. Students come from 13 states and territories; 18 other countries; 0.4% are from out of state; 6% Black or African American, non-Hispanic/Latino; 20% Hispanic/Latino; 2% Asian, non-Hispanic/Latino; 0.2% American Indian or Alaska Native, non-Hispanic/Latino; 4% Two or more races, non-Hispanic/Latino; 7% Race/ethnicity unknown; 0.5% international; 55% transferred in.

Freshmen *Admission:* 4,006 applied, 4,006 admitted, 1,410 enrolled.

Faculty *Total:* 458, 19% full-time, 3% with terminal degrees. *Student/faculty ratio:* 19:1.

Majors Accounting technology and bookkeeping; aeronautics/aviation/aerospace science and technology; airline pilot and flight crew; animation, interactive technology, video graphics and special effects; art; biology/biological sciences; biotechnology; building/construction site management; business administration and management; business/commerce; chemical technology; chemistry; computer and information sciences; computer and information systems security; computer programming; computer programming (specific applications); computer systems networking and telecommunications; construction trades; criminal justice/law enforcement administration; criminal justice/safety; drafting and design technology; early childhood education; education; electrical, electronic and communications engineering technology; engineering; environmental science; fashion/apparel design; game and interactive media design; general studies; geographic information science and cartography; graphic design; health information/medical records technology; health services/allied health/health sciences; heating, air conditioning, ventilation and refrigeration maintenance technology; human resources management; human services; industrial electronics technology; interior design; kinesiology and exercise science; legal assistant/paralegal; liberal arts and sciences/liberal studies; manufacturing engineering technology; mathematics; mechanical engineering/mechanical technology; medical/clinical assistant; nanotechnology; occupational therapist assistant; physical sciences; physical therapy technology; psychology; public administration; radio and television broadcasting technology; recording arts technology; registered nursing/registered nurse; resort management; social work; special education; speech communication and rhetoric; sport and fitness administration/management; teacher assistant/aide; veterinary/animal health technology; web page, digital/multimedia and information resources design.

Academics *Calendar:* semesters. *Degree:* certificates, diplomas, and associate. *Special study options:* academic remediation for entering students, advanced placement credit, cooperative education, distance learning, English as a second language, external degree program, honors programs, independent study, internships, off-campus study, part-time degree program, services for LD students, summer session for credit. *ROTC:* Army (c).

Library Rothrock Library. *Books:* 49,325 (physical), 66,651 (digital/electronic); *Serial titles:* 220 (physical); *Databases:* 44. Weekly public service hours: 71.

Student Life *Housing:* college housing not available. *Activities and Organizations:* drama/theater group, student-run newspaper, choral group, Phi Theta Kappa, Justice Society, PSI BETA (psychology club), Student Government Association, Teacher Education Student Association (TESA). *Campus security:* 24-hour emergency response devices. *Student services:* personal/psychological counseling.

Athletics Member NJCAA. *Intercollegiate sports:* baseball M, basketball M/W, golf M/W, soccer M, softball W, volleyball W. *Intramural sports:* basketball M/W, golf M/W, table tennis M/W, volleyball M/W.

Costs (2017–18) *Tuition:* area resident $3000 full-time, $100 per credit hour part-time; state resident $6270 full-time, $209 per credit hour part-time; nonresident $9540 full-time, $318 per credit hour part-time. *Required fees:* $900 full-time, $40 per credit hour part-time. *Payment plan:* installment. *Waivers:* senior citizens and employees or children of employees.

Applying *Options:* electronic application. *Required for some:* essay or personal statement, high school transcript, interview. *Application deadlines:* rolling (freshmen), rolling (transfers). *Notification:* continuous (freshmen), continuous (transfers).

Freshman Application Contact Ms. Nancy Kelley, Admission Representative, Lehigh Carbon Community College, 4525 Education Park Drive, Schnecksville, PA 18078. *Phone:* 610-799-1558. *Fax:* 610-799-1527. *E-mail:* admissions@lccc.edu. *Website:* http://www.lccc.edu/.

Lincoln Technical Institute
Allentown, Pennsylvania

Freshman Application Contact Admissions Office, Lincoln Technical Institute, 5151 Tilghman Street, Allentown, PA 18104. *Phone:* 610-398-5301. *Toll-free phone:* 844-215-1513. *Website:* http://www.lincolntech.edu/.

Lincoln Technical Institute
Philadelphia, Pennsylvania

Director of Admissions Mr. James Kuntz, Executive Director, Lincoln Technical Institute, 9191 Torresdale Avenue, Philadelphia, PA 19136. *Phone:* 215-335-0800. *Toll-free phone:* 844-215-1513. *Fax:* 215-335-1443. *E-mail:* jkuntz@lincolntech.com. *Website:* http://www.lincolntech.edu/.

Luzerne County Community College
Nanticoke, Pennsylvania

- **County-supported** 2-year, founded 1966
- **Suburban** 122-acre campus with easy access to Philadelphia
- **Coed,** 5,669 undergraduate students, 45% full-time, 61% women, 39% men

Undergraduates 2,526 full-time, 3,143 part-time. 4% Black or African American, non-Hispanic/Latino; 12% Hispanic/Latino; 1% Asian, non-Hispanic/Latino; 0.2% Native Hawaiian or other Pacific Islander, non-Hispanic/Latino; 0.4% American Indian or Alaska Native, non-Hispanic/Latino; 1% Two or more races, non-Hispanic/Latino; 10% Race/ethnicity unknown. *Retention:* 55% of full-time freshmen returned.

Freshmen *Admission:* 2,458 applied, 2,458 admitted, 1,260 enrolled.
Faculty *Total:* 438, 26% full-time. *Student/faculty ratio:* 15:1.
Majors Accounting; administrative assistant and secretarial science; airline pilot and flight crew; architectural engineering; architectural engineering technology; automobile/automotive mechanics technology; aviation/airway management; baking and pastry arts; banking and financial support services; biological and physical sciences; building/property maintenance; business administration and management; child-care provision; commercial and advertising art; commercial photography; computer and information sciences; computer and information sciences related; computer graphics; computer programming related; computer science; computer systems networking and telecommunications; computer technology/computer systems technology; court reporting; criminal justice/law enforcement administration; culinary arts; data entry/microcomputer applications; data processing and data processing technology; dental assisting; dental hygiene; drafting and design technology; drafting/design engineering technologies related; drawing; early childhood education; education; electrical, electronic and communications engineering technology; electrician; emergency medical technology (EMT paramedic); engineering technology; executive assistant/executive secretary; fire science/firefighting; food technology and processing; funeral service and mortuary science; general studies; graphic and printing equipment operation/production; graphic design; health and physical education/fitness; health/health-care administration; heating, air conditioning, ventilation and refrigeration maintenance technology; hospitality and recreation marketing; hotel/motel administration; humanities; human services; industrial and product design; international business/trade/commerce; journalism; legal assistant/paralegal; liberal arts and sciences and humanities related; liberal arts and sciences/liberal studies; mathematics; medical administrative assistant and medical secretary; painting; photography; physical education teaching and coaching; plumbing technology; pre-pharmacy studies; radio and television broadcasting technology; registered nursing/registered nurse; respiratory care therapy; social sciences; surgical technology; tourism and travel services management; tourism and travel services marketing.

Academics *Calendar:* semesters. *Degree:* certificates, diplomas, and associate. *Special study options:* academic remediation for entering students, accelerated degree program, advanced placement credit, distance learning, external degree program, internships, part-time degree program, services for LD students, summer session for credit. *ROTC:* Army (c).

Library Learning Resources Center plus 1 other. Students can reserve study rooms.

Student Life *Housing:* college housing not available. *Activities and Organizations:* drama/theater group, student-run radio and television station, choral group, Student Government, Circle K, Nursing Forum, Science Club, SADAH. *Campus security:* 24-hour patrols.

Athletics Member NJCAA. *Intercollegiate sports:* baseball M, basketball M/W, cross-country running M/W, golf M/W, soccer M/W, softball W, volleyball W. *Intramural sports:* badminton M/W, basketball M/W, bowling M/W, softball M/W, tennis M/W, volleyball M/W.

Applying *Options:* electronic application. *Recommended:* high school transcript.

Freshman Application Contact Mr. James Domzalski, Director of Enrollment Management, Luzerne County Community College, 1333 South Prospect Street, Nanticoke, PA 18634. *Phone:* 570-740-0342. *Toll-free phone:* 800-377-5222 Ext. 7337. *Fax:* 570-740-0238. *E-mail:* admissions@luzerne.edu. *Website:* http://www.luzerne.edu/.

Manor College
Jenkintown, Pennsylvania

- **Independent Byzantine Catholic** 2-year, founded 1947
- **Suburban** 35-acre campus with easy access to Philadelphia
- **Endowment** $2.8 million
- **Coed,** 622 undergraduate students, 64% full-time, 73% women, 27% men

Undergraduates 400 full-time, 222 part-time. Students come from 4 states and territories; 2 other countries; 3% are from out of state; 36% Black or African American, non-Hispanic/Latino; 10% Hispanic/Latino; 3% Asian, non-Hispanic/Latino; 1% American Indian or Alaska Native, non-Hispanic/Latino; 3% Two or more races, non-Hispanic/Latino; 5% Race/ethnicity unknown; 0.2% international; 17% transferred in; 11% live on campus. *Retention:* 65% of full-time freshmen returned.

Freshmen *Admission:* 393 applied, 350 admitted, 120 enrolled. *Average high school GPA:* 2.71. *Test scores:* SAT critical reading scores over 500: 19%; SAT math scores over 500: 20%; SAT writing scores over 500: 13%; ACT scores over 18: 20%; SAT critical reading scores over 600: 3%; SAT math scores over 600: 5%; SAT writing scores over 600: 1%; ACT scores over 24: 10%; SAT critical reading scores over 700: 1%.

Faculty *Total:* 98, 26% full-time, 48% with terminal degrees. *Student/faculty ratio:* 10:1.

Majors Accounting; business administration and management; business, management, and marketing related; communication and media related; computer programming (specific applications); criminal justice/law enforcement administration; dental assisting; dental hygiene; education (specific levels and methods) related; elementary education; health/health-care administration; health/medical preparatory programs related; health professions related; legal assistant/paralegal; liberal arts and sciences/liberal studies; marketing/marketing management; prenursing studies; pre-occupational therapy; pre-pharmacy studies; pre-physical therapy; psychology; sport and fitness administration/management; veterinary/animal health technology.

Academics *Calendar:* semesters. *Degrees:* certificates, associate, and postbachelor's certificates. *Special study options:* academic remediation for entering students, accelerated degree program, advanced placement credit, distance learning, double majors, honors programs, independent study, internships, part-time degree program, services for LD students, summer session for credit.

Library Basileiad Library. *Books:* 28,400 (physical), 5,047 (digital/electronic); *Serial titles:* 8 (physical); *Databases:* 12. Weekly public service hours: 65.

Student Life *Housing Options:* coed. Campus housing is university owned. *Activities and Organizations:* choral group, Rotoract (student service organization), Vet Tech Club, Campus Activities Board, Macrinian Yearbook, Phi Theta Kappa (honor society). *Campus security:* 24-hour emergency response devices and patrols, late-night transport/escort service. *Student services:* personal/psychological counseling.

Athletics Member NJCAA. *Intercollegiate sports:* baseball M, basketball M/W, soccer M/W, volleyball W.

Standardized Tests *Required for some:* SAT or ACT (for admission). *Recommended:* SAT or ACT (for admission).

Costs (2017–18) *Comprehensive fee:* $24,754 includes full-time tuition ($16,428), mandatory fees ($600), and room and board ($7726). Full-time tuition and fees vary according to course load and program. Part-time tuition: $669 per credit hour. Part-time tuition and fees vary according to course load and program. *Required fees:* $100 per term part-time. *Payment plan:* installment. *Waivers:* adult students, senior citizens, and employees or children of employees.

Financial Aid Of all full-time matriculated undergraduates who enrolled in 2009, 35 Federal Work-Study jobs (averaging $3000). 10 state and other part-time jobs (averaging $3600).

Applying *Options:* electronic application, deferred entrance. *Required:* high school transcript. *Recommended:* letters of recommendation. *Application deadlines:* rolling (freshmen), rolling (transfers). *Notification:* continuous (freshmen), continuous (transfers).

Freshman Application Contact Stephanie Walker, Director of Admissions, Manor College, 700 Fox Chase Road, Jenkintown, PA 19046. *Phone:* 215-885-2216 Ext. 205. *Fax:* 215-576-6564. *E-mail:* swalker@manor.edu. *Website:* http://www.manor.edu/.

McCann School of Business & Technology
Hazelton, Pennsylvania

Admissions Office Contact McCann School of Business & Technology, 370 Maplewood Drive, Humboldt Industrial Park, Hazelton, PA 18202. *Toll-free phone:* 866-865-8065. *Website:* http://www.mccann.edu/.

McCann School of Business & Technology
Lewisburg, Pennsylvania

Admissions Office Contact McCann School of Business & Technology, 7495 Westbranch Highway, Lewisburg, PA 17837. *Toll-free phone:* 866-865-8065. *Website:* http://www.mccann.edu/.

McCann School of Business & Technology
Pottsville, Pennsylvania

Freshman Application Contact Mrs. Amelia Hopkins, Director, Pottsville Campus, McCann School of Business & Technology, 2650 Woodglen Road, Pottsville, PA 17901. *Phone:* 570-622-7622. *Toll-free phone:* 866-865-8065. *Fax:* 570-622-7770. *Website:* http://www.mccann.edu/.

Mercyhurst North East
North East, Pennsylvania

Director of Admissions Travis Lindahl, Director of Admissions, Mercyhurst North East, 16 West Division Street, North East, PA 16428. *Phone:* 814-725-6217. *Toll-free phone:* 866-846-6042. *Fax:* 814-725-6251. *E-mail:* neadmiss@mercyhurst.edu. *Website:* http://northeast.mercyhurst.edu/.

Montgomery County Community College
Blue Bell, Pennsylvania

- **County-supported** 2-year, founded 1964
- **Suburban** 186-acre campus with easy access to Philadelphia
- **Coed,** 11,480 undergraduate students, 33% full-time, 57% women, 43% men

Undergraduates 3,773 full-time, 7,707 part-time. Students come from 22 states and territories; 107 other countries; 1% are from out of state; 15% Black or African American, non-Hispanic/Latino; 7% Hispanic/Latino; 6% Asian, non-Hispanic/Latino; 0.3% Native Hawaiian or other Pacific Islander, non-Hispanic/Latino; 0.3% American Indian or Alaska Native, non-Hispanic/Latino; 3% Two or more races, non-Hispanic/Latino; 8% Race/ethnicity unknown; 2% international. *Retention:* 65% of full-time freshmen returned.

Freshmen *Admission:* 7,738 applied, 7,738 admitted, 2,718 enrolled.

Faculty *Total:* 707, 24% full-time. *Student/faculty ratio:* 18:1.

Majors Accounting; accounting technology and bookkeeping; administrative assistant and secretarial science; art; baking and pastry arts; biology/biological sciences; biotechnology; business administration and management; business/commerce; business/corporate communications; child-care and support services management; clinical/medical laboratory technology; commercial and advertising art; communications technologies and support services related; computer and information sciences; computer programming; computer systems networking and telecommunications; criminal justice/police science; culinary arts; dental hygiene; electrical, electronic and communications engineering technology; electromechanical technology; elementary education; engineering science; engineering technologies and engineering related; environmental science; fire prevention and safety technology; health and physical education/fitness; hospitality and recreation marketing; humanities; information science/studies; liberal arts and sciences/liberal studies; management information systems and services related; mathematics; mechanical engineering/mechanical technology; medical/clinical assistant; medical radiologic technology; network and system administration; physical education teaching and coaching; physical sciences; physical therapy technology; psychiatric/mental health services technology; psychology; radiologic technology/science; radio, television, and digital communication related; real estate; recording arts technology; registered nursing/registered nurse; sales, distribution, and marketing operations; secondary education; social sciences; speech communication and rhetoric; surgical technology; teacher assistant/aide; tourism and travel services marketing; web/multimedia management and webmaster.

Academics *Calendar:* semesters plus winter term. *Degree:* certificates and associate. *Special study options:* academic remediation for entering students, accelerated degree program, adult/continuing education programs, advanced placement credit, cooperative education, distance learning, English as a second language, honors programs, independent study, internships, part-time degree program, services for LD students, student-designed majors, study abroad, summer session for credit.

Library The Brendlinger Library. *Books:* 74,157 (physical); *Databases:* 47. Weekly public service hours: 75; students can reserve study rooms.

Student Life *Housing:* college housing not available. *Activities and Organizations:* drama/theater group, student-run newspaper, radio and television station, choral group, West End Student Theater (drama club), Phi Theta Kappa, Gender Sexuality Association, Thrive (Christian fellowship), Student Government. *Campus security:* 24-hour emergency response devices and patrols, late-night transport/escort service, bicycle patrol. *Student services:* health clinic, personal/psychological counseling.

Athletics Member NJCAA. *Intercollegiate sports:* baseball M, basketball M/W, soccer M/W, softball W, volleyball W. *Intramural sports:* badminton M/W, basketball M/W, bowling M/W, cross-country running M/W, football M, racquetball M/W, soccer M/W, table tennis M/W, tennis M/W, volleyball M/W, weight lifting M/W.

Costs (2016–17) *Tuition:* area resident $4320 full-time, $144 per credit part-time; state resident $8940 full-time, $288 per credit part-time; nonresident $13,560 full-time, $432 per credit part-time. Full-time tuition and fees vary according to program. Part-time tuition and fees vary according to program. *Required fees:* $1290 full-time, $43 per credit part-time. *Payment plan:* deferred payment. *Waivers:* senior citizens and employees or children of employees.

Financial Aid Of all full-time matriculated undergraduates who enrolled in 2015, 60 Federal Work-Study jobs (averaging $2500).

Applying *Options:* electronic application, early admission, deferred entrance. *Required:* high school transcript. *Required for some:* interview. *Application deadline:* rolling (transfers). *Notification:* continuous (freshmen), continuous (transfers).

Freshman Application Contact Montgomery County Community College, Blue Bell, PA 19422. *Phone:* 215-641-6551. *Fax:* 215-619-7188. *E-mail:* admrec@admin.mc3.edu. *Website:* http://www.mc3.edu/.

New Castle School of Trades
New Castle, Pennsylvania

- **Independent** 2-year, founded 1945
- **Rural** 20-acre campus with easy access to Pittsburgh
- **Coed, primarily men**

Undergraduates 503 full-time. Students come from 3 states and territories; 45% are from out of state.

Faculty *Student/faculty ratio:* 11:1.

Academics *Calendar:* quarters. *Degree:* diplomas and associate. *Special study options:* part-time degree program.

Library New Castle School of Trades plus 1 other. *Books:* 600 (physical). Weekly public service hours: 60.

Student Life *Campus security:* 24-hour emergency response devices.

Standardized Tests *Required:* Wonderlic aptitude test (for admission).

Applying *Required:* high school transcript, interview. *Required for some:* essay or personal statement.

Freshman Application Contact Mr. Joe Blazak, Admissions Director, New Castle School of Trades, 4117 Pulaski Road, New Castle, PA 16101. *Phone:* 724-964-8811. *Toll-free phone:* 800-837-8299. *Fax:* 724-964-8177. *Website:* http://www.ncstrades.com/.

Northampton Community College
Bethlehem, Pennsylvania

- **State and locally supported** 2-year, founded 1967
- **Suburban** 165-acre campus with easy access to Philadelphia
- **Endowment** $40.9 million
- **Coed,** 10,067 undergraduate students, 44% full-time, 59% women, 41% men

Undergraduates 4,435 full-time, 5,632 part-time. Students come from 23 states and territories; 47 other countries; 2% are from out of state; 13% Black or African American, non-Hispanic/Latino; 21% Hispanic/Latino; 2% Asian, non-Hispanic/Latino; 0.2% Native Hawaiian or other Pacific Islander, non-Hispanic/Latino; 0.2% American Indian or Alaska Native, non-Hispanic/Latino; 3% Two or more races, non-Hispanic/Latino; 1% Race/ethnicity unknown; 1% international; 9% transferred in; 6% live on campus.

Freshmen *Admission:* 4,643 applied, 4,643 admitted, 2,078 enrolled.

Faculty *Total:* 703, 17% full-time, 16% with terminal degrees. *Student/faculty ratio:* 20:1.

Majors Accounting technology and bookkeeping; acting; administrative assistant and secretarial science; applied psychology; architectural engineering technology; athletic training; automobile/automotive mechanics technology; biology/biological sciences; biotechnology; business administration and management; business/commerce; CAD/CADD drafting/design technology; chemistry; computer and information systems security; computer programming; computer science; computer support specialist; computer systems networking and telecommunications; construction management; criminal justice/safety; culinary arts; dental hygiene; diagnostic medical sonography and ultrasound technology; early childhood education; electrical, electronic and communications engineering technology; electrician; electromechanical technology; engineering; environmental science; fine/studio arts; fire science/firefighting; fire services administration; funeral service and mortuary science; general studies; graphic design; heating, air conditioning, ventilation and refrigeration maintenance technology; hotel/motel administration; industrial electronics technology; interior design; international/global studies; journalism; legal assistant/paralegal; liberal arts and sciences and humanities related; liberal arts and sciences/liberal studies; marketing/marketing management; mathematics; medical administrative assistant and medical secretary; meeting and event planning; middle school education; physics; public health education and promotion; quality control technology; radio and television broadcasting technology; radiologic technology/science; registered nursing/registered nurse; restaurant/food services management; secondary education; social work; speech communication and rhetoric; sport and fitness administration/management; teacher assistant/aide; veterinary/animal health technology; web page, digital/multimedia and information resources design; welding technology.

Academics *Calendar:* semesters. *Degree:* certificates, diplomas, and associate. *Special study options:* academic remediation for entering students, adult/continuing education programs, advanced placement credit, distance learning, English as a second language, honors programs, independent study, internships, off-campus study, part-time degree program, services for LD students, student-designed majors, study abroad, summer session for credit.

Library Paul & Harriett Mack Library. *Books:* 72,983 (physical), 23,273 (digital/electronic); *Serial titles:* 275 (physical), 36,998 (digital/electronic); *Databases:* 75. Weekly public service hours: 83; students can reserve study rooms.

Student Life *Housing Options:* coed. Campus housing is university owned. *Activities and Organizations:* student-run newspaper, radio station, choral group, Phi Theta Kappa, Student Senate, Nursing Student Organization, American Dental Hygiene Association (ADHA), International Student Organization. *Campus security:* 24-hour emergency response devices and patrols, controlled dormitory access. *Student services:* health clinic, personal/psychological counseling.

Athletics Member NJCAA. *Intercollegiate sports:* baseball M, basketball M/W, cross-country running M/W, golf M, lacrosse M, soccer M/W, softball W, tennis W, volleyball W. *Intramural sports:* basketball M/W, cheerleading M(c)/W(c), soccer M/W, volleyball M/W.

Costs (2016–17) *Tuition:* area resident $2910 full-time, $97 per credit hour part-time; state resident $5820 full-time, $194 per credit hour part-time; nonresident $8730 full-time, $291 per credit hour part-time. Full-time tuition and fees vary according to course load. Part-time tuition and fees vary according to course load. *Required fees:* $1200 full-time, $40 per credit hour part-time. *Room and board:* $8452; room only: $5150. Room and board charges vary according to board plan and housing facility. *Payment plan:* installment. *Waivers:* senior citizens and employees or children of employees.

Financial Aid Of all full-time matriculated undergraduates who enrolled in 2016, 268 Federal Work-Study jobs (averaging $2400). 149 state and other part-time jobs (averaging $2000).

Applying *Options:* electronic application, deferred entrance. *Application fee:* $25. *Required for some:* high school transcript, minimum 2.5 GPA, interview, interview for radiography and veterinary programs. *Recommended:* high school transcript. *Application deadlines:* rolling (freshmen), rolling (transfers). *Notification:* continuous (freshmen), continuous (transfers).

Freshman Application Contact Mr. James McCarthy, Director of Admissions, Northampton Community College, 3835 Green Pond Road, Bethlehem, PA 18020-7599. *Phone:* 610-861-5506. *Fax:* 610-861-5551. *E-mail:* jrmccarthy@northampton.edu. *Website:* http://www.northampton.edu/.

Penn Commercial Business and Technical School
Washington, Pennsylvania

Director of Admissions Mr. Michael John Joyce, Director of Admissions, Penn Commercial Business and Technical School, 242 Oak Spring Road, Washington, PA 15301. *Phone:* 724-222-5330 Ext. 1. *Toll-free phone:* 888-309-7484. *E-mail:* mjoyce@penn-commercial.com. *Website:* http://www.penncommercial.net/.

Pennco Tech
Bristol, Pennsylvania

Freshman Application Contact Pennco Tech, 3815 Otter Street, Bristol, PA 19007-3696. *Phone:* 215-785-0111. *Toll-free phone:* 800-575-9399. *Website:* http://www.penncotech.com/.

Penn State DuBois
DuBois, Pennsylvania

- **State-related** primarily 2-year, founded 1935, part of Pennsylvania State University
- **Small-town** campus
- **Coed,** 608 undergraduate students, 79% full-time, 43% women, 57% men

Undergraduates 483 full-time, 125 part-time. 3% are from out of state; 2% Black or African American, non-Hispanic/Latino; 2% Hispanic/Latino; 0.6% Asian, non-Hispanic/Latino; 0.2% American Indian or Alaska Native, non-Hispanic/Latino; 0.6% Two or more races, non-Hispanic/Latino; 0.6% Race/ethnicity unknown; 0.8% international; 5% transferred in. *Retention:* 75% of full-time freshmen returned.

Freshmen *Admission:* 373 applied, 320 admitted, 165 enrolled. *Average high school GPA:* 3.1. *Test scores:* SAT critical reading scores over 500: 46%; SAT math scores over 500: 58%; ACT scores over 18: 100%; SAT critical reading scores over 600: 14%; SAT math scores over 600: 18%; SAT critical reading scores over 700: 1%; SAT math scores over 700: 5%.

Faculty *Total:* 60, 70% full-time, 52% with terminal degrees. *Student/faculty ratio:* 11:1.

Majors Accounting; acting; actuarial science; adult and continuing education administration; advertising; aerospace, aeronautical and astronautical/space engineering; African American/Black studies; agribusiness; agricultural and extension education; agricultural business and management related; agricultural engineering; agricultural mechanization; agriculture; agronomy and crop science; animal sciences; animal sciences related; anthropology; applied economics; archeology; architectural engineering; art; art history, criticism and conservation; art teacher education; Asian studies (East); astronomy; atmospheric sciences and meteorology; biochemistry; bioengineering and biomedical engineering; biological and biomedical sciences related; biological and physical sciences; biology/biological sciences; biology/biotechnology laboratory technician; biomedical technology; business administration and management; business/commerce; business/managerial economics; chemical engineering; chemistry; civil engineering; classics and classical languages; clinical/medical laboratory technology; communication and journalism related; communication sciences and disorders; comparative literature; computer and information sciences; computer engineering; criminal justice/law enforcement administration; economics; electrical and electronics engineering; electrical, electronic and communications engineering technology; elementary education; engineering science; English; environmental/environmental health engineering; film/cinema/video studies; finance; food science; foreign language teacher education; forest sciences and biology; forest technology; French; geography; geological and earth sciences/geosciences related; geology/earth science; German; graphic design; health/health-care administration; history; horticultural science; hospitality administration related; human development and family studies; human nutrition; industrial engineering; information science/studies; international business/trade/commerce; international relations and affairs; Italian; Japanese; Jewish/Judaic studies; journalism; kinesiology and exercise science; labor and industrial relations; landscaping and groundskeeping; Latin American studies; liberal arts and sciences/liberal studies; management information systems; marketing/marketing management; materials science; mathematics; mechanical engineering; mechanical engineering/mechanical technology; medical microbiology and bacteriology; medieval and Renaissance studies; metallurgical technology; mining and mineral engineering; music; natural resources and conservation related; natural resources/conservation; nuclear engineering; occupational therapist assistant; organizational behavior; parks, recreation and leisure facilities management; petroleum engineering; philosophy; physical therapy technology; physics; political science and government; premedical studies; psychology; registered nursing/registered nurse; rehabilitation and therapeutic professions related; religious studies; Russian; secondary education; sociology; soil science and agronomy; Spanish; special education; speech communication and rhetoric; statistics; telecommunications technology; theater design and technology; toxicology; turf and turfgrass management; visual and performing arts; wildlife, fish and wildlands science and management; women's studies.

Academics *Calendar:* semesters. *Degrees:* certificates, associate, and bachelor's. *Special study options:* adult/continuing education programs, external degree program.

Student Life *Housing:* college housing not available.

Athletics Member NJCAA. *Intercollegiate sports:* basketball M, cross-country running M/W, golf M/W, volleyball W. *Intramural sports:* basketball M/W, football M, soccer M/W, table tennis M/W, volleyball M/W.

Standardized Tests *Required:* SAT or ACT (for admission).

Costs (2016–17) *Tuition:* state resident $12,718 full-time, $524 per credit hour part-time; nonresident $19,598 full-time, $817 per credit hour part-time. Full-time tuition and fees vary according to course level, degree level, location, program, and student level. Part-time tuition and fees vary according to course level, course load, degree level, location, program, and student level. *Required fees:* $898 full-time. *Payment plan:* deferred payment. *Waivers:* senior citizens and employees or children of employees.

Financial Aid Of all full-time matriculated undergraduates who enrolled in 2015, 447 applied for aid, 391 were judged to have need, 23 had their need fully met. In 2015, 17 non-need-based awards were made. *Average percent of need met:* 65%. *Average financial aid package:* $11,311. *Average need-based loan:* $3865. *Average need-based gift aid:* $6450. *Average non-need-based aid:* $2741. *Average indebtedness upon graduation:* $36,818.

Applying *Options:* electronic application, early admission, deferred entrance. *Application fee:* $65. *Required:* high school transcript. *Required for some:* interview. *Recommended:* essay or personal statement. *Application deadlines:* rolling (freshmen), rolling (transfers). *Notification:* continuous (freshmen), continuous (transfers).

Freshman Application Contact Admissions Office, Penn State DuBois, 1 College Place, DuBois, PA 15801. *Phone:* 814-375-4720. *Toll-free phone:* 800-346-7627. *Fax:* 814-375-4784. *E-mail:* duboisinfo@psi.edu. *Website:* http://www.ds.psu.edu/.

Penn State Fayette, The Eberly Campus
Lemont Furnace, Pennsylvania

- **State-related** primarily 2-year, founded 1934, part of Pennsylvania State University
- **Small-town** campus
- **Coed,** 643 undergraduate students, 87% full-time, 59% women, 41% men

Undergraduates 557 full-time, 86 part-time. 5% are from out of state; 4% Black or African American, non-Hispanic/Latino; 3% Hispanic/Latino; 0.3% Asian, non-Hispanic/Latino; 0.2% Native Hawaiian or other Pacific Islander, non-Hispanic/Latino; 0.3% American Indian or Alaska Native, non-Hispanic/Latino; 4% Two or more races, non-Hispanic/Latino; 0.8% Race/ethnicity unknown; 1% international; 5% transferred in. *Retention:* 74% of full-time freshmen returned.

Freshmen *Admission:* 593 applied, 475 admitted, 194 enrolled. *Average high school GPA:* 3.19. *Test scores:* SAT critical reading scores over 500: 37%; SAT math scores over 500: 51%; ACT scores over 18: 71%; SAT critical reading scores over 600: 7%; SAT math scores over 600: 6%; ACT scores over 24: 29%; SAT math scores over 700: 2%.

Faculty *Total:* 68, 63% full-time, 38% with terminal degrees. *Student/faculty ratio:* 12:1.

Majors Accounting; acting; actuarial science; adult and continuing education administration; advertising; aerospace, aeronautical and astronautical/space engineering; African American/Black studies; agribusiness; agricultural and extension education; agricultural business and management related; agricultural engineering; agricultural mechanization; agriculture; agronomy and crop science; animal sciences; animal sciences related; anthropology; applied economics; archeology; architectural engineering; architectural engineering technology; art; art history, criticism and conservation; art teacher education; Asian studies (East); astronomy; atmospheric sciences and meteorology; biochemistry; bioengineering and biomedical engineering; biological and biomedical sciences related; biological and physical sciences; biology/biological sciences; biology/biotechnology laboratory technician; biomedical technology; business administration and management; business/commerce; business/managerial economics; chemical engineering; chemistry; civil engineering; classics and classical languages; communication and journalism related; communication sciences and disorders; comparative literature; computer and information sciences; computer engineering; criminal justice/law enforcement administration; criminal justice/safety; economics; electrical and electronics engineering; electrical, electronic and communications engineering technology; elementary education; engineering science; English; environmental/environmental health engineering; film/cinema/video studies; finance; food science; foreign language teacher education; forest sciences and biology; forest technology; French; geography; geological and earth sciences/geosciences related; geology/earth science; German; graphic design; health/health-care administration; history; horticultural science; hospitality administration related; human development and family studies; human nutrition; industrial engineering; information science/studies; international relations and affairs; Italian; Japanese; Jewish/Judaic studies; journalism; kinesiology and exercise science; labor and industrial relations; landscaping and groundskeeping; Latin American studies; liberal arts and sciences/liberal studies; logistics, materials, and supply chain management; management information systems; manufacturing engineering; marketing/marketing management; materials science; mathematics; mechanical engineering; medical microbiology and bacteriology; medieval and Renaissance studies; metallurgical technology; mining and mineral engineering; natural resources and conservation related; natural resources/conservation; nuclear engineering; organizational behavior; parks, recreation and leisure facilities management; petroleum engineering; philosophy; physics; political science and government; premedical studies; psychology; registered nursing/registered nurse; rehabilitation and therapeutic professions related; religious studies; Russian; secondary education; sociology; soil science and agronomy; Spanish; special education; speech communication and rhetoric; statistics; telecommunications technology; theater design and technology; toxicology; turf and turfgrass management; visual and performing arts; women's studies.

Academics *Calendar:* semesters. *Degrees:* certificates, associate, and bachelor's. *Special study options:* adult/continuing education programs, external degree program.

Student Life *Housing:* college housing not available. *Campus security:* student patrols, 8-hour patrols by trained security personnel.

Athletics Member NJCAA. *Intercollegiate sports:* baseball M, basketball M, softball W, volleyball W. *Intramural sports:* badminton M/W, basketball M/W, cheerleading M(c)/W(c), equestrian sports M(c)/W(c), football M/W, golf M(c)/W(c), softball M/W, tennis M/W, volleyball M/W, weight lifting M/W.

Standardized Tests *Required:* SAT or ACT (for admission).

Costs (2016–17) *Tuition:* state resident $12,718 full-time, $524 per credit hour part-time; nonresident $19,598 full-time, $817 per credit hour part-time. Full-time tuition and fees vary according to course level, degree level, location, program, and student level. Part-time tuition and fees vary according to course level, course load, degree level, location, program, and student level. *Required fees:* $898 full-time. *Payment plan:* deferred payment. *Waivers:* senior citizens and employees or children of employees.

Financial Aid Of all full-time matriculated undergraduates who enrolled in 2015, 546 applied for aid, 472 were judged to have need, 26 had their need fully met. In 2015, 51 non-need-based awards were made. *Average percent of need met:* 65%. *Average financial aid package:* $10,865. *Average need-based loan:* $3854. *Average need-based gift aid:* $6633. *Average non-need-based aid:* $2743. *Average indebtedness upon graduation:* $35,525.

Applying *Options:* electronic application, early admission, deferred entrance. *Application fee:* $65. *Required:* high school transcript. *Required for some:* interview. *Recommended:* essay or personal statement. *Application deadlines:* rolling (freshmen), rolling (transfers). *Notification:* continuous (freshmen), continuous (transfers).

Freshman Application Contact Admissions Office, Penn State Fayette, The Eberly Campus, 2201 University Drive, Lemont Furnace, PA 15456. *Phone:* 724-430-4130. *Toll-free phone:* 877-568-4130. *Fax:* 724-430-4175. *E-mail:* feadm@psu.edu.
Website: http://www.fe.psu.edu/.

Penn State Mont Alto
Mont Alto, Pennsylvania

- **State-related** primarily 2-year, founded 1929, part of Pennsylvania State University
- **Small-town** campus
- **Coed,** 902 undergraduate students, 76% full-time, 53% women, 47% men

Undergraduates 683 full-time, 219 part-time. 15% are from out of state; 7% Black or African American, non-Hispanic/Latino; 8% Hispanic/Latino; 2% Asian, non-Hispanic/Latino; 4% Two or more races, non-Hispanic/Latino; 0.7% Race/ethnicity unknown; 0.1% international; 5% transferred in; 24% live on campus. *Retention:* 76% of full-time freshmen returned.

Freshmen *Admission:* 711 applied, 552 admitted, 269 enrolled. *Average high school GPA:* 3.21. *Test scores:* SAT critical reading scores over 500: 42%; SAT math scores over 500: 51%; ACT scores over 18: 96%; SAT critical reading scores over 600: 11%; SAT math scores over 600: 14%; ACT scores over 24: 46%; SAT critical reading scores over 700: 2%; SAT math scores over 700: 2%; ACT scores over 30: 17%.

Faculty *Total:* 95, 60% full-time, 34% with terminal degrees. *Student/faculty ratio:* 11:1.

Majors Accounting; acting; actuarial science; adult and continuing education administration; advertising; aerospace, aeronautical and astronautical/space engineering; African American/Black studies; agribusiness; agricultural and extension education; agricultural business and management related; agricultural engineering; agricultural mechanization; agriculture; agronomy and crop science; animal sciences; animal sciences related; anthropology; applied economics; archeology; architectural engineering; art; art history, criticism and conservation; art teacher education; Asian studies (East); astronomy; atmospheric sciences and meteorology; biochemistry; bioengineering and biomedical engineering; biological and biomedical sciences related; biological and physical sciences; biology/biological sciences; biology/biotechnology laboratory technician; business administration and management; business/commerce; business/managerial economics; chemical engineering; chemistry; civil engineering; classics and classical languages; communication and journalism related; communication sciences and disorders; comparative literature; computer and information sciences; computer engineering; criminal justice/law enforcement administration; economics; electrical and electronics engineering; elementary education; engineering science; English; environmental/environmental health engineering; film/cinema/video studies; finance; food science; foreign language teacher education; forest sciences and biology; forest technology; French; geography; geological and earth sciences/geosciences related; geology/earth science; German; graphic design; health/health-care administration; history; horticultural science; hospitality administration related; human development and family studies; human nutrition; industrial engineering; information science/studies; international relations and affairs; Italian; Japanese; Jewish/Judaic studies; journalism; kinesiology and exercise science; labor and industrial relations; landscaping and groundskeeping; Latin American studies; liberal arts and sciences/liberal studies; management information systems; marketing/marketing management; materials science; mathematics; mechanical engineering; medical microbiology and bacteriology; medieval and Renaissance studies; mining and mineral engineering; music; natural resources and conservation related; natural resources/conservation; nuclear engineering; occupational therapist assistant; occupational therapy; organizational behavior; parks, recreation and leisure facilities management; petroleum engineering; philosophy; physical therapy technology; physics; political science and government; premedical studies; psychology; registered nursing/registered nurse; rehabilitation and therapeutic professions related; religious studies; Russian; secondary education; sociology; soil science and

agronomy; Spanish; special education; speech communication and rhetoric; statistics; theater design and technology; toxicology; turf and turfgrass management; visual and performing arts; women's studies.

Academics *Calendar:* semesters. *Degrees:* certificates, associate, and bachelor's. *Special study options:* adult/continuing education programs, external degree program. *ROTC:* Army (c).

Student Life *Housing Options:* coed, special housing for students with disabilities. Campus housing is university owned. Freshman campus housing is guaranteed. *Campus security:* 24-hour patrols, controlled dormitory access.

Athletics Member NJCAA. *Intercollegiate sports:* basketball M/W, cheerleading M/W, cross-country running M/W, golf M/W, soccer M/W, softball W, tennis M/W, volleyball W. *Intramural sports:* badminton M/W, basketball M/W, cheerleading M(c)/W(c), racquetball M/W, soccer M/W, softball W, volleyball M/W.

Standardized Tests *Required:* SAT or ACT (for admission).

Costs (2016–17) *Tuition:* state resident $12,718 full-time, $524 per credit hour part-time; nonresident $19,598 full-time, $817 per credit hour part-time. Full-time tuition and fees vary according to course load, degree level, location, program, and student level. Part-time tuition and fees vary according to course level, course load, degree level, location, program, and student level. *Required fees:* $960 full-time. *Room and board:* $11,860; room only: $5940. Room and board charges vary according to board plan, housing facility, and location. *Payment plan:* deferred payment. *Waivers:* senior citizens and employees or children of employees.

Financial Aid Of all full-time matriculated undergraduates who enrolled in 2015, 602 applied for aid, 522 were judged to have need, 28 had their need fully met. In 2015, 34 non-need-based awards were made. *Average percent of need met:* 62%. *Average financial aid package:* $11,228. *Average need-based loan:* $4068. *Average need-based gift aid:* $6419. *Average non-need-based aid:* $3498. *Average indebtedness upon graduation:* $43,317.

Applying *Options:* electronic application, early admission, deferred entrance. *Application fee:* $65. *Required:* high school transcript. *Required for some:* interview. *Recommended:* essay or personal statement. *Application deadlines:* rolling (freshmen), rolling (transfers). *Notification:* continuous (freshmen), continuous (transfers).

Freshman Application Contact Admissions Office, Penn State Mont Alto, 1 Campus Drive, Mont Alto, PA 17237. *Phone:* 717-749-6130. *Toll-free phone:* 800-392-6173. *Fax:* 717-749-6132. *E-mail:* psuma@psu.edu.
Website: http://www.ma.psu.edu/.

Penn State Shenango
Sharon, Pennsylvania

- **State-related** primarily 2-year, founded 1965, part of Pennsylvania State University
- **Small-town** campus
- **Coed,** 462 undergraduate students, 52% full-time, 71% women, 29% men

Undergraduates 239 full-time, 223 part-time. 23% are from out of state; 8% Black or African American, non-Hispanic/Latino; 3% Hispanic/Latino; 2% Two or more races, non-Hispanic/Latino; 1% Race/ethnicity unknown; 7% transferred in. *Retention:* 60% of full-time freshmen returned.

Freshmen *Admission:* 198 applied, 143 admitted, 77 enrolled. *Average high school GPA:* 3.04. *Test scores:* SAT critical reading scores over 500: 41%; SAT math scores over 500: 26%; ACT scores over 18: 100%; SAT critical reading scores over 600: 11%; SAT math scores over 600: 7%; ACT scores over 24: 50%; ACT scores over 30: 25%.

Faculty *Total:* 51, 53% full-time, 31% with terminal degrees. *Student/faculty ratio:* 9:1.

Majors Accounting; acting; actuarial science; adult and continuing education administration; advertising; aerospace, aeronautical and astronautical/space engineering; African American/Black studies; agribusiness; agricultural and extension education; agricultural business and management related; agricultural engineering; agricultural mechanization; agriculture; agronomy and crop science; animal sciences; animal sciences related; anthropology; applied economics; archeology; architectural engineering; art; art history, criticism and conservation; art teacher education; Asian studies (East); astronomy; atmospheric sciences and meteorology; biochemistry; bioengineering and biomedical engineering; biological and biomedical sciences related; biological and physical sciences; biology/biological sciences; biology/biotechnology laboratory technician; biomedical technology; business administration and management; business/commerce; business/managerial economics; chemical engineering; chemistry; civil engineering; classics and classical languages; communication and journalism related; communication sciences and disorders; comparative literature; computer and information sciences; computer engineering; criminal justice/law enforcement administration; economics; electrical and electronics engineering; electrical, electronic and communications engineering technology; elementary education; engineering science; English; environmental/environmental health engineering; film/cinema/video studies; finance; food science; foreign language teacher education; forest sciences and biology; forest technology;

French; geography; geological and earth sciences/geosciences related; geology/earth science; German; graphic design; health/health-care administration; history; horticultural science; hospitality administration related; human development and family studies; human nutrition; industrial engineering; information science/studies; international relations and affairs; Italian; Japanese; Jewish/Judaic studies; journalism; kinesiology and exercise science; labor and industrial relations; landscaping and groundskeeping; Latin American studies; liberal arts and sciences/liberal studies; logistics, materials, and supply chain management; management information systems; marketing/marketing management; materials science; mathematics; mechanical engineering; mechanical engineering/mechanical technology; medical microbiology and bacteriology; medieval and Renaissance studies; metallurgical technology; mining and mineral engineering; music; natural resources and conservation related; natural resources/conservation; nuclear engineering; organizational behavior; parks, recreation and leisure facilities management; petroleum engineering; philosophy; physical therapy technology; physics; political science and government; premedical studies; psychology; registered nursing/registered nurse; rehabilitation and therapeutic professions related; religious studies; Russian; secondary education; sociology; soil science and agronomy; Spanish; special education; speech communication and rhetoric; statistics; telecommunications technology; theater design and technology; toxicology; turf and turfgrass management; visual and performing arts; women's studies.
Academics *Calendar:* semesters. *Degrees:* certificates, associate, and bachelor's. *Special study options:* adult/continuing education programs, external degree program.
Student Life *Housing:* college housing not available.
Athletics *Intramural sports:* basketball M(c)/W, bowling M/W, football M(c), golf M/W, softball M/W, tennis M/W, volleyball M/W.
Standardized Tests *Required:* SAT or ACT (for admission).
Costs (2016–17) *Tuition:* state resident $12,474 full-time, $504 per credit hour part-time; nonresident $19,220 full-time, $801 per credit hour part-time. Full-time tuition and fees vary according to course level, degree level, location, program, and student level. Part-time tuition and fees vary according to course level, course load, degree level, location, program, and student level. *Required fees:* $822 full-time. *Payment plan:* deferred payment. *Waivers:* senior citizens and employees or children of employees.
Financial Aid Of all full-time matriculated undergraduates who enrolled in 2015, 259 applied for aid, 247 were judged to have need, 12 had their need fully met. In 2015, 15 non-need-based awards were made. *Average percent of need met:* 62%. *Average financial aid package:* $13,323. *Average need-based loan:* $3902. *Average need-based gift aid:* $7384. *Average non-need-based aid:* $2366. *Average indebtedness upon graduation:* $39,706.
Applying *Options:* electronic application, early admission, deferred entrance. *Application fee:* $65. *Required:* high school transcript. *Application deadlines:* rolling (freshmen), rolling (transfers). *Notification:* continuous (freshmen), continuous (transfers).
Freshman Application Contact Admissions Office, Penn State Shenango, 147 Shenango Avenue, Sharon, PA 16146. *Phone:* 724-983-2803. *Fax:* 724-983-2820. *E-mail:* psushenango@psu.edu.
Website: http://www.shenango.psu.edu/.

Pennsylvania Highlands Community College
Johnstown, Pennsylvania

- **State and locally supported** 2-year, founded 1994
- **Small-town** campus
- **Coed**

Undergraduates 866 full-time, 1,590 part-time. 4% Black or African American, non-Hispanic/Latino; 2% Hispanic/Latino; 2% Asian, non-Hispanic/Latino; 0.2% American Indian or Alaska Native, non-Hispanic/Latino; 2% Two or more races, non-Hispanic/Latino; 3% Race/ethnicity unknown; 4% transferred in.
Faculty *Student/faculty ratio:* 26:1.
Academics *Calendar:* semesters. *Degree:* certificates, diplomas, and associate. *Special study options:* academic remediation for entering students, adult/continuing education programs, advanced placement credit, cooperative education, distance learning, independent study, internships, part-time degree program, services for LD students, summer session for credit.
Library Mangarella Library. *Books:* 1,274 (physical), 2,192 (digital/electronic); *Databases:* 35.
Athletics Member NJCAA.
Costs (2016–17) *Tuition:* area resident $3930 full-time, $131 per credit hour part-time; state resident $6090 full-time, $203 per credit hour part-time; nonresident $9150 full-time, $305 per credit hour part-time. Full-time tuition and fees vary according to program. Part-time tuition and fees vary according to course load and program. *Required fees:* $1860 full-time, $62 per credit hour part-time.

Financial Aid Of all full-time matriculated undergraduates who enrolled in 2015, 25 Federal Work-Study jobs (averaging $2500).
Applying *Options:* electronic application. *Application fee:* $20.
Freshman Application Contact Mr. Jeff Maul, Admissions Officer, Pennsylvania Highlands Community College, 101 Community College Way, Johnstown, PA 15904. *Phone:* 814-262-6431. *Toll-free phone:* 888-385-7325. *Fax:* 814-269-9743. *E-mail:* jmaul@pennhighlands.edu.
Website: http://www.pennhighlands.edu/.

Pennsylvania Institute of Health and Technology
Mount Braddock, Pennsylvania

Admissions Office Contact Pennsylvania Institute of Health and Technology, 1015 Mount Braddock Road, Mount Braddock, PA 15465.
Website: http://www.piht.edu/.

Pennsylvania Institute of Technology
Media, Pennsylvania

- **Independent** 2-year, founded 1953
- **Small-town** 12-acre campus with easy access to Philadelphia
- **Coed,** 492 undergraduate students, 28% full-time, 81% women, 19% men

Undergraduates 137 full-time, 355 part-time. 56% Black or African American, non-Hispanic/Latino; 3% Hispanic/Latino; 1% Asian, non-Hispanic/Latino; 0.2% Native Hawaiian or other Pacific Islander, non-Hispanic/Latino; 2% Two or more races, non-Hispanic/Latino; 21% Race/ethnicity unknown.
Freshmen *Admission:* 361 enrolled.
Faculty *Total:* 74, 26% full-time. *Student/faculty ratio:* 14:1.
Majors Allied health and medical assisting services related; biomedical technology; business administration and management; communication; computer science; corrections and criminal justice related; electrical, electronic and communications engineering technology; engineering technology; general studies; health/health-care administration; health information/medical records technology; health services/allied health/health sciences; medical office management; pharmacy technician; physical therapy technology; practical nursing, vocational nursing and nursing assistants related; psychiatric/mental health services technology.
Academics *Calendar:* 4 terms. *Degree:* certificates and associate. *Special study options:* academic remediation for entering students, adult/continuing education programs, advanced placement credit, cooperative education, part-time degree program, summer session for credit.
Library Pennsylvania Institute of Technology Library/Learning Resource Center.
Student Life *Housing:* college housing not available. *Campus security:* 24-hour emergency response devices. *Student services:* personal/psychological counseling.
Costs (2016–17) *Tuition:* $13,500 full-time, $375 per credit hour part-time. Full-time tuition and fees vary according to program. Part-time tuition and fees vary according to course load and program. *Required fees:* $3600 full-time, $100 per credit hour part-time. *Payment plan:* installment. *Waivers:* employees or children of employees.
Financial Aid Of all full-time matriculated undergraduates who enrolled in 2015, 15 Federal Work-Study jobs (averaging $1025). *Financial aid deadline:* 8/1.
Applying *Options:* electronic application, deferred entrance. *Application fee:* $25. *Required:* high school transcript, interview. *Required for some:* 2 letters of recommendation. *Recommended:* essay or personal statement. *Application deadlines:* 10/9 (freshmen), 10/9 (transfers). *Notification:* continuous until 10/9 (freshmen), continuous until 10/9 (transfers).
Freshman Application Contact Mr. Matthew Meyers, Director of Admissions, Pennsylvania Institute of Technology, 800 Manchester Avenue, Media, PA 19063-4036. *Phone:* 610-892-1543. *Toll-free phone:* 800-422-0025. *Fax:* 610-892-1510. *E-mail:* info@pit.edu.
Website: http://www.pit.edu/.

Pittsburgh Career Institute
Pittsburgh, Pennsylvania

- **Proprietary** 2-year, founded 1980
- **Urban** campus
- **Coed,** 200 undergraduate students

Majors Diagnostic medical sonography and ultrasound technology.
Academics *Calendar:* continuous. *Degree:* associate. *Special study options:* academic remediation for entering students, accelerated degree program, adult/continuing education programs, advanced placement credit, cooperative education, English as a second language, internships, services for LD students.

Library Campus Library.

Student Life *Housing:* college housing not available. *Campus security:* 24-hour emergency response devices, 14-hour security patrols Monday through Friday.

Athletics *Intramural sports:* basketball M.

Standardized Tests *Recommended:* SAT or ACT (for admission), SAT Subject Tests (for admission).

Financial Aid Of all full-time matriculated undergraduates who enrolled in 2015, 25 Federal Work-Study jobs (averaging $1200).

Applying *Options:* electronic application, early admission, deferred entrance. *Application fee:* $25. *Required:* high school transcript, interview.

Freshman Application Contact Pittsburgh Career Institute, 421 Seventh Avenue, Pittsburgh, PA 15219-1907. *Phone:* 412-281-2600. *Toll-free phone:* 800-333-6607.

Website: http://www.pci.edu/.

Pittsburgh Institute of Aeronautics
Pittsburgh, Pennsylvania

- **Independent** 2-year, founded 1929
- **Suburban** campus
- **Coed, primarily men,** 368 undergraduate students, 100% full-time, 6% women, 94% men

Undergraduates 368 full-time. Students come from 19 states and territories; 26% are from out of state; 6% Black or African American, non-Hispanic/Latino; 3% Hispanic/Latino; 2% Asian, non-Hispanic/Latino; 0.5% Native Hawaiian or other Pacific Islander, non-Hispanic/Latino; 0.8% American Indian or Alaska Native, non-Hispanic/Latino; 4% Two or more races, non-Hispanic/Latino; 0.3% Race/ethnicity unknown; 8% transferred in.

Freshmen *Admission:* 64 applied, 64 admitted, 131 enrolled.

Faculty *Total:* 32, 91% full-time. *Student/faculty ratio:* 10:1.

Majors Aeronautical/aerospace engineering technology; airframe mechanics and aircraft maintenance technology; avionics maintenance technology; electrical, electronic and communications engineering technology.

Academics *Calendar:* quarters. *Degree:* certificates and associate. *Special study options:* academic remediation for entering students.

Library Technical Library.

Student Life *Housing:* college housing not available. *Student services:* personal/psychological counseling.

Applying *Options:* electronic application, deferred entrance. *Required:* high school transcript, PIA Math Skills Assessment. *Recommended:* interview. *Application deadlines:* rolling (freshmen), rolling (transfers). *Notification:* continuous (freshmen), continuous (transfers).

Freshman Application Contact Steven D. Sabold, Director of Admissions, Pittsburgh Institute of Aeronautics, PO Box 10897, Pittsburgh, PA 15236-0897. *Phone:* 412-346-2100. *Toll-free phone:* 800-444-1440. *Fax:* 412-466-5013. *E-mail:* admissions@pia.edu.

Website: http://www.pia.edu/.

Pittsburgh Institute of Mortuary Science, Incorporated
Pittsburgh, Pennsylvania

- **Independent** 2-year, founded 1939
- **Urban** campus
- **Coed,** 193 undergraduate students, 44% full-time, 43% women, 57% men

Undergraduates 85 full-time, 108 part-time. Students come from 12 states and territories; 1 other country; 37% are from out of state.

Freshmen *Admission:* 68 enrolled.

Faculty *Total:* 24, 8% full-time, 13% with terminal degrees. *Student/faculty ratio:* 13:1.

Majors Funeral service and mortuary science.

Academics *Calendar:* trimesters. *Degree:* diplomas and associate. *Special study options:* academic remediation for entering students, adult/continuing education programs, distance learning, part-time degree program, services for LD students.

Library William J. Musmanno Memorial Library. Weekly public service hours: 12.

Student Life *Housing:* college housing not available. *Campus security:* 24-hour emergency response devices.

Costs (2016–17) *Tuition:* $12,000 full-time, $350 per credit hour part-time. Full-time tuition and fees vary according to program. Part-time tuition and fees vary according to program. *Required fees:* $2005 full-time, $2005 per year part-time. *Waivers:* minority students.

Applying *Options:* electronic application. *Application fee:* $50. *Required:* essay or personal statement, high school transcript, minimum 2.0 GPA, 2 letters of recommendation, interview, immunizations. *Application deadlines:* rolling (freshmen), rolling (transfers). *Notification:* continuous (freshmen), continuous (transfers).

Freshman Application Contact Ms. Karen Rocco, Registrar, Pittsburgh Institute of Mortuary Science, Incorporated, 5808 Baum Boulevard, Pittsburgh, PA 15206-3706. *Phone:* 412-362-8500 Ext. 105. *Fax:* 412-362-1684. *E-mail:* pims5808@aol.com.

Website: http://www.pims.edu/.

Pittsburgh Technical College
Oakdale, Pennsylvania

- **Proprietary** primarily 2-year, founded 1946
- **Suburban** 180-acre campus with easy access to Pittsburgh
- **Coed,** 1,875 undergraduate students, 100% full-time, 42% women, 58% men
- **87%** of applicants were admitted

Undergraduates 1,875 full-time. Students come from 11 states and territories; 19% are from out of state; 8% Black or African American, non-Hispanic/Latino; 0.5% Hispanic/Latino; 0.9% Asian, non-Hispanic/Latino; 0.1% Native Hawaiian or other Pacific Islander, non-Hispanic/Latino; 0.3% American Indian or Alaska Native, non-Hispanic/Latino; 5% Two or more races, non-Hispanic/Latino; 17% Race/ethnicity unknown; 10% transferred in; 44% live on campus.

Freshmen *Admission:* 1,865 applied, 1,615 admitted, 663 enrolled. *Average high school GPA:* 2.47.

Faculty *Total:* 133, 57% full-time, 5% with terminal degrees. *Student/faculty ratio:* 14:1.

Majors Business administration and management; computer graphics; computer programming; computer technology/computer systems technology; cooking and related culinary arts; drafting and design technology; electrical, electronic and communications engineering technology; electrical/electronics equipment installation and repair; heating, air conditioning, ventilation and refrigeration maintenance technology; homeland security, law enforcement, firefighting and protective services related; hotel/motel administration; medical/health management and clinical assistant; medical office assistant; network and system administration; registered nursing/registered nurse; surgical technology; web page, digital/multimedia and information resources design; welding technology.

Academics *Calendar:* quarters. *Degrees:* certificates, associate, and bachelor's. *Special study options:* academic remediation for entering students, adult/continuing education programs, advanced placement credit, cooperative education, distance learning, double majors, internships, services for LD students.

Library Library Resource Center. *Books:* 6,529 (physical), 53 (digital/electronic); *Serial titles:* 133 (physical), 2 (digital/electronic); *Databases:* 7. Weekly public service hours: 58.

Student Life *Housing Options:* coed. Campus housing is university owned and leased by the school. *Activities and Organizations:* drama/theater group, Software Development Club, Drama Club, DECA, Gay-Straight Alliance, Magic Club. *Campus security:* 24-hour emergency response devices and patrols, student patrols, late-night transport/escort service, controlled dormitory access. *Student services:* personal/psychological counseling.

Athletics *Intramural sports:* basketball M/W, sand volleyball M/W, soccer M/W, softball M/W, ultimate Frisbee M/W, volleyball M/W.

Standardized Tests *Required:* entrance exams for practical nursing certificate and nursing and surgical technology Associate degrees (for admission). *Required for some:* SAT or ACT (for admission).

Costs (2017–18) *Comprehensive fee:* $25,811 includes full-time tuition ($16,361) and room and board ($9450). Full-time tuition and fees vary according to degree level and program. No tuition increase for student's term of enrollment. *Room and board:* college room only: $6993. Room and board charges vary according to housing facility. *Payment plans:* installment, deferred payment. *Waivers:* children of alumni and employees or children of employees.

Applying *Options:* electronic application, deferred entrance. *Required:* high school transcript. *Required for some:* essay or personal statement, criminal background check, minimum rank in top 80% of class. *Recommended:* interview. *Application deadlines:* rolling (freshmen), rolling (transfers). *Notification:* continuous (freshmen), continuous (transfers).

Freshman Application Contact Ms. Nancy Goodlin, Admissions Office Assistant, Pittsburgh Technical College, 1111 McKee Road, Oakdale, PA 15071. *Phone:* 412-809-5100. *Toll-free phone:* 800-784-9675. *Fax:* 412-809-5351. *E-mail:* goodlin.nancy@ptcollege.edu.

Website: http://www.ptcollege.edu/.

Reading Area Community College

Reading, Pennsylvania

- **County-supported** 2-year, founded 1971
- **Urban** 14-acre campus with easy access to Philadelphia
- **Endowment** $10.6 million
- **Coed**

Undergraduates 936 full-time, 3,154 part-time. 0.3% are from out of state; 11% Black or African American, non-Hispanic/Latino; 32% Hispanic/Latino; 2% Asian, non-Hispanic/Latino; 0.2% Native Hawaiian or other Pacific Islander, non-Hispanic/Latino; 0.4% American Indian or Alaska Native, non-Hispanic/Latino; 3% Two or more races, non-Hispanic/Latino; 0.6% Race/ethnicity unknown.

Faculty *Student/faculty ratio:* 18:1.

Academics *Calendar:* semesters. *Degree:* certificates, diplomas, and associate. *Special study options:* academic remediation for entering students, adult/continuing education programs, advanced placement credit, cooperative education, distance learning, English as a second language, honors programs, part-time degree program, services for LD students, summer session for credit.

Library Yocum Library.

Student Life *Campus security:* 24-hour emergency response devices, late-night transport/escort service.

Standardized Tests *Required for some:* TOEFL. *Recommended:* SAT (for admission), ACT (for admission).

Costs (2016–17) *Tuition:* area resident $3750 full-time, $125 per credit part-time; state resident $7500 full-time, $250 per credit part-time; nonresident $11,250 full-time, $375 per credit part-time. Full-time tuition and fees vary according to course load and program. Part-time tuition and fees vary according to course load and program. *Required fees:* $1560 full-time, $52 per credit part-time.

Financial Aid Of all full-time matriculated undergraduates who enrolled in 2015, 80 Federal Work-Study jobs (averaging $5400). 20 state and other part-time jobs (averaging $3300).

Applying *Options:* electronic application, early admission. *Required for some:* essay or personal statement, high school transcript, 1 letter of recommendation, interview, background/criminal check, physical exam, proof of insurance for selective admissions programs. *Recommended:* high school transcript.

Freshman Application Contact Ms. Debbie Hettinger, Enrollment Services Coordinator/Communications Specialist, Reading Area Community College, PO Box 1706, Reading, PA 19603-1706. *Phone:* 610-372-4721 Ext. 5130. *E-mail:* dhettinger@racc.edu. *Website:* http://www.racc.edu/.

The Restaurant School at Walnut Hill College

Philadelphia, Pennsylvania

- **Proprietary** primarily 2-year, founded 1974
- **Urban** 2-acre campus
- **Coed**
- 97% of applicants were admitted

Undergraduates 429 full-time. Students come from 2 other countries; 28% are from out of state; 29% Black or African American, non-Hispanic/Latino; 6% Hispanic/Latino; 2% Asian, non-Hispanic/Latino; 0.3% American Indian or Alaska Native, non-Hispanic/Latino; 5% Two or more races, non-Hispanic/Latino; 4% Race/ethnicity unknown; 0.5% international; 10% transferred in.

Faculty *Student/faculty ratio:* 22:1.

Academics *Calendar:* quarters. *Degrees:* associate and bachelor's. *Special study options:* internships, part-time degree program.

Library Alumni Resource Center plus 1 other. Weekly public service hours: 61.

Student Life *Campus security:* 24-hour emergency response devices and patrols, student patrols, controlled dormitory access.

Standardized Tests *Recommended:* SAT or ACT (for admission).

Costs (2016–17) *One-time required fee:* $200. *Tuition:* $19,050 full-time. *Required fees:* $3850 full-time. *Room only:* $5400. Room and board charges vary according to housing facility. *Payment plans:* installment, deferred payment.

Financial Aid Of all full-time matriculated undergraduates who enrolled in 2015, 227 applied for aid, 225 were judged to have need. *Average indebtedness upon graduation:* $46,188.

Applying *Options:* electronic application, early admission, early decision, deferred entrance. *Application fee:* $50. *Required:* essay or personal statement, high school transcript, 2 letters of recommendation, interview. *Recommended:* minimum 2.0 GPA.

Freshman Application Contact Mr. John English, Director of Admissions, The Restaurant School at Walnut Hill College, 4207 Walnut Street, Philadelphia, PA 19104-3518. *Phone:* 267-295-2353. *Fax:* 215-222-4219. *E-mail:* jenglish@walnuthillcollege.edu. *Website:* http://www.walnuthillcollege.edu/.

Rosedale Technical Institute

Pittsburgh, Pennsylvania

Freshman Application Contact Ms. Debbie Bier, Director of Admissions, Rosedale Technical Institute, 215 Beecham Drive, Suite 2, Pittsburgh, PA 15205-9791. *Phone:* 412-521-6200. *Toll-free phone:* 800-521-6262. *Fax:* 412-521-2520. *E-mail:* admissions@rosedaletech.org. *Website:* http://www.rosedaletech.org/.

South Hills School of Business & Technology

Altoona, Pennsylvania

Freshman Application Contact Ms. Holly J. Emerick, Director of Admissions, South Hills School of Business & Technology, 508 58th Street, Altoona, PA 16602. *Phone:* 814-944-6134. *Fax:* 814-944-4684. *E-mail:* hemerick@southhills.edu. *Website:* http://www.southhills.edu/.

South Hills School of Business & Technology

State College, Pennsylvania

Freshman Application Contact Mr. Troy R. Otradovec, Regional Director of Admissions, South Hills School of Business & Technology, 480 Waupelani Drive, State College, PA 16801-4516. *Phone:* 814-234-7755 Ext. 2020. *Toll-free phone:* 888-282-7427. *Fax:* 814-234-0926. *E-mail:* admissions@southhills.edu. *Website:* http://www.southhills.edu/.

Thaddeus Stevens College of Technology

Lancaster, Pennsylvania

- **State-supported** 2-year, founded 1905
- **Urban** 33-acre campus with easy access to Philadelphia
- **Endowment** $696,058
- **Coed**

Undergraduates 45% live on campus. *Retention:* 79% of full-time freshmen returned.

Faculty *Student/faculty ratio:* 12:1.

Academics *Calendar:* semesters. *Degree:* certificates and associate. *Special study options:* academic remediation for entering students, advanced placement credit, internships, services for LD students.

Library K. W. Schuler Learning Resources Center plus 1 other. *Books:* 59,073 (physical), 1,187 (digital/electronic); *Serial titles:* 21 (physical), 2,823 (digital/electronic); *Databases:* 21. Weekly public service hours: 78; students can reserve study rooms.

Student Life *Campus security:* 24-hour emergency response devices and patrols, controlled dormitory access.

Athletics Member NCAA, NJCAA.

Standardized Tests *Required:* ACT, SAT, or ACT Compass (for admission).

Applying *Options:* electronic application, deferred entrance. *Application fee:* $45. *Required:* essay or personal statement, high school transcript, minimum 2.0 GPA. *Required for some:* interview.

Freshman Application Contact Ms. Amy Kwiatkowski, Thaddeus Stevens College of Technology, 750 East King Street, Lancaster, PA 17055. *Phone:* 717-391-3540. *Toll-free phone:* 800-842-3832. *E-mail:* kwiatkowski@stevenscollege.edu. *Website:* http://www.stevenscollege.edu/.

Triangle Tech, Bethlehem

Bethlehem, Pennsylvania

Freshman Application Contact Triangle Tech, Bethlehem, 3184 Airport Road, Bethlehem, PA 18017. *Website:* http://www.triangle-tech.edu/.

Triangle Tech, DuBois

Falls Creek, Pennsylvania

Freshman Application Contact Terry Kucic, Director of Admissions, Triangle Tech, DuBois, PO Box 551, DuBois, PA 15801. *Phone:* 814-371-2090. *Toll-free phone:* 800-874-8324. *Fax:* 814-371-9227. *E-mail:* tkucic@triangle-tech.com. *Website:* http://www.triangle-tech.edu/.

Triangle Tech, Erie

Erie, Pennsylvania

Freshman Application Contact Admissions Representative, Triangle Tech, Erie, 2000 Liberty Street, Erie, PA 16502-2594. *Phone:* 814-453-6016. *Toll-free phone:* 800-874-8324 (in-state); 800-TRI-TECH (out-of-state). *Website:* http://www.triangle-tech.edu/.

Triangle Tech, Greensburg

Greensburg, Pennsylvania

Freshman Application Contact Mr. John Mazzarese, Vice President of Admissions, Triangle Tech, Greensburg, 222 East Pittsburgh Street, Greensburg, PA 15601. *Phone:* 412-359-1000. *Toll-free phone:* 800-874-8324. *Website:* http://www.triangle-tech.edu/.

Triangle Tech, Pittsburgh

Pittsburgh, Pennsylvania

Freshman Application Contact Director of Admissions, Triangle Tech, Pittsburgh, 1940 Perrysville Avenue, Pittsburgh, PA 15214-3897. *Phone:* 412-359-1000. *Toll-free phone:* 800-874-8324. *Fax:* 412-359-1012. *E-mail:* info@triangle-tech.edu. *Website:* http://www.triangle-tech.edu/.

Triangle Tech, Sunbury

Sunbury, Pennsylvania

Freshman Application Contact Triangle Tech, Sunbury, 191 Performance Road, Sunbury, PA 17801. *Phone:* 412-359-1000. *Website:* http://www.triangle-tech.edu/.

University of Pittsburgh at Titusville

Titusville, Pennsylvania

- **State-related** 2-year, founded 1963, part of University of Pittsburgh System
- **Small-town** 10-acre campus
- **Endowment** $850,000
- **Coed,** 388 undergraduate students, 81% full-time, 65% women, 35% men

Undergraduates 313 full-time, 75 part-time. Students come from 15 states and territories; 8% are from out of state; 14% Black or African American, non-Hispanic/Latino; 4% Hispanic/Latino; 2% Asian, non-Hispanic/Latino; 2% Two or more races, non-Hispanic/Latino; 2% Race/ethnicity unknown; 4% transferred in; 57% live on campus.

Freshmen *Admission:* 160 enrolled. *Average high school GPA:* 3.1. *Test scores:* SAT critical reading scores over 500: 22%; SAT math scores over 500: 29%; SAT writing scores over 500: 23%; ACT scores over 18: 69%; SAT critical reading scores over 600: 5%; SAT math scores over 600: 4%; SAT writing scores over 600: 4%; ACT scores over 24: 7%.

Faculty *Total:* 48, 52% full-time. *Student/faculty ratio:* 15:1.

Majors Accounting; biology/biological sciences; business/commerce; criminal justice/law enforcement administration; history related; human services; information technology; liberal arts and sciences/liberal studies; management information systems; natural sciences; physical therapy technology; psychology related; registered nursing/registered nurse.

Academics *Calendar:* semesters. *Degree:* associate. *Special study options:* academic remediation for entering students, advanced placement credit, distance learning, internships, part-time degree program, summer session for credit.

Library Haskell Memorial Library.

Student Life *Housing:* on-campus residence required through sophomore year. *Options:* coed, special housing for students with disabilities. Campus housing is university owned. Freshman campus housing is guaranteed. *Activities and Organizations:* Phi Theta Kappa, BSU, SAB, Dining Club, Diversity Club. *Campus security:* 24-hour emergency response devices and patrols, late-night transport/escort service, controlled dormitory access. *Student services:* health clinic, personal/psychological counseling.

Athletics Member NJCAA. *Intercollegiate sports:* basketball M/W, cheerleading M/W, volleyball W. *Intramural sports:* badminton M/W, basketball M/W, bowling M/W, football M/W, golf M/W, racquetball M/W, sand volleyball M/W, softball M/W, tennis M/W, ultimate Frisbee M/W, volleyball M/W, weight lifting M/W.

Standardized Tests *Required:* SAT or ACT (for admission).

Costs (2016–17) *One-time required fee:* $60. *Tuition:* state resident $10,958 full-time, $456 per credit part-time; nonresident $20,702 full-time, $862 per credit part-time. Full-time tuition and fees vary according to program. Part-time tuition and fees vary according to program. *Required fees:* $830 full-time, $135 per term part-time. *Room and board:* $10,372; room only: $5396.

Room and board charges vary according to board plan. *Payment plan:* installment.

Applying *Required:* high school transcript, minimum 2.0 GPA. *Required for some:* essay or personal statement. *Recommended:* interview.

Freshman Application Contact Ms. Colleen R. Motter, Admissions Counselor, University of Pittsburgh at Titusville, 504 East Main Street, Titusville, PA 16354. *Phone:* 814-827-4408. *Toll-free phone:* 888-878-0462. *Fax:* 814-827-4519. *E-mail:* motter@pitt.edu. *Website:* http://www.upt.pitt.edu/.

Valley Forge Military College

Wayne, Pennsylvania

Freshman Application Contact Maj. Greg Potts, Dean of Enrollment Management, Valley Forge Military College, 1001 Eagle Road, Wayne, PA 19087-3695. *Phone:* 610-989-1300. *Toll-free phone:* 800-234-8362. *Fax:* 610-688-1545. *E-mail:* admissions@vfmac.edu. *Website:* http://www.vfmac.edu/.

Vet Tech Institute

Pittsburgh, Pennsylvania

- **Proprietary** 2-year, founded 1958
- **Urban** campus
- **Coed**
- 64% of applicants were admitted

Academics *Calendar:* semesters. *Degree:* associate. *Special study options:* accelerated degree program, internships.

Freshman Application Contact Admissions Office, Vet Tech Institute, 125 7th Street, Pittsburgh, PA 15222-3400. *Phone:* 412-391-7021. *Toll-free phone:* 800-570-0693. *Website:* http://pittsburgh.vettechinstitute.edu/.

Westmoreland County Community College

Youngwood, Pennsylvania

- **County-supported** 2-year, founded 1970
- **Rural** 85-acre campus with easy access to Pittsburgh
- **Endowment** $1.2 million
- **Coed,** 5,554 undergraduate students, 42% full-time, 61% women, 39% men

Undergraduates 2,340 full-time, 3,214 part-time. Students come from 12 states and territories; 0.3% are from out of state; 3% Black or African American, non-Hispanic/Latino; 2% Hispanic/Latino; 0.6% Asian, non-Hispanic/Latino; 0.1% Native Hawaiian or other Pacific Islander, non-Hispanic/Latino; 0.1% American Indian or Alaska Native, non-Hispanic/Latino; 3% Two or more races, non-Hispanic/Latino; 20% transferred in. *Retention:* 62% of full-time freshmen returned.

Freshmen *Admission:* 3,227 applied, 3,227 admitted, 1,084 enrolled.

Faculty *Total:* 427, 19% full-time. *Student/faculty ratio:* 17:1.

Majors Accounting; accounting technology and bookkeeping; administrative assistant and secretarial science; applied horticulture/horticulture operations; architectural drafting and CAD/CADD; baking and pastry arts; biology/biotechnology laboratory technician; business/commerce; child-care provision; communications systems installation and repair technology; computer and information systems security; computer programming; computer programming (specific applications); computer support specialist; computer systems networking and telecommunications; corrections; criminal justice/police science; criminal justice/safety; criminology; culinary arts; data entry/microcomputer applications; data processing and data processing technology; dental assisting; dental hygiene; design and applied arts related; diagnostic medical sonography and ultrasound technology; dietetic technology; early childhood education; electrical and power transmission installation; electrical, electronic and communications engineering technology; executive assistant/executive secretary; finance; fine and studio arts management; fine arts related; fine/studio arts; fire prevention and safety technology; floriculture/floristry management; food service and dining room management; forensic science and technology; graphic communications related; graphic design; health and medical administrative services related; heating, air conditioning, ventilation and refrigeration maintenance technology; homeland security, law enforcement, firefighting and protective services related; hotel/motel administration; human resources management; human services; industrial mechanics and maintenance technology; industrial technology; legal assistant/paralegal; liberal arts and sciences/liberal studies; machine shop technology; machine tool technology; manufacturing engineering technology; marketing/marketing management; mechanical drafting and CAD/CADD; mechanical engineering/mechanical technology; mechatronics, robotics, and automation engineering; medical/clinical assistant;

medical office assistant; music related; occupational safety and health technology; petroleum technology; phlebotomy technology; psychology; radio and television broadcasting technology; radiologic technology/science; real estate; registered nursing/registered nurse; restaurant, culinary, and catering management; small business administration; tourism and travel services management; turf and turfgrass management; web page, digital/multimedia and information resources design; welding technology.

Academics *Calendar:* semesters. *Degree:* certificates, diplomas, and associate. *Special study options:* academic remediation for entering students, accelerated degree program, adult/continuing education programs, advanced placement credit, cooperative education, distance learning, double majors, English as a second language, honors programs, independent study, internships, off-campus study, part-time degree program, services for LD students, summer session for credit.

Library Westmoreland County Community College Learning Resources Center. *Books:* 41,368 (physical), 168,542 (digital/electronic); *Serial titles:* 71 (physical); *Databases:* 24. Weekly public service hours: 60.

Student Life *Activities and Organizations:* choral group, Phi Theta Kappa, Sigma Alpha Pi Leadership Society, Criminal Justice Fraternity, SNAP, SADAA/SADHA. *Campus security:* 24-hour emergency response devices and patrols, late-night transport/escort service, county police office on campus. *Student services:* personal/psychological counseling.

Athletics Member NJCAA. *Intercollegiate sports:* baseball M, basketball M/W, bowling M/W, cross-country running M/W, golf M/W, soccer M/W, softball W, volleyball W.

Costs (2016–17) *Tuition:* area resident $3660 full-time, $122 per credit part-time; state resident $7320 full-time, $244 per credit part-time; nonresident $10,980 full-time, $366 per credit part-time. Full-time tuition and fees vary according to course load. Part-time tuition and fees vary according to course load. *Required fees:* $1410 full-time, $47 per credit part-time. *Payment plans:* installment, deferred payment. *Waivers:* senior citizens and employees or children of employees.

Applying *Options:* electronic application, early admission. *Application deadlines:* rolling (freshmen), rolling (transfers). *Notification:* continuous (freshmen), continuous (transfers).

Freshman Application Contact Ms. Shawna Little, Admissions Coordinator, Westmoreland County Community College, 145 Pavillon Lane, Youngwood, PA 15697. *Phone:* 724-925-4064. *Toll-free phone:* 800-262-2103. *Fax:* 724-925-4292. *E-mail:* littles@wccc.edu.
Website: http://www.wccc.edu/.

Williamson College of the Trades
Media, Pennsylvania

- **Independent** 2-year, founded 1888
- **Small-town** 222-acre campus with easy access to Philadelphia
- **Men only**

Undergraduates 270 full-time. Students come from 9 states and territories; 24% are from out of state; 100% live on campus.

Faculty *Student/faculty ratio:* 12:1.

Academics *Calendar:* semesters. *Degree:* diplomas and associate. *Special study options:* academic remediation for entering students, independent study, off-campus study.

Library Shrigley Library plus 3 others.

Student Life *Campus security:* evening patrols and gate security.

Athletics Member USCAA, NJCAA.

Standardized Tests *Required:* Armed Services Vocational Aptitude Battery (ASVAB) (for admission).

Costs (2016–17) *Tuition:* $0 full-time. All Williamson students attend on full scholarships covering tuition, room, board, and textbooks. *Required fees:* $800 full-time.

Financial Aid *Financial aid deadline:* 2/22.

Applying *Options:* electronic application. *Required:* essay or personal statement, high school transcript, minimum 2.0 GPA, interview, minimum average performance on the Armed Services Vocational Aptitude Battery (ASVAB).

Freshman Application Contact Mr. Jay Merillat, Dean of Admissions, Williamson College of the Trades, 106 South New Middletown Road, Media, PA 19063. *Phone:* 610-566-1776 Ext. 235.
E-mail: jmerillat@williamson.edu. *Website:* http://www.williamson.edu/.

The Workforce Institute's City College
Philadelphia, Pennsylvania

Freshman Application Contact Admissions Office, The Workforce Institute's City College, 1231 North Broad Street, Philadelphia, PA 19122. *Phone:* 215-568-7861. *Website:* http://www.theworkforce-institute.org/.

WyoTech Blairsville
Blairsville, Pennsylvania

Freshman Application Contact Mr. Tim Smyers, WyoTech Blairsville, 500 Innovation Drive, Blairsville, PA 15717. *Phone:* 724-459-2311. *Toll-free phone:* 888-577-7559. *Fax:* 724-459-6499. *E-mail:* tsmyers@wyotech.edu. *Website:* http://www.wyotech.edu/.

YTI Career Institute–Altoona
Altoona, Pennsylvania

Admissions Office Contact YTI Career Institute–Altoona, 2900 Fairway Drive, Altoona, PA 16602. *Website:* http://www.yti.edu/.

YTI Career Institute–York
York, Pennsylvania

Freshman Application Contact YTI Career Institute–York, 1405 Williams Road, York, PA 17402-9017. *Phone:* 717-757-1100 Ext. 318. *Toll-free phone:* 800-557-6335. *Website:* http://www.yti.edu/.

PUERTO RICO

The Center of Cinematography, Arts and Television
Bayamon, Puerto Rico

Admissions Office Contact The Center of Cinematography, Arts and Television, 51 Dr. Veve Street, Degetau Street Corner, Bayamon, PR 00960. *Website:* http://ccatmiami.com/.

Centro de Estudios Multidisciplinarios
Mayaguez, Puerto Rico

Admissions Office Contact Centro de Estudios Multidisciplinarios, Calle Cristy #56, Mayaguez, PR 00680. *Website:* http://www.cempr.edu/.

Centro de Estudios Multidisciplinarios
Rio Piedras, Puerto Rico

Director of Admissions Admissions Department, Centro de Estudios Multidisciplinarios, Calle 13 #1206, Ext. San Agustin, Rio Piedras, PR 00926. *Phone:* 787-765-4210 Ext. 115. *Toll-free phone:* 877-779-CDEM. *Website:* http://www.cempr.edu/.

Dewey University–Bayamón
Bayamón, Puerto Rico

Admissions Office Contact Dewey University–Bayamón, Carr. #2, Km. 15.9, Parque Industrial Corujo, Hato Tejas, Bayamón, PR 00959. *Website:* http://www.dewey.edu/.

Dewey University–Carolina
Carolina, Puerto Rico

Admissions Office Contact Dewey University–Carolina, Carr. #3, Km. 11, Parque Industrial de Carolina, Lote 7, Carolina, PR 00986. *Website:* http://www.dewey.edu/.

Dewey University–Fajardo
Fajardo, Puerto Rico

Admissions Office Contact Dewey University–Fajardo, 267 Calle General Valero, Fajardo, PR 00910. *Website:* http://www.dewey.edu/.

Dewey University–Hato Rey
Hato Rey, Puerto Rico

Admissions Office Contact Dewey University–Hato Rey, 427 Avenida Barbosa, Hato Rey, PR 00923. *Website:* http://www.dewey.edu/.

Dewey University–Juana Diaz
Juana Diaz, Puerto Rico

Admissions Office Contact Dewey University–Juana Diaz, Carr. 149, Km. 55.9, Parque Industrial Lomas, Juana Diaz, PR 00910. *Website:* http://www.dewey.edu/.

Dewey University–Manati
Manati, Puerto Rico

Admissions Office Contact Dewey University–Manati, Carr. 604, Km. 49.1 Barrio Tierras Nuevas, Salientes, Manati, PR 00674. *Toll-free phone:* 866-773-3939. *Website:* http://www.dewey.edu/.

Dewey University–Mayaguez
Mayaguez, Puerto Rico

Admissions Office Contact Dewey University–Mayaguez, Carr. #64 Km 6.6 Barrio Algarrobo, Mayaguez, PR 00682. *Website:* http://www.dewey.edu/.

EDIC College
Caguas, Puerto Rico

Admissions Office Contact EDIC College, Ave. Rafael Cordero Calle Gnova Urb. Caguas Norte, Caguas, PR 00726. *Website:* http://www.ediccollege.edu/.

Huertas Junior College
Caguas, Puerto Rico

Director of Admissions Mrs. Barbara Hassim López, Director of Admissions, Huertas Junior College, PO Box 8429, Caguas, PR 00726. *Phone:* 787-743-1242. *Fax:* 787-743-0203. *E-mail:* huertas@huertas.org. *Website:* http://www.huertas.edu/.

Humacao Community College
Humacao, Puerto Rico

- **Independent** primarily 2-year
- **Urban** campus
- **Endowment** $865,348
- **Coed,** 516 undergraduate students, 75% full-time, 67% women, 33% men

Undergraduates 388 full-time, 128 part-time. Students come from 1 other state; 100% Hispanic/Latino; 29% transferred in. *Retention:* 54% of full-time freshmen returned.
Freshmen *Admission:* 140 applied, 124 admitted, 94 enrolled. *Average high school GPA:* 2.89.
Faculty *Total:* 27, 48% full-time, 100% with terminal degrees. *Student/faculty ratio:* 30:1.
Majors Biotechnology; business/commerce; chemical technology; computer programming (specific applications); dental assisting; electrical and electronics engineering; environmental science; executive assistant/executive secretary; health information/medical records administration; heating, ventilation, air conditioning and refrigeration engineering technology; medical administrative assistant and medical secretary; microbiology; pharmacy technician; registered nursing/registered nurse.
Academics *Calendar:* trimesters. *Degrees:* certificates, diplomas, associate, and bachelor's. *Special study options:* academic remediation for entering students, adult/continuing education programs, cooperative education, distance learning, internships, part-time degree program, services for LD students.
Library Santiago N. Manuez Educational Resources Center plus 1 other. *Books:* 5,320 (physical); *Serial titles:* 43 (physical), 2 (digital/electronic); *Databases:* 5. Weekly public service hours: 56.
Student Life *Housing:* college housing not available. *Activities and Organizations:* Enactus Humacao Community College, Students Council. *Campus security:* 24-hour emergency response devices and patrols. *Student services:* personal/psychological counseling.
Costs (2017–18) *One-time required fee:* $140. *Tuition:* $4932 full-time, $2466 per year part-time. Full-time tuition and fees vary according to course load and degree level. Part-time tuition and fees vary according to course load and degree level. *Required fees:* $450 full-time, $450 per year part-time. *Payment plan:* installment. *Waivers:* employees or children of employees.
Financial Aid Of all full-time matriculated undergraduates who enrolled in 2015, 64 Federal Work-Study jobs (averaging $546).
Applying *Application fee:* $15. *Required:* high school transcript, interview. *Required for some:* certificate of Immunization for students under 21 years. *Notification:* continuous (freshmen).
Freshman Application Contact Mrs. Adela Aponte, Director of Admissions, Humacao Community College, PO Box 9139, Humacao, PR 00792, Puerto Rico. *Phone:* 787-852-1430 Ext. 225. *Fax:* 787-850-1577. *E-mail:* adela.aponte@hccpr.edu. *Website:* http://www.hccpr.edu/.

ICPR Junior College–Hato Rey Campus
Hato Rey, Puerto Rico

Freshman Application Contact Admissions Office, ICPR Junior College–Hato Rey Campus, 558 Munoz Rivera Avenue, PO Box 190304, Hato Rey, PR 00919-0304. *Phone:* 787-753-6335. *Website:* http://www.icprjc.edu/.

Ponce Paramedical College
Ponce, Puerto Rico

Admissions Office Contact Ponce Paramedical College, L-15 Acacia Street Villa Flores Urbanizacion, Ponce, PR 00731. *Website:* http://www.popac.edu/.

RHODE ISLAND

Community College of Rhode Island
Warwick, Rhode Island

- **State-supported** 2-year, founded 1964
- **Urban** 205-acre campus with easy access to Boston
- **Coed,** 15,101 undergraduate students, 29% full-time, 59% women, 41% men

Undergraduates 4,441 full-time, 10,660 part-time. Students come from 9 states and territories; 4% are from out of state; 9% Black or African American, non-Hispanic/Latino; 20% Hispanic/Latino; 3% Asian, non-Hispanic/Latino; 0.5% American Indian or Alaska Native, non-Hispanic/Latino; 5% Two or more races, non-Hispanic/Latino; 4% Race/ethnicity unknown; 0.1% international; 3% transferred in.
Freshmen *Admission:* 6,271 applied, 6,201 admitted, 2,688 enrolled.
Faculty *Total:* 823, 40% full-time. *Student/faculty ratio:* 18:1.
Majors Accounting; administrative assistant and secretarial science; adult development and aging; art; banking and financial support services; biological and physical sciences; business administration and management; business/commerce; chemical technology; clinical/medical laboratory technology; computer and information sciences; computer engineering technology; computer programming (specific applications); computer support specialist; computer systems networking and telecommunications; criminal justice/police science; crisis/emergency/disaster management; dental hygiene; diagnostic medical sonography and ultrasound technology; dramatic/theater arts; electrical and electronic engineering technologies related; electromechanical technology; engineering; fire science/firefighting; general studies; histologic technician; jazz/jazz studies; kindergarten/preschool education; legal administrative assistant/secretary; legal assistant/paralegal; liberal arts and sciences/liberal studies; licensed practical/vocational nurse training; manufacturing engineering technology; marketing/marketing management; massage therapy; mechanical engineering; medical administrative assistant and medical secretary; mental health counseling; music; occupational therapist assistant; opticianry; physical therapy technology; radiologic technology/science; registered nursing/registered nurse; respiratory care therapy; social work; special education; substance abuse/addiction counseling; surveying engineering; web/multimedia management and webmaster.
Academics *Calendar:* semesters. *Degree:* certificates, diplomas, and associate. *Special study options:* academic remediation for entering students, adult/continuing education programs, advanced placement credit, cooperative education, distance learning, double majors, English as a second language, external degree program, honors programs, independent study, internships, off-campus study, part-time degree program, services for LD students, study abroad, summer session for credit. *ROTC:* Army (c).
Library Community College of Rhode Island Learning Resources Center plus 3 others.
Student Life *Housing:* college housing not available. *Activities and Organizations:* drama/theater group, student-run newspaper, choral group, Distributive Education Clubs of America, Players (theater group), SkillsUSA, Phi Theta Kappa, Student Government. *Campus security:* 24-hour emergency response devices and patrols. *Student services:* health clinic, personal/psychological counseling.
Athletics Member NJCAA. *Intercollegiate sports:* baseball M(s), basketball M(s)/W(s), golf M/W, soccer M(s)/W(s), softball W(s), tennis M/W, track and field M/W, volleyball W(s). *Intramural sports:* basketball M/W, volleyball M/W.

Costs (2016–17) *Tuition:* state resident $3950 full-time, $180 per credit hour part-time; nonresident $11,180 full-time, $534 per credit hour part-time. Full-time tuition and fees vary according to program. Part-time tuition and fees vary according to course load and program. *Required fees:* $316 full-time, $12 per credit hour part-time. *Payment plans:* installment, deferred payment. *Waivers:* senior citizens and employees or children of employees.
Financial Aid Of all full-time matriculated undergraduates who enrolled in 2015, 500 Federal Work-Study jobs (averaging $2500).
Applying *Options:* deferred entrance. *Application fee:* $20. *Application deadlines:* rolling (freshmen), rolling (transfers). *Notification:* continuous (freshmen).
Freshman Application Contact Community College of Rhode Island, Flanagan Campus, 1762 Louisquisset Pike, Lincoln, RI 02865-4585. *Phone:* 401-333-7490. *Fax:* 401-333-7122. *E-mail:* webadmission@ccri.edu. *Website:* http://www.ccri.edu/.

SOUTH CAROLINA

Aiken Technical College
Graniteville, South Carolina

- **State and locally supported** 2-year, founded 1972, part of South Carolina State Board for Technical and Comprehensive Education
- **Rural** 88-acre campus
- **Endowment** $4.7 million
- **Coed**

Undergraduates 694 full-time, 1,663 part-time. 14% are from out of state; 33% Black or African American, non-Hispanic/Latino; 5% Hispanic/Latino; 1% Asian, non-Hispanic/Latino; 0.1% Native Hawaiian or other Pacific Islander, non-Hispanic/Latino; 0.7% American Indian or Alaska Native, non-Hispanic/Latino; 0.9% Two or more races, non-Hispanic/Latino; 2% Race/ethnicity unknown; 36% transferred in. *Retention:* 57% of full-time freshmen returned.
Academics *Calendar:* semesters. *Degree:* certificates, diplomas, and associate. *Special study options:* academic remediation for entering students, accelerated degree program, advanced placement credit, cooperative education, distance learning, double majors, independent study, internships, off-campus study, part-time degree program, services for LD students, summer session for credit.
Library Aiken Technical College Learning Resources Center. *Books:* 29,105 (physical), 133,000 (digital/electronic); *Serial titles:* 124 (physical), 391,523 (digital/electronic); *Databases:* 73. Weekly public service hours: 64; study areas open 24 hours, 5&-7 days a week; students can reserve study rooms.
Student Life *Campus security:* 24-hour emergency response devices and patrols, late-night transport/escort service.
Costs (2016–17) *Tuition:* area resident $4352 full-time; state resident $4712 full-time; nonresident $8224 full-time.
Financial Aid Of all full-time matriculated undergraduates who enrolled in 2015, 48 Federal Work-Study jobs (averaging $3000).
Applying *Options:* electronic application, deferred entrance. *Recommended:* high school transcript.
Freshman Application Contact Jessica Moon, Director of Enrollment Services, Aiken Technical College, 2276 J. Davis Highway, Graniteville, SC 29829. *Phone:* 803-508-7262 Ext. 156. *E-mail:* moonj@atc.edu. *Website:* http://www.atc.edu/.

Central Carolina Technical College
Sumter, South Carolina

Freshman Application Contact Ms. Barbara Wright, Director of Admissions and Counseling, Central Carolina Technical College, 506 North Guignard Drive, Sumter, SC 29150. *Phone:* 803-778-6695. *Toll-free phone:* 800-221-8711. *Fax:* 803-778-6696. *E-mail:* wrightb@cctech.edu. *Website:* http://www.cctech.edu/.

Centura College
Columbia, South Carolina

Admissions Office Contact Centura College, 7500 Two Notch Road, Columbia, SC 29223. *Website:* http://www.centuracollege.edu/.

Clinton College
Rock Hill, South Carolina

Director of Admissions Robert M. Copeland, Vice President for Student Affairs, Clinton College, 1029 Crawford Road, Rock Hill, SC 29730. *Phone:*

803-327-7402. *Toll-free phone:* 877-837-9645. *Fax:* 803-327-3261. *E-mail:* rcopeland@clintonjrcollege.org. *Website:* http://www.clintoncollege.edu/.

Denmark Technical College
Denmark, South Carolina

- **State-supported** 2-year, founded 1948, part of South Carolina State Board for Technical and Comprehensive Education
- **Rural** 53-acre campus
- **Coed**

Undergraduates 655 full-time, 388 part-time. 4% are from out of state; 92% Black or African American, non-Hispanic/Latino; 0.8% Hispanic/Latino; 0.2% Asian, non-Hispanic/Latino; 0.2% American Indian or Alaska Native, non-Hispanic/Latino; 0.4% Race/ethnicity unknown; 0.8% transferred in. *Retention:* 28% of full-time freshmen returned.
Faculty *Student/faculty ratio:* 20:1.
Academics *Calendar:* semesters. *Degree:* certificates, diplomas, and associate. *Special study options:* academic remediation for entering students, adult/continuing education programs, advanced placement credit, cooperative education, distance learning, independent study, internships, off-campus study, part-time degree program, services for LD students, summer session for credit.
Library Denmark Technical College Learning Resources Center. *Books:* 9,810 (physical); *Databases:* 2. Weekly public service hours: 40; study areas open 24 hours, 5&-7 days a week; students can reserve study rooms.
Student Life *Campus security:* 24-hour patrols, late-night transport/escort service, 24-hour emergency contact line/alarm devices.
Athletics Member NJCAA.
Standardized Tests *Required:* ACT ASSET, ACCUPLACER, and TEAS (for nursing) (for admission). *Recommended:* SAT or ACT (for admission).
Costs (2016–17) *Tuition:* state resident $3340 full-time, $111 per credit hour part-time; nonresident $6680 full-time, $223 per credit hour part-time. *Required fees:* $316 full-time. *Room and board:* $4038; room only: $1970.
Financial Aid Of all full-time matriculated undergraduates who enrolled in 2015, 250 Federal Work-Study jobs (averaging $2000).
Applying *Options:* electronic application, early admission, deferred entrance. *Application fee:* $10. *Required:* high school transcript. *Required for some:* essay or personal statement, criminal background check, drug test, PPD test for LPN.
Freshman Application Contact Ms. Kara Troy, Administrative Specialist II, Denmark Technical College, PO Box 327, 1126 Solomon Blatt Boulevard, Denmark, SC 29042. *Phone:* 803-793-5180. *Fax:* 803-793-5942. *E-mail:* troyk@denmarktech.edu. *Website:* http://www.denmarktech.edu/.

Florence-Darlington Technical College
Florence, South Carolina

Director of Admissions Shelley Fortin, Vice President for Enrollment Management and Student Services, Florence-Darlington Technical College, 2715 West Lucas Street, PO Box 100548, Florence, SC 29501-0548. *Phone:* 843-661-8111 Ext. 117. *Toll-free phone:* 800-228-5745. *E-mail:* shelley.fortin@fdtc.edu. *Website:* http://www.fdtc.edu/.

Forrest College
Anderson, South Carolina

- **Proprietary** 2-year, founded 1946
- **Small-town** 3-acre campus
- **Endowment** $60,000
- **Coed**

Undergraduates 85 full-time, 14 part-time. Students come from 1 other state; 31% Black or African American, non-Hispanic/Latino; 2% Hispanic/Latino.
Faculty *Student/faculty ratio:* 4:1.
Academics *Calendar:* quarters. *Degree:* certificates, diplomas, and associate. *Special study options:* advanced placement credit, cooperative education, double majors, independent study, internships, part-time degree program, summer session for credit.
Library Forrest College Library plus 1 other.
Student Life *Campus security:* 24-hour emergency response devices, late-night transport/escort service.
Costs (2016–17) *One-time required fee:* $800. *Tuition:* $10,770 full-time, $245 per credit hour part-time. Full-time tuition and fees vary according to class time, course level, course load, degree level, program, reciprocity agreements, and student level. Part-time tuition and fees vary according to class time, course level, course load, degree level, program, reciprocity agreements, and student level. *Required fees:* $375 full-time, $125 per term part-time.

Applying *Required:* essay or personal statement, high school transcript, interview.

Freshman Application Contact Ms. Janie Turmon, Admissions and Placement Coordinator/Representative, Forrest College, 601 East River Street, Anderson, SC 29624. *Phone:* 864-225-7653. *Fax:* 864-261-7471. *E-mail:* janieturmon@forrestcollege.edu. *Website:* http://www.forrestcollege.edu/.

Fortis College
Columbia, South Carolina

Admissions Office Contact Fortis College, 246 Stoneridge Drive, Suite 101, Columbia, SC 29210. *Toll-free phone:* 855-4-FORTIS. *Website:* http://www.fortis.edu/.

Golf Academy of America
Myrtle Beach, South Carolina

Admissions Office Contact Golf Academy of America, 3268 Waccamaw Boulevard, Myrtle Beach, SC 29579. *Website:* http://www.golfacademy.edu/.

Greenville Technical College
Greenville, South Carolina

- **State-supported** 2-year, founded 1962, part of South Carolina State Board for Technical and Comprehensive Education
- **Urban** 604-acre campus
- **Coed,** 11,932 undergraduate students, 40% full-time, 59% women, 41% men

Undergraduates 4,828 full-time, 7,104 part-time. 22% Black or African American, non-Hispanic/Latino; 9% Hispanic/Latino; 2% Asian, non-Hispanic/Latino; 0.1% Native Hawaiian or other Pacific Islander, non-Hispanic/Latino; 0.3% American Indian or Alaska Native, non-Hispanic/Latino; 3% Two or more races, non-Hispanic/Latino; 3% Race/ethnicity unknown; 0.5% international.

Freshmen *Admission:* 5,014 applied, 5,010 admitted, 2,103 enrolled.

Faculty *Total:* 807, 40% full-time, 9% with terminal degrees. *Student/faculty ratio:* 15:1.

Majors Accounting; administrative assistant and secretarial science; architectural engineering technology; autobody/collision and repair technology; automobile/automotive mechanics technology; business administration and management; child-care and support services management; clinical/medical laboratory technology; computer numerically controlled (CNC) machinist technology; construction engineering technology; criminal justice/safety; culinary arts; data processing and data processing technology; dental hygiene; diagnostic medical sonography and ultrasound technology; electrical, electronic and communications engineering technology; electromechanical and instrumentation and maintenance technologies related; emergency medical technology (EMT paramedic); fire science/firefighting; health information/medical records technology; human services; legal assistant/paralegal; liberal arts and sciences/liberal studies; machine tool technology; mechanical drafting and CAD/CADD; mechanical engineering/mechanical technology; mechanic and repair technologies related; medical radiologic technology; multi/interdisciplinary studies related; occupational therapist assistant; physical therapy technology; purchasing, procurement/acquisitions and contracts management; registered nursing/registered nurse; respiratory care therapy; sales, distribution, and marketing operations.

Academics *Calendar:* semesters. *Degree:* certificates, diplomas, and associate. *Special study options:* academic remediation for entering students, advanced placement credit, cooperative education, distance learning, double majors, English as a second language, honors programs, independent study, internships, part-time degree program, services for LD students, summer session for credit.

Library J. Verne Smith Library plus 3 others. *Books:* 36,932 (physical), 372,967 (digital/electronic); *Serial titles:* 143 (physical), 16 (digital/electronic); *Databases:* 30. Weekly public service hours: 67.

Student Life *Housing:* college housing not available. *Activities and Organizations:* Phi Theta Kappa, AAMLI, Cosmetology Club, Engineering Club, SGA/SAT Club. *Campus security:* 24-hour emergency response devices and patrols, late-night transport/escort service.

Athletics *Intramural sports:* badminton M(c)/W(c), basketball M(c)/W(c), bowling M(c)/W(c), football M(c)/W(c), softball M(c)/W(c), table tennis M(c)/W(c), tennis M(c)/W(c), volleyball M(c)/W(c).

Costs (2017–18) *Tuition:* area resident $5170 full-time; state resident $5630 full-time; nonresident $10,550 full-time. Full-time tuition and fees vary according to course load and program. Part-time tuition and fees vary according to course load and program. *Payment plans:* installment, deferred payment. *Waivers:* senior citizens.

Applying *Options:* electronic application, early admission, deferred entrance. *Required:* high school transcript. *Application deadlines:* rolling (freshmen), rolling (transfers). *Notification:* continuous until 8/18 (freshmen), continuous until 8/18 (transfers).

Freshman Application Contact Greenville Technical College, PO Box 5616, Greenville, SC 29606-5616. *Phone:* 864-250-8107. *Toll-free phone:* 800-992-1183 (in-state); 800-723-0673 (out-of-state). *Website:* http://www.gvltec.edu/.

Horry Georgetown Technical College
Conway, South Carolina

- **State and locally supported** 2-year, founded 1966, part of South Carolina State Board for Technical and Comprehensive Education
- **Small-town** 150-acre campus
- **Endowment** $2.7 million
- **Coed,** 7,018 undergraduate students, 43% full-time, 63% women, 37% men

Undergraduates 3,039 full-time, 3,979 part-time. Students come from 26 states and territories; 38 other countries; 15% are from out of state; 21% Black or African American, non-Hispanic/Latino; 4% Hispanic/Latino; 1% Asian, non-Hispanic/Latino; 0.1% Native Hawaiian or other Pacific Islander, non-Hispanic/Latino; 0.6% American Indian or Alaska Native, non-Hispanic/Latino; 3% Two or more races, non-Hispanic/Latino; 0.9% Race/ethnicity unknown; 0.1% international; 7% transferred in. *Retention:* 57% of full-time freshmen returned.

Freshmen *Admission:* 1,212 enrolled. *Average high school GPA:* 2.5.

Faculty *Total:* 352, 42% full-time. *Student/faculty ratio:* 21:1.

Majors Administrative assistant and secretarial science; business administration and management; criminal justice/safety; culinary arts; electrical, electronic and communications engineering technology; forest technology; legal assistant/paralegal; machine tool technology; registered nursing/registered nurse.

Academics *Calendar:* semesters. *Degree:* certificates, diplomas, and associate. *Special study options:* academic remediation for entering students, adult/continuing education programs, advanced placement credit, cooperative education, distance learning, double majors, independent study, internships, part-time degree program, services for LD students, summer session for credit.

Library Conway Campus Library plus 2 others.

Student Life *Housing:* college housing not available. *Campus security:* 24-hour emergency response devices and patrols. *Student services:* personal/psychological counseling.

Costs (2017–18) *Tuition:* area resident $4710 full-time, $157 per credit hour part-time; state resident $5880 full-time, $196 per credit hour part-time; nonresident $9600 full-time, $320 per credit hour part-time. *Required fees:* $268 full-time, $268 per year part-time. *Payment plan:* installment. *Waivers:* senior citizens and employees or children of employees.

Applying *Options:* early admission. *Application fee:* $25. *Required for some:* high school transcript. *Application deadlines:* rolling (freshmen), rolling (transfers). *Notification:* continuous (freshmen), continuous (transfers).

Freshman Application Contact Cynthia Johnston, Assistant Vice President for Enrollment Services, Horry Georgetown Technical College, 2050 Highway 501 East, PO Box 261966, Conway, SC 29528-6066. *Phone:* 843-349-7835. *Fax:* 843-349-7588. *E-mail:* cynthia.johnston@hgtc.edu. *Website:* http://www.hgtc.edu/.

Midlands Technical College
Columbia, South Carolina

- **State and locally supported** 2-year, founded 1974, part of South Carolina State Board for Technical and Comprehensive Education
- **Suburban** 156-acre campus
- **Endowment** $6.9 million
- **Coed**

Undergraduates 4,981 full-time, 5,965 part-time. Students come from 30 states and territories; 65 other countries; 2% are from out of state; 36% Black or African American, non-Hispanic/Latino; 4% Hispanic/Latino; 2% Asian, non-Hispanic/Latino; 0.1% Native Hawaiian or other Pacific Islander, non-Hispanic/Latino; 0.5% American Indian or Alaska Native, non-Hispanic/Latino; 3% Two or more races, non-Hispanic/Latino; 3% Race/ethnicity unknown; 10% transferred in.

Faculty *Student/faculty ratio:* 20:1.

Academics *Calendar:* semesters. *Degree:* certificates, diplomas, and associate. *Special study options:* academic remediation for entering students, adult/continuing education programs, advanced placement credit, cooperative education, distance learning, double majors, English as a second language, internships, part-time degree program, services for LD students, student-designed majors, summer session for credit. *ROTC:* Army (c), Navy (c), Air Force (c).

Library Midlands Technical College Library plus 5 others. *Books:* 50,329 (physical), 354,481 (digital/electronic); *Serial titles:* 295 (physical); *Databases:* 111. Weekly public service hours: 58; students can reserve study rooms.

Student Life *Campus security:* 24-hour emergency response devices and patrols, late-night transport/escort service.

Standardized Tests *Required for some:* ACT ASSET. *Recommended:* SAT or ACT (for admission).

Costs (2016–17) *One-time required fee:* $35. *Tuition:* area resident $3840 full-time, $160 per credit hour part-time; state resident $4800 full-time, $200 per credit hour part-time; nonresident $11,520 full-time, $480 per credit hour part-time. Full-time tuition and fees vary according to course load. Part-time tuition and fees vary according to course load. *Required fees:* $1044 full-time, $30 per credit hour part-time, $162 per term part-time.

Financial Aid Of all full-time matriculated undergraduates who enrolled in 2011, 4,794 applied for aid, 4,160 were judged to have need, 118 had their need fully met. 154 Federal Work-Study jobs (averaging $2775). *Average percent of need met:* 13. *Average financial aid package:* $6098. *Average need-based loan:* $3089. *Average need-based gift aid:* $4370.

Applying *Options:* electronic application, early admission, deferred entrance. *Application fee:* $35. *Recommended:* high school transcript.

Freshman Application Contact Ms. Sylvia Littlejohn, Director of Admissions, Midlands Technical College, PO Box 2408, Columbia, SC 29202. *Phone:* 803-738-8324. *Toll-free phone:* 800-922-8038. *Fax:* 803-790-7524. *E-mail:* admissions@midlandstech.edu. *Website:* http://www.midlandstech.edu/.

Miller-Motte Technical College
Conway, South Carolina

Admissions Office Contact Miller-Motte Technical College, 2451 Highway 501 East, Conway, SC 29526. *Toll-free phone:* 800-705-9182. *Website:* http://www.miller-motte.edu/.

Miller-Motte Technical College
North Charleston, South Carolina

Freshman Application Contact Ms. Elaine Cue, Campus President, Miller-Motte Technical College, 8085 Rivers Avenue, North Charleston, SC 29406. *Phone:* 843-574-0101. *Toll-free phone:* 800-705-9182. *Fax:* 843-266-3424. *E-mail:* juliasc@miller-mott.net. *Website:* http://www.miller-motte.edu/.

Northeastern Technical College
Cheraw, South Carolina

Freshman Application Contact Mrs. Mary K. Newton, Dean of Students, Northeastern Technical College, 1201 Chesterfield Highway, Cheraw, SC 29520-1007. *Phone:* 843-921-6935. *Toll-free phone:* 800-921-7399. *Fax:* 843-921-1476. *E-mail:* mpace@netc.edu. *Website:* http://www.netc.edu/.

Orangeburg-Calhoun Technical College
Orangeburg, South Carolina

Freshman Application Contact Mr. Dana Rickards, Director of Recruitment, Orangeburg-Calhoun Technical College, 3250 St Matthews Road, NE, Orangeburg, SC 29118-8299. *Phone:* 803-535-1219. *Toll-free phone:* 800-813-6519. *Website:* http://www.octech.edu/.

Piedmont Technical College
Greenwood, South Carolina

Director of Admissions Mr. Steve Coleman, Director of Admissions, Piedmont Technical College, 620 North Emerald Road, PO Box 1467, Greenwood, SC 29648-1467. *Phone:* 864-941-8603. *Toll-free phone:* 800-868-5528. *Website:* http://www.ptc.edu/.

Spartanburg Community College
Spartanburg, South Carolina

- **State-supported** 2-year, founded 1961, part of South Carolina State Board for Technical and Comprehensive Education
- **Suburban** 104-acre campus with easy access to Charlotte
- **Coed,** 4,715 undergraduate students, 46% full-time, 58% women, 42% men

Undergraduates 2,179 full-time, 2,536 part-time. Students come from 7 states and territories; 2 other countries; 2% are from out of state; 21% Black or African American, non-Hispanic/Latino; 7% Hispanic/Latino; 4% Asian, non-Hispanic/Latino; 0.1% Native Hawaiian or other Pacific Islander, non-Hispanic/Latino; 0.4% American Indian or Alaska Native, non-Hispanic/Latino; 3% Two or more races, non-Hispanic/Latino; 2% Race/ethnicity unknown; 8% transferred in. *Retention:* 63% of full-time freshmen returned.

Freshmen *Admission:* 909 enrolled. *Average high school GPA:* 3.2.

Faculty *Total:* 315, 35% full-time. *Student/faculty ratio:* 15:1.

Majors Accounting; administrative assistant and secretarial science; applied horticulture/horticulture operations; automobile/automotive mechanics technology; business administration and management; clinical/medical laboratory technology; data processing and data processing technology; electrical, electronic and communications engineering technology; heating, air conditioning, ventilation and refrigeration maintenance technology; industrial electronics technology; liberal arts and sciences/liberal studies; machine tool technology; manufacturing engineering technology; mechanical engineering/mechanical technology; medical radiologic technology; multi/interdisciplinary studies related; radiation protection/health physics technology; registered nursing/registered nurse; respiratory care therapy.

Academics *Calendar:* semesters condensed semesters plus summer sessions. *Degree:* certificates, diplomas, and associate. *Special study options:* academic remediation for entering students, adult/continuing education programs, advanced placement credit, cooperative education, distance learning, English as a second language, part-time degree program, services for LD students, summer session for credit.

Library Spartanburg Community College Library.

Student Life *Housing:* college housing not available. *Activities and Organizations:* drama/theater group, student-run newspaper. *Campus security:* 24-hour emergency response devices and patrols. *Student services:* personal/psychological counseling, women's center.

Standardized Tests *Required for some:* SAT or ACT (for admission).

Costs (2016–17) *Tuition:* area resident $4200 full-time, $175 per credit hour part-time; state resident $5232 full-time, $218 per credit hour part-time; nonresident $8592 full-time, $358 per credit hour part-time. Full-time tuition and fees vary according to course load and location. Part-time tuition and fees vary according to location. *Required fees:* $100 full-time, $50 per term part-time. *Payment plans:* installment, deferred payment. *Waivers:* senior citizens.

Financial Aid Of all full-time matriculated undergraduates who enrolled in 2014, 41 Federal Work-Study jobs (averaging $3020).

Applying *Options:* electronic application, early admission. *Application fee:* $25. *Required:* high school transcript. *Recommended:* interview. *Application deadlines:* rolling (freshmen), rolling (transfers). *Notification:* continuous (freshmen), continuous (transfers).

Freshman Application Contact Ms. Sabrina Sims, Admissions Counselor, Spartanburg Community College, PO Box 4386, Spartanburg, SC 29305. *Phone:* 864-592-4816. *Toll-free phone:* 866-591-3700. *Fax:* 864-592-4564. *E-mail:* admissions@sccsc.edu. *Website:* http://www.sccsc.edu/.

Spartanburg Methodist College
Spartanburg, South Carolina

- **Independent Methodist** 2-year, founded 1911
- **Suburban** 110-acre campus with easy access to Charlotte
- **Endowment** $22.0 million
- **Coed,** 737 undergraduate students, 99% full-time, 47% women, 53% men

Undergraduates 730 full-time, 7 part-time. Students come from 10 states and territories; 4 other countries; 7% are from out of state; 33% Black or African American, non-Hispanic/Latino; 7% Hispanic/Latino; 0.7% Asian, non-Hispanic/Latino; 0.1% American Indian or Alaska Native, non-Hispanic/Latino; 2% Two or more races, non-Hispanic/Latino; 0.7% international; 4% transferred in; 66% live on campus.

Freshmen *Admission:* 1,373 applied, 895 admitted, 425 enrolled. *Average high school GPA:* 3.39. *Test scores:* SAT critical reading scores over 500: 19%; SAT math scores over 500: 22%; SAT writing scores over 500: 14%; ACT scores over 18: 142%; SAT critical reading scores over 600: 4%; SAT math scores over 600: 4%; SAT writing scores over 600: 1%; ACT scores over 24: 20%; ACT scores over 30: 1%.

Faculty *Total:* 52, 52% full-time, 44% with terminal degrees. *Student/faculty ratio:* 21:1.

Majors Business/commerce; criminal justice/law enforcement administration; liberal arts and sciences/liberal studies; religious studies related; visual and performing arts.

Academics *Calendar:* semesters. *Degree:* associate. *Special study options:* academic remediation for entering students, advanced placement credit, English as a second language, honors programs, independent study, part-time degree program, services for LD students, summer session for credit.

Library Marie Blair Burgess Library. Weekly public service hours: 77; students can reserve study rooms.

Student Life *Housing Options:* coed, men-only, women-only. Campus housing is university owned. Freshman campus housing is guaranteed.

Activities and Organizations: drama/theater group, student-run newspaper, choral group, College Christian Movement, Alpha Phi Omega, Campus Union, Fellowship of Christian Athletes, Kappa Sigma Alpha. *Campus security:* 24-hour emergency response devices and patrols, student patrols, late-night transport/escort service, controlled dormitory access. *Student services:* health clinic, personal/psychological counseling.

Athletics Member NJCAA. *Intercollegiate sports:* baseball M(s), basketball M(s)/W(s), cross-country running M(s)/W(s), golf M(s)/W(s), soccer M(s)/W(s), softball W(s), tennis M(s)/W(s), volleyball W(s), wrestling M(s). *Intramural sports:* basketball M/W, cheerleading M/W, football M/W, softball M/W, table tennis M/W, volleyball M/W.

Standardized Tests *Required:* SAT or ACT (for admission).

Costs (2016–17) *One-time required fee:* $175. *Comprehensive fee:* $25,610 includes full-time tuition ($15,750), mandatory fees ($950), and room and board ($8910). Full-time tuition and fees vary according to course load. Part-time tuition: $425 per credit hour. Part-time tuition and fees vary according to course load. *Room and board:* Room and board charges vary according to board plan. *Payment plan:* installment. *Waivers:* senior citizens and employees or children of employees.

Financial Aid Of all full-time matriculated undergraduates who enrolled in 2015, 80 Federal Work-Study jobs (averaging $1600). 90 state and other part-time jobs (averaging $1600). *Financial aid deadline:* 8/30.

Applying *Options:* electronic application, deferred entrance. *Application fee:* $25. *Required:* essay or personal statement, high school transcript, minimum 2.0 GPA. *Required for some:* interview. *Recommended:* interview. *Application deadlines:* rolling (freshmen), rolling (transfers). *Notification:* continuous (freshmen), continuous (transfers).

Freshman Application Contact Mr. Wells Shepard, Vice President for Enrollment, Spartanburg Methodist College, 1000 Powell Mill Road, Spartanburg, SC 29301-5899. *Phone:* 864-587-4254. *Toll-free phone:* 800-772-7286. *Fax:* 864-587-4355. *E-mail:* admiss@smcsc.edu. *Website:* http://www.smcsc.edu/.

Technical College of the Lowcountry
Beaufort, South Carolina

- **State-supported** 2-year, founded 1972, part of South Carolina Technical and Comprehensive Education System
- **Small-town** 12-acre campus
- **Coed**

Undergraduates 665 full-time, 1,667 part-time. 6% are from out of state; 35% Black or African American, non-Hispanic/Latino; 9% Hispanic/Latino; 1% Asian, non-Hispanic/Latino; 0.5% American Indian or Alaska Native, non-Hispanic/Latino; 2% Two or more races, non-Hispanic/Latino; 1% Race/ethnicity unknown; 12% transferred in.

Faculty *Student/faculty ratio:* 15:1.

Academics *Calendar:* semesters. *Degree:* certificates, diplomas, and associate. *Special study options:* academic remediation for entering students, adult/continuing education programs, advanced placement credit, distance learning, part-time degree program, summer session for credit.

Student Life *Campus security:* security during class hours.

Standardized Tests *Required:* ACT ASSET (for admission). *Recommended:* SAT and SAT Subject Tests or ACT (for admission).

Financial Aid Of all full-time matriculated undergraduates who enrolled in 2015, 56 Federal Work-Study jobs (averaging $1700).

Applying *Options:* early admission, deferred entrance. *Application fee:* $25.

Freshman Application Contact Rhonda Cole, Admissions Services Manager, Technical College of the Lowcountry, 921 Ribaut Road, PO Box 1288, Beaufort, SC 29901-1288. *Phone:* 843-525-8229. *Fax:* 843-525-8285. *E-mail:* rcole@tcl.edu. *Website:* http://www.tcl.edu/.

Tri-County Technical College
Pendleton, South Carolina

- **State-supported** 2-year, founded 1962, part of South Carolina State Board for Technical and Comprehensive Education
- **Rural** 100-acre campus
- **Endowment** $21.8 million
- **Coed**

Undergraduates 3,451 full-time, 2,677 part-time. Students come from 38 states and territories; 35 other countries; 2% are from out of state; 10% Black or African American, non-Hispanic/Latino; 4% Hispanic/Latino; 1% Asian, non-Hispanic/Latino; 0.1% Native Hawaiian or other Pacific Islander, non-Hispanic/Latino; 0.2% American Indian or Alaska Native, non-Hispanic/Latino; 3% Two or more races, non-Hispanic/Latino; 0.8% Race/ethnicity unknown; 6% transferred in. *Retention:* 36% of full-time freshmen returned.

Faculty *Student/faculty ratio:* 21:1.

Academics *Calendar:* semesters. *Degree:* certificates, diplomas, and associate. *Special study options:* academic remediation for entering students, adult/continuing education programs, advanced placement credit, distance learning, part-time degree program, study abroad, summer session for credit. *ROTC:* Army (c), Air Force (c).

Library Tri-County Technical College Library.

Student Life *Campus security:* 24-hour emergency response devices and patrols.

Athletics Member NJCAA.

Costs (2016–17) *One-time required fee:* $40. *Tuition:* area resident $3906 full-time, $169 per credit hour part-time; state resident $5178 full-time, $222 per credit hour part-time; nonresident $8898 full-time, $377 per credit hour part-time. *Required fees:* $144 full-time, $6 per credit hour part-time.

Applying *Options:* early admission. *Application fee:* $30.

Freshman Application Contact Tri-County Technical College, PO Box 587, 7900 Highway 76, Pendleton, SC 29670-0587. *Phone:* 864-646-1550. *Website:* http://www.tctc.edu/.

Trident Technical College
Charleston, South Carolina

- **State and locally supported** 2-year, founded 1964, part of South Carolina State Board for Technical and Comprehensive Education
- **Urban** campus
- **Coed,** 13,561 undergraduate students, 40% full-time, 60% women, 40% men

Undergraduates 5,479 full-time, 8,082 part-time. Students come from 86 other countries; 2% are from out of state; 27% Black or African American, non-Hispanic/Latino; 6% Hispanic/Latino; 2% Asian, non-Hispanic/Latino; 0.3% Native Hawaiian or other Pacific Islander, non-Hispanic/Latino; 0.5% American Indian or Alaska Native, non-Hispanic/Latino; 3% Two or more races, non-Hispanic/Latino; 2% Race/ethnicity unknown; 8% transferred in.

Freshmen *Admission:* 1,956 admitted, 1,956 enrolled.

Faculty *Total:* 617, 50% full-time, 8% with terminal degrees. *Student/faculty ratio:* 20:1.

Majors Accounting; administrative assistant and secretarial science; airframe mechanics and aircraft maintenance technology; automobile/automotive mechanics technology; biological and physical sciences; business administration and management; child-care provision; civil engineering technology; clinical/medical laboratory technology; commercial and advertising art; computer engineering technology; computer graphics; computer/information technology services administration related; computer programming (specific applications); computer systems networking and telecommunications; criminal justice/law enforcement administration; culinary arts; dental hygiene; electrical, electronic and communications engineering technology; engineering technology; horticultural science; hotel/motel administration; human services; industrial technology; legal assistant/paralegal; legal studies; liberal arts and sciences/liberal studies; machine tool technology; marketing/marketing management; mechanical engineering/mechanical technology; medical administrative assistant and medical secretary; occupational therapy; physical therapy; registered nursing/registered nurse; respiratory care therapy; telecommunications technology; veterinary/animal health technology; web/multimedia management and webmaster; web page, digital/multimedia and information resources design.

Academics *Calendar:* semesters. *Degree:* certificates, diplomas, and associate. *Special study options:* academic remediation for entering students, advanced placement credit, cooperative education, distance learning, double majors, English as a second language, internships, off-campus study, part-time degree program, services for LD students, study abroad, summer session for credit.

Library Learning Resource Center plus 2 others. Students can reserve study rooms.

Student Life *Housing:* college housing not available. *Activities and Organizations:* drama/theater group, student-run newspaper, radio station, Phi Theta Kappa, Lex Artis Paralegal Society, Hospitality and Culinary Student Association, Partnership for Change in Communities and Families, Society of Student Leaders. *Campus security:* 24-hour emergency response devices and patrols, late-night transport/escort service. *Student services:* personal/psychological counseling.

Costs (2017–18) *One-time required fee:* $32. *Tuition:* area resident $4124 full-time, $172 per credit hour part-time; state resident $4575 full-time, $191 per credit hour part-time; nonresident $7806 full-time, $325 per credit hour part-time. *Required fees:* $45 full-time. *Payment plan:* installment. *Waivers:* senior citizens.

Applying *Options:* electronic application, early admission. *Application fee:* $30. *Required for some:* high school transcript. *Application deadlines:* 8/6 (freshmen), 8/6 (transfers). *Notification:* continuous (freshmen), continuous (transfers).

Freshman Application Contact Ms. Clara Martin, Admissions Director, Trident Technical College, Charleston, SC 29423-8067. *Phone:* 843-574-6326. *Fax:* 843-574-6109. *E-mail:* clara.martin@tridenttech.edu. *Website:* http://www.tridenttech.edu/.

University of South Carolina Lancaster
Lancaster, South Carolina

Freshman Application Contact Susan Vinson, Admissions Counselor, University of South Carolina Lancaster, PO Box 889, Lancaster, SC 29721. *Phone:* 803-313-7000. *Fax:* 803-313-7116. *E-mail:* vinsons@mailbox.sc.edu. *Website:* http://usclancaster.sc.edu/.

University of South Carolina Salkehatchie
Allendale, South Carolina

- **State-supported** 2-year, founded 1965, part of University of South Carolina System
- **Rural** 95-acre campus
- **Coed,** 1,076 undergraduate students

Undergraduates 5% are from out of state. *Retention:* 45% of full-time freshmen returned.
Freshmen *Admission:* 654 applied, 388 admitted.
Faculty *Student/faculty ratio:* 17:1.
Majors Liberal arts and sciences/liberal studies.
Academics *Calendar:* semesters. *Degree:* associate. *Special study options:* academic remediation for entering students, adult/continuing education programs, advanced placement credit, cooperative education, distance learning, independent study, internships, part-time degree program, services for LD students, study abroad, summer session for credit.
Library Salkehatchie Learning Resource Center.
Student Life *Housing:* college housing not available. *Campus security:* 24-hour emergency response devices, late-night transport/escort service.
Athletics Member NJCAA. *Intercollegiate sports:* baseball M, basketball M, soccer M/W, softball W.
Standardized Tests *Required:* SAT or ACT (for admission).
Costs (2016–17) *One-time required fee:* $100. *Tuition:* state resident $3351 full-time, $279 per credit hour part-time; nonresident $4941 full-time, $412 per credit hour part-time. Full-time tuition and fees vary according to course load, degree level, program, reciprocity agreements, and student level. Part-time tuition and fees vary according to course load, degree level, program, reciprocity agreements, and student level. *Required fees:* $400 full-time, $17 per credit hour part-time. *Room and board:* $4050. *Payment plan:* installment. *Waivers:* senior citizens.
Applying *Options:* electronic application. *Application fee:* $40. *Required:* high school transcript, minimum 2.0 GPA. *Application deadlines:* rolling (freshmen), rolling (transfers).
Freshman Application Contact Ms. Carmen Brown, Admissions Coordinator, University of South Carolina Salkehatchie, PO Box 617, Allendale, SC 29810. *Phone:* 803-584-3446. *Toll-free phone:* 800-922-5500. *Fax:* 803-584-3884. *E-mail:* cdbrown@mailbox.sc.edu. *Website:* http://uscsalkehatchie.sc.edu/.

University of South Carolina Sumter
Sumter, South Carolina

Freshman Application Contact Mr. Keith Britton, Director of Admissions, University of South Carolina Sumter, 200 Miller Road, Sumter, SC 29150-2498. *Phone:* 803-938-3882. *Fax:* 803-938-3901. *E-mail:* kbritton@usc.sumter.edu. *Website:* http://www.uscsumter.edu/.

University of South Carolina Union
Union, South Carolina

- **State-supported** primarily 2-year, founded 1965, part of University of South Carolina System
- **Small-town** 7-acre campus with easy access to Charlotte
- **Endowment** $1.2 million
- **Coed,** 757 undergraduate students, 57% full-time, 60% women, 40% men

Undergraduates 435 full-time, 322 part-time. Students come from 1 other state.
Freshmen *Admission:* 200 applied, 190 admitted. *Average high school GPA:* 3.2.

Faculty *Total:* 38, 26% full-time. *Student/faculty ratio:* 18:1.
Majors Biological and physical sciences; liberal arts and sciences/liberal studies.
Academics *Calendar:* semesters. *Degrees:* associate and bachelor's. *Special study options:* advanced placement credit, cooperative education, distance learning, double majors, independent study, internships, part-time degree program, study abroad, summer session for credit.
Library USC Union Campus Library plus 1 other.
Student Life *Housing:* college housing not available. *Activities and Organizations:* drama/theater group, choral group.
Athletics *Intramural sports:* baseball M, softball W.
Standardized Tests *Required:* SAT or ACT (for admission).
Costs (2017–18) *One-time required fee:* $50. *Tuition:* state resident $3500 full-time, $280 per credit hour part-time; nonresident $8400 full-time, $700 per credit hour part-time. Full-time tuition and fees vary according to class time, course load, degree level, location, program, and student level. Part-time tuition and fees vary according to class time, location, program, and student level. *Required fees:* $315 full-time, $40 per credit hour part-time. *Payment plan:* deferred payment. *Waivers:* senior citizens.
Financial Aid Of all full-time matriculated undergraduates who enrolled in 2015, 16 Federal Work-Study jobs (averaging $3400).
Applying *Options:* electronic application. *Application fee:* $40. *Required:* high school transcript. *Application deadlines:* rolling (freshmen), rolling (out-of-state freshmen), rolling (transfers), rolling (early action). *Early decision deadline:* rolling (for plan 1), rolling (for plan 2). *Notification:* continuous (freshmen), continuous (out-of-state freshmen), continuous (transfers), rolling (early decision plan 1), rolling (early decision plan 2), rolling (early action).
Freshman Application Contact Mr. Michael B. Greer, Director of Enrollment Services, University of South Carolina Union, PO Drawer 729, Union, SC 29379-0729. *Phone:* 864-424-8039. *E-mail:* tyoung@gwm.sc.edu. *Website:* http://uscunion.sc.edu/.

Virginia College in Charleston
North Charleston, South Carolina

Admissions Office Contact Virginia College in Charleston, 6185 Rivers Avenue, North Charleston, SC 29406. *Website:* http://www.vc.edu/.

Virginia College in Columbia
Columbia, South Carolina

Admissions Office Contact Virginia College in Columbia, 7201 Two Notch Road, Suite 1000, Columbia, SC 29223. *Website:* http://www.vc.edu/.

Virginia College in Florence
Florence, South Carolina

Admissions Office Contact Virginia College in Florence, 2400 David H. McLeod Boulevard, Florence, SC 29501. *Website:* http://www.vc.edu/.

Virginia College in Greenville
Greenville, South Carolina

Admissions Office Contact Virginia College in Greenville, 78 Global Drive, Suite 200, Greenville, SC 29607. *Website:* http://www.vc.edu/.

Virginia College in Spartanburg
Spartanburg, South Carolina

Admissions Office Contact Virginia College in Spartanburg, 8150 Warren H. Abernathy Highway, Spartanburg, SC 29301. *Website:* http://www.vc.edu/.

Williamsburg Technical College
Kingstree, South Carolina

- **State-supported** 2-year, founded 1969, part of South Carolina State Board for Technical and Comprehensive Education
- **Rural** 41-acre campus
- **Coed,** 676 undergraduate students, 26% full-time, 59% women, 41% men

Undergraduates 179 full-time, 497 part-time. Students come from 1 other state; 72% Black or African American, non-Hispanic/Latino; 0.1% Hispanic/Latino; 0.3% Asian, non-Hispanic/Latino; 0.1% American Indian or Alaska Native, non-Hispanic/Latino; 1% Race/ethnicity unknown; 4% transferred in. *Retention:* 65% of full-time freshmen returned.
Freshmen *Admission:* 210 enrolled.
Faculty *Total:* 45, 40% full-time. *Student/faculty ratio:* 13:1.

Majors Administrative assistant and secretarial science; business/commerce; child-care and support services management; interdisciplinary studies; liberal arts and sciences/liberal studies.

Academics *Calendar:* semesters. *Degree:* certificates, diplomas, and associate. *Special study options:* academic remediation for entering students, adult/continuing education programs, distance learning, part-time degree program, summer session for credit.

Library Learning Resource Center. *Books:* 20,516 (physical), 372,967 (digital/electronic); *Databases:* 58.

Student Life *Housing:* college housing not available. *Activities and Organizations:* Phi Theta Kappa, Student Government Association. *Student services:* personal/psychological counseling.

Costs (2016–17) *Tuition:* area resident $3888 full-time, $162 per credit hour part-time; state resident $4008 full-time, $167 per credit hour part-time; nonresident $7560 full-time, $315 per credit hour part-time. *Required fees:* $192 full-time, $8 per credit hour part-time. *Payment plan:* deferred payment. *Waivers:* senior citizens and employees or children of employees.

Applying *Options:* electronic application, early admission, deferred entrance. *Required:* high school transcript. *Application deadlines:* rolling (freshmen), rolling (transfers). *Notification:* continuous (freshmen), continuous (transfers).

Freshman Application Contact Ms. Cheryl DuBose, Director of Admissions, Williamsburg Technical College, 601 MLK Jr. Avenue, Kingstree, SC 29556-4197. *Phone:* 843-355-4165. *Toll-free phone:* 800-768-2021. *Fax:* 843-355-4289. *E-mail:* dubosec@wiltech.edu.
Website: http://www.wiltech.edu/.

York Technical College
Rock Hill, South Carolina

Freshman Application Contact Mr. Kenny Aldridge, Admissions Department Manager, York Technical College, Rock Hill, SC 29730. *Phone:* 803-327-8008. *Toll-free phone:* 800-922-8324. *Fax:* 803-981-7237. *E-mail:* kaldridge@yorktech.com. *Website:* http://www.yorktech.com/.

SOUTH DAKOTA

Lake Area Technical Institute
Watertown, South Dakota

- **State-supported** 2-year, founded 1965, part of South Dakota Department of Education
- **Small-town** 40-acre campus
- **Endowment** $2.7 million
- **Coed,** 2,061 undergraduate students, 78% full-time, 47% women, 53% men

Undergraduates 1,600 full-time, 461 part-time. Students come from 16 states and territories; 3 other countries; 18% are from out of state; 0.5% Black or African American, non-Hispanic/Latino; 2% Hispanic/Latino; 0.7% Asian, non-Hispanic/Latino; 0.4% Native Hawaiian or other Pacific Islander, non-Hispanic/Latino; 2% American Indian or Alaska Native, non-Hispanic/Latino; 0.1% Two or more races, non-Hispanic/Latino; 2% Race/ethnicity unknown; 0.2% international. *Retention:* 81% of full-time freshmen returned.

Freshmen *Admission:* 827 enrolled. *Test scores:* ACT scores over 18: 73%; ACT scores over 24: 16%; ACT scores over 30: 1%.

Faculty *Total:* 166, 64% full-time. *Student/faculty ratio:* 16:1.

Majors Agricultural business and management; aircraft powerplant technology; autobody/collision and repair technology; automobile/automotive mechanics technology; banking and financial support services; building construction technology; clinical/medical laboratory technology; community health services counseling; computer science; construction engineering technology; construction/heavy equipment/earthmoving equipment operation; criminal justice/police science; dental assisting; diesel mechanics technology; electrical, electronic and communications engineering technology; emergency medical technology (EMT paramedic); engine machinist; environmental science; human services; machine tool technology; manufacturing engineering technology; marketing/marketing management; medical/clinical assistant; occupational therapist assistant; physical therapy technology; robotics technology; welding technology.

Academics *Calendar:* semesters. *Degree:* certificates, diplomas, and associate. *Special study options:* academic remediation for entering students, advanced placement credit, cooperative education, distance learning, double majors, English as a second language, independent study, internships, off-campus study, part-time degree program, services for LD students, summer session for credit.

Library Leonard H. Timmerman Library plus 1 other. *Books:* 2,500 (physical), 50,000 (digital/electronic); *Serial titles:* 32 (physical); *Databases:* 40. Weekly public service hours: 58.

Student Life *Housing:* college housing not available. *Activities and Organizations:* Campus Crusades, Campus Activities Board, Student Voice, Student Ambassador, SkillsUSA. *Campus security:* 24-hour emergency response devices, partnership with local police department. *Student services:* personal/psychological counseling.

Athletics *Intramural sports:* basketball M/W, bowling M/W, equestrian sports M/W, football M, softball M/W, volleyball M/W.

Standardized Tests *Required for some:* ACCUPLACER. *Recommended:* ACT (for admission).

Costs (2016–17) *Tuition:* state resident $3706 full-time, $109 per credit part-time; nonresident $3706 full-time, $109 per credit part-time. Full-time tuition and fees vary according to course load and program. Part-time tuition and fees vary according to course load and program. *Required fees:* $2607 full-time, $103 per credit part-time. *Payment plan:* installment. *Waivers:* employees or children of employees.

Financial Aid Of all full-time matriculated undergraduates who enrolled in 2016, 1,290 applied for aid, 1,054 were judged to have need, 108 had their need fully met. 121 Federal Work-Study jobs (averaging $1945). In 2016, 87 non-need-based awards were made. *Average percent of need met:* 54%. *Average financial aid package:* $7921. *Average need-based loan:* $3853. *Average need-based gift aid:* $4951. *Average non-need-based aid:* $980.

Applying *Options:* electronic application. *Application fee:* $25. *Required:* high school transcript. *Required for some:* essay or personal statement, interview. *Application deadlines:* rolling (freshmen), rolling (transfers). *Notification:* continuous (freshmen), continuous (transfers).

Freshman Application Contact Ms. LuAnn Strait, Director of Student Services, Lake Area Technical Institute, 1201 Arrow Avenue, PO Box 730, Watertown, SD 57201. *Phone:* 605-882-5284 Ext. 241. *Toll-free phone:* 800-657-4344. *Fax:* 605-882-6299. *E-mail:* straitl@lakeareatech.edu.
Website: http://www.lakeareatech.edu/.

Mitchell Technical Institute
Mitchell, South Dakota

- **State-supported** 2-year, founded 1968, part of South Dakota Board of Technical Education
- **Small-town** 90-acre campus
- **Coed,** 1,253 undergraduate students, 67% full-time, 31% women, 69% men

Undergraduates 843 full-time, 410 part-time. Students come from 22 states and territories; 1 other country; 10% are from out of state; 0.6% Black or African American, non-Hispanic/Latino; 2% Hispanic/Latino; 1% Asian, non-Hispanic/Latino; 0.1% Native Hawaiian or other Pacific Islander, non-Hispanic/Latino; 3% American Indian or Alaska Native, non-Hispanic/Latino; 1% Two or more races, non-Hispanic/Latino; 2% Race/ethnicity unknown; 0.2% international; 11% transferred in. *Retention:* 82% of full-time freshmen returned.

Freshmen *Admission:* 916 applied, 527 admitted, 358 enrolled. *Average high school GPA:* 2.85. *Test scores:* ACT scores over 18: 67%; ACT scores over 24: 13%.

Faculty *Total:* 82, 88% full-time, 1% with terminal degrees. *Student/faculty ratio:* 13:1.

Majors Accounting and business/management; agricultural mechanics and equipment technology; agricultural production; automation engineer technology; building construction technology; business automation/technology/data entry; clinical/medical laboratory technology; computer support specialist; construction trades related; culinary arts; electrician; energy management and systems technology; geographic information science and cartography; heating, air conditioning, ventilation and refrigeration maintenance technology; human services; licensed practical/vocational nurse training; lineworker; magnetic resonance imaging (MRI) technology; medical/clinical assistant; medical office assistant; medical radiologic technology; network and system administration; radiologic technology/science; small engine mechanics and repair technology; speech-language pathology assistant; telecommunications technology; truck and bus driver/commercial vehicle operation/instruction; welding engineering technology.

Academics *Calendar:* semesters. *Degree:* certificates, diplomas, and associate. *Special study options:* academic remediation for entering students, advanced placement credit, cooperative education, distance learning, double majors, internships, part-time degree program, services for LD students, summer session for credit.

Library Center for Student Success. *Books:* 1,657 (physical), 929 (digital/electronic); *Databases:* 17. Weekly public service hours: 45.

Student Life *Housing:* college housing not available. *Activities and Organizations:* Student Representative Board, SkillsUSA, Post-Secondary Agricultural Students, Rodeo Club, Diversity Club. *Campus security:* 24-hour emergency response devices. *Student services:* personal/psychological counseling.

Athletics *Intercollegiate sports:* equestrian sports M/W. *Intramural sports:* basketball M/W, bowling M/W, riflery M/W, softball M/W, volleyball M/W.

Standardized Tests *Required:* ACT (for admission), ACCUPLACER (for admission).

Costs (2016–17) *Tuition:* state resident $3488 full-time, $109 per credit hour part-time; nonresident $3488 full-time, $109 per credit hour part-time. Full-time tuition and fees vary according to course load and program. Part-time tuition and fees vary according to course load and program. *Required fees:* $2944 full-time, $92 per credit hour part-time. *Payment plan:* installment. *Waivers:* employees or children of employees.

Financial Aid Of all full-time matriculated undergraduates who enrolled in 2015, 676 applied for aid, 556 were judged to have need, 10 had their need fully met. *Average financial aid package:* $7486. *Average need-based loan:* $3694. *Average need-based gift aid:* $4002.

Applying *Options:* electronic application. *Required:* high school transcript. *Required for some:* essay or personal statement, interview. *Recommended:* minimum 2.0 GPA. *Application deadlines:* rolling (freshmen), rolling (transfers). *Notification:* continuous (freshmen), continuous (transfers).

Freshman Application Contact Mr. Clayton Deuter, Director of Admissions, Mitchell Technical Institute, 1800 East Spruce Street, Mitchell, SD 57301. *Phone:* 605-995-3025. *Toll-free phone:* 800-684-1969. *Fax:* 605-995-3067. *E-mail:* clayton.deuter@mitchelltech.edu. *Website:* http://www.mitchelltech.edu/.

Sisseton-Wahpeton College
Sisseton, South Dakota

- **Federally supported** 2-year, founded 1979
- **Rural** 2-acre campus
- **Coed,** 165 undergraduate students, 61% full-time, 64% women, 36% men

Undergraduates 101 full-time, 64 part-time. Students come from 165 states and territories; 2% are from out of state; 0.6% Black or African American, non-Hispanic/Latino; 91% American Indian or Alaska Native, non-Hispanic/Latino; 0.6% Two or more races, non-Hispanic/Latino; 0.6% transferred in.

Freshmen *Admission:* 67 applied, 63 admitted, 31 enrolled.

Faculty *Total:* 30, 33% full-time, 33% with terminal degrees. *Student/faculty ratio:* 10:1.

Majors Accounting; American Indian/Native American studies; business administration and management; electrical, electronic and communications engineering technology; hospitality administration; information science/studies; kindergarten/preschool education; liberal arts and sciences/liberal studies; natural sciences; nutrition sciences; registered nursing/registered nurse; substance abuse/addiction counseling.

Academics *Calendar:* semesters. *Degree:* certificates and associate. *Special study options:* academic remediation for entering students, adult/continuing education programs, cooperative education, double majors, internships, off-campus study, part-time degree program, summer session for credit.

Library Sisseton-Wahpeton Community College Library.

Student Life *Activities and Organizations:* AIHEC, AISES, Student Senate, Student Nurses Association, AIBL. *Campus security:* 24-hour emergency response devices. *Student services:* personal/psychological counseling.

Standardized Tests *Required:* ACT Compass (for admission).

Costs (2017–18) *One-time required fee:* $540. *Tuition:* state resident $3250 full-time, $125 per credit hour part-time; nonresident $3250 full-time, $125 per credit hour part-time. Full-time tuition and fees vary according to class time, course level, course load, location, program, and student level. Part-time tuition and fees vary according to class time, course level, course load, location, program, and student level. No tuition increase for student's term of enrollment. *Required fees:* $590 full-time. *Room and board:* $6500; room only: $6500. Room and board charges vary according to student level. *Payment plan:* installment. *Waivers:* minority students, adult students, senior citizens, and employees or children of employees.

Financial Aid Of all full-time matriculated undergraduates who enrolled in 2015, 101 applied for aid, 101 were judged to have need. 10 Federal Work-Study jobs (averaging $785). In 2015, 101 non-need-based awards were made. *Average need-based gift aid:* $800. *Average non-need-based aid:* $800.

Applying *Required:* high school transcript. *Required for some:* Certificate of Indian Blood for enrolled tribal members. *Recommended:* minimum 2.0 GPA, interview. *Application deadlines:* rolling (freshmen), 7/8 (out-of-state freshmen), rolling (transfers).

Freshman Application Contact Sisseton-Wahpeton College, Old Agency Box 689, Sisseton, SD 57262. *Phone:* 605-698-3966 Ext. 1180. *Website:* http://www.swc.tc/.

Southeast Technical Institute
Sioux Falls, South Dakota

- **State-supported** 2-year, founded 1968
- **Urban** 138-acre campus
- **Endowment** $768,716
- **Coed**

Undergraduates 1,304 full-time, 743 part-time. Students come from 11 states and territories; 9% are from out of state; 4% Black or African American, non-Hispanic/Latino; 4% Hispanic/Latino; 2% Asian, non-Hispanic/Latino; 0.2% Native Hawaiian or other Pacific Islander, non-Hispanic/Latino; 2% American Indian or Alaska Native, non-Hispanic/Latino; 2% Two or more races, non-Hispanic/Latino; 2% Race/ethnicity unknown; 14% transferred in; 2% live on campus. *Retention:* 64% of full-time freshmen returned.

Faculty *Student/faculty ratio:* 15:1.

Academics *Calendar:* semesters. *Degree:* certificates, diplomas, and associate. *Special study options:* academic remediation for entering students, advanced placement credit, distance learning, double majors, independent study, internships, part-time degree program, services for LD students, summer session for credit.

Library Southeast Library.

Student Life *Campus security:* 24-hour patrols, late-night transport/escort service, controlled dormitory access.

Standardized Tests *Required for some:* ACT (for admission). *Recommended:* ACT (for admission).

Costs (2016–17) *Tuition:* state resident $3270 full-time, $109 per credit hour part-time; nonresident $3270 full-time, $109 per credit hour part-time. Full-time tuition and fees vary according to program. Part-time tuition and fees vary according to program. *Required fees:* $3630 full-time, $121 per credit hour part-time, $121 per credit hour part-time. *Room and board:* room only: $4750.

Financial Aid Of all full-time matriculated undergraduates who enrolled in 2015, 35 Federal Work-Study jobs (averaging $2550).

Applying *Options:* electronic application. *Application fee:* $35. *Required:* high school transcript, minimum 2.2 GPA. *Required for some:* interview, background check, drug screening.

Freshman Application Contact Mr. Scott Dorman, Recruiter, Southeast Technical Institute, Sioux Falls, SD 57107. *Phone:* 605-367-4458. *Toll-free phone:* 800-247-0789. *Fax:* 605-367-8305. *E-mail:* scott.dorman@ southeasttech.edu. *Website:* http://www.southeasttech.edu/.

Western Dakota Technical Institute
Rapid City, South Dakota

- **State-supported** 2-year, founded 1968
- **Small-town** 5-acre campus
- **Endowment** $171,306
- **Coed,** 1,002 undergraduate students, 65% full-time, 53% women, 47% men

Undergraduates 649 full-time, 353 part-time. Students come from 16 states and territories; 6% are from out of state; 2% Black or African American, non-Hispanic/Latino; 6% Hispanic/Latino; 1% Asian, non-Hispanic/Latino; 0.7% Native Hawaiian or other Pacific Islander, non-Hispanic/Latino; 12% American Indian or Alaska Native, non-Hispanic/Latino; 3% Two or more races, non-Hispanic/Latino; 0.5% Race/ethnicity unknown; 0.4% transferred in. *Retention:* 98% of full-time freshmen returned.

Freshmen *Admission:* 1,041 applied, 787 admitted, 190 enrolled. *Average high school GPA:* 2.54. *Test scores:* ACT scores over 18: 74%; ACT scores over 24: 18%.

Faculty *Total:* 86, 52% full-time, 2% with terminal degrees. *Student/faculty ratio:* 13:1.

Majors Accounting; business administration and management; clinical/medical laboratory technology; computer systems networking and telecommunications; criminal justice/police science; criminal justice/safety; drafting and design technology; electrician; emergency medical technology (EMT paramedic); environmental control technologies related; fire science/firefighting; heating, air conditioning, ventilation and refrigeration maintenance technology; library and archives assisting; licensed practical/vocational nurse training; machine tool technology; medical/clinical assistant; medical transcription; pharmacy technician; precision metal working related; surgical technology; vehicle maintenance and repair technologies related.

Academics *Calendar:* semesters. *Degree:* certificates, diplomas, and associate. *Special study options:* academic remediation for entering students, advanced placement credit, distance learning, independent study, internships, part-time degree program, services for LD students, summer session for credit.

Library Western Dakota Technical Institute Library plus 1 other. *Books:* 3,500 (physical), 158,080 (digital/electronic); *Databases:* 12. Weekly public service hours: 48.

Student Life *Housing:* college housing not available. *Campus security:* 24-hour video surveillance.

Standardized Tests *Recommended:* SAT or ACT (for admission).

Costs (2017–18) *One-time required fee:* $155. *Tuition:* state resident $3270 full-time, $654 per term part-time; nonresident $3270 full-time, $644 per term part-time. Full-time tuition and fees vary according to course load and program. Part-time tuition and fees vary according to course load and program. *Required fees:* $3005 full-time, $576 per term part-time. *Payment plans:* installment, deferred payment. *Waivers:* employees or children of employees.

Financial Aid Of all full-time matriculated undergraduates who enrolled in 2016, 546 applied for aid, 526 were judged to have need, 42 had their need fully met. 48 Federal Work-Study jobs (averaging $1288). In 2016, 5 non-need-based awards were made. *Average percent of need met:* 69%. *Average financial aid package:* $11,067. *Average need-based loan:* $3251. *Average need-based gift aid:* $6300. *Average non-need-based aid:* $900. *Financial aid deadline:* 6/30.

Applying *Options:* electronic application. *Required:* high school transcript. *Required for some:* essay or personal statement, 3 letters of recommendation, interview. *Recommended:* minimum 2.0 GPA. *Application deadlines:* 8/1 (freshmen), 8/1 (transfers). *Notification:* continuous until 8/15 (freshmen), continuous until 8/15 (transfers).

Freshman Application Contact Jill Elder, Admissions Coordinator, Western Dakota Technical Institute, 800 Mickelson Drive, Rapid City, SD 57703. *Phone:* 605-718-2411. *Toll-free phone:* 800-544-8765. *Fax:* 605-394-2204. *E-mail:* jill.elder@wdt.edu.

Website: http://www.wdt.edu/.

TENNESSEE

Brightwood College, Nashville Campus
Nashville, Tennessee

Freshman Application Contact Brightwood College, Nashville Campus, 750 Envious Lane, Nashville, TN 37217. *Phone:* 615-269-9900. *Toll-free phone:* 866-543-0208. *Website:* http://www.brightwood.edu/.

Chattanooga College–Medical, Dental and Technical Careers
Chattanooga, Tennessee

Freshman Application Contact Chattanooga College–Medical, Dental and Technical Careers, 248 Northgate Mall Drive, Suite 130, Chattanooga, TN 37415. *Phone:* 423-305-7781. *Toll-free phone:* 877-313-2373. *Website:* http://www.chattanoogacollege.edu/.

Chattanooga State Community College
Chattanooga, Tennessee

Freshman Application Contact Brad McCormick, Director of Admissions and Records, Chattanooga State Community College, 4501 Amnicola Highway, Chattanooga, TN 37406. *Phone:* 423-697-4401 Ext. 3264. *Toll-free phone:* 866-547-3733. *Fax:* 423-697-4709. *E-mail:* brad.mccormick@chattanoogastate.edu. *Website:* http://www.chattanoogastate.edu/.

Cleveland State Community College
Cleveland, Tennessee

- **State-supported** 2-year, founded 1967, part of Tennessee Board of Regents
- **Suburban** 83-acre campus
- **Endowment** $7.8 million
- **Coed,** 3,315 undergraduate students, 52% full-time, 59% women, 41% men

Undergraduates 1,709 full-time, 1,606 part-time. Students come from 8 states and territories; 1 other country; 1% are from out of state; 5% Black or African American, non-Hispanic/Latino; 8% Hispanic/Latino; 1% Asian, non-Hispanic/Latino; 0.1% Native Hawaiian or other Pacific Islander, non-Hispanic/Latino; 0.1% American Indian or Alaska Native, non-Hispanic/Latino; 2% Two or more races, non-Hispanic/Latino; 4% Race/ethnicity unknown; 11% transferred in.

Freshmen *Admission:* 1,828 applied, 783 admitted, 807 enrolled. *Average high school GPA:* 3.11.

Faculty *Total:* 204, 37% full-time, 15% with terminal degrees. *Student/faculty ratio:* 23:1.

Majors Administrative assistant and secretarial science; business administration and management; child development; community organization and advocacy; criminal justice/police science; general studies; industrial technology; kindergarten/preschool education; liberal arts and sciences and humanities related; liberal arts and sciences/liberal studies; public administration and social service professions related; registered nursing/registered nurse; science technologies related.

Academics *Calendar:* semesters. *Degree:* certificates and associate. *Special study options:* academic remediation for entering students, adult/continuing education programs, advanced placement credit, cooperative education, distance learning, double majors, external degree program, honors programs, independent study, internships, off-campus study, part-time degree program, services for LD students, summer session for credit.

Library Cleveland State Community College Library. *Books:* 181,877 (physical), 260,161 (digital/electronic); *Databases:* 76.

Student Life *Housing:* college housing not available. *Activities and Organizations:* choral group, Human Services/Social Work, Computer-Aided Design, Phi Theta Kappa, Student Nursing Association, Early Childhood Education. *Campus security:* 24-hour emergency response devices and patrols. *Student services:* personal/psychological counseling.

Athletics Member NJCAA. *Intercollegiate sports:* baseball M(s), basketball M(s)/W(s), cross-country running M(s)/W(s), golf M(s)/W(s), softball W(s), volleyball W(s). *Intramural sports:* archery M/W, basketball M/W, bowling M/W, cheerleading M(c)/W(c), softball W, table tennis M/W, volleyball M/W.

Costs (2016–17) *Tuition:* state resident $3930 full-time, $156 per credit hour part-time; nonresident $15,990 full-time, $642 per credit hour part-time. Full-time tuition and fees vary according to course load. *Required fees:* $299 full-time, $14 per credit hour part-time, $37 per term part-time. *Payment plan:* deferred payment. *Waivers:* senior citizens and employees or children of employees.

Financial Aid Of all full-time matriculated undergraduates who enrolled in 2015, 52 Federal Work-Study jobs (averaging $1025).

Applying *Options:* electronic application, early admission, deferred entrance. *Required:* high school transcript. *Application deadlines:* rolling (freshmen), rolling (transfers). *Notification:* continuous (freshmen), continuous (transfers).

Freshman Application Contact Mr. Jason Sewell, Enrollment Services Director, Cleveland State Community College, PO Box 3570, Cleveland, TN 37320-3570. *Phone:* 423-472-7141 Ext. 744. *Toll-free phone:* 800-604-2722. *Fax:* 423-614-8711. *E-mail:* jsewell@clevelandstatecc.edu. *Website:* http://www.clevelandstatecc.edu/.

Columbia State Community College
Columbia, Tennessee

Freshman Application Contact Mr. Joey Scruggs, Coordinator of Recruitment, Columbia State Community College, 1665 Hampshire Pike, Columbia, TN 38401. *Phone:* 931-540-2540. *E-mail:* scruggs@coscc.cc.tn.us. *Website:* http://www.columbiastate.edu/.

Concorde Career College
Memphis, Tennessee

Freshman Application Contact Dee Vickers, Director, Concorde Career College, 5100 Poplar Avenue, Suite 132, Memphis, TN 38137. *Phone:* 901-761-9494. *Fax:* 901-761-3293. *E-mail:* dvickers@concorde.edu. *Website:* http://www.concorde.edu/.

Daymar College
Clarksville, Tennessee

Freshman Application Contact Daymar College, 2691 Trenton Road, Clarksville, TN 37040. *Phone:* 931-552-7600 Ext. 204. *Website:* http://www.daymarcollege.edu/.

Daymar College
Murfreesboro, Tennessee

Admissions Office Contact Daymar College, 415 Golden Bear Court, Murfreesboro, TN 37128. *Website:* http://www.daymarcollege.edu/.

Daymar College
Nashville, Tennessee

Director of Admissions Admissions Office, Daymar College, 560 Royal Parkway, Nashville, TN 37214. *Phone:* 615-361-7555. *Fax:* 615-367-2736. *Website:* http://www.daymarcollege.edu/.

Dyersburg State Community College
Dyersburg, Tennessee

- **State-supported** 2-year, founded 1969, part of Tennessee Board of Regents
- **Small-town** 115-acre campus with easy access to Memphis
- **Endowment** $4.0 million
- **Coed,** 2,857 undergraduate students, 43% full-time, 65% women, 35% men

Undergraduates 1,226 full-time, 1,631 part-time. Students come from 5 states and territories; 1 other country; 23% Black or African American, non-Hispanic/Latino; 2% Hispanic/Latino; 0.7% Asian, non-Hispanic/Latino; 0.1% Native Hawaiian or other Pacific Islander, non-Hispanic/Latino; 0.4% American Indian or Alaska Native, non-Hispanic/Latino; 2% Two or more races, non-Hispanic/Latino; 0.7% Race/ethnicity unknown; 6% transferred in. *Retention:* 45% of full-time freshmen returned.
Freshmen *Admission:* 611 enrolled. *Average high school GPA:* 2.9.
Faculty *Total:* 162, 32% full-time, 10% with terminal degrees. *Student/faculty ratio:* 8:1.
Majors Agriculture; automation engineer technology; business administration and management; child development; computer and information sciences; computer and information systems security; criminal justice/police science; criminal justice/safety; education; emergency medical technology (EMT paramedic); general studies; health information/medical records technology; health services/allied health/health sciences; industrial electronics technology; industrial mechanics and maintenance technology; information science/studies; liberal arts and sciences/liberal studies; registered nursing/registered nurse.
Academics *Calendar:* semesters. *Degree:* certificates and associate. *Special study options:* academic remediation for entering students, accelerated degree program, adult/continuing education programs, advanced placement credit, cooperative education, distance learning, double majors, honors programs, independent study, internships, off-campus study, part-time degree program, services for LD students, study abroad, summer session for credit.
Library Learning Resource Center plus 2 others. *Books:* 17,817 (physical), 225,400 (digital/electronic); *Serial titles:* 29 (digital/electronic); *Databases:* 121. Weekly public service hours: 66; students can reserve study rooms.
Student Life *Activities and Organizations:* drama/theater group, choral group, Psychology Club, Phi Theta Kappa, Student Government, Student Nurses Association, Criminal Justice Association. *Campus security:* 24-hour emergency response devices and patrols. *Student services:* personal/psychological counseling.
Athletics Member NJCAA. *Intercollegiate sports:* baseball M(s), basketball M(s)/W(s), cheerleading M(s)/W(s), softball W(s). *Intramural sports:* soccer M/W, table tennis M/W, ultimate Frisbee M/W, volleyball M/W.
Standardized Tests *Required:* SAT or ACT (for admission). *Required for some:* ACT Compass for students who are over 21.
Costs (2016–17) *Tuition:* state resident $3930 full-time, $156 per credit hour part-time; nonresident $16,176 full-time, $642 per credit hour part-time. Full-time tuition and fees vary according to course load. Part-time tuition and fees vary according to course load. *Required fees:* $299 full-time, $150 per term part-time. *Payment plan:* deferred payment. *Waivers:* senior citizens and employees or children of employees.
Financial Aid Of all full-time matriculated undergraduates who enrolled in 2015, 40 Federal Work-Study jobs (averaging $2175). 142 state and other part-time jobs (averaging $1174).
Applying *Required:* high school transcript.
Freshman Application Contact Mrs. Heather Page, Director of Admissions & Records, Dyersburg State Community College, Dyersburg, TN 38024. *Phone:* 731-286-3331. *Fax:* 731-286-3325. *E-mail:* page@dscc.edu. *Website:* http://www.dscc.edu/.

Fortis Institute
Cookeville, Tennessee

Director of Admissions Ms. Sharon Mellott, Director of Admissions, Fortis Institute, 1025 Highway 111, Cookeville, TN 38501. *Phone:* 931-526-3660. *Toll-free phone:* 855-4-FORTIS. *Website:* http://www.fortis.edu/.

Fortis Institute
Nashville, Tennessee

Admissions Office Contact Fortis Institute, 3354 Perimeter Hill Drive, Suite 105, Nashville, TN 37211. *Toll-free phone:* 855-4-FORTIS. *Website:* http://www.fortis.edu/.

Fountainhead College of Technology
Knoxville, Tennessee

Freshman Application Contact Mr. Joel B. Southern, Director of Admissions, Fountainhead College of Technology, 10208 Technology Drive, Knoxville, TN 37932. *Phone:* 865-688-9422. *Toll-free phone:* 888-218-7335. *Fax:* 865-688-2419. *E-mail:* joel.southern@fountainheadcollege.edu. *Website:* http://www.fountainheadcollege.edu/.

Hiwassee College
Madisonville, Tennessee

Director of Admissions Jamie Williamson, Director of Admission, Hiwassee College, 225 Hiwassee College Drive, Madisonville, TN 37354. *Phone:* 423-420-1891. *Toll-free phone:* 800-356-2187. *Website:* http://www.hiwassee.edu/.

Jackson State Community College
Jackson, Tennessee

Freshman Application Contact Ms. Andrea Winchester, Director of High School Initiatives, Jackson State Community College, 2046 North Parkway, Jackson, TN 38301-3797. *Phone:* 731-424-3520 Ext. 50484. *Toll-free phone:* 800-355-5722. *Fax:* 731-425-9559. *E-mail:* awinchester@jscc.edu. *Website:* http://www.jscc.edu/.

John A. Gupton College
Nashville, Tennessee

- **Independent** 2-year, founded 1946
- **Urban** 1-acre campus with easy access to Nashville
- **Endowment** $60,000
- **Coed**

Undergraduates 70 full-time, 50 part-time. Students come from 5 states and territories; 10% are from out of state; 23% Black or African American, non-Hispanic/Latino; 3% Hispanic/Latino; 0.8% Asian, non-Hispanic/Latino; 18% transferred in; 11% live on campus.
Academics *Calendar:* semesters. *Degree:* certificates, diplomas, and associate. *Special study options:* part-time degree program.
Library Memorial Library plus 1 other.
Student Life *Campus security:* controlled dormitory access, day patrols.
Standardized Tests *Required:* ACT (for admission).
Costs (2016–17) *Tuition:* $10,400 full-time, $325 per semester hour part-time. Full-time tuition and fees vary according to course load. Part-time tuition and fees vary according to course load. *Required fees:* $70 full-time. *Room only:* $4000.
Financial Aid *Financial aid deadline:* 6/1.
Applying *Options:* electronic application, deferred entrance. *Application fee:* $50. *Required:* essay or personal statement, high school transcript, 2 letters of recommendation.
Freshman Application Contact John A. Gupton College, 1616 Church Street, Nashville, TN 37203-2920. *Phone:* 615-327-3927. *Website:* http://www.guptoncollege.edu/.

L'Ecole Culinaire–Memphis
Cordova, Tennessee

Admissions Office Contact L'Ecole Culinaire–Memphis, 1245 North Germantown Parkway, Cordova, TN 38016. *Toll-free phone:* 888-238-2077. *Website:* http://www.lecole.edu/memphis/.

Lincoln College of Technology
Nashville, Tennessee

Freshman Application Contact Ms. Tanya Smith, Director of Admissions, Lincoln College of Technology, 1524 Gallatin Road, Nashville, TN 37206. *Phone:* 615-226-3990 Ext. 71703. *Toll-free phone:* 844-215-1513. *Fax:* 615-262-8466. *E-mail:* tlegg-smith@lincolntech.com. *Website:* http://www.lincolntech.edu/.

Miller-Motte Technical College
Chattanooga, Tennessee

Admissions Office Contact Miller-Motte Technical College, 6397 Lee Highway, Suite 100, Chattanooga, TN 37421. *Toll-free phone:* 800-705-9182. *Website:* http://www.miller-motte.edu/.

Miller-Motte Technical College
Clarksville, Tennessee

Director of Admissions Ms. Jessica Juliano, Director of Admissions, Miller-Motte Technical College, 1820 Business Park Drive, Clarksville, TN 37040. *Phone:* 800-558-0071. *Toll-free phone:* 800-705-9182. *E-mail:* lisateague@hotmail.com. *Website:* http://www.miller-motte.edu/.

Miller-Motte Technical College
Madison, Tennessee

Admissions Office Contact Miller-Motte Technical College, 1515 Gallatin Pike North, Madison, TN 37115. *Toll-free phone:* 800-705-9182. *Website:* http://www.miller-motte.edu/.

Motlow State Community College
Tullahoma, Tennessee

- **State-supported** 2-year, founded 1969, part of Tennessee Board of Regents
- **Rural** 187-acre campus with easy access to Nashville
- **Endowment** $6.1 million
- **Coed,** 5,670 undergraduate students, 57% full-time, 58% women, 42% men

Undergraduates 3,252 full-time, 2,418 part-time. Students come from 17 states and territories; 1% are from out of state; 9% Black or African American, non-Hispanic/Latino; 6% Hispanic/Latino; 3% Asian, non-Hispanic/Latino; 0.2% Native Hawaiian or other Pacific Islander, non-Hispanic/Latino; 0.3% American Indian or Alaska Native, non-Hispanic/Latino; 1% Race/ethnicity unknown; 4% transferred in.
Faculty *Total:* 307, 30% full-time, 6% with terminal degrees.
Majors Business administration and management; education; electromechanical technology; general studies; liberal arts and sciences/liberal studies; registered nursing/registered nurse; special education–early childhood; web page, digital/multimedia and information resources design.
Academics *Calendar:* semesters. *Degree:* certificates and associate. *Special study options:* academic remediation for entering students, accelerated degree program, adult/continuing education programs, advanced placement credit, cooperative education, distance learning, double majors, honors programs, independent study, part-time degree program, services for LD students, study abroad, summer session for credit.
Library Clayton-Glass Library.
Student Life *Housing:* college housing not available. *Activities and Organizations:* drama/theater group, choral group, PTK Club, Communication Club, Student Government Association, Art Club, Baptist Student Union. *Campus security:* 24-hour patrols, late-night transport/escort service. *Student services:* personal/psychological counseling.
Athletics Member NJCAA. *Intercollegiate sports:* baseball M(s), basketball M(s)/W(s), soccer W(s), softball W(s). *Intramural sports:* badminton M/W, basketball M/W, bowling M/W, golf M/W, tennis M/W, volleyball M/W.
Costs (2016–17) *Tuition:* state resident $3744 full-time, $156 per credit hour part-time; nonresident $11,664 full-time, $486 per credit hour part-time. Full-time tuition and fees vary according to course load and program. Part-time tuition and fees vary according to program. *Required fees:* $307 full-time, $31 per credit hour part-time, $97 per credit hour part-time. *Payment plans:* installment, deferred payment. *Waivers:* senior citizens and employees or children of employees.
Financial Aid Of all full-time matriculated undergraduates who enrolled in 2015, 2,418 applied for aid, 1,844 were judged to have need, 210 had their need fully met. In 2015, 524 non-need-based awards were made. *Average percent of need met:* 57%. *Average financial aid package:* $5867. *Average need-based gift aid:* $4968. *Average non-need-based aid:* $3661.
Applying *Options:* electronic application, early admission, deferred entrance. *Required:* high school transcript. *Application deadlines:* 8/27 (freshmen), 8/13 (transfers). *Notification:* continuous (freshmen), continuous (transfers).
Freshman Application Contact Motlow State Community College, PO Box 8500, Lynchburg, TN 37352-8500. *Phone:* 931-393-1597. *Toll-free phone:* 800-654-4877.
Website: http://www.mscc.edu/.

Nashville State Community College
Nashville, Tennessee

- **State-supported** 2-year, founded 1970, part of Tennessee Board of Regents
- **Urban** 85-acre campus
- **Coed,** 8,914 undergraduate students

Undergraduates Students come from 55 other countries; 2% are from out of state; 27% Black or African American, non-Hispanic/Latino; 6% Hispanic/Latino; 4% Asian, non-Hispanic/Latino; 0.2% Native Hawaiian or other Pacific Islander, non-Hispanic/Latino; 0.3% American Indian or Alaska Native, non-Hispanic/Latino; 4% Two or more races, non-Hispanic/Latino; 0.8% Race/ethnicity unknown.
Freshmen *Average high school GPA:* 2.91.
Faculty *Student/faculty ratio:* 19:1.
Majors Accounting; administrative assistant and secretarial science; architectural engineering; architectural engineering technology; art; automobile/automotive mechanics technology; biology/biological sciences; business administration and management; chemistry; child development; civil engineering; civil engineering technology; commercial and advertising art; computer and information sciences related; computer engineering technology; computer science; computer systems networking and telecommunications; computer technology/computer systems technology; construction engineering technology; criminal justice/police science; culinary arts; design and visual communications; early childhood education; economics; electrical, electronic and communications engineering technology; elementary education; English; foreign languages related; geography; health/health-care administration; health information/medical records administration; health professions related; history; industrial engineering; industrial production technologies related; industrial technology; information science/studies; information technology; kindergarten/preschool education; kinesiology and exercise science; legal assistant/paralegal; mathematics; mechanical engineering; medical informatics; middle school education; music; nursing practice; occupational therapist assistant; occupational therapy; philosophy; photography; physics; political science and government; pre-engineering; pre-law studies; premedical studies; prenursing studies; pre-occupational therapy; pre-physical therapy; psychology; secondary education; sign language interpretation and translation; social work; sociology; special education; speech communication and rhetoric.
Academics *Calendar:* semesters. *Degree:* certificates and associate. *Special study options:* academic remediation for entering students, adult/continuing education programs, advanced placement credit, cooperative education, distance learning, double majors, English as a second language, off-campus study, part-time degree program, services for LD students, study abroad, summer session for credit.
Library Jane G. Kisber Memorial Library. Students can reserve study rooms.
Student Life *Housing:* college housing not available. *Activities and Organizations:* drama/theater group, student-run newspaper, choral group, National Society of Leadership and Success, Occupational Therapy Club, Phi Theta Kappa, Student Government Association, Black Student Association. *Campus security:* 24-hour emergency response devices and patrols, late-night transport/escort service. *Student services:* personal/psychological counseling.
Standardized Tests *Required:* SAT or ACT (for admission).
Costs (2016–17) *Tuition:* state resident $3969 full-time, $156 per credit hour part-time; nonresident $15,633 full-time, $642 per credit hour part-time. Full-time tuition and fees vary according to course load. Part-time tuition and fees vary according to course load. *Required fees:* $10 per credit hour part-time. *Payment plan:* deferred payment. *Waivers:* senior citizens and employees or children of employees.
Financial Aid Of all full-time matriculated undergraduates who enrolled in 2015, 3,942 applied for aid, 3,514 were judged to have need, 917 had their need fully met. 188 Federal Work-Study jobs (averaging $5400). 64 state and other part-time jobs (averaging $3600). In 2015, 3 non-need-based awards were made. *Average percent of need met:* 33%. *Average financial aid package:* $6616. *Average need-based loan:* $2970. *Average need-based gift aid:* $3331. *Average non-need-based aid:* $950.
Applying *Options:* electronic application. *Application fee:* $20. *Required:* high school transcript. *Application deadlines:* rolling (freshmen), rolling (out-of-state freshmen), rolling (transfers). *Notification:* continuous (freshmen), continuous (out-of-state freshmen), continuous (transfers).
Freshman Application Contact Mr. Tyler White, Coordinator of Recruitment, Nashville State Community College, 120 White Bridge Road, Nashville, TN 37209-4515. *Phone:* 615-353-3265. *Toll-free phone:* 800-272-7363. *E-mail:* recruiting@nscc.edu.
Website: http://www.nscc.edu/.

National College
Bristol, Tennessee

Freshman Application Contact National College, 1328 Highway 11 West, Bristol, TN 37620. *Phone:* 423-878-4440. *Toll-free phone:* 888-9-JOBREADY. *Website:* http://www.national-college.edu/.

National College
Knoxville, Tennessee

Director of Admissions Frank Alvey, Campus Director, National College, 8415 Kingston Pike, Knoxville, TN 37919. *Phone:* 865-539-2011. *Toll-free phone:* 888-9-JOBREADY. *Fax:* 865-539-2049. *Website:* http://www.national-college.edu/.

National College
Nashville, Tennessee

Director of Admissions Jerry Lafferty, Campus Director, National College, 1638 Bell Road, Nashville, TN 37211. *Phone:* 615-333-3344. *Toll-free phone:* 888-9-JOBREADY. *Website:* http://www.national-college.edu/.

North Central Institute
Clarksville, Tennessee

Freshman Application Contact Dale Wood, Director of Admissions, North Central Institute, 168 Jack Miller Boulevard, Clarksville, TN 37042. *Phone:* 931-431-9700. *Toll-free phone:* 800-603-4116. *Fax:* 931-431-9771. *E-mail:* admissions@nci.edu. *Website:* http://www.nci.edu/.

Northeast State Community College
Blountville, Tennessee

Freshman Application Contact Dr. Jon P. Harr, Vice President for Student Affairs, Northeast State Community College, PO Box 246, Blountville, TN 37617. *Phone:* 423-323-0231. *Toll-free phone:* 800-836-7822. *Fax:* 423-323-0240. *E-mail:* jpharr@northeaststate.edu. *Website:* http://www.northeaststate.edu/.

Pellissippi State Community College
Knoxville, Tennessee

Freshman Application Contact Director of Admissions and Records, Pellissippi State Community College, PO Box 22990, Knoxville, TN 37933-0990. *Phone:* 865-694-6400. *Fax:* 865-539-7217. *Website:* http://www.pstcc.edu/.

Remington College–Memphis Campus
Memphis, Tennessee

Director of Admissions Randal Hayes, Director of Recruitment, Remington College–Memphis Campus, 2710 Nonconnah Boulevard, Memphis, TN 38132. *Phone:* 901-345-1000. *Toll-free phone:* 800-323-8122. *Fax:* 901-396-8310. *E-mail:* randal.hayes@remingtoncollege.edu. *Website:* http://www.remingtoncollege.edu/.

Remington College–Nashville Campus
Nashville, Tennessee

Director of Admissions Mr. Frank Vivelo, Campus President, Remington College–Nashville Campus, 441 Donelson Pike, Suite 150, Nashville, TN 37214. *Phone:* 615-889-5520. *Toll-free phone:* 800-323-8122. *Fax:* 615-889-5528. *E-mail:* frank.vivelo@remingtoncollege.edu. *Website:* http://www.remingtoncollege.edu/.

Roane State Community College
Harriman, Tennessee

Freshman Application Contact Admissions Office, Roane State Community College, 276 Patton Lane, Harriman, TN 37748. *Phone:* 865-882-4523. *Toll-free phone:* 866-462-7722 Ext. 4554. *E-mail:* admissionsrecords@roanestate.edu. *Website:* http://www.roanestate.edu/.

SAE Institute Nashville
Nashville, Tennessee

Admissions Office Contact SAE Institute Nashville, 7 Music Circle N, Nashville, TN 37203. *Website:* http://www.sae.edu/.

Southwest Tennessee Community College
Memphis, Tennessee

- **State-supported** 2-year, founded 2000, part of Tennessee Board of Regents
- **Urban** 100-acre campus
- **Coed**

Undergraduates 4,183 full-time, 5,984 part-time. Students come from 13 states and territories; 8 other countries; 2% are from out of state; 6% transferred in.
Academics *Calendar:* semesters. *Degree:* certificates and associate. *Special study options:* academic remediation for entering students, accelerated degree program, adult/continuing education programs, advanced placement credit, cooperative education, distance learning, double majors, English as a second language, internships, part-time degree program, services for LD students, student-designed majors, summer session for credit. *ROTC:* Army (c), Air Force (c).
Library Infonet Library plus 4 others.
Student Life *Campus security:* 24-hour emergency response devices and patrols, late-night transport/escort service.
Athletics Member NJCAA.
Financial Aid Of all full-time matriculated undergraduates who enrolled in 2015, 201 Federal Work-Study jobs (averaging $2600).
Applying *Options:* early admission, deferred entrance. *Application fee:* $10. *Required:* high school transcript.
Freshman Application Contact Mrs. Vanessa Dowdy, Southwest Tennessee Community College, 5983 Macon Cove, Memphis, TN 38134. *Phone:* 901-333-4275. *Toll-free phone:* 877-717-STCC. *E-mail:* vdowdy@southwest.tn.edu. *Website:* http://www.southwest.tn.edu/.

Vatterott College
Memphis, Tennessee

Admissions Office Contact Vatterott College, 2655 Dividend Drive, Memphis, TN 38132. *Toll-free phone:* 888-553-6627. *Website:* http://www.vatterott.edu/.

Vatterott College
Memphis, Tennessee

Admissions Office Contact Vatterott College, 6991 Appling Farms Parkway, Memphis, TN 38133. *Website:* http://www.vatterott.edu/.

Virginia College in Chattanooga
Chattanooga, Tennessee

Admissions Office Contact Virginia College in Chattanooga, 721 Eastgate Loop Road, Chattanooga, TN 37411. *Website:* http://www.vc.edu/.

Virginia College in Knoxville
Knoxville, Tennessee

Admissions Office Contact Virginia College in Knoxville, 5003 North Broadway Street, Knoxville, TN 37918. *Website:* http://www.vc.edu/.

Volunteer State Community College
Gallatin, Tennessee

- **State-supported** 2-year, founded 1970, part of Tennessee Board of Regents
- **Suburban** 110-acre campus with easy access to Nashville
- **Endowment** $4.4 million
- **Coed,** 8,684 undergraduate students, 55% full-time, 59% women, 41% men

Undergraduates 4,753 full-time, 3,931 part-time. Students come from 12 states and territories; 14 other countries; 1% are from out of state; 10% Black or African American, non-Hispanic/Latino; 6% Hispanic/Latino; 1% Asian, non-Hispanic/Latino; 0.1% Native Hawaiian or other Pacific Islander, non-Hispanic/Latino; 0.4% American Indian or Alaska Native, non-

Hispanic/Latino; 3% Two or more races, non-Hispanic/Latino; 2% Race/ethnicity unknown; 0.5% international; 8% transferred in.

Freshmen *Admission:* 2,255 applied, 2,255 admitted, 2,239 enrolled. *Average high school GPA:* 2.96. *Test scores:* ACT scores over 18: 41%; ACT scores over 24: 8%.

Faculty *Total:* 411, 41% full-time, 13% with terminal degrees. *Student/faculty ratio:* 22:1.

Majors Business administration and management; child development; clinical/medical laboratory technology; computer and information sciences; criminal justice/police science; digital arts; education; electromechanical technology; fire science/firefighting; general studies; health information/medical records technology; health professions related; legal assistant/paralegal; liberal arts and sciences/liberal studies; medical informatics; medical radiologic technology; music performance; ophthalmic technology; physical therapy technology; respiratory care therapy; veterinary/animal health technology.

Academics *Calendar:* semesters. *Degree:* certificates and associate. *Special study options:* academic remediation for entering students, accelerated degree program, adult/continuing education programs, advanced placement credit, cooperative education, distance learning, double majors, English as a second language, honors programs, independent study, internships, part-time degree program, services for LD students, study abroad, summer session for credit.

Library Thigpen Library.

Student Life *Housing:* college housing not available. *Activities and Organizations:* drama/theater group, student-run newspaper, radio station, choral group, Gamma Beta Phi, Returning Woman's Organization, Phi Theta Kappa, Student Government Association, The Settler. *Campus security:* 24-hour emergency response devices and patrols, late-night transport/escort service. *Student services:* personal/psychological counseling.

Athletics Member NJCAA. *Intercollegiate sports:* baseball M(s), basketball M(s)/W(s), softball W(s).

Standardized Tests *Required for some:* SAT or ACT (for admission).

Costs (2016–17) *Tuition:* state resident $3744 full-time, $156 per credit hour part-time; nonresident $15,408 full-time, $642 per credit hour part-time. Full-time tuition and fees vary according to course load. Part-time tuition and fees vary according to course load. *Required fees:* $293 full-time, $9 per hour part-time, $34 per term part-time. *Payment plan:* deferred payment. *Waivers:* senior citizens and employees or children of employees.

Financial Aid Of all full-time matriculated undergraduates who enrolled in 2015, 3,796 applied for aid, 2,754 were judged to have need, 191 had their need fully met. 50 Federal Work-Study jobs (averaging $2301). In 2015, 65 non-need-based awards were made. *Average percent of need met:* 54%. *Average financial aid package:* $5860. *Average need-based loan:* $2861. *Average need-based gift aid:* $4720. *Average non-need-based aid:* $2318.

Applying *Options:* electronic application, early admission, deferred entrance. *Application fee:* $20. *Required:* high school transcript. *Required for some:* minimum 2.0 GPA, interview. *Application deadlines:* 8/25 (freshmen), 8/25 (transfers). *Notification:* continuous (freshmen), continuous (transfers).

Freshman Application Contact Mr. Tim Amyx, Director of Admissions, Volunteer State Community College, 1480 Nashville Pike, Gallatin, TN 37066-3188. *Phone:* 615-452-8600 Ext. 3614. *Toll-free phone:* 888-335-8722. *Fax:* 615-230-4875. *E-mail:* admissions@volstate.edu. *Website:* http://www.volstate.edu/.

Walters State Community College
Morristown, Tennessee

- **State-supported** 2-year, founded 1970, part of Tennessee Board of Regents
- **Small-town** 100-acre campus
- **Coed,** 5,951 undergraduate students, 54% full-time, 61% women, 39% men

Undergraduates 3,184 full-time, 2,767 part-time. 1% are from out of state; 2% Black or African American, non-Hispanic/Latino; 4% Hispanic/Latino; 0.8% Asian, non-Hispanic/Latino; 0.3% American Indian or Alaska Native, non-Hispanic/Latino; 2% Two or more races, non-Hispanic/Latino; 0.1% Race/ethnicity unknown; 0.6% international; 3% transferred in.

Freshmen *Admission:* 3,640 applied, 3,640 admitted, 1,552 enrolled. *Average high school GPA:* 3.16.

Faculty *Total:* 349, 48% full-time, 25% with terminal degrees. *Student/faculty ratio:* 18:1.

Majors Business administration and management; child development; computer and information sciences; criminal justice/police science; criminal justice/safety; data processing and data processing technology; education; energy management and systems technology; general studies; health information/medical records technology; industrial technology; liberal arts and sciences/liberal studies; music performance; occupational therapist assistant; ornamental horticulture; physical therapy technology; registered nursing/registered nurse; respiratory care therapy; surgical technology; web page, digital/multimedia and information resources design.

Academics *Calendar:* semesters. *Degree:* certificates and associate. *Special study options:* academic remediation for entering students, accelerated degree program, advanced placement credit, cooperative education, distance learning, English as a second language, freshman honors college, honors programs, independent study, internships, off-campus study, part-time degree program, services for LD students, student-designed majors, study abroad, summer session for credit. *ROTC:* Army (c).

Library Walters State Library.

Student Life *Housing:* college housing not available. *Activities and Organizations:* drama/theater group, choral group, Baptist Collegiate Ministry, Phi Theta Kappa, Debate Club, Student Government Association, Service Learners Club. *Campus security:* 24-hour emergency response devices and patrols, late-night transport/escort service, security cameras. *Student services:* health clinic, personal/psychological counseling.

Athletics Member NJCAA. *Intercollegiate sports:* baseball M(s), basketball M(s)/W(s), golf M(s), softball W(s), volleyball W(s). *Intramural sports:* baseball M, basketball M/W.

Costs (2016–17) *Tuition:* state resident $4032 full-time, $156 per credit hour part-time; nonresident $15,696 full-time, $642 per credit hour part-time. Full-time tuition and fees vary according to course load and program. Part-time tuition and fees vary according to course load and program. *Required fees:* $288 full-time, $16 per credit hour part-time, $20 per term part-time. *Payment plan:* installment. *Waivers:* senior citizens and employees or children of employees.

Financial Aid Of all full-time matriculated undergraduates who enrolled in 2015, 2,755 applied for aid, 2,258 were judged to have need, 230 had their need fully met. In 2015, 486 non-need-based awards were made. *Average percent of need met:* 59%. *Average financial aid package:* $5909. *Average need-based gift aid:* $4808. *Average non-need-based aid:* $3738.

Applying *Options:* electronic application, early admission. *Required:* high school transcript. *Application deadlines:* rolling (freshmen), rolling (transfers). *Notification:* continuous (freshmen), continuous (transfers).

Freshman Application Contact Mr. Michael Campbell, Assistant Vice President for Student Affairs, Walters State Community College, 500 South Davy Crockett Parkway, Morristown, TN 37813-6899. *Phone:* 423-585-2682. *Toll-free phone:* 800-225-4770. *Fax:* 423-585-6876. *E-mail:* mike.campbell@ws.edu. *Website:* http://www.ws.edu/.

West Tennessee Business College
Jackson, Tennessee

Admissions Office Contact West Tennessee Business College, 1186 Highway 45 Bypass, Jackson, TN 38343. *Website:* http://www.wtbc.edu/.

TEXAS

Alvin Community College
Alvin, Texas

- **State and locally supported** 2-year, founded 1949
- **Suburban** 114-acre campus with easy access to Houston
- **Coed,** 5,677 undergraduate students, 24% full-time, 57% women, 43% men

Undergraduates 1,372 full-time, 4,305 part-time. Students come from 4 states and territories; 12% Black or African American, non-Hispanic/Latino; 32% Hispanic/Latino; 4% Asian, non-Hispanic/Latino; 0.3% Native Hawaiian or other Pacific Islander, non-Hispanic/Latino; 0.5% American Indian or Alaska Native, non-Hispanic/Latino; 1% Race/ethnicity unknown; 0.8% international; 3% transferred in.

Freshmen *Admission:* 707 enrolled.

Faculty *Total:* 361, 29% full-time, 10% with terminal degrees. *Student/faculty ratio:* 17:1.

Majors Accounting; administrative assistant and secretarial science; aeronautics/aviation/aerospace science and technology; art; automobile/automotive mechanics technology; biology/biological sciences; business administration and management; business/commerce; chemical technology; child development; computer engineering technology; computer programming; corrections; court reporting; criminalistics and criminal science; criminal justice/police science; criminal justice/safety; culinary arts; desktop publishing and digital imaging design; diagnostic medical sonography and ultrasound technology; drafting and design technology; dramatic/theater arts; early childhood education; electrical, electronic and communications engineering technology; electroneurodiagnostic/electroencephalographic technology; emergency medical technology (EMT paramedic); executive assistant/executive secretary; general studies; health and physical education/fitness; health services/allied health/health sciences; history; legal administrative assistant/secretary; legal assistant/paralegal; legal studies; liberal arts and sciences/liberal studies; licensed practical/vocational nurse training; marketing/marketing management; mathematics; medical administrative assistant and medical secretary; mental health counseling; middle school education; music; office occupations and clerical services; pharmacy technician; physical education teaching and coaching; physical sciences; psychiatric/mental health services technology; psychology; radio and television; registered nursing/registered nurse; respiratory care therapy; secondary education; sociology; substance abuse/addiction counseling; voice and opera.

Academics *Calendar:* semesters. *Degree:* certificates, diplomas, and associate. *Special study options:* academic remediation for entering students, accelerated degree program, adult/continuing education programs, advanced placement credit, cooperative education, distance learning, double majors, English as a second language, honors programs, independent study, internships, part-time degree program, services for LD students, student-designed majors, study abroad, summer session for credit.

Library Alvin Community College Library. *Books:* 12,400 (physical); *Serial titles:* 34 (physical); *Databases:* 127. Weekly public service hours: 67; students can reserve study rooms.

Student Life *Housing:* college housing not available. *Activities and Organizations:* drama/theater group, student-run radio and television station, choral group. *Campus security:* 24-hour patrols, late-night transport/escort service, Vehicle Assist, emergency messages.

Student services: personal/psychological counseling.

Athletics Member NJCAA. *Intercollegiate sports:* baseball M(s), softball W(s).

Costs (2017–18) *Tuition:* area resident $1104 full-time, $46 per credit hour part-time; state resident $2208 full-time, $92 per credit hour part-time; nonresident $3360 full-time, $140 per credit hour part-time. Full-time tuition and fees vary according to course load and program. Part-time tuition and fees vary according to course load and program. *Required fees:* $518 full-time, $7 per credit hour part-time, $175 per term part-time. *Payment plan:* installment.

Applying *Required for some:* high school transcript.

Freshman Application Contact Alvin Community College, 3110 Mustang Road, Alvin, TX 77511-4898. *Phone:* 281-756-3531.

Website: http://www.alvincollege.edu/.

Amarillo College
Amarillo, Texas

- **State and locally supported** 2-year, founded 1929
- **Urban** 1542-acre campus
- **Endowment** $34.9 million
- **Coed**

Undergraduates 5% Black or African American, non-Hispanic/Latino; 38% Hispanic/Latino; 3% Asian, non-Hispanic/Latino; 0.1% Native Hawaiian or other Pacific Islander, non-Hispanic/Latino; 0.5% American Indian or Alaska Native, non-Hispanic/Latino; 2% Two or more races, non-Hispanic/Latino; 1% Race/ethnicity unknown. *Retention:* 52% of full-time freshmen returned.

Faculty *Total:* 406, 51% full-time, 7% with terminal degrees.

Majors Accounting; administrative assistant and secretarial science; airframe mechanics and aircraft maintenance technology; architectural engineering technology; art; automobile/automotive mechanics technology; behavioral sciences; biblical studies; biology/biological sciences; broadcast journalism; business administration and management; business teacher education; chemical technology; chemistry; child development; clinical laboratory science/medical technology; commercial and advertising art; computer engineering technology; computer programming; computer science; computer systems analysis; corrections; criminal justice/law enforcement administration; criminal justice/police science; dental hygiene; drafting and design technology; dramatic/theater arts; electrical, electronic and communications engineering technology; elementary education; emergency medical technology (EMT paramedic); engineering; English; environmental health; fine/studio arts; fire science/firefighting; funeral service and mortuary science; general studies; geology/earth science; health information/medical records administration; heating, air conditioning, ventilation and refrigeration maintenance technology; heavy equipment maintenance technology; history; industrial radiologic technology; information science/studies; instrumentation technology; interior design; journalism; laser and optical technology; legal administrative assistant/secretary; liberal arts and sciences/liberal studies; licensed practical/vocational nurse training; machine tool technology; mass communication/media; mathematics; medical administrative assistant and medical secretary; modern languages; music; music teacher education; natural sciences; nuclear medical technology; occupational therapy; photography; physical education teaching and coaching; physical sciences; physical therapy; physics; pre-engineering; pre-pharmacy studies; psychology; public relations/image management; radio and television; radiologic technology/science; real estate; registered nursing/registered nurse; religious studies; respiratory care therapy; rhetoric and composition; social sciences;

social work; substance abuse/addiction counseling; telecommunications technology; tourism and travel services management; visual and performing arts.

Academics *Calendar:* semesters. *Degree:* certificates and associate. *Special study options:* academic remediation for entering students, adult/continuing education programs, advanced placement credit, cooperative education, distance learning, English as a second language, freshman honors college, honors programs, part-time degree program, services for LD students, summer session for credit.

Library Lynn Library Learning Center plus 2 others.

Student Life *Housing:* college housing not available. *Activities and Organizations:* drama/theater group, student-run newspaper, radio station, choral group, Student Government Association, College Republicans. *Campus security:* 24-hour emergency response devices, late-night transport/escort service, campus police patrol Monday through Saturday 7 am to 11 pm.

Athletics *Intramural sports:* basketball M/W, soccer M/W, softball M/W, tennis M/W, volleyball M/W.

Costs (2017–18) *Tuition:* area resident $2010 full-time, $84 per semester hour part-time; state resident $3042 full-time, $127 per semester hour part-time; nonresident $4578 full-time, $191 per semester hour part-time. Full-time tuition and fees vary according to course load. Part-time tuition and fees vary according to course load. *Payment plan:* installment. *Waivers:* senior citizens and employees or children of employees.

Financial Aid Of all full-time matriculated undergraduates who enrolled in 2015, 100 Federal Work-Study jobs (averaging $3000).

Applying *Options:* early admission, deferred entrance. *Required:* high school transcript. *Notification:* continuous (freshmen), continuous (transfers).

Freshman Application Contact Amarillo College, PO Box 447, Amarillo, TX 79178-0001. *Phone:* 806-371-5000. *Toll-free phone:* 800-227-8784. *Fax:* 806-371-5497. *E-mail:* askac@actx.edu.

Website: http://www.actx.edu/.

Angelina College
Lufkin, Texas

Freshman Application Contact Angelina College, PO Box 1768, Lufkin, TX 75902-1768. *Phone:* 936-633-5213. *Website:* http://www.angelina.cc.tx.us/.

Auguste Escoffier School of Culinary Arts
Austin, Texas

Admissions Office Contact Auguste Escoffier School of Culinary Arts, 6020-B Dillard, Austin, TX 78752. *Website:* http://www.escoffier.edu/.

Austin Community College District
Austin, Texas

- **State and locally supported** 2-year, founded 1972
- **Urban** campus with easy access to Austin
- **Endowment** $5.3 million
- **Coed,** 41,543 undergraduate students, 22% full-time, 55% women, 45% men

Undergraduates 9,155 full-time, 32,388 part-time. Students come from 53 states and territories; 109 other countries; 2% are from out of state; 7% Black or African American, non-Hispanic/Latino; 36% Hispanic/Latino; 5% Asian, non-Hispanic/Latino; 0.2% Native Hawaiian or other Pacific Islander, non-Hispanic/Latino; 0.8% American Indian or Alaska Native, non-Hispanic/Latino; 4% Two or more races, non-Hispanic/Latino; 0.9% Race/ethnicity unknown; 2% international.

Faculty *Total:* 1,856, 30% full-time, 22% with terminal degrees. *Student/faculty ratio:* 20:1.

Majors Accounting; accounting technology and bookkeeping; administrative assistant and secretarial science; animation, interactive technology, video graphics and special effects; anthropology; Arabic; archeology; art; automobile/automotive mechanics technology; biology/biological sciences; biology/biotechnology laboratory technician; business administration and management; business/commerce; carpentry; chemistry; child development; Chinese; clinical/medical laboratory technology; commercial photography; computer and information sciences; computer programming; computer systems networking and telecommunications; corrections; creative writing; criminal justice/police science; culinary arts; dance; dental hygiene; design and visual communications; diagnostic medical sonography and ultrasound technology; drafting and design technology; dramatic/theater arts; early childhood education; economics; electrical, electronic and communications engineering technology; emergency medical technology (EMT paramedic); engineering; environmental engineering technology; environmental science; fire prevention and safety technology; French; general studies; geographic information science and cartography; geography; geology/earth science; German; health and physical education/fitness; health information/medical records technology; heating, ventilation, air conditioning and refrigeration engineering technology; history; hospitality administration; hotel/motel administration; international business/trade/commerce; Japanese; journalism; kinesiology and exercise science; Latin; legal assistant/paralegal; logistics, materials, and supply chain management; marketing/marketing management; mathematics; mental health counseling; middle school education; multi/interdisciplinary studies related; music; music management; occupational therapist assistant; pharmacy technician; philosophy; photographic and film/video technology; physical therapy technology; physics; political science and government; premedical studies; professional, technical, business, and scientific writing; psychology; radio and television; radiologic technology/science; real estate; registered nursing/registered nurse; rhetoric and composition; Russian; secondary education; sign language interpretation and translation; social work; sociology; Spanish; substance abuse/addiction counseling; surgical technology; surveying technology; therapeutic recreation; tourism and travel services management; veterinary/animal health technology; watchmaking and jewelrymaking; welding technology; writing.

Academics *Calendar:* semesters. *Degrees:* certificates, associate, and postbachelor's certificates. *Special study options:* academic remediation for entering students, accelerated degree program, adult/continuing education programs, advanced placement credit, cooperative education, distance learning, English as a second language, honors programs, independent study, internships, part-time degree program, services for LD students, summer session for credit. *ROTC:* Army (c), Air Force (c).

Library Main Library plus 11 others. *Books:* 125,067 (physical), 37,543 (digital/electronic); *Serial titles:* 577 (physical), 76,999 (digital/electronic); *Databases:* 103. Weekly public service hours: 83; students can reserve study rooms.

Student Life *Housing:* college housing not available. *Activities and Organizations:* student-run newspaper, choral group, Intramurals, Students for Environmental Outreach, Phi Theta Kappa (PTK), National Society of Collegiate Scholars, Students for Community Involvement. *Campus security:* 24-hour emergency response devices, late-night transport/escort service, 24-hour patrols by police officers. *Student services:* personal/psychological counseling.

Athletics *Intramural sports:* basketball M/W, soccer M/W, volleyball W.

Costs (2016–17) *Tuition:* area resident $2010 full-time, $67 per credit hour part-time; state resident $10,350 full-time, $345 per credit hour part-time; nonresident $12,540 full-time, $418 per credit hour part-time. Full-time tuition and fees vary according to course load. Part-time tuition and fees vary according to course load. *Required fees:* $540 full-time, $18 per credit hour part-time. *Payment plan:* installment. *Waivers:* senior citizens and employees or children of employees.

Financial Aid Of all full-time matriculated undergraduates who enrolled in 2016, 4,713 applied for aid, 4,116 were judged to have need. 162 Federal Work-Study jobs (averaging $4179). 36 state and other part-time jobs (averaging $4900). *Average need-based loan:* $2938. *Average need-based gift aid:* $3157.

Applying *Options:* electronic application. *Required:* high school transcript. *Application deadlines:* rolling (freshmen), rolling (transfers).

Freshman Application Contact Ms. Linda Kluck, Director, Admissions and Records, Austin Community College District, 5930 Middle Fiskville Road, Austin, TX 78752. *Phone:* 512-223-7503. *Fax:* 512-223-7665. *E-mail:* admission@austincc.edu. *Website:* http://www.austincc.edu/.

Blinn College
Brenham, Texas

- **State and locally supported** 2-year, founded 1883
- **Small-town** 100-acre campus with easy access to Houston
- **Endowment** $10.3 million
- **Coed**, 19,074 undergraduate students, 55% full-time, 51% women, 48% men

Undergraduates 10,473 full-time, 8,274 part-time. Students come from 42 other countries; 1% are from out of state; 10% Black or African American, non-Hispanic/Latino; 21% Hispanic/Latino; 2% Asian, non-Hispanic/Latino; 0.1% Native Hawaiian or other Pacific Islander, non-Hispanic/Latino; 0.4% American Indian or Alaska Native, non-Hispanic/Latino; 3% Two or more races, non-Hispanic/Latino; 2% Race/ethnicity unknown; 0.7% international; 10% transferred in; 9% live on campus.

Freshmen *Admission:* 6,266 admitted, 6,266 enrolled.

Faculty *Total:* 1,094, 72% full-time.

Majors Accounting; administrative assistant and secretarial science; agriculture; biology/biological sciences; business administration and management; chemistry; child development; comparative literature; computer science; computer systems networking and telecommunications; criminal justice/law enforcement administration; dental hygiene; dramatic/theater arts; English; fire science/firefighting; French; German; health information/medical records technology; history; industrial radiologic technology; legal administrative assistant/secretary; mass communication/media; mathematics; mental health counseling; music; philosophy; physical education teaching and coaching; physical therapy technology; physics; psychology; real estate; registered nursing/registered nurse; rhetoric and composition; Spanish.

Academics *Calendar:* semesters. *Degree:* certificates, diplomas, and associate. *Special study options:* academic remediation for entering students, adult/continuing education programs, advanced placement credit, distance learning, double majors, English as a second language, freshman honors college, part-time degree program, services for LD students, summer session for credit.

Library W. L. Moody, Jr. Library plus 1 other.

Student Life *Housing Options:* coed, men-only, women-only. Campus housing is university owned. *Activities and Organizations:* drama/theater group, student-run newspaper, choral group, marching band, Student Government Association, Phi Theta Kappa, Baptist student ministries, Blinn Ethnic Student Organization, Circle K. *Campus security:* 24-hour emergency response devices and patrols, controlled dormitory access. *Student services:* personal/psychological counseling.

Athletics Member NJCAA. *Intercollegiate sports:* baseball M(s), basketball M(s)/W(s), cheerleading M(s)/W(s), football M(s), softball W(s), volleyball W(s). *Intramural sports:* basketball M/W, bowling M/W, football M, golf M, softball W, table tennis M/W, volleyball M/W, weight lifting M/W.

Costs (2017–18) *Tuition:* area resident $1200 full-time; state resident $2568 full-time; nonresident $6240 full-time. Full-time tuition and fees vary according to course load. Part-time tuition and fees vary according to course load. *Required fees:* $1530 full-time. *Room and board:* $6250; room only: $3750. Room and board charges vary according to board plan, gender, and housing facility. *Payment plan:* installment.

Financial Aid Of all full-time matriculated undergraduates who enrolled in 2015, 110 Federal Work-Study jobs (averaging $1625).

Applying *Options:* electronic application, early admission, deferred entrance. *Required:* high school transcript. *Application deadlines:* rolling (freshmen), rolling (transfers).

Freshman Application Contact Ms. Jennifer Bynum, Director Prospective Student Relations/ Community Outreach, Blinn College, PO Box 6030, Bryan, TX 77805-6030. *Phone:* 979-209-7640. *E-mail:* jennifer.bynum@blinn.edu. *Website:* http://www.blinn.edu/.

Brazosport College
Lake Jackson, Texas

Freshman Application Contact Brazosport College, 500 College Drive, Lake Jackson, TX 77566-3199. *Phone:* 979-230-3020. *Website:* http://www.brazosport.edu/.

Brightwood College, Arlington Campus
Arlington, Texas

Freshman Application Contact Brightwood College, Arlington Campus, 2241 South Watson Road, Suite 181, Arlington, TX 76010. *Phone:* 866-249-2074. *Toll-free phone:* 866-543-0208. *Website:* http://www.brightwood.edu/.

Brightwood College, Beaumont Campus
Beaumont, Texas

Freshman Application Contact Admissions Office, Brightwood College, Beaumont Campus, 6115 Eastex Freeway, Beaumont, TX 77706. *Phone:* 409-833-2722. *Toll-free phone:* 866-543-0208. *Website:* http://www.brightwood.edu/.

Brightwood College, Brownsville Campus
Brownsville, Texas

Freshman Application Contact Director of Admissions, Brightwood College, Brownsville Campus, 1900 North Expressway, Suite O, Brownsville, TX 78521. *Phone:* 956-547-8200. *Toll-free phone:* 866-543-0208. *Website:* http://www.brightwood.edu/.

Brightwood College, Corpus Christi Campus

Corpus Christi, Texas

Freshman Application Contact Admissions Director, Brightwood College, Corpus Christi Campus, 1620 South Padre Island Drive, Suite 600, Corpus Christi, TX 78416. *Phone:* 361-852-2900. *Toll-free phone:* 866-543-0208. *Website:* http://www.brightwood.edu/.

Brightwood College, Dallas Campus

Dallas, Texas

Freshman Application Contact Brightwood College, Dallas Campus, 12005 Ford Road, Suite 100, Dallas, TX 75234. *Phone:* 972-385-1446. *Toll-free phone:* 866-543-0208. *Website:* http://www.brightwood.edu/.

Brightwood College, El Paso Campus

El Paso, Texas

Freshman Application Contact Director of Admissions, Brightwood College, El Paso Campus, 8360 Burnham Road, Suite 100, El Paso, TX 79907. *Toll-free phone:* 866-543-0208. *Website:* http://www.brightwood.edu/.

Brightwood College, Fort Worth Campus

Fort Worth, Texas

Freshman Application Contact Director of Admissions, Brightwood College, Fort Worth Campus, 2001 Beach Street, Suite 201, Fort Worth, TX 76103. *Phone:* 817-413-2000. *Toll-free phone:* 866-543-0208. *Website:* http://www.brightwood.edu/.

Brightwood College, Friendswood Campus

Friendswood, Texas

Freshman Application Contact Admissions Office, Brightwood College, Friendswood Campus, 3208 Farm to Market Road 528, Friendswood, TX 77546. *Toll-free phone:* 866-543-0208. *Website:* http://www.brightwood.edu/.

Brightwood College, Houston Campus

Houston, Texas

Freshman Application Contact Admissions Office, Brightwood College, Houston Campus, 711 East Airtex Drive, Houston, TX 77073. *Phone:* 281-443-8900. *Toll-free phone:* 866-543-0208. *Website:* http://www.brightwood.edu/.

Brightwood College, Laredo Campus

Laredo, Texas

Freshman Application Contact Admissions Office, Brightwood College, Laredo Campus, 6410 McPherson Road, Laredo, TX 78041. *Phone:* 956-717-5909. *Toll-free phone:* 866-543-0208. *Website:* http://www.brightwood.edu/.

Brightwood College, McAllen Campus

McAllen, Texas

Admissions Office Contact Brightwood College, McAllen Campus, 1500 South Jackson Road, McAllen, TX 78503. *Toll-free phone:* 866-543-0208. *Website:* http://www.brightwood.edu/.

Brightwood College, San Antonio Ingram Campus

San Antonio, Texas

Freshman Application Contact Admissions Office, Brightwood College, San Antonio Ingram Campus, 6441 NW Loop 410, San Antonio, TX 78238. *Phone:* 210-308-8584. *Toll-free phone:* 866-543-0208. *Website:* http://www.brightwood.edu/.

Brightwood College, San Antonio San Pedro Campus

San Antonio, Texas

Freshman Application Contact Director of Admissions, Brightwood College, San Antonio San Pedro Campus, 7142 San Pedro Avenue, Suite 100, San Antonio, TX 78216. *Toll-free phone:* 866-543-0208. *Website:* http://www.brightwood.edu/.

Brookhaven College

Farmers Branch, Texas

- **County-supported** 2-year, founded 1978, part of Dallas County Community College District System
- **Suburban** 200-acre campus with easy access to Dallas-Fort Worth
- **Coed,** 13,240 undergraduate students, 18% full-time, 57% women, 43% men

Undergraduates 2,348 full-time, 10,892 part-time. Students come from 34 states and territories; 80 other countries; 0.2% are from out of state; 18% Black or African American, non-Hispanic/Latino; 39% Hispanic/Latino; 12% Asian, non-Hispanic/Latino; 0.2% Native Hawaiian or other Pacific Islander, non-Hispanic/Latino; 2% American Indian or Alaska Native, non-Hispanic/Latino; 2% Two or more races, non-Hispanic/Latino; 7% Race/ethnicity unknown; 2% international; 7% transferred in.
Freshmen *Admission:* 5,600 enrolled.
Faculty *Total:* 587, 22% full-time. *Student/faculty ratio:* 21:1.
Majors Accounting; automobile/automotive mechanics technology; business administration and management; business/commerce; child development; computer engineering technology; computer programming; computer technology/computer systems technology; criminal justice/law enforcement administration; design and visual communications; e-commerce; education (multiple levels); emergency medical technology (EMT paramedic); executive assistant/executive secretary; general studies; geographic information science and cartography; graphic design; humanities; information science/studies; liberal arts and sciences/liberal studies; marketing/marketing management; music; office management; radiologic technology/science; registered nursing/registered nurse; secondary education; speech communication and rhetoric.
Academics *Calendar:* semesters. *Degree:* certificates and associate. *Special study options:* academic remediation for entering students, adult/continuing education programs, advanced placement credit, cooperative education, distance learning, English as a second language, honors programs, independent study, internships, off-campus study, part-time degree program, services for LD students, student-designed majors, study abroad, summer session for credit.
Library Brookhaven College Learning Resources Center plus 1 other.
Student Life *Housing:* college housing not available. *Activities and Organizations:* drama/theater group, student-run newspaper, choral group. *Campus security:* 24-hour emergency response devices and patrols, late-night transport/escort service. *Student services:* health clinic, personal/psychological counseling.
Athletics Member NJCAA. *Intercollegiate sports:* baseball M, basketball M, soccer W, volleyball W.
Costs (2017–18) *Tuition:* area resident $1770 full-time, $59 per credit hour part-time; state resident $3330 full-time, $111 per credit hour part-time; nonresident $5220 full-time, $174 per credit hour part-time. *Payment plan:* installment. *Waivers:* senior citizens and employees or children of employees.
Applying *Options:* electronic application, early admission, deferred entrance. *Required:* high school transcript. *Required for some:* HESI score, minimum GPA in prerequisite courses, completion of support courses for nursing program. *Application deadlines:* rolling (freshmen), rolling (transfers).
Freshman Application Contact Admissions Office, Brookhaven College, 3939 Valley View Lane, Farmers Branch, TX 75244-4997. *Phone:* 972-860-4883. *Fax:* 972-860-4886. *E-mail:* bhcadmissions@dcccd.edu. *Website:* http://www.brookhavencollege.edu/.

Cedar Valley College

Lancaster, Texas

Freshman Application Contact Admissions Office, Cedar Valley College, Lancaster, TX 75134-3799. *Phone:* 972-860-8206. *Fax:* 972-860-8207. *Website:* http://www.cedarvalleycollege.edu/.

Center for Advanced Legal Studies

Houston, Texas

Freshman Application Contact Mr. James Scheffer, Center for Advanced Legal Studies, 3910 Kirby, Suite 200, Houston, TX 77098. *Phone:* 713-529-

2778. *Toll-free phone:* 800-446-6931. *Fax:* 713-523-2715.
E-mail: james.scheffer@paralegal.edu. *Website:* http://www.paralegal.edu/.

Central Texas College
Killeen, Texas

- **State and locally supported** 2-year, founded 1967
- **Suburban** 500-acre campus with easy access to Austin
- **Endowment** $6.4 million
- **Coed,** 19,562 undergraduate students, 22% full-time, 47% women, 53% men

Undergraduates 4,362 full-time, 15,200 part-time. 27% Black or African American, non-Hispanic/Latino; 21% Hispanic/Latino; 3% Asian, non-Hispanic/Latino; 2% Native Hawaiian or other Pacific Islander, non-Hispanic/Latino; 1% American Indian or Alaska Native, non-Hispanic/Latino; 3% Two or more races, non-Hispanic/Latino; 3% Race/ethnicity unknown; 0.3% international; 1% live on campus.
Freshmen *Admission:* 2,625 enrolled.
Faculty *Total:* 1,540, 15% full-time. *Student/faculty ratio:* 16:1.
Majors Administrative assistant and secretarial science; agriculture; airline pilot and flight crew; autobody/collision and repair technology; automobile/automotive mechanics technology; biology/biological sciences; building/property maintenance; business administration and management; business/commerce; chemistry; clinical/medical laboratory technology; clinical/medical social work; commercial and advertising art; computer and information systems security; computer programming; computer technology/computer systems technology; criminal justice/safety; diesel mechanics technology; drafting and design technology; dramatic/theater arts; early childhood education; emergency medical technology (EMT paramedic); engineering; environmental science; farm and ranch management; fine/studio arts; fire services administration; foreign languages and literatures; general studies; geology/earth science; graphic and printing equipment operation/production; heating, air conditioning, ventilation and refrigeration maintenance technology; hospitality administration; journalism; kinesiology and exercise science; legal assistant/paralegal; liberal arts and sciences/liberal studies; licensed practical/vocational nurse training; mathematics; medical administrative assistant and medical secretary; medical insurance coding; music; public administration; radio and television; registered nursing/registered nurse; restaurant/food services management; social sciences; welding technology.
Academics *Calendar:* semesters. *Degree:* certificates and associate. *Special study options:* academic remediation for entering students, accelerated degree program, adult/continuing education programs, advanced placement credit, cooperative education, distance learning, English as a second language, external degree program, internships, part-time degree program, services for LD students, student-designed majors, summer session for credit. *ROTC:* Army (b).
Library Oveta Culp Hobby Memorial Library. *Books:* 64,080 (physical), 32,555 (digital/electronic); *Serial titles:* 65,620 (physical), 32,639 (digital/electronic); *Databases:* 87.
Student Life *Housing Options:* coed. Campus housing is university owned. *Activities and Organizations:* drama/theater group, student-run newspaper, International Student Association, We Can Do It Club, Enactus, Student Nurses Association, NAACP. *Campus security:* 24-hour emergency response devices and patrols.
Athletics *Intramural sports:* basketball M/W, football M/W, soccer M/W, softball M/W, volleyball M/W.
Standardized Tests *Required for some:* TSI Assessment required for those that are not TSI exempt or waived.
Costs (2017–18) *Tuition:* area resident $2400 full-time, $80 per credit hour part-time; state resident $3090 full-time, $103 per credit hour part-time; nonresident $6750 full-time, $225 per credit hour part-time. Full-time tuition and fees vary according to location and program. Part-time tuition and fees vary according to location and program. *Room and board:* $5600. *Payment plan:* installment. *Waivers:* senior citizens and employees or children of employees.
Financial Aid Of all full-time matriculated undergraduates who enrolled in 2015, 68 Federal Work-Study jobs (averaging $3658).
Applying *Options:* electronic application, early admission, deferred entrance. *Required:* high school transcript. *Application deadlines:* rolling (freshmen), rolling (out-of-state freshmen), rolling (transfers).
Freshman Application Contact Admissions Office, Central Texas College, PO Box 1800, Killeen, TX 76540-1800. *Phone:* 254-526-1696. *Toll-free phone:* 800-223-4760 (in-state); 800-792-3348 (out-of-state). *E-mail:* admissions@ctcd.edu.
Website: http://www.ctcd.edu/.

Cisco College
Cisco, Texas

Freshman Application Contact Mr. Olin O. Odom III, Dean of Admission/Registrar, Cisco College, 101 College Heights, Cisco, TX 76437-9321. *Phone:* 254-442-2567 Ext. 5130. *E-mail:* oodom@cjc.edu. *Website:* http://www.cisco.edu/.

Clarendon College
Clarendon, Texas

Freshman Application Contact Ms. Martha Smith, Admissions Director, Clarendon College, PO Box 968, Clarendon, TX 79226. *Phone:* 806-874-3571 Ext. 106. *Toll-free phone:* 800-687-9737. *Fax:* 806-874-3201. *E-mail:* martha.smith@clarendoncollege.edu. *Website:* http://www.clarendoncollege.edu/.

Coastal Bend College
Beeville, Texas

Freshman Application Contact Mrs. Tammy Adams, Director of Admissions/Registrar, Coastal Bend College, Beeville, TX 78102-2197. *Phone:* 361-354-2245. *Toll-free phone:* 866-722-2838 (in-state); 866-262-2838 (out-of-state). *Fax:* 361-354-2254. *E-mail:* tadams@coastalbend.edu. *Website:* http://www.coastalbend.edu/.

The College of Health Care Professions
Austin, Texas

Admissions Office Contact The College of Health Care Professions, 6505 Airport Boulevard, Austin, TX 78752. *Website:* http://www.chcp.edu/.

The College of Health Care Professions
Fort Worth, Texas

Admissions Office Contact The College of Health Care Professions, 4248 North Freeway, Fort Worth, TX 76137-5021. *Website:* http://www.chcp.edu/.

The College of Health Care Professions
Houston, Texas

Freshman Application Contact Admissions Office, The College of Health Care Professions, 240 Northwest Mall Boulevard, Houston, TX 77092. *Phone:* 713-425-3100. *Toll-free phone:* 800-487-6728. *Fax:* 713-425-3193. *Website:* http://www.chcp.edu/.

The College of Health Care Professions
San Antonio, Texas

Admissions Office Contact The College of Health Care Professions, 4738 NW Loop 410, San Antonio, TX 78229. *Website:* http://www.chcp.edu/.

College of the Mainland
Texas City, Texas

Freshman Application Contact Mr. Martin Perez, Director of Admissions/International Affairs, College of the Mainland, 1200 Amburn Road, Texas City, TX 77591. *Phone:* 409-933-8653. *Toll-free phone:* 888-258-8859 Ext. 8264. *E-mail:* mperez@com.edu. *Website:* http://www.com.edu/.

Collin County Community College District
McKinney, Texas

- **State and locally supported** 2-year, founded 1985
- **Suburban** 333-acre campus with easy access to Dallas-Fort Worth
- **Endowment** $9.1 million
- **Coed,** 29,703 undergraduate students, 32% full-time, 55% women, 45% men

Undergraduates 9,642 full-time, 20,061 part-time. Students come from 55 states and territories; 98 other countries; 11% Black or African American, non-Hispanic/Latino; 19% Hispanic/Latino; 10% Asian, non-Hispanic/Latino; 0.2% Native Hawaiian or other Pacific Islander, non-Hispanic/Latino; 0.5% American Indian or Alaska Native, non-Hispanic/Latino; 4% Two or more

races, non-Hispanic/Latino; 1% Race/ethnicity unknown; 4% international; 6% transferred in. *Retention:* 61% of full-time freshmen returned.
Freshmen *Admission:* 4,825 applied, 4,825 admitted, 5,836 enrolled.
Faculty *Total:* 1,277, 31% full-time. *Student/faculty ratio:* 24:1.
Majors Administrative assistant and secretarial science; baking and pastry arts; biology/biotechnology laboratory technician; business administration and management; business/commerce; child-care provision; child development; commercial and advertising art; computer and information sciences; computer and information systems security; computer science; criminal justice/police science; culinary arts; dental hygiene; drafting and design technology; early childhood education; electrical, electronic and communications engineering technology; electroneurodiagnostic/electroencephalographic technology; emergency medical technology (EMT paramedic); engineering; engineering technology; fire prevention and safety technology; fire science/firefighting; game and interactive media design; geographic information science and cartography; graphic design; health information/medical records technology; hospitality administration; illustration; integrated circuit design; interior design; legal assistant/paralegal; liberal arts and sciences/liberal studies; medical insurance coding; middle school education; music; music management; network and system administration; real estate; registered nursing/registered nurse; respiratory care therapy; retail management; secondary education; sign language interpretation and translation; speech communication and rhetoric; surgical technology; system, networking, and LAN/WAN management; telecommunications technology; web page, digital/multimedia and information resources design.
Academics *Calendar:* semesters. *Degree:* certificates and associate. *Special study options:* academic remediation for entering students, adult/continuing education programs, advanced placement credit, cooperative education, distance learning, English as a second language, honors programs, internships, part-time degree program, services for LD students, summer session for credit. *ROTC:* Air Force (c).
Library Collin College Library. *Books:* 226,318 (physical), 37,392 (digital/electronic); *Databases:* 120. Students can reserve study rooms.
Student Life *Housing:* college housing not available. *Activities and Organizations:* drama/theater group, choral group, Student Government, Phi Theta Kappa, Baptist Student Ministry, National Society of Leadership Success, Political Science Club. *Campus security:* 24-hour emergency response devices and patrols, late-night transport/escort service. *Student services:* personal/psychological counseling.
Athletics Member NJCAA. *Intercollegiate sports:* basketball M(s)/W(s), tennis M(s)/W(s).
Costs (2016–17) *Tuition:* area resident $1230 full-time, $41 per credit hour part-time; state resident $2460 full-time, $82 per credit hour part-time; nonresident $4260 full-time, $142 per credit hour part-time. *Required fees:* $34 full-time, $1 per credit hour part-time, $2 per term part-time. *Payment plan:* installment. *Waivers:* senior citizens.
Applying *Options:* electronic application. *Required for some:* high school transcript. *Application deadlines:* rolling (freshmen), rolling (transfers). *Notification:* continuous (freshmen), continuous (transfers).
Freshman Application Contact Mr. Todd Fields, Registrar/Director of Admissions, Collin County Community College District, 2800 E. Spring Creek Parkway, Plano, TX 75074. *Phone:* 972-881-5174. *Fax:* 972-881-5175. *E-mail:* tfields@collin.edu.
Website: http://www.collin.edu/.

Commonwealth Institute of Funeral Service
Houston, Texas

Freshman Application Contact Ms. Patricia Moreno, Registrar, Commonwealth Institute of Funeral Service, 415 Barren Springs Drive, Houston, TX 77090. *Phone:* 281-873-0262. *Toll-free phone:* 800-628-1580. *Fax:* 281-873-5232. *E-mail:* p.moreno@commonwealth.edu. *Website:* http://www.commonwealth.edu/.

Concorde Career College
Dallas, Texas

Admissions Office Contact Concorde Career College, 12606 Greenville Avenue, Suite 130, Dallas, TX 75243. *Website:* http://www.concorde.edu/.

Concorde Career College
Grand Prairie, Texas

Admissions Office Contact Concorde Career College, 3015 West Interstate 20, Grand Prairie, TX 75052. *Toll-free phone:* 800-693-7010. *Website:* http://www.concorde.edu/.

Concorde Career College
San Antonio, Texas

Admissions Office Contact Concorde Career College, 4803 NW Loop 410, Suite 200, San Antonio, TX 78229. *Website:* http://www.concorde.edu/.

Culinary Institute LeNotre
Houston, Texas

- **Proprietary** 2-year, founded 1998
- **Urban** campus with easy access to Houston
- **Coed,** 320 undergraduate students

Undergraduates Students come from 6 other countries.
Faculty *Student/faculty ratio:* 12:1.
Majors Baking and pastry arts; culinary arts; restaurant, culinary, and catering management.
Academics *Degree:* diplomas and associate. *Special study options:* academic remediation for entering students, adult/continuing education programs, cooperative education, internships, part-time degree program, study abroad.
Library Learning Resource Center.
Student Life *Housing:* college housing not available. *Campus security:* late-night transport/escort service, security personnel patrol during class hours. *Student services:* personal/psychological counseling.
Applying *Options:* electronic application. *Application fee:* $50. *Required:* high school transcript, interview.
Freshman Application Contact Ellen Hogaboom, Admissions Manager, Culinary Institute LeNotre, 7070 Allensby Street, Houston, TX 77022. *Phone:* 713-692-0077. *Toll-free phone:* 888-LENOTRE. *Fax:* 713-692-7399. *E-mail:* ehogaboom@ciaml.com.
Website: http://www.culinaryinstitute.edu/.

Dallas Institute of Funeral Service
Dallas, Texas

- **Independent** 2-year, founded 1945, part of Pierce Mortuary Colleges, Inc.
- **Urban** 4-acre campus with easy access to Dallas-Fort Worth
- **Coed,** 141 undergraduate students, 100% full-time, 47% women, 53% men

Undergraduates 141 full-time. Students come from 7 states and territories; 11% are from out of state; 30% Black or African American, non-Hispanic/Latino; 15% Hispanic/Latino. *Retention:* 71% of full-time freshmen returned.
Freshmen *Admission:* 19 applied, 18 admitted, 56 enrolled.
Faculty *Total:* 10, 40% full-time, 10% with terminal degrees. *Student/faculty ratio:* 17:1.
Majors Funeral service and mortuary science.
Academics *Calendar:* quarters. *Degree:* certificates and associate. *Special study options:* distance learning, services for LD students.
Library J. Frank Pierce Library. *Books:* 2,223 (physical).
Student Life *Housing:* college housing not available. *Activities and Organizations:* Lions Club International, Women in Black, Epsilon Chapter of Pi Sigma Eta National Mortician's Honors Fraternity. *Campus security:* 24-hour emergency response devices, electronically locked doors.
Costs (2016–17) *One-time required fee:* $20. *Tuition:* $11,100 full-time, $250 per quarter hour part-time. Full-time tuition and fees vary according to course load and program. Part-time tuition and fees vary according to course load and program. No tuition increase for student's term of enrollment. *Payment plan:* installment.
Applying *Options:* electronic application. *Application fee:* $50. *Required:* high school transcript. *Application deadlines:* rolling (freshmen), rolling (transfers).
Freshman Application Contact Olga Retana, Admissions Representative, Dallas Institute of Funeral Service, 3909 South Buckner Boulevard, Dallas, TX 75227. *Phone:* 214-388-5466 Ext. 817. *Toll-free phone:* 800-235-5444. *Fax:* 214-388-0316. *E-mail:* oretana@dallasinstitute.edu.
Website: http://www.dallasinstitute.edu/.

Dallas Nursing Institute
Dallas, Texas

Admissions Office Contact Dallas Nursing Institute, 12170 N. Abrams Road, Suite 200, Dallas, TX 75243. *Website:* http://www.dni.edu/.

Del Mar College
Corpus Christi, Texas

- **State and locally supported** 2-year, founded 1935
- **Urban** 159-acre campus
- **Coed,** 11,973 undergraduate students, 25% full-time, 57% women, 43% men

Undergraduates 2,983 full-time, 8,990 part-time. Students come from 45 states and territories; 57 other countries; 2% are from out of state; 3% Black or African American, non-Hispanic/Latino; 66% Hispanic/Latino; 2% Asian, non-Hispanic/Latino; 0.2% Native Hawaiian or other Pacific Islander, non-Hispanic/Latino; 0.2% American Indian or Alaska Native, non-Hispanic/Latino; 4% Two or more races, non-Hispanic/Latino; 0.3% Race/ethnicity unknown; 0.1% international; 6% transferred in. *Retention:* 56% of full-time freshmen returned.
Freshmen *Admission:* 1,006 enrolled.
Faculty *Total:* 560, 48% full-time. *Student/faculty ratio:* 18:1.
Majors Accounting; accounting technology and bookkeeping; administrative assistant and secretarial science; architectural engineering technology; art; art teacher education; automobile/automotive mechanics technology; biology/biological sciences; building/property maintenance; business administration and management; business/commerce; business machine repair; chemical technology; chemistry; child development; clinical laboratory science/medical technology; clinical/medical laboratory technology; community organization and advocacy; computer and information sciences and support services related; computer and information sciences related; computer programming; computer programming related; computer programming (specific applications); computer programming (vendor/product certification); computer science; computer systems networking and telecommunications; computer typography and composition equipment operation; consumer merchandising/retailing management; cosmetology; court reporting; criminal justice/law enforcement administration; criminal justice/police science; culinary arts; data entry/microcomputer applications; dental hygiene; design and applied arts related; diagnostic medical sonography and ultrasound technology; drafting and design technology; dramatic/theater arts; e-commerce; education; electrical, electronic and communications engineering technology; elementary education; emergency medical technology (EMT paramedic); English; finance; fine/studio arts; fire prevention and safety technology; fire science/firefighting; geography; geology/earth science; health information/medical records technology; health teacher education; heavy equipment maintenance technology; history; hotel/motel administration; industrial radiologic technology; information science/studies; information technology; interdisciplinary studies; journalism; kindergarten/preschool education; legal administrative assistant/secretary; legal studies; liberal arts and sciences/liberal studies; machine tool technology; management information systems; mathematics; medical administrative assistant and medical secretary; medical radiologic technology; mental health counseling; music; music teacher education; network and system administration; nuclear medical technology; occupational safety and health technology; occupational therapist assistant; office occupations and clerical services; parks, recreation and leisure; physical education teaching and coaching; physics; political science and government; pre-engineering; psychology; public administration; public policy analysis; radio and television; real estate; registered nursing/registered nurse; respiratory care therapy; rhetoric and composition; sign language interpretation and translation; social work; sociology; special products marketing; trade and industrial teacher education; transportation/mobility management; voice and opera; web/multimedia management and webmaster; web page, digital/multimedia and information resources design; welding technology; word processing.
Academics *Calendar:* semesters. *Degree:* certificates and associate. *Special study options:* academic remediation for entering students, accelerated degree program, adult/continuing education programs, advanced placement credit, cooperative education, distance learning, double majors, English as a second language, freshman honors college, honors programs, internships, off-campus study, part-time degree program, services for LD students, summer session for credit. *ROTC:* Army (b).
Library White Library plus 1 other. *Books:* 145,107 (physical), 192,073 (digital/electronic); *Serial titles:* 1,635 (physical), 74,730 (digital/electronic); *Databases:* 172.
Student Life *Housing:* college housing not available. *Activities and Organizations:* drama/theater group, student-run newspaper, radio station, choral group, Phi Theta Kappa, Alpha Beta Gamma, Student Government Association. *Campus security:* 24-hour emergency response devices and patrols. *Student services:* personal/psychological counseling.
Athletics *Intramural sports:* badminton M/W, basketball M/W, bowling M/W, football M/W, golf M/W, racquetball M/W, tennis M/W, track and field M/W, volleyball M/W, weight lifting M/W.
Financial Aid Of all full-time matriculated undergraduates who enrolled in 2015, 259 Federal Work-Study jobs (averaging $960). 449 state and other part-time jobs (averaging $1082).

Applying *Options:* electronic application, early admission, deferred entrance. *Required:* high school transcript. *Application deadlines:* rolling (freshmen), rolling (transfers).
Freshman Application Contact Del Mar College, 101 Baldwin Boulevard, Corpus Christi, TX 78404-3897. *Phone:* 361-698-1248. *Toll-free phone:* 800-652-3357.
Website: http://www.delmar.edu/.

Eastfield College
Mesquite, Texas

Freshman Application Contact Ms. Glynis Miller, Director of Admissions/Registrar, Eastfield College, 3737 Motley Drive, Mesquite, TX 75150-2099. *Phone:* 972-860-7010. *Fax:* 972-860-8306.
E-mail: efc@dcccd.edu. *Website:* http://www.efc.dcccd.edu/.

El Centro College
Dallas, Texas

Freshman Application Contact Ms. Rebecca Garza, Director of Admissions and Registrar, El Centro College, Dallas, TX 75202. *Phone:* 214-860-2618. *Fax:* 214-860-2233. *E-mail:* rgarza@dcccd.edu.
Website: http://www.elcentrocollege.edu/.

El Paso Community College
El Paso, Texas

- **County-supported** 2-year, founded 1969
- **Urban** campus
- **Endowment** $737,859
- **Coed,** 29,460 undergraduate students, 30% full-time, 56% women, 44% men

Undergraduates 8,877 full-time, 20,583 part-time. Students come from 16 states and territories; 32 other countries; 3% are from out of state; 2% Black or African American, non-Hispanic/Latino; 85% Hispanic/Latino; 0.7% Asian, non-Hispanic/Latino; 0.2% Native Hawaiian or other Pacific Islander, non-Hispanic/Latino; 0.2% American Indian or Alaska Native, non-Hispanic/Latino; 0.1% Two or more races, non-Hispanic/Latino; 2% Race/ethnicity unknown; 2% international; 5% transferred in.
Freshmen *Admission:* 4,797 enrolled.
Faculty *Total:* 1,186, 35% full-time, 27% with terminal degrees.
Majors Accounting; administrative assistant and secretarial science; adult development and aging; automobile/automotive mechanics technology; business administration and management; business automation/technology/data entry; business/commerce; child-care and support services management; child development; cinematography and film/video production; clinical/medical laboratory technology; commercial and advertising art; computer and information sciences; computer programming; corrections; corrections and criminal justice related; court reporting; criminal justice/police science; criminal justice/safety; culinary arts; dental assisting; dental hygiene; diagnostic medical sonography and ultrasound technology; dietetics; drafting and design technology; electrical, electronic and communications engineering technology; emergency medical technology (EMT paramedic); engineering; environmental engineering technology; fashion/apparel design; fire prevention and safety technology; general studies; health information/medical records administration; heating, air conditioning, ventilation and refrigeration maintenance technology; homeland security, law enforcement, firefighting and protective services related; hotel/motel administration; institutional food workers; interior design; international business/trade/commerce; kindergarten/preschool education; legal assistant/paralegal; liberal arts and sciences/liberal studies; machine tool technology; medical/clinical assistant; medical radiologic technology; middle school education; multi/interdisciplinary studies related; music; opticianry; optometric technician; pharmacy technician; physical therapy technology; plastics and polymer engineering technology; psychiatric/mental health services technology; radiologic technology/science; real estate; registered nursing/registered nurse; respiratory care therapy; sign language interpretation and translation; social work; speech communication and rhetoric; substance abuse/addiction counseling; surgical technology; system, networking, and LAN/WAN management; tourism and travel services management.
Academics *Calendar:* semesters. *Degree:* certificates and associate. *Special study options:* academic remediation for entering students, adult/continuing education programs, advanced placement credit, cooperative education, distance learning, English as a second language, external degree program, honors programs, independent study, internships, off-campus study, part-time degree program, services for LD students, summer session for credit. *ROTC:* Army (c).

Library El Paso Community College Learning Resource Center plus 4 others. *Books:* 208,580 (physical), 165,600 (digital/electronic); *Databases:* 6. Weekly public service hours: 95.

Student Life *Housing:* college housing not available. *Activities and Organizations:* drama/theater group, student-run newspaper, radio and television station, choral group. *Campus security:* 24-hour patrols, late-night transport/escort service. *Student services:* health clinic, personal/psychological counseling.

Athletics Member NJCAA. *Intercollegiate sports:* baseball M(s), cross-country running M(s)/W(s), softball W(s). *Intramural sports:* baseball M, cross-country running M/W, softball W.

Costs (2017–18) *Tuition:* state resident $2256 full-time, $564 per term part-time; nonresident $4126 full-time, $1055 per term part-time. Full-time tuition and fees vary according to course level, course load, and student level. Part-time tuition and fees vary according to course level, course load, and student level. *Required fees:* $480 full-time, $20 per credit hour part-time. *Payment plan:* installment. *Waivers:* senior citizens and employees or children of employees.

Applying *Options:* electronic application, early admission, deferred entrance. *Application fee:* $10.

Freshman Application Contact Cassandra Lachica-Chavez, Executive Director Admission and Registrar, El Paso Community College, PO Box 20500, El Paso, TX 79998. *Phone:* 915-831-2580. *E-mail:* clachica@epcc.edu. *Website:* http://www.epcc.edu/.

Everest College
Arlington, Texas

Freshman Application Contact Admissions Office, Everest College, 300 Six Flags Drive, Suite 100, Arlington, TX 76011. *Phone:* 817-652-7790. *Toll-free phone:* 888-741-4270. *Fax:* 817-649-6033. *Website:* http://www.everest.edu/.

Everest College
Fort Worth, Texas

Admissions Office Contact Everest College, 4200 South Freeway, Suite 1940, Fort Worth, TX 76115. *Website:* http://www.everest.edu/.

Frank Phillips College
Borger, Texas

Freshman Application Contact Ms. Michele Stevens, Director of Enrollment Management, Frank Phillips College, PO Box 5118, Borger, TX 79008-5118. *Phone:* 806-457-4200 Ext. 707. *Fax:* 806-457-4225. *E-mail:* mstevens@fpctx.edu. *Website:* http://www.fpctx.edu/.

Galen College of Nursing
San Antonio, Texas

Admissions Office Contact Galen College of Nursing, 7411 John Smith Drive, Suite 1400, San Antonio, TX 78229. *Toll-free phone:* 877-223-7040. *Website:* http://www.galencollege.edu/.

Galveston College
Galveston, Texas

- **State and locally supported** 2-year, founded 1967
- **Urban** 11-acre campus with easy access to Houston
- **Coed**

Undergraduates 504 full-time, 1,567 part-time. 13% Black or African American, non-Hispanic/Latino; 37% Hispanic/Latino; 3% Asian, non-Hispanic/Latino; 0.2% Native Hawaiian or other Pacific Islander, non-Hispanic/Latino; 0.5% American Indian or Alaska Native, non-Hispanic/Latino; 0.4% Two or more races, non-Hispanic/Latino; 3% Race/ethnicity unknown; 1% international; 12% transferred in. *Retention:* 53% of full-time freshmen returned.

Faculty *Student/faculty ratio:* 15:1.

Academics *Calendar:* semesters. *Degree:* certificates and associate. *Special study options:* adult/continuing education programs, advanced placement credit, cooperative education, distance learning, internships, off-campus study, part-time degree program, services for LD students, summer session for credit.

Library David Glenn Hunt Memorial Library.

Student Life *Campus security:* 24-hour emergency response devices and patrols, late-night transport/escort service.

Athletics Member NJCAA.

Standardized Tests *Required:* TSI or exemption test scores and documentation (for admission).

Costs (2016–17) *Tuition:* area resident $1200 full-time, $40 per credit hour part-time; state resident $1800 full-time, $60 per credit hour part-time; nonresident $3750 full-time, $125 per credit hour part-time. Full-time tuition and fees vary according to course level, course load, and program. Part-time tuition and fees vary according to course level, course load, and program. *Required fees:* $850 full-time, $22 per credit hour part-time, $95 per term part-time.

Financial Aid Of all full-time matriculated undergraduates who enrolled in 2015, 36 Federal Work-Study jobs (averaging $2000).

Applying *Required for some:* high school transcript.

Freshman Application Contact Galveston College, 4015 Avenue Q, Galveston, TX 77550. *Phone:* 409-944-1216. *Website:* http://www.gc.edu/.

Golf Academy of America
Farmers Branch, Texas

Admissions Office Contact Golf Academy of America, 1861 Valley View Lane, Suite 100, Farmers Branch, TX 75234. *Toll-free phone:* 800-342-7342. *Website:* http://www.golfacademy.edu/.

Grayson College
Denison, Texas

Freshman Application Contact Charles Leslie, Enrollment Advisor, Grayson College, 6101 Grayson Drive, Denison, TX 75020. *Phone:* 903-415-2532. *Fax:* 903-463-5284. *E-mail:* lesliec@grayson.edu. *Website:* http://www.grayson.edu/.

Hill College
Hillsboro, Texas

- **District-supported** 2-year, founded 1923
- **Small-town** 80-acre campus with easy access to Dallas-Fort Worth
- **Coed**, 4,075 undergraduate students

Undergraduates 5% Black or African American, non-Hispanic/Latino; 23% Hispanic/Latino; 0.7% Asian, non-Hispanic/Latino; 0.3% Native Hawaiian or other Pacific Islander, non-Hispanic/Latino; 0.6% American Indian or Alaska Native, non-Hispanic/Latino; 3% Two or more races, non-Hispanic/Latino; 0.9% Race/ethnicity unknown; 1% international. *Retention:* 53% of full-time freshmen returned.

Faculty *Total:* 209. *Student/faculty ratio:* 17:1.

Majors Accounting; administrative assistant and secretarial science; agricultural business and management; agriculture; art; autobody/collision and repair technology; automobile/automotive mechanics technology; behavioral sciences; biology/biological sciences; business administration and management; business/commerce; chemistry; child-care provision; commercial and advertising art; computer and information sciences; computer programming; corrections; corrections and criminal justice related; cosmetology; cosmetology, barber/styling, and nail instruction; criminal justice/law enforcement administration; drafting and design technology; dramatic/theater arts; economics; elementary education; emergency medical technology (EMT paramedic); engineering; English; family and consumer sciences/human sciences; fire science/firefighting; foreign languages and literatures; general studies; geology/earth science; health and physical education/fitness; heating, air conditioning, ventilation and refrigeration maintenance technology; history; industrial electronics technology; industrial mechanics and maintenance technology; mathematics; music; philosophy; physical therapy; physics; political science and government; pre-dentistry studies; pre-law studies; premedical studies; prenursing studies; pre-pharmacy studies; pre-veterinary studies; psychology; registered nursing/registered nurse; religious studies; rhetoric and composition; secondary education; security and loss prevention; sociology; special education; speech communication and rhetoric; system, networking, and LAN/WAN management; teacher assistant/aide; welding technology.

Academics *Calendar:* semesters. *Degree:* certificates and associate. *Special study options:* academic remediation for entering students, advanced placement credit, cooperative education, distance learning, services for LD students, summer session for credit.

Library Hill College Library plus 1 other. *Books:* 55,000 (physical), 203 (digital/electronic); *Serial titles:* 75 (physical); *Databases:* 105. Weekly public service hours: 65.

Student Life *Housing Options:* men-only, women-only. Campus housing is university owned. *Activities and Organizations:* drama/theater group, choral group, Student Government, Phi Theta Kappa. *Campus security:* 24-hour emergency response devices, late-night transport/escort service, security officers.

Athletics Member NJCAA. *Intercollegiate sports:* baseball M(s), basketball M(s)/W(s), soccer M/W(s), softball W(s), volleyball W(s). *Intramural sports:* basketball M/W, volleyball W.

Costs (2017–18) *Tuition:* area resident $924 full-time, $462 per term part-time; state resident $1224 full-time, $612 per term part-time; nonresident $1424 full-time, $812 per term part-time. Full-time tuition and fees vary according to course load. Part-time tuition and fees vary according to course load. *Required fees:* $147 full-time, $66 per term part-time, $15 per term part-time. *Room and board:* $1925; room only: $400. *Payment plan:* installment. *Waivers:* senior citizens and employees or children of employees.

Financial Aid Of all full-time matriculated undergraduates who enrolled in 2015, 51 Federal Work-Study jobs (averaging $858). 20 state and other part-time jobs (averaging $230).

Applying *Options:* electronic application, early admission. *Required:* high school transcript. *Application deadlines:* rolling (freshmen), rolling (transfers).

Freshman Application Contact Enrollment Management, Hill College, 112 Lamar Drive, Hillsboro, TX 76645. *Phone:* 254-659-7600. *Fax:* 254-582-7591. *E-mail:* enrollmentinfo@hillcollege.edu. *Website:* http://www.hillcollege.edu/.

Houston Community College
Houston, Texas

- **State and locally supported** 2-year, founded 1971
- **Urban** campus with easy access to Houston
- **Coed,** 57,032 undergraduate students, 29% full-time, 57% women, 43% men

Undergraduates 16,415 full-time, 40,617 part-time. 28% Black or African American, non-Hispanic/Latino; 33% Hispanic/Latino; 10% Asian, non-Hispanic/Latino; 0.2% Native Hawaiian or other Pacific Islander, non-Hispanic/Latino; 0.2% American Indian or Alaska Native, non-Hispanic/Latino; 2% Two or more races, non-Hispanic/Latino; 2% Race/ethnicity unknown; 11% international; 7% transferred in.

Freshmen *Admission:* 7,559 enrolled.

Faculty *Total:* 2,501, 30% full-time. *Student/faculty ratio:* 22:1.

Majors Accounting; animation, interactive technology, video graphics and special effects; anthropology; applied horticulture/horticulture operations; automobile/automotive mechanics technology; banking and financial support services; biology/biological sciences; biology/biotechnology laboratory technician; business administration and management; business automation/technology/data entry; business/corporate communications; cardiovascular technology; chemical technology; chemistry; child development; cinematography and film/video production; clinical/medical laboratory science and allied professions related; clinical/medical laboratory technology; commercial photography; computer engineering technology; computer programming; computer programming (specific applications); computer science; computer systems networking and telecommunications; construction engineering technology; cosmetology; court reporting; criminal justice/police science; culinary arts; desktop publishing and digital imaging design; drafting and design technology; early childhood education; education (multiple levels); emergency medical technology (EMT paramedic); energy management and systems technology; engineering science; English; fashion/apparel design; fashion merchandising; fine/studio arts; fire prevention and safety technology; general studies; health and physical education/fitness; health information/medical records technology; health services/allied health/health sciences; histologic technician; hotel/motel administration; instrumentation technology; interior design; international business/trade/commerce; legal assistant/paralegal; logistics, materials, and supply chain management; manufacturing engineering technology; marketing/marketing management; mathematics; music management; music performance; music theory and composition; network and system administration; nuclear medical technology; occupational safety and health technology; occupational therapist assistant; petroleum technology; physical therapy technology; physics; psychiatric/mental health services technology; public administration; radio and television broadcasting technology; radiologic technology/science; real estate; registered nursing/registered nurse; respiratory care therapy; secondary education; sign language interpretation and translation; speech communication and rhetoric; tourism and travel services management; turf and turfgrass management.

Academics *Calendar:* semesters. *Degree:* certificates and associate. *Special study options:* academic remediation for entering students, advanced placement credit, cooperative education, distance learning, English as a second language, honors programs, internships, part-time degree program, services for LD students, study abroad, summer session for credit. *ROTC:* Army (c), Air Force (c).

Library Houston Community College Libraries. Students can reserve study rooms.

Student Life *Housing:* college housing not available. *Activities and Organizations:* student-run newspaper. *Campus security:* 24-hour emergency response devices and patrols, late-night transport/escort service, crime prevention services.

Costs (2016–17) *Tuition:* area resident $1632 full-time, $411 per term part-time; state resident $3360 full-time, $843 per term part-time; nonresident $3756 full-time, $942 per term part-time. Full-time tuition and fees vary according to course load. Part-time tuition and fees vary according to course load. *Payment plan:* installment. *Waivers:* senior citizens and employees or children of employees.

Financial Aid Of all full-time matriculated undergraduates who enrolled in 2015, 54,280 applied for aid, 54,280 were judged to have need, 26,217 had their need fully met. 206 state and other part-time jobs (averaging $5500). *Average percent of need met:* 82%. *Average financial aid package:* $6510.

Applying *Options:* electronic application. *Required for some:* high school transcript, interview. *Application deadlines:* rolling (freshmen), rolling (out-of-state freshmen), rolling (transfers).

Freshman Application Contact Ms. Mary Lemburg, Registrar, Houston Community College, 3100 Main Street, PO Box 667517, Houston, TX 77266-7517. *Phone:* 713-718-2000. *Toll-free phone:* 877-422-6111. *Fax:* 713-718-2111. *E-mail:* student.info@hccs.edu. *Website:* http://www.hccs.edu/.

Howard College
Big Spring, Texas

Freshman Application Contact Ms. TaNeal Richardson, Assistant Registrar, Howard College, 1001 Birdwell Lane, Big Spring, TX 79720-3702. *Phone:* 432-264-5105. *Toll-free phone:* 866-HC-HAWKS. *Fax:* 432-264-5604. *E-mail:* trichardson@howardcollege.edu. *Website:* http://www.howardcollege.edu/.

Interactive College of Technology
Houston, Texas

- **Proprietary** 2-year
- **Urban** campus
- **Coed**

Academics *Calendar:* semesters. *Degree:* certificates, diplomas, and associate. *Special study options:* academic remediation for entering students, advanced placement credit, cooperative education, distance learning, English as a second language, internships.

Applying *Required:* high school transcript, interview.

Freshman Application Contact Interactive College of Technology, 4473 I-45 N. Freeway, Airline Plaza, Houston, TX 77022. *Website:* http://ict.edu/.

Interactive College of Technology
Houston, Texas

- **Proprietary** 2-year
- **Coed**

Academics *Calendar:* semesters. *Degree:* certificates, diplomas, and associate. *Special study options:* academic remediation for entering students, cooperative education, distance learning, English as a second language, internships.

Freshman Application Contact Interactive College of Technology, 6200 Hillcroft Avenue, Suite 200, Houston, TX 77081. *Website:* http://ict.edu/.

Interactive College of Technology
Pasadena, Texas

- **Proprietary** 2-year
- **Coed**

Academics *Calendar:* semesters. *Degree:* diplomas and associate. *Special study options:* academic remediation for entering students, advanced placement credit, distance learning, English as a second language, internships, part-time degree program.

Applying *Required:* high school transcript, interview.

Freshman Application Contact Interactive College of Technology, 213 West Southmore Street, Suite 101, Pasadena, TX 77502. *Website:* http://ict.edu/.

International Business College
El Paso, Texas

Admissions Office Contact International Business College, 1155 North Zaragosa Road, El Paso, TX 79907. *Website:* http://www.ibcelpaso.edu/.

International Business College

El Paso, Texas

Admissions Office Contact International Business College, 5700 Cromo Drive, El Paso, TX 79912. *Website:* http://www.ibcelpaso.edu/.

Jacksonville College

Jacksonville, Texas

Freshman Application Contact Danny Morris, Director of Admissions, Jacksonville College, 105 B.J. Albritton Drive, Jacksonville, TX 75766. *Phone:* 903-589-7110. *Toll-free phone:* 800-256-8522. *E-mail:* admissions@jacksonville-college.org. *Website:* http://www.jacksonville-college.edu/.

KD Conservatory College of Film and Dramatic Arts

Dallas, Texas

Freshman Application Contact Mr. T. A. Taylor, Director of Education, KD Conservatory College of Film and Dramatic Arts, 2600 Stemmons Freeway, Suite 117, Dallas, TX 75207. *Phone:* 214-638-0484. *Toll-free phone:* 877-278-2283. *Fax:* 214-630-5140. *E-mail:* tataylor@kdstudio.com. *Website:* http://www.kdstudio.com/.

Kilgore College

Kilgore, Texas

- **State and locally supported** 2-year, founded 1935
- **Small-town** 35-acre campus with easy access to Dallas-Fort Worth
- **Endowment** $10.0 million
- **Coed**

Undergraduates 2,245 full-time, 3,421 part-time. Students come from 25 states and territories; 18 other countries; 2% are from out of state; 19% Black or African American, non-Hispanic/Latino; 18% Hispanic/Latino; 1% Asian, non-Hispanic/Latino; 0.5% American Indian or Alaska Native, non-Hispanic/Latino; 3% Two or more races, non-Hispanic/Latino; 0.9% Race/ethnicity unknown; 0.7% international; 6% transferred in; 7% live on campus. *Retention:* 52% of full-time freshmen returned.
Faculty *Student/faculty ratio:* 17:1.
Academics *Calendar:* semesters. *Degree:* certificates and associate. *Special study options:* academic remediation for entering students, adult/continuing education programs, advanced placement credit, cooperative education, distance learning, honors programs, internships, part-time degree program, services for LD students, summer session for credit.
Library Randolph C. Watson Library plus 1 other. *Books:* 44,165 (physical), 34,163 (digital/electronic); *Serial titles:* 153 (physical), 50,534 (digital/electronic); *Databases:* 106. Weekly public service hours: 62.
Student Life *Campus security:* 24-hour emergency response devices and patrols.
Athletics Member NJCAA.
Financial Aid Of all full-time matriculated undergraduates who enrolled in 2015, 80 Federal Work-Study jobs (averaging $2500). *Financial aid deadline:* 6/1.
Applying *Options:* electronic application, early admission. *Required:* high school transcript. *Required for some:* interview.
Freshman Application Contact Kilgore College, 1100 Broadway Boulevard, Kilgore, TX 75662-3299. *Phone:* 903-983-8200.
E-mail: register@kilgore.cc.tx.us. *Website:* http://www.kilgore.edu/.

Lamar Institute of Technology

Beaumont, Texas

Freshman Application Contact Admissions Office, Lamar Institute of Technology, 855 East Lavaca, Beaumont, TX 77705. *Phone:* 409-880-8354. *Toll-free phone:* 800-950-6989. *Website:* http://www.lit.edu/.

Lamar State College–Orange

Orange, Texas

Freshman Application Contact Kerry Olson, Director of Admissions and Financial Aid, Lamar State College–Orange, 410 Front Street, Orange, TX 77632. *Phone:* 409-882-3362. *Fax:* 409-882-3374.
Website: http://www.lsco.edu/.

Lamar State College–Port Arthur

Port Arthur, Texas

Freshman Application Contact Ms. Connie Nicholas, Registrar, Lamar State College–Port Arthur, PO Box 310, Port Arthur, TX 77641-0310. *Phone:* 409-984-6165. *Toll-free phone:* 800-477-5872. *Fax:* 409-984-6025. *E-mail:* nichoca@lamarpa.edu. *Website:* http://www.lamarpa.edu/.

Laredo Community College

Laredo, Texas

Freshman Application Contact Ms. Josie Soliz, Admissions Records Supervisor, Laredo Community College, Laredo, TX 78040-4395. *Phone:* 956-721-5177. *Fax:* 956-721-5493. *Website:* http://www.laredo.edu/.

Lee College

Baytown, Texas

Director of Admissions Ms. Becki Griffith, Registrar, Lee College, PO Box 818, Baytown, TX 77522-0818. *Phone:* 281-425-6399.
E-mail: bgriffit@lee.edu. *Website:* http://www.lee.edu/.

Lincoln College of Technology

Grand Prairie, Texas

Admissions Office Contact Lincoln College of Technology, 2915 Alouette Drive, Grand Prairie, TX 75052. *Toll-free phone:* 844-215-1513.
Website: http://www.lincolntech.edu/.

Lone Star College–CyFair

Cypress, Texas

- **State and locally supported** 2-year, founded 2002, part of Lone Star College
- **Suburban** campus with easy access to Houston
- **Coed**, 21,636 undergraduate students, 31% full-time, 56% women, 44% men

Undergraduates 6,757 full-time, 14,879 part-time. Students come from 67 other countries; 13% Black or African American, non-Hispanic/Latino; 43% Hispanic/Latino; 11% Asian, non-Hispanic/Latino; 0.2% American Indian or Alaska Native, non-Hispanic/Latino; 3% Two or more races, non-Hispanic/Latino; 3% Race/ethnicity unknown; 25% transferred in.
Freshmen *Admission:* 3,424 applied, 3,424 admitted, 3,424 enrolled.
Faculty *Total:* 658, 22% full-time, 22% with terminal degrees. *Student/faculty ratio:* 37:1.
Majors Accounting; accounting and computer science; animation, interactive technology, video graphics and special effects; business administration and management; computer and information sciences; computer science; criminal justice/law enforcement administration; dance; design and visual communications; diagnostic medical sonography and ultrasound technology; economics; education; electrical, electronic and communications engineering technology; emergency medical technology (EMT paramedic); fire science/firefighting; geographic information science and cartography; health information/medical records technology; industrial technology; information technology; liberal arts and sciences/liberal studies; logistics, materials, and supply chain management; marketing/marketing management; medical radiologic technology; music; office occupations and clerical services; radiation protection/health physics technology; registered nursing/registered nurse; sign language interpretation and translation; speech communication and rhetoric; welding technology.
Academics *Calendar:* semesters. *Degree:* certificates, diplomas, and associate. *Special study options:* academic remediation for entering students, accelerated degree program, adult/continuing education programs, advanced placement credit, cooperative education, distance learning, double majors, English as a second language, honors programs, independent study, internships, part-time degree program, services for LD students, study abroad, summer session for credit.
Library LSC–CyFair Library.
Student Life *Housing:* college housing not available. *Activities and Organizations:* drama/theater group, choral group. *Campus security:* 24-hour emergency response devices and patrols, late-night transport/escort service. *Student services:* personal/psychological counseling.
Costs (2017–18) *Tuition:* area resident $1352 full-time, $44 per credit hour part-time; state resident $3452 full-time, $114 per credit hour part-time; nonresident $3902 full-time, $129 per credit hour part-time. Full-time tuition and fees vary according to course load and program. Part-time tuition and fees vary according to course load and program. *Required fees:* $604 full-time, $18

per credit hour part-time, $32 per term part-time. *Payment plans:* installment, deferred payment. *Waivers:* employees or children of employees.
Applying *Options:* electronic application, early admission. *Recommended:* high school transcript.
Freshman Application Contact Admissions Office, Lone Star College–CyFair, 9191 Barker Cypress Road, Cypress, TX 77433-1383. *Phone:* 281-290-3200. *E-mail:* cfc.info@lonestar.edu.
Website: http://www.lonestar.edu/cyfair.

Lone Star College–Kingwood
Kingwood, Texas

- **State and locally supported** 2-year, founded 1984, part of Lone Star College
- **Suburban** 264-acre campus with easy access to Houston
- **Coed,** 12,287 undergraduate students, 31% full-time, 62% women, 38% men

Undergraduates 3,785 full-time, 8,502 part-time. Students come from 48 other countries; 14% Black or African American, non-Hispanic/Latino; 35% Hispanic/Latino; 4% Asian, non-Hispanic/Latino; 0.3% American Indian or Alaska Native, non-Hispanic/Latino; 3% Two or more races, non-Hispanic/Latino; 4% Race/ethnicity unknown; 28% transferred in.
Freshmen *Admission:* 1,590 applied, 1,590 admitted, 1,590 enrolled.
Faculty *Total:* 684, 19% full-time, 13% with terminal degrees. *Student/faculty ratio:* 21:1.
Majors Administrative assistant and secretarial science; business administration and management; computer and information sciences; computer science; cosmetology; criminal justice/law enforcement administration; dental hygiene; design and visual communications; education; electroneurodiagnostic/electroencephalographic technology; fire science/firefighting; interior design; marketing/marketing management; music; occupational therapy; registered nursing/registered nurse; respiratory care therapy.
Academics *Calendar:* semesters. *Degree:* certificates and associate. *Special study options:* academic remediation for entering students, accelerated degree program, adult/continuing education programs, advanced placement credit, cooperative education, distance learning, double majors, English as a second language, honors programs, independent study, internships, part-time degree program, services for LD students, study abroad, summer session for credit.
Library LSC–Kingwood Library.
Student Life *Housing:* college housing not available. *Activities and Organizations:* drama/theater group, student-run television station, choral group. *Campus security:* 24-hour emergency response devices and patrols, late-night transport/escort service. *Student services:* personal/psychological counseling.
Costs (2017–18) *Tuition:* area resident $1352 full-time, $44 per credit hour part-time; state resident $3452 full-time, $114 per credit hour part-time; nonresident $3902 full-time, $129 per credit hour part-time. Full-time tuition and fees vary according to course load and program. Part-time tuition and fees vary according to course load and program. *Required fees:* $604 full-time, $18 per credit hour part-time, $32 per term part-time. *Payment plans:* installment, deferred payment. *Waivers:* employees or children of employees.
Financial Aid Of all full-time matriculated undergraduates who enrolled in 2009, 28 Federal Work-Study jobs, 6 state and other part-time jobs. *Financial aid deadline:* 4/1.
Applying *Options:* electronic application, early admission. *Recommended:* high school transcript. *Application deadlines:* rolling (freshmen), rolling (transfers).
Freshman Application Contact Admissions Office, Lone Star College–Kingwood, 20000 Kingwood Drive, Kingwood, TX 77339. *Phone:* 281-312-1525. *Fax:* 281-312-1477. *E-mail:* kingwoodadvising@lonestar.edu.
Website: http://www.lonestar.edu/kingwood.htm.

Lone Star College–Montgomery
Conroe, Texas

- **State and locally supported** 2-year, founded 1995, part of Lone Star College
- **Suburban** campus with easy access to Houston
- **Coed,** 14,411 undergraduate students, 31% full-time, 60% women, 40% men

Undergraduates 4,466 full-time, 9,945 part-time. Students come from 63 other countries; 10% Black or African American, non-Hispanic/Latino; 30% Hispanic/Latino; 4% Asian, non-Hispanic/Latino; 0.3% American Indian or Alaska Native, non-Hispanic/Latino; 3% Two or more races, non-Hispanic/Latino; 4% Race/ethnicity unknown; 26% transferred in.
Freshmen *Admission:* 1,852 applied, 1,852 admitted, 1,852 enrolled.
Faculty *Total:* 658, 22% full-time, 22% with terminal degrees. *Student/faculty ratio:* 25:1.

Majors Accounting and business/management; automobile/automotive mechanics technology; biology/biotechnology laboratory technician; business administration and management; computer science; criminal justice/law enforcement administration; education; emergency medical technology (EMT paramedic); fire science/firefighting; human services; information technology; music; physical therapy technology; registered nursing/registered nurse.
Academics *Calendar:* semesters. *Degree:* certificates and associate. *Special study options:* academic remediation for entering students, adult/continuing education programs, advanced placement credit, cooperative education, distance learning, double majors, English as a second language, honors programs, independent study, internships, part-time degree program, services for LD students, study abroad, summer session for credit.
Library LSC–Montgomery Library.
Student Life *Housing:* college housing not available. *Activities and Organizations:* drama/theater group, choral group, Campus Crusade for Christ, Criminal Justice Club, Phi Theta Kappa, Latino-American Student Association, African-American Cultural Awareness. *Campus security:* 24-hour emergency response devices and patrols, late-night transport/escort service. *Student services:* personal/psychological counseling.
Costs (2017–18) *Tuition:* area resident $1362 full-time, $44 per credit hour part-time; state resident $3452 full-time, $114 per credit hour part-time; nonresident $3902 full-time, $129 per credit hour part-time. Full-time tuition and fees vary according to course load and program. Part-time tuition and fees vary according to course load and program. *Required fees:* $604 full-time, $18 per credit hour part-time, $32 per term part-time. *Payment plans:* installment, deferred payment. *Waivers:* employees or children of employees.
Financial Aid Of all full-time matriculated undergraduates who enrolled in 2015, 25 Federal Work-Study jobs (averaging $2500). 4 state and other part-time jobs.
Applying *Options:* electronic application, early admission. *Recommended:* high school transcript. *Application deadlines:* rolling (freshmen), rolling (transfers).
Freshman Application Contact Lone Star College–Montgomery, 3200 College Park Drive, Conroe, TX 77384. *Phone:* 281-290-2721.
Website: http://www.lonestar.edu/montgomery.

Lone Star College–North Harris
Houston, Texas

- **State and locally supported** 2-year, founded 1972, part of Lone Star College
- **Suburban** campus with easy access to Houston
- **Coed,** 16,290 undergraduate students, 29% full-time, 60% women, 40% men

Undergraduates 4,797 full-time, 11,493 part-time. Students come from 49 other countries; 26% Black or African American, non-Hispanic/Latino; 46% Hispanic/Latino; 5% Asian, non-Hispanic/Latino; 0.2% American Indian or Alaska Native, non-Hispanic/Latino; 3% Two or more races, non-Hispanic/Latino; 5% Race/ethnicity unknown; 27% transferred in.
Freshmen *Admission:* 2,228 applied, 2,228 admitted, 2,228 enrolled.
Faculty *Total:* 897, 23% full-time, 17% with terminal degrees. *Student/faculty ratio:* 20:1.
Majors Accounting; automobile/automotive mechanics technology; business administration and management; computer science; cosmetology; criminal justice/law enforcement administration; design and visual communications; drafting and design technology; education; educational/instructional technology; electrical, electronic and communications engineering technology; emergency medical technology (EMT paramedic); health information/medical records technology; heating, air conditioning, ventilation and refrigeration maintenance technology; industrial technology; legal assistant/paralegal; mechanical engineering; music; pharmacy technician; registered nursing/registered nurse; sign language interpretation and translation; welding technology.
Academics *Calendar:* semesters. *Degree:* certificates and associate. *Special study options:* academic remediation for entering students, adult/continuing education programs, advanced placement credit, cooperative education, distance learning, double majors, English as a second language, honors programs, independent study, internships, part-time degree program, services for LD students, study abroad, summer session for credit.
Library LSC–North Harris Library.
Student Life *Activities and Organizations:* drama/theater group, choral group, Student Government Association, Phi Theta Kappa, Ambassadors, Honors Student Organizations, Soccer Club. *Campus security:* 24-hour emergency response devices and patrols, late-night transport/escort service. *Student services:* personal/psychological counseling, women's center.
Athletics *Intramural sports:* badminton M/W, baseball M/W, basketball M/W, bowling M/W, football M/W, golf M/W, gymnastics M/W, racquetball M/W, soccer M/W, softball M/W, table tennis M/W, tennis M/W, track and field M/W, volleyball M/W, weight lifting M/W.

Costs (2017–18) *Tuition:* area resident $1352 full-time, $44 per credit hour part-time; state resident $3452 full-time, $114 per credit hour part-time; nonresident $3902 full-time, $129 per credit hour part-time. Full-time tuition and fees vary according to course load and program. Part-time tuition and fees vary according to course load and program. *Required fees:* $604 full-time, $18 per credit hour part-time, $32 per term part-time. *Payment plans:* installment, deferred payment. *Waivers:* employees or children of employees.
Applying *Options:* electronic application, early admission. *Application deadlines:* rolling (freshmen), rolling (transfers).
Freshman Application Contact Admissions Office, Lone Star College–North Harris, 2700 W. W. Thorne Drive, Houston, TX 77073-3499. *Phone:* 281-618-5410. *E-mail:* nhcounselor@lonestar.edu.
Website: http://www.lonestar.edu/northharris.

Lone Star College–Tomball
Tomball, Texas

- **State and locally supported** 2-year, founded 1988, part of Lone Star College
- **Suburban** campus with easy access to Houston
- **Coed,** 9,013 undergraduate students, 30% full-time, 62% women, 38% men

Undergraduates 2,705 full-time, 6,308 part-time. Students come from 44 other countries; 13% Black or African American, non-Hispanic/Latino; 29% Hispanic/Latino; 5% Asian, non-Hispanic/Latino; 0.3% American Indian or Alaska Native, non-Hispanic/Latino; 3% Two or more races, non-Hispanic/Latino; 5% Race/ethnicity unknown; 31% transferred in.
Freshmen *Admission:* 1,114 applied, 1,114 admitted, 1,114 enrolled.
Faculty *Total:* 393, 26% full-time, 23% with terminal degrees. *Student/faculty ratio:* 24:1.
Majors Accounting; administrative assistant and secretarial science; animation, interactive technology, video graphics and special effects; business administration and management; computer programming; computer science; criminal justice/law enforcement administration; education; electrical, electronic and communications engineering technology; industrial technology; music; registered nursing/registered nurse; surgical technology; system, networking, and LAN/WAN management; veterinary/animal health technology.
Academics *Calendar:* semesters. *Degree:* certificates and associate. *Special study options:* academic remediation for entering students, adult/continuing education programs, advanced placement credit, cooperative education, distance learning, double majors, English as a second language, honors programs, independent study, internships, part-time degree program, services for LD students, study abroad, summer session for credit.
Library LSC–Tomball Community Library.
Student Life *Housing:* college housing not available. *Activities and Organizations:* drama/theater group, choral group, Phi Theta Kappa, Occupational Therapy OTA, Veterinary Technicians Student Organization, STARS, Student Nurses Association. *Campus security:* 24-hour emergency response devices and patrols, late-night transport/escort service, trained security personnel during hours of operation. *Student services:* personal/psychological counseling.
Costs (2017–18) *Tuition:* area resident $1352 full-time, $44 per credit hour part-time; state resident $3452 full-time, $114 per credit part-time; nonresident $3902 full-time, $129 per credit part-time. Full-time tuition and fees vary according to course load and program. Part-time tuition and fees vary according to course load and program. *Required fees:* $604 full-time, $18 per credit hour part-time, $32 per term part-time. *Payment plans:* installment, deferred payment. *Waivers:* employees or children of employees.
Financial Aid Of all full-time matriculated undergraduates who enrolled in 2015, 34 Federal Work-Study jobs (averaging $3000).
Applying *Options:* electronic application, early admission. *Recommended:* high school transcript. *Application deadlines:* rolling (freshmen), rolling (transfers).
Freshman Application Contact Admissions Office, Lone Star College–Tomball, 30555 Tomball Parkway, Tomball, TX 77375-4036. *Phone:* 281-351-3310. *E-mail:* tcinfo@lonestar.edu.
Website: http://www.lonestar.edu/tomball.

Lone Star College–University Park
Houston, Texas

- **State and locally supported** 2-year, founded 2010, part of Lone Star College
- **Suburban** campus with easy access to Houston
- **Coed,** 12,024 undergraduate students, 30% full-time, 57% women, 43% men

Undergraduates 3,645 full-time, 8,379 part-time. Students come from 57 other countries; 13% Black or African American, non-Hispanic/Latino; 38% Hispanic/Latino; 12% Asian, non-Hispanic/Latino; 0.2% American Indian or Alaska Native, non-Hispanic/Latino; 4% Two or more races, non-Hispanic/Latino; 6% Race/ethnicity unknown; 25% transferred in.
Freshmen *Admission:* 1,413 enrolled.
Faculty *Total:* 511, 15% full-time, 19% with terminal degrees. *Student/faculty ratio:* 29:1.
Majors Accounting; business administration and management; criminal justice/law enforcement administration; speech communication and rhetoric.
Academics *Degree:* certificates and associate. *Special study options:* academic remediation for entering students, advanced placement credit, cooperative education, distance learning, English as a second language, honors programs, independent study, internships, off-campus study, part-time degree program, services for LD students, study abroad, summer session for credit.
Student Life *Housing:* college housing not available. *Campus security:* 24-hour emergency response devices and patrols, late-night transport/escort service. *Student services:* personal/psychological counseling.
Costs (2017–18) *Tuition:* area resident $1352 full-time, $44 per credit hour part-time; state resident $3452 full-time, $114 per credit hour part-time; nonresident $3902 full-time, $129 per credit hour part-time. Full-time tuition and fees vary according to course load and program. Part-time tuition and fees vary according to course load and program. *Required fees:* $604 full-time, $18 per credit hour part-time, $32 per term part-time. *Payment plans:* installment, deferred payment. *Waivers:* employees or children of employees.
Applying *Recommended:* high school transcript.
Freshman Application Contact Lone Star College–University Park, 20515 SH 249, Houston, TX 77070. *Phone:* 281-290-2721.
Website: http://www.lonestar.edu/universitypark.

McLennan Community College
Waco, Texas

- **County-supported** 2-year, founded 1965
- **Urban** 200-acre campus
- **Endowment** $15.3 million
- **Coed,** 8,799 undergraduate students, 39% full-time, 55% women, 27% men

Undergraduates 3,471 full-time, 3,678 part-time. Students come from 17 states and territories; 2% are from out of state; 12% Black or African American, non-Hispanic/Latino; 30% Hispanic/Latino; 1% Asian, non-Hispanic/Latino; 0.4% American Indian or Alaska Native, non-Hispanic/Latino; 3% Two or more races, non-Hispanic/Latino; 1% Race/ethnicity unknown; 7% transferred in.
Freshmen *Admission:* 2,362 applied, 2,362 admitted, 1,340 enrolled.
Faculty *Total:* 389, 14% with terminal degrees. *Student/faculty ratio:* 17:1.
Majors Accounting; administrative assistant and secretarial science; art teacher education; business administration and management; clinical/medical laboratory technology; computer engineering technology; criminal justice/law enforcement administration; criminal justice/police science; developmental and child psychology; finance; health information/medical records administration; industrial radiologic technology; information science/studies; kindergarten/preschool education; legal administrative assistant/secretary; legal assistant/paralegal; liberal arts and sciences/liberal studies; medical administrative assistant and medical secretary; mental health counseling; music; physical education teaching and coaching; physical therapy; real estate; registered nursing/registered nurse; respiratory care therapy; sign language interpretation and translation.
Academics *Calendar:* semesters. *Degree:* certificates and associate. *Special study options:* academic remediation for entering students, adult/continuing education programs, advanced placement credit, cooperative education, distance learning, honors programs, internships, off-campus study, part-time degree program, services for LD students, study abroad, summer session for credit. *ROTC:* Air Force (c).
Library McLennan Community College Library. *Books:* 69,255 (physical), 237,879 (digital/electronic); *Serial titles:* 290 (physical), 61 (digital/electronic); *Databases:* 134. Students can reserve study rooms.
Student Life *Housing:* college housing not available. *Activities and Organizations:* drama/theater group, student-run newspaper, choral group. *Campus security:* 24-hour emergency response devices and patrols. *Student services:* personal/psychological counseling.
Athletics Member NCAA, NJCAA. All NCAA Division I. *Intercollegiate sports:* baseball M(s), basketball M(s)/W(s), golf M(s)/W(s), softball W(s). *Intramural sports:* basketball M/W, volleyball M/W.
Costs (2017–18) *Tuition:* area resident $3180 full-time, $106 per semester hour part-time; state resident $3720 full-time, $124 per semester hour part-time; nonresident $5430 full-time, $181 per semester hour part-time. *Required fees:* $270 full-time, $9 per semester hour part-time. *Waivers:* employees or children of employees.
Financial Aid Of all full-time matriculated undergraduates who enrolled in 2015, 265 Federal Work-Study jobs (averaging $850). 35 state and other part-time jobs (averaging $1000).

Applying *Options:* electronic application, early admission. *Required:* high school transcript. *Application deadlines:* rolling (freshmen), rolling (transfers). *Notification:* continuous until 9/2 (freshmen), continuous until 9/2 (transfers).

Freshman Application Contact Amanda Straten, Coordinator of Student Admissions, McLennan Community College, 1400 College Drive, Waco, TX 76708. *Phone:* 254-299-8657. *Fax:* 254-299-8694. *E-mail:* astraten@mclennan.edu.

Website: http://www.mclennan.edu/.

MediaTech Institute
Dallas, Texas

Admissions Office Contact MediaTech Institute, 13300 Branch View Lane, Dallas, TX 75234. *Toll-free phone:* 866-498-1122.

Website: http://www.mediatech.edu/.

Mountain View College
Dallas, Texas

- **State and locally supported** 2-year, founded 1970, part of Dallas County Community College District System
- **Urban** 200-acre campus
- **Coed,** 9,068 undergraduate students, 23% full-time, 58% women, 42% men

Undergraduates 2,066 full-time, 7,002 part-time. Students come from 12 states and territories; 26% Black or African American, non-Hispanic/Latino; 53% Hispanic/Latino; 4% Asian, non-Hispanic/Latino; 0.3% American Indian or Alaska Native, non-Hispanic/Latino; 0.5% Two or more races, non-Hispanic/Latino; 3% Race/ethnicity unknown; 0.3% international; 18% transferred in. *Retention:* 57% of full-time freshmen returned.

Freshmen *Admission:* 2,500 applied, 2,500 admitted, 1,476 enrolled.

Faculty *Total:* 386, 22% full-time. *Student/faculty ratio:* 28:1.

Majors Accounting; business administration and management; computer systems networking and telecommunications; criminal justice/safety; drafting and design technology; education; electrical, electronic and communications engineering technology; liberal arts and sciences/liberal studies; music; speech communication and rhetoric; welding technology.

Academics *Calendar:* semesters. *Degree:* certificates and associate. *Special study options:* academic remediation for entering students, adult/continuing education programs, advanced placement credit, cooperative education, distance learning, double majors, English as a second language, external degree program, freshman honors college, honors programs, independent study, internships, part-time degree program, services for LD students, summer session for credit.

Student Life *Housing:* college housing not available. *Activities and Organizations:* drama/theater group, choral group. *Campus security:* 24-hour patrols, late-night transport/escort service. *Student services:* health clinic, personal/psychological counseling.

Athletics Member NJCAA. *Intercollegiate sports:* baseball M, basketball M/W, soccer M/W, volleyball W.

Costs (2017–18) *Tuition:* $59 per credit hour part-time; state resident $111 per credit hour part-time; nonresident $174 per credit hour part-time. *Payment plan:* installment. *Waivers:* senior citizens and employees or children of employees.

Financial Aid Of all full-time matriculated undergraduates who enrolled in 2015, 145 Federal Work-Study jobs (averaging $2700).

Applying *Options:* electronic application, early admission, deferred entrance. *Required:* high school transcript. *Application deadlines:* rolling (freshmen), rolling (transfers). *Notification:* continuous (freshmen), continuous (transfers).

Freshman Application Contact Ms. Glenda Hall, Director of Admissions, Mountain View College, 4849 West Illinois Avenue, Dallas, TX 75211-6599. *Phone:* 214-860-8666. *Fax:* 214-860-8570. *E-mail:* ghall@dcccd.edu.

Website: http://www.mountainviewcollege.edu/.

Navarro College
Corsicana, Texas

- **State and locally supported** 2-year, founded 1946
- **Small-town** 275-acre campus with easy access to Dallas-Fort Worth
- **Coed,** 9,230 undergraduate students, 34% full-time, 57% women, 43% men

Undergraduates 3,181 full-time, 6,049 part-time. Students come from 36 other countries; 2% are from out of state; 17% Black or African American, non-Hispanic/Latino; 21% Hispanic/Latino; 1% Asian, non-Hispanic/Latino; 0.2% Native Hawaiian or other Pacific Islander, non-Hispanic/Latino; 0.7% American Indian or Alaska Native, non-Hispanic/Latino; 1% Two or more races, non-Hispanic/Latino; 12% international; 25% live on campus.

Freshmen *Admission:* 1,508 enrolled.

Faculty *Total:* 515, 26% full-time, 8% with terminal degrees. *Student/faculty ratio:* 20:1.

Majors Accounting; administrative assistant and secretarial science; agricultural mechanization; art; biological and physical sciences; biology/biological sciences; business administration and management; chemistry; clinical/medical laboratory technology; commercial and advertising art; computer graphics; computer programming; computer science; consumer merchandising/retailing management; corrections; criminal justice/law enforcement administration; criminal justice/police science; data processing and data processing technology; developmental and child psychology; drafting and design technology; dramatic/theater arts; education; elementary education; engineering; English; fire science/firefighting; industrial technology; legal administrative assistant/secretary; legal assistant/paralegal; legal studies; licensed practical/vocational nurse training; marketing/marketing management; mathematics; music; occupational therapy; pharmacy; physical education teaching and coaching; physical sciences; physics; pre-engineering; psychology; registered nursing/registered nurse; rhetoric and composition; social sciences; sociology; voice and opera.

Academics *Calendar:* semesters. *Degree:* certificates, diplomas, and associate. *Special study options:* academic remediation for entering students, adult/continuing education programs, advanced placement credit, cooperative education, distance learning, freshman honors college, honors programs, part-time degree program, services for LD students, student-designed majors, summer session for credit.

Library Richard M. Sanchez Library.

Student Life *Housing Options:* men-only, women-only. Campus housing is university owned. *Activities and Organizations:* drama/theater group, choral group, marching band, Student Government Association, Phi Theta Kappa, Ebony Club, Que Pasa. *Campus security:* 24-hour emergency response devices. *Student services:* personal/psychological counseling.

Athletics Member NJCAA. *Intercollegiate sports:* baseball M(s), basketball M(s), football M(s), soccer W, softball W, volleyball W(s). *Intramural sports:* basketball M/W, bowling M/W, football M, soccer M, softball M/W, volleyball M/W.

Costs (2016–17) *Tuition:* area resident $1260 full-time, $126 per credit hour part-time; state resident $1440 full-time, $144 per credit hour part-time; nonresident $2970 full-time, $297 per credit hour part-time. Full-time tuition and fees vary according to course load. Part-time tuition and fees vary according to course load. *Required fees:* $1140 full-time, $109 per credit hour part-time. *Room and board:* $6621. Room and board charges vary according to board plan. *Payment plan:* installment. *Waivers:* employees or children of employees.

Applying *Options:* electronic application, early admission. *Required:* high school transcript.

Freshman Application Contact Tammy Adams, Registrar, Navarro College, 3200 West 7th Avenue, Corsicana, TX 75110-4899. *Phone:* 903-875-7348. *Toll-free phone:* 800-NAVARRO (in-state); 800-628-2776 (out-of-state). *Fax:* 903-875-7353. *E-mail:* tammy.adams@navarrocollege.edu.

Website: http://www.navarrocollege.edu/.

North Central Texas College
Gainesville, Texas

- **State and locally supported** 2-year, founded 1924
- **Suburban** 132-acre campus with easy access to Dallas-Fort Worth
- **Endowment** $4.3 million
- **Coed**

Undergraduates 3,068 full-time, 6,550 part-time. Students come from 27 states and territories; 31 other countries; 1% are from out of state; 9% Black or African American, non-Hispanic/Latino; 22% Hispanic/Latino; 3% Asian, non-Hispanic/Latino; 0.1% Native Hawaiian or other Pacific Islander, non-Hispanic/Latino; 0.7% American Indian or Alaska Native, non-Hispanic/Latino; 3% Two or more races, non-Hispanic/Latino; 0.4% Race/ethnicity unknown; 1% international; 32% transferred in; 1% live on campus. *Retention:* 55% of full-time freshmen returned.

Faculty *Student/faculty ratio:* 16:1.

Academics *Calendar:* semesters. *Degree:* certificates, diplomas, and associate. *Special study options:* academic remediation for entering students, adult/continuing education programs, advanced placement credit, cooperative education, distance learning, internships, part-time degree program, services for LD students, summer session for credit. *ROTC:* Army (c).

Library North Central Texas College Library plus 1 other.

Student Life *Campus security:* late-night transport/escort service, controlled dormitory access, security cameras.

Athletics Member NJCAA.

Costs (2016–17) *Tuition:* area resident $1824 full-time, $76 per semester hour part-time; state resident $3120 full-time, $130 per semester hour part-time; nonresident $5232 full-time, $218 per semester hour part-time. *Room and* *board:* $1964; room only: $850. Room and board charges vary according to housing facility. *Payment plans:* installment, deferred payment.

Financial Aid Of all full-time matriculated undergraduates who enrolled in 2015, 108 Federal Work-Study jobs (averaging $1253). 29 state and other part-time jobs (averaging $392).

Applying *Options:* electronic application, early admission. *Required:* high school transcript.

Freshman Application Contact Melinda Carroll, Director of Admissions/Registrar, North Central Texas College, 1525 West California, Gainesville, TX 76240-4699. *Phone:* 940-668-7731. *Fax:* 940-668-7075. *E-mail:* mcarroll@nctc.edu. *Website:* http://www.nctc.edu/.

Northeast Texas Community College
Mount Pleasant, Texas

Freshman Application Contact Linda Bond, Admissions Specialist, Northeast Texas Community College, PO Box 1307, Mount Pleasant, TX 75456-1307. *Phone:* 903-434-8140. *Toll-free phone:* 800-870-0142. *E-mail:* lbond@ntcc.edu. *Website:* http://www.ntcc.edu/.

North Lake College
Irving, Texas

Freshman Application Contact Admissions/Registration Office, North Lake College, 5001 North MacArthur Boulevard, Irving, TX 75038. *Phone:* 972-273-3183. *Website:* http://www.northlakecollege.edu/.

Northwest Vista College
San Antonio, Texas

- **State and locally supported** 2-year, founded 1995, part of Alamo Community College District System
- **Urban** 137-acre campus with easy access to San Antonio
- **Coed**

Undergraduates 4,235 full-time, 8,983 part-time. Students come from 24 states and territories; 7% transferred in. *Retention:* 54% of full-time freshmen returned.

Faculty *Student/faculty ratio:* 23:1.

Academics *Calendar:* semesters. *Degree:* certificates and associate. *Special study options:* academic remediation for entering students, advanced placement credit, cooperative education, distance learning, double majors, English as a second language, independent study, internships, off-campus study, part-time degree program, services for LD students, study abroad, summer session for credit. *ROTC:* Army (c).

Library Redbud Learning Center. *Books:* 19,338 (physical), 233,202 (digital/electronic); *Serial titles:* 48 (physical), 33,000 (digital/electronic); *Databases:* 133. Weekly public service hours: 67.

Student Life *Campus security:* 24-hour emergency response devices, student patrols, late-night transport/escort service.

Costs (2016–17) *Tuition:* area resident $1418 full-time; state resident $3962 full-time; nonresident $7777 full-time. Full-time tuition and fees vary according to course load, location, and program. Part-time tuition and fees vary according to course load, location, and program. *Required fees:* $74 full-time.

Applying *Options:* electronic application, early admission. *Required:* high school transcript.

Freshman Application Contact Ms. Robin Sandberg, Director of Enrollment Management, Northwest Vista College, 3535 North Ellison Drive, San Antonio, TX 78251. *Phone:* 210-486-4134. *Fax:* 210-486-9091. *E-mail:* rsandberg@alamo.edu. *Website:* http://www.alamo.edu/nvc/.

Odessa College
Odessa, Texas

- **State and locally supported** 2-year, founded 1946
- **Urban** 87-acre campus
- **Endowment** $844,464
- **Coed**

Undergraduates 1,609 full-time, 3,487 part-time. Students come from 26 states and territories; 2% are from out of state; 4% Black or African American, non-Hispanic/Latino; 59% Hispanic/Latino; 1% Asian, non-Hispanic/Latino; 0.1% Native Hawaiian or other Pacific Islander, non-Hispanic/Latino; 0.6% American Indian or Alaska Native, non-Hispanic/Latino; 0.7% Two or more races, non-Hispanic/Latino; 4% Race/ethnicity unknown; 1% international; 14% transferred in; 5% live on campus. *Retention:* 46% of full-time freshmen returned.

Faculty *Student/faculty ratio:* 18:1.

Academics *Calendar:* semesters. *Degree:* certificates and associate. *Special study options:* academic remediation for entering students, adult/continuing

education programs, advanced placement credit, cooperative education, distance learning, independent study, internships, part-time degree program, services for LD students, summer session for credit.

Library Murry H. Fly Learning Resources Center plus 1 other. *Books:* 29,875 (physical), 179,657 (digital/electronic); *Databases:* 76.

Student Life *Campus security:* 24-hour emergency response devices and patrols, late-night transport/escort service, controlled dormitory access.

Athletics Member NJCAA.

Costs (2016–17) *Tuition:* area resident $2088 full-time; state resident $3144 full-time, $12 per credit hour part-time; nonresident $4512 full-time, $12 per credit hour part-time. *Required fees:* $720 full-time, $87 per credit hour part-time. *Room and board:* $4600. Room and board charges vary according to board plan and housing facility.

Financial Aid Of all full-time matriculated undergraduates who enrolled in 2015, 59 Federal Work-Study jobs (averaging $1527). 8 state and other part-time jobs (averaging $1904).

Applying *Options:* electronic application, early admission, deferred entrance.

Freshman Application Contact Ms. Tracy Avery, Director of Recruitment, Odessa College, 201 West University Avenue, Odessa, TX 79764. *Phone:* 432-335-6765. *Fax:* 432-335-6303. *E-mail:* tavery@odessa.edu. *Website:* http://www.odessa.edu/.

Palo Alto College
San Antonio, Texas

Freshman Application Contact Ms. Elizabeth Aguilar-Villarreal, Director of Enrollment Management, Palo Alto College, 1400 West Villaret Boulevard, San Antonio, TX 78224. *Phone:* 210-486-3713. *E-mail:* eaguilar-villarr@ alamo.edu. *Website:* http://www.alamo.edu/pac/.

Panola College
Carthage, Texas

- **State and locally supported** 2-year, founded 1947
- **Small-town** 35-acre campus
- **Endowment** $3.8 million
- **Coed,** 2,667 undergraduate students, 51% full-time, 69% women, 32% men

Undergraduates 1,372 full-time, 1,340 part-time. Students come from 19 states and territories; 12 other countries; 6% are from out of state; 22% Black or African American, non-Hispanic/Latino; 12% Hispanic/Latino; 0.7% Asian, non-Hispanic/Latino; 0.4% American Indian or Alaska Native, non-Hispanic/Latino; 0.4% Two or more races, non-Hispanic/Latino; 0.9% Race/ethnicity unknown; 2% international; 2% transferred in; 10% live on campus. *Retention:* 2% of full-time freshmen returned.

Freshmen *Admission:* 414 enrolled.

Faculty *Total:* 147, 47% full-time, 5% with terminal degrees. *Student/faculty ratio:* 19:1.

Majors Administrative assistant and secretarial science; agriculture; architecture; art; biology/biological sciences; business administration and management; business automation/technology/data entry; chemistry; clinical/medical laboratory technology; computer/information technology services administration related; computer science; construction engineering technology; criminology; dramatic/theater arts; education; electrician; English; farm and ranch management; foreign languages and literatures; forestry; general studies; geology/earth science; health information/medical records technology; health professions related; history; industrial technology; information science/studies; information technology; journalism; liberal arts and sciences and humanities related; management information systems; mathematics; medical/clinical assistant; middle school education; music; occupational therapist assistant; petroleum technology; physical education teaching and coaching; physics; pre-dentistry studies; pre-law studies; pre-pharmacy studies; pre-veterinary studies; psychology; registered nursing/registered nurse; sociology; speech communication and rhetoric; welding technology.

Academics *Calendar:* semesters. *Degree:* certificates and associate. *Special study options:* academic remediation for entering students, advanced placement credit, cooperative education, distance learning, English as a second language, part-time degree program, services for LD students, summer session for credit.

Library M. P. Baker Library. *Books:* 26,739 (physical), 462,289 (digital/electronic); *Serial titles:* 64 (physical), 14 (digital/electronic); *Databases:* 74. Weekly public service hours: 64; study areas open 24 hours, 5&-7 days a week; students can reserve study rooms.

Student Life *Housing Options:* coed, men-only, special housing for students with disabilities. Campus housing is university owned. *Activities and Organizations:* drama/theater group, student-run newspaper, choral group, marching band, History Club, SOTA (Student Occupational Therapy Assistant), NSLS (National Society of Leadership and Success, PTK (Phi

Theta Kappa), BSM (Baptist Student Ministry). *Campus security:* controlled dormitory access, 24-hour campus police department.

Athletics Member NJCAA. *Intercollegiate sports:* baseball M(s), basketball M(s)/W(s), equestrian sports M(s)/W(s), volleyball W(s). *Intramural sports:* basketball M/W, table tennis M/W, volleyball M/W, weight lifting M/W.

Costs (2016–17) *Tuition:* area resident $750 full-time, $60 per semester hour part-time; state resident $2250 full-time, $110 per semester hour part-time; nonresident $3240 full-time, $283 per semester hour part-time. Full-time tuition and fees vary according to course load and reciprocity agreements. Part-time tuition and fees vary according to course load and reciprocity agreements. *Required fees:* $1530 full-time, $51 per semester hour part-time. *Room and board:* $4840. Room and board charges vary according to housing facility. *Payment plan:* deferred payment. *Waivers:* employees or children of employees.

Applying *Required for some:* high school transcript. *Recommended:* high school transcript.

Freshman Application Contact Mr. Jeremy Dorman, Registrar/Director of Admissions, Panola College, 1109 West Panola Street, Carthage, TX 75633-2397. *Phone:* 903-693-2009. *Fax:* 903-693-2031.
E-mail: bsimpson@panola.edu.
Website: http://www.panola.edu/.

Paris Junior College
Paris, Texas

- **State and locally supported** 2-year, founded 1924
- **Rural** 54-acre campus with easy access to Dallas-Fort Worth
- **Endowment** $20.7 million
- **Coed**, 4,806 undergraduate students, 38% full-time, 59% women, 41% men

Undergraduates 1,831 full-time, 2,975 part-time. Students come from 26 states and territories; 3 other countries; 3% are from out of state; 10% Black or African American, non-Hispanic/Latino; 15% Hispanic/Latino; 1% Asian, non-Hispanic/Latino; 2% American Indian or Alaska Native, non-Hispanic/Latino; 1% Two or more races, non-Hispanic/Latino; 0.1% Race/ethnicity unknown; 0.5% international; 7% transferred in; 6% live on campus.

Freshmen *Admission:* 696 applied, 696 admitted, 895 enrolled.
Faculty *Total:* 266, 31% full-time. *Student/faculty ratio:* 22:1.
Majors Accounting; agricultural mechanization; agriculture; art; biological and physical sciences; biology/biological sciences; business administration and management; business automation/technology/data entry; business/commerce; business teacher education; chemistry; computer and information sciences; computer engineering technology; computer typography and composition equipment operation; cosmetology; criminal justice/safety; criminology; drafting and design technology; dramatic/theater arts; early childhood education; education; education (multiple levels); electrical, electronic and communications engineering technology; electromechanical technology; elementary education; emergency medical technology (EMT paramedic); engineering; English; foreign languages and literatures; general studies; health and physical education/fitness; health information/medical records technology; health services/allied health/health sciences; heating, air conditioning, ventilation and refrigeration maintenance technology; history; information science/studies; journalism; liberal arts and sciences/liberal studies; mathematics; medical insurance coding; metal and jewelry arts; music; nursing administration; physical sciences; physics; political science and government; pre-law studies; premedical studies; prenursing studies; pre-pharmacy studies; psychology; radiologic technology/science; registered nursing/registered nurse; rhetoric and composition; secondary education; social sciences; social work; sociology; surgical technology; system, networking, and LAN/WAN management; watchmaking and jewelrymaking; welding technology.

Academics *Calendar:* semesters. *Degree:* certificates, diplomas, and associate. *Special study options:* academic remediation for entering students, adult/continuing education programs, advanced placement credit, cooperative education, distance learning, double majors, part-time degree program, services for LD students, summer session for credit.

Library Mike Rheudasil Learning Center.

Student Life *Housing Options:* men-only, women-only. Campus housing is university owned. *Activities and Organizations:* drama/theater group, student-run newspaper, choral group, Student Government Organization, Blends Club (for all ethic groups). *Campus security:* 24-hour emergency response devices and patrols, late-night transport/escort service, controlled dormitory access.

Athletics Member NJCAA. *Intercollegiate sports:* baseball M(s), basketball M(s)/W(s), soccer M(s)/W(s), softball W(s). *Intramural sports:* basketball M, football M, table tennis M/W, tennis M/W.

Costs (2017–18) *Tuition:* area resident $1650 full-time, $55 per credit hour part-time; state resident $3150 full-time, $105 per credit hour part-time; nonresident $4650 full-time, $155 per credit hour part-time. Full-time tuition and fees vary according to class time, course level, course load, degree level,

location, program, and student level. Part-time tuition and fees vary according to class time, course level, course load, degree level, location, program, and student level. *Required fees:* $750 full-time, $25 per credit hour part-time. *Room and board:* $5000. Room and board charges vary according to board plan and housing facility. *Payment plan:* installment. *Waivers:* senior citizens and employees or children of employees.

Financial Aid Of all full-time matriculated undergraduates who enrolled in 2015, 57 Federal Work-Study jobs (averaging $3600). 8 state and other part-time jobs (averaging $3600).

Applying *Options:* electronic application, early admission. *Required:* high school transcript. *Application deadlines:* rolling (freshmen), rolling (out-of-state freshmen), rolling (transfers). *Notification:* continuous (freshmen), continuous (out-of-state freshmen), continuous (transfers).

Freshman Application Contact Paris Junior College, 2400 Clarksville Street, Paris, TX 75460-6298. *Phone:* 903-782-0211. *Toll-free phone:* 800-232-5804.
Website: http://www.parisjc.edu/.

Pima Medical Institute
Houston, Texas

Freshman Application Contact Mr. Christopher Luebke, Corporate Director of Admissions, Pima Medical Institute, 2160 South Power Road, Mesa, AZ 85209. *Phone:* 480-610-6063. *Toll-free phone:* 800-477-PIMA.
E-mail: cluebke@pmi.edu. *Website:* http://www.pmi.edu/.

Quest College
San Antonio, Texas

Admissions Office Contact Quest College, 5430 Fredericksburg Road, Suite 310, San Antonio, TX 78229. *Website:* http://www.questcollege.edu/.

Ranger College
Ranger, Texas

Freshman Application Contact Dr. Jim Davis, Dean of Students, Ranger College, 1100 College Circle, Ranger, TX 76470. *Phone:* 254-647-3234 Ext. 110. *Website:* http://www.rangercollege.edu/.

Remington College–Dallas Campus
Garland, Texas

Director of Admissions Ms. Shonda Wisenhunt, Remington College–Dallas Campus, 1800 Eastgate Drive, Garland, TX 75041. *Phone:* 972-686-7878. *Toll-free phone:* 800-323-8122. *Fax:* 972-686-5116.
E-mail: shonda.wisenhunt@remingtoncollege.edu.
Website: http://www.remingtoncollege.edu/.

Remington College–Fort Worth Campus
Fort Worth, Texas

Director of Admissions Marcia Kline, Director of Recruitment, Remington College–Fort Worth Campus, 300 East Loop 820, Fort Worth, TX 76112. *Phone:* 817-451-0017. *Toll-free phone:* 800-323-8122. *Fax:* 817-496-1257.
E-mail: marcia.kline@remingtoncollege.edu.
Website: http://www.remingtoncollege.edu/.

Remington College–Houston Southeast Campus
Webster, Texas

Director of Admissions Lori Minor, Director of Recruitment, Remington College–Houston Southeast Campus, 20985 Gulf Freeway, Webster, TX 77598. *Phone:* 281-554-1700. *Toll-free phone:* 800-323-8122. *Fax:* 281-554-1765. *E-mail:* lori.minor@remingtoncollege.edu.
Website: http://www.remingtoncollege.edu/.

Remington College–North Houston Campus
Houston, Texas

Director of Admissions Edmund Flores, Director of Recruitment, Remington College–North Houston Campus, 11310 Greens Crossing Boulevard, Suite 300, Houston, TX 77067. *Phone:* 281-885-4450. *Toll-free phone:* 800-323-8122. *Fax:* 281-875-9964. *E-mail:* edmund.flores@remingtoncollege.edu. *Website:* http://www.remingtoncollege.edu/.

Richland College
Dallas, Texas

Freshman Application Contact Ms. Carol McKinney, Department Assistant, Richland College, 12800 Abrams Road, Dallas, TX 75243-2199. *Phone:* 972-238-6100. *Website:* http://www.richlandcollege.edu/.

St. Philip's College
San Antonio, Texas

- **District-supported** 2-year, founded 1898, part of Alamo Community College District System
- **Urban** 68-acre campus with easy access to San Antonio
- **Coed,** 11,604 undergraduate students, 12% full-time, 57% women, 43% men

Undergraduates 1,403 full-time, 10,201 part-time. Students come from 10 other countries; 1% are from out of state; 9% Black or African American, non-Hispanic/Latino; 56% Hispanic/Latino; 2% Asian, non-Hispanic/Latino; 0.1% Native Hawaiian or other Pacific Islander, non-Hispanic/Latino; 0.2% American Indian or Alaska Native, non-Hispanic/Latino; 3% Two or more races, non-Hispanic/Latino; 1% Race/ethnicity unknown; 0.6% international; 4% transferred in.

Freshmen *Admission:* 968 enrolled.

Faculty *Total:* 395, 47% full-time, 6% with terminal degrees. *Student/faculty ratio:* 19:1.

Majors Accounting technology and bookkeeping; administrative assistant and secretarial science; aircraft powerplant technology; airframe mechanics and aircraft maintenance technology; American government and politics; art; autobody/collision and repair technology; automobile/automotive mechanics technology; baking and pastry arts; biology/biological sciences; biomedical technology; biotechnology; business administration and management; cardiovascular technology; chemistry; child development; clinical/medical laboratory technology; computer and information systems security; computer programming; computer science; computer technology/computer systems technology; construction engineering technology; criminal justice/safety; culinary arts; data entry/microcomputer applications; design and visual communications; diagnostic medical sonography and ultrasound technology; diesel mechanics technology; dramatic/theater arts; economics; education (multiple levels); electrician; engineering; English; fine/studio arts; foreign languages and literatures; health information/medical records technology; health services/allied health/health sciences; heating, ventilation, air conditioning and refrigeration engineering technology; history; hotel/motel administration; instrumentation technology; kinesiology and exercise science; liberal arts and sciences/liberal studies; machine tool technology; mathematics; mechanical engineering; music; occupational therapist assistant; physical therapy technology; pre-dentistry studies; premedical studies; prenursing studies; pre-pharmacy studies; psychology; radiologic technology/science; registered nursing/registered nurse; respiratory care therapy; restaurant, culinary, and catering management; rhetoric and composition; social work; sociology; surgical technology; system, networking, and LAN/WAN management; tourism and travel services management; welding technology.

Academics *Calendar:* semesters. *Degree:* certificates, diplomas, and associate. *Special study options:* academic remediation for entering students, adult/continuing education programs, advanced placement credit, cooperative education, distance learning, double majors, English as a second language, honors programs, independent study, internships, off-campus study, part-time degree program, services for LD students, study abroad, summer session for credit. *ROTC:* Army (c).

Library St. Philip's College Library plus 1 other. *Books:* 71,242 (physical), 54,973 (digital/electronic); *Serial titles:* 71 (physical), 131,596 (digital/electronic); *Databases:* 120. Weekly public service hours: 68.

Student Life *Housing:* college housing not available. *Activities and Organizations:* drama/theater group, choral group, Student Government, Future United Latino Leaders of Change, Collegiate 100. *Campus security:* 24-hour emergency response devices and patrols, late-night transport/escort service. *Student services:* health clinic.

Athletics *Intramural sports:* basketball M/W, cheerleading M/W, table tennis M/W, volleyball M/W, weight lifting M/W.

Costs (2017–18) *Tuition:* area resident $2580 full-time, $86 per credit hour part-time; state resident $6990 full-time, $233 per credit hour part-time; nonresident $13,590 full-time, $453 per credit hour part-time. Full-time tuition and fees vary according to course load and program. Part-time tuition and fees vary according to course load and program. *Required fees:* $80 full-time, $1 per credit hour part-time, $25 per term part-time. *Payment plan:* installment. *Waivers:* senior citizens and employees or children of employees.

Applying *Options:* electronic application, early admission. *Required:* high school transcript. *Application deadlines:* rolling (freshmen), rolling (transfers). *Notification:* continuous (freshmen), continuous (transfers).

Freshman Application Contact Ms. Angela Molina, Coordinator, Student Success, St. Philip's College, 1801 Martin Luther King Drive, San Antonio,

TX 78203-2098. *Phone:* 210-486-2403. *Fax:* 210-486-2103. *E-mail:* amolina@alamo.edu. *Website:* http://www.alamo.edu/spc/.

San Antonio College
San Antonio, Texas

Director of Admissions Mr. J. Martin Ortega, Director of Admissions and Records, San Antonio College, 1819 North Main Avenue, San Antonio, TX 78212-3941. *Phone:* 210-733-2582. *Toll-free phone:* 844-202-5266. *Website:* http://www.alamo.edu/sac/.

San Jacinto College District
Pasadena, Texas

- **State and locally supported** 2-year, founded 1961
- **Suburban** 445-acre campus with easy access to Houston
- **Endowment** $6.4 million
- **Coed,** 28,998 undergraduate students, 23% full-time, 56% women, 44% men

Undergraduates 6,598 full-time, 22,400 part-time. Students come from 44 states and territories; 76 other countries; 1% are from out of state; 9% Black or African American, non-Hispanic/Latino; 55% Hispanic/Latino; 5% Asian, non-Hispanic/Latino; 0.1% Native Hawaiian or other Pacific Islander, non-Hispanic/Latino; 0.2% American Indian or Alaska Native, non-Hispanic/Latino; 2% Two or more races, non-Hispanic/Latino; 1% Race/ethnicity unknown; 2% international; 6% transferred in. *Retention:* 60% of full-time freshmen returned.

Freshmen *Admission:* 12,939 applied, 6,869 admitted, 5,407 enrolled.

Faculty *Total:* 1,183, 41% full-time, 13% with terminal degrees. *Student/faculty ratio:* 20:1.

Majors Accounting; administrative assistant and secretarial science; agribusiness; agriculture; airline pilot and flight crew; art; autobody/collision and repair technology; automobile/automotive mechanics technology; baking and pastry arts; behavioral sciences; biology/biological sciences; business administration and management; business/commerce; cardiovascular technology; chemical process technology; chemical technology; chemistry; child development; clinical/medical laboratory technology; commercial and advertising art; computer and information sciences; construction engineering technology; cosmetology; cosmetology, barber/styling, and nail instruction; criminal justice/police science; culinary arts; dance; diagnostic medical sonography and ultrasound technology; diesel mechanics technology; digital communication and media/multimedia; drafting and design technology; dramatic/theater arts; electrical and power transmission installation; electrical, electronic and communications engineering technology; emergency medical technology (EMT paramedic); engineering; English; environmental science; fire science/firefighting; food service systems administration; foreign languages and literatures; general studies; geology/earth science; health and physical education/fitness; health information/medical records technology; heating, air conditioning, ventilation and refrigeration maintenance technology; Hispanic-American, Puerto Rican, and Mexican-American/Chicano studies; history; instrumentation technology; interior design; international business/trade/commerce; journalism; legal assistant/paralegal; management information systems; marine science/merchant marine officer; mathematics; medical/clinical assistant; music; occupational safety and health technology; occupational therapy; optometric technician; pharmacy technician; philosophy; physical sciences; physical therapy technology; physics; political science and government; psychology; radio and television broadcasting technology; radiologic technology/science; real estate; registered nursing/registered nurse; respiratory care therapy; restaurant, culinary, and catering management; rhetoric and composition; science teacher education; secondary education; social sciences; sociology; surgical technology; welding technology.

Academics *Calendar:* semesters. *Degree:* certificates, diplomas, and associate. *Special study options:* academic remediation for entering students, accelerated degree program, adult/continuing education programs, advanced placement credit, cooperative education, distance learning, double majors, English as a second language, honors programs, off-campus study, part-time degree program, services for LD students, student-designed majors, study abroad, summer session for credit. *ROTC:* Army (c), Air Force (c).

Library Lee Davis Library. Students can reserve study rooms.

Student Life *Housing:* college housing not available. *Activities and Organizations:* drama/theater group, student-run newspaper, choral group, Phi Theta Kappa honor society, Nurses Association, Student Government Association, ABG Radiography, Texas Student Education Association. *Campus security:* 24-hour emergency response devices and patrols, late-night transport/escort service.

Athletics Member NJCAA. *Intercollegiate sports:* baseball M(s), basketball M(s)/W(s), soccer M(s), softball W(s), volleyball W(s). *Intramural sports:*

basketball M/W, football M/W, soccer M/W, softball M/W, tennis M/W, ultimate Frisbee M/W, volleyball M/W, weight lifting M/W.

Costs (2016–17) *Tuition:* area resident $1500 full-time, $50 per credit hour part-time; state resident $2580 full-time, $95 per credit hour part-time; nonresident $4140 full-time, $160 per credit hour part-time. Full-time tuition and fees vary according to course load. Part-time tuition and fees vary according to course load. *Required fees:* $300 full-time. *Payment plan:* installment. *Waivers:* senior citizens.

Applying *Options:* electronic application, early admission. *Required:* high school transcript. *Required for some:* interview. *Recommended:* interview for nursing and EMT programs. *Application deadlines:* rolling (freshmen), rolling (transfers). *Notification:* continuous (freshmen), continuous (transfers).

Freshman Application Contact San Jacinto College District, 4624 Fairmont Parkway, Pasadena, TX 77504-3323. *Phone:* 281-998-6150.

Website: http://www.sanjac.edu/.

School of Automotive Machinists & Technology
Houston, Texas

Admissions Office Contact School of Automotive Machinists & Technology, 1911 Antoine Drive, Houston, TX 77055. *Website:* http://www.samtech.edu/.

South Plains College
Levelland, Texas

- **State and locally supported** 2-year, founded 1958
- **Small-town** 177-acre campus
- **Endowment** $3.0 million
- **Coed,** 9,053 undergraduate students, 51% full-time, 54% women, 46% men

Undergraduates 4,605 full-time, 4,448 part-time. Students come from 31 states and territories; 28 other countries; 2% are from out of state; 6% Black or African American, non-Hispanic/Latino; 45% Hispanic/Latino; 1% Asian, non-Hispanic/Latino; 0.1% Native Hawaiian or other Pacific Islander, non-Hispanic/Latino; 0.4% American Indian or Alaska Native, non-Hispanic/Latino; 0.9% international; 29% transferred in; 10% live on campus. *Retention:* 8% of full-time freshmen returned.

Freshmen *Admission:* 1,577 applied, 1,577 admitted, 1,577 enrolled.

Faculty *Total:* 454, 60% full-time. *Student/faculty ratio:* 20:1.

Majors Accounting; administrative assistant and secretarial science; advertising; agricultural economics; agriculture; agronomy and crop science; art; automobile/automotive mechanics technology; biological and physical sciences; biology/biological sciences; business administration and management; chemistry; child development; commercial and advertising art; computer engineering technology; computer programming; computer science; consumer merchandising/retailing management; cosmetology; criminal justice/law enforcement administration; criminal justice/police science; data processing and data processing technology; developmental and child psychology; dietetics; drafting and design technology; education; electrical, electronic and communications engineering technology; engineering; fashion merchandising; fire science/firefighting; health/health-care administration; health information/medical records administration; heating, air conditioning, ventilation and refrigeration maintenance technology; industrial radiologic technology; journalism; legal administrative assistant/secretary; liberal arts and sciences/liberal studies; licensed practical/vocational nurse training; machine tool technology; marketing/marketing management; mass communication/media; medical administrative assistant and medical secretary; mental health counseling; music; petroleum technology; physical education teaching and coaching; physical therapy; pre-engineering; real estate; recording arts technology; registered nursing/registered nurse; respiratory care therapy; social work; special products marketing; surgical technology; telecommunications technology; welding technology.

Academics *Calendar:* semesters. *Degree:* certificates and associate. *Special study options:* academic remediation for entering students, accelerated degree program, adult/continuing education programs, advanced placement credit, distance learning, double majors, internships, off-campus study, part-time degree program, services for LD students, study abroad, summer session for credit. *ROTC:* Army (c), Air Force (c).

Library South Plains College Library plus 1 other. Weekly public service hours: 57; students can reserve study rooms.

Student Life *Housing Options:* men-only, women-only. Campus housing is university owned. Freshman applicants given priority for college housing. *Activities and Organizations:* drama/theater group, student-run newspaper, radio and television station, choral group, Student Government, Phi Theta Kappa, Law Enforcement Association. *Campus security:* 24-hour emergency response devices and patrols, controlled dormitory access. *Student services:* health clinic, personal/psychological counseling.

Athletics Member NJCAA. *Intercollegiate sports:* basketball M(s)/W(s), cross-country running M(s)/W(s), track and field M(s)/W(s). *Intramural sports:* basketball M/W, cross-country running M/W, football M/W, golf M/W, racquetball M/W, table tennis M/W, tennis M/W.

Standardized Tests *Recommended:* SAT or ACT (for admission).

Financial Aid Of all full-time matriculated undergraduates who enrolled in 2015, 80 Federal Work-Study jobs (averaging $2000). 22 state and other part-time jobs (averaging $2000).

Applying *Options:* electronic application, early admission. *Required:* high school transcript, proof of meningitis vaccination. *Application deadlines:* rolling (freshmen), rolling (transfers). *Notification:* continuous (freshmen), continuous (transfers).

Freshman Application Contact Mrs. Andrea Rangel, Dean of Admissions and Records, South Plains College, 1401 College Avenue, Levelland, TX 78336. *Phone:* 806-894-9611 Ext. 2370. *Fax:* 806-897-3167.

E-mail: arangel@southplainscollege.edu.

Website: http://www.southplainscollege.edu/.

South Texas College
McAllen, Texas

Freshman Application Contact Mr. Matthew Hebbard, Director of Enrollment Services and Registrar, South Texas College, 3201 West Pecan, McAllen, TX 78501. *Phone:* 956-872-2147. *Toll-free phone:* 800-742-7822. *E-mail:* mshebbar@southtexascollege.edu.

Website: http://www.southtexascollege.edu/.

Southwest Texas Junior College
Uvalde, Texas

- **State and locally supported** 2-year, founded 1946
- **Small-town** 97-acre campus with easy access to San Antonio
- **Coed**

Undergraduates Students come from 2 states and territories; 6 other countries; 1% Black or African American, non-Hispanic/Latino; 84% Hispanic/Latino; 0.5% Asian, non-Hispanic/Latino; 1% American Indian or Alaska Native, non-Hispanic/Latino; 0.9% Race/ethnicity unknown; 0.1% international; 9% live on campus.

Faculty *Total:* 199, 57% full-time.

Majors Agricultural mechanization; automobile/automotive mechanics technology; avionics maintenance technology; biological and physical sciences; business administration and management; computer engineering technology; cosmetology; criminal justice/law enforcement administration; data processing and data processing technology; education; engineering; farm and ranch management; liberal arts and sciences/liberal studies; teacher assistant/aide.

Academics *Calendar:* semesters. *Degree:* certificates and associate. *Special study options:* academic remediation for entering students, adult/continuing education programs, advanced placement credit, English as a second language, external degree program, part-time degree program, summer session for credit.

Library Will C. Miller Memorial Library.

Student Life *Housing Options:* coed, women-only. Campus housing is university owned. *Activities and Organizations:* drama/theater group, student-run newspaper, Catholic Students Club, Business Administration Club. *Campus security:* 24-hour patrols, controlled dormitory access. *Student services:* health clinic, personal/psychological counseling.

Athletics *Intercollegiate sports:* basketball M/W, cross-country running M/W, equestrian sports M/W. *Intramural sports:* basketball M/W, equestrian sports M/W, football M, golf M/W, racquetball M/W, swimming and diving M/W, tennis M/W.

Costs (2016–17) *Tuition:* area resident $1368 full-time, $57 per semester hour part-time; state resident $2832 full-time, $57 per semester hour part-time; nonresident $3720 full-time, $57 per semester hour part-time. Part-time tuition and fees vary according to course load. *Required fees:* $748 full-time. *Room and board:* $4990; room only: $2400. Room and board charges vary according to board plan. *Payment plan:* installment. *Waivers:* employees or children of employees.

Financial Aid Of all full-time matriculated undergraduates who enrolled in 2015, 150 Federal Work-Study jobs (averaging $1250). 75 state and other part-time jobs (averaging $1250).

Applying *Options:* electronic application, early admission, deferred entrance. *Required:* high school transcript. *Application deadlines:* rolling (freshmen), rolling (transfers). *Notification:* continuous (freshmen), continuous (transfers).

Freshman Application Contact Southwest Texas Junior College, 2401 Garner Field Road, Uvalde, TX 78801-6297. *Phone:* 830-278-4401 Ext. 7276.

Website: http://www.swtjc.edu/.

Tarrant County College District
Fort Worth, Texas

- **County-supported** 2-year, founded 1967
- **Urban** 667-acre campus with easy access to Dallas-Fort Worth
- **Endowment** $5.8 million
- **Coed**, 51,688 undergraduate students, 30% full-time, 58% women, 42% men

Undergraduates 15,316 full-time, 36,372 part-time. Students come from 32 states and territories; 64 other countries; 18% Black or African American, non-Hispanic/Latino; 30% Hispanic/Latino; 6% Asian, non-Hispanic/Latino; 0.2% Native Hawaiian or other Pacific Islander, non-Hispanic/Latino; 0.4% American Indian or Alaska Native, non-Hispanic/Latino; 2% Two or more races, non-Hispanic/Latino; 1% Race/ethnicity unknown; 0.8% international; 4% transferred in.

Freshmen *Admission:* 8,054 applied, 8,054 admitted, 8,054 enrolled.

Faculty *Total:* 1,944, 35% full-time. *Student/faculty ratio:* 26:1.

Majors Accounting; administrative assistant and secretarial science; architectural engineering technology; automobile/automotive mechanics technology; avionics maintenance technology; business administration and management; clinical laboratory science/medical technology; clinical/medical laboratory technology; computer programming; computer science; construction engineering technology; consumer merchandising/retailing management; criminal justice/law enforcement administration; dental hygiene; developmental and child psychology; dietetics; drafting and design technology; educational/instructional technology; electrical, electronic and communications engineering technology; electromechanical technology; emergency medical technology (EMT paramedic); fashion merchandising; fire science/firefighting; food technology and processing; graphic and printing equipment operation/production; health information/medical records administration; heating, air conditioning, ventilation and refrigeration maintenance technology; horticultural science; industrial radiologic technology; legal assistant/paralegal; liberal arts and sciences/liberal studies; machine tool technology; marketing/marketing management; mechanical engineering/mechanical technology; mental health counseling; physical therapy; quality control technology; registered nursing/registered nurse; respiratory care therapy; sign language interpretation and translation; surgical technology; welding technology.

Academics *Calendar:* semesters. *Degree:* certificates and associate. *Special study options:* academic remediation for entering students, adult/continuing education programs, advanced placement credit, distance learning, English as a second language, honors programs, part-time degree program, services for LD students, summer session for credit. *ROTC:* Army (c), Air Force (c).

Library Main Library plus 5 others. *Books:* 161,173 (physical), 83,268 (digital/electronic); *Databases:* 139.

Student Life *Housing:* college housing not available. *Activities and Organizations:* drama/theater group, student-run newspaper, choral group. *Campus security:* 24-hour emergency response devices and patrols, late-night transport/escort service. *Student services:* health clinic, personal/psychological counseling.

Athletics *Intramural sports:* basketball M/W, football M/W, golf M, sailing M/W, table tennis M, tennis M/W, volleyball M/W.

Costs (2017–18) *Tuition:* area resident $1593 full-time, $59 per credit hour part-time; state resident $2862 full-time, $106 per credit hour part-time; nonresident $6885 full-time, $255 per credit hour part-time. Full-time tuition and fees vary according to course load and program. Part-time tuition and fees vary according to course load and program. *Payment plans:* installment, deferred payment. *Waivers:* senior citizens and employees or children of employees.

Financial Aid Of all full-time matriculated undergraduates who enrolled in 2015, 7,613 applied for aid, 6,970 were judged to have need. 539 Federal Work-Study jobs (averaging $1482). 97 state and other part-time jobs (averaging $3550). In 2015, 78 non-need-based awards were made. *Average need-based loan:* $1374. *Average need-based gift aid:* $6194. *Average non-need-based aid:* $1415.

Applying *Options:* electronic application. *Application deadlines:* rolling (freshmen), rolling (transfers).

Freshman Application Contact Ms. Nichole Mancone, District Director of Admissions and Records, Tarrant County College District, 300 Trinity Campus Circle, Fort Worth, TX 76102-6599. *Phone:* 817-515-1581.
E-mail: nichole.mancone@tccd.edu.
Website: http://www.tccd.edu/.

Temple College
Temple, Texas

Freshman Application Contact Ms. Toni Cuellar, Director of Admissions and Records, Temple College, 2600 South First Street, Temple, TX 76504.

Phone: 254-298-8303. *Toll-free phone:* 800-460-4636. *E-mail:* carey.rose@templejc.edu. *Website:* http://www.templejc.edu/.

Texarkana College
Texarkana, Texas

- **State and locally supported** 2-year, founded 1927
- **Urban** 105-acre campus
- **Coed**, 4,296 undergraduate students, 33% full-time, 61% women, 39% men

Undergraduates 1,426 full-time, 2,870 part-time. Students come from 8 states and territories; 2 other countries; 12% are from out of state; 20% Black or African American, non-Hispanic/Latino; 7% Hispanic/Latino; 1% Asian, non-Hispanic/Latino; 0.1% Native Hawaiian or other Pacific Islander, non-Hispanic/Latino; 0.6% American Indian or Alaska Native, non-Hispanic/Latino; 4% Two or more races, non-Hispanic/Latino; 2% Race/ethnicity unknown; 0.8% international; 1% live on campus.

Faculty *Total:* 191, 48% full-time. *Student/faculty ratio:* 21:1.

Majors Administrative assistant and secretarial science; agriculture; art; automobile/automotive mechanics technology; biology/biological sciences; business administration and management; business/commerce; chemistry; child-care and support services management; child development; computer and information sciences; cosmetology; criminal justice/law enforcement administration; criminal justice/safety; culinary arts; diesel mechanics technology; drafting and design technology; dramatic/theater arts; electrical, electronic and communications engineering technology; emergency medical technology (EMT paramedic); engineering; foreign languages and literatures; health aide; heating, air conditioning, ventilation and refrigeration maintenance technology; history; humanities; industrial mechanics and maintenance technology; journalism; liberal arts and sciences/liberal studies; licensed practical/vocational nurse training; marketing/marketing management; mathematics; music; pharmacy technician; physics; political science and government; registered nursing/registered nurse; social sciences; substance abuse/addiction counseling; welding technology.

Academics *Calendar:* semesters. *Degree:* certificates and associate. *Special study options:* academic remediation for entering students, adult/continuing education programs, advanced placement credit, cooperative education, distance learning, freshman honors college, honors programs, independent study, internships, part-time degree program, services for LD students, study abroad, summer session for credit.

Library Palmer Memorial Library.

Student Life *Housing Options:* coed. Campus housing is university owned. *Activities and Organizations:* drama/theater group, student-run newspaper, choral group, Black Student Association, Earth Club, Culinary Arts Club, Cultural Awareness Student Association, Cosmetology Club. *Campus security:* 24-hour patrols. *Student services:* personal/psychological counseling.

Athletics *Intramural sports:* basketball M/W, racquetball M/W, soccer M/W, tennis M/W, volleyball M/W.

Costs (2017–18) *Tuition:* area resident $1176 full-time, $49 per credit hour part-time; state resident $2448 full-time, $102 per credit hour part-time; nonresident $3648 full-time, $152 per credit hour part-time. Full-time tuition and fees vary according to program. Part-time tuition and fees vary according to program. *Required fees:* $840 full-time, $35 per credit hour part-time, $50 per term part-time. *Room and board:* $6150; room only: $2000. *Payment plan:* installment. *Waivers:* employees or children of employees.

Financial Aid Of all full-time matriculated undergraduates who enrolled in 2015, 30 Federal Work-Study jobs (averaging $3090).

Applying *Options:* electronic application, early admission, deferred entrance. *Required:* high school transcript. *Recommended:* interview for nursing program, meningitis vaccine. *Application deadlines:* rolling (freshmen), rolling (transfers).

Freshman Application Contact Mr. Lee Williams, Director of Admissions, Texarkana College, 2500 North Robison Road, Texarkana, TX 75599-0001. *Phone:* 903-823-3016. *Fax:* 903-823-3451.
E-mail: lee.williams@texarkanacollege.edu.
Website: http://www.texarkanacollege.edu/.

Texas Southmost College
Brownsville, Texas

Freshman Application Contact New Student Relations, Texas Southmost College, 80 Fort Brown, Brownsville, TX 78520-4991. *Phone:* 956-882-8860. *Toll-free phone:* 877-882-8721. *Fax:* 956-882-8959.
Website: http://www.utb.edu/.

Texas State Technical College
Waco, Texas

- **State-supported** 2-year, founded 1965
- **Suburban** 200-acre campus
- **Coed,** 10,689 undergraduate students, 44% full-time, 36% women, 64% men

Undergraduates 4,665 full-time, 6,024 part-time. 1% are from out of state; 7% Black or African American, non-Hispanic/Latino; 53% Hispanic/Latino; 0.7% Asian, non-Hispanic/Latino; 0.1% Native Hawaiian or other Pacific Islander, non-Hispanic/Latino; 0.3% American Indian or Alaska Native, non-Hispanic/Latino; 0.2% Two or more races, non-Hispanic/Latino; 3% Race/ethnicity unknown; 7% transferred in. *Retention:* 18% of full-time freshmen returned.

Freshmen *Admission:* 1,286 applied, 1,286 admitted, 1,597 enrolled.

Faculty *Total:* 283, 89% full-time, 3% with terminal degrees. *Student/faculty ratio:* 17:1.

Majors Aircraft powerplant technology; airframe mechanics and aircraft maintenance technology; airline pilot and flight crew; air traffic control; autobody/collision and repair technology; automobile/automotive mechanics technology; avionics maintenance technology; biomedical technology; chemical technology; computer and information systems security; computer programming; computer technology/computer systems technology; construction trades; culinary arts; diesel mechanics technology; drafting and design technology; educational/instructional technology; electrical, electronic and communications engineering technology; electromechanical technology; environmental engineering technology; game and interactive media design; graphic design; heating, ventilation, air conditioning and refrigeration engineering technology; instrumentation technology; laser and optical technology; manufacturing engineering technology; mechanical engineering/mechanical technology; network and system administration; nuclear/nuclear power technology; occupational safety and health technology; robotics technology; solar energy technology; surveying technology; system, networking, and LAN/WAN management; telecommunications technology; turf and turfgrass management; viticulture and enology; web page, digital/multimedia and information resources design.

Academics *Calendar:* trimesters. *Degree:* certificates and associate. *Special study options:* academic remediation for entering students, adult/continuing education programs, cooperative education, distance learning, internships, part-time degree program, services for LD students, summer session for credit.

Library Texas State Technical College-Waco Campus Library.

Student Life *Housing:* on-campus residence required for freshman year. *Options:* coed, men-only, women-only, special housing for students with disabilities. Campus housing is university owned. *Activities and Organizations:* Student Ambassador Association, SkillsUSA, Student Leadership Council, Phi Theta Kappa, Hispanic Student Association. *Campus security:* 24-hour emergency response devices and patrols, late-night transport/escort service, controlled dormitory access. *Student services:* health clinic, personal/psychological counseling, women's center.

Athletics *Intramural sports:* basketball M/W, football M, golf M/W, racquetball M/W, softball M/W, volleyball M/W, weight lifting M.

Standardized Tests *Required:* Texas Success Initiative assessment (for admission).

Costs (2016–17) *Tuition:* state resident $4665 full-time, $156 per credit hour part-time; nonresident $10,080 full-time, $322 per credit hour part-time. Full-time tuition and fees vary according to class time, course load, and program. Part-time tuition and fees vary according to class time, course load, and program. *Room and board:* $6620; room only: $3780. Room and board charges vary according to board plan, housing facility, and location. *Payment plan:* installment. *Waivers:* senior citizens and employees or children of employees.

Financial Aid Of all full-time matriculated undergraduates who enrolled in 2016, 4,274 applied for aid, 4,247 were judged to have need, 320 had their need fully met. 129 Federal Work-Study jobs (averaging $1480). 27 state and other part-time jobs (averaging $955). In 2016, 5 non-need-based awards were made. *Average percent of need met:* 32%. *Average financial aid package:* $2787. *Average need-based loan:* $1246. *Average need-based gift aid:* $2787. *Average non-need-based aid:* $250.

Applying *Options:* electronic application, early admission. *Required:* high school transcript. *Required for some:* interview. *Application deadlines:* rolling (freshmen), rolling (transfers). *Notification:* continuous (freshmen), continuous (transfers).

Freshman Application Contact Mrs. Paula Arredondo, Registrar/Director of Admission and Records, Texas State Technical College, 3801 Campus Drive, Waco, TX 76705. *Phone:* 254-867-3363. *Toll-free phone:* 800-792-8784 Ext. 2362. *E-mail:* mary.daniel@tstc.edu.

Website: http://www.tstc.edu/.

Trinity Valley Community College
Athens, Texas

- **State and locally supported** 2-year, founded 1946
- **Rural** 65-acre campus with easy access to Dallas-Fort Worth
- **Coed,** 7,120 undergraduate students, 32% full-time, 57% women, 43% men

Undergraduates 2,262 full-time, 4,858 part-time. Students come from 27 states and territories; 18 other countries; 4% are from out of state; 16% Black or African American, non-Hispanic/Latino; 7% Hispanic/Latino; 0.7% Asian, non-Hispanic/Latino; 0.1% Native Hawaiian or other Pacific Islander, non-Hispanic/Latino; 0.5% American Indian or Alaska Native, non-Hispanic/Latino; 15% Two or more races, non-Hispanic/Latino; 3% Race/ethnicity unknown; 0.1% international; 21% transferred in; 14% live on campus.

Freshmen *Admission:* 651 enrolled.

Faculty *Total:* 252, 65% full-time. *Student/faculty ratio:* 20:1.

Majors Accounting; agricultural teacher education; animal sciences; art; automobile/automotive mechanics technology; biology/biological sciences; business administration and management; business teacher education; chemistry; child development; commercial photography; computer science; corrections; cosmetology; criminal justice/law enforcement administration; criminal justice/police science; dance; data processing and data processing technology; developmental and child psychology; drafting and design technology; dramatic/theater arts; education; elementary education; emergency medical technology (EMT paramedic); English; farm and ranch management; fashion merchandising; finance; geology/earth science; heating, air conditioning, ventilation and refrigeration maintenance technology; history; horticultural science; insurance; journalism; kindergarten/preschool education; legal administrative assistant/secretary; liberal arts and sciences/liberal studies; licensed practical/vocational nurse training; marketing/marketing management; mathematics; music; physical education teaching and coaching; physical sciences; political science and government; pre-engineering; psychology; range science and management; real estate; registered nursing/registered nurse; religious studies; rhetoric and composition; sociology; Spanish; surgical technology; welding technology.

Academics *Calendar:* semesters. *Degree:* certificates, diplomas, and associate. *Special study options:* academic remediation for entering students, adult/continuing education programs, advanced placement credit, cooperative education, distance learning, double majors, English as a second language, honors programs, independent study, internships, part-time degree program, services for LD students, summer session for credit.

Library Ginger Murchison Learning Resource Center plus 3 others. *Books:* 47,319 (physical), 49,836 (digital/electronic); *Serial titles:* 124 (physical), 3 (digital/electronic); *Databases:* 68.

Student Life *Housing Options:* coed, men-only, women-only. Campus housing is university owned. *Activities and Organizations:* drama/theater group, student-run newspaper, choral group, marching band, Student Senate, Phi Theta Kappa, Delta Epsilon Chi. *Campus security:* 24-hour emergency response devices and patrols, controlled dormitory access. *Student services:* personal/psychological counseling.

Athletics Member NJCAA. *Intercollegiate sports:* basketball M(s)/W(s), cheerleading M(s)/W(s), football M(s), softball W(s), volleyball W(s). *Intramural sports:* baseball M/W, basketball M/W, football M, table tennis M/W, volleyball M/W.

Costs (2016–17) *Tuition:* area resident $1080 full-time, $36 per credit hour part-time; state resident $2940 full-time, $98 per credit hour part-time; nonresident $3540 full-time, $118 per credit hour part-time. Full-time tuition and fees vary according to course load. Part-time tuition and fees vary according to course load. *Required fees:* $1380 full-time, $46 per credit hour part-time. *Room and board:* $5650. Room and board charges vary according to board plan. *Payment plan:* installment. *Waivers:* employees or children of employees.

Financial Aid Of all full-time matriculated undergraduates who enrolled in 2014, 90 Federal Work-Study jobs (averaging $1176). 56 state and other part-time jobs (averaging $660).

Applying *Options:* electronic application, early admission. *Required:* high school transcript. *Application deadlines:* rolling (freshmen), rolling (transfers). *Notification:* continuous (freshmen), continuous (transfers).

Freshman Application Contact Dr. Colette Hilliard, Dean of Enrollment Management and Registrar, Trinity Valley Community College, 100 Cardinal Drive, Athens, TX 75751. *Phone:* 903-675-6209 Ext. 209.

Website: http://www.tvcc.edu/.

Tyler Junior College
Tyler, Texas

- **State and locally supported** primarily 2-year, founded 1926
- **Suburban** 137-acre campus
- **Endowment** $42.2 million
- **Coed,** 11,478 undergraduate students, 51% full-time, 58% women, 42% men

Undergraduates 5,904 full-time, 5,574 part-time. Students come from 27 states and territories; 31 other countries; 3% are from out of state; 20% Black or African American, non-Hispanic/Latino; 20% Hispanic/Latino; 1% Asian, non-Hispanic/Latino; 0.2% Native Hawaiian or other Pacific Islander, non-Hispanic/Latino; 0.5% American Indian or Alaska Native, non-Hispanic/Latino; 3% Two or more races, non-Hispanic/Latino; 1% Race/ethnicity unknown; 0.8% international; 5% transferred in; 11% live on campus. *Retention:* 54% of full-time freshmen returned.
Freshmen *Admission:* 10,778 applied, 10,778 admitted, 2,995 enrolled.
Faculty *Total:* 559, 56% full-time, 9% with terminal degrees. *Student/faculty ratio:* 20:1.
Majors Animation, interactive technology, video graphics and special effects; art; athletic training; automobile/automotive mechanics technology; biology/biological sciences; business administration and management; business/commerce; chemistry; child development; clinical/medical laboratory technology; computer science; computer systems networking and telecommunications; criminalistics and criminal science; criminal justice/safety; dance; dental hygiene; diagnostic medical sonography and ultrasound technology; drafting and design technology; dramatic/theater arts; economics; education (multiple levels); electromechanical technology; emergency medical technology (EMT paramedic); engineering; family and consumer sciences/human sciences; fire prevention and safety technology; foreign languages and literatures; forest/forest resources management; general studies; geology/earth science; graphic design; health and physical education/fitness; health information/medical records technology; heating, air conditioning, ventilation and refrigeration maintenance technology; history; industrial electronics technology; journalism; legal assistant/paralegal; literature; mathematics; medical administrative assistant and medical secretary; middle school education; music; natural sciences; occupational therapist assistant; physical education teaching and coaching; physical therapy technology; physics; political science and government; psychology; public administration; radio and television; radiologic technology/science; registered nursing/registered nurse; respiratory care therapy; secondary education; sign language interpretation and translation; social work; sociology; speech communication and rhetoric; substance abuse/addiction counseling; surgical technology; surveying technology; system, networking, and LAN/WAN management; veterinary/animal health technology; welding technology.
Academics *Calendar:* semesters. *Degrees:* certificates, diplomas, associate, and bachelor's. *Special study options:* academic remediation for entering students, accelerated degree program, adult/continuing education programs, advanced placement credit, distance learning, freshman honors college, honors programs, part-time degree program, services for LD students, study abroad, summer session for credit.
Library Vaughn Library and Learning Resource Center. *Books:* 85,418 (physical), 135,816 (digital/electronic); *Databases:* 100. Weekly public service hours: 74.
Student Life *Housing Options:* coed, men-only, women-only. Campus housing is university owned and is provided by a third party. *Activities and Organizations:* drama/theater group, student-run newspaper, choral group, marching band, Student Government, Religious Affiliation Clubs, Phi Theta Kappa, national sororities. *Campus security:* 24-hour emergency response devices and patrols, controlled dormitory access. *Student services:* health clinic, personal/psychological counseling.
Athletics Member NJCAA. *Intercollegiate sports:* baseball M, basketball M(s)/W(s), cheerleading W(s), football M(s), golf M/W, soccer M(s)/W(s), softball W(s), tennis M(s)/W(s), volleyball W(s). *Intramural sports:* basketball M/W, cheerleading W, racquetball M/W, volleyball M/W, weight lifting M/W.
Costs (2016–17) *Tuition:* area resident $900 full-time, $30 per credit hour part-time; state resident $2550 full-time, $85 per credit hour part-time; nonresident $3240 full-time, $108 per credit hour part-time. *Required fees:* $1538 full-time, $7 per credit hour part-time, $106 per term part-time. *Room and board:* $8320; room only: $5940. Room and board charges vary according to housing facility. *Payment plan:* installment. *Waivers:* senior citizens and employees or children of employees.
Financial Aid Of all full-time matriculated undergraduates who enrolled in 2015, 4,408 applied for aid, 3,832 were judged to have need, 59 had their need fully met. 41 Federal Work-Study jobs (averaging $1707). 33 state and other part-time jobs (averaging $1869). In 2015, 687 non-need-based awards were made. *Average percent of need met:* 59%. *Average financial aid package:* $6573. *Average need-based loan:* $3346. *Average need-based gift aid:* $4481.

Average non-need-based aid: $1061. *Average indebtedness upon graduation:* $14,743. *Financial aid deadline:* 6/1.
Applying *Options:* electronic application, early admission. *Required:* high school transcript. *Application deadlines:* rolling (freshmen), rolling (transfers). *Notification:* continuous (freshmen), continuous (transfers).
Freshman Application Contact Ms. Janna Chancey, Director of Enrollment Management, Tyler Junior College, PO Box 9020, Tyler, TX 75711-9020. *Phone:* 903-510-3325. *Toll-free phone:* 800-687-5680.
E-mail: jcha@tjc.edu.
Website: http://www.tjc.edu/.

Vernon College
Vernon, Texas

Director of Admissions Mr. Joe Hite, Dean of Admissions/Registrar, Vernon College, 4400 College Drive, Vernon, TX 76384-4092. *Phone:* 940-552-6291 Ext. 2204. *Website:* http://www.vernoncollege.edu/.

Vet Tech Institute of Houston
Houston, Texas

- **Proprietary** 2-year, founded 1958
- **Suburban** campus
- **Coed**
- 62% of applicants were admitted

Academics *Calendar:* semesters. *Degree:* associate. *Special study options:* accelerated degree program, internships.
Freshman Application Contact Admissions Office, Vet Tech Institute of Houston, 4669 Southwest Freeway, Suite 100, Houston, TX 77027.
Phone: 800-275-2736. *Toll-free phone:* 800-275-2736.
Website: http://houston.vettechinstitute.edu/.

Victoria College
Victoria, Texas

- **County-supported** 2-year, founded 1925
- **Rural** 80-acre campus
- **Coed,** 4,000 undergraduate students, 26% full-time, 66% women, 34% men

Undergraduates 1,053 full-time, 2,947 part-time. Students come from 5 states and territories; 0.1% are from out of state; 6% Black or African American, non-Hispanic/Latino; 48% Hispanic/Latino; 2% Asian, non-Hispanic/Latino; 0.1% Native Hawaiian or other Pacific Islander, non-Hispanic/Latino; 0.2% American Indian or Alaska Native, non-Hispanic/Latino; 1% Two or more races, non-Hispanic/Latino; 0.5% Race/ethnicity unknown; 6% transferred in.
Freshmen *Admission:* 765 applied, 765 admitted, 765 enrolled.
Faculty *Total:* 370, 24% full-time. *Student/faculty ratio:* 11:1.
Majors Administrative assistant and secretarial science; business administration and management; chemical technology; clinical/medical laboratory technology; criminal justice/police science; electrical, electronic and communications engineering technology; emergency medical technology (EMT paramedic); fire science/firefighting; general studies; industrial technology; machine tool technology; physical therapy technology; registered nursing/registered nurse; respiratory care therapy.
Academics *Calendar:* semesters. *Degree:* certificates and associate. *Special study options:* academic remediation for entering students, advanced placement credit, distance learning, English as a second language, off-campus study, part-time degree program, services for LD students, summer session for credit.
Library Victoria College/University of Houston-Victoria Library plus 1 other. *Books:* 166,027 (physical), 75,644 (digital/electronic); *Serial titles:* 133 (physical), 48,862 (digital/electronic); *Databases:* 124. Weekly public service hours: 76; students can reserve study rooms.
Student Life *Housing:* college housing not available. *Activities and Organizations:* choral group, Student Government Association. *Campus security:* 24-hour emergency response devices. *Student services:* personal/psychological counseling.
Athletics *Intercollegiate sports:* basketball M/W, volleyball W. *Intramural sports:* basketball M/W, sand volleyball M/W, soccer M/W, tennis M/W, volleyball M/W.
Costs (2017–18) *Tuition:* area resident $1380 full-time, $46 per credit hour part-time; state resident $2790 full-time, $93 per credit hour part-time; nonresident $3390 full-time, $113 per credit hour part-time. Full-time tuition and fees vary according to program. Part-time tuition and fees vary according to program. *Required fees:* $1260 full-time, $42 per credit hour part-time. *Payment plan:* installment. *Waivers:* employees or children of employees.

Applying *Options:* electronic application, early admission. *Required:* high school transcript. *Application deadlines:* rolling (freshmen), rolling (transfers).

Freshman Application Contact Edrel Stoneham, Registrar, Victoria College, 2200 E. Red River, Victoria, TX 77901. *Phone:* 361-573-3291 Ext. 6407. *Toll-free phone:* 877-843-4369. *Fax:* 361-582-2525.
E-mail: registrar@victoriacollege.edu.
Website: http://www.victoriacollege.edu/.

Virginia College in Austin
Austin, Texas

Admissions Office Contact Virginia College in Austin, 14200 North Interstate Highway 35, Austin, TX 78728. *Website:* http://www.vc.edu/.

Virginia College in Lubbock
Lubbock, Texas

Admissions Office Contact Virginia College in Lubbock, 5005 50th Street, Lubbock, TX 79414. *Website:* http://www.vc.edu/.

Vista College
El Paso, Texas

Director of Admissions Ms. Sarah Hernandez, Registrar, Vista College, 6101 Montana Avenue, El Paso, TX 79925. *Phone:* 915-779-8031. *Toll-free phone:* 866-442-4197. *Website:* http://www.vistacollege.edu/.

Vista College–Online Campus
Richardson, Texas

Admissions Office Contact Vista College–Online Campus, 300 North Coit Road, Suite 300, Richardson, TX 75080.
Website: http://www.vistacollege.edu/.

Wade College
Dallas, Texas

Freshman Application Contact Wade College, INFOMart, 1950 Stemmons Freeway, Suite 4080, LB 562, Dallas, TX 75207. *Phone:* 214-637-3530. *Toll-free phone:* 800-624-4850. *Website:* http://www.wadecollege.edu/.

Weatherford College
Weatherford, Texas

- **State and locally supported** 2-year, founded 1869
- **Small-town** 94-acre campus with easy access to Dallas-Fort Worth
- **Coed,** 5,637 undergraduate students

Undergraduates 7% live on campus.
Faculty *Total:* 220, 43% full-time. *Student/faculty ratio:* 22:1.
Majors Administrative assistant and secretarial science; biological and physical sciences; business administration and management; computer graphics; computer programming; cosmetology; criminal justice/law enforcement administration; diagnostic medical sonography and ultrasound technology; emergency medical technology (EMT paramedic); fire science/firefighting; information science/studies; liberal arts and sciences/liberal studies; occupational therapist assistant; pharmacy technician; physical therapy technology; radiologic technology/science; registered nursing/registered nurse; respiratory care therapy.
Academics *Calendar:* semesters. *Degree:* certificates, diplomas, and associate. *Special study options:* academic remediation for entering students, adult/continuing education programs, cooperative education, distance learning, freshman honors college, honors programs, internships, part-time degree program, services for LD students, student-designed majors, summer session for credit. *ROTC:* Army (c), Air Force (c).
Library Weatherford College Library. *Books:* 50,220 (physical). Students can reserve study rooms.
Student Life *Housing Options:* coed. Campus housing is university owned. *Activities and Organizations:* drama/theater group, choral group, Black Awareness Student Organization, Criminal Justice Club, Phi Theta Kappa. *Campus security:* 24-hour emergency response devices and patrols, late-night transport/escort service. *Student services:* personal/psychological counseling.
Athletics Member NJCAA. *Intercollegiate sports:* baseball M(s), basketball M(s)/W(s), cheerleading M(s)/W(s), equestrian sports M(s)/W(s), softball W(s).
Costs (2016–17) *Tuition:* area resident $1920 full-time, $80 per semester hour part-time; state resident $2976 full-time, $124 per semester hour part-time;

nonresident $4224 full-time, $176 per semester hour part-time. Full-time tuition and fees vary according to course load and program. Part-time tuition and fees vary according to course load and program. *Room and board:* $7450; room only: $4980. Room and board charges vary according to board plan. *Payment plan:* installment. *Waivers:* senior citizens and employees or children of employees.
Applying *Options:* electronic application, early admission. *Recommended:* high school transcript. *Application deadline:* rolling (transfers). *Notification:* continuous (freshmen), continuous (transfers).
Freshman Application Contact Mr. Ralph Willingham, Director of Admissions, Weatherford College, 225 College Park Drive, Weatherford, TX 76086-5699. *Phone:* 817-598-6248. *Toll-free phone:* 800-287-5471. *Fax:* 817-598-6205. *E-mail:* rwillingham@wc.edu.
Website: http://www.wc.edu/.

Western Technical College
El Paso, Texas

Freshman Application Contact Ms. Laura Pena, Director of Admissions, Western Technical College, 9451 Diana Drive, El Paso, TX 79930-2610. *Phone:* 915-566-9621. *Toll-free phone:* 800-201-9232. *E-mail:* lpena@westerntech.edu. *Website:* http://www.westerntech.edu/.

Western Technical College
El Paso, Texas

Freshman Application Contact Mr. Bill Terrell, Chief Admissions Officer, Western Technical College, 9624 Plaza Circle, El Paso, TX 79927. *Phone:* 915-532-3737 Ext. 117. *Fax:* 915-532-6946.
E-mail: bterrell@wtc-ep.edu. *Website:* http://www.westerntech.edu/.

Western Texas College
Snyder, Texas

- **State and locally supported** 2-year, founded 1969
- **Small-town** 165-acre campus
- **Coed**

Undergraduates 543 full-time, 1,582 part-time. Students come from 34 states and territories; 17 other countries; 6% are from out of state; 15% Black or African American, non-Hispanic/Latino; 35% Hispanic/Latino; 0.2% Asian, non-Hispanic/Latino; 0.6% Native Hawaiian or other Pacific Islander, non-Hispanic/Latino; 0.2% American Indian or Alaska Native, non-Hispanic/Latino; 2% Two or more races, non-Hispanic/Latino; 6% international; 3% transferred in; 100% live on campus.
Faculty *Student/faculty ratio:* 19:1.
Academics *Calendar:* semesters. *Degree:* certificates and associate. *Special study options:* academic remediation for entering students, adult/continuing education programs, advanced placement credit, distance learning, independent study, internships, part-time degree program, services for LD students, student-designed majors, summer session for credit.
Library Western Texas College Resource Center. *Books:* 30,884 (physical), 28,077 (digital/electronic); *Serial titles:* 95 (physical); *Databases:* 23. Weekly public service hours: 56.
Student Life *Campus security:* 24-hour emergency response devices and patrols, late-night transport/escort service.
Athletics Member NCAA, NJCAA. All NCAA Division I.
Costs (2016–17) *Tuition:* area resident $2370 full-time, $52 per credit hour part-time; state resident $3780 full-time, $93 per credit hour part-time; nonresident $4890 full-time, $130 per credit hour part-time. Full-time tuition and fees vary according to course load, location, and program. Part-time tuition and fees vary according to course load, location, and program. *Required fees:* $450 full-time, $30 per credit hour part-time. *Room and board:* $2550. Room and board charges vary according to housing facility.
Financial Aid Of all full-time matriculated undergraduates who enrolled in 2015, 19 Federal Work-Study jobs (averaging $1600).
Applying *Options:* electronic application, early admission, deferred entrance. *Required:* high school transcript.
Freshman Application Contact Western Texas College, 6200 College Avenue, Snyder, TX 79549. *Phone:* 325-573-8511. *Toll-free phone:* 888-GO-TO-WTC. *Website:* http://www.wtc.edu/.

Wharton County Junior College
Wharton, Texas

Freshman Application Contact Mr. Albert Barnes, Dean of Admissions and Registration, Wharton County Junior College, 911 Boling Highway, Wharton, TX 77488-3298. *Phone:* 979-532-6381. *E-mail:* albertb@wcjc.edu. *Website:* http://www.wcjc.edu/.

UTAH

AmeriTech College
Draper, Utah
- **Proprietary** primarily 2-year
- **Coed**

Academics *Degrees:* associate and bachelor's.
Admissions Office Contact AmeriTech College, 12257 South Business Park Drive, Suite 108, Draper, UT 84020-6545.
Website: http://www.ameritech.edu/.

Fortis College
Salt Lake City, Utah

Admissions Office Contact Fortis College, 3949 South 700 East, Suite 150, Salt Lake City, UT 84107. *Toll-free phone:* 855-4-FORTIS.
Website: http://www.fortis.edu/.

LDS Business College
Salt Lake City, Utah
- **Independent** 2-year, founded 1886, affiliated with The Church of Jesus Christ of Latter-day Saints, part of Church Education System (CES) of The Church of Jesus Christ of Latter-day Saints
- **Urban** 2-acre campus with easy access to Salt Lake City
- **Endowment** $8.5 million
- **Coed**

Undergraduates 1,589 full-time, 602 part-time. Students come from 60 other countries; 45% are from out of state; 0.2% Black or African American, non-Hispanic/Latino; 11% Hispanic/Latino; 1% Asian, non-Hispanic/Latino; 2% Native Hawaiian or other Pacific Islander, non-Hispanic/Latino; 0.5% American Indian or Alaska Native, non-Hispanic/Latino; 4% Two or more races, non-Hispanic/Latino; 3% Race/ethnicity unknown; 13% international; 34% transferred in. *Retention:* 48% of full-time freshmen returned.
Faculty *Student/faculty ratio:* 25:1.
Academics *Calendar:* semesters. *Degree:* certificates and associate. *Special study options:* academic remediation for entering students, adult/continuing education programs, advanced placement credit, distance learning, English as a second language, internships, part-time degree program, services for LD students, summer session for credit. *ROTC:* Army (c), Air Force (c).
Library LDS Business College Library.
Student Life *Campus security:* 24-hour emergency response devices and patrols.
Standardized Tests *Recommended:* SAT or ACT (for admission).
Applying *Options:* electronic application, deferred entrance. *Application fee:* $35. *Required:* essay or personal statement, high school transcript, interview.
Freshman Application Contact Miss Dawn Fellows, Assistant Director of Admissions, LDS Business College, 95 North 300 West, Salt Lake City, UT 84101-3500. *Phone:* 801-524-8146. *Toll-free phone:* 800-999-5767. *Fax:* 801-524-1900. *E-mail:* dfellows@ldsbc.edu. *Website:* http://www.ldsbc.edu/.

Nightingale College
Ogden, Utah
- **Proprietary** primarily 2-year
- **Suburban** campus with easy access to Salt Lake City
- **Coed**
- 75% of applicants were admitted

Undergraduates *Retention:* 95% of full-time freshmen returned.
Academics *Calendar:* semesters. *Degrees:* diplomas, associate, and bachelor's. *Special study options:* part-time degree program.
Standardized Tests *Required:* Nightingale Entrance Exam (for admission).
Costs (2016–17) *Tuition:* $20,040 full-time, $835 per credit hour part-time. Full-time tuition and fees vary according to class time, course load, degree level, location, and program. Part-time tuition and fees vary according to class time, course load, degree level, location, and program. *Required fees:* $2200 full-time.
Applying *Options:* electronic application, early admission. *Application fee:* $100. *Required:* essay or personal statement, high school transcript, interview.
Freshman Application Contact Nightingale College, 4155 Harrison Boulevard #100, Ogden, UT 84403. *Website:* http://www.nightingale.edu/.

Provo College
Provo, Utah

Director of Admissions Mr. Gordon Peters, College Director, Provo College, 1450 West 820 North, Provo, UT 84601. *Phone:* 801-375-1861. *Toll-free phone:* 877-777-5886. *Fax:* 801-375-9728.
E-mail: gordonp@provocollege.org. *Website:* http://www.provocollege.edu/.

Salt Lake Community College
Salt Lake City, Utah
- **State-supported** 2-year, founded 1948, part of Utah System of Higher Education
- **Urban** 114-acre campus with easy access to Salt Lake City
- **Endowment** $833,883
- **Coed,** 29,901 undergraduate students, 26% full-time, 51% women, 49% men

Undergraduates 7,762 full-time, 22,139 part-time. 2% Black or African American, non-Hispanic/Latino; 17% Hispanic/Latino; 4% Asian, non-Hispanic/Latino; 1% Native Hawaiian or other Pacific Islander, non-Hispanic/Latino; 0.8% American Indian or Alaska Native, non-Hispanic/Latino; 3% Two or more races, non-Hispanic/Latino; 2% Race/ethnicity unknown; 1% international; 7% transferred in.
Freshmen *Admission:* 4,303 applied, 4,303 admitted, 4,303 enrolled.
Faculty *Total:* 1,577, 21% full-time. *Student/faculty ratio:* 18:1.
Majors Accounting technology and bookkeeping; airline pilot and flight crew; architectural engineering technology; autobody/collision and repair technology; avionics maintenance technology; biology/biological sciences; biology/biotechnology laboratory technician; building/construction finishing, management, and inspection related; business administration and management; chemistry; clinical/medical laboratory technology; computer and information sciences; computer science; criminal justice/law enforcement administration; culinary arts; dental hygiene; design and visual communications; diesel mechanics technology; drafting and design technology; economics; electrical, electronic and communications engineering technology; engineering; engineering technology; English; entrepreneurship; environmental engineering technology; finance; general studies; geology/earth science; graphic design; health professions related; heating, air conditioning, ventilation and refrigeration maintenance technology; history; human development and family studies; humanities; industrial radiologic technology; information science/studies; information technology; instrumentation technology; international/global studies; international relations and affairs; kinesiology and exercise science; legal assistant/paralegal; marketing/marketing management; mass communication/media; medical/clinical assistant; medical radiologic technology; music; occupational therapist assistant; photographic and film/video technology; physical sciences; physical therapy technology; physics; political science and government; psychology; public health related; quality control technology; radio and television broadcasting technology; registered nursing/registered nurse; sign language interpretation and translation; social work; sociology; speech communication and rhetoric; sport and fitness administration/management; surveying technology; teacher assistant/aide; telecommunications technology; welding technology.
Academics *Calendar:* semesters. *Degree:* certificates, diplomas, and associate. *Special study options:* academic remediation for entering students, advanced placement credit, cooperative education, distance learning, double majors, English as a second language, internships, part-time degree program, services for LD students, student-designed majors, study abroad, summer session for credit. *ROTC:* Army (c), Air Force (c).
Library Markosian Library plus 2 others.
Student Life *Housing:* college housing not available. *Activities and Organizations:* drama/theater group, student-run newspaper, radio and television station, choral group, marching band. *Campus security:* 24-hour emergency response devices and patrols, late-night transport/escort service. *Student services:* health clinic, personal/psychological counseling.
Athletics Member NJCAA. *Intercollegiate sports:* baseball M(s), basketball M(s)/W(s), cheerleading M(s)/W(s), soccer M(c)/W(c), softball W(s), volleyball W(s).
Costs (2016–17) *Tuition:* state resident $134 per credit hour part-time; nonresident $469 per credit hour part-time. *Payment plan:* installment. *Waivers:* senior citizens and employees or children of employees.
Applying *Options:* electronic application, early admission. *Application fee:* $40. *Application deadlines:* rolling (freshmen), rolling (transfers).
Freshman Application Contact Salt Lake Community College, PO Box 30808, Salt Lake City, UT 84130-0808. *Phone:* 801-957-4136.
Website: http://www.slcc.edu/.

Snow College
Ephraim, Utah

Freshman Application Contact Ms. Lorie Parry, Admissions Advisor, Snow College, 150 East College Avenue, Ephraim, UT 84627. *Phone:* 435-283-7144. *Fax:* 435-283-7157. *E-mail:* snowcollege@snow.edu. *Website:* http://www.snow.edu/.

VERMONT

Community College of Vermont
Montpelier, Vermont

- **State-supported** 2-year, founded 1973, part of Vermont State Colleges System
- **Rural** campus
- **Coed,** 6,385 undergraduate students, 14% full-time, 67% women, 33% men

Undergraduates 862 full-time, 5,489 part-time. Students come from 25 states and territories; 4% are from out of state. *Retention:* 57% of full-time freshmen returned.
Freshmen *Admission:* 1,695 applied, 1,008 admitted.
Faculty *Total:* 735, 11% with terminal degrees. *Student/faculty ratio:* 13:1.
Majors Accounting; administrative assistant and secretarial science; art; business administration and management; child development; community organization and advocacy; computer and information sciences; computer science; computer systems networking and telecommunications; criminal justice/law enforcement administration; data entry/microcomputer applications; developmental and child psychology; digital communication and media/multimedia; early childhood education; education; environmental science; graphic design; hospitality administration; human services; industrial technology; information technology; liberal arts and sciences/liberal studies; medical/clinical assistant; science technologies related; social sciences; teacher assistant/aide.
Academics *Calendar:* semesters. *Degree:* certificates and associate. *Special study options:* academic remediation for entering students, accelerated degree program, adult/continuing education programs, advanced placement credit, cooperative education, distance learning, double majors, English as a second language, external degree program, independent study, internships, part-time degree program, services for LD students, student-designed majors, study abroad, summer session for credit.
Library Hartness Library plus 1 other.
Student Life *Housing:* college housing not available.
Standardized Tests *Required for some:* ACCUPLACER or SAT/ACT. *Recommended:* SAT or ACT (for admission).
Costs (2017–18) *Tuition:* state resident $7830 full-time, $261 per credit hour part-time; nonresident $15,660 full-time, $522 per credit hour part-time. *Required fees:* $150 full-time, $75 per term part-time. *Payment plan:* installment. *Waivers:* senior citizens and employees or children of employees.
Applying *Options:* electronic application. *Application deadlines:* rolling (freshmen), rolling (out-of-state freshmen), rolling (transfers). *Notification:* continuous (freshmen), continuous (out-of-state freshmen), continuous (transfers).
Freshman Application Contact Community College of Vermont, 660 Elm Street, Montpelier, VT 05602. *Phone:* 802-654-0505. *Toll-free phone:* 800-CCV-6686.
Website: http://www.ccv.edu/.

Landmark College
Putney, Vermont

Freshman Application Contact Admissions Main Desk, Landmark College, Admissions Office, River Road South, Putney, VT 05346. *Phone:* 802-387-6718. *Fax:* 802-387-6868. *E-mail:* admissions@landmark.edu. *Website:* http://www.landmark.edu/.

New England Culinary Institute
Montpelier, Vermont

- **Proprietary** primarily 2-year, founded 1980
- **Small-town** campus
- **Coed,** 300 undergraduate students, 86% full-time, 45% women, 55% men

Undergraduates 257 full-time, 43 part-time. Students come from 39 states and territories; 6 other countries; 80% are from out of state; 8% Black or African American, non-Hispanic/Latino; 5% Hispanic/Latino; 4% Asian, non-Hispanic/Latino; 1% American Indian or Alaska Native, non-Hispanic/Latino; 1% Two or more races, non-Hispanic/Latino; 13% Race/ethnicity unknown; 6% transferred in; 80% live on campus. *Retention:* 86% of full-time freshmen returned.
Freshmen *Admission:* 52 enrolled.
Faculty *Total:* 27, 59% full-time. *Student/faculty ratio:* 15:1.
Majors Baking and pastry arts; culinary arts; restaurant, culinary, and catering management.
Academics *Calendar:* quarters. *Degrees:* certificates, associate, and bachelor's. *Special study options:* academic remediation for entering students, accelerated degree program, advanced placement credit, cooperative education, distance learning, honors programs, internships, services for LD students.
Library New England Culinary Institute Library.
Student Life *Housing:* on-campus residence required for freshman year. *Options:* coed, men-only, women-only. Campus housing is leased by the school. Freshman applicants given priority for college housing. *Activities and Organizations:* American Culinary Federation, Slow Food, Student Council, Special Guest Lecture Series, Student Ambassadors (leadership program). *Campus security:* 24-hour emergency response devices, student patrols.
Standardized Tests *Recommended:* SAT or ACT (for admission).
Costs (2016–17) *Comprehensive fee:* $31,165 includes full-time tuition ($20,625), mandatory fees ($2540), and room and board ($8000). Full-time tuition and fees vary according to course load, degree level, program, reciprocity agreements, and student level. Part-time tuition and fees vary according to course load, degree level, program, reciprocity agreements, and student level. *Payment plan:* installment. *Waivers:* employees or children of employees.
Financial Aid Of all full-time matriculated undergraduates who enrolled in 2015, 320 Federal Work-Study jobs (averaging $1000).
Applying *Options:* electronic application, early admission, deferred entrance. *Application fee:* $35. *Required:* essay or personal statement, high school transcript, 1 letter of recommendation, interview. *Recommended:* culinary experience. *Application deadline:* rolling (freshmen).
Freshman Application Contact Adonica Williams, New England Culinary Institute, 7 School Street, Montpelier, VT 05602-3115. *Phone:* 802-225-3210. *Toll-free phone:* 877-223-6324. *Fax:* 802-225-3280.
E-mail: admissions@neci.edu.
Website: http://www.neci.edu/.

VIRGINIA

Advanced Technology Institute
Virginia Beach, Virginia

Freshman Application Contact Admissions Office, Advanced Technology Institute, 5700 Southern Boulevard, Suite 100, Virginia Beach, VA 23462. *Phone:* 757-490-1241. *Toll-free phone:* 888-468-1093. *Website:* http://www.auto.edu/.

American National University
Charlottesville, Virginia

Director of Admissions Kimberly Moore, Campus Director, American National University, 3926 Seminole Trail, Charlottesville, VA 22911. *Phone:* 434-295-0136. *Toll-free phone:* 888-9-JOBREADY. *Fax:* 434-979-8061. *Website:* http://www.an.edu/.

American National University
Danville, Virginia

Freshman Application Contact Admissions Office, American National University, 336 Old Riverside Drive, Danville, VA 24541. *Phone:* 434-793-6822. *Toll-free phone:* 888-9-JOBREADY. *Website:* http://www.an.edu/.

American National University
Harrisonburg, Virginia

Director of Admissions Jack Evey, Campus Director, American National University, 1515 Country Club Road, Harrisonburg, VA 22802. *Phone:* 540-432-0943. *Toll-free phone:* 888-9-JOBREADY. *Website:* http://www.an.edu/.

American National University
Lynchburg, Virginia

Freshman Application Contact Admissions Representative, American National University, 104 Candlewood Court, Lynchburg, VA 24502. *Phone:* 804-239-3500. *Toll-free phone:* 888-9-JOBREADY. *Website:* http://www.an.edu/.

American National University
Martinsville, Virginia

Director of Admissions Mr. John Scott, Campus Director, American National University, 905 North Memorial Boulevard, Martinsville, VA 24112. *Phone:* 276-632-5621. *Toll-free phone:* 888-9-JOBREADY. *Website:* http://www.an.edu/.

Blue Ridge Community College
Weyers Cave, Virginia

Freshman Application Contact Blue Ridge Community College, PO Box 80, Weyers Cave, VA 24486-0080. *Phone:* 540-453-2217. *Toll-free phone:* 888-750-2722. *Website:* http://www.brcc.edu/.

Bryant & Stratton College–Richmond Campus
Richmond, Virginia

Freshman Application Contact Mr. David K. Mayle, Director of Admissions, Bryant & Stratton College–Richmond Campus, 8141 Hull Street Road, Richmond, VA 23235-6411. *Phone:* 804-745-2444. *Fax:* 804-745-6884. *E-mail:* tlawson@bryanstratton.edu. *Website:* http://www.bryantstratton.edu/.

Bryant & Stratton College–Virginia Beach Campus
Virginia Beach, Virginia

Freshman Application Contact Bryant & Stratton College–Virginia Beach Campus, 301 Centre Pointe Drive, Virginia Beach, VA 23462. *Phone:* 757-499-7900 Ext. 173. *Website:* http://www.bryantstratton.edu/.

Centra College of Nursing
Lynchburg, Virginia

Admissions Office Contact Centra College of Nursing, 905 Lakeside Drive, Suite A, Lynchburg, VA 24501. *Website:* http://www.centrahealth.com/college-of-nursing.

Central Virginia Community College
Lynchburg, Virginia

- **State-supported** 2-year, founded 1966, part of Virginia Community College System
- **Suburban** 104-acre campus
- **Coed,** 4,125 undergraduate students, 33% full-time, 55% women, 45% men

Undergraduates 1,357 full-time, 2,768 part-time. Students come from 12 states and territories; 1% are from out of state; 17% Black or African American, non-Hispanic/Latino; 3% Hispanic/Latino; 2% Asian, non-Hispanic/Latino; 0.1% Native Hawaiian or other Pacific Islander, non-Hispanic/Latino; 0.3% American Indian or Alaska Native, non-Hispanic/Latino; 4% Two or more races, non-Hispanic/Latino; 0.6% Race/ethnicity unknown.
Freshmen *Admission:* 1,062 applied, 1,062 admitted.
Faculty *Total:* 302, 21% full-time. *Student/faculty ratio:* 18:1.
Majors Business administration and management; business/commerce; business operations support and secretarial services related; computer and information sciences; criminal justice/law enforcement administration; culinary arts; design and visual communications; education; emergency medical technology (EMT paramedic); engineering; engineering technology; industrial technology; liberal arts and sciences/liberal studies; management science; medical/clinical assistant; radiologic technology/science; respiratory care therapy; science technologies.
Academics *Calendar:* semesters. *Degree:* certificates, diplomas, and associate. *Special study options:* academic remediation for entering students, advanced placement credit, cooperative education, distance learning, independent study, internships, part-time degree program, services for LD students, summer session for credit.
Library Bedford Learning Resources Center.
Student Life *Housing:* college housing not available. *Activities and Organizations:* drama/theater group. *Campus security:* 24-hour emergency response devices.
Costs (2016–17) *Tuition:* state resident $4598 full-time, $153 per credit hour part-time; nonresident $10,496 full-time, $350 per credit hour part-time. *Payment plan:* installment. *Waivers:* senior citizens.
Financial Aid Of all full-time matriculated undergraduates who enrolled in 2015, 65 Federal Work-Study jobs (averaging $2700).
Applying *Options:* electronic application, early admission, deferred entrance. *Application deadlines:* rolling (freshmen), rolling (transfers). *Notification:* continuous (freshmen), continuous (transfers).
Freshman Application Contact Admissions Office, Central Virginia Community College, 3506 Wards Road, Lynchburg, VA 24502. *Phone:* 434-832-7633. *Toll-free phone:* 800-562-3060. *Fax:* 434-832-7793. *Website:* http://www.cvcc.vccs.edu/.

Centura College
Chesapeake, Virginia

Director of Admissions Director of Admissions, Centura College, 932 Ventures Way, Chesapeake, VA 23320. *Phone:* 757-549-2121. *Toll-free phone:* 877-575-5627. *Fax:* 575-549-1196. *Website:* http://www.centuracollege.edu/.

Centura College
Newport News, Virginia

Director of Admissions Victoria Whitehead, Director of Admissions, Centura College, 616 Denbigh Boulevard, Newport News, VA 23608. *Phone:* 757-874-2121. *Toll-free phone:* 877-575-5627. *Fax:* 757-874-3857. *E-mail:* admdircpen@centura.edu. *Website:* http://www.centuracollege.edu/.

Centura College
Norfolk, Virginia

Director of Admissions Director of Admissions, Centura College, 7020 North Military Highway, Norfolk, VA 23518. *Phone:* 757-853-2121. *Toll-free phone:* 877-575-5627. *Fax:* 757-852-9017. *Website:* http://www.centuracollege.edu/.

Centura College
North Chesterfield, Virginia

Freshman Application Contact Admissions Office, Centura College, 7914 Midlothian Turnpike, North Chesterfield, VA 23235-5230. *Phone:* 804-330-0111. *Toll-free phone:* 877-575-5627. *Fax:* 804-330-3809. *Website:* http://www.centuracollege.edu/.

Centura College
Virginia Beach, Virginia

Freshman Application Contact Admissions Office, Centura College, 2697 Dean Drive, Suite 100, Virginia Beach, VA 23452. *Phone:* 757-340-2121. *Toll-free phone:* 877-575-5627. *Fax:* 757-340-9704. *Website:* http://www.centuracollege.edu/.

Columbia College
Vienna, Virginia

Admissions Office Contact Columbia College, 8620 Westwood Center Drive, Vienna, VA 22182. *Website:* http://www.ccdc.edu/.

Dabney S. Lancaster Community College
Clifton Forge, Virginia

- **State-supported** 2-year, founded 1964, part of Virginia Community College System
- **Rural** 117-acre campus
- **Endowment** $5.7 million
- **Coed**

Undergraduates Students come from 4 states and territories; 2% are from out of state; 6% Black or African American, non-Hispanic/Latino; 2% Hispanic/Latino; 0.6% Asian, non-Hispanic/Latino; 0.9% American Indian or

Alaska Native, non-Hispanic/Latino; 3% Two or more races, non-Hispanic/Latino; 0.8% Race/ethnicity unknown.
Faculty *Student/faculty ratio:* 16:1.
Academics *Calendar:* semesters. *Degree:* certificates and associate. *Special study options:* academic remediation for entering students, adult/continuing education programs, advanced placement credit, cooperative education, distance learning, honors programs, independent study, internships, part-time degree program, services for LD students, study abroad, summer session for credit.
Library DSLCC Library plus 1 other.
Student Life *Campus security:* 24-hour emergency response devices.
Standardized Tests *Required for some:* SAT and SAT Subject Tests or ACT (for admission), SAT Subject Tests (for admission).
Costs (2016–17) *Tuition:* state resident $4133 full-time, $138 per credit part-time; nonresident $9431 full-time, $314 per credit part-time. Full-time tuition and fees vary according to reciprocity agreements. Part-time tuition and fees vary according to reciprocity agreements. *Required fees:* $345 full-time, $12 per credit part-time.
Applying *Recommended:* high school transcript.
Freshman Application Contact Mrs. Lorrie Wilhelm Ferguson, Registrar, Dabney S. Lancaster Community College, Backels Hall, Clifton Forge, VA 24422. *Phone:* 540-863-2823. *Toll-free phone:* 877-73-DSLCC. *Fax:* 540-863-2915. *E-mail:* lwferguson@dslcc.edu. *Website:* http://www.dslcc.edu/.

Danville Community College
Danville, Virginia
Freshman Application Contact Cathy Pulliam, Coordinator of Student Recruitment and Enrollment, Danville Community College, 1008 South Main Street, Danville, VA 24541-4088. *Phone:* 434-797-8538. *Toll-free phone:* 800-560-4291. *E-mail:* cpulliam@dcc.vccs.edu. *Website:* http://www.dcc.vccs.edu/.

Eastern Shore Community College
Melfa, Virginia
Freshman Application Contact P. Bryan Smith, Dean of Student Services, Eastern Shore Community College, 29300 Lankford Highway, Melfa, VA 23410. *Phone:* 757-789-1732. *Toll-free phone:* 877-871-8455. *Fax:* 757-789-1737. *E-mail:* bsmith@es.vccs.edu. *Website:* http://www.es.vccs.edu/.

Eastern Virginia Career College
Fredericksburg, Virginia
Admissions Office Contact Eastern Virginia Career College, 10304 Spotsylvania Avenue, Suite 400, Fredericksburg, VA 22408. *Website:* http://www.evcc.edu/.

Everest College
Chesapeake, Virginia
Admissions Office Contact Everest College, 825 Greenbrier Circle, Suite 100, Chesapeake, VA 23320. *Website:* http://www.everest.edu/.

Fortis College
Norfolk, Virginia
Admissions Office Contact Fortis College, 6300 Center Drive, Suite 100, Norfolk, VA 23502. *Toll-free phone:* 855-4-FORTIS. *Website:* http://www.fortis.edu/.

Fortis College
Richmond, Virginia
Admissions Office Contact Fortis College, 2000 Westmoreland Street, Suite A, Richmond, VA 23230. *Toll-free phone:* 855-4-FORTIS. *Website:* http://www.fortis.edu/.

Germanna Community College
Locust Grove, Virginia
Freshman Application Contact Ms. Rita Dunston, Registrar, Germanna Community College, 10000 Germanna Point Drive, Fredericksburg, VA 22408. *Phone:* 540-891-3020. *Fax:* 540-891-3092. *Website:* http://www.germanna.edu/.

Global Health College
Alexandria, Virginia
Admissions Office Contact Global Health College, 25 South Quaker Lane, 1st Floor, Alexandria, VA 22314. *Website:* http://www.global.edu/.

John Tyler Community College
Chester, Virginia
- **State-supported** 2-year, founded 1967, part of Virginia Community College System
- **Suburban** 160-acre campus with easy access to Richmond
- **Coed,** 10,021 undergraduate students, 24% full-time, 57% women, 43% men

Undergraduates 2,402 full-time, 7,619 part-time. Students come from 34 states and territories; 8 other countries; 1% are from out of state; 23% Black or African American, non-Hispanic/Latino; 8% Hispanic/Latino; 3% Asian, non-Hispanic/Latino; 0.2% Native Hawaiian or other Pacific Islander, non-Hispanic/Latino; 0.4% American Indian or Alaska Native, non-Hispanic/Latino; 5% Two or more races, non-Hispanic/Latino; 0.7% Race/ethnicity unknown; 5% transferred in.
Freshmen *Admission:* 1,317 enrolled.
Faculty *Total:* 574. *Student/faculty ratio:* 19:1.
Majors Accounting related; architectural technology; business administration and management; business administration, management and operations related; child-care provision; computer and information sciences; criminal justice/law enforcement administration; emergency medical technology (EMT paramedic); engineering; funeral service and mortuary science; general studies; humanities; industrial technology; information technology; mechanical engineering technologies related; mental and social health services and allied professions related; registered nursing/registered nurse; visual and performing arts related.
Academics *Calendar:* semesters. *Degree:* certificates and associate. *Special study options:* academic remediation for entering students, adult/continuing education programs, advanced placement credit, distance learning, external degree program, honors programs, off-campus study, part-time degree program, services for LD students, study abroad, summer session for credit. *ROTC:* Army (c).
Library John Tyler Community College Learning Resource and Technology Center.
Student Life *Housing:* college housing not available. *Activities and Organizations:* drama/theater group, choral group, Phi Theta Kappa, Human Services Club, Future Teachers Club, Student Nurses' Association, Student Veteran's Organization. *Campus security:* 24-hour emergency response devices and patrols.
Athletics *Intramural sports:* basketball M(c)/W(c), golf M(c)/W(c), ultimate Frisbee M(c)/W(c).
Costs (2016–17) *Tuition:* state resident $4148 full-time, $147 per credit hour part-time; nonresident $9446 full-time, $343 per credit hour part-time. Full-time tuition and fees vary according to course load. Part-time tuition and fees vary according to course load. *Required fees:* $325 full-time, $35 per term part-time. *Payment plan:* installment. *Waivers:* senior citizens.
Financial Aid Of all full-time matriculated undergraduates who enrolled in 2015, 63 Federal Work-Study jobs (averaging $2092).
Applying *Options:* electronic application, early admission, deferred entrance. *Recommended:* high school transcript. *Application deadline:* rolling (freshmen). *Notification:* continuous (freshmen).
Freshman Application Contact Mr. Leigh Baxter, Interim Director Admission and Records and Registrar, John Tyler Community College, 13101 Jefferson Davis Highway, Chester, VA 23831. *Phone:* 804-706-5214. *Toll-free phone:* 800-552-3490. *Fax:* 804-796-4362. *E-mail:* jjames@jtcc.edu. *Website:* http://www.jtcc.edu/.

J. Sargeant Reynolds Community College
Richmond, Virginia
- **State-supported** 2-year, founded 1972, part of Virginia Community College System
- **Suburban** 207-acre campus with easy access to Richmond
- **Endowment** $10.0 million
- **Coed,** 10,375 undergraduate students, 27% full-time, 60% women, 40% men

Undergraduates 2,851 full-time, 7,524 part-time. Students come from 23 states and territories; 17 other countries; 1% are from out of state; 34% Black or African American, non-Hispanic/Latino; 3% Hispanic/Latino; 6% Asian, non-Hispanic/Latino; 0.2% Native Hawaiian or other Pacific Islander, non-Hispanic/Latino; 0.5% American Indian or Alaska Native, non-

Hispanic/Latino; 8% Two or more races, non-Hispanic/Latino; 0.8% Race/ethnicity unknown; 3% transferred in. *Retention:* 50% of full-time freshmen returned.

Freshmen *Admission:* 1,552 enrolled.

Faculty *Total:* 589, 23% full-time, 5% with terminal degrees. *Student/faculty ratio:* 19:1.

Majors Accounting related; applied horticulture/horticulture operations; architectural and building sciences; automobile/automotive mechanics technology; baking and pastry arts; biological and physical sciences; building/construction site management; business administration and management; child-care provision; clinical/medical laboratory technology; computer and information sciences; computer programming; computer systems networking and telecommunications; consumer merchandising/retailing management; cooking and related culinary arts; criminal justice/law enforcement administration; dental laboratory technology; emergency medical technology (EMT paramedic); engineering; fire science/firefighting; floriculture/floristry management; hospitality administration; hospitality administration related; hotel/motel administration; legal assistant/paralegal; liberal arts and sciences and humanities related; licensed practical/vocational nurse training; mathematics; mental and social health services and allied professions related; opticianry; pharmacy technician; respiratory care therapy; restaurant/food services management; sign language interpretation and translation; small business administration; social sciences; substance abuse/addiction counseling; web page, digital/multimedia and information resources design.

Academics *Calendar:* semesters. *Degree:* certificates and associate. *Special study options:* academic remediation for entering students, adult/continuing education programs, advanced placement credit, distance learning, double majors, English as a second language, independent study, internships, off-campus study, part-time degree program, services for LD students, summer session for credit.

Library J. Sargeant Reynolds Community College Library plus 2 others. *Books:* 82,000 (physical), 52,000 (digital/electronic); *Serial titles:* 5,142 (physical), 22,781 (digital/electronic); *Databases:* 119. Weekly public service hours: 26.

Student Life *Housing:* college housing not available. *Campus security:* 24-hour emergency response devices and patrols, late-night transport/escort service, security during hours of operation. *Student services:* personal/psychological counseling.

Costs (2017–18) *Tuition:* state resident $4241 full-time, $159 per credit hour part-time; nonresident $10,139 full-time, $355 per credit hour part-time. Full-time tuition and fees vary according to course load and program. Part-time tuition and fees vary according to course load and program. *Required fees:* $524 full-time, $22 per credit hour part-time. *Payment plan:* installment. *Waivers:* senior citizens.

Financial Aid Of all full-time matriculated undergraduates who enrolled in 2015, 3,417 applied for aid, 1,964 were judged to have need. *Average financial aid package:* $2496. *Average need-based gift aid:* $5741.

Applying *Options:* electronic application. *Required:* high school transcript. *Required for some:* interview, interview, criminal background check and/or drug screening, physical standard minimum. *Application deadlines:* rolling (freshmen), rolling (transfers). *Notification:* continuous (freshmen), continuous (transfers).

Freshman Application Contact Ms. Karen Pettis-Walden, Director of Admissions and Records, J. Sargeant Reynolds Community College, PO Box 85622, Richmond, VA 23285-5622. *Phone:* 804-523-5029. *Fax:* 804-371-3650. *E-mail:* kpettis-walden@reynolds.edu. *Website:* http://www.reynolds.edu/.

Lord Fairfax Community College
Middletown, Virginia

Freshman Application Contact Karen Bucher, Director of Enrollment Management, Lord Fairfax Community College, 173 Skirmisher Lane, Middletown, VA 22645. *Phone:* 540-868-7132. *Toll-free phone:* 800-906-LFCC. *Fax:* 540-868-7005. *E-mail:* kbucher@lfcc.edu. *Website:* http://www.lfcc.edu/.

Miller-Motte Technical College
Lynchburg, Virginia

Director of Admissions Ms. Betty J. Dierstein, Director, Miller-Motte Technical College, 1011 Creekside Lane, Lynchburg, VA 24502. *Phone:* 434-239-5222. *Toll-free phone:* 800-705-9182. *Fax:* 434-239-1069. *E-mail:* bjdierstein@miller-mott.com. *Website:* http://www.miller-motte.edu/.

Miller-Motte Technical College
Roanoke, Virginia

Admissions Office Contact Miller-Motte Technical College, 4444 Electric Road, Roanoke, VA 24018. *Toll-free phone:* 800-705-9182. *Website:* http://www.miller-motte.edu/.

Mountain Empire Community College
Big Stone Gap, Virginia

Freshman Application Contact Mountain Empire Community College, 3441 Mountain Empire Road, Big Stone Gap, VA 24219. *Phone:* 276-523-2400 Ext. 219. *Website:* http://www.mecc.edu/.

New River Community College
Dublin, Virginia

- **State-supported** 2-year, founded 1969, part of Virginia Community College System
- **Rural** 100-acre campus
- **Coed,** 4,477 undergraduate students

Majors Accounting; administrative assistant and secretarial science; architectural engineering technology; automobile/automotive mechanics technology; biological and physical sciences; business administration and management; child development; community organization and advocacy; computer engineering technology; computer graphics; criminal justice/law enforcement administration; criminal justice/police science; drafting and design technology; education; electrical, electronic and communications engineering technology; engineering; forensic science and technology; general studies; information science/studies; instrumentation technology; liberal arts and sciences/liberal studies; licensed practical/vocational nurse training; machine tool technology; marketing/marketing management; mental and social health services and allied professions related; registered nursing/registered nurse; welding technology.

Academics *Calendar:* semesters. *Degree:* certificates, diplomas, and associate. *Special study options:* academic remediation for entering students, adult/continuing education programs, advanced placement credit, cooperative education, distance learning, double majors, internships, part-time degree program, services for LD students, summer session for credit.

Library New River Community College Library plus 1 other.

Student Life *Housing:* college housing not available. *Activities and Organizations:* Phi Theta Kappa, Phi Beta Lambda, NRCC Computer Club. *Campus security:* 24-hour patrols.

Athletics Member NJCAA. *Intercollegiate sports:* baseball M. *Intramural sports:* basketball M/W, soccer M/W, table tennis M/W.

Costs (2016–17) *Tuition:* state resident $149 per credit hour part-time; nonresident $345 per credit hour part-time. Full-time tuition and fees vary according to course load and program. Part-time tuition and fees vary according to course load and program. *Payment plans:* installment, deferred payment. *Waivers:* senior citizens.

Applying *Options:* electronic application, early admission. *Required for some:* high school transcript. *Application deadlines:* rolling (freshmen), rolling (transfers). *Notification:* continuous (freshmen), continuous (transfers).

Freshman Application Contact Mrs. Tammy L. Smith, Coordinator, Admissions and Records, New River Community College, 5251 College Drive, Dublin, VA 24084. *Phone:* 540-674-3600 Ext. 4203. *Toll-free phone:* 866-462-6722. *Fax:* 540-674-3644. *E-mail:* tsmith@nr.edu. *Website:* http://www.nr.edu/.

Northern Virginia Community College
Annandale, Virginia

Freshman Application Contact Northern Virginia Community College, 8333 Little River Turnpike, Annandale, VA 22003. *Phone:* 703-323-3195. *Website:* http://www.nvcc.edu/.

Patrick Henry Community College
Martinsville, Virginia

- **State-supported** 2-year, founded 1962, part of Virginia Community College System
- **Rural** 137-acre campus with easy access to Greensboro
- **Endowment** $10.6 million
- **Coed,** 2,405 undergraduate students, 50% full-time, 59% women, 41% men

Undergraduates 1,214 full-time, 1,191 part-time. Students come from 6 states and territories; 1% are from out of state; 19% Black or African American, non-Hispanic/Latino; 7% Hispanic/Latino; 0.8% Asian, non-Hispanic/Latino; 0.1%

American Indian or Alaska Native, non-Hispanic/Latino; 3% Two or more races, non-Hispanic/Latino; 0.3% Race/ethnicity unknown; 0.4% international. *Retention:* 65% of full-time freshmen returned.

Freshmen *Admission:* 415 enrolled.

Faculty *Total:* 237, 23% full-time. *Student/faculty ratio:* 20:1.

Majors Accounting; administrative assistant and secretarial science; agricultural business and management; automobile/automotive mechanics technology; biological and physical sciences; business administration and management; criminal justice/law enforcement administration; emergency medical technology (EMT paramedic); engineering technology; industrial electronics technology; industrial technology; information technology; legal assistant/paralegal; liberal arts and sciences/liberal studies; medical office assistant; registered nursing/registered nurse; teacher assistant/aide.

Academics *Calendar:* semesters. *Degree:* certificates and associate. *Special study options:* academic remediation for entering students, adult/continuing education programs, advanced placement credit, cooperative education, distance learning, independent study, internships, part-time degree program, services for LD students, summer session for credit.

Library Lester Library. *Books:* 25,464 (physical), 197,427 (digital/electronic); *Serial titles:* 174 (physical), 73,546 (digital/electronic); *Databases:* 190.

Student Life *Housing:* college housing not available. *Activities and Organizations:* drama/theater group, Student Government Association, Student Support Services, Phi Theta Kappa, Multi Cutural, Cross Cultural Club. *Campus security:* 24-hour emergency response devices and patrols, late-night transport/escort service. *Student services:* personal/psychological counseling.

Athletics Member NJCAA. *Intercollegiate sports:* baseball M, basketball M/W, cross-country running M/W, golf M/W, soccer M/W, softball W, volleyball W. *Intramural sports:* cheerleading W(c).

Costs (2016–17) *Tuition:* state resident $4473 full-time, $138 per credit hour part-time; nonresident $10,370 full-time, $314 per credit hour part-time. Full-time tuition and fees vary according to course load. Part-time tuition and fees vary according to course load. *Required fees:* $340 full-time, $11 per credit hour part-time, $11 per credit hour part-time. *Payment plans:* installment, deferred payment. *Waivers:* senior citizens.

Applying *Options:* electronic application, early admission. *Required:* high school transcript. *Application deadlines:* rolling (freshmen), rolling (transfers). *Notification:* continuous (freshmen), continuous (transfers).

Freshman Application Contact Mr. Travis Tisdale, Coordinator, Admissions and Records, Patrick Henry Community College, 645 Patriot Avenue, Martinsville, VA 24112. *Phone:* 276-656-0311. *Toll-free phone:* 800-232-7997. *Fax:* 276-656-0352.

Website: http://www.ph.vccs.edu/.

Paul D. Camp Community College
Franklin, Virginia

Freshman Application Contact Mrs. Trina Jones, Dean Student Services, Paul D. Camp Community College, PO Box 737, 100 N. College Drive, Franklin, VA 23851. *Phone:* 757-569-6720. *E-mail:* tjones@pdc.edu. *Website:* http://www.pdc.edu/.

Piedmont Virginia Community College
Charlottesville, Virginia

- **State-supported** 2-year, founded 1972, part of Virginia Community College System
- **Suburban** 114-acre campus with easy access to Richmond
- **Endowment** $6.8 million
- **Coed,** 5,438 undergraduate students, 23% full-time, 59% women, 41% men

Undergraduates 1,232 full-time, 4,206 part-time.

Academics *Calendar:* semesters. *Degree:* certificates and associate. *Special study options:* academic remediation for entering students, adult/continuing education programs, advanced placement credit, cooperative education, distance learning, English as a second language, honors programs, independent study, internships, part-time degree program, services for LD students, summer session for credit. *ROTC:* Army (c), Air Force (c).

Library Jessup Library.

Student Life *Housing:* college housing not available. *Activities and Organizations:* drama/theater group, student-run newspaper, choral group. *Campus security:* 24-hour emergency response devices and patrols, late-night transport/escort service, establishment of Campus Police.

Athletics *Intramural sports:* basketball M/W, golf M/W, soccer M/W, table tennis M/W, tennis M/W, ultimate Frisbee M/W, volleyball M/W, weight lifting M/W.

Costs (2017–18) *Tuition:* state resident $4163 full-time; nonresident $9461 full-time. Full-time tuition and fees vary according to course load. Part-time tuition and fees vary according to course load. *Required fees:* $395 full-time.

Payment plan: installment. *Waivers:* senior citizens and employees or children of employees.

Applying *Options:* electronic application, early admission, deferred entrance. *Required for some:* high school transcript, prerequisite courses for nursing, practical nursing, radiography, sonography, surgical technology, emergency medical services, health information management, and patient admissions coordination. *Application deadlines:* rolling (freshmen), rolling (transfers). *Notification:* continuous (freshmen), continuous (transfers).

Freshman Application Contact Ms. Mary Lee Walsh, Dean of Student Services, Piedmont Virginia Community College, 501 College Drive, Charlottesville, VA 22902-7589. *Phone:* 434-961-6540. *Fax:* 434-961-5425. *E-mail:* mwalsh@pvcc.edu.

Website: http://www.pvcc.edu/.

Rappahannock Community College
Glenns, Virginia

- **State and locally supported** 2-year, founded 1970, part of Virginia Community College System
- **Rural** campus
- **Coed,** 3,463 undergraduate students, 23% full-time, 62% women, 38% men

Undergraduates 793 full-time, 2,670 part-time.

Majors Accounting; administrative assistant and secretarial science; biological and physical sciences; business administration and management; business administration, management and operations related; criminal justice/law enforcement administration; criminal justice/police science; engineering technology; information science/studies; liberal arts and sciences/liberal studies; registered nursing/registered nurse.

Academics *Calendar:* semesters. *Degree:* certificates and associate. *Special study options:* academic remediation for entering students, adult/continuing education programs, distance learning, honors programs, internships, off-campus study, part-time degree program, services for LD students, summer session for credit.

Student Life *Student services:* personal/psychological counseling.

Athletics *Intercollegiate sports:* softball W.

Costs (2016–17) *Tuition:* state resident $4133 full-time, $138 per credit hour part-time; nonresident $9431 full-time, $314 per credit hour part-time. Full-time tuition and fees vary according to course load. Part-time tuition and fees vary according to course load. *Required fees:* $455 full-time, $15 per credit hour part-time. *Payment plan:* deferred payment. *Waivers:* senior citizens.

Financial Aid Of all full-time matriculated undergraduates who enrolled in 2015, 40 Federal Work-Study jobs (averaging $1015).

Applying *Options:* electronic application, early admission. *Application deadlines:* rolling (freshmen), rolling (transfers). *Notification:* continuous (freshmen), continuous (transfers).

Freshman Application Contact Ms. Felicia Packett, Admissions and Records Officer, Rappahannock Community College, 12745 College Drive, Glenns, VA 23149-0287. *Phone:* 804-758-6740. *Toll-free phone:* 800-836-9381. *Website:* http://www.rappahannock.edu/.

Richard Bland College of The College of William and Mary
Petersburg, Virginia

Freshman Application Contact Office of Admissions, Richard Bland College of The College of William and Mary, 8311 Halifax Road, Petersburg, VA 23805. *Phone:* 804-862-6100 Ext. 6249. *E-mail:* apply@rbc.edu. *Website:* http://www.rbc.edu/.

Riverside College of Health Careers
Newport News, Virginia

Admissions Office Contact Riverside College of Health Careers, 316 Main Street, Newport News, VA 23601.

Website: http://www.riversideonline.com/rshc/.

Southside Regional Medical Center Professional Schools
Colonial Heights, Virginia

Admissions Office Contact Southside Regional Medical Center Professional Schools, 430 Clairmont Court, Suite 200, Colonial Heights, VA 23834. *Website:* http://www.srmconline.com/Southside-Regional-Medical-Center/nursingeducation.aspx.

Southside Virginia Community College
Alberta, Virginia

Freshman Application Contact Mr. Brent Richey, Dean of Enrollment Management, Southside Virginia Community College, 109 Campus Drive, Alberta, VA 23821. *Phone:* 434-949-1012. *Fax:* 434-949-7863. *E-mail:* rhina.jones@sv.vccs.edu. *Website:* http://www.southside.edu/.

Southwest Virginia Community College
Richlands, Virginia

- **State-supported** 2-year, founded 1968, part of Virginia Community College System
- **Rural** 100-acre campus
- **Endowment** $18.0 million
- **Coed,** 2,481 undergraduate students, 47% full-time, 61% women, 39% men

Undergraduates 1,159 full-time, 1,322 part-time. Students come from 7 states and territories; 1% are from out of state; 2% Black or African American, non-Hispanic/Latino; 0.7% Hispanic/Latino; 0.4% Asian, non-Hispanic/Latino; 0.3% American Indian or Alaska Native, non-Hispanic/Latino; 1% Two or more races, non-Hispanic/Latino; 0.2% Race/ethnicity unknown; 27% transferred in. *Retention:* 56% of full-time freshmen returned.
Freshmen *Admission:* 478 enrolled.
Faculty *Total:* 116, 38% full-time. *Student/faculty ratio:* 29:1.
Majors Accounting related; business administration, management and operations related; business operations support and secretarial services related; child-care provision; computer and information sciences; criminal justice/law enforcement administration; electrical, electronic and communications engineering technology; emergency medical technology (EMT paramedic); liberal arts and sciences/liberal studies; mental and social health services and allied professions related; radiologic technology/science; registered nursing/registered nurse.
Academics *Calendar:* semesters. *Degree:* certificates, diplomas, and associate. *Special study options:* academic remediation for entering students, accelerated degree program, adult/continuing education programs, advanced placement credit, distance learning, double majors, honors programs, internships, off-campus study, part-time degree program, summer session for credit.
Library Southwest Virginia Community College Library. *Books:* 42,207 (physical), 62,566 (digital/electronic); *Serial titles:* 275 (physical), 118,007 (digital/electronic); *Databases:* 118. Students can reserve study rooms.
Student Life *Housing:* college housing not available. *Activities and Organizations:* choral group, Phi Theta Kappa, Phi Beta Lambda, Intervoice, Helping Minds Club, Project ACHEIVE. *Campus security:* 24-hour emergency response devices and patrols, student patrols, extensive security camera system. *Student services:* personal/psychological counseling.
Standardized Tests *Required:* VCCS Math and English Assessments (for admission).
Costs (2016–17) *Tuition:* state resident $4133 full-time, $138 per credit hour part-time; nonresident $9431 full-time, $314 per credit hour part-time. Full-time tuition and fees vary according to reciprocity agreements. Part-time tuition and fees vary according to reciprocity agreements. *Required fees:* $330 full-time, $11 per credit hour part-time. *Payment plan:* installment. *Waivers:* senior citizens.
Financial Aid Of all full-time matriculated undergraduates who enrolled in 2015, 150 Federal Work-Study jobs (averaging $1140).
Applying *Options:* electronic application, early admission, deferred entrance. *Required:* high school transcript, interview. *Application deadlines:* rolling (freshmen), rolling (transfers).
Freshman Application Contact Ms. Dionne Cook, Admissions Counselor, Southwest Virginia Community College, Box SVCC, Richlands, VA 24641. *Phone:* 276-964-7301. *Toll-free phone:* 800-822-7822. *Fax:* 276-964-7716. *E-mail:* dionne.cook@sw.edu.
Website: http://www.sw.edu/.

Standard Healthcare Services, College of Nursing
Falls Church, Virginia

Admissions Office Contact Standard Healthcare Services, College of Nursing, 7704 Leesburg Pike, Suite 1000, Falls Church, VA 22043. *Website:* http://www.standardcollege.edu/.

Thomas Nelson Community College
Hampton, Virginia

Freshman Application Contact Ms. Geraldine Newson, Sr. Admission Specialist, Thomas Nelson Community College, PO Box 9407, Hampton, VA 23670-0407. *Phone:* 757-825-2800. *Fax:* 757-825-2763. *E-mail:* admissions@tncc.edu. *Website:* http://www.tncc.edu/.

Tidewater Community College
Norfolk, Virginia

- **State-supported** 2-year, founded 1968, part of Virginia Community College System
- **Suburban** 520-acre campus
- **Endowment** $7.1 million
- **Coed,** 23,946 undergraduate students, 36% full-time, 59% women, 41% men

Undergraduates 8,667 full-time, 15,279 part-time. 15% are from out of state; 32% Black or African American, non-Hispanic/Latino; 8% Hispanic/Latino; 4% Asian, non-Hispanic/Latino; 0.5% Native Hawaiian or other Pacific Islander, non-Hispanic/Latino; 0.5% American Indian or Alaska Native, non-Hispanic/Latino; 5% Two or more races, non-Hispanic/Latino; 0.8% Race/ethnicity unknown; 0.6% international. *Retention:* 58% of full-time freshmen returned.
Faculty *Total:* 1,314, 27% full-time. *Student/faculty ratio:* 20:1.
Majors Accounting; administrative assistant and secretarial science; advertising; automobile/automotive mechanics technology; biological and physical sciences; business administration and management; civil engineering; commercial and advertising art; computer programming; drafting and design technology; education; electrical, electronic and communications engineering technology; engineering; finance; fine/studio arts; graphic design; horticultural science; information technology; interior design; kindergarten/preschool education; legal assistant/paralegal; liberal arts and sciences/liberal studies; marketing/marketing management; music; real estate; registered nursing/registered nurse.
Academics *Calendar:* semesters. *Degree:* certificates and associate. *Special study options:* academic remediation for entering students, accelerated degree program, adult/continuing education programs, advanced placement credit, cooperative education, distance learning, English as a second language, honors programs, independent study, internships, off-campus study, part-time degree program, services for LD students, summer session for credit.
Library Main Library plus 5 others.
Student Life *Housing:* college housing not available. *Activities and Organizations:* drama/theater group, student-run newspaper. *Campus security:* 24-hour patrols. *Student services:* personal/psychological counseling, women's center.
Athletics *Intramural sports:* basketball M/W, soccer M, softball W, tennis M/W, volleyball W.
Costs (2016–17) *Tuition:* state resident $3354 full-time, $140 per credit hour part-time; nonresident $7592 full-time, $316 per credit hour part-time. *Required fees:* $884 full-time, $37 per credit hour part-time. *Payment plan:* installment. *Waivers:* senior citizens.
Financial Aid Of all full-time matriculated undergraduates who enrolled in 2015, 64 Federal Work-Study jobs (averaging $2000).
Applying *Options:* electronic application, early admission, deferred entrance. *Application deadlines:* rolling (freshmen), rolling (transfers). *Notification:* continuous (freshmen), continuous (transfers).
Freshman Application Contact Registrar, Tidewater Community College, Norfolk, VA 23510. *Phone:* 757-822-1900. *E-mail:* centralrecords@tcc.edu. *Website:* http://www.tcc.edu/.

Virginia College in Richmond
Richmond, Virginia

Admissions Office Contact Virginia College in Richmond, 7200 Midlothian Turnpike, Richmond, VA 23225. *Website:* http://www.vc.edu/.

Virginia Highlands Community College
Abingdon, Virginia

Freshman Application Contact Karen Cheers, Acting Director of Admissions, Records, and Financial Aid, Virginia Highlands Community College, PO Box 828, 100 VHCC Drive Abingdon, Abingdon, VA 24212. *Phone:* 276-739-2490. *Toll-free phone:* 877-207-6115. *E-mail:* kcheers@vhcc.edu. *Website:* http://www.vhcc.edu/.

Virginia Western Community College
Roanoke, Virginia

- **State-supported** 2-year, founded 1966, part of Virginia Community College System
- **Suburban** 70-acre campus
- **Coed,** 8,632 undergraduate students, 29% full-time, 55% women, 45% men

Undergraduates 2,527 full-time, 6,105 part-time. Students come from 34 states and territories; 62 other countries; 2% are from out of state; 15% Black or African American, non-Hispanic/Latino; 3% Hispanic/Latino; 3% Asian, non-Hispanic/Latino; 0.1% Native Hawaiian or other Pacific Islander, non-Hispanic/Latino; 0.3% American Indian or Alaska Native, non-Hispanic/Latino; 3% Two or more races, non-Hispanic/Latino; 0.6% Race/ethnicity unknown; 0.3% international; 3% transferred in. *Retention:* 53% of full-time freshmen returned.
Freshmen *Admission:* 2,770 applied, 1,376 enrolled.
Faculty *Student/faculty ratio:* 34:1.
Majors Accounting; administrative assistant and secretarial science; art; automobile/automotive mechanics technology; biological and physical sciences; business administration and management; child development; civil engineering technology; commercial and advertising art; computer science; criminal justice/law enforcement administration; data processing and data processing technology; dental hygiene; education; electrical, electronic and communications engineering technology; engineering; industrial radiologic technology; kindergarten/preschool education; liberal arts and sciences/liberal studies; mechanical engineering/mechanical technology; mental health counseling; pre-engineering; radio and television; radiologic technology/science; registered nursing/registered nurse.
Academics *Calendar:* semesters. *Degree:* certificates and associate. *Special study options:* academic remediation for entering students, advanced placement credit, cooperative education, distance learning, double majors, English as a second language, honors programs, independent study, internships, part-time degree program, services for LD students, summer session for credit.
Library Brown Library.
Student Life *Housing:* college housing not available. *Activities and Organizations:* drama/theater group, student-run newspaper. *Campus security:* 24-hour emergency response devices and patrols, late-night transport/escort service. *Student services:* personal/psychological counseling.
Athletics *Intramural sports:* basketball M/W, soccer M, volleyball W.
Costs (2016–17) *Tuition:* state resident $4193 full-time, $140 per credit hour part-time; nonresident $9491 full-time, $316 per credit hour part-time. *Required fees:* $900 full-time. *Payment plan:* installment. *Waivers:* senior citizens and employees or children of employees.
Applying *Options:* electronic application, early admission, deferred entrance. *Required for some:* high school transcript. *Recommended:* high school transcript. *Application deadlines:* rolling (freshmen), rolling (transfers). *Notification:* continuous (freshmen), continuous (transfers).
Freshman Application Contact Admissions Office, Virginia Western Community College, PO Box 14007, Roanoke, VA 24038. *Phone:* 540-857-7231.
Website: http://www.virginiawestern.edu/.

Wytheville Community College
Wytheville, Virginia

- **State-supported** 2-year, founded 1963, part of Virginia Community College System
- **Rural** 141-acre campus
- **Coed,** 2,745 undergraduate students, 34% full-time, 61% women, 39% men

Undergraduates 940 full-time, 1,805 part-time. Students come from 9 states and territories; 2% are from out of state; 4% Black or African American, non-Hispanic/Latino; 2% Hispanic/Latino; 0.8% Asian, non-Hispanic/Latino; 0.1% Native Hawaiian or other Pacific Islander, non-Hispanic/Latino; 0.4% American Indian or Alaska Native, non-Hispanic/Latino; 4% Two or more races, non-Hispanic/Latino; 0.2% Race/ethnicity unknown. *Retention:* 62% of full-time freshmen returned.
Faculty *Total:* 137, 29% full-time. *Student/faculty ratio:* 23:1.
Majors Accounting; administrative assistant and secretarial science; biological and physical sciences; business administration and management; civil engineering technology; clinical/medical laboratory technology; corrections; criminal justice/law enforcement administration; criminal justice/police science; dental hygiene; drafting and design technology; education; electrical, electronic and communications engineering technology; information science/studies; liberal arts and sciences/liberal studies; machine tool technology; mass communication/media; mechanical

engineering/mechanical technology; medical administrative assistant and medical secretary; physical therapy; registered nursing/registered nurse.
Academics *Calendar:* semesters. *Degree:* certificates, diplomas, and associate. *Special study options:* academic remediation for entering students, adult/continuing education programs, advanced placement credit, distance learning, external degree program, independent study, part-time degree program, services for LD students, summer session for credit.
Library Wytheville Community College Library. *Books:* 33,041 (physical), 51,770 (digital/electronic); *Serial titles:* 3,319 (physical), 3,418 (digital/electronic); *Databases:* 101.
Student Life *Housing:* college housing not available. *Activities and Organizations:* drama/theater group, student-run newspaper. *Campus security:* 24-hour emergency response devices and patrols.
Athletics *Intercollegiate sports:* volleyball W.
Costs (2016–17) *Tuition:* state resident $4133 full-time, $138 per credit hour part-time; nonresident $9431 full-time, $314 per credit hour part-time. *Required fees:* $360 full-time, $12 per credit hour part-time.
Financial Aid Of all full-time matriculated undergraduates who enrolled in 2015, 125 Federal Work-Study jobs (averaging $2592).
Applying *Options:* electronic application, early admission. *Required:* high school transcript. *Required for some:* interview. *Application deadlines:* rolling (freshmen), rolling (transfers). *Notification:* continuous (freshmen), continuous (transfers).
Freshman Application Contact Wytheville Community College, 1000 East Main Street, Wytheville, VA 24382-3308. *Phone:* 276-223-4701.
Toll-free phone: 800-468-1195.
Website: http://www.wcc.vccs.edu/.

WASHINGTON

Bates Technical College
Tacoma, Washington

Director of Admissions Director of Admissions, Bates Technical College, 1101 South Yakima Avenue, Tacoma, WA 98405-4895. *Phone:* 253-680-7000. *E-mail:* registration@bates.ctc.edu. *Website:* http://www.bates.ctc.edu/.

Bellevue College
Bellevue, Washington

Freshman Application Contact Morenika Jacobs, Associate Dean of Enrollment Services, Bellevue College, 3000 Landerholm Circle, SE, Bellevue, WA 98007-6484. *Phone:* 425-564-2205. *Fax:* 425-564-4065. *Website:* http://www.bcc.ctc.edu/.

Bellingham Technical College
Bellingham, Washington

- **State-supported** 2-year, founded 1957, part of Washington State Board for Community and Technical Colleges
- **Suburban** 21-acre campus with easy access to Vancouver, BC; Seattle, WA
- **Coed**

Faculty *Student/faculty ratio:* 24:1.
Academics *Calendar:* quarters. *Degree:* certificates and associate. *Special study options:* academic remediation for entering students, distance learning, English as a second language, internships, part-time degree program, services for LD students, summer session for credit.
Library Bellingham Technical College Library. *Books:* 15,500 (physical), 120,000 (digital/electronic); *Serial titles:* 90 (physical); *Databases:* 13. Weekly public service hours: 70; students can reserve study rooms.
Standardized Tests *Required:* ACCUPLACER or waiver (for admission).
Costs (2016–17) *Tuition:* state resident $3401 full-time, $102 per credit part-time; nonresident $4300 full-time, $279 per credit part-time. Full-time tuition and fees vary according to course load. Part-time tuition and fees vary according to course load.
Financial Aid Of all full-time matriculated undergraduates who enrolled in 2015, 16 Federal Work-Study jobs (averaging $2565). 28 state and other part-time jobs (averaging $2600).
Applying *Options:* electronic application, early admission, deferred entrance. *Required for some:* high school transcript, prerequisite courses.
Freshman Application Contact Bellingham Technical College, 3028 Lindbergh Avenue, Bellingham, WA 98225. *Phone:* 360-752-8324. *Website:* http://www.btc.edu/.

Big Bend Community College
Moses Lake, Washington

- **State-supported** 2-year, founded 1962
- **Small-town** 159-acre campus
- **Coed**

Undergraduates 1,458 full-time, 558 part-time. 1% Black or African American, non-Hispanic/Latino; 35% Hispanic/Latino; 2% Asian, non-Hispanic/Latino; 0.6% American Indian or Alaska Native, non-Hispanic/Latino; 2% Two or more races, non-Hispanic/Latino; 3% Race/ethnicity unknown; 0.5% international; 7% live on campus.
Faculty *Student/faculty ratio:* 22:1.
Academics *Calendar:* quarters. *Degree:* certificates and associate. *Special study options:* academic remediation for entering students, advanced placement credit, cooperative education, distance learning, English as a second language, part-time degree program, services for LD students, summer session for credit.
Library William C. Bonaudi Library. *Books:* 37,906 (physical), 3,484 (digital/electronic); *Serial titles:* 102 (physical); *Databases:* 29. Weekly public service hours: 68; students can reserve study rooms.
Student Life *Campus security:* 24-hour emergency response devices, late-night transport/escort service, daytime security during the week, dorm security six evenings/week, Enhanced Campus Notification System, video surveillance on campus.
Applying *Options:* electronic application, early admission, deferred entrance. *Application fee:* $30. *Required for some:* high school transcript.
Freshman Application Contact Candis Lacher, Associate Vice President of Student Services, Big Bend Community College, 7662 Chanute Street NE, Moses Lake, WA 98837. *Phone:* 509-793-2061. *Toll-free phone:* 877-745-1212. *Fax:* 509-793-6243. *E-mail:* admissions@bigbend.edu. *Website:* http://www.bigbend.edu/.

Carrington College–Spokane
Spokane, Washington

- **Proprietary** 2-year, founded 1976, part of Carrington Colleges Group, Inc.
- **Coed**

Undergraduates 413 full-time. 18% are from out of state; 2% Black or African American, non-Hispanic/Latino; 9% Hispanic/Latino; 1% Asian, non-Hispanic/Latino; 1% Native Hawaiian or other Pacific Islander, non-Hispanic/Latino; 2% American Indian or Alaska Native, non-Hispanic/Latino; 4% Two or more races, non-Hispanic/Latino; 1% Race/ethnicity unknown; 18% transferred in.
Faculty *Student/faculty ratio:* 35:1.
Academics *Degree:* certificates and associate.
Applying *Required:* essay or personal statement, high school transcript, interview, institutional entrance test.
Freshman Application Contact Carrington College–Spokane, 10102 East Knox Avenue, Suite 200, Spokane, WA 99206. *Website:* http://carrington.edu/.

Cascadia College
Bothell, Washington

- **State-supported** primarily 2-year, founded 1999, part of Washington State Board for Community and Technical Colleges
- **Suburban** 128-acre campus
- **Coed**

Undergraduates 1,529 full-time, 1,230 part-time. Students come from 12 states and territories; 3% Black or African American, non-Hispanic/Latino; 18% Hispanic/Latino; 15% Asian, non-Hispanic/Latino; 0.4% Native Hawaiian or other Pacific Islander, non-Hispanic/Latino; 0.8% American Indian or Alaska Native, non-Hispanic/Latino; 16% Two or more races, non-Hispanic/Latino; 17% Race/ethnicity unknown; 12% international.
Academics *Calendar:* quarters. *Degrees:* certificates, diplomas, associate, and bachelor's. *Special study options:* academic remediation for entering students, accelerated degree program, adult/continuing education programs, advanced placement credit, cooperative education, distance learning, double majors, English as a second language, independent study, internships, off-campus study, part-time degree program, services for LD students, study abroad, summer session for credit.
Library Campus Library. *Books:* 90,000 (physical), 600,000 (digital/electronic); *Serial titles:* 600 (physical), 100,000 (digital/electronic); *Databases:* 600. Weekly public service hours: 86; students can reserve study rooms.
Student Life *Campus security:* 24-hour emergency response devices, late-night transport/escort service.

Costs (2016–17) *One-time required fee:* $30. *Tuition:* state resident $3852 full-time, $103 per credit hour part-time; nonresident $4265 full-time, $116 per credit hour part-time. Full-time tuition and fees vary according to course load, degree level, and program. Part-time tuition and fees vary according to course load, degree level, and program. *Required fees:* $420 full-time, $11 per credit hour part-time.
Applying *Options:* electronic application. *Application fee:* $30.
Freshman Application Contact Ms. Erin Blakeney, Dean for Student Success, Cascadia College, 18345 Campus Way, NE, Bothell, WA 98011. *Phone:* 425-352-8000. *Fax:* 425-352-8137. *E-mail:* admissions@cascadia.edu. *Website:* http://www.cascadia.edu/.

Centralia College
Centralia, Washington

Freshman Application Contact Admissions Office, Centralia College, Centralia, WA 98531. *Phone:* 360-736-9391 Ext. 221. *Fax:* 360-330-7503. *E-mail:* admissions@centralia.edu. *Website:* http://www.centralia.edu/.

Clark College
Vancouver, Washington

- **State-supported** primarily 2-year, founded 1933, part of Washington State Board for Community and Technical Colleges
- **Urban** 101-acre campus with easy access to Portland
- **Coed**

Undergraduates 5,035 full-time, 5,442 part-time. 4% are from out of state; 2% Black or African American, non-Hispanic/Latino; 9% Hispanic/Latino; 4% Asian, non-Hispanic/Latino; 0.1% Native Hawaiian or other Pacific Islander, non-Hispanic/Latino; 0.6% American Indian or Alaska Native, non-Hispanic/Latino; 8% Two or more races, non-Hispanic/Latino; 6% Race/ethnicity unknown; 1% international; 3% transferred in.
Faculty *Student/faculty ratio:* 24:1.
Academics *Calendar:* quarters. *Degrees:* certificates, diplomas, associate, and bachelor's. *Special study options:* adult/continuing education programs, part-time degree program. *ROTC:* Army (c), Air Force (c).
Library Lewis D. Cannell Library.
Student Life *Campus security:* 24-hour patrols, late-night transport/escort service, security staff during hours of operation.
Costs (2016–17) *Tuition:* area resident $4023 full-time, $107 per credit hour part-time; state resident $5436 full-time, $153 per credit hour part-time; nonresident $9432 full-time, $283 per credit hour part-time. Full-time tuition and fees vary according to course level, course load, degree level, program, and reciprocity agreements. Part-time tuition and fees vary according to course level, course load, degree level, program, and reciprocity agreements.
Applying *Options:* electronic application, early admission, deferred entrance. *Application fee:* $25.
Freshman Application Contact Ms. Sheryl Anderson, Director of Admissions, Clark College, Vancouver, WA 98663. *Phone:* 360-992-2308. *Fax:* 360-992-2867. *E-mail:* admissions@clark.edu. *Website:* http://www.clark.edu/.

Clover Park Technical College
Lakewood, Washington

Director of Admissions Ms. Judy Richardson, Registrar, Clover Park Technical College, 4500 Steilacoom Boulevard, SW, Lakewood, WA 98499. *Phone:* 253-589-5570. *Website:* http://www.cptc.edu/.

Columbia Basin College
Pasco, Washington

Freshman Application Contact Admissions Department, Columbia Basin College, 2600 North 20th Avenue, Pasco, WA 99301-3397. *Phone:* 509-542-4524. *Fax:* 509-544-2023. *E-mail:* admissions@columbiabasin.edu. *Website:* http://www.columbiabasin.edu/.

Edmonds Community College
Lynnwood, Washington

Freshman Application Contact Ms. Nancy Froemming, Enrollment Services Office Manager, Edmonds Community College, 20000 68th Avenue West, Lynwood, WA 98036-5999. *Phone:* 425-640-1853. *Fax:* 425-640-1159. *E-mail:* nanci.froemming@edcc.edu. *Website:* http://www.edcc.edu/.

Everest College
Tacoma, Washington

Admissions Office Contact Everest College, 2156 Pacific Avenue, Tacoma, WA 98402. *Website:* http://www.everest.edu/.

Everett Community College
Everett, Washington

Freshman Application Contact Ms. Linda Baca, Entry Services Manager, Everett Community College, 2000 Tower Street, Everett, WA 98201-1327. *Phone:* 425-388-9219. *Fax:* 425-388-9173. *E-mail:* admissions@everettcc.edu. *Website:* http://www.everettcc.edu/.

Grays Harbor College
Aberdeen, Washington

Freshman Application Contact Ms. Brenda Dell, Admissions Officer, Grays Harbor College, 1620 Edward P. Smith Drive, Aberdeen, WA 98520. *Phone:* 360-532-4216. *Toll-free phone:* 800-562-4830. *Website:* http://www.ghc.edu/.

Green River College
Auburn, Washington

Freshman Application Contact Ms. Peggy Morgan, Program Support Supervisor, Green River College, 12401 Southeast 320th Street, Auburn, WA 98092-3699. *Phone:* 253-833-9111. *Fax:* 253-288-3454. *Website:* http://www.greenriver.edu/.

Highline College
Des Moines, Washington

Freshman Application Contact Ms. Michelle Kuwasaki, Director of Admissions, Highline College, 2400 South 240th Street, Des Moines, WA 98198-9800. *Phone:* 206-878-3710 Ext. 9800. *Website:* http://www.highline.edu/.

Lake Washington Institute of Technology
Kirkland, Washington

Freshman Application Contact Shawn Miller, Registrar, Enrollment Services, Lake Washington Institute of Technology, 11605 132nd Avenue NE, Kirkland, WA 98034-8506. *Phone:* 425-739-8104. *E-mail:* info@lwtc.edu. *Website:* http://www.lwtech.edu/.

Lower Columbia College
Longview, Washington

Freshman Application Contact Ms. Nichole Seroshek, Director of Registration, Lower Columbia College, 1600 Maple Street, Longview, WA 98632. *Phone:* 360-442-2372. *Toll-free phone:* 866-900-2311. *Fax:* 360-442-2379. *E-mail:* registration@lowercolumbia.edu. *Website:* http://www.lowercolumbia.edu/.

North Seattle College
Seattle, Washington

Freshman Application Contact Ms. Betsy Abts, Registrar, North Seattle College, Seattle, WA 98103-3599. *Phone:* 206-934-3663. *Fax:* 206-934-3671. *E-mail:* arrc@seattlecolleges.edu. *Website:* http://www.northseattle.edu/.

Northwest Indian College
Bellingham, Washington

Freshman Application Contact Office of Admissions, Northwest Indian College, 2522 Kwina Road, Bellingham, WA 98226. *Phone:* 360-676-2772. *Toll-free phone:* 866-676-2772. *Fax:* 360-392-4333. *E-mail:* admissions@nwic.edu. *Website:* http://www.nwic.edu/.

Northwest School of Wooden Boatbuilding
Port Hadlock, Washington

- **Independent** 2-year, founded 1980
- **Small-town** 6-acre campus
- **Coed**

Undergraduates Students come from 20 states and territories; 3 other countries; 59% are from out of state.
Faculty *Total:* 8, 75% full-time. *Student/faculty ratio:* 12:1.
Majors Marine maintenance and ship repair technology.
Academics *Calendar:* quarters. *Degree:* diplomas and associate.
Library School Library.
Student Life *Housing:* college housing not available.
Costs (2017–18) *Tuition:* $19,400 full-time. No tuition increase for student's term of enrollment. *Required fees:* $100 full-time.
Applying *Options:* electronic application. *Required:* essay or personal statement, high school transcript.
Freshman Application Contact Northwest School of Wooden Boatbuilding, 42 North Water Street, Port Hadlock, WA 98339. *Phone:* 360-385-4948 Ext. 305. *Website:* http://www.nwswb.edu/.

Olympic College
Bremerton, Washington

- **State-supported** primarily 2-year, founded 1946, part of Washington State Board for Community and Technical Colleges
- **Suburban** 33-acre campus with easy access to Seattle, Tacoma
- **Coed**, 7,253 undergraduate students

Undergraduates 5% Black or African American, non-Hispanic/Latino; 8% Hispanic/Latino; 10% Asian, non-Hispanic/Latino; 2% American Indian or Alaska Native, non-Hispanic/Latino; 2% international; 1% live on campus.
Faculty *Total:* 473, 27% full-time.
Majors Accounting technology and bookkeeping; administrative assistant and secretarial science; business administration and management; chemical engineering; computer systems networking and telecommunications; cosmetology; crisis/emergency/disaster management; culinary arts; drafting and design technology; early childhood education; electrical and electronics engineering; electrical, electronic and communications engineering technology; engineering technology; industrial technology; information technology; liberal arts and sciences/liberal studies; marine maintenance and ship repair technology; mechanical engineering; medical/clinical assistant; mental and social health services and allied professions related; organizational leadership; photographic and film/video technology; physical sciences; physical therapy technology; registered nursing/registered nurse; substance abuse/addiction counseling; welding technology.
Academics *Calendar:* quarters. *Degrees:* certificates, diplomas, associate, and bachelor's. *Special study options:* academic remediation for entering students, adult/continuing education programs, advanced placement credit, cooperative education, distance learning, English as a second language, independent study, internships, off-campus study, part-time degree program, services for LD students, study abroad, summer session for credit.
Library Haselwood Library plus 1 other. Students can reserve study rooms.
Student Life *Housing Options:* coed. Campus housing is university owned. *Activities and Organizations:* drama/theater group, student-run newspaper, choral group, International Club, Armed Forces Club, Gay/Straight Alliance, Engineering Club, Clay Club. *Campus security:* 24-hour emergency response devices and patrols, student patrols, late-night transport/escort service. *Student services:* personal/psychological counseling.
Athletics *Intercollegiate sports:* baseball M(s), basketball M(s)/W(s), cross-country running M(s)/W(s), golf M(s)/W(s), softball W(s), track and field M(s)/W, volleyball W(s). *Intramural sports:* basketball M/W.
Financial Aid Of all full-time matriculated undergraduates who enrolled in 2015, 105 Federal Work-Study jobs (averaging $2380). 31 state and other part-time jobs (averaging $2880).
Applying *Options:* electronic application. *Required for some:* essay or personal statement, high school transcript, 2 letters of recommendation. *Application deadlines:* rolling (freshmen), rolling (transfers).
Freshman Application Contact Ms. Nora Downard, Program Manager, Olympic College, 1600 Chester Avenue, Bremerton, WA 98337-1699. *Phone:* 360-475-7445. *Toll-free phone:* 800-259-6718. *Fax:* 360-475-7202. *E-mail:* ndownard@olympic.edu. *Website:* http://www.olympic.edu/.

Peninsula College
Port Angeles, Washington

Freshman Application Contact Ms. Pauline Marvin, Peninsula College, 1502 East Lauridsen Boulevard, Port Angeles, WA 98362. *Phone:* 360-417-6596. *Toll-free phone:* 877-452-9277. *Fax:* 360-457-8100. *E-mail:* admissions@pencol.edu. *Website:* http://www.pc.ctc.edu/.

Pierce College at Fort Steilacoom
Lakewood, Washington

Freshman Application Contact Admissions Office, Pierce College at Fort Steilacoom, 9401 Farwest Drive SW, Lakewood, WA 98498. *Phone:* 253-964-6501. *E-mail:* admiss1@pierce.ctc.edu. *Website:* http://www.pierce.ctc.edu/.

Pierce College at Puyallup
Puyallup, Washington

Freshman Application Contact Pierce College at Puyallup, 1601 39th Avenue Southeast, Puyallup, WA 98374. *Phone:* 253-840-8400. *Website:* http://www.pierce.ctc.edu/.

Pima Medical Institute
Renton, Washington

Freshman Application Contact Pima Medical Institute, 555 South Renton Village Place, Renton, WA 98057. *Phone:* 425-228-9600. *Toll-free phone:* 800-477-PIMA. *Website:* http://www.pmi.edu/.

Pima Medical Institute
Seattle, Washington

Freshman Application Contact Admissions Office, Pima Medical Institute, 9709 Third Avenue NE, Suite 400, Seattle, WA 98115. *Phone:* 206-322-6100. *Toll-free phone:* 800-477-PIMA. *Website:* http://www.pmi.edu/.

Renton Technical College
Renton, Washington

- **State-supported** primarily 2-year, founded 1942, part of Washington State Board for Community and Technical Colleges
- **Suburban** 30-acre campus with easy access to Seattle
- **Endowment** $818,276
- **Coed,** 3,961 undergraduate students, 31% full-time, 30% women, 70% men

Undergraduates 1,238 full-time, 2,723 part-time. Students come from 8 states and territories; 0.1% are from out of state; 8% Black or African American, non-Hispanic/Latino; 7% Hispanic/Latino; 11% Asian, non-Hispanic/Latino; 0.5% Native Hawaiian or other Pacific Islander, non-Hispanic/Latino; 0.9% American Indian or Alaska Native, non-Hispanic/Latino; 3% Two or more races, non-Hispanic/Latino; 34% Race/ethnicity unknown; 0.2% international; 15% transferred in. *Retention:* 73% of full-time freshmen returned.
Freshmen *Admission:* 184 enrolled.
Faculty *Total:* 247, 37% full-time. *Student/faculty ratio:* 17:1.
Majors Accounting and business/management; anesthesiologist assistant; appliance installation and repair technology; autobody/collision and repair technology; automobile/automotive mechanics technology; building/property maintenance; business automation/technology/data entry; civil drafting and CAD/CADD; computer science; computer systems networking and telecommunications; construction management; culinary arts; dental assisting; drafting and design technology; early childhood education; heating, air conditioning, ventilation and refrigeration maintenance technology; legal administrative assistant/secretary; machine tool technology; massage therapy; medical administrative assistant and medical secretary; medical/clinical assistant; medical insurance coding; musical instrument fabrication and repair; office management; ophthalmic technology; pharmacy technician; registered nursing/registered nurse; surgical technology; surveying technology; welding technology.
Academics *Calendar:* quarters. *Degrees:* certificates, diplomas, associate, and bachelor's. *Special study options:* academic remediation for entering students, adult/continuing education programs, advanced placement credit, cooperative education, distance learning, English as a second language, internships, off-campus study, part-time degree program, services for LD students, summer session for credit.
Library Renton Technical College Library.
Student Life *Housing:* college housing not available. *Campus security:* patrols by security, security system. *Student services:* personal/psychological counseling.

Standardized Tests *Required for some:* ACT ASSET, CLEP, ACCUPLACER, DSP.
Costs (2016–17) *Tuition:* state resident $4167 full-time, $110 per credit hour part-time; nonresident $4580 full-time, $123 per credit hour part-time. Full-time tuition and fees vary according to course load, degree level, and program. Part-time tuition and fees vary according to course load, degree level, and program. *Payment plan:* installment.
Applying *Options:* electronic application, early admission. *Application fee:* $30. *Required for some:* essay or personal statement, high school transcript, interview. *Application deadlines:* rolling (freshmen), rolling (transfers). *Notification:* continuous (freshmen), continuous (transfers).
Freshman Application Contact Linh Bracking, Student Success Advisor, Renton Technical College, 3000 NE 4th Street, Renton, WA 98056. *Phone:* 425-235-2352 Ext. 5543. *E-mail:* lbracking@rtc.edu. *Website:* http://www.rtc.edu/.

Seattle Central College
Seattle, Washington

Freshman Application Contact Admissions Office, Seattle Central College, 1701 Broadway, Seattle, WA 98122-2400. *Phone:* 206-587-5450. *Website:* http://www.seattlecentral.edu/.

Shoreline Community College
Shoreline, Washington

Freshman Application Contact Shoreline Community College, 16101 Greenwood Avenue North, Shoreline, WA 98133-5696. *Phone:* 206-546-4613. *Website:* http://www.shoreline.edu/.

Skagit Valley College
Mount Vernon, Washington

Freshman Application Contact Ms. Karen Marie Bade, Admissions and Recruitment Coordinator, Skagit Valley College, 2405 College Way, Mount Vernon, WA 98273-5899. *Phone:* 360-416-7620. *E-mail:* karenmarie.bade@skagit.edu. *Website:* http://www.skagit.edu/.

South Puget Sound Community College
Olympia, Washington

Freshman Application Contact Ms. Heidi Dearborn, South Puget Sound Community College, 2011 Mottman Road, SW, Olympia, WA 98512-6292. *Phone:* 360-754-7711 Ext. 5358. *E-mail:* hdearborn@spcc.edu. *Website:* http://www.spscc.edu/.

South Seattle College
Seattle, Washington

Director of Admissions Ms. Kim Manderbach, Dean of Student Services/Registration, South Seattle College, 6000 16th Avenue, SW, Seattle, WA 98106-1499. *Phone:* 206-764-5378. *Fax:* 206-764-7947. *E-mail:* kimmanderb@sccd.ctc.edu. *Website:* http://southseattle.edu/.

Spokane Community College
Spokane, Washington

Freshman Application Contact Ann Hightower-Chavez, Researcher, District Institutional Research, Spokane Community College, Spokane, WA 99217-5399. *Phone:* 509-434-5242. *Toll-free phone:* 800-248-5644. *Fax:* 509-434-5249. *E-mail:* mlee@ccs.spokane.edu. *Website:* http://www.scc.spokane.edu/.

Spokane Falls Community College
Spokane, Washington

Freshman Application Contact Admissions Office, Spokane Falls Community College, Admissions MS 3011, 3410 West Fort George Wright Drive, Spokane, WA 99224. *Phone:* 509-533-3401. *Toll-free phone:* 888-509-7944. *Fax:* 509-533-3852. *Website:* http://www.spokanefalls.edu/.

Tacoma Community College
Tacoma, Washington

Freshman Application Contact Enrollment Services, Tacoma Community College, 6501 South 19th Street, Tacoma, WA 98466. *Phone:* 253-566-5325. *Fax:* 253-566-6034. *Website:* http://www.tacomacc.edu/.

Walla Walla Community College
Walla Walla, Washington

Freshman Application Contact Walla Walla Community College, 500 Tausick Way, Walla Walla, WA 99362-9267. *Phone:* 509-522-2500. *Toll-free phone:* 877-992-9922. *Website:* http://www.wwcc.edu/.

Wenatchee Valley College
Wenatchee, Washington

- **State and locally supported** 2-year, founded 1939, part of Washington State Board for Community and Technical Colleges
- **Small-town** 56-acre campus
- **Coed**

Undergraduates 2,334 full-time, 884 part-time. 0.8% Black or African American, non-Hispanic/Latino; 36% Hispanic/Latino; 1% Asian, non-Hispanic/Latino; 2% American Indian or Alaska Native, non-Hispanic/Latino; 3% Two or more races, non-Hispanic/Latino; 3% Race/ethnicity unknown; 0.1% international.

Academics *Calendar:* quarters. *Degree:* certificates, diplomas, and associate. *Special study options:* academic remediation for entering students, adult/continuing education programs, advanced placement credit, cooperative education, distance learning, English as a second language, external degree program, independent study, internships, part-time degree program, services for LD students, study abroad, summer session for credit.

Library John Brown Library plus 1 other.

Student Life *Campus security:* 24-hour patrols, controlled dormitory access.

Costs (2016–17) *Tuition:* state resident $3801 full-time; nonresident $4234 full-time. Full-time tuition and fees vary according to course load.

Applying *Options:* electronic application, early admission, deferred entrance. *Required for some:* high school transcript.

Freshman Application Contact Wenatchee Valley College, 1300 Fifth Street, Wenatchee, WA 98801-1799. *Phone:* 509-682-6835. *Toll-free phone:* 877-982-4968. *Website:* http://www.wvc.edu/.

Whatcom Community College
Bellingham, Washington

Freshman Application Contact Entry and Advising Center, Whatcom Community College, 237 West Kellogg Road, Bellingham, WA 98226-8003. *Phone:* 360-676-2170. *Fax:* 360-676-2171. *E-mail:* admit@whatcom.ctc.edu. *Website:* http://www.whatcom.ctc.edu/.

Yakima Valley Community College
Yakima, Washington

Freshman Application Contact Ms. Denise Anderson, Registrar and Director for Enrollment Services, Yakima Valley Community College, PO Box 1647, Yakima, WA 98907-1647. *Phone:* 509-574-4702. *Fax:* 509-574-6879. *E-mail:* admis@yvcc.edu. *Website:* http://www.yvcc.edu/.

WEST VIRGINIA

Blue Ridge Community and Technical College
Martinsburg, West Virginia

- **State-supported** 2-year, founded 1974, part of Community and Technical College System of West Virginia
- **Small-town** 46-acre campus
- **Coed,** 5,599 undergraduate students, 19% full-time, 64% women, 36% men

Undergraduates 1,052 full-time, 4,547 part-time. 5% are from out of state; 6% Black or African American, non-Hispanic/Latino; 2% Hispanic/Latino; 2% Asian, non-Hispanic/Latino; 0.1% Native Hawaiian or other Pacific Islander, non-Hispanic/Latino; 0.3% American Indian or Alaska Native, non-Hispanic/Latino; 3% Two or more races, non-Hispanic/Latino; 0.1% Race/ethnicity unknown; 4% transferred in. *Retention:* 51% of full-time freshmen returned.

Freshmen *Admission:* 423 enrolled. *Test scores:* SAT critical reading scores over 500: 45%; SAT critical reading scores over 600: 10%.

Faculty *Total:* 181, 36% full-time, 9% with terminal degrees. *Student/faculty ratio:* 25:1.

Majors Accounting; allied health and medical assisting services related; automation engineer technology; baking and pastry arts; business administration and management; business administration, management and operations related; clinical/medical laboratory technology; computer and information systems security; criminal justice/safety; culinary arts; data entry/microcomputer applications related; electrical and electronic engineering technologies related; emergency medical technology (EMT paramedic); general studies; information technology; legal assistant/paralegal; liberal arts and sciences/liberal studies; medical/clinical assistant; multi/interdisciplinary studies related; operations management; physical therapy technology; registered nursing/registered nurse; restaurant, culinary, and catering management; science technologies related; system, networking, and LAN/WAN management.

Academics *Calendar:* semesters. *Degree:* certificates and associate. *Special study options:* academic remediation for entering students, accelerated degree program, adult/continuing education programs, advanced placement credit, double majors, English as a second language, independent study, internships, part-time degree program, services for LD students.

Student Life *Housing:* college housing not available. *Activities and Organizations:* drama/theater group, Student Leadership Academy, Drama Club, Phi Theta Kappa, SkillsUSA, Student Nurses Association, national fraternities. *Campus security:* late-night transport/escort service. *Student services:* personal/psychological counseling.

Standardized Tests *Recommended:* SAT and SAT Subject Tests or ACT (for admission).

Costs (2016–17) *Tuition:* state resident $3864 full-time, $161 per credit hour part-time; nonresident $6984 full-time, $291 per credit hour part-time. Full-time tuition and fees vary according to class time and course load. Part-time tuition and fees vary according to class time and course load. *Payment plan:* installment. *Waivers:* employees or children of employees.

Applying *Options:* electronic application, deferred entrance. *Application fee:* $25. *Required:* high school transcript. *Required for some:* interview.

Freshman Application Contact Brenda K. Neal, Dean of Students, Blue Ridge Community and Technical College, 13650 Apple Harvest Drive, Martinsburg, WV 25403. *Phone:* 304-260-4380 Ext. 2109. *Fax:* 304-260-4376. *E-mail:* bneal@blueridgectc.edu. *Website:* http://www.blueridgectc.edu/.

BridgeValley Community and Technical College
Montgomery, West Virginia

Director of Admissions Ms. Lisa Graham, Director of Admissions, BridgeValley Community and Technical College, 619 2nd Avenue, Montgomery, WV 25136. *Phone:* 304-442-3167. *Website:* http://www.bridgevalley.edu/.

BridgeValley Community and Technical College
South Charleston, West Virginia

Freshman Application Contact Mr. Bryce Casto, Vice President, Student Affairs, BridgeValley Community and Technical College, 2001 Union Carbide Drive, South Charleston, WV 25303. *Phone:* 304-766-3140. *Fax:* 304-766-4158. *E-mail:* castosb@wvstateu.edu. *Website:* http://www.bridgevalley.edu/.

Eastern West Virginia Community and Technical College
Moorefield, West Virginia

Freshman Application Contact Learner Support Services, Eastern West Virginia Community and Technical College, HC 65 Box 402, Moorefield, WV 26836. *Phone:* 304-434-8000. *Toll-free phone:* 877-982-2322. *Fax:* 304-434-7000. *E-mail:* askeast@eastern.wvnet.edu. *Website:* http://www.eastern.wvnet.edu/.

Huntington Junior College
Huntington, West Virginia

Director of Admissions Mr. James Garrett, Educational Services Director, Huntington Junior College, 900 Fifth Avenue, Huntington, WV 25701-2004. *Phone:* 304-697-7550. *Toll-free phone:* 800-344-4522. *Website:* http://www.huntingtonjuniorcollege.com/.

Mountain State College
Parkersburg, West Virginia

- **Proprietary** 2-year, founded 1888
- **Small-town** campus
- **Coed**

Undergraduates 174 full-time, 2 part-time. Students come from 2 states and territories; 3% transferred in. *Retention:* 70% of full-time freshmen returned.
Faculty *Student/faculty ratio:* 17:1.
Academics *Calendar:* quarters. *Degree:* diplomas and associate. *Special study options:* distance learning, independent study, internships, part-time degree program, services for LD students.
Library Mountain State College Library.
Standardized Tests *Required:* CPAt (for admission).
Applying *Required:* interview.
Freshman Application Contact Ms. Judith Sutton, President, Mountain State College, 1508 Spring Street, Parkersburg, WV 26101-3993. *Phone:* 304-485-5487. *Toll-free phone:* 800-841-0201. *Fax:* 304-485-3524. *E-mail:* jsutton@msc.edu. *Website:* http://www.msc.edu/.

Mountwest Community & Technical College
Huntington, West Virginia

Freshman Application Contact Dr. Tammy Johnson, Admissions Director, Mountwest Community & Technical College, 1 John Marshall Drive, Huntington, WV 25755. *Phone:* 304-696-3160. *Toll-free phone:* 866-676-5533. *Fax:* 304-696-3135. *E-mail:* admissions@marshall.edu. *Website:* http://www.mctc.edu/.

New River Community and Technical College
Beaver, West Virginia

Director of Admissions Dr. Allen B. Withers, Vice President, Student Services, New River Community and Technical College, 280 University Drive, Beaver, WV 25813. *Phone:* 304-929-5011. *Toll-free phone:* 866-349-3739. *E-mail:* awithers@newriver.edu. *Website:* http://www.newriver.edu/.

Pierpont Community & Technical College
Fairmont, West Virginia

Freshman Application Contact Mr. Steve Leadman, Director of Admissions and Recruiting, Pierpont Community & Technical College, 1201 Locust Avenue, Fairmont, WV 26554. *Phone:* 304-367-4892. *Toll-free phone:* 800-641-5678. *Fax:* 304-367-4789. *Website:* http://www.pierpont.edu/.

Potomac State College of West Virginia University
Keyser, West Virginia

- **State-supported** primarily 2-year, founded 1901, part of West Virginia Higher Education Policy Commission
- **Small-town** 18-acre campus
- **Coed**

Undergraduates 1,156 full-time, 319 part-time. Students come from 24 states and territories; 2 other countries; 37% are from out of state; 21% Black or African American, non-Hispanic/Latino; 3% Hispanic/Latino; 0.2% Asian, non-Hispanic/Latino; 0.2% Native Hawaiian or other Pacific Islander, non-Hispanic/Latino; 0.5% American Indian or Alaska Native, non-Hispanic/Latino; 4% Two or more races, non-Hispanic/Latino; 1% Race/ethnicity unknown; 0.6% international; 3% transferred in; 52% live on campus. *Retention:* 44% of full-time freshmen returned.
Faculty *Student/faculty ratio:* 22:1.
Academics *Calendar:* semesters. *Degrees:* associate and bachelor's. *Special study options:* academic remediation for entering students, adult/continuing education programs, advanced placement credit, cooperative education, distance learning, double majors, honors programs, independent study, internships, part-time degree program, services for LD students, study abroad, summer session for credit.
Library Mary F. Shipper Library.
Student Life *Campus security:* 24-hour patrols, late-night transport/escort service, controlled dormitory access.
Athletics Member NJCAA.

Standardized Tests *Recommended:* SAT or ACT (for admission).
Costs (2016–17) *Tuition:* state resident $4056 full-time, $169 per credit hour part-time; nonresident $10,416 full-time, $434 per credit hour part-time. Full-time tuition and fees vary according to course load and degree level. Part-time tuition and fees vary according to course load and degree level. *Room and board:* $8752; room only: $4620. Room and board charges vary according to board plan and housing facility.
Financial Aid Of all full-time matriculated undergraduates who enrolled in 2015, 70 Federal Work-Study jobs (averaging $1300).
Applying *Options:* electronic application. *Required:* high school transcript.
Freshman Application Contact Ms. Beth Little, Director of Enrollment Services, Potomac State College of West Virginia University, 75 Arnold Street, Keyser, WV 26726. *Phone:* 304-788-6820. *Toll-free phone:* 800-262-7332 Ext. 6820. *Fax:* 304-788-6939. *E-mail:* go2psc@mail.wvu.edu. *Website:* http://www.potomacstatecollege.edu/.

Southern West Virginia Community and Technical College
Mount Gay, West Virginia

Freshman Application Contact Mr. Roy Simmons, Registrar, Southern West Virginia Community and Technical College, PO Box 2900, Mt. Gay, WV 25637. *Phone:* 304-792-7160 Ext. 120. *Fax:* 304-792-7096. *E-mail:* admissions@southern.wvnet.edu. *Website:* http://southernwv.edu/.

Valley College
Beckley, West Virginia

Director of Admissions Kerri Cline, Admissions Director, Valley College, 120 New River Town Center, Beckley, WV 25801. *Phone:* 304-252-9547. *Toll-free phone:* 888-53LEARN. *Fax:* 304-252-1694. *Website:* http://www.valley.edu/.

West Virginia Business College
Wheeling, West Virginia

Freshman Application Contact Ms. Karen D. Shaw, Director, West Virginia Business College, 1052 Main Street, Wheeling, WV 26003. *Phone:* 304-232-0361. *Fax:* 304-232-0363. *E-mail:* wvbcwheeling@stratuswave.net. *Website:* http://www.wvbc.edu/.

West Virginia Junior College–Bridgeport
Bridgeport, West Virginia

- **Proprietary** 2-year, founded 1922
- **Small-town** 3-acre campus
- **Coed,** 150 undergraduate students, 100% full-time, 87% women, 13% men

Undergraduates 150 full-time. Students come from 4 states and territories; 7% transferred in. *Retention:* 80% of full-time freshmen returned.
Freshmen *Admission:* 150 enrolled. *Average high school GPA:* 2.5.
Faculty *Total:* 10, 50% full-time, 30% with terminal degrees. *Student/faculty ratio:* 15:1.
Majors Dental assisting; information technology; medical/clinical assistant; medical office management; pharmacy technician.
Academics *Calendar:* quarters. *Degree:* diplomas and associate. *Special study options:* academic remediation for entering students, cooperative education, distance learning, independent study, internships, services for LD students, summer session for credit.
Library WVJC Library plus 1 other. *Books:* 350 (physical), 15 (digital/electronic); *Serial titles:* 12 (physical); *Databases:* 5. Weekly public service hours: 50.
Student Life *Housing:* college housing not available. *Activities and Organizations:* Medical Club, Business Club, Computer Club, Dental Assisting Club, Pharmacy Tech Club. *Campus security:* 24-hour emergency response devices.
Financial Aid Of all full-time matriculated undergraduates who enrolled in 2015, 10 Federal Work-Study jobs.
Applying *Options:* electronic application. *Application fee:* $25. *Required:* minimum 2.5 GPA, interview, meeting with an Admissions Representative. *Required for some:* essay or personal statement, 1 letter of recommendation. *Recommended:* high school transcript. *Application deadline:* rolling (freshmen). *Notification:* continuous (freshmen).
Freshman Application Contact Ms. Kristen Kirk, High School Admissions Representative, West Virginia Junior College–Bridgeport, 176 Thompson Drive, Bridgeport, WV 26330. *Phone:* 304-842-4007. *Toll-free phone:* 800-470-5627. *Fax:* 304-842-8191. *E-mail:* kkirk@wvjc.edu. *Website:* http://www.wvjc.edu/.

West Virginia Junior College–Charleston
Charleston, West Virginia

Freshman Application Contact West Virginia Junior College–Charleston, 1000 Virginia Street East, Charleston, WV 25301-2817. *Phone:* 304-345-2820. *Toll-free phone:* 800-924-5208. *Website:* http://www.wvjc.edu/.

West Virginia Junior College–Morgantown
Morgantown, West Virginia

Freshman Application Contact Admissions Office, West Virginia Junior College–Morgantown, 148 Willey Street, Morgantown, WV 26505-5521. *Phone:* 304-296-8282. *Website:* http://www.wvjcmorgantown.edu/.

West Virginia Northern Community College
Wheeling, West Virginia

Freshman Application Contact Mrs. Janet Fike, Vice President of Student Services, West Virginia Northern Community College, 1704 Market Street, Wheeling, WV 26003. *Phone:* 304-214-8837. *E-mail:* jfike@northern.wvnet.edu. *Website:* http://www.wvncc.edu/.

West Virginia University at Parkersburg
Parkersburg, West Virginia

Freshman Application Contact Christine Post, Associate Dean of Enrollment Management, West Virginia University at Parkersburg, 300 Campus Drive, Parkersburg, WV 26104. *Phone:* 304-424-8223 Ext. 223. *Toll-free phone:* 800-WVA-WVUP. *Fax:* 304-424-8332. *E-mail:* christine.post@mail.wvu.edu. *Website:* http://www.wvup.edu/.

WISCONSIN

Blackhawk Technical College
Janesville, Wisconsin

- **District-supported** 2-year, founded 1968, part of Wisconsin Technical College System
- **Small-town** 84-acre campus
- **Coed,** 2,034 undergraduate students, 40% full-time, 58% women, 42% men

Undergraduates 822 full-time, 1,212 part-time. Students come from 3 states and territories; 1% are from out of state; 6% Black or African American, non-Hispanic/Latino; 10% Hispanic/Latino; 1% Asian, non-Hispanic/Latino; 0.6% American Indian or Alaska Native, non-Hispanic/Latino; 2% Two or more races, non-Hispanic/Latino; 2% Race/ethnicity unknown. *Retention:* 54% of full-time freshmen returned.
Freshmen *Admission:* 316 enrolled.
Faculty *Total:* 290, 31% full-time, 1% with terminal degrees. *Student/faculty ratio:* 8:1.
Majors Accounting; administrative assistant and secretarial science; agribusiness; biology/biotechnology laboratory technician; business administration and management; clinical/medical laboratory technology; computer systems networking and telecommunications; criminal justice/police science; culinary arts; diagnostic medical sonography and ultrasound technology; early childhood education; electromechanical technology; fire science/firefighting; human resources management; interdisciplinary studies; legal administrative assistant/secretary; marketing/marketing management; medical administrative assistant and medical secretary; physical therapy technology; radiologist assistant; registered nursing/registered nurse; web page, digital/multimedia and information resources design.
Academics *Calendar:* semesters. *Degree:* certificates, diplomas, and associate. *Special study options:* academic remediation for entering students, accelerated degree program, adult/continuing education programs, advanced placement credit, cooperative education, distance learning, English as a second language, independent study, internships, part-time degree program, services for LD students, student-designed majors, summer session for credit.
Library Blackhawk Technical College Library. *Books:* 12,369 (physical), 89,551 (digital/electronic); *Serial titles:* 109 (physical), 13 (digital/electronic); *Databases:* 68. Weekly public service hours: 57.
Student Life *Housing:* college housing not available. *Activities and Organizations:* student-run newspaper, Student Government Association,

Public Safety Association, Epicurean Club, Veterans Club, Phi Theta Kappa Honor Society. *Campus security:* student patrols.
Costs (2016–17) *Tuition:* state resident $3911 full-time, $130 per credit hour part-time; nonresident $5866 full-time, $196 per credit hour part-time. Full-time tuition and fees vary according to course load. Part-time tuition and fees vary according to course load. *Required fees:* $338 full-time, $7 per credit hour part-time. *Payment plans:* installment, deferred payment. *Waivers:* senior citizens.
Financial Aid Of all full-time matriculated undergraduates who enrolled in 2015, 33 Federal Work-Study jobs (averaging $1150).
Applying *Options:* electronic application. *Required:* high school transcript. *Application deadlines:* rolling (freshmen), rolling (transfers). *Notification:* continuous (freshmen), continuous (transfers).
Freshman Application Contact Blackhawk Technical College, 6004 South County Road G, Janesville, WI 53546-9458. *Phone:* 608-757-7713. *Website:* http://www.blackhawk.edu/.

Bryant & Stratton College–Bayshore Campus
Glendale, Wisconsin

Admissions Office Contact Bryant & Stratton College–Bayshore Campus, 500 West Silver Spring Drive, Bayshore Town Center, Suite K340, Glendale, WI 53217. *Website:* http://www.bryantstratton.edu/.

Bryant & Stratton College–Milwaukee Campus
Milwaukee, Wisconsin

Freshman Application Contact Mr. Dan Basile, Director of Admissions, Bryant & Stratton College–Milwaukee Campus, 310 West Wisconsin Avenue, Suite 500 East, Milwaukee, WI 53203-2214. *Phone:* 414-276-5200. *Website:* http://www.bryantstratton.edu/.

Chippewa Valley Technical College
Eau Claire, Wisconsin

- **District-supported** 2-year, founded 1912, part of Wisconsin Technical College System
- **Suburban** 255-acre campus
- **Coed**

Faculty *Total:* 411, 54% full-time.
Majors Accounting; administrative assistant and secretarial science; agronomy and crop science; animal/livestock husbandry and production; applied horticulture/horticultural business services related; business administration and management; civil engineering technology; clinical/medical laboratory technology; computer programming; computer systems networking and telecommunications; criminal justice/police science; dental hygiene; diagnostic medical sonography and ultrasound technology; digital communication and media/multimedia; early childhood education; electromechanical technology; emergency medical technology (EMT paramedic); health information/medical records technology; heating, ventilation, air conditioning and refrigeration engineering technology; human resources management; industrial mechanics and maintenance technology; legal assistant/paralegal; liberal arts and sciences/liberal studies; library and information science; manufacturing engineering technology; marketing/marketing management; mechanical drafting and CAD/CADD; medical radiologic technology; multi/interdisciplinary studies related; nanotechnology; operations management; physical therapy technology; public relations, advertising, and applied communication; registered nursing/registered nurse; respiratory care therapy; sales, distribution, and marketing operations; substance abuse/addiction counseling.
Academics *Calendar:* semesters. *Degree:* certificates, diplomas, and associate. *Special study options:* academic remediation for entering students, accelerated degree program, adult/continuing education programs, advanced placement credit, cooperative education, distance learning, double majors, English as a second language, honors programs, independent study, internships, part-time degree program, services for LD students, student-designed majors, summer session for credit.
Library The Learning Center. *Books:* 10,758 (physical), 158,463 (digital/electronic); *Serial titles:* 110 (physical), 3,589 (digital/electronic); *Databases:* 116. Weekly public service hours: 66; students can reserve study rooms.
Student Life *Housing:* college housing not available. *Activities and Organizations:* The Chippewa Valley Nurses, Phi Theta Kappa, Welding Club, IMAGERS, Auto Club. *Campus security:* 24-hour emergency response

devices, late-night transport/escort service, security cameras. *Student services:* health clinic, personal/psychological counseling.

Costs (2016–17) *Tuition:* state resident $3911 full-time, $130 per credit part-time; nonresident $5866 full-time, $196 per credit part-time. Full-time tuition and fees vary according to course load and reciprocity agreements. Part-time tuition and fees vary according to course load and reciprocity agreements. *Required fees:* $338 full-time, $338 per year part-time. *Payment plans:* installment, deferred payment. *Waivers:* senior citizens.

Financial Aid Of all full-time matriculated undergraduates who enrolled in 2015, 218 Federal Work-Study jobs (averaging $875).

Applying *Options:* electronic application, early admission, deferred entrance. *Application fee:* $30. *Application deadlines:* rolling (freshmen), rolling (transfers). *Notification:* continuous (freshmen), continuous (transfers).

Freshman Application Contact Admissions Office, Chippewa Valley Technical College, 620 W. Clairemont Avenue, Eau Claire, WI 54701. *Phone:* 715-833-6200. *Toll-free phone:* 800-547-2882. *Fax:* 715-833-6470. *E-mail:* infocenter@cvtc.edu. *Website:* http://www.cvtc.edu/.

College of Menominee Nation
Keshena, Wisconsin

Director of Admissions Tessa James, Admissions Coordinator, College of Menominee Nation, PO Box 1179, Keshena, WI 54135. *Phone:* 715-799-5600 Ext. 3053. *Toll-free phone:* 800-567-2344. *E-mail:* tjames@menominee.edu. *Website:* http://www.menominee.edu/.

Fox Valley Technical College
Appleton, Wisconsin

- **State and locally supported** 2-year, founded 1967, part of Wisconsin Technical College System
- **Suburban** 100-acre campus
- **Endowment** $3.3 million
- **Coed,** 10,889 undergraduate students, 22% full-time, 47% women, 53% men
- **67% of applicants were admitted**

Undergraduates 2,393 full-time, 8,496 part-time. Students come from 13 states and territories; 4 other countries; 1% are from out of state; 3% Black or African American, non-Hispanic/Latino; 4% Hispanic/Latino; 5% Asian, non-Hispanic/Latino; 0.2% Native Hawaiian or other Pacific Islander, non-Hispanic/Latino; 1% American Indian or Alaska Native, non-Hispanic/Latino; 0.5% Two or more races, non-Hispanic/Latino; 9% Race/ethnicity unknown; 0.1% international.

Freshmen *Admission:* 1,523 applied, 1,017 admitted, 807 enrolled.

Faculty *Total:* 802, 38% full-time. *Student/faculty ratio:* 11:1.

Majors Accounting; administrative assistant and secretarial science; agricultural/farm supplies retailing and wholesaling; agricultural mechanization; airline pilot and flight crew; autobody/collision and repair technology; automation engineer technology; automobile/automotive mechanics technology; avionics maintenance technology; banking and financial support services; biology/biotechnology laboratory technician; building/construction site management; business administration and management; computer and information systems security; computer programming; computer support specialist; computer systems networking and telecommunications; court reporting; criminal justice/police science; culinary arts; dental hygiene; diesel mechanics technology; early childhood education; electrical and electronic engineering technologies related; electrical, electronic and communications engineering technology; electromechanical technology; emergency medical technology (EMT paramedic); energy management and systems technology; fire science/firefighting; forensic science and technology; health information/medical records technology; homeland security related; hospitality administration; human resources management; industrial safety technology; interior design; legal assistant/paralegal; logistics, materials, and supply chain management; manufacturing engineering technology; marketing/marketing management; mechanical drafting and CAD/CADD; medical office management; meeting and event planning; multi/interdisciplinary studies related; natural resources/conservation; occupational therapist assistant; office management; professional, technical, business, and scientific writing; radio, television, and digital communication related; registered nursing/registered nurse; substance abuse/addiction counseling; web/multimedia management and webmaster; welding technology.

Academics *Calendar:* semesters. *Degree:* certificates, diplomas, and associate. *Special study options:* academic remediation for entering students, accelerated degree program, advanced placement credit, cooperative education, distance learning, double majors, English as a second language, independent study, internships, off-campus study, part-time degree program, services for LD students, student-designed majors, study abroad, summer session for credit.

Library Student Success Center Library. *Books:* 8,288 (physical), 1.2 million (digital/electronic); *Serial titles:* 50 (physical), 37,572 (digital/electronic); *Databases:* 141. Weekly public service hours: 65; students can reserve study rooms.

Student Life *Housing:* college housing not available. *Activities and Organizations:* student-run newspaper, Student Government Association, Phi Theta Kappa, Culinary Arts Club, Machine Tool Club, Post Secondary Agribusiness Club. *Campus security:* 24-hour emergency response devices, late-night transport/escort service, trained security personnel patrol during hours of operation. *Student services:* health clinic, personal/psychological counseling.

Athletics *Intercollegiate sports:* basketball M/W. *Intramural sports:* table tennis M/W.

Standardized Tests *Required for some:* ACT or ACCUPLACER, TEAS, Bennett Mechanical Comprehension Test.

Costs (2016–17) *Tuition:* state resident $3911 full-time, $130 per credit part-time; nonresident $5866 full-time, $196 per credit part-time. *Required fees:* $525 full-time, $18 per credit part-time, $18 per credit part-time. *Payment plan:* installment.

Applying *Options:* electronic application. *Application fee:* $30. *Required for some:* high school transcript, interview. *Application deadlines:* rolling (freshmen), rolling (transfers).

Freshman Application Contact Admissions Center, Fox Valley Technical College, 1825 North Bluemound Drive, PO Box 2277, Appleton, WI 54912-2277. *Phone:* 920-735-5643. *Toll-free phone:* 800-735-3882. *Fax:* 920-735-2582. *Website:* http://www.fvtc.edu/.

Gateway Technical College
Kenosha, Wisconsin

- **State and locally supported** 2-year, founded 1911, part of Wisconsin Technical College System
- **Urban** 10-acre campus with easy access to Chicago, Milwaukee
- **Endowment** $4.6 million
- **Coed,** 8,722 undergraduate students, 16% full-time, 56% women, 44% men

Undergraduates 1,379 full-time, 7,343 part-time. Students come from 5 states and territories; 2% are from out of state; 10% Black or African American, non-Hispanic/Latino; 15% Hispanic/Latino; 1% Asian, non-Hispanic/Latino; 0.1% Native Hawaiian or other Pacific Islander, non-Hispanic/Latino; 0.5% American Indian or Alaska Native, non-Hispanic/Latino; 3% Two or more races, non-Hispanic/Latino; 7% Race/ethnicity unknown; 10% transferred in. *Retention:* 57% of full-time freshmen returned.

Freshmen *Admission:* 1,598 applied, 1,571 admitted, 1,202 enrolled.

Faculty *Total:* 699, 35% full-time, 3% with terminal degrees. *Student/faculty ratio:* 10:1.

Majors Accounting; administrative assistant and secretarial science; airline pilot and flight crew; applied horticulture/horticulture operations; architectural engineering technology; automation engineer technology; automobile/automotive mechanics technology; business administration and management; computer programming; computer support specialist; computer systems networking and telecommunications; criminal justice/police science; culinary arts; diesel mechanics technology; early childhood education; electrical, electronic and communications engineering technology; electromechanical technology; emergency medical technology (EMT paramedic); graphic design; health information/medical records technology; heating, air conditioning, ventilation and refrigeration maintenance technology; hospitality administration; interdisciplinary studies; interior design; marketing/marketing management; mechanical drafting and CAD/CADD; physical therapy technology; professional, technical, business, and scientific writing; psychiatric/mental health services technology; registered nursing/registered nurse; surgical technology; surveying technology; teacher assistant/aide; transportation and highway engineering; veterinary/animal health technology; water resources engineering; web/multimedia management and webmaster.

Academics *Calendar:* semesters. *Degree:* certificates, diplomas, and associate. *Special study options:* academic remediation for entering students, advanced placement credit, cooperative education, distance learning, double majors, English as a second language, independent study, internships, off-campus study, part-time degree program, services for LD students, student-designed majors, summer session for credit.

Library Library/Learning Resources Center plus 2 others. *Books:* 23,575 (physical), 4,369 (digital/electronic); *Serial titles:* 131 (physical); *Databases:* 41. Weekly public service hours: 59; students can reserve study rooms.

Student Life *Housing:* college housing not available. *Activities and Organizations:* student-run newspaper, International Club, United Student Government, Outdoor Adventure Club, Team EXCEED, Collegiate DECA. *Campus security:* 24-hour emergency response devices, late-night transport/escort service, patrols by trained security when open, locked/alarmed when closed. *Student services:* personal/psychological counseling.

Costs (2017–18) *Tuition:* state resident $4123 full-time, $130 per credit part-time; nonresident $6078 full-time, $196 per credit part-time. Full-time tuition and fees vary according to course level, course load, program, and reciprocity agreements. Part-time tuition and fees vary according to course level, course load, program, and reciprocity agreements. *Required fees:* $345 full-time. *Payment plans:* installment, deferred payment. *Waivers:* senior citizens and employees or children of employees.

Applying *Options:* electronic application, early admission, deferred entrance. *Application fee:* $30. *Required:* high school transcript. *Required for some:* interview. *Application deadlines:* rolling (freshmen), rolling (transfers). *Notification:* continuous (freshmen), continuous (transfers).

Freshman Application Contact Admissions, Gateway Technical College, 3520 30th Avenue, Kenosha, WI 53144-1690. *Phone:* 262-564-2300. *Fax:* 262-564-2301. *E-mail:* admissions@gtc.edu.

Website: http://www.gtc.edu/.

Lac Courte Oreilles Ojibwa Community College
Hayward, Wisconsin

Freshman Application Contact Ms. Annette Wiggins, Registrar, Lac Courte Oreilles Ojibwa Community College, 13466 West Trepania Road, Hayward, WI 54843-2181. *Phone:* 715-634-4790 Ext. 104. *Toll-free phone:* 888-526-6221. *Website:* http://www.lco.edu/.

Lakeshore Technical College
Cleveland, Wisconsin

Freshman Application Contact Lakeshore Technical College, 1290 North Avenue, Cleveland, WI 53015. *Phone:* 920-693-1339. *Toll-free phone:* 888-GO TO LTC. *Fax:* 920-693-3561. *Website:* http://www.gotoltc.com/.

Madison Area Technical College
Madison, Wisconsin

- **District-supported** 2-year, founded 1911, part of Wisconsin Technical College System
- **Urban** 150-acre campus
- **Coed**, 16,537 undergraduate students, 30% full-time, 59% women, 41% men

Undergraduates 5,037 full-time, 11,500 part-time. Students come from 10 states and territories; 5 other countries; 3% are from out of state; 6% Black or African American, non-Hispanic/Latino; 9% Hispanic/Latino; 4% Asian, non-Hispanic/Latino; 0.1% Native Hawaiian or other Pacific Islander, non-Hispanic/Latino; 0.5% American Indian or Alaska Native, non-Hispanic/Latino; 4% Two or more races, non-Hispanic/Latino; 1% Race/ethnicity unknown; 1% international; 5% transferred in.

Freshmen *Admission:* 2,280 enrolled.

Faculty *Total:* 1,476, 32% full-time. *Student/faculty ratio:* 13:1.

Majors Accounting; administrative assistant and secretarial science; agricultural mechanization; architectural engineering technology; automobile/automotive mechanics technology; biology/biotechnology laboratory technician; business administration and management; business teacher education; child development; civil engineering technology; clinical/medical laboratory technology; commercial and advertising art; communications technology; computer engineering technology; computer programming; computer typography and composition equipment operation; court reporting; criminal justice/police science; culinary arts; data processing and data processing technology; dental hygiene; dietetics; drafting/design engineering technologies related; electrical, electronic and communications engineering technology; emergency medical technology (EMT paramedic); fashion merchandising; finance; fire science/firefighting; graphic and printing equipment operation/production; hospitality administration; human services; industrial radiologic technology; insurance; interior design; liberal arts and sciences/liberal studies; marketing/marketing management; medical administrative assistant and medical secretary; occupational therapy; parks, recreation and leisure; photography; real estate; registered nursing/registered nurse; respiratory care therapy; tourism and travel services management; veterinary/animal health technology; welding technology.

Academics *Calendar:* semesters. *Degree:* certificates, diplomas, and associate. *Special study options:* academic remediation for entering students, accelerated degree program, adult/continuing education programs, cooperative education, distance learning, English as a second language, internships, off-campus study, part-time degree program, services for LD students, summer session for credit.

Library Truax-Information Resource Center.

Student Life *Housing:* college housing not available. *Activities and Organizations:* drama/theater group, student-run newspaper, choral group, Marketing Club, Minority Networking Groups, Data Processing Management Association, Student Nurses Association, Business Professionals of America. *Campus security:* 24-hour emergency response devices and patrols, late-night transport/escort service. *Student services:* health clinic, personal/psychological counseling, women's center.

Athletics Member NJCAA. *Intercollegiate sports:* baseball M, basketball M/W, bowling M/W, cross-country running M/W, softball W, tennis M/W, track and field M/W, volleyball M/W, wrestling M. *Intramural sports:* basketball M/W, bowling M/W, softball M/W, tennis M/W, volleyball M/W.

Costs (2016–17) *One-time required fee:* $35. *Tuition:* state resident $3911 full-time, $130 per credit hour part-time; nonresident $5866 full-time, $196 per credit hour part-time. Full-time tuition and fees vary according to course load. Part-time tuition and fees vary according to course load. *Required fees:* $365 full-time, $12 per credit part-time.

Financial Aid Of all full-time matriculated undergraduates who enrolled in 2015, 200 Federal Work-Study jobs (averaging $2000). 300 state and other part-time jobs (averaging $2000).

Applying *Options:* electronic application, early admission. *Application fee:* $25. *Required for some:* high school transcript. *Application deadlines:* 7/1 (freshmen), 7/1 (transfers). *Notification:* continuous (freshmen), continuous (transfers).

Freshman Application Contact Ms. Lori Sebranek, Dean - Enrollment Services, Madison Area Technical College, 1701 Wright Street, Madison, WI 53704. *Phone:* 608-243-4185. *Toll-free phone:* 800-322-6282. *Fax:* 608-243-4353. *E-mail:* enrollmentservices@madisoncollege.edu.

Website: http://madisoncollege.edu/.

Madison Media Institute
Madison, Wisconsin

Freshman Application Contact Mr. Chris K. Hutchings, President/Director, Madison Media Institute, 2702 Agriculture Drive, Madison, WI 53718. *Phone:* 608-237-8301. *Toll-free phone:* 800-236-4997.

Website: http://www.mediainstitute.edu/.

Mid-State Technical College
Wisconsin Rapids, Wisconsin

Freshman Application Contact Ms. Carole Prochnow, Admissions Assistant, Mid-State Technical College, 500 32nd Street North, Wisconsin Rapids, WI 54494-5599. *Phone:* 715-422-5444. *Website:* http://www.mstc.edu/.

Milwaukee Area Technical College
Milwaukee, Wisconsin

Freshman Application Contact Sarah Adams, Director, Enrollment Services, Milwaukee Area Technical College, 700 West State Street, Milwaukee, WI 53233-1443. *Phone:* 414-297-6595. *Fax:* 414-297-7800. *E-mail:* adamss4@matc.edu. *Website:* http://www.matc.edu/.

Milwaukee Career College
Milwaukee, Wisconsin

Admissions Office Contact Milwaukee Career College, 3077 N. Mayfair Road, Suite 300, Milwaukee, WI 53222. *Website:* http://www.mkecc.edu/.

Moraine Park Technical College
Fond du Lac, Wisconsin

Freshman Application Contact Karen Jarvis, Student Services, Moraine Park Technical College, 235 North National Avenue, Fond du Lac, WI 54935. *Phone:* 920-924-3200. *Toll-free phone:* 800-472-4554. *Fax:* 920-924-3421. *E-mail:* kjarvis@morainepark.edu. *Website:* http://www.morainepark.edu/.

Nicolet Area Technical College
Rhinelander, Wisconsin

Freshman Application Contact Ms. Susan Kordula, Director of Admissions, Nicolet Area Technical College, PO Box 518, Rhinelander, WI 54501. *Phone:* 715-365-4451. *Toll-free phone:* 800-544-3039. *E-mail:* inquire@nicoletcollege.edu. *Website:* http://www.nicoletcollege.edu/.

Northcentral Technical College
Wausau, Wisconsin

- **District-supported** 2-year, founded 1912, part of Wisconsin Technical College System
- **Rural** 96-acre campus
- **Coed**, 4,158 undergraduate students, 35% full-time, 61% women, 39% men

Undergraduates 1,437 full-time, 2,721 part-time. 1% Black or African American, non-Hispanic/Latino; 2% Hispanic/Latino; 6% Asian, non-Hispanic/Latino; 0.1% Native Hawaiian or other Pacific Islander, non-Hispanic/Latino; 1% American Indian or Alaska Native, non-Hispanic/Latino; 1% Two or more races, non-Hispanic/Latino; 11% Race/ethnicity unknown.
Freshmen *Admission:* 750 enrolled.
Faculty *Student/faculty ratio:* 23:1.
Majors Accounting; administrative assistant and secretarial science; agribusiness; agronomy and crop science; architectural engineering technology; automobile/automotive mechanics technology; business administration and management; cinematography and film/video production; clinical/medical laboratory technology; computer and information sciences and support services related; computer systems analysis; computer systems networking and telecommunications; criminal justice/police science; culinary arts; dental hygiene; diesel mechanics technology; early childhood education; electromechanical technology; emergency medical technology (EMT paramedic); entrepreneurship; furniture design and manufacturing; general studies; graphic communications; manufacturing engineering technology; marketing/marketing management; mechanical drafting and CAD/CADD; medical insurance/medical billing; medical radiologic technology; mental and social health services and allied professions related; merchandising, sales, and marketing operations related (general); multi/interdisciplinary studies related; operations management; registered nursing/registered nurse; sign language interpretation and translation; substance abuse/addiction counseling; teacher assistant/aide.
Academics *Calendar:* semesters. *Degree:* certificates, diplomas, and associate. *Special study options:* academic remediation for entering students, accelerated degree program, adult/continuing education programs, advanced placement credit, cooperative education, distance learning, double majors, English as a second language, independent study, internships, off-campus study, part-time degree program, services for LD students, student-designed majors, summer session for credit.
Library Northcentral Technical College, Wausau Campus Library.
Student Life *Housing Options:* Campus housing is provided by a third party. *Campus security:* 24-hour emergency response devices, student patrols, late-night transport/escort service. *Student services:* personal/psychological counseling, women's center.
Athletics *Intramural sports:* basketball M/W, field hockey M/W, football M/W, soccer M/W, softball M/W, volleyball M/W.
Costs (2016–17) *Tuition:* state resident $4313 full-time; nonresident $6208 full-time. Full-time tuition and fees vary according to course level, course load, and program. Part-time tuition and fees vary according to course level, course load, and program. *Payment plans:* installment, deferred payment. *Waivers:* senior citizens.
Financial Aid Of all full-time matriculated undergraduates who enrolled in 2015, 1,146 applied for aid, 923 were judged to have need, 923 had their need fully met. 159 Federal Work-Study jobs (averaging $3000). In 2015, 156 non-need-based awards were made. *Average financial aid package:* $5911. *Average need-based loan:* $3076. *Average need-based gift aid:* $5279. *Average non-need-based aid:* $795.
Applying *Options:* electronic application, early admission, deferred entrance. *Application fee:* $30. *Required:* high school transcript. *Required for some:* interview. *Application deadlines:* rolling (freshmen), rolling (transfers). *Notification:* continuous (freshmen), continuous (transfers).
Freshman Application Contact Northcentral Technical College, 1000 West Campus Drive, Wausau, WI 54401-1899. *Phone:* 715-675-3331. *Website:* http://www.ntc.edu/.

Northeast Wisconsin Technical College
Green Bay, Wisconsin

Freshman Application Contact Christine Lemerande, Program Enrollment Supervisor, Northeast Wisconsin Technical College, 2740 W Mason Street, PO Box 19042, Green Bay, WI 54307-9042. *Phone:* 920-498-5444. *Toll-free phone:* 888-385-6982. *Fax:* 920-498-6882. *Website:* http://www.nwtc.edu/.

Southwest Wisconsin Technical College
Fennimore, Wisconsin

Freshman Application Contact Student Services, Southwest Wisconsin Technical College, 1800 Bronson Boulevard, Fennimore, WI 53809-9778.

Phone: 608-822-2354. *Toll-free phone:* 800-362-3322. *Fax:* 608-822-6019. *E-mail:* student-services@swtc.edu. *Website:* http://www.swtc.edu/.

University of Wisconsin–Baraboo/Sauk County
Baraboo, Wisconsin

Freshman Application Contact Ms. Jan Gerlach, Assistant Director of Student Services, University of Wisconsin–Baraboo/Sauk County, Baraboo, WI 53913-1015. *Phone:* 608-355-5270. *E-mail:* booinfo@uwc.edu. *Website:* http://www.baraboo.uwc.edu/.

University of Wisconsin–Barron County
Rice Lake, Wisconsin

Freshman Application Contact Assistant Dean for Student Services, University of Wisconsin–Barron County, 1800 College Drive, Rice Lake, WI 54868-2497. *Phone:* 715-234-8024. *Fax:* 715-234-8024. *Website:* http://www.barron.uwc.edu/.

University of Wisconsin–Fond du Lac
Fond du Lac, Wisconsin

Freshman Application Contact University of Wisconsin–Fond du Lac, 400 University Drive, Fond du Lac, WI 54935. *Phone:* 920-929-1122. *Website:* http://www.fdl.uwc.edu/.

University of Wisconsin–Fox Valley
Menasha, Wisconsin

- **State-supported** 2-year, founded 1933, part of University of Wisconsin System
- **Urban** 33-acre campus
- **Coed**, 1,399 undergraduate students

Undergraduates Students come from 5 states and territories; 5 other countries; 1% are from out of state. *Retention:* 60% of full-time freshmen returned.
Freshmen *Average high school GPA:* 2.5.
Faculty *Total:* 91, 34% full-time. *Student/faculty ratio:* 20:1.
Majors Liberal arts and sciences/liberal studies.
Academics *Calendar:* semesters. *Degree:* certificates and associate. *Special study options:* academic remediation for entering students, accelerated degree program, adult/continuing education programs, advanced placement credit, cooperative education, distance learning, honors programs, independent study, internships, off-campus study, part-time degree program, services for LD students, study abroad, summer session for credit.
Library UW Fox Library. Students can reserve study rooms.
Student Life *Housing:* college housing not available. *Activities and Organizations:* drama/theater group, student-run newspaper, radio and television station, choral group, Business Club, Education Club, Ballroom Dance Club, Campus Crusade for Christ, Computer Science Club. *Campus security:* 24-hour emergency response devices, late-night transport/escort service. *Student services:* personal/psychological counseling.
Athletics Member NJCAA. *Intercollegiate sports:* basketball M/W, golf M/W, soccer M/W, tennis M/W, volleyball M/W. *Intramural sports:* baseball M(c), basketball M/W, volleyball M/W, wrestling M(c).
Standardized Tests *Required:* ACT (for admission).
Costs (2017–18) *Tuition:* state resident $5035 full-time; nonresident $12,018 full-time. Full-time tuition and fees vary according to course load. Part-time tuition and fees vary according to course load. *Payment plan:* installment. *Waivers:* senior citizens.
Applying *Required:* high school transcript. *Required for some:* interview. *Recommended:* essay or personal statement.
Freshman Application Contact University of Wisconsin–Fox Valley, 1478 Midway Road, Menasha, WI 54952. *Phone:* 920-832-2620. *Website:* http://www.uwfox.uwc.edu/.

University of Wisconsin–Manitowoc
Manitowoc, Wisconsin

Freshman Application Contact Dr. Christopher Lewis, Assistant Campus Dean for Student Services, University of Wisconsin–Manitowoc, 705 Viebahn Street, Manitowoc, WI 54220-6699. *Phone:* 920-683-4707. *Fax:* 920-683-4776. *E-mail:* christopher.lewis@uwc.edu. *Website:* http://www.manitowoc.uwc.edu/.

University of Wisconsin–Marathon County
Wausau, Wisconsin

Freshman Application Contact Dr. Nolan Beck, Director of Student Services, University of Wisconsin–Marathon County, 518 South Seventh Avenue, Wausau, WI 54401-5396. *Phone:* 715-261-6238. *Toll-free phone:* 888-367-8962. *Fax:* 715-848-3568. *Website:* http://www.uwmc.uwc.edu/.

University of Wisconsin–Marinette
Marinette, Wisconsin

Freshman Application Contact Ms. Cynthia M. Bailey, Assistant Campus Dean for Student Services, University of Wisconsin–Marinette, 750 West Bay Shore, Marinette, WI 54143-4299. *Phone:* 715-735-4301. *E-mail:* cynthia.bailey@uwc.edu. *Website:* http://www.marinette.uwc.edu/.

University of Wisconsin–Marshfield/Wood County
Marshfield, Wisconsin

Freshman Application Contact Ms. Brittany Lueth, Director of Student Services, University of Wisconsin–Marshfield/Wood County, 2000 West 5th Street, Marshfield, WI 54449. *Phone:* 715-389-6500. *Fax:* 715-384-1718. *Website:* http://marshfield.uwc.edu/.

University of Wisconsin–Richland
Richland Center, Wisconsin

Freshman Application Contact Mr. John D. Poole, Assistant Campus Dean, University of Wisconsin–Richland, 1200 Highway 14 West, Richland Center, WI 53581. *Phone:* 608-647-8422. *Fax:* 608-647-2275. *E-mail:* john.poole@uwc.edu. *Website:* http://richland.uwc.edu/.

University of Wisconsin–Rock County
Janesville, Wisconsin

Freshman Application Contact University of Wisconsin–Rock County, 2909 Kellogg Avenue, Janesville, WI 53546-5699. *Phone:* 608-758-6523. *Toll-free phone:* 888-INFO-UWC. *Website:* http://rock.uwc.edu/.

University of Wisconsin–Sheboygan
Sheboygan, Wisconsin

Freshman Application Contact Mrs. Elisa Carr, High School Relations and Recruitment Coordinator, University of Wisconsin–Sheboygan, One University Drive, Sheboygan, WI 53081. *Phone:* 920-459-5956. *Fax:* 920-459-6602. *E-mail:* elisa.carr@uwc.edu. *Website:* http://www.sheboygan.uwc.edu/.

University of Wisconsin–Washington County
West Bend, Wisconsin

Freshman Application Contact Mr. Dan Cebrario, Associate Director of Student Services, University of Wisconsin–Washington County, Student Services Office, 400 University Drive, West Bend, WI 53095. *Phone:* 262-335-5201. *Fax:* 262-335-5220. *E-mail:* dan.cibrario@uwc.edu. *Website:* http://www.washington.uwc.edu/.

University of Wisconsin–Waukesha
Waukesha, Wisconsin

Freshman Application Contact Ms. Deb Kusick, Sr. Admission Specialist, University of Wisconsin–Waukesha, 1500 North University Drive, Waukesha, WI 53188-2799. *Phone:* 262-521-5040. *Fax:* 262-521-5530. *E-mail:* deborah.kusick@uwc.edu. *Website:* http://www.waukesha.uwc.edu/.

Waukesha County Technical College
Pewaukee, Wisconsin

- **State and locally supported** 2-year, founded 1923, part of Wisconsin Technical College System
- **Suburban** 137-acre campus with easy access to Milwaukee
- **Coed,** 7,947 undergraduate students, 21% full-time, 50% women, 50% men

Undergraduates 1,642 full-time, 6,305 part-time. 6% Black or African American, non-Hispanic/Latino; 7% Hispanic/Latino; 3% Asian, non-Hispanic/Latino; 0.3% Native Hawaiian or other Pacific Islander, non-Hispanic/Latino; 0.3% American Indian or Alaska Native, non-Hispanic/Latino; 2% Two or more races, non-Hispanic/Latino; 3% Race/ethnicity unknown; 0.1% international.
Freshmen *Admission:* 658 enrolled.
Faculty *Total:* 797, 24% full-time. *Student/faculty ratio:* 16:1.
Majors Accounting; administrative assistant and secretarial science; architectural drafting and CAD/CADD; automation engineer technology; automobile/automotive mechanics technology; baking and pastry arts; biomedical technology; business administration and management; business administration, management and operations related; clinical/medical laboratory technology; computer programming; computer support specialist; computer systems networking and telecommunications; criminal justice/police science; dental hygiene; digital arts; early childhood education; electrical, electronic and communications engineering technology; emergency medical technology (EMT paramedic); fire science/firefighting; graphic design; health information/medical records technology; hospitality administration; human resources management; interior design; international business/trade/commerce; international marketing; marketing/marketing management; mechanical drafting and CAD/CADD; medical radiologic technology; metal fabricator; multi/interdisciplinary studies related; office management; physical therapy technology; psychiatric/mental health services technology; real estate; registered nursing/registered nurse; restaurant, culinary, and catering management; surgical technology; teacher assistant/aide; web/multimedia management and webmaster.
Academics *Calendar:* semesters. *Degree:* certificates, diplomas, and associate. *Special study options:* academic remediation for entering students, accelerated degree program, adult/continuing education programs, advanced placement credit, cooperative education, distance learning, double majors, English as a second language, independent study, internships, part-time degree program, services for LD students, student-designed majors, study abroad, summer session for credit.
Student Life *Housing:* college housing not available. *Campus security:* patrols by police officers 8 am to 10 pm.
Costs (2016–17) *Tuition:* state resident $3911 full-time, $130 per credit hour part-time; nonresident $5866 full-time, $196 per credit hour part-time. Full-time tuition and fees vary according to program. Part-time tuition and fees vary according to program. *Required fees:* $234 full-time, $8 per credit hour part-time. *Payment plans:* installment, deferred payment. *Waivers:* senior citizens.
Financial Aid Of all full-time matriculated undergraduates who enrolled in 2015, 177 Federal Work-Study jobs (averaging $2864). 219 state and other part-time jobs (averaging $1398).
Applying *Options:* electronic application. *Application fee:* $30. *Required:* high school transcript. *Required for some:* interview. *Application deadlines:* rolling (freshmen), rolling (transfers).
Freshman Application Contact Waukesha County Technical College, 800 Main Street, Pewaukee, WI 53072-4601. *Phone:* 262-691-5464. *Website:* http://www.wctc.edu/.

Western Technical College
La Crosse, Wisconsin

Freshman Application Contact Ms. Jane Wells, Manager of Admissions, Registration, and Records, Western Technical College, PO Box 908, La Crosse, WI 54602-0908. *Phone:* 608-785-9158. *Toll-free phone:* 800-322-9982. *Fax:* 608-785-9094. *E-mail:* mildes@wwtc.edu. *Website:* http://www.westerntc.edu/.

Wisconsin Indianhead Technical College
Shell Lake, Wisconsin

- **District-supported** 2-year, founded 1912, part of Wisconsin Technical College System
- **Urban** 118-acre campus
- **Endowment** $3.8 million
- **Coed,** 2,944 undergraduate students, 39% full-time, 61% women, 39% men

Undergraduates 1,134 full-time, 1,810 part-time. Students come from 9 states and territories; 8% are from out of state; 1% Black or African American, non-

Hispanic/Latino; 0.6% Hispanic/Latino; 0.9% Asian, non-Hispanic/Latino; 0.1% Native Hawaiian or other Pacific Islander, non-Hispanic/Latino; 2% American Indian or Alaska Native, non-Hispanic/Latino; 2% Two or more races, non-Hispanic/Latino; 2% Race/ethnicity unknown.

Freshmen *Admission:* 455 enrolled.

Faculty *Total:* 328, 47% full-time. *Student/faculty ratio:* 8:1.

Majors Accounting; administrative assistant and secretarial science; architectural engineering technology; business administration and management; computer programming; computer support specialist; computer systems networking and telecommunications; early childhood education; emergency medical technology (EMT paramedic); finance; gerontology; health information/medical records technology; human resources management; interdisciplinary studies; medical administrative assistant and medical secretary; occupational therapist assistant; office management; psychiatric/mental health services technology; registered nursing/registered nurse.

Academics *Calendar:* semesters. *Degree:* certificates, diplomas, and associate. *Special study options:* academic remediation for entering students, adult/continuing education programs, cooperative education, distance learning, double majors, English as a second language, independent study, part-time degree program, services for LD students, summer session for credit.

Student Life *Housing:* college housing not available. *Student services:* health clinic.

Costs (2016–17) *Tuition:* state resident $4171 full-time, $130 per credit part-time; nonresident $6257 full-time, $196 per credit part-time. Full-time tuition and fees vary according to course load, program, and reciprocity agreements. Part-time tuition and fees vary according to course load, program, and reciprocity agreements. *Required fees:* $427 full-time. *Payment plans:* installment, deferred payment.

Applying *Options:* electronic application. *Application fee:* $30. *Application deadline:* rolling (freshmen).

Freshman Application Contact Mr. Steve Bitzer, Vice President, Student Affairs and Campus Administrator, Wisconsin Indianhead Technical College, 2100 Beaser Avenue, Ashland, WI 54806. *Phone:* 715-468-2815 Ext. 3149. *Toll-free phone:* 800-243-9482. *Fax:* 715-468-2819.

E-mail: steve.bitzer@witc.edu.

Website: http://www.witc.edu/.

WYOMING

Casper College
Casper, Wyoming

- **State and locally supported** 2-year, founded 1945
- **Small-town** 200-acre campus
- **Coed**, 3,626 undergraduate students, 48% full-time, 56% women, 44% men

Undergraduates 1,733 full-time, 1,893 part-time. Students come from 37 states and territories; 17 other countries; 10% are from out of state; 1% Black or African American, non-Hispanic/Latino; 7% Hispanic/Latino; 0.8% Asian, non-Hispanic/Latino; 0.2% Native Hawaiian or other Pacific Islander, non-Hispanic/Latino; 0.6% American Indian or Alaska Native, non-Hispanic/Latino; 3% Two or more races, non-Hispanic/Latino; 2% Race/ethnicity unknown; 0.9% international; 2% transferred in; 16% live on campus.

Freshmen *Admission:* 1,097 applied, 1,097 admitted, 623 enrolled. *Average high school GPA:* 3.1.

Faculty *Total:* 246, 57% full-time, 19% with terminal degrees. *Student/faculty ratio:* 14:1.

Majors Accounting; accounting technology and bookkeeping; acting; administrative assistant and secretarial science; agricultural business and management; agricultural communication/journalism; agriculture; airline pilot and flight crew; animal sciences; anthropology; art; art teacher education; athletic training; autobody/collision and repair technology; automobile/automotive mechanics technology; biology/biological sciences; business administration and management; business automation/technology/data entry; chemistry; clinical laboratory science/medical technology; computer and information systems security; computer programming; construction management; construction trades; criminal justice/law enforcement administration; dance; diesel mechanics technology; drafting and design technology; economics; electrical, electronic and communications engineering technology; elementary education; emergency medical technology (EMT paramedic); energy management and systems technology; engineering; English; entrepreneurship; environmental science; fine/studio arts; fire science/firefighting; foreign languages and literatures; forensic science and technology; general studies; geographic information science and cartography; geology/earth science; graphic design;

health services/allied health/health sciences; history; hospitality administration; industrial mechanics and maintenance technology; international relations and affairs; journalism; kindergarten/preschool education; legal assistant/paralegal; liberal arts and sciences/liberal studies; machine tool technology; manufacturing engineering technology; marketing/marketing management; mass communication/media; mathematics; mining technology; museum studies; music; musical theater; music performance; music teacher education; nutrition sciences; occupational therapist assistant; pharmacy technician; photography; physical education teaching and coaching; physics; political science and government; pre-dentistry studies; pre-law studies; premedical studies; pre-occupational therapy; pre-optometry; pre-pharmacy studies; pre-physical therapy; pre-veterinary studies; psychology; radiologic technology/science; range science and management; registered nursing/registered nurse; respiratory care therapy; retailing; robotics technology; social studies teacher education; social work; sociology; speech communication and rhetoric; statistics related; substance abuse/addiction counseling; technology/industrial arts teacher education; theater design and technology; web/multimedia management and webmaster; web page, digital/multimedia and information resources design; welding technology; wildlife, fish and wildlands science and management; women's studies.

Academics *Calendar:* semesters. *Degree:* certificates and associate. *Special study options:* academic remediation for entering students, accelerated degree program, advanced placement credit, cooperative education, distance learning, English as a second language, honors programs, independent study, internships, off-campus study, part-time degree program, services for LD students, summer session for credit.

Library Goodstein Foundation Library. *Books:* 66,488 (physical), 184,000 (digital/electronic); *Serial titles:* 4,300 (physical); *Databases:* 415. Weekly public service hours: 82; students can reserve study rooms.

Student Life *Housing Options:* coed. Campus housing is university owned. *Activities and Organizations:* drama/theater group, student-run newspaper, choral group, Student Senate, Student Activities Board, Agriculture Club, Theater Club, Phi Theta Kappa. *Campus security:* 24-hour emergency response devices and patrols, late-night transport/escort service. *Student services:* health clinic, personal/psychological counseling, legal services.

Athletics Member NJCAA. *Intercollegiate sports:* basketball M(s)/W(s), equestrian sports M/W, volleyball W(s). *Intramural sports:* basketball M/W, bowling M/W, football M/W, golf M/W, racquetball M/W, soccer M/W, softball M/W, tennis M/W.

Costs (2016–17) *Tuition:* state resident $2136 full-time, $89 per credit hour part-time; nonresident $6408 full-time, $267 per credit hour part-time. Part-time tuition and fees vary according to course load. *Required fees:* $696 full-time, $29 per credit hour part-time. *Room and board:* $6520. Room and board charges vary according to board plan and housing facility. *Payment plan:* installment. *Waivers:* senior citizens and employees or children of employees.

Financial Aid Of all full-time matriculated undergraduates who enrolled in 2015, 80 Federal Work-Study jobs (averaging $2000).

Applying *Options:* electronic application, early admission. *Required:* high school transcript. *Application deadlines:* 8/15 (freshmen), 8/15 (transfers). *Notification:* continuous until 8/15 (freshmen), continuous until 8/15 (transfers).

Freshman Application Contact Ms. Kyla Foltz, Director of Admissions Services, Casper College, 125 College Drive, Casper, WY 82601. *Phone:* 307-268-2111. *Toll-free phone:* 800-442-2963. *Fax:* 307-268-2611.

E-mail: kfoltz@caspercollege.edu.

Website: http://www.caspercollege.edu/.

Central Wyoming College
Riverton, Wyoming

- **State and locally supported** 2-year, founded 1966, part of Wyoming Community College Commission
- **Small-town** 200-acre campus
- **Endowment** $20.0 million
- **Coed**, 2,020 undergraduate students, 34% full-time, 54% women, 46% men

Undergraduates 688 full-time, 1,328 part-time. Students come from 41 states and territories; 6 other countries; 13% are from out of state; 0.8% Black or African American, non-Hispanic/Latino; 9% Hispanic/Latino; 0.8% Asian, non-Hispanic/Latino; 0.0% Native Hawaiian or other Pacific Islander, non-Hispanic/Latino; 10% American Indian or Alaska Native, non-Hispanic/Latino; 3% Two or more races, non-Hispanic/Latino; 2% Race/ethnicity unknown; 0.3% international; 5% transferred in; 18% live on campus. *Retention:* 54% of full-time freshmen returned.

Freshmen *Admission:* 453 applied, 453 admitted, 286 enrolled. *Average high school GPA:* 3.06.

Faculty *Total:* 168, 29% full-time, 52% with terminal degrees. *Student/faculty ratio:* 13:1.

Majors Accounting; accounting technology and bookkeeping; acting; administrative assistant and secretarial science; agricultural business and management; American Indian/Native American studies; anthropology; art; athletic training; automobile/automotive mechanics technology; biology/biological sciences; building/property maintenance; business administration and management; business/commerce; carpentry; child-care and support services management; commercial photography; computer science; computer technology/computer systems technology; criminal justice/law enforcement administration; culinary arts; customer service support/call center/teleservice operation; dramatic/theater arts; early childhood education; elementary education; engineering; English; entrepreneurship; environmental/environmental health engineering; environmental science; equestrian studies; fire science/firefighting; general studies; geographic information science and cartography; health and wellness; health/medical preparatory programs related; health professions related; homeland security, law enforcement, firefighting and protective services related; hotel/motel administration; international/global studies; liberal arts and sciences/liberal studies; mathematics; medical office assistant; multi/interdisciplinary studies related; music; parks, recreation and leisure; parks, recreation and leisure facilities management; physical sciences; pre-law studies; psychology; radio and television; range science and management; registered nursing/registered nurse; rehabilitation and therapeutic professions related; science, technology and society; secondary education; social sciences; teacher assistant/aide; theater design and technology; visual and performing arts; welding technology.

Academics *Calendar:* semesters. *Degree:* certificates, diplomas, and associate. *Special study options:* academic remediation for entering students, adult/continuing education programs, advanced placement credit, cooperative education, distance learning, double majors, English as a second language, honors programs, independent study, internships, off-campus study, part-time degree program, services for LD students, summer session for credit.

Library Central Wyoming College Library. *Books:* 53,204 (physical), 5 (digital/electronic); *Serial titles:* 152 (physical), 8 (digital/electronic); *Databases:* 141. Weekly public service hours: 82.

Student Life *Housing Options:* coed. Campus housing is university owned. *Activities and Organizations:* drama/theater group, student-run radio and television station, choral group, Multi-Cultural Club, La Vida Nueva Club, Fellowship of College Christians, Quality Leaders, Science Club. *Campus security:* 24-hour emergency response devices, late-night transport/escort service, controlled dormitory access. *Student services:* personal/psychological counseling.

Athletics Member NJCAA. *Intercollegiate sports:* basketball M(s)/W(s), cross-country running M(s)/W(s), equestrian sports M(s)/W(s), golf M(s)/W(s), volleyball W(s). *Intramural sports:* badminton M/W, basketball M/W, football M/W, rock climbing M/W, skiing (cross-country) M/W, skiing (downhill) M/W, soccer M/W, softball M/W, swimming and diving M/W, table tennis M/W, tennis M/W, ultimate Frisbee M/W, volleyball M/W, weight lifting M/W.

Costs (2017–18) *Tuition:* state resident $2256 full-time, $94 per credit part-time; nonresident $6768 full-time, $282 per credit part-time. Full-time tuition and fees vary according to course load, program, and reciprocity agreements. Part-time tuition and fees vary according to course load, program, and reciprocity agreements. *Required fees:* $768 full-time, $32 per credit part-time. *Room and board:* Room and board charges vary according to board plan and housing facility. *Payment plans:* installment, deferred payment. *Waivers:* senior citizens and employees or children of employees.

Financial Aid Of all full-time matriculated undergraduates who enrolled in 2015, 410 applied for aid, 336 were judged to have need. 89 Federal Work-Study jobs (averaging $1673). *Financial aid deadline:* 6/30.

Applying *Options:* electronic application, early admission, deferred entrance. *Recommended:* high school transcript. *Application deadlines:* rolling (freshmen), rolling (transfers).

Freshman Application Contact Ms. Tawnie DeJong, Student Recruiter, Central Wyoming College, 2660 Peck Avenue, Riverton, WY 82501-2273. *Phone:* 307-855-2231. *Toll-free phone:* 800-735-8418. *Fax:* 307-855-2065. *E-mail:* tdejong@cwc.edu. *Website:* http://www.cwc.edu/.

Eastern Wyoming College
Torrington, Wyoming

- **State and locally supported** 2-year, founded 1948, part of Wyoming Community College Commission
- **Rural** 40-acre campus
- **Endowment** $4.6 million
- **Coed**, 1,604 undergraduate students, 38% full-time, 58% women, 42% men

Undergraduates 602 full-time, 1,002 part-time. Students come from 20 states and territories; 9 other countries; 26% are from out of state; 1% Black or African American, non-Hispanic/Latino; 6% Hispanic/Latino; 0.3% Asian, non-Hispanic/Latino; 0.8% Native Hawaiian or other Pacific Islander, non-

Hispanic/Latino; 2% American Indian or Alaska Native, non-Hispanic/Latino; 0.2% Two or more races, non-Hispanic/Latino; 3% international; 8% transferred in; 21% live on campus.

Freshmen *Admission:* 211 enrolled.

Faculty *Total:* 71, 48% full-time. *Student/faculty ratio:* 20:1.

Majors Accounting; administrative assistant and secretarial science; agribusiness; agricultural teacher education; art; biology/biological sciences; business administration and management; business teacher education; computer systems networking and telecommunications; corrections administration; cosmetology; criminal justice/law enforcement administration; criminal justice/police science; criminal justice/safety; early childhood education; economics; elementary education; English; environmental biology; farm and ranch management; foreign languages and literatures; general studies; health/medical preparatory programs related; liberal arts and sciences/liberal studies; mathematics; mathematics teacher education; music; music teacher education; office management; physical education teaching and coaching; pre-dentistry studies; premedical studies; pre-pharmacy studies; pre-veterinary studies; range science and management; registered nursing/registered nurse; secondary education; social sciences; speech communication and rhetoric; statistics; veterinary/animal health technology; welding technology; wildlife, fish and wildlands science and management.

Academics *Calendar:* semesters. *Degree:* certificates, diplomas, and associate. *Special study options:* academic remediation for entering students, accelerated degree program, advanced placement credit, distance learning, double majors, English as a second language, independent study, internships, part-time degree program, services for LD students, student-designed majors, summer session for credit.

Library Eastern Wyoming College Library. *Books:* 30,339 (physical), 681,514 (digital/electronic); *Serial titles:* 86 (physical); *Databases:* 268. Weekly public service hours: 61.

Student Life *Housing Options:* coed, special housing for students with disabilities. Campus housing is university owned. *Activities and Organizations:* drama/theater group, choral group, Veterinary Technology Club, Rodeo Club, Student Senate, Block and Bridle Club, SkillsUSA. *Campus security:* 24-hour emergency response devices, controlled dormitory access. *Student services:* personal/psychological counseling.

Athletics Member NJCAA. *Intercollegiate sports:* basketball M/W, equestrian sports M/W, golf M, volleyball W.

Costs (2017–18) *Tuition:* state resident $2136 full-time, $89 per credit hour part-time; nonresident $6408 full-time, $267 per credit hour part-time. Full-time tuition and fees vary according to course load, location, and program. Part-time tuition and fees vary according to course load, location, and program. *Required fees:* $672 full-time, $28 per credit hour part-time. *Room and board:* $6136; room only: $3292. Room and board charges vary according to board plan and housing facility. *Payment plan:* installment. *Waivers:* senior citizens and employees or children of employees.

Applying *Recommended:* high school transcript.

Freshman Application Contact Dr. Rex Cogdill, Vice President for Students Services, Eastern Wyoming College, 3200 West C Street, Torrington, WY 82240. *Phone:* 307-532-8257. *Toll-free phone:* 866-327-8996. *Fax:* 307-532-8222. *E-mail:* rex.cogdill@ewc.wy.edu. *Website:* http://www.ewc.wy.edu/.

Laramie County Community College
Cheyenne, Wyoming

- **District-supported** 2-year, founded 1968, part of Wyoming Community College Commission
- **Small-town** 271-acre campus
- **Coed**, 4,132 undergraduate students, 42% full-time, 58% women, 42% men

Undergraduates 1,719 full-time, 2,413 part-time. 14% are from out of state; 2% Black or African American, non-Hispanic/Latino; 11% Hispanic/Latino; 1% Asian, non-Hispanic/Latino; 0.4% Native Hawaiian or other Pacific Islander, non-Hispanic/Latino; 1% American Indian or Alaska Native, non-Hispanic/Latino; 1% Two or more races, non-Hispanic/Latino; 5% Race/ethnicity unknown; 0.9% international; 20% transferred in; 12% live on campus.

Freshmen *Admission:* 1,982 applied, 1,982 admitted, 514 enrolled. *Average high school GPA:* 2.96.

Faculty *Total:* 264, 45% full-time, 10% with terminal degrees. *Student/faculty ratio:* 16:1.

Majors Accounting; agribusiness; agricultural business technology; agricultural production; agriculture; anthropology; art; autobody/collision and repair technology; automobile/automotive mechanics technology; biological and physical sciences; biology/biological sciences; business administration and management; business/commerce; chemistry; computer programming; computer science; corrections; criminal justice/law enforcement administration; dental hygiene; diagnostic medical sonography and ultrasound technology; diesel mechanics technology; digital communication and media/multimedia; drafting and design technology; early childhood education; economics; education; emergency medical technology (EMT paramedic); energy management and systems technology; engineering; English; entrepreneurship; equestrian studies; fire science/firefighting; general studies; heating, air conditioning, ventilation and refrigeration maintenance technology; history; homeland security, law enforcement, firefighting and protective services related; humanities; human services; kinesiology and exercise science; legal assistant/paralegal; mass communication/media; mathematics; mechanic and repair technologies related; medical insurance coding; music; physical education teaching and coaching; physical therapy technology; political science and government; pre-law studies; pre-pharmacy studies; psychology; public administration; radiologic technology/science; registered nursing/registered nurse; religious studies; social sciences; sociology; Spanish; speech communication and rhetoric; surgical technology; wildlife, fish and wildlands science and management.

Academics *Calendar:* semesters. *Degree:* certificates, diplomas, and associate. *Special study options:* academic remediation for entering students, adult/continuing education programs, advanced placement credit, cooperative education, distance learning, double majors, English as a second language, honors programs, independent study, internships, off-campus study, part-time degree program, services for LD students, summer session for credit. *ROTC:* Army (c), Air Force (c).

Library Ludden Library.

Student Life *Housing Options:* coed. Campus housing is university owned. *Activities and Organizations:* drama/theater group, student-run newspaper, choral group, Student Government Association, Phi Theta Kappa, Block and Bridle, Student Nursing Club, SkillsUSA. *Campus security:* 24-hour emergency response devices and patrols, late-night transport/escort service, controlled dormitory access. *Student services:* health clinic, personal/psychological counseling.

Athletics Member NJCAA. *Intercollegiate sports:* basketball M(s), cheerleading M(s)/W(s), equestrian sports M(s)/W(s), soccer M(s)/W(s), volleyball W(s). *Intramural sports:* basketball M/W, equestrian sports M/W, racquetball M/W, rock climbing M/W, skiing (cross-country) M/W, soccer M/W, softball M/W, table tennis M/W, ultimate Frisbee M/W, volleyball M/W.

Costs (2017–18) *Tuition:* state resident $2136 full-time, $89 per credit hour part-time; nonresident $6408 full-time, $267 per credit hour part-time. Full-time tuition and fees vary according to course load. Part-time tuition and fees vary according to course load. *Required fees:* $1170 full-time, $49 per credit hour part-time. *Room and board:* $7988. Room and board charges vary according to board plan and housing facility. *Payment plan:* installment. *Waivers:* senior citizens and employees or children of employees.

Financial Aid Of all full-time matriculated undergraduates who enrolled in 2015, 1,355 applied for aid, 1,022 were judged to have need, 116 had their need fully met. In 2015, 557 non-need-based awards were made. *Average percent of need met:* 66%. *Average financial aid package:* $6652. *Average need-based loan:* $3219. *Average need-based gift aid:* $2500. *Average non-need-based aid:* $1482.

Applying *Options:* electronic application, deferred entrance. *Required for some:* high school transcript, interview.

Freshman Application Contact Ms. Holly Bruegman, Director of Admissions, Laramie County Community College, 1400 East College Drive, Cheyenne, WY 82007. *Phone:* 307-778-1117. *Toll-free phone:* 800-522-2993 Ext. 1357. *Fax:* 307-778-1360. *E-mail:* learnmore@lccc.wy.edu. *Website:* http://www.lccc.wy.edu/.

Northwest College
Powell, Wyoming

- **State and locally supported** 2-year, founded 1946, part of Wyoming Community College System
- **Rural** 132-acre campus
- **Coed,** 1,664 undergraduate students, 61% full-time, 59% women, 41% men

Undergraduates 1,007 full-time, 657 part-time. Students come from 31 states and territories; 24 other countries; 20% are from out of state; 0.5% Black or African American, non-Hispanic/Latino; 7% Hispanic/Latino; 0.4% Asian, non-Hispanic/Latino; 0.3% Native Hawaiian or other Pacific Islander, non-Hispanic/Latino; 0.7% American Indian or Alaska Native, non-Hispanic/Latino; 2% Two or more races, non-Hispanic/Latino; 0.1% Race/ethnicity unknown; 4% international. *Retention:* 62% of full-time freshmen returned.

Freshmen *Admission:* 405 enrolled.

Faculty *Total:* 141, 54% full-time. *Student/faculty ratio:* 13:1.

Majors Accounting; administrative assistant and secretarial science; aeronautics/aviation/aerospace science and technology; agribusiness; agricultural communication/journalism; agricultural production; agricultural teacher education; allied health and medical assisting services related; animal sciences; anthropology; archeology; art; athletic training; biology/biological sciences; business administration and management; business/commerce;

CAD/CADD drafting/design technology; chemistry; commercial and advertising art; commercial photography; criminal justice/law enforcement administration; crop production; elementary education; engineering; English; equestrian studies; farm and ranch management; general studies; health and physical education/fitness; health/medical preparatory programs related; history; international relations and affairs; kindergarten/preschool education; liberal arts and sciences/liberal studies; mathematics; music; natural resources management and policy; parks, recreation and leisure; physics; political science and government; pre-pharmacy studies; psychology; range science and management; registered nursing/registered nurse; secondary education; social sciences; sociology; Spanish; speech communication and rhetoric; veterinary/animal health technology; visual and performing arts related; welding technology.

Academics *Calendar:* semesters. *Degree:* certificates and associate. *Special study options:* academic remediation for entering students, adult/continuing education programs, advanced placement credit, cooperative education, distance learning, double majors, English as a second language, external degree program, independent study, internships, off-campus study, part-time degree program, services for LD students, study abroad, summer session for credit.

Library John Taggart Hinckley Library.

Student Life *Housing:* on-campus residence required for freshman year. *Options:* coed, women-only, special housing for students with disabilities. Campus housing is university owned. Freshman campus housing is guaranteed. *Activities and Organizations:* drama/theater group, choral group. *Campus security:* 24-hour emergency response devices and patrols, late-night transport/escort service, controlled dormitory access. *Student services:* health clinic, personal/psychological counseling.

Athletics Member NJCAA. *Intercollegiate sports:* basketball M(s)/W(s), equestrian sports M(s)/W(s), soccer M(s)/W(s), volleyball W(s), wrestling M(s). *Intramural sports:* basketball M/W, football M/W, golf M/W, softball M/W, ultimate Frisbee M/W, volleyball M/W.

Costs (2016–17) *Tuition:* state resident $2136 full-time, $89 per credit hour part-time; nonresident $6408 full-time, $267 per credit hour part-time. Full-time tuition and fees vary according to course load, location, and program. Part-time tuition and fees vary according to course load, location, and program. *Required fees:* $1065 full-time, $45 per credit hour part-time. *Room and board:* $5512. Room and board charges vary according to board plan and housing facility. *Payment plan:* installment. *Waivers:* children of alumni, senior citizens, and employees or children of employees.

Financial Aid Of all full-time matriculated undergraduates who enrolled in 2015, 115 Federal Work-Study jobs (averaging $2700). 215 state and other part-time jobs (averaging $2700).

Applying *Options:* electronic application. *Required:* high school transcript. *Required for some:* minimum 2.0 GPA. *Recommended:* minimum 2.0 GPA. *Application deadlines:* rolling (freshmen), rolling (transfers). *Notification:* continuous (freshmen), continuous (transfers).

Freshman Application Contact Mr. West Hernandez, Admissions Manager, Northwest College, 231 W 6th Street, Orendorff Building 1, Powell, WY 82435-1898. *Phone:* 307-754-6103. *Toll-free phone:* 800-560-4692. *Fax:* 307-754-6249. *E-mail:* west.hernandez@nwc.edu. *Website:* http://www.nwc.edu/.

Sheridan College
Sheridan, Wyoming

- **State and locally supported** 2-year, founded 1948, part of Wyoming Community College Commission
- **Small-town** 145-acre campus
- **Endowment** $29.6 million
- **Coed**

Undergraduates 1,398 full-time, 2,909 part-time. Students come from 37 states and territories; 11 other countries; 18% are from out of state; 1% Black or African American, non-Hispanic/Latino; 7% Hispanic/Latino; 0.6% Asian, non-Hispanic/Latino; 0.2% Native Hawaiian or other Pacific Islander, non-Hispanic/Latino; 2% American Indian or Alaska Native, non-Hispanic/Latino; 3% Two or more races, non-Hispanic/Latino; 0.8% international; 3% transferred in; 10% live on campus. *Retention:* 59% of full-time freshmen returned.

Faculty *Student/faculty ratio:* 17:1.

Academics *Calendar:* semesters. *Degree:* certificates and associate. *Special study options:* academic remediation for entering students, accelerated degree program, advanced placement credit, cooperative education, distance learning, double majors, English as a second language, independent study, internships, off-campus study, part-time degree program, services for LD students, summer session for credit.

Library Mary Brown Kooi Library plus 1 other.

Student Life *Campus security:* 24-hour emergency response devices, student patrols, controlled dormitory access, night patrols by certified officers.

Athletics Member NJCAA.

Costs (2016–17) *Tuition:* state resident $2136 full-time, $89 per credit part-time; nonresident $6408 full-time, $267 per credit part-time. Full-time tuition and fees vary according to course load, location, and reciprocity agreements. Part-time tuition and fees vary according to location and reciprocity agreements. *Required fees:* $1020 full-time, $34 per credit part-time. *Room and board:* $6907. Room and board charges vary according to board plan, housing facility, and location.

Applying *Options:* electronic application, early admission, deferred entrance. *Required for some:* high school transcript. *Recommended:* high school transcript.

Freshman Application Contact Mr. Matt Adams, Admissions Coordinator, Sheridan College, PO Box 1500, Sheridan, WY 82801-1500. *Phone:* 307-674-6446 Ext. 2005. *Toll-free phone:* 800-913-9139 Ext. 2002. *Fax:* 307-674-3373. *E-mail:* madams@sheridan.edu. *Website:* http://www.sheridan.edu/.

Western Wyoming Community College
Rock Springs, Wyoming

- **State and locally supported** 2-year, founded 1959
- **Small-town** 342-acre campus
- **Endowment** $21.8 million
- **Coed,** 3,392 undergraduate students, 35% full-time, 53% women, 47% men

Undergraduates 1,183 full-time, 2,209 part-time. Students come from 27 states and territories; 16 other countries; 7% are from out of state; 0.9% Black or African American, non-Hispanic/Latino; 12% Hispanic/Latino; 0.6% Asian, non-Hispanic/Latino; 0.2% Native Hawaiian or other Pacific Islander, non-Hispanic/Latino; 0.5% American Indian or Alaska Native, non-Hispanic/Latino; 3% Two or more races, non-Hispanic/Latino; 2% international; 2% transferred in; 11% live on campus.

Freshmen *Admission:* 203 applied, 203 admitted, 239 enrolled. *Average high school GPA:* 2.97.

Faculty *Total:* 313, 25% full-time. *Student/faculty ratio:* 16:1.

Majors Accounting; administrative assistant and secretarial science; anthropology; archeology; art; automobile/automotive mechanics technology; biological and physical sciences; biology/biological sciences; business administration and management; chemistry; computer and information sciences; computer programming (specific applications); computer science; criminal justice/law enforcement administration; criminology; dance; data entry/microcomputer applications; data processing and data processing technology; diesel mechanics technology; dramatic/theater arts; early childhood education; economics; education; education (multiple levels); electrical, electronic and communications engineering technology; electrical/electronics equipment installation and repair; electrician; elementary education; engineering technology; English; environmental science; forestry; general studies; geology/earth science; health/medical preparatory programs related; health services/allied health/health sciences; heavy equipment maintenance technology; history; humanities; human services; industrial electronics technology; industrial mechanics and maintenance technology; information science/studies; information technology; instrumentation technology; international relations and affairs; journalism; kinesiology and exercise science; legal administrative assistant/secretary; liberal arts and sciences/liberal studies; licensed practical/vocational nurse training; marketing/marketing management; mathematics; mechanics and repair; medical administrative assistant and medical secretary; medical/clinical assistant; medical office assistant; medical office computer specialist; mining technology; music; nursing assistant/aide and patient care assistant/aide; photography; political science and government; pre-dentistry studies; pre-engineering; pre-law studies; premedical studies; prenursing studies; pre-pharmacy studies; pre-veterinary studies; psychology; secondary education; social sciences; social work; sociology; Spanish; speech communication and rhetoric; theater design and technology; visual and performing arts; web/multimedia management and webmaster; web page, digital/multimedia and information resources design; welding technology; wildlife, fish and wildlands science and management; word processing.

Academics *Calendar:* semesters. *Degree:* certificates, diplomas, and associate. *Special study options:* academic remediation for entering students, advanced placement credit, cooperative education, distance learning, English as a second language, honors programs, independent study, internships, part-time degree program, services for LD students, summer session for credit.

Library Hay Library. *Books:* 49,787 (physical), 125,000 (digital/electronic); *Serial titles:* 136 (physical); *Databases:* 147. Weekly public service hours: 33.

Student Life *Housing Options:* coed, special housing for students with disabilities. Campus housing is university owned. *Activities and Organizations:* drama/theater group, student-run newspaper, radio station, choral group, Association of Non-Traditional Students (ANTS), Spanish Club, Residence Hall Association, International Club, Latter Day Saints Student Association. *Campus security:* 24-hour emergency response devices and patrols, late-night transport/escort service, controlled dormitory access, patrols by trained security personnel from 4 pm to 8 am, 24-hour patrols on weekends and holidays. *Student services:* personal/psychological counseling.

Athletics Member NJCAA. *Intercollegiate sports:* basketball M(s)/W(s), cheerleading M(s)/W(s), soccer M(s)/W(s), volleyball W(s), wrestling M(s).

Costs (2017–18) *Tuition:* state resident $2136 full-time, $89 per credit hour part-time; nonresident $6408 full-time, $267 per credit hour part-time. *Required fees:* $440 full-time, $19 per credit hour part-time. *Room and board:* $5212; room only: $2632. Room and board charges vary according to board plan and housing facility. *Waivers:* senior citizens and employees or children of employees.

Financial Aid Of all full-time matriculated undergraduates who enrolled in 2015, 20 Federal Work-Study jobs (averaging $1500).

Applying *Options:* electronic application, early admission, deferred entrance. *Recommended:* high school transcript. *Application deadlines:* rolling (freshmen), rolling (transfers).

Freshman Application Contact Ms. Erin M. Grey, Director of Admissions, Western Wyoming Community College, 2500 College Drive, PO Box 428, Rock Springs, WY 82901. *Phone:* 307-382-1647. *Toll-free phone:* 800-226-1181. *Fax:* 307-382-1636. *E-mail:* admissions@westernwyoming.edu. *Website:* http://www.westernwyoming.edu/.

WyoTech Laramie
Laramie, Wyoming

Director of Admissions Director of Admissions, WyoTech Laramie, 1889 Venture Drive, Laramie, WY 82070. *Phone:* 307-742-3776. *Toll-free phone:* 888-577-7559. *Fax:* 307-721-4854. *Website:* http://www.wyotech.edu/.

CANADA

CANADA

Southern Alberta Institute of Technology
Calgary, Alberta, Canada

Freshman Application Contact Southern Alberta Institute of Technology, 1301 16th Avenue NW, Calgary, AB T2M 0L4, Canada. *Phone:* 403-284-8857. *Toll-free phone:* 877-284-SAIT. *Website:* http://www.sait.ca/.

INTERNATIONAL

PALAU

Palau Community College
Koror, Palau

- **Territory-supported** 2-year, founded 1969
- **Small-town** 30-acre campus
- **Endowment** $1.3 million
- **Coed**

Undergraduates 347 full-time, 280 part-time. 0.3% transferred in; 20% live on campus. *Retention:* 58% of full-time freshmen returned.
Faculty *Student/faculty ratio:* 10:1.
Academics *Calendar:* semesters. *Degree:* certificates and associate. *Special study options:* academic remediation for entering students, adult/continuing education programs, cooperative education, double majors, English as a second language, honors programs, internships, part-time degree program, summer session for credit.
Library Palau Community College Library.
Student Life *Campus security:* 24-hour emergency response devices and patrols, late-night transport/escort service, evening patrols by trained security personnel.
Financial Aid *Financial aid deadline:* 6/30.
Applying *Options:* early admission, deferred entrance. *Application fee:* $10. *Required:* high school transcript, minimum 2.0 GPA.
Freshman Application Contact Ms. Dahlia Katosang, Director of Admissions and Financial Aid, Palau Community College, PO Box 9, Koror, PW 96940-0009. *Phone:* 680-488-2471 Ext. 233. *Fax:* 680-488-4468. *E-mail:* dahliapcc@palaunet.com. *Website:* http://www.palau.edu/.

Institutional Changes Since *Peterson's® Two-Year Colleges 2017*

The following is an alphabetical listing of institutions that have closed, merged with other institutions, or changed their names or status since the release of *Peterson's® Two-Year Coleges 2017*.

Academy of Couture Art (Beverly Hills, CA): *name changed to Beverly Hills Design Institute.*

Alabama Southern Community College (Monroeville, AL): *merged into a new single entry for Coastal Alabama Community College (Bay Minette, AL).*

The Art Institute of Cincinnati (Cincinnati, OH): *name changed to AIC College of Design.*

Ashdown College of Health Sciences (Redlands, CA): *closed.*

Aviation & Electronic Schools of America (Colfax, CA): *closed.*

Berkeley College–White Plains Campus (White Plains, NY): *now classified as a 4-year college.*

Blake Austin College (Vacaville, CA): *no longer degree granting.*

Blue Cliff College–Shreveport (Shreveport, LA): *closed.*

Bramson ORT College (Forest Hills, NY): *no longer degree granting.*

Brightwood College, Hammond Campus (Hammond, IN): *no longer degree granting.*

Brown Mackie College–Akron (Akron, OH): *closed.*

Brown Mackie College–Albuquerque (Albuquerque, NM): *closed.*

Brown Mackie College–Atlanta (Atlanta, GA): *closed.*

Brown Mackie College–Boise (Boise, ID): *closed.*

Brown Mackie College–Cincinnati (Cincinnati, OH): *closed.*

Brown Mackie College–Findlay (Findlay, OH): *closed.*

Brown Mackie College–Fort Wayne (Fort Wayne, IN): *closed.*

Brown Mackie College–Greenville (Greenville, SC): *closed.*

Brown Mackie College–Hopkinsville (Hopkinsville, KY): *name changed to Ross College.*

Brown Mackie College–Indianapolis (Indianapolis, IN): *closed.*

Brown Mackie College–Kansas City (Lenexa, KS): *closed.*

Brown Mackie College–Louisville (Louisville, KY): *closed.*

Brown Mackie College–Merrillville (Merrillville, IN): *closed.*

Brown Mackie College–Miami (Miramar, FL): *closed.*

Brown Mackie College–Michigan City (Michigan City, IN): *closed.*

Brown Mackie College–North Canton (Canton, OH): *name changed to Ross College.*

Brown Mackie College–Northern Kentucky (Fort Mitchell, KY): *closed.*

Brown Mackie College–Oklahoma City (Oklahoma City, OK): *closed.*

Brown Mackie College–Phoenix (Phoenix, AZ): *closed.*

Brown Mackie College–Quad Cities (Bettendorf, IA): *name changed to Ross College.*

Brown Mackie College–St. Louis (Fenton, MO): *closed.*

Brown Mackie College–Salina (Salina, KS): *closed.*

Brown Mackie College–South Bend (South Bend, IN): *closed.*

Brown Mackie College–Tucson (Tucson, AZ): *closed.*

Brown Mackie College–Tulsa (Tulsa, OK): *closed.*

Bryan College (Gold River, CA): *closed.*

Bryant & Stratton College–Liverpool Campus (Liverpool, NY): *name changed to Bryant & Stratton College–Syracuse North Campus.*

Cambria-Rowe Business College (Indiana, PA): *closed.*

Cambria-Rowe Business College (Johnstown, PA): *closed.*

Cambridge Institute of Allied Health and Technology (Delray Beach, FL): *name changed to Cambridge College of Healthcare & Technology.*

Career Point College (Tulsa, OK): *closed.*

Carrington College–Phoenix West (Phoenix, AZ): *name changed to Carrington College–Phoenix East.*

Charter College (Canyon Country, CA): *no longer degree granting.*

Comanche Nation College (Lawton, OK): *no longer accredited by agency recognized by USDE or CHEA.*

Darton State College (Albany, GA): *merged into a single 4-year college entry for Albany State University (Albany, GA).*

Daymar College (Madisonville, KY): *closed.*

Daymar College (Owensboro, KY): *closed.*

Dean College (Franklin, MA): *now classified as a 4-year college.*

Dewey University–Arroyo (Arroyo, PR): *closed.*

Dewey University–Hatillo (Hatillo, PR): *closed.*

DuBois Business College (DuBois, PA): *closed.*

DuBois Business College (Huntingdon, PA): *closed.*

DuBois Business College (Oil City, PA): *closed.*

ECPI University (Charlotte, NC): *merged into a single entry for ECPI University (Virginia Beach, VA) classified as a 4-year college.*

ECPI University (Greensboro, NC): *merged into a single entry for ECPI University (Virginia Beach, VA) classified as a 4-year college.*

ECPI University (Columbia, SC): *merged into a single entry for ECPI University (Virginia Beach, VA) classified as a 4-year college.*

ECPI University (Greenville, SC): *merged into a single entry for ECPI University (Virginia Beach, VA) classified as a 4-year college.*

ECPI University (North Charleston, SC): *merged into a single entry for ECPI University (Virginia Beach, VA) classified as a 4-year college.*

ECPI University (Richmond, VA): *merged into a single entry for ECPI University (Virginia Beach, VA) classified as a 4-year college.*

Edison Community College (Piqua, OH): *name changed to Edison State Community College.*

Everest College (Springfield, MO): *closed.*

Everest Institute (Norcross, GA): *no longer degree granting.*

Florida Technical College (DeLand, FL): *merged into a single entry for Florida Technical College (Orlando, FL).*

Fortis College (Largo, FL): *closed.*

Fortis College (Winter Park, FL): *closed.*

Fortis Institute (Fort Lauderdale, FL): *closed.*

Fortis Institute (Palm Springs, FL): *closed.*

Fremont College (Los Angeles, CA: *merged into a single entry for Fremont College (Cerritos, CA).*

Graduate School USA (Washington, DC): *no longer degree granting.*

Heritage College (Denver, CO): *closed.*

Heritage College (Wichita, KS): *closed.*

Heritage College (Kansas City, MO): *closed.*

Heritage College (Oklahoma City, OK): *closed.*

Heritage Institute (Fort Myers, FL): *closed.*

Heritage Institute (Jacksonville, FL): *closed.*

Horry-Georgetown Technical College (Conway, SC): *name changed to Horry Georgetown Technical College.*

Hussian College, School of Art (Philadelphia, PA): *now classified as a 4-year college.*

ICDC College (Huntington Park, CA): *closed.*

IHM Academy of EMS (St. Louis, MO): *no longer degree granting.*

ITT Technical Institute (Bessemer, AL): *closed.*

ITT Technical Institute (Madison, AL): *closed.*

ITT Technical Institute (Mobile, AL): *closed.*

ITT Technical Institute (Little Rock, AR): *closed.*

ITT Technical Institute (Phoenix, AZ): *closed.*

ITT Technical Institute (Phoenix, AZ): *closed.*

ITT Technical Institute (Tucson, AZ): *closed.*

ITT Technical Institute (Lathrop, CA): *closed.*

ITT Technical Institute (National City, CA): *closed.*
ITT Technical Institute (Oakland, CA): *closed.*
ITT Technical Institute (Orange, CA): *closed.*
ITT Technical Institute (Oxnard, CA): *closed.*
ITT Technical Institute (Rancho Cordova, CA): *closed.*
ITT Technical Institute (San Bernardino, CA): *closed.*
ITT Technical Institute (San Dimas, CA): *closed.*
ITT Technical Institute (Sylmar, CA): *closed.*
ITT Technical Institute (Torrance, CA): *closed.*
ITT Technical Institute (Aurora, CO): *closed.*
ITT Technical Institute (Fort Lauderdale, FL): *closed.*
ITT Technical Institute (Fort Myers, FL): *closed.*
ITT Technical Institute (Hialeah, FL): *closed.*
ITT Technical Institute (Jacksonville, FL): *closed.*
ITT Technical Institute (Lake Mary, FL): *closed.*
ITT Technical Institute (Pensacola, FL): *closed.*
ITT Technical Institute (Tallahassee, FL): *closed.*
ITT Technical Institute (Tampa, FL): *closed.*
ITT Technical Institute (Atlanta, GA): *closed.*
ITT Technical Institute (Duluth, GA): *closed.*
ITT Technical Institute (Kennesaw, GA): *closed.*
ITT Technical Institute (Boise, ID): *closed.*
ITT Technical Institute (Arlington Heights, IL): *closed.*
ITT Technical Institute (Oak Brook, IL): *closed.*
ITT Technical Institute (Orland Park, IL): *closed.*
ITT Technical Institute (Fort Wayne, IN): *closed.*
ITT Technical Institute (Merrillville, IN): *closed.*
ITT Technical Institute (Newburgh, IN): *closed.*
ITT Technical Institute (Louisville, KY): *closed.*
ITT Technical Institute (Baton Rouge, LA): *closed.*
ITT Technical Institute (St. Rose, LA): *closed.*
ITT Technical Institute (Norwood, MA): *closed.*
ITT Technical Institute (Wilmington, MA): *closed.*
ITT Technical Institute (Owings Mills, MD): *closed.*
ITT Technical Institute (Canton, MI): *closed.*
ITT Technical Institute (Dearborn, MI): *closed.*
ITT Technical Institute (Swartz Creek, MI): *closed.*
ITT Technical Institute (Troy, MI): *closed.*
ITT Technical Institute (Wyoming, MI): *closed.*
ITT Technical Institute (Brooklyn Center, MN): *closed.*
ITT Technical Institute (Arnold, MO): *closed.*
ITT Technical Institute (Earth City, MO): *closed.*
ITT Technical Institute (Kansas City, MO): *closed.*
ITT Technical Institute (Charlotte, NC): *closed.*
ITT Technical Institute (High Point, NC): *closed.*
ITT Technical Institute (Omaha, NE): *closed.*
ITT Technical Institute (Marlton, NJ): *closed.*
ITT Technical Institute (Albuquerque, NM): *closed.*
ITT Technical Institute (Henderson, NV): *closed.*
ITT Technical Institute (North Las Vegas, NV): *closed.*
ITT Technical Institute (Albany, NY): *closed.*
ITT Technical Institute (Getzville, NY): *closed.*
ITT Technical Institute (Liverpool, NY): *closed.*
ITT Technical Institute (Akron, OH): *closed.*
ITT Technical Institute (Columbus, OH): *closed.*
ITT Technical Institute (Dayton, OH): *closed.*
ITT Technical Institute (Hilliard, OH): *closed.*
ITT Technical Institute (Maumee, OH): *closed.*
ITT Technical Institute (Norwood, OH): *closed.*
ITT Technical Institute (Strongsville, OH): *closed.*
ITT Technical Institute (Warrensville Heights, OH): *closed.*
ITT Technical Institute (Youngstown, OH): *closed.*
ITT Technical Institute (Tulsa, OK): *closed.*
ITT Technical Institute (Portland, OR): *closed.*
ITT Technical Institute (Harrisburg, PA): *closed.*
ITT Technical Institute (Levittown, PA): *closed.*
ITT Technical Institute (Philadelphia, PA): *closed.*
ITT Technical Institute (Pittsburgh, PA): *closed.*
ITT Technical Institute (Plymouth Meeting, PA): *closed.*
ITT Technical Institute (Columbia, SC): *closed.*
ITT Technical Institute (Greenville, SC): *closed.*
ITT Technical Institute (North Charleston, SC): *closed.*
ITT Technical Institute (Chattanooga, TN): *closed.*
ITT Technical Institute (Cordova, TN): *closed.*
ITT Technical Institute (Knoxville, TN): *closed.*
ITT Technical Institute (Nashville, TN): *closed.*

ITT Technical Institute (Arlington, TX): *closed.*
ITT Technical Institute (Austin, TX): *closed.*
ITT Technical Institute (DeSoto, TX): *closed.*
ITT Technical Institute (Houston, TX): *closed.*
ITT Technical Institute (Houston, TX): *closed.*
ITT Technical Institute (Richardson, TX): *closed.*
ITT Technical Institute (San Antonio, TX): *closed.*
ITT Technical Institute (San Antonio, TX): *closed.*
ITT Technical Institute (Waco, TX): *closed.*
ITT Technical Institute (Webster, TX): *closed.*
ITT Technical Institute (Murray, UT): *closed.*
ITT Technical Institute (Chantilly, VA): *closed.*
ITT Technical Institute (Norfolk, VA): *closed.*
ITT Technical Institute (Richmond, VA): *closed.*
ITT Technical Institute (Salem, VA): *closed.*
ITT Technical Institute (Springfield, VA): *closed.*
ITT Technical Institute (Everett, WA): *closed.*
ITT Technical Institute (Seattle, WA): *closed.*
ITT Technical Institute (Spokane Valley, WA): *closed.*
ITT Technical Institute (Greenfield, WI): *closed.*
Ivy Tech Community College–Southern Indiana (Sellersburg, IN): *name changed to Ivy Tech Community College–Sellersburg.*
James H. Faulkner State Community College (Bay Minette, AL): *merged into a new single entry for Coastal Alabama Community College (Bay Minette, AL).*
Jefferson Davis Community College (Brewton, AL): *merged into a new single entry for Coastal Alabama Community College (Bay Minette, AL).*
Lassen Community College District (Susanville, CA): *name changed to Lassen Community College.*
Lincoln College of Technology (West Palm Beach, FL): *closed.*
Lincoln Technical Institute (Fern Park, FL): *closed.*
Lincoln Technical Institute (Philadelphia, PA): *closed.*
Management Resources College (Miami, FL): *name changed to Miami Regional University and now classified as a 4-year college.*
Manthano Christian College (Westland, MI): *no longer accredited by agency recognized by USDE or CHEA.*
Medtech College (Orlando, FL): *name changed to Gwinnett Institute.*
Medtech College (Ft. Wayne, IN): *closed.*
Medtech College (Greenwood, IN): *closed.*
Medtech College (Indianapolis, IN): *closed.*
Medtech College (Lexington, KY): *closed.*
Medtech College (Falls Church, VA): *closed.*
Memorial Hospital School of Nursing (Albany, NY): *name changed to Memorial College of Nursing.*
Metropolitan Career Center Computer Technology Institute (Philadelphia, PA): *name changed to The Workforce Institute's City College.*
Miami-Jacobs Career College (Columbus, OH): *closed.*
Miami-Jacobs Career College (Dayton, OH): *closed.*
Miami-Jacobs Career College (Independence, OH): *closed.*
Miami-Jacobs Career College (Sharonville, OH): *closed.*
Miami-Jacobs Career College (Springboro, OH): *closed.*
Miami-Jacobs Career College (Troy, OH): *closed.*
Minneapolis Media Institute (Edina, MN): *closed.*
Minnesota School of Business–Brooklyn Center (Brooklyn Center, MN): *closed.*
Minnesota School of Business–Plymouth (Plymouth, MN): *closed.*
Missouri College (Brentwood, MO): *closed.*
National American University (Overland Park, KS): *now classified as a 4-year college.*
National American University (Bloomington, MN): *now classified as a 4-year college.*
National American University (Brooklyn Center, MN): *now classified as a 4-year college.*
National American University (Albuquerque, NM): *now classified as a 4-year college.*
National American University (Ellsworth AFB, SD): *now classified as a 4-year college.*
New York Career Institute (New York, NY): *closed.*
Ohio College of Massotherapy (Akron, OH): *closed.*
Oklahoma State University, Oklahoma City (Oklahoma City, OK): *name changed to Oklahoma State University–Oklahoma City.*
Pima Medical Institute (Albuquerque, NM): *West Campus no longer degree granting.*

Pittsburgh Technical Institute (Oakdale, PA): *name changed to Pittsburgh Technical College.*

Radians College (Washington, DC): *closed.*

Redstone College–Denver (Broomfield, CO): *name changed to Spartan College of Aeronautics and Technology.*

Riverside School of Health Careers (Newport News, VA): *name changed to Riverside College of Health Careers.*

San Joaquin Valley College (Chula Vista, CA): *closed.*

School of Automotive Machinists (Houston, TX): *name changed to School of Automotive Machinists & Technology.*

South College–Asheville (Asheville, NC): *merged into a single 4-year college entry for South College (Knoxville, TN) by request from the institution.*

Southeastern College–Jacksonville (Jacksonville, FL): *closed.*

Southwestern Oklahoma State University at Sayre (Sayre, OK): *merged into a single 4-year college entry for Southwestern Oklahoma State University (Weatherford, OK) by request from the institution.*

Stanbridge College (Irvine, CA): *name changed to Stanbridge University and now classified as a 4-year college.*

Ultimate Medical Academy Tampa (Tampa, FL): *closed.*

Utica School of Commerce (Utica, NY): *closed.*

Vista College (Clearfield, UT): *name changed to Vista College–Online Campus and relocated to Richardson, TX.*

Westhill University (Sante Fe, Mexico): *no longer degree granting.*

West Virginia Business College (Nutter Fort, WV): *merged into a single entry for West Virginia Business College (Wheeling, WV) by request from the institution.*

Featured Two-Year Colleges

BAY STATE COLLEGE
BOSTON, MASSACHUSETTS

 To read more about this school, visit http://petersons.to/baystatecollege

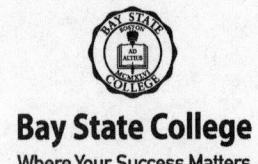

Bay State College
Where Your Success Matters.

The College and Its Mission

Founded in 1946, Bay State College is an independent, co-educational institution located in Boston's historic Back Bay. Since its founding, Bay State College has been preparing graduates for outstanding careers and continued education.

Bay State College is a small, private college focused on passionate students who want to turn their interests into rewarding careers. The College offers associate, bachelor's degrees, and one certificate program in a number of rewarding fields. Everyone at Bay State—from admissions representatives and professors to the career services team—helps to assist, guide, and advise students, from the moment they step on campus. Located in Boston's Back Bay, the College offers the city of Boston as a campus, small classes, and one-on-one attention. For students seeking a career in one of the many professional opportunities offered by Bay State, a degree program at the College could be a strong first step on their career path.

The College offers day, evening, and online courses. Students can receive associate and bachelor's degrees, as well as a certificate in medical assisting. The educational experience offered through the variety of programs prepares students to excel in the careers of their choice. Personalized attention is the cornerstone of a Bay State College education. Through the transformative power of its core values of quality, respect, and support, Bay State College has, for the past seventy years, assisted students with setting and achieving goals that prepare them for careers and continued education.

Recognizing that one of the most important aspects of college is life outside the classroom, the Office of Student Affairs seeks to provide services from orientation through graduation. Special events throughout the year include an annual fashion show and a host of events produced by the Entertainment Management Association. Students also enjoy nearby professional sports teams such as the Boston Celtics and Boston Red Sox.

Bay State College's campus experience can be whatever the student chooses it to be. It's not the typical college campus—its residence halls are actually brownstones along Boston's trendy Commonwealth Avenue and Bay State's "quad" could be Boston Common, the banks of the Charles River by the Esplanade, or Copley Square. That's the advantage of being located in Boston's Back Bay, which is also one of the safest neighborhood in the city. Students can relax at a favorite coffee shop, bike along the Charles River, ice skate on the Frog Pond, check out the city's nightlife, or take in a ball game at Fenway Park.

Bay State College is accredited by the New England Association of Schools and Colleges and is authorized to award the Associate in Science, Associate in Applied Science, and three Bachelor of Science degrees by the Commonwealth of Massachusetts. Bay State is a member of several professional educational associations. Its medical assisting program is accredited by the Accrediting Bureau of Health Education Schools (ABHES). The physical therapist assistant program is accredited by the Commission on Accreditation in Physical Therapy Education (CAPTE) of the American Physical Therapy Association (APTA). Bay State College's Associate of Science in Nursing program is accredited by the Accreditation Commission for Education in Nursing (ACEN). ACEN is located at 3343 Peachtree Road NE, Suite 850, Atlanta, Georgia 30326. The Associate Degree in Nursing program was granted full approval status by the Massachusetts Board of Registration in Nursing on November 12, 2014.

Academic Programs

Bay State College's Day Division operates on a semester calendar. The fall semester typically runs from early September to mid-December. The spring semester runs from mid-January until mid-May.

Associate degrees are offered in accounting, business administration, criminal justice, health studies, information technology, medical assisting, nursing, physical therapist assistant, and retail management.

Bachelor's degrees are offered in criminal justice, management, management–fashion industry concentration, management–music

industry concentration, finance, healthcare management, hospitality management, human resource management, management information systems, marketing, information technology, and RN to B.S.N.

Bay State College's Evening and Online Division offers courses to working adults. The courses are offered in eight-week sessions and allow more flexibility for students who must balance work and family commitments while pursuing their education.

Bay State College's additional location in Taunton, Massachusetts, offers evening programs to working adults.

Bay State College reviews, enhances, and adds new programs to help graduates remain industry-current in their respective fields.

Off-Campus Programs

Many students cite Bay State's internship program as a turning point for them. Bay State internships allow students to gain hands-on experience and spend time working in their chosen fields. These valuable opportunities can give students an advantage when they apply for positions after they have completed their studies.

Bay State's Boston location allows the College to offer internships at many well-known companies and organizations. Students are able to apply what they've learned in the classroom and do meaningful work in their field of study. In addition, they build working relationships with people in their chosen profession. For more information on internships, prospective students may contact Career Services at 617-217-9000.

Costs

Tuition charges are assessed on a per-credit-hour basis and vary depending upon program of study. This provides students with maximum flexibility based on individual financial and academic needs, making a Bay State College education more accommodating and affordable. Rates quoted below by program are for the 2016–17 academic year. Charges are not prorated unless noted. Program flow sheets may require more or less than 30 credits per academic year.

Medical assisting certificate: $550 per credit, $15,950 (29 credits). Medical assisting, and health studies: $810 per credit, $24,300 (30 credits). Business, criminal justice, fashion merchandising, fashion design, entertainment management, and hospitality management: $905 per credit, $27,150 (30 credits). Nursing and physical therapy assistant: $905 per credit, $27,150 (30 credits).

Room and board are $13,000 per year, the student services fee is $400 (for day students only), and the student activity fee is $50. The cost of books and additional fees vary by major. A residence hall security deposit of $300 and a technology fee of $300 are required of all resident students.

The fall tuition payment due date is July 1; the spring tuition payment is due December 1.

Financial Aid

Each student works with a personal advocate to thoroughly explain financial options and guide them through the financial aid application process. Many options are available to those who qualify: aid, grants and scholarships, federal programs, and private loans. Bay State College's Financial Aid Department and tuition planners can help students determine what aid may apply. Approximately 85 percent of students receive some form of financial assistance. Bay State College requires a completed Free Application for Federal Student Aid (FAFSA) form and signed federal tax forms. The College's institutional financial aid priority deadline is March 31. Financial aid is granted on a rolling basis.

Faculty

There are approximately 100 faculty members, many holding advanced degrees and several holding doctoral degrees. The student-faculty ratio is 18:1.

Student Body Profile

There are approximately 800 students in degree programs in the day, evening, and online divisions.

Student Activities

Bay State College students participate in a number of activities offered by the College through existing student organizations. Students also have the opportunity to create clubs and organizations that meet their interests. Existing organizations include the Student Government Association, Entertainment Management Association, and the Justice Society. Fashion Design and Merchandising students produce an annual fashion show that showcases student work from the College's fashion design program. An annual literary magazine also features the work of students throughout the College.

Facilities and Resources

Advisement/Counseling: Trained staff members assist students in selecting courses and programs of study. A counseling center is available to provide mental and physical health referrals to all students in need of such services. Referral networks are extensive, within a wide range of geographic areas, and provide access to a variety of public and private health agencies.

Specialized Services: The Office of Academic Development at Bay State College is designed to meet and support the various academic needs of the student body and serve as a resource for supplemental instruction, academic plans, learning accommodations, and other types of support. The Office of Academic Development operates on the belief that all students can achieve success in their courses by accessing support services and creating individual academic plans.

The Center for Learning and Academic Success (CLAS) at Bay State College is a key component available to help students achieve academic success. Students come to CLAS to get support in specific subject areas as well as study skills such as note-taking, reading comprehension, writing research papers, time management, and coping with exam anxiety. They utilize CLAS to develop study plans and strategies that positively impact their grades in all subjects. Students can also take advantage of the tutoring and seminars CLAS offers. CLAS's goal is to ensure that students are provided with exceptional academic support in all areas of study.

Career Planning/Placement: For many college students, the transition from student life to professional life is filled with questions and uncharted realities. Bay State College's Career Services Department can help students learn to write a resume and cover letter, use social networks, practice interviewing skills, find the right job opportunity, and learn other career-related functions. The Career Services Department is determined to help each student succeed and offers valuable instruction that will serve students throughout their professional careers.

Library and Audiovisual Services: The library is staffed with trained librarians who are available to guide students in their research process. The library's resources include 7,500 books, eighty-five periodical subscriptions, and a dramatically increased reach through its online library resource databases that include ProQuest, InfoTrac, and LexisNexis. In addition, the library provides computer access and study space for students. The library catalog and databases are accessible from any Internet-ready terminal.

First-Year Experience: The First-Year Experience (FYE) is an orientation that is required of all first-year students. FYE combines social activities with an academic syllabus that is designed to ease the transition into the college experience. Through FYE, students have the opportunity to connect with their academic advisers as well as with other students in their academic programs. At the conclusion of FYE, students are on the road to mapping out their personal action plan for success. The plan, designed by students, guided by academic advisers, and revisited each semester, helps students set, monitor, and achieve academic and life goals.

Location

Located in the historic city of Boston, Massachusetts, and surrounded by dozens of colleges and universities, Bay State College is an ideal setting in which to pursue a college degree. Tree-lined streets around the school are mirrored in the skyscrapers of the Back Bay. The College is located within walking distance of several major league sport franchises, concert halls, museums, the Freedom Trail, Boston Symphony Hall, the Boston Public Library, and the Boston Public Garden. World-class shopping and major cultural and sporting events help make college life a memorable experience. The College is accessible by the MBTA and commuter rail and bus, and it is near Boston Logan International Airport.

Admission Requirements

Applicants must be a high school graduate, a current high school student working toward graduation, or a recipient of a GED certificate. The Office of Admissions requires that applicants to the associate degree programs have a minimum of a 2.0 GPA (on a 4.0 scale); if available, applicants may submit SAT and/or ACT scores. Applicants to bachelor's degree programs must have a minimum 2.3 GPA (on a 4.0 scale) and must also submit SAT or ACT scores. International applicants must also submit high school transcripts translated to English with an explanation of the grading system, financial documentation, and official TOEFL score of 183 or a 6.0 on the IELTS if native language is not English (or language school affiliate equivalent). The College also accepts iTEP test scores. If students are taking a different test, they need to check with the admissions team to ensure that test is accepted for admission.

The physical therapist assistant and nursing programs require a minimum 2.7 GPA (on a 4.0 scale) and the Evening Division has different or additional admission requirements. For more information about these programs, interested students should visit the website at http://www.baystate.edu.

A personal interview is required for all prospective students—parents are encouraged to attend. Applicants must receive the recommendation of a Bay State College Admissions Officer.

Application and Information

Applications are accepted on a rolling basis. Students are responsible for arranging for their official high school transcripts, test scores, and letters of recommendation to be submitted to Bay State College.

The Bay State College Admissions Office notifies applicants of a decision within one week of receipt of the transcript and other required documents. There is a $100 nonrefundable tuition deposit required upon acceptance to ensure a place in the class; the deposit is credited toward the tuition fee. Deposits are due within thirty days of acceptance. Once a student is accepted, a Bay State College representative creates a personalized financial plan that provides payment options for a Bay State College education.

Applications should be submitted to:

Admissions Office
Bay State College
122 Commonwealth Avenue
Boston, Massachusetts 02116
Phone: 800-81-LEARN (53276)
Fax: 617-249-0400 (eFax)
E-mail: admissions@baystate.edu
Website: http://www.baystate.edu
      http://www.facebook.com/baystatecollege
      http://twitter.com/baystatecollege

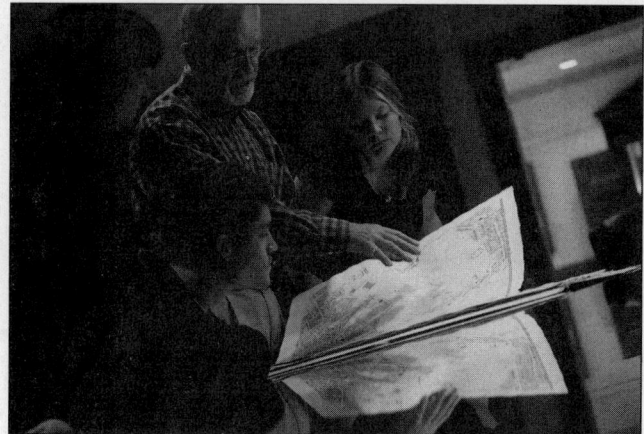

Giving students access is an essential part of a Bay State College education. Students have access to a community of support, experiential learning, faculty with real-world experience, and a dynamic location in the heart of the city.

FASHION INSTITUTE OF TECHNOLOGY
State University of New York
NEW YORK, NEW YORK

 To read more about this school, visit http://petersons.to/fit

The College and Its Mission

The Fashion Institute of Technology, a college of the State University of New York, has been a leader in career education in art, design, business, and technology for more than 70 years. FIT infuses its nearly 50 majors with a comprehensive liberal arts education, providing a singular blend of practical experience and a pioneering curriculum that prepares students for success and leadership in the competitive global marketplace. FIT offers a range of innovative programs that are affordable and relevant to today's rapidly changing industries. Internationally renowned, FIT draws on its New York City location to provide a vibrant, creative community in which to learn. The schools of Art and Design, Business and Technology, and Liberal Arts offer Associate in Applied Science (A.A.S.), Bachelor of Fine Arts (B.F.A.), and Bachelor of Science (B.S.) degrees. The School of Graduate Studies offers Master of Arts (M.A.), Master of Fine Arts (M.F.A.), and Master of Professional Studies (M.P.S.) degrees. The college is accredited by the Middle States Commission on Higher Education, the National Association of Schools of Art and Design, and the Council for Interior Design Accreditation. FIT serves approximately 9,500 students from the greater metropolitan area, New York State, across the country, and around the world, providing full- and part-time study, evening/weekend degree programs, noncredit, certificate, and online courses.

FIT's faculty members bring high-level industry experience to the classroom, working as corporate executives, entrepreneurs, consultants, designers, artists, filmmakers, and authors. Both practitioners and scholars, they connect students with real-world practice, fostering collaboration, innovation, and a global perspective. Academic departments consult with industry leaders to ensure that curricula and classroom technology remain current with evolving professional practice.

FIT offers a complete college experience, with a vibrant campus life that includes over 60 clubs and organizations, athletic teams, and an active student government. Four residence halls house 2,300 undergraduate students in traditional and apartment-style rooms. Professional staff and residence assistants live in each hall to ensure that students are fully enjoying their residential experience.

Academic Programs

Each undergraduate program includes a core of liberal arts courses, providing students with a global perspective, critical-thinking skills, and the ability to communicate effectively. All degree programs are designed to prepare students for careers in the creative industries and to provide them with the prerequisite studies to go on to baccalaureate, master's, or doctoral degrees.

Typically, undergraduate students apply to and enroll in the two-year A.A.S. degree program. For those who have already earned a degree or have taken the requisite general education courses at other institutions, FIT also offers one-year A.A.S. degree programs. Upon earning the A.A.S. degree (either at FIT or another institution), students apply to FIT's bachelor's programs to earn the B.F.A. or B.S. degree.

Associate Degree Programs: For the A.A.S. degree, FIT offers ten majors through the School of Art and Design, four through the Jay and Patty Baker School of Business and Technology, and one through the School of Liberal Arts. The A.A.S. programs are accessories design*, advertising and marketing communications*, communication design foundation*, fashion design*, fashion business management* (with an online option), film and media, fine arts, illustration, interior design, jewelry design, menswear, photography and related media, production management: fashion and related industries, textile development and marketing*, and textile/surface design*. Programs with an asterisk (*) also offer a one-year A.A.S. degree for eligible transfer applicants.

Bachelor's Degree Programs: The majority of FIT's A.A.S. graduates choose to pursue a related baccalaureate program at the college. FIT offers twenty-six baccalaureate programs—fourteen B.F.A. programs through the School of Art and Design, ten B.S. programs through the Baker School of Business and Technology, and two B.S. programs through the School of Liberal Arts. The B.F.A. programs are accessories design,

advertising design, computer animation and interactive media, fabric styling, fashion design (with specializations in children's wear, intimate apparel, knitwear, special occasion, and sportswear), fine arts, graphic design, illustration, interior design, packaging design, photography and related media, textile/surface design, toy design, and visual presentation and exhibition design. The B.S. programs are advertising and marketing communications, art history and museum professions, cosmetics and fragrance marketing, direct and interactive marketing, entrepreneurship for the fashion and design industries, fashion business management, film and media, home products development, international trade and marketing for the fashion industries, production management: fashion and related industries, technical design, and textile development and marketing.

Minors: FIT's curriculum offers a range of subject-based and interdisciplinary minors that let students expand and deepen their major studies or explore additional interests. Liberal Arts minors include communication studies, dance, film and media, economics, international politics, Latin American studies, Mandarin Chinese, and women and gender studies; Art and Design minors are creative technology and design thinking; the Business and Technology minor is international trade and marketing; and the ethics and sustainability minor is offered jointly through all three schools.

Evening/Weekend Programs: FIT provides evening and weekend credit and noncredit classes to students and working professionals interested in pursuing a degree or furthering their knowledge of a particular industry, while balancing the demands of career or family.

Certificate Programs: FIT's Center for Continuing and Professional Studies offers credit and noncredit certificates through its two divisions: Enterprise Studies and Digital Design and Professional Studies. Certificate programs include leather apparel, millinery, retail management, fashion styling, pet product design and marketing, and sustainable design entrepreneurship. The center also provides career and personal development courses designed for adults with busy schedules.

Honors Program: The Presidential Scholars honors program, available to academically exceptional students in all majors, offers special courses, projects, colloquia, and off-campus activities that broaden horizons and stimulate discourse. Presidential Scholars receive priority course registration and an annual merit stipend.

Internships: Internships are a required element of most programs and are available to all matriculated students. Nearly one third of FIT student interns are offered employment on completion of their internships; past sponsors include American Eagle Outfitters, Bloomingdale's, Calvin Klein, Estée Lauder, Hearst Magazines, MTV, and Saatchi & Saatchi.

Precollege Programs: Precollege programs are available to middle and high school students during the fall, spring, and summer. More than 100 courses provide the chance to learn in an innovative environment, develop art and design portfolios, explore the business and technological sides of many creative careers, and discover natural talents and abilities.

Off-Campus Programs

The study-abroad experience lets students immerse themselves in diverse cultures and prepares them to live and work in a global community. FIT has two campuses in Italy—one in Milan, one in Florence—and one near Seoul, South Korea, where students study fashion design or fashion business management and gain firsthand experience in the dynamics of global fashion. FIT also offers study-abroad opportunities on six continents. Students can study abroad during the winter or summer sessions, for a semester, or for a full academic year.

Costs

As a SUNY college, FIT offers affordable tuition for both New York State residents and nonresidents. The 2016–17 associate-level tuition per semester for in-state residents was $2,295; for nonresidents, $6,885. Baccalaureate-level tuition per semester was $3,235 for in-state residents and $9,796 for nonresidents. Per-semester housing costs were $6,693–$6,892 for traditional residence hall accommodations with mandatory meal plan and $6,175–$10,289 for apartment-style accommodations. Meal plans ranged from $1,851 to $2,369 per semester. Textbook costs and other nominal fees, such as locker rental or laboratory use, vary per program. All costs are subject to change.

Financial Aid

FIT offers scholarships, grants, loans, and federal work-study employment for students with financial need. Overall, two-thirds of full-time, matriculated undergraduate students who complete the Free Application for Federal Student Aid (FAFSA) receive some type of assistance through loans and/or grants. The college directly administers its own institutional grants and scholarships, which are provided by the FIT Foundation.

College-administered funding includes Federal Pell Grants, Federal Perkins Loans, Federal Supplemental Educational Opportunity Grants, Federal Work-Study, and the Federal Family Educational Loan Program, which includes student and parent loans. New York State residents who meet eligibility guidelines may also receive grants from the Tuition Assistance Program (TAP) and/or Educational Opportunity Program (EOP). To be considered for need-based federal financial aid, U.S. citizens and permanent residents must file the FAFSA prior to February 15 for fall admission or November 1 for spring admission. Additional documentation may be requested by Financial Aid Services.

Faculty

FIT's faculty is drawn from top professionals in academia, art, design, communications, and business, providing a curriculum rich in real-world experience and traditional educational values. Student-instructor interaction is encouraged, with a maximum class size of 25, and courses are structured to foster collaboration, independent thinking, and self-expression.

Student Body Profile

Fall 2016 enrollment was 9,272 with 8,455 students enrolled in degree programs. Thirty-six percent of degree-seeking students are enrolled in the School of Art and Design; 50 percent were in the Baker School of Business and Technology. The average age of full-time degree seekers was 23. Thirty-six percent of FIT's students were New York City residents, 25 percent were New York State (non–New York City) residents, and 38 percent were out-of-state residents or international students. The ethnic/racial makeup of the student body was approximately 11 percent Asian; 9 percent black; 18 percent Hispanic; 3 percent multiracial; and 45 percent white. There were 1,139 international students.

Student Activities

Participation in campus life is encouraged, and the college is home to more than sixty student organizations, societies, athletic teams, major-related groups, and special-interest clubs. Each organization is open to all students who have paid their activity fee.

Student Government: The FIT Student Government Association grants all students the privileges and responsibilities of citizens in a self-governing college community. Faculty committees often include student representatives, and the president of the student government sits on FIT's Board of Trustees.

Athletics: FIT has intercollegiate teams in cross-country and half marathon, track and field, table tennis, women's tennis, women's soccer, swimming and diving, and women's volleyball; there is also a coed dance company. Athletics and Recreation offers a full array of group fitness classes, including aerobics, dance, spin, and yoga at no extra cost. Students can also work out on their own in a 5,000-square-foot fitness center. Open gym activities allow students to participate in both team and individual sports.

Events: Concerts, dances, field trips, films, flea markets, and other events are planned by the FIT Student Government Association and Programming Board and various clubs. Student-run publications include a campus newspaper, a fashion and beauty magazine, and a literary and art magazine.

Facilities and Resources

FIT's campus provides its students with classrooms, laboratories, and studios that reflect the most advanced educational and industry practices. The Fred P. Pomerantz Art and Design Center houses drawing, painting, photography, printmaking, and sculpture studios; display and exhibition design rooms; a model-making workshop; and a graphics printing service bureau. The Peter G. Scotese Computer-Aided Design and Communications Center provides the latest technology in computer graphics, design, photography, and animation.

Other cutting-edge facilities include a professionally equipped fragrance-development laboratory—the only one of its kind on a U.S. college campus—cutting and sewing labs, a design/research lighting laboratory, knitting lab, broadcasting studio, multimedia foreign languages laboratory, and forty-six computer labs containing Mac and PC workstations.

The Museum at FIT, New York City's only museum dedicated to fashion, contains one of the most important collections of fashion and textiles in the world. The museum, which is accredited by the American Alliance of Museums, operates year-round, and its exhibitions are free and open to the public. The Gladys Marcus Library provides more than 300,000 volumes of print, nonprint, and digital materials. The periodicals collection includes over 500 current subscriptions, with a specialization in international design and trade publications; online resources include more than 90 searchable databases. Students also have access to the library's Special Collections, a highly specialized repository of primary-source research materials related to fashion and design.

The David Dubinsky Student Center offers student lounges, a game room, a student radio station, the Style Shop (a student-run boutique), a full-service dining hall and Starbucks, student government and club offices, disability services, comprehensive health services and a counseling center, two gyms, a state-of-the-art fitness center, and a dance studio.

Location

Occupying an entire block in Manhattan's Chelsea neighborhood, FIT makes extensive use of the city's creative, commercial, and cultural resources, providing students with unrivaled internship opportunities and professional connections. A wide range of cultural and entertainment options are available within a short walk of the campus, as is convenient access to several subway and bus lines and the city's major rail and bus transportation hubs.

Admission Requirements

Applicants for admission must be either candidates for or recipients of a high school diploma or a General Educational Development (GED) certificate. Admission is based on performance in college-preparatory coursework and the student essay. A portfolio evaluation is required for art and design majors. Specific portfolio requirements are explained on FIT's website. SAT and ACT scores are required for placement in math and English classes and students applying to the Presidential Scholars honors program. International applicants whose native language is not English must submit scores from either the TOEFL, PTE, or IELTS examinations.

Transfer applicants must submit official transcripts for all coursework previously taken at an accredited college/university. Transfer applicants may qualify either for the one-year A.A.S. program if they hold a bachelor's degree or have a minimum of 30 transferable college credits, including 24 credits equivalent to FIT's liberal arts degree requirements.

Students seeking admission to a B.F.A. or B.S. program must hold an A.A.S. degree from FIT or an equivalent college degree and must meet the prerequisites for the specific major. A portfolio is required for applicants to B.F.A. programs. Any student who applies for baccalaureate-level transfer to FIT from a four-year bachelor's-level program must have completed a minimum of 60 credits, including the requisite art or technical courses and the liberal arts requirements.

Application and Information

Prospective students wishing to visit FIT are encouraged to attend an admissions information session and a student-led tour of FIT's campus. The visit schedule, including open houses, portfolio review days, and Junior Days for high school juniors, is available online at fitnyc. edu/visitfit. A virtual tour of the campus can be found at fitnyc.edu/virtualtour. Candidates may apply for undergraduate admission online at fitnyc.edu/admissions. More information is available by contacting:
Undergraduate Admissions
Fashion Institute of Technology
227 West 27 Street, Room C139
New York, New York 10001-5992
Phone: 212-217-3760
E-mail: fitinfo@fitnyc.edu
Website: http://www.fitnyc.edu/admissions
http://www.facebook.com/FashionInstituteofTechnology
instagram.com/fitnyc
twitter.com/fit

MIAMI DADE COLLEGE
MIAMI, FLORIDA

 To read more about this school, visit http://petersons.to/miami-dade-college

Miami Dade
College

The College and Its Mission

With 165,000 students currently enrolled and more than 2 million students admitted, Miami Dade College (MDC) is the largest campus-based institution of higher education in the United States. MDC's eight campuses are located in and around Miami, Florida, and include the Hialeah Campus, Homestead Campus, InterAmerican Campus, Kendall Campus, Medical Campus, North Campus, West Campus, and Wolfson Campus. In addition, MDC has a major outreach center: The Carrie P. Meek Entrepreneurial Education Center.

The College's multiple locations throughout Miami-Dade County allow it to offer students highly flexible scheduling options for its more than 300 study pathways. Students may pursue four-year bachelor's degrees and two-year associate degrees, as well as various vocational and college-credit certificates. MDC offers evening and weekend courses, many of which can be completed online through MDC's Virtual College at http://www.mdc.edu/virtual/.

Miami Dade College, its students, faculty, and staff have been recognized through numerous prestigious awards and honors. Recent examples include the 2017 Leah Meyer Austin Award from Achieving the Dream, the 2016 Higher Education Excellence in Diversity award from Insight into Diversity, and the Presidential Medal of Freedom, which was presented to MDC President Eduardo J. Padrón by former U.S. President Barack Obama.

In addition to being one of the top colleges in the region, MDC also serves the community as the backbone of several of South Florida's most prominent cultural institutions. MDC's Department of Cultural Affairs presents and produces nationally acclaimed events including Miami Book Fair and the Miami Film Festival, as well as cultural venues such as the MDC Museum of Art + Design, MDC Live Arts, Tower Theater, Koubek Center, the National Historic Landmark Freedom Tower, The Center for Writing and Literature at MDC, and Teatro Prometeo.

Graduates from MDC include many notable professionals, performers, political figures, and celebrities, including: U.S. Congresswoman Ileana Ros-Lehtinen, Emilio Estefan, Andy Garcia, Oscar-winning playwright Tarell Alvin McCraney, Pulitzer Prize-winning journalist Mirta Ojito, The Related Group co-founder and CEO Jorge M. Perez, National Baseball Hall of Fame inductee Mike Piazza, Miami-Dade County State Attorney Katherine Fernández Rundle, Sylvester Stallone, and *Miami Herald* president and publisher Alexandra Villoch.

Academic Programs

Associate Degree Programs: Two-year associate degree programs at Miami Dade College prepare students to enter into junior-year studies at universities or immediate employment in certain career fields. MDC offers hundreds of associate degree pathways in areas such as accounting, architecture, biology, computer science, criminal justice, dietetics, education, fashion, hospitality, interior design, journalism, social work, theater and entertainment, and translation to name a few. MDC awards more associate degrees to Hispanics than any other institution of higher education in the United States.

A student graduating with an associate degree from MDC is guaranteed admission into any public university in Florida, as well as dozens of other universities nationwide with which MDC has articulation agreements. Graduates of Miami Dade College have transferred into such prestigious institutions as Harvard, Yale, Georgetown, Columbia, and Boston University among numerous others.

Specialized Training and Certificate Options: Miami Dade College offers several options for students looking to start new careers, improve their job skills, or learn a specialty. MDC's technical certification programs prepare students for specific vocations in more than 40 areas, including real estate, practical nursing, massage therapy, firefighting, legal secretary, insurance marketing, and business computer programming.

For students who want to hone their knowledge in a specific area but are not seeking particular technical certifications or a degree, the College also offers college credit programs that focus on a unique industry or a specific job.

Noncredit options and alternative education options at MDC include courses open to accelerated high school students, GED preparation, and English as a second language (ESL) courses.

Bachelor's Degree Programs: Miami Dade College offers bachelor's degree programs in select majors, including biological sciences; data analytics; education; electronics engineering technology; film, TV, and digital production; information systems technology; nursing; physician assistant studies; public safety management; supervision and management; and supply chain management. All bachelor's degree programs at MDC are workforce-driven and coursework is designed to prepare students for a specific career.

Students considering MDC have the option to apply to The Honors College, a division of Miami Dade College that is open to high school graduates with exceptionally high GPA and SAT scores. Benefits of admission to The Honors College include small classes, study-travel opportunities, and development of capstone projects for potential publication and personalized educational planning.

Study-Abroad Opportunities

Students at MDC can study abroad in other countries while earning credits toward an MDC degree. MDC sponsors study-abroad programs on six continents, as well as numerous faculty-led programs to destinations around the world. As a member of the College Consortium for International Students (CCIS), MDC students also are able to participate in study-abroad programs sponsored by other CCIS partner institutions.

Costs

For the 2016–17 academic year, the full-time (24 credits) associate degree cost for in-state students was $2,837.28 and $9,660.24 for out-of-state students. Career and Technical Education Programs cost $2,185.92 per term for in-state students and $8,527.44 for out-of-state students. Up-to-date tuition and fees information can be found online at http://www. mdc.edu/about/tuition.aspx.

To pay in-state tuition rates, prospective students need to provide proof of Florida residency. More information is available at www.mdc.edu/main/flresidency/.

Financial Aid and Scholarships

Ample financial aid opportunities are awarded based on financial need and/or academic record, and include direct loan programs, scholarships, federal student aid, Pell Grants, the Florida Bright Futures Scholarship Program, and MDC's American Dream Scholarship, which covers two years of tuition for qualified high-achieving students.

Student Activities

Each MDC campus has a culture that is as diverse its student body. Each offers an opportunity for teamwork and leadership. All club and organization information can be found on SharkNet, MDC's virtual connection to Student Life (http://sharknet.mdc.edu). Here students can browse existing organizations, create a new organization, submit event requests, and more.

Miami Dade College is home to five intercollegiate athletic teams: women's basketball, softball, and volleyball; and men's basketball and baseball. Since 1961, the Miami Dade College Sharks have won multiple championship games and various recognitions and honors. MDC is a member of the National Junior College Athletic Association (NJCAA) and the Florida Community College Activities Association's (FCCAA) Southern Conference.

Facilities and Resources

Learning Resources at Miami Dade College provides a stimulating learning environment that enhances the classroom experience through a variety of services such as face-to-face tutoring, information literacy instruction, and informative workshops. Its facilities enable students to study collaboratively as well as individually and access MDC's specialized collections of print and electronic resources.

MDC's Learning Resources Labs and Courtyards offer students and faculty a wide array of supplemental assistance to ensure academic success, from state-of-the-art technology and software to knowledgeable tutors who can provide instruction in a variety of courses such as math, writing, reading, business,

natural science, health sciences, speech and test preparation, and more.

Library liaisons work with discipline faculty to ensure that resources needed to support the curriculum are available collegewide. These resources may include such things as LibGuides, books, online databases, or eBooks. In addition, the library liaison can design instructional sessions or work with faculty to design assignments that teach students information literacy skills.

Location

Miami Dade College has eight Florida campuses: Hialeah, Homestead, InterAmerican (Miami), Kendall (Miami), Medical (Miami), North (Miami), West (Doral), Wolfson (Miami), along with its Entrepreneurial Education Center (Miami).

Details on each of the campuses can be found at www.mdc.edu/about/campuses.aspx.

Application and Information

The online application is the fastest, easiest way to apply for admission to Miami Dade College, which has rolling admissions and an acceptance rate of 100 percent. There is a $30 application fee, and a transcript of the student's high school record is required.

Additional information, including the link to apply online, can be found at http://www.mdc.edu/admissions/.

For more information, prospective students should contact:

Ms. Ferne Creary, Interim College Registrar
Miami Dade College
300 Northeast Second Avenue
Miami, Florida 33132
United States
Phone: 305-237-2206
Fax: 305-237-2532
E-mail: fcreary@mdc.edu
Website: http://www.mdc.edu

Miami Dade College—North Campus, Science Complex Building
Photo credit: Cristian Lazzari

MIRACOSTA COLLEGE
OCEANSIDE, CALIFORNIA

The College and Its Mission

MiraCosta College offers a friendly and safe suburban environment within easy driving distance of world famous attractions in Southern California. The sunny climate and ocean views make the campus a great place to study. Facilities include library and technology center, student computer labs, free academic tutoring and writing center, cafeteria and patio, an outdoor amphitheater, tennis courts, track, gymnasium, and fitness center.

The MiraCosta Community College District is located in North San Diego County, along the Southern California coast between Orange County to the north and the metropolitan area of San Diego to the south. Classes and resources are available in four separate locations within the district.

The MiraCosta Community College District's mission is to provide superior educational opportunities and student support services to a diverse population of learners with a focus on their success. MiraCosta offers associate degrees, university transfer courses, career and technical education, certificate programs, basic skills education, and lifelong learning opportunities that strengthen the economic, cultural, social, and educational well-being of the communities it serves.

Academic Programs

MiraCosta Community College offers students a wide range of subjects to pursue. Most classes are also available online. Academic programs include:

Accounting
Administration of justice
Anthropology
Art
Astronomy
Athletics
Automotive technology
Biology
Biotechnology
Business administration
Business office technology
Career and life planning
Chemistry
Child development
Chinese
Communication
Computer studies and information technology
Computer science
Counseling
Dance
Design
Dramatic arts
Earth science
Economics
English
English as a second language
Film
French
Geography
Geology
German
Gerontology
Health education
History
Horticulture
Hospitality management
Humanities
Internship studies and cooperative education
Italian
Japanese
Kinesiology
Linguistics
Literature
Mathematics
Media arts and technologies
Medical administrative professional
Massage therapy
Music
Nursing
Nutrition
Oceanography
Philosophy
Physical science
Physics
Political science
Psychology
Reading
Real estate
Religious studies
Sociology
Spanish
Surgical technology

Costs

For the 2017–18 academic year, tuition at MiraCosta College is $46 per credit unit for California residents and $280 per credit unit for nonresident and international students.

Financial Aid

In fiscal year 2014, a total of $11,321,677 in financial aid was distributed to 11,330 students.

Faculty

The College has 178 full-time faculty members and 540 part-time faculty members.

Student Body Profile

There are approximately 18,500 students enrolled at MiraCosta College. The diverse student body includes people from a variety of ages, ethnicities, and cultural backgrounds. Fifty-six percent of the students are women and 44 percent are men; 64 percent are age 24 or younger, while 36 percent are 25 and older. Ethnicity of the student body is 46 percent white, 34 percent Hispanic, 8 percent Asian/Pacific Islander, 4 percent African American, and 8 percent multiethnic or other.

Student Activities

The Offices of Student Activities supports a wide range of activities and events, provides information and resources centers, and serves as a focal point for service and leadership development programs. MiraCosta has more than forty active student clubs including the Accounting and Business

Club, the International Club, the Black Student Union, the Dance Club, the Martial Arts Club, the Performance Writers Club, and many others.

Facilities and Resources

Advisement/Counseling: MiraCosta College offers individualized academic, career, and personal counseling to assist both prospective and current students develop their educational programs; coordinate their career and academic goals; and understand graduation, major, certificate, and transfer requirements.

Specialized Services: With an average class size of about 30 to 45, MiraCosta students rave about their professors and the personal attention they receive. Both students and staff enjoy a friendly atmosphere and a shared belief in helping one another.

Career Planning/Placement: The mission of the Center for Career Studies and Services is to empower students to make informed, intentional career decisions. Career Center resources include a computer lab, resource library, workshops, and career counseling by appointment.

Library and Audiovisual Services: Maintaining thousands of academic research databases, periodicals, reference materials, and professional research guides, the Library and Information Hub is the center for learning and academic support for MiraCosta students. The Library is also home to the Academic Tutoring Center, the Math Learning Center, the Writing Center, and a large computer lab. All services are free to MiraCosta students.

Location

MiraCosta College's district is coastal North San Diego County, approximately 35 miles north of San Diego and 90 miles south of Los Angeles. The Oceanside Campus is a 121-acre hilltop location with coastal and mountain views; the San Elijo Campus is on 42 acres in Cardiff facing the San Elijo Lagoon and Nature Preserve.

Students enjoy MiraCosta's friendly and safe environment. MiraCosta is within driving distance of Los Angeles, Mexico, Disneyland, Hollywood, La Jolla, San Diego Zoo, SeaWorld, and other world famous attractions in Southern California. Facilities include a new library and technology center, student computer labs, cafeteria and patio, an outdoor amphitheater, tennis courts, track, gymnasium, and fitness center.

Admission Requirements

U.S. adults and high school students (sophomore level and higher) are able to enroll. International students who are at least 18 years old with a high school diploma and English proficiency can apply with a written application and supporting documents. International students should contact the International Office for application procedures. MiraCosta College also offers intensive English language training for students seeking to improve their English skills.

Application and Information

For more information, prospective students should contact:

Admissions Office
MiraCosta College
1 Barnard Drive
Oceanside, California 92056
Phone: 760-757-2121
Website: www.miracosta.edu
www.miracosta.edu/iip (for international students)
www.facebook.com/MiraCostaCC
www.twitter.com/MiraCosta
https://www.instagram.com/miracostacollege
https://www.youtube.com/user/MiraCostaCC

Students at MiraCosta College enjoying the first day of fall semester.

PIONEER PACIFIC COLLEGE
WILSONVILLE, OREGON

 For more information, visit http://petersons.to/pioneerpacific

The College and Its Mission

Since 1981, Pioneer Pacific College has been one of the most notable trade schools in Oregon. The College is dedicated to improving individuals' lives through quality programs that give them the foundation to succeed.

Pioneer Pacific College offers programs in four of the most in-demand fields: business, culinary arts, healthcare, and paralegal. These programs are offered at four campuses located throughout western Oregon in some of the state's most popular destinations: Beaverton, Portland, Springfield, and Wilsonville.

Students who wish to pursue careers in the healthcare field have many degree, diploma, and certificate programs to choose from. Because Pioneer Pacific College offers one of the most accessible healthcare schools in Oregon, its programs typically have no waiting lists and provide easier acceptance than programs at surrounding healthcare schools.

The high demand for healthcare professionals across the country including in Oregon provides many employment opportunities for graduates. The Bureau of Labor Statistics projected that demand for the following healthcare occupations will grow much faster than the average for all occupations from 2014 through 2024. Expected increases in demand are as follows:

- Licensed Practical and Licensed Vocational Nurses: 16 percent

- Medical and clinical laboratory technologists and technicians: 16 percent

- Medical and health services managers: 17 percent

- Medical assistants: 23 percent

- Medical records and health information technicians: 15 percent

- Phlebotomists: 25 percent

Healthcare Programs

The Associate of Occupational Science (A.O.S.) in Medical Assisting program emphasizes both the administrative and clinical tasks that keep medical offices running smoothly. It focuses on computer skills; a full-range of clinical competencies; and comprehensive laboratory work that simulates the equipment, facilities, and records associated with ambulatory care centers. It also includes a 180-hour externship that provides real-word training and a limited x-ray training option.

The A.O.S. in Medical Assisting with Limited X-ray program focuses on the same areas as the standard program and also includes a 180-hour externship. It also provides limited X-Ray training concerning the chest, head, spine, and upper and lower extremities.

Upon graduation, students from both programs are eligible to take the National Certified Medical Assisting exam. Graduates of the A.O.S. in Medical Assisting with Limited X-ray must pass the American Registry of Radiologic Technologist's Limited Scope Exam to obtain limiting licensing from the state of Oregon.

The Medical Assisting Diploma includes all of the elements of the A.O.S. in Medical Assisting program including emphasis on both clinical and administrative skills, a 180-hour externship, a limited x-ray training option, and qualification for certification and licensure. However, unlike the A.O.S. program, it doesn't include an additional emphasis on computer skills and a full-range of clinical and lab competencies.

The Licensed Practical Nursing (LPN) Diploma program is one of the best practical nursing programs in Oregon. In addition to classroom learning, the program provides clinical training in interdisciplinary settings at community health facilities, hospitals, and long-term care facilities.

Upon graduation, students are eligible to apply to the Oregon State Board of Nursing to take the National Council of State Boards of Nursing's certification exam for practical nurses (NCLEX-PN). According to the Oregon State Board of Nursing the first-time pass/fail rate for graduates at the Springfield campus was 93 percent in 2012, 91 percent in 2013, 85 percent in 2014, and 85 percent in 2016; and the Wilsonville campus was 90 percent in 2012, 82 percent in 2013, 78 percent in 2014, 83 percent in 2015, and 80 percent in 2016.

Additional healthcare programs: In addition to the medical assisting and LPN programs, Pacific Pioneer College offers the following healthcare programs:

- Associate of Applied Science (A.A.S.) in Healthcare Administration

- A.A.S. in Radiologic Technology

- A.O.S. in Medical Coding

- A.O.S. in Medical Office Administration

- Bachelor of Science (B.S.) in Healthcare Administration

- Certificate in EKG and Phlebotomy

- Certificate in Limited X-ray

- Certificate in Medical Transcription

- Diploma in Medical Billing

Costs

Tuition and fees vary by program: Medical Coding (A.O.S.), $27,500; Medical Office Administration (A.O.S.), $27,800; Medical Billing (diploma), $14,900; EKG and Phlebotomy Technician (certificate), $9,500; Limited X-ray (certificate),

$13,100; Medical Transcription (certificate), $3,500; Radiologic Technology (A.A.S.), $37,435; Healthcare Administration (A.A.S.), $27,650; Healthcare Administration (B.S.), $53,650; Medical Assisting (diploma), $19,700; Medical Assisting (A.O.S.), $27,650; Medical Assisting with Limited X-ray (A.O.S.), $34,500; Medical Assisting with Limited X-ray (diploma), $25,100; and Practical Nursing (diploma), $30,160.

Financial aid

Students at Pioneer Pacific College may qualify for one or more of the following financial aid sources: Federal Pell Grants, Federal Direct Plus Student Loans, Federal Direct Stafford Student Loans, high school scholarships, high school tuition credits, and periodic payment plans.

Faculty members

Healthcare faculty members at Pioneer Pacific College are skilled practitioners and excellent instructors who are committed to making a difference in their students' lives.

For example, Brianne Ene, a Certified Medical Assistant, teaches medical assisting at the Beaverton campus. She has worked as a medical assistant at primary care and specialty clinics throughout the Portland metropolitan area. She loves teaching and spending time with students.

Locations

Pioneer Pacific College's main campus is located in Wilsonville, Oregon in the northwestern region of the United States. It also has campuses in Beaverton, Portland, and Springfield (near Eugene). Its campuses offer state-of-the-art facilities and equipment and resources like career services, academic guidance, and library services. Its locations provide many recreational options.

Beaverton, a city with nearly 90,000 residents, offers museums; nightlife; restaurants; and shopping as well as events like Bike Beaverton, Beaverton Fun Run, and Flicks by the Fountain. Portland, the largest city in Oregon, has a myriad of recreational options including parks and gardens; museums and historic sites; visual arts, music, and film; restaurants and shopping; and events and spectator sports.

Springfield, a smaller city with more than 60,000 residents, offers many shopping outlets including antique and thrift stores. It also has parks, museums, art centers, and events. Wilsonville, the smallest of the four cities with 22,000 residents, provides restaurants, attractions like the Wilsonville Farmers Market, shopping, nightlife, and outdoor

Admission Requirements

To be eligible for admission to any program at Pioneer Pacific College, an applicant must have a high school diploma or a general equivalency diploma (GED). Students who have completed an associate degree or above at an accredited

institution may submit official college transcripts in lieu of a high school diploma or GED.

In addition to meeting the general requirements above, applicants are required to take an assessment for placement purposes. The exam measures basic skills in reading, writing, and mathematics, and are used to ensure that applicants accepted have the requisite skills and support to meet the rigors of 100-level English and Algebra.

Practical Nursing and Radiologic Technology students are required to take the placement assessment regardless of prior post-secondary education or test scores.

For additional information regarding admissions requirements, prospective students can call an Admissions Officer toll-free at 866-772-4636.

Application and Information

Prospective students are encouraged to visit one of Pioneer Pacific College's campuses, tour the facilities, and talk with an Admissions Officer about their interests and goals. This visit allows students to learn more and to ask specific questions regarding the curriculum and career field(s) being considered.

Once the application process has been completed, applicants are scheduled to meet with a Financial Aid Officer regarding the details of their personalized financial assistance plan. Financial Aid Officers are available to meet with students at any time, from pre-application and beyond. Once students have been accepted, they are then scheduled for orientation and can begin taking the first steps toward their career.

Pioneer Pacific College Health Career Institute
27375 SW Parkway Avenue
Wilsonville, Oregon 97070
Phone: 503-682-1862
Fax: 503-682-6801
E-mail:
Website: http://www.pioneerpacific.edu/.

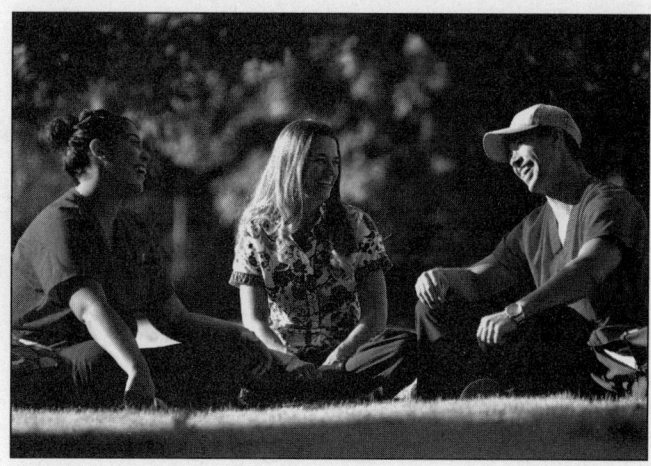

WESTCHESTER COMMUNITY COLLEGE
VALHALLA, NEW YORK

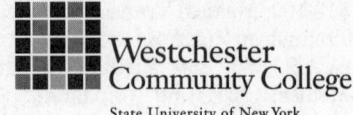
Westchester Community College
State University of New York

The College and Its Mission

Westchester Community College is a public, 2-year college and one of the largest community colleges affiliated with the State University of New York (SUNY) system. It was founded in 1946, and in 1957 it relocated its main campus to 218 acres of the former John A. Harford estate in Valhalla, New York.

Today the college has an annual part- and full-time credit student enrollment of approximately 13,000 individuals who attend classes at the main campus in Valhalla or at extension sites or locations including Mount Vernon, Yonkers, Ossining, Peekskill, and White Plains. The college's Division of Workforce Development and Community Education is the largest in the SUNY system and raises the college's total student enrollment above 26,000.

Westchester Community College is recognized as a Veteran Friendly Campus with extensive services geared toward veterans. The college also has been recognized for its commitment to student diversity. The college has more than 60 associate degree and certificate programs.

Academic Programs

Westchester Community College is dedicated to the belief that growth and adaptation through educational experience are possible for individuals and organizations at all stages of development.

The college offers three types of associate degrees in more than thirty subject areas: the Associate in Arts (A.A.) degree for students transferring to 4-year institutions in the liberal arts; the Associate in Science (A.S.) degree for those transferring to 4-year institutions for business, math, science, or health careers; and the Associate in Applied Science (A.A.S) degree for students preparing to seek immediate employment, change careers, or transfer.

In addition, Westchester Community College offers certificate programs in approximately 20 career fields.

The college's Continuing Education Division offers programming for people of every age considering career choices, changes, or personal development. These programs include customized training for businesses, innovative programming for older adults, and an arts and culture series open to the public. The continuing education division is the largest in the state university of New York system.

Associate of Arts (A.A.) Degree Program: There are 4 A.A. degree programs at Westchester Community College: the Communications and Media Arts A.A. degree program; the Liberal Arts and Sciences/Childhood Education (Teacher Transfer) A.A. degree program; the Liberal Arts and Sciences/ Humanities A.A.; and Liberal Arts and Sciences/Social Science A.A. Requirements for the A.A. degree at Westchester Community College are equivalent to the first two years at an accredited 4-year institution and emphasize the liberal arts and sciences. Graduates typically transfer to baccalaureate-granting institutions.

Associate of Science (A.S.) Degree Program: A.S. degrees are granted in a wide range of disciplines including various aspects of accounting, business, and computers; digital filmmaking; engineering; food service, food, and nutrition; human services; liberal arts, sciences/mathematics, and science; and individual studies. Requirements for the A.S. degree at the college are equivalent to the first two years at an accredited 4-year institution; they are designed to balance a professional orientation with the liberal arts and sciences. Graduates typically transfer to baccalaureate-granting institutions.

Associate of Applied Science (A.A.S.) Degree Program: The college offers 29 A.A.S. degree programs in a wide range of disciplines in business, criminal justice, education, energy, food service, healthcare, human services, technology, and veterinary technology. The curriculum for the A.A.S. degree prepares graduates for immediate employment within specific technical fields. The requirements combine specific career preparations with a firm foundation in the liberal arts and sciences. Although the A.A.S. is not intended as a transfer degree, graduates in some professions do transfer to baccalaureate-granting institutions.

Certificate Programs: The college offers 22 certificate programs covering virtually every sector of business, profession, and service that comprise today's economy. Certificate programs prepare students for immediate employment in a variety of skilled occupations. College credits earned in certificate programs can often be applied to parallel associate degrees offered at the college. Certificates provide a well-rounded course of study which may include English, mathematics, and science courses, in addition to occupational training.

Continuing Education: The Division of Workforce Development and Community Education at Westchester Community College offers a large variety of affordable, high-quality credit and non-credit classes for all ages at numerous locations and online. The division's commitment to lifelong learning and professional development is exemplified by its comprehensive offering of programs and support. Continuing education students at the college can not only improve career or language skills but also explore the creative side of life through a variety of workshops ranging from music, dance, and yoga to cooking, local history, and folklore.

Costs

For the 2017–18 academic year, tuition is $4,280 for in-state students and $11,770 for non-residents.

Fees for full-time students total $462.50 per year.

Financial Aid

Westchester Community College participates in both federal and state financial aid programs. Most financial aid is based on income, and students are required to complete an application form and provide documentation of family income. Financial aid workshops are held to take students through the application process step by step.

The Westchester Community College Foundation provides many scholarships to students. In addition to monies given to incoming and graduating students, many scholarships are offered for continuing students who have demonstrated success while attending Westchester Community College.

Faculty

Westchester Community College's faculty members and professional staff members have received more SUNY Chancellors Awards for Excellence than those of any other community college in the SUNY system. More than 98 percent of faculty members hold master's or doctorate degrees in their fields. The student-faculty ratio is 16:1.

Student Activities

The Student Affairs Office is one of the busiest places on the main campus. This is where a student can access almost 80 different student clubs and organizations that cater to a wide variety of cultural, career, and personal interest fields. The office also is the hub for all student information on campus from bus schedules and voter registration forms to a variety of student services, athletics, scholarships, counseling, and employment services.

Westchester Community College is a member of the National Junior College Athletic Association (NJCAA). Intercollegiate sports include men's baseball, bowling, golf, and soccer and women's basketball, bowling, softball, and volleyball. Intramural sports include men's and women's badminton, basketball, softball, swimming, tennis, volleyball, and weightlifting.

For details on the various clubs and organizations, visit http://www.sunywcc.edu/student-services/getinvolved/clubs/.

Facilities and Resources

Advisement/Counseling:

The Center for Student provides a variety of services in order to aid student success. Personal, career, and educational goals are identified and discussed through one-on-one Counseling. Academic Counselors are available days and evenings, on campus and at extension sites. The goal is to increase student success and assist students in developing educational plans, selecting and scheduling courses, assessing abilities and interests, addressing personal concerns, career planning and job placement, attending to any special needs, and helping with available financial programs.

Specialized Services:

The professional staff of Westchester Community College's expanded Academic Support Center (ASC) offers students free tutoring and support in reading and math. An extensive series of academic workshops in test-taking, note taking and study skills are offered each semester to help sharpen students' academic skills. In addition to the ASC, tutoring centers for many other areas such as science and writing are available.

The Veterans Resource Office at Westchester Community College is committed to providing Veterans and Reserve component personnel, as well as active duty, family members, and dependents, the support they need through a variety of programs and services, intended to make a seamless transition into the college environment. Veterans are encouraged and supported to strengthen their existing foundation built through their military careers with additional career and internship opportunities, utilizing campus, community and national resources The College is devoted to assisting veterans and their dependents reach personal, professional, and academic goals, and is committed to guide each from admissions to graduation, and beyond.

Career Planning/Placement:

Counselors are available to help students with career and college decisions. Transfer Services include one-on-one college counseling, college searches, scholarship availability, and more. Career Services includes, one-on-one career counseling, on-campus recruitment, interviewing skill building, resume writing, and much more.

Location

The main campus of the college in Valhalla, New York, is located in Westchester County. The county is located 11 miles from Columbus Circle in New York City and has almost 1 million residents. Its geographical setting is beautiful, with the Long Island Sound on the southeast and the Hudson River on the west. Within the county's borders, the terrain is largely rolling hills, intersected by the Croton, Bronx, and Saw Mill rivers. It has retained much of its rural character, while adopting the urban and suburban lifestyles dictated by its proximity to New York City.

Application and Information

The Online Application may be used to apply as a matriculated student (for Admission to an Associate Degree/Certificate program) or for Non-matriculated/Summer Visiting Student Status. There is a $35 application fee.
Visit http://www.sunywcc.edu/admissions/apply/.

For more information, prospective students should contact:
Ms. Gloria Leon, Director of Admissions
Westchester Community College
75 Grasslands Road
Valhalla, New York 10595-1698
United States
Phone: 914-606-6735
Fax: 914-606-6540
E-mail: admissions@sunywcc.edu
Website: http://www.sunywcc.edu

Indexes

Associate Degree Programs at Two-Year Colleges

ACCOUNTING
Adirondack Comm Coll (NY)
Albany Tech Coll (GA)
Alexandria Tech and
  Comm Coll (MN)
Allen Comm Coll (KS)
Alvin Comm Coll (TX)
Amarillo Coll (TX)
American Samoa Comm Coll (AS)
Anoka-Ramsey Comm Coll (MN)
Anoka Tech Coll (MN)
Arizona Western Coll (AZ)
Athens Tech Coll (GA)
Atlanta Tech Coll (GA)
Augusta Tech Coll (GA)
Austin Comm Coll District (TX)
Bainbridge State Coll (GA)
Blackhawk Tech Coll (WI)
Blinn Coll (TX)
Blue Ridge Comm and Tech
  Coll (WV)
Borough of Manhattan Comm Coll of
  the City U of New York (NY)
Brookhaven Coll (TX)
Bunker Hill Comm Coll (MA)
Caldwell Comm Coll and Tech
  Inst (NC)
Casper Coll (WY)
Central Georgia Tech Coll (GA)
Central Maine Comm Coll (ME)
Central New Mexico Comm Coll
  (NM)
Central Oregon Comm Coll (OR)
Central Wyoming Coll (WY)
Century Coll (MN)
Cerritos Coll (CA)
Chandler-Gilbert Comm Coll (AZ)
Chattahoochee Tech Coll (GA)
Chippewa Valley Tech Coll (WI)
Clinton Comm Coll (NY)
Coll of the Ouachitas (AR)
The Coll of Westchester (NY)
Colorado Northwestern Comm
  Coll (CO)
Columbus Tech Coll (GA)
Comm Coll of Philadelphia (PA)
Comm Coll of Rhode Island (RI)
Comm Coll of Vermont (VT)
Craven Comm Coll (NC)
Dakota Coll at Bottineau (ND)
Daytona State Coll (FL)
De Anza Coll (CA)
Del Mar Coll (TX)
Des Moines Area Comm Coll (IA)
Dodge City Comm Coll (KS)
Dutchess Comm Coll (NY)
Eastern Idaho Tech Coll (ID)
Eastern Wyoming Coll (WY)
Edison State Comm Coll (OH)
Elgin Comm Coll (IL)
El Paso Comm Coll (TX)
Fayetteville Tech Comm Coll (NC)
Finger Lakes Comm Coll (NY)
Fox Valley Tech Coll (WI)
Frederick Comm Coll (MD)
Gateway Tech Coll (WI)
Genesee Comm Coll (NY)
Georgia Northwestern Tech
  Coll (GA)
Georgia Piedmont Tech Coll (GA)
Golden West Coll (CA)
Greenville Tech Coll (SC)
Guam Comm Coll (GU)
Gwinnett Tech Coll (GA)
Harford Comm Coll (MD)
Harper Coll (IL)
Hawkeye Comm Coll (IA)
Haywood Comm Coll (NC)
Hennepin Tech Coll (MN)

Highland Comm Coll (IL)
Hill Coll (TX)
Housatonic Comm Coll (CT)
Houston Comm Coll (TX)
Howard Comm Coll (MD)
Hudson County Comm Coll (NJ)
Illinois Central Coll (IL)
Illinois Eastern Comm Colls, Olney
  Central College (IL)
Illinois Valley Comm Coll (IL)
Imperial Valley Coll (CA)
Iowa Central Comm Coll (IA)
James Sprunt Comm Coll (NC)
Jefferson Comm Coll (NY)
Johnston Comm Coll (NC)
Kaskaskia Coll (IL)
Kingsborough Comm Coll of the City
  U of New York (NY)
Lackawanna Coll (PA)
Lakeland Comm Coll (OH)
Lake Superior Coll (MN)
Lanier Tech Coll (GA)
Laramie County Comm Coll (WY)
Lenoir Comm Coll (NC)
Lone Star Coll–CyFair (TX)
Lone Star Coll–North Harris (TX)
Lone Star Coll–Tomball (TX)
Lone Star Coll–U Park (TX)
Long Island Business Inst (NY)
Lorain County Comm Coll (OH)
Los Angeles City Coll (CA)
Luzerne County Comm Coll (PA)
Macomb Comm Coll (MI)
Madison Area Tech Coll (WI)
Manchester Comm Coll (CT)
Manor Coll (PA)
Massachusetts Bay Comm Coll (MA)
McHenry County Coll (IL)
McLennan Comm Coll (TX)
Mercer County Comm Coll (NJ)
Metropolitan Comm Coll (NE)
Middlesex County Coll (NJ)
Minnesota State Coll–Southeast
  Tech (MN)
Minnesota State Comm and Tech
  Coll (MN)
Minnesota State Comm and Tech
  Coll–Detroit Lakes (MN)
Minnesota State Comm and Tech
  Coll–Moorhead (MN)
Minnesota West Comm and Tech
  Coll (MN)
Mitchell Comm Coll (NC)
Mohave Comm Coll (AZ)
Monroe Comm Coll (NY)
Monroe County Comm Coll (MI)
Montgomery County Comm Coll (PA)
Morton Coll (IL)
Mountain View Coll (TX)
Mt. San Antonio Coll (CA)
Nashville State Comm Coll (TN)
Nassau Comm Coll (NY)
Navarro Coll (TX)
New Mexico Jr Coll (NM)
New River Comm Coll (VA)
NHTI, Concord's Comm Coll,
  Concord (NH)
Niagara County Comm Coll (NY)
North Central Missouri Coll (MO)
Northcentral Tech Coll (WI)
Northeast Comm Coll (NE)
Northeastern Jr Coll (CO)
Northeast Iowa Comm Coll (IA)
Northern Essex Comm Coll (MA)
Northern Maine Comm Coll (ME)
North Shore Comm Coll (MA)
NorthWest Arkansas Comm
  Coll (AR)
Northwest Coll (WY)

Norwalk Comm Coll (CT)
Oconee Fall Line Tech Coll (GA)
Ogeechee Tech Coll (GA)
Oklahoma State U–
  Oklahoma City (OK)
Orange Coast Coll (CA)
Ozarks Tech Comm Coll (MO)
Paris Jr Coll (TX)
Patrick Henry Comm Coll (VA)
Penn Foster Coll (AZ)
Pensacola State Coll (FL)
Piedmont Comm Coll (NC)
Queensborough Comm Coll of the
  City U of New York (NY)
Randolph Comm Coll (NC)
Rappahannock Comm Coll (VA)
Richmond Comm Coll (NC)
Rockingham Comm Coll (NC)
Rock Valley Coll (IL)
Rowan-Cabarrus Comm Coll (NC)
San Jacinto Coll District (TX)
San Joaquin Delta Coll (CA)
Santa Fe Comm Coll (NM)
Santa Monica Coll (CA)
Savannah Tech Coll (GA)
Scottsdale Comm Coll (AZ)
Seminole State Coll (OK)
Seminole State Coll of Florida (FL)
Shawnee Comm Coll (IL)
Sierra Coll (CA)
Sisseton-Wahpeton Coll (SD)
Southeastern Comm Coll (IA)
Southeastern Tech Coll (GA)
Southern Crescent Tech Coll (GA)
Southern Regional Tech Coll (GA)
Southern U at Shreveport (LA)
South Florida State Coll (FL)
South Georgia Tech Coll (GA)
South Plains Coll (TX)
South Suburban Coll (IL)
Southwestern Comm Coll (NC)
Spartanburg Comm Coll (SC)
Springfield Tech Comm Coll (MA)
Stark State Coll (OH)
Sullivan County Comm Coll (NY)
Sussex County Comm Coll (NJ)
Tarrant County Coll District (TX)
Three Rivers Comm Coll (CT)
Tidewater Comm Coll (VA)
Trident Tech Coll (SC)
Trinity Valley Comm Coll (TX)
U of Cincinnati Clermont Coll (OH)
U of Pittsburgh at Titusville (PA)
Virginia Western Comm Coll (VA)
Waukesha County Tech Coll (WI)
Westchester Comm Coll (NY)
Western Dakota Tech Inst (SD)
Western Nevada Coll (NV)
Western Wyoming Comm Coll (WY)
West Georgia Tech Coll (GA)
Westmoreland County Comm
  Coll (PA)
White Mountains Comm Coll (NH)
Wiregrass Georgia Tech Coll (GA)
Wisconsin Indianhead Tech Coll (WI)
Wytheville Comm Coll (VA)
York County Comm Coll (ME)

ACCOUNTING AND BUSINESS/
MANAGEMENT
Des Moines Area Comm Coll (IA)
Lansdale School of Business (PA)
Lone Star Coll–Montgomery (TX)
Mitchell Tech Inst (SD)
Renton Tech Coll (WA)

ACCOUNTING AND
COMPUTER SCIENCE
Lone Star Coll–CyFair (TX)

ACCOUNTING AND FINANCE
Oklahoma City Comm Coll (OK)
Stark State Coll (OH)

ACCOUNTING RELATED
Dakota Coll at Bottineau (ND)
John Tyler Comm Coll (VA)
J. Sargeant Reynolds Comm
  Coll (VA)
Lansing Comm Coll (MI)
Raritan Valley Comm Coll (NJ)
Southwest Virginia Comm Coll (VA)

ACCOUNTING TECHNOLOGY
AND BOOKKEEPING
Adirondack Comm Coll (NY)
Alamance Comm Coll (NC)
Anne Arundel Comm Coll (MD)
Anoka-Ramsey Comm Coll (MN)
Arapahoe Comm Coll (CO)
Asnuntuck Comm Coll (CT)
Austin Comm Coll District (TX)
Borough of Manhattan Comm Coll of
  the City U of New York (NY)
Bucks County Comm Coll (PA)
Camden County Cañada Coll (CA)
  Coll (NJ)
Cape Fear Comm Coll (NC)
Carroll Comm Coll (MD)
Casper Coll (WY)
Cayuga County Comm Coll (NY)
Central Wyoming Coll (WY)
Chandler-Gilbert Comm Coll (AZ)
Chesapeake Coll (MD)
Coconino Comm Coll (AZ)
Coll of Central Florida (FL)
Coll of Marin (CA)
Coll of the Canyons (CA)
Columbia-Greene Comm Coll (NY)
Columbus State Comm Coll (OH)
Comm Care Coll (OK)
Comm Coll of Allegheny County (PA)
Comm Coll of Aurora (CO)
Comm Coll of Baltimore County
  (MD)
Dakota Coll at Bottineau (ND)
Danville Area Comm Coll (IL)
Del Mar Coll (TX)
Delta Coll (MI)
Des Moines Area Comm Coll (IA)
Dutchess Comm Coll (NY)
East Central Coll (MO)
Feather River Coll (CA)
Fiorello H. LaGuardia Comm Coll of
  the City U of New York (NY)
Florida SouthWestern State Coll (FL)
Front Range Comm Coll (CO)
Fullerton Coll (CA)
Great Basin Coll (NV)
Great Falls Coll Montana
  State U (MT)
Gulf Coast State Coll (FL)
Hagerstown Comm Coll (MD)
Harrisburg Area Comm Coll (PA)
Haywood Comm Coll (NC)
H. Councill Trenholm State Comm
  Coll (AL)
Hinds Comm Coll (MS)
Holyoke Comm Coll (MA)
Hudson County Comm Coll (NJ)
IBMC Coll, Fort Collins (CO)
Ivy Tech Comm Coll–
  Bloomington (IN)
Ivy Tech Comm Coll–
  Central Indiana (IN)
Ivy Tech Comm Coll–Columbus (IN)
Ivy Tech Comm Coll–East
  Central (IN)
Ivy Tech Comm Coll–Kokomo (IN)

Ivy Tech Comm Coll–Lafayette (IN)
Ivy Tech Comm Coll–North
  Central (IN)
Ivy Tech Comm Coll–Northeast (IN)
Ivy Tech Comm Coll–Northwest (IN)
Ivy Tech Comm Coll–Richmond (IN)
Ivy Tech Comm Coll–Sellersburg (IN)
Ivy Tech Comm Coll–Southeast (IN)
Ivy Tech Comm Coll–Southwest (IN)
Ivy Tech Comm Coll–Wabash
  Valley (IN)
Jamestown Comm Coll (NY)
Jefferson Comm Coll (NY)
Jefferson State Comm Coll (AL)
Johnson County Comm Coll (KS)
Kellogg Comm Coll (MI)
Kent State U at Ashtabula (OH)
Kent State U at East Liverpool (OH)
Kent State U at Salem (OH)
Kent State U at Trumbull (OH)
Kent State U at Tuscarawas (OH)
Lackawanna Coll (PA)
Lake Superior Coll (MN)
Lansing Comm Coll (MI)
Lehigh Carbon Comm Coll (PA)
Manhattan Area Tech Coll (KS)
Merced Coll (CA)
Miami Dade Coll (FL)
Minnesota State Coll–Southeast
  Tech (MN)
Mohawk Valley Comm Coll (NY)
Montgomery Coll (MD)
Montgomery County Comm Coll (PA)
Mott Comm Coll (MI)
Nassau Comm Coll (NY)
Naugatuck Valley Comm Coll (CT)
Northampton Comm Coll (PA)
Northland Comm and Tech Coll (MN)
Oakton Comm Coll (IL)
Olympic Coll (WA)
Orange Coast Coll (CA)
Oregon Coast Comm Coll (OR)
Palomar Coll (CA)
Pensacola State Coll (FL)
Pueblo Comm Coll (CO)
Queensborough Comm Coll of the
  City U of New York (NY)
Raritan Valley Comm Coll (NJ)
Rogue Comm Coll (OR)
St. Charles Comm Coll (MO)
St. Clair County Comm Coll (MI)
St. Philip's Coll (TX)
Salt Lake Comm Coll (UT)
San Juan Coll (NM)
Santa Monica Coll (CA)
Schoolcraft Coll (MI)
Southern U at Shreveport (LA)
South Florida State Coll (FL)
South Suburban Coll (IL)
Southwestern Indian
  Polytechnic Inst (NM)
Southwestern Michigan Coll (MI)
Sowela Tech Comm Coll (LA)
State U of New York Coll of
  Technology at Alfred (NY)
Tallahassee Comm Coll (FL)
Three Rivers Comm Coll (CT)
Three Rivers Comm Coll (MO)
Tompkins Cortland Comm Coll (NY)
Ulster County Comm Coll (NY)
U of Cincinnati Blue Ash Coll (OH)
Vincennes U (IN)
Wayne County Comm Coll
  District (MI)
Westchester Comm Coll (NY)
Westmoreland County Comm
  Coll (PA)
Williston State Coll (ND)

ACTING
Casper Coll (WY)
Central Wyoming Coll (WY)
Northampton Comm Coll (PA)

ACTUARIAL SCIENCE
South Florida State Coll (FL)

ADMINISTRATIVE ASSISTANT AND SECRETARIAL SCIENCE
Allen Comm Coll (KS)
Alvin Comm Coll (TX)
Amarillo Coll (TX)
Anoka Tech Coll (MN)
Athens Tech Coll (GA)
Augusta Tech Coll (GA)
Austin Comm Coll District (TX)
Bainbridge State Coll (GA)
Bevill State Comm Coll (AL)
Bismarck State Coll (ND)
Blackhawk Tech Coll (WI)
Blinn Coll (TX)
Borough of Manhattan Comm Coll of the City U of New York (NY)
Bossier Parish Comm Coll (LA)
Camden County Coll (NJ)
Cañada Coll (CA)
Carroll Comm Coll (MD)
Casper Coll (WY)
Cecil Coll (MD)
Central Georgia Tech Coll (GA)
Central Maine Comm Coll (ME)
Central New Mexico Comm Coll (NM)
Central Texas Coll (TX)
Central Wyoming Coll (WY)
Century Coll (MN)
Cerritos Coll (CA)
Chattahoochee Tech Coll (GA)
Chippewa Valley Tech Coll (WI)
Citrus Coll (CA)
Cleveland State Comm Coll (TN)
Cloud County Comm Coll (KS)
Coastal Pines Tech Coll (GA)
Cochise County Comm Coll District (AZ)
Coll of The Albemarle (NC)
Coll of the Canyons (CA)
Coll of the Ouachitas (AR)
Collin County Comm Coll District (TX)
Columbia-Greene Comm Coll (NY)
Columbus State Comm Coll (OH)
Columbus Tech Coll (GA)
Comm Coll of Allegheny County (PA)
Comm Coll of Baltimore County (MD)
Comm Coll of Rhode Island (RI)
Comm Coll of Vermont (VT)
Crowder Coll (MO)
Dakota Coll at Bottineau (ND)
Daytona State Coll (FL)
De Anza Coll (CA)
Del Mar Coll (TX)
Delta Coll (MI)
Dodge City Comm Coll (KS)
Eastern Idaho Tech Coll (ID)
Eastern Wyoming Coll (WY)
Elgin Comm Coll (IL)
El Paso Comm Coll (TX)
Feather River Coll (CA)
Finger Lakes Comm Coll (NY)
Fiorello H. LaGuardia Comm Coll of the City U of New York (NY)
Fox Valley Tech Coll (WI)
Fullerton Coll (CA)
Gateway Tech Coll (WI)
Georgia Piedmont Tech Coll (GA)
Golden West Coll (CA)
Greenville Tech Coll (SC)
Gwinnett Tech Coll (GA)
Harford Comm Coll (MD)
Harper Coll (IL)
Harrisburg Area Comm Coll (PA)
H. Councill Trenholm State Comm Coll (AL)
Hennepin Tech Coll (MN)
Highland Comm Coll (IL)
Hill Coll (TX)
Hinds Comm Coll (MS)
Holyoke Comm Coll (MA)
Horry Georgetown Tech Coll (SC)
Housatonic Comm Coll (CT)
Hutchinson Comm Coll (KS)
Illinois Central Coll (IL)
Imperial Valley Coll (CA)
Iowa Central Comm Coll (IA)
Ivy Tech Comm Coll–Bloomington (IN)
Ivy Tech Comm Coll–Columbus (IN)
Ivy Tech Comm Coll–East Central (IN)
Ivy Tech Comm Coll–Kokomo (IN)
Ivy Tech Comm Coll–Sellersburg (IN)
Ivy Tech Comm Coll–Southeast (IN)
Ivy Tech Comm Coll–Southwest (IN)
Jamestown Business Coll (NY)
Jamestown Comm Coll (NY)
Jefferson Comm Coll (NY)
Jefferson State Comm Coll (AL)
Johnson County Comm Coll (KS)
Johnston Comm Coll (NC)
Kellogg Comm Coll (MI)
Kent State U at Ashtabula (OH)
Kent State U at Salem (OH)
Kent State U at Trumbull (OH)
Kent State U at Tuscarawas (OH)
Kingsborough Comm Coll of the City U of New York (NY)
Kishwaukee Coll (IL)
Lackawanna Coll (PA)
Lakeland Comm Coll (OH)
Lake Region State Coll (ND)
Lanier Tech Coll (GA)
Lansing Comm Coll (MI)
Lone Star Coll–Kingwood (TX)
Lone Star Coll–Tomball (TX)
Los Angeles City Coll (CA)
Lurleen B. Wallace Comm Coll (AL)
Luzerne County Comm Coll (PA)
Macomb Comm Coll (MI)
Madison Area Tech Coll (WI)
Manchester Comm Coll (CT)
Manhattan Area Tech Coll (KS)
McHenry County Coll (IL)
McLennan Comm Coll (TX)
Merced Coll (CA)
Mercer County Comm Coll (NJ)
Meridian Comm Coll (MS)
Mesabi Range Coll (MN)
Mesa Comm Coll (AZ)
Metropolitan Comm Coll (NE)
Miami Dade Coll (FL)
Middlesex County Coll (NJ)
Mid-Plains Comm Coll, North Platte (NE)
Minnesota State Coll–Southeast Tech (MN)
Minnesota State Comm and Tech Coll (MN)
Minnesota State Comm and Tech Coll–Detroit Lakes (MN)
Minnesota State Comm and Tech Coll–Moorhead (MN)
Minnesota West Comm and Tech Coll (MN)
Mohawk Valley Comm Coll (NY)
Monroe Comm Coll (NY)
Monroe County Comm Coll (MI)
Montgomery County Comm Coll (PA)
Morton Coll (IL)
Mt. San Antonio Coll (CA)
Nashville State Comm Coll (TN)
Nassau Comm Coll (NY)
Navarro Coll (TX)
New Mexico Jr Coll (NM)
New River Comm Coll (VA)
Niagara County Comm Coll (NY)
Northampton Comm Coll (PA)
North Central Missouri Coll (MO)
Northcentral Tech Coll (WI)
Northeast Comm Coll (NE)
Northeast Iowa Comm Coll (IA)
North Georgia Tech Coll (GA)
Northland Comm and Tech Coll (MN)
North Shore Comm Coll (MA)
Northwest Coll (WY)
Northwest-Shoals Comm Coll (AL)
Norwalk Comm Coll (CT)
Oakton Comm Coll (IL)
Oconee Fall Line Tech Coll (GA)
Ogeechee Tech Coll (GA)
Oklahoma City Comm Coll (OK)
Olympic Coll (WA)
Oregon Coast Comm Coll (OR)
Otero Jr Coll (CO)
Ozarks Tech Comm Coll (MO)
Palomar Coll (CA)
Panola Coll (TX)
Patrick Henry Comm Coll (VA)
Pensacola State Coll (FL)
Queensborough Comm Coll of the City U of New York (NY)
Rainy River Comm Coll (MN)
Rappahannock Comm Coll (VA)
Raritan Valley Comm Coll (NJ)
Reid State Tech Coll (AL)
Rend Lake Coll (IL)
Rock Valley Coll (IL)
St. Philip's Coll (TX)
Salina Area Tech Coll (KS)
San Jacinto Coll District (TX)
Santa Fe Comm Coll (NM)
Santa Monica Coll (CA)
Savannah Tech Coll (GA)
Scottsdale Comm Coll (AZ)
Seminole State Coll of Florida (FL)
Shawnee Comm Coll (IL)
Sierra Coll (CA)
Southeast Comm Coll, Lincoln Campus (NE)
Southeastern Comm Coll (IA)
Southeastern Tech Coll (GA)
Southern Crescent Tech Coll (GA)
Southern Regional Tech Coll (GA)
South Georgia Tech Coll (GA)
South Plains Coll (TX)
Sowela Tech Comm Coll (LA)
Spartanburg Comm Coll (SC)
Springfield Tech Comm Coll (MA)
Stark State Coll (OH)
Sullivan County Comm Coll (NY)
Tarrant County Coll District (TX)
Texarkana Coll (TX)
Three Rivers Comm Coll (MO)
Tidewater Comm Coll (VA)
Trident Tech Coll (SC)
Victoria Coll (TX)
Vincennes U (IN)
Virginia Western Comm Coll (VA)
Waukesha County Tech Coll (WI)
Weatherford Coll (TX)
Westchester Comm Coll (NY)
Western Wyoming Comm Coll (WY)
West Georgia Tech Coll (GA)
Westmoreland County Comm Coll (PA)
Williamsburg Tech Coll (SC)
Wiregrass Georgia Tech Coll (GA)
Wisconsin Indianhead Tech Coll (WI)
Wor-Wic Comm Coll (MD)
Wytheville Comm Coll (VA)

ADULT AND CONTINUING EDUCATION
Cochise County Comm Coll District (AZ)

ADULT DEVELOPMENT AND AGING
Albany Tech Coll (GA)
Central Georgia Tech Coll (GA)
Comm Coll of Rhode Island (RI)
Dakota Coll at Bottineau (ND)
El Paso Comm Coll (TX)
Fiorello H. LaGuardia Comm Coll of the City U of New York (NY)
Wayne County Comm Coll District (MI)

ADVERTISING
Coll of Central Florida (FL)
Dakota Coll at Bottineau (ND)
Fashion Inst of Technology (NY)
Harford Comm Coll (MD)
Mohawk Valley Comm Coll (NY)
Mt. San Antonio Coll (CA)
Palomar Coll (CA)
Santa Monica Coll (CA)
South Florida State Coll (FL)
South Plains Coll (TX)
Tidewater Comm Coll (VA)

AERONAUTICAL/AEROSPACE ENGINEERING TECHNOLOGY
Columbus State Comm Coll (OH)
Lenoir Comm Coll (NC)
Mohawk Valley Comm Coll (NY)
Oklahoma City Comm Coll (OK)
Pittsburgh Inst of Aeronautics (PA)

AERONAUTICS/AVIATION/ AEROSPACE SCIENCE AND TECHNOLOGY
Alvin Comm Coll (TX)
Cecil Coll (MD)
Comm Coll of Baltimore County (MD)
Comm Coll of the Air Force (AL)
Hesston Coll (KS)
Hinds Comm Coll (MS)
Lehigh Carbon Comm Coll (PA)
Miami Dade Coll (FL)
Naugatuck Valley Comm Coll (CT)
Northwest Coll (WY)
U of Cincinnati Clermont Coll (OH)

AEROSPACE, AERONAUTICAL AND ASTRONAUTICAL/SPACE ENGINEERING
Kent State U at Ashtabula (OH)
South Florida State Coll (FL)

AESTHETICIAN/ESTHETICIAN AND SKIN CARE
Southeastern Coll–West Palm Beach (FL)

AFRICAN AMERICAN/BLACK STUDIES
Lansing Comm Coll (MI)
Nassau Comm Coll (NY)

AGRIBUSINESS
Bainbridge State Coll (GA)
Blackhawk Tech Coll (WI)
Coll of Central Florida (FL)
Coll of the Desert (CA)
Crowder Coll (MO)
Eastern Wyoming Coll (WY)
Harford Comm Coll (MD)
Hinds Comm Coll (MS)
James Sprunt Comm Coll (NC)
Laramie County Comm Coll (WY)
Merced Coll (CA)
Mesa Comm Coll (AZ)
Minnesota West Comm and Tech Coll (MN)
Mitchell Comm Coll (NC)
Northcentral Tech Coll (WI)
Northeast Comm Coll (NE)
Northeast Iowa Comm Coll (IA)
Northwest Coll (WY)
Ogeechee Tech Coll (GA)
The Ohio State U Ag Tech Inst (OH)
San Jacinto Coll District (TX)
South Florida State Coll (FL)
State U of New York Coll of Technology at Alfred (NY)

AGRICULTURAL AND FOOD PRODUCTS PROCESSING
Minnesota State Comm and Tech Coll (MN)
Minnesota West Comm and Tech Coll (MN)
Northeast Iowa Comm Coll (IA)
Rockingham Comm Coll (NC)

AGRICULTURAL BUSINESS AND MANAGEMENT
American Samoa Comm Coll (AS)
Arizona Western Coll (AZ)
Bismarck State Coll (ND)
Casper Coll (WY)
Central Wyoming Coll (WY)
Cloud County Comm Coll (KS)
Cochise County Comm Coll District (AZ)
County Coll of Morris (NJ)
Danville Area Comm Coll (IL)
Dodge City Comm Coll (KS)
Hill Coll (TX)
Illinois Central Coll (IL)
Illinois Eastern Comm Colls, Wabash Valley College (IL)
Imperial Valley Coll (CA)
Lake Area Tech Inst (SD)
Lake Region State Coll (ND)
Lamar Comm Coll (CO)
Lansing Comm Coll (MI)
Mt. San Antonio Coll (CA)
North Central Missouri Coll (MO)
Northeastern Jr Coll (CO)
The Ohio State U Ag Tech Inst (OH)
Otero Jr Coll (CO)
Patrick Henry Comm Coll (VA)
Pensacola State Coll (FL)
Rend Lake Coll (IL)
San Joaquin Delta Coll (CA)
Santa Rosa Jr Coll (CA)
Shawnee Comm Coll (IL)
Southeastern Comm Coll (IA)
Spoon River Coll (IL)
Treasure Valley Comm Coll (OR)
Vincennes U (IN)

AGRICULTURAL BUSINESS AND MANAGEMENT RELATED
Penn State DuBois (PA)
Penn State Fayette, The Eberly Campus (PA)
Penn State Mont Alto (PA)
Penn State Shenango (PA)
Wayne County Comm Coll District (MI)

AGRICULTURAL BUSINESS TECHNOLOGY
Laramie County Comm Coll (WY)
The Ohio State U Ag Tech Inst (OH)

AGRICULTURAL COMMUNICATION/ JOURNALISM
Casper Coll (WY)
Northwest Coll (WY)
The Ohio State U Ag Tech Inst (OH)
Santa Rosa Jr Coll (CA)

AGRICULTURAL ECONOMICS
Dodge City Comm Coll (KS)
The Ohio State U Ag Tech Inst (OH)
South Florida State Coll (FL)
South Plains Coll (TX)
Treasure Valley Comm Coll (OR)

AGRICULTURAL ENGINEERING
South Florida State Coll (FL)
Vincennes U (IN)

AGRICULTURAL/FARM SUPPLIES RETAILING AND WHOLESALING
Cloud County Comm Coll (KS)
Des Moines Area Comm Coll (IA)
Fox Valley Tech Coll (WI)
Hawkeye Comm Coll (IA)
Illinois Central Coll (IL)
Minnesota West Comm and Tech Coll (MN)

AGRICULTURAL MECHANICS AND EQUIPMENT TECHNOLOGY
Hutchinson Comm Coll (KS)
Illinois Central Coll (IL)
Merced Coll (CA)
Mitchell Tech Inst (SD)
Northland Comm and Tech Coll (MN)
Rend Lake Coll (IL)
Spoon River Coll (IL)

AGRICULTURAL MECHANIZATION
Crowder Coll (MO)
Dodge City Comm Coll (KS)
Fox Valley Tech Coll (WI)
Imperial Valley Coll (CA)
Ivy Tech Comm Coll–Wabash Valley (IN)
Kishwaukee Coll (IL)
Madison Area Tech Coll (WI)
Navarro Coll (TX)
The Ohio State U Ag Tech Inst (OH)
Paris Jr Coll (TX)
Rend Lake Coll (IL)
San Joaquin Delta Coll (CA)
Southern Regional Tech Coll (GA)
Southwest Texas Jr Coll (TX)
Spoon River Coll (IL)
Three Rivers Comm Coll (MO)

AGRICULTURAL MECHANIZATION RELATED
Hinds Comm Coll (MS)

AGRICULTURAL POWER MACHINERY OPERATION
Hawkeye Comm Coll (IA)
Northeast Iowa Comm Coll (IA)
The Ohio State U Ag Tech Inst (OH)

AGRICULTURAL PRODUCTION
Allen Comm Coll (KS)
Chesapeake Coll (MD)
Illinois Eastern Comm Colls, Wabash Valley College (IL)
Laramie County Comm Coll (WY)
Minnesota West Comm and Tech Coll (MN)
Mitchell Tech Inst (SD)
Northeast Iowa Comm Coll (IA)
Northwest Coll (WY)
Owensboro Comm and Tech Coll (KY)
Rend Lake Coll (IL)
Southwestern Michigan Coll (MI)
Three Rivers Comm Coll (MO)

AGRICULTURAL TEACHER EDUCATION
Eastern Wyoming Coll (WY)
Murray State Coll (OK)
Northeastern Jr Coll (CO)
Northwest Coll (WY)
The Ohio State U Ag Tech Inst (OH)

South Florida State Coll (FL)
Trinity Valley Comm Coll (TX)

AGRICULTURE
American Samoa Comm Coll (AS)
Ancilla Coll (IN)
Arizona Western Coll (AZ)
Bainbridge State Coll (GA)
Blinn Coll (TX)
Casper Coll (WY)
Central Texas Coll (TX)
Coll of Central Florida (FL)
Coll of the Desert (CA)
Crowder Coll (MO)
Dakota Coll at Bottineau (ND)
Dyersburg State Comm Coll (TN)
Feather River Coll (CA)
Georgia Highlands Coll (GA)
Harford Comm Coll (MD)
Hill Coll (TX)
Hutchinson Comm Coll (KS)
Imperial Valley Coll (CA)
Ivy Tech Comm Coll–Columbus (IN)
Ivy Tech Comm Coll–East Central (IN)
Ivy Tech Comm Coll–Kokomo (IN)
Ivy Tech Comm Coll–Lafayette (IN)
Ivy Tech Comm Coll–Northeast (IN)
Ivy Tech Comm Coll–Richmond (IN)
Ivy Tech Comm Coll–Southwest (IN)
Ivy Tech Comm Coll–Wabash Valley (IN)
Kaskaskia Coll (IL)
Laramie County Comm Coll (WY)
Macomb Coll (MI)
Merced Coll (CA)
Miami Dade Coll (FL)
Minnesota West Comm and Tech Coll (MN)
Missouri State U–West Plains (MO)
Mt. San Antonio Coll (CA)
Murray State Coll (OK)
New Mexico Jr Coll (NM)
Northeast Comm Coll (NE)
Northeastern Jr Coll (CO)
Northland Comm and Tech Coll (MN)
Panola Coll (TX)
Paris Jr Coll (TX)
Pensacola State Coll (FL)
San Jacinto Coll District (TX)
San Joaquin Delta Coll (CA)
Shawnee Comm Coll (IL)
Sierra Coll (CA)
South Florida State Coll (FL)
South Plains Coll (TX)
State U of New York Coll of Technology at Alfred (NY)
Texarkana Coll (TX)
Treasure Valley Comm Coll (OR)
Vincennes U (IN)
Williston State Coll (ND)

AGROECOLOGY AND SUSTAINABLE AGRICULTURE
Lenoir Comm Coll (NC)
Lorain County Comm Coll (OH)
Mesa Comm Coll (AZ)
Santa Rosa Jr Coll (CA)
Tompkins Cortland Comm Coll (NY)

AGRONOMY AND CROP SCIENCE
Chippewa Valley Tech Coll (WI)
Dodge City Comm Coll (KS)
Merced Coll (CA)
Minnesota West Comm and Tech Coll (MN)
Northcentral Tech Coll (WI)
Northeast Comm Coll (NE)
Northeastern Jr Coll (CO)
The Ohio State U Ag Tech Inst (OH)
Shawnee Comm Coll (IL)
Southeastern Comm Coll (IA)
South Plains Coll (TX)
Treasure Valley Comm Coll (OR)

AIR AND SPACE OPERATIONS TECHNOLOGY
Cochise County Comm Coll District (AZ)

AIRCRAFT POWERPLANT TECHNOLOGY
Colorado Northwestern Comm Coll (CO)
Lake Area Tech Inst (SD)
Lansing Comm Coll (MI)
Middlesex Comm Coll (MA)
Orange Coast Coll (CA)
St. Philip's Coll (TX)
Somerset Comm Coll (KY)
Southern Arkansas U Tech (AR)

Sowela Tech Comm Coll (LA)
Texas State Tech Coll (TX)
Vincennes U (IN)
Wayne County Comm Coll District (MI)

AIRFRAME MECHANICS AND AIRCRAFT MAINTENANCE TECHNOLOGY
Amarillo Coll (TX)
Central New Mexico Comm Coll (NM)
Comm Coll of the Air Force (AL)
Craven Comm Coll (NC)
Hinds Comm Coll (MS)
Ivy Tech Comm Coll–Wabash Valley (IN)
Lake Superior Coll (MN)
Lansing Comm Coll (MI)
Mohawk Valley Comm Coll (NY)
Mt. San Antonio Coll (CA)
Northland Comm and Tech Coll (MN)
Orange Coast Coll (CA)
Pittsburgh Inst of Aeronautics (PA)
St. Philip's Coll (TX)
Texas State Tech Coll (TX)
Trident Tech Coll (SC)
Wayne County Comm Coll District (MI)

AIRLINE FLIGHT ATTENDANT
Mercer County Comm Coll (NJ)
Orange Coast Coll (CA)

AIRLINE PILOT AND FLIGHT CREW
Casper Coll (WY)
Central Oregon Comm Coll (OR)
Central Texas Coll (TX)
Chandler-Gilbert Comm Coll (AZ)
Cochise County Comm Coll District (AZ)
Colorado Northwestern Comm Coll (CO)
Comm Coll of Allegheny County (PA)
Comm Coll of Baltimore County (MD)
Dutchess Comm Coll (NY)
Fox Valley Tech Coll (WI)
Gateway Tech Coll (WI)
Hesston Coll (KS)
Iowa Central Comm Coll (IA)
Jamestown Comm Coll (NY)
Kishwaukee Coll (IL)
Lake Superior Coll (MN)
Lansing Comm Coll (MI)
Lehigh Carbon Comm Coll (PA)
Lenoir Comm Coll (NC)
Luzerne County Comm Coll (PA)
Mercer County Comm Coll (NJ)
Miami Dade Coll (FL)
Morgan Comm Coll (CO)
Mt. San Antonio Coll (CA)
North Shore Comm Coll (MA)
Salt Lake Comm Coll (UT)
San Jacinto Coll District (TX)
Texas State Tech Coll (TX)
Treasure Valley Comm Coll (OR)
Vincennes U (IN)

AIR TRAFFIC CONTROL
Cecil Coll (MD)
Comm Coll of Baltimore County (MD)
Comm Coll of the Air Force (AL)
Hesston Coll (KS)
Miami Dade Coll (FL)
Mt. San Antonio Coll (CA)
Texas State Tech Coll (TX)

AIR TRANSPORTATION RELATED
Cochise County Comm Coll District (AZ)

ALLIED HEALTH AND MEDICAL ASSISTING SERVICES RELATED
Blue Ridge Comm and Tech Coll (WV)
Bowling Green State U–Firelands Coll (OH)
CollAmerica–Fort Collins (CO)
Mount Wachusett Comm Coll (MA)
Northwest Coll (WY)
Pennsylvania Inst of Technology (PA)

ALTERNATIVE AND COMPLEMENTARY MEDICAL SUPPORT SERVICES RELATED
Mount Wachusett Comm Coll (MA)

ALTERNATIVE AND COMPLEMENTARY MEDICINE RELATED
Quinsigamond Comm Coll (MA)

ALTERNATIVE FUEL VEHICLE TECHNOLOGY
Cerritos Coll (CA)

AMERICAN GOVERNMENT AND POLITICS
Oklahoma City Comm Coll (OK)
St. Philip's Coll (TX)

AMERICAN INDIAN/NATIVE AMERICAN STUDIES
Aaniiih Nakoda Coll (MT)
Arizona Western Coll (AZ)
Central Wyoming Coll (WY)
Nebraska Indian Comm Coll (NE)
Saginaw Chippewa Tribal Coll (MI)
San Juan Coll (NM)
Sisseton-Wahpeton Coll (SD)

AMERICAN SIGN LANGUAGE (ASL)
Montgomery Coll (MD)
Oklahoma State U–Oklahoma City (OK)
Santa Rosa Jr Coll (CA)
Sierra Coll (CA)
Vincennes U (IN)
Wayne County Comm Coll District (MI)

AMERICAN STUDIES
Lansing Comm Coll (MI)
Miami Dade Coll (FL)
South Florida State Coll (FL)

ANESTHESIOLOGIST ASSISTANT
Renton Tech Coll (WA)
Wayne County Comm Coll District (MI)

ANIMAL/LIVESTOCK HUSBANDRY AND PRODUCTION
Chippewa Valley Tech Coll (WI)
Hawkeye Comm Coll (IA)
Illinois Central Coll (IL)
Jefferson Comm Coll (NY)
Merced Coll (CA)
Mt. San Antonio Coll (CA)
The Ohio State U Ag Tech Inst (OH)
Sierra Coll (CA)

ANIMAL PHYSIOLOGY
Massachusetts Bay Comm Coll (MA)

ANIMAL SCIENCES
Alamance Comm Coll (NC)
Casper Coll (WY)
Coll of Central Florida (FL)
Dodge City Comm Coll (KS)
James Sprunt Comm Coll (NC)
Kaskaskia Coll (IL)
Mt. San Antonio Coll (CA)
Niagara County Comm Coll (NY)
Northeast Comm Coll (NE)
Northeastern Jr Coll (CO)
Northwest Coll (WY)
The Ohio State U Ag Tech Inst (OH)
San Joaquin Delta Coll (CA)
Santa Rosa Jr Coll (CA)
Shawnee Comm Coll (IL)
South Florida State Coll (FL)
Treasure Valley Comm Coll (OR)
Trinity Valley Comm Coll (TX)
Westchester Comm Coll (NY)

ANIMAL TRAINING
Lamar Comm Coll (CO)

ANIMATION, INTERACTIVE TECHNOLOGY, VIDEO GRAPHICS AND SPECIAL EFFECTS
Austin Comm Coll District (TX)
Borough of Manhattan Comm Coll of the City U of New York (NY)
Cañada Coll (CA)
Cecil Coll (MD)
Century Coll (MN)
Cerritos Coll (CA)
Coll of Marin (CA)
Coll of the Canyons (CA)
Elgin Comm Coll (IL)
Finger Lakes Comm Coll (NY)
Front Range Comm Coll (CO)
Hagerstown Comm Coll (MD)
Houston Comm Coll (TX)
Kellogg Comm Coll (MI)
Lansing Comm Coll (MI)
Lehigh Carbon Comm Coll (PA)
Lone Star Coll–CyFair (TX)

Lone Star Coll–Tomball (TX)
McHenry County Coll (IL)
Miami Dade Coll (FL)
Missouri State U–West Plains (MO)
Montgomery Coll (MD)
Morgan Comm Coll (CO)
NHTI, Concord's Comm Coll, Concord (NH)
Oklahoma City Comm Coll (OK)
Orange Coast Coll (CA)
Palomar Coll (CA)
Pueblo Comm Coll (CO)
Raritan Valley Comm Coll (NJ)
Santa Monica Coll (CA)
Springfield Tech Comm Coll (MA)
State U of New York Coll of Technology at Alfred (NY)
Tyler Jr Coll (TX)
York County Comm Coll (ME)

ANTHROPOLOGY
Austin Comm Coll District (TX)
Cañada Coll (CA)
Casper Coll (WY)
Central New Mexico Comm Coll (NM)
Central Wyoming Coll (WY)
Cerritos Coll (CA)
Coconino Comm Coll (AZ)
Coll of the Desert (CA)
Eastern Arizona Coll (AZ)
Feather River Coll (CA)
Fullerton Coll (CA)
Harford Comm Coll (MD)
Houston Comm Coll (TX)
Imperial Valley Coll (CA)
Lansing Comm Coll (MI)
Laramie County Comm Coll (WY)
Merced Coll (CA)
Miami Dade Coll (FL)
Northeastern Jr Coll (CO)
Northwest Coll (WY)
Orange Coast Coll (CA)
San Joaquin Delta Coll (CA)
Santa Monica Coll (CA)
Santa Rosa Jr Coll (CA)
South Florida State Coll (FL)
Truckee Meadows Comm Coll (NV)
Vincennes U (IN)
Western Wyoming Comm Coll (WY)

APPAREL AND ACCESSORIES MARKETING
Des Moines Area Comm Coll (IA)

APPAREL AND TEXTILE MANUFACTURING
Cañada Coll (CA)
Fashion Inst of Technology (NY)
Orange Coast Coll (CA)
Sierra Coll (CA)

APPAREL AND TEXTILE MARKETING MANAGEMENT
Comm Coll of the Air Force (AL)
FIDM/Fashion Inst of Design & Merchandising, Orange County Campus (CA)
Fullerton Coll (CA)
Orange Coast Coll (CA)
Palomar Coll (CA)
Santa Monica Coll (CA)
Sierra Coll (CA)

APPAREL AND TEXTILES
Fullerton Coll (CA)
Mt. San Antonio Coll (CA)

APPLIANCE INSTALLATION AND REPAIR TECHNOLOGY
Renton Tech Coll (WA)

APPLIED HORTICULTURE/ HORTICULTURAL BUSINESS SERVICES RELATED
Chippewa Valley Tech Coll (WI)
Dakota Coll at Bottineau (ND)
Des Moines Area Comm Coll (IA)
Hinds Comm Coll (MS)
Northeast Comm Coll (NE)

APPLIED HORTICULTURE/ HORTICULTURE OPERATIONS
Alamance Comm Coll (NC)
Cecil Coll (MD)
Century Coll (MN)
Coll of the Desert (CA)
Comm Coll of Allegheny County (PA)
Comm Coll of Baltimore County (MD)
Dakota Coll at Bottineau (ND)
Fayetteville Tech Comm Coll (NC)
Front Range Comm Coll (CO)
Fullerton Coll (CA)

Gateway Tech Coll (WI)
Haywood Comm Coll (NC)
Houston Comm Coll (TX)
Illinois Central Coll (IL)
J. Sargeant Reynolds Comm Coll (VA)
Kaskaskia Coll (IL)
Kishwaukee Coll (IL)
Lenoir Comm Coll (NC)
McHenry County Coll (IL)
Merced Coll (CA)
Montgomery Coll (MD)
Mt. San Antonio Coll (CA)
Orange Coast Coll (CA)
Sierra Coll (CA)
Spartanburg Comm Coll (SC)
Vincennes U (IN)
Westmoreland County Comm Coll (PA)

APPLIED MATHEMATICS
South Florida State Coll (FL)

APPLIED PSYCHOLOGY
Northampton Comm Coll (PA)

AQUACULTURE
Carteret Comm Coll (NC)
Hillsborough Comm Coll (FL)

ARABIC
Austin Comm Coll District (TX)

ARCHEOLOGY
Austin Comm Coll District (TX)
Cañada Coll (CA)
Northwest Coll (WY)
Palomar Coll (CA)
Western Wyoming Comm Coll (WY)

ARCHITECTURAL AND BUILDING SCIENCES
J. Sargeant Reynolds Comm Coll (VA)
Springfield Tech Comm Coll (MA)

ARCHITECTURAL DRAFTING AND CAD/CADD
American Samoa Comm Coll (AS)
Anne Arundel Comm Coll (MD)
Anoka Tech Coll (MN)
Carroll Comm Coll (MD)
Central New Mexico Comm Coll (NM)
Coconino Comm Coll (AZ)
Coll of the Canyons (CA)
Comm Coll of Allegheny County (PA)
Comm Coll of Baltimore County (MD)
Des Moines Area Comm Coll (IA)
Dunwoody Coll of Technology (MN)
Guam Comm Coll (GU)
Harper Coll (IL)
Hennepin Tech Coll (MN)
Hutchinson Comm Coll (KS)
Kaskaskia Coll (IL)
Lake Superior Coll (MN)
Macomb Coll (MI)
Merced Coll (CA)
Mesa Comm Coll (AZ)
Miami Dade Coll (FL)
Minnesota State Comm and Tech Coll (MN)
Minnesota State Comm and Tech Coll–Detroit Lakes (MN)
Montgomery Coll (MD)
Northeast Comm Coll (NE)
Northland Comm and Tech Coll (MN)
Oakton Comm Coll (IL)
Oklahoma City Comm Coll (OK)
Oklahoma State U–Oklahoma City (OK)
Palomar Coll (CA)
Rend Lake Coll (IL)
Santa Fe Comm Coll (NM)
Sierra Coll (CA)
South Suburban Coll (IL)
Three Rivers Comm Coll (CT)
Truckee Meadows Comm Coll (NV)
Vincennes U (IN)
Waukesha County Tech Coll (WI)
Westmoreland County Comm Coll (PA)
York County Comm Coll (ME)

ARCHITECTURAL ENGINEERING
Luzerne County Comm Coll (PA)
Nashville State Comm Coll (TN)

ARCHITECTURAL ENGINEERING TECHNOLOGY
Amarillo Coll (TX)
Arapahoe Comm Coll (CO)

Cape Fear Comm Coll (NC)
Cerritos Coll (CA)
Coconino Comm Coll (AZ)
Coll of The Albemarle (NC)
Columbus State Comm Coll (OH)
Daytona State Coll (FL)
Del Mar Coll (TX)
Delta Coll (MI)
Dutchess Comm Coll (NY)
Erie Comm Coll, South Campus (NY)
Fayetteville Tech Comm Coll (NC)
Finger Lakes Comm Coll (NY)
Front Range Comm Coll (CO)
Gateway Tech Coll (WI)
Golden West Coll (CA)
Greenville Tech Coll (SC)
Harper Coll (IL)
Harrisburg Area Comm Coll (PA)
Hillsborough Comm Coll (FL)
Hinds Comm Coll (MS)
Lansing Comm Coll (MI)
Luzerne County Comm Coll (PA)
Madison Area Tech Coll (WI)
Mercer County Comm Coll (NJ)
Metropolitan Comm Coll (NE)
Miami Dade Coll (FL)
Monroe County Comm Coll (MI)
Mott Comm Coll (MI)
Mt. San Antonio Coll (CA)
Nashville State Comm Coll (TN)
New River Comm Coll (VA)
NHTI, Concord's Comm Coll, Concord (NH)
Northampton Comm Coll (PA)
Northcentral Tech Coll (WI)
Norwalk Comm Coll (CT)
Oklahoma State U–Oklahoma City (OK)
Penn State Fayette, The Eberly Campus (PA)
Salt Lake Comm Coll (UT)
Seminole State Coll of Florida (FL)
Southeast Comm Coll, Milford Campus (NE)
State U of New York Coll of Technology at Alfred (NY)
Tarrant County Coll District (TX)
Three Rivers Comm Coll (CT)
Wisconsin Indianhead Tech Coll (WI)

ARCHITECTURAL TECHNOLOGY

Arizona Western Coll (AZ)
Coconino Comm Coll (AZ)
Coll of Marin (CA)
Coll of the Desert (CA)
Dunwoody Coll of Technology (MN)
Florida SouthWestern State Coll (FL)
Fullerton Coll (CA)
Grand Rapids Comm Coll (MI)
John Tyler Comm Coll (VA)
Lansing Comm Coll (MI)
Miami Dade Coll (FL)
Minnesota State Comm and Tech Coll–Detroit Lakes (MN)
Orange Coast Coll (CA)
Palomar Coll (CA)

ARCHITECTURE

Allen Comm Coll (KS)
Coll of Central Florida (FL)
Grand Rapids Comm Coll (MI)
Harrisburg Area Comm Coll (PA)
Panola Coll (TX)
South Florida State Coll (FL)
Truckee Meadows Comm Coll (NV)

AREA STUDIES RELATED

Coconino Comm Coll (AZ)
Fullerton Coll (CA)

ART

Allen Comm Coll (KS)
Alvin Comm Coll (TX)
Amarillo Coll (TX)
American Samoa Comm Coll (AS)
Austin Comm Coll District (TX)
Bainbridge State Coll (GA)
Bunker Hill Comm Coll (MA)
Cañada Coll (CA)
Carroll Comm Coll (MD)
Casper Coll (WY)
Cayuga County Comm Coll (NY)
Central New Mexico Comm Coll (NM)
Central Oregon Comm Coll (OR)
Central Wyoming Coll (WY)
Cerritos Coll (CA)
Citrus Coll (CA)

Cochise County Comm Coll District (AZ)
Coll of Central Florida (FL)
Coll of Marin (CA)
Coll of The Albemarle (NC)
Coll of the Canyons (CA)
Coll of the Desert (CA)
Columbia-Greene Comm Coll (NY)
Comm Coll of Allegheny County (PA)
Comm Coll of Philadelphia (PA)
Comm Coll of Rhode Island (RI)
Comm Coll of Vermont (VT)
Crowder Coll (MO)
De Anza Coll (CA)
Del Mar Coll (TX)
Dodge City Comm Coll (KS)
Dutchess Comm Coll (NY)
Eastern Arizona Coll (AZ)
Eastern Wyoming Coll (WY)
Edison State Comm Coll (OH)
Frederick Comm Coll (MD)
Fullerton Coll (CA)
Georgia Highlands Coll (GA)
Golden West Coll (CA)
Gordon State Coll (GA)
Grand Rapids Comm Coll (MI)
Harper Coll (IL)
Hill Coll (TX)
Holyoke Comm Coll (MA)
Housatonic Comm Coll (CT)
Howard Comm Coll (MD)
Imperial Valley Coll (CA)
Kingsborough Comm Coll of the City U of New York (NY)
Kishwaukee Coll (IL)
Lansing Comm Coll (MI)
Laramie County Comm Coll (WY)
Lehigh Carbon Comm Coll (PA)
Los Angeles City Coll (CA)
Merced Coll (CA)
Mercer County Comm Coll (NJ)
Miami Dade Coll (FL)
Middlesex Comm Coll (MA)
Minnesota State Comm and Tech Coll (MN)
Mohave Comm Coll (AZ)
Mohawk Valley Comm Coll (NY)
Monroe Comm Coll (NY)
Monroe County Comm Coll (MI)
Montgomery Coll (MD)
Montgomery County Comm Coll (PA)
Morton Coll (IL)
Mount Wachusett Comm Coll (MA)
Nashville State Comm Coll (TN)
Nassau Comm Coll (NY)
Naugatuck Valley Comm Coll (CT)
Navarro Coll (TX)
New Mexico Jr Coll (NM)
Northeast Comm Coll (NE)
Northeastern Jr Coll (CO)
Northwest Coll (WY)
Norwalk Comm Coll (CT)
Oklahoma City Comm Coll (OK)
Orange Coast Coll (CA)
Palomar Coll (CA)
Panola Coll (TX)
Paris Jr Coll (TX)
Pensacola State Coll (FL)
St. Philip's Coll (TX)
San Jacinto Coll District (TX)
San Joaquin Delta Coll (CA)
Santa Fe Comm Coll (NM)
Santa Monica Coll (CA)
Santa Rosa Jr Coll (CA)
Seminole State Coll (OK)
Sierra Coll (CA)
South Florida State Coll (FL)
South Plains Coll (TX)
Texarkana Coll (TX)
Trinity Valley Comm Coll (TX)
Tyler Jr Coll (TX)
Vincennes U (IN)
Virginia Western Comm Coll (VA)
Westchester Comm Coll (NY)
Western Wyoming Comm Coll (WY)

ART HISTORY, CRITICISM AND CONSERVATION

Borough of Manhattan Comm Coll of the City U of New York (NY)
Bucks County Comm Coll (PA)
De Anza Coll (CA)
Lansing Comm Coll (MI)
Mercer County Comm Coll (NJ)
Northeastern Jr Coll (CO)
Santa Fe Comm Coll (NM)
Santa Rosa Jr Coll (CA)
South Florida State Coll (FL)

ARTIFICIAL INTELLIGENCE

Southeastern Comm Coll (IA)

ARTS, ENTERTAINMENT, AND MEDIA MANAGEMENT RELATED

Hinds Comm Coll (MS)

ART TEACHER EDUCATION

Casper Coll (WY)
Del Mar Coll (TX)
Eastern Arizona Coll (AZ)
McLennan Comm Coll (TX)
Pensacola State Coll (FL)
South Florida State Coll (FL)
Vincennes U (IN)

ART THERAPY

Vincennes U (IN)

ASIAN STUDIES

Miami Dade Coll (FL)

ASTRONOMY

Fullerton Coll (CA)
Gordon State Coll (GA)
Palomar Coll (CA)
South Florida State Coll (FL)

ATHLETIC TRAINING

Allen Comm Coll (KS)
Casper Coll (WY)
Central Wyoming Coll (WY)
Coll of the Canyons (CA)
Comm Coll of Allegheny County (PA)
Dodge City Comm Coll (KS)
Northampton Comm Coll (PA)
Northeast Comm Coll (NE)
Northwest Coll (WY)
Tyler Jr Coll (TX)
Westchester Comm Coll (NY)

ATMOSPHERIC SCIENCES AND METEOROLOGY

Comm Coll of the Air Force (AL)
South Florida State Coll (FL)

AUDIOLOGY AND SPEECH-LANGUAGE PATHOLOGY

Cerritos Coll (CA)
Miami Dade Coll (FL)
Orange Coast Coll (CA)
South Florida State Coll (FL)
U of Cincinnati Clermont Coll (OH)

AUDIOVISUAL COMMUNICATIONS TECHNOLOGIES RELATED

Bossier Parish Comm Coll (LA)
International Coll of Broadcasting (OH)
Northeast Comm Coll (NE)

AUTOBODY/COLLISION AND REPAIR TECHNOLOGY

American Samoa Comm Coll (AS)
Bismarck State Coll (ND)
Casper Coll (WY)
Central Texas Coll (TX)
Cerritos Coll (CA)
Coll of Marin (CA)
Crowder Coll (MO)
Des Moines Area Comm Coll (IA)
Dunwoody Coll of Technology (MN)
Erie Comm Coll, South Campus (NY)
Fayetteville Tech Comm Coll (NC)
Fox Valley Tech Coll (WI)
Greenville Tech Coll (SC)
Hawkeye Comm Coll (IA)
Haywood Comm Coll (NC)
Hennepin Tech Coll (MN)
Highland Comm Coll (IL)
Hill Coll (TX)
Hutchinson Comm Coll (KS)
Illinois Eastern Comm Colls, Olney Central College (IL)
Kishwaukee Coll (IL)
Lake Area Tech Inst (SD)
Lake Superior Coll (MN)
Lansing Comm Coll (MI)
Laramie County Comm Coll (WY)
Lenoir Comm Coll (NC)
Manhattan Area Tech Coll (KS)
Merced Coll (CA)
Mid-Plains Comm Coll, North Platte (NE)
Minnesota State Coll–Southeast Tech (MN)
Minnesota State Comm and Tech Coll (MN)

Morgan Comm Coll (CO)
Northeast Comm Coll (NE)
Northland Comm and Tech Coll (MN)
Ohio Tech Coll (OH)
Oklahoma State U Inst of Technology (OK)
Ozarks Tech Comm Coll (MO)
Palomar Coll (CA)
Pueblo Comm Coll (CO)
Randolph Comm Coll (NC)
Renton Tech Coll (WA)
St. Philip's Coll (TX)
Salina Area Tech Coll (KS)
Salt Lake Comm Coll (UT)
San Jacinto Coll District (TX)
San Juan Coll (NM)
Southeast Comm Coll, Milford Campus (NE)
State U of New York Coll of Technology at Alfred (NY)
Texas State Tech Coll (TX)
U of Arkansas Comm Coll at Morrilton (AR)
Vincennes U (IN)
Wayne County Comm Coll District (MI)

AUTOMATION ENGINEER TECHNOLOGY

Alexandria Tech and Comm Coll (MN)
Blue Ridge Comm and Tech Coll (WV)
Dyersburg State Comm Coll (TN)
Fox Valley Tech Coll (WI)
Gateway Tech Coll (WI)
Gulf Coast State Coll (FL)
Hawkeye Comm Coll (IA)
Hennepin Tech Coll (MN)
Hutchinson Comm Coll (KS)
Lake Superior Coll (MN)
Miami Dade Coll (FL)
Mitchell Tech Inst (SD)
Mott Comm Coll (MI)
Northland Comm and Tech Coll (MN)
St. Clair County Comm Coll (MI)
Southwestern Michigan Coll (MI)
Waukesha County Tech Coll (WI)

AUTOMOBILE/AUTOMOTIVE MECHANICS TECHNOLOGY

Alamance Comm Coll (NC)
Alvin Comm Coll (TX)
Amarillo Coll (TX)
American Samoa Comm Coll (AS)
Anoka Tech Coll (MN)
Arapahoe Comm Coll (CO)
Arizona Western Coll (AZ)
Austin Comm Coll District (TX)
Bismarck State Coll (ND)
Brookhaven Coll (TX)
Caldwell Comm Coll and Tech Inst (NC)
Cape Fear Comm Coll (NC)
Casper Coll (WY)
Central Maine Comm Coll (ME)
Central Oregon Comm Coll (OR)
Central Texas Coll (TX)
Central Wyoming Coll (WY)
Cerritos Coll (CA)
Chattahoochee Tech Coll (GA)
Citrus Coll (CA)
City Colls of Chicago, Kennedy-King College (IL)
City Colls of Chicago, Olive-Harvey College (IL)
Cochise County Comm Coll District (AZ)
Coll of Marin (CA)
Coll of the Canyons (CA)
Coll of the Desert (CA)
Coll of the Ouachitas (AR)
Colorado Northwestern Comm Coll (CO)
Columbia-Greene Comm Coll (NY)
Columbus Tech Coll (GA)
Comm Coll of Baltimore County (MD)
Comm Coll of Philadelphia (PA)
Comm Coll of the Air Force (AL)
Craven Comm Coll (NC)
Crowder Coll (MO)
Danville Area Comm Coll (IL)
Daytona State Coll (FL)
De Anza Coll (CA)
Del Mar Coll (TX)
Delta Coll (MI)
Des Moines Area Comm Coll (IA)
Dodge City Comm Coll (KS)
Dunwoody Coll of Technology (MN)

East Central Coll (MO)
Eastern Arizona Coll (AZ)
Eastern Idaho Tech Coll (ID)
Elgin Comm Coll (IL)
El Paso Comm Coll (TX)
Erie Comm Coll, South Campus (NY)
Fayetteville Tech Comm Coll (NC)
Fox Valley Tech Coll (WI)
Front Range Comm Coll (CO)
Fullerton Coll (CA)
Gateway Tech Coll (WI)
Georgia Piedmont Tech Coll (GA)
Golden West Coll (CA)
Grand Rapids Comm Coll (MI)
Greenville Tech Coll (SC)
Guam Comm Coll (GU)
Gwinnett Tech Coll (GA)
Harrisburg Area Comm Coll (PA)
Hawkeye Comm Coll (IA)
Haywood Comm Coll (NC)
Hennepin Tech Coll (MN)
Highland Comm Coll (IL)
Hill Coll (TX)
Houston Comm Coll (TX)
Hutchinson Comm Coll (KS)
Illinois Central Coll (IL)
Illinois Eastern Comm Colls, Frontier Community College (IL)
Illinois Eastern Comm Colls, Olney Central College (IL)
Illinois Valley Comm Coll (IL)
Imperial Valley Coll (CA)
Iowa Central Comm Coll (IA)
Ivy Tech Comm Coll–Central Indiana (IN)
Ivy Tech Comm Coll–Columbus (IN)
Ivy Tech Comm Coll–East Central (IN)
Ivy Tech Comm Coll–Kokomo (IN)
Ivy Tech Comm Coll–Lafayette (IN)
Ivy Tech Comm Coll–Northeast (IN)
Ivy Tech Comm Coll–Northwest (IN)
Ivy Tech Comm Coll–Richmond (IN)
Ivy Tech Comm Coll–Sellersburg (IN)
Ivy Tech Comm Coll–Southwest (IN)
Ivy Tech Comm Coll–Wabash Valley (IN)
Johnson County Comm Coll (KS)
J. Sargeant Reynolds Comm Coll (VA)
Kaskaskia Coll (IL)
Kirtland Comm Coll (MI)
Kishwaukee Coll (IL)
Lake Area Tech Inst (SD)
Lake Region State Coll (ND)
Lake Superior Coll (MN)
Lansing Comm Coll (MI)
Laramie County Comm Coll (WY)
Lenoir Comm Coll (NC)
Lone Star Coll–Montgomery (TX)
Lone Star Coll–North Harris (TX)
Luzerne County Comm Coll (PA)
Macomb Comm Coll (MI)
Madison Area Tech Coll (WI)
Manhattan Area Tech Coll (KS)
Massachusetts Bay Comm Coll (MA)
Merced Coll (CA)
Metropolitan Comm Coll (NE)
Middlesex Comm Coll (MA)
Mid-Plains Comm Coll, North Platte (NE)
Minnesota State Comm and Tech Coll (MN)
Minnesota State Comm and Tech Coll–Moorhead (MN)
Minnesota West Comm and Tech Coll (MN)
Mohave Comm Coll (AZ)
Monroe Comm Coll (NY)
Montgomery Coll (MD)
Morgan Comm Coll (CO)
Morton Coll (IL)
Mott Comm Coll (MI)
Mount Wachusett Comm Coll (MA)
Nashville State Comm Coll (TN)
Naugatuck Valley Comm Coll (CT)
New Mexico Jr Coll (NM)
New River Comm Coll (VA)
Northampton Comm Coll (PA)
North Central Missouri Coll (MO)
Northcentral Tech Coll (WI)
Northeast Comm Coll (NE)
Northeastern Jr Coll (CO)
Northeast Iowa Comm Coll (IA)
Northern Maine Comm Coll (ME)
Northland Comm and Tech Coll (MN)
Oakton Comm Coll (IL)
Ogeechee Tech Coll (GA)
Ohio Tech Coll (OH)

Oklahoma City Comm Coll (OK)
Otero Jr Coll (CO)
Owensboro Comm and Tech Coll (KY)
Ozarks Tech Comm Coll (MO)
Palomar Coll (CA)
Patrick Henry Comm Coll (VA)
Pueblo Comm Coll (CO)
Quinsigamond Comm Coll (MA)
Randolph Comm Coll (NC)
Rend Lake Coll (IL)
Renton Tech Coll (WA)
Rock Valley Coll (IL)
Rogue Comm Coll (OR)
Rowan-Cabarrus Comm Coll (NC)
St. Philip's Coll (TX)
Salina Area Tech Coll (KS)
San Jacinto Coll District (TX)
San Joaquin Delta Coll (CA)
San Juan Coll (NM)
Santa Fe Comm Coll (NM)
Santa Rosa Jr Coll (CA)
Savannah Tech Coll (GA)
Seminole State Coll of Florida (FL)
Shawnee Comm Coll (IL)
Sierra Coll (CA)
Southeast Comm Coll, Lincoln Campus (NE)
Southeast Comm Coll, Milford Campus (NE)
Southeastern Comm Coll (IA)
Southern Crescent Tech Coll (GA)
South Plains Coll (TX)
Southwestern Comm Coll (NC)
Southwestern Michigan Coll (MI)
Southwest Texas Jr Coll (TX)
Spartanburg Comm Coll (SC)
Springfield Tech Comm Coll (MA)
State U of New York Coll of Technology at Alfred (NY)
Tarrant County Coll District (TX)
Texarkana Coll (TX)
Texas State Tech Coll (TX)
Tidewater Comm Coll (VA)
Trident Tech Coll (SC)
Trinity Valley Comm Coll (TX)
Truckee Meadows Comm Coll (NV)
Tyler Jr Coll (TX)
U of Arkansas Comm Coll at Morrilton (AR)
Vincennes U (IN)
Virginia Western Comm Coll (VA)
Waukesha County Tech Coll (WI)
Wayne County Comm Coll District (MI)
Western Nevada Coll (NV)
Western Wyoming Comm Coll (WY)
West Georgia Tech Coll (GA)
White Mountains Comm Coll (NH)

AUTOMOTIVE ENGINEERING TECHNOLOGY
Arizona Western Coll (AZ)
Camden County Coll (NJ)
Columbus State Comm Coll (OH)
Comm Coll of Allegheny County (PA)
H. Councill Trenholm State Comm Coll (AL)
Macomb Comm Coll (MI)
Mercer County Comm Coll (NJ)
Middlesex County Coll (NJ)
Minnesota State Comm and Tech Coll–Moorhead (MN)
Oklahoma State U Inst of Technology (OK)
Raritan Valley Comm Coll (NJ)
Sussex County Comm Coll (NJ)

AVIATION/AIRWAY MANAGEMENT
Comm Coll of Allegheny County (PA)
Comm Coll of Baltimore County (MD)
Dutchess Comm Coll (NY)
Hinds Comm Coll (MS)
Iowa Central Comm Coll (IA)
Lake Superior Coll (MN)
Luzerne County Comm Coll (PA)
Mercer County Comm Coll (NJ)
Miami Dade Coll (FL)
Orange Coast Coll (CA)

AVIONICS MAINTENANCE TECHNOLOGY
Cochise County Comm Coll District (AZ)
Comm Coll of the Air Force (AL)
Fox Valley Tech Coll (WI)
Housatonic Comm Coll (CT)
Lansing Comm Coll (MI)
Mt. San Antonio Coll (CA)
Pittsburgh Inst of Aeronautics (PA)
Rock Valley Coll (IL)

Salt Lake Comm Coll (UT)
Southern U at Shreveport (LA)
Southwest Texas Jr Coll (TX)
Tarrant County Coll District (TX)
Texas State Tech Coll (TX)

BAKING AND PASTRY ARTS
Blue Ridge Comm and Tech Coll (WV)
Bucks County Comm Coll (PA)
Cape Fear Comm Coll (NC)
Carteret Comm Coll (NC)
Collin County Comm Coll District (TX)
Culinary Inst LeNotre (TX)
Elgin Comm Coll (IL)
Hudson County Comm Coll (NJ)
J. Sargeant Reynolds Comm Coll (VA)
Luzerne County Comm Coll (PA)
Montgomery County Comm Coll (PA)
Mott Comm Coll (MI)
New England Culinary Inst (VT)
Niagara County Comm Coll (NY)
St. Philip's Coll (TX)
San Jacinto Coll District (TX)
Sullivan County Comm Coll (NY)
Waukesha County Tech Coll (WI)
Westmoreland County Comm Coll (PA)
White Mountains Comm Coll (NH)

BANKING AND FINANCIAL SUPPORT SERVICES
Alamance Comm Coll (NC)
Allen Comm Coll (KS)
Asnuntuck Comm Coll (CT)
Central Georgia Tech Coll (GA)
Comm Coll of Allegheny County (PA)
Comm Coll of Rhode Island (RI)
Craven Comm Coll (NC)
Fayetteville Tech Comm Coll (NC)
Fox Valley Tech Coll (WI)
Harper Coll (IL)
Hinds Comm Coll (MS)
Houston Comm Coll (TX)
Illinois Central Coll (IL)
Lackawanna Coll (PA)
Lake Area Tech Inst (SD)
Lanier Tech Coll (GA)
Lansing Comm Coll (MI)
Luzerne County Comm Coll (PA)
Miami Dade Coll (FL)
Minnesota State Comm and Tech Coll (MN)
Mohawk Valley Comm Coll (NY)
Oakton Comm Coll (IL)
Ogeechee Tech Coll (GA)
Oklahoma City Comm Coll (OK)
Rockingham Comm Coll (NC)
Seminole State Coll of Florida (FL)
South Florida State Coll (FL)
Southern U at Shreveport (LA)
Three Rivers Comm Coll (CT)
Wiregrass Georgia Tech Coll (GA)

BARBERING
Rend Lake Coll (IL)

BEHAVIORAL SCIENCES
Amarillo Coll (TX)
Ancilla Coll (IN)
Citrus Coll (CA)
De Anza Coll (CA)
Dodge City Comm Coll (KS)
Hill Coll (TX)
Imperial Valley Coll (CA)
Miami Dade Coll (FL)
Monroe Comm Coll (NY)
Naugatuck Valley Comm Coll (CT)
San Jacinto Coll District (TX)
Santa Fe Comm Coll (NM)
Santa Rosa Jr Coll (CA)
Seminole State Coll (OK)
Vincennes U (IN)

BIBLICAL STUDIES
Amarillo Coll (TX)
Hesston Coll (KS)
Rosedale Bible Coll (OH)

BIOCHEMISTRY
Pensacola State Coll (FL)
South Florida State Coll (FL)
Vincennes U (IN)

BIOCHEMISTRY AND MOLECULAR BIOLOGY
Minnesota State Comm and Tech Coll (MN)

BIOENGINEERING AND BIOMEDICAL ENGINEERING
Bunker Hill Comm Coll (MA)
Quinsigamond Comm Coll (MA)

BIOINFORMATICS
Massachusetts Bay Comm Coll (MA)

BIOLOGICAL AND BIOMEDICAL SCIENCES RELATED
Massachusetts Bay Comm Coll (MA)
Murray State Coll (OK)
Seminole State Coll (OK)
Vincennes U (IN)

BIOLOGICAL AND PHYSICAL SCIENCES
Ancilla Coll (IN)
Caldwell Comm Coll and Tech Inst (NC)
Cañada Coll (CA)
Central Oregon Comm Coll (OR)
Cerritos Coll (CA)
Citrus Coll (CA)
City Colls of Chicago, Kennedy-King College (IL)
City Colls of Chicago, Olive-Harvey College (IL)
Clinton Comm Coll (NY)
Coll of Marin (CA)
Coll of the Canyons (CA)
Coll of the Desert (CA)
Comm Coll of Baltimore County (MD)
Comm Coll of Rhode Island (RI)
Dodge City Comm Coll (KS)
Elgin Comm Coll (IL)
Finger Lakes Comm Coll (NY)
Fullerton Coll (CA)
Golden West Coll (CA)
Highland Comm Coll (IL)
Howard Comm Coll (MD)
Hudson County Comm Coll (NJ)
Illinois Eastern Comm Colls, Frontier Community College (IL)
Illinois Eastern Comm Colls, Lincoln Trail College (IL)
Illinois Eastern Comm Colls, Olney Central College (IL)
Illinois Eastern Comm Colls, Wabash Valley College (IL)
Illinois Valley Comm Coll (IL)
Imperial Valley Coll (CA)
Iowa Central Comm Coll (IA)
J. Sargeant Reynolds Comm Coll (VA)
Kaskaskia Coll (IL)
Kishwaukee Coll (IL)
Laramie County Comm Coll (WY)
Luzerne County Comm Coll (PA)
McHenry County Coll (IL)
Monroe Comm Coll (NY)
Morton Coll (IL)
Mt. San Antonio Coll (CA)
Navarro Coll (TX)
New Mexico Jr Coll (NM)
New River Comm Coll (VA)
Niagara County Comm Coll (NY)
Oakton Comm Coll (IL)
Otero Jr Coll (CO)
Palomar Coll (CA)
Paris Jr Coll (TX)
Patrick Henry Comm Coll (VA)
Penn State DuBois (PA)
Penn State Fayette, The Eberly Campus (PA)
Penn State Shenango (PA)
Rainy River Comm Coll (MN)
Rappahannock Comm Coll (VA)
Rend Lake Coll (IL)
Santa Monica Coll (CA)
Shawnee Comm Coll (IL)
Sierra Coll (CA)
South Florida State Coll (FL)
South Plains Coll (TX)
South Suburban Coll (IL)
Southwest Texas Jr Coll (TX)
Spoon River Coll (IL)
Sussex County Comm Coll (NJ)
Tidewater Comm Coll (VA)
Trident Tech Coll (SC)
U of South Carolina Union (SC)
Vincennes U (IN)
Virginia Western Comm Coll (VA)
Weatherford Coll (TX)
Western Wyoming Comm Coll (WY)
Wor-Wic Comm Coll (MD)
Wytheville Comm Coll (VA)

BIOLOGY/BIOLOGICAL SCIENCES
Allen Comm Coll (KS)
Alvin Comm Coll (TX)

Amarillo Coll (TX)
Anoka-Ramsey Comm Coll (MN)
Arizona Western Coll (AZ)
Austin Comm Coll District (TX)
Bainbridge State Coll (GA)
Blinn Coll (TX)
Bunker Hill Comm Coll (MA)
Cañada Coll (CA)
Carl Albert State Coll (OK)
Casper Coll (WY)
Cecil Coll (MD)
Central Maine Comm Coll (ME)
Central New Mexico Comm Coll (NM)
Central Oregon Comm Coll (OR)
Central Texas Coll (TX)
Central Wyoming Coll (WY)
Cerritos Coll (CA)
Chesapeake Coll (MD)
Citrus Coll (CA)
Cochise County Comm Coll District (AZ)
Coll of Central Florida (FL)
Coll of Marin (CA)
Coll of the Desert (CA)
Comm Coll of Allegheny County (PA)
Crowder Coll (MO)
Dakota Coll at Bottineau (ND)
De Anza Coll (CA)
Del Mar Coll (TX)
Dodge City Comm Coll (KS)
Eastern Arizona Coll (AZ)
Eastern Wyoming Coll (WY)
Edison State Comm Coll (OH)
Feather River Coll (CA)
Finger Lakes Comm Coll (NY)
Fiorello H. LaGuardia Comm Coll of the City U of New York (NY)
Frederick Comm Coll (MD)
Fullerton Coll (CA)
Genesee Comm Coll (NY)
Georgia Highlands Coll (GA)
Georgia Military Coll (GA)
Golden West Coll (CA)
Great Basin Coll (NV)
Harford Comm Coll (MD)
Harper Coll (IL)
Harrisburg Area Comm Coll (PA)
Hill Coll (TX)
Holyoke Comm Coll (MA)
Houston Comm Coll (TX)
Hutchinson Comm Coll (KS)
Kingsborough Comm Coll of the City U of New York (NY)
Lackawanna Coll (PA)
Lansing Comm Coll (MI)
Laramie County Comm Coll (WY)
Lehigh Carbon Comm Coll (PA)
Macomb Comm Coll (MI)
Merced Coll (CA)
Mercer County Comm Coll (NJ)
Miami Dade Coll (FL)
Middlesex Comm Coll (MA)
Minnesota State Comm and Tech Coll (MN)
Minnesota State Comm and Tech Coll–Moorhead (MN)
Monroe Comm Coll (NY)
Monroe County Comm Coll (MI)
Montgomery County Comm Coll (PA)
Mott Comm Coll (MI)
Murray State Coll (OK)
Nashville State Comm Coll (TN)
Navarro Coll (TX)
New Mexico Jr Coll (NM)
Northampton Comm Coll (PA)
Northeast Comm Coll (NE)
Northeastern Jr Coll (CO)
Northern Essex Comm Coll (MA)
Northwest Coll (WY)
Oklahoma City Comm Coll (OK)
Orange Coast Coll (CA)
Otero Jr Coll (CO)
Palomar Coll (CA)
Panola Coll (TX)
Paris Jr Coll (TX)
Pensacola State Coll (FL)
Quinsigamond Comm Coll (MA)
St. Charles Comm Coll (MO)
St. Philip's Coll (TX)
Salt Lake Comm Coll (UT)
San Jacinto Coll District (TX)
San Joaquin Delta Coll (CA)
San Juan Coll (NM)
Santa Fe Comm Coll (NM)
Santa Rosa Jr Coll (CA)
Seminole State Coll (OK)
Sierra Coll (CA)
Southern U at Shreveport (LA)
South Florida State Coll (FL)
South Plains Coll (TX)
Springfield Tech Comm Coll (MA)

State U of New York Coll of Technology at Alfred (NY)
Texarkana Coll (TX)
Trinity Valley Comm Coll (TX)
Truckee Meadows Comm Coll (NV)
Tyler Jr Coll (TX)
U of Cincinnati Clermont Coll (OH)
U of Pittsburgh at Titusville (PA)
Vincennes U (IN)
Western Wyoming Comm Coll (WY)

BIOLOGY/BIOTECHNOLOGY LABORATORY TECHNICIAN
Athens Tech Coll (GA)
Austin Comm Coll District (TX)
Blackhawk Tech Coll (WI)
Bucks County Comm Coll (PA)
Camden County Coll (NJ)
Collin County Comm Coll District (TX)
County Coll of Morris (NJ)
East Central Coll (MO)
Elgin Comm Coll (IL)
Erie Comm Coll, North Campus (NY)
Finger Lakes Comm Coll (NY)
Florida SouthWestern State Coll (FL)
Fox Valley Tech Coll (WI)
Genesee Comm Coll (NY)
Hagerstown Comm Coll (MD)
Hillsborough Comm Coll (FL)
Houston Comm Coll (TX)
Hutchinson Comm Coll (KS)
Jamestown Comm Coll (NY)
Johnson County Comm Coll (KS)
Lone Star Coll–Montgomery (TX)
Madison Area Tech Coll (WI)
Manhattan Area Tech Coll (KS)
Massachusetts Bay Comm Coll (MA)
Mercer County Comm Coll (NJ)
Middlesex Comm Coll (MA)
Middlesex County Coll (NJ)
Minnesota West Comm and Tech Coll (MN)
Monroe Comm Coll (NY)
Montgomery Coll (MD)
North Shore Comm Coll (MA)
The Ohio State U Ag Tech Inst (OH)
Rockingham Comm Coll (NC)
Salt Lake Comm Coll (UT)
Tompkins Cortland Comm Coll (NY)
Westmoreland County Comm Coll (PA)

BIOLOGY TEACHER EDUCATION
Bucks County Comm Coll (PA)
Ulster County Comm Coll (NY)

BIOMEDICAL TECHNOLOGY
Anoka-Ramsey Comm Coll (MN)
Anoka Tech Coll (MN)
Caldwell Comm Coll and Tech Inst (NC)
Cerritos Coll (CA)
Chattahoochee Tech Coll (GA)
Comm Coll of the Air Force (AL)
Des Moines Area Comm Coll (IA)
Fullerton Coll (CA)
Howard Comm Coll (MD)
Merced Coll (CA)
Miami Dade Coll (FL)
Minnesota State Coll–Southeast Tech (MN)
Penn State DuBois (PA)
Penn State Fayette, The Eberly Campus (PA)
Penn State Shenango (PA)
Pennsylvania Inst of Technology (PA)
Quinsigamond Comm Coll (MA)
Rend Lake Coll (IL)
St. Philip's Coll (TX)
Schoolcraft Coll (MI)
Southeastern Comm Coll (IA)
South Florida State Coll (FL)
Stark State Coll (OH)
Texas State Tech Coll (TX)
Waukesha County Tech Coll (WI)
Wayne County Comm Coll District (MI)

BIOTECHNOLOGY
Alamance Comm Coll (NC)
Augusta Tech Coll (GA)
Borough of Manhattan Comm Coll of the City U of New York (NY)
Bunker Hill Comm Coll (MA)
Cecil Coll (MD)
Central New Mexico Comm Coll (NM)
Coll of The Albemarle (NC)
Genesee Comm Coll (NY)
Holyoke Comm Coll (MA)
Howard Comm Coll (MD)

Humacao Comm Coll (PR)
Ivy Tech Comm Coll–Bloomington (IN)
Ivy Tech Comm Coll–Central Indiana (IN)
Ivy Tech Comm Coll–Lafayette (IN)
Ivy Tech Comm Coll–North Central (IN)
Ivy Tech Comm Coll–Southwest (IN)
Lackawanna Coll (PA)
Lakeland Comm Coll (OH)
Lansing Comm Coll (MI)
Lehigh Carbon Comm Coll (PA)
Mesa Comm Coll (AZ)
Miami Dade Coll (FL)
Middlesex County Coll (NJ)
Montgomery County Comm Coll (PA)
Mount Wachusett Comm Coll (MA)
Northampton Comm Coll (PA)
Oklahoma City Comm Coll (OK)
Queensborough Comm Coll of the City U of New York (NY)
Quinsigamond Comm Coll (MA)
St. Philip's Coll (TX)
Springfield Tech Comm Coll (MA)
Vincennes U (IN)

BOILERMAKING
Ivy Tech Comm Coll–Southwest (IN)

BOTANY/PLANT BIOLOGY
Pensacola State Coll (FL)
South Florida State Coll (FL)

BROADCAST JOURNALISM
Amarillo Coll (TX)
Cerritos Coll (CA)
Dodge City Comm Coll (KS)
Iowa Central Comm Coll (IA)
Kingsborough Comm Coll of the City U of New York (NY)
Oklahoma City Comm Coll (OK)
Palomar Coll (CA)
San Joaquin Delta Coll (CA)
Sussex County Comm Coll (NJ)

BUILDING/CONSTRUCTION FINISHING, MANAGEMENT, AND INSPECTION RELATED
Comm Coll of Baltimore County (MD)
Delta Coll (MI)
Fayetteville Tech Comm Coll (NC)
Frederick Comm Coll (MD)
Gwinnett Tech Coll (GA)
Haywood Comm Coll (NC)
Manhattan Area Tech Coll (KS)
Mid-Plains Comm Coll, North Platte (NE)
Mohave Comm Coll (AZ)
Montgomery Coll (MD)
Mt. San Antonio Coll (CA)
Nebraska Indian Comm Coll (NE)
Northeast Comm Coll (NE)
Oakton Comm Coll (IL)
Salt Lake Comm Coll (UT)
Seminole State Coll of Florida (FL)
Southeast Comm Coll, Milford Campus (NE)
Springfield Tech Comm Coll (MA)

BUILDING/CONSTRUCTION SITE MANAGEMENT
Arapahoe Comm Coll (CO)
Coll of the Canyons (CA)
Coll of the Desert (CA)
Comm Coll of Baltimore County (MD)
Dunwoody Coll of Technology (MN)
Erie Comm Coll, North Campus (NY)
Fox Valley Tech Coll (WI)
Fullerton Coll (CA)
Ivy Tech Comm Coll–Kokomo (IN)
J. Sargeant Reynolds Comm Coll (VA)
Lehigh Carbon Comm Coll (PA)
Lorain County Comm Coll (OH)
Minnesota State Comm and Tech Coll (MN)
The Ohio State U Ag Tech Inst (OH)

BUILDING CONSTRUCTION TECHNOLOGY
Central Maine Comm Coll (ME)
Central New Mexico Comm Coll (NM)
Cochise County Comm Coll District (AZ)
Coconino Comm Coll (AZ)
Lake Area Tech Inst (SD)

Lake Superior Coll (MN)
Mitchell Tech Inst (SD)
Penn Foster Coll (AZ)
Western Nevada Coll (NV)

BUILDING/HOME/ CONSTRUCTION INSPECTION
Bucks County Comm Coll (PA)
Fullerton Coll (CA)
Oklahoma State U–Oklahoma City (OK)
Palomar Coll (CA)
South Suburban Coll (IL)
Vincennes U (IN)

BUILDING/PROPERTY MAINTENANCE
Cape Fear Comm Coll (NC)
Central Texas Coll (TX)
Central Wyoming Coll (WY)
Century Coll (MN)
Columbus State Comm Coll (OH)
Comm Coll of Allegheny County (PA)
Del Mar Coll (TX)
Delta Coll (MI)
Erie Comm Coll (NY)
Ivy Tech Comm Coll–Bloomington (IN)
Ivy Tech Comm Coll–East Central (IN)
Ivy Tech Comm Coll–Kokomo (IN)
Ivy Tech Comm Coll–Lafayette (IN)
Ivy Tech Comm Coll–North Central (IN)
Ivy Tech Comm Coll–Northeast (IN)
Ivy Tech Comm Coll–Northwest (IN)
Ivy Tech Comm Coll–Richmond (IN)
Ivy Tech Comm Coll–Sellersburg (IN)
Ivy Tech Comm Coll–Southwest (IN)
Ivy Tech Comm Coll–Wabash Valley (IN)
Luzerne County Comm Coll (PA)
Manhattan Area Tech Coll (KS)
Mohawk Valley Comm Coll (NY)
Pensacola State Coll (FL)
Renton Tech Coll (WA)
Rowan-Cabarrus Comm Coll (NC)
Wayne County Comm Coll District (MI)

BUSINESS ADMINISTRATION AND MANAGEMENT
Adirondack Comm Coll (NY)
Alamance Comm Coll (NC)
Alexandria Tech and Comm Coll (MN)
Allen Comm Coll (KS)
Alvin Comm Coll (TX)
Amarillo Coll (TX)
American Samoa Comm Coll (AS)
Ancilla Coll (IN)
Anne Arundel Comm Coll (MD)
Anoka-Ramsey Comm Coll (MN)
Arapahoe Comm Coll (CO)
Arizona Western Coll (AZ)
Augusta Tech Coll (GA)
Austin Comm Coll District (TX)
Bainbridge State Coll (GA)
Berkshire Comm Coll (MA)
Blackhawk Tech Coll (WI)
Blinn Coll (TX)
Blue Ridge Comm and Tech Coll (WV)
Borough of Manhattan Comm Coll of the City U of New York (NY)
Bowling Green State U–Firelands Coll (OH)
Brookhaven Coll (TX)
Bucks County Comm Coll (PA)
Bunker Hill Comm Coll (MA)
Caldwell Comm Coll and Tech Inst (NC)
Camden County Coll (NJ)
Cañada Coll (CA)
Cape Fear Comm Coll (NC)
Carl Albert State Coll (OK)
Carroll Comm Coll (MD)
Carteret Comm Coll (NC)
Casper Coll (WY)
Cayuga County Comm Coll (NY)
Cecil Coll (MD)
Central Georgia Tech Coll (GA)
Central Maine Comm Coll (ME)
Central New Mexico Comm Coll (NM)
Central Oregon Comm Coll (OR)
Central Texas Coll (TX)
Central Virginia Comm Coll (VA)
Central Wyoming Coll (WY)
Century Coll (MN)

Cerritos Coll (CA)
Chandler-Gilbert Comm Coll (AZ)
Chattahoochee Tech Coll (GA)
Chesapeake Coll (MD)
Chippewa Valley Tech Coll (WI)
Citrus Coll (CA)
City Colls of Chicago, Kennedy-King College (IL)
City Colls of Chicago, Olive-Harvey College (IL)
Cleveland State Comm Coll (TN)
Clinton Comm Coll (NY)
Cloud County Comm Coll (KS)
Cochise County Comm Coll District (AZ)
Coconino Comm Coll (AZ)
Coll of Business and Technology– Cutler Bay Campus (FL)
Coll of Business and Technology– Flagler Campus (FL)
Coll of Business and Technology– Main Campus (FL)
Coll of Business and Technology– Miami Gardens (FL)
Coll of Central Florida (FL)
Coll of Marin (CA)
Coll of The Albemarle (NC)
Coll of the Canyons (CA)
Coll of the Desert (CA)
Coll of the Marshall Islands (MH)
Coll of the Ouachitas (AR)
The Coll of Westchester (NY)
Collin County Comm Coll District (TX)
Columbia-Greene Comm Coll (NY)
Columbus State Comm Coll (OH)
Comm Coll of Allegheny County (PA)
Comm Coll of Baltimore County (MD)
Comm Coll of Philadelphia (PA)
Comm Coll of Rhode Island (RI)
County Coll of Morris (NJ)
Craven Comm Coll (NC)
Crowder Coll (MO)
Dakota Coll at Bottineau (ND)
Daytona State Coll (FL)
De Anza Coll (CA)
Del Mar Coll (TX)
Delta Coll (MI)
Des Moines Area Comm Coll (IA)
Dodge City Comm Coll (KS)
Duluth Business U (MN)
Dutchess Comm Coll (NY)
Dyersburg State Comm Coll (TN)
Eastern Arizona Coll (AZ)
Eastern Wyoming Coll (WY)
Edison State Comm Coll (OH)
Elgin Comm Coll (IL)
El Paso Comm Coll (TX)
Erie Comm Coll (NY)
Erie Comm Coll, North Campus (NY)
Erie Comm Coll, South Campus (NY)
Fayetteville Tech Comm Coll (NC)
Finger Lakes Comm Coll (NY)
Fiorello H. LaGuardia Comm Coll of the City U of New York (NY)
Florida Keys Comm and Coll (FL)
Florida SouthWestern State Coll (FL)
Fox Valley Tech Coll (WI)
Frederick Comm Coll (MD)
Front Range Comm Coll (CO)
Fullerton Coll (CA)
Garrett Coll (MD)
Gateway Comm and Tech Coll (KY)
Gateway Tech Coll (WI)
Genesee Comm Coll (NY)
Georgia Highlands Coll (GA)
Golden West Coll (CA)
Gordon State Coll (GA)
Grand Rapids Comm Coll (MI)
Great Basin Coll (NV)
Greenville Tech Coll (SC)
Gulf Coast State Coll (FL)
Gwinnett Tech Coll (GA)
Hagerstown Comm Coll (MD)
Halifax Comm Coll (NC)
Harford Comm Coll (MD)
Harper Coll (IL)
Harrisburg Area Comm Coll (PA)
Haywood Comm Coll (NC)
Hennepin Tech Coll (MN)
Hesston Coll (KS)
Highland Comm Coll (IL)
Hill Coll (TX)
Hillsborough Comm Coll (FL)
Holyoke Comm Coll (MA)
Horry Georgetown Tech Coll (SC)
Housatonic Comm Coll (CT)

Houston Comm Coll (TX)
Howard Comm Coll (MD)
Hudson County Comm Coll (NJ)
IBMC Coll, Fort Collins (CO)
Illinois Central Coll (IL)
Illinois Eastern Comm Colls, Olney Central College (IL)
Illinois Eastern Comm Colls, Wabash Valley College (IL)
Illinois Valley Comm Coll (IL)
Imperial Valley Coll (CA)
Iowa Central Comm Coll (IA)
Ivy Tech Comm Coll–Bloomington (IN)
Ivy Tech Comm Coll–Central Indiana (IN)
Ivy Tech Comm Coll–Columbus (IN)
Ivy Tech Comm Coll–East Central (IN)
Ivy Tech Comm Coll–Kokomo (IN)
Ivy Tech Comm Coll–Lafayette (IN)
Ivy Tech Comm Coll–North Central (IN)
Ivy Tech Comm Coll–Northeast (IN)
Ivy Tech Comm Coll–Northwest (IN)
Ivy Tech Comm Coll–Richmond (IN)
Ivy Tech Comm Coll–Sellersburg (IN)
Ivy Tech Comm Coll–Southeast (IN)
Ivy Tech Comm Coll–Southwest (IN)
Ivy Tech Comm Coll–Wabash Valley (IN)
James Sprunt Comm Coll (NC)
Jamestown Business Coll (NY)
Jamestown Comm Coll (NY)
Jefferson Comm Coll (NY)
Johnson County Comm Coll (KS)
Johnston Comm Coll (NC)
John Tyler Comm Coll (VA)
J. Sargeant Reynolds Comm Coll (VA)
Kellogg Comm Coll (MI)
Kingsborough Comm Coll of the City U of New York (NY)
Kirtland Comm Coll (MI)
Kishwaukee Coll (IL)
Lackawanna Coll (PA)
Lakeland Comm Coll (OH)
Lake Region State Coll (ND)
Lake Superior Coll (MN)
Lansing Comm Coll (MI)
Laramie County Comm Coll (WY)
Lehigh Carbon Comm Coll (PA)
Lone Star Coll–CyFair (TX)
Lone Star Coll–Kingwood (TX)
Lone Star Coll–Montgomery (TX)
Lone Star Coll–North Harris (TX)
Lone Star Coll–Tomball (TX)
Lone Star Coll–U Park (TX)
Long Island Business Inst (NY)
Lorain County Comm Coll (OH)
Los Angeles City Coll (CA)
Louisiana State U at Eunice (LA)
Luzerne County Comm Coll (PA)
Macomb Comm Coll (MI)
Madison Area Tech Coll (WI)
Manchester Comm Coll (CT)
Manor Coll (PA)
Massachusetts Bay Comm Coll (MA)
Maysville Comm and Tech Coll, Maysville (KY)
McHenry County Coll (IL)
McLennan Comm Coll (TX)
Merced Coll (CA)
Mercer County Comm Coll (NJ)
Metropolitan Comm Coll (NE)
Miami Dade Coll (FL)
Middlesex Comm Coll (MA)
Middlesex County Coll (NJ)
Mid-Plains Comm Coll, North Platte (NE)
Minnesota State Coll–Southeast Tech (MN)
Minnesota State Comm and Tech Coll (MN)
Minnesota State Comm and Tech Coll–Moorhead (MN)
Minnesota West Comm and Tech Coll (MN)
Mitchell Comm Coll (NC)
Mohave Comm Coll (AZ)
Mohawk Valley Comm Coll (NY)
Monroe Comm Coll (NY)
Monroe County Comm Coll (MI)
Montgomery Comm Coll (NC)
Montgomery County Comm Coll (PA)
Morgan Comm Coll (CO)
Morton Coll (IL)
Motlow State Comm Coll (TN)
Mott Comm Coll (MI)
Mountain View Coll (TX)

Mt. San Antonio Coll (CA)
Mount Wachusett Comm Coll (MA)
Nashville State Comm Coll (TN)
Nassau Comm Coll (NY)
Naugatuck Valley Comm Coll (CT)
Navarro Coll (TX)
Nebraska Indian Comm Coll (NE)
New Mexico Jr Coll (NM)
New River Comm Coll (VA)
NHTI, Concord's Comm Coll, Concord (NH)
Niagara County Comm Coll (NY)
Northampton Comm Coll (PA)
North Central Missouri Coll (MO)
Northcentral Tech Coll (WI)
Northeast Comm Coll (NE)
Northeastern Jr Coll (CO)
Northeast Iowa Comm Coll (IA)
Northern Essex Comm Coll (MA)
Northern Maine Comm Coll (ME)
Northland Comm and Tech Coll (MN)
North Shore Comm Coll (MA)
NorthWest Arkansas Comm Coll (AR)
Northwest Coll (WY)
Norwalk Comm Coll (CT)
Oklahoma City Comm Coll (OK)
Oklahoma State U–Oklahoma City (OK)
Olympic Coll (WA)
Orange Coast Coll (CA)
Otero Jr Coll (CO)
Owensboro Comm and Tech Coll (KY)
Ozarks Tech Comm Coll (MO)
Palomar Coll (CA)
Panola Coll (TX)
Paris Jr Coll (TX)
Patrick Henry Comm Coll (VA)
Penn Foster Coll (AZ)
Pennsylvania Inst of Technology (PA)
Pensacola State Coll (FL)
Piedmont Comm Coll (NC)
Pittsburgh Tech Coll (PA)
Pueblo Comm Coll (CO)
Queensborough Comm Coll of the City U of New York (NY)
Quinsigamond Comm Coll (MA)
Rainy River Comm Coll (MN)
Randolph Comm Coll (NC)
Rappahannock Comm Coll (VA)
Raritan Valley Comm Coll (NJ)
Richmond Comm Coll (NC)
Rio Salado Coll (AZ)
Rockingham Comm Coll (NC)
Rock Valley Coll (IL)
Rogue Comm Coll (OR)
Rowan-Cabarrus Comm Coll (NC)
St. Philip's Coll (TX)
Salt Lake Comm Coll (UT)
San Jacinto Coll District (TX)
San Joaquin Delta Coll (CA)
San Juan Coll (NM)
Santa Fe Comm Coll (NM)
Santa Monica Coll (CA)
Santa Rosa Jr Coll (CA)
Schoolcraft Coll (MI)
Scottsdale Comm Coll (AZ)
Seminole State Coll (OK)
Seminole State Coll of Florida (FL)
Shawnee Comm Coll (IL)
Sierra Coll (CA)
Sisseton-Wahpeton Coll (SD)
Snead State Comm Coll (AL)
Somerset Comm Coll (KY)
Southeast Comm Coll, Lincoln Campus (NE)
Southeast Comm Coll, Milford Campus (NE)
Southeastern Comm Coll (IA)
Southern Arkansas U Tech (AR)
Southern Crescent Tech Coll (GA)
South Florida State Coll (FL)
South Plains Coll (TX)
Southwestern Comm Coll (NC)
Southwestern Indian Polytechnic Inst (NM)
Southwestern Michigan Coll (MI)
Southwest Texas Jr Coll (TX)
Spartanburg Comm Coll (SC)
Springfield Tech Comm Coll (MA)
Stark State Coll (OH)
State U of New York Coll of Technology at Alfred (NY)
Sullivan County Comm Coll (NY)
Sussex County Comm Coll (NJ)
Tarrant County Coll District (TX)
Texarkana Coll (TX)
Tidewater Comm Coll (VA)
Tohono O'odham Comm Coll (AZ)

Tompkins Cortland Comm Coll (NY)
Trident Tech Coll (SC)
Trinity Valley Comm Coll (TX)
Tyler Jr Coll (TX)
Ulster County Comm Coll (NY)
U of Cincinnati Blue Ash Coll (OH)
U of Cincinnati Clermont Coll (OH)
Victoria Coll (TX)
Vincennes U (IN)
Virginia Western Comm Coll (VA)
Volunteer State Comm Coll (TN)
Walters State Comm Coll (TN)
Waukesha County Tech Coll (WI)
Wayne County Comm Coll District (MI)
Weatherford Coll (TX)
Westchester Comm Coll (NY)
Western Dakota Tech Inst (SD)
Western Nevada Coll (NV)
Western Wyoming Comm Coll (WY)
White Mountains Comm Coll (NH)
Wisconsin Indianhead Tech Coll (WI)
Wor-Wic Comm Coll (MD)
Wytheville Comm Coll (VA)
York County Comm Coll (ME)

BUSINESS ADMINISTRATION, MANAGEMENT AND OPERATIONS RELATED
Ancilla Coll (IN)
Anne Arundel Comm Coll (MD)
Blue Ridge Comm and Tech Coll (WV)
Bunker Hill Comm Coll (MA)
Chandler-Gilbert Comm Coll (AZ)
Coll of Central Florida (FL)
Comm Care Coll (OK)
Genesee Comm Coll (NY)
John Tyler Comm Coll (VA)
Lackawanna Coll (PA)
Pensacola State Coll (FL)
Rappahannock Comm Coll (VA)
Rowan-Cabarrus Comm Coll (NC)
Southwest Virginia Comm Coll (VA)
U of Cincinnati Blue Ash Coll (OH)
Waukesha County Tech Coll (WI)
Williston State Coll (ND)

BUSINESS AND PERSONAL/ FINANCIAL SERVICES MARKETING
Hutchinson Comm Coll (KS)

BUSINESS AUTOMATION/ TECHNOLOGY/DATA ENTRY
Berkshire Comm Coll (MA)
Bismarck State Coll (ND)
Casper Coll (WY)
Comm Coll of Allegheny County (PA)
Crowder Coll (MO)
Dakota Coll at Bottineau (ND)
Danville Area Comm Coll (IL)
El Paso Comm Coll (TX)
Garrett Coll (MD)
Guam Comm Coll (GU)
Houston Comm Coll (TX)
Illinois Eastern Comm Colls, Frontier Community College (IL)
Illinois Eastern Comm Colls, Lincoln Trail College (IL)
Illinois Eastern Comm Colls, Olney Central College (IL)
Illinois Eastern Comm Colls, Wabash Valley College (IL)
Illinois Valley Comm Coll (IL)
Ivy Tech Comm Coll–Bloomington (IN)
Ivy Tech Comm Coll–Central Indiana (IN)
Ivy Tech Comm Coll–Columbus (IN)
Ivy Tech Comm Coll–Lafayette (IN)
Ivy Tech Comm Coll–North Central (IN)
Ivy Tech Comm Coll–Northeast (IN)
Ivy Tech Comm Coll–Northwest (IN)
Ivy Tech Comm Coll–Richmond (IN)
Ivy Tech Comm Coll–Sellersburg (IN)
Ivy Tech Comm Coll–Southeast (IN)
Ivy Tech Comm Coll–Southwest (IN)
Kaskaskia Coll (IL)
Lake Superior Coll (MN)
Lamar Comm Coll (CO)
Lansdale School of Business (PA)
Macomb Comm Coll (MI)
Miami Dade Coll (FL)
Minnesota State Comm and Tech Coll (MN)
Mitchell Tech Inst (SD)
Northeast Iowa Comm Coll (IA)
Panola Coll (TX)
Paris Jr Coll (TX)
Pueblo Comm Coll (CO)

Renton Tech Coll (WA)
Schoolcraft Coll (MI)
Shawnee Comm Coll (IL)

BUSINESS/COMMERCE
Aaniiih Nakoda Coll (MT)
Allen Comm Coll (KS)
Alvin Comm Coll (TX)
Anne Arundel Comm Coll (MD)
Anoka-Ramsey Comm Coll (MN)
Arkansas Northeastern Coll (AR)
Asnuntuck Comm Coll (CT)
Austin Comm Coll District (TX)
Berkshire Comm Coll (MA)
Bismarck State Coll (ND)
Bossier Parish Comm Coll (LA)
Brookhaven Coll (TX)
Carl Albert State Coll (OK)
Cecil Coll (MD)
Central Texas Coll (TX)
Central Virginia Comm Coll (VA)
Central Wyoming Coll (WY)
Chandler-Gilbert Comm Coll (AZ)
Chesapeake Coll (MD)
Citrus Coll (CA)
Coconino Comm Coll (AZ)
Coll of Central Florida (FL)
Coll of Marin (CA)
Coll of the Desert (CA)
Collin County Comm Coll District (TX)
Colorado Northwestern Comm Coll (CO)
Columbia-Greene Comm Coll (NY)
Comm Coll of Baltimore County (MD)
Comm Coll of Rhode Island (RI)
Del Mar Coll (TX)
East Central Coll (MO)
El Paso Comm Coll (TX)
Feather River Coll (CA)
Garrett Coll (MD)
Georgia Military Coll (GA)
Georgia Piedmont Tech Coll (GA)
Great Basin Coll (NV)
Hagerstown Comm Coll (MD)
Harrisburg Area Comm Coll (PA)
Hill Coll (TX)
Humacao Comm Coll (PR)
Hutchinson Comm Coll (KS)
Kaskaskia Coll (IL)
Kent State U at Ashtabula (OH)
Kent State U at East Liverpool (OH)
Kent State U at Salem (OH)
Kent State U at Trumbull (OH)
Kent State U at Tuscarawas (OH)
Lackawanna Coll (PA)
Lansing Comm Coll (MI)
Laramie County Comm Coll (WY)
Lehigh Carbon Comm Coll (PA)
Macomb Comm Coll (MI)
Massachusetts Bay Comm Coll (MA)
Merced Coll (CA)
Mesabi Range Coll (MN)
Mesa Comm Coll (AZ)
Minnesota State Comm and Tech Coll (MN)
Minnesota State Comm and Tech Coll–Moorhead (MN)
Minnesota West Comm and Tech Coll (MN)
Missouri State U–West Plains (MO)
Montgomery Coll (MD)
Montgomery County Comm Coll (PA)
Mott Comm Coll (MI)
Mount Wachusett Comm Coll (MA)
Naugatuck Valley Comm Coll (CT)
Northampton Comm Coll (PA)
Northeast Comm Coll (NE)
Northern Essex Comm Coll (MA)
Northwest Coll (WY)
Nunez Comm Coll (LA)
Oklahoma City Comm Coll (OK)
Oklahoma State U Inst of Technology (OK)
Orange Coast Coll (CA)
Palomar Coll (CA)
Paris Jr Coll (TX)
Penn State DuBois (PA)
Penn State Fayette, The Eberly Campus (PA)
Penn State Mont Alto (PA)
Penn State Shenango (PA)
Pensacola State Coll (FL)
Quinsigamond Comm Coll (MA)
Raritan Valley Comm Coll (NJ)
Rend Lake Coll (IL)
Rogue Comm Coll (OR)
Saginaw Chippewa Tribal Coll (MI)
St. Clair County Comm Coll (MI)
San Jacinto Coll District (TX)
Schoolcraft Coll (MI)

Seminole State Coll (OK)
Sierra Coll (CA)
Southern U at Shreveport (LA)
South Florida State Coll (FL)
Southwestern Indian Polytechnic Inst (NM)
Sowela Tech Comm Coll (LA)
Spartanburg Methodist Coll (SC)
Springfield Tech Comm Coll (MA)
Texarkana Coll (TX)
Three Rivers Comm Coll (CT)
Treasure Valley Comm Coll (OR)
Truckee Meadows Comm Coll (NV)
Tyler Jr Coll (TX)
U of Arkansas Comm Coll at Morrilton (AR)
U of Cincinnati Blue Ash Coll (OH)
U of Cincinnati Clermont Coll (OH)
U of Pittsburgh at Titusville (PA)
Vincennes U (IN)
Western Nevada Coll (NV)
Westmoreland County Comm Coll (PA)
Williamsburg Tech Coll (SC)
Wor-Wic Comm Coll (MD)

BUSINESS/CORPORATE COMMUNICATIONS
Cecil Coll (MD)
Houston Comm Coll (TX)
Montgomery County Comm Coll (PA)

BUSINESS MACHINE REPAIR
Comm Coll of Allegheny County (PA)
De Anza Coll (CA)
Del Mar Coll (TX)
Ozarks Tech Comm Coll (MO)

BUSINESS, MANAGEMENT, AND MARKETING RELATED
Bucks County Comm Coll (PA)
Chandler-Gilbert Comm Coll (AZ)
Cloud County Comm Coll (KS)
County Coll of Morris (NJ)
Eastern Arizona Coll (AZ)
Genesee Comm Coll (NY)
Long Island Business Inst (NY)
Manor Coll (PA)
Niagara County Comm Coll (NY)
Queensborough Comm Coll of the City U of New York (NY)
Southeastern Coll–West Palm Beach (FL)

BUSINESS/MANAGERIAL ECONOMICS
South Florida State Coll (FL)

BUSINESS OPERATIONS SUPPORT AND SECRETARIAL SERVICES RELATED
Bunker Hill Comm Coll (MA)
Central Virginia Comm Coll (VA)
Eastern Arizona Coll (AZ)
Genesee Comm Coll (NY)
Southwest Virginia Comm Coll (VA)

BUSINESS TEACHER EDUCATION
Allen Comm Coll (KS)
Amarillo Coll (TX)
Bainbridge State Coll (GA)
Eastern Arizona Coll (AZ)
Eastern Wyoming Coll (WY)
Iowa Central Comm Coll (IA)
Madison Area Tech Coll (WI)
Mt. San Antonio Coll (CA)
Northern Essex Comm Coll (MA)
Paris Jr Coll (TX)
Rio Hondo Coll (CA)
South Florida State Coll (FL)
Trinity Valley Comm Coll (TX)

CABINETMAKING AND MILLWORK
Bucks County Comm Coll (PA)
Central Georgia Tech Coll (GA)
Cerritos Coll (CA)
Columbus State Comm Coll (OH)
Ivy Tech Comm Coll–Bloomington (IN)
Ivy Tech Comm Coll–Central Indiana (IN)
Ivy Tech Comm Coll–Columbus (IN)
Ivy Tech Comm Coll–Lafayette (IN)
Ivy Tech Comm Coll–North Central (IN)
Ivy Tech Comm Coll–Northeast (IN)
Ivy Tech Comm Coll–Northwest (IN)
Ivy Tech Comm Coll–Richmond (IN)
Ivy Tech Comm Coll–Sellersburg (IN)
Ivy Tech Comm Coll–Southwest (IN)

Ivy Tech Comm Coll–Wabash Valley (IN)
Macomb Comm Coll (MI)
Palomar Coll (CA)
Sierra Coll (CA)

CAD/CADD DRAFTING/DESIGN TECHNOLOGY
Arizona Western Coll (AZ)
Central Oregon Comm Coll (OR)
Century Coll (MN)
Danville Area Comm Coll (IL)
Dunwoody Coll of Technology (MN)
Elgin Comm Coll (IL)
Erie Comm Coll, South Campus (NY)
Front Range Comm Coll (CO)
Gulf Coast State Coll (FL)
Hennepin Tech Coll (MN)
Illinois Valley Comm Coll (IL)
Johnson County Comm Coll (KS)
Kellogg Comm Coll (MI)
Kent State U at Tuscarawas (OH)
Kishwaukee Coll (IL)
Lake Superior Coll (MN)
Manhattan Area Tech Coll (KS)
Miami Dade Coll (FL)
Minnesota State Coll–Southeast Tech (MN)
Mohawk Valley Comm Coll (NY)
Morton Coll (IL)
Northampton Comm Coll (PA)
Northwest Coll (WY)
Salina Area Tech Coll (KS)
South Suburban Coll (IL)
Tallahassee Comm Coll (FL)
Wayne County Comm Coll District (MI)

CARDIOPULMONARY TECHNOLOGY
Lackawanna Coll (PA)

CARDIOVASCULAR TECHNOLOGY
Augusta Tech Coll (GA)
Bunker Hill Comm Coll (MA)
Central Georgia Tech Coll (GA)
Comm Coll of the Air Force (AL)
Florida SouthWestern State Coll (FL)
Harper Coll (IL)
Harrisburg Area Comm Coll (PA)
Houston Comm Coll (TX)
Howard Comm Coll (MD)
Kirtland Comm Coll (MI)
Minnesota State Comm and Tech Coll (MN)
Minnesota State Comm and Tech Coll–Moorhead (MN)
Oklahoma State U–Oklahoma City (OK)
Orange Coast Coll (CA)
St. Philip's Coll (TX)
San Jacinto Coll District (TX)
Southern U at Shreveport (LA)

CARPENTRY
Alamance Comm Coll (NC)
Arizona Western Coll (AZ)
Austin Comm Coll District (TX)
Bismarck State Coll (ND)
Central Georgia Tech Coll (GA)
Central Wyoming Coll (WY)
Coconino Comm Coll (AZ)
Columbus State Comm Coll (OH)
Comm Coll of Allegheny County (PA)
Delta Coll (MI)
Fullerton Coll (CA)
Hawkeye Comm Coll (IA)
Hennepin Tech Coll (MN)
Hutchinson Comm Coll (KS)
Iowa Central Comm Coll (IA)
Ivy Tech Comm Coll–Central Indiana (IN)
Ivy Tech Comm Coll–East Central (IN)
Ivy Tech Comm Coll–Lafayette (IN)
Ivy Tech Comm Coll–North Central (IN)
Ivy Tech Comm Coll–Northwest (IN)
Ivy Tech Comm Coll–Sellersburg (IN)
Ivy Tech Comm Coll–Southwest (IN)
Ivy Tech Comm Coll–Wabash Valley (IN)
Kaskaskia Coll (IL)
Lake Superior Coll (MN)
Lansing Comm Coll (MI)
Manhattan Area Tech Coll (KS)
Minnesota State Coll–Southeast Tech (MN)
Minnesota State Comm and Tech Coll (MN)
North Central Missouri Coll (MO)

Ivy Tech Comm Coll–Wabash Valley (IN)
Macomb Comm Coll (MI)
Palomar Coll (CA)
Sierra Coll (CA)

CERAMIC ARTS AND CERAMICS
De Anza Coll (CA)
Mercer County Comm Coll (NJ)
Palomar Coll (CA)
Santa Fe Comm Coll (NM)

CHEMICAL ENGINEERING
Monroe Comm Coll (NY)
Olympic Coll (WA)
South Florida State Coll (FL)

CHEMICAL PROCESS TECHNOLOGY
San Jacinto Coll District (TX)

CHEMICAL TECHNOLOGY
Alvin Comm Coll (TX)
Amarillo Coll (TX)
Bucks County Comm Coll (PA)
Cape Fear Comm Coll (NC)
Comm Coll of Allegheny County (PA)
Comm Coll of Rhode Island (RI)
County Coll of Morris (NJ)
Del Mar Coll (TX)
Delta Coll (MI)
Fullerton Coll (CA)
Houston Comm Coll (TX)
Humacao Comm Coll (PR)
Ivy Tech Comm Coll–Lafayette (IN)
Ivy Tech Comm Coll–Wabash Valley (IN)
Lansing Comm Coll (MI)
Lehigh Carbon Comm Coll (PA)
Mohawk Valley Comm Coll (NY)
Niagara County Comm Coll (NY)
Pensacola State Coll (FL)
San Jacinto Coll District (TX)
Sowela Tech Comm Coll (LA)
Texas State Tech Coll (TX)
U of Cincinnati Blue Ash Coll (OH)
Victoria Coll (TX)

CHEMISTRY
Allen Comm Coll (KS)
Amarillo Coll (TX)
Arizona Western Coll (AZ)
Austin Comm Coll District (TX)
Bainbridge State Coll (GA)
Blinn Coll (TX)
Bunker Hill Comm Coll (MA)
Cañada Coll (CA)
Casper Coll (WY)
Cecil Coll (MD)
Central New Mexico Comm Coll (NM)
Central Texas Coll (TX)
Cerritos Coll (CA)
Cochise County Comm Coll District (AZ)
Coll of Central Florida (FL)
Coll of Marin (CA)
Coll of the Desert (CA)
Comm Coll of Allegheny County (PA)
Dakota Coll at Bottineau (ND)
Del Mar Coll (TX)
Dodge City Comm Coll (KS)
Eastern Arizona Coll (AZ)
Finger Lakes Comm Coll (NY)
Frederick Comm Coll (MD)
Fullerton Coll (CA)
Genesee Comm Coll (NY)
Georgia Highlands Coll (GA)
Gordon State Coll (GA)
Grand Rapids Comm Coll (MI)
Harford Comm Coll (MD)
Harper Coll (IL)
Harrisburg Area Comm Coll (PA)
Hill Coll (TX)
Holyoke Comm Coll (MA)
Houston Comm Coll (TX)
Kingsborough Comm Coll of the City U of New York (NY)
Lansing Comm Coll (MI)
Laramie County Comm Coll (WY)
Lehigh Carbon Comm Coll (PA)
Los Angeles City Coll (CA)
Macomb Comm Coll (MI)
Merced Coll (CA)
Mercer County Comm Coll (NJ)
Miami Dade Coll (FL)
Minnesota State Comm and Tech Coll (MN)
Minnesota State Comm and Tech Coll–Moorhead (MN)
Monroe Comm Coll (NY)
Murray State Coll (OK)

Nashville State Comm Coll (TN)
Navarro Coll (TX)
New Mexico Jr Coll (NM)
Northampton Comm Coll (PA)
Northeast Comm Coll (NE)
Northeastern Jr Coll (CO)
Northwest Coll (WY)
Oklahoma City Comm Coll (OK)
Orange Coast Coll (CA)
Palomar Coll (CA)
Panola Coll (TX)
Paris Jr Coll (TX)
Pensacola State Coll (FL)
Queensborough Comm Coll of the City U of New York (NY)
Quinsigamond Comm Coll (MA)
St. Charles Comm Coll (MO)
St. Philip's Coll (TX)
Salt Lake Comm Coll (UT)
San Jacinto Coll District (TX)
San Joaquin Delta Coll (CA)
San Juan Coll (NM)
Santa Rosa Jr Coll (CA)
Sierra Coll (CA)
Southern U at Shreveport (LA)
South Florida State Coll (FL)
South Plains Coll (TX)
Springfield Tech Comm Coll (MA)
Texarkana Coll (TX)
Trinity Valley Comm Coll (TX)
Truckee Meadows Comm Coll (NV)
Tyler Jr Coll (TX)
U of Cincinnati Clermont Coll (OH)
Vincennes U (IN)
Western Wyoming Comm Coll (WY)

CHEMISTRY RELATED
South Florida State Coll (FL)
Vincennes U (IN)

CHEMISTRY TEACHER EDUCATION
Anne Arundel Comm Coll (MD)
Carroll Comm Coll (MD)
Chesapeake Coll (MD)
Comm Coll of Baltimore County (MD)
Harford Comm Coll (MD)
Montgomery Coll (MD)
Ulster County Comm Coll (NY)
Vincennes U (IN)

CHILD-CARE AND SUPPORT SERVICES MANAGEMENT
Anne Arundel Comm Coll (MD)
Bevill State Comm Coll (AL)
Carroll Comm Coll (MD)
Cayuga County Comm Coll (NY)
Cecil Coll (MD)
Central Georgia Tech Coll (GA)
Central Oregon Comm Coll (OR)
Central Wyoming Coll (WY)
Chesapeake Coll (MD)
Cloud County Comm Coll (KS)
Coll of the Desert (CA)
Coll of the Ouachitas (AR)
Columbus State Comm Coll (OH)
Comm Coll of Baltimore County (MD)
Dakota Coll at Bottineau (ND)
Dutchess Comm Coll (NY)
East Central Coll (MO)
El Paso Comm Coll (TX)
Erie Comm Coll (NY)
Grand Rapids Comm Coll (MI)
Greenville Tech Coll (SC)
Hagerstown Comm Coll (MD)
Haywood Comm Coll (NC)
H. Councill Trenholm State Comm Coll (AL)
Hillsborough Comm Coll (FL)
Holyoke Comm Coll (MA)
Hutchinson Comm Coll (KS)
Ivy Tech Comm Coll–North Central (IN)
Ivy Tech Comm Coll–Northwest (IN)
Jefferson Comm Coll (NY)
Jefferson State Comm Coll (AL)
Johnson County Comm Coll (KS)
Kellogg Comm Coll (MI)
Kishwaukee Coll (IL)
Lurleen B. Wallace Comm Coll (AL)
Macomb Comm Coll (MI)
Minnesota West Comm and Tech Coll (MN)
Mitchell Comm Coll (NC)
Montgomery County Comm Coll (PA)
Mount Wachusett Comm Coll (MA)
Nebraska Indian Comm Coll (NE)
Northwest-Shoals Comm Coll (AL)

Orange Coast Coll (CA)
Palomar Coll (CA)
Pensacola State Coll (FL)
Piedmont Comm Coll (NC)
Rogue Comm Coll (OR)
St. Charles Comm Coll (MO)
Snead State Comm Coll (AL)
Southeast Comm Coll, Lincoln Campus (NE)
Texarkana Coll (TX)
Three Rivers Comm Coll (CT)
Three Rivers Comm Coll (MO)
Tompkins Cortland Comm Coll (NY)
Vincennes U (IN)
Wayne County Comm Coll District (MI)
Westchester Comm Coll (NY)
Williamsburg Tech Coll (SC)
Wor-Wic Comm Coll (MD)

CHILD-CARE PROVISION
Bossier Parish Comm Coll (LA)
Bucks County Comm Coll (PA)
Cañada Coll (CA)
City Colls of Chicago, Kennedy-King College (IL)
City Colls of Chicago, Olive-Harvey College (IL)
Coll of Marin (CA)
Coll of the Canyons (CA)
Collin County Comm Coll District (TX)
Comm Coll of Allegheny County (PA)
Dakota Coll at Bottineau (ND)
Danville Area Comm Coll (IL)
Delta Coll (MI)
Des Moines Area Comm Coll (IA)
Feather River Coll (CA)
Florida SouthWestern State Coll (FL)
Fullerton Coll (CA)
Gulf Coast State Coll (FL)
Harper Coll (IL)
Hawkeye Comm Coll (IA)
Highland Comm Coll (IL)
Hill Coll (TX)
Hinds Comm Coll (MS)
Hudson County Comm Coll (NJ)
Illinois Central Coll (IL)
Illinois Valley Comm Coll (IL)
John Tyler Comm Coll (VA)
J. Sargeant Reynolds Comm Coll (VA)
Kaskaskia Coll (IL)
Kishwaukee Coll (IL)
Lakeland Comm Coll (OH)
Lake Region State Coll (ND)
Lansing Comm Coll (MI)
Louisiana State U at Eunice (LA)
Luzerne County Comm Coll (PA)
McHenry County Coll (IL)
Merced Coll (CA)
Meridian Comm Coll (MS)
Miami Dade Coll (FL)
Montgomery Coll (MD)
Morgan Comm Coll (CO)
Morton Coll (IL)
Mott Comm Coll (MI)
Murray State Coll (OK)
Nunez Comm Coll (LA)
Oakton Comm Coll (IL)
Orange Coast Coll (CA)
Owensboro Comm and Tech Coll (KY)
Palomar Coll (CA)
Pensacola State Coll (FL)
Raritan Valley Comm Coll (NJ)
Rend Lake Coll (IL)
St. Charles Comm Coll (MO)
San Juan Coll (NM)
Santa Monica Coll (CA)
Somerset Comm Coll (KY)
Southern Arkansas U Tech (AR)
South Suburban Coll (IL)
Southwest Virginia Comm Coll (VA)
Trident Tech Coll (SC)
Vincennes U (IN)
Westmoreland County Comm Coll (PA)

CHILD DEVELOPMENT
Albany Tech Coll (GA)
Allen Comm Coll (KS)
Alvin Comm Coll (TX)
Amarillo Coll (TX)
Athens Tech Coll (GA)
Atlanta Tech Coll (GA)
Augusta Tech Coll (GA)
Austin Comm Coll District (TX)
Blinn Coll (TX)
Brookhaven Coll (TX)

Carl Albert State Coll (OK)
Central Georgia Tech Coll (GA)
Chattahoochee Tech Coll (GA)
Citrus Coll (CA)
Cleveland State Comm Coll (TN)
Cloud County Comm Coll (KS)
Coastal Pines Tech Coll (GA)
Collin County Comm Coll District (TX)
Columbus Tech Coll (GA)
Comm Coll of Allegheny County (PA)
Comm Coll of Aurora (CO)
Comm Coll of Vermont (VT)
Daytona State Coll (FL)
De Anza Coll (CA)
Del Mar Coll (TX)
Dodge City Comm Coll (KS)
Dyersburg State Comm Coll (TN)
Edison State Comm Coll (OH)
El Paso Comm Coll (TX)
Frederick Comm Coll (MD)
Georgia Northwestern Tech Coll (GA)
Hennepin Tech Coll (MN)
Housatonic Comm Coll (CT)
Houston Comm Coll (TX)
Howard Comm Coll (MD)
Illinois Eastern Comm Colls, Wabash Valley College (IL)
Illinois Valley Comm Coll (IL)
Ivy Tech Comm Coll–Central Indiana (IN)
James Sprunt Comm Coll (NC)
Jefferson Comm Coll (NY)
Lanier Tech Coll (GA)
Los Angeles City Coll (CA)
Madison Area Tech Coll (WI)
Mesa Comm Coll (AZ)
Metropolitan Comm Coll (NE)
Miami Dade Coll (FL)
Monroe County Comm Coll (MI)
Mt. San Antonio Coll (CA)
Mount Wachusett Comm Coll (MA)
Murray State Coll (OK)
Nashville State Comm Coll (TN)
New River Comm Coll (VA)
Northeastern Jr Coll (CO)
North Shore Comm Coll (MA)
Northwest-Shoals Comm Coll (AL)
Oconee Fall Line Tech Coll (GA)
Ogeechee Tech Coll (GA)
Oklahoma City Comm Coll (OK)
Otero Jr Coll (CO)
Rock Valley Coll (IL)
St. Philip's Coll (TX)
San Jacinto Coll District (TX)
Santa Monica Coll (CA)
Santa Rosa Jr Coll (CA)
Savannah Tech Coll (GA)
Schoolcraft Coll (MI)
Seminole State Coll (OK)
Seminole State Coll of Florida (FL)
Shawnee Comm Coll (IL)
Sierra Coll (CA)
Southeastern Comm Coll (IA)
Southeastern Tech Coll (GA)
Southern Crescent Tech Coll (GA)
Southern Regional Tech Coll (GA)
South Georgia Tech Coll (GA)
South Plains Coll (TX)
Southwestern Comm Coll (NC)
Texarkana Coll (TX)
Tohono O'odham Comm Coll (AZ)
Trinity Valley Comm Coll (TX)
Tyler Jr Coll (TX)
U of Arkansas Comm Coll at Morrilton (AR)
Virginia Western Comm Coll (VA)
Volunteer State Comm Coll (TN)
Walters State Comm Coll (TN)
West Georgia Tech Coll (GA)
Wiregrass Georgia Tech Coll (GA)

CHINESE
Austin Comm Coll District (TX)

CINEMATOGRAPHY AND FILM/ VIDEO PRODUCTION
Bucks County Comm Coll (PA)
Camden County Coll (NJ)
Cape Fear Comm Coll (NC)
Central New Mexico Comm Coll (NM)
Century Coll (MN)
Cerritos Coll (CA)
Coll of Marin (CA)
Coll of the Canyons (CA)
Comm Coll of Aurora (CO)
El Paso Comm Coll (TX)
Hillsborough Comm Coll (FL)

Houston Comm Coll (TX)
Lansing Comm Coll (MI)
Miami Dade Coll (FL)
Mott Comm Coll (MI)
Northcentral Tech Coll (WI)
Oklahoma City Comm Coll (OK)
Orange Coast Coll (CA)
Piedmont Comm Coll (NC)
Raritan Valley Comm Coll (NJ)
Santa Fe Comm Coll (NM)
Santa Monica Coll (CA)

CITY/URBAN, COMMUNITY AND REGIONAL PLANNING
South Florida State Coll (FL)

CIVIL DRAFTING AND CAD/ CADD
Comm Coll of Allegheny County (PA)
Genesee Comm Coll (NY)
Harford Comm Coll (MD)
Renton Tech Coll (WA)

CIVIL ENGINEERING
American Samoa Comm Coll (AS)
Fiorello H. LaGuardia Comm Coll of the City U of New York (NY)
Nashville State Comm Coll (TN)
St. Charles Comm Coll (MO)
South Florida State Coll (FL)
Tidewater Comm Coll (VA)
Truckee Meadows Comm Coll (NV)
Vincennes U (IN)

CIVIL ENGINEERING TECHNOLOGY
Arizona Western Coll (AZ)
Central Maine Comm Coll (ME)
Chattahoochee Tech Coll (GA)
Chippewa Valley Tech Coll (WI)
Columbus State Comm Coll (OH)
Comm Coll of Allegheny County (PA)
Des Moines Area Comm Coll (IA)
Dunwoody Coll of Technology (MN)
Eastern Arizona Coll (AZ)
Erie Comm Coll, North Campus (NY)
Fayetteville Tech Comm Coll (NC)
Florida SouthWestern State Coll (FL)
Gulf Coast State Coll (FL)
Harrisburg Area Comm Coll (PA)
Hawkeye Comm Coll (IA)
Johnson County Comm Coll (KS)
Lakeland Comm Coll (OH)
Lake Superior Coll (MN)
Lansing Comm Coll (MI)
Macomb Comm Coll (MI)
Madison Area Tech Coll (WI)
Mercer County Comm Coll (NJ)
Metropolitan Comm Coll (NE)
Miami Dade Coll (FL)
Middlesex County Coll (NJ)
Minnesota State Comm and Tech Coll (MN)
Minnesota State Comm and Tech Coll–Detroit Lakes (MN)
Mohawk Valley Comm Coll (NY)
Monroe Comm Coll (NY)
Mt. San Antonio Coll (CA)
Nashville State Comm Coll (TN)
Nassau Comm Coll (NY)
Northern Essex Comm Coll (MA)
Pensacola State Coll (FL)
San Joaquin Delta Coll (CA)
Santa Rosa Jr Coll (CA)
Seminole State Coll of Florida (FL)
Southeast Comm Coll, Milford Campus (NE)
South Florida State Coll (FL)
Springfield Tech Comm Coll (MA)
Stark State Coll (OH)
Trident Tech Coll (SC)
Virginia Western Comm Coll (VA)
Westchester Comm Coll (NY)
Wytheville Comm Coll (VA)

CLINICAL LABORATORY SCIENCE/MEDICAL TECHNOLOGY
Amarillo Coll (TX)
Athens Tech Coll (GA)
Casper Coll (WY)
Coll of Central Florida (FL)
Del Mar Coll (TX)
Dodge City Comm Coll (KS)
Howard Comm Coll (MD)
Monroe County Comm Coll (MI)
Southeast Comm Coll, Lincoln Campus (NE)
South Florida State Coll (FL)
Tarrant County Coll District (TX)

CLINICAL/MEDICAL LABORATORY ASSISTANT
Somerset Comm Coll (KY)

CLINICAL/MEDICAL LABORATORY SCIENCE AND ALLIED PROFESSIONS RELATED
Columbus State Comm Coll (OH)
Houston Comm Coll (TX)

CLINICAL/MEDICAL LABORATORY TECHNOLOGY
Alamance Comm Coll (NC)
Alexandria Tech and Comm Coll (MN)
Anne Arundel Comm Coll (MD)
Arapahoe Comm Coll (CO)
Austin Comm Coll District (TX)
Bismarck State Coll (ND)
Blackhawk Tech Coll (WI)
Blue Ridge Comm and Tech Coll (WV)
Bunker Hill Comm Coll (MA)
Camden County Coll (NJ)
Central Georgia Tech Coll (GA)
Central New Mexico Comm Coll (NM)
Central Texas Coll (TX)
Chippewa Valley Tech Coll (WI)
Coastal Pines Tech Coll (GA)
Coll of the Canyons (CA)
Columbus State Comm Coll (OH)
Comm Coll of Allegheny County (PA)
Comm Coll of Baltimore County (MD)
Comm Coll of Philadelphia (PA)
Comm Coll of Rhode Island (RI)
Comm Coll of the Air Force (AL)
Del Mar Coll (TX)
Des Moines Area Comm Coll (IA)
Dutchess Comm Coll (NY)
Edison State Comm Coll (OH)
Elgin Comm Coll (IL)
El Paso Comm Coll (TX)
Erie Comm Coll, North Campus (NY)
Genesee Comm Coll (NY)
Georgia Piedmont Tech Coll (GA)
Greenville Tech Coll (SC)
Halifax Comm Coll (NC)
Harrisburg Area Comm Coll (PA)
Hawkeye Comm Coll (IA)
Hinds Comm Coll (MS)
Housatonic Comm Coll (CT)
Houston Comm Coll (TX)
Hutchinson Comm Coll (KS)
Illinois Central Coll (IL)
Iowa Central Comm Coll (IA)
Ivy Tech Comm Coll–Lafayette (IN)
Ivy Tech Comm Coll–North Central (IN)
Ivy Tech Comm Coll–Sellersburg (IN)
Ivy Tech Comm Coll–Wabash Valley (IN)
Jefferson State Comm Coll (AL)
J. Sargeant Reynolds Comm Coll (VA)
Kaskaskia Coll (IL)
Lake Area Tech Inst (SD)
Lakeland Comm Coll (OH)
Lake Superior Coll (MN)
Lorain County Comm Coll (OH)
Madison Area Tech Coll (WI)
Manchester Comm Coll (CT)
Manhattan Area Tech Coll (KS)
McLennan Comm Coll (TX)
Mercer County Comm Coll (NJ)
Meridian Comm Coll (MS)
Miami Dade Coll (FL)
Middlesex Comm Coll (MA)
Middlesex County Coll (NJ)
Mid-Plains Comm Coll, North Platte (NE)
Minnesota State Comm and Tech Coll (MN)
Minnesota West Comm and Tech Coll (MN)
Mitchell Tech Inst (SD)
Montgomery County Comm Coll (PA)
Mount Wachusett Comm Coll (MA)
Nassau Comm Coll (NY)
Navarro Coll (TX)
New Mexico Jr Coll (NM)
Northcentral Tech Coll (WI)
Northeast Iowa Comm Coll (IA)
Oakton Comm Coll (IL)
Orange Coast Coll (CA)
Panola Coll (TX)
Queensborough Comm Coll of the City U of New York (NY)

Rend Lake Coll (IL)
St. Philip's Coll (TX)
Salt Lake Comm Coll (UT)
San Jacinto Coll District (TX)
San Juan Coll (NM)
Santa Monica Coll (CA)
Seminole State Coll (OK)
Shawnee Comm Coll (IL)
Southeast Comm Coll, Lincoln Campus (NE)
Southern U at Shreveport (LA)
Southwestern Comm Coll (NC)
Spartanburg Comm Coll (SC)
Spencerian Coll (KY)
Spencerian Coll–Lexington (KY)
Springfield Tech Comm Coll (MA)
Stark State Coll (OH)
Tarrant County Coll District (TX)
Three Rivers Comm Coll (MO)
Trident Tech Coll (SC)
Tyler Jr Coll (TX)
Victoria Coll (TX)
Volunteer State Comm Coll (TN)
Waukesha County Tech Coll (WI)
Western Dakota Tech Inst (SD)
Wytheville Comm Coll (VA)

CLINICAL/MEDICAL SOCIAL WORK
Central Texas Coll (TX)
Nebraska Indian Comm Coll (NE)
Southeast Comm Coll, Lincoln Campus (NE)

COMMERCIAL AND ADVERTISING ART
Alamance Comm Coll (NC)
Alexandria Tech and Comm Coll (MN)
Amarillo Coll (TX)
Bismarck State Coll (ND)
Bucks County Comm Coll (PA)
Central Texas Coll (TX)
Collin County Comm Coll District (TX)
Comm Coll of Allegheny County (PA)
Comm Coll of Baltimore County (MD)
Comm Coll of the Air Force (AL)
De Anza Coll (CA)
Des Moines Area Comm Coll (IA)
Dutchess Comm Coll (NY)
East Central Coll (MO)
Eastern Arizona Coll (AZ)
El Paso Comm Coll (TX)
Fashion Inst of Technology (NY)
Fayetteville Tech Comm Coll (NC)
Finger Lakes Comm Coll (NY)
Golden West Coll (CA)
Hagerstown Comm Coll (MD)
Halifax Comm Coll (NC)
Hill Coll (TX)
Housatonic Comm Coll (CT)
James Sprunt Comm Coll (NC)
Kingsborough Comm Coll of the City U of New York (NY)
Lakeland Comm Coll (OH)
Luzerne County Comm Coll (PA)
Macomb Comm Coll (MI)
Madison Area Tech Coll (WI)
Manchester Comm Coll (CT)
Mercer County Comm Coll (NJ)
Metropolitan Comm Coll (NE)
Miami Dade Coll (FL)
Middlesex Comm Coll (MA)
Mid-Plains Comm Coll, North Platte (NE)
Mohawk Valley Comm Coll (NY)
Monroe Comm Coll (NY)
Montgomery Coll (MD)
Montgomery County Comm Coll (PA)
Mt. San Antonio Coll (CA)
Nashville State Comm Coll (TN)
Nassau Comm Coll (NY)
Navarro Coll (TX)
New Mexico Jr Coll (NM)
Northern Essex Comm Coll (MA)
NorthWest Arkansas Comm Coll (AR)
Northwest Coll (WY)
Norwalk Comm Coll (CT)
Oklahoma City Comm Coll (OK)
Orange Coast Coll (CA)
Palomar Coll (CA)
Pensacola State Coll (FL)
Randolph Comm Coll (NC)
St. Charles Comm Coll (MO)
St. Clair County Comm Coll (MI)
San Jacinto Coll District (TX)
San Joaquin Delta Coll (CA)
San Juan Coll (NM)
School of Advertising Art (OH)

Southeast Comm Coll, Lincoln Campus (NE)
South Plains Coll (TX)
Southwestern Comm Coll (NC)
Sowela Tech Comm Coll (LA)
Springfield Tech Comm Coll (MA)
Sullivan County Comm Coll (NY)
Sussex County Comm Coll (NJ)
Tallahassee Comm Coll (FL)
Tidewater Comm Coll (VA)
Tompkins Cortland Comm Coll (NY)
Trident Tech Coll (SC)
Truckee Meadows Comm Coll (NV)
Ulster County Comm Coll (NY)
U of Cincinnati Blue Ash Coll (OH)
Vincennes U (IN)
Virginia Marti Coll of Art and Design (OH)
Virginia Western Comm Coll (VA)
Westchester Comm Coll (NY)
Western Nevada Coll (NV)

COMMERCIAL PHOTOGRAPHY
Austin Comm Coll District (TX)
Bucks County Comm Coll (PA)
Cecil Coll (MD)
Central Wyoming Coll (WY)
Century Coll (MN)
Columbus State Comm Coll (OH)
Fashion Inst of Technology (NY)
Fiorello H. LaGuardia Comm Coll of the City U of New York (NY)
Hawkeye Comm Coll (IA)
Houston Comm Coll (TX)
Luzerne County Comm Coll (PA)
McHenry County Coll (IL)
Mohawk Valley Comm Coll (NY)
Montgomery Coll (MD)
Northwest Coll (WY)
Randolph Comm Coll (NC)
Santa Fe Comm Coll (NM)
Santa Monica Coll (CA)
Sierra Coll (CA)
Springfield Tech Comm Coll (MA)
Trinity Valley Comm Coll (TX)

COMMUNICATION
Arizona Western Coll (AZ)
Asnuntuck Comm Coll (CT)
Central New Mexico Comm Coll (NM)
Northeastern Jr Coll (CO)
Pennsylvania Inst of Technology (PA)
Santa Rosa Jr Coll (CA)

COMMUNICATION AND JOURNALISM RELATED
Cayuga County Comm Coll (NY)
Harrisburg Area Comm Coll (PA)
Ivy Tech Comm Coll–Kokomo (IN)
Queensborough Comm Coll of the City U of New York (NY)

COMMUNICATION AND MEDIA RELATED
County Coll of Morris (NJ)
Manor Coll (PA)
Raritan Valley Comm Coll (NJ)

COMMUNICATIONS SYSTEMS INSTALLATION AND REPAIR TECHNOLOGY
Cayuga County Comm Coll (NY)
Des Moines Area Comm Coll (IA)
Dutchess Comm Coll (NY)
Erie Comm Coll, South Campus (NY)
Westmoreland County Comm Coll (PA)

COMMUNICATIONS TECHNOLOGIES AND SUPPORT SERVICES RELATED
Anne Arundel Comm Coll (MD)
Bowling Green State U–Firelands Coll (OH)
Comm Coll of Allegheny County (PA)
Comm Coll of Baltimore County (MD)
Middlesex County Coll (NJ)
Montgomery Coll (MD)
Montgomery County Comm Coll (PA)

COMMUNICATIONS TECHNOLOGY
Athens Tech Coll (GA)
Comm Coll of the Air Force (AL)
Daytona State Coll (FL)
Dodge City Comm Coll (KS)
Gulf Coast State Coll (FL)
Hutchinson Comm Coll (KS)
Lackawanna Coll (PA)
Madison Area Tech Coll (WI)
Mott Comm Coll (MI)
Pensacola State Coll (FL)

Pueblo Comm Coll (CO)
Vincennes U (IN)

COMMUNITY HEALTH AND PREVENTIVE MEDICINE
Anoka-Ramsey Comm Coll (MN)
Arizona Western Coll (AZ)
Massachusetts Bay Comm Coll (MA)
Quinsigamond Comm Coll (MA)

COMMUNITY HEALTH SERVICES COUNSELING
Comm Coll of Allegheny County (PA)
Dutchess Comm Coll (NY)
Florida SouthWestern State Coll (FL)
Illinois Central Coll (IL)
Kingsborough Comm Coll of the City U of New York (NY)
Lake Area Tech Inst (SD)
Miami Dade Coll (FL)
Mott Comm Coll (MI)
Santa Rosa Jr Coll (CA)

COMMUNITY ORGANIZATION AND ADVOCACY
Berkshire Comm Coll (MA)
Borough of Manhattan Comm Coll of the City U of New York (NY)
Cleveland State Comm Coll (TN)
Clinton Comm Coll (NY)
Comm Coll of Vermont (VT)
Del Mar Coll (TX)
Iowa Central Comm Coll (IA)
Jefferson Comm Coll (NY)
Kellogg Comm Coll (MI)
Lansing Comm Coll (MI)
Mercer County Comm Coll (NJ)
New River Comm Coll (VA)
Ulster County Comm Coll (NY)
Westchester Comm Coll (NY)

COMPARATIVE LITERATURE
Blinn Coll (TX)
Miami Dade Coll (FL)
Otero Jr Coll (CO)
San Joaquin Delta Coll (CA)

COMPUTER AND INFORMATION SCIENCES
Aaniiih Nakoda Coll (MT)
Albany Tech Coll (GA)
Ancilla Coll (IN)
Anne Arundel Comm Coll (MD)
Arapahoe Comm Coll (CO)
Arizona Western Coll (AZ)
Austin Comm Coll District (TX)
Berkshire Comm Coll (MA)
Bevill State Comm Coll (AL)
Borough of Manhattan Comm Coll of the City U of New York (NY)
Bucks County Comm Coll (PA)
Camden County Coll (NJ)
Carl Albert State Coll (OK)
Cayuga County Comm Coll (NY)
Central New Mexico Comm Coll (NM)
Central Virginia Comm Coll (VA)
Chandler-Gilbert Comm Coll (AZ)
Coll of Central Florida (FL)
Coll of the Ouachitas (AR)
Collin County Comm Coll District (TX)
Columbia-Greene Comm Coll (NY)
Columbus State Comm Coll (OH)
Comm Coll of Baltimore County (MD)
Comm Coll of Rhode Island (RI)
Comm Coll of Vermont (VT)
Dakota Coll at Bottineau (ND)
Dyersburg State Comm Coll (TN)
Edison State Comm Coll (OH)
El Paso Comm Coll (TX)
Erie Comm Coll, North Campus (NY)
Finger Lakes Comm Coll (NY)
Front Range Comm Coll (CO)
Gateway Comm and Tech Coll (KY)
Georgia Highlands Coll (GA)
Grand Rapids Comm Coll (MI)
Great Basin Coll (NV)
Hagerstown Comm Coll (MD)
Harford Comm Coll (MD)
Harper Coll (IL)
Harrisburg Area Comm Coll (PA)
H. Councill Trenholm State Comm Coll (AL)
Hill Coll (TX)
Hudson County Comm Coll (NJ)
Hutchinson Comm Coll (KS)
Ivy Tech Comm Coll–Bloomington (IN)
Ivy Tech Comm Coll–Central Indiana (IN)
Ivy Tech Comm Coll–Columbus (IN)

Ivy Tech Comm Coll–East Central (IN)
Ivy Tech Comm Coll–Kokomo (IN)
Ivy Tech Comm Coll–Lafayette (IN)
Ivy Tech Comm Coll–North Central (IN)
Ivy Tech Comm Coll–Northeast (IN)
Ivy Tech Comm Coll–Northwest (IN)
Ivy Tech Comm Coll–Richmond (IN)
Ivy Tech Comm Coll–Sellersburg (IN)
Ivy Tech Comm Coll–Southeast (IN)
Ivy Tech Comm Coll–Southwest (IN)
Ivy Tech Comm Coll–Wabash Valley (IN)
Jamestown Comm Coll (NY)
Jefferson Comm Coll (NY)
Jefferson State Comm Coll (AL)
John Tyler Comm Coll (VA)
J. Sargeant Reynolds Comm Coll (VA)
Kingsborough Comm Coll of the City U of New York (NY)
Lackawanna Coll (PA)
Lansing Comm Coll (MI)
Lehigh Carbon Comm Coll (PA)
Lone Star Coll–CyFair (TX)
Lone Star Coll–Kingwood (TX)
Lurleen B. Wallace Comm Coll (AL)
Luzerne County Comm Coll (PA)
Maysville Comm and Tech Coll, Maysville (KY)
Mesa Comm Coll (AZ)
Middlesex Comm Coll (MA)
Middlesex County Coll (NJ)
Mid-Plains Comm Coll, North Platte (NE)
Mohawk Valley Comm Coll (NY)
Montgomery Coll (MD)
Montgomery County Comm Coll (PA)
Mt. San Antonio Coll (CA)
Mount Wachusett Comm Coll (MA)
Murray State Coll (OK)
Nassau Comm Coll (NY)
NHTI, Concord's Comm Coll, Concord (NH)
Northeast Comm Coll (NE)
Northern Essex Comm Coll (MA)
Northwest-Shoals Comm Coll (AL)
Owensboro Comm and Tech Coll (KY)
Paris Jr Coll (TX)
Penn Foster Coll (AZ)
Pensacola State Coll (FL)
Pueblo Comm Coll (CO)
Quinsigamond Comm Coll (MA)
Rogue Comm Coll (OR)
Salt Lake Comm Coll (UT)
San Jacinto Coll District (TX)
Santa Fe Comm Coll (NM)
Snead State Comm Coll (AL)
Somerset Comm Coll (KY)
Southeast Comm Coll, Lincoln Campus (NE)
Southern Arkansas U Tech (AR)
South Florida State Coll (FL)
Southwest Virginia Comm Coll (VA)
Stark State Coll (OH)
State U of New York Coll of Technology at Alfred (NY)
Sussex County Comm Coll (NJ)
Texarkana Coll (TX)
Tompkins Cortland Comm Coll (NY)
Treasure Valley Comm Coll (OR)
Ulster County Comm Coll (NY)
Vincennes U (IN)
Volunteer State Comm Coll (TN)
Walters State Comm Coll (TN)
Westchester Comm Coll (NY)
Western Nevada Coll (NV)
Western Wyoming Comm Coll (WY)
White Mountains Comm Coll (NH)
Wor-Wic Comm Coll (MD)

COMPUTER AND INFORMATION SCIENCES AND SUPPORT SERVICES RELATED
Bowling Green State U–Firelands Coll (OH)
Bunker Hill Comm Coll (MA)
Cayuga County Comm Coll (NY)
Chandler-Gilbert Comm Coll (AZ)
Chesapeake Coll (MD)
Dakota Coll at Bottineau (ND)
Del Mar Coll (TX)
Des Moines Area Comm Coll (IA)
Fiorello H. LaGuardia Comm Coll of the City U of New York (NY)
Jefferson Comm Coll (NY)
Los Angeles City Coll (CA)
Massachusetts Bay Comm Coll (MA)
Middlesex Comm Coll (MA)

Mohawk Valley Comm Coll (NY)
Monroe Comm Coll (NY)
Northcentral Tech Coll (WI)
Raritan Valley Comm Coll (NJ)
Rio Salado Coll (AZ)
Seminole State Coll of Florida (FL)
Sierra Coll (CA)
Southeastern Coll–West Palm Beach (FL)
Westchester Comm Coll (NY)

COMPUTER AND INFORMATION SCIENCES RELATED
Central Oregon Comm Coll (OR)
Citrus Coll (CA)
Daytona State Coll (FL)
Del Mar Coll (TX)
Delta Coll (MI)
Genesee Comm Coll (NY)
Howard Comm Coll (MD)
Los Angeles City Coll (CA)
Luzerne County Comm Coll (PA)
Mohave Comm Coll (AZ)
Monroe Comm Coll (NY)
Monroe County Comm Coll (MI)
Nashville State Comm Coll (TN)
Nassau Comm Coll (NY)
North Shore Comm Coll (MA)
Pensacola State Coll (FL)
Rio Salado Coll (AZ)
Seminole State Coll of Florida (FL)

COMPUTER AND INFORMATION SYSTEMS SECURITY
Anne Arundel Comm Coll (MD)
Blue Ridge Comm and Tech Coll (WV)
Bunker Hill Comm Coll (MA)
Casper Coll (WY)
Central Texas Coll (TX)
Century Coll (MN)
Chattahoochee Tech Coll (GA)
Chesapeake Coll (MD)
Cochise County Comm Coll District (AZ)
Collin County Comm Coll District (TX)
Comm Coll of Baltimore County (MD)
Craven Comm Coll (NC)
Delta Coll (MI)
Donnelly Coll (KS)
Dyersburg State Comm Coll (TN)
Edison State Comm Coll (OH)
Elgin Comm Coll (IL)
Fayetteville Tech Comm Coll (NC)
Fox Valley Tech Coll (WI)
Georgia Military Coll (GA)
Grand Rapids Comm Coll (MI)
Hagerstown Comm Coll (MD)
Harrisburg Area Comm Coll (PA)
Hinds Comm Coll (MS)
Lanier Tech Coll (GA)
Lehigh Carbon Comm Coll (PA)
Massachusetts Bay Comm Coll (MA)
Minnesota State Comm and Tech Coll (MN)
Minnesota State Comm and Tech Coll–Detroit Lakes (MN)
Minnesota West Comm and Tech Coll (MN)
Mohawk Valley Comm Coll (NY)
Montgomery Coll (MD)
Northampton Comm Coll (PA)
Norwalk Comm Coll (CT)
Pensacola State Coll (FL)
Quinsigamond Comm Coll (MA)
Rowan-Cabarrus Comm Coll (NC)
St. Philip's Coll (TX)
Seminole State Coll of Florida (FL)
Southern Crescent Tech Coll (GA)
Springfield Tech Comm Coll (MA)
Texas State Tech Coll (TX)
Westchester Comm Coll (NY)
Westmoreland County Comm Coll (PA)
Wiregrass Georgia Tech Coll (GA)

COMPUTER ENGINEERING
Carroll Comm Coll (MD)
Comm Coll of Baltimore County (MD)
Daytona State Coll (FL)
Pensacola State Coll (FL)
South Florida State Coll (FL)

COMPUTER ENGINEERING RELATED
Columbus Tech Coll (GA)
Daytona State Coll (FL)
Monroe Comm Coll (NY)
Seminole State Coll of Florida (FL)

COMPUTER ENGINEERING TECHNOLOGIES RELATED
Lorain County Comm Coll (OH)

COMPUTER ENGINEERING TECHNOLOGY
Alvin Comm Coll (TX)
Amarillo Coll (TX)
Brookhaven Coll (TX)
Carteret Comm Coll (NC)
Coll of The Albemarle (NC)
Comm Coll of Allegheny County (PA)
Comm Coll of Rhode Island (RI)
Des Moines Area Comm Coll (IA)
Georgia Piedmont Tech Coll (GA)
Houston Comm Coll (TX)
Hudson County Comm Coll (NJ)
Iowa Central Comm Coll (IA)
Lakeland Comm Coll (OH)
Lenoir Comm Coll (NC)
Lorain County Comm Coll (OH)
Los Angeles City Coll (CA)
Madison Area Tech Coll (WI)
McLennan Comm Coll (TX)
Miami Dade Coll (FL)
Middlesex Comm Coll (MA)
Minnesota State Comm and Tech
   Coll (MN)
Minnesota West Comm and Tech
   Coll (MN)
Monroe Comm Coll (NY)
Monroe County Comm Coll (MI)
Mt. San Antonio Coll (CA)
Nashville State Comm Coll (TN)
Naugatuck Valley Comm Coll (CT)
New River Comm Coll (VA)
NHTI, Concord's Comm Coll,
   Concord (NH)
North Central Missouri Coll (MO)
Northern Essex Comm Coll (MA)
North Shore Comm Coll (MA)
Oklahoma City Comm Coll (OK)
Paris Jr Coll (TX)
Queensborough Comm Coll of the
   City U of New York (NY)
Quinsigamond Comm Coll (MA)
Richmond Comm Coll (NC)
Rock Valley Coll (IL)
Seminole State Coll of Florida (FL)
South Florida State Coll (FL)
South Plains Coll (TX)
Southwestern Comm Coll (NC)
Southwest Texas Jr Coll (TX)
Springfield Tech Comm Coll (MA)
State U of New York Coll of
   Technology at Alfred (NY)
Three Rivers Comm Coll (CT)
Trident Tech Coll (SC)

COMPUTER GRAPHICS
Arizona Western Coll (AZ)
Carroll Comm Coll (MD)
Citrus Coll (CA)
Coll of the Desert (CA)
Daytona State Coll (FL)
De Anza Coll (CA)
Genesee Comm Coll (NY)
Great Basin Coll (NV)
Howard Comm Coll (MD)
Hudson County Comm Coll (NJ)
Kellogg Comm Coll (MI)
Lansdale School of Business (PA)
Luzerne County Comm Coll (PA)
Mercer County Comm Coll (NJ)
Mesabi Range Coll (MN)
Miami Dade Coll (FL)
Monroe County Comm Coll (MI)
Mt. San Antonio Coll (CA)
Mount Wachusett Comm Coll (MA)
Nassau Comm Coll (NY)
Navarro Coll (TX)
New Mexico Jr Coll (NM)
New River Comm Coll (VA)
Northern Essex Comm Coll (MA)
North Shore Comm Coll (MA)
Orange Coast Coll (CA)
Palomar Coll (CA)
Pittsburgh Tech Coll (PA)
Quinsigamond Comm Coll (MA)
Schoolcraft Coll (MI)
Seminole State Coll of Florida (FL)
Shawnee Comm Coll (IL)
Sullivan County Comm Coll (NY)
Tallahassee Comm Coll (FL)
Trident Tech Coll (SC)
Weatherford Coll (TX)

COMPUTER HARDWARE ENGINEERING
Seminole State Coll of Florida (FL)

COMPUTER/INFORMATION TECHNOLOGY SERVICES ADMINISTRATION RELATED
Bossier Parish Comm Coll (LA)
Bunker Hill Comm Coll (MA)
Clinton Comm Coll (NY)
Daytona State Coll (FL)
Dutchess Comm Coll (NY)
Hawkeye Comm Coll (IA)
Hesston Coll (KS)
Howard Comm Coll (MD)
Jefferson Comm Coll (NY)
Massachusetts Bay Comm Coll (MA)
Mesabi Range Coll (MN)
Panola Coll (TX)
Seminole State Coll of Florida (FL)
Trident Tech Coll (SC)
Vincennes U (IN)

COMPUTER INSTALLATION AND REPAIR TECHNOLOGY
Delta Coll (MI)
Fiorello H. LaGuardia Comm Coll of
   the City U of New York (NY)
Genesee Comm Coll (NY)
Hinds Comm Coll (MS)
Lake Region State Coll (ND)
Merced Coll (CA)
Miami Dade Coll (FL)
Orange Coast Coll (CA)
Penn Foster Coll (AZ)
Queensborough Comm Coll of the
   City U of New York (NY)
Sierra Coll (CA)

COMPUTER NUMERICALLY CONTROLLED (CNC) MACHINIST TECHNOLOGY
Anoka Tech Coll (MN)
Dunwoody Coll of Technology (MN)
Greenville Tech Coll (SC)
Hennepin Tech Coll (MN)
Lake Superior Coll (MN)
Wayne County Comm Coll District
   (MI)

COMPUTER PROGRAMMING
Alvin Comm Coll (TX)
Amarillo Coll (TX)
Athens Tech Coll (GA)
Atlanta Tech Coll (GA)
Augusta Tech Coll (GA)
Austin Comm Coll District (TX)
Brookhaven Coll (TX)
Bunker Hill Comm Coll (MA)
Caldwell Comm Coll and Tech Inst
   (NC)
Casper Coll (WY)
Central Georgia Tech Coll (GA)
Central Texas Coll (TX)
Cerritos Coll (CA)
Chandler-Gilbert Comm Coll (AZ)
Chattahoochee Tech Coll (GA)
Chippewa Valley Tech Coll (WI)
Cochise County Comm Coll District
   (AZ)
Coll of The Albemarle (NC)
Daytona State Coll (FL)
De Anza Coll (CA)
Del Mar Coll (TX)
Delta Coll (MI)
Dodge City Comm Coll (KS)
Edison State Comm Coll (OH)
El Paso Comm Coll (TX)
Fayetteville Tech Comm Coll (NC)
Feather River Coll (CA)
Fiorello H. LaGuardia Comm Coll of
   the City U of New York (NY)
Florida Keys Comm Coll (FL)
Florida SouthWestern State Coll (FL)
Fox Valley Tech Coll (WI)
Gateway Tech Coll (WI)
Georgia Northwestern Tech Coll
   (GA)
Georgia Piedmont Tech Coll (GA)
Grand Rapids Comm Coll (MI)
Gulf Coast State Coll (FL)
Gwinnett Tech Coll (GA)
Harper Coll (IL)
Hennepin Tech Coll (MN)
Hill Coll (TX)
Hinds Comm Coll (MS)
Houston Comm Coll (TX)
Illinois Central Coll (IL)
Illinois Valley Comm Coll (IL)
Johnson County Comm Coll (KS)
J. Sargeant Reynolds Comm Coll
   (VA)
Kellogg Comm Coll (MI)
Lanier Tech Coll (GA)

Laramie County Comm Coll (WY)
Lehigh Carbon Comm Coll (PA)
Lone Star Coll–Tomball (TX)
Louisiana State U at Eunice (LA)
Macomb Comm Coll (MI)
Madison Area Tech Coll (WI)
Metropolitan Comm Coll (NE)
Miami Dade Coll (FL)
Middlesex Comm Coll (MA)
Minnesota State Coll–Southeast
   Tech (MN)
Minnesota State Comm and Tech
   Coll (MN)
Minnesota State Comm and Tech
   Coll–Moorhead (MN)
Mitchell Comm Coll (NC)
Mohawk Valley Comm Coll (NY)
Montgomery County Comm Coll (PA)
Mott Comm Coll (MI)
Navarro Coll (TX)
New Mexico Jr Coll (NM)
Northampton Comm Coll (PA)
Northern Essex Comm Coll (MA)
North Shore Comm Coll (MA)
NorthWest Arkansas Comm Coll
   (AR)
Oakton Comm Coll (IL)
Orange Coast Coll (CA)
Palomar Coll (CA)
Pensacola State Coll (FL)
Pittsburgh Tech Coll (PA)
Rend Lake Coll (IL)
Rowan-Cabarrus Comm Coll (NC)
St. Charles Comm Coll (MO)
St. Clair County Comm Coll (MI)
St. Philip's Coll (TX)
Santa Fe Comm Coll (NM)
Santa Monica Coll (CA)
Schoolcraft Coll (MI)
Seminole State Coll of Florida (FL)
Sierra Coll (CA)
Southeastern Comm Coll (IA)
Southern Crescent Tech Coll (GA)
South Florida State Coll (FL)
South Plains Coll (TX)
Southwestern Michigan Coll (MI)
Sowela Tech Comm Coll (LA)
Tallahassee Comm Coll (FL)
Tarrant County Coll District (TX)
Texas State Tech Coll (TX)
Tidewater Comm Coll (VA)
Vincennes U (IN)
Waukesha County Tech Coll (WI)
Wayne County Comm Coll District
   (MI)
Weatherford Coll (TX)
Westmoreland County Comm Coll
   (PA)
Wiregrass Georgia Tech Coll (GA)
Wisconsin Indianhead Tech Coll (WI)

COMPUTER PROGRAMMING RELATED
Del Mar Coll (TX)
Genesee Comm Coll (NY)
Lorain County Comm Coll (OH)
Luzerne County Comm Coll (PA)
Mesabi Range Coll (MN)
Northern Essex Comm Coll (MA)
Rio Salado Coll (AZ)
Seminole State Coll of Florida (FL)

COMPUTER PROGRAMMING (SPECIFIC APPLICATIONS)
Bunker Hill Comm Coll (MA)
Coll of The Albemarle (NC)
Columbus State Comm Coll (OH)
Comm Coll of Rhode Island (RI)
Craven Comm Coll (NC)
Danville Area Comm Coll (IL)
Daytona State Coll (FL)
Del Mar Coll (TX)
Des Moines Area Comm Coll (IA)
Grand Rapids Comm Coll (MI)
Harper Coll (IL)
Hillsborough Comm Coll (FL)
Holyoke Comm Coll (MA)
Houston Comm Coll (TX)
Humacao Comm Coll (PR)
Johnson County Comm Coll (KS)
Kellogg Comm Coll (MI)
Kent State U at Ashtabula (OH)
Kent State U at East Liverpool (OH)
Kent State U at Salem (OH)
Kent State U at Trumbull (OH)
Kent State U at Tuscarawas (OH)
Lakeland Comm Coll (OH)
Lansing Comm Coll (MI)
Lehigh Carbon Comm Coll (PA)
Macomb Comm Coll (MI)

Manor Coll (PA)
Mesabi Range Coll (MN)
Miami Dade Coll (FL)
Mitchell Comm Coll (NC)
Mohave Comm Coll (AZ)
Monroe County Comm Coll (MI)
Mott Comm Coll (MI)
NHTI, Concord's Comm Coll,
   Concord (NH)
Northeast Iowa Comm Coll (IA)
Northern Essex Comm Coll (MA)
North Shore Comm Coll (MA)
Pensacola State Coll (FL)
Quinsigamond Comm Coll (MA)
Schoolcraft Coll (OH)
Seminole State Coll of Florida (FL)
Springfield Tech Comm Coll (MA)
Stark State Coll (OH)
Sullivan County Comm Coll (NY)
Tallahassee Comm Coll (FL)
Trident Tech Coll (SC)
Truckee Meadows Comm Coll (NV)
Western Wyoming Comm Coll (WY)
Westmoreland County Comm Coll
   (PA)

COMPUTER PROGRAMMING (VENDOR/PRODUCT CERTIFICATION)
Chandler-Gilbert Comm Coll (AZ)
Del Mar Coll (TX)
Gulf Coast State Coll (FL)
Miami Dade Coll (FL)
Pensacola State Coll (FL)
Raritan Valley Comm Coll (NJ)
Seminole State Coll of Florida (FL)

COMPUTER SCIENCE
Adirondack Comm Coll (NY)
Allen Comm Coll (KS)
Amarillo Coll (TX)
Anoka-Ramsey Comm Coll (MN)
Blinn Coll (TX)
Borough of Manhattan Comm Coll of
   the City U of New York (NY)
Bunker Hill Comm Coll (MA)
Cañada Coll (CA)
Central New Mexico Comm Coll
   (NM)
Central Oregon Comm Coll (OR)
Central Wyoming Coll (WY)
Century Coll (MN)
Cerritos Coll (CA)
Chesapeake Coll (MD)
Citrus Coll (CA)
Cochise County Comm Coll District
   (AZ)
Coll of Marin (CA)
Coll of the Canyons (CA)
Coll of the Desert (CA)
Collin County Comm Coll District
   (TX)
Comm Coll of Philadelphia (PA)
Comm Coll of Vermont (VT)
County Coll of Morris (NJ)
Daytona State Coll (FL)
De Anza Coll (CA)
Del Mar Coll (TX)
Dodge City Comm Coll (KS)
Dutchess Comm Coll (NY)
Finger Lakes Comm Coll (NY)
Fiorello H. LaGuardia Comm Coll of
   the City U of New York (NY)
Frederick Comm Coll (MD)
Fullerton Coll (CA)
Genesee Comm Coll (NY)
Georgia Military Coll (GA)
Gordon State Coll (GA)
Guam Comm Coll (GU)
Gwinnett Tech Coll (GA)
Harford Comm Coll (MD)
Harper Coll (IL)
Harrisburg Area Comm Coll (PA)
Houston Comm Coll (TX)
Howard Comm Coll (MD)
Ivy Tech Comm Coll–Bloomington
   (IN)
Ivy Tech Comm Coll–Central Indiana
   (IN)
Ivy Tech Comm Coll–Columbus (IN)
Ivy Tech Comm Coll–East Central
   (IN)
Ivy Tech Comm Coll–Kokomo (IN)
Ivy Tech Comm Coll–Lafayette (IN)
Ivy Tech Comm Coll–Northeast (IN)
Ivy Tech Comm Coll–Richmond (IN)
Ivy Tech Comm Coll–Sellersburg (IN)
Ivy Tech Comm Coll–Southeast (IN)
Ivy Tech Comm Coll–Southwest (IN)

Ivy Tech Comm Coll–Wabash Valley
   (IN)
Jefferson Comm Coll (NY)
Kingsborough Comm Coll of the City
   U of New York (NY)
Lake Area Tech Inst (SD)
Lanier Tech Coll (GA)
Laramie County Comm Coll (WY)
Lone Star Coll–CyFair (TX)
Lone Star Coll–Kingwood (TX)
Lone Star Coll–Montgomery (TX)
Lone Star Coll–North Harris (TX)
Lone Star Coll–Tomball (TX)
Luzerne County Comm Coll (PA)
Massachusetts Bay Comm Coll (MA)
Merced Coll (CA)
Mercer County Comm Coll (NJ)
Miami Dade Coll (FL)
Minnesota West Comm and Tech
   Coll (MN)
Mohave Comm Coll (AZ)
Monroe Comm Coll (NY)
Mt. San Antonio Coll (CA)
Nashville State Comm Coll (TN)
Nassau Comm Coll (NY)
Navarro Coll (TX)
New Mexico Jr Coll (NM)
Niagara County Comm Coll (NY)
Northampton Comm Coll (PA)
Northeast Comm Coll (NE)
Northern Essex Comm Coll (MA)
North Shore Comm Coll (MA)
Oklahoma City Comm Coll (OK)
Orange Coast Coll (CA)
Panola Coll (TX)
Pennsylvania Inst of Technology (PA)
Pensacola State Coll (FL)
Quinsigamond Comm Coll (MA)
Renton Tech Coll (WA)
Rio Salado Coll (AZ)
Rock Valley Coll (IL)
Rogue Comm Coll (OR)
St. Philip's Coll (TX)
Salt Lake Comm Coll (UT)
San Joaquin Delta Coll (CA)
Santa Monica Coll (CA)
Santa Rosa Jr Coll (CA)
Seminole State Coll (OK)
Southern Arkansas U Tech (AR)
Southern U at Shreveport (LA)
South Plains Coll (TX)
Springfield Tech Comm Coll (MA)
Tarrant County Coll District (TX)
Trinity Valley Comm Coll (TX)
Tyler Jr Coll (TX)
Vincennes U (IN)
Virginia Western Comm Coll (VA)
Western Wyoming Comm Coll (WY)
York County Comm Coll (ME)

COMPUTER SOFTWARE AND MEDIA APPLICATIONS RELATED
Carteret Comm Coll (NC)
The Coll of Westchester (NY)
Dakota Coll at Bottineau (ND)
Genesee Comm Coll (NY)
Lansdale School of Business (PA)
Mesabi Range Coll (MN)
Seminole State Coll of Florida (FL)
Southern Arkansas U Tech (AR)

COMPUTER SOFTWARE ENGINEERING
Seminole State Coll of Florida (FL)

COMPUTER SOFTWARE TECHNOLOGY
Coconino Comm Coll (AZ)
Miami Dade Coll (FL)
Rogue Comm Coll (OR)

COMPUTER SUPPORT SPECIALIST
Comm Coll of Rhode Island (RI)
Fox Valley Tech Coll (WI)
Gateway Tech Coll (WI)
Genesee Comm Coll (NY)
Grand Rapids Comm Coll (MI)
Lake Superior Coll (MN)
Miami Dade Coll (FL)
Mitchell Tech Inst (SD)
Morton Coll (IL)
Northampton Comm Coll (PA)
Northland Comm and Tech Coll (MN)
Tompkins Cortland Comm Coll (NY)
Waukesha County Tech Coll (WI)
Westmoreland County Comm Coll
   (PA)
Wisconsin Indianhead Tech Coll (WI)

COMPUTER SYSTEMS ANALYSIS

Amarillo Coll (TX)
Cerritos Coll (CA)
Chandler-Gilbert Comm Coll (AZ)
Crowder Coll (MO)
Florida Keys Comm Coll (FL)
Hillsborough Comm Coll (FL)
Hutchinson Comm Coll (KS)
Lakeland Comm Coll (OH)
Mesa Comm Coll (AZ)
Mitchell Comm Coll (NC)
Northcentral Tech Coll (WI)
Oklahoma City Comm Coll (OK)
Pensacola State Coll (FL)
Quinsigamond Comm Coll (MA)
Tohono O'odham Comm Coll (AZ)
Wor-Wic Comm Coll (MD)

COMPUTER SYSTEMS NETWORKING AND TELECOMMUNICATIONS

Adirondack Comm Coll (NY)
Alexandria Tech and Comm Coll (MN)
Allen Comm Coll (KS)
Anne Arundel Comm Coll (MD)
Anoka-Ramsey Comm Coll (MN)
Arapahoe Comm Coll (CO)
Athens Tech Coll (GA)
Augusta Tech Coll (GA)
Austin Comm Coll District (TX)
Bismarck State Coll (ND)
Blackhawk Tech Coll (WI)
Blinn Coll (TX)
Bowling Green State U–Firelands Coll (OH)
Bucks County Comm Coll (PA)
Bunker Hill Comm Coll (MA)
Cañada Coll (CA)
Cape Fear Comm Coll (NC)
Carteret Comm Coll (NC)
Central Georgia Tech Coll (GA)
Central Oregon Comm Coll (OR)
Century Coll (MN)
Cerritos Coll (CA)
Chandler-Gilbert Comm Coll (AZ)
Chattahoochee Tech Coll (GA)
Chippewa Valley Tech Coll (WI)
Coastal Pines Tech Coll (GA)
Cochise County Comm Coll District (AZ)
Coll of Business and Technology–Flagler Campus (FL)
Coll of Business and Technology–Miami Gardens (FL)
Coll of Marin (CA)
Coll of the Canyons (CA)
Columbus Tech Coll (GA)
Comm Coll of Allegheny County (PA)
Comm Coll of Baltimore County (MD)
Comm Coll of Rhode Island (RI)
Comm Coll of Vermont (VT)
Craven Comm Coll (NC)
Crowder Coll (MO)
Danville Area Comm Coll (IL)
Daytona State Coll (FL)
Del Mar Coll (TX)
Delta Coll (MI)
Dunwoody Coll of Technology (MN)
East Central Coll (MO)
Eastern Idaho Tech Coll (ID)
Eastern Wyoming Coll (WY)
Edison State Comm Coll (OH)
Fayetteville Tech Comm Coll (NC)
Fiorello H. LaGuardia Comm Coll of the City U of New York (NY)
Florida SouthWestern State Coll (FL)
Fox Valley Tech Coll (WI)
Front Range Comm Coll (CO)
Gateway Tech Coll (WI)
Genesee Comm Coll (NY)
Georgia Piedmont Tech Coll (GA)
Grand Rapids Comm Coll (MI)
Great Basin Coll (NV)
Great Falls Coll Montana State U (MT)
Guam Comm Coll (GU)
Gulf Coast State Coll (FL)
Gwinnett Tech Coll (GA)
Harrisburg Area Comm Coll (PA)
Hawkeye Comm Coll (IA)
Haywood Comm Coll (NC)
Hennepin Tech Coll (MN)
Hinds Comm Coll (MS)
Houston Comm Coll (TX)
Howard Comm Coll (MD)
Hutchinson Comm Coll (KS)
Illinois Central Coll (IL)
Illinois Eastern Comm Colls, Lincoln Trail College (IL)

Illinois Valley Comm Coll (IL)
Ivy Tech Comm Coll–Bloomington (IN)
Ivy Tech Comm Coll–East Central (IN)
Ivy Tech Comm Coll–Kokomo (IN)
Ivy Tech Comm Coll–Lafayette (IN)
Ivy Tech Comm Coll–Sellersburg (IN)
Ivy Tech Comm Coll–Wabash Valley (IN)
Johnson County Comm Coll (KS)
J. Sargeant Reynolds Comm Coll (VA)
Lakeland Comm Coll (OH)
Lake Superior Coll (MN)
Lanier Tech Coll (GA)
Lansdale School of Business (PA)
Lansing Comm Coll (MI)
Lehigh Carbon Comm Coll (PA)
Lenoir Comm Coll (NC)
Lorain County Comm Coll (OH)
Luzerne County Comm Coll (PA)
Manhattan Area Tech Coll (KS)
McHenry County Coll (IL)
Mercer County Comm Coll (NJ)
Mesabi Range Coll (MN)
Mesa Comm Coll (AZ)
Miami Dade Coll (FL)
Minnesota State Coll–Southeast Tech (MN)
Minnesota State Comm and Tech Coll (MN)
Minnesota State Comm and Tech Coll–Moorhead (MN)
Minnesota West Comm and Tech Coll (MN)
Montgomery County Comm Coll (PA)
Mott Comm Coll (MI)
Mountain View Coll (TX)
Nashville State Comm Coll (TN)
Nassau Comm Coll (NY)
NHTI, Concord's Comm Coll, Concord (NH)
Northampton Comm Coll (PA)
Northcentral Tech Coll (WI)
Northern Essex Comm Coll (MA)
Northern Maine Comm Coll (ME)
North Georgia Tech Coll (GA)
Northland Comm and Tech Coll (MN)
Norwalk Comm Coll (CT)
Oconee Fall Line Tech Coll (GA)
Ogeechee Tech Coll (GA)
Oklahoma City Comm Coll (OK)
Olympic Coll (WA)
Ozarks Tech Comm Coll (MO)
Palomar Coll (CA)
Randolph Comm Coll (NC)
Raritan Valley Comm Coll (NJ)
Renton Tech Coll (WA)
Rock Valley Coll (IL)
St. Clair County Comm Coll (MI)
Savannah Tech Coll (GA)
Seminole State Coll of Florida (FL)
Shawnee Comm Coll (IL)
Sierra Coll (CA)
Southeastern Coll–West Palm Beach (FL)
Southeastern Tech Coll (GA)
Southern Crescent Tech Coll (GA)
Southern Regional Tech Coll (GA)
South Georgia Tech Coll (GA)
Southwestern Michigan Coll (MI)
Sowela Tech Comm Coll (LA)
Stark State Coll (OH)
Tallahassee Comm Coll (FL)
Three Rivers Comm Coll (MO)
Trident Tech Coll (SC)
Truckee Meadows Comm Coll (NV)
Tyler Jr Coll (TX)
Vincennes U (IN)
Waukesha County Tech Coll (WI)
Western Dakota Tech Inst (SD)
West Georgia Tech Coll (GA)
Westmoreland County Comm Coll (PA)
Wiregrass Georgia Tech Coll (GA)
Wisconsin Indianhead Tech Coll (WI)

COMPUTER TECHNOLOGY/ COMPUTER SYSTEMS TECHNOLOGY

Aaniiih Nakoda Coll (MT)
Anoka Tech Coll (MN)
Brookhaven Coll (TX)
Cape Fear Comm Coll (NC)
Central Texas Coll (TX)
Central Wyoming Coll (WY)
Century Coll (MN)
Coastal Pines Tech Coll (GA)
Coconino Comm Coll (AZ)
Comm Coll of Allegheny County (PA)

Dakota Coll at Bottineau (ND)
Daytona State Coll (FL)
Erie Comm Coll, South Campus (NY)
Hillsborough Comm Coll (FL)
ITI Tech Coll (LA)
Jefferson Comm Coll (NY)
Kellogg Comm Coll (MI)
Lakeland Comm Coll (OH)
Lake Superior Coll (MN)
Lansing Comm Coll (MI)
Lorain County Comm Coll (OH)
Luzerne County Comm Coll (PA)
Manhattan Area Tech Coll (KS)
Miami Dade Coll (FL)
Minnesota State Coll–Southeast Tech (MN)
Minnesota State Comm and Tech Coll (MN)
Minnesota West Comm and Tech Coll (MN)
Montgomery Coll (MD)
Nashville State Comm Coll (TN)
Pittsburgh Tech Coll (PA)
Rend Lake Coll (IL)
St. Philip's Coll (TX)
Southern Arkansas U Tech (AR)
Texas State Tech Coll (TX)
U of Arkansas Comm Coll at Morrilton (AR)
U of Cincinnati Blue Ash Coll (OH)
U of Cincinnati Clermont Coll (OH)

COMPUTER TYPOGRAPHY AND COMPOSITION EQUIPMENT OPERATION

Del Mar Coll (TX)
Housatonic Comm Coll (CT)
Madison Area Tech Coll (WI)
Northern Essex Comm Coll (MA)
Paris Jr Coll (TX)
U of Cincinnati Clermont Coll (OH)

CONSTRUCTION ENGINEERING

Bossier Parish Comm Coll (LA)

CONSTRUCTION ENGINEERING TECHNOLOGY

Arizona Western Coll (AZ)
Bossier Parish Comm Coll (LA)
Coll of Central Florida (FL)
Columbus State Comm Coll (OH)
Comm Coll of Allegheny County (PA)
Comm Coll of Philadelphia (PA)
Comm Coll of the Air Force (AL)
Crowder Coll (MO)
De Anza Coll (CA)
Delta Coll (MI)
Dodge City Comm Coll (KS)
Greenville Tech Coll (SC)
Gulf Coast State Coll (FL)
Harrisburg Area Comm Coll (PA)
Houston Comm Coll (TX)
Illinois Central Coll (IL)
Jefferson State Comm Coll (AL)
Lake Area Tech Inst (SD)
Lorain County Comm Coll (OH)
Macomb Comm Coll (MI)
Metropolitan Comm Coll (NE)
Miami Dade Coll (FL)
Mid-Plains Comm Coll, North Platte (NE)
Monroe Comm Coll (NY)
Nashville State Comm Coll (TN)
North Central Missouri Coll (MO)
Norwalk Comm Coll (CT)
The Ohio State U Ag Tech Inst (OH)
Oklahoma State U Inst of Technology (OK)
Oklahoma State U–Oklahoma City (OK)
Ozarks Tech Comm Coll (MO)
Panola Coll (TX)
Pensacola State Coll (FL)
Raritan Valley Comm Coll (NJ)
Rock Valley Coll (IL)
Rogue Comm Coll (OR)
St. Philip's Coll (TX)
San Jacinto Coll District (TX)
San Joaquin Delta Coll (CA)
Santa Fe Comm Coll (NM)
Seminole State Coll of Florida (FL)
Southeastern Comm Coll (IA)
South Florida State Coll (FL)
South Suburban Coll (IL)
State U of New York Coll of Technology at Alfred (NY)
Sullivan County Comm Coll (NY)
Tallahassee Comm Coll (FL)
Tarrant County Coll District (TX)
Tompkins Cortland Comm Coll (NY)

CONSTRUCTION/HEAVY EQUIPMENT/EARTHMOVING EQUIPMENT OPERATION

Ivy Tech Comm Coll–Southwest (IN)
Ivy Tech Comm Coll–Wabash Valley (IN)
Lake Area Tech Inst (SD)
Lansing Comm Coll (MI)
Mesa Comm Coll (AZ)

CONSTRUCTION MANAGEMENT

Arizona Western Coll (AZ)
Casper Coll (WY)
Central New Mexico Comm Coll (NM)
Coconino Comm Coll (AZ)
Dunwoody Coll of Technology (MN)
Kaskaskia Coll (IL)
Lansing Comm Coll (MI)
McHenry County Coll (IL)
Middlesex Comm Coll (MA)
Minnesota State Comm and Tech Coll (MN)
Minnesota State Comm and Tech Coll–Moorhead (MN)
Northampton Comm Coll (PA)
The Ohio State U Ag Tech Inst (OH)
Oklahoma State U–Oklahoma City (OK)
Renton Tech Coll (WA)
State U of New York Coll of Technology at Alfred (NY)
Three Rivers Comm Coll (CT)

CONSTRUCTION TRADES

American Samoa Comm Coll (AS)
Casper Coll (WY)
Coll of The Albemarle (NC)
Columbus State Comm Coll (OH)
Crowder Coll (MO)
East Central Coll (MO)
Harrisburg Area Comm Coll (PA)
Illinois Eastern Comm Colls, Frontier Community College (IL)
Illinois Eastern Comm Colls, Lincoln Trail College (IL)
Ivy Tech Comm Coll–East Central (IN)
Ivy Tech Comm Coll–Northeast (IN)
Ivy Tech Comm Coll–Northwest (IN)
Ivy Tech Comm Coll–Richmond (IN)
Lamar Comm Coll (CO)
Lehigh Carbon Comm Coll (PA)
Northeast Iowa Comm Coll (IA)
Ogeechee Tech Coll (GA)
Oklahoma State U–Oklahoma City (OK)
Orange Coast Coll (CA)
Rogue Comm Coll (OR)
Sierra Coll (CA)
Texas State Tech Coll (TX)
Vincennes U (IN)

CONSTRUCTION TRADES RELATED

Central Maine Comm Coll (ME)
Citrus Coll (CA)
Coconino Comm Coll (AZ)
Comm Coll of Allegheny County (PA)
Dutchess Comm Coll (NY)
East Central Coll (MO)
Fullerton Coll (CA)
Ivy Tech Comm Coll–East Central (IN)
Ivy Tech Comm Coll–Kokomo (IN)
Ivy Tech Comm Coll–Northeast (IN)
Ivy Tech Comm Coll–Richmond (IN)
Mitchell Tech Inst (SD)
Northern Maine Comm Coll (ME)
Palomar Coll (CA)
State U of New York Coll of Technology at Alfred (NY)
York County Comm Coll (ME)

CONSUMER MERCHANDISING/ RETAILING MANAGEMENT

Clinton Comm Coll (NY)
Del Mar Coll (TX)
Golden West Coll (CA)
J. Sargeant Reynolds Comm Coll (VA)
Monroe Comm Coll (NY)
Navarro Coll (TX)
Niagara County Comm Coll (NY)
South Plains Coll (TX)
Sullivan County Comm Coll (NY)
Tarrant County Coll District (TX)
Westchester Comm Coll (NY)

CONSUMER SERVICES AND ADVOCACY

Pensacola State Coll (FL)

Rio Salado Coll (AZ)

COOKING AND RELATED CULINARY ARTS

Adirondack Comm Coll (NY)
Central Oregon Comm Coll (OR)
Cerritos Coll (CA)
Feather River Coll (CA)
Hinds Comm Coll (MS)
J. Sargeant Reynolds Comm Coll (VA)
Kingsborough Comm Coll of the City U of New York (NY)
Merced Coll (CA)
Miami Dade Coll (FL)
Minnesota State Comm and Tech Coll (MN)
Mitchell Comm Coll (NC)
Orange Coast Coll (CA)
Pensacola State Coll (FL)
Pittsburgh Tech Coll (PA)
Pueblo Comm Coll (CO)
Truckee Meadows Comm Coll (NV)

CORRECTIONS

Alvin Comm Coll (TX)
Amarillo Coll (TX)
Austin Comm Coll District (TX)
Cayuga County Comm Coll (NY)
Coconino Comm Coll (AZ)
Comm Coll of Allegheny County (PA)
Danville Area Comm Coll (IL)
De Anza Coll (CA)
Delta Coll (MI)
El Paso Comm Coll (TX)
Garrett Coll (MD)
Grand Rapids Comm Coll (MI)
Hill Coll (TX)
Illinois Eastern Comm Colls, Frontier Community College (IL)
Illinois Eastern Comm Colls, Lincoln Trail College (IL)
Illinois Valley Comm Coll (IL)
Kellogg Comm Coll (MI)
Lakeland Comm Coll (OH)
Lansing Comm Coll (MI)
Laramie County Comm Coll (WY)
Lorain County Comm Coll (OH)
Mercer County Comm Coll (NJ)
Miami Dade Coll (FL)
Monroe Comm Coll (NY)
Mott Comm Coll (MI)
Mt. San Antonio Coll (CA)
Mount Wachusett Comm Coll (MA)
Navarro Coll (TX)
Northeast Comm Coll (NE)
Raritan Valley Comm Coll (NJ)
St. Clair County Comm Coll (MI)
San Joaquin Delta Coll (CA)
Sierra Coll (CA)
Tallahassee Comm Coll (FL)
Trinity Valley Comm Coll (TX)
Wayne County Comm Coll District (MI)
Westchester Comm Coll (NY)
Westmoreland County Comm Coll (PA)
Wytheville Comm Coll (VA)

CORRECTIONS ADMINISTRATION

Eastern Wyoming Coll (WY)

CORRECTIONS AND CRIMINAL JUSTICE RELATED

Albany Tech Coll (GA)
Chesapeake Coll (MD)
Coconino Comm Coll (AZ)
El Paso Comm Coll (TX)
Feather River Coll (CA)
Genesee Comm Coll (NY)
Hill Coll (TX)
Hinds Comm Coll (MS)
Miami Dade Coll (FL)
Murray State Coll (OK)
Pennsylvania Inst of Technology (PA)
Rockingham Comm Coll (NC)
Sussex County Comm Coll (NJ)

COSMETOLOGY

Caldwell Comm Coll and Tech Inst (NC)
Cape Fear Comm Coll (NC)
Central New Mexico Comm Coll (NM)
Century Coll (MN)
Cerritos Coll (CA)
Citrus Coll (CA)
Colorado Northwestern Comm Coll (CO)
Del Mar Coll (TX)
Dodge City Comm Coll (KS)
Eastern Arizona Coll (AZ)

Eastern Wyoming Coll (WY)
Fayetteville Tech Comm Coll (NC)
Fullerton Coll (CA)
Golden West Coll (CA)
Haywood Comm Coll (NC)
Hill Coll (TX)
Houston Comm Coll (TX)
Johnson County Comm Coll (KS)
Kaskaskia Coll (IL)
Kirtland Comm Coll (MI)
Lamar Comm Coll (CO)
Lenoir Comm Coll (NC)
Lone Star Coll–Kingwood (TX)
Lone Star Coll–North Harris (TX)
Minnesota State Coll–Southeast
    Tech (MN)
Minnesota State Comm and Tech
    Coll (MN)
New Mexico Jr Coll (NM)
Northeastern Jr Coll (CO)
Northeast Iowa Comm Coll (IA)
Olympic Coll (WA)
Paris Jr Coll (TX)
Pueblo Comm Coll (CO)
Randolph Comm Coll (NC)
Rend Lake Coll (IL)
Rowan-Cabarrus Comm Coll (NC)
San Jacinto Coll District (TX)
San Juan Coll (NM)
Santa Monica Coll (CA)
Shawnee Comm Coll (IL)
Southeastern Comm Coll (IA)
South Plains Coll (TX)
Southwestern Comm Coll (NC)
Southwest Texas Jr Coll (TX)
Texarkana Coll (TX)
Trinity Valley Comm Coll (TX)
Vincennes U (IN)
Weatherford Coll (TX)

**COSMETOLOGY AND
PERSONAL GROOMING ARTS
RELATED**
Comm Coll of Allegheny County (PA)

**COSMETOLOGY, BARBER/
STYLING, AND NAIL
INSTRUCTION**
Hill Coll (TX)
San Jacinto Coll District (TX)

COURT REPORTING
Alvin Comm Coll (TX)
Anoka Tech Coll (MN)
Cerritos Coll (CA)
Coll of Marin (CA)
Comm Coll of Allegheny County (PA)
Del Mar Coll (TX)
El Paso Comm Coll (TX)
Fox Valley Tech Coll (WI)
Hinds Comm Coll (MS)
Houston Comm Coll (TX)
Long Island Business Inst (NY)
Luzerne County Comm Coll (PA)
Madison Area Tech Coll (WI)
Miami Dade Coll (FL)
South Suburban Coll (IL)
Stark State Coll (OH)
State U of New York Coll of
    Technology at Alfred (NY)

**CRAFTS, FOLK ART AND
ARTISANRY**
Coll of The Albemarle (NC)
Haywood Comm Coll (NC)

CREATIVE WRITING
Adirondack Comm Coll (NY)
Anoka-Ramsey Comm Coll (MN)
Austin Comm Coll District (TX)
Coll of the Desert (CA)
Tompkins Cortland Comm Coll (NY)

**CRIMINALISTICS AND
CRIMINAL SCIENCE**
Alvin Comm Coll (TX)
Tyler Jr Coll (TX)

**CRIMINAL JUSTICE/LAW
ENFORCEMENT
ADMINISTRATION**
Allen Comm Coll (KS)
Amarillo Coll (TX)
Anne Arundel Comm Coll (MD)
Arapahoe Comm Coll (CO)
Arizona Western Coll (AZ)
Athens Tech Coll (GA)
Bainbridge State Coll (GA)
Blinn Coll (TX)
Brookhaven Coll (TX)
Bunker Hill Comm Coll (MA)

Carteret Comm Coll (NC)
Casper Coll (WY)
Central Maine Comm Coll (ME)
Central New Mexico Comm Coll
    (NM)
Central Virginia Comm Coll (VA)
Central Wyoming Coll (WY)
Citrus Coll (CA)
Clinton Comm Coll (NY)
Coconino Comm Coll (AZ)
Coll of Central Florida (FL)
Coll of The Albemarle (NC)
Columbia-Greene Comm Coll (NY)
Comm Coll of Aurora (CO)
Comm Coll of Philadelphia (PA)
Comm Coll of the Air Force (AL)
Comm Coll of Vermont (VT)
Craven Comm Coll (NC)
Daytona State Coll (FL)
De Anza Coll (CA)
Del Mar Coll (TX)
Des Moines Area Comm Coll (IA)
Dodge City Comm Coll (KS)
Eastern Arizona Coll (AZ)
Eastern Wyoming Coll (WY)
Erie Comm Coll (NY)
Erie Comm Coll, North Campus (NY)
Erie Comm Coll, South Campus
    (NY)
Finger Lakes Comm Coll (NY)
Florida SouthWestern State Coll (FL)
Frederick Comm Coll (MD)
Gateway Comm and Tech Coll (KY)
Genesee Comm Coll (NY)
Georgia Military Coll (GA)
Golden West Coll (CA)
Grand Rapids Comm Coll (MI)
Guam Comm Coll (GU)
Gulf Coast State Coll (FL)
Harper Coll (IL)
Harrisburg Area Comm Coll (PA)
Haywood Comm Coll (NC)
Hill Coll (TX)
Hillsborough Comm Coll (FL)
Housatonic Comm Coll (CT)
Howard Comm Coll (MD)
Illinois Valley Comm Coll (IL)
Imperial Valley Coll (CA)
Jamestown Comm Coll (NY)
Jefferson Comm Coll (NY)
John Tyler Comm Coll (VA)
J. Sargeant Reynolds Comm Coll
    (VA)
Kaskaskia Coll (IL)
Kingsborough Comm Coll of the City
    U of New York (NY)
Kirtland Comm Coll (MI)
Laramie County Comm Coll (WY)
Lehigh Carbon Comm Coll (PA)
Lone Star Coll–CyFair (TX)
Lone Star Coll–Kingwood (TX)
Lone Star Coll–Montgomery (TX)
Lone Star Coll–North Harris (TX)
Lone Star Coll–Tomball (TX)
Lone Star Coll–U Park (TX)
Los Angeles City Coll (CA)
Luzerne County Comm Coll (PA)
Macomb Comm Coll (MI)
Manchester Comm Coll (CT)
Manor Coll (PA)
Massachusetts Bay Comm Coll (MA)
McLennan Comm Coll (TX)
Miami Dade Coll (FL)
Middlesex Comm Coll (MA)
Minnesota State Comm and Tech
    Coll–Moorhead (MN)
Mitchell Comm Coll (NC)
Mohawk Valley Comm Coll (NY)
Monroe Comm Coll (NY)
Mount Wachusett Comm Coll (MA)
Nassau Comm Coll (NY)
Navarro Coll (TX)
New River Comm Coll (VA)
NHTI, Concord's Comm Coll,
    Concord (NH)
Niagara County Comm Coll (NY)
North Central Missouri Coll (MO)
Northern Essex Comm Coll (MA)
North Shore Comm Coll (MA)
NorthWest Arkansas Comm Coll
    (AR)
Northwest Coll (WY)
Norwalk Comm Coll (CT)
Owensboro Comm and Tech Coll
    (KY)
Patrick Henry Comm Coll (VA)
Penn Foster Coll (AZ)
Pensacola State Coll (FL)
Pueblo Comm Coll (CO)

Queensborough Comm Coll of the
    City U of New York (NY)
Rappahannock Comm Coll (VA)
Raritan Valley Comm Coll (NJ)
Rio Hondo Coll (CA)
Rock Valley Coll (IL)
Rowan-Cabarrus Comm Coll (NC)
St. Clair County Comm Coll (MI)
Salt Lake Comm Coll (UT)
Santa Rosa Jr Coll (CA)
Scottsdale Comm Coll (AZ)
Seminole State Coll (OK)
Seminole State Coll of Florida (FL)
Somerset Comm Coll (KY)
Southeastern Comm Coll (IA)
Southern U at Shreveport (LA)
South Florida State Coll (FL)
South Plains Coll (TX)
Southwest Texas Jr Coll (TX)
Southwest Virginia Comm Coll (VA)
Spartanburg Methodist Coll (SC)
Tallahassee Comm Coll (FL)
Tarrant County Coll District (TX)
Texarkana Coll (TX)
Tompkins Cortland Comm Coll (NY)
Trident Tech Coll (SC)
Trinity Valley Comm Coll (TX)
Ulster County Comm Coll (NY)
U of Arkansas Comm Coll at
    Morrilton (AR)
U of Pittsburgh at Titusville (PA)
Virginia Western Comm Coll (VA)
Weatherford Coll (TX)
Western Nevada Coll (NV)
Western Wyoming Comm Coll (WY)
Wytheville Comm Coll (VA)

**CRIMINAL JUSTICE/POLICE
SCIENCE**
Adirondack Comm Coll (NY)
Alexandria Tech and Comm Coll
    (MN)
Alvin Comm Coll (TX)
Amarillo Coll (TX)
Anne Arundel Comm Coll (MD)
Arkansas Northeastern Coll (AR)
Asnuntuck Comm Coll (CT)
Austin Comm Coll District (TX)
Blackhawk Tech Coll (WI)
Borough of Manhattan Comm Coll of
    the City U of New York (NY)
Bunker Hill Comm Coll (MA)
Camden County Coll (NJ)
Cape Fear Comm Coll (NC)
Carroll Comm Coll (MD)
Cayuga County Comm Coll (NY)
Cecil Coll (MD)
Century Coll (MN)
Cerritos Coll (CA)
Chippewa Valley Tech Coll (WI)
Citrus Coll (CA)
Cleveland State Comm Coll (TN)
Clinton Comm Coll (NY)
Cloud County Comm Coll (KS)
Coastal Pines Tech Coll (GA)
Cochise County Comm Coll District
    (AZ)
Coll of Marin (CA)
Coll of the Canyons (CA)
Coll of the Desert (CA)
Collin County Comm Coll District
    (TX)
Columbus State Comm Coll (OH)
Comm Coll of Allegheny County (PA)
Comm Coll of Baltimore County
    (MD)
Comm Coll of Rhode Island (RI)
County Coll of Morris (NJ)
Danville Area Comm Coll (IL)
Daytona State Coll (FL)
De Anza Coll (CA)
Del Mar Coll (TX)
Delta Coll (MI)
Dutchess Comm Coll (NY)
Dyersburg State Comm Coll (TN)
Eastern Arizona Coll (AZ)
Eastern Wyoming Coll (WY)
Edison State Comm Coll (OH)
Elgin Comm Coll (IL)
El Paso Comm Coll (TX)
Erie Comm Coll, North Campus (NY)
Finger Lakes Comm Coll (NY)
Fox Valley Tech Coll (WI)
Fullerton Coll (CA)
Gateway Tech Coll (WI)
Genesee Comm Coll (NY)
Georgia Highlands Coll (GA)
Golden West Coll (CA)
Grand Rapids Comm Coll (MI)
Hagerstown Comm Coll (MD)

Harford Comm Coll (MD)
Harrisburg Area Comm Coll (PA)
Hawkeye Comm Coll (IA)
Houston Comm Coll (TX)
Hudson County Comm Coll (NJ)
Hutchinson Comm Coll (KS)
Illinois Central Coll (IL)
Illinois Valley Comm Coll (IL)
Iowa Central Comm Coll (IA)
Jamestown Comm Coll (NY)
Jefferson State Comm Coll (AL)
Johnson County Comm Coll (KS)
Johnston Comm Coll (NC)
Kirtland Comm Coll (MI)
Kishwaukee Coll (IL)
Lake Area Tech Inst (SD)
Lakeland Comm Coll (OH)
Lake Region State Coll (ND)
Lansing Comm Coll (MI)
Lorain County Comm Coll (OH)
Louisiana State U at Eunice (LA)
Macomb Comm Coll (MI)
Madison Area Tech Coll (WI)
McHenry County Coll (IL)
McLennan Comm Coll (TX)
Merced Coll (CA)
Mercer County Comm Coll (NJ)
Mesa Comm Coll (AZ)
Metropolitan Comm Coll (NE)
Miami Dade Coll (FL)
Middlesex County Coll (NJ)
Minnesota West Comm and Tech
    Coll (MN)
Missouri State U–West Plains (MO)
Mohave Comm Coll (AZ)
Monroe Comm Coll (NY)
Monroe County Comm Coll (MI)
Montgomery Coll (MD)
Montgomery County Comm Coll (PA)
Morton Coll (IL)
Mott Comm Coll (MI)
Mt. San Antonio Coll (CA)
Nashville State Comm Coll (TN)
Naugatuck Valley Comm Coll (CT)
Navarro Coll (TX)
New Mexico Jr Coll (NM)
New River Comm Coll (VA)
Northcentral Tech Coll (WI)
Northeast Comm Coll (NE)
Northeastern Jr Coll (CO)
Northland Comm and Tech Coll (MN)
Northwest-Shoals Comm Coll (AL)
Oakton Comm Coll (IL)
Oklahoma State U–Oklahoma City
    (OK)
Quinsigamond Comm Coll (MA)
Rappahannock Comm Coll (VA)
Raritan Valley Comm Coll (NJ)
Rend Lake Coll (IL)
Rockingham Comm Coll (NC)
Rogue Comm Coll (OR)
St. Charles Comm Coll (MO)
San Jacinto Coll District (TX)
San Joaquin Delta Coll (CA)
San Juan Coll (NM)
Santa Fe Comm Coll (NM)
Schoolcraft Coll (MI)
Seminole State Coll (OK)
Shawnee Comm Coll (IL)
Sierra Coll (CA)
South Plains Coll (TX)
Southwestern Comm Coll (NC)
Springfield Tech Comm Coll (MA)
Sullivan County Comm Coll (NY)
Tallahassee Comm Coll (FL)
Three Rivers Comm Coll (CT)
Three Rivers Comm Coll (MO)
Tompkins Cortland Comm Coll (NY)
Treasure Valley Comm Coll (OR)
Trinity Valley Comm Coll (TX)
Truckee Meadows Comm Coll (NV)
Victoria Coll (TX)
Vincennes U (IN)
Volunteer State Comm Coll (TN)
Walters State Comm Coll (TN)
Waukesha County Tech Coll (WI)
Wayne County Comm Coll District
    (MI)
Western Dakota Tech Inst (SD)
Westmoreland County Comm Coll
    (PA)
Wor-Wic Comm Coll (MD)
Wytheville Comm Coll (VA)

CRIMINAL JUSTICE/SAFETY
Alamance Comm Coll (NC)
Alvin Comm Coll (TX)
American Samoa Comm Coll (AS)
Ancilla Coll (IN)
Augusta Tech Coll (GA)

Berkshire Comm Coll (MA)
Bismarck State Coll (ND)
Blue Ridge Comm and Tech Coll
    (WV)
Bossier Parish Comm Coll (LA)
Bowling Green State U–Firelands
    Coll (OH)
Bucks County Comm Coll (PA)
Central Georgia Tech Coll (GA)
Central Maine Comm Coll (ME)
Central Texas Coll (TX)
Century Coll (MN)
Chandler-Gilbert Comm Coll (AZ)
Chattahoochee Tech Coll (GA)
City Colls of Chicago, Kennedy-King
    College (IL)
City Colls of Chicago, Olive-Harvey
    College (IL)
Craven Comm Coll (NC)
Dyersburg State Comm Coll (TN)
Eastern Wyoming Coll (WY)
El Paso Comm Coll (TX)
Fayetteville Tech Comm Coll (NC)
Fiorello H. LaGuardia Comm Coll of
    the City U of New York (NY)
Genesee Comm Coll (NY)
Georgia Northwestern Tech Coll
    (GA)
Georgia Piedmont Tech Coll (GA)
Gordon State Coll (GA)
Great Basin Coll (NV)
Greenville Tech Coll (SC)
Halifax Comm Coll (NC)
Haywood Comm Coll (NC)
Holyoke Comm Coll (MA)
Horry Georgetown Tech Coll (SC)
Ivy Tech Comm Coll–Bloomington
    (IN)
Ivy Tech Comm Coll–Central Indiana
    (IN)
Ivy Tech Comm Coll–Columbus (IN)
Ivy Tech Comm Coll–East Central
    (IN)
Ivy Tech Comm Coll–Kokomo (IN)
Ivy Tech Comm Coll–Lafayette (IN)
Ivy Tech Comm Coll–North Central
    (IN)
Ivy Tech Comm Coll–Northeast (IN)
Ivy Tech Comm Coll–Northwest (IN)
Ivy Tech Comm Coll–Richmond (IN)
Ivy Tech Comm Coll–Southeast (IN)
Ivy Tech Comm Coll–Southwest (IN)
Ivy Tech Comm Coll–Wabash Valley
    (IN)
James Sprunt Comm Coll (NC)
Kellogg Comm Coll (MI)
Kent State U at Ashtabula (OH)
Kent State U at East Liverpool (OH)
Kent State U at Trumbull (OH)
Kent State U at Tuscarawas (OH)
Kishwaukee Coll (IL)
Lackawanna Coll (PA)
Lanier Tech Coll (GA)
Lehigh Carbon Comm Coll (PA)
Lenoir Comm Coll (NC)
Mesa Comm Coll (AZ)
Middlesex Comm Coll (MA)
Minnesota State Coll–Southeast
    Tech (MN)
Minnesota State Comm and Tech
    Coll (MN)
Minnesota State Comm and Tech
    Coll–Moorhead (MN)
Monroe County Comm Coll (MI)
Montgomery Comm Coll (NC)
Mountain View Coll (TX)
Nassau Comm Coll (NY)
Northampton Comm Coll (PA)
North Georgia Tech Coll (GA)
NorthWest Arkansas Comm Coll
    (AR)
Oregon Coast Comm Coll (OR)
Paris Jr Coll (TX)
Piedmont Comm Coll (NC)
Randolph Comm Coll (NC)
Richmond Comm Coll (NC)
St. Philip's Coll (TX)
Santa Fe Comm Coll (NM)
Savannah Tech Coll (GA)
Southeast Comm Coll, Lincoln
    Campus (NE)
Southeastern Tech Coll (GA)
Southern Crescent Tech Coll (GA)
Southern Regional Tech Coll (GA)
South Florida State Coll (FL)
South Georgia Tech Coll (GA)
South Suburban Coll (IL)
Southwestern Michigan Coll (MI)
Sowela Tech Comm Coll (LA)
Texarkana Coll (TX)

Truckee Meadows Comm Coll (NV)
Tyler Jr Coll (TX)
U of Cincinnati Blue Ash Coll (OH)
U of Cincinnati Clermont Coll (OH)
Walters State Comm Coll (TN)
Western Dakota Tech Inst (SD)
West Georgia Tech Coll (GA)
Westmoreland County Comm Coll (PA)
White Mountains Comm Coll (NH)
Wiregrass Georgia Tech Coll (GA)
York County Comm Coll (ME)

CRIMINOLOGY
Central New Mexico Comm Coll (NM)
Coll of Central Florida (FL)
Genesee Comm Coll (NY)
Panola Coll (TX)
Paris Jr Coll (TX)
State U of New York Coll of Technology at Alfred (NY)
Western Wyoming Comm Coll (WY)
Westmoreland County Comm Coll (PA)

CRISIS/EMERGENCY/DISASTER MANAGEMENT
Comm Coll of Rhode Island (RI)
Erie Comm Coll (NY)
Fayetteville Tech Comm Coll (NC)
Guam Comm Coll (GU)
Montgomery Coll (MD)
Olympic Coll (WA)
Sullivan County Comm Coll (NY)

CRITICAL INCIDENT RESPONSE/SPECIAL POLICE OPERATIONS
Raritan Valley Comm Coll (NJ)

CROP PRODUCTION
Arizona Western Coll (AZ)
Cochise County Comm Coll District (AZ)
Coll of the Desert (CA)
Dakota Coll at Bottineau (ND)
Illinois Central Coll (IL)
Merced Coll (CA)
Northeast Iowa Comm Coll (IA)
Northwest (WY)
The Ohio State U Ag Tech Inst (OH)
San Joaquin Delta Coll (CA)

CULINARY ARTS
Alamance Comm Coll (NC)
Albany Tech Coll (GA)
Alvin Comm Coll (TX)
Arizona Western Coll (AZ)
Atlanta Tech Coll (GA)
Augusta Tech Coll (GA)
Austin Comm Coll District (TX)
Blackhawk Tech Coll (WI)
Blue Ridge Comm and Tech Coll (WV)
Bossier Parish Comm Coll (LA)
Bucks County Comm Coll (PA)
Bunker Hill Comm Coll (MA)
Caldwell Comm Coll and Tech Inst (NC)
Cape Fear Comm Coll (NC)
Carteret Comm Coll (NC)
Central New Mexico Comm Coll (NM)
Central Virginia Comm Coll (VA)
Central Wyoming Coll (WY)
Chattahoochee Tech Coll (GA)
City Colls of Chicago, Kennedy-King College (IL)
Cochise County Comm Coll District (AZ)
Coll of The Albemarle (NC)
Coll of the Desert (CA)
Collin County Comm Coll District (TX)
Columbus State Comm Coll (OH)
Comm Coll of Allegheny County (PA)
Comm Coll of Philadelphia (PA)
County Coll of Morris (NJ)
Culinary Inst LeNotre (TX)
Daytona State Coll (FL)
Del Mar Coll (TX)
Des Moines Area Comm Coll (IA)
East Central Coll (MO)
Elgin Comm Coll (IL)
El Paso Comm Coll (TX)
Erie Comm Coll (NY)
Erie Comm Coll, North Campus (NY)
Fayetteville Tech Comm Coll (NC)
Finger Lakes Comm Coll (NY)
Fox Valley Tech Coll (WI)
Gateway Tech Coll (WI)
Grand Rapids Comm Coll (MI)
Greenville Tech Coll (SC)

Harrisburg Area Comm Coll (PA)
H. Councill Trenholm State Comm Coll (AL)
Horry Georgetown Tech Coll (SC)
Houston Comm Coll (TX)
Hudson County Comm Coll (NJ)
Illinois Central Coll (IL)
Illinois Eastern Comm Colls, Olney Central College (IL)
Johnson County Comm Coll (KS)
Kaskaskia Coll (IL)
Lenoir Comm Coll (NC)
Lorain County Comm Coll (OH)
Luzerne County Comm Coll (PA)
Macomb Comm Coll (MI)
Madison Area Tech Coll (WI)
Mercer County Comm Coll (NJ)
Metropolitan Comm Coll (NE)
Miami Dade Coll (FL)
Mitchell Tech Inst (SD)
Mohave Comm Coll (AZ)
Monroe County Comm Coll (MI)
Montgomery County Comm Coll (PA)
Mott Comm Coll (MI)
Nashville State Comm Coll (TN)
New England Culinary Inst (VT)
Niagara County Comm Coll (NY)
Northampton Comm Coll (PA)
Northcentral Tech Coll (WI)
North Georgia Tech Coll (GA)
North Shore Comm Coll (MA)
NorthWest Arkansas Comm Coll (AR)
Ogeechee Tech Coll (GA)
Olympic Coll (WA)
Orange Coast Coll (CA)
Ozarks Tech Comm Coll (MO)
Rend Lake Coll (IL)
Renton Tech Coll (WA)
St. Philip's Coll (TX)
Salt Lake Comm Coll (UT)
San Jacinto Coll District (TX)
San Joaquin Delta Coll (CA)
Santa Fe Comm Coll (NM)
Santa Rosa Jr Coll (CA)
Savannah Tech Coll (GA)
Schoolcraft Coll (MI)
Scottsdale Comm Coll (AZ)
South Georgia Tech Coll (GA)
Southwestern Comm Coll (NC)
Sowela Tech Comm Coll (LA)
State U of New York Coll of Technology at Alfred (NY)
Sullivan County Comm Coll (NY)
Texarkana Coll (TX)
Texas State Tech Coll (TX)
Tompkins Cortland Comm Coll (NY)
Trident Tech Coll (SC)
Vincennes U (IN)
Westmoreland County Comm Coll (PA)
White Mountains Comm Coll (NH)
York County Comm Coll (ME)

CULINARY ARTS RELATED
Ancilla Coll (IN)
Guam Comm Coll (GU)
Oklahoma State U Inst of Technology (OK)

CUSTOMER SERVICE MANAGEMENT
Central Oregon Comm Coll (OR)

CUSTOMER SERVICE SUPPORT/CALL CENTER/TELESERVICE OPERATION
Central Wyoming Coll (WY)
Lansing Comm Coll (MI)
Miami Dade Coll (FL)

CYBER/COMPUTER FORENSICS AND COUNTERTERRORISM
Century Coll (MN)
Columbia-Greene Comm Coll (NY)
Harper Coll (IL)
Pensacola State Coll (FL)

CYBER/ELECTRONIC OPERATIONS AND WARFARE
Oklahoma City Comm Coll (OK)

DAIRY HUSBANDRY AND PRODUCTION
Northeast Iowa Comm Coll (IA)
The Ohio State U Ag Tech Inst (OH)

DAIRY SCIENCE
Mt. San Antonio Coll (CA)
The Ohio State U Ag Tech Inst (OH)

DANCE
Austin Comm Coll District (TX)
Casper Coll (WY)
Cerritos Coll (CA)
Citrus Coll (CA)
Coll of Marin (CA)
Fullerton Coll (CA)
Lone Star Coll–CyFair (TX)
Mercer County Comm Coll (NJ)
Miami Dade Coll (FL)
Nassau Comm Coll (NY)
Northern Essex Comm Coll (MA)
Orange Coast Coll (CA)
Palomar Coll (CA)
Raritan Valley Comm Coll (NJ)
San Jacinto Coll District (TX)
San Joaquin Delta Coll (CA)
Santa Monica Coll (CA)
Santa Rosa Jr Coll (CA)
Trinity Valley Comm Coll (TX)
Tyler Jr Coll (TX)
Western Wyoming Comm Coll (WY)

DANCE RELATED
Citrus Coll (CA)
Orange Coast Coll (CA)

DATA ENTRY/MICROCOMPUTER APPLICATIONS
Arizona Western Coll (AZ)
Bunker Hill Comm Coll (MA)
Cerritos Coll (CA)
Chandler-Gilbert Comm Coll (AZ)
Coll of The Albemarle (NC)
Comm Coll of Vermont (VT)
Del Mar Coll (TX)
Elgin Comm Coll (IL)
Fiorello H. LaGuardia Comm Coll of the City U of New York (NY)
Luzerne County Comm Coll (PA)
Montgomery Coll (MD)
North Shore Comm Coll (MA)
Rio Salado Coll (AZ)
St. Philip's Coll (TX)
Santa Monica Coll (CA)
Seminole State Coll of Florida (FL)
Sierra Coll (CA)
Sullivan County Comm Coll (NY)
Western Wyoming Comm Coll (WY)
Westmoreland County Comm Coll (PA)

DATA ENTRY/MICROCOMPUTER APPLICATIONS RELATED
Blue Ridge Comm and Tech Coll (WV)
Seminole State Coll of Florida (FL)

DATA MODELING/WAREHOUSING AND DATABASE ADMINISTRATION
Chandler-Gilbert Comm Coll (AZ)
Coll of Marin (CA)
Ivy Tech Comm Coll–Bloomington (IN)
Ivy Tech Comm Coll–Central Indiana (IN)
Ivy Tech Comm Coll–Columbus (IN)
Ivy Tech Comm Coll–East Central (IN)
Ivy Tech Comm Coll–Kokomo (IN)
Ivy Tech Comm Coll–Lafayette (IN)
Ivy Tech Comm Coll–Northeast (IN)
Ivy Tech Comm Coll–Richmond (IN)
Ivy Tech Comm Coll–Sellersburg (IN)
Ivy Tech Comm Coll–Southeast (IN)
Ivy Tech Comm Coll–Southwest (IN)
Ivy Tech Comm Coll–Wabash Valley (IN)
Lansing Comm Coll (MI)
Quinsigamond Comm Coll (MA)
Santa Monica Coll (CA)
Seminole State Coll of Florida (FL)
Wayne County Comm Coll District (MI)

DATA PROCESSING AND DATA PROCESSING TECHNOLOGY
Allen Comm Coll (KS)
Anoka Tech Coll (MN)
Bainbridge State Coll (GA)
Citrus Coll (CA)
City Colls of Chicago, Kennedy-King College (IL)
Dodge City Comm Coll (KS)
Finger Lakes Comm Coll (NY)
Great Basin Coll (NV)
Greenville Tech Coll (SC)
Housatonic Comm Coll (CT)
Illinois Valley Comm Coll (IL)

Iowa Central Comm Coll (IA)
Kingsborough Comm Coll of the City U of New York (NY)
Louisiana State U at Eunice (LA)
Luzerne County Comm Coll (PA)
Madison Area Tech Coll (WI)
Monroe Comm Coll (NY)
Monroe County Comm Coll (MI)
Morton Coll (IL)
Mt. San Antonio Coll (CA)
Nassau Comm Coll (NY)
Navarro Coll (TX)
North Central Missouri Coll (MO)
Northern Essex Comm Coll (MA)
NorthWest Arkansas Comm Coll (AR)
Otero Jr Coll (CO)
Queensborough Comm Coll of the City U of New York (NY)
St. Clair County Comm Coll (MI)
San Juan Coll (NM)
Seminole State Coll of Florida (FL)
South Plains Coll (TX)
Southwest Texas Jr Coll (TX)
Spartanburg Comm Coll (SC)
Trinity Valley Comm Coll (TX)
U of Cincinnati Clermont Coll (OH)
Virginia Western Comm Coll (VA)
Walters State Comm Coll (TN)
Western Wyoming Comm Coll (WY)
Westmoreland County Comm Coll (PA)

DEAF STUDIES
Quinsigamond Comm Coll (MA)
Western Nevada Coll (NV)

DENTAL ASSISTING
Athens Tech Coll (GA)
Camden County Coll (NJ)
Central Oregon Comm Coll (OR)
Century Coll (MN)
Citrus Coll (CA)
Coll of Central Florida (FL)
Coll of Marin (CA)
Comm Care Coll (OK)
Comm Coll of the Air Force (AL)
Delta Coll (MI)
El Paso Comm Coll (TX)
H. Councill Trenholm State Comm Coll (AL)
Hennepin Tech Coll (MN)
Hinds Comm Coll (MS)
Humacao Comm Coll (PR)
IBMC Coll, Fort Collins (CO)
Ivy Tech Comm Coll–Columbus (IN)
Ivy Tech Comm Coll–East Central (IN)
Ivy Tech Comm Coll–Kokomo (IN)
Ivy Tech Comm Coll–Lafayette (IN)
Kaskaskia Coll (IL)
Lake Area Tech Inst (SD)
Luzerne County Comm Coll (PA)
Manor Coll (PA)
Middlesex Comm Coll (MA)
Mid-Plains Comm Coll, North Platte (NE)
Minnesota State Comm and Tech Coll (MN)
Minnesota State Comm and Tech Coll–Moorhead (MN)
Minnesota West Comm and Tech Coll (MN)
Mohave Comm Coll (AZ)
Mott Comm Coll (MI)
NHTI, Concord's Comm Coll, Concord (NH)
Northern Essex Comm Coll (MA)
Orange Coast Coll (CA)
Palomar Coll (CA)
Pueblo Comm Coll (CO)
Raritan Valley Comm Coll (NJ)
Renton Tech Coll (WA)
Salina Area Tech Coll (KS)
Santa Fe Comm Coll (NM)
Tallahassee Comm Coll (FL)
Truckee Meadows Comm Coll (NV)
Wayne County Comm Coll District (MI)
Westmoreland County Comm Coll (PA)
West Virginia Jr Coll–Bridgeport (WV)

DENTAL HYGIENE
Amarillo Coll (TX)
Athens Tech Coll (GA)
Atlanta Tech Coll (GA)
Austin Comm Coll District (TX)
Blinn Coll (TX)
Camden County Coll (NJ)
Cape Fear Comm Coll (NC)

Central Georgia Tech Coll (GA)
Century Coll (MN)
Cerritos Coll (CA)
Chippewa Valley Tech Coll (WI)
Collin County Comm Coll District (TX)
Colorado Northwestern Comm Coll (CO)
Columbus State Comm Coll (OH)
Columbus Tech Coll (GA)
Comm Coll of Baltimore County (MD)
Comm Coll of Philadelphia (PA)
Comm Coll of Rhode Island (RI)
Daytona State Coll (FL)
Del Mar Coll (TX)
Delta Coll (MI)
Des Moines Area Comm Coll (IA)
El Paso Comm Coll (TX)
Erie Comm Coll, North Campus (NY)
Fayetteville Tech Comm Coll (NC)
Florida SouthWestern State Coll (FL)
Fox Valley Tech Coll (WI)
Georgia Highlands Coll (GA)
Grand Rapids Comm Coll (MI)
Great Falls Coll Montana State U (MT)
Greenville Tech Coll (SC)
Gulf Coast State Coll (FL)
Hagerstown Comm Coll (MD)
Halifax Comm Coll (NC)
Harper Coll (IL)
Harrisburg Area Comm Coll (PA)
Hawkeye Comm Coll (IA)
Hillsborough Comm Coll (FL)
Illinois Central Coll (IL)
Ivy Tech Comm Coll–East Central (IN)
Ivy Tech Comm Coll–Kokomo (IN)
Johnson County Comm Coll (KS)
Kellogg Comm Coll (MI)
Lakeland Comm Coll (OH)
Lake Superior Coll (MN)
Lansing Comm Coll (MI)
Laramie County Comm Coll (WY)
Lone Star Coll–Kingwood (TX)
Lorain County Comm Coll (OH)
Luzerne County Comm Coll (PA)
Madison Area Tech Coll (WI)
Manor Coll (PA)
Meridian Comm Coll (MS)
Mesa Comm Coll (AZ)
Miami Dade Coll (FL)
Middlesex Comm Coll (MA)
Middlesex County Coll (NJ)
Minnesota State Comm and Tech Coll (MN)
Minnesota State Comm and Tech Coll–Moorhead (MN)
Mohave Comm Coll (AZ)
Monroe Comm Coll (NY)
Montgomery County Comm Coll (PA)
Mott Comm Coll (MI)
Mount Wachusett Comm Coll (MA)
NHTI, Concord's Comm Coll, Concord (NH)
Northampton Comm Coll (PA)
Northcentral Tech Coll (WI)
Ogeechee Tech Coll (GA)
Pensacola State Coll (FL)
Pueblo Comm Coll (CO)
Quinsigamond Comm Coll (MA)
Raritan Valley Comm Coll (NJ)
Rio Salado Coll (AZ)
Rock Valley Coll (IL)
Salt Lake Comm Coll (UT)
San Juan Coll (NM)
Santa Rosa Jr Coll (CA)
Southeastern Tech Coll (GA)
Southern U at Shreveport (LA)
South Florida State Coll (FL)
Springfield Tech Comm Coll (MA)
Stark State Coll (OH)
Tallahassee Comm Coll (FL)
Tarrant County Coll District (TX)
Trident Tech Coll (SC)
Truckee Meadows Comm Coll (NV)
Tyler Jr Coll (TX)
U of Cincinnati Blue Ash Coll (OH)
Virginia Western Comm Coll (VA)
Waukesha County Tech Coll (WI)
Wayne County Comm Coll District (MI)
Westmoreland County Comm Coll (PA)
Wytheville Comm Coll (VA)

DENTAL LABORATORY TECHNOLOGY
Comm Coll of the Air Force (AL)
Erie Comm Coll, South Campus (NY)

J. Sargeant Reynolds Comm Coll (VA)
Middlesex Comm Coll (MA)

DENTAL SERVICES AND ALLIED PROFESSIONS RELATED
Gordon State Coll (GA)
Quinsigamond Comm Coll (MA)

DESIGN AND APPLIED ARTS RELATED
County Coll of Morris (NJ)
Del Mar Coll (TX)
Howard Comm Coll (MD)
Kingsborough Comm Coll of the City U of New York (NY)
Niagara County Comm Coll (NY)
Oklahoma City Comm Coll (OK)
Raritan Valley Comm Coll (NJ)
Vincennes U (IN)
Westchester Comm Coll (NY)
Westmoreland County Comm Coll (PA)

DESIGN AND VISUAL COMMUNICATIONS
Adirondack Comm Coll (NY)
Austin Comm Coll District (TX)
Brookhaven Coll (TX)
Bunker Hill Comm Coll (MA)
Cecil Coll (MD)
Central Virginia Comm Coll (VA)
Coll of Marin (CA)
Elgin Comm Coll (IL)
FIDM/Fashion Inst of Design & Merchandising, Orange County Campus (CA)
FIDM/Fashion Inst of Design & Merchandising, San Diego Campus (CA)
Guam Comm Coll (GU)
Harrisburg Area Comm Coll (PA)
Hutchinson Comm Coll (KS)
Ivy Tech Comm Coll–Central Indiana (IN)
Ivy Tech Comm Coll–Columbus (IN)
Ivy Tech Comm Coll–Kokomo (IN)
Ivy Tech Comm Coll–North Central (IN)
Ivy Tech Comm Coll–Sellersburg (IN)
Ivy Tech Comm Coll–Southwest (IN)
Ivy Tech Comm Coll–Wabash Valley (IN)
Lone Star Coll–CyFair (TX)
Lone Star Coll–Kingwood (TX)
Lone Star Coll–North Harris (TX)
Mesa Comm Coll (AZ)
Nashville State Comm Coll (TN)
Nassau Comm Coll (NY)
Oklahoma City Comm Coll (OK)
Palomar Coll (CA)
St. Philip's Coll (TX)
Salt Lake Comm Coll (UT)
Santa Fe Comm Coll (NM)
Southeastern Tech Coll (GA)

DESKTOP PUBLISHING AND DIGITAL IMAGING DESIGN
Alvin Comm Coll (TX)
Camden County Coll (NJ)
Coconino Comm Coll (AZ)
Des Moines Area Comm Coll (IA)
Dunwoody Coll of Technology (MN)
Hawkeye Comm Coll (IA)
Hennepin Tech Coll (MN)
Houston Comm Coll (TX)
Northeast Iowa Comm Coll (IA)
Palomar Coll (CA)

DEVELOPMENTAL AND CHILD PSYCHOLOGY
Comm Coll of Vermont (VT)
De Anza Coll (CA)
McLennan Comm Coll (TX)
Navarro Coll (TX)
South Plains Coll (TX)
Tarrant County Coll District (TX)
Trinity Valley Comm Coll (TX)

DEVELOPMENTAL SERVICES WORKER
Anoka Tech Coll (MN)

DIAGNOSTIC MEDICAL SONOGRAPHY AND ULTRASOUND TECHNOLOGY
Alvin Comm Coll (TX)
Athens Tech Coll (GA)
Austin Comm Coll District (TX)
Blackhawk Tech Coll (WI)

Bowling Green State U–Firelands Coll (OH)
Bunker Hill Comm Coll (MA)
Caldwell Comm Coll and Tech Inst (NC)
Cape Fear Comm Coll (NC)
Central New Mexico Comm Coll (NM)
Chippewa Valley Tech Coll (WI)
Columbus Tech Coll (GA)
Comm Coll of Allegheny County (PA)
Comm Coll of Rhode Island (RI)
Del Mar Coll (TX)
Delta Coll (MI)
El Paso Comm Coll (TX)
Greenville Tech Coll (SC)
Gulf Coast State Coll (FL)
Harper Coll (IL)
Harrisburg Area Comm Coll (PA)
H. Council Trenholm State Comm Coll (AL)
Hillsborough Comm Coll (FL)
Hinds Comm Coll (MS)
Howard Comm Coll (MD)
Lackawanna Coll (PA)
Lansing Comm Coll (MI)
Laramie County Comm Coll (WY)
Lone Star Coll–CyFair (TX)
Lorain County Comm Coll (OH)
Lurleen B. Wallace Comm Coll (AL)
Merced Coll (CA)
Miami Dade Coll (FL)
Middlesex Comm Coll (MA)
Montgomery Coll (MD)
NHTI, Concord's Comm Coll, Concord (NH)
Northampton Comm Coll (PA)
Orange Coast Coll (CA)
Pensacola State Coll (FL)
Pittsburgh Career Inst (PA)
St. Philip's Coll (TX)
San Jacinto Coll District (TX)
Springfield Tech Comm Coll (MA)
Tallahassee Comm Coll (FL)
Tyler Jr Coll (TX)
Weatherford Coll (TX)
Westmoreland County Comm Coll (PA)

DIESEL MECHANICS TECHNOLOGY
Alexandria Tech and Comm Coll (MN)
Casper Coll (WY)
Central Texas Coll (TX)
Citrus Coll (CA)
City Colls of Chicago, Olive-Harvey College (IL)
Delta Coll (MI)
Des Moines Area Comm Coll (IA)
Eastern Arizona Coll (AZ)
Eastern Idaho Tech Coll (ID)
Fox Valley Tech Coll (WI)
Gateway Tech Coll (WI)
Great Basin Coll (NV)
Hawkeye Comm Coll (IA)
Hinds Comm Coll (MS)
Illinois Central Coll (IL)
Illinois Eastern Comm Colls, Wabash Valley College (IL)
Johnston Comm Coll (NC)
Kishwaukee Coll (IL)
Lake Area Tech Inst (SD)
Laramie County Comm Coll (WY)
Mid-Plains Comm Coll, North Platte (NE)
Minnesota State Comm and Tech Coll (MN)
Minnesota State Comm and Tech Coll–Moorhead (MN)
Minnesota West Comm and Tech Coll (MN)
Northcentral Tech Coll (WI)
Northeast Comm Coll (NE)
Ohio Tech Coll (OH)
Oklahoma City Comm Coll (OK)
Oklahoma State U Inst of Technology (OK)
Owensboro Comm and Tech Coll (KY)
Ozarks Tech Comm Coll (MO)
Palomar Coll (CA)
Raritan Valley Comm Coll (NJ)
Rogue Comm Coll (OR)
St. Philip's Coll (TX)
Salt Lake Comm Coll (UT)
San Jacinto Coll District (TX)
San Juan Coll (NM)
Santa Rosa Jr Coll (CA)

Southeast Comm Coll, Milford Campus (NE)
State U of New York Coll of Technology at Alfred (NY)
Texarkana Coll (TX)
Texas State Tech Coll (TX)
Three Rivers Comm Coll (MO)
Truckee Meadows Comm Coll (NV)
Vincennes U (IN)
Western Wyoming Comm Coll (WY)
White Mountains Comm Coll (NH)
Williston State Coll (ND)

DIETETICS
Camden County Coll (NJ)
Central Oregon Comm Coll (OR)
Comm Coll of the Air Force (AL)
El Paso Comm Coll (TX)
Harper Coll (IL)
Harrisburg Area Comm Coll (PA)
Los Angeles City Coll (CA)
Madison Area Tech Coll (WI)
Miami Dade Coll (FL)
Northeast Comm Coll (NE)
Pensacola State Coll (FL)
South Florida State Coll (FL)
South Plains Coll (TX)
Tarrant County Coll District (TX)
Truckee Meadows Comm Coll (NV)
Vincennes U (IN)

DIETETICS AND CLINICAL NUTRITION SERVICES RELATED
Oklahoma State U–Oklahoma City (OK)

DIETETIC TECHNOLOGY
Camden County Coll (NJ)
Chandler-Gilbert Comm Coll (AZ)
Coll of the Desert (CA)
Fiorello H. LaGuardia Comm Coll of the City U of New York (NY)
Harper Coll (IL)
Hudson County Comm Coll (NJ)
Miami Dade Coll (FL)
Mohawk Valley Comm Coll (NY)
Northland Comm and Tech Coll (MN)
Orange Coast Coll (CA)
Santa Rosa Jr Coll (CA)
Westmoreland County Comm Coll (PA)

DIETITIAN ASSISTANT
Chandler-Gilbert Comm Coll (AZ)
Comm Coll of Allegheny County (PA)
Erie Comm Coll, North Campus (NY)
Hillsborough Comm Coll (FL)
Middlesex County Coll (NJ)
Westchester Comm Coll (NY)

DIGITAL ARTS
Fiorello H. LaGuardia Comm Coll of the City U of New York (NY)
Genesee Comm Coll (NY)
Gulf Coast State Coll (FL)
Harford Comm Coll (MD)
Mohawk Valley Comm Coll (NY)
Queensborough Comm Coll of the City U of New York (NY)
Volunteer State Comm Coll (TN)
Waukesha County Tech Coll (WI)
Westchester Comm Coll (NY)

DIGITAL COMMUNICATION AND MEDIA/MULTIMEDIA
Chippewa Valley Tech Coll (WI)
Cochise County Comm Coll District (AZ)
Comm Coll of Vermont (VT)
Finger Lakes Comm Coll (NY)
Gulf Coast State Coll (FL)
Hawkeye Comm Coll (IA)
Laramie County Comm Coll (WY)
Naugatuck Valley Comm Coll (CT)
Oklahoma City Comm Coll (OK)
Raritan Valley Comm Coll (NJ)
San Jacinto Coll District (TX)
Santa Monica Coll (CA)
Santa Rosa Jr Coll (CA)
Sierra Coll (CA)
Tompkins Cortland Comm Coll (NY)
Virginia Marti Coll of Art and Design (OH)
Wayne County Comm Coll District (MI)
Westchester Comm Coll (NY)

DIRECTING AND THEATRICAL PRODUCTION
Quinsigamond Comm Coll (MA)

DRAFTING AND DESIGN TECHNOLOGY
Albany Tech Coll (GA)
Allen Comm Coll (KS)
Alvin Comm Coll (TX)
Amarillo Coll (TX)
Austin Comm Coll District (TX)
Bainbridge State Coll (GA)
Bevill State Comm Coll (AL)
Bossier Parish Comm Coll (LA)
Camden County Coll (NJ)
Casper Coll (WY)
Cayuga County Comm Coll (NY)
Central Georgia Tech Coll (GA)
Central Oregon Comm Coll (OR)
Central Texas Coll (TX)
Cerritos Coll (CA)
Chattahoochee Tech Coll (GA)
Citrus Coll (CA)
Coll of Central Florida (FL)
Coll of the Desert (CA)
Collin County Comm Coll District (TX)
Columbus Tech Coll (GA)
Comm Coll of Allegheny County (PA)
Comm Coll of Philadelphia (PA)
Crowder Coll (MO)
Daytona State Coll (FL)
Del Mar Coll (TX)
Eastern Arizona Coll (AZ)
El Paso Comm Coll (TX)
Finger Lakes Comm Coll (NY)
Florida SouthWestern State Coll (FL)
Frederick Comm Coll (MD)
Fullerton Coll (CA)
Genesee Comm Coll (NY)
Georgia Piedmont Tech Coll (GA)
Golden West Coll (CA)
Gwinnett Tech Coll (GA)
H. Council Trenholm State Comm Coll (AL)
Hill Coll (TX)
Hinds Comm Coll (MS)
Houston Comm Coll (TX)
Hutchinson Comm Coll (KS)
Illinois Valley Comm Coll (IL)
Iowa Central Comm Coll (IA)
ITI Tech Coll (LA)
Ivy Tech Comm Coll–Bloomington (IN)
Ivy Tech Comm Coll–Central Indiana (IN)
Ivy Tech Comm Coll–Columbus (IN)
Ivy Tech Comm Coll–East Central (IN)
Ivy Tech Comm Coll–Kokomo (IN)
Ivy Tech Comm Coll–Lafayette (IN)
Ivy Tech Comm Coll–Northeast (IN)
Ivy Tech Comm Coll–Northwest (IN)
Ivy Tech Comm Coll–Sellersburg (IN)
Ivy Tech Comm Coll–Southeast (IN)
Ivy Tech Comm Coll–Southwest (IN)
Ivy Tech Comm Coll–Wabash Valley (IN)
Kellogg Comm Coll (MI)
Lanier Tech Coll (GA)
Laramie County Comm Coll (WY)
Lehigh Carbon Comm Coll (PA)
Lone Star Coll–North Harris (TX)
Luzerne County Comm Coll (PA)
Macomb Comm Coll (MI)
Manhattan Area Tech Coll (KS)
Meridian Comm Coll (MS)
Metropolitan Comm Coll (NE)
Miami Dade Coll (FL)
Mohave Comm Coll (AZ)
Monroe County Comm Coll (MI)
Morton Coll (IL)
Mott Comm Coll (MI)
Mountain View Coll (TX)
Mt. San Antonio Coll (CA)
Navarro Coll (TX)
New River Comm Coll (VA)
Niagara County Comm Coll (NY)
North Central Missouri Coll (MO)
Northern Maine Comm Coll (ME)
NorthWest Arkansas Comm Coll (AR)
Northwest-Shoals Comm Coll (AL)
Oklahoma City Comm Coll (OK)
Olympic Coll (WA)
Palomar Coll (CA)
Paris Jr Coll (TX)
Pensacola State Coll (FL)
Pittsburgh Tech Coll (PA)
Renton Tech Coll (WA)
St. Charles Comm Coll (MO)
St. Clair County Comm Coll (MI)
Salt Lake Comm Coll (UT)
San Jacinto Coll District (TX)

San Juan Coll (NM)
Santa Fe Comm Coll (NM)
Schoolcraft Coll (MI)
Seminole State Coll of Florida (FL)
Southeast Comm Coll, Lincoln Campus (NE)
Southeastern Comm Coll (IA)
Southern Crescent Tech Coll (GA)
South Georgia Tech Coll (GA)
South Plains Coll (TX)
Sowela Tech Comm Coll (LA)
State U of New York Coll of Technology at Alfred (NY)
Tallahassee Comm Coll (FL)
Tarrant County Coll District (TX)
Texarkana Coll (TX)
Texas State Tech Coll (TX)
Tidewater Comm Coll (VA)
Treasure Valley Comm Coll (OR)
Trinity Valley Comm Coll (TX)
Truckee Meadows Comm Coll (NV)
Tyler Jr Coll (TX)
U of Arkansas Comm Coll at Morrilton (AR)
Westchester Comm Coll (NY)
Western Dakota Tech Inst (SD)
Wiregrass Georgia Tech Coll (GA)
Wytheville Comm Coll (VA)
York County Comm Coll (ME)

DRAFTING/DESIGN ENGINEERING TECHNOLOGIES RELATED
Coll of The Albemarle (NC)
Comm Coll of Allegheny County (PA)
De Anza Coll (CA)
Genesee Comm Coll (NY)
Hennepin Tech Coll (MN)
Illinois Valley Comm Coll (IL)
Luzerne County Comm Coll (PA)
Macomb Comm Coll (MI)
Madison Area Tech Coll (WI)
Mt. San Antonio Coll (CA)
Niagara County Comm Coll (NY)
Rock Valley Coll (IL)
Ulster County Comm Coll (NY)

DRAMA AND DANCE TEACHER EDUCATION
Hutchinson Comm Coll (KS)

DRAMATIC/THEATER ARTS
Allen Comm Coll (KS)
Alvin Comm Coll (TX)
Amarillo Coll (TX)
American Academy of Dramatic Arts–New York (NY)
Anoka-Ramsey Comm Coll (MN)
Arizona Western Coll (AZ)
Austin Comm Coll District (TX)
Bainbridge State Coll (GA)
Blinn Coll (TX)
Bossier Parish Comm Coll (LA)
Bunker Hill Comm Coll (MA)
Cañada Coll (CA)
Central New Mexico Comm Coll (NM)
Central Texas Coll (TX)
Central Wyoming Coll (WY)
Cerritos Coll (CA)
Chandler-Gilbert Comm Coll (AZ)
Citrus Coll (CA)
Cochise County Comm Coll District (AZ)
Coll of Central Florida (FL)
Coll of Marin (CA)
Coll of The Albemarle (NC)
Coll of the Canyons (CA)
Coll of the Desert (CA)
Comm Coll of Allegheny County (PA)
Comm Coll of Rhode Island (RI)
Crowder Coll (MO)
De Anza Coll (CA)
Del Mar Coll (TX)
Dodge City Comm Coll (KS)
Eastern Arizona Coll (AZ)
Edison State Comm Coll (OH)
Finger Lakes Comm Coll (NY)
Fiorello H. LaGuardia Comm Coll of the City U of New York (NY)
Fullerton Coll (CA)
Genesee Comm Coll (NY)
Gordon State Coll (GA)
Harrisburg Area Comm Coll (PA)
Hill Coll (TX)
Howard Comm Coll (MD)
Kingsborough Comm Coll of the City U of New York (NY)
Lansing Comm Coll (MI)
Manchester Comm Coll (CT)

Merced Coll (CA)
Mercer County Comm Coll (NJ)
Miami Dade Coll (FL)
Nassau Comm Coll (NY)
Navarro Coll (TX)
Niagara County Comm Coll (NY)
Northeast Comm Coll (NE)
Northeastern Jr Coll (CO)
Northern Essex Comm Coll (MA)
Oklahoma City Comm Coll (OK)
Orange Coast Coll (CA)
Otero Jr Coll (CO)
Owensboro Comm and Tech Coll (KY)
Palomar Coll (CA)
Panola Coll (TX)
Paris Jr Coll (TX)
Pensacola State Coll (FL)
St. Philip's Coll (TX)
San Jacinto Coll District (TX)
San Joaquin Delta Coll (CA)
Santa Monica Coll (CA)
Santa Rosa Jr Coll (CA)
Scottsdale Comm Coll (AZ)
South Florida State Coll (FL)
Texarkana Coll (TX)
Trinity Valley Comm Coll (TX)
Tyler Jr Coll (TX)
Ulster County Comm Coll (NY)
Vincennes U (IN)
Western Wyoming Comm Coll (WY)

DRAMATIC/THEATER ARTS AND STAGECRAFT RELATED
Genesee Comm Coll (NY)

DRAWING
Cecil Coll (MD)
De Anza Coll (CA)
Luzerne County Comm Coll (PA)
Palomar Coll (CA)

DRYWALL INSTALLATION
Palomar Coll (CA)

EARLY CHILDHOOD EDUCATION
Aaniiih Nakoda Coll (MT)
Alexandria Tech and Comm Coll (MN)
Alvin Comm Coll (TX)
Ancilla Coll (IN)
Anne Arundel Comm Coll (MD)
Arizona Western Coll (AZ)
Asnuntuck Comm Coll (CT)
Austin Comm Coll District (TX)
Blackhawk Tech Coll (WI)
Bucks County Comm Coll (PA)
Bunker Hill Comm Coll (MA)
Caldwell Comm Coll and Tech Inst (NC)
Camden County Coll (NJ)
Cape Fear Comm Coll (NC)
Carroll Comm Coll (MD)
Carteret Comm Coll (NC)
Central Maine Comm Coll (ME)
Central New Mexico Comm Coll (NM)
Central Oregon Comm Coll (OR)
Central Texas Coll (TX)
Central Wyoming Coll (WY)
Chesapeake Coll (MD)
Chippewa Valley Tech Coll (WI)
Cochise County Comm Coll District (AZ)
Coconino Comm Coll (AZ)
Coll of Central Florida (FL)
Collin County Comm Coll District (TX)
Colorado Northwestern Comm Coll (CO)
Comm Care Coll (OK)
Comm Coll of Baltimore County (MD)
Comm Coll of Vermont (VT)
Craven Comm Coll (NC)
Eastern Arizona Coll (AZ)
Eastern Wyoming Coll (WY)
Fayetteville Tech Comm Coll (NC)
Finger Lakes Comm Coll (NY)
Florida SouthWestern State Coll (FL)
Fox Valley Tech Coll (WI)
Frederick Comm Coll (MD)
Front Range Comm Coll (CO)
Garrett Coll (MD)
Gateway Comm and Tech Coll (KY)
Gateway Tech Coll (WI)
Georgia Military Coll (GA)
Great Basin Coll (NV)
Guam Comm Coll (GU)
Gulf Coast State Coll (FL)
Hagerstown Comm Coll (MD)
Halifax Comm Coll (NC)
Harford Comm Coll (MD)

Harper Coll (IL)
Harrisburg Area Comm Coll (PA)
Haywood Comm Coll (NC)
Hesston Coll (KS)
Highland Comm Coll (IL)
Houston Comm Coll (TX)
Illinois Valley Comm Coll (IL)
Ivy Tech Comm Coll–Bloomington (IN)
Ivy Tech Comm Coll–Central Indiana (IN)
Ivy Tech Comm Coll–Columbus (IN)
Ivy Tech Comm Coll–East Central (IN)
Ivy Tech Comm Coll–Kokomo (IN)
Ivy Tech Comm Coll–Lafayette (IN)
Ivy Tech Comm Coll–North Central (IN)
Ivy Tech Comm Coll–Northeast (IN)
Ivy Tech Comm Coll–Northwest (IN)
Ivy Tech Comm Coll–Richmond (IN)
Ivy Tech Comm Coll–Sellersburg (IN)
Ivy Tech Comm Coll–Southeast (IN)
Ivy Tech Comm Coll–Southwest (IN)
Ivy Tech Comm Coll–Wabash Valley (IN)
James Sprunt Comm Coll (NC)
Jefferson Comm Coll (NY)
Johnston Comm Coll (NC)
Kingsborough Comm Coll of the City U of New York (NY)
Lackawanna Coll (PA)
Laramie County Comm Coll (WY)
Lehigh Carbon Comm Coll (PA)
Lorain County Comm Coll (OH)
Luzerne County Comm Coll (PA)
Massachusetts Bay Comm Coll (MA)
Miami Dade Coll (FL)
Minnesota State Coll–Southeast Tech (MN)
Minnesota State Comm and Tech Coll–Detroit Lakes (MN)
Mitchell Comm Coll (NC)
Montgomery Coll (MD)
Montgomery Comm Coll (NC)
Morton Coll (IL)
Mott Comm Coll (MI)
Nashville State Comm Coll (TN)
Naugatuck Valley Comm Coll (CT)
Northampton Comm Coll (PA)
North Central Missouri Coll (MO)
Northcentral Tech Coll (WI)
Northeast Comm Coll (NE)
NorthWest Arkansas Comm Coll (AR)
Norwalk Comm Coll (CT)
Oklahoma State U–Oklahoma City (OK)
Olympic Coll (WA)
Paris Jr Coll (TX)
Penn Foster Coll (AZ)
Pensacola State Coll (FL)
Piedmont Comm Coll (NC)
Pueblo Comm Coll (CO)
Randolph Comm Coll (NC)
Renton Tech Coll (WA)
Richmond Comm Coll (NC)
Rockingham Comm Coll (NC)
Rowan-Cabarrus Comm Coll (NC)
Santa Rosa Jr Coll (CA)
South Florida State Coll (FL)
Southwestern Indian Polytechnic Inst (NM)
Southwestern Michigan Coll (MI)
Springfield Tech Comm Coll (MA)
Tallahassee Comm Coll (FL)
Tohono O'odham Comm Coll (AZ)
Vincennes U (IN)
Waukesha County Tech Coll (WI)
Western Wyoming Comm Coll (WY)
Westmoreland County Comm Coll (PA)
White Mountains Comm Coll (NH)
Wisconsin Indianhead Tech Coll (WI)
Wor-Wic Comm Coll (MD)
York County Comm Coll (ME)

E-COMMERCE
Augusta Tech Coll (GA)
Brookhaven Coll (TX)
Central Georgia Tech Coll (GA)
Century Coll (MN)
Del Mar Coll (TX)
Finger Lakes Comm Coll (NY)
Genesee Comm Coll (NY)
Lansing Comm Coll (MI)
North Central Missouri Coll (MO)
Wayne County Comm Coll District (MI)
Wiregrass Georgia Tech Coll (GA)

ECONOMICS
Allen Comm Coll (KS)
Austin Comm Coll District (TX)
Cañada Coll (CA)
Casper Coll (WY)
Cerritos Coll (CA)
Cochise County Comm Coll District (AZ)
Coll of Central Florida (FL)
Coll of the Desert (CA)
De Anza Coll (CA)
Eastern Wyoming Coll (WY)
Edison State Comm Coll (OH)
Fullerton Coll (CA)
Hill Coll (TX)
Lansing Comm Coll (MI)
Laramie County Comm Coll (WY)
Lone Star Coll–CyFair (TX)
Miami Dade Coll (FL)
Nashville State Comm Coll (TN)
Northeastern Jr Coll (CO)
Orange Coast Coll (CA)
Palomar Coll (CA)
St. Philip's Coll (TX)
Salt Lake Comm Coll (UT)
San Joaquin Delta Coll (CA)
Santa Monica Coll (CA)
Santa Rosa Jr Coll (CA)
South Florida State Coll (FL)
Tyler Jr Coll (TX)
Vincennes U (IN)
Western Wyoming Comm Coll (WY)

EDUCATION
American Samoa Comm Coll (AS)
Bainbridge State Coll (GA)
Bossier Parish Comm Coll (LA)
Bowling Green State U–Firelands Coll (OH)
Bunker Hill Comm Coll (MA)
Caldwell Comm Coll and Tech Inst (NC)
Cañada Coll (CA)
Carroll Comm Coll (MD)
Cecil Coll (MD)
Central Oregon Comm Coll (OR)
Central Virginia Comm Coll (VA)
Century Coll (MN)
Chesapeake Coll (MD)
Coll of The Albemarle (NC)
Comm Coll of Baltimore County (MD)
Comm Coll of Philadelphia (PA)
Comm Coll of Vermont (VT)
Crowder Coll (MO)
Dakota Coll at Bottineau (ND)
Del Mar Coll (TX)
Dodge City Comm Coll (KS)
Dyersburg State Comm Coll (TN)
East Central Coll (MO)
Edison State Comm Coll (OH)
Frederick Comm Coll (MD)
Garrett Coll (MD)
Genesee Comm Coll (NY)
Georgia Highlands Coll (GA)
Guam Comm Coll (GU)
Hagerstown Comm Coll (MD)
Harford Comm Coll (MD)
Hutchinson Comm Coll (KS)
Illinois Valley Comm Coll (IL)
Iowa Central Comm Coll (IA)
Ivy Tech Comm Coll–Bloomington (IN)
Ivy Tech Comm Coll–Central Indiana (IN)
Ivy Tech Comm Coll–Columbus (IN)
Ivy Tech Comm Coll–East Central (IN)
Ivy Tech Comm Coll–Kokomo (IN)
Ivy Tech Comm Coll–Lafayette (IN)
Ivy Tech Comm Coll–Richmond (IN)
Ivy Tech Comm Coll–Sellersburg (IN)
Ivy Tech Comm Coll–Southeast (IN)
Ivy Tech Comm Coll–Southwest (IN)
Ivy Tech Comm Coll–Wabash Valley (IN)
Kingsborough Comm Coll of the City U of New York (NY)
Lackawanna Coll (PA)
Laramie County Comm Coll (WY)
Lehigh Carbon Comm Coll (PA)
Lone Star Coll–CyFair (TX)
Lone Star Coll–Kingwood (TX)
Lone Star Coll–Montgomery (TX)
Lone Star Coll–North Harris (TX)
Lone Star Coll–Tomball (TX)
Luzerne County Comm Coll (PA)
Miami Dade Coll (FL)
Mohave Comm Coll (AZ)
Motlow State Comm Coll (TN)
Mountain View Coll (TX)
Navarro Coll (TX)

New Mexico Jr Coll (NM)
New River Comm Coll (VA)
Northeast Comm Coll (NE)
Northern Essex Comm Coll (MA)
NorthWest Arkansas Comm Coll (AR)
Nunez Comm Coll (LA)
Palomar Coll (CA)
Panola Coll (TX)
Paris Jr Coll (TX)
Pensacola State Coll (FL)
Santa Fe Comm Coll (NM)
Schoolcraft Coll (MI)
South Plains Coll (TX)
Southwest Texas Jr Coll (TX)
Three Rivers Comm Coll (CT)
Tidewater Comm Coll (VA)
Trinity Valley Comm Coll (TX)
U of Cincinnati Blue Ash Coll (OH)
Vincennes U (IN)
Virginia Western Comm Coll (VA)
Volunteer State Comm Coll (TN)
Walters State Comm Coll (TN)
Western Wyoming Comm Coll (WY)
White Mountains Comm Coll (NH)
Wor-Wic Comm Coll (MD)
Wytheville Comm Coll (VA)
York County Comm Coll (ME)

EDUCATIONAL/ INSTRUCTIONAL TECHNOLOGY
Bossier Parish Comm Coll (LA)
Comm Coll of the Air Force (AL)
Gateway Comm and Tech Coll (KY)
Ivy Tech Comm Coll–North Central (IN)
Lone Star Coll–North Harris (TX)
Tarrant County Coll District (TX)
Texas State Tech Coll (TX)

EDUCATIONAL LEADERSHIP AND ADMINISTRATION
Comm Coll of the Air Force (AL)

EDUCATION (MULTIPLE LEVELS)
Brookhaven Coll (TX)
Camden County Coll (NJ)
Cayuga County Comm Coll (NY)
Central New Mexico Comm Coll (NM)
Genesee Comm Coll (NY)
Houston Comm Coll (TX)
Kishwaukee Coll (IL)
Lorain County Comm Coll (OH)
Oklahoma State U Inst of Technology (OK)
Paris Jr Coll (TX)
St. Philip's Coll (TX)
Southern Arkansas U Tech (AR)
Three Rivers Comm Coll (MO)
Tyler Jr Coll (TX)
Westchester Comm Coll (NY)
Western Wyoming Comm Coll (WY)

EDUCATION RELATED
Genesee Comm Coll (NY)
Kent State U at Salem (OH)
Kent State U at Tuscarawas (OH)
Miami Dade Coll (FL)

EDUCATION (SPECIFIC LEVELS AND METHODS) RELATED
Comm Coll of Allegheny County (PA)
Harford Comm Coll (MD)
Manor Coll (PA)
Miami Dade Coll (FL)

EDUCATION (SPECIFIC SUBJECT AREAS) RELATED
Comm Coll of Allegheny County (PA)
Harford Comm Coll (MD)
St. Charles Comm Coll (MO)
Three Rivers Comm Coll (MO)

ELECTRICAL AND ELECTRONIC ENGINEERING TECHNOLOGIES RELATED
Albany Tech Coll (GA)
Blue Ridge Comm and Tech Coll (WV)
Columbus State Comm Coll (OH)
Comm Coll of Rhode Island (RI)
Fox Valley Tech Coll (WI)
Kent State U at Trumbull (OH)
Kent State U at Tuscarawas (OH)
Lake Region State Coll (ND)
Massachusetts Bay Comm Coll (MA)
Miami Dade Coll (FL)
Minnesota State Comm and Tech Coll (MN)

Owensboro Comm and Tech Coll (KY)
Wayne County Comm Coll District (MI)

ELECTRICAL AND ELECTRONICS ENGINEERING
Allen Comm Coll (KS)
Anne Arundel Comm Coll (MD)
Caldwell Comm Coll and Tech Inst (NC)
Carroll Comm Coll (MD)
Comm Coll of Baltimore County (MD)
Fiorello H. LaGuardia Comm Coll of the City U of New York (NY)
Garrett Coll (MD)
Humacao Comm Coll (PR)
Olympic Coll (WA)
South Florida State Coll (FL)

ELECTRICAL AND POWER TRANSMISSION INSTALLATION
Delta Coll (MI)
Ivy Tech Comm Coll–Columbus (IN)
Lansing Comm Coll (MI)
Lorain County Comm Coll (OH)
Manhattan Area Tech Coll (KS)
Minnesota West Comm and Tech Coll (MN)
Oklahoma State U–Oklahoma City (OK)
Piedmont Comm Coll (NC)
Richmond Comm Coll (NC)
Rogue Comm Coll (OR)
San Jacinto Coll District (TX)
State U of New York Coll of Technology at Alfred (NY)
Westmoreland County Comm Coll (PA)

ELECTRICAL AND POWER TRANSMISSION INSTALLATION RELATED
Manhattan Area Tech Coll (KS)
Minnesota State Comm and Tech Coll–Wadena (MN)
Minnesota West Comm and Tech Coll (MN)
Oklahoma State U–Oklahoma City (OK)

ELECTRICAL, ELECTRONIC AND COMMUNICATIONS ENGINEERING TECHNOLOGY
Adirondack Comm Coll (NY)
Alamance Comm Coll (NC)
Allen Comm Coll (KS)
Alvin Comm Coll (TX)
Amarillo Coll (TX)
American Samoa Comm Coll (AS)
Anne Arundel Comm Coll (MD)
Anoka Tech Coll (MN)
Arizona Western Coll (AZ)
Athens Tech Coll (GA)
Augusta Tech Coll (GA)
Austin Comm Coll District (TX)
Bainbridge State Coll (GA)
Berkshire Comm Coll (MA)
Bismarck State Coll (ND)
Camden County Coll (NJ)
Cape Fear Comm Coll (NC)
Casper Coll (WY)
Cayuga County Comm Coll (NY)
Cecil Coll (MD)
Central Georgia Tech Coll (GA)
Central Oregon Comm Coll (OR)
Cerritos Coll (CA)
Chattahoochee Tech Coll (GA)
Citrus Coll (CA)
Clinton Comm Coll (NY)
Cochise County Comm Coll District (AZ)
Coconino Comm Coll (AZ)
Collin County Comm Coll District (TX)
Columbus State Comm Coll (OH)
Columbus Tech Coll (GA)
Comm Coll of Allegheny County (PA)
Comm Coll of the Air Force (AL)
County of Morris (NJ)
Craven Comm Coll (NC)
Crowder Coll (MO)
Daytona State Coll (FL)
Del Mar Coll (TX)
Des Moines Area Comm Coll (IA)
Dodge City Comm Coll (KS)
Dunwoody Coll of Technology (MN)
Dutchess Comm Coll (NY)
Edison State Comm Coll (OH)
El Paso Comm Coll (TX)
Erie Comm Coll, North Campus (NY)
Fayetteville Tech Comm Coll (NC)

Fox Valley Tech Coll (WI)
Gateway Tech Coll (WI)
Georgia Piedmont Tech Coll (GA)
Golden West Coll (CA)
Grand Rapids Comm Coll (MI)
Great Basin Coll (NV)
Greenville Tech Coll (SC)
Gulf Coast State Coll (FL)
Gwinnett Tech Coll (GA)
Harper Coll (IL)
Harrisburg Area Comm Coll (PA)
Hawkeye Comm Coll (IA)
Haywood Comm Coll (NC)
Hennepin Tech Coll (MN)
Hillsborough Comm Coll (FL)
Hinds Comm Coll (MS)
Horry Georgetown Tech Coll (SC)
Howard Comm Coll (MD)
Hudson County Comm Coll (NJ)
Hutchinson Comm Coll (KS)
Illinois Central Coll (IL)
Illinois Valley Comm Coll (IL)
Iowa Central Comm Coll (IA)
ITI Tech Coll (LA)
Ivy Tech Comm Coll–Bloomington (IN)
Ivy Tech Comm Coll–Central Indiana (IN)
Ivy Tech Comm Coll–Columbus (IN)
Ivy Tech Comm Coll–East Central (IN)
Ivy Tech Comm Coll–Kokomo (IN)
Ivy Tech Comm Coll–Lafayette (IN)
Ivy Tech Comm Coll–North Central (IN)
Ivy Tech Comm Coll–Northeast (IN)
Ivy Tech Comm Coll–Northwest (IN)
Ivy Tech Comm Coll–Richmond (IN)
Ivy Tech Comm Coll–Sellersburg (IN)
Ivy Tech Comm Coll–Southeast (IN)
Ivy Tech Comm Coll–Southwest (IN)
Ivy Tech Comm Coll–Wabash Valley (IN)
Kaskaskia Coll (IL)
Kirtland Comm Coll (MI)
Kishwaukee Coll (IL)
Lake Area Tech Inst (SD)
Lakeland Comm Coll (OH)
Lake Superior Coll (MN)
Lanier Tech Coll (GA)
Lehigh Carbon Comm Coll (PA)
Lone Star Coll–CyFair (TX)
Lone Star Coll–North Harris (TX)
Lone Star Coll–Tomball (TX)
Lorain County Comm Coll (OH)
Luzerne County Comm Coll (PA)
Macomb Comm Coll (MI)
Madison Area Tech Coll (WI)
Massachusetts Bay Comm Coll (MA)
Mercer County Comm Coll (NJ)
Meridian Comm Coll (MS)
Mesa Comm Coll (AZ)
Metropolitan Comm Coll (NE)
Miami Dade Coll (FL)
Middlesex Comm Coll (MA)
Middlesex County Coll (NJ)
Minnesota State Coll–Southeast Tech (MN)
Minnesota State Comm and Tech Coll (MN)
Mitchell Comm Coll (NC)
Mohawk Valley Comm Coll (NY)
Monroe Comm Coll (NY)
Monroe County Comm Coll (MI)
Montgomery County Comm Coll (PA)
Mott Comm Coll (MI)
Mountain View Coll (TX)
Mt. San Antonio Coll (CA)
Nashville State Comm Coll (TN)
Naugatuck Valley Comm Coll (CT)
New River Comm Coll (VA)
NHTI, Concord's Comm Coll, Concord (NH)
Northampton Comm Coll (PA)
North Central Missouri Coll (MO)
Northeast Iowa Comm Coll (IA)
Northern Essex Comm Coll (MA)
Northern Maine Comm Coll (ME)
NorthWest Arkansas Comm Coll (AR)
Oakton Comm Coll (IL)
Oklahoma State U–Oklahoma City (OK)
Olympic Coll (WA)
Ozarks Tech Comm Coll (MO)
Paris Jr Coll (TX)
Penn State DuBois (PA)
Penn State Fayette, The Eberly Campus (PA)
Penn State Shenango (PA)

Pennsylvania Inst of Technology (PA)
Pensacola State Coll (FL)
Pittsburgh Inst of Aeronautics (PA)
Pittsburgh Tech Coll (PA)
Pueblo Comm Coll (CO)
Queensborough Comm Coll of the City U of New York (NY)
Quinsigamond Comm Coll (MA)
Reid State Tech Coll (AL)
Rend Lake Coll (IL)
Richmond Comm Coll (NC)
Rockingham Comm Coll (NC)
Rock Valley Coll (IL)
Rogue Comm Coll (OR)
Rowan-Cabarrus Comm Coll (NC)
St. Clair County Comm Coll (MI)
Salt Lake Comm Coll (UT)
San Jacinto Coll District (TX)
San Joaquin Delta Coll (CA)
San Juan Coll (NM)
Santa Fe Comm Coll (NM)
Santa Rosa Jr Coll (CA)
Savannah Tech Coll (GA)
Schoolcraft Coll (MI)
Scottsdale Comm Coll (AZ)
Seminole State Coll of Florida (FL)
Shawnee Comm Coll (IL)
Sisseton-Wahpeton Coll (SD)
Southeast Comm Coll, Lincoln Campus (NE)
Southeast Comm Coll, Milford Campus (NE)
Southeastern Comm Coll (IA)
Southeastern Tech Coll (GA)
Southern Crescent Tech Coll (GA)
Southern U at Shreveport (LA)
South Florida State Coll (FL)
South Georgia Tech Coll (GA)
South Plains Coll (TX)
South Suburban Coll (IL)
Southwestern Comm Coll (NC)
Southwest Virginia Comm Coll (VA)
Spartanburg Comm Coll (SC)
Springfield Tech Comm Coll (MA)
State U of New York Coll of Technology at Alfred (NY)
Sullivan County Comm Coll (NY)
Tarrant County Coll District (TX)
Texarkana Coll (TX)
Texas State Tech Coll (TX)
Three Rivers Comm Coll (CT)
Three Rivers Comm Coll (MO)
Tidewater Comm Coll (VA)
Trident Tech Coll (SC)
Victoria Coll (TX)
Vincennes U (IN)
Virginia Western Comm Coll (VA)
Waukesha County Tech Coll (WI)
Wayne County Comm Coll District (MI)
Westchester Comm Coll (NY)
Western Wyoming Comm Coll (WY)
West Georgia Tech Coll (GA)
Westmoreland County Comm Coll (PA)
Wytheville Comm Coll (VA)

ELECTRICAL/ELECTRONICS DRAFTING AND CAD/CADD
Dunwoody Coll of Technology (MN)
Middlesex Comm Coll (MA)
Palomar Coll (CA)

ELECTRICAL/ELECTRONICS EQUIPMENT INSTALLATION AND REPAIR
Cape Fear Comm Coll (NC)
Fullerton Coll (CA)
Hinds Comm Coll (MS)
Hutchinson Comm Coll (KS)
Johnson County Comm Coll (KS)
Macomb Comm Coll (MI)
Merced Coll (CA)
Mesabi Range Coll (MN)
Orange Coast Coll (CA)
Pittsburgh Tech Coll (PA)
Sierra Coll (CA)
Western Wyoming Comm Coll (WY)

ELECTRICAL/ELECTRONICS MAINTENANCE AND REPAIR TECHNOLOGY RELATED
Bunker Hill Comm Coll (MA)
Mohawk Valley Comm Coll (NY)

ELECTRICIAN
Adirondack Comm Coll (NY)
Bevill State Comm Coll (AL)
Central New Mexico Comm Coll (NM)

Coll of Business and Technology–Cutler Bay Campus (FL)
Coll of Business and Technology–Flagler Campus (FL)
Coll of Business and Technology–Hialeah Campus (FL)
Coll of Business and Technology–Miami Gardens (FL)
Danville Area Comm Coll (IL)
Delta Coll (MI)
Dunwoody Coll of Technology (MN)
Eastern Idaho Tech Coll (ID)
Fayetteville Tech Comm Coll (NC)
Harrisburg Area Comm Coll (PA)
Haywood Comm Coll (NC)
H. Councill Trenholm State Comm Coll (AL)
Hinds Comm Coll (MS)
Illinois Valley Comm Coll (IL)
Ivy Tech Comm Coll–Bloomington (IN)
Ivy Tech Comm Coll–Central Indiana (IN)
Ivy Tech Comm Coll–East Central (IN)
Ivy Tech Comm Coll–Kokomo (IN)
Ivy Tech Comm Coll–Lafayette (IN)
Ivy Tech Comm Coll–North Central (IN)
Ivy Tech Comm Coll–Northeast (IN)
Ivy Tech Comm Coll–Northwest (IN)
Ivy Tech Comm Coll–Richmond (IN)
Ivy Tech Comm Coll–Sellersburg (IN)
Ivy Tech Comm Coll–Southwest (IN)
Ivy Tech Comm Coll–Wabash Valley (IN)
Johnson County Comm Coll (KS)
Kellogg Comm Coll (MI)
Lake Superior Coll (MN)
Lansing Comm Coll (MI)
Luzerne County Comm Coll (PA)
Merced Coll (CA)
Miami Dade Coll (FL)
Minnesota West Comm and Tech Coll (MN)
Mitchell Comm Coll (NC)
Mitchell Tech Inst (SD)
Montgomery Comm Coll (NC)
Northampton Comm Coll (PA)
Northeast Comm Coll (NE)
Northeast Iowa Comm Coll (IA)
Palomar Coll (CA)
Panola Coll (TX)
Piedmont Comm Coll (NC)
Randolph Comm Coll (NC)
Rend Lake Coll (IL)
Rockingham Comm Coll (NC)
Rock Valley Coll (IL)
Rowan-Cabarrus Comm Coll (NC)
St. Philip's Coll (TX)
Salina Area Tech Coll (KS)
Three Rivers Comm Coll (MO)
Western Dakota Tech Inst (SD)
Western Wyoming Comm Coll (WY)

ELECTROCARDIOGRAPH TECHNOLOGY
Oklahoma State U–Oklahoma City (OK)
Orange Coast Coll (CA)

ELECTROMECHANICAL AND INSTRUMENTATION AND MAINTENANCE TECHNOLOGIES RELATED
Cape Fear Comm Coll (NC)
Greenville Tech Coll (SC)
Halifax Comm Coll (NC)
Haywood Comm Coll (NC)
Mitchell Comm Coll (NC)
Montgomery Comm Coll (NC)
Piedmont Comm Coll (NC)
Pueblo Comm Coll (CO)
Richmond Comm Coll (NC)

ELECTROMECHANICAL TECHNOLOGY
Blackhawk Tech Coll (WI)
Camden County Coll (NJ)
Central Maine Comm Coll (ME)
Chandler-Gilbert Comm Coll (AZ)
Chippewa Valley Tech Coll (WI)
Coll of the Ouachitas (AR)
Columbus State Comm Coll (OH)
Comm Coll of Rhode Island (RI)
Craven Comm Coll (NC)
Edison State Comm Coll (OH)
Fox Valley Tech Coll (WI)
Gateway Tech Coll (WI)
Georgia Piedmont Tech Coll (GA)

Hawkeye Comm Coll (IA)
Kirtland Comm Coll (MI)
Lansing Comm Coll (MI)
Macomb Comm Coll (MI)
Maysville Comm and Tech Coll, Maysville (KY)
Mesa Comm Coll (AZ)
Montgomery County Comm Coll (PA)
Motlow State Comm Coll (TN)
Northampton Comm Coll (PA)
Northcentral Tech Coll (WI)
Northeast Comm Coll (NE)
Paris Jr Coll (TX)
Quinsigamond Comm Coll (MA)
Randolph Comm Coll (NC)
Richmond Comm Coll (NC)
Springfield Tech Comm Coll (MA)
Tarrant County Coll District (TX)
Texas State Tech Coll (TX)
Tyler Jr Coll (TX)
Volunteer State Comm Coll (TN)

ELECTRONEURODIAGNOSTIC/ELECTROENCEPHALOGRAPHIC TECHNOLOGY
Alvin Comm Coll (TX)
Collin County Comm Coll District (TX)
Comm Coll of Allegheny County (PA)
Harford Comm Coll (MD)
Lone Star Coll–Kingwood (TX)
Orange Coast Coll (CA)

ELEMENTARY EDUCATION
Aaniiih Nakoda Coll (MT)
Allen Comm Coll (KS)
Amarillo Coll (TX)
Ancilla Coll (IN)
Arizona Western Coll (AZ)
Bainbridge State Coll (GA)
Carl Albert State Coll (OK)
Carroll Comm Coll (MD)
Casper Coll (WY)
Cecil Coll (MD)
Central Wyoming Coll (WY)
Chandler-Gilbert Comm Coll (AZ)
Chesapeake Coll (MD)
Cochise County Comm Coll District (AZ)
Coconino Comm Coll (AZ)
Coll of Central Florida (FL)
Coll of the Marshall Islands (MH)
Comm Coll of Baltimore County (MD)
Craven Comm Coll (NC)
Crowder Coll (MO)
Del Mar Coll (TX)
Dodge City Comm Coll (KS)
Eastern Arizona Coll (AZ)
Eastern Wyoming Coll (WY)
Fayetteville Tech Comm Coll (NC)
Frederick Comm Coll (MD)
Garrett Coll (MD)
Genesee Comm Coll (NY)
Grand Rapids Comm Coll (MI)
Great Basin Coll (NV)
Hagerstown Comm Coll (MD)
Harford Comm Coll (MD)
Harper Coll (IL)
Haywood Comm Coll (NC)
Hill Coll (TX)
Howard Comm Coll (MD)
Illinois Valley Comm Coll (IL)
James Sprunt Comm Coll (NC)
Kellogg Comm Coll (MI)
Kingsborough Comm Coll of the City U of New York (NY)
Lansing Comm Coll (MI)
Lenoir Comm Coll (NC)
Manor Coll (PA)
Massachusetts Bay Comm Coll (MA)
Miami Dade Coll (FL)
Middlesex Comm Coll (MA)
Missouri State U–West Plains (MO)
Mitchell Comm Coll (NC)
Monroe County Comm Coll (MI)
Montgomery Coll (MD)
Montgomery County Comm Coll (PA)
Murray State Coll (OK)
Nashville State Comm Coll (TN)
Navarro Coll (TX)
New Mexico Jr Coll (NM)
Niagara County Comm Coll (NY)
Northeast Comm Coll (NE)
Northeastern Jr Coll (CO)
Northern Essex Comm Coll (MA)
Northwest Coll (WY)
Oklahoma City Comm Coll (OK)
Orange Coast Coll (CA)
Otero Jr Coll (CO)

Paris Jr Coll (TX)
Pensacola State Coll (FL)
Quinsigamond Comm Coll (MA)
Richmond Comm Coll (NC)
Rowan-Cabarrus Comm Coll (NC)
San Juan Coll (NM)
Seminole State Coll (OK)
South Florida State Coll (FL)
Springfield Tech Comm Coll (MA)
Sullivan County Comm Coll (NY)
Treasure Valley Comm Coll (OR)
Trinity Valley Comm Coll (TX)
Truckee Meadows Comm Coll (NV)
U of Cincinnati Clermont Coll (OH)
Vincennes U (IN)
Wayne County Comm Coll District (MI)
Western Wyoming Comm Coll (WY)
Wor-Wic Comm Coll (MD)

EMERGENCY CARE ATTENDANT (EMT AMBULANCE)
Coconino Comm Coll (AZ)
Illinois Eastern Comm Colls, Frontier Community College (IL)
Mohawk Valley Comm Coll (NY)
Salina Area Tech Coll (KS)

EMERGENCY MEDICAL TECHNOLOGY (EMT PARAMEDIC)
Allen Comm Coll (KS)
Alvin Comm Coll (TX)
Amarillo Coll (TX)
Arapahoe Comm Coll (CO)
Arizona Western Coll (AZ)
Athens Tech Coll (GA)
Augusta Tech Coll (GA)
Austin Comm Coll District (TX)
Bevill State Comm Coll (AL)
Bismarck State Coll (ND)
Blue Ridge Comm and Tech Coll (WV)
Borough of Manhattan Comm Coll of the City U of New York (NY)
Bossier Parish Comm Coll (LA)
Brookhaven Coll (TX)
Bunker Hill Comm Coll (MA)
Caldwell Comm Coll and Tech Inst (NC)
Camden County Coll (NJ)
Cape Fear Comm Coll (NC)
Carroll Comm Coll (MD)
Carteret Comm Coll (NC)
Casper Coll (WY)
Cecil Coll (MD)
Central New Mexico Comm Coll (NM)
Central Oregon Comm Coll (OR)
Central Texas Coll (TX)
Central Virginia Comm Coll (VA)
Century Coll (MN)
Chesapeake Coll (MD)
Chippewa Valley Tech Coll (WI)
Cochise County Comm Coll District (AZ)
Coll of Central Florida (FL)
Collin County Comm Coll District (TX)
Colorado Northwestern Comm Coll (CO)
Columbus State Comm Coll (OH)
Columbus Tech Coll (GA)
Comm Coll of Aurora (CO)
Comm Coll of Baltimore County (MD)
Crowder Coll (MO)
Daytona State Coll (FL)
Del Mar Coll (TX)
Dutchess Comm Coll (NY)
Dyersburg State Comm Coll (TN)
East Central Coll (MO)
Eastern Arizona Coll (AZ)
El Paso Comm Coll (TX)
Erie Comm Coll, South Campus (NY)
Fayetteville Tech Comm Coll (NC)
Finger Lakes Comm Coll (NY)
Fiorello H. LaGuardia Comm Coll of the City U of New York (NY)
Florida SouthWestern State Coll (FL)
Fox Valley Tech Coll (WI)
Frederick Comm Coll (MD)
Gateway Tech Coll (WI)
Great Basin Coll (NV)
Great Falls Coll Montana State U (MT)
Greenville Tech Coll (SC)
Gulf Coast State Coll (FL)

Gwinnett Tech Coll (GA)
Hagerstown Comm Coll (MD)
Harper Coll (IL)
Harrisburg Area Comm Coll (PA)
Hawkeye Comm Coll (IA)
H. Councill Trenholm State Comm Coll (AL)
Highland Comm Coll (IL)
Hill Coll (TX)
Hillsborough Comm Coll (FL)
Hinds Comm Coll (MS)
Houston Comm Coll (TX)
Howard Comm Coll (MD)
Hudson County Comm Coll (NJ)
Hutchinson Comm Coll (KS)
Illinois Central Coll (IL)
Ivy Tech Comm Coll–Bloomington (IN)
Ivy Tech Comm Coll–Columbus (IN)
Ivy Tech Comm Coll–Kokomo (IN)
Ivy Tech Comm Coll–North Central (IN)
Ivy Tech Comm Coll–Richmond (IN)
Ivy Tech Comm Coll–Southwest (IN)
Ivy Tech Comm Coll–Wabash Valley (IN)
Jefferson Comm Coll (NY)
Jefferson State Comm Coll (AL)
Johnson County Comm Coll (KS)
John Tyler Comm Coll (VA)
J. Sargeant Reynolds Comm Coll (VA)
Kaskaskia Coll (IL)
Kellogg Comm Coll (MI)
Kent State U at Trumbull (OH)
Kirtland Comm Coll (MI)
Kishwaukee Coll (IL)
Lackawanna Coll (PA)
Lake Area Tech Inst (SD)
Lansing Comm Coll (MI)
Laramie County Comm Coll (WY)
Lenoir Comm Coll (NC)
Lone Star Coll–CyFair (TX)
Lone Star Coll–Montgomery (TX)
Lone Star Coll–North Harris (TX)
Lorain County Comm Coll (OH)
Lurleen B. Wallace Comm Coll (AL)
Luzerne County Comm Coll (PA)
Macomb Comm Coll (MI)
Madison Area Tech Coll (WI)
McHenry County Coll (IL)
Merced Coll (CA)
Meridian Comm Coll (MS)
Mesa Comm Coll (AZ)
Miami Dade Coll (FL)
Mohave Comm Coll (AZ)
Mott Comm Coll (MI)
Mt. San Antonio Coll (CA)
NHTI, Concord's Comm Coll, Concord (NH)
North Central Missouri Coll (MO)
Northcentral Tech Coll (WI)
Northeast Comm Coll (NE)
Northeastern Jr Coll (CO)
Northeast Iowa Comm Coll (IA)
Northern Essex Comm Coll (MA)
Northern Maine Comm Coll (ME)
Northland Comm and Tech Coll (MN)
NorthWest Arkansas Comm Coll (AR)
Northwest-Shoals Comm Coll (AL)
Oklahoma City Comm Coll (OK)
Oklahoma State U–Oklahoma City (OK)
Owensboro Comm and Tech Coll (KY)
Ozarks Tech Comm Coll (MO)
Palomar Coll (CA)
Paris Jr Coll (TX)
Patrick Henry Comm Coll (VA)
Pensacola State Coll (FL)
Pueblo Comm Coll (CO)
Quinsigamond Comm Coll (MA)
Rend Lake Coll (IL)
Rogue Comm Coll (OR)
St. Charles Comm Coll (MO)
St. Clair County Comm Coll (MI)
San Jacinto Coll District (TX)
San Juan Coll (NM)
Santa Rosa Jr Coll (CA)
Schoolcraft Coll (MI)
Seminole State Coll of Florida (FL)
Southeast Comm Coll, Lincoln Campus (NE)
Southeastern Coll–West Palm Beach (FL)
Southeastern Comm Coll (IA)
Southern Crescent Tech Coll (GA)
South Florida State Coll (FL)
Southwestern Comm Coll (NC)

Southwest Virginia Comm Coll (VA)
Tallahassee Comm Coll (FL)
Tarrant County Comm Coll District (TX)
Texarkana Coll (TX)
Three Rivers Comm Coll (MO)
Trinity Valley Comm Coll (TX)
Tyler Jr Coll (TX)
Victoria Coll (TX)
Vincennes U (IN)
Waukesha County Tech Coll (WI)
Wayne County Comm Coll District (MI)
Weatherford Coll (TX)
Westchester Comm Coll (NY)
Western Dakota Tech Inst (SD)
Wisconsin Indianhead Tech Coll (WI)
Wor-Wic Comm Coll (MD)

ENERGY MANAGEMENT AND SYSTEMS TECHNOLOGY
Casper Coll (WY)
Century Coll (MN)
Clinton Comm Coll (NY)
Comm Coll of Allegheny County (PA)
Crowder Coll (MO)
Danville Area Comm Coll (IL)
Delta Coll (MI)
Fiorello H. LaGuardia Comm Coll of the City U of New York (NY)
Fox Valley Tech Coll (WI)
Front Range Comm Coll (CO)
Hawkeye Comm Coll (IA)
Houston Comm Coll (TX)
Illinois Central Coll (IL)
Illinois Eastern Comm Colls, Wabash Valley College (IL)
Ivy Tech Comm Coll–East Central (IN)
Ivy Tech Comm Coll–Sellersburg (IN)
Ivy Tech Comm Coll–Southwest (IN)
Ivy Tech Comm Coll–Wabash Valley (IN)
Lakeland Comm Coll (OH)
Lamar Comm Coll (CO)
Lansing Comm Coll (MI)
Laramie County Comm Coll (WY)
Lenoir Comm Coll (NC)
Lorain County Comm Coll (OH)
Macomb Comm Coll (MI)
Middlesex County Coll (NJ)
Minnesota West Comm and Tech Coll (MN)
Mitchell Tech Inst (SD)
Mount Wachusett Comm Coll (MA)
Northeast Comm Coll (NE)
Northeast Iowa Comm Coll (IA)
Oklahoma State U–Oklahoma City (OK)
Quinsigamond Comm Coll (MA)
The Refrigeration School (AZ)
Rock Valley Coll (IL)
St. Clair County Comm Coll (MI)
Santa Monica Coll (CA)
Southeast Comm Coll, Milford Campus (NE)
Truckee Meadows Comm Coll (NV)
Walters State Comm Coll (TN)

ENGINEERING
Adirondack Comm Coll (NY)
Allen Comm Coll (KS)
Amarillo Coll (TX)
Anne Arundel Comm Coll (MD)
Arizona Western Coll (AZ)
Austin Comm Coll District (TX)
Berkshire Comm Coll (MA)
Borough of Manhattan Comm Coll of the City U of New York (NY)
Bossier Parish Comm Coll (LA)
Bunker Hill Comm Coll (MA)
Cañada Coll (CA)
Carl Albert State Coll (OK)
Casper Coll (WY)
Central Oregon Comm Coll (OR)
Central Texas Coll (TX)
Central Virginia Comm Coll (VA)
Central Wyoming Coll (WY)
Citrus Coll (CA)
Cochise County Comm Coll District (AZ)
Coll of Central Florida (FL)
Coll of Marin (CA)
Collin County Comm Coll District (TX)
Comm Coll of Baltimore County (MD)
Comm Coll of Philadelphia (PA)
Comm Coll of Rhode Island (RI)
Danville Area Comm Coll (IL)
Daytona State Coll (FL)
De Anza Coll (CA)
Dodge City Comm Coll (KS)

Dutchess Comm Coll (NY)
East Central Coll (MO)
Elgin Comm Coll (IL)
El Paso Comm Coll (TX)
Erie Comm Coll, North Campus (NY)
Frederick Comm Coll (MD)
Fullerton Coll (CA)
Genesee Comm Coll (NY)
Georgia Highlands Coll (GA)
Gordon State Coll (GA)
Grand Rapids Comm Coll (MI)
Hagerstown Comm Coll (MD)
Harford Comm Coll (MD)
Harper Coll (IL)
Harrisburg Area Comm Coll (PA)
Highland Comm Coll (IL)
Hill Coll (TX)
Holyoke Comm Coll (MA)
Howard Comm Coll (MD)
Hutchinson Comm Coll (KS)
Illinois Central Coll (IL)
Illinois Eastern Comm Colls, Frontier Community College (IL)
Illinois Eastern Comm Colls, Olney Central College (IL)
Illinois Eastern Comm Colls, Wabash Valley College (IL)
Illinois Valley Comm Coll (IL)
Jamestown Comm Coll (NY)
Jefferson Comm Coll (NY)
John Tyler Comm Coll (VA)
J. Sargeant Reynolds Comm Coll (VA)
Kaskaskia Coll (IL)
Kishwaukee Coll (IL)
Lansing Comm Coll (MI)
Laramie County Comm Coll (WY)
Lehigh Carbon Comm Coll (PA)
Los Angeles City Coll (CA)
McHenry County Coll (IL)
Miami Dade Coll (FL)
Minnesota State Comm and Tech Coll–Moorhead (MN)
Missouri State U–West Plains (MO)
Mohawk Valley Comm Coll (NY)
Montgomery Coll (MD)
Nassau Comm Coll (NY)
Navarro Coll (TX)
New Mexico Jr Coll (NM)
New River Comm Coll (VA)
Northampton Comm Coll (PA)
Northeast Comm Coll (NE)
Northwest Coll (WY)
Oakton Comm Coll (IL)
Paris Jr Coll (TX)
Pensacola State Coll (FL)
Queensborough Comm Coll of the City U of New York (NY)
Rend Lake Coll (IL)
St. Charles Comm Coll (MO)
St. Clair County Comm Coll (MI)
St. Philip's Coll (TX)
Salt Lake Comm Coll (UT)
San Jacinto Coll District (TX)
San Joaquin Delta Coll (CA)
San Juan Coll (NM)
Santa Fe Comm Coll (NM)
Santa Rosa Jr Coll (CA)
Schoolcraft Coll (MI)
Seminole State Coll (OK)
Sierra Coll (CA)
South Florida State Coll (FL)
South Plains Coll (TX)
Southwestern Indian Polytechnic Inst (NM)
Southwest Texas Jr Coll (TX)
Springfield Tech Comm Coll (MA)
State U of New York Coll of Technology at Alfred (NY)
Texarkana Coll (TX)
Tidewater Comm Coll (VA)
Tompkins Cortland Comm Coll (NY)
Truckee Meadows Comm Coll (NV)
Tyler Jr Coll (TX)
Ulster County Comm Coll (NY)
Virginia Western Comm Coll (VA)
Westchester Comm Coll (NY)

ENGINEERING/INDUSTRIAL MANAGEMENT
Mitchell Comm Coll (NC)

ENGINEERING PHYSICS/ APPLIED PHYSICS
Lansing Comm Coll (MI)

ENGINEERING RELATED
Macomb Comm Coll (MI)
Miami Dade Coll (FL)
San Joaquin Delta Coll (CA)
Southeastern Comm Coll (IA)

ENGINEERING-RELATED TECHNOLOGIES
Chesapeake Coll (MD)

ENGINEERING SCIENCE
Asnuntuck Comm Coll (CT)
Camden County Coll (NJ)
County Coll of Morris (NJ)
Finger Lakes Comm Coll (NY)
Genesee Comm Coll (NY)
Houston Comm Coll (TX)
Hudson County Comm Coll (NJ)
Jefferson Comm Coll (NY)
Kingsborough Comm Coll of the City U of New York (NY)
Manchester Comm Coll (CT)
Mercer County Comm Coll (NJ)
Middlesex County Coll (NJ)
Monroe Comm Coll (NY)
Montgomery County Comm Coll (PA)
Naugatuck Valley Comm Coll (CT)
Northern Essex Comm Coll (MA)
North Shore Comm Coll (MA)
Norwalk Comm Coll (CT)
Queensborough Comm Coll of the City U of New York (NY)
Raritan Valley Comm Coll (NJ)
South Florida State Coll (FL)
Three Rivers Comm Coll (CT)

ENGINEERING TECHNOLOGIES AND ENGINEERING RELATED
Camden County Coll (NJ)
Carl Albert State Coll (OK)
Chesapeake Coll (MD)
Clinton Comm Coll (NY)
Comm Coll of Allegheny County (PA)
Comm Coll of Baltimore County (MD)
County Coll of Morris (NJ)
Hagerstown Comm Coll (MD)
Harrisburg Area Comm Coll (PA)
Hudson County Comm Coll (NJ)
Massachusetts Bay Comm Coll (MA)
Middlesex Comm Coll (MA)
Middlesex County Coll (NJ)
Montgomery County Comm Coll (PA)
Mott Comm Coll (MI)
Oklahoma City Comm Coll (OK)
Orange Coast Coll (CA)
Quinsigamond Comm Coll (MA)
Raritan Valley Comm Coll (NJ)
Southern Arkansas U Tech (AR)
Truckee Meadows Comm Coll (NV)

ENGINEERING TECHNOLOGY
Allen Comm Coll (KS)
Arapahoe Comm Coll (CO)
Asnuntuck Comm Coll (CT)
Bismarck State Coll (ND)
Bucks County Comm Coll (PA)
Central Virginia Comm Coll (VA)
Century Coll (MN)
Citrus Coll (CA)
Coll of Central Florida (FL)
Coll of Marin (CA)
Collin County Comm Coll District (TX)
Comm Coll of Philadelphia (PA)
De Anza Coll (CA)
Dodge City Comm Coll (KS)
Gateway Comm and Tech Coll (KY)
Georgia Piedmont Tech Coll (GA)
Golden West Coll (CA)
Gulf Coast State Coll (FL)
Harford Comm Coll (MD)
Ivy Tech Comm Coll–Bloomington (IN)
Ivy Tech Comm Coll–Columbus (IN)
Ivy Tech Comm Coll–East Central (IN)
Ivy Tech Comm Coll–Kokomo (IN)
Ivy Tech Comm Coll–Richmond (IN)
Ivy Tech Comm Coll–Sellersburg (IN)
Ivy Tech Comm Coll–Southwest (IN)
Ivy Tech Comm Coll–Wabash Valley (IN)
Jefferson State Comm Coll (AL)
Luzerne County Comm Coll (PA)
Massachusetts Bay Comm Coll (MA)
Maysville Comm and Tech Coll, Maysville (KY)
Merced Coll (CA)
Miami Dade Coll (FL)
Minnesota State Comm and Tech Coll–Detroit Lakes (MN)
Mt. San Antonio Coll (CA)
Naugatuck Valley Comm Coll (CT)
NHTI, Concord's Comm Coll, Concord (NH)
Oklahoma State U Inst of Technology (OK)

Oklahoma State U–Oklahoma City (OK)
Olympic Coll (WA)
Patrick Henry Comm Coll (VA)
Penn Foster Coll (AZ)
Pennsylvania Inst of Technology (PA)
Pensacola State Coll (FL)
Pueblo Comm Coll (CO)
Rappahannock Comm Coll (VA)
Salt Lake Comm Coll (UT)
San Joaquin Delta Coll (CA)
San Juan Coll (NM)
Snead State Comm Coll (AL)
Somerset Comm Coll (KY)
South Florida State Coll (FL)
Southwestern Michigan Coll (MI)
Three Rivers Comm Coll (CT)
Trident Tech Coll (SC)
Vincennes U (IN)
Western Wyoming Comm Coll (WY)

ENGINE MACHINIST
Lake Area Tech Inst (SD)

ENGLISH
Amarillo Coll (TX)
Ancilla Coll (IN)
Arizona Western Coll (AZ)
Bainbridge State Coll (GA)
Blinn Coll (TX)
Borough of Manhattan Comm Coll of the City U of New York (NY)
Bucks County Comm Coll (PA)
Bunker Hill Comm Coll (MA)
Cañada Coll (CA)
Carl Albert State Coll (OK)
Casper Coll (WY)
Central New Mexico Comm Coll (NM)
Central Wyoming Coll (WY)
Cerritos Coll (CA)
Citrus Coll (CA)
Cochise County Comm Coll District (AZ)
Coll of Central Florida (FL)
Coll of Marin (CA)
Coll of the Canyons (CA)
Coll of the Desert (CA)
Comm Coll of Allegheny County (PA)
De Anza Coll (CA)
Del Mar Coll (TX)
Dodge City Comm Coll (KS)
Eastern Arizona Coll (AZ)
Eastern Wyoming Coll (WY)
Edison State Comm Coll (OH)
Feather River Coll (CA)
Fiorello H. LaGuardia Comm Coll of the City U of New York (NY)
Fullerton Coll (CA)
Georgia Highlands Coll (GA)
Georgia Military Coll (GA)
Grand Rapids Comm Coll (MI)
Harford Comm Coll (MD)
Harper Coll (IL)
Hill Coll (TX)
Houston Comm Coll (TX)
Hutchinson Comm Coll (KS)
Illinois Valley Comm Coll (IL)
Imperial Valley Coll (CA)
Lansing Comm Coll (MI)
Laramie County Comm Coll (WY)
Lincoln Coll (IL)
Los Angeles City Coll (CA)
Massachusetts Bay Comm Coll (MA)
Merced Coll (CA)
Miami Dade Coll (FL)
Mohave Comm Coll (AZ)
Monroe County Comm Coll (MI)
Nashville State Comm Coll (TN)
Navarro Coll (TX)
New Mexico Jr Coll (NM)
Northeast Comm Coll (NE)
Northeastern Jr Coll (CO)
Northwest Coll (WY)
Palomar Coll (CA)
Panola Coll (TX)
Paris Jr Coll (TX)
Pensacola State Coll (FL)
Raritan Valley Comm Coll (NJ)
St. Philip's Coll (TX)
Salt Lake Comm Coll (UT)
San Jacinto Coll District (TX)
San Joaquin Delta Coll (CA)
Santa Rosa Jr Coll (CA)
Seminole State Coll (OK)
Sierra Coll (CA)
South Florida State Coll (FL)
Sussex County Comm Coll (NJ)
Trinity Valley Comm Coll (TX)
Truckee Meadows Comm Coll (NV)
Vincennes U (IN)
Western Wyoming Comm Coll (WY)

ENGLISH AS A SECOND/ FOREIGN LANGUAGE (TEACHING)
Gordon State Coll (GA)

ENGLISH LANGUAGE AND LITERATURE RELATED
Citrus Coll (CA)
Mt. San Antonio Coll (CA)

ENGLISH/LANGUAGE ARTS TEACHER EDUCATION
Anne Arundel Comm Coll (MD)
Carroll Comm Coll (MD)
Cecil Coll (MD)
Chesapeake Coll (MD)
Hagerstown Comm Coll (MD)
Harford Comm Coll (MD)
Montgomery Coll (MD)
South Florida State Coll (FL)
Vincennes U (IN)

ENTOMOLOGY
South Florida State Coll (FL)

ENTREPRENEURIAL AND SMALL BUSINESS RELATED
Dakota Coll at Bottineau (ND)
Truckee Meadows Comm Coll (NV)

ENTREPRENEURSHIP
Anne Arundel Comm Coll (MD)
Bunker Hill Comm Coll (MA)
Casper Coll (WY)
Cayuga County Comm Coll (NY)
Central Oregon Comm Coll (OR)
Central Wyoming Coll (WY)
Columbus State Comm Coll (OH)
Comm Coll of Allegheny County (PA)
Craven Comm Coll (NC)
Eastern Arizona Coll (AZ)
Elgin Comm Coll (IL)
Genesee Comm Coll (NY)
Great Falls Coll Montana State U (MT)
Harford Comm Coll (MD)
Haywood Comm Coll (NC)
Johnson County Comm Coll (KS)
Laramie County Comm Coll (WY)
Lorain County Comm Coll (OH)
Miami Dade Coll (FL)
Minnesota State Comm and Tech Coll–Detroit Lakes (MN)
Mott Comm Coll (MI)
Nassau Comm Coll (NY)
Northcentral Tech Coll (WI)
Richmond Comm Coll (NC)
Salt Lake Comm Coll (UT)
Spoon River Coll (IL)
Tallahassee Comm Coll (FL)
Tompkins Cortland Comm Coll (NY)
Wayne County Comm Coll District (MI)

ENVIRONMENTAL BIOLOGY
Eastern Arizona Coll (AZ)
Eastern Wyoming Coll (WY)

ENVIRONMENTAL CONTROL TECHNOLOGIES RELATED
Bismarck State Coll (ND)
Hillsborough Comm Coll (FL)
Holyoke Comm Coll (MA)
Massachusetts Bay Comm Coll (MA)
Middlesex County Coll (NJ)
Ulster County Comm Coll (NY)
Westchester Comm Coll (NY)
Western Dakota Tech Inst (SD)

ENVIRONMENTAL DESIGN/ ARCHITECTURE
Central New Mexico Comm Coll (NM)
Queensborough Comm Coll of the City U of New York (NY)
Scottsdale Comm Coll (AZ)

ENVIRONMENTAL ENGINEERING TECHNOLOGY
Austin Comm Coll District (TX)
Columbus State Comm Coll (OH)
Comm Coll of Allegheny County (PA)
Crowder Coll (MO)
Dakota Coll at Bottineau (ND)
Delta Coll (MI)
El Paso Comm Coll (TX)
Erie Comm Coll, North Campus (NY)
Georgia Northwestern Tech Coll (GA)
Harford Comm Coll (MD)
Kent State U at Trumbull (OH)

Lansing Comm Coll (MI)
Miami Dade Coll (FL)
Naugatuck Valley Comm Coll (CT)
Northwest-Shoals Comm Coll (AL)
Queensborough Comm Coll of the City U of New York (NY)
Salt Lake Comm Coll (UT)
Schoolcraft Coll (MI)
Southern Arkansas U Tech (AR)
State U of New York Coll of Technology at Alfred (NY)
Texas State Tech Coll (TX)
Three Rivers Comm Coll (CT)

ENVIRONMENTAL/ ENVIRONMENTAL HEALTH ENGINEERING
Central Wyoming Coll (WY)
South Florida State Coll (FL)

ENVIRONMENTAL HEALTH
Amarillo Coll (TX)
Comm Coll of the Air Force (AL)
Queensborough Comm Coll of the City U of New York (NY)
St. Charles Comm Coll (MO)
Three Rivers Comm Coll (MO)

ENVIRONMENTAL SCIENCE
Anoka-Ramsey Comm Coll (MN)
Arizona Western Coll (AZ)
Austin Comm Coll District (TX)
Bucks County Comm Coll (PA)
Casper Coll (WY)
Central Texas Coll (TX)
Central Wyoming Coll (WY)
Chesapeake Coll (MD)
Coconino Comm Coll (AZ)
Coll of the Desert (CA)
Comm Coll of Vermont (VT)
Erie Comm Coll, North Campus (NY)
Fiorello H. LaGuardia Comm Coll of the City U of New York (NY)
Gordon State Coll (GA)
Harford Comm Coll (MD)
Harrisburg Area Comm Coll (PA)
Humacao Comm Coll (PR)
Jamestown Comm Coll (NY)
Lake Area Tech Inst (SD)
Lehigh Carbon Comm Coll (PA)
Miami Dade Coll (FL)
Montgomery County Comm Coll (PA)
Northampton Comm Coll (PA)
NorthWest Arkansas Comm Coll (AR)
The Ohio State U Ag Tech Inst (OH)
Quinsigamond Comm Coll (MA)
San Jacinto Coll District (TX)
Santa Monica Coll (CA)
South Florida State Coll (FL)
State U of New York Coll of Technology at Alfred (NY)
Tallahassee Comm Coll (FL)
Truckee Meadows Comm Coll (NV)
Westchester Comm Coll (NY)
Western Wyoming Comm Coll (WY)

ENVIRONMENTAL STUDIES
Ancilla Coll (IN)
Berkshire Comm Coll (MA)
Coll of Central Florida (FL)
Coll of the Desert (CA)
Columbia-Greene Comm Coll (NY)
Comm Coll of the Air Force (AL)
De Anza Coll (CA)
Feather River Coll (CA)
Finger Lakes Comm Coll (NY)
Fullerton Coll (CA)
Harper Coll (IL)
Housatonic Comm Coll (CT)
Howard Comm Coll (MD)
Hudson County Comm Coll (NJ)
Lackawanna Coll (PA)
Minnesota State Comm and Tech Coll (MN)
Minnesota State Comm and Tech Coll–Moorhead (MN)
Monroe Comm Coll (NY)
Mt. San Antonio Coll (CA)
Mount Wachusett Comm Coll (MA)
New Mexico Jr Coll (NM)
Santa Fe Comm Coll (NM)
Santa Monica Coll (CA)
Santa Rosa Jr Coll (CA)
Southwestern Comm Coll (NC)
Sullivan County Comm Coll (NY)
Sussex County Comm Coll (NJ)
Tompkins Cortland Comm Coll (NY)
Ulster County Comm Coll (NY)
U of Cincinnati Clermont Coll (OH)

Westchester Comm Coll (NY)
White Mountains Comm Coll (NH)

EQUESTRIAN STUDIES
Allen Comm Coll (KS)
Central Wyoming Coll (WY)
Cochise County Comm Coll District (AZ)
Coll of Central Florida (FL)
Colorado Northwestern Comm Coll (CO)
Dodge City Comm Coll (KS)
Highland Comm Coll (IL)
Laramie County Comm Coll (WY)
Minnesota State Comm and Tech Coll (MN)
Northeastern Jr Coll (CO)
Northwest Coll (WY)
The Ohio State U Ag Tech Inst (OH)
Scottsdale Comm Coll (AZ)
Sierra Coll (CA)

ETHNIC, CULTURAL MINORITY, GENDER, AND GROUP STUDIES RELATED
Coll of Marin (CA)
Fullerton Coll (CA)
Santa Fe Comm Coll (NM)

ETHNIC STUDIES
Santa Monica Coll (CA)

EXECUTIVE ASSISTANT/ EXECUTIVE SECRETARY
Alamance Comm Coll (NC)
Alvin Comm Coll (TX)
Brookhaven Coll (TX)
Cape Fear Comm Coll (NC)
Crowder Coll (MO)
Dakota Coll at Bottineau (ND)
Danville Area Comm Coll (IL)
Edison State Comm Coll (OH)
Elgin Comm Coll (IL)
Hawkeye Comm Coll (IA)
Hillsborough Comm Coll (FL)
Humacao Comm Coll (PR)
Illinois Eastern Comm Colls, Frontier Community College (IL)
Illinois Eastern Comm Colls, Wabash Valley College (IL)
Ivy Tech Comm Coll–Bloomington (IN)
Ivy Tech Comm Coll–Central Indiana (IN)
Ivy Tech Comm Coll–Columbus (IN)
Ivy Tech Comm Coll–East Central (IN)
Ivy Tech Comm Coll–Kokomo (IN)
Ivy Tech Comm Coll–Lafayette (IN)
Ivy Tech Comm Coll–North Central (IN)
Ivy Tech Comm Coll–Northeast (IN)
Ivy Tech Comm Coll–Northwest (IN)
Ivy Tech Comm Coll–Richmond (IN)
Ivy Tech Comm Coll–Sellersburg (IN)
Ivy Tech Comm Coll–Southeast (IN)
Ivy Tech Comm Coll–Southwest (IN)
Ivy Tech Comm Coll–Wabash Valley (IN)
Kaskaskia Coll (IL)
Lamar Comm Coll (CO)
Luzerne County Comm Coll (PA)
Maysville Comm and Tech Coll, Maysville (KY)
Mitchell Comm Coll (NC)
Owensboro Comm and Tech Coll (KY)
Quinsigamond Comm Coll (MA)
St. Clair County Comm Coll (MI)
Schoolcraft Coll (MI)
Somerset Comm Coll (KY)
South Suburban Coll (IL)
U of Cincinnati Blue Ash Coll (OH)
Westmoreland County Comm Coll (PA)

FACILITIES PLANNING AND MANAGEMENT
Comm Coll of Philadelphia (PA)

FAMILY AND COMMUNITY SERVICES
Merced Coll (CA)
Palomar Coll (CA)
Rogue Comm Coll (OR)

FAMILY AND CONSUMER ECONOMICS RELATED
American Samoa Comm Coll (AS)

FAMILY AND CONSUMER SCIENCES/HOME ECONOMICS TEACHER EDUCATION
South Florida State Coll (FL)
Vincennes U (IN)

FAMILY AND CONSUMER SCIENCES/HUMAN SCIENCES
Allen Comm Coll (KS)
Arizona Western Coll (AZ)
Bainbridge State Coll (GA)
Coll of Central Florida (FL)
Hill Coll (TX)
Hutchinson Comm Coll (KS)
Monroe Comm Coll (NY)
Mt. San Antonio Coll (CA)
Orange Coast Coll (CA)
Palomar Coll (CA)
San Joaquin Delta Coll (CA)
Tyler Jr Coll (TX)
Vincennes U (IN)

FAMILY SYSTEMS
Maysville Comm and Tech Coll, Maysville (KY)

FARM AND RANCH MANAGEMENT
Allen Comm Coll (KS)
Bismarck State Coll (ND)
Central Texas Coll (TX)
Crowder Coll (MO)
Dodge City Comm Coll (KS)
Eastern Wyoming Coll (WY)
Hutchinson Comm Coll (KS)
North Central Missouri Coll (MO)
Northeast Comm Coll (NE)
Northeastern Jr Coll (CO)
Northwest Coll (WY)
Panola Coll (TX)
Southwest Texas Jr Coll (TX)
Treasure Valley Comm Coll (OR)
Trinity Valley Comm Coll (TX)

FASHION AND FABRIC CONSULTING
Harper Coll (IL)

FASHION/APPAREL DESIGN
Cañada Coll (CA)
Cerritos Coll (CA)
El Paso Comm Coll (TX)
Fashion Inst of Technology (NY)
FIDM/Fashion Inst of Design & Merchandising, Orange County Campus (CA)
FIDM/Fashion Inst of Design & Merchandising, San Diego Campus (CA)
Fullerton Coll (CA)
Genesee Comm Coll (NY)
Harper Coll (IL)
Houston Comm Coll (TX)
Johnson County Comm Coll (KS)
Lehigh Carbon Comm Coll (PA)
Monroe Comm Coll (NY)
Nassau Comm Coll (NY)
Orange Coast Coll (CA)
Palomar Coll (CA)
Santa Fe Comm Coll (NM)
Santa Monica Coll (CA)
Santa Rosa Jr Coll (CA)
Ulster County Comm Coll (NY)
Virginia Marti Coll of Art and Design (OH)

FASHION MERCHANDISING
Alexandria Tech and Comm Coll (MN)
Fashion Inst of Technology (NY)
FIDM/Fashion Inst of Design & Merchandising, Orange County Campus (CA)
FIDM/Fashion Inst of Design & Merchandising, San Diego Campus (CA)
Genesee Comm Coll (NY)
Grand Rapids Comm Coll (MI)
Harper Coll (IL)
Hinds Comm Coll (MS)
Houston Comm Coll (TX)
Johnson County Comm Coll (KS)
Kingsborough Comm Coll of the City U of New York (NY)
Lansing Comm Coll (MI)
Madison Area Tech Coll (WI)
Mesa Comm Coll (AZ)
Middlesex Comm Coll (MA)
Minnesota State Comm and Tech Coll (MN)

Monroe Comm Coll (NY)
Mt. San Antonio Coll (CA)
Nassau Comm Coll (NY)
Penn Foster Coll (AZ)
San Joaquin Delta Coll (CA)
Santa Rosa Jr Coll (CA)
Scottsdale Comm Coll (AZ)
South Plains Coll (TX)
Tarrant County Coll District (TX)
Trinity Valley Comm Coll (TX)
Vincennes U (IN)
Virginia Marti Coll of Art and Design (OH)

FASHION MODELING
Fashion Inst of Technology (NY)

FIBER, TEXTILE AND WEAVING ARTS
Haywood Comm Coll (NC)

FILM/CINEMA/VIDEO STUDIES
Coll of Marin (CA)
De Anza Coll (CA)
Fashion Inst of Technology (NY)
Palomar Coll (CA)
Santa Fe Comm Coll (NM)
Santa Monica Coll (CA)

FINANCE
Bunker Hill Comm Coll (MA)
Comm Coll of the Air Force (AL)
Del Mar Coll (TX)
Dodge City Comm Coll (KS)
Harper Coll (IL)
Los Angeles City Coll (CA)
Macomb Comm Coll (MI)
Madison Area Tech Coll (WI)
McLennan Comm Coll (TX)
Mesa Comm Coll (AZ)
Miami Dade Coll (FL)
Monroe County Comm Coll (MI)
Morton Coll (IL)
Mt. San Antonio Coll (CA)
Naugatuck Valley Comm Coll (CT)
New Mexico Jr Coll (NM)
Northeast Comm Coll (NE)
Northern Essex Comm Coll (MA)
NorthWest Arkansas Comm Coll (AR)
Norwalk Comm Coll (CT)
Penn Foster Coll (AZ)
Salt Lake Comm Coll (UT)
Scottsdale Comm Coll (AZ)
Seminole State Coll of Florida (FL)
South Florida State Coll (FL)
Stark State Coll (OH)
Tidewater Comm Coll (VA)
Trinity Valley Comm Coll (TX)
Vincennes U (IN)
Westmoreland County Comm Coll (PA)
Wisconsin Indianhead Tech Coll (WI)

FINANCE AND FINANCIAL MANAGEMENT SERVICES RELATED
Columbus State Comm Coll (OH)

FINANCIAL PLANNING AND SERVICES
Cecil Coll (MD)
Howard Comm Coll (MD)
Minnesota State Comm and Tech Coll (MN)
Raritan Valley Comm Coll (NJ)

FINE AND STUDIO ARTS MANAGEMENT
Santa Fe Comm Coll (NM)
Westmoreland County Comm Coll (PA)

FINE ARTS RELATED
Bunker Hill Comm Coll (MA)
County Coll of Morris (NJ)
Mid-Plains Comm Coll, North Platte (NE)
Murray State Coll (OK)
Schoolcraft Coll (MI)
Seminole State Coll (OK)
Truckee Meadows Comm Coll (NV)
Westmoreland County Comm Coll (PA)

FINE/STUDIO ARTS
Amarillo Coll (TX)
Anoka-Ramsey Comm Coll (MN)
Arizona Western Coll (AZ)
Caldwell Comm Coll and Tech Inst (NC)

Camden County Coll (NJ)
Casper Coll (WY)
Cayuga County Comm Coll (NY)
Cecil Coll (MD)
Central Texas Coll (TX)
Century Coll (MN)
Chandler-Gilbert Comm Coll (AZ)
Coconino Comm Coll (AZ)
Del Mar Coll (TX)
Delta Coll (MI)
East Central Coll (MO)
Elgin Comm Coll (IL)
Erie Comm Coll (NY)
Erie Comm Coll, North Campus (NY)
Erie Comm Coll, South Campus (NY)
Fashion Inst of Technology (NY)
Finger Lakes Comm Coll (NY)
Fiorello H. LaGuardia Comm Coll of the City U of New York (NY)
Genesee Comm Coll (NY)
Harford Comm Coll (MD)
Harper Coll (IL)
Houston Comm Coll (TX)
Hudson County Comm Coll (NJ)
Ivy Tech Comm Coll–Bloomington (IN)
Jamestown Comm Coll (NY)
Kishwaukee Coll (IL)
Lake Superior Coll (MN)
Lansing Comm Coll (MI)
Manchester Comm Coll (CT)
McHenry County Coll (IL)
Middlesex Comm Coll (MA)
Morton Coll (IL)
Niagara County Comm Coll (NY)
Northampton Comm Coll (PA)
Northeastern Jr Coll (CO)
Norwalk Comm Coll (CT)
Oklahoma City Comm Coll (OK)
Owensboro Comm and Tech Coll (KY)
Queensborough Comm Coll of the City U of New York (NY)
Raritan Valley Comm Coll (NJ)
Rend Lake Coll (IL)
St. Philip's Coll (TX)
South Florida State Coll (FL)
South Suburban Coll (IL)
Springfield Tech Comm Coll (MA)
Sussex County Comm Coll (NJ)
Three Rivers Comm Coll (CT)
Tidewater Comm Coll (VA)
Westmoreland County Comm Coll (PA)

FIRE PREVENTION AND SAFETY TECHNOLOGY

Anne Arundel Comm Coll (MD)
Austin Comm Coll District (TX)
Bunker Hill Comm Coll (MA)
Camden County Coll (NJ)
Cape Fear Comm Coll (NC)
Coll of the Canyons (CA)
Collin County Comm Coll District (TX)
Comm Coll of Allegheny County (PA)
County Coll of Morris (NJ)
Del Mar Coll (TX)
Delta Coll (MI)
Des Moines Area Comm Coll (IA)
El Paso Comm Coll (TX)
Fayetteville Tech Comm Coll (NC)
Florida SouthWestern State Coll (FL)
Gulf Coast State Coll (FL)
Hillsborough Comm Coll (FL)
Houston Comm Coll (TX)
Jefferson Comm Coll (NY)
Lakeland Comm Coll (OH)
Lake Superior Coll (MN)
Macomb Comm Coll (MI)
Merced Coll (CA)
Miami Dade Coll (FL)
Middlesex Comm Coll (MA)
Middlesex County Coll (NJ)
Montgomery Coll (MD)
Montgomery County Comm Coll (PA)
Mott Comm Coll (MI)
Mount Wachusett Comm Coll (MA)
Northland Comm and Tech Coll (MN)
Palomar Coll (CA)
Rogue Comm Coll (OR)
South Florida State Coll (FL)
Springfield Tech Comm Coll (MA)
Sullivan County Comm Coll (NY)
Treasure Valley Comm Coll (OR)
Truckee Meadows Comm Coll (NV)
Tyler Jr Coll (TX)
Wayne County Comm Coll District (MI)
Westmoreland County Comm Coll (PA)

FIRE PROTECTION RELATED

Sussex County Comm Coll (NJ)

FIRE SCIENCE/FIREFIGHTING

Amarillo Coll (TX)
Arizona Western Coll (AZ)
Augusta Tech Coll (GA)
Berkshire Comm Coll (MA)
Blackhawk Tech Coll (WI)
Blinn Coll (TX)
Casper Coll (WY)
Cecil Coll (MD)
Central New Mexico Comm Coll (NM)
Central Oregon Comm Coll (OR)
Central Wyoming Coll (WY)
Chattahoochee Tech Coll (GA)
Cochise County Comm Coll District (AZ)
Coconino Comm Coll (AZ)
Coll of Central Florida (FL)
Coll of the Desert (CA)
Collin County Comm Coll District (TX)
Columbus State Comm Coll (OH)
Comm Coll of Aurora (CO)
Comm Coll of Philadelphia (PA)
Comm Coll of Rhode Island (RI)
Comm Coll of the Air Force (AL)
Crowder Coll (MO)
Danville Area Comm Coll (IL)
Daytona State Coll (FL)
Del Mar Coll (TX)
Delta Coll (MI)
Dodge City Comm Coll (KS)
East Central Coll (MO)
Eastern Arizona Coll (AZ)
Eastern Idaho Tech Coll (ID)
Elgin Comm Coll (IL)
Fox Valley Tech Coll (WI)
Frederick Comm Coll (MD)
Gateway Comm and Tech Coll (KY)
Georgia Northwestern Tech Coll (GA)
Greenville Tech Coll (SC)
Harper Coll (IL)
Harrisburg Area Comm Coll (PA)
Hawkeye Comm Coll (IA)
Hennepin Tech Coll (MN)
Hill Coll (TX)
Hutchinson Comm Coll (KS)
Illinois Central Coll (IL)
Illinois Eastern Comm Colls, Frontier Community College (IL)
Imperial Valley Coll (CA)
Johnson County Comm Coll (KS)
J. Sargeant Reynolds Comm Coll (VA)
Lake Superior Coll (MN)
Lanier Tech Coll (GA)
Lansing Comm Coll (MI)
Laramie County Comm Coll (WY)
Lone Star Coll–CyFair (TX)
Lone Star Coll–Kingwood (TX)
Lone Star Coll–Montgomery (TX)
Lorain County Comm Coll (OH)
Louisiana State U at Eunice (LA)
Luzerne County Comm Coll (PA)
Madison Area Tech Coll (WI)
McHenry County Coll (IL)
Mercer County Comm Coll (NJ)
Meridian Comm Coll (MS)
Mesa Comm Coll (AZ)
Miami Dade Coll (FL)
Middlesex Comm Coll (MA)
Mid-Plains Comm Coll, North Platte (NE)
Mohave Comm Coll (AZ)
Monroe Comm Coll (NY)
Morton Coll (IL)
Mt. San Antonio Coll (CA)
Navarro Coll (TX)
Northampton Comm Coll (PA)
Northeast Iowa Comm Coll (IA)
North Shore Comm Coll (MA)
Norwalk Comm Coll (CT)
Oakton Comm Coll (IL)
Oklahoma State U–Oklahoma City (OK)
Owensboro Comm and Tech Coll (KY)
Ozarks Tech Comm Coll (MO)
Pueblo Comm Coll (CO)
Rock Valley Coll (IL)
St. Clair County Comm Coll (MI)
San Jacinto Coll District (TX)
San Joaquin Delta Coll (CA)
San Juan Coll (NM)
Santa Rosa Jr Coll (CA)
Savannah Tech Coll (GA)
Schoolcraft Coll (MI)
Seminole State Coll of Florida (FL)
Sierra Coll (CA)

Southeast Comm Coll, Lincoln Campus (NE)
Southern Arkansas U Tech (AR)
South Plains Coll (TX)
Southwestern Michigan Coll (MI)
Tallahassee Comm Coll (FL)
Tarrant County Coll District (TX)
Three Rivers Comm Coll (MO)
Treasure Valley Comm Coll (OR)
Victoria Coll (TX)
Vincennes U (IN)
Volunteer State Comm Coll (TN)
Waukesha County Tech Coll (WI)
Weatherford Coll (TX)
Western Dakota Tech Inst (SD)
West Georgia Tech Coll (GA)
Wiregrass Georgia Tech Coll (GA)

FIRE SERVICES ADMINISTRATION

Camden County Coll (NJ)
Central Texas Coll (TX)
Delta Coll (MI)
Dutchess Comm Coll (NY)
Erie Comm Coll, South Campus (NY)
Jefferson Comm Coll (NY)
Jefferson State Comm Coll (AL)
Lake Superior Coll (MN)
Minnesota State Comm and Tech Coll (MN)
Mohawk Valley Comm Coll (NY)
Naugatuck Valley Comm Coll (CT)
Northampton Comm Coll (PA)
NorthWest Arkansas Comm Coll (AR)
Quinsigamond Comm Coll (MA)
Southern Arkansas U Tech (AR)

FISHING AND FISHERIES SCIENCES AND MANAGEMENT

Central Oregon Comm Coll (OR)
Dakota Coll at Bottineau (ND)
Finger Lakes Comm Coll (NY)
Florida Keys Comm Coll (FL)

FLORICULTURE/FLORISTRY MANAGEMENT

Dakota Coll at Bottineau (ND)
Danville Area Comm Coll (IL)
Illinois Valley Comm Coll (IL)
J. Sargeant Reynolds Comm Coll (VA)
The Ohio State U Ag Tech Inst (OH)
Santa Rosa Jr Coll (CA)
Westmoreland County Comm Coll (PA)

FOOD SCIENCE

Miami Dade Coll (FL)
Missouri State U–West Plains (MO)
South Florida State Coll (FL)
Vincennes U (IN)

FOOD SERVICE AND DINING ROOM MANAGEMENT

Kaskaskia Coll (IL)
Westmoreland County Comm Coll (PA)

FOOD SERVICE SYSTEMS ADMINISTRATION

Bucks County Comm Coll (PA)
Comm Coll of Allegheny County (PA)
Harper Coll (IL)
Mesa Comm Coll (AZ)
Mott Comm Coll (MI)
Pensacola State Coll (FL)
San Jacinto Coll District (TX)
Wayne County Comm Coll District (MI)
Westchester Comm Coll (NY)

FOODS, NUTRITION, AND WELLNESS

Bossier Parish Comm Coll (LA)
Carl Albert State Coll (OK)
Central New Mexico Comm Coll (NM)
Fullerton Coll (CA)
North Shore Comm Coll (MA)
Orange Coast Coll (CA)
Pensacola State Coll (FL)
Truckee Meadows Comm Coll (NV)

FOOD TECHNOLOGY AND PROCESSING

Adirondack Comm Coll (NY)
Cerritos Coll (CA)
Genesee Comm Coll (NY)
Luzerne County Comm Coll (PA)
Monroe Comm Coll (NY)
Tarrant County Coll District (TX)

FOREIGN LANGUAGES AND LITERATURES

Borough of Manhattan Comm Coll of the City U of New York (NY)
Bunker Hill Comm Coll (MA)
Casper Coll (WY)
Central New Mexico Comm Coll (NM)
Central Oregon Comm Coll (OR)
Central Texas Coll (TX)
Coll of Central Florida (FL)
Coll of Marin (CA)
Comm Coll of Allegheny County (PA)
Eastern Arizona Coll (AZ)
Eastern Wyoming Coll (WY)
Fullerton Coll (CA)
Georgia Highlands Coll (GA)
Gordon State Coll (GA)
Grand Rapids Comm Coll (MI)
Hill Coll (TX)
Hutchinson Comm Coll (KS)
Lansing Comm Coll (MI)
Oklahoma City Comm Coll (OK)
Orange Coast Coll (CA)
Palomar Coll (CA)
Panola Coll (TX)
Paris Jr Coll (TX)
St. Philip's Coll (TX)
San Jacinto Coll District (TX)
South Florida State Coll (FL)
Texarkana Coll (TX)
Tyler Jr Coll (TX)
Vincennes U (IN)

FOREIGN LANGUAGES RELATED

Genesee Comm Coll (NY)
Nashville State Comm Coll (TN)
Vincennes U (IN)

FOREIGN LANGUAGE TEACHER EDUCATION

South Florida State Coll (FL)

FORENSIC SCIENCE AND TECHNOLOGY

American Samoa Comm Coll (AS)
Borough of Manhattan Comm Coll of the City U of New York (NY)
Carroll Comm Coll (MD)
Casper Coll (WY)
Coconino Comm Coll (AZ)
Fayetteville Tech Comm Coll (NC)
Florida SouthWestern State Coll (FL)
Fox Valley Tech Coll (WI)
Gulf Coast State Coll (FL)
Illinois Valley Comm Coll (IL)
Kishwaukee Coll (IL)
Macomb Comm Coll (MI)
Miami Dade Coll (FL)
Middlesex Comm Coll (MA)
New River Comm Coll (VA)
Palomar Coll (CA)
Pensacola State Coll (FL)
Queensborough Comm Coll of the City U of New York (NY)
South Florida State Coll (FL)
Sullivan County Comm Coll (NY)
U of Arkansas Comm Coll at Morrilton (AR)
Westmoreland County Comm Coll (PA)

FOREST/FOREST RESOURCES MANAGEMENT

Three Rivers Comm Coll (MO)
Tyler Jr Coll (TX)

FORESTRY

Allen Comm Coll (KS)
Central Oregon Comm Coll (OR)
Coll of Central Florida (FL)
Dodge City Comm Coll (KS)
Eastern Arizona Coll (AZ)
Gordon State Coll (GA)
Grand Rapids Comm Coll (MI)
Miami Dade Coll (FL)
Monroe Comm Coll (NY)
Panola Coll (TX)
Sierra Coll (CA)
South Florida State Coll (FL)
Western Wyoming Comm Coll (WY)

FOREST TECHNOLOGY

Albany Tech Coll (GA)
Central Oregon Comm Coll (OR)
Coastal Pines Tech Coll (GA)
Haywood Comm Coll (NC)
Horry Georgetown Tech Coll (SC)
Lurleen B. Wallace Comm Coll (AL)
Montgomery Comm Coll (NC)
Mt. San Antonio Coll (CA)
Ogeechee Tech Coll (GA)

Penn State Mont Alto (PA)
Three Rivers Comm Coll (MO)

FRENCH

Austin Comm Coll District (TX)
Blinn Coll (TX)
Cerritos Coll (CA)
Citrus Coll (CA)
Coll of Marin (CA)
Coll of the Canyons (CA)
Coll of the Desert (CA)
Imperial Valley Coll (CA)
Lansing Comm Coll (MI)
Los Angeles City Coll (CA)
Merced Coll (CA)
Miami Dade Coll (FL)
Palomar Coll (CA)
Santa Rosa Jr Coll (CA)
South Florida State Coll (FL)

FUNERAL SERVICE AND MORTUARY SCIENCE

Amarillo Coll (TX)
Arapahoe Comm Coll (CO)
Comm Coll of Baltimore County (MD)
Dallas Inst of Funeral Service (TX)
Des Moines Area Comm Coll (IA)
Fayetteville Tech Comm Coll (NC)
FINE Mortuary Coll, LLC (MA)
Ivy Tech Comm Coll–Northwest (IN)
Jefferson State Comm Coll (AL)
John Tyler Comm Coll (VA)
Luzerne County Comm Coll (PA)
Mercer County Comm Coll (NJ)
Miami Dade Coll (FL)
Monroe County Comm Coll (MI)
Nassau Comm Coll (NY)
Northampton Comm Coll (PA)
Northeast Comm Coll (NE)
Ogeechee Tech Coll (GA)
Pittsburgh Inst of Mortuary Science, Incorporated (PA)
Randolph Comm Coll (NC)
Vincennes U (IN)

FURNITURE DESIGN AND MANUFACTURING

Northcentral Tech Coll (WI)

GAME AND INTERACTIVE MEDIA DESIGN

Arapahoe Comm Coll (CO)
Cayuga County Comm Coll (NY)
Collin County Comm Coll District (TX)
Columbus State Comm Coll (OH)
Fayetteville Tech Comm Coll (NC)
Hinds Comm Coll (MS)
Lehigh Carbon Comm Coll (PA)
Miami Dade Coll (FL)
Oklahoma City Comm Coll (OK)
Quinsigamond Comm Coll (MA)
Texas State Tech Coll (TX)
Wayne County Comm Coll District (MI)

GENERAL STUDIES

Allen Comm Coll (KS)
Alvin Comm Coll (TX)
Amarillo Coll (TX)
Ancilla Coll (IN)
Arapahoe Comm Coll (CO)
Arizona Western Coll (AZ)
Arkansas Northeastern Coll (AR)
Asnuntuck Comm Coll (CT)
Austin Comm Coll District (TX)
Bevill State Comm Coll (AL)
Blue Ridge Comm and Tech Coll (WV)
Borough of Manhattan Comm Coll of the City U of New York (NY)
Bossier Parish Comm Coll (LA)
Brookhaven Coll (TX)
Bunker Hill Comm Coll (MA)
Carroll Comm Coll (MD)
Casper Coll (WY)
Cayuga County Comm Coll (NY)
Cecil Coll (MD)
Central New Mexico Comm Coll (NM)
Central Texas Coll (TX)
Central Wyoming Coll (WY)
Chandler-Gilbert Comm Coll (AZ)
Chesapeake Coll (MD)
City Colls of Chicago, Kennedy-King College (IL)
City Colls of Chicago, Olive-Harvey College (IL)
Cleveland State Comm Coll (TN)
Cochise County Comm Coll District (AZ)
Coconino Comm Coll (AZ)

Colorado Northwestern Comm Coll (CO)
Columbia-Greene Comm Coll (NY)
Columbus State Comm Coll (OH)
Comm Coll of Allegheny County (PA)
Comm Coll of Aurora (CO)
Comm Coll of Rhode Island (RI)
Craven Comm Coll (NC)
Crowder Coll (MO)
Dakota Coll at Bottineau (ND)
Danville Area Comm Coll (IL)
Delta Coll (MI)
Dutchess Comm Coll (NY)
Dyersburg State Comm Coll (TN)
East Central Coll (MO)
Eastern Wyoming Coll (WY)
El Paso Comm Coll (TX)
Erie Comm Coll (NY)
Erie Comm Coll, North Campus (NY)
Erie Comm Coll, South Campus (NY)
Estrella Mountain Comm Coll (AZ)
Fayetteville Tech Comm Coll (NC)
Frederick Comm Coll (MD)
Front Range Comm Coll (CO)
Gateway Comm and Tech Coll (KY)
Genesee Comm Coll (NY)
Georgia Highlands Coll (GA)
Georgia Military Coll (GA)
Gordon State Coll (GA)
Great Basin Coll (NV)
Harford Comm Coll (MD)
Harrisburg Area Comm Coll (PA)
Hesston Coll (KS)
Highland Comm Coll (IL)
Hill Coll (TX)
Hinds Comm Coll (MS)
Houston Comm Coll (TX)
Howard Comm Coll (MD)
Illinois Central Coll (IL)
Illinois Eastern Comm Colls, Frontier Community College (IL)
Illinois Eastern Comm Colls, Lincoln Trail College (IL)
Illinois Eastern Comm Colls, Olney Central College (IL)
Illinois Eastern Comm Colls, Wabash Valley College (IL)
Illinois Valley Comm Coll (IL)
Ivy Tech Comm Coll–Bloomington (IN)
Ivy Tech Comm Coll–Central Indiana (IN)
Ivy Tech Comm Coll–Columbus (IN)
Ivy Tech Comm Coll–East Central (IN)
Ivy Tech Comm Coll–Kokomo (IN)
Ivy Tech Comm Coll–Lafayette (IN)
Ivy Tech Comm Coll–North Central (IN)
Ivy Tech Comm Coll–Northwest (IN)
Ivy Tech Comm Coll–Richmond (IN)
Ivy Tech Comm Coll–Sellersburg (IN)
Ivy Tech Comm Coll–Southeast (IN)
Ivy Tech Comm Coll–Southwest (IN)
Ivy Tech Comm Coll–Wabash Valley (IN)
James Sprunt Comm Coll (NC)
Jamestown Comm Coll (NY)
Jefferson State Comm Coll (AL)
John Tyler Comm Coll (VA)
Kaskaskia Coll (IL)
Kellogg Comm Coll (MI)
Kirtland Comm Coll (MI)
Lackawanna Coll (PA)
Laramie County Comm Coll (WY)
Lehigh Carbon Comm Coll (PA)
Lincoln Coll (IL)
Louisiana State U at Eunice (LA)
Lurleen B. Wallace Comm Coll (AL)
Luzerne County Comm Coll (PA)
Macomb Comm Coll (MI)
Manchester Comm Coll (CT)
Massachusetts Bay Comm Coll (MA)
McHenry County Coll (IL)
Miami Dade Coll (FL)
Middlesex Comm Coll (MA)
Missouri State U–West Plains (MO)
Mitchell Comm Coll (NC)
Mohawk Valley Comm Coll (NY)
Morgan Comm Coll (CO)
Motlow State Comm Coll (TN)
Mott Comm Coll (MI)
Mount Wachusett Comm Coll (MA)
Murray State Coll (OK)
Nassau Comm Coll (NY)
Naugatuck Valley Comm Coll (CT)
New River Comm Coll (VA)
NHTI, Concord's Comm Coll, Concord (NH)

Niagara County Comm Coll (NY)
Northampton Comm Coll (PA)
Northcentral Tech Coll (WI)
Northeast Comm Coll (NE)
Northern Essex Comm Coll (MA)
Northern Maine Comm Coll (ME)
Northwest Coll (WY)
Northwest-Shoals Comm Coll (AL)
Norwalk Comm Coll (CT)
Nunez Comm Coll (LA)
Oklahoma City Comm Coll (OK)
Oklahoma State U–Oklahoma City (OK)
Oregon Coast Comm Coll (OR)
Panola Coll (TX)
Paris Jr Coll (TX)
Pennsylvania Inst of Technology (PA)
Piedmont Comm Coll (NC)
Pueblo Comm Coll (CO)
Queensborough Comm Coll of the City U of New York (NY)
Quinsigamond Comm Coll (MA)
Rockingham Comm Coll (NC)
Rogue Comm Coll (OR)
Rowan-Cabarrus Comm Coll (NC)
St. Charles Comm Coll (MO)
St. Vincent's Coll (CT)
Salt Lake Comm Coll (UT)
San Jacinto Coll District (TX)
San Juan Coll (NM)
Santa Fe Comm Coll (NM)
Schoolcraft Coll (MI)
Seminole State Coll (OK)
Sierra Coll (CA)
Snead State Comm Coll (AL)
Southern Arkansas U Tech (AR)
Southern U at Shreveport (LA)
South Florida State Coll (FL)
Southwestern Michigan Coll (MI)
Sowela Tech Comm Coll (LA)
Spoon River Coll (IL)
State U of New York Coll of Technology at Alfred (NY)
Three Rivers Comm Coll (CT)
Three Rivers Comm Coll (MO)
Truckee Meadows Comm Coll (NV)
Tyler Jr Coll (TX)
U of Arkansas Comm Coll at Morrilton (AR)
U of Cincinnati Blue Ash Coll (OH)
U of Cincinnati Clermont Coll (OH)
Victoria Coll (TX)
Volunteer State Comm Coll (TN)
Walters State Comm Coll (TN)
Western Nevada Coll (NV)
Western Wyoming Comm Coll (WY)
White Mountains Comm Coll (NH)

GEOGRAPHIC INFORMATION SCIENCE AND CARTOGRAPHY
Austin Comm Coll District (TX)
Borough of Manhattan Comm Coll of the City U of New York (NY)
Brookhaven Coll (TX)
Casper Coll (WY)
Central New Mexico Comm Coll (NM)
Central Wyoming Coll (WY)
Collin County Comm Coll District (TX)
Columbus State Comm Coll (OH)
Front Range Comm Coll (CO)
Harrisburg Area Comm Coll (PA)
Hinds Comm Coll (MS)
Hudson County Comm Coll (NJ)
Lehigh Carbon Comm Coll (PA)
Lone Star Coll–CyFair (TX)
Mitchell Tech Inst (SD)
Oklahoma City Comm Coll (OK)
Southwestern Indian Polytechnic Inst (NM)
Three Rivers Comm Coll (MO)

GEOGRAPHY
Allen Comm Coll (KS)
Austin Comm Coll District (TX)
Cañada Coll (CA)
Cayuga County Comm Coll (NY)
Central New Mexico Comm Coll (NM)
Cerritos Coll (CA)
Coll of Marin (CA)
Coll of the Canyons (CA)
Coll of the Desert (CA)
Comm Coll of Baltimore County (MD)
Del Mar Coll (TX)
Fullerton Coll (CA)
Lansing Comm Coll (MI)
Merced Coll (CA)

Mesa Comm Coll (AZ)
Montgomery Coll (MD)
Nashville State Comm Coll (TN)
Northeastern Jr Coll (CO)
Orange Coast Coll (CA)
Palomar Coll (CA)
Santa Monica Coll (CA)
South Florida State Coll (FL)

GEOGRAPHY RELATED
Palomar Coll (CA)

GEOLOGICAL AND EARTH SCIENCES/GEOSCIENCES RELATED
Great Basin Coll (NV)

GEOLOGY/EARTH SCIENCE
Amarillo Coll (TX)
Arizona Western Coll (AZ)
Austin Comm Coll District (TX)
Casper Coll (WY)
Central New Mexico Comm Coll (NM)
Central Texas Coll (TX)
Cerritos Coll (CA)
Coll of Marin (CA)
Coll of the Canyons (CA)
Coll of the Desert (CA)
Del Mar Coll (TX)
Eastern Arizona Coll (AZ)
Edison State Comm Coll (OH)
Fullerton Coll (CA)
Georgia Highlands Coll (GA)
Grand Rapids Comm Coll (MI)
Hill Coll (TX)
Merced Coll (CA)
Miami Dade Coll (FL)
Middlesex County Coll (NJ)
Northeastern Jr Coll (CO)
Orange Coast Coll (CA)
Palomar Coll (CA)
Panola Coll (TX)
Pensacola State Coll (FL)
Salt Lake Comm Coll (UT)
San Jacinto Coll District (TX)
San Joaquin Delta Coll (CA)
San Juan Coll (NM)
Sierra Coll (CA)
South Florida State Coll (FL)
Trinity Valley Comm Coll (TX)
Truckee Meadows Comm Coll (NV)
Tyler Jr Coll (TX)
Vincennes U (IN)
Western Wyoming Comm Coll (WY)

GERMAN
Austin Comm Coll District (TX)
Blinn Coll (TX)
Cerritos Coll (CA)
Citrus Coll (CA)
Los Angeles City Coll (CA)
Merced Coll (CA)
Miami Dade Coll (FL)

GERMANIC LANGUAGES
Lansing Comm Coll (MI)

GERONTOLOGY
Anne Arundel Comm Coll (MD)
Borough of Manhattan Comm Coll of the City U of New York (NY)
Genesee Comm Coll (NY)
North Shore Comm Coll (MA)
South Florida State Coll (FL)
Wisconsin Indianhead Tech Coll (WI)
York County Comm Coll (ME)

GOLF COURSE OPERATION AND GROUNDS MANAGEMENT
Anoka Tech Coll (MN)
Hawkeye Comm Coll (IA)

GRAPHIC AND PRINTING EQUIPMENT OPERATION/ PRODUCTION
Central Maine Comm Coll (ME)
Central Texas Coll (TX)
Columbus State Comm Coll (OH)
Erie Comm Coll, South Campus (NY)
Fullerton Coll (CA)
Golden West Coll (CA)
Luzerne County Comm Coll (PA)
Macomb Comm Coll (MI)
Madison Area Tech Coll (WI)
Metropolitan Comm Coll (NE)
Monroe Comm Coll (NY)
Ozarks Tech Comm Coll (MO)
Palomar Coll (CA)
Rock Valley Coll (IL)

Tarrant County Coll District (TX)
Vincennes U (IN)

GRAPHIC COMMUNICATIONS
Central Maine Comm Coll (ME)
Hutchinson Comm Coll (KS)
Northcentral Tech Coll (WI)
Oklahoma City Comm Coll (OK)
Piedmont Comm Coll (NC)

GRAPHIC COMMUNICATIONS RELATED
H. Councill Trenholm State Comm Coll (AL)
Middlesex County Coll (NJ)
Westmoreland County Comm Coll (PA)

GRAPHIC DESIGN
Anne Arundel Comm Coll (MD)
Arapahoe Comm Coll (CO)
Brookhaven Coll (TX)
Casper Coll (WY)
Cayuga County Comm Coll (NY)
Century Coll (MN)
Cloud County Comm Coll (KS)
Coll of Business and Technology–Miami Gardens (FL)
Coll of the Canyons (CA)
Collin County Comm Coll District (TX)
Comm Coll of Vermont (VT)
County Coll of Morris (NJ)
Dunwoody Coll of Technology (MN)
Elgin Comm Coll (IL)
FIDM/Fashion Inst of Design & Merchandising, Orange County Campus (CA)
Fullerton Coll (CA)
Gateway Tech Coll (WI)
Genesee Comm Coll (NY)
Harford Comm Coll (MD)
Harrisburg Area Comm Coll (PA)
Hennepin Tech Coll (MN)
Highland Comm Coll (IL)
Hinds Comm Coll (MS)
Illinois Central Coll (IL)
Illinois Valley Comm Coll (IL)
Johnson County Comm Coll (KS)
Kellogg Comm Coll (MI)
Kirtland Comm Coll (MI)
Lansing Comm Coll (MI)
Lehigh Carbon Comm Coll (PA)
Lenoir Comm Coll (NC)
Luzerne County Comm Coll (PA)
Minnesota State Comm and Tech Coll (MN)
Minnesota State Comm and Tech Coll–Moorhead (MN)
Mott Comm Coll (MI)
Northampton Comm Coll (PA)
Northeast Comm Coll (NE)
Norwalk Comm Coll (CT)
Oakton Comm Coll (IL)
Oklahoma State U Inst of Technology (OK)
Palomar Coll (CA)
Penn Foster Coll (AZ)
Pensacola State Coll (FL)
Rend Lake Coll (IL)
Salina Area Tech Coll (KS)
Salt Lake Comm Coll (UT)
Santa Monica Coll (CA)
Santa Rosa Jr Coll (CA)
Sierra Coll (CA)
South Florida State Coll (FL)
Southwestern Michigan Coll (MI)
State U of New York Coll of Technology at Alfred (NY)
Texas State Tech Coll (TX)
Three Rivers Comm Coll (CT)
Tidewater Comm Coll (VA)
Tyler Jr Coll (TX)
Waukesha County Tech Coll (WI)
Westmoreland County Comm Coll (PA)

GREENHOUSE MANAGEMENT
Comm Coll of Allegheny County (PA)
Dakota Coll at Bottineau (ND)
Hennepin Tech Coll (MN)
The Ohio State U Ag Tech Inst (OH)

GROUND TRANSPORTATION RELATED
Johnson County Comm Coll (KS)

GUNSMITHING
Fayetteville Tech Comm Coll (NC)
Lenoir Comm Coll (NC)

Montgomery Comm Coll (NC)
Murray State Coll (OK)

HAZARDOUS MATERIALS MANAGEMENT AND WASTE TECHNOLOGY
Fullerton Coll (CA)
Pensacola State Coll (FL)
Santa Monica Coll (CA)
Sierra Coll (CA)

HEALTH AIDE
Allen Comm Coll (KS)
Ivy Tech Comm Coll–Kokomo (IN)
Ivy Tech Comm Coll–Lafayette (IN)
Ivy Tech Comm Coll–Wabash Valley (IN)
Texarkana Coll (TX)

HEALTH AND MEDICAL ADMINISTRATIVE SERVICES RELATED
Hinds Comm Coll (MS)
Kent State U at Ashtabula (OH)
Kent State U at Salem (OH)
Owensboro Comm and Tech Coll (KY)
Westmoreland County Comm Coll (PA)

HEALTH AND PHYSICAL EDUCATION/FITNESS
Allen Comm Coll (KS)
Alvin Comm Coll (TX)
Anne Arundel Comm Coll (MD)
Arapahoe Comm Coll (CO)
Arizona Western Coll (AZ)
Austin Comm Coll District (TX)
Cañada Coll (CA)
Central New Mexico Comm Coll (NM)
Central Oregon Comm Coll (OR)
Citrus Coll (CA)
Cochise County Comm Coll District (AZ)
Coll of Marin (CA)
Coll of the Canyons (CA)
Coll of the Desert (CA)
Columbus State Comm Coll (OH)
Comm Care Coll (OK)
Comm Coll of Allegheny County (PA)
Dakota Coll at Bottineau (ND)
Eastern Arizona Coll (AZ)
Elgin Comm Coll (IL)
Erie Comm Coll (NY)
Erie Comm Coll, North Campus (NY)
Erie Comm Coll, South Campus (NY)
Feather River Coll (CA)
Fullerton Coll (CA)
Genesee Comm Coll (NY)
Gordon State Coll (GA)
Harrisburg Area Comm Coll (PA)
Hill Coll (TX)
Holyoke Comm Coll (MA)
Houston Comm Coll (TX)
Illinois Central Coll (IL)
Jamestown Comm Coll (NY)
Lansing Comm Coll (MI)
Lincoln Coll (IL)
Luzerne County Comm Coll (PA)
McHenry County Coll (IL)
Merced Coll (CA)
Montgomery County Comm Coll (PA)
Mt. San Antonio Coll (CA)
Northeast Comm Coll (NE)
Northwest Coll (WY)
Orange Coast Coll (CA)
Paris Jr Coll (TX)
Raritan Valley Comm Coll (NJ)
San Jacinto Coll District (TX)
San Juan Coll (NM)
Santa Fe Comm Coll (NM)
Santa Monica Coll (CA)
Santa Rosa Jr Coll (CA)
Sierra Coll (CA)
Tyler Jr Coll (TX)
Vincennes U (IN)

HEALTH AND PHYSICAL EDUCATION RELATED
Chesapeake Coll (MD)
Fayetteville Tech Comm Coll (NC)
Genesee Comm Coll (NY)
Kingsborough Comm Coll of the City U of New York (NY)

HEALTH AND WELLNESS
Central Wyoming Coll (WY)
Erie Comm Coll (NY)

Erie Comm Coll, North Campus (NY)
Erie Comm Coll, South Campus (NY)

HEALTH/HEALTH-CARE ADMINISTRATION
Comm Care Coll (OK)
Comm Coll of the Air Force (AL)
Des Moines Area Comm Coll (IA)
Harrisburg Area Comm Coll (PA)
Kent State U at Trumbull (OH)
Luzerne County Comm Coll (PA)
Manor Coll (PA)
Nashville State Comm Coll (TN)
Oklahoma State U–Oklahoma City (OK)
Penn Foster Coll (AZ)
Pennsylvania Inst of Technology (PA)
Pensacola State Coll (FL)
Rockingham Comm Coll (NC)
Southeast Comm Coll, Lincoln Campus (NE)
South Florida State Coll (FL)
South Plains Coll (TX)
Ultimate Medical Academy Online (FL)

HEALTH INFORMATION/ MEDICAL RECORDS ADMINISTRATION
Amarillo Coll (TX)
Bunker Hill Comm Coll (MA)
Camden County Coll (NJ)
Central New Mexico Comm Coll (NM)
The Coll of Westchester (NY)
Columbus State Comm Coll (OH)
Daytona State Coll (FL)
Dodge City Comm Coll (KS)
El Paso Comm Coll (TX)
Georgia Highlands Coll (GA)
Humacao Comm Coll (PR)
Illinois Eastern Comm Colls, Lincoln Trail College (IL)
McLennan Comm Coll (TX)
Miami Dade Coll (FL)
Monroe Comm Coll (NY)
Mount Wachusett Comm Coll (MA)
Nashville State Comm Coll (TN)
Northern Essex Comm Coll (MA)
Oakton Comm Coll (IL)
Oklahoma City Comm Coll (OK)
Pensacola State Coll (FL)
Southern U at Shreveport (LA)
South Florida State Coll (FL)
South Plains Coll (TX)
Southwestern Comm Coll (NC)
Spoon River Coll (IL)
Stark State Coll (OH)
Tarrant County Coll District (TX)

HEALTH INFORMATION/ MEDICAL RECORDS TECHNOLOGY
Anne Arundel Comm Coll (MD)
Anoka Tech Coll (MN)
Arapahoe Comm Coll (CO)
Atlanta Tech Coll (GA)
Austin Comm Coll District (TX)
Bainbridge State Coll (GA)
Blinn Coll (TX)
Borough of Manhattan Comm Coll of the City U of New York (NY)
Carroll Comm Coll (MD)
Central New Mexico Comm Coll (NM)
Central Oregon Comm Coll (OR)
Chippewa Valley Tech Coll (WI)
Coll of Business and Technology–Cutler Bay Campus (FL)
Coll of Business and Technology–Miami Gardens (FL)
Coll of Central Florida (FL)
Collin County Comm Coll District (TX)
Columbus Tech Coll (GA)
Comm Coll of Allegheny County (PA)
Craven Comm Coll (NC)
Crowder Coll (MO)
Danville Area Comm Coll (IL)
Del Mar Coll (TX)
Duluth Business U (MN)
Dyersburg State Comm Coll (TN)
East Central Coll (MO)
Erie Comm Coll, North Campus (NY)
Florida SouthWestern State Coll (FL)
Fox Valley Tech Coll (WI)
Front Range Comm Coll (CO)
Gateway Tech Coll (WI)
Great Falls Coll Montana State U (MT)
Greenville Tech Coll (SC)
Highland Comm Coll (IL)
Hinds Comm Coll (MS)
Houston Comm Coll (TX)

Hudson County Comm Coll (NJ)
Hutchinson Comm Coll (KS)
Illinois Eastern Comm Colls, Frontier Community College (IL)
Ivy Tech Comm Coll–Central Indiana (IN)
Ivy Tech Comm Coll–East Central (IN)
Ivy Tech Comm Coll–Kokomo (IN)
Ivy Tech Comm Coll–Lafayette (IN)
Ivy Tech Comm Coll–Wabash Valley (IN)
Jamestown Comm Coll (NY)
Kaskaskia Coll (IL)
Kirtland Comm Coll (MI)
Lehigh Carbon Comm Coll (PA)
Lone Star Coll–CyFair (TX)
Lone Star Coll–North Harris (TX)
Miami Dade Coll (FL)
Minnesota State Comm and Tech Coll (MN)
Mohawk Valley Comm Coll (NY)
Montgomery Coll (MD)
Morton Coll (IL)
Northeast Comm Coll (NE)
Northeast Iowa Comm Coll (IA)
NorthWest Arkansas Comm Coll (AR)
Ogeechee Tech Coll (GA)
Ozarks Tech Comm Coll (MO)
Panola Coll (TX)
Paris Jr Coll (TX)
Penn Foster Coll (AZ)
Pennsylvania Inst of Technology (PA)
Pensacola State Coll (FL)
Quinsigamond Comm Coll (MA)
Raritan Valley Comm Coll (NJ)
Rend Lake Coll (IL)
Richmond Comm Coll (NC)
St. Charles Comm Coll (MO)
St. Clair County Comm Coll (MI)
St. Philip's Coll (TX)
San Jacinto Coll District (TX)
San Juan Coll (NM)
Schoolcraft Coll (MI)
Shawnee Comm Coll (IL)
Southern U at Shreveport (LA)
Southwestern Comm Coll (NC)
Southwestern Michigan Coll (MI)
State U of New York Coll of Technology at Alfred (NY)
Tallahassee Comm Coll (FL)
Tyler Jr Coll (TX)
Ultimate Medical Academy Online (FL)
U of Cincinnati Clermont Coll (OH)
Vincennes U (IN)
Volunteer State Comm Coll (TN)
Walters State Comm Coll (TN)
Waukesha County Tech Coll (WI)
West Georgia Tech Coll (GA)
Wisconsin Indianhead Tech Coll (WI)
York County Comm Coll (ME)

HEALTH/MEDICAL PREPARATORY PROGRAMS RELATED
Ancilla Coll (IN)
Central Wyoming Coll (WY)
Coll of Central Florida (FL)
Eastern Arizona Coll (AZ)
Eastern Wyoming Coll (WY)
Edison State Comm Coll (OH)
Fullerton Coll (CA)
Gordon State Coll (GA)
Manor Coll (PA)
Merced Coll (CA)
Miami Dade Coll (FL)
Missouri State U–West Plains (MO)
Northeast Comm Coll (NE)
Northwest Coll (WY)
Three Rivers Comm Coll (MO)
U of Cincinnati Blue Ash Coll (OH)
Western Wyoming Comm Coll (WY)

HEALTH PROFESSIONS RELATED
Berkshire Comm Coll (MA)
Bowling Green State U–Firelands Coll (OH)
Bucks County Comm Coll (PA)
Carl Albert State Coll (OK)
Carroll Comm Coll (MD)
Central Wyoming Coll (WY)
Coll of the Marshall Islands (MH)
Comm Coll of Allegheny County (PA)
Comm Coll of Philadelphia (PA)
Gateway Comm and Tech Coll (KY)
Genesee Comm Coll (NY)
Harrisburg Area Comm Coll (PA)
Lakeland Comm Coll (OH)
Lanier Tech Coll (GA)

Manor Coll (PA)
Mercer County Comm Coll (NJ)
Miami Dade Coll (FL)
Middlesex County Coll (NJ)
Mitchell Comm Coll (NC)
Nashville State Comm Coll (TN)
New Mexico Jr Coll (NM)
North Shore Comm Coll (MA)
Panola Coll (TX)
Piedmont Comm Coll (NC)
Queensborough Comm Coll of the City U of New York (NY)
Richmond Comm Coll (NC)
Salt Lake Comm Coll (UT)
Southeastern Coll–West Palm Beach (FL)
Sussex County Comm Coll (NJ)
U of Cincinnati Clermont Coll (OH)
Volunteer State Comm Coll (TN)

HEALTH SERVICES ADMINISTRATION
Harrisburg Area Comm Coll (PA)

HEALTH SERVICES/ALLIED HEALTH/HEALTH SCIENCES
Aaniiih Nakoda Coll (MT)
Alvin Comm Coll (TX)
American Samoa Comm Coll (AS)
Ancilla Coll (IN)
Anoka-Ramsey Comm Coll (MN)
Borough of Manhattan Comm Coll of the City U of New York (NY)
Camden County Coll (NJ)
Carl Albert State Coll (OK)
Casper Coll (WY)
Cayuga County Comm Coll (NY)
Cecil Coll (MD)
Central New Mexico Comm Coll (NM)
Century Coll (MN)
Coll of Central Florida (FL)
Dakota Coll at Bottineau (ND)
Dyersburg State Comm Coll (TN)
Georgia Highlands Coll (GA)
Georgia Military Coll (GA)
Gulf Coast State Coll (FL)
Holyoke Comm Coll (MA)
Houston Comm Coll (TX)
Hudson County Comm Coll (NJ)
Lake Superior Coll (MN)
Lehigh Carbon Comm Coll (PA)
Miami Dade Coll (FL)
Middlesex County Coll (NJ)
Missouri State U–West Plains (MO)
Northland Comm and Tech Coll (MN)
Oklahoma State U Inst of Technology (OK)
Orange Coast Coll (CA)
Paris Jr Coll (TX)
Pennsylvania Inst of Technology (PA)
Queensborough Comm Coll of the City U of New York (NY)
Quinsigamond Comm Coll (MA)
Raritan Valley Comm Coll (NJ)
St. Philip's Coll (TX)
Schoolcraft Coll (MI)
South Florida State Coll (FL)
Ultimate Medical Academy Clearwater (FL)
Ultimate Medical Academy Online (FL)
Western Wyoming Comm Coll (WY)
White Mountains Comm Coll (NH)
York County Comm Coll (ME)

HEALTH TEACHER EDUCATION
Bainbridge State Coll (GA)
Del Mar Coll (TX)
Georgia Military Coll (GA)
Harper Coll (IL)
Howard Comm Coll (MD)
South Florida State Coll (FL)

HEALTH UNIT COORDINATOR/ WARD CLERK
Comm Coll of Allegheny County (PA)

HEATING, AIR CONDITIONING, VENTILATION AND REFRIGERATION MAINTENANCE TECHNOLOGY
Amarillo Coll (TX)
Arizona Western Coll (AZ)
Bismarck State Coll (ND)
Central New Mexico Comm Coll (NM)
Central Texas Coll (TX)
Century Coll (MN)
City Colls of Chicago, Kennedy-King College (IL)
Coll of the Desert (CA)
Comm Coll of Allegheny County (PA)
Craven Comm Coll (NC)

Delta Coll (MI)
Des Moines Area Comm Coll (IA)
Dunwoody Coll of Technology (MN)
East Central Coll (MO)
Elgin Comm Coll (IL)
El Paso Comm Coll (TX)
Fayetteville Tech Comm Coll (NC)
Gateway Tech Coll (WI)
Grand Rapids Comm Coll (MI)
Harper Coll (IL)
Harrisburg Area Comm Coll (PA)
Hennepin Tech Coll (MN)
Hill Coll (TX)
Hinds Comm Coll (MS)
Illinois Central Coll (IL)
Ivy Tech Comm Coll–Bloomington (IN)
Ivy Tech Comm Coll–Central Indiana (IN)
Ivy Tech Comm Coll–Columbus (IN)
Ivy Tech Comm Coll–Kokomo (IN)
Ivy Tech Comm Coll–Lafayette (IN)
Ivy Tech Comm Coll–North Central (IN)
Ivy Tech Comm Coll–Northeast (IN)
Ivy Tech Comm Coll–Northwest (IN)
Ivy Tech Comm Coll–Richmond (IN)
Ivy Tech Comm Coll–Sellersburg (IN)
Ivy Tech Comm Coll–Southwest (IN)
Ivy Tech Comm Coll–Wabash Valley (IN)
Johnston Comm Coll (NC)
Kaskaskia Coll (IL)
Kellogg Comm Coll (MI)
Kirtland Comm Coll (MI)
Lansing Comm Coll (MI)
Laramie County Comm Coll (WY)
Lehigh Carbon Comm Coll (PA)
Lone Star Coll–North Harris (TX)
Luzerne County Comm Coll (PA)
Macomb Comm Coll (MI)
Manhattan Area Tech Coll (KS)
Metropolitan Comm Coll (NE)
Miami Dade Coll (FL)
Mid-Plains Comm Coll, North Platte (NE)
Minnesota State Coll–Southeast Tech (MN)
Mitchell Tech Inst (SD)
Mohave Comm Coll (AZ)
Mohawk Valley Comm Coll (NY)
Monroe Comm Coll (NY)
Montgomery Comm Coll (NC)
Morton Coll (IL)
Mt. San Antonio Coll (CA)
Northampton Comm Coll (PA)
Northeast Comm Coll (NE)
Northern Maine Comm Coll (ME)
Northland Comm and Tech Coll (MN)
Oklahoma State U Inst of Technology (OK)
Ozarks Tech Comm Coll (MO)
Paris Jr Coll (TX)
Pittsburgh Tech Coll (PA)
Renton Tech Coll (WA)
Richmond Comm Coll (NC)
Salina Area Tech Coll (KS)
Salt Lake Comm Coll (UT)
San Jacinto Coll District (TX)
San Joaquin Delta Coll (CA)
Southeast Comm Coll, Milford Campus (NE)
South Plains Coll (TX)
Spartanburg Comm Coll (SC)
Springfield Tech Comm Coll (MA)
State U of New York Coll of Technology at Alfred (NY)
Tarrant County Coll District (TX)
Texarkana Coll (TX)
Three Rivers Comm Coll (MO)
Trinity Valley Comm Coll (TX)
Truckee Meadows Comm Coll (NV)
Tyler Jr Coll (TX)
U of Arkansas Comm Coll at Morrilton (AR)
Wayne County Comm Coll District (MI)
Western Dakota Tech Inst (SD)
Westmoreland County Comm Coll (PA)

HEATING, VENTILATION, AIR CONDITIONING AND REFRIGERATION ENGINEERING TECHNOLOGY
Alamance Comm Coll (NC)
Arizona Western Coll (AZ)
Austin Comm Coll District (TX)
Bevill State Comm Coll (AL)
Chippewa Valley Tech Coll (WI)

Coll of Business and Technology–Flagler Campus (FL)
Coll of Business and Technology–Hialeah Campus (FL)
Columbus State Comm Coll (OH)
Comm Coll of Baltimore County (MD)
Dunwoody Coll of Technology (MN)
Front Range Comm Coll (CO)
Georgia Piedmont Tech Coll (GA)
H. Councill Trenholm State Comm Coll (AL)
Humacao Comm Coll (PR)
Johnson County Comm Coll (KS)
Macomb Comm Coll (MI)
Manhattan Area Tech Coll (KS)
Merced Coll (CA)
Mercer County Comm Coll (NJ)
Miami Dade Coll (FL)
Minnesota State Comm and Tech Coll (MN)
Mott Comm Coll (MI)
North Georgia Tech Coll (GA)
Oakton Comm Coll (IL)
Raritan Valley Comm Coll (NJ)
St. Philip's Coll (TX)
Savannah Tech Coll (GA)
Southern Crescent Tech Coll (GA)
South Georgia Tech Coll (GA)
Texas State Tech Coll (TX)

HEAVY EQUIPMENT MAINTENANCE TECHNOLOGY
Amarillo Coll (TX)
Comm Coll of Aurora (CO)
Del Mar Coll (TX)
Highland Comm Coll (IL)
Mesa Comm Coll (AZ)
Metropolitan Comm Coll (NE)
The Ohio State U Ag Tech Inst (OH)
Ozarks Tech Comm Coll (MO)
Rend Lake Coll (IL)
Western Wyoming Comm Coll (WY)

HEAVY/INDUSTRIAL EQUIPMENT MAINTENANCE TECHNOLOGIES RELATED
East Central Coll (MO)
Southern Arkansas U Tech (AR)
State U of New York Coll of Technology at Alfred (NY)

HEMATOLOGY TECHNOLOGY
Comm Coll of the Air Force (AL)

HIGHER EDUCATION/HIGHER EDUCATION ADMINISTRATION
Lansing Comm Coll (MI)

HIGH PERFORMANCE AND CUSTOM ENGINE TECHNOLOGY
Ohio Tech Coll (OH)

HISPANIC-AMERICAN, PUERTO RICAN, AND MEXICAN-AMERICAN/CHICANO STUDIES
Cerritos Coll (CA)
San Jacinto Coll District (TX)

HISTOLOGIC TECHNICIAN
Comm Coll of Rhode Island (RI)
Houston Comm Coll (TX)
Lansing Comm Coll (MI)
Miami Dade Coll (FL)
Mott Comm Coll (MI)

HISTOLOGIC TECHNOLOGY/ HISTOTECHNOLOGIST
Miami Dade Coll (FL)

HISTORIC PRESERVATION AND CONSERVATION
Piedmont Comm Coll (NC)

HISTORY
Allen Comm Coll (KS)
Alvin Comm Coll (TX)
Amarillo Coll (TX)
Ancilla Coll (IN)
Arizona Western Coll (AZ)
Austin Comm Coll District (TX)
Bainbridge State Coll (GA)
Blinn Coll (TX)
Borough of Manhattan Comm Coll of the City U of New York (NY)
Bucks County Comm Coll (PA)
Bunker Hill Comm Coll (MA)
Cañada Coll (CA)
Casper Coll (WY)
Central New Mexico Comm Coll (NM)
Cerritos Coll (CA)
Citrus Coll (CA)

Coll of Central Florida (FL)
Coll of Marin (CA)
Coll of the Canyons (CA)
Coll of the Desert (CA)
Dakota Coll at Bottineau (ND)
De Anza Coll (CA)
Del Mar Coll (TX)
Dodge City Comm Coll (KS)
Eastern Arizona Coll (AZ)
Edison State Comm Coll (OH)
Feather River Coll (CA)
Fullerton Coll (CA)
Georgia Highlands Coll (GA)
Georgia Military Coll (GA)
Harford Comm Coll (MD)
Harper Coll (IL)
Hill Coll (TX)
Lansing Comm Coll (MI)
Laramie County Comm Coll (WY)
Lincoln Coll (IL)
Merced Coll (CA)
Miami Dade Coll (FL)
Mohave Comm Coll (AZ)
Monroe Comm Coll (NY)
Murray State Coll (OK)
Nashville State Comm Coll (TN)
New Mexico Jr Coll (NM)
Northeastern Jr Coll (CO)
Northern Essex Comm Coll (MA)
Northwest Coll (WY)
Oklahoma City Comm Coll (OK)
Orange Coast Coll (CA)
Otero Jr Coll (CO)
Panola Coll (TX)
Paris Jr Coll (TX)
Pensacola State Coll (FL)
St. Philip's Coll (TX)
Salt Lake Comm Coll (UT)
San Jacinto Coll District (TX)
San Joaquin Delta Coll (CA)
Santa Monica Coll (CA)
Santa Rosa Jr Coll (CA)
South Florida State Coll (FL)
Texarkana Coll (TX)
Trinity Valley Comm Coll (TX)
Truckee Meadows Comm Coll (NV)
Tyler Jr Coll (TX)
Vincennes U (IN)
Western Wyoming Comm Coll (WY)

HISTORY RELATED
U of Pittsburgh at Titusville (PA)

HISTORY TEACHER EDUCATION
Bucks County Comm Coll (PA)

HOLISTIC HEALTH
Anoka-Ramsey Comm Coll (MN)
Front Range Comm Coll (CO)

HOME HEALTH AIDE/HOME ATTENDANT
Allen Comm Coll (KS)

HOMELAND SECURITY
Arizona Western Coll (AZ)
Georgia Military Coll (GA)
Harper Coll (IL)
Long Island Business Inst (NY)
Palomar Coll (CA)

HOMELAND SECURITY, LAW ENFORCEMENT, FIREFIGHTING AND PROTECTIVE SERVICES RELATED
Central Wyoming Coll (WY)
Century Coll (MN)
El Paso Comm Coll (TX)
Lakeland Comm Coll (OH)
Laramie County Comm Coll (WY)
Pittsburgh Tech Coll (PA)
Schoolcraft Coll (MI)
Wayne County Comm Coll District (MI)
Westmoreland County Comm Coll (PA)

HOMELAND SECURITY RELATED
Fox Valley Tech Coll (WI)
Pensacola State Coll (FL)
Tallahassee Comm Coll (FL)

HORSE HUSBANDRY/EQUINE SCIENCE AND MANAGEMENT
Cecil Coll (MD)
Feather River Coll (CA)
Merced Coll (CA)
Minnesota State Comm and Tech Coll (MN)

Mt. San Antonio Coll (CA)
The Ohio State U Ag Tech Inst (OH)
Santa Rosa Jr Coll (CA)
Treasure Valley Comm Coll (OR)

HORTICULTURAL SCIENCE
Century Coll (MN)
Chattahoochee Tech Coll (GA)
Columbus Tech Coll (GA)
Dakota Coll at Bottineau (ND)
Gwinnett Tech Coll (GA)
Mesa Comm Coll (AZ)
Miami Dade Coll (FL)
Mt. San Antonio Coll (CA)
Naugatuck Valley Comm Coll (CT)
North Georgia Tech Coll (GA)
The Ohio State U Ag Tech Inst (OH)
Oklahoma State U–Oklahoma City (OK)
Southern Crescent Tech Coll (GA)
South Florida State Coll (FL)
South Georgia Tech Coll (GA)
Tarrant County Coll District (TX)
Tidewater Comm Coll (VA)
Treasure Valley Comm Coll (OR)
Trident Tech Coll (SC)
Trinity Valley Comm Coll (TX)

HOSPITAL AND HEALTH-CARE FACILITIES ADMINISTRATION
Allen Comm Coll (KS)
Bossier Parish Comm Coll (LA)
Minnesota West Comm and Tech Coll (MN)

HOSPITALITY ADMINISTRATION
Adirondack Comm Coll (NY)
Arizona Western Coll (AZ)
Austin Comm Coll District (TX)
Berkshire Comm Coll (MA)
Bunker Hill Comm Coll (MA)
Casper Coll (WY)
Central New Mexico Comm Coll (NM)
Central Texas Coll (TX)
Chesapeake Coll (MD)
Coconino Comm Coll (AZ)
Coll of the Canyons (CA)
Coll of the Desert (CA)
Collin County Comm Coll District (TX)
Columbus State Comm Coll (OH)
Comm Coll of Vermont (VT)
County Coll of Morris (NJ)
Daytona State Coll (FL)
Des Moines Area Comm Coll (IA)
Fox Valley Tech Coll (WI)
Front Range Comm Coll (CO)
Gateway Tech Coll (WI)
Genesee Comm Coll (NY)
Gulf Coast State Coll (FL)
Harper Coll (IL)
Hawkeye Comm Coll (IA)
Highland Comm Coll (IL)
Hillsborough Comm Coll (FL)
Hinds Comm Coll (MS)
Hudson County Comm Coll (NJ)
Ivy Tech Comm Coll–Bloomington (IN)
Ivy Tech Comm Coll–Columbus (IN)
Ivy Tech Comm Coll–East Central (IN)
Ivy Tech Comm Coll–North Central (IN)
Ivy Tech Comm Coll–Northeast (IN)
Ivy Tech Comm Coll–Northwest (IN)
Ivy Tech Comm Coll–Southwest (IN)
Jefferson Comm Coll (NY)
Jefferson State Comm Coll (AL)
J. Sargeant Reynolds Comm Coll (VA)
Lakeland Comm Coll (OH)
Madison Area Tech Coll (WI)
Massachusetts Bay Comm Coll (MA)
Miami Dade Coll (FL)
Naugatuck Valley Comm Coll (CT)
Niagara County Comm Coll (NY)
North Shore Comm Coll (MA)
Penn Foster Coll (AZ)
Pensacola State Coll (FL)
Quinsigamond Comm Coll (MA)
Santa Fe Comm Coll (NM)
Scottsdale Comm Coll (AZ)
Sisseton-Wahpeton Coll (SD)
Southern U at Shreveport (LA)
South Florida State Coll (FL)
Sullivan County Comm Coll (NY)
Three Rivers Comm Coll (CT)
Three Rivers Comm Coll (MO)

Vincennes U (IN)
Waukesha County Tech Coll (WI)
Wor-Wic Comm Coll (MD)
York County Comm Coll (ME)

HOSPITALITY ADMINISTRATION RELATED
Ancilla Coll (IN)
Bunker Hill Comm Coll (MA)
Chesapeake Coll (MD)
Holyoke Comm Coll (MA)
Ivy Tech Comm Coll–Central Indiana (IN)
Ivy Tech Comm Coll–East Central (IN)
Ivy Tech Comm Coll–Northeast (IN)
J. Sargeant Reynolds Comm Coll (VA)
Long Island Business Inst (NY)

HOSPITALITY AND RECREATION MARKETING
Dakota Coll at Bottineau (ND)
Iowa Central Comm Coll (IA)
Luzerne County Comm Coll (PA)
Montgomery County Comm Coll (PA)

HOTEL/MOTEL ADMINISTRATION
Albany Tech Coll (GA)
Anne Arundel Comm Coll (MD)
Athens Tech Coll (GA)
Atlanta Tech Coll (GA)
Austin Comm Coll District (TX)
Cape Fear Comm Coll (NC)
Carl Albert State Coll (OK)
Central Georgia Tech Coll (GA)
Central Oregon Comm Coll (OR)
Central Wyoming Coll (WY)
Coll of the Canyons (CA)
Comm Coll of Allegheny County (PA)
Comm Coll of Baltimore County (MD)
Comm Coll of Philadelphia (PA)
Comm Coll of the Air Force (AL)
Daytona State Coll (FL)
Del Mar Coll (TX)
El Paso Comm Coll (TX)
Finger Lakes Comm Coll (NY)
Genesee Comm Coll (NY)
Guam Comm Coll (GU)
Gwinnett Tech Coll (GA)
Houston Comm Coll (TX)
Johnson County Comm Coll (KS)
J. Sargeant Reynolds Comm Coll (VA)
Lansing Comm Coll (MI)
Luzerne County Comm Coll (PA)
Manchester Comm Coll (CT)
Mercer County Comm Coll (NJ)
Miami Dade Coll (FL)
Middlesex Comm Coll (MA)
Middlesex County Coll (NJ)
Mohawk Valley Comm Coll (NY)
Monroe Comm Coll (NY)
Montgomery Coll (MD)
Mt. San Antonio Coll (CA)
Nassau Comm Coll (NY)
Naugatuck Valley Comm Coll (CT)
NHTI, Concord's Comm Coll, Concord (NH)
Northampton Comm Coll (PA)
Northern Essex Comm Coll (MA)
Norwalk Comm Coll (CT)
Ogeechee Tech Coll (GA)
Orange Coast Coll (CA)
Ozarks Tech Comm Coll (MO)
Pensacola State Coll (FL)
Pittsburgh Tech Coll (PA)
St. Philip's Coll (TX)
Savannah Tech Coll (GA)
Scottsdale Comm Coll (AZ)
Southern U at Shreveport (LA)
Trident Tech Coll (SC)
Vincennes U (IN)
Westmoreland County Comm Coll (PA)

HOTEL, MOTEL, AND RESTAURANT MANAGEMENT
Caldwell Comm Coll and Tech Inst (NC)
Carteret Comm Coll (NC)
Craven Comm Coll (NC)
Fayetteville Tech Comm Coll (NC)
Pensacola State Coll (FL)
Tompkins Cortland Comm Coll (NY)
Wayne County Comm Coll District (MI)

HOUSING AND HUMAN ENVIRONMENTS RELATED
Comm Coll of Allegheny County (PA)

HUMAN DEVELOPMENT AND FAMILY STUDIES
Bucks County Comm Coll (PA)
Central New Mexico Comm Coll (NM)
Imperial Valley Coll (CA)
Missouri State U–West Plains (MO)
Penn State DuBois (PA)
Penn State Fayette, The Eberly Campus (PA)
Penn State Mont Alto (PA)
Penn State Shenango (PA)
Salt Lake Comm Coll (UT)

HUMAN DEVELOPMENT AND FAMILY STUDIES RELATED
Albany Tech Coll (GA)
Comm Coll of Allegheny County (PA)

HUMANITIES
Allen Comm Coll (KS)
Brookhaven Coll (TX)
Bucks County Comm Coll (PA)
Cañada Coll (CA)
Cayuga County Comm Coll (NY)
Central Oregon Comm Coll (OR)
Clinton Comm Coll (NY)
Cochise County Comm Coll District (AZ)
Coll of Central Florida (FL)
Coll of Marin (CA)
Coll of the Canyons (CA)
Coll of the Desert (CA)
Columbia-Greene Comm Coll (NY)
Comm Coll of Allegheny County (PA)
Dakota Coll at Bottineau (ND)
De Anza Coll (CA)
Dodge City Comm Coll (KS)
Dutchess Comm Coll (NY)
Erie Comm Coll (NY)
Erie Comm Coll, North Campus (NY)
Erie Comm Coll, South Campus (NY)
Feather River Coll (CA)
Finger Lakes Comm Coll (NY)
Fullerton Coll (CA)
Genesee Comm Coll (NY)
Golden West Coll (CA)
Harper Coll (IL)
Housatonic Comm Coll (CT)
Imperial Valley Coll (CA)
Jamestown Comm Coll (NY)
Jefferson Comm Coll (NY)
John Tyler Comm Coll (VA)
Lackawanna Coll (PA)
Lansing Comm Coll (MI)
Laramie County Comm Coll (WY)
Luzerne County Comm Coll (PA)
Merced Coll (CA)
Mercer County Comm Coll (NJ)
Miami Dade Coll (FL)
Mohawk Valley Comm Coll (NY)
Montgomery County Comm Coll (PA)
Mt. San Antonio Coll (CA)
Murray State Coll (OK)
Niagara County Comm Coll (NY)
Oklahoma City Comm Coll (OK)
Orange Coast Coll (CA)
Otero Jr Coll (CO)
Palomar Coll (CA)
Salt Lake Comm Coll (UT)
San Joaquin Delta Coll (CA)
Santa Fe Comm Coll (NM)
Santa Monica Coll (CA)
Santa Rosa Jr Coll (CA)
Seminole State Coll (OK)
South Florida State Coll (FL)
State U of New York Coll of Technology at Alfred (NY)
Texarkana Coll (TX)
Tompkins Cortland Comm Coll (NY)
Ulster County Comm Coll (NY)
Westchester Comm Coll (NY)
Western Wyoming Comm Coll (WY)

HUMAN RESOURCES DEVELOPMENT
Minnesota State Comm and Tech Coll–Moorhead (MN)

HUMAN RESOURCES MANAGEMENT
Anoka-Ramsey Comm Coll (MN)
Blackhawk Tech Coll (WI)
Cecil Coll (MD)
Chippewa Valley Tech Coll (WI)

Columbus State Comm Coll (OH)
Comm Coll of Allegheny County (PA)
Comm Coll of the Air Force (AL)
Edison State Comm Coll (OH)
Fayetteville Tech Comm Coll (NC)
Fox Valley Tech Coll (WI)
Harford Comm Coll (MD)
Hawkeye Comm Coll (IA)
Illinois Eastern Comm Colls, Olney Central College (IL)
Lansing Comm Coll (MI)
Lehigh Carbon Comm Coll (PA)
Lorain County Comm Coll (OH)
Minnesota State Comm and Tech Coll (MN)
Minnesota State Comm and Tech Coll–Moorhead (MN)
NHTI, Concord's Comm Coll, Concord (NH)
Penn Foster Coll (AZ)
Santa Rosa Jr Coll (CA)
South Florida State Coll (FL)
Waukesha County Tech Coll (WI)
Westmoreland County Comm Coll (PA)
Wisconsin Indianhead Tech Coll (WI)

HUMAN SERVICES
Aaniiih Nakoda Coll (MT)
Alexandria Tech and Comm Coll (MN)
American Samoa Comm Coll (AS)
Berkshire Comm Coll (MA)
Bismarck State Coll (ND)
Bowling Green State U–Firelands Coll (OH)
Bunker Hill Comm Coll (MA)
Cañada Coll (CA)
Central Maine Comm Coll (ME)
Century Coll (MN)
Cerritos Coll (CA)
Coll of Central Florida (FL)
Columbia-Greene Comm Coll (NY)
Comm Coll of Philadelphia (PA)
Comm Coll of Vermont (VT)
Daytona State Coll (FL)
Dutchess Comm Coll (NY)
Finger Lakes Comm Coll (NY)
Frederick Comm Coll (MD)
Genesee Comm Coll (NY)
Georgia Highlands Coll (GA)
Great Basin Coll (NV)
Greenville Tech Coll (SC)
Guam Comm Coll (GU)
Harper Coll (IL)
Harrisburg Area Comm Coll (PA)
Housatonic Comm Coll (CT)
Ivy Tech Comm Coll–Bloomington (IN)
Ivy Tech Comm Coll–Central Indiana (IN)
Ivy Tech Comm Coll–Columbus (IN)
Ivy Tech Comm Coll–East Central (IN)
Ivy Tech Comm Coll–Kokomo (IN)
Ivy Tech Comm Coll–Lafayette (IN)
Ivy Tech Comm Coll–North Central (IN)
Ivy Tech Comm Coll–Northeast (IN)
Ivy Tech Comm Coll–Northwest (IN)
Ivy Tech Comm Coll–Richmond (IN)
Ivy Tech Comm Coll–Sellersburg (IN)
Ivy Tech Comm Coll–Southeast (IN)
Ivy Tech Comm Coll–Southwest (IN)
Ivy Tech Comm Coll–Wabash Valley (IN)
Jamestown Comm Coll (NY)
Jefferson Comm Coll (NY)
Kingsborough Comm Coll of the City U of New York (NY)
Lackawanna Coll (PA)
Lake Area Tech Inst (SD)
Laramie County Comm Coll (WY)
Lehigh Carbon Comm Coll (PA)
Lone Star Coll–Montgomery (TX)
Los Angeles City Coll (CA)
Luzerne County Comm Coll (PA)
Madison Area Tech Coll (WI)
Manchester Comm Coll (CT)
Massachusetts Bay Comm Coll (MA)
Merced Coll (CA)
Mesabi Range Coll (MN)
Metropolitan Comm Coll (NE)
Miami Dade Coll (FL)
Minnesota West Comm and Tech Coll (MN)
Mitchell Tech Inst (SD)
Mohawk Valley Comm Coll (NY)
Monroe Comm Coll (NY)
Mount Wachusett Comm Coll (MA)

NHTI, Concord's Comm Coll, Concord (NH)
Niagara County Comm Coll (NY)
North Central Missouri Coll (MO)
Northeast Comm Coll (NE)
Northern Essex Comm Coll (MA)
Norwalk Comm Coll (CT)
Owensboro Comm and Tech Coll (KY)
Quinsigamond Comm Coll (MA)
Randolph Comm Coll (NC)
Rock Valley Coll (IL)
St. Charles Comm Coll (MO)
Santa Rosa Jr Coll (CA)
Shawnee Comm Coll (IL)
Southern U at Shreveport (LA)
Stark State Coll (OH)
State U of New York Coll of Technology at Alfred (NY)
Sullivan County Comm Coll (NY)
Sussex County Comm Coll (NJ)
Tohono O'odham Comm Coll (AZ)
Tompkins Cortland Comm Coll (NY)
Trident Tech Coll (SC)
Ulster County Comm Coll (NY)
Ultimate Medical Academy Online (FL)
U of Pittsburgh at Titusville (PA)
Western Wyoming Comm Coll (WY)
Westmoreland County Comm Coll (PA)
White Mountains Comm Coll (NH)
York County Comm Coll (ME)

HYDRAULICS AND FLUID POWER TECHNOLOGY
Comm Coll of Baltimore County (MD)
Hennepin Tech Coll (MN)
Minnesota West Comm and Tech Coll (MN)
The Ohio State U Ag Tech Inst (OH)

HYDROLOGY AND WATER RESOURCES SCIENCE
Citrus Coll (CA)
Dodge City Comm Coll (KS)
Imperial Valley Coll (CA)

ILLUSTRATION
Collin County Comm Coll District (TX)
Fashion Inst of Technology (NY)

INDUSTRIAL AND PRODUCT DESIGN
Fiorello H. LaGuardia Comm Coll of the City U of New York (NY)
Luzerne County Comm Coll (PA)
Mt. San Antonio Coll (CA)
Rock Valley Coll (IL)

INDUSTRIAL ELECTRONICS TECHNOLOGY
Bevill State Comm Coll (AL)
Danville Area Comm Coll (IL)
Des Moines Area Comm Coll (IA)
Dyersburg State Comm Coll (TN)
Eastern Arizona Coll (AZ)
Hill Coll (TX)
Lackawanna Coll (PA)
Lehigh Carbon Comm Coll (PA)
Lenoir Comm Coll (NC)
Lurleen B. Wallace Comm Coll (AL)
Northampton Comm Coll (PA)
Northwest-Shoals Comm Coll (AL)
Patrick Henry Comm Coll (VA)
Penn Foster Coll (AZ)
Sierra Coll (CA)
Spartanburg Comm Coll (SC)
Tyler Jr Coll (TX)
Western Wyoming Comm Coll (WY)

INDUSTRIAL ENGINEERING
Manchester Comm Coll (CT)
Nashville State Comm Coll (TN)
South Florida State Coll (FL)

INDUSTRIAL MECHANICS AND MAINTENANCE TECHNOLOGY
Arkansas Northeastern Coll (AR)
Bevill State Comm Coll (AL)
Bismarck State Coll (ND)
Bossier Parish Comm Coll (LA)
Casper Coll (WY)
Chippewa Valley Tech Coll (WI)
Danville Area Comm Coll (IL)
Delta Coll (MI)
Des Moines Area Comm Coll (IA)
Dyersburg State Comm Coll (TN)
Eastern Arizona Coll (AZ)
Elgin Comm Coll (IL)

H. Councill Trenholm State Comm Coll (AL)
Hill Coll (TX)
Illinois Eastern Comm Colls, Olney Central College (IL)
Ivy Tech Comm Coll–East Central (IN)
Johnson County Comm Coll (KS)
Kaskaskia Coll (IL)
Macomb Comm Coll (MI)
Minnesota State Coll–Southeast Tech (MN)
Minnesota State Comm and Tech Coll (MN)
Minnesota State Comm and Tech Coll–Wadena (MN)
Northwest-Shoals Comm Coll (AL)
Owensboro Comm and Tech Coll (KY)
Rend Lake Coll (IL)
San Juan Coll (NM)
Somerset Comm Coll (KY)
Southwestern Michigan Coll (MI)
Texarkana Coll (TX)
Three Rivers Comm Coll (MO)
U of Arkansas Comm Coll at Morrilton (AR)
Western Wyoming Comm Coll (WY)
Westmoreland County Comm Coll (PA)

INDUSTRIAL PRODUCTION TECHNOLOGIES RELATED
Arkansas Northeastern Coll (AR)
Bismarck State Coll (ND)
Camden County Coll (NJ)
Ivy Tech Comm Coll–Central Indiana (IN)
Ivy Tech Comm Coll–East Central (IN)
Ivy Tech Comm Coll–Kokomo (IN)
Ivy Tech Comm Coll–Lafayette (IN)
Ivy Tech Comm Coll–North Central (IN)
Ivy Tech Comm Coll–Northeast (IN)
Ivy Tech Comm Coll–Richmond (IN)
Ivy Tech Comm Coll–Southwest (IN)
Ivy Tech Comm Coll–Wabash Valley (IN)
Kellogg Comm Coll (MI)
Kent State U at Trumbull (OH)
Lansing Comm Coll (MI)
Middlesex County Coll (NJ)
Missouri State U–West Plains (MO)
Murray State Coll (OK)
Nashville State Comm Coll (TN)

INDUSTRIAL RADIOLOGIC TECHNOLOGY
Amarillo Coll (TX)
Blinn Coll (TX)
Daytona State Coll (FL)
Del Mar Coll (TX)
Iowa Central Comm Coll (IA)
Los Angeles City Coll (CA)
Madison Area Tech Coll (WI)
McLennan Comm Coll (TX)
Monroe Comm Coll (NY)
Mt. San Antonio Coll (CA)
Northern Essex Comm Coll (MA)
Salt Lake Comm Coll (UT)
Southeastern Comm Coll (IA)
South Plains Coll (TX)
Tarrant County Coll District (TX)
Virginia Western Comm Coll (VA)

INDUSTRIAL SAFETY TECHNOLOGY
Fox Valley Tech Coll (WI)

INDUSTRIAL TECHNOLOGY
Albany Tech Coll (GA)
Allen Comm Coll (KS)
Arizona Western Coll (AZ)
Arkansas Northeastern Coll (AR)
Bismarck State Coll (ND)
Bossier Parish Comm Coll (LA)
Bowling Green State U–Firelands Coll (OH)
Bucks County Comm Coll (PA)
Central Georgia Tech Coll (GA)
Central Oregon Comm Coll (OR)
Central Virginia Comm Coll (VA)
Cerritos Coll (CA)
Cleveland State Comm Coll (TN)
Coll of the Ouachitas (AR)
Columbus Tech Coll (GA)
Comm Coll of Allegheny County (PA)
Comm Coll of the Air Force (AL)
Comm Coll of Vermont (VT)
Crowder Coll (MO)
Daytona State Coll (FL)

De Anza Coll (CA)
Dodge City Comm Coll (KS)
Edison State Comm Coll (OH)
Erie Comm Coll, North Campus (NY)
Gateway Comm and Tech Coll (KY)
Georgia Piedmont Tech Coll (GA)
Grand Rapids Comm Coll (MI)
Great Basin Coll (NV)
Hagerstown Comm Coll (MD)
Highland Comm Coll (IL)
Illinois Central Coll (IL)
Illinois Eastern Comm Colls, Wabash Valley College (IL)
Illinois Valley Comm Coll (IL)
Ivy Tech Comm Coll–Bloomington (IN)
Ivy Tech Comm Coll–Central Indiana (IN)
Ivy Tech Comm Coll–Columbus (IN)
Ivy Tech Comm Coll–East Central (IN)
Ivy Tech Comm Coll–Kokomo (IN)
Ivy Tech Comm Coll–Lafayette (IN)
Ivy Tech Comm Coll–North Central (IN)
Ivy Tech Comm Coll–Northeast (IN)
Ivy Tech Comm Coll–Northwest (IN)
Ivy Tech Comm Coll–Richmond (IN)
Ivy Tech Comm Coll–Sellersburg (IN)
Ivy Tech Comm Coll–Southeast (IN)
Ivy Tech Comm Coll–Southwest (IN)
Ivy Tech Comm Coll–Wabash Valley (IN)
John Tyler Comm Coll (VA)
Kellogg Comm Coll (MI)
Kent State U at Trumbull (OH)
Kent State U at Tuscarawas (OH)
Lackawanna Coll (PA)
Lanier Tech Coll (GA)
Lone Star Coll–CyFair (TX)
Lone Star Coll–North Harris (TX)
Lone Star Coll–Tomball (TX)
Macomb Comm Coll (MI)
Manchester Comm Coll (CT)
Mesa Comm Coll (AZ)
Miami Dade Coll (FL)
Monroe Comm Coll (NY)
Monroe County Comm Coll (MI)
Nashville State Comm Coll (TN)
Navarro Coll (TX)
North Georgia Tech Coll (GA)
Nunez Comm Coll (LA)
The Ohio State U Ag Tech Inst (OH)
Olympic Coll (WA)
Ozarks Tech Comm Coll (MO)
Panola Coll (TX)
Patrick Henry Comm Coll (VA)
Piedmont Comm Coll (NC)
Rock Valley Coll (IL)
Rowan-Cabarrus Comm Coll (NC)
San Juan Coll (NM)
Savannah Tech Coll (GA)
Seminole State Coll of Florida (FL)
Southern Arkansas U Tech (AR)
Southern Crescent Tech Coll (GA)
South Georgia Tech Coll (GA)
Stark State Coll (OH)
Trident Tech Coll (SC)
Victoria Coll (TX)
Walters State Comm Coll (TN)
Western Nevada Coll (NV)
West Georgia Tech Coll (GA)
Westmoreland County Comm Coll (PA)

INFORMATICS
Ivy Tech Comm Coll–Bloomington (IN)
Ivy Tech Comm Coll–Central Indiana (IN)
Ivy Tech Comm Coll–Columbus (IN)
Ivy Tech Comm Coll–East Central (IN)
Ivy Tech Comm Coll–Kokomo (IN)
Ivy Tech Comm Coll–Lafayette (IN)
Ivy Tech Comm Coll–Richmond (IN)
Ivy Tech Comm Coll–Sellersburg (IN)
Ivy Tech Comm Coll–Southeast (IN)
Ivy Tech Comm Coll–Southwest (IN)
Ivy Tech Comm Coll–Wabash Valley (IN)

INFORMATION SCIENCE/ STUDIES
Alamance Comm Coll (NC)
Alexandria Tech and Comm Coll (MN)
Allen Comm Coll (KS)
Amarillo Coll (TX)
Athens Tech Coll (GA)
Augusta Tech Coll (GA)
Bainbridge State Coll (GA)

Bossier Parish Comm Coll (LA)
Brookhaven Coll (TX)
Bucks County Comm Coll (PA)
Cayuga County Comm Coll (NY)
Central Georgia Tech Coll (GA)
Century Coll (MN)
Chattahoochee Tech Coll (GA)
Coastal Pines Tech Coll (GA)
Cochise County Comm Coll District (AZ)
Coll of The Albemarle (NC)
Columbus Tech Coll (GA)
Dakota Coll at Bottineau (ND)
De Anza Coll (CA)
Del Mar Coll (TX)
Dodge City Comm Coll (KS)
Dutchess Comm Coll (NY)
Dyersburg State Comm Coll (TN)
Eastern Arizona Coll (AZ)
Fayetteville Tech Comm Coll (NC)
Genesee Comm Coll (NY)
Georgia Highlands Coll (GA)
Georgia Northwestern Tech Coll (GA)
Georgia Piedmont Tech Coll (GA)
Gwinnett Tech Coll (GA)
Harford Comm Coll (MD)
Howard Comm Coll (MD)
Imperial Valley Coll (CA)
ITI Tech Coll (LA)
Ivy Tech Comm Coll–Bloomington (IN)
Ivy Tech Comm Coll–Central Indiana (IN)
Ivy Tech Comm Coll–Columbus (IN)
Ivy Tech Comm Coll–East Central (IN)
Ivy Tech Comm Coll–Kokomo (IN)
Ivy Tech Comm Coll–Lafayette (IN)
Ivy Tech Comm Coll–Richmond (IN)
Ivy Tech Comm Coll–Sellersburg (IN)
Ivy Tech Comm Coll–Southeast (IN)
Ivy Tech Comm Coll–Southwest (IN)
Ivy Tech Comm Coll–Wabash Valley (IN)
Jamestown Comm Coll (NY)
Jefferson Comm Coll (NY)
Lanier Tech Coll (GA)
Manchester Comm Coll (CT)
McLennan Comm Coll (TX)
Miami Dade Coll (FL)
Mitchell Comm Coll (NC)
Monroe Comm Coll (NY)
Montgomery County Comm Coll (PA)
Murray State Coll (OK)
Nashville State Comm Coll (TN)
New River Comm Coll (VA)
Niagara County Comm Coll (NY)
North Shore Comm Coll (MA)
Norwalk Comm Coll (CT)
Oconee Fall Line Tech Coll (GA)
Ogeechee Tech Coll (GA)
Oklahoma State U–Oklahoma City (OK)
Ozarks Tech Comm Coll (MO)
Panola Coll (TX)
Paris Jr Coll (TX)
Penn State DuBois (PA)
Pensacola State Coll (FL)
Queensborough Comm Coll of the City U of New York (NY)
Rappahannock Comm Coll (VA)
Rio Salado Coll (AZ)
Rowan-Cabarrus Comm Coll (NC)
Salt Lake Comm Coll (UT)
Scottsdale Comm Coll (AZ)
Seminole State Coll of Florida (FL)
Shawnee Comm Coll (IL)
Sisseton-Wahpeton Coll (SD)
Southeastern Comm Coll (IA)
Southeastern Tech Coll (GA)
Southern Regional Tech Coll (GA)
South Florida State Coll (FL)
South Georgia Tech Coll (GA)
Southwestern Comm Coll (NC)
State U of New York Coll of Technology at Alfred (NY)
Sullivan County Comm Coll (NY)
Tompkins Cortland Comm Coll (NY)
U of Cincinnati Clermont Coll (OH)
Weatherford Coll (TX)
Westchester Comm Coll (NY)
Western Wyoming Comm Coll (WY)
West Georgia Tech Coll (GA)
Wytheville Comm Coll (VA)

INFORMATION TECHNOLOGY
Adirondack Comm Coll (NY)
Atlanta Tech Coll (GA)
Blue Ridge Comm and Tech Coll (WV)

Caldwell Comm Coll and Tech Inst (NC)
Carteret Comm Coll (NC)
Chandler-Gilbert Comm Coll (AZ)
City Colls of Chicago, Kennedy-King College (IL)
City Colls of Chicago, Olive-Harvey College (IL)
Coll of Central Florida (FL)
Coll of The Albemarle (NC)
Coll of the Desert (CA)
Columbia-Greene Comm Coll (NY)
Comm Coll of Vermont (VT)
County Coll of Morris (NJ)
Craven Comm Coll (NC)
Dakota Coll at Bottineau (ND)
Daytona State Coll (FL)
Del Mar Coll (TX)
Des Moines Area Comm Coll (IA)
Erie Comm Coll, South Campus (NY)
Fayetteville Tech Comm Coll (NC)
Florida SouthWestern State Coll (FL)
Frederick Comm Coll (MD)
Fullerton Coll (CA)
Georgia Military Coll (GA)
Gordon State Coll (GA)
Great Falls Coll Montana State U (MT)
Halifax Comm Coll (NC)
Haywood Comm Coll (NC)
Highland Comm Coll (IL)
Howard Comm Coll (MD)
Illinois Eastern Comm Colls, Frontier Community College (IL)
Illinois Eastern Comm Colls, Olney Central College (IL)
Illinois Valley Comm Coll (IL)
ITI Tech Coll (LA)
Ivy Tech Comm Coll–Bloomington (IN)
Ivy Tech Comm Coll–Central Indiana (IN)
Ivy Tech Comm Coll–Columbus (IN)
Ivy Tech Comm Coll–East Central (IN)
Ivy Tech Comm Coll–Kokomo (IN)
Ivy Tech Comm Coll–Lafayette (IN)
Ivy Tech Comm Coll–Richmond (IN)
Ivy Tech Comm Coll–Sellersburg (IN)
Ivy Tech Comm Coll–Southeast (IN)
Ivy Tech Comm Coll–Southwest (IN)
Ivy Tech Comm Coll–Wabash Valley (IN)
James Sprunt Comm Coll (NC)
Jamestown Comm Coll (NY)
John Tyler Comm Coll (VA)
Kishwaukee Coll (IL)
Lenoir Comm Coll (NC)
Lone Star Coll–CyFair (TX)
Lone Star Coll–Montgomery (TX)
McHenry County Coll (IL)
Merced Coll (CA)
Mesabi Range Coll (MN)
Miami Dade Coll (FL)
Minnesota State Comm and Tech Coll (MN)
Minnesota State Comm and Tech Coll–Moorhead (MN)
Minnesota West Comm and Tech Coll (MN)
Mitchell Comm Coll (NC)
Mohave Comm Coll (AZ)
Monroe Comm Coll (NY)
Monroe County Comm Coll (MI)
Montgomery Comm Coll (NC)
Morton Coll (IL)
Nashville State Comm Coll (TN)
Norwalk Comm Coll (CT)
Oakton Comm Coll (IL)
Oklahoma State U Inst of Technology (OK)
Oklahoma State U–Oklahoma City (OK)
Palomar Coll (CA)
Panola Coll (TX)
Patrick Henry Comm Coll (VA)
Piedmont Comm Coll (NC)
Queensborough Comm Coll of the City U of New York (NY)
Randolph Comm Coll (NC)
Raritan Valley Comm Coll (NJ)
Richmond Comm Coll (NC)
Rio Salado Coll (AZ)
Rockingham Comm Coll (NC)
Rowan-Cabarrus Comm Coll (NC)
Salt Lake Comm Coll (UT)
Savannah Tech Coll (GA)
Seminole State Coll of Florida (FL)
Sierra Coll (CA)
South Suburban Coll (IL)
Tallahassee Comm Coll (FL)

Tidewater Comm Coll (VA)
U of Pittsburgh at Titusville (PA)
Western Wyoming Comm Coll (WY)
West Virginia Jr Coll–Bridgeport (WV)

INSTITUTIONAL FOOD WORKERS
El Paso Comm Coll (TX)
James Sprunt Comm Coll (NC)
Southwestern Indian Polytechnic Inst (NM)

INSTRUMENTATION TECHNOLOGY
Amarillo Coll (TX)
Bevill State Comm Coll (AL)
Bismarck State Coll (ND)
Cape Fear Comm Coll (NC)
Finger Lakes Comm Coll (NY)
Georgia Piedmont Tech Coll (GA)
Hagerstown Comm Coll (MD)
Houston Comm Coll (TX)
ITI Tech Coll (LA)
Lakeland Comm Coll (OH)
Merced Coll (CA)
Mesabi Range Coll (MN)
Monroe Comm Coll (NY)
Nassau Comm Coll (NY)
New River Comm Coll (VA)
Ozarks Tech Comm Coll (MO)
St. Philip's Coll (TX)
Salt Lake Comm Coll (UT)
San Jacinto Coll District (TX)
San Juan Coll (NM)
Sowela Tech Comm Coll (LA)
Texas State Tech Coll (TX)
Western Wyoming Comm Coll (WY)

INSURANCE
Cerritos Coll (CA)
Comm Coll of Allegheny County (PA)
Madison Area Tech Coll (WI)
Mesa Comm Coll (AZ)
Nassau Comm Coll (NY)
Palomar Coll (CA)
Santa Monica Coll (CA)
South Florida State Coll (FL)
Trinity Valley Comm Coll (TX)

INTEGRATED CIRCUIT DESIGN
Collin County Comm Coll District (TX)

INTELLIGENCE
Cochise County Comm Coll District (AZ)

INTERDISCIPLINARY STUDIES
Anoka-Ramsey Comm Coll (MN)
Blackhawk Tech Coll (WI)
Bowling Green State U–Firelands Coll (OH)
Del Mar Coll (TX)
Gateway Tech Coll (WI)
Great Basin Coll (NV)
Maysville Comm and Tech Coll, Maysville (KY)
North Shore Comm Coll (MA)
Williamsburg Tech Coll (SC)
Wisconsin Indianhead Tech Coll (WI)

INTERIOR ARCHITECTURE
Coll of Central Florida (FL)

INTERIOR DESIGN
Alexandria Tech and Comm Coll (MN)
Amarillo Coll (TX)
Arapahoe Comm Coll (CO)
Cañada Coll (CA)
Cape Fear Comm Coll (NC)
Century Coll (MN)
Coll of Marin (CA)
Coll of the Canyons (CA)
Collin County Comm Coll District (TX)
Daytona State Coll (FL)
El Paso Comm Coll (TX)
Fashion Inst of Technology (NY)
FIDM/Fashion Inst of Design & Merchandising, Orange County Campus (CA)
Fox Valley Tech Coll (WI)
Front Range Comm Coll (CO)
Fullerton Coll (CA)
Gateway Tech Coll (WI)
Gwinnett Tech Coll (GA)
Harford Comm Coll (MD)
Harper Coll (IL)
Houston Comm Coll (TX)

Ivy Tech Comm Coll–Columbus (IN)
Ivy Tech Comm Coll–East Central (IN)
Ivy Tech Comm Coll–North Central (IN)
Ivy Tech Comm Coll–Southwest (IN)
Johnson County Comm Coll (KS)
Lanier Tech Coll (GA)
Lansing Comm Coll (MI)
Lehigh Carbon Comm Coll (PA)
Lone Star Coll–Kingwood (TX)
Madison Area Tech Coll (WI)
Mesa Comm Coll (AZ)
Metropolitan Comm Coll (NE)
Miami Dade Coll (FL)
Monroe Comm Coll (NY)
Montgomery Coll (MD)
Mt. San Antonio Coll (CA)
Nassau Comm Coll (NY)
Northampton Comm Coll (PA)
Norwalk Comm Coll (CT)
Ogeechee Tech Coll (GA)
Orange Coast Coll (CA)
Palomar Coll (CA)
Randolph Comm Coll (NC)
Raritan Valley Comm Coll (NJ)
San Jacinto Coll District (TX)
Santa Fe Comm Coll (NM)
Santa Monica Coll (CA)
Santa Rosa Jr Coll (CA)
Scottsdale Comm Coll (AZ)
Seminole State Coll of Florida (FL)
State U of New York Coll of Technology at Alfred (NY)
Tidewater Comm Coll (VA)
Virginia Marti Coll of Art and Design (OH)
Waukesha County Tech Coll (WI)

INTERMEDIA/MULTIMEDIA
Oklahoma State U Inst of Technology (OK)
Santa Fe Comm Coll (NM)

INTERNATIONAL BUSINESS/TRADE/COMMERCE
Austin Comm Coll District (TX)
Bunker Hill Comm Coll (MA)
Columbus State Comm Coll (OH)
El Paso Comm Coll (TX)
Fullerton Coll (CA)
Harper Coll (IL)
Houston Comm Coll (TX)
Lansing Comm Coll (MI)
Luzerne County Comm Coll (PA)
Massachusetts Bay Comm Coll (MA)
Monroe Comm Coll (NY)
Orange Coast Coll (CA)
Palomar Coll (CA)
Raritan Valley Comm Coll (NJ)
San Jacinto Coll District (TX)
South Florida State Coll (FL)
Tompkins Cortland Comm Coll (NY)
Waukesha County Tech Coll (WI)
Westchester Comm Coll (NY)

INTERNATIONAL/GLOBAL STUDIES
Berkshire Comm Coll (MA)
Central Wyoming Coll (WY)
Jamestown Comm Coll (NY)
Macomb Comm Coll (MI)
Massachusetts Bay Comm Coll (MA)
Northampton Comm Coll (PA)
Salt Lake Comm Coll (UT)
Three Rivers Comm Coll (MO)
Tompkins Cortland Comm Coll (NY)

INTERNATIONAL MARKETING
Waukesha County Tech Coll (WI)

INTERNATIONAL RELATIONS AND AFFAIRS
Cañada Coll (CA)
Casper Coll (WY)
Cerritos Coll (CA)
Coll of Marin (CA)
De Anza Coll (CA)
Harford Comm Coll (MD)
Harrisburg Area Comm Coll (PA)
Lansing Comm Coll (MI)
Merced Coll (CA)
Miami Dade Coll (FL)
Northern Essex Comm Coll (MA)
Northwest Coll (WY)
Salt Lake Comm Coll (UT)
Santa Monica Coll (CA)
South Florida State Coll (FL)
Western Wyoming Comm Coll (WY)

IRONWORKING
Ivy Tech Comm Coll–North Central (IN)
Ivy Tech Comm Coll–Northeast (IN)
Ivy Tech Comm Coll–Northwest (IN)
Ivy Tech Comm Coll–Southwest (IN)
Ivy Tech Comm Coll–Wabash Valley (IN)

ITALIAN
Coll of the Desert (CA)
Miami Dade Coll (FL)

JAPANESE
Austin Comm Coll District (TX)
Citrus Coll (CA)
Fiorello H. LaGuardia Comm Coll of the City U of New York (NY)
Lansing Comm Coll (MI)

JAZZ/JAZZ STUDIES
Comm Coll of Rhode Island (RI)
Santa Rosa Jr Coll (CA)
South Florida State Coll (FL)

JOURNALISM
Allen Comm Coll (KS)
Amarillo Coll (TX)
Arapahoe Comm Coll (CO)
Austin Comm Coll District (TX)
Bucks County Comm Coll (PA)
Casper Coll (WY)
Central Texas Coll (TX)
Cerritos Coll (CA)
Citrus Coll (CA)
Cloud County Comm Coll (KS)
Cochise County Comm Coll District (AZ)
Coll of Central Florida (FL)
Coll of the Canyons (CA)
Coll of the Desert (CA)
Comm Coll of Allegheny County (PA)
De Anza Coll (CA)
Del Mar Coll (TX)
Delta Coll (MI)
Dodge City Comm Coll (KS)
Fullerton Coll (CA)
Georgia Highlands Coll (GA)
Golden West Coll (CA)
Grand Rapids Comm Coll (MI)
Housatonic Comm Coll (CT)
Illinois Valley Comm Coll (IL)
Imperial Valley Coll (CA)
Iowa Central Comm Coll (IA)
Kingsborough Comm Coll of the City U of New York (NY)
Los Angeles City Coll (CA)
Luzerne County Comm Coll (PA)
Manchester Comm Coll (CT)
Mesa Comm Coll (AZ)
Miami Dade Coll (FL)
Monroe County Comm Coll (MI)
Mt. San Antonio Coll (CA)
Northampton Comm Coll (PA)
Northeastern Jr Coll (CO)
Northern Essex Comm Coll (MA)
Orange Coast Coll (CA)
Palomar Coll (CA)
Panola Coll (TX)
Paris Jr Coll (TX)
Pensacola State Coll (FL)
San Jacinto Coll District (TX)
San Joaquin Delta Coll (CA)
Santa Monica Coll (CA)
South Florida State Coll (FL)
South Plains Coll (TX)
Sussex County Comm Coll (NJ)
Texarkana Coll (TX)
Trinity Valley Comm Coll (TX)
Tyler Jr Coll (TX)
Vincennes U (IN)
Westchester Comm Coll (NY)
Western Wyoming Comm Coll (WY)

JUVENILE CORRECTIONS
Danville Area Comm Coll (IL)
Illinois Valley Comm Coll (IL)
Kaskaskia Coll (IL)
Lansing Comm Coll (MI)

KINDERGARTEN/PRESCHOOL EDUCATION
Aaniiih Nakoda Coll (MT)
Alamance Comm Coll (NC)
Bainbridge State Coll (GA)
Casper Coll (WY)
Cerritos Coll (CA)
Cleveland State Comm Coll (TN)
Comm Coll of Philadelphia (PA)
Comm Coll of Rhode Island (RI)

County Coll of Morris (NJ)
Daytona State Coll (FL)
Del Mar Coll (TX)
El Paso Comm Coll (TX)
Finger Lakes Comm Coll (NY)
Genesee Comm Coll (NY)
Hesston Coll (KS)
Howard Comm Coll (MD)
Imperial Valley Coll (CA)
Manchester Comm Coll (CT)
McLennan Comm Coll (TX)
Metropolitan Comm Coll (NE)
Miami Dade Coll (FL)
Middlesex Comm Coll (MA)
Mitchell Comm Coll (NC)
Mt. San Antonio Coll (CA)
Nashville State Comm Coll (TN)
Nassau Comm Coll (NY)
NHTI, Concord's Comm Coll, Concord (NH)
Northern Essex Comm Coll (MA)
Northern Maine Comm Coll (ME)
North Shore Comm Coll (MA)
Northwest Coll (WY)
Nunez Comm Coll (LA)
Otero Jr Coll (CO)
Ozarks Tech Comm Coll (MO)
Quinsigamond Comm Coll (MA)
Raritan Valley Comm Coll (NJ)
Santa Fe Comm Coll (NM)
Sisseton-Wahpeton Coll (SD)
Southern U at Shreveport (LA)
Sullivan County Comm Coll (NY)
Tidewater Comm Coll (VA)
Trinity Valley Comm Coll (TX)
Truckee Meadows Comm Coll (NV)
Ulster County Comm Coll (NY)
U of Cincinnati Blue Ash Coll (OH)
U of Cincinnati Clermont Coll (OH)
Virginia Western Comm Coll (VA)

KINESIOLOGY AND EXERCISE SCIENCE
Ancilla Coll (IN)
Austin Comm Coll District (TX)
Bucks County Comm Coll (PA)
Carroll Comm Coll (MD)
Central Oregon Comm Coll (OR)
Central Texas Coll (TX)
Cerritos Coll (CA)
Chandler-Gilbert Comm Coll (AZ)
Columbus State Comm Coll (OH)
County Coll of Morris (NJ)
Feather River Coll (CA)
Ivy Tech Comm Coll–East Central (IN)
Ivy Tech Comm Coll–Sellersburg (IN)
Laramie County Comm Coll (WY)
Lehigh Carbon Comm Coll (PA)
Merced Coll (CA)
Mesa Comm Coll (AZ)
Nashville State Comm Coll (TN)
Northeast Comm Coll (NE)
Norwalk Comm Coll (CT)
Orange Coast Coll (CA)
Palomar Coll (CA)
Raritan Valley Comm Coll (NJ)
St. Philip's Coll (TX)
Salt Lake Comm Coll (UT)
Santa Monica Coll (CA)
Santa Rosa Jr Coll (CA)
South Florida State Coll (FL)
South Suburban Coll (IL)
Three Rivers Comm Coll (CT)
Western Wyoming Comm Coll (WY)

LABOR AND INDUSTRIAL RELATIONS
Kingsborough Comm Coll of the City U of New York (NY)

LANDSCAPE ARCHITECTURE
Caldwell Comm Coll and Tech Inst (NC)
Chesapeake Coll (MD)
Monroe Comm Coll (NY)
Mt. San Antonio Coll (CA)
Truckee Meadows Comm Coll (NV)

LANDSCAPING AND GROUNDSKEEPING
Anoka Tech Coll (MN)
Cape Fear Comm Coll (NC)
Coll of Central Florida (FL)
Coll of Marin (CA)
Comm Coll of Allegheny County (PA)
Dakota Coll at Bottineau (ND)
Danville Area Comm Coll (IL)
Fullerton Coll (CA)
Grand Rapids Comm Coll (MI)

Hawkeye Comm Coll (IA)
Hennepin Tech Coll (MN)
Hinds Comm Coll (MS)
Illinois Valley Comm Coll (IL)
Kishwaukee Coll (IL)
Miami Dade Coll (FL)
The Ohio State U Ag Tech Inst (OH)
Pensacola State Coll (FL)
San Juan Coll (NM)
Santa Rosa Jr Coll (CA)
South Florida State Coll (FL)
Springfield Tech Comm Coll (MA)

LAND USE PLANNING AND MANAGEMENT
Dakota Coll at Bottineau (ND)

LANGUAGE INTERPRETATION AND TRANSLATION
Allen Comm Coll (KS)
Cape Fear Comm Coll (NC)
Century Coll (MN)
Des Moines Area Comm Coll (IA)
Lake Region State Coll (ND)

LASER AND OPTICAL TECHNOLOGY
Amarillo Coll (TX)
Monroe Comm Coll (NY)
Queensborough Comm Coll of the City U of New York (NY)
Quinsigamond Comm Coll (MA)
Springfield Tech Comm Coll (MA)
Texas State Tech Coll (TX)
Three Rivers Comm Coll (CT)

LATIN
Austin Comm Coll District (TX)

LATIN AMERICAN STUDIES
Central New Mexico Comm Coll (NM)
Miami Dade Coll (FL)
Santa Rosa Jr Coll (CA)

LAW ENFORCEMENT INVESTIGATION AND INTERVIEWING
Arizona Western Coll (AZ)
Mohawk Valley Comm Coll (NY)

LEGAL ADMINISTRATIVE ASSISTANT/SECRETARY
Alamance Comm Coll (NC)
Alexandria Tech and Comm Coll (MN)
Alvin Comm Coll (TX)
Amarillo Coll (TX)
Anoka Tech Coll (MN)
Bismarck State Coll (ND)
Blackhawk Tech Coll (WI)
Blinn Coll (TX)
Cerritos Coll (CA)
Coll of the Ouachitas (AR)
Comm Coll of Allegheny County (PA)
Comm Coll of Rhode Island (RI)
Craven Comm Coll (NC)
Crowder Coll (MO)
Del Mar Coll (TX)
Dodge City Comm Coll (KS)
Fullerton Coll (CA)
Georgia Piedmont Tech Coll (GA)
Golden West Coll (CA)
Harper Coll (IL)
Howard Comm Coll (MD)
Johnson County Comm Coll (KS)
Kellogg Comm Coll (MI)
Lake Superior Coll (MN)
Los Angeles City Coll (CA)
Manchester Comm Coll (CT)
McLennan Comm Coll (TX)
Metropolitan Comm Coll (NE)
Miami Dade Coll (FL)
Minnesota State Coll–Southeast Tech (MN)
Minnesota State Comm and Tech Coll (MN)
Monroe Comm Coll (NY)
Monroe County Comm Coll (MI)
Morton Coll (IL)
Mt. San Antonio Coll (CA)
Nassau Comm Coll (NY)
Navarro Coll (TX)
North Shore Comm Coll (MA)
Oklahoma City Comm Coll (OK)
Otero Jr Coll (CO)
Pensacola State Coll (FL)
Renton Tech Coll (WA)
Santa Monica Coll (CA)
Shawnee Comm Coll (IL)
South Plains Coll (TX)

Stark State Coll (OH)
Treasure Valley Comm Coll (OR)
Trinity Valley Comm Coll (TX)
Western Wyoming Comm Coll (WY)

LEGAL ASSISTANT/PARALEGAL
Alexandria Tech and Comm Coll (MN)
Alvin Comm Coll (TX)
Anne Arundel Comm Coll (MD)
Arapahoe Comm Coll (CO)
Arizona Western Coll (AZ)
Athens Tech Coll (GA)
Atlanta Tech Coll (GA)
Austin Comm Coll District (TX)
Blue Ridge Comm and Tech Coll (WV)
Bunker Hill Comm Coll (MA)
Caldwell Comm Coll and Tech Inst (NC)
Camden County Coll (NJ)
Cañada Coll (CA)
Carteret Comm Coll (NC)
Casper Coll (WY)
Central Georgia Tech Coll (GA)
Central New Mexico Comm Coll (NM)
Central Texas Coll (TX)
Cerritos Coll (CA)
Chesapeake Coll (MD)
Chippewa Valley Tech Coll (WI)
Cloud County Comm Coll (KS)
Coll of Central Florida (FL)
Coll of the Canyons (CA)
Coll of the Ouachitas (AR)
Collin County Comm Coll District (TX)
Columbus State Comm Coll (OH)
Comm Care Coll (OK)
Comm Coll of Allegheny County (PA)
Comm Coll of Baltimore County (MD)
Comm Coll of Rhode Island (RI)
Comm Coll of the Air Force (AL)
Daytona State Coll (FL)
De Anza Coll (CA)
Delta Coll (MI)
Des Moines Area Comm Coll (IA)
Dutchess Comm Coll (NY)
Eastern Idaho Tech Coll (ID)
Edison State Comm Coll (OH)
Elgin Comm Coll (IL)
El Paso Comm Coll (TX)
Erie Comm Coll (NY)
Fayetteville Tech Comm Coll (NC)
Finger Lakes Comm Coll (NY)
Fiorello H. LaGuardia Comm Coll of the City U of New York (NY)
Florida SouthWestern State Coll (FL)
Fox Valley Tech Coll (WI)
Frederick Comm Coll (MD)
Front Range Comm Coll (CO)
Fullerton Coll (CA)
Genesee Comm Coll (NY)
Georgia Military Coll (GA)
Georgia Northwestern Tech Coll (GA)
Georgia Piedmont Tech Coll (GA)
Greenville Tech Coll (SC)
Halifax Comm Coll (NC)
Harford Comm Coll (MD)
Harper Coll (IL)
Harrisburg Area Comm Coll (PA)
Hillsborough Comm Coll (FL)
Hinds Comm Coll (MS)
Horry Georgetown Tech Coll (SC)
Houston Comm Coll (TX)
Hudson County Comm Coll (NJ)
Hutchinson Comm Coll (KS)
IBMC Coll, Fort Collins (CO)
Illinois Central Coll (IL)
Illinois Eastern Comm Colls, Wabash Valley College (IL)
Ivy Tech Comm Coll–Bloomington (IN)
Ivy Tech Comm Coll–Central Indiana (IN)
Ivy Tech Comm Coll–Columbus (IN)
Ivy Tech Comm Coll–East Central (IN)
Ivy Tech Comm Coll–Kokomo (IN)
Ivy Tech Comm Coll–Lafayette (IN)
Ivy Tech Comm Coll–North Central (IN)
Ivy Tech Comm Coll–Northeast (IN)
Ivy Tech Comm Coll–Northwest (IN)
Ivy Tech Comm Coll–Richmond (IN)
Ivy Tech Comm Coll–Sellersburg (IN)
Ivy Tech Comm Coll–Southeast (IN)
Ivy Tech Comm Coll–Southwest (IN)
Ivy Tech Comm Coll–Wabash Valley (IN)
Jefferson Comm Coll (NY)
Johnson County Comm Coll (KS)

Johnston Comm Coll (NC)
J. Sargeant Reynolds Comm Coll (VA)
Kent State U at East Liverpool (OH)
Kent State U at Trumbull (OH)
Lackawanna Coll (PA)
Lakeland Comm Coll (OH)
Lake Superior Coll (MN)
Lansdale School of Business (PA)
Lansing Comm Coll (MI)
Laramie County Comm Coll (WY)
Lehigh Carbon Comm Coll (PA)
Lone Star Coll–North Harris (TX)
Luzerne County Comm Coll (PA)
Macomb Comm Coll (MI)
Manchester Comm Coll (CT)
Manor Coll (PA)
Massachusetts Bay Comm Coll (MA)
McLennan Comm Coll (TX)
Mercer County Comm Coll (NJ)
Metropolitan Comm Coll (NE)
Miami Dade Coll (FL)
Middlesex Comm Coll (MA)
Middlesex County Coll (NJ)
Mohave Comm Coll (AZ)
Montgomery Coll (MD)
Mt. San Antonio Coll (CA)
Mount Wachusett Comm Coll (MA)
Nashville State Comm Coll (TN)
Nassau Comm Coll (NY)
Naugatuck Valley Comm Coll (CT)
Navarro Coll (TX)
NHTI, Concord's Comm Coll, Concord (NH)
Northampton Comm Coll (PA)
Northern Essex Comm Coll (MA)
North Shore Comm Coll (MA)
NorthWest Arkansas Comm Coll (AR)
Norwalk Comm Coll (CT)
Nunez Comm Coll (LA)
Ogeechee Tech Coll (GA)
Patrick Henry Comm Coll (VA)
Penn Foster Coll (AZ)
Pensacola State Coll (FL)
Raritan Valley Comm Coll (NJ)
Salt Lake Comm Coll (UT)
San Jacinto Coll District (TX)
San Juan Coll (NM)
Santa Fe Comm Coll (NM)
Santa Rosa Jr Coll (CA)
Seminole State Coll of Florida (FL)
Southern Crescent Tech Coll (GA)
Southern U at Shreveport (LA)
South Florida State Coll (FL)
South Georgia Tech Coll (GA)
South Suburban Coll (IL)
Southwestern Comm Coll (NC)
Sullivan County Comm Coll (NY)
Sussex County Comm Coll (NJ)
Tallahassee Comm Coll (FL)
Tarrant County Coll District (TX)
Tidewater Comm Coll (VA)
Tompkins Cortland Comm Coll (NY)
Trident Tech Coll (SC)
Truckee Meadows Comm Coll (NV)
Tyler Jr Coll (TX)
U of Cincinnati Clermont Coll (OH)
Vincennes U (IN)
Volunteer State Comm Coll (TN)
Wayne County Comm Coll District (MI)
Westchester Comm Coll (NY)
Westmoreland County Comm Coll (PA)

LEGAL PROFESSIONS AND STUDIES RELATED
Bucks County Comm Coll (PA)

LEGAL STUDIES
Alvin Comm Coll (TX)
Carroll Comm Coll (MD)
Del Mar Coll (TX)
Macomb Comm Coll (MI)
Metropolitan Comm Coll (NE)
Navarro Coll (TX)
Palomar Coll (CA)
Trident Tech Coll (SC)

LIBERAL ARTS AND SCIENCES AND HUMANITIES RELATED
Anne Arundel Comm Coll (MD)
Arapahoe Comm Coll (CO)
Bossier Parish Comm Coll (LA)
Bucks County Comm Coll (PA)
Chandler-Gilbert Comm Coll (AZ)
Chesapeake Coll (MD)

Cleveland State Comm Coll (TN)
Coll of Central Florida (FL)
Comm Coll of Aurora (CO)
Comm Coll of Baltimore County (MD)
Craven Comm Coll (NC)
Dakota Coll at Bottineau (ND)
Dutchess Comm Coll (NY)
Erie Comm Coll (NY)
Fayetteville Tech Comm Coll (NC)
Front Range Comm Coll (CO)
Garrett Coll (MD)
Genesee Comm Coll (NY)
Great Falls Coll Montana State U (MT)
Hagerstown Comm Coll (MD)
Halifax Comm Coll (NC)
Haywood Comm Coll (NC)
Holyoke Comm Coll (MA)
Ivy Tech Comm Coll–Richmond (IN)
James Sprunt Comm Coll (NC)
Jamestown Comm Coll (NY)
J. Sargeant Reynolds Comm Coll (VA)
Kellogg Comm Coll (MI)
Kent State U at Ashtabula (OH)
Kent State U at East Liverpool (OH)
Kent State U at Salem (OH)
Kent State U at Trumbull (OH)
Kent State U at Tuscarawas (OH)
Lenoir Comm Coll (NC)
Louisiana State U at Eunice (LA)
Luzerne County Comm Coll (PA)
Minnesota West Comm and Tech Coll (MN)
Mitchell Comm Coll (NC)
Mohawk Valley Comm Coll (NY)
Montgomery Coll (MD)
Morgan Comm Coll (CO)
Northampton Comm Coll (PA)
Northern Maine Comm Coll (ME)
Nunez Comm Coll (LA)
Panola Coll (TX)
Piedmont Comm Coll (NC)
Pueblo Comm Coll (CO)
Randolph Comm Coll (NC)
Southern U at Shreveport (LA)
South Florida State Coll (FL)
Sowela Tech Comm Coll (LA)
State U of New York Coll of Technology at Alfred (NY)
Tompkins Cortland Comm Coll (NY)
Wor-Wic Comm Coll (MD)

LIBERAL ARTS AND SCIENCES/ LIBERAL STUDIES
Aaniiih Nakoda Coll (MT)
Adirondack Comm Coll (NY)
Alamance Comm Coll (NC)
Alexandria Tech and Comm Coll (MN)
Alvin Comm Coll (TX)
Amarillo Coll (TX)
American Samoa Comm Coll (AS)
Ancilla Coll (IN)
Anne Arundel Comm Coll (MD)
Anoka-Ramsey Comm Coll (MN)
Arapahoe Comm Coll (CO)
Asnuntuck Comm Coll (CT)
Bainbridge State Coll (GA)
Berkshire Comm Coll (MA)
Bevill State Comm Coll (AL)
Bismarck State Coll (ND)
Blue Ridge Comm and Tech Coll (WV)
Borough of Manhattan Comm Coll of the City U of New York (NY)
Bossier Parish Comm Coll (LA)
Bowling Green State U–Firelands Coll (OH)
Brookhaven Coll (TX)
Bucks County Comm Coll (PA)
Caldwell Comm Coll and Tech Inst (NC)
Camden County Coll (NJ)
Cañada Coll (CA)
Cape Fear Comm Coll (NC)
Carroll Comm Coll (MD)
Carteret Comm Coll (NC)
Casper Coll (WY)
Cayuga County Comm Coll (NY)
Cecil Coll (MD)
Central Maine Comm Coll (ME)
Central New Mexico Comm Coll (NM)
Central Oregon Comm Coll (OR)
Central Texas Coll (TX)
Central Virginia Comm Coll (VA)
Central Wyoming Coll (WY)
Century Coll (MN)
Cerritos Coll (CA)
Chandler-Gilbert Comm Coll (AZ)
Chesapeake Coll (MD)

Chippewa Valley Tech Coll (WI)
Citrus Coll (CA)
City Colls of Chicago, Kennedy-King College (IL)
City Colls of Chicago, Olive-Harvey College (IL)
Cleveland State Comm Coll (TN)
Clinton Comm Coll (NY)
Cloud County Comm Coll (KS)
Coastline Comm Coll (CA)
Coll of Central Florida (FL)
Coll of Marin (CA)
Coll of The Albemarle (NC)
Coll of the Canyons (CA)
Coll of the Desert (CA)
Coll of the Marshall Islands (MH)
Coll of the Ouachitas (AR)
Collin County Comm Coll District (TX)
Colorado Northwestern Comm Coll (CO)
Columbia-Greene Comm Coll (NY)
Columbus State Comm Coll (OH)
Comm Coll of Allegheny County (PA)
Comm Coll of Aurora (CO)
Comm Coll of Baltimore County (MD)
Comm Coll of Philadelphia (PA)
Comm Coll of Rhode Island (RI)
Comm Coll of Vermont (VT)
County Coll of Morris (NJ)
Craven Comm Coll (NC)
Crowder Coll (MO)
Dakota Coll at Bottineau (ND)
Danville Area Comm Coll (IL)
De Anza Coll (CA)
Del Mar Coll (TX)
Delta Coll (MI)
Des Moines Area Comm Coll (IA)
Dodge City Comm Coll (KS)
Donnelly Coll (KS)
Dutchess Comm Coll (NY)
Dyersburg State Comm Coll (TN)
Eastern Arizona Coll (AZ)
Eastern Wyoming Coll (WY)
East Georgia State Coll (GA)
Edison State Comm Coll (OH)
Elgin Comm Coll (IL)
El Paso Comm Coll (TX)
Erie Comm Coll (NY)
Erie Comm Coll, North Campus (NY)
Erie Comm Coll, South Campus (NY)
Estrella Mountain Comm Coll (AZ)
Fayetteville Tech Comm Coll (NC)
Feather River Coll (CA)
Finger Lakes Comm Coll (NY)
Fiorello H. LaGuardia Comm Coll of the City U of New York (NY)
Florida Keys Comm Coll (FL)
Florida SouthWestern State Coll (FL)
Frederick Comm Coll (MD)
Front Range Comm Coll (CO)
Fullerton Coll (CA)
Garrett Coll (MD)
Genesee Comm Coll (NY)
Golden West Coll (CA)
Gordon State Coll (GA)
Grand Rapids Comm Coll (MI)
Great Basin Coll (NV)
Greenville Tech Coll (SC)
Guam Comm Coll (GU)
Gulf Coast State Coll (FL)
Hagerstown Comm Coll (MD)
Halifax Comm Coll (NC)
Harper Coll (IL)
Hawaii Tokai International Coll (HI)
Hawkeye Comm Coll (IA)
Haywood Comm Coll (NC)
Hesston Coll (KS)
Highland Comm Coll (IL)
Hillsborough Comm Coll (FL)
Holyoke Comm Coll (MA)
Housatonic Comm Coll (CT)
Howard Comm Coll (MD)
Hudson County Comm Coll (NJ)
Hutchinson Comm Coll (KS)
Illinois Central Coll (IL)
Illinois Eastern Comm Colls, Frontier Community College (IL)
Illinois Eastern Comm Colls, Lincoln Trail College (IL)
Illinois Eastern Comm Colls, Olney Central College (IL)
Illinois Eastern Comm Colls, Wabash Valley College (IL)
Illinois Valley Comm Coll (IL)
Imperial Valley Coll (CA)
Iowa Central Comm Coll (IA)
Ivy Tech Comm Coll–Bloomington (IN)
Ivy Tech Comm Coll–Central Indiana (IN)

Ivy Tech Comm Coll–Columbus (IN)
Ivy Tech Comm Coll–East Central (IN)
Ivy Tech Comm Coll–Kokomo (IN)
Ivy Tech Comm Coll–Lafayette (IN)
Ivy Tech Comm Coll–North Central (IN)
Ivy Tech Comm Coll–Northeast (IN)
Ivy Tech Comm Coll–Northwest (IN)
Ivy Tech Comm Coll–Richmond (IN)
Ivy Tech Comm Coll–Sellersburg (IN)
Ivy Tech Comm Coll–Southeast (IN)
Ivy Tech Comm Coll–Wabash Valley (IN)
James Sprunt Comm Coll (NC)
Jamestown Comm Coll (NY)
Jefferson Comm Coll (NY)
Jefferson State Comm Coll (AL)
Johnson County Comm Coll (KS)
Johnston Comm Coll (NC)
Kaskaskia Coll (IL)
Kellogg Comm Coll (MI)
Kingsborough Comm Coll of the City U of New York (NY)
Kirtland Comm Coll (MI)
Kishwaukee Coll (IL)
Lackawanna Coll (PA)
Lakeland Comm Coll (OH)
Lake Region State Coll (ND)
Lake Superior Coll (MN)
Lamar Comm Coll (CO)
Lansing Comm Coll (MI)
Lehigh Carbon Comm Coll (PA)
Lenoir Comm Coll (NC)
Lone Star Coll–CyFair (TX)
Lorain County Comm Coll (OH)
Lurleen B. Wallace Comm Coll (AL)
Luzerne County Comm Coll (PA)
Macomb Comm Coll (MI)
Madison Area Tech Coll (WI)
Manchester Comm Coll (CT)
Manor Coll (PA)
Massachusetts Bay Comm Coll (MA)
Maysville Comm and Tech Coll, Maysville (KY)
McHenry County Coll (IL)
McLennan Comm Coll (TX)
Merced Coll (CA)
Mercer County Comm Coll (NJ)
Mesabi Range Coll (MN)
Mesa Comm Coll (AZ)
Metropolitan Comm Coll (NE)
Miami Dade Coll (FL)
Middlesex Comm Coll (MA)
Middlesex County Coll (NJ)
Mid-Plains Comm Coll, North Platte (NE)
Minnesota State Comm and Tech Coll (MN)
Minnesota State Comm and Tech Coll–Detroit Lakes (MN)
Minnesota State Comm and Tech Coll–Moorhead (MN)
Minnesota State Comm and Tech Coll–Wadena (MN)
Minnesota West Comm and Tech Coll (MN)
Mitchell Comm Coll (NC)
Mohave Comm Coll (AZ)
Mohawk Valley Comm Coll (NY)
Monroe Comm Coll (NY)
Monroe County Comm Coll (MI)
Montgomery Coll (MD)
Montgomery Comm Coll (NC)
Montgomery County Comm Coll (PA)
Morgan Comm Coll (CO)
Morton Coll (IL)
Motlow State Comm Coll (TN)
Mott Comm Coll (MI)
Mountain View Coll (TX)
Mount Wachusett Comm Coll (MA)
Nassau Comm Coll (NY)
Naugatuck Valley Comm Coll (CT)
New Mexico Jr Coll (NM)
New River Comm Coll (VA)
NHTI, Concord's Comm Coll, Concord (NH)
Niagara County Comm Coll (NY)
Northampton Comm Coll (PA)
North Central Missouri Coll (MO)
Northeast Comm Coll (NE)
Northeastern Jr Coll (CO)
Northeast Iowa Comm Coll (IA)
Northern Essex Comm Coll (MA)
Northland Comm and Tech Coll (MN)
North Shore Comm Coll (MA)
NorthWest Arkansas Comm Coll (AR)
Northwest Coll (WY)
Northwest-Shoals Comm Coll (AL)
Norwalk Comm Coll (CT)

Oakton Comm Coll (IL)
Oklahoma City Comm Coll (OK)
Olympic Coll (WA)
Orange Coast Coll (CA)
Oregon Coast Comm Coll (OR)
Otero Jr Coll (CO)
Owensboro Comm and Tech Coll (KY)
Ozarks Tech Comm Coll (MO)
Palomar Coll (CA)
Paris Jr Coll (TX)
Patrick Henry Comm Coll (VA)
Penn State DuBois (PA)
Penn State Fayette, The Eberly Campus (PA)
Penn State Mont Alto (PA)
Penn State Shenango (PA)
Pensacola State Coll (FL)
Piedmont Comm Coll (NC)
Pueblo Comm Coll (CO)
Queensborough Comm Coll of the City U of New York (NY)
Quinsigamond Comm Coll (MA)
Rainy River Comm Coll (MN)
Randolph Comm Coll (NC)
Rappahannock Comm Coll (VA)
Raritan Valley Comm Coll (NJ)
Rend Lake Coll (IL)
Richmond Comm Coll (NC)
Rio Hondo Coll (CA)
Rockingham Comm Coll (NC)
Rock Valley Coll (IL)
Rogue Comm Coll (OR)
Rowan-Cabarrus Comm Coll (NC)
Saginaw Chippewa Tribal Coll (MI)
St. Charles Comm Coll (MO)
St. Clair County Comm Coll (MI)
St. Philip's Coll (TX)
San Joaquin Delta Coll (CA)
San Juan Coll (NM)
Santa Monica Coll (CA)
Santa Rosa Jr Coll (CA)
Seminole State Coll (OK)
Seminole State Coll of Florida (FL)
Shawnee Comm Coll (IL)
Sierra Coll (CA)
Sisseton-Wahpeton Coll (SD)
Somerset Comm Coll (KY)
Southeast Comm Coll, Lincoln Campus (NE)
Southeastern Comm Coll (IA)
South Florida State Coll (FL)
South Plains Coll (TX)
South Suburban Coll (IL)
Southwestern Comm Coll (NC)
Southwestern Indian Polytechnic Inst (NM)
Southwestern Michigan Coll (MI)
Southwest Texas Jr Coll (TX)
Southwest Virginia Comm Coll (VA)
Spartanburg Comm Coll (SC)
Spartanburg Methodist Coll (SC)
Spoon River Coll (IL)
Springfield Tech Comm Coll (MA)
State U of New York Coll of Technology at Alfred (NY)
Sullivan County Comm Coll (NY)
Sussex County Comm Coll (NJ)
Tallahassee Comm Coll (FL)
Tarrant County Coll District (TX)
Texarkana Coll (TX)
Three Rivers Comm Coll (CT)
Three Rivers Comm Coll (MO)
Tidewater Comm Coll (VA)
Tohono O'odham Comm Coll (AZ)
Tompkins Cortland Comm Coll (NY)
Trident Tech Coll (SC)
Trinity Valley Comm Coll (TX)
Truckee Meadows Comm Coll (NV)
Ulster County Comm Coll (NY)
U of Arkansas Comm Coll at Morrilton (AR)
U of Cincinnati Blue Ash Coll (OH)
U of Cincinnati Clermont Coll (OH)
U of Pittsburgh at Titusville (PA)
U of South Carolina Salkehatchie (SC)
U of South Carolina Union (SC)
U of Wisconsin–Fox Valley (WI)
Vincennes U (IN)
Virginia Western Comm Coll (VA)
Volunteer State Comm Coll (TN)
Walters State Comm Coll (TN)
Wayne County Comm Coll District (MI)
Weatherford Coll (TX)
Westchester Comm Coll (NY)
Western Nevada Coll (NV)
Western Wyoming Comm Coll (WY)

Westmoreland County Comm Coll (PA)
White Mountains Comm Coll (NH)
Williamsburg Tech Coll (SC)
Williston State Coll (ND)
Wor-Wic Comm Coll (MD)
Wytheville Comm Coll (VA)
York County Comm Coll (ME)

LIBRARY AND ARCHIVES ASSISTING
Citrus Coll (CA)
Illinois Central Coll (IL)
Ivy Tech Comm Coll–Bloomington (IN)
Ivy Tech Comm Coll–Columbus (IN)
Ivy Tech Comm Coll–East Central (IN)
Ivy Tech Comm Coll–Kokomo (IN)
Ivy Tech Comm Coll–Lafayette (IN)
Ivy Tech Comm Coll–North Central (IN)
Ivy Tech Comm Coll–Northeast (IN)
Ivy Tech Comm Coll–Northwest (IN)
Ivy Tech Comm Coll–Richmond (IN)
Ivy Tech Comm Coll–Sellersburg (IN)
Ivy Tech Comm Coll–Southwest (IN)
Ivy Tech Comm Coll–Wabash Valley (IN)
Kaskaskia Coll (IL)
Northeast Comm Coll (NE)
Palomar Coll (CA)
Pueblo Comm Coll (CO)
Western Dakota Tech Inst (SD)

LIBRARY AND INFORMATION SCIENCE
Allen Comm Coll (KS)
Chippewa Valley Tech Coll (WI)
Citrus Coll (CA)
Coll of Central Florida (FL)
Grand Rapids Comm Coll (MI)
Mesa Comm Coll (AZ)
Northeast Comm Coll (NE)
U of Cincinnati Blue Ash Coll (OH)

LICENSED PRACTICAL/ VOCATIONAL NURSE TRAINING
Alvin Comm Coll (TX)
Amarillo Coll (TX)
Athens Tech Coll (GA)
Bainbridge State Coll (GA)
Carroll Comm Coll (MD)
Central Maine Comm Coll (ME)
Central Oregon Comm Coll (OR)
Central Texas Coll (TX)
Citrus Coll (CA)
Coll of The Albemarle (NC)
Coll of the Desert (CA)
Coll of the Ouachitas (AR)
Comm Coll of Allegheny County (PA)
Comm Coll of Rhode Island (RI)
Dakota Coll at Bottineau (ND)
De Anza Coll (CA)
Des Moines Area Comm Coll (IA)
Dodge City Comm Coll (KS)
Feather River Coll (CA)
Fiorello H. LaGuardia Comm Coll of the City U of New York (NY)
Grand Rapids Comm Coll (MI)
Great Falls Coll Montana State U (MT)
Hennepin Tech Coll (MN)
Howard Comm Coll (MD)
Hudson County Comm Coll (NJ)
Imperial Valley Coll (CA)
Iowa Central Comm Coll (IA)
J. Sargeant Reynolds Comm Coll (VA)
Lake Superior Coll (MN)
Lansing Comm Coll (MI)
Manhattan Area Tech Coll (KS)
Metropolitan Comm Coll (NE)
Mid-Plains Comm Coll, North Platte (NE)
Minnesota State Comm and Tech Coll (MN)
Minnesota State Comm and Tech Coll–Detroit Lakes (MN)
Minnesota State Comm and Tech Coll–Moorhead (MN)
Minnesota State Comm and Tech Coll–Wadena (MN)
Mitchell Tech Inst (SD)
Morgan Comm Coll (CO)
Navarro Coll (TX)
New Mexico Jr Coll (NM)
New River Comm Coll (VA)
Northeastern Jr Coll (CO)

San Joaquin Delta Coll (CA)
Santa Rosa Jr Coll (CA)
Sierra Coll (CA)
Southeastern Coll–West Palm Beach (FL)
Southeastern Comm Coll (IA)
South Plains Coll (TX)
Texarkana Coll (TX)
Three Rivers Comm Coll (MO)
Trinity Valley Comm Coll (TX)
Western Dakota Tech Inst (SD)
Western Wyoming Comm Coll (WY)
Williston State Coll (ND)

LINEWORKER
Bismarck State Coll (ND)
Chandler-Gilbert Comm Coll (AZ)
Ivy Tech Comm Coll–Lafayette (IN)
Minnesota State Comm and Tech Coll (MN)
Minnesota State Comm and Tech Coll–Wadena (MN)
Minnesota West Comm and Tech Coll (MN)
Mitchell Tech Inst (SD)
Northeast Comm Coll (NE)
Raritan Valley Comm Coll (NJ)

LINGUISTICS
Cañada Coll (CA)
Santa Monica Coll (CA)
South Florida State Coll (FL)

LITERATURE
Oklahoma City Comm Coll (OK)
Tyler Jr Coll (TX)

LITERATURE RELATED
Cayuga County Comm Coll (NY)

LIVESTOCK MANAGEMENT
The Ohio State U Ag Tech Inst (OH)

LOGISTICS, MATERIALS, AND SUPPLY CHAIN MANAGEMENT
Ancilla Coll (IN)
Arizona Western Coll (AZ)
Athens Tech Coll (GA)
Austin Comm Coll District (TX)
Cecil Coll (MD)
Chattahoochee Tech Coll (GA)
City Colls of Chicago, Olive-Harvey College (IL)
Cochise County Comm Coll District (AZ)
Columbus State Comm Coll (OH)
Comm Coll of the Air Force (AL)
Edison State Comm Coll (OH)
Fayetteville Tech Comm Coll (NC)
Fox Valley Tech Coll (WI)
Georgia Military Coll (GA)
Hinds Comm Coll (MS)
Houston Comm Coll (TX)
Ivy Tech Comm Coll–Bloomington (IN)
Ivy Tech Comm Coll–Central Indiana (IN)
Ivy Tech Comm Coll–Columbus (IN)
Ivy Tech Comm Coll–East Central (IN)
Ivy Tech Comm Coll–Richmond (IN)
Ivy Tech Comm Coll–Sellersburg (IN)
Ivy Tech Comm Coll–Southeast (IN)
Ivy Tech Comm Coll–Southwest (IN)
Ivy Tech Comm Coll–Wabash Valley (IN)
Lenoir Comm Coll (NC)
Lone Star Coll–CyFair (TX)
Miami Dade Coll (FL)
Northern Essex Comm Coll (MA)
Rockingham Comm Coll (NC)
Santa Monica Coll (CA)
Wayne County Comm Coll District (MI)

MACHINE SHOP TECHNOLOGY
Cape Fear Comm Coll (NC)
Comm Coll of Allegheny County (PA)
Craven Comm Coll (NC)
Daytona State Coll (FL)
Delta Coll (MI)
Eastern Arizona Coll (AZ)
Fayetteville Tech Comm Coll (NC)
Haywood Comm Coll (NC)
Ivy Tech Comm Coll–Central Indiana (IN)
Ivy Tech Comm Coll–East Central (IN)
Ivy Tech Comm Coll–Kokomo (IN)
Ivy Tech Comm Coll–Richmond (IN)

Ivy Tech Comm Coll–Wabash Valley (IN)
Lenoir Comm Coll (NC)
Maysville Comm and Tech Coll, Maysville (KY)
Mitchell Comm Coll (NC)
Owensboro Comm and Tech Coll (KY)
Pueblo Comm Coll (CO)
Randolph Comm Coll (NC)
Rockingham Comm Coll (NC)
State U of New York Coll of Technology at Alfred (NY)
Westmoreland County Comm Coll (PA)

MACHINE TOOL TECHNOLOGY
Alamance Comm Coll (NC)
Amarillo Coll (TX)
Casper Coll (WY)
Central Maine Comm Coll (ME)
Central New Mexico Comm Coll (NM)
Cerritos Coll (CA)
Coll of Marin (CA)
Coll of the Ouachitas (AR)
Columbus Tech Coll (GA)
De Anza Coll (CA)
Del Mar Coll (TX)
Des Moines Area Comm Coll (IA)
East Central Coll (MO)
Elgin Comm Coll (IL)
El Paso Comm Coll (TX)
Georgia Piedmont Tech Coll (GA)
Greenville Tech Coll (SC)
Gwinnett Tech Coll (GA)
Hawkeye Comm Coll (IA)
H. Councill Trenholm State Comm Coll (AL)
Hennepin Tech Coll (MN)
Horry Georgetown Tech Coll (SC)
Hutchinson Comm Coll (KS)
Illinois Eastern Comm Colls, Wabash Valley College (IL)
Iowa Central Comm Coll (IA)
Ivy Tech Comm Coll–Bloomington (IN)
Ivy Tech Comm Coll–Central Indiana (IN)
Ivy Tech Comm Coll–Columbus (IN)
Ivy Tech Comm Coll–East Central (IN)
Ivy Tech Comm Coll–Kokomo (IN)
Ivy Tech Comm Coll–Lafayette (IN)
Ivy Tech Comm Coll–North Central (IN)
Ivy Tech Comm Coll–Northwest (IN)
Ivy Tech Comm Coll–Richmond (IN)
Ivy Tech Comm Coll–Sellersburg (IN)
Ivy Tech Comm Coll–Southwest (IN)
Ivy Tech Comm Coll–Wabash Valley (IN)
Kellogg Comm Coll (MI)
Lake Area Tech Inst (SD)
Lake Superior Coll (MN)
Lansing Comm Coll (MI)
Macomb Comm Coll (MI)
Meridian Comm Coll (MS)
Mesa Comm Coll (AZ)
Mt. San Antonio Coll (CA)
New River Comm Coll (VA)
Northern Essex Comm Coll (MA)
Northern Maine Comm Coll (ME)
Orange Coast Coll (CA)
Ozarks Tech Comm Coll (MO)
Renton Tech Coll (WA)
St. Philip's Coll (TX)
Salina Area Tech Coll (KS)
San Joaquin Delta Coll (CA)
Southeast Comm Coll, Milford Campus (NE)
Southeastern Comm Coll (IA)
South Plains Coll (TX)
Southwestern Michigan Coll (MI)
Spartanburg Comm Coll (SC)
Tarrant County Coll District (TX)
Trident Tech Coll (SC)
Victoria Coll (TX)
Western Dakota Tech Inst (SD)
Western Nevada Coll (NV)
Westmoreland County Comm Coll (PA)
Wiregrass Georgia Tech Coll (GA)
Wytheville Comm Coll (VA)
York County Comm Coll (ME)

MAGNETIC RESONANCE IMAGING (MRI) TECHNOLOGY
Lansing Comm Coll (MI)
Mitchell Tech Inst (SD)

MANAGEMENT INFORMATION SYSTEMS
Anne Arundel Comm Coll (MD)
Asnuntuck Comm Coll (CT)
Camden County Coll (NJ)
Carl Albert State Coll (OK)
Carroll Comm Coll (MD)
Cecil Coll (MD)
Central Oregon Comm Coll (OR)
Coll of the Ouachitas (AR)
Columbus State Comm Coll (OH)
Comm Coll of Allegheny County (PA)
Comm Coll of Aurora (CO)
Comm Coll of Baltimore County (MD)
Comm Coll of the Air Force (AL)
County Coll of Morris (NJ)
Del Mar Coll (TX)
Florida SouthWestern State Coll (FL)
Garrett Coll (MD)
Georgia Military Coll (GA)
Gulf Coast State Coll (FL)
Gwinnett Tech Coll (GA)
Hagerstown Comm Coll (MD)
Hennepin Tech Coll (MN)
Lackawanna Coll (PA)
Lakeland Comm Coll (OH)
Lake Region State Coll (ND)
Lake Superior Coll (MN)
Lansing Comm Coll (MI)
Manchester Comm Coll (CT)
Manhattan Area Tech Coll (KS)
Mercer County Comm Coll (NJ)
Miami Dade Coll (FL)
Nassau Comm Coll (NY)
Ozarks Tech Comm Coll (MO)
Panola Coll (TX)
Pensacola State Coll (FL)
Raritan Valley Comm Coll (NJ)
San Jacinto Coll District (TX)
South Florida State Coll (FL)
Three Rivers Comm Coll (CT)
Treasure Valley Comm Coll (OR)
U of Pittsburgh at Titusville (PA)
Western Nevada Coll (NV)

MANAGEMENT INFORMATION SYSTEMS AND SERVICES RELATED
Anne Arundel Comm Coll (MD)
Bowling Green State U–Firelands Coll (OH)
Hillsborough Comm Coll (FL)
Montgomery County Comm Coll (PA)
Pensacola State Coll (FL)
Seminole State Coll (OK)
Truckee Meadows Comm Coll (NV)
Ulster County Comm Coll (NY)

MANAGEMENT SCIENCE
Central Virginia Comm Coll (VA)
Murray State Coll (OK)
Oklahoma State U–Oklahoma City (OK)
Pensacola State Coll (FL)
South Florida State Coll (FL)

MANUFACTURING ENGINEERING
Mesa Comm Coll (AZ)
Mitchell Comm Coll (NC)
Penn State Fayette, The Eberly Campus (PA)
Southeast Comm Coll, Milford Campus (NE)

MANUFACTURING ENGINEERING TECHNOLOGY
Albany Tech Coll (GA)
Arizona Western Coll (AZ)
Casper Coll (WY)
Central Oregon Comm Coll (OR)
Cerritos Coll (CA)
Chippewa Valley Tech Coll (WI)
Comm Coll of Baltimore County (MD)
Comm Coll of Rhode Island (RI)
Crowder Coll (MO)
Danville Area Comm Coll (IL)
Delta Coll (MI)
Edison State Comm Coll (OH)
Fox Valley Tech Coll (WI)
Gateway Comm and Tech Coll (KY)
Gulf Coast State Coll (FL)
H. Councill Trenholm State Comm Coll (AL)
Hennepin Tech Coll (MN)
Houston Comm Coll (TX)
Hutchinson Comm Coll (KS)
Illinois Central Coll (IL)

Illinois Eastern Comm Colls, Wabash Valley College (IL)
ITI Tech Coll (LA)
Ivy Tech Comm Coll–Bloomington (IN)
Ivy Tech Comm Coll–Central Indiana (IN)
Ivy Tech Comm Coll–Columbus (IN)
Ivy Tech Comm Coll–East Central (IN)
Ivy Tech Comm Coll–Kokomo (IN)
Ivy Tech Comm Coll–Lafayette (IN)
Ivy Tech Comm Coll–Richmond (IN)
Ivy Tech Comm Coll–Southeast (IN)
Ivy Tech Comm Coll–Southwest (IN)
Ivy Tech Comm Coll–Wabash Valley (IN)
Lake Area Tech Inst (SD)
Lehigh Carbon Comm Coll (PA)
Lorain County Comm Coll (OH)
Macomb Comm Coll (MI)
Mesa Comm Coll (AZ)
Miami Dade Coll (FL)
Minnesota State Comm and Tech Coll (MN)
Minnesota West Comm and Tech Coll (MN)
Mitchell Comm Coll (NC)
Morgan Comm Coll (CO)
Northcentral Tech Coll (WI)
Northland Comm and Tech Coll (MN)
Oakton Comm Coll (IL)
Pueblo Comm Coll (CO)
Quinsigamond Comm Coll (MA)
Raritan Valley Comm Coll (NJ)
Rend Lake Coll (IL)
Rogue Comm Coll (OR)
St. Clair County Comm Coll (MI)
Schoolcraft Coll (MI)
Sierra Coll (CA)
Southern Crescent Tech Coll (GA)
South Florida State Coll (FL)
South Georgia Tech Coll (GA)
Spartanburg Comm Coll (SC)
Tallahassee Comm Coll (FL)
Texas State Tech Coll (TX)
Three Rivers Comm Coll (CT)
Truckee Meadows Comm Coll (NV)
U of Cincinnati Clermont Coll (OH)
Vincennes U (IN)
Wayne County Comm Coll District (MI)
Western Nevada Coll (NV)
Westmoreland County Comm Coll (PA)

MARINE BIOLOGY AND BIOLOGICAL OCEANOGRAPHY
Oregon Coast Comm Coll (OR)
South Florida State Coll (FL)

MARINE MAINTENANCE AND SHIP REPAIR TECHNOLOGY
Cape Fear Comm Coll (NC)
Coll of The Albemarle (NC)
Kingsborough Comm Coll of the City U of New York (NY)
Minnesota State Comm and Tech Coll (MN)
Minnesota State Comm and Tech Coll–Detroit Lakes (MN)
Northwest School of Wooden Boatbuilding (WA)
Olympic Coll (WA)

MARINE SCIENCE/MERCHANT MARINE OFFICER
American Samoa Comm Coll (AS)
San Jacinto Coll District (TX)

MARINE TRANSPORTATION RELATED
Orange Coast Coll (CA)

MARKETING/MARKETING MANAGEMENT
Adirondack Comm Coll (NY)
Albany Tech Coll (GA)
Alvin Comm Coll (TX)
Arkansas Northeastern Coll (AR)
Athens Tech Coll (GA)
Atlanta Tech Coll (GA)
Augusta Tech Coll (GA)
Austin Comm Coll District (TX)
Bainbridge State Coll (GA)
Blackhawk Tech Coll (WI)
Brookhaven Coll (TX)
Camden County Coll (NJ)
Casper Coll (WY)
Cecil Coll (MD)
Central Georgia Tech Coll (GA)
Central Oregon Comm Coll (OR)

Century Coll (MN)
Cerritos Coll (CA)
Chattahoochee Tech Coll (GA)
Chippewa Valley Tech Coll (WI)
Coll of Central Florida (FL)
Coll of the Ouachitas (AR)
Columbus State Comm Coll (OH)
Comm Coll of Allegheny County (PA)
Comm Coll of Rhode Island (RI)
Dakota Coll at Bottineau (ND)
De Anza Coll (CA)
Delta Coll (MI)
Des Moines Area Comm Coll (IA)
Dodge City Comm Coll (KS)
Eastern Idaho Tech Coll (ID)
Edison State Comm Coll (OH)
Elgin Comm Coll (IL)
Fayetteville Tech Comm Coll (NC)
Finger Lakes Comm Coll (NY)
Fox Valley Tech Coll (WI)
Gateway Tech Coll (WI)
Genesee Comm Coll (NY)
Georgia Northwestern Tech Coll (GA)
Georgia Piedmont Tech Coll (GA)
Golden West Coll (CA)
Guam Comm Coll (GU)
Gwinnett Tech Coll (GA)
Harford Comm Coll (MD)
Harper Coll (IL)
Hinds Comm Coll (MS)
Houston Comm Coll (TX)
Illinois Valley Comm Coll (IL)
Imperial Valley Coll (CA)
Johnson County Comm Coll (KS)
Kingsborough Comm Coll of the City U of New York (NY)
Lake Area Tech Inst (SD)
Lakeland Comm Coll (OH)
Lamar Comm Coll (CO)
Lanier Tech Coll (GA)
Lansdale School of Business (PA)
Lenoir Comm Coll (NC)
Lone Star Coll–CyFair (TX)
Lone Star Coll–Kingwood (TX)
Los Angeles City Coll (CA)
Macomb Comm Coll (MI)
Madison Area Tech Coll (WI)
Manchester Comm Coll (CT)
Manor Coll (PA)
Meridian Comm Coll (MS)
Mesa Comm Coll (AZ)
Miami Dade Coll (FL)
Middlesex County Coll (NJ)
Minnesota State Comm and Tech Coll (MN)
Minnesota State Comm and Tech Coll–Detroit Lakes (MN)
Monroe Comm Coll (NY)
Monroe County Comm Coll (MI)
Morton Coll (IL)
Mott Comm Coll (MI)
Mt. San Antonio Coll (CA)
Nassau Comm Coll (NY)
Naugatuck Valley Comm Coll (CT)
Navarro Coll (TX)
New Mexico Jr Coll (NM)
New River Comm Coll (VA)
NHTI, Concord's Comm Coll, Concord (NH)
Northampton Comm Coll (PA)
North Central Missouri Coll (MO)
Northcentral Tech Coll (WI)
Northeastern Jr Coll (CO)
Northern Essex Comm Coll (MA)
North Shore Comm Coll (MA)
Norwalk Comm Coll (CT)
Oakton Comm Coll (IL)
Ogeechee Tech Coll (GA)
Penn Foster Coll (AZ)
Raritan Valley Comm Coll (NJ)
Rock Valley Coll (IL)
Rogue Comm Coll (OR)
Rowan-Cabarrus Comm Coll (NC)
St. Charles Comm Coll (MO)
St. Clair County Comm Coll (MI)
Salt Lake Comm Coll (UT)
Savannah Tech Coll (GA)
Schoolcraft Coll (MI)
Seminole State Coll of Florida (FL)
Southeastern Tech Coll (GA)
Southern Crescent Tech Coll (GA)
South Florida State Coll (FL)
South Georgia Tech Coll (GA)
South Plains Coll (TX)
Springfield Tech Comm Coll (MA)
Stark State Coll (OH)
Sullivan County Comm Coll (NY)
Tarrant County Coll District (TX)
Texarkana Coll (TX)
Three Rivers Comm Coll (CT)
Three Rivers Comm Coll (MO)

Tidewater Comm Coll (VA)
Trident Tech Coll (SC)
Trinity Valley Comm Coll (TX)
Vincennes U (IN)
Waukesha County Tech Coll (WI)
Western Wyoming Comm Coll (WY)
West Georgia Tech Coll (GA)
Westmoreland County Comm Coll (PA)
Wiregrass Georgia Tech Coll (GA)

MARKETING RELATED
Columbus State Comm Coll (OH)
Dakota Coll at Bottineau (ND)
Westchester Comm Coll (NY)

MARKETING RESEARCH
Penn Foster Coll (AZ)

MASONRY
Ivy Tech Comm Coll–Central Indiana (IN)
Ivy Tech Comm Coll–Columbus (IN)
Ivy Tech Comm Coll–East Central (IN)
Ivy Tech Comm Coll–Lafayette (IN)
Ivy Tech Comm Coll–Northeast (IN)
Ivy Tech Comm Coll–Northwest (IN)
Ivy Tech Comm Coll–Southwest (IN)
Ivy Tech Comm Coll–Wabash Valley (IN)
Palomar Coll (CA)
State U of New York Coll of Technology at Alfred (NY)
Tallahassee Comm Coll (FL)

MASSAGE THERAPY
Arizona Western Coll (AZ)
Camden County Coll (NJ)
Carteret Comm Coll (NC)
Central Oregon Comm Coll (OR)
Chandler-Gilbert Comm Coll (AZ)
Columbus State Comm Coll (OH)
Comm Coll of Baltimore County (MD)
Comm Coll of Rhode Island (RI)
Illinois Valley Comm Coll (IL)
Ivy Tech Comm Coll–Northeast (IN)
Lake Superior Coll (MN)
Lenoir Comm Coll (NC)
Miami Dade Coll (FL)
Minnesota State Coll–Southeast Tech (MN)
Morton Coll (IL)
Niagara County Comm Coll (NY)
Queensborough Comm Coll of the City U of New York (NY)
Renton Tech Coll (WA)
St. Clair County Comm Coll (MI)
Schoolcraft Coll (MI)
Southeastern Coll–West Palm Beach (FL)
Southwestern Comm Coll (NC)
Spencerian Coll (KY)
Vincennes U (IN)
Williston State Coll (ND)

MASS COMMUNICATION/ MEDIA
Amarillo Coll (TX)
Ancilla Coll (IN)
Blinn Coll (TX)
Bunker Hill Comm Coll (MA)
Casper Coll (WY)
Coll of Marin (CA)
Coll of the Desert (CA)
Crowder Coll (MO)
De Anza Coll (CA)
Dodge City Comm Coll (KS)
Finger Lakes Comm Coll (NY)
Fullerton Coll (CA)
Genesee Comm Coll (NY)
Georgia Military Coll (GA)
Harford Comm Coll (MD)
Iowa Central Comm Coll (IA)
Lackawanna Coll (PA)
Laramie County Comm Coll (WY)
Mercer County Comm Coll (NJ)
Miami Dade Coll (FL)
Monroe Comm Coll (NY)
Monroe County Comm Coll (MI)
Nassau Comm Coll (NY)
Niagara County Comm Coll (NY)
Northeast Comm Coll (NE)
Oklahoma City Comm Coll (OK)
Orange Coast Coll (CA)
Salt Lake Comm Coll (UT)
South Plains Coll (TX)
Wytheville Comm Coll (VA)

MATERIALS ENGINEERING
South Florida State Coll (FL)

MATERIALS SCIENCE
Mt. San Antonio Coll (CA)
Northern Essex Comm Coll (MA)

MATHEMATICS
Allen Comm Coll (KS)
Alvin Comm Coll (TX)
Amarillo Coll (TX)
Anne Arundel Comm Coll (MD)
Arizona Western Coll (AZ)
Austin Comm Coll District (TX)
Bainbridge State Coll (GA)
Blinn Coll (TX)
Borough of Manhattan Comm Coll of the City U of New York (NY)
Bucks County Comm Coll (PA)
Bunker Hill Comm Coll (MA)
Cañada Coll (CA)
Carl Albert State Coll (OK)
Casper Coll (WY)
Cecil Coll (MD)
Central New Mexico Comm Coll (NM)
Central Oregon Comm Coll (OR)
Central Texas Coll (TX)
Central Wyoming Coll (WY)
Cerritos Coll (CA)
Citrus Coll (CA)
Cochise County Comm Coll District (AZ)
Coll of Central Florida (FL)
Coll of Marin (CA)
Coll of the Canyons (CA)
Coll of the Desert (CA)
Comm Coll of Allegheny County (PA)
Crowder Coll (MO)
Dakota Coll at Bottineau (ND)
De Anza Coll (CA)
Del Mar Coll (TX)
Dodge City Comm Coll (KS)
Eastern Arizona Coll (AZ)
Eastern Wyoming Coll (WY)
Edison State Comm Coll (OH)
Feather River Coll (CA)
Finger Lakes Comm Coll (NY)
Frederick Comm Coll (MD)
Fullerton Coll (CA)
Genesee Comm Coll (NY)
Georgia Highlands Coll (GA)
Georgia Military Coll (GA)
Golden West Coll (CA)
Harford Comm Coll (MD)
Harper Coll (IL)
Harrisburg Area Comm Coll (PA)
Hill Coll (TX)
Holyoke Comm Coll (MA)
Housatonic Comm Coll (CT)
Houston Comm Coll (TX)
Hutchinson Comm Coll (KS)
Imperial Valley Coll (CA)
Jefferson Comm Coll (NY)
J. Sargeant Reynolds Comm Coll (VA)
Kingsborough Comm Coll of the City U of New York (NY)
Lansing Comm Coll (MI)
Laramie County Comm Coll (WY)
Lehigh Carbon Comm Coll (PA)
Lincoln Coll (IL)
Los Angeles City Coll (CA)
Luzerne County Comm Coll (PA)
Macomb Comm Coll (MI)
Massachusetts Bay Comm Coll (MA)
Merced Coll (CA)
Mercer County Comm Coll (NJ)
Mesa Comm Coll (AZ)
Miami Dade Coll (FL)
Mohave Comm Coll (AZ)
Monroe Comm Coll (NY)
Monroe County Comm Coll (MI)
Montgomery County Comm Coll (PA)
Mt. San Antonio Coll (CA)
Murray State Coll (OK)
Nashville State Comm Coll (TN)
Nassau Comm Coll (NY)
Navarro Coll (TX)
New Mexico Jr Coll (NM)
Niagara County Comm Coll (NY)
Northampton Comm Coll (PA)
Northeast Comm Coll (NE)
Northeastern Jr Coll (CO)
Northwest Coll (WY)
Oklahoma City Comm Coll (OK)
Orange Coast Coll (CA)
Otero Jr Coll (CO)
Palomar Coll (CA)
Panola Coll (TX)
Paris Jr Coll (TX)
Pensacola State Coll (FL)
St. Philip's Coll (TX)
San Jacinto Coll District (TX)
San Joaquin Delta Coll (CA)

San Juan Coll (NM)
Santa Monica Coll (CA)
Santa Rosa Jr Coll (CA)
Scottsdale Comm Coll (AZ)
Seminole State Coll (OK)
Sierra Coll (CA)
Southern U at Shreveport (LA)
South Florida State Coll (FL)
Springfield Tech Comm Coll (MA)
Sullivan County Comm Coll (NY)
Texarkana Coll (TX)
Trinity Valley Comm Coll (TX)
Truckee Meadows Comm Coll (NV)
Tyler Jr Coll (TX)
Vincennes U (IN)
Western Wyoming Comm Coll (WY)

MATHEMATICS AND COMPUTER SCIENCE
Crowder Coll (MO)

MATHEMATICS RELATED
Cayuga County Comm Coll (NY)
Genesee Comm Coll (NY)
Middlesex Comm Coll (MA)

MATHEMATICS TEACHER EDUCATION
Anne Arundel Comm Coll (MD)
Bucks County Comm Coll (PA)
Carroll Comm Coll (MD)
Chesapeake Coll (MD)
Comm Coll of Baltimore County (MD)
Eastern Wyoming Coll (WY)
Frederick Comm Coll (MD)
Harford Comm Coll (MD)
Highland Comm Coll (IL)
Montgomery Coll (MD)
South Florida State Coll (FL)
Ulster County Comm Coll (NY)
Vincennes U (IN)

MECHANICAL DRAFTING AND CAD/CADD
Alexandria Tech and Comm Coll (MN)
Anoka Tech Coll (MN)
Chippewa Valley Tech Coll (WI)
Comm Coll of Allegheny County (PA)
Des Moines Area Comm Coll (IA)
Edison State Comm Coll (OH)
Fox Valley Tech Coll (WI)
Gateway Tech Coll (WI)
Greenville Tech Coll (SC)
Hutchinson Comm Coll (KS)
Lake Superior Coll (MN)
Lansing Comm Coll (MI)
Macomb Comm Coll (MI)
Merced Coll (CA)
Minnesota State Comm and Tech Coll (MN)
Minnesota State Comm and Tech Coll–Moorhead (MN)
Mitchell Comm Coll (NC)
Northcentral Tech Coll (WI)
Ozarks Tech Comm Coll (MO)
Queensborough Comm Coll of the City U of New York (NY)
Sierra Coll (CA)
Vincennes U (IN)
Waukesha County Tech Coll (WI)
Westmoreland County Comm Coll (PA)

MECHANICAL ENGINEERING
Cayuga County Comm Coll (NY)
Comm Coll of Rhode Island (RI)
Fiorello H. LaGuardia Comm Coll of the City U of New York (NY)
Lone Star Coll–North Harris (TX)
Nashville State Comm Coll (TN)
Olympic Coll (WA)
St. Philip's Coll (TX)
South Florida State Coll (FL)

MECHANICAL ENGINEERING/ MECHANICAL TECHNOLOGY
Alamance Comm Coll (NC)
Augusta Tech Coll (GA)
Bowling Green State U–Firelands Coll (OH)
Caldwell Comm Coll and Tech Inst (NC)
Camden County Coll (NJ)
Cape Fear Comm Coll (NC)
Cayuga County Comm Coll (NY)
Citrus Coll (CA)
Clinton Comm Coll (NY)
Columbus State Comm Coll (OH)
Columbus Tech Coll (GA)
County Coll of Morris (NJ)
Craven Comm Coll (NC)

Delta Coll (MI)
Erie Comm Coll, North Campus (NY)
Finger Lakes Comm Coll (NY)
Fullerton Coll (CA)
Greenville Tech Coll (SC)
Hagerstown Comm Coll (MD)
Harrisburg Area Comm Coll (PA)
Illinois Central Coll (IL)
Illinois Eastern Comm Colls, Lincoln Trail College (IL)
Illinois Valley Comm Coll (IL)
Ivy Tech Comm Coll–Lafayette (IN)
Jamestown Comm Coll (NY)
Kent State U at Trumbull (OH)
Kent State U at Tuscarawas (OH)
Lakeland Comm Coll (OH)
Lehigh Carbon Comm Coll (PA)
Macomb Comm Coll (MI)
Massachusetts Bay Comm Coll (MA)
Merced Coll (CA)
Middlesex County Coll (NJ)
Mitchell Comm Coll (NC)
Mohawk Valley Comm Coll (NY)
Monroe Comm Coll (NY)
Montgomery County Comm Coll (PA)
Mott Comm Coll (MI)
NHTI, Concord's Comm Coll, Concord (NH)
Oakton Comm Coll (IL)
Oklahoma State U Inst of Technology (OK)
Penn State DuBois (PA)
Penn State Shenango (PA)
Queensborough Comm Coll of the City U of New York (NY)
Richmond Comm Coll (NC)
San Joaquin Delta Coll (CA)
Southeastern Comm Coll (IA)
Southern U at Shreveport (LA)
Spartanburg Comm Coll (SC)
Springfield Tech Comm Coll (MA)
Stark State Coll (OH)
State U of New York Coll of Technology at Alfred (NY)
Tarrant County Coll District (TX)
Texas State Tech Coll (TX)
Three Rivers Comm Coll (CT)
Trident Tech Coll (SC)
Vincennes U (IN)
Virginia Western Comm Coll (VA)
Westchester Comm Coll (NY)
Westmoreland County Comm Coll (PA)
Wytheville Comm Coll (VA)

MECHANICAL ENGINEERING TECHNOLOGIES RELATED

Camden County Coll (NJ)
Florida Keys Comm Coll (FL)
Jefferson Comm Coll (NY)
John Tyler Comm Coll (VA)
Middlesex County Coll (NJ)
Mohawk Valley Comm Coll (NY)

MECHANIC AND REPAIR TECHNOLOGIES RELATED

Chandler-Gilbert Comm Coll (AZ)
Cloud County Comm Coll (KS)
Greenville Tech Coll (SC)
Ivy Tech Comm Coll–Bloomington (IN)
Ivy Tech Comm Coll–Columbus (IN)
Ivy Tech Comm Coll–Kokomo (IN)
Ivy Tech Comm Coll–Lafayette (IN)
Ivy Tech Comm Coll–North Central (IN)
Ivy Tech Comm Coll–Northwest (IN)
Ivy Tech Comm Coll–Southwest (IN)
Johnson County Comm Coll (KS)
Laramie County Comm Coll (WY)
Macomb Comm Coll (MI)
Ohio Tech Coll (OH)
Oklahoma State U Inst of Technology (OK)
Three Rivers Comm Coll (MO)

MECHANICS AND REPAIR

Ivy Tech Comm Coll–Bloomington (IN)
Ivy Tech Comm Coll–Central Indiana (IN)
Ivy Tech Comm Coll–Columbus (IN)
Ivy Tech Comm Coll–Kokomo (IN)
Ivy Tech Comm Coll–Lafayette (IN)
Ivy Tech Comm Coll–North Central (IN)
Ivy Tech Comm Coll–Northeast (IN)
Ivy Tech Comm Coll–Northwest (IN)
Ivy Tech Comm Coll–Richmond (IN)
Ivy Tech Comm Coll–Sellersburg (IN)

Ivy Tech Comm Coll–Southwest (IN)
Ivy Tech Comm Coll–Wabash Valley (IN)
Rogue Comm Coll (OR)
Western Wyoming Comm Coll (WY)

MECHATRONICS, ROBOTICS, AND AUTOMATION ENGINEERING

Anne Arundel Comm Coll (MD)
Cochise County Comm Coll District (AZ)
Delta Coll (MI)
Harrisburg Area Comm Coll (PA)
Lorain County Comm Coll (OH)
Mitchell Comm Coll (NC)
Randolph Comm Coll (NC)
Schoolcraft Coll (MI)
Westmoreland County Comm Coll (PA)

MEDICAL ADMINISTRATIVE ASSISTANT AND MEDICAL SECRETARY

Alamance Comm Coll (NC)
Alexandria Tech and Comm Coll (MN)
Alvin Comm Coll (TX)
Amarillo Coll (TX)
Anne Arundel Comm Coll (MD)
Anoka Tech Coll (MN)
Bismarck State Coll (ND)
Blackhawk Tech Coll (WI)
Bunker Hill Comm Coll (MA)
Carteret Comm Coll (NC)
Central Texas Coll (TX)
Century Coll (MN)
Coll of Marin (CA)
Coll of The Albemarle (NC)
Coll of the Ouachitas (AR)
Comm Coll of Allegheny County (PA)
Comm Coll of Baltimore County (MD)
Comm Coll of Rhode Island (RI)
Craven Comm Coll (NC)
Crowder Coll (MO)
Dakota Coll at Bottineau (ND)
Danville Area Comm Coll (IL)
Daytona State Coll (FL)
Del Mar Coll (TX)
Delta Coll (MI)
Des Moines Area Comm Coll (IA)
Dodge City Comm Coll (KS)
Edison State Comm Coll (OH)
Erie Comm Coll, North Campus (NY)
Frederick Comm Coll (MD)
Genesee Comm Coll (NY)
Grand Rapids Comm Coll (MI)
Gulf Coast State Coll (FL)
Halifax Comm Coll (NC)
Harper Coll (IL)
Hawkeye Comm Coll (IA)
Hennepin Tech Coll (MN)
Howard Comm Coll (MD)
Humacao Comm Coll (PR)
IBMC Coll, Fort Collins (CO)
Illinois Eastern Comm Colls, Olney Central College (IL)
Jefferson Comm Coll (NY)
Kellogg Comm Coll (MI)
Lackawanna Coll (PA)
Lake Superior Coll (MN)
Luzerne County Comm Coll (PA)
Madison Area Tech Coll (WI)
Manchester Comm Coll (CT)
McLennan Comm Coll (TX)
Merced Coll (CA)
Mesa Comm Coll (AZ)
Minnesota State Coll–Southeast Tech (MN)
Minnesota State Comm and Tech Coll (MN)
Minnesota State Comm and Tech Coll–Moorhead (MN)
Minnesota State Comm and Tech Coll–Wadena (MN)
Minnesota West Comm and Tech Coll (MN)
Monroe County Comm Coll (MI)
Morton Coll (IL)
Mt. San Antonio Coll (CA)
Nassau Comm Coll (NY)
New Mexico Jr Coll (NM)
Northampton Comm Coll (PA)
Northeast Comm Coll (NE)
Northern Essex Comm Coll (MA)
Northland Comm and Tech Coll (MN)
North Shore Comm Coll (MA)
Otero Jr Coll (CO)

MEDICAL/CLINICAL ASSISTANT

Alamance Comm Coll (NC)
Anoka Tech Coll (MN)
Blue Ridge Comm and Tech Coll (WV)
Bossier Parish Comm Coll (LA)
Bucks County Comm Coll (PA)
Caldwell Comm Coll and Tech Inst (NC)
Cañada Coll (CA)
Carteret Comm Coll (NC)
Central Maine Comm Coll (ME)
Central Oregon Comm Coll (OR)
Central Virginia Comm Coll (VA)
Cerritos Coll (CA)
Coll of Business and Technology–Cutler Bay Campus (FL)
Coll of Marin (CA)
The Coll of Westchester (NY)
Columbia-Greene Comm Coll (NY)
Columbus State Comm Coll (OH)
Comm Care Coll (OK)
Comm Coll of Allegheny County (PA)
Comm Coll of Vermont (VT)
Craven Comm Coll (NC)
Dakota Coll at Bottineau (ND)
De Anza Coll (CA)
Des Moines Area Comm Coll (IA)
East Central Coll (MO)
Eastern Idaho Tech Coll (ID)
East Georgia State Coll (GA)
Edison State Comm Coll (OH)
El Paso Comm Coll (TX)
Frederick Comm Coll (MD)
Georgia Piedmont Tech Coll (GA)
Great Falls Coll Montana State U (MT)
Guam Comm Coll (GU)
Gwinnett Tech Coll (GA)
Harper Coll (IL)
Harrisburg Area Comm Coll (PA)
Haywood Comm Coll (NC)
H. Councill Trenholm State Comm Coll (AL)
Highland Comm Coll (IL)
Hinds Comm Coll (MS)
Hudson County Comm Coll (NJ)
IBMC Coll, Fort Collins (CO)
Illinois Eastern Comm Colls, Lincoln Trail College (IL)
Iowa Central Comm Coll (IA)
Ivy Tech Comm Coll–Central Indiana (IN)
Ivy Tech Comm Coll–Columbus (IN)
Ivy Tech Comm Coll–East Central (IN)
Ivy Tech Comm Coll–Kokomo (IN)
Ivy Tech Comm Coll–Lafayette (IN)
Ivy Tech Comm Coll–North Central (IN)
Ivy Tech Comm Coll–Northeast (IN)
Ivy Tech Comm Coll–Northwest (IN)
Ivy Tech Comm Coll–Richmond (IN)
Ivy Tech Comm Coll–Sellersburg (IN)
Ivy Tech Comm Coll–Southeast (IN)
Ivy Tech Comm Coll–Southwest (IN)
Ivy Tech Comm Coll–Wabash Valley (IN)
James Sprunt Comm Coll (NC)
Jamestown Business Coll (NY)
Johnston Comm Coll (NC)
Kirtland Comm Coll (MI)
Lake Area Tech Inst (SD)
Lake Superior Coll (MN)
Lansdale School of Business (PA)

Owensboro Comm and Tech Coll (KY)
Palomar Coll (CA)
Piedmont Comm Coll (NC)
Quinsigamond Comm Coll (MA)
Renton Tech Coll (WA)
Santa Monica Coll (CA)
Scottsdale Comm Coll (AZ)
Shawnee Comm Coll (IL)
Somerset Comm Coll (KY)
South Plains Coll (TX)
Spoon River Coll (IL)
Springfield Tech Comm Coll (MA)
Treasure Valley Comm Coll (OR)
Trident Tech Coll (SC)
Tyler Jr Coll (TX)
Ultimate Medical Academy Online (FL)
U of Cincinnati Blue Ash Coll (OH)
Westchester Comm Coll (NY)
Western Wyoming Comm Coll (WY)
Wisconsin Indianhead Tech Coll (WI)
Wytheville Comm Coll (VA)

MEDICAL/HEALTH MANAGEMENT AND CLINICAL ASSISTANT

Ivy Tech Comm Coll–Bloomington (IN)
Ivy Tech Comm Coll–Central Indiana (IN)
Ivy Tech Comm Coll–East Central (IN)
Ivy Tech Comm Coll–Lafayette (IN)
Ivy Tech Comm Coll–Richmond (IN)
Ivy Tech Comm Coll–Sellersburg (IN)
Ivy Tech Comm Coll–Southeast (IN)
Ivy Tech Comm Coll–Southwest (IN)
Ivy Tech Comm Coll–Wabash Valley (IN)
Pittsburgh Tech Coll (PA)

MEDICAL INFORMATICS

Borough of Manhattan Comm Coll of the City U of New York (NY)
Comm Coll of Baltimore County (MD)
Harrisburg Area Comm Coll (PA)
Nashville State Comm Coll (TN)
Volunteer State Comm Coll (TN)

MEDICAL INSURANCE CODING

Berkshire Comm Coll (MA)
Bucks County Comm Coll (PA)
Central Texas Coll (TX)
Collin County Comm Coll District (TX)
Comm Care Coll (OK)
Dakota Coll at Bottineau (ND)
Hawkeye Comm Coll (IA)
Lake Superior Coll (MN)
Laramie County Comm Coll (WY)
Minnesota West Comm and Tech Coll (MN)
Northland Comm and Tech Coll (MN)
Paris Jr Coll (TX)
Renton Tech Coll (WA)
Southeastern Coll–West Palm Beach (FL)

Lehigh Carbon Comm Coll (PA)
Lenoir Comm Coll (NC)
Lorain County Comm Coll (OH)
Macomb Comm Coll (MI)
Miami Dade Coll (FL)
Middlesex Comm Coll (MA)
Minnesota West Comm and Tech Coll (MN)
Mitchell Comm Coll (NC)
Mitchell Tech Inst (SD)
Mohave Comm Coll (AZ)
Mohawk Valley Comm Coll (NY)
Montgomery Comm Coll (NC)
Montgomery County Comm Coll (PA)
Morgan Comm Coll (CO)
Mount Wachusett Comm Coll (MA)
New Mexico Jr Coll (NM)
Niagara County Comm Coll (NY)
North Central Missouri Coll (MO)
Northwest-Shoals Comm Coll (AL)
Oklahoma City Comm Coll (OK)
Olympic Coll (WA)
Orange Coast Coll (CA)
Panola Coll (TX)
Penn Foster Coll (AZ)
Piedmont Comm Coll (NC)
Queensborough Comm Coll of the City U of New York (NY)
Randolph Comm Coll (NC)
Raritan Valley Comm Coll (NJ)
Rend Lake Coll (IL)
Renton Tech Coll (WA)
Richmond Comm Coll (NC)
Salina Area Tech Coll (KS)
Salt Lake Comm Coll (UT)
San Jacinto Coll District (TX)
Santa Monica Coll (CA)
Santa Rosa Jr Coll (CA)
Southeastern Coll–West Palm Beach (FL)
Southeastern Comm Coll (IA)
Southwestern Michigan Coll (MI)
Springfield Tech Comm Coll (MA)
Stark State Coll (OH)
Sullivan County Comm Coll (NY)
U of Cincinnati Blue Ash Coll (OH)
Western Dakota Tech Inst (SD)
Western Wyoming Comm Coll (WY)
Westmoreland County Comm Coll (PA)
West Virginia Jr Coll–Bridgeport (WV)
White Mountains Comm Coll (NH)
York County Comm Coll (ME)

MEDICAL INSURANCE/ MEDICAL BILLING

Coconino Comm Coll (AZ)
Northcentral Tech Coll (WI)
Southeastern Coll–West Palm Beach (FL)
Ultimate Medical Academy Online (FL)

MEDICAL MICROBIOLOGY AND BACTERIOLOGY

South Florida State Coll (FL)

MEDICAL OFFICE ASSISTANT

Central Wyoming Coll (WY)
Coconino Comm Coll (AZ)
Dakota Coll at Bottineau (ND)
Front Range Comm Coll (CO)
Harford Comm Coll (MD)
Johnson County Comm Coll (KS)
Lake Superior Coll (MN)
Manhattan Area Tech Coll (KS)
Mitchell Tech Inst (SD)
Patrick Henry Comm Coll (VA)
Pittsburgh Tech Coll (PA)
Western Wyoming Comm Coll (WY)
Westmoreland County Comm Coll (PA)
White Mountains Comm Coll (NH)

MEDICAL OFFICE COMPUTER SPECIALIST

Carteret Comm Coll (NC)
Richmond Comm Coll (NC)
Rogue Comm Coll (OR)
Western Wyoming Comm Coll (WY)

MEDICAL OFFICE MANAGEMENT

Caldwell Comm Coll and Tech Inst (NC)
Cape Fear Comm Coll (NC)
Columbus Tech Coll (GA)
Craven Comm Coll (NC)
Fayetteville Tech Comm Coll (NC)
Fox Valley Tech Coll (WI)
Georgia Northwestern Tech Coll (GA)
Halifax Comm Coll (NC)
Haywood Comm Coll (NC)
Johnston Comm Coll (NC)
Lenoir Comm Coll (NC)
Long Island Business Inst (NY)
Norwalk Comm Coll (CT)
Pennsylvania Inst of Technology (PA)
Piedmont Comm Coll (NC)
Pueblo Comm Coll (CO)
Queensborough Comm Coll of the City U of New York (NY)
Randolph Comm Coll (NC)
Richmond Comm Coll (NC)
Rockingham Comm Coll (NC)
Rowan-Cabarrus Comm Coll (NC)
Spencerian Coll–Lexington (KY)
West Virginia Jr Coll–Bridgeport (WV)

MEDICAL RADIOLOGIC TECHNOLOGY

Albany Tech Coll (GA)
Anne Arundel Comm Coll (MD)
Athens Tech Coll (GA)
Augusta Tech Coll (GA)
Bowling Green State U–Firelands Coll (OH)
Bunker Hill Comm Coll (MA)
Cape Fear Comm Coll (NC)
Carolinas Coll of Health Sciences (NC)
Central Georgia Tech Coll (GA)
Chattahoochee Tech Coll (GA)
Chesapeake Coll (MD)
Chippewa Valley Tech Coll (WI)
Coll of Central Florida (FL)
Columbus State Comm Coll (OH)
Columbus Tech Coll (GA)
Comm Coll of Allegheny County (PA)
Comm Coll of Baltimore County (MD)
Comm Coll of Philadelphia (PA)
Comm Coll of the Air Force (AL)
Del Mar Coll (TX)
Delta Coll (MI)
Dunwoody Coll of Technology (MN)
East Central Coll (MO)
El Paso Comm Coll (TX)
Erie Comm Coll (NY)

Spencerian Coll (KY)
Springfield Tech Comm Coll (MA)

Fiorello H. LaGuardia Comm Coll of the City U of New York (NY)
Florida SouthWestern State Coll (FL)
Greenville Tech Coll (SC)
Gulf Coast State Coll (FL)
Gwinnett Tech Coll (GA)
Hagerstown Comm Coll (MD)
Hillsborough Comm Coll (FL)
Holyoke Comm Coll (MA)
Hutchinson Comm Coll (KS)
Illinois Eastern Comm Colls, Olney Central College (IL)
Ivy Tech Comm Coll–Bloomington (IN)
Ivy Tech Comm Coll–Central Indiana (IN)
Ivy Tech Comm Coll–Columbus (IN)
Ivy Tech Comm Coll–East Central (IN)
Ivy Tech Comm Coll–Richmond (IN)
Ivy Tech Comm Coll–Southeast (IN)
Ivy Tech Comm Coll–Wabash Valley (IN)
Kellogg Comm Coll (MI)
Kent State U at Ashtabula (OH)
Kent State U at Salem (OH)
Lakeland Comm Coll (OH)
Lanier Tech Coll (GA)
Lone Star Coll–CyFair (TX)
Lorain County Comm Coll (OH)
Mercer County Comm Coll (NJ)
Miami Dade Coll (FL)
Middlesex Comm Coll (MA)
Middlesex County Coll (NJ)
Mitchell Tech Inst (SD)
Mohawk Valley Comm Coll (NY)
Montgomery Coll (MD)
Montgomery County Comm Coll (PA)
Mott Comm Coll (MI)
Nassau Comm Coll (NY)
Naugatuck Valley Comm Coll (CT)
Niagara County Comm Coll (NY)
Northcentral Tech Coll (WI)
Northeast Comm Coll (NE)
North Shore Comm Coll (MA)
Pensacola State Coll (FL)
Rend Lake Coll (IL)
St. Clair County Comm Coll (MI)
Salt Lake Comm Coll (UT)
Somerset Comm Coll (KY)
Southeast Comm Coll, Lincoln Campus (NE)
Southeastern Tech Coll (GA)
Southern Crescent Tech Coll (GA)
Southern Regional Tech Coll (GA)
Southern U at Shreveport (LA)
South Florida State Coll (FL)
Southwestern Comm Coll (NC)
Spartanburg Comm Coll (SC)
Tallahassee Comm Coll (FL)
Truckee Meadows Comm Coll (NV)
U of Cincinnati Blue Ash Coll (OH)
Vincennes U (IN)
Volunteer State Comm Coll (TN)
Waukesha County Tech Coll (WI)
Westchester Comm Coll (NY)
West Georgia Tech Coll (GA)
Wiregrass Georgia Tech Coll (GA)
Wor-Wic Comm Coll (MD)

MEDICAL RECEPTION
Lake Superior Coll (MN)

MEDICAL STAFF SERVICES TECHNOLOGY
Rend Lake Coll (IL)

MEDICAL TRANSCRIPTION
Hudson County Comm Coll (NJ)
Lake Superior Coll (MN)
Northern Essex Comm Coll (MA)
Treasure Valley Comm Coll (OR)
Western Dakota Tech Inst (SD)

MEDICATION AIDE
Salina Area Tech Coll (KS)

MEDIUM/HEAVY VEHICLE AND TRUCK TECHNOLOGY
Edison State Comm Coll (OH)
Hennepin Tech Coll (MN)
Salina Area Tech Coll (KS)
Williston State Coll (ND)

MEETING AND EVENT PLANNING
Fox Valley Tech Coll (WI)
Northampton Comm Coll (PA)
Raritan Valley Comm Coll (NJ)

MENTAL AND SOCIAL HEALTH SERVICES AND ALLIED PROFESSIONS RELATED
Carteret Comm Coll (NC)
Chesapeake Coll (MD)
Halifax Comm Coll (NC)
John Tyler Comm Coll (VA)
J. Sargeant Reynolds Comm Coll (VA)
Lenoir Comm Coll (NC)
Montgomery Comm Coll (NC)
New River Comm Coll (VA)
Northcentral Tech Coll (WI)
Olympic Coll (WA)
Piedmont Comm Coll (NC)
Richmond Comm Coll (NC)
Southwest Virginia Comm Coll (VA)

MENTAL HEALTH COUNSELING
Alvin Comm Coll (TX)
Austin Comm Coll District (TX)
Blinn Coll (TX)
Comm Coll of Rhode Island (RI)
Comm Coll of the Air Force (AL)
Del Mar Coll (TX)
Housatonic Comm Coll (CT)
Kingsborough Comm Coll of the City U of New York (NY)
Lackawanna Coll (PA)
Macomb Comm Coll (MI)
McLennan Comm Coll (TX)
Metropolitan Comm Coll (NE)
Mt. San Antonio Coll (CA)
NHTI, Concord's Comm Coll, Concord (NH)
Northern Essex Comm Coll (MA)
North Shore Comm Coll (MA)
Orange Coast Coll (CA)
Southern U at Shreveport (LA)
South Plains Coll (TX)
Southwestern Comm Coll (NC)
Tarrant County Coll District (TX)
Truckee Meadows Comm Coll (NV)
Virginia Western Comm Coll (VA)

MERCHANDISING
Delta Coll (MI)

MERCHANDISING, SALES, AND MARKETING OPERATIONS RELATED (GENERAL)
Lake Region State Coll (ND)
Minnesota State Comm and Tech Coll (MN)
Northcentral Tech Coll (WI)
Orange Coast Coll (CA)

MERCHANDISING, SALES, AND MARKETING OPERATIONS RELATED (SPECIALIZED)
Middlesex County Coll (NJ)

METAL AND JEWELRY ARTS
Coll of The Albemarle (NC)
Fashion Inst of Technology (NY)
Haywood Comm Coll (NC)
Palomar Coll (CA)
Paris Jr Coll (TX)
Santa Fe Comm Coll (NM)

METAL FABRICATOR
Waukesha County Tech Coll (WI)

METALLURGICAL TECHNOLOGY
Arkansas Northeastern Coll (AR)
Comm Coll of the Air Force (AL)
Macomb Comm Coll (MI)
Penn State DuBois (PA)
Penn State Fayette, The Eberly Campus (PA)
Penn State Shenango (PA)
Schoolcraft Coll (MI)

MICROBIOLOGY
Fullerton Coll (CA)
Humacao Comm Coll (PR)

MIDDLE SCHOOL EDUCATION
Alvin Comm Coll (TX)
Arkansas Northeastern Coll (AR)
Austin Comm Coll District (TX)
Collin County Comm Coll District (TX)
El Paso Comm Coll (TX)
Georgia Military Coll (GA)
Miami Dade Coll (FL)
Nashville State Comm Coll (TN)
Northampton Comm Coll (PA)
Panola Coll (TX)
Southern Arkansas U Tech (AR)

South Florida State Coll (FL)
Tyler Jr Coll (TX)
U of Arkansas Comm Coll at Morrilton (AR)
U of Cincinnati Clermont Coll (OH)

MINING TECHNOLOGY
Casper Coll (WY)
Eastern Arizona Coll (AZ)
Illinois Eastern Comm Colls, Wabash Valley College (IL)
Rend Lake Coll (IL)
Western Wyoming Comm Coll (WY)

MODERN LANGUAGES
Amarillo Coll (TX)
Citrus Coll (CA)
Imperial Valley Coll (CA)
Otero Jr Coll (CO)

MORTUARY SCIENCE AND EMBALMING
Gupton-Jones Coll of Funeral Service (GA)
Wayne County Comm Coll District (MI)

MULTI/INTERDISCIPLINARY STUDIES RELATED
Alexandria Tech and Comm Coll (MN)
Anne Arundel Comm Coll (MD)
Arkansas Northeastern Coll (AR)
Austin Comm Coll District (TX)
Bismarck State Coll (ND)
Blue Ridge Comm and Tech Coll (WV)
Bucks County Comm Coll (PA)
Carroll Comm Coll (MD)
Central Maine Comm Coll (ME)
Central Wyoming Coll (WY)
Century Coll (MN)
Chippewa Valley Tech Coll (WI)
Coll of the Desert (CA)
County Coll of Morris (NJ)
Eastern Arizona Coll (AZ)
El Paso Comm Coll (TX)
Fox Valley Tech Coll (WI)
Greenville Tech Coll (SC)
Hawkeye Comm Coll (IA)
Hinds Comm Coll (MS)
Lake Superior Coll (MN)
Manhattan Area Tech Coll (KS)
Minnesota State Coll–Southeast Tech (MN)
Minnesota State Comm and Tech Coll (MN)
Minnesota State Comm and Tech Coll–Detroit Lakes (MN)
Minnesota State Comm and Tech Coll–Moorhead (MN)
Minnesota State Comm and Tech Coll–Wadena (MN)
Northcentral Tech Coll (WI)
Northwest-Shoals Comm Coll (AL)
Oklahoma City Comm Coll (OK)
Oklahoma State U Inst of Technology (OK)
Owensboro Comm and Tech Coll (KY)
Raritan Valley Comm Coll (NJ)
Somerset Comm Coll (KY)
Southern Arkansas U Tech (AR)
South Florida State Coll (FL)
Spartanburg Comm Coll (SC)
U of Cincinnati Clermont Coll (OH)
Waukesha County Tech Coll (WI)
Williston State Coll (ND)
York County Comm Coll (ME)

MUSEUM STUDIES
Casper Coll (WY)
Queensborough Comm Coll of the City U of New York (NY)

MUSIC
Adirondack Comm Coll (NY)
Allen Comm Coll (KS)
Alvin Comm Coll (TX)
Amarillo Coll (TX)
American Samoa Comm Coll (AS)
Anoka-Ramsey Comm Coll (MN)
Arizona Western Coll (AZ)
Austin Comm Coll District (TX)
Blinn Coll (TX)
Bossier Parish Comm Coll (LA)
Brookhaven Coll (TX)
Bucks County Comm Coll (PA)
Bunker Hill Comm Coll (MA)
Cañada Coll (CA)
Carroll Comm Coll (MD)
Casper Coll (WY)

Central Texas Coll (TX)
Central Wyoming Coll (WY)
Century Coll (MN)
Cerritos Coll (CA)
Citrus Coll (CA)
Cochise County Comm Coll District (AZ)
Coll of Central Florida (FL)
Coll of Marin (CA)
Coll of The Albemarle (NC)
Coll of the Canyons (CA)
Coll of the Desert (CA)
Collin County Comm Coll District (TX)
Comm Coll of Allegheny County (PA)
Comm Coll of Philadelphia (PA)
Comm Coll of Rhode Island (RI)
Crowder Coll (MO)
De Anza Coll (CA)
Del Mar Coll (TX)
Dodge City Comm Coll (KS)
East Central Coll (MO)
Eastern Arizona Coll (AZ)
Eastern Wyoming Coll (WY)
Elgin Comm Coll (IL)
El Paso Comm Coll (TX)
Finger Lakes Comm Coll (NY)
Fullerton Coll (CA)
Georgia Highlands Coll (GA)
Golden West Coll (CA)
Gordon State Coll (GA)
Grand Rapids Comm Coll (MI)
Harford Comm Coll (MD)
Harper Coll (IL)
Hill Coll (TX)
Holyoke Comm Coll (MA)
Howard Comm Coll (MD)
Imperial Valley Coll (CA)
Jamestown Comm Coll (NY)
Kaskaskia Coll (IL)
Kingsborough Comm Coll of the City U of New York (NY)
Lansing Comm Coll (MI)
Laramie County Comm Coll (WY)
Lincoln Coll (IL)
Lone Star Coll–CyFair (TX)
Lone Star Coll–Kingwood (TX)
Lone Star Coll–Montgomery (TX)
Lone Star Coll–North Harris (TX)
Lone Star Coll–Tomball (TX)
Los Angeles City Coll (CA)
Manchester Comm Coll (CT)
McHenry County Coll (IL)
McLennan Comm Coll (TX)
Merced Coll (CA)
Mercer County Comm Coll (NJ)
Mesa Comm Coll (AZ)
Miami Dade Coll (FL)
Minnesota State Comm and Tech Coll (MN)
Monroe Comm Coll (NY)
Morton Coll (IL)
Mountain View Coll (TX)
Mt. San Antonio Coll (CA)
Nashville State Comm Coll (TN)
Navarro Coll (TX)
New Mexico Jr Coll (NM)
Niagara County Comm Coll (NY)
Northeastern Jr Coll (CO)
Northern Essex Comm Coll (MA)
Northwest Coll (WY)
Oakton Comm Coll (IL)
Oklahoma City Comm Coll (OK)
Orange Coast Coll (CA)
Palomar Coll (CA)
Panola Coll (TX)
Paris Jr Coll (TX)
Pensacola State Coll (FL)
Quinsigamond Comm Coll (MA)
Raritan Valley Comm Coll (NJ)
Rend Lake Coll (IL)
St. Philip's Coll (TX)
Salt Lake Comm Coll (UT)
San Jacinto Coll District (TX)
San Joaquin Delta Coll (CA)
Santa Monica Coll (CA)
Sierra Coll (CA)
South Florida State Coll (FL)
South Plains Coll (TX)
Texarkana Coll (TX)
Tidewater Comm Coll (VA)
Trinity Valley Comm Coll (TX)
Truckee Meadows Comm Coll (NV)
Tyler Jr Coll (TX)
Ulster County Comm Coll (NY)
Vincennes U (IN)
Western Wyoming Comm Coll (WY)

MUSICAL INSTRUMENT FABRICATION AND REPAIR
Queensborough Comm Coll of the City U of New York (NY)
Renton Tech Coll (WA)

MUSICAL THEATER
Casper Coll (WY)
Coll of the Canyons (CA)

MUSIC HISTORY, LITERATURE, AND THEORY
South Florida State Coll (FL)

MUSIC MANAGEMENT
Austin Comm Coll District (TX)
Chandler-Gilbert Comm Coll (AZ)
Collin County Comm Coll District (TX)
Georgia Highlands Coll (GA)
Harrisburg Area Comm Coll (PA)
Houston Comm Coll (TX)
Mesa Comm Coll (AZ)
Northeast Comm Coll (NE)

MUSIC PERFORMANCE
Adirondack Comm Coll (NY)
Casper Coll (WY)
Comm Coll of the Air Force (AL)
Houston Comm Coll (TX)
Lansing Comm Coll (MI)
Macomb Comm Coll (MI)
Miami Dade Coll (FL)
Nassau Comm Coll (NY)
Northeast Comm Coll (NE)
South Florida State Coll (FL)
Truckee Meadows Comm Coll (NV)
Volunteer State Comm Coll (TN)
Walters State Comm Coll (TN)

MUSIC RELATED
Cayuga County Comm Coll (NY)
County Coll of Morris (NJ)
Santa Rosa Jr Coll (CA)
Westmoreland County Comm Coll (PA)

MUSIC TEACHER EDUCATION
Amarillo Coll (TX)
Casper Coll (WY)
Coll of Central Florida (FL)
Del Mar Coll (TX)
Dodge City Comm Coll (KS)
Eastern Wyoming Coll (WY)
Grand Rapids Comm Coll (MI)
Miami Dade Coll (FL)
Northeast Comm Coll (NE)
Pensacola State Coll (FL)
South Florida State Coll (FL)
Vincennes U (IN)

MUSIC TECHNOLOGY
Arapahoe Comm Coll (CO)
Gulf Coast State Coll (FL)
Miami Dade Coll (FL)
Mott Comm Coll (MI)

MUSIC THEORY AND COMPOSITION
Houston Comm Coll (TX)
South Florida State Coll (FL)

MUSIC THERAPY
South Florida State Coll (FL)

NANOTECHNOLOGY
Chippewa Valley Tech Coll (WI)
Erie Comm Coll, North Campus (NY)
Genesee Comm Coll (NY)
Harper Coll (IL)
Lehigh Carbon Comm Coll (PA)

NATURAL RESOURCES AND CONSERVATION RELATED
Murray State Coll (OK)
Southwestern Indian Polytechnic Inst (NM)

NATURAL RESOURCES/ CONSERVATION
American Samoa Comm Coll (AS)
Central Oregon Comm Coll (OR)
Coll of the Desert (CA)
Dakota Coll at Bottineau (ND)
Feather River Coll (CA)
Finger Lakes Comm Coll (NY)
Fox Valley Tech Coll (WI)
Niagara County Comm Coll (NY)
Santa Rosa Jr Coll (CA)
Treasure Valley Comm Coll (OR)
Truckee Meadows Comm Coll (NV)
Ulster County Comm Coll (NY)
Vincennes U (IN)

NATURAL RESOURCES LAW ENFORCEMENT AND PROTECTIVE SERVICES
Finger Lakes Comm Coll (NY)

NATURAL RESOURCES MANAGEMENT AND POLICY
Aaniiih Nakoda Coll (MT)
Finger Lakes Comm Coll (NY)
Hawkeye Comm Coll (IA)
Hutchinson Comm Coll (KS)
Northwest Coll (WY)
The Ohio State U Ag Tech Inst (OH)
Pensacola State Coll (FL)
San Joaquin Delta Coll (CA)
Spoon River Coll (IL)

NATURAL RESOURCES MANAGEMENT AND POLICY RELATED
Finger Lakes Comm Coll (NY)
Great Basin Coll (NV)
The Ohio State U Ag Tech Inst (OH)

NATURAL SCIENCES
Amarillo Coll (TX)
Bossier Parish Comm Coll (LA)
Citrus Coll (CA)
Golden West Coll (CA)
Miami Dade Coll (FL)
Northeastern Jr Coll (CO)
San Joaquin Delta Coll (CA)
Santa Rosa Jr Coll (CA)
Sisseton-Wahpeton Coll (SD)
Tyler Jr Coll (TX)
U of Pittsburgh at Titusville (PA)

NETWORK AND SYSTEM ADMINISTRATION
Bucks County Comm Coll (PA)
Cañada Coll (CA)
Central Maine Comm Coll (ME)
The Coll of Westchester (NY)
Collin County Comm Coll District (TX)
Dakota Coll at Bottineau (ND)
Del Mar Coll (TX)
Florida SouthWestern State Coll (FL)
Genesee Comm Coll (NY)
Gulf Coast State Coll (FL)
Hillsborough Comm Coll (FL)
Houston Comm Coll (TX)
Illinois Valley Comm Coll (IL)
Ivy Tech Comm Coll–Bloomington (IN)
Ivy Tech Comm Coll–Central Indiana (IN)
Ivy Tech Comm Coll–East Central (IN)
Ivy Tech Comm Coll–Kokomo (IN)
Ivy Tech Comm Coll–Richmond (IN)
Ivy Tech Comm Coll–Sellersburg (IN)
Ivy Tech Comm Coll–Southeast (IN)
Ivy Tech Comm Coll–Southwest (IN)
Ivy Tech Comm Coll–Wabash Valley (IN)
Kaskaskia Coll (IL)
Kishwaukee Coll (IL)
Lake Superior Coll (MN)
Manhattan Area Tech Coll (KS)
Massachusetts Bay Comm Coll (MA)
Miami Dade Coll (FL)
Minnesota State Comm and Tech Coll–Wadena (MN)
Mitchell Tech Inst (SD)
Montgomery County Comm Coll (PA)
Pittsburgh Tech Coll (PA)
Rio Salado Coll (AZ)
Seminole State Coll of Florida (FL)
Sierra Coll (CA)
Southeast Comm Coll, Lincoln Campus (NE)
Southeast Comm Coll, Milford Campus (NE)
South Florida State Coll (FL)
Texas State Tech Coll (TX)
York County Comm Coll (ME)

NEUROSCIENCE
Bucks County Comm Coll (PA)

NONPROFIT MANAGEMENT
Miami Dade Coll (FL)

NUCLEAR ENGINEERING
South Florida State Coll (FL)

NUCLEAR ENGINEERING TECHNOLOGY
Bismarck State Coll (ND)

NUCLEAR MEDICAL TECHNOLOGY
Amarillo Coll (TX)
Caldwell Comm Coll and Tech Inst (NC)
Comm Coll of Allegheny County (PA)
Comm Coll of the Air Force (AL)
Del Mar Coll (TX)
Frederick Comm Coll (MD)
Gulf Coast State Coll (FL)
Harrisburg Area Comm Coll (PA)
Hillsborough Comm Coll (FL)
Houston Comm Coll (TX)
Howard Comm Coll (MD)
Lakeland Comm Coll (OH)
Maine Coll of Health Professions (ME)
Miami Dade Coll (FL)
Vincennes U (IN)

NUCLEAR/NUCLEAR POWER TECHNOLOGY
Allen Comm Coll (KS)
Cape Fear Comm Coll (NC)
Texas State Tech Coll (TX)
Three Rivers Comm Coll (CT)

NURSING ADMINISTRATION
Paris Jr Coll (TX)
South Suburban Coll (IL)

NURSING ASSISTANT/AIDE AND PATIENT CARE ASSISTANT/AIDE
Allen Comm Coll (KS)
Central New Mexico Comm Coll (NM)
Coconino Comm Coll (AZ)
Comm Coll of Allegheny County (PA)
Lake Superior Coll (MN)
Morgan Comm Coll (CO)
Pensacola State Coll (FL)
Salina Area Tech Coll (KS)
Tallahassee Comm Coll (FL)
Western Wyoming Comm Coll (WY)

NURSING PRACTICE
Genesee Comm Coll (NY)
Minnesota State Comm and Tech Coll–Detroit Lakes (MN)
Minnesota State Comm and Tech Coll–Moorhead (MN)
Minnesota State Comm and Tech Coll–Wadena (MN)
Nashville State Comm Coll (TN)

NUTRITION SCIENCES
Casper Coll (WY)
Santa Rosa Jr Coll (CA)
Sisseton-Wahpeton Coll (SD)

OCCUPATIONAL HEALTH AND INDUSTRIAL HYGIENE
Niagara County Comm Coll (NY)

OCCUPATIONAL SAFETY AND HEALTH TECHNOLOGY
Anne Arundel Comm Coll (MD)
Coastal Pines Tech Coll (GA)
Comm Coll of Baltimore County (MD)
Comm Coll of the Air Force (AL)
Del Mar Coll (TX)
Houston Comm Coll (TX)
Ivy Tech Comm Coll–Central Indiana (IN)
Ivy Tech Comm Coll–Northwest (IN)
Ivy Tech Comm Coll–Wabash Valley (IN)
Lanier Tech Coll (GA)
Mt. San Antonio Coll (CA)
NorthWest Arkansas Comm Coll (AR)
San Jacinto Coll District (TX)
San Juan Coll (NM)
Texas State Tech Coll (TX)
Three Rivers Comm Coll (MO)
Westmoreland County Comm Coll (PA)

OCCUPATIONAL THERAPIST ASSISTANT
Anoka Tech Coll (MN)
Augusta Tech Coll (GA)
Austin Comm Coll District (TX)
Bossier Parish Comm Coll (LA)
Cape Fear Comm Coll (NC)
Casper Coll (WY)
Cayuga County Comm Coll (NY)
Comm Coll of Allegheny County (PA)
Comm Coll of Rhode Island (RI)

County Coll of Morris (NJ)
Crowder Coll (MO)
Daytona State Coll (FL)
Del Mar Coll (TX)
East Central Coll (MO)
Erie Comm Coll, North Campus (NY)
Fiorello H. LaGuardia Comm Coll of the City U of New York (NY)
Fox Valley Tech Coll (WI)
Greenville Tech Coll (SC)
Hawkeye Comm Coll (IA)
Houston Comm Coll (TX)
Illinois Central Coll (IL)
Jamestown Comm Coll (NY)
Kaskaskia Coll (IL)
Kent State U at Ashtabula (OH)
Kent State U at East Liverpool (OH)
Lake Area Tech Inst (SD)
Lehigh Carbon Comm Coll (PA)
Lorain County Comm Coll (OH)
Macomb Comm Coll (MI)
Manchester Comm Coll (CT)
McHenry County Coll (IL)
Mott Comm Coll (MI)
Murray State Coll (OK)
Nashville State Comm Coll (TN)
Northland Comm and Tech Coll (MN)
Ozarks Tech Comm Coll (MO)
Panola Coll (TX)
Penn State DuBois (PA)
Penn State Mont Alto (PA)
Pueblo Comm Coll (CO)
Quinsigamond Comm Coll (MA)
Rend Lake Coll (IL)
St. Charles Comm Coll (MO)
St. Philip's Coll (TX)
Salt Lake Comm Coll (UT)
San Juan Coll (NM)
Shawnee Comm Coll (IL)
South Suburban Coll (IL)
Springfield Tech Comm Coll (MA)
Three Rivers Comm Coll (MO)
Tyler Jr Coll (TX)
Walters State Comm Coll (TN)
Weatherford Coll (TX)
Wisconsin Indianhead Tech Coll (WI)
Wor-Wic Comm Coll (MD)

OCCUPATIONAL THERAPY
Amarillo Coll (TX)
Coll of Central Florida (FL)
Comm Coll of Baltimore County (MD)
Iowa Central Comm Coll (IA)
Lone Star Coll–Kingwood (TX)
Madison Area Tech Coll (WI)
Nashville State Comm Coll (TN)
Navarro Coll (TX)
North Shore Comm Coll (MA)
Oklahoma City Comm Coll (OK)
Ozarks Tech Comm Coll (MO)
San Jacinto Coll District (TX)
South Florida State Coll (FL)
Stark State Coll (OH)
Trident Tech Coll (SC)

OCEAN ENGINEERING
South Florida State Coll (FL)

OCEANOGRAPHY (CHEMICAL AND PHYSICAL)
Cape Fear Comm Coll (NC)

OFFICE MANAGEMENT
Alexandria Tech and Comm Coll (MN)
Anoka Tech Coll (MN)
Brookhaven Coll (TX)
Carteret Comm Coll (NC)
Cecil Coll (MD)
Coll of Central Florida (FL)
Coll of Marin (CA)
Coll of the Desert (CA)
Comm Coll of Allegheny County (PA)
Comm Coll of Aurora (CO)
Comm Coll of the Air Force (AL)
Craven Comm Coll (NC)
Dakota Coll at Bottineau (ND)
Des Moines Area Comm Coll (IA)
Eastern Wyoming Coll (WY)
Erie Comm Coll, North Campus (NY)
Fayetteville Tech Comm Coll (NC)
Fox Valley Tech Coll (WI)
Guam Comm Coll (GU)
Gulf Coast State Coll (FL)
Halifax Comm Coll (NC)
Howard Comm Coll (MD)
Jamestown Business Coll (NY)
Jefferson Comm Coll (NY)
Jefferson State Comm Coll (AL)

Johnston Comm Coll (NC)
Lake Superior Coll (MN)
Lansing Comm Coll (MI)
Lenoir Comm Coll (NC)
Merced Coll (CA)
Miami Dade Coll (FL)
Minnesota State Comm and Tech Coll (MN)
Minnesota State Comm and Tech Coll–Detroit Lakes (MN)
Minnesota State Comm and Tech Coll–Moorhead (MN)
Minnesota State Comm and Tech Coll–Wadena (MN)
Mitchell Comm Coll (NC)
Montgomery Comm Coll (NC)
Piedmont Comm Coll (NC)
Renton Tech Coll (WA)
Richmond Comm Coll (NC)
Rockingham Comm Coll (NC)
Rowan-Cabarrus Comm Coll (NC)
St. Charles Comm Coll (MO)
St. Clair County Comm Coll (MI)
Santa Monica Coll (CA)
Southern Arkansas U Tech (AR)
South Florida State Coll (FL)
South Suburban Coll (IL)
Tallahassee Comm Coll (FL)
Three Rivers Comm Coll (MO)
Treasure Valley Comm Coll (OR)
Waukesha County Tech Coll (WI)
Wayne County Comm Coll District (MI)
White Mountains Comm Coll (NH)
Wisconsin Indianhead Tech Coll (WI)

OFFICE OCCUPATIONS AND CLERICAL SERVICES
Alamance Comm Coll (NC)
Alvin Comm Coll (TX)
American Samoa Comm Coll (AS)
Caldwell Comm Coll and Tech Inst (NC)
Cloud County Comm Coll (KS)
Dakota Coll at Bottineau (ND)
Del Mar Coll (TX)
Gateway Comm and Tech Coll (KY)
Great Basin Coll (NV)
IBMC Coll, Fort Collins (CO)
ITI Tech Coll (LA)
Jefferson Comm Coll (NY)
Lake Superior Coll (MN)
Lone Star Coll–CyFair (TX)
Middlesex Comm Coll (MA)
Northeast Comm Coll (NE)

OPERATIONS MANAGEMENT
Blue Ridge Comm and Tech Coll (WV)
Bunker Hill Comm Coll (MA)
Chippewa Valley Tech Coll (WI)
Fayetteville Tech Comm Coll (NC)
Georgia Piedmont Tech Coll (GA)
Great Basin Coll (NV)
Hillsborough Comm Coll (FL)
Lenoir Comm Coll (NC)
Macomb Comm Coll (MI)
McHenry County Coll (IL)
Miami Dade Coll (FL)
Mitchell Comm Coll (NC)
Mohawk Valley Comm Coll (NY)
Northcentral Tech Coll (WI)
Oakton Comm Coll (IL)
South Florida State Coll (FL)
Stark State Coll (OH)

OPHTHALMIC AND OPTOMETRIC SUPPORT SERVICES AND ALLIED PROFESSIONS RELATED
Vincennes U (IN)

OPHTHALMIC LABORATORY TECHNOLOGY
Comm Coll of the Air Force (AL)
Georgia Piedmont Tech Coll (GA)

OPHTHALMIC TECHNOLOGY
Lakeland Comm Coll (OH)
Miami Dade Coll (FL)
Renton Tech Coll (WA)
Volunteer State Comm Coll (TN)

OPTICIANRY
Camden County Coll (NJ)
Central New Mexico Comm Coll (NM)
Comm Coll of Rhode Island (RI)
El Paso Comm Coll (TX)
Erie Comm Coll, North Campus (NY)

Florida SouthWestern State Coll (FL)
Georgia Piedmont Tech Coll (GA)
Hillsborough Comm Coll (FL)
J. Sargeant Reynolds Comm Coll (VA)
Miami Dade Coll (FL)
Ogeechee Tech Coll (GA)
Raritan Valley Comm Coll (NJ)
Southwestern Indian Polytechnic Inst (NM)

OPTOMETRIC TECHNICIAN
El Paso Comm Coll (TX)
Hillsborough Comm Coll (FL)
Raritan Valley Comm Coll (NJ)
San Jacinto Coll District (TX)

ORGANIZATIONAL BEHAVIOR
Chandler-Gilbert Comm Coll (AZ)
Mesa Comm Coll (AZ)
U of Cincinnati Clermont Coll (OH)

ORGANIZATIONAL LEADERSHIP
Lake Superior Coll (MN)
Olympic Coll (WA)

ORNAMENTAL HORTICULTURE
Comm Coll of Allegheny County (PA)
Dakota Coll at Bottineau (ND)
Finger Lakes Comm Coll (NY)
Golden West Coll (CA)
Gwinnett Tech Coll (GA)
Kishwaukee Coll (IL)
Mercer County Comm Coll (NJ)
Mesa Comm Coll (AZ)
Metropolitan Comm Coll (NE)
Miami Dade Coll (FL)
Mt. San Antonio Coll (CA)
Pensacola State Coll (FL)
San Joaquin Delta Coll (CA)
Walters State Comm Coll (TN)

ORTHOTICS/PROSTHETICS
Century Coll (MN)
Oklahoma State U Inst of Technology (OK)

PAINTING
Luzerne County Comm Coll (PA)

PAINTING AND WALL COVERING
Ivy Tech Comm Coll–Central Indiana (IN)
Ivy Tech Comm Coll–East Central (IN)
Ivy Tech Comm Coll–Lafayette (IN)
Ivy Tech Comm Coll–North Central (IN)
Ivy Tech Comm Coll–Northeast (IN)
Ivy Tech Comm Coll–Northwest (IN)
Ivy Tech Comm Coll–Southwest (IN)
Ivy Tech Comm Coll–Wabash Valley (IN)

PARKS, RECREATION AND LEISURE
Central Wyoming Coll (WY)
Coll of Central Florida (FL)
Coll of the Canyons (CA)
Comm Coll of the Air Force (AL)
Dakota Coll at Bottineau (ND)
Del Mar Coll (TX)
Feather River Coll (CA)
Florida Keys Comm Coll (FL)
Fullerton Coll (CA)
Kingsborough Comm Coll of the City U of New York (NY)
Madison Area Tech Coll (WI)
Mesa Comm Coll (AZ)
Miami Dade Coll (FL)
Monroe Comm Coll (NY)
Mt. San Antonio Coll (CA)
Niagara County Comm Coll (NY)
Northern Essex Comm Coll (MA)
Northwest Coll (WY)
Norwalk Comm Coll (CT)
Palomar Coll (CA)
San Juan Coll (NM)
Santa Fe Comm Coll (NM)
Sierra Coll (CA)
Sullivan County Comm Coll (NY)
Tompkins Cortland Comm Coll (NY)
Vincennes U (IN)

PARKS, RECREATION AND LEISURE FACILITIES MANAGEMENT
Adirondack Comm Coll (NY)

Allen Comm Coll (KS)
Arizona Western Coll (AZ)
Augusta Tech Coll (GA)
Central Wyoming Coll (WY)
Chattahoochee Tech Coll (GA)
Coll of the Desert (CA)
Dakota Coll at Bottineau (ND)
Mohawk Valley Comm Coll (NY)
Mt. San Antonio Coll (CA)
North Georgia Tech Coll (GA)
Santa Rosa Jr Coll (CA)
South Florida State Coll (FL)
Tompkins Cortland Comm Coll (NY)
Ulster County Comm Coll (NY)

PARKS, RECREATION, LEISURE, AND FITNESS STUDIES RELATED
Comm Coll of Baltimore County (MD)
Dakota Coll at Bottineau (ND)
Genesee Comm Coll (NY)
Southwestern Comm Coll (NC)

PASTORAL STUDIES/ COUNSELING
Hesston Coll (KS)

PEACE STUDIES AND CONFLICT RESOLUTION
Delta Coll (MI)

PERIOPERATIVE/OPERATING ROOM AND SURGICAL NURSING
Comm Coll of Allegheny County (PA)

PERSONAL AND CULINARY SERVICES RELATED
Mohave Comm Coll (AZ)

PETROLEUM TECHNOLOGY
Bismarck State Coll (ND)
Bossier Parish Comm Coll (LA)
Houston Comm Coll (TX)
Lackawanna Coll (PA)
New Mexico Jr Coll (NM)
Oklahoma State U Inst of Technology (OK)
Panola Coll (TX)
Rend Lake Coll (IL)
South Plains Coll (TX)
U of Arkansas Comm Coll at Morrilton (AR)
Westmoreland County Comm Coll (PA)
Williston State Coll (ND)

PHARMACY
Cerritos Coll (CA)
Navarro Coll (TX)
South Florida State Coll (FL)

PHARMACY TECHNICIAN
Albany Tech Coll (GA)
Alvin Comm Coll (TX)
Anoka-Ramsey Comm Coll (MN)
Augusta Tech Coll (GA)
Austin Comm Coll District (TX)
Bossier Parish Comm Coll (LA)
Casper Coll (WY)
Columbus Tech Coll (GA)
Comm Care Coll (OK)
Comm Coll of Allegheny County (PA)
Comm Coll of the Air Force (AL)
Eastern Arizona Coll (AZ)
El Paso Comm Coll (TX)
Fayetteville Tech Comm Coll (NC)
Humacao Comm Coll (PR)
Hutchinson Comm Coll (KS)
J. Sargeant Reynolds Comm Coll (VA)
Lone Star Coll–North Harris (TX)
Miami Dade Coll (FL)
Minnesota State Comm and Tech Coll (MN)
Mohave Comm Coll (AZ)
Northland Comm and Tech Coll (MN)
Pennsylvania Inst of Technology (PA)
Pensacola State Coll (FL)
Renton Tech Coll (WA)
San Jacinto Coll District (TX)
Santa Rosa Jr Coll (CA)
Southeastern Coll–West Palm Beach (FL)
Southern Crescent Tech Coll (GA)
Tallahassee Comm Coll (FL)
Texarkana Coll (TX)
Ultimate Medical Academy Online (FL)
Vincennes U (IN)
Wayne County Comm Coll District (MI)

Weatherford Coll (TX)
Western Dakota Tech Inst (SD)
West Georgia Tech Coll (GA)
West Virginia Jr Coll–Bridgeport (WV)

PHILOSOPHY
Allen Comm Coll (KS)
Arizona Western Coll (AZ)
Austin Comm Coll District (TX)
Blinn Coll (TX)
Cañada Coll (CA)
Cerritos Coll (CA)
Cochise County Comm Coll District (AZ)
Coll of Central Florida (FL)
Coll of the Canyons (CA)
Coll of the Desert (CA)
De Anza Coll (CA)
Fiorello H. LaGuardia Comm Coll of the City U of New York (NY)
Fullerton Coll (CA)
Georgia Highlands Coll (GA)
Harford Comm Coll (MD)
Harper Coll (IL)
Harrisburg Area Comm Coll (PA)
Hill Coll (TX)
Lansing Comm Coll (MI)
Merced Coll (CA)
Miami Dade Coll (FL)
Nashville State Comm Coll (TN)
Northeastern Jr Coll (CO)
Oklahoma City Comm Coll (OK)
Orange Coast Coll (CA)
Pensacola State Coll (FL)
San Jacinto Coll District (TX)
San Joaquin Delta Coll (CA)
Santa Rosa Jr Coll (CA)
Sierra Coll (CA)
South Florida State Coll (FL)
Truckee Meadows Comm Coll (NV)
Vincennes U (IN)

PHILOSOPHY AND RELIGIOUS STUDIES RELATED
Edison State Comm Coll (OH)
South Florida State Coll (FL)

PHLEBOTOMY TECHNOLOGY
Coconino Comm Coll (AZ)
Lake Superior Coll (MN)
Miami Dade Coll (FL)
Wayne County Comm Coll District (MI)
Westmoreland County Comm Coll (PA)

PHOTOGRAPHIC AND FILM/ VIDEO TECHNOLOGY
Austin Comm Coll District (TX)
Carteret Comm Coll (NC)
Daytona State Coll (FL)
Eastern Arizona Coll (AZ)
Hinds Comm Coll (MS)
Miami Dade Coll (FL)
Oklahoma City Comm Coll (OK)
Olympic Coll (WA)
Orange Coast Coll (CA)
Palomar Coll (CA)
Randolph Comm Coll (NC)
Salt Lake Comm Coll (UT)
Santa Monica Coll (CA)
Tompkins Cortland Comm Coll (NY)
U of Cincinnati Blue Ash Coll (OH)

PHOTOGRAPHY
Amarillo Coll (TX)
Casper Coll (WY)
Cecil Coll (MD)
Cerritos Coll (CA)
Citrus Coll (CA)
Coll of the Canyons (CA)
Comm Coll of Philadelphia (PA)
County Coll of Morris (NJ)
Dakota Coll at Bottineau (ND)
De Anza Coll (CA)
Gwinnett Tech Coll (GA)
Harford Comm Coll (MD)
Harrisburg Area Comm Coll (PA)
Howard Comm Coll (MD)
Lansing Comm Coll (MI)
Los Angeles City Coll (CA)
Luzerne County Comm Coll (PA)
Madison Area Tech Coll (WI)
Merced Coll (CA)
Mercer County Comm Coll (NJ)
Metropolitan Comm Coll (NE)
Miami Dade Coll (FL)
Mott Comm Coll (MI)
Mt. San Antonio Coll (CA)
Nashville State Comm Coll (TN)
Nassau Comm Coll (NY)

Oklahoma State U Inst of Technology (OK)
Orange Coast Coll (CA)
Pensacola State Coll (FL)
San Joaquin Delta Coll (CA)
Santa Fe Comm Coll (NM)
Scottsdale Comm Coll (AZ)
Sullivan County Comm Coll (NY)
Western Wyoming Comm Coll (WY)

PHOTOJOURNALISM
Randolph Comm Coll (NC)
Vincennes U (IN)

PHYSICAL EDUCATION TEACHING AND COACHING
Alvin Comm Coll (TX)
Amarillo Coll (TX)
Blinn Coll (TX)
Bucks County Comm Coll (PA)
Carl Albert State Coll (OK)
Casper Coll (WY)
Cerritos Coll (CA)
Citrus Coll (CA)
Clinton Comm Coll (NY)
Coll of Central Florida (FL)
Crowder Coll (MO)
De Anza Coll (CA)
Del Mar Coll (TX)
Dodge City Comm Coll (KS)
Dutchess Comm Coll (NY)
Eastern Wyoming Coll (WY)
Finger Lakes Comm Coll (NY)
Genesee Comm Coll (NY)
Grand Rapids Comm Coll (MI)
Harper Coll (IL)
Imperial Valley Coll (CA)
Laramie County Comm Coll (WY)
Luzerne County Comm Coll (PA)
McLennan Comm Coll (TX)
Miami Dade Coll (FL)
Monroe Comm Coll (NY)
Montgomery County Comm Coll (PA)
Murray State Coll (OK)
Navarro Coll (TX)
New Mexico Jr Coll (NM)
Niagara County Comm Coll (NY)
Northeastern Jr Coll (CO)
Northern Essex Comm Coll (MA)
Panola Coll (TX)
San Joaquin Delta Coll (CA)
Seminole State Coll (OK)
South Plains Coll (TX)
Trinity Valley Comm Coll (TX)
Tyler Jr Coll (TX)
Vincennes U (IN)

PHYSICAL FITNESS TECHNICIAN
Alexandria Tech and Comm Coll (MN)
Anoka-Ramsey Comm Coll (MN)
Central Maine Comm Coll (ME)
Lake Region State Coll (ND)
Orange Coast Coll (CA)
Schoolcraft Coll (MI)
Tallahassee Comm Coll (FL)

PHYSICAL SCIENCES
Alvin Comm Coll (TX)
Amarillo Coll (TX)
Borough of Manhattan Comm Coll of the City U of New York (NY)
Carl Albert State Coll (OK)
Central Oregon Comm Coll (OR)
Central Wyoming Coll (WY)
Chandler-Gilbert Comm Coll (AZ)
Citrus Coll (CA)
Coll of Marin (CA)
Crowder Coll (MO)
Dakota Coll at Bottineau (ND)
Dodge City Comm Coll (KS)
Feather River Coll (CA)
Golden West Coll (CA)
Harper Coll (IL)
Harrisburg Area Comm Coll (PA)
Howard Comm Coll (MD)
Hutchinson Comm Coll (KS)
Imperial Valley Coll (CA)
Lehigh Carbon Comm Coll (PA)
Mesa Comm Coll (AZ)
Miami Dade Coll (FL)
Middlesex Comm Coll (MA)
Middlesex County Coll (NJ)
Montgomery County Comm Coll (PA)
Navarro Coll (TX)
Northeastern Jr Coll (CO)
Olympic Coll (WA)
Ozarks Tech Comm Coll (MO)
Paris Jr Coll (TX)
Queensborough Comm Coll of the City U of New York (NY)

Salt Lake Comm Coll (UT)
San Jacinto Coll District (TX)
San Joaquin Delta Coll (CA)
San Juan Coll (NM)
Santa Fe Comm Coll (NM)
Seminole State Coll (OK)
Trinity Valley Comm Coll (TX)
Vincennes U (IN)
Western Nevada Coll (NV)

PHYSICAL SCIENCES RELATED
Cerritos Coll (CA)
Dakota Coll at Bottineau (ND)
Mt. San Antonio Coll (CA)
Naugatuck Valley Comm Coll (CT)

PHYSICAL THERAPY
Allen Comm Coll (KS)
Amarillo Coll (TX)
Athens Tech Coll (GA)
Bossier Parish Comm Coll (LA)
Central Oregon Comm Coll (OR)
Cerritos Coll (CA)
Chesapeake Coll (MD)
Coll of Central Florida (FL)
Daytona State Coll (FL)
De Anza Coll (CA)
Dodge City Comm Coll (KS)
Genesee Comm Coll (NY)
Gwinnett Tech Coll (GA)
Hill Coll (TX)
Housatonic Comm Coll (CT)
Iowa Central Comm Coll (IA)
Kingsborough Comm Coll of the City U of New York (NY)
McLennan Comm Coll (TX)
Monroe County Comm Coll (MI)
Morton Coll (IL)
NorthWest Arkansas Comm Coll (AR)
Oklahoma City Comm Coll (OK)
Seminole State Coll of Florida (FL)
South Plains Coll (TX)
Stark State Coll (OH)
Tarrant County Coll District (TX)
Trident Tech Coll (SC)
Wytheville Comm Coll (VA)

PHYSICAL THERAPY TECHNOLOGY
Anne Arundel Comm Coll (MD)
Anoka-Ramsey Comm Coll (MN)
Arapahoe Comm Coll (CO)
Austin Comm Coll District (TX)
Berkshire Comm Coll (MA)
Blackhawk Tech Coll (WI)
Blinn Coll (TX)
Blue Ridge Comm and Tech Coll (WV)
Bossier Parish Comm Coll (LA)
Caldwell Comm Coll and Tech Inst (NC)
Carl Albert State Coll (OK)
Carroll Comm Coll (MD)
Central New Mexico Comm Coll (NM)
Chesapeake Coll (MD)
Chippewa Valley Tech Coll (WI)
Coll of Central Florida (FL)
Comm Coll of Allegheny County (PA)
Comm Coll of Rhode Island (RI)
Comm Coll of the Air Force (AL)
Craven Comm Coll (NC)
Delta Coll (MI)
Edison State Comm Coll (OH)
Elgin Comm Coll (IL)
El Paso Comm Coll (TX)
Fayetteville Tech Comm Coll (NC)
Fiorello H. LaGuardia Comm Coll of the City U of New York (NY)
Florida SouthWestern State Coll (FL)
Gateway Tech Coll (WI)
Genesee Comm Coll (NY)
Great Falls Coll Montana State U (MT)
Greenville Tech Coll (SC)
Gulf Coast State Coll (FL)
Gwinnett Tech Coll (GA)
Hawkeye Comm Coll (IA)
Hinds Comm Coll (MS)
Houston Comm Coll (TX)
Howard Comm Coll (MD)
Hutchinson Comm Coll (KS)
Illinois Central Coll (IL)
Ivy Tech Comm Coll–East Central (IN)
Ivy Tech Comm Coll–Kokomo (IN)
Ivy Tech Comm Coll–Sellersburg (IN)
Jefferson State Comm Coll (AL)
Kaskaskia Coll (IL)
Kellogg Comm Coll (MI)
Kent State U at Ashtabula (OH)
Kent State U at East Liverpool (OH)

Kingsborough Comm Coll of the City U of New York (NY)
Lake Area Tech Inst (SD)
Lake Superior Coll (MN)
Laramie County Comm Coll (WY)
Lehigh Carbon Comm Coll (PA)
Lone Star Coll–Montgomery (TX)
Lorain County Comm Coll (OH)
Macomb Comm Coll (MI)
Manchester Comm Coll (CT)
Mercer County Comm Coll (NJ)
Miami Dade Coll (FL)
Mohave Comm Coll (AZ)
Montgomery Coll (MD)
Montgomery County Comm Coll (PA)
Morgan Comm Coll (CO)
Morton Coll (IL)
Mott Comm Coll (MI)
Mount Wachusett Comm Coll (MA)
Murray State Coll (OK)
Nassau Comm Coll (NY)
Naugatuck Valley Comm Coll (CT)
Niagara County Comm Coll (NY)
Northeast Comm Coll (NE)
Northland Comm and Tech Coll (MN)
North Shore Comm Coll (MA)
Oakton Comm Coll (IL)
Olympic Coll (WA)
Ozarks Tech Comm Coll (MO)
Penn State DuBois (PA)
Penn State Mont Alto (PA)
Penn State Shenango (PA)
Pennsylvania Inst of Technology (PA)
Pensacola State Coll (FL)
Pueblo Comm Coll (CO)
Randolph Comm Coll (NC)
St. Philip's Coll (TX)
Salt Lake Comm Coll (UT)
San Jacinto Coll District (TX)
San Juan Coll (NM)
Somerset Comm Coll (KY)
Southeast Comm Coll, Lincoln Campus (NE)
Southern U at Shreveport (LA)
Southwestern Comm Coll (NC)
Springfield Tech Comm Coll (MA)
Three Rivers Comm Coll (MO)
Tyler Jr Coll (TX)
U of Cincinnati Clermont Coll (OH)
U of Pittsburgh at Titusville (PA)
Victoria Coll (TX)
Vincennes U (IN)
Volunteer State Comm Coll (TN)
Walters State Comm Coll (TN)
Waukesha County Tech Coll (WI)
Weatherford Coll (TX)
Wor-Wic Comm Coll (MD)

PHYSICIAN ASSISTANT
Miami Dade Coll (FL)
Wayne County Comm Coll District (MI)

PHYSICS
Allen Comm Coll (KS)
Amarillo Coll (TX)
Arizona Western Coll (AZ)
Austin Comm Coll District (TX)
Blinn Coll (TX)
Bunker Hill Comm Coll (MA)
Cañada Coll (CA)
Casper Coll (WY)
Cecil Coll (MD)
Central New Mexico Comm Coll (NM)
Cerritos Coll (CA)
Cochise County Comm Coll District (AZ)
Coll of Central Florida (FL)
Coll of Marin (CA)
Coll of the Canyons (CA)
Coll of the Desert (CA)
Comm Coll of Allegheny County (PA)
De Anza Coll (CA)
Del Mar Coll (TX)
Dodge City Comm Coll (KS)
Eastern Arizona Coll (AZ)
Finger Lakes Comm Coll (NY)
Fullerton Coll (CA)
Georgia Highlands Coll (GA)
Gordon State Coll (GA)
Harford Comm Coll (MD)
Hill Coll (TX)
Holyoke Comm Coll (MA)
Houston Comm Coll (TX)
Kingsborough Comm Coll of the City U of New York (NY)
Los Angeles City Coll (CA)
Merced Coll (CA)
Mercer County Comm Coll (NJ)
Miami Dade Coll (FL)
Monroe Comm Coll (NY)
Nashville State Comm Coll (TN)

Navarro Coll (TX)
Northampton Comm Coll (PA)
Northeast Comm Coll (NE)
Northwest Coll (WY)
Oklahoma City Comm Coll (OK)
Orange Coast Coll (CA)
Panola Coll (TX)
Paris Jr Coll (TX)
Pensacola State Coll (FL)
Salt Lake Comm Coll (UT)
San Jacinto Coll District (TX)
San Juan Coll (NM)
Santa Rosa Jr Coll (CA)
Sierra Coll (CA)
South Florida State Coll (FL)
Springfield Tech Comm Coll (MA)
Texarkana Coll (TX)
Truckee Meadows Comm Coll (NV)
Tyler Jr Coll (TX)

PHYSICS RELATED
South Florida State Coll (FL)

PHYSICS TEACHER EDUCATION
Anne Arundel Comm Coll (MD)
Chesapeake Coll (MD)
Comm Coll of Baltimore County (MD)
Harford Comm Coll (MD)
Montgomery Coll (MD)

PHYSIOLOGY
Comm Coll of the Air Force (AL)

PIPEFITTING AND SPRINKLER FITTING
Delta Coll (MI)
Ivy Tech Comm Coll–Bloomington (IN)
Ivy Tech Comm Coll–Central Indiana (IN)
Ivy Tech Comm Coll–Columbus (IN)
Ivy Tech Comm Coll–East Central (IN)
Ivy Tech Comm Coll–Lafayette (IN)
Ivy Tech Comm Coll–North Central (IN)
Ivy Tech Comm Coll–Northeast (IN)
Ivy Tech Comm Coll–Northwest (IN)
Ivy Tech Comm Coll–Richmond (IN)
Ivy Tech Comm Coll–Sellersburg (IN)
Ivy Tech Comm Coll–Wabash Valley (IN)
Kellogg Comm Coll (MI)
Miami Dade Coll (FL)
Northern Maine Comm Coll (ME)

PLANT NURSERY MANAGEMENT
Coll of Marin (CA)
Comm Coll of Allegheny County (PA)
Fullerton Coll (CA)
Miami Dade Coll (FL)
The Ohio State U Ag Tech Inst (OH)

PLANT PROTECTION AND INTEGRATED PEST MANAGEMENT
Hinds Comm Coll (MS)

PLANT SCIENCES
Mercer County Comm Coll (NJ)
South Florida State Coll (FL)

PLASTICS AND POLYMER ENGINEERING TECHNOLOGY
Cerritos Coll (CA)
Daytona State Coll (FL)
El Paso Comm Coll (TX)
Grand Rapids Comm Coll (MI)
Hennepin Tech Coll (MN)
Macomb Comm Coll (MI)
Mount Wachusett Comm Coll (MA)
West Georgia Tech Coll (GA)

PLATEMAKING/IMAGING
Illinois Central Coll (IL)

PLUMBING TECHNOLOGY
Arizona Western Coll (AZ)
Delta Coll (MI)
Hinds Comm Coll (MS)
Luzerne County Comm Coll (PA)
Macomb Comm Coll (MI)
Miami Dade Coll (FL)
Minnesota State Comm and Tech Coll (MN)
Minnesota State Comm and Tech Coll–Moorhead (MN)

Minnesota West Comm and Tech Coll (MN)
Northeast Iowa Comm Coll (IA)
Three Rivers Comm Coll (MO)

POLITICAL SCIENCE AND GOVERNMENT
Allen Comm Coll (KS)
American Samoa Comm Coll (AS)
Arizona Western Coll (AZ)
Austin Comm Coll District (TX)
Bainbridge State Coll (GA)
Cañada Coll (CA)
Casper Coll (WY)
Cerritos Coll (CA)
Coll of Marin (CA)
Coll of the Canyons (CA)
Coll of the Desert (CA)
De Anza Coll (CA)
Del Mar Coll (TX)
Dodge City Comm Coll (KS)
Eastern Arizona Coll (AZ)
Feather River Coll (CA)
Finger Lakes Comm Coll (NY)
Frederick Comm Coll (MD)
Fullerton Coll (CA)
Georgia Highlands Coll (GA)
Georgia Military Coll (GA)
Gordon State Coll (GA)
Harford Comm Coll (MD)
Hill Coll (TX)
Lansing Comm Coll (MI)
Laramie County Comm Coll (WY)
Miami Dade Coll (FL)
Monroe Comm Coll (NY)
Nashville State Comm Coll (TN)
Northeastern Jr Coll (CO)
Northern Essex Comm Coll (MA)
Northwest Coll (WY)
Oklahoma City Comm Coll (OK)
Orange Coast Coll (CA)
Otero Jr Coll (CO)
Paris Jr Coll (TX)
Salt Lake Comm Coll (UT)
San Jacinto Coll District (TX)
San Joaquin Delta Coll (CA)
Santa Monica Coll (CA)
Santa Rosa Jr Coll (CA)
South Florida State Coll (FL)
Texarkana Coll (TX)
Trinity Valley Comm Coll (TX)
Tyler Jr Coll (TX)
Vincennes U (IN)
Western Wyoming Comm Coll (WY)

POLYMER/PLASTICS ENGINEERING
Central Oregon Comm Coll (OR)

POLYSOMNOGRAPHY
Genesee Comm Coll (NY)
Lenoir Comm Coll (NC)

PORTUGUESE
Miami Dade Coll (FL)

POULTRY SCIENCE
Hinds Comm Coll (MS)

PRACTICAL NURSING, VOCATIONAL NURSING AND NURSING ASSISTANTS RELATED
Pennsylvania Inst of Technology (PA)
Westchester Comm Coll (NY)

PRECISION METAL WORKING RELATED
Delta Coll (MI)
Western Dakota Tech Inst (SD)

PRECISION PRODUCTION RELATED
Delta Coll (MI)
East Central Coll (MO)
Mott Comm Coll (MI)
St. Charles Comm Coll (MO)

PRE-DENTISTRY STUDIES
Allen Comm Coll (KS)
Casper Coll (WY)
Eastern Wyoming Coll (WY)
Hill Coll (TX)
Northeast Comm Coll (NE)
Panola Coll (TX)
Pensacola State Coll (FL)
St. Philip's Coll (TX)
Vincennes U (IN)
Western Wyoming Comm Coll (WY)

PRE-ENGINEERING
Alexandria Tech and Comm Coll (MN)
Amarillo Coll (TX)
Anoka-Ramsey Comm Coll (MN)
Central New Mexico Comm Coll (NM)
Century Coll (MN)
Cerritos Coll (CA)
Coll of the Canyons (CA)
Craven Comm Coll (NC)
Crowder Coll (MO)
De Anza Coll (CA)
Del Mar Coll (TX)
Dodge City Comm Coll (KS)
Fayetteville Tech Comm Coll (NC)
Finger Lakes Comm Coll (NY)
Gordon State Coll (GA)
Haywood Comm Coll (NC)
Housatonic Comm Coll (CT)
Illinois Valley Comm Coll (IL)
Imperial Valley Coll (CA)
Ivy Tech Comm Coll–Columbus (IN)
Ivy Tech Comm Coll–Lafayette (IN)
Ivy Tech Comm Coll–Southwest (IN)
Macomb Comm Coll (MI)
Merced Coll (CA)
Mesabi Range Coll (MN)
Mesa Comm Coll (AZ)
Metropolitan Comm Coll (NE)
Miami Dade Coll (FL)
Minnesota State Comm and Tech Coll (MN)
Minnesota State Comm and Tech Coll–Moorhead (MN)
Monroe County Comm Coll (MI)
Mt. San Antonio Coll (CA)
Nashville State Comm Coll (TN)
Navarro Coll (TX)
Northeastern Jr Coll (CO)
North Shore Comm Coll (MA)
Oklahoma City Comm Coll (OK)
Orange Coast Coll (CA)
Otero Jr Coll (CO)
Palomar Coll (CA)
Rainy River Comm Coll (MN)
Rock Valley Coll (IL)
St. Charles Comm Coll (MO)
Seminole State Coll (OK)
South Plains Coll (TX)
Three Rivers Comm Coll (MO)
Trinity Valley Comm Coll (TX)
Virginia Western Comm Coll (VA)
Wayne County Comm Coll District (MI)
Western Wyoming Comm Coll (WY)

PRE-LAW STUDIES
Allen Comm Coll (KS)
American Samoa Comm Coll (AS)
Anne Arundel Comm Coll (MD)
Carl Albert State Coll (OK)
Casper Coll (WY)
Central New Mexico Comm Coll (NM)
Central Oregon Comm Coll (OR)
Central Wyoming Coll (WY)
Coll of Central Florida (FL)
Hill Coll (TX)
Laramie County Comm Coll (WY)
Nashville State Comm Coll (TN)
Northeast Comm Coll (NE)
Panola Coll (TX)
Paris Jr Coll (TX)
Pensacola State Coll (FL)
U of Cincinnati Blue Ash Coll (OH)
U of Cincinnati Clermont Coll (OH)
Western Wyoming Comm Coll (WY)

PREMEDICAL STUDIES
Allen Comm Coll (KS)
Austin Comm Coll District (TX)
Casper Coll (WY)
Central Oregon Comm Coll (OR)
Coll of Central Florida (FL)
Dakota Coll at Bottineau (ND)
Eastern Arizona Coll (AZ)
Eastern Wyoming Coll (WY)
Hill Coll (TX)
Howard Comm Coll (MD)
Lansing Comm Coll (MI)
Nashville State Comm Coll (TN)
Northeast Comm Coll (NE)
Paris Jr Coll (TX)
Pensacola State Coll (FL)
St. Philip's Coll (TX)
San Juan Coll (NM)
Springfield Tech Comm Coll (MA)
Vincennes U (IN)
Western Wyoming Comm Coll (WY)

PRENURSING STUDIES
Arizona Western Coll (AZ)
Dakota Coll at Bottineau (ND)
Edison State Comm Coll (OH)
Georgia Military Coll (GA)
Hill Coll (TX)
Lincoln Coll (IL)
Manor Coll (PA)
Nashville State Comm Coll (TN)
Northeast Comm Coll (NE)
Paris Jr Coll (TX)
Pensacola State Coll (FL)
St. Philip's Coll (TX)
Southwestern Michigan Coll (MI)
Three Rivers Comm Coll (MO)
Western Wyoming Comm Coll (WY)

PRE-OCCUPATIONAL THERAPY
Casper Coll (WY)
Gordon State Coll (GA)
Manor Coll (PA)
Nashville State Comm Coll (TN)

PRE-OPTOMETRY
Casper Coll (WY)
Three Rivers Comm Coll (MO)

PRE-PHARMACY STUDIES
Allen Comm Coll (KS)
Amarillo Coll (TX)
Casper Coll (WY)
Central Oregon Comm Coll (OR)
Coll of Central Florida (FL)
Dodge City Comm Coll (KS)
Eastern Arizona Coll (AZ)
Eastern Wyoming Coll (WY)
Gordon State Coll (GA)
Hill Coll (TX)
Howard Comm Coll (MD)
Laramie County Comm Coll (WY)
Luzerne County Comm Coll (PA)
Manor Coll (PA)
Monroe Comm Coll (NY)
Northeast Comm Coll (NE)
Northwest Coll (WY)
Panola Coll (TX)
Paris Jr Coll (TX)
Pensacola State Coll (FL)
Quinsigamond Comm Coll (MA)
St. Charles Comm Coll (MO)
St. Philip's Coll (TX)
Schoolcraft Coll (MI)
Three Rivers Comm Coll (MO)
U of Cincinnati Blue Ash Coll (OH)
U of Cincinnati Clermont Coll (OH)
Vincennes U (IN)
Western Wyoming Comm Coll (WY)

PRE-PHYSICAL THERAPY
Casper Coll (WY)
Gordon State Coll (GA)
Manor Coll (PA)
Nashville State Comm Coll (TN)

PRE-VETERINARY STUDIES
Allen Comm Coll (KS)
Casper Coll (WY)
Coll of Central Florida (FL)
Dakota Coll at Bottineau (ND)
Eastern Wyoming Coll (WY)
Hill Coll (TX)
Northeast Comm Coll (NE)
Panola Coll (TX)
Pensacola State Coll (FL)
Vincennes U (IN)
Western Wyoming Comm Coll (WY)

PRINTING PRESS OPERATION
Dunwoody Coll of Technology (MN)

PRINTMAKING
De Anza Coll (CA)
Santa Fe Comm Coll (NM)

PROFESSIONAL, TECHNICAL, BUSINESS, AND SCIENTIFIC WRITING
Austin Comm Coll District (TX)
De Anza Coll (CA)
Fox Valley Tech Coll (WI)
Gateway Tech Coll (WI)
Southwestern Michigan Coll (MI)

PSYCHIATRIC/MENTAL HEALTH SERVICES TECHNOLOGY
Alvin Comm Coll (TX)
Anne Arundel Comm Coll (MD)
Asnuntuck Comm Coll (CT)
Columbus State Comm Coll (OH)
Comm Coll of Allegheny County (PA)

Comm Coll of Baltimore County (MD)
El Paso Comm Coll (TX)
Fiorello H. LaGuardia Comm Coll of the City U of New York (NY)
Gateway Tech Coll (WI)
Hagerstown Comm Coll (MD)
Hillsborough Comm Coll (FL)
Houston Comm Coll (TX)
Ivy Tech Comm Coll–Bloomington (IN)
Ivy Tech Comm Coll–Central Indiana (IN)
Ivy Tech Comm Coll–Columbus (IN)
Ivy Tech Comm Coll–Lafayette (IN)
Ivy Tech Comm Coll–Northeast (IN)
Ivy Tech Comm Coll–Northwest (IN)
Ivy Tech Comm Coll–Richmond (IN)
Ivy Tech Comm Coll–Sellersburg (IN)
Ivy Tech Comm Coll–Southeast (IN)
Ivy Tech Comm Coll–Southwest (IN)
Kingsborough Comm Coll of the City U of New York (NY)
Middlesex Comm Coll (MA)
Montgomery Coll (MD)
Montgomery County Comm Coll (PA)
Naugatuck Valley Comm Coll (CT)
Pennsylvania Inst of Technology (PA)
Pueblo Comm Coll (CO)
Three Rivers Comm Coll (CT)
Waukesha County Tech Coll (WI)
Wayne County Comm Coll District (MI)
Williston State Coll (ND)
Wisconsin Indianhead Tech Coll (WI)

PSYCHOLOGY
Aaniiih Nakoda Coll (MT)
Allen Comm Coll (KS)
Alvin Comm Coll (TX)
Amarillo Coll (TX)
Arizona Western Coll (AZ)
Austin Comm Coll District (TX)
Bainbridge State Coll (GA)
Blinn Coll (TX)
Borough of Manhattan Comm Coll of the City U of New York (NY)
Bucks County Comm Coll (PA)
Bunker Hill Comm Coll (MA)
Cañada Coll (CA)
Carroll Comm Coll (MD)
Casper Coll (WY)
Central New Mexico Comm Coll (NM)
Central Wyoming Coll (WY)
Cerritos Coll (CA)
Chandler-Gilbert Comm Coll (AZ)
Citrus Coll (CA)
Coconino Comm Coll (AZ)
Coll of Central Florida (FL)
Coll of Marin (CA)
Coll of the Canyons (CA)
Coll of the Desert (CA)
Comm Coll of Allegheny County (PA)
Comm Coll of Philadelphia (PA)
Crowder Coll (MO)
Dakota Coll at Bottineau (ND)
De Anza Coll (CA)
Del Mar Coll (TX)
Dodge City Comm Coll (KS)
Eastern Arizona Coll (AZ)
Edison State Comm Coll (OH)
Finger Lakes Comm Coll (NY)
Fiorello H. LaGuardia Comm Coll of the City U of New York (NY)
Frederick Comm Coll (MD)
Fullerton Coll (CA)
Genesee Comm Coll (NY)
Georgia Highlands Coll (GA)
Georgia Military Coll (GA)
Gordon State Coll (GA)
Harford Comm Coll (MD)
Harper Coll (IL)
Harrisburg Area Comm Coll (PA)
Hill Coll (TX)
Hutchinson Comm Coll (KS)
Imperial Valley Coll (CA)
Lansing Comm Coll (MI)
Laramie County Comm Coll (WY)
Lehigh Carbon Comm Coll (PA)
Manor Coll (PA)
Merced Coll (CA)
Miami Dade Coll (FL)
Mohave Comm Coll (AZ)
Monroe County Comm Coll (MI)
Montgomery County Comm Coll (PA)
Nashville State Comm Coll (TN)
Navarro Coll (TX)
Northeast Comm Coll (NE)
Northeastern Jr Coll (CO)

Northern Essex Comm Coll (MA)
Northwest Coll (WY)
Norwalk Comm Coll (CT)
Oklahoma City Comm Coll (OK)
Orange Coast Coll (CA)
Otero Jr Coll (CO)
Palomar Coll (CA)
Panola Coll (TX)
Paris Jr Coll (TX)
Pensacola State Coll (FL)
Quinsigamond Comm Coll (MA)
St. Philip's Coll (TX)
Salt Lake Comm Coll (UT)
San Jacinto Coll District (TX)
San Joaquin Delta Coll (CA)
San Juan Coll (NM)
Santa Fe Comm Coll (NM)
Santa Rosa Jr Coll (CA)
Sierra Coll (CA)
South Florida State Coll (FL)
Sullivan County Comm Coll (NY)
Trinity Valley Comm Coll (TX)
Truckee Meadows Comm Coll (NV)
Tyler Jr Coll (TX)
U of Cincinnati Blue Ash Coll (OH)
U of Cincinnati Clermont Coll (OH)
Vincennes U (IN)
Western Wyoming Comm Coll (WY)
Westmoreland County Comm Coll (PA)

PSYCHOLOGY RELATED
Cayuga County Comm Coll (NY)
Genesee Comm Coll (NY)
Murray State Coll (OK)
Seminole State Coll (OK)
U of Pittsburgh at Titusville (PA)

PUBLIC ADMINISTRATION
Central Texas Coll (TX)
Citrus Coll (CA)
County Coll of Morris (NJ)
Del Mar Coll (TX)
Fayetteville Tech Comm Coll (NC)
Housatonic Comm Coll (CT)
Houston Comm Coll (TX)
Laramie County Comm Coll (WY)
Lehigh Carbon Comm Coll (PA)
Lenoir Comm Coll (NC)
Lorain County Comm Coll (OH)
Miami Dade Coll (FL)
Palomar Coll (CA)
Rio Salado Coll (AZ)
Scottsdale Comm Coll (AZ)
Southern U at Shreveport (LA)
South Florida State Coll (FL)
Tyler Jr Coll (TX)

PUBLIC ADMINISTRATION AND SOCIAL SERVICE PROFESSIONS RELATED
Cleveland State Comm Coll (TN)
Oklahoma State U–Oklahoma City (OK)

PUBLIC HEALTH
Anne Arundel Comm Coll (MD)
County Coll of Morris (NJ)
Northern Essex Comm Coll (MA)

PUBLIC HEALTH EDUCATION AND PROMOTION
Borough of Manhattan Comm Coll of the City U of New York (NY)
Northampton Comm Coll (PA)
U of Cincinnati Blue Ash Coll (OH)

PUBLIC HEALTH RELATED
Salt Lake Comm Coll (UT)

PUBLIC POLICY ANALYSIS
Del Mar Coll (TX)

PUBLIC RELATIONS, ADVERTISING, AND APPLIED COMMUNICATION
Chippewa Valley Tech Coll (WI)
Oklahoma City Comm Coll (OK)

PUBLIC RELATIONS, ADVERTISING, AND APPLIED COMMUNICATION RELATED
Harper Coll (IL)

PUBLIC RELATIONS/IMAGE MANAGEMENT
Amarillo Coll (TX)
Bismarck State Coll (ND)
Comm Coll of the Air Force (AL)
Crowder Coll (MO)
Mesa Comm Coll (AZ)

South Florida State Coll (FL)
Vincennes U (IN)

PURCHASING, PROCUREMENT/ ACQUISITIONS AND CONTRACTS MANAGEMENT
Cecil Coll (MD)
Comm Coll of the Air Force (AL)
De Anza Coll (CA)
Greenville Tech Coll (SC)

QUALITY CONTROL AND SAFETY TECHNOLOGIES RELATED
Ivy Tech Comm Coll–Lafayette (IN)
Ivy Tech Comm Coll–Wabash Valley (IN)
Lake Superior Coll (MN)
Macomb Comm Coll (MI)
Mount Wachusett Comm Coll (MA)

QUALITY CONTROL TECHNOLOGY
Columbus State Comm Coll (OH)
Comm Coll of Allegheny County (PA)
Grand Rapids Comm Coll (MI)
Illinois Eastern Comm Colls, Lincoln Trail College (IL)
Lakeland Comm Coll (OH)
Macomb Comm Coll (MI)
Mesa Comm Coll (AZ)
Monroe Comm Coll (NY)
Mt. San Antonio Coll (CA)
Northampton Comm Coll (PA)
Rock Valley Coll (IL)
Salt Lake Comm Coll (UT)
Southeast Comm Coll, Milford Campus (NE)
Tarrant County Coll District (TX)
Three Rivers Comm Coll (MO)

RADIATION PROTECTION/ HEALTH PHYSICS TECHNOLOGY
Lone Star Coll–CyFair (TX)
Spartanburg Comm Coll (SC)

RADIO AND TELEVISION
Alvin Comm Coll (TX)
Amarillo Coll (TX)
Austin Comm Coll District (TX)
Central Texas Coll (TX)
Central Wyoming Coll (WY)
City Colls of Chicago, Kennedy-King College (IL)
Daytona State Coll (FL)
De Anza Coll (CA)
Del Mar Coll (TX)
Delta Coll (MI)
Dodge City Comm Coll (KS)
Fullerton Coll (CA)
Genesee Comm Coll (NY)
Golden West Coll (CA)
Illinois Eastern Comm Colls, Wabash Valley College (IL)
Iowa Central Comm Coll (IA)
Los Angeles City Coll (CA)
Miami Dade Coll (FL)
Mt. San Antonio Coll (CA)
Palomar Coll (CA)
Santa Monica Coll (CA)
South Florida State Coll (FL)
Sullivan County Comm Coll (NY)
Tyler Jr Coll (TX)
Virginia Western Comm Coll (VA)

RADIO AND TELEVISION BROADCASTING TECHNOLOGY
Adirondack Comm Coll (NY)
Arizona Western Coll (AZ)
Borough of Manhattan Comm Coll of the City U of New York (NY)
Camden County Coll (NJ)
Cloud County Comm Coll (KS)
Genesee Comm Coll (NY)
Hinds Comm Coll (MS)
Houston Comm Coll (TX)
Hutchinson Comm Coll (KS)
International Coll of Broadcasting (OH)
Lake Superior Coll (MN)
Lansing Comm Coll (MI)
Lehigh Carbon Comm Coll (PA)
Luzerne County Comm Coll (PA)
Mercer County Comm Coll (NJ)
Miami Dade Coll (FL)
Mount Wachusett Comm Coll (MA)
Northampton Comm Coll (PA)
Ozarks Tech Comm Coll (MO)
Salt Lake Comm Coll (UT)
San Jacinto Coll District (TX)
Santa Fe Comm Coll (NM)

Schoolcraft Coll (MI)
Springfield Tech Comm Coll (MA)
Tompkins Cortland Comm Coll (NY)
Vincennes U (IN)
Westmoreland County Comm Coll (PA)

RADIOLOGIC TECHNOLOGY/ SCIENCE
Amarillo Coll (TX)
Arizona Western Coll (AZ)
Austin Comm Coll District (TX)
Brookhaven Coll (TX)
Bucks County Comm Coll (PA)
Caldwell Comm Coll and Tech Inst (NC)
Cañada Coll (CA)
Carolinas Coll of Health Sciences (NC)
Carteret Comm Coll (NC)
Casper Coll (WY)
Central New Mexico Comm Coll (NM)
Central Oregon Comm Coll (OR)
Central Virginia Comm Coll (VA)
Century Coll (MN)
Comm Coll of Rhode Island (RI)
County Coll of Morris (NJ)
Danville Area Comm Coll (IL)
Elgin Comm Coll (IL)
El Paso Comm Coll (TX)
Fayetteville Tech Comm Coll (NC)
Gordon State Coll (GA)
Great Basin Coll (NV)
Great Falls Coll Montana State U (MT)
Harper Coll (IL)
Harrisburg Area Comm Coll (PA)
H. Councill Trenholm State Comm Coll (AL)
Hinds Comm Coll (MS)
Houston Comm Coll (TX)
Hudson County Comm Coll (NJ)
Hutchinson Comm Coll (KS)
Illinois Central Coll (IL)
Jefferson State Comm Coll (AL)
Kaskaskia Coll (IL)
Kishwaukee Coll (IL)
Lake Superior Coll (MN)
Lansing Comm Coll (MI)
Laramie County Comm Coll (WY)
Lenoir Comm Coll (NC)
Louisiana State U at Eunice (LA)
Maine Coll of Health Professions (ME)
Massachusetts Bay Comm Coll (MA)
Merced Coll (CA)
Miami Dade Coll (FL)
Minnesota State Coll–Southeast Tech (MN)
Minnesota State Comm and Tech Coll (MN)
Minnesota State Comm and Tech Coll–Detroit Lakes (MN)
Minnesota West Comm and Tech Coll (MN)
Mitchell Tech Inst (SD)
Montgomery County Comm Coll (PA)
Northampton Comm Coll (PA)
Northeast Iowa Comm Coll (IA)
Northern Essex Comm Coll (MA)
Northland Comm and Tech Coll (MN)
Oklahoma State U–Oklahoma City (OK)
Owensboro Comm and Tech Coll (KY)
Paris Jr Coll (TX)
Pueblo Comm Coll (CO)
Quinsigamond Comm Coll (MA)
Randolph Comm Coll (NC)
Rowan-Cabarrus Comm Coll (NC)
St. Luke's Coll (IA)
St. Philip's Coll (TX)
St. Vincent's Coll (CT)
San Jacinto Coll District (TX)
Santa Fe Comm Coll (NM)
Santa Rosa Jr Coll (CA)
Southern U at Shreveport (LA)
South Suburban Coll (IL)
Southwest Virginia Comm Coll (VA)
Spencerian Coll (KY)
Spencerian Coll–Lexington (KY)
Springfield Tech Comm Coll (MA)
State U of New York Coll of Technology at Alfred (NY)
Tyler Jr Coll (TX)
Virginia Western Comm Coll (VA)
Weatherford Coll (TX)
Westmoreland County Comm Coll (PA)

RADIOLOGIST ASSISTANT
Blackhawk Tech Coll (WI)

RADIO, TELEVISION, AND DIGITAL COMMUNICATION RELATED
Cayuga County Comm Coll (NY)
Fox Valley Tech Coll (WI)
Genesee Comm Coll (NY)
Montgomery County Comm Coll (PA)
Sullivan County Comm Coll (NY)

RANGE SCIENCE AND MANAGEMENT
Casper Coll (WY)
Central Wyoming Coll (WY)
Eastern Wyoming Coll (WY)
Northwest Coll (WY)
Treasure Valley Comm Coll (OR)
Trinity Valley Comm Coll (TX)

REAL ESTATE
Amarillo Coll (TX)
Austin Comm Coll District (TX)
Blinn Coll (TX)
Cerritos Coll (CA)
Citrus Coll (CA)
Coll of Marin (CA)
Coll of the Canyons (CA)
Collin County Comm Coll District (TX)
Columbus State Comm Coll (OH)
Comm Coll of Allegheny County (PA)
De Anza Coll (CA)
Del Mar Coll (TX)
Dodge City Comm Coll (KS)
El Paso Comm Coll (TX)
Fullerton Coll (CA)
Golden West Coll (CA)
Hinds Comm Coll (MS)
Houston Comm Coll (TX)
Lansing Comm Coll (MI)
Los Angeles City Coll (CA)
Madison Area Tech Coll (WI)
McLennan Comm Coll (TX)
Merced Coll (CA)
Mesa Comm Coll (AZ)
Miami Dade Coll (FL)
Montgomery County Comm Coll (PA)
Mt. San Antonio Coll (CA)
Nassau Comm Coll (NY)
NHTI, Concord's Comm Coll, Concord (NH)
Oakton Comm Coll (IL)
Orange Coast Coll (CA)
Palomar Coll (CA)
San Jacinto Coll District (TX)
Santa Rosa Jr Coll (CA)
Scottsdale Comm Coll (AZ)
Sierra Coll (CA)
South Florida State Coll (FL)
South Plains Coll (TX)
Tidewater Comm Coll (VA)
Trinity Valley Comm Coll (TX)
U of Cincinnati Blue Ash Coll (OH)
Waukesha County Tech Coll (WI)
Westmoreland County Comm Coll (PA)

RECEPTIONIST
Dakota Coll at Bottineau (ND)

RECORDING ARTS TECHNOLOGY
Bismarck State Coll (ND)
Bossier Parish Comm Coll (LA)
Citrus Coll (CA)
Comm Coll of Philadelphia (PA)
Finger Lakes Comm Coll (NY)
Fiorello H. LaGuardia Comm Coll of the City U of New York (NY)
Front Range Comm Coll (CO)
Fullerton Coll (CA)
Grand Rapids Comm Coll (MI)
Hennepin Tech Coll (MN)
Lehigh Carbon Comm Coll (PA)
Mesa Comm Coll (AZ)
Miami Dade Coll (FL)
Montgomery County Comm Coll (PA)
Orange Coast Coll (CA)
Queensborough Comm Coll of the City U of New York (NY)
Schoolcraft Coll (MI)
South Plains Coll (TX)
Springfield Tech Comm Coll (MA)
Vincennes U (IN)

REGISTERED NURSING, NURSING ADMINISTRATION, NURSING RESEARCH AND CLINICAL NURSING RELATED
Genesee Comm Coll (NY)
Harford Comm Coll (MD)

REGISTERED NURSING/ REGISTERED NURSE
Adirondack Comm Coll (NY)
Alamance Comm Coll (NC)
Alexandria Tech and Comm Coll (MN)
Alvin Comm Coll (TX)
Amarillo Coll (TX)
Ancilla Coll (IN)
Anne Arundel Comm Coll (MD)
Anoka-Ramsey Comm Coll (MN)
Arapahoe Comm Coll (CO)
Arizona Western Coll (AZ)
Arkansas Northeastern Coll (AR)
Athens Tech Coll (GA)
Austin Comm Coll District (TX)
Bainbridge State Coll (GA)
The Belanger School of Nursing (NY)
Berkshire Comm Coll (MA)
Bevill State Comm Coll (AL)
Bismarck State Coll (ND)
Blackhawk Tech Coll (WI)
Blinn Coll (TX)
Blue Ridge Comm and Tech Coll (WV)
Borough of Manhattan Comm Coll of the City U of New York (NY)
Bossier Parish Comm Coll (LA)
Bowling Green State U–Firelands Coll (OH)
Brookhaven Coll (TX)
Bucks County Comm Coll (PA)
Bunker Hill Comm Coll (MA)
Caldwell Comm Coll and Tech Inst (NC)
Camden County Coll (NJ)
Cape Fear Comm Coll (NC)
Carl Albert State Coll (OK)
Carolinas Coll of Health Sciences (NC)
Carroll Comm Coll (MD)
Carteret Comm Coll (NC)
Casper Coll (WY)
Cayuga County Comm Coll (NY)
Cecil Coll (MD)
Central Maine Comm Coll (ME)
Central New Mexico Comm Coll (NM)
Central Oregon Comm Coll (OR)
Central Texas Coll (TX)
Central Wyoming Coll (WY)
Century Coll (MN)
Cerritos Coll (CA)
Chandler-Gilbert Comm Coll (AZ)
Chesapeake Coll (MD)
Chippewa Valley Tech Coll (WI)
Citrus Coll (CA)
Cleveland State Comm Coll (TN)
Clinton Comm Coll (NY)
Cloud County Comm Coll (KS)
Cochise County Comm Coll District (AZ)
Cochran School of Nursing (NY)
Coconino Comm Coll (AZ)
Coll of Central Florida (FL)
Coll of Marin (CA)
Coll of The Albemarle (NC)
Coll of the Canyons (CA)
Coll of the Desert (CA)
Coll of the Marshall Islands (MH)
Collin County Comm Coll District (TX)
Colorado Northwestern Comm Coll (CO)
Columbia-Greene Comm Coll (NY)
Columbus State Comm Coll (OH)
Columbus Tech Coll (GA)
Comm Coll of Allegheny County (PA)
Comm Coll of Baltimore County (MD)
Comm Coll of Philadelphia (PA)
Comm Coll of Rhode Island (RI)
County Coll of Morris (NJ)
Craven Comm Coll (NC)
Crowder Coll (MO)
Dakota Coll at Bottineau (ND)
Danville Area Comm Coll (IL)
Daytona State Coll (FL)
De Anza Coll (CA)
Del Mar Coll (TX)
Delta Coll (MI)
Des Moines Area Comm Coll (IA)
Dodge City Comm Coll (KS)
Dutchess Comm Coll (NY)
Dyersburg State Comm Coll (TN)
East Central Coll (MO)
Eastern Arizona Coll (AZ)
Eastern Idaho Tech Coll (ID)
Eastern Wyoming Coll (WY)
Edison State Comm Coll (OH)
Elgin Comm Coll (IL)
El Paso Comm Coll (TX)
Erie Comm Coll (NY)

Erie Comm Coll, North Campus (NY)
Fayetteville Tech Comm Coll (NC)
Finger Lakes Comm Coll (NY)
Fiorello H. LaGuardia Comm Coll of the City U of New York (NY)
Florida Keys Comm Coll (FL)
Florida SouthWestern State Coll (FL)
Fox Valley Tech Coll (WI)
Frederick Comm Coll (MD)
Front Range Comm Coll (CO)
Gateway Comm and Tech Coll (KY)
Gateway Tech Coll (WI)
Genesee Comm Coll (NY)
Georgia Highlands Coll (GA)
Golden West Coll (CA)
Gordon State Coll (GA)
Grand Rapids Comm Coll (MI)
Great Basin Coll (NV)
Greenville Tech Coll (SC)
Hagerstown Comm Coll (MD)
Halifax Comm Coll (NC)
Harper Coll (IL)
Harrisburg Area Comm Coll (PA)
Hawkeye Comm Coll (IA)
Haywood Comm Coll (NC)
Hesston Coll (KS)
Highland Comm Coll (IL)
Hill Coll (TX)
Hillsborough Comm Coll (FL)
Hinds Comm Coll (MS)
Holyoke Comm Coll (MA)
Horry Georgetown Tech Coll (SC)
Houston Comm Coll (TX)
Howard Comm Coll (MD)
Hudson County Comm Coll (NJ)
Hutchinson Comm Coll (KS)
Illinois Central Coll (IL)
Illinois Eastern Comm Colls, Frontier Community College (IL)
Illinois Eastern Comm Colls, Olney Central College (IL)
Illinois Valley Comm Coll (IL)
Imperial Valley Coll (CA)
Iowa Central Comm Coll (IA)
Ivy Tech Comm Coll–Bloomington (IN)
Ivy Tech Comm Coll–Central Indiana (IN)
Ivy Tech Comm Coll–East Central (IN)
Ivy Tech Comm Coll–Kokomo (IN)
Ivy Tech Comm Coll–Lafayette (IN)
Ivy Tech Comm Coll–North Central (IN)
Ivy Tech Comm Coll–Northeast (IN)
Ivy Tech Comm Coll–Northwest (IN)
Ivy Tech Comm Coll–Richmond (IN)
Ivy Tech Comm Coll–Sellersburg (IN)
Ivy Tech Comm Coll–Southeast (IN)
Ivy Tech Comm Coll–Southwest (IN)
Ivy Tech Comm Coll–Wabash Valley (IN)
James Sprunt Comm Coll (NC)
Jamestown Comm Coll (NY)
Jefferson Comm Coll (NY)
Jefferson State Comm Coll (AL)
Jersey Coll (NJ)
Johnson County Comm Coll (KS)
Johnston Comm Coll (NC)
John Tyler Comm Coll (VA)
Kaskaskia Coll (IL)
Kellogg Comm Coll (MI)
Kent State U at Ashtabula (OH)
Kent State U at East Liverpool (OH)
Kent State U at Tuscarawas (OH)
Kingsborough Comm Coll of the City U of New York (NY)
Kirtland Comm Coll (MI)
Kishwaukee Coll (IL)
Lakeland Comm Coll (OH)
Lake Region State Coll (ND)
Lake Superior Coll (MN)
Lamar Comm Coll (CO)
Lansing Comm Coll (MI)
Laramie County Comm Coll (WY)
Lehigh Carbon Comm Coll (PA)
Lenoir Comm Coll (NC)
Lone Star Coll–CyFair (TX)
Lone Star Coll–Kingwood (TX)
Lone Star Coll–Montgomery (TX)
Lone Star Coll–North Harris (TX)
Lone Star Coll–Tomball (TX)
Lorain County Comm Coll (OH)
Louisiana State U at Eunice (LA)
Lurleen B. Wallace Comm Coll (AL)
Luzerne County Comm Coll (PA)
Macomb Comm Coll (MI)
Madison Area Tech Coll (WI)
Maine Coll of Health Professions (ME)

Manhattan Area Tech Coll (KS)
Massachusetts Bay Comm Coll (MA)
Maysville Comm and Tech Coll, Maysville (KY)
McHenry County Coll (IL)
McLennan Comm Coll (TX)
Merced Coll (CA)
Mercer County Comm Coll (NJ)
Meridian Comm Coll (MS)
Mesa Comm Coll (AZ)
Metropolitan Comm Coll (NE)
Miami Dade Coll (FL)
Middlesex Comm Coll (MA)
Middlesex County Coll (NJ)
Mid-Plains Comm Coll, North Platte (NE)
Minnesota State Coll–Southeast Tech (MN)
Minnesota State Comm and Tech Coll (MN)
Minnesota State Comm and Tech Coll–Detroit Lakes (MN)
Minnesota State Comm and Tech Coll–Moorhead (MN)
Minnesota State Comm and Tech Coll–Wadena (MN)
Minnesota West Comm and Tech Coll (MN)
Missouri State U–West Plains (MO)
Mitchell Comm Coll (NC)
Mohave Comm Coll (AZ)
Mohawk Valley Comm Coll (NY)
Monroe Comm Coll (NY)
Monroe County Comm Coll (MI)
Montgomery Coll (MD)
Montgomery County Comm Coll (PA)
Morton Coll (IL)
Motlow State Comm Coll (TN)
Mott Comm Coll (MI)
Mt. San Antonio Coll (CA)
Mount Wachusett Comm Coll (MA)
Murray State Coll (OK)
Nassau Comm Coll (NY)
Naugatuck Valley Comm Coll (CT)
Navarro Coll (TX)
New Mexico Jr Coll (NM)
New River Comm Coll (VA)
NHTI, Concord's Comm Coll, Concord (NH)
Niagara County Comm Coll (NY)
Northampton Comm Coll (PA)
North Central Missouri Coll (MO)
Northcentral Tech Coll (WI)
Northeast Comm Coll (NE)
Northeastern Jr Coll (CO)
Northeast Iowa Comm Coll (IA)
Northern Essex Comm Coll (MA)
Northern Maine Comm Coll (ME)
Northland Comm and Tech Coll (MN)
North Shore Comm Coll (MA)
NorthWest Arkansas Comm Coll (AR)
Northwest Coll (WY)
Northwest-Shoals Comm Coll (AL)
Norwalk Comm Coll (CT)
Oakton Comm Coll (IL)
Oklahoma City Comm Coll (OK)
Oklahoma State U Inst of Technology (OK)
Oklahoma State U–Oklahoma City (OK)
Olympic Coll (WA)
Oregon Coast Comm Coll (OR)
Otero Jr Coll (CO)
Owensboro Comm and Tech Coll (KY)
Palomar Coll (CA)
Panola Coll (TX)
Paris Jr Coll (TX)
Patrick Henry Comm Coll (VA)
Penn State Fayette, The Eberly Campus (PA)
Penn State Mont Alto (PA)
Pensacola State Coll (FL)
Piedmont Comm Coll (NC)
Pittsburgh Tech Coll (PA)
Pueblo Comm Coll (CO)
Queensborough Comm Coll of the City U of New York (NY)
Quinsigamond Comm Coll (MA)
Randolph Comm Coll (NC)
Rappahannock Comm Coll (VA)
Raritan Valley Comm Coll (NJ)
Rend Lake Coll (IL)
Renton Tech Coll (WA)
Richmond Comm Coll (NC)
Rio Hondo Coll (CA)
Rockingham Comm Coll (NC)
Rock Valley Coll (IL)
Rogue Comm Coll (OR)

Rowan-Cabarrus Comm Coll (NC)
St. Charles Comm Coll (MO)
St. Clair County Comm Coll (MI)
St. Luke's Coll (IA)
St. Philip's Coll (TX)
St. Vincent's Coll (CT)
Salt Lake Comm Coll (UT)
San Jacinto Coll District (TX)
San Joaquin Delta Coll (CA)
San Juan Coll (NM)
Santa Fe Comm Coll (NM)
Santa Monica Coll (CA)
Santa Rosa Jr Coll (CA)
Schoolcraft Coll (MI)
Scottsdale Comm Coll (AZ)
Seminole State Coll (OK)
Seminole State Coll of Florida (FL)
Shawnee Comm Coll (IL)
Sierra Coll (CA)
Sisseton-Wahpeton Coll (SD)
Somerset Comm Coll (KY)
Southeast Comm Coll, Lincoln Campus (NE)
Southeastern Comm Coll (IA)
Southern Regional Tech Coll (GA)
Southern U at Shreveport (LA)
South Florida State Coll (FL)
South Plains Coll (TX)
Southwestern Comm Coll (NC)
Southwestern Michigan Coll (MI)
Southwest Virginia Comm Coll (VA)
Spartanburg Comm Coll (SC)
Spencerian Coll (KY)
Spoon River Coll (IL)
Springfield Tech Comm Coll (MA)
Stark State Coll (OH)
State U of New York Coll of Technology at Alfred (NY)
Sullivan County Comm Coll (NY)
Tallahassee Comm Coll (FL)
Tarrant County Coll District (TX)
Texarkana Coll (TX)
Three Rivers Comm Coll (CT)
Three Rivers Comm Coll (MO)
Tidewater Comm Coll (VA)
Tompkins Cortland Comm Coll (NY)
Treasure Valley Comm Coll (OR)
Trident Tech Coll (SC)
Trinity Valley Comm Coll (TX)
Truckee Meadows Comm Coll (NV)
Tyler Jr Coll (TX)
Ulster County Comm Coll (NY)
U of Arkansas Comm Coll at Morrilton (AR)
U of Cincinnati Blue Ash Coll (OH)
U of Pittsburgh at Titusville (PA)
Victoria Coll (TX)
Vincennes U (IN)
Virginia Western Comm Coll (VA)
Walters State Comm Coll (TN)
Waukesha County Tech Coll (WI)
Wayne County Comm Coll District (MI)
Weatherford Coll (TX)
Westchester Comm Coll (NY)
Western Nevada Coll (NV)
Westmoreland County Comm Coll (PA)
White Mountains Comm Coll (NH)
Williston State Coll (ND)
Wisconsin Indianhead Tech Coll (WI)
Wor-Wic Comm Coll (MD)
Wytheville Comm Coll (VA)

REHABILITATION AIDE
Salina Area Tech Coll (KS)

REHABILITATION AND THERAPEUTIC PROFESSIONS RELATED
Camden County Coll (NJ)
Central Wyoming Coll (WY)
Middlesex County Coll (NJ)
Nassau Comm Coll (NY)

RELIGIOUS STUDIES
Allen Comm Coll (KS)
Amarillo Coll (TX)
Cerritos Coll (CA)
Coll of Central Florida (FL)
Fullerton Coll (CA)
Hill Coll (TX)
Lansing Comm Coll (MI)
Laramie County Comm Coll (WY)
Orange Coast Coll (CA)
San Joaquin Delta Coll (CA)
Santa Rosa Jr Coll (CA)
South Florida State Coll (FL)
Trinity Valley Comm Coll (TX)

RELIGIOUS STUDIES RELATED
Ancilla Coll (IN)
Spartanburg Methodist Coll (SC)

RENAL/DIALYSIS TECHNOLOGY
Lake Superior Coll (MN)

RESORT MANAGEMENT
Coll of the Desert (CA)
Finger Lakes Comm Coll (NY)
Lehigh Carbon Comm Coll (PA)
White Mountains Comm Coll (NH)

RESPIRATORY CARE THERAPY
Alvin Comm Coll (TX)
Amarillo Coll (TX)
Athens Tech Coll (GA)
Augusta Tech Coll (GA)
Berkshire Comm Coll (MA)
Bossier Parish Comm Coll (LA)
Bowling Green State U–Firelands Coll (OH)
Carteret Comm Coll (NC)
Casper Coll (WY)
Central New Mexico Comm Coll (NM)
Central Virginia Comm Coll (VA)
Chippewa Valley Tech Coll (WI)
Cochise County Comm Coll District (AZ)
Collin County Comm Coll District (TX)
Columbus State Comm Coll (OH)
Comm Coll of Allegheny County (PA)
Comm Coll of Baltimore County (MD)
Comm Coll of Philadelphia (PA)
Comm Coll of Rhode Island (RI)
County Coll of Morris (NJ)
Daytona State Coll (FL)
Del Mar Coll (TX)
Delta Coll (MI)
Des Moines Area Comm Coll (IA)
Dodge City Comm Coll (KS)
East Central Coll (MO)
El Paso Comm Coll (TX)
Erie Comm Coll, North Campus (NY)
Fayetteville Tech Comm Coll (NC)
Florida SouthWestern State Coll (FL)
Frederick Comm Coll (MD)
Genesee Comm Coll (NY)
Great Falls Coll Montana State U (MT)
Greenville Tech Coll (SC)
Gulf Coast State Coll (FL)
Gwinnett Tech Coll (GA)
Harrisburg Area Comm Coll (PA)
Hawkeye Comm Coll (IA)
Hillsborough Comm Coll (FL)
Hinds Comm Coll (MS)
Houston Comm Coll (TX)
Hudson County Comm Coll (NJ)
Hutchinson Comm Coll (KS)
Illinois Central Coll (IL)
Ivy Tech Comm Coll–Central Indiana (IN)
Ivy Tech Comm Coll–Lafayette (IN)
Ivy Tech Comm Coll–Northeast (IN)
Ivy Tech Comm Coll–Northwest (IN)
Ivy Tech Comm Coll–Richmond (IN)
Ivy Tech Comm Coll–Sellersburg (IN)
Ivy Tech Comm Coll–Wabash Valley (IN)
Johnson County Comm Coll (KS)
J. Sargeant Reynolds Comm Coll (VA)
Kaskaskia Coll (IL)
Kent State U at Ashtabula (OH)
Lakeland Comm Coll (OH)
Lake Superior Coll (MN)
Lone Star Coll–Kingwood (TX)
Louisiana State U at Eunice (LA)
Luzerne County Comm Coll (PA)
Macomb Comm Coll (MI)
Madison Area Tech Coll (WI)
Manchester Comm Coll (CT)
Maysville Comm and Tech Coll, Maysville (KY)
McLennan Comm Coll (TX)
Mercer County Comm Coll (NJ)
Meridian Comm Coll (MS)
Metropolitan Comm Coll (NE)
Miami Dade Coll (FL)
Middlesex County Coll (NJ)
Missouri State U–West Plains (MO)
Mohawk Valley Comm Coll (NY)
Monroe County Comm Coll (MI)
Mott Comm Coll (MI)
Mt. San Antonio Coll (CA)

Nassau Comm Coll (NY)
Naugatuck Valley Comm Coll (CT)
Northeast Comm Coll (NE)
Northeast Iowa Comm Coll (IA)
Northern Essex Comm Coll (MA)
Northland Comm and Tech Coll (MN)
North Shore Comm Coll (MA)
NorthWest Arkansas Comm Coll (AR)
Norwalk Comm Coll (CT)
Oklahoma City Comm Coll (OK)
Orange Coast Coll (CA)
Ozarks Tech Comm Coll (MO)
Pueblo Comm Coll (CO)
Quinsigamond Comm Coll (MA)
Raritan Valley Comm Coll (NJ)
Rockingham Comm Coll (NC)
Rock Valley Coll (IL)
St. Luke's Coll (IA)
St. Philip's Coll (TX)
San Jacinto Coll District (TX)
San Juan Coll (NM)
Santa Fe Comm Coll (NM)
Santa Monica Coll (CA)
Seminole State Coll of Florida (FL)
Somerset Comm Coll (KY)
Southeast Comm Coll, Lincoln Campus (NE)
Southeastern Comm Coll (IA)
Southern Regional Tech Coll (GA)
Southern U at Shreveport (LA)
South Florida State Coll (FL)
South Plains Coll (TX)
Southwestern Comm Coll (NC)
Spartanburg Comm Coll (SC)
Spencerian Coll (KY)
Springfield Tech Comm Coll (MA)
Stark State Coll (OH)
Sullivan County Comm Coll (NY)
Tallahassee Comm Coll (FL)
Tarrant County Coll District (TX)
Trident Tech Coll (SC)
Tyler Jr Coll (TX)
U of Cincinnati Clermont Coll (OH)
Victoria Coll (TX)
Volunteer State Comm Coll (TN)
Walters State Comm Coll (TN)
Weatherford Coll (TX)
Westchester Comm Coll (NY)

RESPIRATORY THERAPY TECHNICIAN
Augusta Tech Coll (GA)
Borough of Manhattan Comm Coll of the City U of New York (NY)
Bunker Hill Comm Coll (MA)
Coastal Pines Tech Coll (GA)
Columbus Tech Coll (GA)
Florida SouthWestern State Coll (FL)
Georgia Northwestern Tech Coll (GA)
Hutchinson Comm Coll (KS)
Miami Dade Coll (FL)
Northern Essex Comm Coll (MA)
Southeastern Tech Coll (GA)
Southern Crescent Tech Coll (GA)

RESTAURANT, CULINARY, AND CATERING MANAGEMENT
Blue Ridge Comm and Tech Coll (WV)
Central New Mexico Comm Coll (NM)
Coll of Central Florida (FL)
Coll of the Canyons (CA)
Comm Coll of Allegheny County (PA)
Culinary Inst LeNotre (TX)
Elgin Comm Coll (IL)
Grand Rapids Comm Coll (MI)
Guam Comm Coll (GU)
Gulf Coast State Coll (FL)
Hillsborough Comm Coll (FL)
JNA Inst of Culinary Arts (PA)
Johnson County Comm Coll (KS)
Lakeland Comm Coll (OH)
McHenry County Coll (IL)
Miami Dade Coll (FL)
Missouri State U–West Plains (MO)
Mohawk Valley Comm Coll (NY)
New England Culinary Inst (VT)
Orange Coast Coll (CA)
Pensacola State Coll (FL)
Raritan Valley Comm Coll (NJ)
St. Philip's Coll (TX)
San Jacinto Coll District (TX)
Southeast Comm Coll, Lincoln Campus (NE)
Vincennes U (IN)
Waukesha County Tech Coll (WI)

Westchester Comm Coll (NY)
Westmoreland County Comm
Coll (PA)

**RESTAURANT/FOOD SERVICES
MANAGEMENT**
Central Texas Coll (TX)
Erie Comm Coll, North Campus (NY)
Fiorello H. LaGuardia Comm Coll of
the City U of New York (NY)
Hillsborough Comm Coll (FL)
J. Sargeant Reynolds Comm Coll
(VA)
Miami Dade Coll (FL)
Naugatuck Valley Comm Coll (CT)
Northampton Comm Coll (PA)
Norwalk Comm Coll (CT)
Quinsigamond Comm Coll (MA)
Santa Rosa Jr Coll (CA)

RETAILING
Alamance Comm Coll (NC)
Arapahoe Comm Coll (CO)
Bucks County Comm Coll (PA)
Cañada Coll (CA)
Casper Coll (WY)
Central Oregon Comm Coll (OR)
Comm Coll of Allegheny County (PA)
Delta Coll (MI)
Elgin Comm Coll (IL)
Holyoke Comm Coll (MA)
Hutchinson Comm Coll (KS)
Illinois Central Coll (IL)
Minnesota State Coll–Southeast
Tech (MN)
Nassau Comm Coll (NY)
U of Cincinnati Blue Ash Coll (OH)
Westchester Comm Coll (NY)

RETAIL MANAGEMENT
Collin County Comm Coll District
(TX)
Orange Coast Coll (CA)
Penn Foster Coll (AZ)

RHETORIC AND COMPOSITION
Allen Comm Coll (KS)
Amarillo Coll (TX)
Austin Comm Coll District (TX)
Bainbridge State Coll (GA)
Blinn Coll (TX)
Carl Albert State Coll (OK)
De Anza Coll (CA)
Del Mar Coll (TX)
Dodge City Comm Coll (KS)
Hill Coll (TX)
Monroe County Comm Coll (MI)
Navarro Coll (TX)
Paris Jr Coll (TX)
St. Philip's Coll (TX)
San Jacinto Coll District (TX)
San Joaquin Delta Coll (CA)
Santa Monica Coll (CA)
Sierra Coll (CA)
South Florida State Coll (FL)
Trinity Valley Comm Coll (TX)

ROBOTICS TECHNOLOGY
Casper Coll (WY)
Comm Coll of Allegheny County (PA)
Daytona State Coll (FL)
Dunwoody Coll of Technology (MN)
Illinois Central Coll (IL)
Kaskaskia Coll (IL)
Kirtland Comm Coll (MI)
Lake Area Tech Inst (SD)
Macomb Comm Coll (MI)
McHenry County Coll (IL)
Minnesota West Comm and Tech
Coll (MN)
Southern U at Shreveport (LA)
Texas State Tech Coll (TX)
Vincennes U (IN)

ROOFING
Penn Foster Coll (AZ)

RUSSIAN
Austin Comm Coll District (TX)

**SALES, DISTRIBUTION, AND
MARKETING OPERATIONS**
Alexandria Tech and Comm Coll
(MN)
Anoka-Ramsey Comm Coll (MN)
Chippewa Valley Tech Coll (WI)
Coll of the Canyons (CA)
Des Moines Area Comm Coll (IA)
Fullerton Coll (CA)
Greenville Tech Coll (SC)
Guam Comm Coll (GU)
Harper Coll (IL)

Harrisburg Area Comm Coll (PA)
Hawkeye Comm Coll (IA)
Johnson County Comm Coll (KS)
Lansing Comm Coll (MI)
Merced Coll (CA)
Minnesota State Coll–Southeast
Tech (MN)
Minnesota State Comm and Tech
Coll (MN)
Minnesota State Comm and Tech
Coll–Detroit Lakes (MN)
Minnesota State Comm and Tech
Coll–Moorhead (MN)
Montgomery County Comm Coll (PA)
Northeast Iowa Comm Coll (IA)
Northland Comm and Tech Coll (MN)
Oakton Comm Coll (IL)
Orange Coast Coll (CA)
Santa Monica Coll (CA)
Sierra Coll (CA)
State U of New York Coll of
Technology at Alfred (NY)

**SALON/BEAUTY SALON
MANAGEMENT**
Bevill State Comm Coll (AL)
Delta Coll (MI)
Mott Comm Coll (MI)
Northwest-Shoals Comm Coll (AL)
Schoolcraft Coll (MI)

**SCIENCE TEACHER
EDUCATION**
Iowa Central Comm Coll (IA)
San Jacinto Coll District (TX)
South Florida State Coll (FL)
Ulster County Comm Coll (NY)
Vincennes U (IN)

SCIENCE TECHNOLOGIES
Central Virginia Comm Coll (VA)
Great Basin Coll (NV)
Northern Essex Comm Coll (MA)

**SCIENCE TECHNOLOGIES
RELATED**
Arapahoe Comm Coll (CO)
Blue Ridge Comm and Tech Coll
(WV)
Cayuga County Comm Coll (NY)
Cleveland State Comm Coll (TN)
Comm Coll of Allegheny County (PA)
Comm Coll of Aurora (CO)
Comm Coll of Vermont (VT)
Dakota Coll at Bottineau (ND)
Front Range Comm Coll (CO)
Lamar Comm Coll (CO)
Morgan Comm Coll (CO)
Pueblo Comm Coll (CO)
Sullivan County Comm Coll (NY)
U of Cincinnati Blue Ash Coll (OH)
U of Cincinnati Clermont Coll (OH)

**SCIENCE, TECHNOLOGY AND
SOCIETY**
Central Wyoming Coll (WY)
Truckee Meadows Comm Coll (NV)

SCULPTURE
De Anza Coll (CA)
Mercer County Comm Coll (NJ)
Palomar Coll (CA)
Santa Fe Comm Coll (NM)

SECONDARY EDUCATION
Allen Comm Coll (KS)
Alvin Comm Coll (TX)
Ancilla Coll (IN)
Arizona Western Coll (AZ)
Austin Comm Coll District (TX)
Brookhaven Coll (TX)
Carl Albert State Coll (OK)
Cecil Coll (MD)
Central Wyoming Coll (WY)
Coll of Central Florida (FL)
Collin County Comm Coll District
(TX)
Eastern Arizona Coll (AZ)
Eastern Wyoming Coll (WY)
Georgia Military Coll (GA)
Gordon State Coll (GA)
Grand Rapids Comm Coll (MI)
Harrisburg Area Comm Coll (PA)
Hill Coll (TX)
Houston Comm Coll (TX)
Howard Coll (TX)
Lansing Comm Coll (MI)
Montgomery County Comm Coll (PA)
Nashville State Comm Coll (TN)
Northampton Comm Coll (PA)
Northeast Comm Coll (NE)
Northwest Coll (WY)

Paris Jr Coll (TX)
San Jacinto Coll District (TX)
San Juan Coll (NM)
South Florida State Coll (FL)
Springfield Tech Comm Coll (MA)
Tyler Jr Coll (TX)
U of Cincinnati Blue Ash Coll (OH)
U of Cincinnati Clermont Coll (OH)
Vincennes U (IN)
Western Wyoming Comm Coll (WY)

**SECURITIES SERVICES
ADMINISTRATION**
Vincennes U (IN)

**SECURITY AND LOSS
PREVENTION**
Citrus Coll (CA)
Comm Coll of the Air Force (AL)
Delta Coll (MI)
Hill Coll (TX)
Miami Dade Coll (FL)
Tallahassee Comm Coll (FL)
Vincennes U (IN)
Wayne County Comm Coll District
(MI)

SELLING SKILLS AND SALES
Danville Area Comm Coll (IL)
Illinois Valley Comm Coll (IL)
Lansing Comm Coll (MI)
McHenry County Coll (IL)
Minnesota State Coll–Southeast
Tech (MN)
Santa Monica Coll (CA)

**SEMICONDUCTOR
MANUFACTURING
TECHNOLOGY**
Mohawk Valley Comm Coll (NY)

SHEET METAL TECHNOLOGY
Coconino Comm Coll (AZ)
Columbus State Comm Coll (OH)
Comm Coll of Allegheny County (PA)
Delta Coll (MI)
Ivy Tech Comm Coll–Central Indiana
(IN)
Ivy Tech Comm Coll–Lafayette (IN)
Ivy Tech Comm Coll–North Central
(IN)
Ivy Tech Comm Coll–Northeast (IN)
Ivy Tech Comm Coll–Northwest (IN)
Ivy Tech Comm Coll–Sellersburg (IN)
Ivy Tech Comm Coll–Southwest (IN)
Ivy Tech Comm Coll–Wabash Valley
(IN)
Lake Superior Coll (MN)
Macomb Comm Coll (MI)
Miami Dade Coll (FL)
Palomar Coll (CA)
Rock Valley Coll (IL)
Shawnee Comm Coll (IL)
Vincennes U (IN)

**SIGNAL/GEOSPATIAL
INTELLIGENCE**
Northland Comm and Tech Coll (MN)

**SIGN LANGUAGE
INTERPRETATION AND
TRANSLATION**
Austin Comm Coll District (TX)
Camden County Coll (NJ)
Coconino Comm Coll (AZ)
Coll of the Canyons (CA)
Collin County Comm Coll District
(TX)
Columbus State Comm Coll (OH)
Comm Coll of Allegheny County (PA)
Comm Coll of Baltimore County (MD)
Comm Coll of Philadelphia (PA)
Del Mar Coll (TX)
El Paso Comm Coll (TX)
Front Range Comm Coll (CO)
Golden West Coll (CA)
Hinds Comm Coll (MS)
Houston Comm Coll (TX)
Illinois Central Coll (IL)
Johnson County Comm Coll (KS)
J. Sargeant Reynolds Comm Coll
(VA)
Lakeland Comm Coll (OH)
Lansing Comm Coll (MI)
Lone Star Coll–CyFair (TX)
Lone Star Coll–North Harris (TX)
McLennan Comm Coll (TX)
Miami Dade Coll (FL)
Minnesota State Comm and Tech
Coll (MN)
Minnesota State Comm and Tech
Coll–Moorhead (MN)

Mohawk Valley Comm Coll (NY)
Mott Comm Coll (MI)
Mt. San Antonio Coll (CA)
Nashville State Comm Coll (TN)
Northcentral Tech Coll (WI)
Northern Essex Comm Coll (MA)
Oklahoma State U–Oklahoma City
(OK)
Palomar Coll (CA)
Salt Lake Comm Coll (UT)
Santa Fe Comm Coll (NM)
Tarrant County Coll District (TX)
Tyler Jr Coll (TX)

**SMALL BUSINESS
ADMINISTRATION**
Borough of Manhattan Comm Coll of
the City U of New York (NY)
Bucks County Comm Coll (PA)
Cañada Coll (CA)
Cerritos Coll (CA)
Coll of the Canyons (CA)
Colorado Northwestern Comm Coll
(CO)
Dakota Coll at Bottineau (ND)
Delta Coll (MI)
Fullerton Coll (CA)
Harper Coll (IL)
J. Sargeant Reynolds Comm Coll
(VA)
Merced Coll (CA)
Middlesex County Coll (NJ)
Raritan Valley Comm Coll (NJ)
Schoolcraft Coll (MI)
Sierra Coll (CA)
South Suburban Coll (IL)
Springfield Tech Comm Coll (MA)
Westchester Comm Coll (NY)
Westmoreland County Comm Coll
(PA)

**SMALL ENGINE MECHANICS
AND REPAIR TECHNOLOGY**
Mitchell Tech Inst (SD)

SOCIAL PSYCHOLOGY
Macomb Comm Coll (MI)
South Florida State Coll (FL)

SOCIAL SCIENCES
Amarillo Coll (TX)
Arizona Western Coll (AZ)
Carl Albert State Coll (OK)
Central Oregon Comm Coll (OR)
Central Texas Coll (TX)
Central Wyoming Coll (WY)
Citrus Coll (CA)
Clinton Comm Coll (NY)
Cochise County Comm Coll District
(AZ)
Coll of Central Florida (FL)
Coll of Marin (CA)
Coll of the Canyons (CA)
Coll of the Desert (CA)
Comm Coll of Allegheny County (PA)
Comm Coll of Vermont (VT)
Dakota Coll at Bottineau (ND)
De Anza Coll (CA)
Dodge City Comm Coll (KS)
Eastern Wyoming Coll (WY)
Feather River Coll (CA)
Finger Lakes Comm Coll (NY)
Genesee Comm Coll (NY)
Harrisburg Area Comm Coll (PA)
Housatonic Comm Coll (CT)
Howard Comm Coll (MD)
Hutchinson Comm Coll (KS)
Imperial Valley Coll (CA)
J. Sargeant Reynolds Comm Coll
(VA)
Lansing Comm Coll (MI)
Laramie County Comm Coll (WY)
Luzerne County Comm Coll (PA)
Massachusetts Bay Comm Coll (MA)
Merced Coll (CA)
Miami Dade Coll (FL)
Middlesex Comm Coll (MA)
Monroe Comm Coll (NY)
Montgomery County Comm Coll (PA)
Mt. San Antonio Coll (CA)
Navarro Coll (TX)
Niagara County Comm Coll (NY)
Northeast Comm Coll (NE)
Northeastern Jr Coll (CO)
Northwest Coll (WY)
Orange Coast Coll (CA)
Otero Jr Coll (CO)
Palomar Coll (CA)
Paris Jr Coll (TX)
San Jacinto Coll District (TX)
San Joaquin Delta Coll (CA)
Santa Rosa Jr Coll (CA)

Seminole State Coll (OK)
Sierra Coll (CA)
South Florida State Coll (FL)
Texarkana Coll (TX)
U of Cincinnati Clermont Coll (OH)
Western Wyoming Comm Coll (WY)

SOCIAL SCIENCES RELATED
Genesee Comm Coll (NY)

**SOCIAL SCIENCE TEACHER
EDUCATION**
South Florida State Coll (FL)

**SOCIAL STUDIES TEACHER
EDUCATION**
Casper Coll (WY)
Ulster County Comm Coll (NY)

SOCIAL WORK
Allen Comm Coll (KS)
Amarillo Coll (TX)
Austin Comm Coll District (TX)
Bowling Green State U–Firelands
Coll (OH)
Camden County Coll (NJ)
Casper Coll (WY)
Chandler-Gilbert Comm Coll (AZ)
City Colls of Chicago, Kennedy-King
College (IL)
Coll of Central Florida (FL)
Comm Coll of Allegheny County (PA)
Comm Coll of Rhode Island (RI)
Comm Coll of the Air Force (AL)
Del Mar Coll (TX)
Dodge City Comm Coll (KS)
Edison State Comm Coll (OH)
Elgin Comm Coll (IL)
El Paso Comm Coll (TX)
Genesee Comm Coll (NY)
Georgia Military Coll (GA)
Gordon State Coll (GA)
Harford Comm Coll (MD)
Harrisburg Area Comm Coll (PA)
Holyoke Comm Coll (MA)
Hudson County Comm Coll (NJ)
Illinois Eastern Comm Colls, Wabash
Valley College (IL)
Illinois Valley Comm Coll (IL)
Iowa Central Comm Coll (IA)
Lakeland Comm Coll (OH)
Lehigh Carbon Comm Coll (PA)
Lorain County Comm Coll (OH)
Manchester Comm Coll (CT)
Miami Dade Coll (FL)
Monroe County Comm Coll (MI)
Nashville State Comm Coll (TN)
Northampton Comm Coll (PA)
Northeast Iowa Comm Coll (IA)
Oakton Comm Coll (IL)
Paris Jr Coll (TX)
Rogue Comm Coll (OR)
St. Philip's Coll (TX)
Salt Lake Comm Coll (UT)
San Juan Coll (NM)
Santa Fe Comm Coll (NM)
Shawnee Comm Coll (IL)
South Florida State Coll (FL)
South Plains Coll (TX)
South Suburban Coll (IL)
Southwestern Michigan Coll (MI)
Tyler Jr Coll (TX)
U of Cincinnati Blue Ash Coll (OH)
U of Cincinnati Clermont Coll (OH)
Vincennes U (IN)
Wayne County Comm Coll District
(MI)
Western Wyoming Comm Coll (WY)
West Georgia Tech Coll (GA)

SOCIAL WORK RELATED
Genesee Comm Coll (NY)

SOCIOLOGY
Allen Comm Coll (KS)
Alvin Comm Coll (TX)
Austin Comm Coll District (TX)
Bainbridge State Coll (GA)
Borough of Manhattan Comm Coll of
the City U of New York (NY)
Bunker Hill Comm Coll (MA)
Cañada Coll (CA)
Casper Coll (WY)
Central New Mexico Comm Coll (NM)
Cerritos Coll (CA)
Citrus Coll (CA)
Coconino Comm Coll (AZ)
Coll of Central Florida (FL)
Coll of the Canyons (CA)
Coll of the Desert (CA)
Comm Coll of Allegheny County (PA)
De Anza Coll (CA)

Del Mar Coll (TX)
Eastern Arizona Coll (AZ)
Feather River Coll (CA)
Finger Lakes Comm Coll (NY)
Fullerton Coll (CA)
Georgia Highlands Coll (GA)
Georgia Military Coll (GA)
Gordon State Coll (GA)
Harford Comm Coll (MD)
Hill Coll (TX)
Iowa Central Comm Coll (IA)
Lansing Comm Coll (MI)
Laramie County Comm Coll (WY)
Merced Coll (CA)
Miami Dade Coll (FL)
Mohave Comm Coll (AZ)
Nashville State Comm Coll (TN)
Navarro Coll (TX)
Northeastern Jr Coll (CO)
Northwest Coll (WY)
Oklahoma City Comm Coll (OK)
Orange Coast Coll (CA)
Palomar Coll (CA)
Panola Coll (TX)
Paris Jr Coll (TX)
Pensacola State Coll (FL)
St. Philip's Coll (TX)
Salt Lake Comm Coll (UT)
San Jacinto Coll District (TX)
San Joaquin Delta Coll (CA)
Santa Rosa Jr Coll (CA)
Southern U at Shreveport (LA)
South Florida State Coll (FL)
Three Rivers Comm Coll (MO)
Trinity Valley Comm Coll (TX)
Tyler Jr Coll (TX)
Vincennes U (IN)
Western Wyoming Comm Coll (WY)

SOCIOLOGY AND ANTHROPOLOGY
Harper Coll (IL)

SOIL SCIENCE AND AGRONOMY
The Ohio State U Ag Tech Inst (OH)
South Florida State Coll (FL)
Treasure Valley Comm Coll (OR)

SOLAR ENERGY TECHNOLOGY
Arizona Western Coll (AZ)
Coconino Comm Coll (AZ)
Comm Coll of Allegheny County (PA)
Crowder Coll (MO)
Lorain County Comm Coll (OH)
Texas State Tech Coll (TX)
Treasure Valley Comm Coll (OR)

SPANISH
Arizona Western Coll (AZ)
Austin Comm Coll District (TX)
Blinn Coll (TX)
Cañada Coll (CA)
Cerritos Coll (CA)
Citrus Coll (CA)
Coll of Marin (CA)
Coll of the Canyons (CA)
Coll of the Desert (CA)
De Anza Coll (CA)
Fiorello H. LaGuardia Comm Coll of the City U of New York (NY)
Imperial Valley Coll (CA)
Lansing Comm Coll (MI)
Laramie County Comm Coll (WY)
Los Angeles City Coll (CA)
Merced Coll (CA)
Miami Dade Coll (FL)
Northwest Coll (WY)
Orange Coast Coll (CA)
Santa Fe Comm Coll (NM)
Santa Monica Coll (CA)
Santa Rosa Jr Coll (CA)
South Florida State Coll (FL)
Trinity Valley Comm Coll (TX)
Western Wyoming Comm Coll (WY)

SPANISH LANGUAGE TEACHER EDUCATION
Anne Arundel Comm Coll (MD)
Carroll Comm Coll (MD)
Comm Coll of Baltimore County (MD)
Frederick Comm Coll (MD)
Harford Comm Coll (MD)
Montgomery Coll (MD)
Ulster County Comm Coll (NY)

SPECIAL EDUCATION
Coll of Central Florida (FL)
Comm Coll of Rhode Island (RI)

Craven Comm Coll (NC)
Harford Comm Coll (MD)
Highland Comm Coll (IL)
Hill Coll (TX)
Lehigh Carbon Comm Coll (PA)
McHenry County Coll (IL)
Miami Dade Coll (FL)
Nashville State Comm Coll (TN)
Pensacola State Coll (FL)
San Juan Coll (NM)
South Florida State Coll (FL)
U of Cincinnati Clermont Coll (OH)
Vincennes U (IN)

SPECIAL EDUCATION–EARLY CHILDHOOD
Harford Comm Coll (MD)
Merced Coll (CA)
Mitchell Comm Coll (NC)
Motlow State Comm Coll (TN)
Orange Coast Coll (CA)
Palomar Coll (CA)
Santa Monica Coll (CA)

SPECIAL EDUCATION– ELEMENTARY SCHOOL
Harford Comm Coll (MD)

SPECIAL EDUCATION– INDIVIDUALS WITH EMOTIONAL DISTURBANCES
South Florida State Coll (FL)

SPECIAL EDUCATION– INDIVIDUALS WITH HEARING IMPAIRMENTS
Miami Dade Coll (FL)

SPECIAL EDUCATION– INDIVIDUALS WITH INTELLECTUAL DISABILITIES
South Florida State Coll (FL)

SPECIAL EDUCATION– INDIVIDUALS WITH SPECIFIC LEARNING DISABILITIES
South Florida State Coll (FL)

SPECIAL EDUCATION– INDIVIDUALS WITH VISION IMPAIRMENTS
South Florida State Coll (FL)

SPECIAL PRODUCTS MARKETING
Del Mar Coll (TX)
Monroe Comm Coll (NY)
Northland Comm and Tech Coll (MN)
Scottsdale Comm Coll (AZ)
South Plains Coll (TX)
Tompkins Cortland Comm Coll (NY)

SPEECH COMMUNICATION AND RHETORIC
Ancilla Coll (IN)
Brookhaven Coll (TX)
Bucks County Comm Coll (PA)
Bunker Hill Comm Coll (MA)
Camden County Coll (NJ)
Cañada Coll (CA)
Casper Coll (WY)
Central Oregon Comm Coll (OR)
Cerritos Coll (CA)
Citrus Coll (CA)
Cochise County Comm Coll District (AZ)
Coll of Marin (CA)
Coll of the Canyons (CA)
Coll of the Desert (CA)
Collin County Comm Coll District (TX)
Dutchess Comm Coll (NY)
Eastern Arizona Coll (AZ)
Eastern Wyoming Coll (WY)
Edison State Comm Coll (OH)
El Paso Comm Coll (TX)
Erie Comm Coll, South Campus (NY)
Fiorello H. LaGuardia Comm Coll of the City U of New York (NY)
Fullerton Coll (CA)
Georgia Highlands Coll (GA)
Harper Coll (IL)
Hill Coll (TX)
Houston Comm Coll (TX)
Hutchinson Comm Coll (KS)
Jamestown Comm Coll (NY)
Lackawanna Coll (PA)
Lansing Comm Coll (MI)
Laramie County Comm Coll (WY)
Lehigh Carbon Comm Coll (PA)

Lone Star Coll–CyFair (TX)
Lone Star Coll–U Park (TX)
Macomb Comm Coll (MI)
Manchester Comm Coll (CT)
Merced Coll (CA)
Montgomery Coll (MD)
Montgomery County Comm Coll (PA)
Mountain View Coll (TX)
Nashville State Comm Coll (TN)
Nassau Comm Coll (NY)
Northampton Comm Coll (PA)
Northeast Comm Coll (NE)
Northwest Coll (WY)
Norwalk Comm Coll (CT)
Orange Coast Coll (CA)
Palomar Coll (CA)
Panola Coll (TX)
Salt Lake Comm Coll (UT)
Santa Monica Coll (CA)
South Florida State Coll (FL)
Tompkins Cortland Comm Coll (NY)
Tyler Jr Coll (TX)
Ulster County Comm Coll (NY)
U of Cincinnati Blue Ash Coll (OH)
Westchester Comm Coll (NY)
Western Wyoming Comm Coll (WY)

SPEECH-LANGUAGE PATHOLOGY
Lake Region State Coll (ND)
Williston State Coll (ND)

SPEECH-LANGUAGE PATHOLOGY ASSISTANT
Alexandria Tech and Comm Coll (MN)
Caldwell Comm Coll and Tech Inst (NC)
Fayetteville Tech Comm Coll (NC)
Mitchell Tech Inst (SD)
Oklahoma City Comm Coll (OK)

SPORT AND FITNESS ADMINISTRATION/ MANAGEMENT
Adirondack Comm Coll (NY)
Arizona Western Coll (AZ)
Bucks County Comm Coll (PA)
Bunker Hill Comm Coll (MA)
Camden County Coll (NJ)
Cañada Coll (CA)
Cayuga County Comm Coll (NY)
Central Oregon Comm Coll (OR)
Cerritos Coll (CA)
Columbus State Comm Coll (OH)
Delta Coll (MI)
Des Moines Area Comm Coll (IA)
Fullerton Coll (CA)
Garrett Coll (MD)
Holyoke Comm Coll (MA)
Howard Comm Coll (MD)
Hutchinson Comm Coll (KS)
Illinois Eastern Comm Colls, Frontier Community College (IL)
Illinois Eastern Comm Colls, Lincoln Trail College (IL)
Illinois Eastern Comm Colls, Wabash Valley College (IL)
Jefferson Comm Coll (NY)
Kingsborough Comm Coll of the City U of New York (NY)
Lehigh Carbon Comm Coll (PA)
Lorain County Comm Coll (OH)
Manor Coll (PA)
NHTI, Concord's Comm Coll, Concord (NH)
Niagara County Comm Coll (NY)
Northampton Comm Coll (PA)
Northern Essex Comm Coll (MA)
Rock Valley Coll (IL)
Salt Lake Comm Coll (UT)
Santa Monica Coll (CA)
Southwestern Michigan Coll (MI)
Springfield Tech Comm Coll (MA)
State U of New York Coll of Technology at Alfred (NY)
Sullivan County Comm Coll (NY)
Three Rivers Comm Coll (CT)
Tompkins Cortland Comm Coll (NY)
U of Cincinnati Clermont Coll (OH)
Vincennes U (IN)

SPORTS COMMUNICATION
Illinois Eastern Comm Colls, Wabash Valley College (IL)

SPORTS STUDIES
Finger Lakes Comm Coll (NY)
Genesee Comm Coll (NY)

STATISTICS
Coll of Central Florida (FL)
Eastern Wyoming Coll (WY)
South Florida State Coll (FL)

STATISTICS RELATED
Casper Coll (WY)

STRUCTURAL ENGINEERING
Harrisburg Area Comm Coll (PA)

SUBSTANCE ABUSE/ ADDICTION COUNSELING
Adirondack Comm Coll (NY)
Alvin Comm Coll (TX)
Amarillo Coll (TX)
Anne Arundel Comm Coll (MD)
Austin Comm Coll District (TX)
Camden County Coll (NJ)
Casper Coll (WY)
Central Oregon Comm Coll (OR)
Century Coll (MN)
Chippewa Valley Tech Coll (WI)
City Colls of Chicago, Kennedy-King College (IL)
Coll of the Desert (CA)
Comm Coll of Allegheny County (PA)
Comm Coll of Baltimore County (MD)
Comm Coll of Rhode Island (RI)
El Paso Comm Coll (TX)
Erie Comm Coll (NY)
Finger Lakes Comm Coll (NY)
Florida SouthWestern State Coll (FL)
Fox Valley Tech Coll (WI)
Genesee Comm Coll (NY)
Housatonic Comm Coll (CT)
Howard Comm Coll (MD)
Illinois Central Coll (IL)
J. Sargeant Reynolds Comm Coll (VA)
Mesabi Range Coll (MN)
Miami Dade Coll (FL)
Mohave Comm Coll (AZ)
Mohawk Valley Comm Coll (NY)
Naugatuck Valley Comm Coll (CT)
NHTI, Concord's Comm Coll, Concord (NH)
Northcentral Tech Coll (WI)
North Shore Comm Coll (MA)
Oakton Comm Coll (IL)
Oklahoma State U–Oklahoma City (OK)
Olympic Coll (WA)
Palomar Coll (CA)
Rio Salado Coll (AZ)
Sisseton-Wahpeton Coll (SD)
Southeastern Comm Coll (IA)
Southwestern Comm Coll (NC)
Stark State Coll (OH)
Texarkana Coll (TX)
Tompkins Cortland Comm Coll (NY)
Treasure Valley Comm Coll (OR)
Tyler Jr Coll (TX)
Wayne County Comm Coll District (MI)
Westchester Comm Coll (NY)
Wor-Wic Comm Coll (MD)

SURGICAL TECHNOLOGY
Anne Arundel Comm Coll (MD)
Anoka Tech Coll (MN)
Athens Tech Coll (GA)
Augusta Tech Coll (GA)
Austin Comm Coll District (TX)
Bismarck State Coll (ND)
Cape Fear Comm Coll (NC)
Central New Mexico Comm Coll (NM)
Coastal Pines Tech Coll (GA)
Collin County Comm Coll District (TX)
Columbus State Comm Coll (OH)
Columbus Tech Coll (GA)
Comm Care Coll (OK)
Comm Coll of Allegheny County (PA)
Comm Coll of the Air Force (AL)
Delta Coll (MI)
Eastern Idaho Tech Coll (ID)
El Paso Comm Coll (TX)
Fayetteville Tech Comm Coll (NC)
Frederick Comm Coll (MD)
Front Range Comm Coll (CO)
Gateway Tech Coll (WI)
Georgia Northwestern Tech Coll (GA)
Georgia Piedmont Tech Coll (GA)
Great Falls Coll Montana State U (MT)
Gulf Coast State Coll (FL)

Harrisburg Area Comm Coll (PA)
Hinds Comm Coll (MS)
Hutchinson Comm Coll (KS)
Illinois Central Coll (IL)
Ivy Tech Comm Coll–Central Indiana (IN)
Ivy Tech Comm Coll–Columbus (IN)
Ivy Tech Comm Coll–East Central (IN)
Ivy Tech Comm Coll–Kokomo (IN)
Ivy Tech Comm Coll–Lafayette (IN)
Ivy Tech Comm Coll–Northwest (IN)
Ivy Tech Comm Coll–Southwest (IN)
Ivy Tech Comm Coll–Wabash Valley (IN)
Kirtland Comm Coll (MI)
Lackawanna Coll (PA)
Lakeland Comm Coll (OH)
Lake Superior Coll (MN)
Lanier Tech Coll (GA)
Lansing Comm Coll (MI)
Laramie County Comm Coll (WY)
Lone Star Coll–Tomball (TX)
Lorain County Comm Coll (OH)
Luzerne County Comm Coll (PA)
Macomb Comm Coll (MI)
Manchester Comm Coll (CT)
Metropolitan Comm Coll (NE)
Minnesota State Comm and Tech Coll (MN)
Minnesota State Comm and Tech Coll–Moorhead (MN)
Minnesota West Comm and Tech Coll (MN)
Mohave Comm Coll (AZ)
Montgomery Coll (MD)
Montgomery County Comm Coll (PA)
Nassau Comm Coll (NY)
Niagara County Comm Coll (NY)
Northeast Comm Coll (NE)
Northland Comm and Tech Coll (MN)
Oklahoma City Comm Coll (OK)
Owensboro Comm and Tech Coll (KY)
Paris Jr Coll (TX)
Pittsburgh Tech Coll (PA)
Pueblo Comm Coll (CO)
Renton Tech Coll (WA)
Rock Valley Coll (IL)
St. Philip's Coll (TX)
San Jacinto Coll District (TX)
San Juan Coll (NM)
Savannah Tech Coll (GA)
Somerset Comm Coll (KY)
Southeast Comm Coll, Lincoln Campus (NE)
Southeastern Coll–West Palm Beach (FL)
Southern Crescent Tech Coll (GA)
Southern Regional Tech Coll (GA)
Southern U at Shreveport (LA)
South Plains Coll (TX)
Spencerian Coll (KY)
Springfield Tech Comm Coll (MA)
Tallahassee Comm Coll (FL)
Tarrant County Coll District (TX)
Trinity Valley Comm Coll (TX)
Tyler Jr Coll (TX)
U of Cincinnati Clermont Coll (OH)
Vincennes U (IN)
Walters State Comm Coll (TN)
Waukesha County Tech Coll (WI)
Wayne County Comm Coll District (MI)
Western Dakota Tech Inst (SD)

SURVEYING ENGINEERING
Central New Mexico Comm Coll (NM)
Comm Coll of Rhode Island (RI)
Des Moines Area Comm Coll (IA)

SURVEYING TECHNOLOGY
Austin Comm Coll District (TX)
Bismarck State Coll (ND)
Coll of the Canyons (CA)
Columbus State Comm Coll (OH)
Comm Coll of Baltimore County (MD)
Fayetteville Tech Comm Coll (NC)
Gateway Tech Coll (WI)
Guam Comm Coll (GU)
Lansing Comm Coll (MI)
Macomb Comm Coll (MI)
Middlesex County Coll (NJ)
Mt. San Antonio Coll (CA)
Oklahoma State U–Oklahoma City (OK)
Rend Lake Coll (IL)
Renton Tech Coll (WA)

Salt Lake Comm Coll (UT)
Santa Fe Comm Coll (NM)
Santa Rosa Jr Coll (CA)
South Florida State Coll (FL)
State U of New York Coll of
Technology at Alfred (NY)
Texas State Tech Coll (TX)
Three Rivers Comm Coll (MO)
Tyler Jr Coll (TX)
U of Arkansas Comm Coll at
Morrilton (AR)
Vincennes U (IN)

SYSTEM, NETWORKING, AND LAN/WAN MANAGEMENT
Blue Ridge Comm and Tech Coll
(WV)
Cloud County Comm Coll (KS)
Collin County Comm Coll District
(TX)
Craven Comm Coll (NC)
El Paso Comm Coll (TX)
Hill Coll (TX)
Lamar Comm Coll (CO)
Lone Star Coll–Tomball (TX)
Oklahoma City Comm Coll (OK)
Paris Jr Coll (TX)
Rowan-Cabarrus Comm Coll (NC)
St. Philip's Coll (TX)
Southwestern Comm Coll (NC)
Southwestern Indian Polytechnic Inst
(NM)
Texas State Tech Coll (TX)
Tyler Jr Coll (TX)
Ulster County Comm Coll (NY)
Wayne County Comm Coll District
(MI)
Williston State Coll (ND)

SYSTEMS ENGINEERING
South Florida State Coll (FL)

TEACHER ASSISTANT/AIDE
Alamance Comm Coll (NC)
Borough of Manhattan Comm Coll of
the City U of New York (NY)
Central Wyoming Coll (WY)
Century Coll (MN)
Cloud County Comm Coll (KS)
Coll of The Albemarle (NC)
Comm Coll of Vermont (VT)
Dakota Coll at Bottineau (ND)
Danville Area Comm Coll (IL)
Fiorello H. LaGuardia Comm Coll of
the City U of New York (NY)
Gateway Comm and Tech Coll (KY)
Gateway Tech Coll (WI)
Genesee Comm Coll (NY)
Harford Comm Coll (MD)
Highland Comm Coll (IL)
Hill Coll (TX)
Illinois Central Coll (IL)
Illinois Eastern Comm Colls, Lincoln
Trail College (IL)
Illinois Valley Comm Coll (IL)
Jamestown Comm Coll (NY)
Jefferson Comm Coll (NY)
Kaskaskia Coll (IL)
Kingsborough Comm Coll of the City
U of New York (NY)
Kishwaukee Coll (IL)
Lake Superior Coll (MN)
Lansing Comm Coll (MI)
Lehigh Carbon Comm Coll (PA)
Manchester Comm Coll (CT)
Mercer County Comm Coll (NJ)
Mesa Comm Coll (AZ)
Miami Dade Coll (FL)
Middlesex County Coll (NJ)
Minnesota State Comm and Tech
Coll (MN)
Minnesota State Comm and Tech
Coll–Detroit Lakes (MN)
Mitchell Comm Coll (NC)
Montgomery County Comm Coll (PA)
NHTI, Concord's Comm Coll,
Concord (NH)
Northampton Comm Coll (PA)
Northcentral Tech Coll (WI)
Northland Comm and Tech Coll (MN)
Patrick Henry Comm Coll (VA)
St. Charles Comm Coll (MO)
Salt Lake Comm Coll (UT)
Somerset Comm Coll (KY)
Southern U at Shreveport (LA)
Southwest Texas Jr Coll (TX)
Vincennes U (IN)
Waukesha County Tech Coll (WI)
Westchester Comm Coll (NY)

TECHNICAL TEACHER EDUCATION
East Central Coll (MO)

TECHNOLOGY/INDUSTRIAL ARTS TEACHER EDUCATION
Allen Comm Coll (KS)
Casper Coll (WY)
Central New Mexico Comm Coll (NM)
Cerritos Coll (CA)
Delta Coll (MI)
Eastern Arizona Coll (AZ)
Fullerton Coll (CA)

TELECOMMUNICATIONS TECHNOLOGY
Amarillo Coll (TX)
Arapahoe Comm Coll (CO)
Carl Albert State Coll (OK)
Cayuga County Comm Coll (NY)
Collin County Comm Coll District
(TX)
County Coll of Morris (NJ)
Georgia Piedmont Tech Coll (GA)
Hinds Comm Coll (MS)
Howard Comm Coll (MD)
Illinois Eastern Comm Colls, Lincoln
Trail College (IL)
Iowa Central Comm Coll (IA)
Ivy Tech Comm Coll–Lafayette (IN)
Ivy Tech Comm Coll–North Central
(IN)
Ivy Tech Comm Coll–Northwest (IN)
Ivy Tech Comm Coll–Sellersburg (IN)
Ivy Tech Comm Coll–Southwest (IN)
Meridian Comm Coll (MS)
Miami Dade Coll (FL)
Minnesota State Comm and Tech
Coll (MN)
Mitchell Tech Inst (SD)
Monroe Comm Coll (NY)
Northern Essex Comm Coll (MA)
Penn State DuBois (PA)
Penn State Fayette, The Eberly
Campus (PA)
Penn State Shenango (PA)
Pensacola State Coll (FL)
Queensborough Comm Coll of the
City U of New York (NY)
Quinsigamond Comm Coll (MA)
Salt Lake Comm Coll (UT)
Seminole State Coll of Florida (FL)
South Plains Coll (TX)
Springfield Tech Comm Coll (MA)
Texas State Tech Coll (TX)
Trident Tech Coll (SC)

THEATER DESIGN AND TECHNOLOGY
Carroll Comm Coll (MD)
Casper Coll (WY)
Central Wyoming Coll (WY)
Genesee Comm Coll (NY)
Harford Comm Coll (MD)
Howard Comm Coll (MD)
Lansing Comm Coll (MI)
Miami Dade Coll (FL)
Nassau Comm Coll (NY)
San Juan Coll (NM)
Santa Monica Coll (CA)
Vincennes U (IN)
Western Wyoming Comm Coll (WY)

THEATER/THEATER ARTS MANAGEMENT
Genesee Comm Coll (NY)
Harper Coll (IL)

THEOLOGY AND RELIGIOUS VOCATIONS RELATED
Ancilla Coll (IN)

THERAPEUTIC RECREATION
Austin Comm Coll District (TX)
Comm Coll of Allegheny County (PA)

TOOL AND DIE TECHNOLOGY
Bevill State Comm Coll (AL)
Craven Comm Coll (NC)
Delta Coll (MI)
Des Moines Area Comm Coll (IA)
Dunwoody Coll of Technology (MN)
Hennepin Tech Coll (MN)
Ivy Tech Comm Coll–Bloomington
(IN)
Ivy Tech Comm Coll–Central Indiana
(IN)
Ivy Tech Comm Coll–Columbus (IN)
Ivy Tech Comm Coll–East Central
(IN)
Ivy Tech Comm Coll–Kokomo (IN)

Ivy Tech Comm Coll–North Central
(IN)
Ivy Tech Comm Coll–Northeast (IN)
Ivy Tech Comm Coll–Northwest (IN)
Ivy Tech Comm Coll–Richmond (IN)
Ivy Tech Comm Coll–Sellersburg (IN)
Ivy Tech Comm Coll–Southwest (IN)
Ivy Tech Comm Coll–Wabash Valley
(IN)
Macomb Comm Coll (MI)
Rock Valley Coll (IL)
Vincennes U (IN)

TOURISM AND TRAVEL SERVICES MANAGEMENT
Adirondack Comm Coll (NY)
Albany Tech Coll (GA)
Amarillo Coll (TX)
Athens Tech Coll (GA)
Atlanta Tech Coll (GA)
Austin Comm Coll District (TX)
Bucks County Comm Coll (PA)
Bunker Hill Comm Coll (MA)
Central Georgia Tech Coll (GA)
Columbus State Comm Coll (OH)
Daytona State Coll (FL)
El Paso Comm Coll (TX)
Finger Lakes Comm Coll (NY)
Fiorello H. LaGuardia Comm Coll of
the City U of New York (NY)
Genesee Comm Coll (NY)
Guam Comm Coll (GU)
Gwinnett Tech Coll (GA)
Hinds Comm Coll (MS)
Houston Comm Coll (TX)
Kingsborough Comm Coll of the City
U of New York (NY)
Lakeland Comm Coll (OH)
Lansing Comm Coll (MI)
Lorain County Comm Coll (OH)
Luzerne County Comm Coll (PA)
Madison Area Tech Coll (WI)
Miami Dade Coll (FL)
Monroe Comm Coll (NY)
NHTI, Concord's Comm Coll,
Concord (NH)
Niagara County Comm Coll (NY)
North Shore Comm Coll (MA)
Ogeechee Tech Coll (GA)
St. Philip's Coll (TX)
Savannah Tech Coll (GA)
Southern U at Shreveport (LA)
Sullivan County Comm Coll (NY)
Westmoreland County Comm Coll
(PA)

TOURISM AND TRAVEL SERVICES MARKETING
Luzerne County Comm Coll (PA)
Montgomery County Comm Coll (PA)
Orange Coast Coll (CA)

TOURISM PROMOTION
Comm Coll of Allegheny County (PA)
Genesee Comm Coll (NY)
Jefferson Comm Coll (NY)

TRADE AND INDUSTRIAL TEACHER EDUCATION
Del Mar Coll (TX)
Lenoir Comm Coll (NC)
Quinsigamond Comm Coll (MA)
Southeastern Comm Coll (IA)
South Florida State Coll (FL)
Southwestern Comm Coll (NC)

TRANSPORTATION AND HIGHWAY ENGINEERING
Gateway Tech Coll (WI)

TRANSPORTATION AND MATERIALS MOVING RELATED
Cecil Coll (MD)
Mid-Plains Comm Coll, North Platte
(NE)
Mt. San Antonio Coll (CA)
Nassau Comm Coll (NY)

TRANSPORTATION/MOBILITY MANAGEMENT
Cecil Coll (MD)
Del Mar Coll (TX)
Gulf Coast State Coll (FL)
Hagerstown Comm Coll (MD)
Ivy Tech Comm Coll–Central Indiana
(IN)
South Florida State Coll (FL)

TRUCK AND BUS DRIVER/ COMMERCIAL VEHICLE OPERATION/INSTRUCTION
Lake Superior Coll (MN)

Mitchell Tech Inst (SD)
Mohave Comm Coll (AZ)
Salina Area Tech Coll (KS)
Spoon River Coll (IL)

TURF AND TURFGRASS MANAGEMENT
Coll of the Desert (CA)
Comm Coll of Allegheny County (PA)
Danville Area Comm Coll (IL)
Florida SouthWestern State Coll (FL)
Houston Comm Coll (TX)
North Georgia Tech Coll (GA)
The Ohio State U Ag Tech Inst (OH)
Ozarks Tech Comm Coll (MO)
Texas State Tech Coll (TX)
Westmoreland County Comm Coll
(PA)

URBAN FORESTRY
Dakota Coll at Bottineau (ND)
Hennepin Tech Coll (MN)
Kent State U at Trumbull (OH)

VEHICLE MAINTENANCE AND REPAIR TECHNOLOGIES
Bevill State Comm Coll (AL)
Coll of the Desert (CA)
Ohio Tech Coll (OH)

VEHICLE MAINTENANCE AND REPAIR TECHNOLOGIES RELATED
Central New Mexico Comm Coll (NM)
State U of New York Coll of
Technology at Alfred (NY)
Western Dakota Tech Inst (SD)

VETERINARY/ANIMAL HEALTH TECHNOLOGY
Athens Tech Coll (GA)
Austin Comm Coll District (TX)
Bel–Rea Inst of Animal Technology
(CO)
Camden County Coll (NJ)
Central Georgia Tech Coll (GA)
Central New Mexico Comm Coll (NM)
Coll of Central Florida (FL)
Columbus State Comm Coll (OH)
Comm Care Coll (OK)
Comm Coll of Baltimore County (MD)
Crowder Coll (MO)
Des Moines Area Comm Coll (IA)
Duluth Business U (MN)
Eastern Wyoming Coll (WY)
Fiorello H. LaGuardia Comm Coll of
the City U of New York (NY)
Front Range Comm Coll (CO)
Gateway Tech Coll (WI)
Genesee Comm Coll (NY)
Gwinnett Tech Coll (GA)
Hillsborough Comm Coll (FL)
Hinds Comm Coll (MS)
Holyoke Comm Coll (MA)
Jefferson State Comm Coll (AL)
Kaskaskia Coll (IL)
Kent State U at Tuscarawas (OH)
Lansing Comm Coll (MI)
Lehigh Carbon Comm Coll (PA)
Lone Star Coll–Tomball (TX)
Macomb Comm Coll (MI)
Madison Area Tech Coll (WI)
Manor Coll (PA)
Mesa Comm Coll (AZ)
Miami Dade Coll (FL)
Murray State Coll (OK)
Northampton Comm Coll (PA)
Northeast Comm Coll (NE)
North Shore Comm Coll (MA)
Northwest Coll (WY)
Ogeechee Tech Coll (GA)
Oklahoma State U–Oklahoma City
(OK)
Owensboro Comm and Tech Coll
(KY)
Penn Foster Coll (AZ)
Pensacola State Coll (FL)
Rend Lake Coll (IL)
San Juan Coll (NM)
Shawnee Comm Coll (IL)
State U of New York Coll of
Technology at Alfred (NY)
Trident Tech Coll (SC)
Truckee Meadows Comm Coll (NV)
Tyler Jr Coll (TX)
Ulster County Comm Coll (NY)
U of Cincinnati Blue Ash Coll (OH)
Volunteer State Comm Coll (TN)
York County Comm Coll (ME)

VISUAL AND PERFORMING ARTS
Amarillo Coll (TX)
Berkshire Comm Coll (MA)
Borough of Manhattan Comm Coll of
the City U of New York (NY)
Bucks County Comm Coll (PA)
Central Wyoming Coll (WY)
Cerritos Coll (CA)
Chandler-Gilbert Comm Coll (AZ)
Citrus Coll (CA)
Coconino Comm Coll (AZ)
Comm Coll of Baltimore County (MD)
Dutchess Comm Coll (NY)
Feather River Coll (CA)
Fiorello H. LaGuardia Comm Coll of
the City U of New York (NY)
Gordon State Coll (GA)
Harrisburg Area Comm Coll (PA)
Hutchinson Comm Coll (KS)
Middlesex County Coll (NJ)
Mott Comm Coll (MI)
Mt. San Antonio Coll (CA)
Nassau Comm Coll (NY)
NHTI, Concord's Comm Coll,
Concord (NH)
Queensborough Comm Coll of the
City U of New York (NY)
Rogue Comm Coll (OR)
Santa Monica Coll (CA)
Sierra Coll (CA)
Spartanburg Methodist Coll (SC)
Ulster County Comm Coll (NY)
Westchester Comm Coll (NY)
Western Wyoming Comm Coll (WY)

VISUAL AND PERFORMING ARTS RELATED
Bossier Parish Comm Coll (LA)
Comm Coll of Allegheny County (PA)
John Tyler Comm Coll (VA)
Northwest Coll (WY)

VITICULTURE AND ENOLOGY
Finger Lakes Comm Coll (NY)
Harrisburg Area Comm Coll (PA)
James Sprunt Comm Coll (NC)
Kent State U at Ashtabula (OH)
Missouri State U–West Plains (MO)
Santa Rosa Jr Coll (CA)
Texas State Tech Coll (TX)

VOCATIONAL REHABILITATION COUNSELING
South Florida State Coll (FL)

VOICE AND OPERA
Alvin Comm Coll (TX)
Del Mar Coll (TX)
Navarro Coll (TX)

WATCHMAKING AND JEWELRYMAKING
Austin Comm Coll District (TX)
Paris Jr Coll (TX)

WATER QUALITY AND WASTEWATER TREATMENT MANAGEMENT AND RECYCLING TECHNOLOGY
Arizona Western Coll (AZ)
Citrus Coll (CA)
Coll of the Canyons (CA)
Delta Coll (MI)
Ogeechee Tech Coll (GA)
Palomar Coll (CA)
Santa Fe Comm Coll (NM)

WATER RESOURCES ENGINEERING
Gateway Tech Coll (WI)

WATER, WETLANDS, AND MARINE RESOURCES MANAGEMENT
South Florida State Coll (FL)

WEB/MULTIMEDIA MANAGEMENT AND WEBMASTER
Casper Coll (WY)
City Colls of Chicago, Olive-Harvey
College (IL)
Comm Coll of Rhode Island (RI)
Del Mar Coll (TX)
Delta Coll (MI)
Fox Valley Tech Coll (WI)
Gateway Tech Coll (WI)
Illinois Central Coll (IL)
Kaskaskia Coll (IL)
Lansdale School of Business (PA)

Monroe County Comm Coll (MI)
Montgomery County Comm Coll (PA)
Morton Coll (IL)
Northern Essex Comm Coll (MA)
Rio Salado Coll (AZ)
St. Clair County Comm Coll (MI)
Seminole State Coll of Florida (FL)
Trident Tech Coll (SC)
Vincennes U (IN)
Waukesha County Tech Coll (WI)
Wayne County Comm Coll District (MI)
Western Wyoming Comm Coll (WY)

WEB PAGE, DIGITAL/ MULTIMEDIA AND INFORMATION RESOURCES DESIGN
Bismarck State Coll (ND)
Blackhawk Tech Coll (WI)
Borough of Manhattan Comm Coll of the City U of New York (NY)
Bucks County Comm Coll (PA)
Bunker Hill Comm Coll (MA)
Casper Coll (WY)
Cecil Coll (MD)
Central Georgia Tech Coll (GA)
Century Coll (MN)
Chattahoochee Tech Coll (GA)
Cloud County Comm Coll (KS)
The Coll of Westchester (NY)
Collin County Comm Coll District (TX)
Columbus Tech Coll (GA)
County Coll of Morris (NJ)
Del Mar Coll (TX)
Dunwoody Coll of Technology (MN)
Eastern Idaho Tech Coll (ID)
Florida SouthWestern State Coll (FL)
Genesee Comm Coll (NY)
Georgia Northwestern Tech Coll (GA)
Gulf Coast State Coll (FL)
Hagerstown Comm Coll (MD)
Harper Coll (IL)
Harrisburg Area Comm Coll (PA)
Hawkeye Comm Coll (IA)
Hennepin Tech Coll (MN)
Highland Comm Coll (IL)
Hutchinson Comm Coll (KS)
Illinois Central Coll (IL)
Illinois Eastern Comm Colls, Frontier Community College (IL)
Johnson County Comm Coll (KS)
J. Sargeant Reynolds Comm Coll (VA)
Lake Superior Coll (MN)
Lanier Tech Coll (GA)

Lansdale School of Business (PA)
Lansing Comm Coll (MI)
Lehigh Carbon Comm Coll (PA)
Lorain County Comm Coll (OH)
Mesabi Range Coll (MN)
Mesa Comm Coll (AZ)
Miami Dade Coll (FL)
Middlesex Comm Coll (MA)
Minnesota State Coll–Southeast Tech (MN)
Minnesota State Comm and Tech Coll (MN)
Mohawk Valley Comm Coll (NY)
Monroe County Comm Coll (MI)
Montgomery Coll (MD)
Motlow State Comm Coll (TN)
Mount Wachusett Comm Coll (MA)
Niagara County Comm Coll (NY)
Northampton Comm Coll (PA)
Northern Essex Comm Coll (MA)
North Georgia Tech Coll (GA)
North Shore Comm Coll (MA)
Norwalk Comm Coll (CT)
Palomar Coll (CA)
Pittsburgh Tech Coll (PA)
Pueblo Comm Coll (CO)
Quinsigamond Comm Coll (MA)
Raritan Valley Comm Coll (NJ)
Rio Salado Coll (AZ)
Schoolcraft Coll (MI)
Seminole State Coll of Florida (FL)
Sierra Coll (CA)
Southeastern Tech Coll (GA)
Southern Crescent Tech Coll (GA)
Stark State Coll (OH)
Tallahassee Comm Coll (FL)
Texas State Tech Coll (TX)
Trident Tech Coll (SC)
Walters State Comm Coll (TN)
Western Wyoming Comm Coll (WY)
West Georgia Tech Coll (GA)
Westmoreland County Comm Coll (PA)
Wiregrass Georgia Tech Coll (GA)

WELDING ENGINEERING TECHNOLOGY
Arizona Western Coll (AZ)
Mitchell Tech Inst (SD)
St. Clair County Comm Coll (MI)

WELDING TECHNOLOGY
Alamance Comm Coll (NC)
American Samoa Comm Coll (AS)
Anoka Tech Coll (MN)
Austin Comm Coll District (TX)
Bainbridge State Coll (GA)
Bismarck State Coll (ND)
Casper Coll (WY)

Central New Mexico Comm Coll (NM)
Central Texas Coll (TX)
Central Wyoming Coll (WY)
Cerritos Coll (CA)
Cochise County Comm Coll District (AZ)
Coll of the Canyons (CA)
Columbus State Comm Coll (OH)
Comm Coll of Allegheny County (PA)
Craven Comm Coll (NC)
Crowder Coll (MO)
Del Mar Coll (TX)
Delta Coll (MI)
Dodge City Comm Coll (KS)
Dunwoody Coll of Technology (MN)
East Central Coll (MO)
Eastern Arizona Coll (AZ)
Eastern Idaho Tech Coll (ID)
Eastern Wyoming Coll (WY)
Fox Valley Tech Coll (WI)
Front Range Comm Coll (CO)
Grand Rapids Comm Coll (MI)
Great Basin Coll (NV)
Great Falls Coll Montana State U (MT)
Halifax Comm Coll (NC)
Haywood Comm Coll (NC)
Highland Comm Coll (IL)
Hill Coll (TX)
Hutchinson Comm Coll (KS)
Illinois Central Coll (IL)
Imperial Valley Coll (CA)
Iowa Central Comm Coll (IA)
Jamestown Comm Coll (NY)
Johnson County Comm Coll (KS)
Kaskaskia Coll (IL)
Kellogg Comm Coll (MI)
Kirtland Comm Coll (MI)
Lake Area Tech Inst (SD)
Lake Superior Coll (MN)
Lansing Comm Coll (MI)
Lenoir Comm Coll (NC)
Lone Star Coll–CyFair (TX)
Lone Star Coll–North Harris (TX)
Lorain County Comm Coll (OH)
Macomb Comm Coll (MI)
Madison Area Tech Coll (WI)
Manhattan Area Tech Coll (KS)
Maysville Comm and Tech Coll, Maysville (KY)
Merced Coll (CA)
Mesa Comm Coll (AZ)
Metropolitan Comm Coll (NE)
Mid-Plains Comm Coll, North Platte (NE)
Mohave Comm Coll (AZ)
Mohawk Valley Comm Coll (NY)

Monroe County Comm Coll (MI)
Morgan Comm Coll (CO)
Mountain View Coll (TX)
Mt. San Antonio Coll (CA)
New Mexico Jr Coll (NM)
New River Comm Coll (VA)
Northampton Comm Coll (PA)
Northwest Coll (WY)
Ohio Tech Coll (OH)
Olympic Coll (WA)
Orange Coast Coll (CA)
Owensboro Comm and Tech Coll (KY)
Ozarks Tech Comm Coll (MO)
Palomar Coll (CA)
Panola Coll (TX)
Paris Jr Coll (TX)
Pittsburgh Tech Coll (PA)
Pueblo Comm Coll (CO)
Rend Lake Coll (IL)
Renton Tech Coll (WA)
Rock Valley Coll (IL)
Rogue Comm Coll (OR)
St. Charles Comm Coll (MO)
St. Philip's Coll (TX)
Salina Area Tech Coll (KS)
Salt Lake Comm Coll (UT)
San Jacinto Coll District (TX)
San Juan Coll (NM)
Schoolcraft Coll (MI)
Shawnee Comm Coll (IL)
Southeast Comm Coll, Lincoln Campus (NE)
Southeastern Comm Coll (IA)
South Plains Coll (TX)
State U of New York Coll of Technology at Alfred (NY)
Tallahassee Comm Coll (FL)
Tarrant County Coll District (TX)
Texarkana Coll (TX)
Three Rivers Comm Coll (MO)
Treasure Valley Comm Coll (OR)
Trinity Valley Comm Coll (TX)
Truckee Meadows Comm Coll (NV)
Tyler Jr Coll (TX)
Wayne County Comm Coll District (MI)
Western Nevada Coll (NV)
Western Wyoming Comm Coll (WY)
Westmoreland County Comm Coll (PA)
White Mountains Comm Coll (NH)
Williston State Coll (ND)

WILDLIFE BIOLOGY
Dodge City Comm Coll (KS)

WILDLIFE, FISH AND WILDLANDS SCIENCE AND MANAGEMENT
Casper Coll (WY)
Dakota Coll at Bottineau (ND)
Eastern Wyoming Coll (WY)
Feather River Coll (CA)
Front Range Comm Coll (CO)
Garrett Coll (MD)
Haywood Comm Coll (NC)
Laramie County Comm Coll (WY)
Mt. San Antonio Coll (CA)
Ogeechee Tech Coll (GA)
Penn State DuBois (PA)
Shawnee Comm Coll (IL)
Treasure Valley Comm Coll (OR)
Western Wyoming Comm Coll (WY)

WINE STEWARD/SOMMELIER
Cayuga County Comm Coll (NY)
Niagara County Comm Coll (NY)

WOMEN'S STUDIES
Casper Coll (WY)
Cerritos Coll (CA)
Palomar Coll (CA)
Santa Monica Coll (CA)
Santa Rosa Jr Coll (CA)
Sierra Coll (CA)

WOOD SCIENCE AND WOOD PRODUCTS/PULP AND PAPER TECHNOLOGY
Ogeechee Tech Coll (GA)

WOODWORKING
Santa Fe Comm Coll (NM)
Vincennes U (IN)

WORD PROCESSING
Del Mar Coll (TX)
Monroe County Comm Coll (MI)
Seminole State Coll of Florida (FL)
Western Wyoming Comm Coll (WY)

WRITING
Allen Comm Coll (KS)
Austin Comm Coll District (TX)
Cayuga County Comm Coll (NY)
Eastern Arizona Coll (AZ)

YOUTH MINISTRY
Hesston Coll (KS)

ZOOLOGY/ANIMAL BIOLOGY
Cerritos Coll (CA)
Dakota Coll at Bottineau (ND)
South Florida State Coll (FL)

Associate Degree Programs at Four-Year Colleges

ACCOUNTING
Academy Coll (MN)
Berkeley Coll–New York City
   Campus (NY)
California U of Pennsylvania (PA)
Calumet Coll of Saint Joseph (IN)
Caribbean U (PR)
Central Penn Coll (PA)
Champlain Coll (VT)
Davenport U, Grand Rapids (MI)
DeVry U–Miramar Campus (FL)
DeVry U Online (IL)
Franciscan U of Steubenville (OH)
Hawai`i Pacific U (HI)
Hobe Sound Bible Coll (FL)
Husson U (ME)
Immaculata U (PA)
Inter American U of Puerto Rico,
   Aguadilla Campus (PR)
Inter American U of Puerto Rico,
   Barranquitas Campus (PR)
Inter American U of Puerto Rico,
   Bayamón Campus (PR)
Inter American U of Puerto Rico,
   Fajardo Campus (PR)
Inter American U of Puerto Rico,
   Guayama Campus (PR)
Inter American U of Puerto Rico,
   Metropolitan Campus (PR)
Inter American U of Puerto Rico,
   Ponce Campus (PR)
Inter American U of Puerto Rico, San
   Germán Campus (PR)
Liberty U (VA)
Morrisville State Coll (NY)
Mount Aloysius Coll (PA)
Mount Marty Coll (SD)
Muhlenberg Coll (PA)
Oakland City U (IN)
Point Park U (PA)
Rasmussen Coll Aurora (IL)
Rasmussen Coll Blaine (MN)
Rasmussen Coll Bloomington (MN)
Rasmussen Coll Brooklyn Park (MN)
Rasmussen Coll Eagan (MN)
Rasmussen Coll Fort Myers (FL)
Rasmussen Coll Green Bay (WI)
Rasmussen Coll Kansas City/
   Overland Park (KS)
Rasmussen Coll Lake Elmo/
   Woodbury (MN)
Rasmussen Coll Land O' Lakes (FL)
Rasmussen Coll Mankato (MN)
Rasmussen Coll Mokena/Tinley Park
   (IL)
Rasmussen Coll Moorhead (MN)
Rasmussen Coll New Port Richey
   (FL)
Rasmussen Coll Ocala (FL)
Rasmussen Coll Romeoville/Joliet
   (IL)
Rasmussen Coll St. Cloud (MN)
Rasmussen Coll Tampa/Brandon
   (FL)
Rasmussen Coll Topeka (KS)
Rasmussen Coll Wausau (WI)
Rogers State U (OK)
Saint Francis U (PA)
Saint Mary-of-the-Woods Coll (IN)
Shawnee State U (OH)
Southern New Hampshire U (NH)
State Coll of Florida Manatee-
   Sarasota (FL)
Thomas More Coll (KY)
Tiffin U (OH)
Trine U (IN)
Union Coll (NE)
The U of Findlay (OH)
U of Northwestern Ohio (OH)
U of the Potomac (DC)
Utah Valley U (UT)
Walsh U (OH)
Webber International U (FL)
Wilson Coll (PA)
Youngstown State U (OH)

ACCOUNTING AND BUSINESS/ MANAGEMENT
Kansas State U (KS)

ACCOUNTING AND FINANCE
Ohio Christian U (OH)

ACCOUNTING RELATED
Bayamón Central U (PR)
Florida National U (FL)
Montana State U Billings (MT)

ACCOUNTING TECHNOLOGY AND BOOKKEEPING
American Public U System (WV)
Ferris State U (MI)
Florida National U (FL)
Hilbert Coll (NY)
Kent State U at Geauga (OH)
Montana State U Billings (MT)
Montana Tech of The U of Montana
   (MT)
Morrisville State Coll (NY)
New York City Coll of Technology of
   the City U of New York (NY)
Pennsylvania Coll of Technology
   (PA)
Polk State Coll (FL)
State U of New York Coll of
   Agriculture and Technology at
   Cobleskill (NY)
State U of New York Coll of
   Technology at Canton (NY)
Sullivan (KY)
The U of Akron (OH)
U of Alaska Fairbanks (AK)
The U of Toledo (OH)
Valencia Coll (FL)

ACTING
Academy of Art U (CA)
New York Film Academy (CA)

ADMINISTRATIVE ASSISTANT AND SECRETARIAL SCIENCE
Arkansas Tech U (AR)
Ball State U (IN)
Bayamón Central U (PR)
Black Hills State U (SD)
Campbellsville U (KY)
Clarion U of Pennsylvania (PA)
Concordia Coll–New York (NY)
Dickinson State U (ND)
EDP U of Puerto Rico (PR)
EDP U of Puerto Rico–San
   Sebastian (PR)
Faith Baptist Bible Coll and
   Theological Seminary (IA)
Hobe Sound Bible Coll (FL)
Idaho State U (ID)
Inter American U of Puerto Rico, San
   Germán Campus (PR)
Kuyper Coll (MI)
Montana State U Billings (MT)
Montana Tech of The U of Montana
   (MT)
Morrisville State Coll (NY)
State Coll of Florida Manatee-
   Sarasota (FL)
Tennessee State U (TN)
Universidad Adventista de las
   Antillas (PR)

The U of Akron (OH)
U of Northwestern Ohio (OH)
Washburn U (KS)
Weber State U (UT)
Welch Coll (TN)
Williams Baptist Coll (AR)

ADULT AND CONTINUING EDUCATION ADMINISTRATION
Concordia Coll–New York (NY)

ADULT DEVELOPMENT AND AGING
Madonna U (MI)

ADVERTISING
Academy of Art U (CA)
Fashion Inst of Technology (NY)
State Coll of Florida Manatee-
   Sarasota (FL)

AERONAUTICAL/AEROSPACE ENGINEERING TECHNOLOGY
Idaho State U (ID)
Purdue U (IN)
Vaughn Coll of Aeronautics and
   Technology (NY)

AERONAUTICS/AVIATION/ AEROSPACE SCIENCE AND TECHNOLOGY
Embry-Riddle Aeronautical U–
   Worldwide (FL)
Liberty U (VA)
Montana State U (MT)
Ohio U (OH)
Vaughn Coll of Aeronautics and
   Technology (NY)
Walla Walla U (WA)

AEROSPACE, AERONAUTICAL AND ASTRONAUTICAL/SPACE ENGINEERING
Embry-Riddle Aeronautical U–
   Worldwide (FL)

AFRICAN AMERICAN/BLACK STUDIES
State Coll of Florida Manatee-
   Sarasota (FL)

AGRIBUSINESS
Southern Arkansas U–Magnolia
   (AR)
State U of New York Coll of
   Agriculture and Technology at
   Cobleskill (NY)
Vermont Tech Coll (VT)

AGRICULTURAL BUSINESS AND MANAGEMENT
Coll of Coastal Georgia (GA)
Colorado Mesa U (CO)
Morrisville State Coll (NY)
North Carolina State U (NC)
State U of New York Coll of
   Agriculture and Technology at
   Cobleskill (NY)
U of New Hampshire (NH)
U of Northwestern Ohio (OH)

AGRICULTURAL BUSINESS AND MANAGEMENT RELATED
Penn State Abington (PA)
Penn State Altoona (PA)
Penn State Beaver (PA)
Penn State Berks (PA)
Penn State Brandywine (PA)

Penn State Erie, The Behrend
   Coll (PA)
Penn State Greater Allegheny (PA)
Penn State Hazleton (PA)
Penn State Lehigh Valley (PA)
Penn State New Kensington (PA)
Penn State Schuylkill (PA)
Penn State Wilkes-Barre (PA)
Penn State Worthington
   Scranton (PA)
Penn State York (PA)
U of Guelph (ON, Canada)

AGRICULTURAL ENGINEERING
Morrisville State Coll (NY)

AGRICULTURAL/FARM SUPPLIES RETAILING AND WHOLESALING
Dickinson State U (ND)

AGRICULTURAL MECHANICS AND EQUIPMENT TECHNOLOGY
Montana State U–Northern (MT)
Morrisville State Coll (NY)

AGRICULTURAL PRODUCTION
U of the Fraser Valley (BC, Canada)
Western Kentucky U (KY)

AGRICULTURE
Morrisville State Coll (NY)
North Carolina State U (NC)
South Dakota State U (SD)
State U of New York Coll of
   Agriculture and Technology at
   Cobleskill (NY)
U of Delaware (DE)
U of Guelph (ON, Canada)

AGRICULTURE AND AGRICULTURE OPERATIONS RELATED
Murray State U (KY)

AGRONOMY AND CROP SCIENCE
State U of New York Coll of
   Agriculture and Technology at
   Cobleskill (NY)

AIRCRAFT POWERPLANT TECHNOLOGY
Embry-Riddle Aeronautical U–
   Daytona (FL)
Embry-Riddle Aeronautical U–
   Worldwide (FL)
Hallmark U (TX)
Idaho State U (ID)
Midland Coll (TX)
Pennsylvania Coll of Technology
   (PA)
U of Alaska Fairbanks (AK)

AIRFRAME MECHANICS AND AIRCRAFT MAINTENANCE TECHNOLOGY
Hallmark U (TX)
Lewis U (IL)
Midland Coll (TX)
St. Petersburg Coll (FL)

AIRLINE FLIGHT ATTENDANT
Liberty U (VA)

AIRLINE PILOT AND FLIGHT CREW
Academy Coll (MN)
Lewis U (IL)

Polk State Coll (FL)
Purdue U (IN)
Southern Illinois U Carbondale (IL)
Southern Utah U (UT)
U of Alaska Fairbanks (AK)
Utah Valley U (UT)

AIR TRAFFIC CONTROL
LeTourneau U (TX)
Lewis U (IL)

ALLIED HEALTH AND MEDICAL ASSISTING SERVICES RELATED
Clarion U of Pennsylvania (PA)
Eastern U (PA)
Florida National U (FL)
Nebraska Methodist Coll (NE)
Thomas Edison State U (NJ)
Widener U (PA)

ALLIED HEALTH DIAGNOSTIC, INTERVENTION, AND TREATMENT PROFESSIONS RELATED
Ball State U (IN)
Cameron U (OK)
Cox Coll (MO)
Pennsylvania Coll of Technology
   (PA)

AMERICAN GOVERNMENT AND POLITICS
State Coll of Florida Manatee-
   Sarasota (FL)

AMERICAN INDIAN/NATIVE AMERICAN STUDIES
Inst of American Indian Arts (NM)

AMERICAN NATIVE/NATIVE AMERICAN LANGUAGES
Idaho State U (ID)
U of Alaska Fairbanks (AK)

AMERICAN SIGN LANGUAGE (ASL)
Bethel Coll (IN)
Idaho State U (ID)
Madonna U (MI)
Weber State U (UT)

AMERICAN STUDIES
State Coll of Florida Manatee-
   Sarasota (FL)

ANIMAL/LIVESTOCK HUSBANDRY AND PRODUCTION
North Carolina State U (NC)
Southern Utah U (UT)
U of the Fraser Valley (BC, Canada)

ANIMAL SCIENCES
Becker Coll (MA)
State U of New York Coll of
   Agriculture and Technology at
   Cobleskill (NY)
U of New Hampshire (NH)

ANIMAL TRAINING
Becker Coll (MA)

ANIMATION, INTERACTIVE TECHNOLOGY, VIDEO GRAPHICS AND SPECIAL EFFECTS
Academy of Art U (CA)
Colorado Mesa U (CO)
Ferris State U (MI)
New England Inst of Technology (RI)

APPAREL AND TEXTILE MANUFACTURING
Academy of Art U (CA)
Fashion Inst of Technology (NY)

APPAREL AND TEXTILE MARKETING MANAGEMENT
Academy of Art U (CA)

APPLIED HORTICULTURE/ HORTICULTURAL BUSINESS SERVICES RELATED
Morrisville State Coll (NY)
U of Massachusetts Amherst (MA)

APPLIED HORTICULTURE/ HORTICULTURE OPERATIONS
Pennsylvania Coll of Technology (PA)
U of Massachusetts Amherst (MA)
U of the Fraser Valley (BC, Canada)

APPLIED MATHEMATICS
Central Methodist U (MO)

APPLIED PSYCHOLOGY
Christian Brothers U (TN)

AQUACULTURE
Morrisville State Coll (NY)

ARCHEOLOGY
Weber State U (UT)

ARCHITECTURAL DRAFTING AND CAD/CADD
Academy of Art U (CA)
Morrisville State Coll (NY)
New York City Coll of Technology of the City U of New York (NY)

ARCHITECTURAL ENGINEERING TECHNOLOGY
Bluefield State Coll (WV)
Brigham Young U–Idaho (ID)
Ferris State U (MI)
Morrisville State Coll (NY)
New England Inst of Technology (RI)
Northern Kentucky U (KY)
Penn State Worthington Scranton (PA)
Vermont Tech Coll (VT)

ARCHITECTURAL TECHNOLOGY
New York Inst of Technology (NY)
Pennsylvania Coll of Technology (PA)

ARCHITECTURE
Morrisville State Coll (NY)
U of Detroit Mercy (MI)

ARCHITECTURE RELATED
Abilene Christian U (TX)

ARMY ROTC/MILITARY SCIENCE
Brigham Young U–Idaho (ID)

ART
Coll of Coastal Georgia (GA)
Felician U (NJ)
Hannibal-LaGrange U (MO)
Lourdes U (OH)
Oakland City U (IN)
State Coll of Florida Manatee-Sarasota (FL)
State U of New York Empire State Coll (NY)
Villa Maria Coll (NY)

ART HISTORY, CRITICISM AND CONSERVATION
State Coll of Florida Manatee-Sarasota (FL)
Thomas More Coll (KY)

ASIAN STUDIES
State Coll of Florida Manatee-Sarasota (FL)

ASTRONOMY
State Coll of Florida Manatee-Sarasota (FL)

ATHLETIC TRAINING
Dean Coll (MA)
Limestone Coll (SC)
Shawnee State U (OH)
The U of Akron (OH)

AUTOBODY/COLLISION AND REPAIR TECHNOLOGY
Academy of Art U (CA)
Idaho State U (ID)
Montana State U Billings (MT)
Morrisville State Coll (NY)
New England Inst of Technology (RI)
Pennsylvania Coll of Technology (PA)
Utah Valley U (UT)

AUTOMATION ENGINEER TECHNOLOGY
Weber State U (UT)

AUTOMOBILE/AUTOMOTIVE MECHANICS TECHNOLOGY
Arkansas Tech U (AR)
Brigham Young U–Idaho (ID)
Colorado Mesa U (CO)
Dixie State U (UT)
Ferris State U (MI)
Idaho State U (ID)
Midland Coll (TX)
Montana State U Billings (MT)
Montana State U–Northern (MT)
Montana Tech of The U of Montana (MT)
Morrisville State Coll (NY)
New England Inst of Technology (RI)
Pennsylvania Coll of Technology (PA)
Pittsburg State U (KS)
State U of New York Coll of Technology at Canton (NY)
U of Northwestern Ohio (OH)
Utah Valley U (UT)
Walla Walla U (WA)
Weber State U (UT)

AUTOMOTIVE ENGINEERING TECHNOLOGY
Farmingdale State Coll (NY)
Vermont Tech Coll (VT)

AVIATION/AIRWAY MANAGEMENT
Academy Coll (MN)
Embry-Riddle Aeronautical U–Worldwide (FL)
Polk State Coll (FL)
Purdue U (IN)
Vaughn Coll of Aeronautics and Technology (NY)

AVIONICS MAINTENANCE TECHNOLOGY
Hallmark U (TX)
Vaughn Coll of Aeronautics and Technology (NY)

BAKING AND PASTRY ARTS
Colorado Mesa U (CO)
The Culinary Inst of America (NY)
Kendall Coll (IL)
Pennsylvania Coll of Technology (PA)
Southern New Hampshire U (NH)
Stratford U (MD)
Stratford U, Alexandria (VA)
Stratford U, Falls Church (VA)
Stratford U, Glen Allen (VA)
Stratford U, Newport News (VA)
Stratford U, Virginia Beach (VA)
Stratford U, Woodbridge (VA)
Sullivan U (KY)
Valencia Coll (FL)

BANKING AND FINANCIAL SUPPORT SERVICES
Brescia U (KY)
Hilbert Coll (NY)
Northern State U (SD)
St. Petersburg Coll (FL)

BEHAVIORAL SCIENCES
Granite State Coll (NH)
Loyola U Chicago (IL)

BIBLICAL STUDIES
Alaska Bible Coll (AK)
Barclay Coll (KS)
Bethel Coll (IN)
Calvary U (MO)
Campbellsville U (KY)
Carolina Christian Coll (NC)
Carver Coll (GA)
Corban U (OR)
Dallas Baptist U (TX)
Davis Coll (NY)
Eastern Mennonite U (VA)

Ecclesia Coll (AR)
Emmaus Bible Coll (IA)
Faith Baptist Bible Coll and Theological Seminary (IA)
Grace Coll (IN)
Houghton Coll (NY)
Howard Payne U (TX)
Johnson U (TN)
Johnson U Florida (FL)
John Wesley U (NC)
Kentucky Mountain Bible Coll (KY)
Kuyper Coll (MI)
Lincoln Christian U (IL)
Mid-Atlantic Christian U (NC)
Nyack Coll (NY)
Piedmont International U (NC)
Point U (GA)
Simpson U (CA)
Southwestern Assemblies of God U (TX)
Trinity Coll of Florida (FL)
U of Valley Forge (PA)
Welch Coll (TN)

BIOLOGICAL AND BIOMEDICAL SCIENCES RELATED
Roberts Wesleyan Coll (NY)

BIOLOGICAL AND PHYSICAL SCIENCES
Ferris State U (MI)
Ohio U–Zanesville (OH)
Penn State Altoona (PA)
Penn State Beaver (PA)
Penn State Greater Allegheny (PA)
Penn State New Kensington (PA)
Penn State Schuylkill (PA)
Thomas Edison State U (NJ)
Trine U (IN)
Valparaiso U (IN)
Welch Coll (TN)

BIOLOGY/BIOLOGICAL SCIENCES
Brewton-Parker Coll (GA)
Dallas Baptist U (TX)
Dalton State Coll (GA)
Dean Coll (MA)
Immaculata U (PA)
Lourdes U (OH)
Pine Manor Coll (MA)
Rogers State U (OK)
Shawnee State U (OH)
State Coll of Florida Manatee-Sarasota (FL)
State U of New York Coll of Agriculture and Technology at Cobleskill (NY)
Thomas More Coll (KY)
U of New Hampshire at Manchester (NH)
Utah Valley U (UT)
Welch Coll (TN)
Wright State U (OH)
Wright State U–Lake Campus (OH)
York Coll of Pennsylvania (PA)

BIOLOGY/BIOTECHNOLOGY LABORATORY TECHNICIAN
State U of New York Coll of Agriculture and Technology at Cobleskill (NY)
Valencia Coll (FL)
Weber State U (UT)

BIOLOGY TEACHER EDUCATION
State Coll of Florida Manatee-Sarasota (FL)

BIOMEDICAL TECHNOLOGY
Indiana U–Purdue U Indianapolis (IN)
Penn State Altoona (PA)
Penn State Berks (PA)
Penn State Erie, The Behrend Coll (PA)
Penn State Hazleton (PA)
Penn State New Kensington (PA)
Penn State Schuylkill (PA)
Penn State York (PA)

BIOTECHNOLOGY
EDP U of Puerto Rico (PR)
Inter American U of Puerto Rico, Barranquitas Campus (PR)
Northern State U (SD)

BLOOD BANK TECHNOLOGY
Rasmussen Coll St. Cloud (MN)

BROADCAST JOURNALISM
Evangel U (MO)
Ohio U–Zanesville (OH)

BUILDING/CONSTRUCTION FINISHING, MANAGEMENT, AND INSPECTION RELATED
Pratt Inst (NY)
Weber State U (UT)

BUILDING/CONSTRUCTION SITE MANAGEMENT
State U of New York Coll of Technology at Canton (NY)
Wentworth Inst of Technology (MA)

BUILDING CONSTRUCTION TECHNOLOGY
Southern Utah U (UT)
Wentworth Inst of Technology (MA)

BUILDING/HOME/ CONSTRUCTION INSPECTION
Utah Valley U (UT)

BUILDING/PROPERTY MAINTENANCE
Utah Valley U (UT)

BUSINESS ADMINISTRATION AND MANAGEMENT
Academy Coll (MN)
Alaska Pacific U (AK)
Albertus Magnus Coll (CT)
The American U of Rome (Italy)
Anderson U (IN)
Austin Peay State U (TN)
Bay Path U (MA)
Beacon Coll (FL)
Berkeley Coll–New York City Campus (NY)
Berkeley Coll–White Plains Campus (NY)
Berkeley Coll–Woodland Park Campus (NJ)
Bethel Coll (IN)
Brewton-Parker Coll (GA)
Bryan Coll (TN)
Calumet Coll of Saint Joseph (IN)
Cameron U (OK)
Campbellsville U (KY)
Caribbean U (PR)
Carroll Coll (MT)
Cazenovia Coll (NY)
Central Baptist Coll (AR)
Chaminade U of Honolulu (HI)
City Vision U (MO)
Clarion U of Pennsylvania (PA)
Coll of Saint Mary (NE)
Columbia Southern U (AL)
Concordia Coll–New York (NY)
Corban U (OR)
Cornerstone U (MI)
Dakota State U (SD)
Dallas Baptist U (TX)
Dallas Christian Coll (TX)
Dalton State Coll (GA)
Dean Coll (MA)
Defiance Coll (OH)
Dixie State U (UT)
EDP U of Puerto Rico (PR)
EDP U of Puerto Rico–San Sebastian (PR)
Elmira Coll (NY)
Embry-Riddle Aeronautical U–Worldwide (FL)
Excelsior Coll (NY)
Faulkner U (AL)
Felician U (NJ)
Ferris State U (MI)
Fisher Coll (MA)
Florida National U (FL)
Franciscan U of Steubenville (OH)
Geneva Coll (PA)
Granite State Coll (NH)
Hallmark U (TX)
Hampton U (VA)
Hawai`i Pacific U (HI)
Hilbert Coll (NY)
Husson U (ME)
Immaculata U (PA)
Inter American U of Puerto Rico, Aguadilla Campus (PR)
Inter American U of Puerto Rico, Barranquitas Campus (PR)
Inter American U of Puerto Rico, Bayamón Campus (PR)
Inter American U of Puerto Rico, Fajardo Campus (PR)

Inter American U of Puerto Rico, Guayama Campus (PR)
Inter American U of Puerto Rico, Ponce Campus (PR)
Inter American U of Puerto Rico, San Germán Campus (PR)
Lincoln Coll of New England, Southington (CT)
Lock Haven U of Pennsylvania (PA)
Loyola U Chicago (IL)
Madonna U (MI)
Marian U (IN)
Marietta Coll (OH)
Medgar Evers Coll of the City U of New York (NY)
MidAmerica Nazarene U (KS)
Missouri Baptist U (MO)
Montana State U Billings (MT)
Morrisville State Coll (NY)
Mount Aloysius Coll (PA)
Mount Marty Coll (SD)
Mount Saint Mary's U (CA)
Mount Vernon Nazarene U (OH)
Muhlenberg Coll (PA)
National U (CA)
New England Coll (NH)
New England Inst of Technology (RI)
Newman U (KS)
New Mexico Inst of Mining and Technology (NM)
New York Inst of Technology (NY)
Niagara U (NY)
Nichols Coll (MA)
Northern State U (SD)
Northwood U, Michigan Campus (MI)
Nyack Coll (NY)
Oakland City U (IN)
Ohio Christian U (OH)
Ohio Dominican U (OH)
Peirce Coll (PA)
Pennsylvania Coll of Technology (PA)
Pine Manor Coll (MA)
Point Park U (PA)
Point U (GA)
Providence Coll (RI)
Rasmussen Coll Aurora (IL)
Rasmussen Coll Blaine (MN)
Rasmussen Coll Bloomington (MN)
Rasmussen Coll Brooklyn Park (MN)
Rasmussen Coll Eagan (MN)
Rasmussen Coll Fort Myers (FL)
Rasmussen Coll Green Bay (WI)
Rasmussen Coll Kansas City/ Overland Park (KS)
Rasmussen Coll Lake Elmo/ Woodbury (MN)
Rasmussen Coll Land O' Lakes (FL)
Rasmussen Coll Mankato (MN)
Rasmussen Coll Mokena/Tinley Park (IL)
Rasmussen Coll Moorhead (MN)
Rasmussen Coll New Port Richey (FL)
Rasmussen Coll Ocala (FL)
Rasmussen Coll Romeoville/Joliet (IL)
Rasmussen Coll St. Cloud (MN)
Rasmussen Coll Tampa/Brandon (FL)
Rasmussen Coll Topeka (KS)
Rasmussen Coll Wausau (WI)
Regent U (VA)
Robert Morris U Illinois (IL)
Rogers State U (OK)
Rust Coll (MS)
Saint Augustine's U (NC)
Saint Francis U (PA)
St. Gregory's U, Shawnee (OK)
St. John's U (NY)
Saint Joseph's U (PA)
Saint Leo U (FL)
St. Petersburg Coll (FL)
Saint Peter's U (NJ)
St. Thomas Aquinas Coll (NY)
Shawnee State U (OH)
Shorter U (GA)
Southern New Hampshire U (NH)
Southwestern Assemblies of God U (TX)
Southwestern Oklahoma State U (OK)
State Coll of Florida Manatee-Sarasota (FL)
State U of New York Coll of Agriculture and Technology at Cobleskill (NY)
State U of New York Coll of Technology at Canton (NY)
Sullivan U (KY)

Taylor U (IN)
Thomas Edison State U (NJ)
Thomas More Coll (KY)
Tiffin U (OH)
Toccoa Falls Coll (GA)
Trevecca Nazarene U (TN)
Trine U (IN)
Tulane U (LA)
Union Coll (NE)
Universidad Adventista de las Antillas (PR)
The U of Akron (OH)
U of Alaska Fairbanks (AK)
U of Maine at Fort Kent (ME)
U of Maine at Presque Isle (ME)
U of Management and Technology (VA)
The U of Montana Western (MT)
U of New Hampshire at Manchester (NH)
U of New Haven (CT)
U of Northwestern Ohio (OH)
U of Pennsylvania (PA)
U of Pikeville (KY)
The U of Scranton (PA)
U of the Cumberlands (KY)
U of the Fraser Valley (BC, Canada)
U of the Incarnate Word (TX)
U of the Potomac (DC)
The U of Toledo (OH)
Upper Iowa U (IA)
Utah Valley U (UT)
Valencia Coll (FL)
Vermont Tech Coll (VT)
Villa Maria Coll (NY)
Walla Walla U (WA)
Walsh U (OH)
Wayland Baptist U (TX)
Webber International U (FL)
Welch Coll (TN)
Western Kentucky U (KY)
Williams Baptist Coll (AR)
Wilson Coll (PA)
Wright State U (OH)
Wright State U–Lake Campus (OH)
York Coll of Pennsylvania (PA)
Youngstown State U (OH)

BUSINESS ADMINISTRATION, MANAGEMENT AND OPERATIONS RELATED
Bay Path U (MA)
Dixie State U (UT)
Eastern Oregon U (OR)
Embry-Riddle Aeronautical U–Worldwide (FL)

BUSINESS AND PERSONAL/ FINANCIAL SERVICES MARKETING
Dixie State U (UT)

BUSINESS AUTOMATION/ TECHNOLOGY/DATA ENTRY
Colorado Mesa U (CO)
Hallmark U (TX)
Montana State U Billings (MT)
Montana State U–Northern (MT)
The U of Akron (OH)
Utah Valley U (UT)

BUSINESS/COMMERCE
Academy Coll (MN)
Adams State U (CO)
Alderson Broaddus U (WV)
Alvernia U (PA)
American Public U System (WV)
Bayamón Central U (PR)
Bethel Coll (IN)
Brescia U (KY)
Champlain Coll (VT)
Christian Brothers U (TN)
Coll of Staten Island of the City U of New York (NY)
Columbia Coll (MO)
Davenport U, Grand Rapids (MI)
Delaware Valley U (PA)
Eastern Nazarene Coll (MA)
Ferris State U (MI)
Gannon U (PA)
Hawai`i Pacific U (HI)
Idaho State U (ID)
Kent State U at Geauga (OH)
Liberty U (VA)
Limestone Coll (SC)
Lourdes U (OH)
Metropolitan Coll of New York (NY)
MidAmerica Nazarene U (KS)
Midland Coll (TX)
Montana State U Billings (MT)
Murray State U (KY)
New Mexico State U (NM)

Niagara U (NY)
Northern Kentucky U (KY)
Penn State Abington (PA)
Penn State Altoona (PA)
Penn State Beaver (PA)
Penn State Berks (PA)
Penn State Brandywine (PA)
Penn State Erie, The Behrend Coll (PA)
Penn State Greater Allegheny (PA)
Penn State Harrisburg (PA)
Penn State Hazleton (PA)
Penn State Lehigh Valley (PA)
Penn State New Kensington (PA)
Penn State Schuylkill (PA)
Penn State Wilkes-Barre (PA)
Penn State Worthington Scranton (PA)
Penn State York (PA)
Saint Mary-of-the-Woods Coll (IN)
Southern Arkansas U–Magnolia (AR)
Southwest Baptist U (MO)
Southwestern Assemblies of God U (TX)
Spalding U (KY)
State Coll of Florida Manatee-Sarasota (FL)
State U of New York Empire State Coll (NY)
Stratford U, Falls Church (VA)
Stratford U, Glen Allen (VA)
Stratford U, Newport News (VA)
Stratford U, Woodbridge (VA)
Tabor Coll (KS)
Thomas More Coll (KY)
Thomas U (GA)
Tulane U (LA)
U of Bridgeport (CT)
U of Maine at Fort Kent (ME)
U of Massachusetts Lowell (MA)
U of Southern Indiana (IN)
The U of Toledo (OH)
Villa Maria Coll (NY)
Waldorf U (IA)
Wright State U (OH)
Youngstown State U (OH)

BUSINESS/CORPORATE COMMUNICATIONS
Waldorf U (IA)

BUSINESS, MANAGEMENT, AND MARKETING RELATED
Florida National U (FL)

BUSINESS/MANAGERIAL ECONOMICS
Campbellsville U (KY)
Niagara U (NY)
Saint Peter's U (NJ)
State Coll of Florida Manatee-Sarasota (FL)

BUSINESS OPERATIONS SUPPORT AND SECRETARIAL SERVICES RELATED
Thomas Edison State U (NJ)

CABINETMAKING AND MILLWORK
Utah Valley U (UT)

CAD/CADD DRAFTING/DESIGN TECHNOLOGY
Academy of Art U (CA)
Ferris State U (MI)
Idaho State U (ID)
Montana Tech of The U of Montana (MT)
Morrisville State Coll (NY)
Shawnee State U (OH)
Southern Utah U (UT)

CARDIOPULMONARY TECHNOLOGY
Inter American U of Puerto Rico, Barranquitas Campus (PR)

CARDIOVASCULAR TECHNOLOGY
Arkansas Tech U (AR)
Mercy Coll of Ohio (OH)
Molloy Coll (NY)
Nebraska Methodist Coll (NE)
Pennsylvania Coll of Health Sciences (PA)
Polk State Coll (FL)
Sentara Coll of Health Sciences (VA)
Valencia Coll (FL)

CARPENTRY
Montana State U Billings (MT)

Montana State U–Northern (MT)
Montana Tech of The U of Montana (MT)
New England Inst of Technology (RI)
Southern Utah U (UT)
U of Alaska Fairbanks (AK)

CELL BIOLOGY AND ANATOMICAL SCIENCES RELATED
National U (CA)

CHEMICAL ENGINEERING
Brigham Young U–Idaho (ID)

CHEMICAL TECHNOLOGY
Ferris State U (MI)
Inter American U of Puerto Rico, Guayama Campus (PR)
Lawrence Technological U (MI)
New York City Coll of Technology of the City U of New York (NY)
State U of New York Coll of Agriculture and Technology at Cobleskill (NY)
Weber State U (UT)

CHEMISTRY
Central Methodist U (MO)
Coll of Coastal Georgia (GA)
Dalton State Coll (GA)
Lindsey Wilson Coll (KY)
Ohio Dominican U (OH)
Southern Arkansas U–Magnolia (AR)
State Coll of Florida Manatee-Sarasota (FL)
Thomas More Coll (KY)
U of Saint Francis (IN)
Utah Valley U (UT)
Wright State U (OH)
Wright State U–Lake Campus (OH)
York Coll of Pennsylvania (PA)

CHEMISTRY TEACHER EDUCATION
State Coll of Florida Manatee-Sarasota (FL)

CHILD-CARE AND SUPPORT SERVICES MANAGEMENT
Ferris State U (MI)
Idaho State U (ID)
Morrisville State Coll (NY)
Polk State Coll (FL)
Southeast Missouri State U (MO)
State U of New York Coll of Agriculture and Technology at Cobleskill (NY)
State U of New York Coll of Technology at Canton (NY)
U of the Fraser Valley (BC, Canada)
Youngstown State U (OH)

CHILD-CARE PROVISION
American Public U System (WV)
Louisiana State U at Alexandria (LA)
Pennsylvania Coll of Technology (PA)

CHILD DEVELOPMENT
Arkansas Tech U (AR)
Evangel U (MO)
Franciscan U of Steubenville (OH)
Kuyper Coll (MI)
Madonna U (MI)
Midland Coll (TX)
Ohio U (OH)
Point U (GA)
Polk State Coll (FL)
Southern Utah U (UT)
State Coll of Florida Manatee-Sarasota (FL)
Weber State U (UT)
Youngstown State U (OH)

CHINESE
Brigham Young U–Idaho (ID)
Weber State U (UT)

CHRISTIAN STUDIES
Heritage Bible Coll (NC)
Huntington U (IN)
Oklahoma Baptist U (OK)
Ouachita Baptist U (AR)
Regent U (VA)

CINEMATOGRAPHY AND FILM/ VIDEO PRODUCTION
Academy of Art U (CA)
Clayton State U (GA)
FIDM/Fashion Inst of Design & Merchandising, Los Angeles Campus (CA)
Inst of American Indian Arts (NM)

New England Inst of Technology (RI)
New York Film Academy (CA)
U of Advancing Technology (AZ)
Valencia Coll (FL)

CIVIL ENGINEERING TECHNOLOGY
Bluefield State Coll (WV)
Ferris State U (MI)
Idaho State U (ID)
Montana State U–Northern (MT)
Montana Tech of The U of Montana (MT)
Murray State U (KY)
New England Inst of Technology (RI)
New York City Coll of Technology of the City U of New York (NY)
Pennsylvania Coll of Technology (PA)
Point Park U (PA)
State Coll of Florida Manatee-Sarasota (FL)
State U of New York Coll of Technology at Canton (NY)
U of New Hampshire (NH)
U of Puerto Rico in Bayamón (PR)
Valencia Coll (FL)
Vermont Tech Coll (VT)
Youngstown State U (OH)

CLINICAL LABORATORY SCIENCE/MEDICAL TECHNOLOGY
Dalton State Coll (GA)
Dixie State U (UT)
New England Inst of Technology (RI)
Shawnee State U (OH)
U of Wisconsin–Parkside (WI)

CLINICAL/MEDICAL LABORATORY ASSISTANT
Brigham Young U–Idaho (ID)
New England Inst of Technology (RI)
U of Alaska Fairbanks (AK)
U of Maine at Presque Isle (ME)

CLINICAL/MEDICAL LABORATORY SCIENCE AND ALLIED PROFESSIONS RELATED
State U of New York Coll of Agriculture and Technology at Cobleskill (NY)
Youngstown State U (OH)

CLINICAL/MEDICAL LABORATORY TECHNOLOGY
Coll of Coastal Georgia (GA)
Colorado Mesa U (CO)
Dalton State Coll (GA)
Farmingdale State Coll (NY)
Ferris State U (MI)
The George Washington U (DC)
Louisiana State U at Alexandria (LA)
Marshall U (WV)
Mount Aloysius Coll (PA)
Penn State Hazleton (PA)
Penn State Schuylkill (PA)
Rasmussen Coll Green Bay (WI)
Rasmussen Coll Lake Elmo/ Woodbury (MN)
Rasmussen Coll Mankato (MN)
Rasmussen Coll Moorhead (MN)
Rasmussen Coll St. Cloud (MN)
St. Petersburg Coll (FL)
Southwestern Oklahoma State U (OK)
Tarleton State U (TX)
U of Maine at Presque Isle (ME)
U of Saint Francis (IN)
Weber State U (UT)
Youngstown State U (OH)

COMMERCIAL AND ADVERTISING ART
Academy Coll (MN)
Academy of Art U (CA)
California U of Pennsylvania (PA)
Fashion Inst of Technology (NY)
Montana State U–Northern (MT)
Mount Saint Mary's U (CA)
New York City Coll of Technology of the City U of New York (NY)
Northern State U (SD)
Nossi Coll of Art (TN)
Pennsylvania Coll of Technology (PA)
Pratt Inst (NY)
Robert Morris U Illinois (IL)
State Coll of Florida Manatee-Sarasota (FL)
State U of New York Coll of Agriculture and Technology at Cobleskill (NY)
U of Advancing Technology (AZ)

COMMERCIAL PHOTOGRAPHY
Fashion Inst of Technology (NY)
Nossi Coll of Art (TN)

COMMUNICATION
Inter American U of Puerto Rico, Ponce Campus (PR)
Thomas More Coll (KY)

COMMUNICATION AND JOURNALISM RELATED
Immaculata U (PA)
Madonna U (MI)
Tulane U (LA)
Valparaiso U (IN)

COMMUNICATION DISORDERS SCIENCES AND SERVICES RELATED
Granite State Coll (NH)

COMMUNICATIONS TECHNOLOGY
Colorado Mesa U (CO)
East Stroudsburg U of Pennsylvania (PA)

COMMUNITY HEALTH AND PREVENTIVE MEDICINE
Utah Valley U (UT)

COMMUNITY HEALTH SERVICES COUNSELING
State Coll of Florida Manatee-Sarasota (FL)

COMMUNITY ORGANIZATION AND ADVOCACY
Elmira Coll (NY)
Metropolitan Coll of New York (NY)
Montana State U–Northern (MT)
Morrisville State Coll (NY)
State U of New York Empire State Coll (NY)
The U of Akron (OH)
U of Alaska Fairbanks (AK)
Wright State U (OH)
Wright State U–Lake Campus (OH)

COMPUTER AND INFORMATION SCIENCES
Beacon Coll (FL)
Black Hills State U (SD)
Columbia Coll (MO)
Faulkner U (AL)
Husson U (ME)
Inter American U of Puerto Rico, Barranquitas Campus (PR)
Inter American U of Puerto Rico, Fajardo Campus (PR)
Lincoln U (MO)
Manchester U (IN)
Montana State U Billings (MT)
Montana State U–Northern (MT)
Morrisville State Coll (NY)
New England Inst of Technology (RI)
New York City Coll of Technology of the City U of New York (NY)
Penn State Schuylkill (PA)
Rogers State U (OK)
Southern New Hampshire U (NH)
State Coll of Florida Manatee-Sarasota (FL)
State U of New York Coll of Agriculture and Technology at Cobleskill (NY)
Troy U (AL)
Tulane U (LA)
Union Coll (NE)
Utah Valley U (UT)
Washburn U (KS)
Webber International U (FL)
Youngstown State U (OH)

COMPUTER AND INFORMATION SCIENCES AND SUPPORT SERVICES RELATED
Academy Coll (MN)
Inter American U of Puerto Rico, Guayama Campus (PR)
Montana State U Billings (MT)
Pace U (NY)
Pace U, Pleasantville Campus (NY)
U of the Potomac (DC)

COMPUTER AND INFORMATION SCIENCES RELATED
Limestone Coll (SC)
Lindsey Wilson Coll (KY)
Madonna U (MI)
State Coll of Florida Manatee-Sarasota (FL)

COMPUTER AND INFORMATION SYSTEMS SECURITY
Academy Coll (MN)
Davenport U, Grand Rapids (MI)
St. John's U (NY)
Stratford U, Falls Church (VA)
Stratford U, Glen Allen (VA)
Stratford U, Newport News (VA)
Stratford U, Woodbridge (VA)
Sullivan U (KY)
U of Maine at Fort Kent (ME)
U of the Potomac (DC)

COMPUTER ENGINEERING
New England Inst of Technology (RI)
The U of Scranton (PA)

COMPUTER ENGINEERING TECHNOLOGY
California U of Pennsylvania (PA)
Dalton State Coll (GA)
Morrisville State Coll (NY)
Penn State New Kensington (PA)
Polk State Coll (FL)
St. Petersburg Coll (FL)
State Coll of Florida Manatee-Sarasota (FL)
U of Hartford (CT)
Valencia Coll (FL)
Vermont Tech Coll (VT)
Weber State U (UT)

COMPUTER GRAPHICS
Academy Coll (MN)
Academy of Art U (CA)
EDP U of Puerto Rico (PR)
Purdue U (IN)
State Coll of Florida Manatee-Sarasota (FL)
U of Advancing Technology (AZ)
Valencia Coll (FL)

COMPUTER/INFORMATION TECHNOLOGY SERVICES ADMINISTRATION RELATED
Berkeley Coll–New York City Campus (NY)
Berkeley Coll–Woodland Park Campus (NJ)
Limestone Coll (SC)
Pennsylvania Coll of Technology (PA)
St. Petersburg Coll (FL)
The U of Toledo (OH)

COMPUTER INSTALLATION AND REPAIR TECHNOLOGY
Dalton State Coll (GA)
Inter American U of Puerto Rico, Aguadilla Campus (PR)
Inter American U of Puerto Rico, Bayamón Campus (PR)
Inter American U of Puerto Rico, Fajardo Campus (PR)
U of Alaska Fairbanks (AK)

COMPUTER PROGRAMMING
Academy Coll (MN)
Bayamón Central U (PR)
Black Hills State U (SD)
Caribbean U (PR)
Champlain Coll (VT)
Coll of Staten Island of the City U of New York (NY)
EDP U of Puerto Rico (PR)
Limestone Coll (SC)
Medgar Evers Coll of the City U of New York (NY)
Morrisville State Coll (NY)
New England Inst of Technology (RI)
Polk State Coll (FL)
Rasmussen Coll Fargo (ND)
Saint Francis U (PA)
St. Petersburg Coll (FL)
State Coll of Florida Manatee-Sarasota (FL)
U of Advancing Technology (AZ)
U of Northwestern Ohio (OH)
The U of Toledo (OH)
Walla Walla U (WA)
Youngstown State U (OH)

COMPUTER PROGRAMMING RELATED
Inter American U of Puerto Rico, Metropolitan Campus (PR)
State Coll of Florida Manatee-Sarasota (FL)

COMPUTER PROGRAMMING (SPECIFIC APPLICATIONS)
Academy of Art U (CA)
Central Penn Coll (PA)
Kent State U at Geauga (OH)
Valencia Coll (FL)

COMPUTER SCIENCE
Black Hills State U (SD)
Carroll Coll (MT)
Central Methodist U (MO)
Creighton U (NE)
Dalton State Coll (GA)
Faulkner U (AL)
Felician U (NJ)
Florida National U (FL)
Hawai`i Pacific U (HI)
Inter American U of Puerto Rico, Aguadilla Campus (PR)
Inter American U of Puerto Rico, Barranquitas Campus (PR)
Inter American U of Puerto Rico, Bayamón Campus (PR)
Inter American U of Puerto Rico, Ponce Campus (PR)
Inter American U of Puerto Rico, San Germán Campus (PR)
Madonna U (MI)
Morrisville State Coll (NY)
New England Inst of Technology (RI)
New York City Coll of Technology of the City U of New York (NY)
Southwest Baptist U (MO)
Southwestern Oklahoma State U (OK)
Universidad Adventista de las Antillas (PR)
The U of Findlay (OH)
U of Maine at Fort Kent (ME)
U of Management and Technology (VA)
U of New Haven (CT)
U of the Virgin Islands (VI)
Utah Valley U (UT)
Walsh U (OH)
Weber State U (UT)

COMPUTER SOFTWARE AND MEDIA APPLICATIONS RELATED
Academy of Art U (CA)
American Public U System (WV)
Champlain Coll (VT)
Hobe Sound Bible Coll (FL)
Pace U (NY)
Pace U, Pleasantville Campus (NY)
Polytechnic U of Puerto Rico (PR)

COMPUTER SOFTWARE ENGINEERING
Rasmussen Coll Blaine (MN)
Rasmussen Coll Bloomington (MN)
Rasmussen Coll Brooklyn Park (MN)
Rasmussen Coll Eagan (MN)
Rasmussen Coll Fargo (ND)
Rasmussen Coll Fort Myers (FL)
Rasmussen Coll Green Bay (WI)
Rasmussen Coll Kansas City/Overland Park (KS)
Rasmussen Coll Lake Elmo/Woodbury (MN)
Rasmussen Coll Land O' Lakes (FL)
Rasmussen Coll Mankato (MN)
Rasmussen Coll Moorhead (MN)
Rasmussen Coll New Port Richey (FL)
Rasmussen Coll Ocala (FL)
Rasmussen Coll St. Cloud (MN)
Rasmussen Coll Tampa/Brandon (FL)
Rasmussen Coll Topeka (KS)
Rasmussen Coll Wausau (WI)
Vermont Tech Coll (VT)

COMPUTER SOFTWARE TECHNOLOGY
The U of Toledo (OH)

COMPUTER SUPPORT SPECIALIST
Sullivan U (KY)
U of Alaska Fairbanks (AK)

COMPUTER SYSTEMS ANALYSIS
Caribbean U (PR)
Davenport U, Grand Rapids (MI)
U of Advancing Technology (AZ)
The U of Akron (OH)

COMPUTER SYSTEMS NETWORKING AND TELECOMMUNICATIONS
Academy Coll (MN)
Colorado Mesa U (CO)
Davenport U, Grand Rapids (MI)
DeVry U–Arlington Campus (VA)
DeVry U–Chicago Campus (IL)
DeVry U–Columbus Campus (OH)
DeVry U–Decatur Campus (GA)
DeVry U–Irving Campus (TX)
DeVry U–Kansas City Campus (MO)
DeVry U–Miramar Campus (FL)
DeVry U–North Brunswick Campus (NJ)
DeVry U Online (IL)
DeVry U–Orlando Campus (FL)
DeVry U–Phoenix Campus (AZ)
DeVry U–Pomona Campus (CA)
DeVry U–Westminster Campus (CO)
Idaho State U (ID)
Montana Tech of The U of Montana (MT)
Pace U (NY)
Pace U, Pleasantville Campus (NY)
Robert Morris U Illinois (IL)
Stratford U, Falls Church (VA)
The U of Akron (OH)
Weber State U (UT)

COMPUTER TECHNOLOGY/COMPUTER SYSTEMS TECHNOLOGY
Dalton State Coll (GA)
Morrisville State Coll (NY)
New England Inst of Technology (RI)
Southeast Missouri State U (MO)

CONSTRUCTION ENGINEERING TECHNOLOGY
Ferris State U (MI)
Lawrence Technological U (MI)
New York City Coll of Technology of the City U of New York (NY)
Pennsylvania Coll of Technology (PA)
Southern Utah U (UT)
State Coll of Florida Manatee-Sarasota (FL)
The U of Akron (OH)
Valencia Coll (FL)
Vermont Tech Coll (VT)

CONSTRUCTION MANAGEMENT
John Brown U (AR)
U of Alaska Fairbanks (AK)
Utah Valley U (UT)
Vermont Tech Coll (VT)
Wentworth Inst of Technology (MA)

CONSTRUCTION TRADES
Colorado Mesa U (CO)
Liberty U (VA)
Morrisville State Coll (NY)

CONSTRUCTION TRADES RELATED
Morrisville State Coll (NY)

CONSUMER MERCHANDISING/RETAILING MANAGEMENT
Academy of Art U (CA)
Madonna U (MI)

COOKING AND RELATED CULINARY ARTS
Colorado Mesa U (CO)

CORRECTIONS
California U of Pennsylvania (PA)
Langston U (OK)
Mount Aloysius Coll (PA)
Youngstown State U (OH)

CORRECTIONS AND CRIMINAL JUSTICE RELATED
Cameron U (OK)
EDP U of Puerto Rico (PR)
EDP U of Puerto Rico–San Sebastian (PR)
Inter American U of Puerto Rico, Aguadilla Campus (PR)
Inter American U of Puerto Rico, Metropolitan Campus (PR)
Morrisville State Coll (NY)
Rasmussen Coll Aurora (IL)
Rasmussen Coll Blaine (MN)
Rasmussen Coll Bloomington (MN)
Rasmussen Coll Brooklyn Park (MN)
Rasmussen Coll Eagan (MN)

Rasmussen Coll Fort Myers (FL)
Rasmussen Coll Green Bay (WI)
Rasmussen Coll Kansas City/Overland Park (KS)
Rasmussen Coll Lake Elmo/Woodbury (MN)
Rasmussen Coll Land O' Lakes (FL)
Rasmussen Coll Mankato (MN)
Rasmussen Coll Mokena/Tinley Park (IL)
Rasmussen Coll Moorhead (MN)
Rasmussen Coll New Port Richey (FL)
Rasmussen Coll Ocala (FL)
Rasmussen Coll Rockford (IL)
Rasmussen Coll Romeoville/Joliet (IL)
Rasmussen Coll St. Cloud (MN)
Rasmussen Coll Tampa/Brandon (FL)
Rasmussen Coll Topeka (KS)
Rasmussen Coll Wausau (WI)

COSMETOLOGY
Midland Coll (TX)

COSTUME DESIGN
FIDM/Fashion Inst of Design & Merchandising, Los Angeles Campus (CA)

COUNSELING PSYCHOLOGY
Hobe Sound Bible Coll (FL)

CREATIVE WRITING
Inst of American Indian Arts (NM)
National U (CA)
Trevecca Nazarene U (TN)

CRIMINALISTICS AND CRIMINAL SCIENCE
Faulkner U (AL)

CRIMINAL JUSTICE/LAW ENFORCEMENT ADMINISTRATION
American Public U System (WV)
Anderson U (IN)
Bemidji State U (MN)
Boise State U (ID)
Campbellsville U (KY)
Clarion U of Pennsylvania (PA)
Coll of Coastal Georgia (GA)
Colorado Mesa U (CO)
Columbia Coll (MO)
Dalton State Coll (GA)
Excelsior Coll (NY)
Hannibal-LaGrange U (MO)
Hawai`i Pacific U (HI)
Husson U (ME)
Lincoln Coll of New England, Southington (CT)
Lincoln U (MO)
Lock Haven U of Pennsylvania (PA)
MacMurray Coll (IL)
Mansfield U of Pennsylvania (PA)
Morrisville State Coll (NY)
New England Inst of Technology (RI)
Peirce Coll (PA)
Polk State Coll (FL)
Regent U (VA)
Roger Williams U (RI)
St. John's U (NY)
St. Petersburg Coll (FL)
Salve Regina U (RI)
Thomas U (GA)
Tiffin U (OH)
Toccoa Falls Coll (GA)
Trevecca Nazarene U (TN)
Trine U (IN)
U of Maine at Fort Kent (ME)
U of Maine at Presque Isle (ME)
U of Management and Technology (VA)
Utah Valley U (UT)
Valencia Coll (FL)
Washburn U (KS)
Webber International U (FL)
York Coll of Pennsylvania (PA)
Youngstown State U (OH)

CRIMINAL JUSTICE/POLICE SCIENCE
Armstrong State U (GA)
Berkeley Coll–New York City Campus (NY)
Berkeley Coll–White Plains Campus (NY)
Berkeley Coll–Woodland Park Campus (NJ)

Caribbean U (PR)
Columbia Southern U (AL)
Dalton State Coll (GA)
Farmingdale State Coll (NY)
Ferris State U (MI)
Hilbert Coll (NY)
Idaho State U (ID)
Inter American U of Puerto Rico, Guayama Campus (PR)
Inter American U of Puerto Rico, Metropolitan Campus (PR)
Inter American U of Puerto Rico, Ponce Campus (PR)
MacMurray Coll (IL)
Midland Coll (TX)
Missouri Western State U (MO)
Rasmussen Coll Blaine (MN)
Rasmussen Coll Bloomington (MN)
Rasmussen Coll Brooklyn Park (MN)
Rasmussen Coll Eagan (MN)
Rasmussen Coll Lake Elmo/Woodbury (MN)
Rasmussen Coll Mankato (MN)
Rasmussen Coll St. Cloud (MN)
Rogers State U (OK)
Southern Utah U (UT)
State U of New York Coll of Technology at Canton (NY)
Sullivan U (KY)
The U of Akron (OH)
U of New Haven (CT)
U of the Virgin Islands (VI)
Youngstown State U (OH)

CRIMINAL JUSTICE/SAFETY
American Public U System (WV)
Arkansas Tech U (AR)
Augusta U (GA)
Ball State U (IN)
Bethel Coll (IN)
Calumet Coll of Saint Joseph (IN)
Cazenovia Coll (NY)
Central Penn Coll (PA)
Chaminade U of Honolulu (HI)
Columbus State U (GA)
Dean Coll (MA)
Defiance Coll (OH)
Dixie State U (UT)
Eastern Nazarene Coll (MA)
Fisher Coll (MA)
Florida National U (FL)
Gannon U (PA)
Hilbert Coll (NY)
Husson U (ME)
Idaho State U (ID)
Inter American U of Puerto Rico, Aguadilla Campus (PR)
Inter American U of Puerto Rico, Barranquitas Campus (PR)
Inter American U of Puerto Rico, Fajardo Campus (PR)
Inter American U of Puerto Rico, Ponce Campus (PR)
Kansas Wesleyan U (KS)
Kent State U at Stark (OH)
Liberty U (VA)
Lourdes U (OH)
Madonna U (MI)
Manchester U (IN)
Morrisville State Coll (NY)
New Mexico State U (NM)
Oakland City U (IN)
Penn State Altoona (PA)
Point U (GA)
Southwestern Oklahoma State U (OK)
State Coll of Florida Manatee-Sarasota (FL)
Thomas More Coll (KY)
U of Pikeville (KY)
U of Saint Francis (IN)
The U of Scranton (PA)
U of the Cumberlands (KY)
U of the Fraser Valley (BC, Canada)
Waldorf U (IA)
Weber State U (UT)
Youngstown State U (OH)

CRIMINOLOGY
LeTourneau U (TX)

CRISIS/EMERGENCY/DISASTER MANAGEMENT
Waldorf U (IA)

CRITICAL INFRASTRUCTURE PROTECTION
Idaho State U (ID)

CROP PRODUCTION
North Carolina State U (NC)
U of Massachusetts Amherst (MA)

CULINARY ARTS
Coll of Coastal Georgia (GA)
The Culinary Inst of America (NY)
Inter American U of Puerto Rico, Barranquitas Campus (PR)
Kendall Coll (IL)
Pennsylvania Coll of Technology (PA)
Robert Morris U Illinois (IL)
Southern New Hampshire U (NH)
State U of New York Coll of Agriculture and Technology at Cobleskill (NY)
Stratford U (MD)
Stratford U, Alexandria (VA)
Stratford U, Falls Church (VA)
Stratford U, Glen Allen (VA)
Stratford U, Newport News (VA)
Stratford U, Virginia Beach (VA)
Stratford U, Woodbridge (VA)
Sullivan U (KY)
The U of Akron (OH)
U of Alaska Fairbanks (AK)
Utah Valley U (UT)
Valencia Coll (FL)

CULINARY ARTS RELATED
Morrisville State Coll (NY)
U of New Hampshire (NH)

CYBER/COMPUTER FORENSICS AND COUNTERTERRORISM
Sullivan U (KY)

DAIRY HUSBANDRY AND PRODUCTION
Morrisville State Coll (NY)

DAIRY SCIENCE
Vermont Tech Coll (VT)

DANCE
Dean Coll (MA)
Dixie State U (UT)
U of Saint Francis (IN)
Utah Valley U (UT)

DATA MODELING/WAREHOUSING AND DATABASE ADMINISTRATION
American Public U System (WV)
Central Penn Coll (PA)
Limestone Coll (SC)

DATA PROCESSING AND DATA PROCESSING TECHNOLOGY
Academy Coll (MN)
American Public U System (WV)
Campbellsville U (KY)
Hallmark U (TX)
Montana State U Billings (MT)
Pace U, Pleasantville Campus (NY)
U of Advancing Technology (AZ)
Youngstown State U (OH)

DENTAL ASSISTING
Lincoln Coll of New England, Southington (CT)
U of Alaska Fairbanks (AK)
U of Southern Indiana (IN)

DENTAL HYGIENE
Dixie State U (UT)
Farmingdale State Coll (NY)
Ferris State U (MI)
Florida National U (FL)
Indiana U–Purdue U Indianapolis (IN)
Mount Ida Coll (MA)
New York City Coll of Technology of the City U of New York (NY)
Pennsylvania Coll of Technology (PA)
Rutgers U–New Brunswick (NJ)
St. Petersburg Coll (FL)
Shawnee State U (OH)
State U of New York Coll of Technology at Canton (NY)
Tennessee State U (TN)
U of Alaska Fairbanks (AK)
U of Arkansas for Medical Sciences (AR)
U of Bridgeport (CT)
U of New Haven (CT)
Utah Valley U (UT)
Valencia Coll (FL)
Vermont Tech Coll (VT)
Weber State U (UT)
Western Kentucky U (KY)

DENTAL LABORATORY TECHNOLOGY
Florida National U (FL)
Louisiana State U Health Sciences Center (LA)
New York City Coll of Technology of the City U of New York (NY)

DENTAL SERVICES AND ALLIED PROFESSIONS RELATED
Valdosta State U (GA)

DESIGN AND APPLIED ARTS RELATED
U of Maine at Presque Isle (ME)
Washburn U (KS)

DESIGN AND VISUAL COMMUNICATIONS
Academy Coll (MN)
FIDM/Fashion Inst of Design & Merchandising, Los Angeles Campus (CA)
FIDM/Fashion Inst of Design & Merchandising, San Francisco Campus (CA)
U of Advancing Technology (AZ)
U of Saint Francis (IN)
Utah Valley U (UT)

DESKTOP PUBLISHING AND DIGITAL IMAGING DESIGN
New England Inst of Technology (RI)

DIAGNOSTIC MEDICAL SONOGRAPHY AND ULTRASOUND TECHNOLOGY
Adventist U of Health Sciences (FL)
Ferris State U (MI)
Florida National U (FL)
Lincoln U (CA)
Mercy Coll of Health Sciences (IA)
Midland Coll (TX)
Nebraska Methodist Coll (NE)
Pennsylvania Coll of Health Sciences (PA)
Polk State Coll (FL)
St. Catherine U (MN)
U of Arkansas for Medical Sciences (AR)
The U of Findlay (OH)
Valencia Coll (FL)

DIESEL MECHANICS TECHNOLOGY
Idaho State U (ID)
Midland Coll (TX)
Montana State U Billings (MT)
Montana State U–Northern (MT)
Morrisville State Coll (NY)
Pennsylvania Coll of Technology (PA)
State U of New York Coll of Agriculture and Technology at Cobleskill (NY)
U of Northwestern Ohio (OH)
Utah Valley U (UT)
Vermont Tech Coll (VT)
Weber State U (UT)

DIETETICS
Ferris State U (MI)
State Coll of Florida Manatee-Sarasota (FL)

DIETETIC TECHNOLOGY
Morrisville State Coll (NY)
Youngstown State U (OH)

DIETITIAN ASSISTANT
Youngstown State U (OH)

DIGITAL ARTS
Academy of Art U (CA)
Oakland City U (IN)

DIGITAL COMMUNICATION AND MEDIA/MULTIMEDIA
Vaughn Coll of Aeronautics and Technology (NY)

DISPUTE RESOLUTION
Life U (GA)

DIVINITY/MINISTRY
Johnson U (TN)
Messenger Coll (TX)
Ohio Christian U (OH)
Piedmont International U (NC)
Providence Coll (RI)

DOG/PET/ANIMAL GROOMING
Becker Coll (MA)

DRAFTING AND DESIGN TECHNOLOGY
Academy of Art U (CA)
Black Hills State U (SD)
California U of Pennsylvania (PA)
Caribbean U (PR)
Dalton State Coll (GA)
Langston U (OK)
LeTourneau U (TX)
Lincoln U (MO)
Montana State U (MT)
Montana State U Billings (MT)
Montana State U–Northern (MT)
Morrisville State Coll (NY)
State Coll of Florida Manatee-Sarasota (FL)
The U of Akron (OH)
U of Alaska Fairbanks (AK)
Utah Valley U (UT)
Valencia Coll (FL)
Weber State U (UT)
Youngstown State U (OH)

DRAFTING/DESIGN ENGINEERING TECHNOLOGIES RELATED
Morrisville State Coll (NY)
Pennsylvania Coll of Technology (PA)
Weber State U (UT)

DRAMATIC/THEATER ARTS
Adams State U (CO)
Dean Coll (MA)
Pine Manor Coll (MA)
State Coll of Florida Manatee-Sarasota (FL)
Thomas More Coll (KY)
U of the Fraser Valley (BC, Canada)
Utah Valley U (UT)

DRAWING
Aquinas Coll (MI)
Pratt Inst (NY)

EARLY CHILDHOOD EDUCATION
Adams State U (CO)
Becker Coll (MA)
Bethel Coll (IN)
Boise State U (ID)
Chaminade U of Honolulu (HI)
Clarion U of Pennsylvania (PA)
Coll of Saint Mary (NE)
Cornerstone U (MI)
Davis Coll (NY)
Dean Coll (MA)
Dixie State U (UT)
Eastern Nazarene Coll (MA)
Fisher Coll (MA)
Gannon U (PA)
Granite State Coll (NH)
Liberty U (VA)
Lindsey Wilson Coll (KY)
Manchester U (IN)
Maranatha Baptist U (WI)
Morrisville State Coll (NY)
Mount Aloysius Coll (PA)
Mount Saint Mary's U (CA)
Nazarene Bible Coll (CO)
Nova Southeastern U (FL)
Oakland City U (IN)
Piedmont International U (NC)
Pine Manor Coll (MA)
Rasmussen Coll Aurora (IL)
Rasmussen Coll Blaine (MN)
Rasmussen Coll Bloomington (MN)
Rasmussen Coll Brooklyn Park (MN)
Rasmussen Coll Eagan (MN)
Rasmussen Coll Fargo (ND)
Rasmussen Coll Fort Myers (FL)
Rasmussen Coll Green Bay (WI)
Rasmussen Coll Kansas City/Overland Park (KS)
Rasmussen Coll Lake Elmo/Woodbury (MN)
Rasmussen Coll Land O' Lakes (FL)
Rasmussen Coll Mankato (MN)
Rasmussen Coll Mokena/Tinley Park (IL)
Rasmussen Coll Moorhead (MN)
Rasmussen Coll New Port Richey (FL)
Rasmussen Coll Ocala (FL)
Rasmussen Coll Rockford (IL)
Rasmussen Coll Romeoville/Joliet (IL)
Rasmussen Coll St. Cloud (MN)
Rasmussen Coll Tampa/Brandon (FL)
Rasmussen Coll Topeka (KS)
Rasmussen Coll Wausau (WI)
Rust Coll (MS)

St. Gregory's U, Shawnee (OK)
St. Petersburg Coll (FL)
Southwestern Assemblies of God U (TX)
Texas Coll (TX)
U of Alaska Fairbanks (AK)
U of Cincinnati (OH)
U of Great Falls (MT)
The U of Montana Western (MT)
U of the Virgin Islands (VI)
U of Valley Forge (PA)
Utah Valley U (UT)
Washburn U (KS)
Wayland Baptist U (TX)
Weber State U (UT)
Western Kentucky U (KY)
Wilmington U (DE)

E-COMMERCE
Limestone Coll (SC)

ECONOMICS
State Coll of Florida Manatee-Sarasota (FL)
Thomas More Coll (KY)
U of Wisconsin–Parkside (WI)

EDUCATION
Alderson Broaddus U (WV)
Central Baptist Coll (AR)
Corban U (OR)
Dalton State Coll (GA)
Eastern Oregon U (OR)
Florida National U (FL)
Lincoln Christian U (IL)
Montana State U Billings (MT)
Morrisville State Coll (NY)
Ohio Christian U (OH)
Saint Francis U (PA)
Southwestern Assemblies of God U (TX)
State U of New York Empire State Coll (NY)
Union Coll (KY)

EDUCATIONAL/INSTRUCTIONAL TECHNOLOGY
Bayamón Central U (PR)

EDUCATION (MULTIPLE LEVELS)
Coll of Coastal Georgia (GA)
Midland Coll (TX)

EDUCATION RELATED
Colorado Christian U (CO)
Liberty U (VA)
The U of Akron (OH)
Weber State U (UT)

EDUCATION (SPECIFIC SUBJECT AREAS) RELATED
Penn State U Park (PA)

ELECTRICAL AND ELECTRONIC ENGINEERING TECHNOLOGIES RELATED
Point Park U (PA)
Rochester Inst of Technology (NY)
Thomas Edison State U (NJ)
Vaughn Coll of Aeronautics and Technology (NY)
Youngstown State U (OH)

ELECTRICAL AND ELECTRONICS ENGINEERING
New England Inst of Technology (RI)
The U of Scranton (PA)

ELECTRICAL AND POWER TRANSMISSION INSTALLATION
Polk State Coll (FL)

ELECTRICAL, ELECTRONIC AND COMMUNICATIONS ENGINEERING TECHNOLOGY
Bluefield State Coll (WV)
Brigham Young U–Idaho (ID)
California U of Pennsylvania (PA)
Dalton State Coll (GA)
DeVry U–Arlington Campus (VA)
DeVry U–Chicago Campus (IL)
DeVry U–Columbus Campus (OH)
DeVry U–Irving Campus (TX)
DeVry U–Kansas City Campus (MO)
DeVry U–Miramar Campus (FL)
DeVry U–North Brunswick Campus (NJ)
DeVry U Online (IL)
DeVry U–Orlando Campus (FL)
DeVry U–Phoenix Campus (AZ)
DeVry U–Pomona Campus (CA)

DeVry U–Westminster Campus (CO)
Hallmark U (TX)
Idaho State U (ID)
Inter American U of Puerto Rico, Aguadilla Campus (PR)
Inter American U of Puerto Rico, San Germán Campus (PR)
Langston U (OK)
Lawrence Technological U (MI)
Morrisville State Coll (NY)
New York City Coll of Technology of the City U of New York (NY)
Northwestern State U of Louisiana (LA)
Penn State Altoona (PA)
Penn State Berks (PA)
Penn State Brandywine (PA)
Penn State Erie, The Behrend Coll (PA)
Penn State Hazleton (PA)
Penn State New Kensington (PA)
Penn State Schuylkill (PA)
Penn State Wilkes-Barre (PA)
Penn State Worthington Scranton (PA)
Penn State York (PA)
Pennsylvania Coll of Technology (PA)
Purdue U (IN)
State Coll of Florida Manatee-Sarasota (FL)
State U of New York Coll of Technology at Canton (NY)
The U of Akron (OH)
U of Massachusetts Lowell (MA)
Valencia Coll (FL)
Vermont Tech Coll (VT)
Weber State U (UT)
Youngstown State U (OH)

ELECTRICAL/ELECTRONICS EQUIPMENT INSTALLATION AND REPAIR
New England Inst of Technology (RI)
Pittsburg State U (KS)

ELECTRICIAN
Pennsylvania Coll of Technology (PA)
Weber State U (UT)

ELECTROCARDIOGRAPH TECHNOLOGY
Pennsylvania Coll of Health Sciences (PA)

ELECTROMECHANICAL AND INSTRUMENTATION AND MAINTENANCE TECHNOLOGIES RELATED
Excelsior Coll (NY)

ELECTROMECHANICAL TECHNOLOGY
Excelsior Coll (NY)
John Brown U (AR)
Midland Coll (TX)
New York City Coll of Technology of the City U of New York (NY)
Pennsylvania Coll of Technology (PA)
Shawnee State U (OH)

ELEMENTARY EDUCATION
Adams State U (CO)
Dalton State Coll (GA)
Ferris State U (MI)
Inter American U of Puerto Rico, Metropolitan Campus (PR)
Morrisville State Coll (NY)
New Mexico Highlands U (NM)
Rogers State U (OK)
Saint Mary-of-the-Woods Coll (IN)
Wilson Coll (PA)

EMERGENCY MEDICAL TECHNOLOGY (EMT PARAMEDIC)
Arkansas Tech U (AR)
Colorado Mesa U (CO)
Creighton U (NE)
Dixie State U (UT)
EDP U of Puerto Rico (PR)
EDP U of Puerto Rico–San Sebastian (PR)
Idaho State U (ID)
Indiana U–Purdue U Indianapolis (IN)
Mercy Coll of Health Sciences (IA)
Midland Coll (TX)
Montana State U Billings (MT)
New England Inst of Technology (RI)
Pennsylvania Coll of Technology (PA)
Polk State Coll (FL)
Purdue U Northwest (IN)
Rogers State U (OK)

St. Petersburg Coll (FL)
Shawnee State U (OH)
Southwest Baptist U (MO)
State U of New York Coll of
 Agriculture and Technology at
 Cobleskill (NY)
The U of Akron (OH)
U of Alaska Fairbanks (AK)
U of Arkansas for Medical Sciences
 (AR)
U of New Haven (CT)
The U of West Alabama (AL)
Valencia Coll (FL)
Weber State U (UT)
Youngstown State U (OH)

ENERGY MANAGEMENT AND SYSTEMS TECHNOLOGY
Idaho State U (ID)
Montana State U Billings (MT)

ENGINEERING
Brescia U (KY)
Brigham Young U–Idaho (ID)
Cameron U (OK)
Coll of Staten Island of the City U of
 New York (NY)
Dixie State U (UT)
Ferris State U (MI)
Lindsey Wilson Coll (KY)
Morrisville State Coll (NY)
St. Thomas U (FL)
State Coll of Florida Manatee-
 Sarasota (FL)
State U of New York Coll of
 Technology at Canton (NY)
Union Coll (NE)
Weber State U (UT)

ENGINEERING/INDUSTRIAL MANAGEMENT
U of Management and Technology
 (VA)

ENGINEERING SCIENCE
Rochester Inst of Technology (NY)

ENGINEERING TECHNOLOGIES AND ENGINEERING RELATED
Excelsior Coll (NY)
Morrisville State Coll (NY)
Rogers State U (OK)
State U of New York Coll of
 Agriculture and Technology at
 Cobleskill (NY)
State U of New York Coll of
 Technology at Canton (NY)
State U of New York Maritime Coll
 (NY)
U of Puerto Rico in Bayamón (PR)

ENGINEERING TECHNOLOGY
Austin Peay State U (TN)
Brescia U (KY)
Brigham Young U–Idaho (ID)
Kansas State U (KS)
Lincoln U (MO)
Morehead State U (KY)
National U (CA)
New Mexico State U (NM)
Northwestern State U of Louisiana
 (LA)
Polk State Coll (FL)
St. Petersburg Coll (FL)
Wentworth Inst of Technology (MA)
Wright State U (OH)
Wright State U–Lake Campus (OH)
Youngstown State U (OH)

ENGLISH
Calumet Coll of Saint Joseph (IN)
Carroll Coll (MT)
Central Methodist U (MO)
Dalton State Coll (GA)
Dean Coll (MA)
Felician U (NJ)
Hannibal-LaGrange U (MO)
Immaculata U (PA)
Lourdes U (OH)
Madonna U (MI)
Pine Manor Coll (MA)
Southwestern Assemblies of God U
 (TX)
State Coll of Florida Manatee-
 Sarasota (FL)
Thomas More Coll (KY)
Utah Valley U (UT)

ENGLISH AS A SECOND/ FOREIGN LANGUAGE (TEACHING)
Cornerstone U (MI)
Union Coll (NE)

ENGLISH LANGUAGE AND LITERATURE RELATED
State U of New York Empire State
 Coll (NY)

ENGLISH/LANGUAGE ARTS TEACHER EDUCATION
State Coll of Florida Manatee-
 Sarasota (FL)

ENTREPRENEURSHIP
Central Penn Coll (PA)
Inter American U of Puerto Rico,
 Barranquitas Campus (PR)
Missouri Valley Coll (MO)
The U of Findlay (OH)

ENVIRONMENTAL CONTROL TECHNOLOGIES RELATED
Montana Tech of The U of Montana
 (MT)

ENVIRONMENTAL ENGINEERING TECHNOLOGY
New York City Coll of Technology of
 the City U of New York (NY)

ENVIRONMENTAL SCIENCE
Georgia Gwinnett Coll (GA)
Madonna U (MI)
U of Saint Francis (IN)

ENVIRONMENTAL STUDIES
Columbia Coll (MO)
Dean Coll (MA)
State U of New York Coll of
 Agriculture and Technology at
 Cobleskill (NY)

EQUESTRIAN STUDIES
Centenary U (NJ)
Morrisville State Coll (NY)
Saint Mary-of-the-Woods Coll (IN)
The U of Findlay (OH)
U of Massachusetts Amherst (MA)
The U of Montana Western (MT)

EXECUTIVE ASSISTANT/ EXECUTIVE SECRETARY
Sullivan U (KY)

FAMILY AND CONSUMER SCIENCES/HOME ECONOMICS TEACHER EDUCATION
State Coll of Florida Manatee-
 Sarasota (FL)

FASHION AND FABRIC CONSULTING
Academy of Art U (CA)

FASHION/APPAREL DESIGN
Academy of Art U (CA)
Centenary U (NJ)
EDP U of Puerto Rico (PR)
EDP U of Puerto Rico–San
 Sebastian (PR)
Fashion Inst of Technology (NY)
FIDM/Fashion Inst of Design &
 Merchandising, San Francisco
 Campus (CA)
Parsons School of Design (NY)

FASHION MERCHANDISING
Academy of Art U (CA)
Berkeley Coll–New York City
 Campus (NY)
Berkeley Coll–White Plains Campus
 (NY)
Berkeley Coll–Woodland Park
 Campus (NJ)
Fashion Inst of Technology (NY)
FIDM/Fashion Inst of Design &
 Merchandising, Los Angeles
 Campus (CA)
Fisher Coll (MA)
Immaculata U (PA)
LIM Coll (NY)
New York City Coll of Technology of
 the City U of New York (NY)
Parsons School of Design (NY)
Southern New Hampshire U (NH)
The U of Akron (OH)
U of Bridgeport (CT)

FASHION MODELING
Fashion Inst of Technology (NY)

FILM/CINEMA/VIDEO STUDIES
Fashion Inst of Technology (NY)
Los Angeles Film School (CA)

FINANCE
Academy Coll (MN)
Davenport U, Grand Rapids (MI)
Saint Peter's U (NJ)
State Coll of Florida Manatee-
 Sarasota (FL)
The U of Findlay (OH)
Youngstown State U (OH)

FINANCIAL PLANNING AND SERVICES
Berkeley Coll–New York City
 Campus (NY)
Berkeley Coll–Woodland Park
 Campus (NJ)

FINE ARTS RELATED
Academy of Art U (CA)
Madonna U (MI)
Pennsylvania Coll of Technology
 (PA)
Saint Francis U (PA)

FINE/STUDIO ARTS
Academy of Art U (CA)
Adams State U (CO)
Beacon Coll (FL)
Fashion Inst of Technology (NY)
Inst of American Indian Arts (NM)
Lindsey Wilson Coll (KY)
Pratt Inst (NY)
State Coll of Florida Manatee-
 Sarasota (FL)
Thomas More Coll (KY)
U of Saint Francis (IN)
Villa Maria Coll (NY)
York Coll of Pennsylvania (PA)

FIRE PREVENTION AND SAFETY TECHNOLOGY
Montana State U Billings (MT)
Polk State Coll (FL)
The U of Akron (OH)
U of New Haven (CT)
Valencia Coll (FL)

FIRE SCIENCE/FIREFIGHTING
American Public U System (WV)
Columbia Southern U (AL)
Idaho State U (ID)
Madonna U (MI)
Midland Coll (TX)
Polk State Coll (FL)
St. Petersburg Coll (FL)
Southwestern Adventist U (TX)
Southwestern Oklahoma State U
 (OK)
State Coll of Florida Manatee-
 Sarasota (FL)
U of Alaska Fairbanks (AK)
U of Cincinnati (OH)
U of New Haven (CT)
Utah Valley U (UT)
Vermont Tech Coll (VT)

FIRE SERVICES ADMINISTRATION
American Public U System (WV)
Columbia Coll (MO)
Waldorf U (IA)

FISHING AND FISHERIES SCIENCES AND MANAGEMENT
State U of New York Coll of
 Agriculture and Technology at
 Cobleskill (NY)

FOOD PREPARATION
Washburn U (KS)

FOODS AND NUTRITION RELATED
U of Guelph (ON, Canada)

FOOD SERVICE SYSTEMS ADMINISTRATION
Inter American U of Puerto Rico,
 Aguadilla Campus (PR)
Morrisville State Coll (NY)
Wright State U (OH)
Wright State U–Lake Campus (OH)

FOODS, NUTRITION, AND WELLNESS
Huntington Coll of Health Sciences
 (TN)
Madonna U (MI)
Morrisville State Coll (NY)
Youngstown State U (OH)

FOREIGN LANGUAGES RELATED
U of Alaska Fairbanks (AK)

FOREIGN LANGUAGE TEACHER EDUCATION
State Coll of Florida Manatee-
 Sarasota (FL)

FORENSIC SCIENCE AND TECHNOLOGY
St. Petersburg Coll (FL)

FORESTRY
Coll of Coastal Georgia (GA)

FOREST TECHNOLOGY
Pennsylvania Coll of Technology
 (PA)
State U of New York Coll of
 Environmental Science and
 Forestry (NY)
U of Maine at Fort Kent (ME)
U of New Hampshire (NH)

FRENCH
State Coll of Florida Manatee-
 Sarasota (FL)
Thomas More Coll (KY)
Weber State U (UT)

FUNERAL SERVICE AND MORTUARY SCIENCE
Ferris State U (MI)
Lincoln Coll of New England,
 Southington (CT)
Mount Ida Coll (MA)
St. Petersburg Coll (FL)

GAME AND INTERACTIVE MEDIA DESIGN
Academy of Art U (CA)
New England Inst of Technology (RI)

GENERAL STUDIES
Adventist U of Health Sciences (FL)
Alderson Broaddus U (WV)
Alverno Coll (WI)
American Public U System (WV)
Arkansas Tech U (AR)
Asbury U (KY)
Austin Peay State U (TN)
Ball State U (IN)
Barclay Coll (KS)
Belhaven U (MS)
Bethel Coll (IN)
Black Hills State U (SD)
Bluefield Coll (VA)
Brandman U (CA)
Brenau U (GA)
Brewton-Parker Coll (GA)
Cabarrus Coll of Health Sciences
 (NC)
California Christian Coll (CA)
Calumet Coll of Saint Joseph (IN)
Cameron U (OK)
Cardinal Stritch U (WI)
Central Baptist Coll (AR)
Chaminade U of Honolulu (HI)
Christian Brothers U (TN)
Colorado Christian U (CO)
Columbia Coll (MO)
Columbia Southern U (AL)
Concordia U, St. Paul (MN)
Criswell Coll (TX)
Dakota State U (SD)
Dalton State Coll (GA)
Dean Coll (MA)
Dixie State U (UT)
Eastern Mennonite U (VA)
Ecclesia Coll (AR)
Fisher Coll (MA)
Franciscan U of Steubenville (OH)
Granite State Coll (NH)
Hampton U (VA)
Hawai`i Pacific U (HI)
Hope International U (CA)
Idaho State U (ID)
John Brown U (AR)
La Salle U (PA)
Lawrence Technological U (MI)

Lincoln Christian U (IL)
Lipscomb U (TN)
Louisiana Tech U (LA)
McNeese State U (LA)
Mercy Coll of Ohio (OH)
Midland Coll (TX)
Monmouth U (NJ)
Montana State U Billings (MT)
Morehead State U (KY)
Morrisville State Coll (NY)
Mount Aloysius Coll (PA)
Mount Marty Coll (SD)
Mount Vernon Nazarene U (OH)
National U (CA)
New Mexico Inst of Mining and
 Technology (NM)
New York City Coll of Technology of
 the City U of New York (NY)
Northern Kentucky U (KY)
Northern State U (SD)
Northwest Christian U (OR)
Northwestern State U of Louisiana
 (LA)
Northwest U (WA)
Oakland City U (IN)
The Ohio State U (OH)
The Ohio State U at Lima (OH)
The Ohio State U at Marion (OH)
The Ohio State U–Mansfield
 Campus (OH)
The Ohio State U–Newark Campus
 (OH)
Ouachita Baptist U (AR)
Our Lady of the Lake Coll (LA)
Pace U (NY)
Pace U, Pleasantville Campus (NY)
Peirce Coll (PA)
Point U (GA)
Regent U (VA)
Sacred Heart U (CT)
Shawnee State U (OH)
Simpson U (CA)
South Dakota School of Mines and
 Technology (SD)
South Dakota State U (SD)
Southern Arkansas U–Magnolia
 (AR)
Southern Utah U (UT)
Southwest Baptist U (MO)
Southwestern Adventist U (TX)
Southwestern Assemblies of God U
 (TX)
Southwestern Coll (KS)
Southwestern Oklahoma State U
 (OK)
State U of New York Coll of
 Technology at Canton (NY)
Temple U (PA)
Texas Coll (TX)
Tiffin U (OH)
Toccoa Falls Coll (GA)
Trevecca Nazarene U (TN)
Trinity Coll of Florida (FL)
U of Bridgeport (CT)
U of Central Arkansas (AR)
U of Hartford (CT)
U of Louisiana at Monroe (LA)
U of Maine at Fort Kent (ME)
U of Management and Technology
 (VA)
U of Mobile (AL)
U of North Georgia (GA)
U of Saint Francis (IN)
U of South Florida Sarasota-
 Manatee (FL)
U of the Fraser Valley (BC, Canada)
U of the Incarnate Word (TX)
The U of Toledo (OH)
U of Wisconsin–Superior (WI)
Utah State U (UT)
Utah Valley U (UT)
Viterbo U (WI)
Wayland Baptist U (TX)
Weber State U (UT)
Western Kentucky U (KY)
Widener U (DE)
Wilmington U (DE)
York Coll of Pennsylvania (PA)

GEOGRAPHIC INFORMATION SCIENCE AND CARTOGRAPHY
The U of Akron (OH)

GEOGRAPHY
Wright State U (OH)
Wright State U–Lake Campus (OH)

GEOGRAPHY RELATED
Adams State U (CO)

GEOLOGY/EARTH SCIENCE
Wright State U (OH)
Wright State U–Lake Campus (OH)

GERMAN
State Coll of Florida Manatee-
  Sarasota (FL)
Weber State U (UT)

GERONTOLOGY
Madonna U (MI)
Manchester U (IN)
Northern State U (SD)
Ohio Dominican U (OH)
Thomas More Coll (KY)

GRAPHIC AND PRINTING EQUIPMENT OPERATION/ PRODUCTION
Chowan U (NC)
Dixie State U (UT)

GRAPHIC COMMUNICATIONS
Ferris State U (MI)
New England Inst of Technology (RI)
Walla Walla U (WA)

GRAPHIC COMMUNICATIONS RELATED
Rasmussen Coll Moorhead (MN)

GRAPHIC DESIGN
Academy Coll (MN)
Academy of Art U (CA)
Brescia U (KY)
California U of Pennsylvania (PA)
Creative Center (NE)
Defiance Coll (OH)
Ferris State U (MI)
FIDM/Fashion Inst of Design & Merchandising, Los Angeles Campus (CA)
FIDM/Fashion Inst of Design & Merchandising, San Francisco Campus (CA)
Inter American U of Puerto Rico, San Germán Campus (PR)
Madonna U (MI)
Montana State U–Northern (MT)
Northern State U (SD)
Parsons School of Design (NY)
Pratt Inst (NY)
State U of New York Coll of Agriculture and Technology at Cobleskill (NY)
Union Coll (NE)
U of the Fraser Valley (BC, Canada)
Villa Maria Coll (NY)
Wright State U (OH)
Wright State U–Lake Campus (OH)

HEALTH AND PHYSICAL EDUCATION/FITNESS
Dean Coll (MA)
Robert Morris U Illinois (IL)
Utah Valley U (UT)

HEALTH AND PHYSICAL EDUCATION RELATED
Dean Coll (MA)
Pennsylvania Coll of Technology (PA)

HEALTH AND WELLNESS
Dean Coll (MA)
Northwest U (WA)
U of Wisconsin–Superior (WI)

HEALTH/HEALTH-CARE ADMINISTRATION
Berkeley Coll–New York City Campus (NY)
Berkeley Coll–White Plains Campus (NY)
Berkeley Coll–Woodland Park Campus (NJ)
LeTourneau U (TX)
Mount Saint Mary's U (CA)
State Coll of Florida Manatee-Sarasota (FL)
U of Northwestern Ohio (OH)
The U of Scranton (PA)
Waldorf U (IA)
Washburn U (KS)

HEALTH INFORMATION/ MEDICAL RECORDS ADMINISTRATION
Dalton State Coll (GA)
Lincoln Coll of New England, Southington (CT)
Montana State U Billings (MT)
St. Petersburg Coll (FL)

HEALTH INFORMATION/ MEDICAL RECORDS TECHNOLOGY
Berkeley Coll–New York City Campus (NY)
Berkeley Coll–White Plains Campus (NY)
Berkeley Coll–Woodland Park Campus (NJ)
Boise State U (ID)
Dakota State U (SD)
Davenport U, Grand Rapids (MI)
DeVry U Online (IL)
Ferris State U (MI)
Fisher Coll (MA)
Idaho State U (ID)
Indiana U Northwest (IN)
Lincoln Coll of New England, Southington (CT)
Louisiana Tech U (LA)
Mercy Coll of Ohio (OH)
Midland Coll (TX)
Peirce Coll (PA)
Pennsylvania Coll of Technology (PA)
Rasmussen Coll Aurora (IL)
Rasmussen Coll Blaine (MN)
Rasmussen Coll Bloomington (MN)
Rasmussen Coll Brooklyn Park (MN)
Rasmussen Coll Eagan (MN)
Rasmussen Coll Fort Myers (FL)
Rasmussen Coll Green Bay (WI)
Rasmussen Coll Kansas City/ Overland Park (KS)
Rasmussen Coll Lake Elmo/ Woodbury (MN)
Rasmussen Coll Land O' Lakes (FL)
Rasmussen Coll Mankato (MN)
Rasmussen Coll Mokena/Tinley Park (IL)
Rasmussen Coll Moorhead (MN)
Rasmussen Coll New Port Richey (FL)
Rasmussen Coll Ocala (FL)
Rasmussen Coll Rockford (IL)
Rasmussen Coll Romeoville/Joliet (IL)
Rasmussen Coll St. Cloud (MN)
Rasmussen Coll Tampa/Brandon (FL)
Rasmussen Coll Topeka (KS)
Rasmussen Coll Wausau (WI)
St. Catherine U (MN)
Sullivan U (KY)
U of Arkansas for Medical Sciences (AR)
Valencia Coll (FL)
Washburn U (KS)
Weber State U (UT)
Western Kentucky U (KY)

HEALTH/MEDICAL PREPARATORY PROGRAMS RELATED
Cornerstone U (MI)
Mount Saint Mary's U (CA)
Northwest U (WA)
Ohio Valley U (WV)

HEALTH PROFESSIONS RELATED
American Public U System (WV)
Caribbean U (PR)
Ferris State U (MI)
Fisher Coll (MA)
Hawai`i Pacific U (HI)
Life U (GA)
Lock Haven U of Pennsylvania (PA)
Morrisville State Coll (NY)
Newman U (KS)
Northwest U (WA)
Saint Peter's U (NJ)
U of Hartford (CT)

HEALTH SERVICES ADMINISTRATION
Florida National U (FL)

HEALTH SERVICES/ALLIED HEALTH/HEALTH SCIENCES
Aultman Coll of Nursing and Health Sciences (OH)
Berkeley Coll–Woodland Park Campus (NJ)
Excelsior Coll (NY)
Fisher Coll (MA)
Henderson State U (AR)
Howard Payne U (TX)
Lindsey Wilson Coll (KY)
Nebraska Methodist Coll (NE)
Ohio Dominican U (OH)
Pine Manor Coll (MA)

HEALTH TEACHER EDUCATION
State Coll of Florida Manatee-Sarasota (FL)

HEATING, AIR CONDITIONING, VENTILATION AND REFRIGERATION MAINTENANCE TECHNOLOGY
Arkansas Tech U (AR)
Montana State U Billings (MT)
New England Inst of Technology (RI)
U of Northwestern Ohio (OH)

HEATING, VENTILATION, AIR CONDITIONING AND REFRIGERATION ENGINEERING TECHNOLOGY
Ferris State U (MI)
Midland Coll (TX)
Pennsylvania Coll of Technology (PA)
State U of New York Coll of Technology at Canton (NY)

HEAVY EQUIPMENT MAINTENANCE TECHNOLOGY
Pennsylvania Coll of Technology (PA)

HISTOLOGIC TECHNICIAN
Indiana U–Purdue U Indianapolis (IN)
Tarleton State U (TX)

HISTOLOGIC TECHNOLOGY/ HISTOTECHNOLOGIST
Tarleton State U (TX)

HISTORIC PRESERVATION AND CONSERVATION
Montana Tech of The U of Montana (MT)

HISTORY
American Public U System (WV)
Dalton State Coll (GA)
Dean Coll (MA)
Immaculata U (PA)
Lindsey Wilson Coll (KY)
Lourdes U (OH)
Regent U (VA)
Rogers State U (OK)
State Coll of Florida Manatee-Sarasota (FL)
State U of New York Empire State Coll (NY)
Thomas More Coll (KY)
Utah Valley U (UT)
Wright State U (OH)
Wright State U–Lake Campus (OH)

HOMELAND SECURITY
U of Management and Technology (VA)
Waldorf U (IA)

HOMELAND SECURITY, LAW ENFORCEMENT, FIREFIGHTING AND PROTECTIVE SERVICES RELATED
Idaho State U (ID)
St. Petersburg Coll (FL)

HORSE HUSBANDRY/EQUINE SCIENCE AND MANAGEMENT
Delaware Valley U (PA)
Southern Utah U (UT)
U of Guelph (ON, Canada)

HORTICULTURAL SCIENCE
Andrews U (MI)
Morrisville State Coll (NY)
Temple U (PA)
U of Guelph (ON, Canada)
U of New Hampshire (NH)

HOSPITAL AND HEALTH-CARE FACILITIES ADMINISTRATION
State Coll of Florida Manatee-Sarasota (FL)

HOSPITALITY ADMINISTRATION
Coll of Coastal Georgia (GA)
Colorado Mesa U (CO)
Florida National U (FL)
Morrisville State Coll (NY)

State U of New York Coll of Agriculture and Technology at Cobleskill (NY)
U of Hartford (CT)
U of Maine at Fort Kent (ME)
U of the Incarnate Word (TX)
Weber State U (UT)

New York City Coll of Technology of the City U of New York (NY)
St. Petersburg Coll (FL)
Stratford U (MD)
The U of Akron (OH)
Utah Valley U (UT)
Valencia Coll (FL)
Webber International U (FL)
Youngstown State U (OH)

HOSPITALITY ADMINISTRATION RELATED
Morrisville State Coll (NY)
Penn State Beaver (PA)
Penn State Berks (PA)

HOSPITALITY AND RECREATION MARKETING
Ferris State U (MI)

HOTEL/MOTEL ADMINISTRATION
Ferris State U (MI)
State U of New York Coll of Agriculture and Technology at Cobleskill (NY)
Stratford U, Woodbridge (VA)
The U of Akron (OH)
Valencia Coll (FL)

HOTEL, MOTEL, AND RESTAURANT MANAGEMENT
Sullivan U (KY)

HUMAN DEVELOPMENT AND FAMILY STUDIES
Penn State Abington (PA)
Penn State Altoona (PA)
Penn State Berks (PA)
Penn State Brandywine (PA)
Penn State Erie, The Behrend Coll (PA)
Penn State New Kensington (PA)
Penn State Schuylkill (PA)
Penn State Worthington Scranton (PA)
Penn State York (PA)
South Dakota State U (SD)

HUMAN DEVELOPMENT AND FAMILY STUDIES RELATED
Utah State U (UT)

HUMANITIES
Aquinas Coll (TN)
Fisher Coll (MA)
Michigan Technological U (MI)
Ohio U (OH)
Saint Mary-of-the-Woods Coll (IN)
Saint Peter's U (NJ)
State Coll of Florida Manatee-Sarasota (FL)
State U of New York Coll of Agriculture and Technology at Cobleskill (NY)
Thomas More Coll (KY)
Utah Valley U (UT)
Valparaiso U (IN)
Washburn U (KS)

HUMAN RESOURCES MANAGEMENT
Montana State U Billings (MT)
Rasmussen Coll Blaine (MN)
Rasmussen Coll Bloomington (MN)
Rasmussen Coll Brooklyn Park (MN)
Rasmussen Coll Eagan (MN)
Rasmussen Coll Fargo (ND)
Rasmussen Coll Fort Myers (FL)
Rasmussen Coll Green Bay (WI)
Rasmussen Coll Kansas City/ Overland Park (KS)
Rasmussen Coll Lake Elmo/ Woodbury (MN)
Rasmussen Coll Land O' Lakes (FL)
Rasmussen Coll Mankato (MN)
Rasmussen Coll Moorhead (MN)
Rasmussen Coll New Port Richey (FL)
Rasmussen Coll Ocala (FL)
Rasmussen Coll Tampa/Brandon (FL)
Rasmussen Coll Topeka (KS)
Rasmussen Coll Wausau (WI)
The U of Findlay (OH)
The U of Scranton (PA)
Waldorf U (IA)

HUMAN RESOURCES MANAGEMENT AND SERVICES RELATED
American Public U System (WV)
Oakland City U (IN)

HUMAN SERVICES
Arkansas Tech U (AR)
Beacon Coll (FL)
Bethel Coll (IN)
Brescia U (KY)
Calumet Coll of Saint Joseph (IN)
Caribbean U (PR)
The Catholic U of America (DC)
Cazenovia Coll (NY)
Columbia Coll (MO)
Cornerstone U (MI)
Excelsior Coll (NY)
Hilbert Coll (NY)
Lincoln Coll of New England, Southington (CT)
Morrisville State Coll (NY)
Mount Saint Mary's U (CA)
New York City Coll of Technology of the City U of New York (NY)
Ohio Christian U (OH)
Rasmussen Coll Blaine (MN)
Rasmussen Coll Bloomington (MN)
Rasmussen Coll Brooklyn Park (MN)
Rasmussen Coll Eagan (MN)
Rasmussen Coll Fargo (ND)
Rasmussen Coll Fort Myers (FL)
Rasmussen Coll Green Bay (WI)
Rasmussen Coll Kansas City/ Overland Park (KS)
Rasmussen Coll Lake Elmo/ Woodbury (MN)
Rasmussen Coll Land O' Lakes (FL)
Rasmussen Coll Mankato (MN)
Rasmussen Coll Moorhead (MN)
Rasmussen Coll New Port Richey (FL)
Rasmussen Coll Ocala (FL)
Rasmussen Coll St. Cloud (MN)
Rasmussen Coll Tampa/Brandon (FL)
Rasmussen Coll Topeka (KS)
Rasmussen Coll Wausau (WI)
Thomas Edison State U (NJ)
U of Great Falls (MT)
U of Maine at Fort Kent (ME)
The U of Scranton (PA)
U of the Cumberlands (KY)
U of Valley Forge (PA)
Walsh U (OH)
Wayland Baptist U (TX)

ILLUSTRATION
Academy of Art U (CA)
Fashion Inst of Technology (NY)
Pratt Inst (NY)

INDUSTRIAL AND PRODUCT DESIGN
Academy of Art U (CA)

INDUSTRIAL ELECTRONICS TECHNOLOGY
Dalton State Coll (GA)
Ferris State U (MI)
Pennsylvania Coll of Technology (PA)

INDUSTRIAL MECHANICS AND MAINTENANCE TECHNOLOGY
Pennsylvania Coll of Technology (PA)
The U of West Alabama (AL)

INDUSTRIAL PRODUCTION TECHNOLOGIES RELATED
California U of Pennsylvania (PA)
Clarion U of Pennsylvania (PA)
U of Alaska Fairbanks (AK)

INDUSTRIAL RADIOLOGIC TECHNOLOGY
The George Washington U (DC)
Our Lady of the Lake Coll (LA)
Widener U (PA)

INDUSTRIAL TECHNOLOGY
Arkansas Tech U (AR)
Dalton State Coll (GA)
Millersville U of Pennsylvania (PA)
Montana State U–Northern (MT)
Murray State U (KY)
Penn State York (PA)
Pittsburg State U (KS)
St. Petersburg Coll (FL)
Southeastern Louisiana U (LA)
U of Puerto Rico in Bayamón (PR)
Washburn U (KS)

INFORMATION RESOURCES MANAGEMENT
Rasmussen Coll Fort Myers (FL)
Rasmussen Coll Land O' Lakes (FL)
Rasmussen Coll New Port Richey (FL)
Rasmussen Coll Ocala (FL)
Rasmussen Coll Tampa/Brandon (FL)

INFORMATION SCIENCE/ STUDIES
Campbellsville U (KY)
Clayton State U (GA)
Immaculata U (PA)
Mansfield U of Pennsylvania (PA)
Morrisville State Coll (NY)
Newman U (KS)
Penn State Abington (PA)
Penn State Altoona (PA)
Penn State Berks (PA)
Penn State Erie, The Behrend Coll (PA)
Penn State Hazleton (PA)
Penn State Lehigh Valley (PA)
Penn State New Kensington (PA)
Penn State Schuylkill (PA)
Penn State U Park (PA)
Saint Peter's U (NJ)
State Coll of Florida Manatee-Sarasota (FL)
State U of New York Coll of Agriculture and Technology at Cobleskill (NY)
State U of New York Coll of Technology at Canton (NY)
Tulane U (LA)
U of Management and Technology (VA)
U of Massachusetts Lowell (MA)
U of Pittsburgh at Bradford (PA)
The U of Scranton (PA)

INFORMATION TECHNOLOGY
Arkansas Tech U (AR)
Cameron U (OK)
EDP U of Puerto Rico–San Sebastian (PR)
Ferris State U (MI)
Florida National U (FL)
Hallmark U (TX)
Liberty U (VA)
Life U (GA)
Limestone Coll (SC)
New England Inst of Technology (RI)
Peirce Coll (PA)
Purdue U (IN)
Regent U (VA)
Southern Utah U (UT)
Thomas More Coll (KY)
Tiffin U (OH)
Trevecca Nazarene U (TN)
U of Management and Technology (VA)
U of the Incarnate Word (TX)
The U of Toledo (OH)
Valencia Coll (FL)
Vermont Tech Coll (VT)
Youngstown State U (OH)

INSTRUMENTATION TECHNOLOGY
Idaho State U (ID)
U of Puerto Rico in Bayamón (PR)

INSURANCE
Inter American U of Puerto Rico, Metropolitan Campus (PR)

INTERCULTURAL/ MULTICULTURAL AND DIVERSITY STUDIES
Baptist U of the Americas (TX)
Nyack Coll (NY)
Waldorf U (IA)

INTERDISCIPLINARY STUDIES
Central Methodist U (MO)
Lesley U (MA)
Ohio Christian U (OH)
Ohio Dominican U (OH)
Trinity Baptist Coll (FL)
U of North Florida (FL)

INTERIOR DESIGN
Academy of Art U (CA)
Bay Path U (MA)
Berkeley Coll–Woodland Park Campus (NJ)
Chaminade U of Honolulu (HI)

EDP U of Puerto Rico (PR)
EDP U of Puerto Rico–San Sebastian (PR)
Fashion Inst of Technology (NY)
FIDM/Fashion Inst of Design & Merchandising, Los Angeles Campus (CA)
FIDM/Fashion Inst of Design & Merchandising, San Francisco Campus (CA)
Indiana U–Purdue U Indianapolis (IN)
Montana State U (MT)
New England Inst of Technology (RI)
Parsons School of Design (NY)
Robert Morris U Illinois (IL)
Villa Maria Coll (NY)
Weber State U (UT)

INTERMEDIA/MULTIMEDIA
Academy Coll (MN)

INTERNATIONAL BUSINESS/ TRADE/COMMERCE
The American U of Rome (Italy)
Berkeley Coll–New York City Campus (NY)
Berkeley Coll–Woodland Park Campus (NJ)
Saint Peter's U (NJ)
U of the Potomac (DC)

INTERNATIONAL/GLOBAL STUDIES
Sacred Heart U (CT)
Thomas More Coll (KY)

JAPANESE
Weber State U (UT)

JAZZ/JAZZ STUDIES
State Coll of Florida Manatee-Sarasota (FL)

JEWISH/JUDAIC STUDIES
State Coll of Florida Manatee-Sarasota (FL)

JOURNALISM
Academy of Art U (CA)
Madonna U (MI)
Manchester U (IN)
Morrisville State Coll (NY)
State Coll of Florida Manatee-Sarasota (FL)
U of Maine (ME)

JOURNALISM RELATED
Adams State U (CO)

KINDERGARTEN/PRESCHOOL EDUCATION
Brigham Young U–Idaho (ID)
Eastern Nazarene Coll (MA)
Fisher Coll (MA)
Mount Saint Mary's U (CA)
Piedmont International U (NC)
Shawnee State U (OH)
State Coll of Florida Manatee-Sarasota (FL)
Tennessee State U (TN)
U of Great Falls (MT)

KINESIOLOGY AND EXERCISE SCIENCE
Dean Coll (MA)
Southwestern Adventist U (TX)

LABOR AND INDUSTRIAL RELATIONS
State U of New York Empire State Coll (NY)

LABOR STUDIES
Indiana U Bloomington (IN)
Indiana U Northwest (IN)
Indiana U–Purdue U Indianapolis (IN)

LANDSCAPE ARCHITECTURE
Academy of Art U (CA)
Morrisville State Coll (NY)

LANDSCAPING AND GROUNDSKEEPING
Pennsylvania Coll of Technology (PA)
U of Massachusetts Amherst (MA)
Valencia Coll (FL)
Vermont Tech Coll (VT)

LATIN AMERICAN STUDIES
State Coll of Florida Manatee-Sarasota (FL)

LAY MINISTRY
Howard Payne U (TX)
Maranatha Baptist U (WI)
U of Saint Francis (IN)

LEGAL ADMINISTRATIVE ASSISTANT/SECRETARY
Clarion U of Pennsylvania (PA)
Shawnee State U (OH)
Sullivan U (KY)
U of Northwestern Ohio (OH)
Washburn U (KS)

LEGAL ASSISTANT/PARALEGAL
American Public U System (WV)
Bay Path U (MA)
Central Penn Coll (PA)
Champlain Coll (VT)
Clayton State U (GA)
Coll of Saint Mary (NE)
Davenport U, Grand Rapids (MI)
Elms Coll (MA)
Ferris State U (MI)
Florida National U (FL)
Gannon U (PA)
Hilbert Coll (NY)
Husson U (ME)
Idaho State U (ID)
Liberty U (VA)
Madonna U (MI)
Marian U (IN)
McNeese State U (LA)
Midland Coll (TX)
Missouri Western State U (MO)
Mount Aloysius Coll (PA)
National Paralegal Coll (AZ)
National U (CA)
Newman U (KS)
New York City Coll of Technology of the City U of New York (NY)
Peirce Coll (PA)
Pennsylvania Coll of Technology (PA)
Rasmussen Coll Aurora (IL)
Rasmussen Coll Blaine (MN)
Rasmussen Coll Bloomington (MN)
Rasmussen Coll Brooklyn Park (MN)
Rasmussen Coll Eagan (MN)
Rasmussen Coll Fargo (ND)
Rasmussen Coll Fort Myers (FL)
Rasmussen Coll Green Bay (WI)
Rasmussen Coll Kansas City/ Overland Park (KS)
Rasmussen Coll Lake Elmo/ Woodbury (MN)
Rasmussen Coll Land O' Lakes (FL)
Rasmussen Coll Mankato (MN)
Rasmussen Coll Mokena/Tinley Park (IL)
Rasmussen Coll Moorhead (MN)
Rasmussen Coll New Port Richey (FL)
Rasmussen Coll Ocala (FL)
Rasmussen Coll Rockford (IL)
Rasmussen Coll Romeoville/Joliet (IL)
Rasmussen Coll St. Cloud (MN)
Rasmussen Coll Tampa/Brandon (FL)
Rasmussen Coll Topeka (KS)
Rasmussen Coll Wausau (WI)
Robert Morris U Illinois (IL)
Saint Mary-of-the-Woods Coll (IN)
St. Petersburg Coll (FL)
Shawnee State U (OH)
Southern Utah U (UT)
State Coll of Florida Manatee-Sarasota (FL)
Suffolk U (MA)
Sullivan U (KY)
Tulane U (LA)
The U of Akron (OH)
U of Alaska Fairbanks (AK)
U of Great Falls (MT)
U of Hartford (CT)
U of Louisville (KY)
U of North Georgia (GA)
U of Northwestern Ohio (OH)
The U of Toledo (OH)
Utah Valley U (UT)
Valencia Coll (FL)
Washburn U (KS)
Western Kentucky U (KY)
Widener U (PA)

LEGAL PROFESSIONS AND STUDIES RELATED
Berkeley Coll–New York City Campus (NY)
Berkeley Coll–Woodland Park Campus (NJ)

LEGAL STUDIES
Faulkner U (AL)
St. John's U (NY)
U of Hartford (CT)
U of New Haven (CT)

LIBERAL ARTS AND SCIENCES AND HUMANITIES RELATED
Adams State U (CO)
Anderson U (IN)
Ball State U (IN)
Becker Coll (MA)
Coll of Saint Mary (NE)
Colorado Mesa U (CO)
Ferris State U (MI)
Florida National U (FL)
Kent State U at Geauga (OH)
Kent State U at Stark (OH)
Marymount California U (CA)
Morrisville State Coll (NY)
Mount Aloysius Coll (PA)
Pennsylvania Coll of Technology (PA)
Talladega Coll (AL)
Taylor U (IN)
U of Maryland U Coll (MD)
U of Wisconsin–Green Bay (WI)
U of Wisconsin–La Crosse (WI)
Walsh U (OH)
Wayland Baptist U (TX)
William Penn U (IA)
Williamson Coll (TN)

LIBERAL ARTS AND SCIENCES/ LIBERAL STUDIES
Adams State U (CO)
Adelphi U (NY)
Alverno Coll (WI)
American International Coll (MA)
American U (DC)
The American U of Rome (Italy)
Amridge U (AL)
Aquinas Coll (MI)
Arizona Christian U (AZ)
Armstrong State U (GA)
Augusta U (GA)
Averett U (VA)
Bard Coll (NY)
Bay Path U (MA)
Beacon Coll (FL)
Bemidji State U (MN)
Bethel Coll (IN)
Bethel U (MN)
Boise State U (ID)
Brescia U (KY)
Briar Cliff U (IA)
Brigham Young U–Idaho (ID)
Bryan Coll (TN)
Bryn Athyn Coll of the New Church (PA)
California U of Pennsylvania (PA)
Cazenovia Coll (NY)
Centenary U (NJ)
Central Baptist Coll (AR)
Charter Oak State Coll (CT)
Chestnut Hill Coll (PA)
Christendom Coll (VA)
Clarion U of Pennsylvania (PA)
Clarke U (IA)
Clayton State U (GA)
Colby-Sawyer Coll (NH)
Coll of Coastal Georgia (GA)
Coll of Staten Island of the City U of New York (NY)
Colorado Mesa U (CO)
Columbia Coll (MO)
Columbus State U (GA)
Concordia Coll–New York (NY)
Concordia U Irvine (CA)
Corban U (OR)
Dallas Baptist U (TX)
Dalton State Coll (GA)
Dickinson State U (ND)
Dominican Coll (NY)
Eastern U (PA)
Elmira Coll (NY)
Emmanuel Coll (GA)
Endicott Coll (MA)
Excelsior Coll (NY)
Fairleigh Dickinson U, Metropolitan Campus (NJ)
Farmingdale State Coll (NY)
Faulkner U (AL)

Felician U (NJ)
Ferris State U (MI)
Fisher Coll (MA)
Florida A&M U (FL)
Florida Atlantic U (FL)
Florida Coll (FL)
Florida State U (FL)
Gannon U (PA)
Gwynedd Mercy U (PA)
Hilbert Coll (NY)
Hobe Sound Bible Coll (FL)
Holy Cross Coll (IN)
Houghton Coll (NY)
Huston-Tillotson U (TX)
Indiana U of Pennsylvania (PA)
Judson U (IL)
Kentucky State U (KY)
Kuyper Coll (MI)
Limestone Coll (SC)
Loras Coll (IA)
Louisiana State U at Alexandria (LA)
Lourdes U (OH)
Loyola U Chicago (IL)
Mansfield U of Pennsylvania (PA)
Maria Coll (NY)
Marian U (IN)
Marietta Coll (OH)
Marymount California U (CA)
Medgar Evers Coll of the City U of New York (NY)
Mercy Coll (NY)
Mercy Coll of Health Sciences (IA)
MidAmerica Nazarene U (KS)
Minnesota State U Mankato (MN)
Minnesota State U Moorhead (MN)
Missouri Valley Coll (MO)
Molloy Coll (NY)
Montana State U (MT)
Montana State U Billings (MT)
Morrisville State Coll (NY)
Mount Aloysius Coll (PA)
Mount Marty Coll (SD)
Mount Saint Mary's U (CA)
Murray State U (KY)
Neumann U (PA)
New England Coll (NH)
Newman U (KS)
New Saint Andrews Coll (ID)
New York City Coll of Technology of the City U of New York (NY)
Niagara U (NY)
Northern Kentucky U (KY)
Northwest U (WA)
Nyack Coll (NY)
The Ohio State U at Marion (OH)
The Ohio State U–Mansfield Campus (OH)
The Ohio State U–Newark Campus (OH)
Ohio U (OH)
Ohio U–Eastern (OH)
Ohio Valley U (WV)
Penn State Abington (PA)
Penn State Altoona (PA)
Penn State Beaver (PA)
Penn State Berks (PA)
Penn State Brandywine (PA)
Penn State Erie, The Behrend Coll (PA)
Penn State Greater Allegheny (PA)
Penn State Harrisburg (PA)
Penn State Hazleton (PA)
Penn State Lehigh Valley (PA)
Penn State New Kensington (PA)
Penn State Schuylkill (PA)
Penn State U Park (PA)
Penn State Wilkes-Barre (PA)
Penn State Worthington Scranton (PA)
Penn State York (PA)
Pine Manor Coll (MA)
Polk State Coll (FL)
Providence Coll (RI)
Rocky Mountain Coll (MT)
Rogers State U (OK)
St. Catherine U (MN)
St. Cloud State U (MN)
St. Gregory's U, Shawnee (OK)
St. John's U (NY)
Saint Joseph's U (PA)
Saint Leo U (FL)
Saint Louis Christian Coll (MO)
St. Petersburg Coll (FL)
St. Thomas Aquinas Coll (NY)
Salve Regina U (RI)
Schreiner U (TX)
Shiloh U (IA)
State Coll of Florida Manatee-Sarasota (FL)

State U of New York Coll of
Agriculture and Technology at
Cobleskill (NY)
Suffolk U (MA)
Syracuse U (NY)
Tabor Coll (KS)
Thomas Edison State U (NJ)
Thomas More Coll (KY)
Thomas U (GA)
Trine U (IN)
Troy U (AL)
Unity Coll (ME)
The U of Akron (OH)
U of Alaska Fairbanks (AK)
U of Delaware (DE)
U of Hartford (CT)
U of Maine at Fort Kent (ME)
U of Maine at Presque Isle (ME)
The U of Montana Western (MT)
U of New Hampshire at Manchester
(NH)
U of North Georgia (GA)
U of Pittsburgh at Bradford (PA)
U of Saint Francis (IN)
The U of South Dakota (SD)
U of South Florida, St. Petersburg
(FL)
U of the Fraser Valley (BC, Canada)
U of the Incarnate Word (TX)
U of Wisconsin–Eau Claire (WI)
U of Wisconsin–Parkside (WI)
U of Wisconsin–Stevens Point (WI)
U of Wisconsin–Superior (WI)
U of Wisconsin–Whitewater (WI)
Upper Iowa U (IA)
Valdosta State U (GA)
Valencia Coll (FL)
Villa Maria Coll (NY)
Waldorf U (IA)
Washburn U (KS)
Western Connecticut State U (CT)
Western New England U (MA)
Wichita State U (KS)
Williams Baptist Coll (AR)
William Woods U (MO)
Wilson Coll (PA)
Winona State U (MN)
Youngstown State U (OH)

**LIBRARY AND ARCHIVES
ASSISTING**
U of the Fraser Valley (BC, Canada)

**LICENSED PRACTICAL/
VOCATIONAL NURSE TRAINING**
Arkansas Tech U (AR)
Campbellsville U (KY)
Dickinson State U (ND)
Inter American U of Puerto Rico,
Aguadilla Campus (PR)
Inter American U of Puerto Rico,
Bayamón Campus (PR)
Inter American U of Puerto Rico,
Metropolitan Campus (PR)
Inter American U of Puerto Rico,
Ponce Campus (PR)
Inter American U of Puerto Rico, San
Germán Campus (PR)
Maria Coll (NY)
Medgar Evers Coll of the City U of
New York (NY)
Montana State U Billings (MT)
U of the Fraser Valley (BC, Canada)

**LINGUISTIC AND
COMPARATIVE LANGUAGE
STUDIES RELATED**
Northwest U (WA)

**LOGISTICS, MATERIALS, AND
SUPPLY CHAIN MANAGEMENT**
Arkansas Tech U (AR)
Embry-Riddle Aeronautical U–
Worldwide (FL)
FIDM/Fashion Inst of Design &
Merchandising, Los Angeles
Campus (CA)
Polytechnic U of Puerto Rico (PR)
Sullivan U (KY)

MACHINE TOOL TECHNOLOGY
Colorado Mesa U (CO)
Idaho State U (ID)
Pennsylvania Coll of Technology (PA)

**MANAGEMENT INFORMATION
SYSTEMS**
Academy Coll (MN)
Bayamón Central U (PR)
Lindsey Wilson Coll (KY)
Morehead State U (KY)
Shawnee State U (OH)

The U of Findlay (OH)
U of the Incarnate Word (TX)
Weber State U (UT)
Wilson Coll (PA)
Wright State U (OH)
Wright State U–Lake Campus (OH)

**MANAGEMENT INFORMATION
SYSTEMS AND SERVICES
RELATED**
Mount Aloysius Coll (PA)
Rasmussen Coll Aurora (IL)
Rasmussen Coll Blaine (MN)
Rasmussen Coll Bloomington (MN)
Rasmussen Coll Brooklyn Park (MN)
Rasmussen Coll Eagan (MN)
Rasmussen Coll Fargo (ND)
Rasmussen Coll Fort Myers (FL)
Rasmussen Coll Green Bay (WI)
Rasmussen Coll Kansas City/
Overland Park (KS)
Rasmussen Coll Lake Elmo/
Woodbury (MN)
Rasmussen Coll Land O' Lakes (FL)
Rasmussen Coll Mankato (MN)
Rasmussen Coll Mokena/Tinley Park
(IL)
Rasmussen Coll Moorhead (MN)
Rasmussen Coll New Port Richey
(FL)
Rasmussen Coll Ocala (FL)
Rasmussen Coll Rockford (IL)
Rasmussen Coll Romeoville/Joliet
(IL)
Rasmussen Coll St. Cloud (MN)
Rasmussen Coll Tampa/Brandon
(FL)
Rasmussen Coll Wausau (WI)

**MANUFACTURING
ENGINEERING**
Penn State Greater Allegheny (PA)
Penn State Hazleton (PA)
Penn State Wilkes-Barre (PA)
Penn State York (PA)

**MANUFACTURING
ENGINEERING TECHNOLOGY**
Colorado Mesa U (CO)
Idaho State U (ID)
Lawrence Technological U (MI)
Missouri Western State U (MO)
Morehead State U (KY)
New England Inst of Technology (RI)
Pennsylvania Coll of Technology (PA)
South Dakota State U (SD)
The U of Akron (OH)
Weber State U (UT)

**MARINE MAINTENANCE AND
SHIP REPAIR TECHNOLOGY**
New England Inst of Technology (RI)

**MARKETING/MARKETING
MANAGEMENT**
Berkeley Coll–New York City Campus
(NY)
Berkeley Coll–White Plains Campus
(NY)
Berkeley Coll–Woodland Park
Campus (NJ)
Central Penn Coll (PA)
Dalton State Coll (GA)
Ferris State U (MI)
FIDM/Fashion Inst of Design &
Merchandising, Los Angeles
Campus (CA)
Hawai`i Pacific U (HI)
Madonna U (MI)
New York City Coll of Technology of
the City U of New York (NY)
Rasmussen Coll Blaine (MN)
Rasmussen Coll Bloomington (MN)
Rasmussen Coll Brooklyn Park (MN)
Rasmussen Coll Eagan (MN)
Rasmussen Coll Fargo (ND)
Rasmussen Coll Fort Myers (FL)
Rasmussen Coll Green Bay (WI)
Rasmussen Coll Kansas City/
Overland Park (KS)
Rasmussen Coll Lake Elmo/
Woodbury (MN)
Rasmussen Coll Land O' Lakes (FL)
Rasmussen Coll Mankato (MN)
Rasmussen Coll Moorhead (MN)
Rasmussen Coll New Port Richey
(FL)
Rasmussen Coll Ocala (FL)
Rasmussen Coll St. Cloud (MN)
Rasmussen Coll Tampa/Brandon
(FL)
Rasmussen Coll Topeka (KS)

Rasmussen Coll Wausau (WI)
Saint Peter's U (NJ)
Southern New Hampshire U (NH)
Tulane U (LA)
The U of Akron (OH)
U of Northwestern Ohio (OH)
Walsh U (OH)
Webber International U (FL)
Youngstown State U (OH)

MASONRY
Pennsylvania Coll of Technology (PA)

MASSAGE THERAPY
Idaho State U (ID)
Morrisville State Coll (NY)

**MASS COMMUNICATION/
MEDIA**
Adams State U (CO)
Black Hills State U (SD)
Dean Coll (MA)
Southwestern Assemblies of God U
(TX)
State Coll of Florida Manatee-
Sarasota (FL)
Wright State U–Lake Campus (OH)
York Coll of Pennsylvania (PA)

MATHEMATICS
Creighton U (NE)
Dalton State Coll (GA)
Dean Coll (MA)
Hawai`i Pacific U (HI)
Idaho State U (ID)
Inter American U of Puerto Rico,
Metropolitan Campus (PR)
Shawnee State U (OH)
State U of New York Coll of
Agriculture and Technology at
Cobleskill (NY)
Taylor U (IN)
Thomas More Coll (KY)
Thomas U (GA)
Trevecca Nazarene U (TN)
Trine U (IN)
U of Great Falls (MT)
Utah Valley U (UT)

**MATHEMATICS TEACHER
EDUCATION**
State Coll of Florida Manatee-
Sarasota (FL)

**MECHANICAL DRAFTING AND
CAD/CADD**
Midland Coll (TX)
New York City Coll of Technology of
the City U of New York (NY)

MECHANICAL ENGINEERING
New England Inst of Technology (RI)

**MECHANICAL ENGINEERING/
MECHANICAL TECHNOLOGY**
Bluefield State Coll (WV)
Brigham Young U–Idaho (ID)
Farmingdale State Coll (NY)
Ferris State U (MI)
Idaho State U (ID)
Lawrence Technological U (MI)
Morrisville State Coll (NY)
New York City Coll of Technology of
the City U of New York (NY)
Penn State Altoona (PA)
Penn State Berks (PA)
Penn State Erie, The Behrend Coll
(PA)
Penn State Hazleton (PA)
Penn State New Kensington (PA)
Penn State York (PA)
Point Park U (PA)
Purdue U (IN)
State U of New York Coll of
Agriculture and Technology at
Cobleskill (NY)
State U of New York Coll of
Technology at Canton (NY)
Syracuse U (NY)
The U of Akron (OH)
Vermont Tech Coll (VT)
Weber State U (UT)
Youngstown State U (OH)

**MECHANICAL ENGINEERING
TECHNOLOGIES RELATED**
Polytechnic U of Puerto Rico (PR)
U of Massachusetts Lowell (MA)

**MECHANIC AND REPAIR
TECHNOLOGIES RELATED**
Inter American U of Puerto Rico,
Guayama Campus (PR)
Pennsylvania Coll of Technology (PA)
Thomas Edison State U (NJ)
Washburn U (KS)

MECHANICS AND REPAIR
Idaho State U (ID)
Utah Valley U (UT)
Weber State U (UT)

**MECHATRONICS, ROBOTICS,
AND AUTOMATION
ENGINEERING**
U of the Fraser Valley (BC, Canada)
Utah Valley U (UT)

**MEDICAL ADMINISTRATIVE
ASSISTANT AND MEDICAL
SECRETARY**
Arkansas Tech U (AR)
Florida National U (FL)
Hallmark U (TX)
Montana State U Billings (MT)
Morrisville State Coll (NY)
Rasmussen Coll Aurora (IL)
Rasmussen Coll Blaine (MN)
Rasmussen Coll Bloomington (MN)
Rasmussen Coll Brooklyn Park (MN)
Rasmussen Coll Eagan (MN)
Rasmussen Coll Fargo (ND)
Rasmussen Coll Fort Myers (FL)
Rasmussen Coll Green Bay (WI)
Rasmussen Coll Kansas City/
Overland Park (KS)
Rasmussen Coll Lake Elmo/
Woodbury (MN)
Rasmussen Coll Land O' Lakes (FL)
Rasmussen Coll Mankato (MN)
Rasmussen Coll Mokena/Tinley Park
(IL)
Rasmussen Coll Moorhead (MN)
Rasmussen Coll New Port Richey
(FL)
Rasmussen Coll Ocala (FL)
Rasmussen Coll Rockford (IL)
Rasmussen Coll Romeoville/Joliet
(IL)
Rasmussen Coll St. Cloud (MN)
Rasmussen Coll Tampa/Brandon
(FL)
Rasmussen Coll Wausau (WI)
U of Northwestern Ohio (OH)

MEDICAL/CLINICAL ASSISTANT
Arkansas Tech U (AR)
Berkeley Coll–Woodland Park
Campus (NJ)
Brigham Young U–Idaho (ID)
Cabarrus Coll of Health Sciences
(NC)
Central Penn Coll (PA)
Colorado Mesa U (CO)
Cox Coll (MO)
Davenport U, Grand Rapids (MI)
Fisher Coll (MA)
Florida National U (FL)
Hallmark U (TX)
Idaho State U (ID)
Mercy Coll of Health Sciences (IA)
Montana State U Billings (MT)
Montana Tech of The U of
Montana (MT)
Mount Aloysius Coll (PA)
New England Inst of Technology (RI)
Rasmussen Coll Aurora (IL)
Rasmussen Coll Blaine (MN)
Rasmussen Coll Bloomington (MN)
Rasmussen Coll Brooklyn Park (MN)
Rasmussen Coll Eagan (MN)
Rasmussen Coll Fort Myers (FL)
Rasmussen Coll Green Bay (WI)
Rasmussen Coll Kansas City/
Overland Park (KS)
Rasmussen Coll Lake Elmo/
Woodbury (MN)
Rasmussen Coll Land O' Lakes (FL)
Rasmussen Coll Mankato (MN)
Rasmussen Coll Mokena/Tinley Park
(IL)
Rasmussen Coll Moorhead (MN)
Rasmussen Coll New Port Richey
(FL)
Rasmussen Coll Ocala (FL)
Rasmussen Coll Rockford (IL)
Rasmussen Coll Romeoville/Joliet
(IL)
Rasmussen Coll St. Cloud (MN)
Rasmussen Coll Tampa/Brandon
(FL)

Rasmussen Coll Topeka (KS)
Rasmussen Coll Wausau (WI)
Robert Morris U Illinois (IL)
Stratford U, Alexandria (VA)
Stratford U, Falls Church (VA)
Stratford U, Glen Allen (VA)
Stratford U, Newport News (VA)
Stratford U, Virginia Beach (VA)
Stratford U, Woodbridge (VA)
Sullivan U (KY)
The U of Akron (OH)
U of Alaska Fairbanks (AK)
U of Northwestern Ohio (OH)
Youngstown State U (OH)

**MEDICAL/HEALTH
MANAGEMENT AND CLINICAL
ASSISTANT**
Florida National U (FL)
Stratford U, Woodbridge (VA)

MEDICAL INFORMATICS
Montana Tech of The U of Montana
(MT)

MEDICAL INSURANCE CODING
Columbia Southern U (AL)
Fisher Coll (MA)

**MEDICAL INSURANCE/MEDICAL
BILLING**
Cox Coll (MO)
Stratford U, Falls Church (VA)
Stratford U, Glen Allen (VA)
Stratford U, Woodbridge (VA)

**MEDICAL MICROBIOLOGY AND
BACTERIOLOGY**
Florida National U (FL)

MEDICAL OFFICE ASSISTANT
Liberty U (VA)
Sullivan U (KY)

**MEDICAL OFFICE
MANAGEMENT**
Dalton State Coll (GA)
The U of Akron (OH)

**MEDICAL RADIOLOGIC
TECHNOLOGY**
Ball State U (IN)
Bluefield State Coll (WV)
Coll of Coastal Georgia (GA)
Drexel U (PA)
Ferris State U (MI)
Inter American U of Puerto Rico,
Aguadilla Campus (PR)
Inter American U of Puerto Rico,
Ponce Campus (PR)
Inter American U of Puerto Rico, San
Germán Campus (PR)
La Roche Coll (PA)
Morehead State U (KY)
Mount Aloysius Coll (PA)
Newman U (KS)
New York City Coll of Technology of
the City U of New York (NY)
Penn State New Kensington (PA)
Penn State Schuylkill (PA)
Pennsylvania Coll of Health Sciences
(PA)
Pennsylvania Coll of Technology (PA)
Polk State Coll (FL)
St. Catherine U (MN)
Shawnee State U (OH)
Southwestern Oklahoma State U
(OK)
State Coll of Florida Manatee-
Sarasota (FL)
The U of Akron (OH)
U of Arkansas for Medical Sciences
(AR)
U of Charleston (WV)
Valencia Coll (FL)
Weber State U (UT)

**MEETING AND EVENT
PLANNING**
Sullivan U (KY)

**MENTAL AND SOCIAL HEALTH
SERVICES AND ALLIED
PROFESSIONS RELATED**
Clarion U of Pennsylvania (PA)
U of Alaska Fairbanks (AK)
Washburn U (KS)

**MENTAL HEALTH
COUNSELING**
Stephen F. Austin State U (TX)

MERCHANDISING
The U of Akron (OH)

MERCHANDISING, SALES, AND MARKETING OPERATIONS RELATED (GENERAL)
Inter American U of Puerto Rico, Aguadilla Campus (PR)
Inter American U of Puerto Rico, Ponce Campus (PR)

METAL AND JEWELRY ARTS
Academy of Art U (CA)
Fashion Inst of Technology (NY)
FIDM/Fashion Inst of Design & Merchandising, Los Angeles Campus (CA)

METALLURGICAL TECHNOLOGY
Penn State Altoona (PA)
Penn State Berks (PA)
Penn State Erie, The Behrend Coll (PA)
Penn State Hazleton (PA)
Penn State New Kensington (PA)
Penn State Schuylkill (PA)
Penn State Wilkes-Barre (PA)
Penn State York (PA)

MICROBIOLOGY
Weber State U (UT)

MIDDLE SCHOOL EDUCATION
East Stroudsburg U of Pennsylvania (PA)

MILITARY HISTORY
American Public U System (WV)

MILITARY TECHNOLOGIES AND APPLIED SCIENCES RELATED
Central Baptist Coll (AR)
Thomas Edison State U (NJ)

MINING AND PETROLEUM TECHNOLOGIES RELATED
U of the Virgin Islands (VI)

MISSIONARY STUDIES AND MISSIOLOGY
Faith Baptist Bible Coll and Theological Seminary (IA)
Hobe Sound Bible Coll (FL)
Ohio Christian U (OH)
Piedmont International U (NC)
Southwestern Assemblies of God U (TX)
U of the Cumberlands (KY)

MULTI/INTERDISCIPLINARY STUDIES RELATED
Arkansas Tech U (AR)
Dallas Baptist U (TX)
Dallas Christian Coll (TX)
John Brown U (AR)
Liberty U (VA)
Montana Tech of The U of Montana (MT)
Northwest Missouri State U (MO)
Ohio U (OH)
Pennsylvania Coll of Technology (PA)
State U of New York Empire State Coll (NY)
Thomas Edison State U (NJ)
The U of Akron (OH)
U of Alaska Fairbanks (AK)
The U of Montana Western (MT)
Utah Valley U (UT)
Washburn U (KS)
Wright State U (OH)
Wright State U–Lake Campus (OH)

MUSEUM STUDIES
Inst of American Indian Arts (NM)
U of Saint Francis (IN)

MUSIC
Hannibal-LaGrange U (MO)
Marian U (IN)
Mount Vernon Nazarene U (OH)
Nyack Coll (NY)
St. Petersburg Coll (FL)
Southwestern Assemblies of God U (TX)
State Coll of Florida Manatee-Sarasota (FL)
Thomas More Coll (KY)
Utah Valley U (UT)

Williams Baptist Coll (AR)
York Coll of Pennsylvania (PA)

MUSICAL INSTRUMENT FABRICATION AND REPAIR
Indiana U Bloomington (IN)

MUSIC HISTORY, LITERATURE, AND THEORY
Cairn U (PA)

MUSIC PERFORMANCE
Inter American U of Puerto Rico, Metropolitan Campus (PR)
State Coll of Florida Manatee-Sarasota (FL)
Trevecca Nazarene U (TN)

MUSIC RELATED
Alverno Coll (WI)
Hobe Sound Bible Coll (FL)
Trevecca Nazarene U (TN)

MUSIC TEACHER EDUCATION
State Coll of Florida Manatee-Sarasota (FL)

MUSIC TECHNOLOGY
U of Saint Francis (IN)

MUSIC THEORY AND COMPOSITION
State Coll of Florida Manatee-Sarasota (FL)

NANOTECHNOLOGY
Lock Haven U of Pennsylvania (PA)

NATURAL RESOURCES/CONSERVATION
Morrisville State Coll (NY)
State U of New York Coll of Environmental Science and Forestry (NY)

NATURAL RESOURCES MANAGEMENT AND POLICY
Morrisville State Coll (NY)
U of Alaska Fairbanks (AK)

NATURAL RESOURCES MANAGEMENT AND POLICY RELATED
U of Guelph (ON, Canada)

NATURAL SCIENCES
Fresno Pacific U (CA)
Gwynedd Mercy U (PA)
Lourdes U (OH)
Madonna U (MI)
Roberts Wesleyan Coll (NY)
St. Petersburg Coll (FL)
U of Alaska Fairbanks (AK)
Washburn U (KS)

NETWORK AND SYSTEM ADMINISTRATION
Academy Coll (MN)
Central Penn Coll (PA)
Florida National U (FL)
Polk State Coll (FL)
Valencia Coll (FL)

NUCLEAR ENGINEERING TECHNOLOGY
Arkansas Tech U (AR)
Idaho State U (ID)

NUCLEAR MEDICAL TECHNOLOGY
Ball State U (IN)
The George Washington U (DC)
Molloy Coll (NY)
Pennsylvania Coll of Health Sciences (PA)
The U of Findlay (OH)

NUCLEAR/NUCLEAR POWER TECHNOLOGY
Excelsior Coll (NY)

NURSING SCIENCE
Dixie State U (UT)
EDP U of Puerto Rico (PR)
EDP U of Puerto Rico–San Sebastian (PR)
Emmaus Bible Coll (IA)
Inter American U of Puerto Rico, Barranquitas Campus (PR)

NUTRITION SCIENCES
U of the Incarnate Word (TX)

OCCUPATIONAL SAFETY AND HEALTH TECHNOLOGY
Columbia Southern U (AL)
Waldorf U (IA)

OCCUPATIONAL THERAPIST ASSISTANT
Adventist U of Health Sciences (FL)
Arkansas Tech U (AR)
Cabarrus Coll of Health Sciences (NC)
California U of Pennsylvania (PA)
Central Penn Coll (PA)
Idaho State U (ID)
Inter American U of Puerto Rico, Ponce Campus (PR)
Lincoln Coll of New England, Southington (CT)
Maria Coll (NY)
Mercy Coll (NY)
New England Inst of Technology (RI)
Newman U (KS)
Penn State Berks (PA)
Pennsylvania Coll of Technology (PA)
Polk State Coll (FL)
Rutgers U–New Brunswick (NJ)
St. Catherine U (MN)
Southwestern Oklahoma State U (OK)
State Coll of Florida Manatee-Sarasota (FL)
U of Charleston (WV)
U of Louisiana at Monroe (LA)
U of Southern Indiana (IN)
Villa Maria Coll (NY)
Washburn U (KS)

OCCUPATIONAL THERAPY
Shawnee State U (OH)
State Coll of Florida Manatee-Sarasota (FL)

OFFICE MANAGEMENT
Academy Coll (MN)
Dalton State Coll (GA)
Emmanuel Coll (GA)
Inter American U of Puerto Rico, Aguadilla Campus (PR)
Inter American U of Puerto Rico, Barranquitas Campus (PR)
Inter American U of Puerto Rico, Bayamón Campus (PR)
Inter American U of Puerto Rico, Fajardo Campus (PR)
Inter American U of Puerto Rico, Guayama Campus (PR)
Inter American U of Puerto Rico, Ponce Campus (PR)
Inter American U of Puerto Rico, San Germán Campus (PR)
Maranatha Baptist U (WI)
Morrisville State Coll (NY)
Shawnee State U (OH)
The U of Akron (OH)
Valencia Coll (FL)

OFFICE OCCUPATIONS AND CLERICAL SERVICES
Midland Coll (TX)
Morrisville State Coll (NY)

OPERATIONS MANAGEMENT
Polk State Coll (FL)

OPTICIANRY
New York City Coll of Technology of the City U of New York (NY)

OPTOMETRIC TECHNICIAN
Indiana U Bloomington (IN)
Inter American U of Puerto Rico, Ponce Campus (PR)

ORGANIZATIONAL BEHAVIOR
Waldorf U (IA)

ORGANIZATIONAL COMMUNICATION
Creighton U (NE)

ORGANIZATIONAL LEADERSHIP
Grace Coll (IN)
Hawai`i Pacific U (HI)
Huntington U (IN)
Point U (GA)
Purdue U (IN)

ORNAMENTAL HORTICULTURE
Farmingdale State Coll (NY)
State U of New York Coll of Agriculture and Technology at Cobleskill (NY)
U of the Fraser Valley (BC, Canada)
Vermont Tech Coll (VT)

PAINTING
Pratt Inst (NY)

PALLIATIVE CARE NURSING
Madonna U (MI)

PARKS, RECREATION AND LEISURE
St. Petersburg Coll (FL)

PASTORAL STUDIES/COUNSELING
Marian U (IN)

PETROLEUM TECHNOLOGY
Mansfield U of Pennsylvania (PA)
Montana State U Billings (MT)
U of Pittsburgh at Bradford (PA)

PHARMACY, PHARMACEUTICAL SCIENCES, AND ADMINISTRATION RELATED
EDP U of Puerto Rico (PR)
EDP U of Puerto Rico–San Sebastian (PR)

PHARMACY TECHNICIAN
Cabarrus Coll of Health Sciences (NC)
Inter American U of Puerto Rico, Aguadilla Campus (PR)
Inter American U of Puerto Rico, Guayama Campus (PR)
Inter American U of Puerto Rico, Metropolitan Campus (PR)
Rasmussen Coll Aurora (IL)
Rasmussen Coll Blaine (MN)
Rasmussen Coll Bloomington (MN)
Rasmussen Coll Brooklyn Park (MN)
Rasmussen Coll Eagan (MN)
Rasmussen Coll Fort Myers (FL)
Rasmussen Coll Green Bay (WI)
Rasmussen Coll Kansas City/Overland Park (KS)
Rasmussen Coll Lake Elmo/Woodbury (MN)
Rasmussen Coll Land O' Lakes (FL)
Rasmussen Coll Mankato (MN)
Rasmussen Coll Mokena/Tinley Park (IL)
Rasmussen Coll Moorhead (MN)
Rasmussen Coll New Port Richey (FL)
Rasmussen Coll Ocala (FL)
Rasmussen Coll Rockford (IL)
Rasmussen Coll Romeoville/Joliet (IL)
Rasmussen Coll St. Cloud (MN)
Rasmussen Coll Tampa/Brandon (FL)
Rasmussen Coll Topeka (KS)
Rasmussen Coll Wausau (WI)
Robert Morris U Illinois (IL)
Stratford U, Falls Church (VA)
Stratford U, Glen Allen (VA)
Stratford U, Newport News (VA)
Stratford U, Virginia Beach (VA)
Sullivan U (KY)

PHILOSOPHY
Carroll Coll (MT)
State Coll of Florida Manatee-Sarasota (FL)
Thomas More Coll (KY)
Utah Valley U (UT)

PHOTOGRAPHIC AND FILM/VIDEO TECHNOLOGY
St. John's U (NY)
Villa Maria Coll (NY)

PHOTOGRAPHY
St. Petersburg Coll (FL)

PHYSICAL EDUCATION TEACHING AND COACHING
Fresno Pacific U (CA)
State Coll of Florida Manatee-Sarasota (FL)

PHYSICAL FITNESS TECHNICIAN
The U of Findlay (OH)

PHYSICAL SCIENCES
Coll of Staten Island of the City U of New York (NY)
New York City Coll of Technology of the City U of New York (NY)
Roberts Wesleyan Coll (NY)
U of the Fraser Valley (BC, Canada)
Utah Valley U (UT)

PHYSICAL SCIENCES RELATED
Lock Haven U of Pennsylvania (PA)
State U of New York Empire State Coll (NY)

PHYSICAL THERAPY
State Coll of Florida Manatee-Sarasota (FL)

PHYSICAL THERAPY TECHNOLOGY
Arkansas Tech U (AR)
California U of Pennsylvania (PA)
Central Penn Coll (PA)
Dixie State U (UT)
EDP U of Puerto Rico (PR)
EDP U of Puerto Rico–San Sebastian (PR)
Florida National U (FL)
Idaho State U (ID)
Inter American U of Puerto Rico, Ponce Campus (PR)
Louisiana Coll (LA)
Mercy Coll of Health Sciences (IA)
Missouri Western State U (MO)
Mount Aloysius Coll (PA)
Nebraska Methodist Coll (NE)
New England Inst of Technology (RI)
Our Lady of the Lake Coll (LA)
Penn State Hazleton (PA)
Polk State Coll (FL)
St. Catherine U (MN)
St. Petersburg Coll (FL)
Shawnee State U (OH)
Southern Illinois U Carbondale (IL)
Southwestern Oklahoma State U (OK)
State Coll of Florida Manatee-Sarasota (FL)
State U of New York Coll of Technology at Canton (NY)
U of Evansville (IN)
U of Indianapolis (IN)
U of Maine at Presque Isle (ME)
U of Saint Francis (IN)
Villa Maria Coll (NY)
Washburn U (KS)

PHYSICIAN ASSISTANT
State Coll of Florida Manatee-Sarasota (FL)

PHYSICS
Dalton State Coll (GA)
Idaho State U (ID)
Rogers State U (OK)
State Coll of Florida Manatee-Sarasota (FL)
Thomas More Coll (KY)
U of the Virgin Islands (VI)
U of Wisconsin–Parkside (WI)
Utah Valley U (UT)
York Coll of Pennsylvania (PA)

PHYSICS TEACHER EDUCATION
State Coll of Florida Manatee-Sarasota (FL)

PIPEFITTING AND SPRINKLER FITTING
New England Inst of Technology (RI)

PLANT NURSERY MANAGEMENT
Dalhousie U (NS, Canada)

PLANT PROTECTION AND INTEGRATED PEST MANAGEMENT
Dalhousie U (NS, Canada)

PLANT SCIENCES
State U of New York Coll of Agriculture and Technology at Cobleskill (NY)

PLASTICS AND POLYMER ENGINEERING TECHNOLOGY
Ferris State U (MI)
Penn State Erie, The Behrend Coll (PA)
Pennsylvania Coll of Technology (PA)
Shawnee State U (OH)

PLUMBING TECHNOLOGY
Montana State U–Northern (MT)

POLITICAL SCIENCE AND GOVERNMENT
Adams State U (CO)
Dalton State Coll (GA)
Immaculata U (PA)
Liberty U (VA)
Thomas More Coll (KY)

POULTRY SCIENCE
State U of New York Coll of Agriculture and Technology at Cobleskill (NY)

PRACTICAL NURSING, VOCATIONAL NURSING AND NURSING ASSISTANTS RELATED
Caribbean U (PR)
Rasmussen Coll Ocala School of Nursing (FL)

PRECISION METAL WORKING RELATED
Montana Tech of The U of Montana (MT)

PRE-DENTISTRY STUDIES
Concordia U Wisconsin (WI)

PRE-ENGINEERING
Columbia Coll (MO)
Dixie State U (UT)
Newman U (KS)
Southern Utah U (UT)
Utah Valley U (UT)
Weber State U (UT)

PRE-LAW STUDIES
Ferris State U (MI)
Florida National U (FL)
Thomas More Coll (KY)
Wayland Baptist U (TX)

PREMEDICAL STUDIES
Concordia U Wisconsin (WI)

PRENURSING STUDIES
Concordia U Wisconsin (WI)
Dean Coll (MA)
Lincoln Christian U (IL)
Missouri Baptist U (MO)

PRE-PHARMACY STUDIES
Dalton State Coll (GA)
Ferris State U (MI)
Madonna U (MI)
State Coll of Florida Manatee-Sarasota (FL)

PRE-THEOLOGY/PRE-MINISTERIAL STUDIES
Eastern Mennonite U (VA)
Nazarene Bible Coll (CO)
Tabor Coll (KS)
Theological U of the Caribbean (PR)

PSYCHIATRIC/MENTAL HEALTH SERVICES TECHNOLOGY
Pennsylvania Coll of Technology (PA)

PSYCHOLOGY
Beacon Coll (FL)
Calumet Coll of Saint Joseph (IN)
Central Methodist U (MO)
Dalton State Coll (GA)
Dean Coll (MA)
Ferris State U (MI)
Fisher Coll (MA)
Fresno Pacific U (CA)
Liberty U (VA)
Life U (GA)
Montana State U Billings (MT)
Muhlenberg Coll (PA)
New England Coll (NH)
Point U (GA)
Regent U (VA)
Southwestern Assemblies of God U (TX)
State Coll of Florida Manatee-Sarasota (FL)

State U of New York Empire State Coll (NY)
Thomas More Coll (KY)
U of the Cumberlands (KY)
Utah Valley U (UT)
Waldorf U (IA)
Wright State U (OH)
Wright State U–Lake Campus (OH)

PSYCHOLOGY RELATED
Morrisville State Coll (NY)

PUBLIC ADMINISTRATION
Central Methodist U (MO)
Florida National U (FL)
Point Park U (PA)
State Coll of Florida Manatee-Sarasota (FL)

PUBLIC ADMINISTRATION AND SOCIAL SERVICE PROFESSIONS RELATED
Metropolitan Coll of New York (NY)
Point Park U (PA)
Thomas More Coll (KY)
Trevecca Nazarene U (TN)
The U of Akron (OH)

PUBLIC HEALTH
American Public U System (WV)
U of Alaska Fairbanks (AK)

PUBLIC POLICY ANALYSIS
Saint Peter's U (NJ)

PUBLIC RELATIONS, ADVERTISING, AND APPLIED COMMUNICATION RELATED
U of Maine at Presque Isle (ME)

PURCHASING, PROCUREMENT/ ACQUISITIONS AND CONTRACTS MANAGEMENT
Trevecca Nazarene U (TN)

QUALITY CONTROL AND SAFETY TECHNOLOGIES RELATED
Madonna U (MI)

QUALITY CONTROL TECHNOLOGY
Weber State U (UT)

RADIO AND TELEVISION
Lawrence Technological U (MI)
Ohio U–Zanesville (OH)
State Coll of Florida Manatee-Sarasota (FL)

RADIO AND TELEVISION BROADCASTING TECHNOLOGY
New England Inst of Technology (RI)
State Coll of Florida Manatee-Sarasota (FL)

RADIOLOGIC TECHNOLOGY/ SCIENCE
Adventist U of Health Sciences (FL)
Allen Coll (IA)
Alvernia U (PA)
Aultman Coll of Nursing and Health Sciences (OH)
Champlain Coll (VT)
Coll of Coastal Georgia (GA)
Colorado Mesa U (CO)
Cox Coll (MO)
Dalton State Coll (GA)
Dixie State U (UT)
Fairleigh Dickinson U, Metropolitan Campus (NJ)
Florida National U (FL)
Gannon U (PA)
Henderson State U (AR)
Holy Family U (PA)
Indiana U Kokomo (IN)
Indiana U Northwest (IN)
Indiana U–Purdue U Indianapolis (IN)
Indiana U South Bend (IN)
Inter American U of Puerto Rico, Barranquitas Campus (PR)
Louisiana State U at Alexandria (LA)
Mansfield U of Pennsylvania (PA)
Mercy Coll of Health Sciences (IA)
Mercy Coll of Ohio (OH)
Montana Tech of The U of Montana (MT)
Nebraska Methodist Coll (NE)
Newman U (KS)
Pennsylvania Coll of Health Sciences (PA)
St. Petersburg Coll (FL)

State Coll of Florida Manatee-Sarasota (FL)
U of Saint Francis (IN)
Washburn U (KS)
Weber State U (UT)
Widener U (PA)

RADIO, TELEVISION, AND DIGITAL COMMUNICATION RELATED
Madonna U (MI)

REAL ESTATE
American Public U System (WV)
Saint Francis U (PA)

RECORDING ARTS TECHNOLOGY
Academy of Art U (CA)
Indiana U Bloomington (IN)
Los Angeles Film School (CA)
New England Inst of Technology (RI)

REGIONAL STUDIES
Arkansas Tech U (AR)

REGISTERED NURSING, NURSING ADMINISTRATION, NURSING RESEARCH AND CLINICAL NURSING RELATED
Rasmussen Coll Ocala School of Nursing (FL)

REGISTERED NURSING/ REGISTERED NURSE
Alcorn State U (MS)
Aquinas Coll (TN)
Arkansas Tech U (AR)
Aultman Coll of Nursing and Health Sciences (OH)
Bayamón Central U (PR)
Becker Coll (MA)
Bethel Coll (IN)
Bluefield State Coll (WV)
Brigham Young U–Idaho (ID)
Cabarrus Coll of Health Sciences (NC)
California U of Pennsylvania (PA)
Campbellsville U (KY)
Clarion U of Pennsylvania (PA)
Coll of Coastal Georgia (GA)
Coll of Staten Island of the City U of New York (NY)
Colorado Mesa U (CO)
Columbia Coll (MO)
Cox Coll (MO)
Dalton State Coll (GA)
Dixie State U (UT)
Excelsior Coll (NY)
Florida National U (FL)
Gardner-Webb U (NC)
Hallmark U (TX)
Hannibal-LaGrange U (MO)
Idaho State U (ID)
Inter American U of Puerto Rico, Barranquitas Campus (PR)
Inter American U of Puerto Rico, Guayama Campus (PR)
Inter American U of Puerto Rico, Metropolitan Campus (PR)
Kent State U at Geauga (OH)
Kentucky State U (KY)
La Roche Coll (PA)
Lock Haven U of Pennsylvania (PA)
Louisiana State U at Alexandria (LA)
Louisiana Tech U (LA)
Maria Coll (NY)
Marshall U (WV)
Mercy Coll of Health Sciences (IA)
Mercy Coll of Ohio (OH)
Midland Coll (TX)
Montana State U Billings (MT)
Montana State U–Northern (MT)
Morehead State U (KY)
Morrisville State Coll (NY)
Mount Aloysius Coll (PA)
Mount Saint Mary's U (CA)
New England Inst of Technology (RI)
New York City Coll of Technology of the City U of New York (NY)
Northwestern State U of Louisiana (LA)
Our Lady of the Lake Coll (LA)
Penn State Altoona (PA)
Penn State Berks (PA)
Penn State Erie, The Behrend Coll (PA)
Penn State Worthington Scranton (PA)
Pennsylvania Coll of Health Sciences (PA)
Pennsylvania Coll of Technology (PA)

Polk State Coll (FL)
Robert Morris U Illinois (IL)
Rogers State U (OK)
St. Petersburg Coll (FL)
Shawnee State U (OH)
Southern Arkansas U–Magnolia (AR)
Southwest Baptist U (MO)
State Coll of Florida Manatee-Sarasota (FL)
State U of New York Coll of Technology at Canton (NY)
Stratford U, Glen Allen (VA)
Tennessee State U (TN)
Thomas U (GA)
Troy U (AL)
Universidad Adventista de las Antillas (PR)
U of Charleston (WV)
U of Pikeville (KY)
U of Pittsburgh at Bradford (PA)
U of Saint Francis (IN)
The U of South Dakota (SD)
U of the Virgin Islands (VI)
The U of West Alabama (AL)
Utah Valley U (UT)
Valencia Coll (FL)
Vermont Tech Coll (VT)
Weber State U (UT)
Western Kentucky U (KY)

REHABILITATION AND THERAPEUTIC PROFESSIONS RELATED
Rutgers U–Newark (NJ)
Rutgers U–New Brunswick (NJ)

RELIGIOUS EDUCATION
Dallas Baptist U (TX)
Heritage Bible Coll (NC)
Kuyper Coll (MI)
Marian U (IN)
Nazarene Bible Coll (CO)
Piedmont International U (NC)

RELIGIOUS/SACRED MUSIC
Calvary U (MO)
Mount Vernon Nazarene U (OH)
Ohio Christian U (OH)
Saint Louis Christian Coll (MO)
Trevecca Nazarene U (TN)

RELIGIOUS STUDIES
Brewton-Parker Coll (GA)
Concordia Coll–New York (NY)
Corban U (OR)
Criswell Coll (TX)
Global U (MO)
Huntington U (IN)
Inter American U of Puerto Rico, Metropolitan Campus (PR)
Liberty U (VA)
Lourdes U (OH)
Madonna U (MI)
Mount Marty Coll (SD)
Mount Vernon Nazarene U (OH)
Northwest U (WA)
Oakland City U (IN)
State Coll of Florida Manatee-Sarasota (FL)
Thomas More Coll (KY)

RESPIRATORY CARE THERAPY
Boise State U (ID)
Clarion U of Pennsylvania (PA)
Dakota State U (SD)
Dixie State U (UT)
Ferris State U (MI)
Gannon U (PA)
Idaho State U (ID)
Inter American U of Puerto Rico, Guayama Campus (PR)
Mansfield U of Pennsylvania (PA)
Midland Coll (TX)
Molloy Coll (NY)
Morehead State U (KY)
Nebraska Methodist Coll (NE)
New England Inst of Technology (RI)
Newman U (KS)
Pennsylvania Coll of Health Sciences (PA)
Polk State Coll (FL)
Rutgers U–New Brunswick (NJ)
St. Petersburg Coll (FL)
Shawnee State U (OH)
State Coll of Florida Manatee-Sarasota (FL)
Universidad Adventista de las Antillas (PR)
U of Pittsburgh at Johnstown (PA)
Valencia Coll (FL)
Vermont Tech Coll (VT)
Washburn U (KS)

Weber State U (UT)
York Coll of Pennsylvania (PA)

RESPIRATORY THERAPY TECHNICIAN
Dalton State Coll (GA)
Florida National U (FL)
U of the Incarnate Word (TX)

RESTAURANT, CULINARY, AND CATERING MANAGEMENT
Arkansas Tech U (AR)
Ferris State U (MI)
Morrisville State Coll (NY)
St. Petersburg Coll (FL)
State U of New York Coll of Agriculture and Technology at Cobleskill (NY)
Stratford U (MD)

RESTAURANT/FOOD SERVICES MANAGEMENT
Morrisville State Coll (NY)
Pennsylvania Coll of Technology (PA)
Stratford U (MD)
Stratford U, Falls Church (VA)
The U of Akron (OH)
Valencia Coll (FL)

RETAILING
American Public U System (WV)
The U of Findlay (OH)
Weber State U (UT)

RHETORIC AND COMPOSITION
Ferris State U (MI)
State Coll of Florida Manatee-Sarasota (FL)

ROBOTICS TECHNOLOGY
Idaho State U (ID)
Pennsylvania Coll of Technology (PA)
Utah Valley U (UT)

RUSSIAN
Idaho State U (ID)

RUSSIAN, CENTRAL EUROPEAN, EAST EUROPEAN AND EURASIAN STUDIES
State Coll of Florida Manatee-Sarasota (FL)

RUSSIAN STUDIES
State Coll of Florida Manatee-Sarasota (FL)

SALES, DISTRIBUTION, AND MARKETING OPERATIONS
Academy Coll (MN)
Dalton State Coll (GA)
Inter American U of Puerto Rico, Aguadilla Campus (PR)
Sullivan U (KY)

SCIENCE TEACHER EDUCATION
State Coll of Florida Manatee-Sarasota (FL)
Wright State U (OH)
Wright State U–Lake Campus (OH)

SCIENCE TECHNOLOGIES
Washburn U (KS)

SCIENCE TECHNOLOGIES RELATED
Madonna U (MI)
Maria Coll (NY)
Ohio Valley U (WV)
State U of New York Coll of Agriculture and Technology at Cobleskill (NY)
U of Alaska Fairbanks (AK)

SECONDARY EDUCATION
Ferris State U (MI)
Rogers State U (OK)

SELLING SKILLS AND SALES
Inter American U of Puerto Rico, San Germán Campus (PR)
The U of Akron (OH)

SHEET METAL TECHNOLOGY
Montana State U Billings (MT)

SIGN LANGUAGE INTERPRETATION AND TRANSLATION
Mount Aloysius Coll (PA)
St. Catherine U (MN)

SMALL BUSINESS ADMINISTRATION
Central Penn Coll (PA)
The U of Akron (OH)

SOCIAL PSYCHOLOGY
State Coll of Florida Manatee-Sarasota (FL)

SOCIAL SCIENCES
Campbellsville U (KY)
Marymount Manhattan Coll (NY)
Ohio U–Zanesville (OH)
Rogers State U (OK)
St. Gregory's U, Shawnee (OK)
Saint Peter's U (NJ)
Shawnee State U (OH)
Southwestern Assemblies of God U (TX)
State Coll of Florida Manatee-Sarasota (FL)
State U of New York Empire State Coll (NY)
Trine U (IN)
U of Southern Indiana (IN)
Valparaiso U (IN)
Wayland Baptist U (TX)

SOCIAL SCIENCES RELATED
U of Wisconsin–Parkside (WI)

SOCIAL SCIENCE TEACHER EDUCATION
Montana State U (MT)

SOCIAL STUDIES TEACHER EDUCATION
State Coll of Florida Manatee-Sarasota (FL)

SOCIAL WORK
Ferris State U (MI)
State Coll of Florida Manatee-Sarasota (FL)
State U of New York Coll of Agriculture and Technology at Cobleskill (NY)
U of the Fraser Valley (BC, Canada)
Youngstown State U (OH)

SOCIAL WORK RELATED
The U of Akron (OH)

SOCIOLOGY
Dean Coll (MA)
Fresno Pacific U (CA)
Lourdes U (OH)
Montana State U Billings (MT)
New England Coll (NH)
Thomas More Coll (KY)
The U of Scranton (PA)
Wright State U (OH)
Wright State U–Lake Campus (OH)

SOLAR ENERGY TECHNOLOGY
Pennsylvania Coll of Technology (PA)

SPANISH
Fresno Pacific U (CA)
State Coll of Florida Manatee-Sarasota (FL)
Thomas More Coll (KY)
Weber State U (UT)

SPECIAL EDUCATION
Inter American U of Puerto Rico, Barranquitas Campus (PR)
Montana State U Billings (MT)
U of Maine at Presque Isle (ME)

SPECIAL EDUCATION–INDIVIDUALS WHO ARE DEVELOPMENTALLY DELAYED
Saint Mary-of-the-Woods Coll (IN)

SPECIAL EDUCATION RELATED
Minot State U (ND)

SPEECH COMMUNICATION AND RHETORIC
American Public U System (WV)
Dean Coll (MA)
Lincoln Coll of New England, Southington (CT)
State U of New York Coll of Agriculture and Technology at Cobleskill (NY)
Trevecca Nazarene U (TN)
Trine U (IN)
Tulane U (LA)
Utah Valley U (UT)
Waldorf U (IA)
Wright State U (OH)
Wright State U–Lake Campus (OH)

SPEECH-LANGUAGE PATHOLOGY
Elms Coll (MA)

SPORT AND FITNESS ADMINISTRATION/MANAGEMENT
Dean Coll (MA)
Inter American U of Puerto Rico, Metropolitan Campus (PR)
Morrisville State Coll (NY)
Mount Vernon Nazarene U (OH)
Southwestern Adventist U (TX)
Waldorf U (IA)
Webber International U (FL)
William Paterson U of New Jersey (NJ)

STATISTICS
State Coll of Florida Manatee-Sarasota (FL)

STRATEGIC STUDIES
U of Wisconsin–Parkside (WI)

SUBSTANCE ABUSE/ADDICTION COUNSELING
Midland Coll (TX)
National U (CA)
St. Petersburg Coll (FL)
Southwestern Assemblies of God U (TX)
U of Great Falls (MT)
Washburn U (KS)

SURGICAL TECHNOLOGY
Berkeley Coll–Woodland Park Campus (NJ)
Cabarrus Coll of Health Sciences (NC)
Mercy Coll of Health Sciences (IA)
Montana State U Billings (MT)
Mount Aloysius Coll (PA)
Nebraska Methodist Coll (NE)
New England Inst of Technology (RI)
Pennsylvania Coll of Health Sciences (PA)
Pennsylvania Coll of Technology (PA)
Rasmussen Coll Brooklyn Park (MN)
Rasmussen Coll St. Cloud (MN)
Robert Morris U Illinois (IL)
Sentara Coll of Health Sciences (VA)
The U of Akron (OH)
U of Arkansas for Medical Sciences (AR)
U of Pittsburgh at Johnstown (PA)
U of Saint Francis (IN)
Washburn U (KS)

SURVEYING TECHNOLOGY
Ferris State U (MI)
Penn State Wilkes-Barre (PA)
Pennsylvania Coll of Technology (PA)
Polytechnic U of Puerto Rico (PR)
State U of New York Coll of Environmental Science and Forestry (NY)
The U of Akron (OH)
Utah Valley U (UT)

SUSTAINABILITY STUDIES
Lock Haven U of Pennsylvania (PA)

SYSTEM, NETWORKING, AND LAN/WAN MANAGEMENT
Academy Coll (MN)
Dakota State U (SD)
Midland Coll (TX)

TEACHER ASSISTANT/AIDE
Alverno Coll (WI)
Corban U (OR)
Eastern Mennonite U (VA)
Johnson U (TN)
Saint Mary-of-the-Woods Coll (IN)
State U of New York Coll of Agriculture and Technology at Cobleskill (NY)
U of Maine at Presque Isle (ME)
Valparaiso U (IN)
Waldorf U (IA)

TECHNICAL TEACHER EDUCATION
Western Kentucky U (KY)

TECHNOLOGY/INDUSTRIAL ARTS TEACHER EDUCATION
State Coll of Florida Manatee-Sarasota (FL)

TELECOMMUNICATIONS TECHNOLOGY
New York City Coll of Technology of the City U of New York (NY)
Pace U (NY)
Penn State Hazleton (PA)
Penn State New Kensington (PA)
Penn State Schuylkill (PA)
Penn State Wilkes-Barre (PA)
Penn State York (PA)

TERRORISM AND COUNTERTERRORISM OPERATIONS
American Public U System (WV)

THEATER DESIGN AND TECHNOLOGY
Utah Valley U (UT)

THEOLOGICAL AND MINISTERIAL STUDIES RELATED
California Christian Coll (CA)
Lincoln Christian U (IL)
Northwest U (WA)

THEOLOGY
Briar Cliff U (IA)
Calvary U (MO)
Creighton U (NE)
Franciscan U of Steubenville (OH)
Immaculata U (PA)
Marian U (IN)
Ohio Dominican U (OH)
Piedmont International U (NC)
Williams Baptist Coll (AR)

THEOLOGY AND RELIGIOUS VOCATIONS RELATED
Anderson U (IN)
Missouri Baptist U (MO)
Southeastern U (FL)
Trevecca Nazarene U (TN)
U of Valley Forge (PA)

TOOL AND DIE TECHNOLOGY
Ferris State U (MI)

TOURISM AND TRAVEL SERVICES MANAGEMENT
Black Hills State U (SD)
Morrisville State Coll (NY)
U of Northwestern Ohio (OH)

TOURISM AND TRAVEL SERVICES MARKETING
Morrisville State Coll (NY)
State U of New York Coll of Agriculture and Technology at Cobleskill (NY)

TRADE AND INDUSTRIAL TEACHER EDUCATION
Murray State U (KY)
State Coll of Florida Manatee-Sarasota (FL)

TRANSPORTATION AND HIGHWAY ENGINEERING
The U of Toledo (OH)

TRANSPORTATION/MOBILITY MANAGEMENT
Polk State Coll (FL)

TURF AND TURFGRASS MANAGEMENT
North Carolina State U (NC)
U of Guelph (ON, Canada)
U of Massachusetts Amherst (MA)

URBAN MINISTRY
Tabor Coll (KS)

URBAN STUDIES/AFFAIRS
Saint Peter's U (NJ)

VEHICLE AND VEHICLE PARTS AND ACCESSORIES MARKETING
Pennsylvania Coll of Technology (PA)

VETERINARY/ANIMAL HEALTH TECHNOLOGY
Becker Coll (MA)
Brigham Young U–Idaho (ID)
Dalhousie U (NS, Canada)
Morehead State U (KY)
Mount Ida Coll (MA)
New England Inst of Technology (RI)
Northwestern State U of Louisiana (LA)
Purdue U (IN)
St. Petersburg Coll (FL)
State U of New York Coll of Technology at Canton (NY)
U of Guelph (ON, Canada)
U of New Hampshire (NH)
Vermont Tech Coll (VT)

VISUAL AND PERFORMING ARTS
Pine Manor Coll (MA)

VOCATIONAL REHABILITATION COUNSELING
State Coll of Florida Manatee-Sarasota (FL)

WATER QUALITY AND WASTEWATER TREATMENT MANAGEMENT AND RECYCLING TECHNOLOGY
Colorado Mesa U (CO)

WEAPONS OF MASS DESTRUCTION
American Public U System (WV)

WEB/MULTIMEDIA MANAGEMENT AND WEBMASTER
Academy Coll (MN)
American Public U System (WV)
Montana Tech of The U of Montana (MT)
St. Petersburg Coll (FL)

WEB PAGE, DIGITAL/MULTIMEDIA AND INFORMATION RESOURCES DESIGN
Academy Coll (MN)
Academy of Art U (CA)
Beacon Coll (FL)
Brigham Young U–Idaho (ID)
DeVry U–Arlington Campus (VA)
DeVry U–Chicago Campus (IL)
DeVry U–Columbus Campus (OH)
DeVry U–Decatur Campus (GA)

DeVry U–Irving Campus (TX)
DeVry U–Kansas City Campus (MO)
DeVry U–Miramar Campus (FL)
DeVry U–North Brunswick Campus (NJ)
DeVry U Online (IL)
DeVry U–Orlando Campus (FL)
DeVry U–Phoenix Campus (AZ)
DeVry U–Pomona Campus (CA)
DeVry U–Westminster Campus (CO)
Florida National U (FL)
Limestone Coll (SC)
New England Inst of Technology (RI)
Polk State Coll (FL)
Rasmussen Coll Aurora (IL)
Rasmussen Coll Blaine (MN)
Rasmussen Coll Bloomington (MN)
Rasmussen Coll Brooklyn Park (MN)
Rasmussen Coll Eagan (MN)
Rasmussen Coll Fargo (ND)
Rasmussen Coll Fort Myers (FL)
Rasmussen Coll Green Bay (WI)
Rasmussen Coll Kansas City/Overland Park (KS)
Rasmussen Coll Lake Elmo/Woodbury (MN)
Rasmussen Coll Land O' Lakes (FL)
Rasmussen Coll Mankato (MN)
Rasmussen Coll Mokena/Tinley Park (IL)
Rasmussen Coll Moorhead (MN)
Rasmussen Coll New Port Richey (FL)
Rasmussen Coll Ocala (FL)
Rasmussen Coll Romeoville/Joliet (IL)
Rasmussen Coll St. Cloud (MN)
Rasmussen Coll Tampa/Brandon (FL)
Rasmussen Coll Topeka (KS)
Rasmussen Coll Wausau (WI)
St. Petersburg Coll (FL)
Thomas More Coll (KY)
The U of Toledo (OH)
Utah Valley U (UT)
Weber State U (UT)
Wilmington U (DE)

WELDING ENGINEERING TECHNOLOGY
New England Inst of Technology (RI)

WELDING TECHNOLOGY
Arkansas Tech U (AR)
Brigham Young U–Idaho (ID)
Ferris State U (MI)
Idaho State U (ID)
Midland Coll (TX)
Pennsylvania Coll of Technology (PA)
Weber State U (UT)

WILDLAND/FOREST FIREFIGHTING AND INVESTIGATION
Colorado Mesa U (CO)

WILDLIFE, FISH AND WILDLANDS SCIENCE AND MANAGEMENT
State U of New York Coll of Agriculture and Technology at Cobleskill (NY)

WOMEN'S STUDIES
Providence Coll (RI)
State Coll of Florida Manatee-Sarasota (FL)

WOOD SCIENCE AND WOOD PRODUCTS/PULP AND PAPER TECHNOLOGY
Morrisville State Coll (NY)

WRITING
Carroll Coll (MT)

YOUTH MINISTRY
Calvary U (MO)
Piedmont International U (NC)
U of Valley Forge (PA)

Alphabetical Listing of Two-Year Colleges

NOTES

NOTES

NOTES

NOTES

NOTES

NOTES

NOTES

NOTES

NOTES

NOTES

NOTES

NOTES

NOTES

NOTES

NOTES